CASES AND MATERIALS

Energy, Economics and the Environment

Second Edition

by

FRED BOSSELMAN
Professor of Law Emeritus
Chicago–Kent College of Law

JOEL B. EISEN
Professor of Law
University of Richmond School of Law

JIM ROSSI
Harry M. Walborsky Professor of Law
Florida State University College of Law

DAVID B. SPENCE
Professor of Law, Politics & Regulation
McCombs School of Business, University of Texas at Austin

JACQUELINE WEAVER
A.A. White Professor of Law
University of Houston Law Center

FOUNDATION PRESS

2006

THOMSON
———*———™
WEST

© 2000 FOUNDATION PRESS
© 2006 By FOUNDATION PRESS
　　　　395 Hudson Street
　　　　New York, NY 10014
　　　　Phone Toll Free 1–877–888–1330
　　　　Fax (212) 367–6799
　　　　foundation-press.com
Printed in the United States of America
ISBN–13: 978–1–58778–924–3
ISBN–10: 1–58778–924–8

 TEXT IS PRINTED ON 10% POST CONSUMER RECYCLED PAPER

INTRODUCTION

PREFACE

In both law and business schools, Energy courses were common after the oil price shocks of the 1970s. A number of fine casebooks were written in the early 1980s, responding to the sense of "energy crisis" and "environmental crisis" during that period.

As the 1980s progressed, however, declining energy prices, improving economic and environmental conditions, and diminishing Cold War tensions alleviated the sense of crisis. Gradually, schools began to lose interest. The 1990s brought about increasing attention to energy issues. The collapse of communism created worldwide interest in the privatization and deregulation of monopolies. Information technology facilitated international business combinations, and increased worldwide awareness about energy alternatives. Meanwhile, confidence about environmental progress faded in the face of worries about the ozone layer, climate change, an asthma epidemic, biogenetics, and our inability to get a handle on air and water pollution from small sources.

During the 1990s, law schools created an increasing number of courses on "regulated industries" – an ironic title given the diminishing role of economic regulation. The law and economics movement continued to expand its influence. Environmental law programs spawned a growing number of subspecialties, and interest in international law boomed. Natural resources law continued to be dominated by intense political and ideological controversy over the use of public lands, by concern about the long-term supply of resources, and by worries about our reliance on overseas suppliers.

In response, there have been excellent new treatises, such as Energy Law and Policy for the 21st Century (Rocky Mountain Mineral Law Foundation 2000) and Environmental Law: From Resources to Recovery (West Group 1993), and a valuable "Nutshell" by Joseph Tomain and Judge Richard Cudahy (Energy Law, West 2004) but no new casebooks. All of these factors contributed to the authors' belief that the beginning of the new century was an appropriate time for a new casebook on energy, economics and the environment. The first edition of this casebook, published in 2000, responded to that need. The second edition of this casebook builds on that effort, with a particular emphasis on recent issues such as increased attention to the environmental concerns surrounding the use of energy resources and energy reliability.

iii

OVERVIEW OF THE CASEBOOK

This book is organized roughly on a chronological basis according to the periods in history within which the issues arose. Thus water power is followed by coal, then oil and gas, electricity, nuclear power and motor vehicles. The book locates energy law at the intersection of economic issues and environmental concerns, so stand-alone chapters discuss both economic and environmental regulation, such as rate regulation and the sustainable development of energy resources. We believe that the material can be taught in many different variations, depending on whether the course is approached with an emphasis on regulated industries, on deregulation, on the environment, or an emphasis on traditional natural resources issues.

Chapter One provides an overview of some of the major energy issues facing us in the new century, a review of the regulatory context in which the energy sector operates, and points out some key energy policy failures of the past.

Chapter Two introduces the concept of the public utility, central to common law and statutory approaches to energy regulation. Public utility principles are grounded in the history and economics of regulation. The chapter introduces basic aspects of public utility regulation and its limitations, laying the groundwork for the discussions of competition and rate deregulation in later chapters.

Chapter Three covers the basic principles of the rise of market power that accompanied the traditional public utility concept. Most of the chapter focuses on rate regulation, with an eye towards the issues introduced by competition, and rate deregulation, in later chapters. The chapter introduces traditional ratemaking principles, such as rate base, operating expenses, and rate of return, and also discusses legal constraints on rate regulation.

Chapter Four traces the history of water power from the early water mill to modern hydroelectric power. Many of the basic property issues underlying energy law today arose in the context of the early water mills. The chapter introduces the role of the Federal Energy Regulatory Commission in licensing hydroelectric projects, particularly the long struggle before the FERC over the resolution of environmental issues in hydroelectric licensing proceedings.

Chapter Five covers the earliest of the fossil fuels to become widely used, coal, and the politics of clean air. This chapter examines the regulation of coal mining, regulatory takings case law arising from regulation of the coal industry, and the major Clean Air Act pollution battles triggered by coal-fired power plants over the last two decades.

Chapter Six explores oil, the energy source most familiar to a population of gas-guzzling consumers. It describes how the rule of capture led to wasteful production processes and ultimately to conservation regulation by state commissions, such as compulsory unitization of oil fields to maximize recovery. The final two sections of the chapter discuss the application of the Clean Water Act to oil and gas operations and the remedial legislation used to address oil spills following the Exxon Valdez catastrophe and pipeline safety after a tragic pipeline explosion in New Mexico

Chapter Seven launches the reader into the geopolitics of international oil and to the legal doctrines which govern arbitration and litigation against multinational oil companies exploring and developing oil and gas abroad. The chapter first traces the nationalistic birth of OPEC, the rise and fall of oil prices during the 1970s and 1980s, and a statistical overview of the international oil industry. It also discusses the Peak Oil debate that is often headlined in today's media: Are we running out of oil? The chapter then compares the early concession agreements used by the major oil companies to exploit foreign reserves with the modern forms of agreements used today. The chapter concludes with a discussion of our national energy security in a troubled global world.

Chapter Eight introduces the reader to the "golden fuel" of natural gas, prized for its cleaner-burning qualities. The chapter first presents a sweep of the changing gas industry landscape, especially its resource base and price trends. The chapter discusses the pre-1985 regulatory and business models that governed gas production and pipelines before restructuring and then takes up the gas industry's post-1985 transition to competitive markets and open access pipelines, as a precursor to the same transition in the electricity industry. The materials illustrate the major problems encountered on the rocky road to restructuring the natural gas industry: industrial bypass; protecting the residential consumer; resolving billions of dollars of "stranded costs" in the form of take-or-pay liabilities; and preventing affiliate abuse. The chapter concludes with a look at LNG, the imported gas that is to rescue us from declining domestic production and record-high natural gas prices.

Chapter Nine explores an issue that cuts across all sectors of the energy business: how to provide energy services without creating serious environmental damage to sensitive areas. The chapter discusses four examples, two involving specific regions of international significance—the Amazon basin and the North Slope of Alaska—and two relating to more common and diffuse resources—wetlands and coastlines—where the cumulative impact of energy development poses significant issues.

Chapter Ten introduces electricity. The structure of the existing industry is discussed, along with some explanation of the historical debates that led to the current structure. The chapter discusses the ways in which government laws and policies have tried to promote conservation of electricity. It reviews some of the problems associated with electricity transmission, and it explores the growing interest in small scale, on-site electricity generation. This chapter serves as background for the next four chapters which explore changes taking place in the electricity business.

Chapter Eleven discusses wholesale competition in the electric power industry in the U.S., a major change to the traditional natural monopoly structure of the industry. Given the jurisdictional split between federal and state regulators under federal electric power statutes, most wholesale regulation decisions occur at the federal level. The chapter discusses the major regulatory decisions to date that will define the nature of power competition. In addition, the chapter introduces federal approaches to regulating power transmission and emerging new power generators and brokers in a competitive power industry.

Chapter Twelve discusses retail competition in the U.S. electric power industry. After exploring the complex issues posed by restructuring at the retail level, the chapter looks at the structure of retail competition plans, with in-depth analyses of such issues as consumer protection. The chapter analyzes the failure of retail competition in California and summarizes the current status of and prospects for the future of retail competition across the nation, with a discussion of innovations such as aggregation and net metering that could play a role in a competitive future.

Chapter Thirteen discusses environmental issues in electric power generation. The chapter focuses on the role of renewable energy resources and energy conservation in the changing utility landscape. The chapter also surveys new approaches to environmental regulation, such as green pricing, and discusses limitations on state regulation, such as those presented by the Commerce Clause.

Chapter Fourteen explores the use of nuclear power to generate electricity. It reviews the development of new nuclear facilities overseas and discusses the laws that affect the outlook for any resumption of nuclear construction in this country. It reviews some of the problems faced by the nuclear industry in the past, and explores the issues associated with the disposal of radioactive waste, which present the most serious obstacle to the growth of nuclear power.

Chapter Fifteen looks at energy in transportation. Each year, every ship, plane, train and motor vehicle in the United States becomes increasingly dependent on imported oil. Burning all that oil is growing more expensive, and is contributing to air pollution and climate change. Are there realistic measures that can be adopted to reduce these economic and environmental impacts? The chapter looks at existing and proposed legal and technological ways of addressing this problem.

Chapter Sixteen examines briefly one of the most complex and contentious scientific issues that presents a major problem for the energy sector – the concern about climate change. After reviewing the scientific consensus about the continuing increase in global average temperatures, the chapter summarizes some potential impacts and looks at the efforts of domestic and international bodies to curb or reduce greenhouse gas emissions.

A NOTE ON EDITING

In common with traditional casebook practice, excerpts from cases, books and other sources have usually been edited to eliminate material not directly relevant to the topic of discussion. Ellipses are routinely used to designate omitted material, but footnotes and citations have often been excised without so indicating. Asterisks are also used to indicate the deletion of substantial amounts of material. Where footnotes have been included the footnote number from the original sometimes precedes our footnote number. Where multiple citations are found in the original, only the West citation of U.S. citation has been included. A reader who plans to rely on any of the excerpted material for research purposes is advised to consult the original.

*

ACKNOWLEDGEMENTS

Fred Bosselman acknowledges the help of Katherine Hausrath, Jayne Hoffman, Rey Phillips and Rebecca Schanz in the preparation of material for the book.

Joel B. Eisen wishes to thank Crista Whitman, Michael Wall, Anne Haith, and Heather Lyons and the outstanding librarians of the University of Richmond School of Law for their research assistance, and the School of Law for summer research grants which supported work on articles in this field and on this book. The Robert R. Merhige Jr. Center of Environmental Law at the School of Law supported an energy law symposium which featured an exchange of ideas that improved the book. Thanks are also due to the judges and staff of the Virginia State Corporation Commission (especially Allison Held) for their support and assistance.

Jim Rossi thanks Tandy Blackburn and Laura Rushin for their research assistance in the preparation of chapters. He also thanks his current and former students for their insights about the materials and Dean Don Weidner for providing support for preparation of the manuscript.

David Spence wishes to thank colleagues, students and especially research assistants (particularly Reece Norris) at the University of Texas at Austin for their support and assistance in the preparation of this book.

Jacqueline Weaver thanks the University of Houston Law Foundation, its many donors, and especially the A.A. White family for providing funds for research support for this casebook. Pete Egler, Public Reference librarian extraordinaire at the Law Center, never failed to provide the timely information, reports, and citations needed to keep abreast of all relevant developments since the first edition. Two gifted law students, Jeff Sinclair and Carrie Clark, Class of 2007 researched, wrote synopses, updated data, proofed and did "just one more emergency request" in a short time period with great skill. The energy seminar presentation on LNG terminals by Irena Agalliu, Class of 2005, made the new LNG section easy to add. Professor Steve Arbogast at the Bauer School of Business at the University of Houston commented on drafts and added key insights based on his extensive knowledge of international energy projects. And, for infinite patience, especially with late-night computer bugaboos, my deepest thanks go to my husband Kirk Weaver.

All five authors thank Craig Hartman for his diligent support in coordinating the manuscript and in obtaining copyright permissions for the materials excerpted in the book.

*

SUMMARY OF CONTENTS

*

TABLE OF CONTENTS

*

TABLE OF CASES

Principal cases are in bold type. Non-principal cases are in roman type. References are to Pages.

CASES AND MATERIALS

ENERGY, ECONOMICS AND THE ENVIRONMENT

*

CHAPTER 1

INTRODUCTION

A. THE IMPORTANCE OF ENERGY

The energy sector of the economy is undergoing major changes. Old systems of regulation are being supplanted by policies that emphasize competition. Scientific and technological advances, and wildly fluctuating markets, make companies' long-range plans obsolete quickly. Older firms merge and consolidate across traditional sector boundaries in order to meet the competition of entrepreneurial new entrants. The environmental sciences raise new and increasingly complex issues, such as climate change and the meaning of sustainable development, that impact the energy industries significantly. Privatization of state-owned energy companies reaches to all corners of the globe. It is an exciting time to be working in energy.

1. EMERGING ISSUES: A TOP 10 LIST

We recognize that in approaching a subject such as energy law, students are often overwhelmed with the specialized nature of the materials. Without pandering to popular culture or to the false comfort that

1

knowledge about the quickly evolving area of energy law and policy can be conveyed in sound bites or consensus predictions, we nonetheless believe that lawyers practicing in this area do confront common themes, and that it is possible to speculate about the major issues they are likely to face in the coming decade.

As co-authors, we have developed our own consensus about some emerging themes. Everyone seems to love "top ten lists." So we offer our own "top ten" list of issues in energy law for the coming decade. First, a quick formulation in the polemical style in which they often appear in debate. Then, a more nuanced explanation:

1. Are we "locking up" too many of our energy resources—making them unavailable for what may be dubious environmental reasons?

2. Are we blindly following a path toward fossil fuel exhaustion and global overheating while giving only token support to the development of renewable resources?

3. Has our fear of too much federal government power created gridlock in which each state or local government, Indian tribe or neighborhood association can block economically efficient energy policies?

4. Can we attract capital to develop energy resources if constant changes in laws and regulatory policy create an atmosphere of insecurity?

5. Have we failed to create enough incentives for the private sector to build the transmission networks that get energy to where it is needed?

6. Can we meaningfully address the problem of global warming without radically altering our lifestyles and destroying our economic competitiveness?

7. With deregulated energy markets causing increasingly volatile price swings, will elected officials be able to resist the public backlash, especially if rolling brownouts and blackouts accompany the transition?

8. Does our existing regulatory system impose needless roadblocks that hamper the introduction of more efficient energy technologies, such as fuel cells and gas microturbines?

9. Are mega-mergers and cartels in the energy sector producing greedy behemoths that are beyond effective government control?

10. At the local level, will urban sprawl, dying species, traffic congestion and choking air pollution arouse a public desire for a less frantic pace of life and greener communities?

1) *Land availability.* Since so many energy resources are tied to land use, one issue that will undeniably be at the fore is whether land is available for resource exploitation. In the U.S., the predominant issue is public land availability. Will the U.S. decide to open up the Arctic National Wildlife Refuge or other areas of Alaska to oil and gas

leasing? Similarly, will offshore areas (on the East and West Coasts) be open to federal leasing, and will this be with or without the support of the coastal states? The flip side: Will additional areas of public lands be preserved for wilderness or national parks as recreation and preservation uses triumph over development uses? Outside of the U.S., land availability will also be of great significance. Will leasing and development proceed abroad in areas of fragile and unique ecosystems, such as rainforests, coral reefs, and tundra? Or will international pressures from environmental and human rights groups, debt-for-nature swaps, and lack of World Bank or IMF financing result in certain areas being considered "lands unsuitable" for exploitation? A related question: Will the principle of sustainable development become an international norm for oil and gas development? If so, can it work in practice in the oil and gas industry?

2) *Renewable energy.* Will green energy and renewables be able to compete in the marketplace for energy without government subsidies? Should they be subsidized, or are subsidies just boondoggles for special interest groups? What other methods exist, aside from PURPA's avoided cost rates, for encouraging renewable power? Will consumers be willing to pay extra for a "green energy" provider when retail competition in energy comes to their door?

3) *Federalism.* Will the rights or desires of the local population (states, provinces, tribes, and cities) ultimately trump federal development (or nondevelopment) policies? How will the tension be resolved between federal and state jurisdiction over energy resources and over the emerging players in industry? In the electricity context, these players include brokers, marketers, power exchanges, and regional transmission organizations ("RTOs"). How does the dormant Commerce Clause limit the scope of state regulation—and how does international law limit the scope of national regulation—in a competitive environment?

4) *Regulatory transitions.* Will stable contract and property norms exist to attract energy project financing, especially in light of regulatory transitions in the industry? In recent years, as competition has evolved in the electric power and natural gas industries, restructuring has had to confront the "stranded cost" issue. However, the issue of stability also arises in more traditional applications of contract law and takings jurisprudence in other energy industry sectors, such as coal and oil.

5) *Network regulation.* How will network access for electricity transmission and natural gas pipelines be priced in a competitive environment? Will there be adequate incentives for transmission capacity expansion? Will economic regulation encourage new transmission facilities, such as pipelines to bring the natural gas in Alaska to market in the lower forty-eight states, and how will new construction hurdle political and environmental opposition?

6) *International climate change.* Will the science of climate change have developed enough so that we will know the full extent to which

human use of energy is responsible for global warming? Even if the science is not fully developed, will the precautionary principle result in real reductions in greenhouse gas emissions? Can this be accomplished without significant reductions in energy use? How will the burden of reducing greenhouse gas emissions be allocated between developed and developing nations?

7) *Market volatility.* With increased reliance on markets to deliver energy products and services, will there be greater price and service quality volatility? In the electricity sector, regulators need to address transmission expansion and reliability in electric power because neither federal nor state regulators have the authority to order more transmission. What impact, if any, will this have on reliability? Will there be adequate supplies of natural gas at current prices to meet all of the demands projected for it? Will OPEC continue to have market power over oil prices?

8) *New technologies and the mix of energy uses.* Will small-scale, gas-fired electric generating plants, known as distributed generation, make increasing inroads in the market, and how will this affect the electric power industry? Will the technology for the use of fuel cells in automotive engines continue to improve, and what fuel and fuel distribution system will prove to be the most effective? Does the government have a role to play in encouraging the development of new technologies? Will the growing cost of natural gas and increasing environmental regulation of coal stimulate interest in a new generation of nuclear power plants? What will be the pace of technological change in clean coal combustion processes, and will coal have a future in the U.S. under the Clean Air Act and the Surface Mining Control and Reclamation Act?

9) *Merger policy and antitrust.* What are the legal and economic issues associated with unbundling the formerly integrated functions of energy companies? Will competitive restructuring ultimately result in antitrust problems due to affiliate transactions, spinoffs, and mergers? How will affiliate transactions be regulated? Do monopoly bottlenecks simply move to gas gathering pipelines at the state level once open access to interstate pipelines succeeds at the federal level? Will the power of private codes of conduct for multinational companies and organizations result in an effective system of corporate and country monitoring of environmental, health and human rights effects of energy development? What antitrust issues will be raised by voluntary regulation? Can antitrust law effectively guard the marketplace against international cartels and mega-mergers?

10) *Emerging environmental issues.* Will concern about salmon and other species at risk force the shutdown of significant amounts of hydroelectric energy? Will growing traffic congestion due to urban sprawl increase the demand for less energy-intensive patterns of land development? Are higher energy prices a necessary predicate to inducing conservation?

2. Scope of the Book

This book is intended to provide an overview of the legal issues raised in regulation of the energy sector. "Energy law" has been defined as "the allocation of rights and duties concerning the exploitation of all energy resources between individuals, between individuals and governments, between governments and between states." Adrian J. Bradbrook, Energy Law as an Academic Discipline, 14 J. Energy & Nat. Res. L. 193, 194 (1996). At the beginning of the twenty-first century, energy law sits at the intersection of environmental law, natural resources law, and regulated industries.

It also sits at the epicenter of a clash of public values. In fact, the title of this casebook should perhaps be rearranged to Economics, Energy, and the Environment, to place energy in the center of a tug-of-war between the two other forces. We want clean energy, but we don't want high energy prices. We want pristine coasts and coral reefs, untouched tundra and rainforests, and clean air and water, but also, comfortable cars, heat and light at our fingertips, and cold beer. Will technological changes in the energy industry bridge the near-schizophrenic gap between the two sets of values? Will the clash between environmental regulation and competition in the global marketplace lead us to "greener" energy or to less energy, to production at home or imports from foreign lands, to the rebirth of nuclear energy or to planting trees as carbon sinks? What are the lessons of history here?

This casebook provides a framework for readers to use in assessing and analyzing the many forces directed at the energy industry today. It is an interdisciplinary blend of history and future projection, of science and technology, of policies made by many levels of political bodies—local, regional, national, and international—and of legal doctrines as ancient as the common law of custom and as new as the internet-posted administrative rulings of state and federal energy commissioners on energy restructuring. All private actors within this framework—energy producers, distributors, traders, endusers, shareholders, and consumers—will be jostled in this tug-of-war for the "public interest," the balance between clean energy and cheap energy. Some will emerge as winners; others as losers. None will escape the pull of these forces.

Much of the environmental law movement of the last three decades was sparked by energy-related events: the Santa Barbara oil spill, the Exxon Valdez, Chernobyl and Three Mile Island. Much of our legal framework for regulated industries and antitrust law derives from our now century-old experiences with problems of monopoly in the energy industry. Much of our current energy policy is directed at adjusting our policy framework from an era of energy crisis (the 1970s and early 1980s) to an era of energy availability in the 1990s and now back to an era of scarcity and market turmoil. Energy law and policy plays on a large stage. It deserves its own casebook.

a. ENVIRONMENTAL LAW

In most U.S. law schools, the traditional environmental law course surveys the major federal statutes, such as the National Environmental Policy Act, the Clean Air Act, the Federal Water Pollution Control Act, and the various hazardous and solid waste disposal statutes. Many law schools supplement this offering with natural resource courses, which cover water issues. wetlands preservation, wildlife management, biodiversity, and the protection of national parks and other resources, such as timber. These courses focus on the statutory and common-law bases for regulation across a variety of activities and uses threatening to the environment.

This casebook is designed to bridge the gap between the environmental, natural resources, and regulated industries curriculums. The materials comprise the core readings for an introductory survey of the legal and policy issues concerning energy resources, conservation, and use. Such a course should be of interest to students of both environmental law and economic regulation. Like traditional courses in environmental and natural resources law, this book addresses problems of conservation, externalities, and pollution control. The surveyed topics include: ownership of and access to energy resources; siting of energy facilities, such as pipelines and power plants; and the mechanisms for regulating pollution emission by existing energy sources. In addition, the book introduces long-term planning mechanisms, such as integrated resource planning, and conservation-minded mechanisms, such as demand-side management.

But the scope of this book also departs significantly from the traditional environmental law curriculum offering. First, by providing an in-depth, context-specific study of the environmental issues affecting energy resources, this book provides a focused lens through which to examine the issues raised by environmental regulation. Students are more likely to grasp with depth the basics of environmental regulation if they see the issues recur in similar contexts, as opposed to an unrelated variety of waste-emitting contexts. One commentator has observed that the relationship between energy and environmental law is interesting because "energy issues sometimes divide the environmental movement" and energy law "concentrates on the causes, rather than the effects, of environmental problems." Bradbrook, *supra*, at 215–16.

Second, this book promotes a greater awareness of the economic issues affecting the environment than the traditional environmental course, both because of its context-specific approach and because of the history of our regulatory scheme. Many of the topics covered in this book have traditionally been studied as public utility law because most energy sources were believed to possess natural monopoly characteristics and were regulated as public utilities. Natural monopoly conditions exist where a single firm can provide a good or service at a lower average cost than two or more firms. To capture these economies of scale, a single firm is often awarded a monopoly franchise to provide service, but then regulators must prevent the franchised monopoly from earning excess profits at the expense of the consumer. In fact, one way to approach this book is to use it as an example of applied public utility or regulatory law.

Although some may question whether the study of economic regulation has a place in the environmental curriculum, we obviously think it does. An economic approach to resource allocation gives students an understanding of resource use and cost, an approach often slighted or missing from the traditional environmental curriculum. Many environmental law teachers complain that students lack a context for understanding the opportunity costs of environmental regulation. We find that those persons with environmental protection sympathies, sympathies with which we intuitively agree, tend instinctively to favor government regulation—often outright prohibition—of activities that produce any perceived harmful effect on the environment. However, regulation has costs. The material presented here provides a more pragmatic context for the study of environmental issues than often found in the traditional curriculum.

b. NATURAL RESOURCES

The energy industries increasingly employ highly entrepreneurial and creative people. But they do not "create" energy. The laws of thermodynamics tell us that we cannot create energy; we can only *transform* it. We must start with the resources found in nature and convert them to forms suitable to meet our needs.

Energy law can effectively be studied in coordination with courses in natural resources law or oil and gas law that focus on the private and public law relating to the extraction of energy resources. While this book does not include a detailed analysis of the leases, concession agreements, and conservation laws applicable to energy extraction, it does provide a solid overview of the different systems used to grant and regulate rights to produce minerals, particularly petroleum, both in the United States and abroad. Energy is only one of the natural resources valued by citizens today. We also value, and indeed put price tags on, otters and sea turtles, whales and wetlands, wilderness and ocean views. Indeed, we swap "debt for nature" internationally to preserve other nations' rainforests. Of all industries in the world, issues of sustainable development most pervade the extractive industries which exploit nonrenewable resources like oil, gas and coal. The classic resource paradigm of the Tragedy of the Commons often appears as an energy policy issue.

Many of these natural resources issues are addressed through national policies, often advanced by presidential administrations. To date, none of these policies have successfully addressed the complex range of energy issues the nation confronts in anything approaching a comprehensive manner. As one author notes in his criticism of national efforts to integrate energy policy:

> Law schools, often the laboratories of future policy, now appear poised to go where presidential administrations have floundered—by integrating energy, environmental, and natural resource policy. The growth of environmental law programs in law schools throughout the 1990s is

well known, accompanied by an escalating number of environmental law journals and available textbooks—whether for environmental law in general or more recently for specific areas that embrace natural resources, such as Wildlife Law or The Law of Biodiversity and Ecosystem Management. But in the past few years, an increasing number of law schools are now also offering energy law (non-oil and gas or mineral law) courses to complement their environmental and natural resource law program.... We can expect this trend to continue, and eventually metamorphose into multidisciplinary programs.

Sam Kalen, Replacing a National Energy Policy With a National Resource Policy, Natural Resources and the Environment, Winter 2005, at 9.

c.　REGULATED INDUSTRIES

Regulated industries courses in most law schools address many of the problems associated with markets in vital industries such as health care, transportation, food and drug, telecommunications, and banking. Two very different bodies of economic laws—one general, the other more specific—govern most of these industries. At the general level, each industry is subject to some degree of regulation under state and federal antitrust statutes which promote competition and guard against monopolistic abuses. In terms of doctrine and principles, antitrust law varies little from industry to industry since each industry is subject to the same statutes and case law. More specifically, public utility law, implemented by courts and administrative agencies also applies to many key industries. Public utility law varies more than antitrust law from industry to industry. Industry-specific statutes and regulations usually guide the application of public law principles.

This book provides a fertile context for discussion of reforms in economic and environmental regulation. In recent years the energy industry has moved away from the natural monopoly model and toward market-based mechanisms. This movement provides an excellent context in which to study the interplay between economic competition and environmental protection. How, for instance, can regulators ensure that a competitive electricity industry—one which uses the lowest-priced energy source—does not abuse our air, land, or water, or prematurely deplete our supply of non-renewable resources? What is the relationship between market-based mechanisms for energy resource allocation and the market-based mechanisms reformers have embraced in environmental law, such as tradable air emissions allowances? Are environment-sensitive mechanisms such as integrated resource planning and demand-side management necessarily at odds with competition? By giving students exposure to environmental regulatory mechanisms in the context of energy resource use, this book will supplement—certainly not displace or undermine—the traditional environmental curriculum.

In turn, the complexity of the real environmental issues facing the energy sector present a challenge to students who approach regulation from a theoretical economic perspective. The values that people attach to the environment are often hard to quantify, and sometimes even hard to define. Recent history is replete with expert economists' prescriptions for addressing environmental issues that died on the vine because they failed to understand public attitudes. An understanding of the history of environmental law brings increasing humility to teacher and student alike.

Last, but certainly not least, this book aspires to prepare students for the practice of energy law—not in the narrower economic context of a traditional public utility law course, but with a fuller sense of responsibility for the environment. The field of energy law promises to be a growing one for years to come as changing regulatory conditions create new legal problems and opportunities. As a specialty, energy law offers a challenging and productive opportunity for lawyers throughout the country. Some students will want to follow up on the materials covered in this book with more specialized courses in topics such as oil and gas law, mining law, federal land and resources law, international energy transactions, international environmental law, government regulation, and administrative law. The world of energy spans all of these.

3. ENERGY RESOURCES AND POLICY

> "Energy can be neither created nor destroyed, only converted from one form to another."
>
> —The First Law of Thermodynamics.
>
> "All physical processes proceed in such a way that the availability of the energy involved decreases."
>
> —The Second Law of Thermodynamics.

Energy is "the power by which anything or anybody acts effectively to move or change other things or persons." Howard Mumford Jones, The Age of Energy 104–05 (1971). This is a physical definition of energy, but one which needs some qualification as we begin to immerse ourselves in the legal problems posed by the energy sector of the economy. We cannot live without physical energy, either alone as individuals or together in our society. Even a Robinson Crusoe, stranded alone on a deserted island, is dependent upon energy. After a day of hard work (the exertion of energy), a Crusoe, feeling low on energy, may eat a meal of bananas to energize his body, and that meal will give energy to a whole set of digestive processes—(thankfully) far beyond the scope of this book.

This book is concerned with the societal—not the individual—implications of physical energy. Although burn-out is a low-energy feeling we each may at times have experienced, we happily leave this problem to the doctors, dieticians, psychologists, or astrologists of the world. We will focus our attention in this book on human beings' discovery, creation, transfer, and distribution of physical energy among themselves to improve their collective social lives.

Can you live your daily life without physical energy, so conceived? Think about your daily routine. You wake up to the noise of an alarm clock—powered perhaps by electricity, perhaps by batteries, but even if it is a wind-up mechanical clock it was made in a factory using a variety of energy sources. You turn on the shower. The fact that water comes out of the faucet is impossible without some use of energy to move the water and create pressure. You like your water hot, heated by natural gas, oil, or electricity. You have not left your home and may not have seen another individual, yet you have used a variety of energy resources.

As your day goes on you will rely even more on energy resources. Perhaps you drive a car fueled by gasoline, or take a train powered by electricity or a bus that runs on natural gas. You will sit in a classroom with lights, powered by electricity generated at a nuclear, hydro, or fossil fuel plant. You will eat a warm lunch, or perhaps a cold salad kept crisp by some form of energy. While writing a paper, you—like us—will rely on electricity to power your computer. You will go home and listen to the radio or a compact disk or the TV, or call a friend, perhaps leaving a message on an answering machine. Virtually every minute of your day requires you to use energy resources. Our daily lives would be dull, inefficient, and downright difficult without energy.

a.   ENERGY RESOURCES

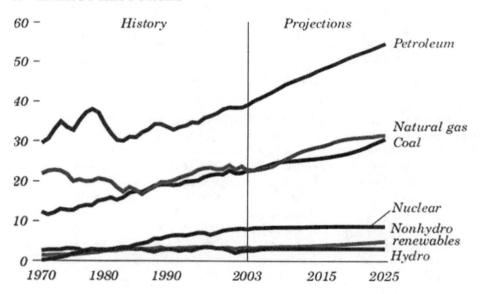

Figure 1–1
Annual Energy Use By Source, 1970–2025 (Energy Information Administration)

The predominant energy resources—both in terms of supply and demand—are fossil fuels, such as oil, coal, and natural gas. Nonetheless, renewable energy resources have historically been important as well. Renewable energy resources are of two different types. "Cool" renewable resources do not require burning to convert energy. For example, the Niagara Dam generates electricity by turning turbines with natural water pressure. Similarly, the sun, wind, or underground pressure or heat may generate electricity without the burning of a primary resource. Non-cool renewable resources, such as wood, biomass or waste, must be burned to convert energy.

Electricity is an extremely important energy resource, but it differs fundamentally from the resources mentioned above. Unlike fossil fuel and renewable resources, which can be either primary or secondary resources, electricity is a secondary resource that is dependent on a primary energy resource as an input. Electricity can only be produced by converting any of the primary resources.

Before introducing the legal and policy themes addressed in this book, it is useful to begin by reviewing some facts about the U.S.'s position in the world-wide energy scenario. First, the U.S. has historically had abundant and accessible energy resources, a fact that has no doubt contributed to our economic growth. According to the Energy Information Administration, as of 2004 almost all of the coal and almost 90 percent of the natural gas consumed in the U.S. was produced from domestic sources. Petroleum imports were a relatively small portion of U.S. demand until the 1970s, when rising demand and falling supply sharply increased oil imports. There is some question as to whether our reliance on domestic resources can continue, but any examination of energy law and policy issues in the U.S. must recognize that this issue is closely intertwined with our economic and industry growth.

Second, the U.S. is the largest consumer of energy resources in the world. The U.S. consumes about one-fourth of worldwide energy consumption each year. One author notes, "[c]ompared with people elsewhere, Americans are less self-conscious about how unsustainable a high-energy society is and, historically speaking, less aware of the anomaly of high energy use...." David E. Nye, Path Insistence: Comparing European and American Attitudes Toward Energy, 53 J. Intl. Affairs 129, 130 (1999). According to the same author, "Americans have become so 'path dependent' that they only become aware of energy during a blackout or gasoline shortage." *Id.* If this is true, policymakers need to reflect seriously on how the behavior of Americans will change in reaction to legal and economic incentives.

Third, since the energy crises of the 1970s, the U.S. has grown increasingly dependent on fossil fuel imports, particularly petroleum. As **Figure 1–2** illustrates, the U.S. is a net energy importer. Overall, the U.S. consumes more energy resources than it produces, and this disparity between demand and supply is particularly large with respect to oil. We consume more oil than any of the other primary energy resources. Over a third of the oil produced in the world is consumed in the United States. As the 1991 Persian Gulf war reminded us, the U.S. is increasingly dependent upon other countries for its oil supply. While oil imports comprised only one-third of U.S. consumption in 1983, by 1990 imports supplied one-half of the oil consumed in the U.S. and the percentage continues to increase steadily. Net gas imports are also growing significantly. Increasingly any discussion of energy law and policy—even if limited to the U.S.—takes on global ramifications.

Figure 1-2

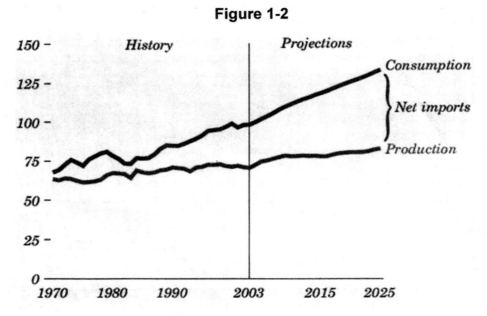

Figure 1–2
Total U.S. Energy Production and Consumption, 1970–2025 (Energy Information Administration)

Fourth, the fact that we are increasingly so dependent on imported petroleum means that attention is focused on the sector of the economy that uses most of that petroleum, the transportation sector. Automobiles, trucks, airplanes and railroad trains all run on fuels derived from petroleum. The transportation sector in the United States uses a much higher amount of petroleum per person that in any other country. This has led to a reexamination of our standards for engines, motor vehicles, and fuels, and even to a reconsideration of the patterns of "urban sprawl" that make us so dependent on the automobile.

Fifth, our integrated electricity transmission network ties the United States together and makes possible the dramatic changes in information technology that are fueling the economy. Electricity generation utilizes more than one-third of the primary energy resources consumed in the U.S. The debates about the choice of resources used to produce electricity have been some of the most volatile in American politics, and have produced a complex array of laws that attempt to balance the economic benefits, safety risks, and environmental attributes, of the competing fuels: coal, oil, natural gas, uranium, hydro, and various other renewable resources.

Finally, energy resources have had an extensive influence on economic growth and development in the U.S. The estimated value of primary energy sources (inputs) in the U.S. economy is 5 percent of GNP. These primary energy resources have significant uses in the residential, commercial, industrial, and transportation sectors of the economy. With end-use products and services, energy sources comprise as much as 12 percent of GNP. Although the materials in this book may seem specialized at times, their ramifications reverberate far throughout the economy.

b. U.S. ENERGY POLICY AND LEGISLATION

The vast majority of U.S. energy production, transportation, and distribution resources are privately owned. Why regulate energy resources? Here suffice it to say that this will be a topic we return to time and time again throughout the book. For now, let us limit ourselves to some historical background. For an excellent survey of the history of energy legislation, see David Howard Davis, Energy Politics (4th ed. 1993).

Regulation of energy resources by state and local governments began late in the nineteenth century. The production of oil and gas was regulated by state agencies to avoid physical waste and, not coincidentally, to keep up the price. At the consumption end, local governments typically authorized a private company to sell gas and electricity to the consumer by issuing a franchise that provided that the company's rates and service were subject to local regulation. As these franchises proliferated, state legislatures often preempted the regulation of rates and services by creating a public utility commission.

Until the New Deal era, most energy resources were regulated at the state or local level. This early regulation, primarily by state utility boards, focused on setting the rates for a local monopoly-franchised utility. In 1920, Congress took some nominal steps by passing what is known today as Part I of the Federal Power Act ("FPA"), which established the Federal Power Commission ("FPC") and gave it authority to establish hydroelectric projects on navigable waters. *See* 16 U.S.C. § 791a *et seq.* That year, Congress also passed the Mineral Leasing Act, which brought some consistency to oil and gas leasing on federal lands. *See* 30 U.S.C. § 181.

The New Deal marked the dawn of the era of contemporary federal energy regulation, as well as the growth of economic regulation more generally. In 1935, Congress passed the Public Utility Holding Company Act ("PUHCA"), to monitor and regulate ownership interests and stock holdings of public utilities. *See* 15 U.S.C. § 79–79z. (PUHCA had a major impact on the structure of the industry for 70 years but was repealed in the Energy Policy Act of 2005.) That same year, Congress added Part II to the FPA, which gave the FPC the authority to regulate wholesale electric utility rates. *See* 16 U.S.C. § 824 *et seq.* In 1938, Congress enacted the Natural Gas Act ("NGA"), which gave the FPC the authority to regulate the rates of interstate natural gas pipelines. *See* 15 U.S.C. § 717–717z. In 1954, the U.S. Supreme Court extended the FPC's jurisdiction to wellhead prices for interstate natural gas. *See Phillips Petroleum Co. v. Wisconsin*, 347 U.S. 672 (1954). Since then, Congress has continued to address major energy issues in a complex array of environmental and economic statutes that make up the "working capital" of today's energy lawyers, such as the 2005 Energy Policy Act.

c. LAW AND POLICY THEMES

As the previous discussion suggests, the regulation of energy resources takes place within a legislative tangle of state and federal statutes, often reviewed by courts using administrative law principles of judicial review. However, many energy issues are also addressed under common-law rules of property and contracts, even in the global arena where private companies contract with government entities for the right to develop state-owned resources. Certain legal and policy themes have a tendency to recur, regardless of the energy source or particular statutory scheme at issue. We will often return to the constitutional themes of federalism under the Commerce Clause and Takings under the Fifth Amendment. Environmental law, antitrust law, and economic regulation appear in every individual resource chapter. International law—both the "hard" law of treaties and international custom and the "softer" law of United Nations resolutions on expropriation, human rights, the rights of indigenous peoples—already plays an important role in the development of petroleum reserves overseas by multinational companies, many of which have headquarters in the United States. International public law, particularly in the environmental arena, will increasingly affect all of the energy sources, not just petroleum.

B. GOVERNMENT REGULATION

Throughout the history of the United States, the development of new types of energy resources brought questions about whether these resources were appropriate subjects for control as natural monopolies or whether a competitive market could be developed. John D. Rockefeller's success in monopolizing the oil business led to the antitrust laws in the nineteenth century. Samuel Insull's similar success in the electricity business encouraged strict regulation of that industry. But over time, technological advances have made competition among different parts of the energy sector more feasible, and this has revived these age-old questions about the proper system of economic regulation. Meanwhile, however, new layers of environmental and conservation regulation have been added to the regulatory mix.

1. MULTIPLICITY OF REGULATORY AGENCIES

One feature of the energy industries that poses constant problems is the overlapping jurisdiction of a wide variety of regulatory agencies. During the same period as the federal government added regulatory programs specifically addressing energy issues, it also created a wide range of environmental regulatory programs that impacted the energy industries. And in many cases these programs paralleled but did not preempt similar regulatory programs adopted by the state and local governments.

a.   FEDERAL AGENCIES

Since many energy issues are addressed at the national policy level, federal agencies pay an important role in the energy sector. Among the federal agencies, the ones that most directly affect the energy industries are the Department of Energy ("DOE"), the Department of Interior ("DOI"), the Federal Energy Regulatory Commission ("FERC"), the Nuclear Regulatory Commission ("NRC") and the Environmental Protection Agency ("EPA").

The DOE sponsors energy research and plays a key role in international issues. DOI controls the federal lands, both onshore and offshore, from which much of our coal, oil and gas resources are extracted, and regulates the surface mining of coal. FERC regulates the construction of hydroelectric facilities and oversees the rates of natural gas and electricity to the extent they are transported in interstate commerce. FERC also articulates policies for the structure of natural gas and electric power markets.

The NRC regulates the construction and operation of nuclear power plants. EPA administers a variety of environmental programs that affect energy: for example, the Clean Air Act has a major impact on electric power plants and oil refineries and the Oil Pollution Act affects the operation of oil tankers.

By no means is this a complete list of federal regulatory programs that affect the energy industries. For example, the Department of Transportation has played some roles in the regulation of oil pipelines and Department of Labor implements safety standards for coal mines. Most of the larger energy companies maintain Washington D.C. offices, or employ legal counsel, to keep track of these regulatory programs.

b.   STATE AGENCIES

The state systems of public utility regulation have not been replaced by the new federal regulatory programs. Public utility commissions continue to regulate the rates, facilities and services of the private utilities that supply natural gas and electricity within the state. As we will see, definition of the precise line between state and federal jurisdiction over rates and service has produced a great deal of litigation.

The state governments also have environmental regulatory agencies that administer state programs and cooperate with the EPA in the administration of federal programs. For example, state agencies set water quality standards that have a major impact on the disposal of wastes from the production of energy resources.

c.   LOCAL AGENCIES

At the local level, energy companies often must comply with a wide range of land use regulations. Construction of new power lines, for example, is likely to run into local concerns that may be expressed through prohibitory regulations. In some states many such regulations have been preempted by state law.

Local governments also exercise power over electric and gas companies through control over the local streets which the companies need to use for delivery of services. In many places, local governments also use regulatory programs as a revenue-raising device through the addition of various fees to consumers' utility bills.

2.   FEDERALISM ISSUES

In view of the overlapping nature of the regulatory systems at the federal, state and local levels, it is not surprising that many of the key issues of energy law involve issues of federalism policy. Because the Supreme Court has begun to cast new attention to issues of "states' rights," energy lawyers are beginning to reexamine the constitutionality of some long-accepted balances between state and federal authority.

a.   IMPACTS BEYOND JURISDICTIONAL BOUNDARIES

Decisions involving energy resources are subject to the assertion of authority by three sovereigns: the state, the federal government, and the international community. It is useful to ask why the federal government should involve itself in the regulation of energy resources. Don't the states adequately regulate energy resources themselves? As a general matter, local regulation has the advantage of providing a regulatory solution that is most likely to respect and reflect the views of those individuals closest to the energy resources at issue.

However, state regulation may create negative spillover costs—a type of externality—for other states or regions that outweigh the benefits of localized control. In the Northeast, for example, pollution from automobiles may spill over from one state to another, and this may invite some type of federal or regional solution. In addition, economies of scale in production may transcend state borders. For example, although the pollution from automobiles may not drift from one state to another outside of the densely populated Northeast, automobile production does exhibit significant economies of scale: the cost per vehicle of meeting one uniform regulation is much lower than the costs of meeting multiple regulations in multiple states. *See* Margaret A. Walls, U.S. Energy and Environmental Policies: Problems of Federalism and Conflicting Goals, in Making National Energy Policy 95 (Hans H. Landsberg, ed. 1993); *but see* Richard L. Revesz, Rehabilitating Interstate Competition: Rethinking the "Race to the Bottom" Rationale for Federal Environmental Regulation, 67 N.Y.U. L. Rev. 1210 (1992).

b.   THE COMMERCE CLAUSE

The U.S. government's authority to regulate energy resources is far reaching under the Commerce Clause. Since 1937, Congress has had the authority to regulate purely intrastate activities that affect interstate commerce, such as electricity and natural gas generation, transmission, distribution.

In many instances, Congress has chosen not to regulate certain energy resource uses. For example, FERC's rate jurisdiction over electricity rates under the FPA extends to only wholesale transactions; Congress has left most matters of retail rate regulation to the states.

This dual regulatory scheme inevitably creates a conflict and has led to much litigation in the energy and environmental areas. As a legal matter, in some instances Congress may explicitly preempt state law, as it is normally allowed to do under the Supremacy Clause. Absent explicit preemption, dual federal and state regulation of energy resources is permissible provided none of the following occurs: state regulation does not frustrate congressional purposes (*Florida Lime & Avocado Growers, Inc. v. Paul*, 373 U.S. 132 (1963)); state law does not regulate conduct in a field Congress intended federal law to occupy exclusively (*California v. ARC America Corp.*, 490 U.S. 93 (1989)); or state law does not conflict directly with federal law. *Transcontinental Gas Pipe Line Corp. v. State Oil and Gas Bd. of Mississippi*, 474 U.S. 409 (1986).

Even in the absence of a federal statute, courts may strike down state statutes that discriminate against out-of-state commerce under the "dormant" Commerce Clause. For example, in *New England Power Co. v. New Hampshire*, 455 U.S. 331 (1982) the Supreme Court held that a state prohibition on the export of locally generated hydropower was unconstitutional for favoring New Hampshire citizens at the expense of out-of-state citizens. The Illinois legislature passed a law that required air quality compliance plans filed by large in-state utilities to consider scrubber installation at their power plants, favoring the usage of Illinois coal in electricity generation facilities. The U.S. Court of Appeals for Seventh Circuit struck the statute down because it discriminated against out-of-state coal producers in *Alliance for Clean Coal v. Miller*, 44 F.3d 591 (7th Cir. 1995). As the states become more concerned about air pollution flowing between the states, dormant commerce clause challenges are likely to become more common in the electricity regulation context.

Finally, federal or state regulation of energy resources may conflict with U.S. obligations under international law. Among these obligations are: the General Agreement on Tariffs and Trade and the North American Free Trade Agreement, which constitute an international obligation by the U.S. not to unilaterally impose impediments to trade with most of its energy trading partners; the International Energy Program Agreement, which commits the U.S. to plan for energy emergencies by maintaining oil reserves and supplies, and to provide assistance through the International Energy Agency in case of emergency situations; and the Nuclear Non–Proliferation Treaty and the programs of the International Atomic Energy Agency, which require the U.S. to restrict certain nuclear and related exports to nonsignatory countries and provide for international inspection systems. The U.S. also has entered into bilateral treaties and agreements with significant obligations concerning energy resources with Canada, Mexico, Venezuela, and Israel. The U.S. has assumed further obligations, particularly concerning global warming and CO_2 emissions, under international environmental treaties.

3.   COMPETITION

One way of understanding the economic and environmental regulation of the energy industry is to view it as governmental reaction to private market failure. Because a market with two or more firms may fail to provide energy resources at a price and quantity which would maximize consumer welfare, the government grants a monopoly franchise to a single firm and regulates its price to guard against monopolist abuses. Similarly, because the market fails to internalize many of the costs of energy resource extraction, conversion, and distribution processes, it is necessary to internalize these costs through environmental controls such as emissions standards, siting proceedings, demand-side management, and resource planning procedures.

In addition, in recent years, public choice theory, which applies economic analysis to government institutions and decisionmaking processes, has raised the concern that government regulation itself may be prone to certain failures. If the purpose of government regulation is to correct market failures, but regulation results in solutions that do not approximate the results of a perfectly functioning market, then regulation itself may have imposed unnecessary costs or inhibited self-correcting incentives.

a.   THE LIMITS OF REGULATION

Price and environmental regulation of energy resources is not without costs, for resource title holders and users as well as society. Regulation often has the unintended effect of falling short of its intended goals for several reasons.

First, the regulatory process may be susceptible to capture by the very interests it is designed to regulate and thus may fall short of its public interest objectives. This has been a recurring problem in the energy regulatory sector. Many of the New Deal modifications to electric utility regulation which extended federal jurisdiction were a reaction to this concern. However, as public choice scholars have recently reminded us, promotion of the public interest continues to be thwarted by rent seeking through the regulatory process. *See* George Stigler, The Theory of Economic Regulation, 2 Bell J. Econ. & Management Sci. 137 (1971); Sam Pelzman, Towards a More General Theory of Regulation, 19 J. L. & Econ. 211 (1976).

Second, regulation may cause regulated firms to incur excessive costs or adopt inefficient methods of operation. Economists sometimes refer to this as"X-Inefficiency." *See* John R. Meyer & William B. Tye, Toward Achieving Workable Competition in Industries Undergoing a Transition to Deregulation: A Contractual Equilibrium Approach, 5 Yale J. Reg. 273, 277–79 (1988). For example, to the extent that regulated firms expend their resources to capture the regulatory process, this creates an inefficiency. Richard A. Posner, The Social Costs of Regulation and Monopoly, 83 J. Pol.

Econ. 207 (1975). However, even if the "capture" theory of regulation is not entirely descriptive of the actual process, regulation creates artificial—and sometimes costly—incentives for behavior. A regulated public utility's rates are calculated on the basis of its revenue requirements, which include both rate base and operating expenses. Some economists have suggested that price regulation has induced many public utilities to artificially inflate their rate base and to overinvest in certain capital assets—e.g., to build too many power plants for their customer base. Harvey Averch & Leland L. Johnson, Behavior of the Firm Under Regulatory Constraint, 52 Am. Econ. Rev. 1052 (1962).

Third, jurisdictional conflicts may create controversies. Perhaps the most familiar of these is the conflict between state and federal regulators, creating the unsatisfactory situation "in which two different persons seek to drive one car." *See Louisiana Pub. Serv. Comm'n v. Fed. Communications Commission*, 476 U.S. 355 (1986). Such controversies may lead to overregulation, uncertainty, protracted litigation, and an inability to implement a regulatory scheme.

Jurisdictional problems are not limited to conflicts between the federal government and the states. There are also potential conflicts at the same level of government, as frequently occurs in developing and implementing national energy policy. One author sums up the problem:

> Past experience amply demonstrates that establishing a meaningful energy policy requires at the outset effective coordination of economic, national security, environmental, and natural resource policies. Today, many federal agencies are involved in responding to aspects of any energy policy. The Federal Energy Regulatory Commission (FERC) for the most part implements energy policy; a role it wrestled from the Department of Energy (DOE) during the mid–1970s when Congress created DOE. And while the U.S. Environmental Protection Agency (EPA) is considered the principal federal agency entrusted with environmental protection, the Department of the Interior (DOI), the National Marine Fisheries Service, the U.S. Forest Service, and the U.S. Army Corps of Engineers all implement aspects of environmental policy along with natural resource policy. Interior Secretary Gayle A. Norton, for instance, recently discussed the Bush administration's National Energy Policy, and in doing so conveyed her department's role, commenting that in addition to alternative energy sources "[w]e must also increase domestic production of traditional energy sources, especially natural gas," and recommended the use of best management practices to address environmental effects.

Kalen, *supra*. As this author suggests, "Establishing an energy policy that transcends each of the agencies involved is difficult, no matter how sound the policy may be. Each federal agency acts in accordance with its own statutory mission and responsibilities." *Id*. For example, "Any goal of promoting greater reliance on natural gas utilization similarly requires coordination among, and appreciation for, other agency mandates and concerns." This could require the coordination of DOE, DOI, and FERC, as "the infrastructure for transporting any new gas must be present, sufficient natural gas fields must be accessible, and the market and economic structure must allow for it." In some cases, congressional action may even be necessary to implement national goals.

b.   COMPETITIVE RESTRUCTURING

Failures in the regulation of energy resources have led regulators to consider market-oriented reforms of the regulatory process. In recent years, this market-oriented approach has driven massive reforms in the natural gas and electric utility contexts. In both contexts, federal regulators have taken a similar approach: unbundling and open access restructuring. In addition, regulators have considered mechanisms such as market-based rates, competitive bidding, and incentive regulation.

Many markets that have been subjected to cost-of-service regulation on the public utility model share a common trait: they are in fact several different markets with varying characteristics. For example, consider the natural gas market. There are thousands of producers and literally millions of consumers of natural gas. Apart from the need to transport gas, the gas sales market is as close to the economist's competitive ideal as any market. Transportation, however, is subject to large economies of scale and is a natural monopoly. Yet historically, sales and transportation have been bundled within a single rate-regulated service. Similarly, electric power generation and electricity transmission have traditionally been bundled into a single rate-regulated service, even though power generation, like natural gas sales, possesses characteristics of a competitive market.

Recognizing the benefits of markets where an industry possesses structurally competitive characteristics, in recent years FERC has implemented unbundling/equal access restructuring in the natural gas industry and has launched similar initiatives in the electric utility industry. This approach has two steps: first, the recognition that, rather than a single market, there are two or more distinctive markets, only one of which is a natural monopoly; second, the implementation of an equal-access regulatory scheme that applies only to the natural monopoly market.

Perhaps the simplest example of this two-step approach has already been implemented on a mass scale in the U.S. telecommunications industry. Beginning with the break-up of AT&T in the early 1980s, long-distance and local telephone services were "unbundled", so that regulators and firms were forced to treat them as distinctive markets, rather than as a single product provided by a single firm. Long-distance service was deemed to be structurally competitive. However, because AT&T continued to exercise monopoly power over long-distance transmission facilities, AT&T's monopoly was broken up and regulated separately to ensure open access to new long-distance firms. Today, consumers can choose among a variety of long-distance providers, but are usually captive to local service provision by a single firm.

Similarly, in the natural gas context, FERC completely unbundled pipeline sale and transportation in what has become to be known as "Order

636." Order 636 prohibited pipelines from providing a bundled service of sales and transportation. At the same time, however, interstate pipelines were required to provide equal access to storage and transportation services and to file a plan for implementing this new regime. *Pipeline Service Obligations and Revisions to Regulations Governing Self–Implementing Transportation and Regulation of Natural Gas Pipelines After Partial Wellhead Decontrol,* 57 Fed. Reg. 13,267 (1992), *order on reh'g,* 57 Fed. Reg. 36,128 (1992), *order on reh'g,* 57 Fed. Reg. 57,911 (1992), *remanded in part, United Distribution Co. v. FERC,* 88 F.3d 1105 (1996). This has led to an increase in competition for pipeline sales which, many suggest, was accrued to accrue to the benefit of consumers. *E.g.,* Robert J. Michaels, The New Age of Natural Gas: How the Regulators Brought Competition, Regulation, Winter 1993, at 68. However, it has also been observed that the costs of implementing Order 636, amounting to about $4.8 billion (General Accounting Office, Costs, Benefits and Concerns Related to FERC's Order 636 16 (1993)), are likely to be disproportionately borne by small consumers. *E.g.,* Joseph Fagan, Note, From Regulation to Deregulation: The Diminishing Role of the Small Consumer Within the Natural Gas Industry, 29 Tulsa L.J. 707 (1994).

FERC has recently made similar steps towards restructuring the electric utility industry. Congress gave FERC a clear signal that it would like to see more competition in wholesale electric power markets in the Energy Policy Act of 1992. In spring 1996, FERC approved a series of regulations that prohibit utilities from bundling wholesale electricity generation and transmission service. FERC regulations also require electric utilities to file an equal access transmission plan, which would facilitate competition in power generation markets. *Promoting Wholesale Competition Through Open Access Non-discriminatory Transmission Services by Public Utilities, Recovery of Stranded Costs by Public Utilities and Transmitting Utilities,* Docket No. RM95–8–000, RM94–7–001, 61 Fed. Reg. 21,539 (May 10, 1996). However, because FERC jurisdiction over electric utilities does not extend as far as its jurisdiction over natural gas pipelines, states retain jurisdiction over many aspects of the industry. Some states, such as California, Texas and Pennsylvania, have experimented with new regulatory regimes that give consumers a choice of their retail power provider, much as consumers are able to chose their long-distance provider. California's experiment was a notorious failure, but others state retail plans have not suffered the same fate.

In addition, FERC and state utility commissions have embarked upon a series of incremental changes to traditional utility price regulation. More than thirty states have instituted competitive bidding regimes for electric utilities, which require utilities to solicit and consider bids before building new power plants. FERC has approved market-based rates, which displace traditional cost-of-service filings, for power sellers that meet certain conditions. FERC and many state commissions have also adopted incentive regulation to encourage a variety of non-traditional utilities to enter into power markets. Together, these new regulatory efforts have sparked a considerable growth of new firms in traditional markets as well as the emergence of new pricing markets, such as spot and futures markets.

Regulators have not only used market-based mechanisms to displace price regulation. In the sulfur dioxide context, mandated technologies for coal-fired utility plants have been replaced with tradeable emissions allowances. In implementing a tradeable emissions program, the government gives a limited number of pollution permits to each emitter but allows the permit holder to trade them, effectively moving them to their highest valued use. However, to date the application of market mechanisms in the traditional pollution context has been limited.

It is unclear how competitive reform of the energy industry will affect environmental regulation mechanisms in the electricity context. Some have challenged the ability of competitive markets to co-exist with centralized decisionmaking mechanisms such as integrated resource planning. *E.g.*, Bernard S. Black and Richard J. Pierce, The Choice Between Markets and Central Planning in Regulating the U.S. Electricity Industry, 93 Colum. L. Rev. 1339 (1993). Others, however, maintain that there is a continued need for such mechanisms to correct market failures (*See* FERC: Electricity Demand Side Bidding: Hearing Before the Subcommittee on Energy and Power of the House Committee on Energy and Commerce, 100th Cong., 2d Sess. 3 (1988) (Statement of Ralph J. Cavanagh)) and to provide critical information for markets to succeed. *See* Carl Pechman, Regulating Power: The Economics of Electricity in the Information Age (1993). The tension between price competition and environmental regulation in the energy resource context is likely to dominate the agenda of federal and state decisionmakers for decades to come.

C.   THE GLOBAL ENVIRONMENT

Energy law is rapidly outgrowing national boundaries. Multinational oil companies have long operated throughout the world, but other parts of the energy industry have expanded internationally as well. American electric companies have expanded by buying electric companies in Europe, and European companies have expanded operations in the United States.

The environmental issues facing the energy sector are also increasingly global in nature. Development of energy resources in the tropical rainforest has implications for global biodiversity. And the most troublesome issue for the energy sector is the widespread and increasingly strong argument that the combustion of fossil fuels threatens to increase global temperatures and cause rising sea levels.

The speed and ubiquity of communication across international boundaries on the internet has brought increasing awareness of international human rights issues. International energy companies working as joint venturers with foreign government entities will have to address the concerns of indigenous people who argue that their own national governments and state-owned oil companies are violating international human rights. The world of energy spans the globe.

D. The Top 5 List of Worst Mistakes

While the top 10 list of emerging issues was forward looking, their solutions will often draw on the past. Throughout the book, we use the past as a reference point for understanding the future, in the belief that we should be able to learn from our mistakes. In this spirit, we also offer our consensus view of the five worst mistakes in energy law and regulation over the past century.

1) *Using price predictions to make policy.* Irrevocable and long-term policy choices have often been based on price forecasts which failed to account for the power of market forces or technological change. For instance, in the 1970s, the energy industry and government supported programs and investments based on the assumption that oil prices would climb relentlessly to $100 a barrel by the year 2000. This assumption contributed to decisions to build nuclear plants that later proved uneconomic relative to alternative energy resources.

2) *Smyth v. Ames*, 169 U.S. 466 (1898). This case endorsed a substantive due process approach to regulation, one that since has been overruled but still lingers in some regulators' decisions, such as recent decisions to compensate stranded costs in the electric power and natural gas industries.

3) *Different environmental standards for incumbents.* The congressional decision to grandfather existing power plants, exempting them from certain requirements of the Clean Air Act, has resulted in thirty years of delay in progress toward cleaner air, as has the failure to regulate diesel fuel at an earlier time.

4) *Reluctance to endorse the common carrier concept in natural gas and electricity transmission.* Until recently, federal regulators failed to recognize that natural gas pipelines and electricity transmission companies are common carriers. Oil pipelines, by contrast, were recognized as common carriers in1906. As a result, the gas and electricity sectors have required restructuring, often painful to both industry and consumers.

5) *Phillips Petroleum Co. v. Wisconsin,* 347 U.S. 672 (1954). In this case, the Supreme Court regulated the price of natural gas sold by producers into interstate commerce, transforming a competitive industry into a regulated industry. The approach of federal regulators led to a regulatory morass of gas shortages, enduse allocation, and take-or-pay liabilities. The natural gas precedent has influenced judicial limitations on federal regulation of electricity.

We welcome our readers to amend our lists with "hits" of their own as they make their way through the material in this casebook. Time will tell us whether our top issues and mistakes stay on the list as the 21st century counts down.

CHAPTER 2

THE RISE OF MARKET POWER IN ENERGY

A. Historical Origins
    1. The English Common Law
    2. The Classic American Cases
B. Regulatory Objectives
    1. Theories of Regulation
    2. Natural Monopoly
    3. Price Regulation
C. The Rise of Market Power and the Traditional Tasks of the Regulatory Commission
D. General Legal Limits on Regulation
    1. Constitutional Limitations
    2. Statutory and Jurisdictional Limitations
    3. The Intersection of Regulation and Antitrust Law

Public utilities are often privately owned. Yet, historically public utilities have been controlled by a different set of economic and legal expectations than other privately owned businesses Today, statutes and regulations largely determine the definition of as well the benefits and burdens that attach to public utilities, but the concept of public utilities has a rich history in the common law. Even in the modern so-called "age of statutes," these common law principles are of importance in determining whether certain energy businesses meet the definition of a public utility. More important, common law principles are of relevance in determining the extent of benefits and burdens for modern public utilities. This chapter will provide a basic introduction to the history of these principles in American law, their economic rationales, and their modern analogs.

A. HISTORICAL ORIGINS

Regulation of ferries, sewers, mills, bridges, and railroads provide the historical origins for modern public utility regulation. Although sometimes these were government owned and operated, in many, if not most instances, they were privately-owned in England and early America.

One particularly prominent example of public utility regulation involves gasoline prices. As prices at the pump have risen, it has become commonplace for some politicians to suggest that gasoline should be regulated as a public utility. Such regulation would treat gasoline as a public utility, setting the price for gas based on cost and a reasonable rate of return, to avoid firms manipulating market power in the gasoline industry. Hawaii, for example, has passed a law that places a cap on gasoline prices. While proposals to regulate the price of gas at the pump have been floated in political discussions—and some have been passed into law—their success is questionable.

Why is gasoline not considered a public utility? Why would its treatment differ from other energy resources, such as natural gas and electric power, which are treated as public utilities? Looking to the historical examples of public utilities, can you identify aspects of these business services that differ from other private businesses, such as farming, calculator manufacturing, or hotel and restaurant operation?

1. The English Common Law

Humphry W. Woolrych, A Treatise on the Law of Waters and Sewers 108–09

(London, W. Benning 1830).

In ancient times, before the necessaries and conveniences of life were supplied in such profusion as at present, it became important to the settlers in and inhabitants of different districts, that they should have free access to some mill for the purpose of grinding their corn. This easement was indispensable, because they required, in the first instance sustenance for their families; and in some cases there might have been an obligation to grind the lord's wheat for his use. Lords of manors, therefore, for the purpose of meeting this exigency, erected mills on their respective domains for the public advantage; but they fettered their gift with this condition that the inhabitants and residents within their respective seignories should bring their corn to be ground at the mill so built up; and this custom, which thus had a reasonable commencement, was called doing suit to the mill. Consequently, whether the millers to whom the respective lords conceded these advantages, make their claim by prescription, which supposes a grant from the lords, or by custom, it seems clear, that this old practice arose originally from a sense of general convenience; and in so strong a point of view does this seem to have been considered, that a man might have claimed the suit by prescription, even from the villeins of a stranger.

In process of years, however, when commerce began to spread, and new erections were prospering on every side, many of the tenants and inhabitants, whose ancestors had derived benefit from the ancient mills, began to employ their own particular workmen, and the old millers found themselves deserted by degrees by those whose duty it was to have continued their support. They were, therefore, necessitated to seek redress, and the writ of *secta ad molendinum,* or *secta molendini,* was the ordinary remedy which they employed upon those occasions. The enforcing of this writ, which is now superseded by the modern action on the case, brought back the inhabitants to the suit and service which they owed.

Again, on the other hand, the millers would sometimes stretch their prerogative too far; and not content with the suit of the tenants and neighbours, would endeavour to lay claim to a more extensive limit than they ought, and thus it was that they were now and then defeated upon actions brought on the one side or the other to try the validity of their customs; or they would even trespass on the rights of the inhabitants, and instead of confining themselves to the usual demand of having all the corn ground at their mills which should be afterwards used in the family, they strove to include within their custom all the corn sold or spent in the neighborhood. This, being an unreasonable custom, was rejected by the courts.■

Tripp v. Frank

100 Eng. Rep. 1234 (1792).

This was an action on the case, wherein the plaintiff declared, that he was possessed of South Ferry, over the Humber; and that the defendant wrongfully carried persons and cattle from Kingston upon Hull to Barton, and other parts of the coast, whereby the plaintiff was injured in his right to his ferry, and lost his tolls.... At the trial before Buller, J. at the last assizes for York, it appeared that the defendant, who was the owner of a marketboat at Barrow, had carried over persons.... from Kingston upon Hull to Barrow, to which place they were going, and which lies two miles lower down the Humber than Barton, upon the same coast. It was shown that there was a daily ferry between Kingston and Barton, but none to any other part of the Lincolnshire coast. A verdict was taken for the plaintiff of 1 shilling with liberty for the defendant to enter a nonsuit in case the Court should be of opinion that the plaintiff was not entitled to recover under these circumstances.

[Plaintiff's counsel argued] that if the conduct of the defendant could be justified in this instance, it would render a right of ferry perfectly nugatory. Every person then, by going a little to the right or left of the usual track of the ferry, may equally avoid the ferry: but that would annihilate the right itself. Ferries in general must have some considerable extent upon which their right may operate, otherwise the exclusive privilege would be of no avail.... The owners of ferries are bound at their peril to supply them for the public use; and are therefore fairly entitled to preserve the exclusive advantage arising from them. But they admitted, on a question being asked by the Court, that the ferryman was not compellable to provide boats to any place on the Lincolnshire coasts besides Barton.

■ LORD KENYON, CH.J. It seems to me that the evidence does not support this action. If certain persons wishing to go to Barton had applied to the defendant, and he had carried them at a little distance above or below the ferry, it would have been a fraud on the plaintiff's right, and would be the ground of an action. But here these persons were substantially, and not colourably merely, carried over to a different place; and it is absurd to say that no person shall be permitted to go to any other place on the Humber than that to which the plaintiff chooses to carry them. It is now admitted that the ferryman cannot be compelled to carry passengers to any other place than Barton: then his right must be commensurate with his duty.

■ ASHHURST, J. The plaintiff's claim is so unreasonable, that it cannot be supported. According to his argument, if a passenger wishes to cross over from Kingston to the Lincolnshire coast three miles eastward, he must necessarily be first carried to Barton, where he would be many miles distant from his place of destination; whereas, if it were not for this ferry, he might go over directly. But the admission which the counsel have made is decisive against the plaintiff.

■ BULLER, J. The question here is, what right the plaintiff has established by evidence; and that extends only from Hull to Barton, and back again. The question of fraud might arise in this way; by saying that, though the defendant really meant to go to Barton, he went in fraud of the plaintiff's claim a little above or below the ferry. But in this case the defendant had no intention of going to Barton: his place of destination was Barrow, at the distance of two miles from Barton; to which place the plaintiff's right does not extend, and to which he says he is not compellable to go.

■ GROSE, J. of the same opinion.

Rule discharged.■

NOTES AND COMMENTS

1. The feudal system in England allowed the monarchy and the aristocracy to grant themselves and their friends a wide range of privileges. These frequently included the privilege of operating some type of business, such as a flour mill or a ferry, on a monopoly basis—no competition allowed. *See* Matthew Hale, Prerogatives of the King (edited for the Selden Society by D.E.C. Yale, 1976). The courts tempered these privileges by requiring the monopolist to serve all potential customers that requested service.

Consider the following account of the duty to serve in American law:

[T]he common law duty to serve is as ancient as the Anglo–American concept of equality and, indeed, predates the equal protection language of the federal Constitution by more than seven hundred years of conscious judicial effort. The veneration of the equality norm . . . can be traced to the writings of Henry de Bracton, legal counselor to Henry III. Here we first discover the judge-created concept that, at a fundamental level of social organization, all persons similarly situated in terms of need have an enforceable claim of equal, adequate, and nondiscriminatory access to essential services; in addition, this doctrine makes such access largely a governmental responsibility. . . .

The founding of the American Republic coincided with a second great upheaval . . .—the Industrial Revolution. The energy harnessed by Watt transformed the law as it remade the industrial world. Turnpike interests may have doomed the steam coaches, or "teakettles," which sought to traverse conventional road surfaces, but this triumph stamped upon them new obligations to the public. The railroads then emerged as the focus of legal and ideological struggles concerning the duty to serve, much as even now their tracks often divide the more from the less desirable parts of town. . . .

The emergence of legislative action, and even dominance in railway affairs, did not undercut the doctrine of the duty to serve. The courts remained the prophets of the equality norm. In fact, the appearance of state and, with the 1887 Interstate Commerce Act, federal regulatory legislation meant the enhancement, not eclipse of the common law duty to serve, as the new branch of government drew on common law precedents for its regulatory activities.

Charles M. Haar & Daniel W. Fessler, The Wrong Side of the Tracks 21–23 (Simon & Schuster 1986). This requirement still plays an important law in American law today: the common law "duty to serve" is presumed to apply to any charter or franchise from the government to operate as a monopoly. *See* Jim Rossi, The Common Law "Duty to Serve" and Protection of Consumers in an Age of Competitive Retail Public Utility Restructuring, 51 Vand. L. Rev. 1233 (1998). Today, however, the nature and extent of the duty is often spelled out in statutes in regulations, and the company often charges customers for the cost of extending service to remote areas. *See, e.g., Deerfield Estates, Inc. v. Twp. of East Brunswick*, 286 A.2d 498 (N.J. 1972).

2.   Whenever the government grants someone a monopoly to provide a particular service, the definition of the extent of the monopoly becomes an issue. The problem addressed by the court in *Tripp v. Frank* commonly occurs today in the context of increasing urbanization or technological advancements. For example, when a city expands into formerly rural areas, does the company that provided service to the city automatically expand its territory too? Or does the company that provided service to the rural area retain that privilege? *See, e.g., City of Wichita v. State Corp. Comm'n*, 592 P.2d 880 (Kan. 1979).

3.   During the seventeenth and eighteenth centuries, the power of the English crown diminished. Following the "glorious revolution" of the seventeenth century, parliament became the supreme power in the English government. *See* Christopher Hill, The Century of Revolution, 1603–1714 (New York, Norton, rev. ed. 1980). The result was the loss of privilege for many of the old monopolists whose powers were granted by the king. The term "monopoly" began to carry connotations of decadence. *See* Vernon A. Mund, Open Markets: An Essential of Free Enterprise (Harper 1948).

2.   THE CLASSIC AMERICAN CASES

In America, the basic common law concepts, such as the duty to serve, were endorsed by most state courts. One of the early issues courts were required to address during the early industrial age was whether the grant of a monopoly franchise guaranteed the monopolist protection against later entrants. The U.S. Supreme Court spoke to the issue in the classic Charles

River Bridge case in 1837. Today, the case and the principles it stands for remains of great importance; we will return to it in several later chapters.

The Proprietors of the Charles River Bridge v. The Proprietors of the Warren Bridge

36 U.S. 420 (1837).

■ TANEY, J. [In 1785], a petition was presented to the legislature, by Thomas Russell and others, stating the inconvenience of the transportation by ferries, over Charles river, and the public advantages that would result from a bridge; and praying to be incorporated, for the purpose of erecting a bridge in the place where the ferry between Boston and Charlestown was then kept. Pursuant to this petition, the legislature, on the 9th of March 1785, passed an act incorporating a company, by the name of "The Proprietors of the Charles River Bridge," for the purposes mentioned in the petition. Under this charter, the company were empowered to erect a bridge, in "the place where the ferry was then kept;" certain tolls were granted, and the charter was limited to forty years from the first opening of the bridge for passengers; and from the time the toll commenced, until the expiration of this term ... and at the expiration of the forty years, the bridge was to be the property of the commonwealth [of Massachusetts].

The bridge was accordingly built, and was opened for passengers on the 17th of June 1786. In 1792, the charter was extended to seventy years from the opening of the bridge; and at the expiration of that time, it was to belong to the commonwealth.

In 1828, the legislature of Massachusetts incorporated a company by the name of "The Proprietors of the Warren Bridge," for the purpose of erecting another bridge over Charles river. This bridge is only sixteen rods, at its commencement, on the Charlestown side, from the commencement of the bridge of the plaintiffs; and they are about fifty rods apart, at their termination on the Boston side.

The Warren bridge, by the terms of its charter, was to be surrendered to the state, as soon as the expenses of the proprietors in building and supporting it should be reimbursed; but this period was not, in any event, to exceed six years from the time the company commenced receiving toll.

The bill, among other things, charged as a ground for relief, that the act for the erection of the Warren bridge impaired the obligation of the contract between the commonwealth and the proprietors of the Charles River bridge; and was, therefore, repugnant to the constitution of the United States.

In the argument here, it was admitted, that since the filing of the supplemental bill, a sufficient amount of toll had been reserved by the proprietors of the Warren bridge to reimburse all their expenses, and that the bridge is now the property of the state, and has been made a free bridge; and that the value of the franchise granted to the proprietors of the Charles River bridge, has by this means been entirely destroyed.

The plaintiffs in error insist [t]hat the acts of the legislature of Massachusetts, of 1785 and 1792, by their true construction, necessarily implied, that the legislature would not authorize another bridge, and especially, a free one, by the side of this, and placed in the same line of travel, whereby the franchise granted to the "Proprietors of the Charles River Bridge" should be rendered of no value.

The act of the legislature of Massachusetts, of 1785, by which the plaintiffs were incorporated ... is the grant of certain franchises, by the public, to a private corporation, and in a matter where the public interest is concerned. The rule of construction in such cases is well settled, both in England, and by the decisions of our own tribunals. In the case of the *Proprietors of the Stourbridge Canal v. Wheeley and others*, 2 B. & Ad. 793, the court say, "the canal having been made under an act of parliament, the rights of the plaintiffs are derived entirely from that act." This, like many other cases, is a bargain between a company of adventurers and the public, the terms of which are expressed in the statute; and the rule of construction in all such cases, is now fully established to be this, that any ambiguity in the terms of the contract, must operate against the adventurers, and in favor of the public, and the plaintiffs can claim nothing that is not clearly given them by the act.

Borrowing, as we have done, our system of jurisprudence from the English law; and having adopted, in every other case, civil and criminal, its rules for the construction of statutes; is there anything in our local situation, or in the nature of our political institutions, which should lead us to depart from the principle, where corporations are concerned? We think not; and it would present a singular spectacle, if, while the courts in England are restraining, within the strictest limits, the spirit of monopoly, and exclusive privileges in nature of monopolies, and confining corporations to the privileges plainly given to them in their charter, the courts of this country should be found enlarging these privileges by implication and construing a statute more unfavorably to the public, and to the rights of community, than would be done in a like case in an English court of justice.

Adopting the rule of construction above stated as the settled one, we proceed to apply it to the charter of 1785, to the proprietors of the Charles River bridge. This act of incorporation is in the usual form, and the privileges such as are commonly given to corporations of that kind. It confers on them the ordinary faculties of a corporation, for the purpose of building the bridge; and establishes certain rates of toll, which the company are authorized to take: this is the whole grant. There is no exclusive privilege given to them over the waters of Charles river, above or below their bridge; no right to erect another bridge themselves, nor to prevent other persons from erecting one, no engagement from the state, that another shall not be erected; and no undertaking not to sanction competition, nor to make improvements that may diminish the amount of its income. Upon all these subject, the charter is silent; and nothing is said in it about a line of travel, so much insisted on in the argument, in which they are to have exclusive privileges.

Can such an agreement be implied? The rule of construction before stated is an answer to the question: in charters of this description, no rights are taken from the public, or given to the corporation, beyond those which the words of the charter, by their natural and proper construction, purport to convey.

Indeed, the practice and usage of almost every state in the Union, old enough to have commenced the work of internal improvement, is opposed to the doctrine contended for on the part of the plaintiffs in error. Turnpike roads have been made in succession, on the same line of travel; the later ones interfering materially with the profits of the first. These corporations have, in some instances, been utterly ruined by the introduction of newer and better modes of transportation and traveling. In some cases, railroads have rendered the turnpike roads on the same line of travel so entirely useless, that the franchise of the turnpike corporation is not worth preserving. Yet in none of these cases have the corporation supposed that their privileges were invaded, or any contract violated on the part of the state. The absence of any such controversy, when there must have been so many occasions to give rise to it, proves, that neither states, nor individuals, nor corporations, ever imagined that such a contract could be implied from such charters.

And what would be the fruits of this doctrine of implied contracts, on the part of the states, and of property in a line of travel, by a corporation, if it would now be sanctioned by this court? To what results would it lead us? If it is to be found in the charter to this bridge, the same process of reasoning must discover it, in the various acts which have been passed, within the last forty years, for turnpike companies. If this court should establish the principles now contended for, what is to become of the numerous railroads established on the same line of travel with turnpike companies; and which have rendered the franchises of the turnpike corporations of no value? Let it once be understood, that such charters carry with them these implied contracts, and give this unknown and undefined property in a line of traveling; and you will soon find the old turnpike corporations awakening from their sleep, and calling upon this court to put down the improvements which have taken their place. The millions of property which have been invested in railroads and canals, upon lines of travel which had been before occupied by turnpike corporations, will be put in jeopardy. We shall be thrown back to the improvements of the last century, and obliged to stand still, until the claims of the old turnpike corporations shall be satisfied; and they shall consent to permit these states to avail themselves of the lights of modern science, and to partake of the benefit of those improvements which are now adding to the wealth and prosperity, and the convenience and comfort, of every other part of the civilized world.

The judgment of the supreme judicial court of the commonwealth of Massachusetts, dismissing the plaintiffs' bill, must, therefore, be affirmed, with costs.

■ STORY, J., dissenting: [W]ith a view to induce the court to withdraw from all the common rules of reasonable and liberal interpretation in favor of grants, we have been told at the argument, that this very charter is a restriction upon the legislative power; that it is in derogation of the rights and interests of the state, and the people; that it tends to promote monopolies and exclusive privileges; and that it will interpose an insuperable barrier to the progress of improvement. Now, upon every one of these propositions, which are assumed, and not proved, I entertain a directly opposite opinion; and if I did not, I am not prepared to admit the conclusion for which they are adduced. If the legislature has made a grant, which involves any or all of these consequences, it is not for courts of justice to overturn the plain sense of the grant, because it has been improvidently or injuriously made.

But I deny the very ground-work of the argument. This charter is not any restriction upon the legislative power; unless it be true, that because the legislature cannot grant again, what it has already granted, the legislative power is restricted. If so, then every grant of the public land is a restriction upon that power; a doctrine, that has never yet been established, nor (so far as I know) ever contended for. Every grant of a franchise is, so far as that grant extends, necessarily exclusive; and cannot be resumed or interfered with.

Then, again, how is it established, that this is a grant in derogation of the rights and interests of the people? No individual citizen has any right to build a bridge over navigable waters; and consequently, he is deprived of no right, when a grant is made to any other persons for that purpose. . . .

The erection of a bridge may be of the highest utility to the people. It may essentially promote the public convenience, and aid the public interests, and protect the public property. And if no persons can be found willing to undertake such a work, unless they receive in return the exclusive privilege of erecting it, and taking toll; surely, it cannot be said, as of course, that such a grant, under such circumstances, is, per se, against the interests of the people.

Again, it is argued, that the present grant is a grant of a monopoly, and of exclusive privileges; and therefore, to be construed by the most narrow mode of interpretation.

There is great virtue in particular phrases; and when it is once suggested, that a grant is of the nature or tendency of a monopoly, the mind almost instantaneously prepares itself to reject every construction which does not pare it down to the narrowest limits. It is an honest prejudice, which grew up, in former times, from the gross abuses of the royal prerogatives; to which, in America, there are no analogous authorities. But what is a monopoly, as understood in law? It is an exclusive right, granted to a few, of something which was before of common right. Thus, a privilege granted by the king for the sole buying, selling, making, working or using a thing, whereby the subject, in general, is restrained from that liberty of manufacturing or trading, which before he had, is a monopoly.

No sound lawyer will, I presume, assert that the grant of a right to erect a bridge over a navigable stream is a grant of a common right. It was neither a monopoly; nor, in a legal sense, had it any tendency to a monopoly. It took from no citizen what he possessed before; and had no tendency to take it from him. It took, indeed, from the legislature the power of granting the same identical privilege or franchise to any other persons. But this made it no more a monopoly, than the grant of the public stock or funds of a state for a valuable consideration.

But it has been argued, and the argument has been pressed in every form which ingenuity could suggest, that if grants of this nature are to be construed liberally, as conferring any exclusive rights on the grantees, it will interpose an effectual barrier against all general improvements of the country. This is a subject upon which different minds may well arrive at different conclusions, both as to policy and principle. For my own part, I can conceive of no surer plan to arrest all public improvements, founded on private capital and enterprise, that to make the outlay of that capital uncertain and questionable, both as to security and as to productiveness. No man will hazard his capital in any enterprise, in which, if there be a loss, it must be borne exclusively by himself; and if there be success, he has not the slightest security of enjoying the rewards of that success, for a single moment. If the government means to invite its citizens to enlarge the public comforts and conveniences, to establish bridges, or turnpikes, or canals, or railroads, there must be some pledge, that the property will be safe; that the enjoyment will be co-extensive with the grant; and that success will not be the signal of a general combination to overthrow its rights and to take away its profits. And yet, we are told, that all such exclusive grants are to the detriment of the public.

But if there were any foundation for the argument itself, in a general view, it would totally fail in its application to the present case. Here, the grant, however exclusive, is but for a short and limited period, more than two-thirds of which have already elapsed; and when it is gone, the whole property and franchise are to revert to the state. The legislature exercised a wholesome foresight on the subject; and within a reasonable period, it will have an unrestricted authority to do whatever it may choose, in the appropriation of the bridge and its tolls. There is not, then, under any fair aspect of the case, the slightest reason to presume that public improvements either can, or will, be injuriously retarded by a liberal construction of the present grant.

In order to entertain a just view of this subject, we must go back to that period of general bankruptcy, and distress and difficulty. The constitution of the United States was not only not then in existence, but it was not then even dreamed of. The union of the states was crumbling into ruins, under the old confederation. Agriculture, manufactures and commerce were at their lowest ebb. There was infinite danger to all the states, from local interests and jealousies, and from the apparent impossibility of a much longer adherence to that shadow of a government, the continental congress.

This is not all. It is well known, historically, that this was the very first bridge ever constructed, in New England, over navigable tide-waters so near the sea. The rigors of our climate, the dangers from sudden thaws and freezing, and the obstructions from ice in a rapid current, were deemed by many persons to be insuperable obstacles to the success of such a project. . . .

Now, I put it to the common sense of every man, whether if, at the moment of granting the charter, the legislature had said to the proprietors; you shall build the bridge; you shall bear the burdens; you shall be bound by the charges; and your sole reimbursement shall be from the tolls of forty years: and yet we will not even guaranty you any certainty of receiving any tolls; on the contrary; we reserve to ourselves the full power and authority to erect other bridges, toll or free bridges, according to our own free will and pleasure, contiguous to yours, and having the same termini with yours; and if you are successful, we may thus supplant you, divide, destroy your profits, and annihilate your tolls, without annihilating your burdens: if, I say, such had been the language of the legislature, is there a man living, of ordinary discretion or prudence, who would have accepted such a charter, upon such terms?

But it is said, if this is the law, what then is to become of turnpikes and canals? Is the legislature precluded from authorizing new turnpikes or new canals, simply because they cross the path of the old ones, and incidentally diminish their receipt of tolls? The answer is plain. Every turnpike has its local limits and local termini; its points of beginning and of end. No one ever imagined, that the legislature might grant a new turnpike, with exactly the same location and termini. That would be to rescind its first grant. And the opinion of Mr. Chancellor Kent, and all the old authorities on the subject of ferries, support me in the doctrine.

But then again, it is said, that all this rests upon implication, and not upon the words of the charter. What objection can there be to implications, if they arise from the very nature and objects of the grant? If it be indispensable to the full enjoyment of the right to take toll, that it should be exclusive within certain limits, is it not just and reasonable, that it should be so construed? . . . If the public exigencies and interests require that the franchise of Charles River bridge should be taken away, or impaired, it may be lawfully done, upon making due compensation to the proprietors.

I maintain, that, upon the principles of common reason and legal interpretation, the present grant carries with it a necessary implication, that the legislature shall do no act to destroy or essentially to impair the franchise; that (as one of the learned judges of the state court expressed it) there is an implied agreement that the state will not grant another bridge between Boston and Charlestown, so near as to draw away the custom from the old one; and (as another learned judge expressed it) that there is an implied agreement of the state to grant the undisturbed use of the bridge and its tolls, so far as respects any acts of its own, or of any persons acting under its authority. . . .

Upon the whole, my judgment is, that the act of the legislature of Massachusetts granting the charter of Warren Bridge, is an act impairing the obligation of the prior contract and grant to the proprietors of Charles River bridge; and, by the constitution of the United States, it is, therefore, utterly void. I am for reversing the decree to the state court (dismissing the bill); and for remanding the cause to the state court for further proceedings, as to law and justice shall appertain.■

Stanley I. Kutler, Privilege and Creative Destruction: The Charles River Bridge Case

(Lippincott 1971).

On Bunker Hill Day, 1786, residents of Boston and Charlestown gathered to celebrate their new fortune. At last the two areas were linked by a bridge across the Charles River. Technical skills and entrepreneurial resources, encouraged by the state, had mastered formidable barriers to construct the span. While men had envisioned such a bridge for nearly a century, the costs and physical hazards always made it a risky proposition. But in 1785 the Massachusetts legislature granted a charter to a group of Charlestown businessmen who assumed the risks in exchange for a forty-year guarantee of tolls. With the bridge's completion a year later, the proprietors and townspeople alike could well congratulate themselves on their happy circumstance. There was a steady and sizable flow of goods and persons between the two towns. In place of the old and unreliable ferry, and despite the tolls, communications now were faster and cheaper. And with the successful engineering feat, the proprietors knew that their bridge would continue to provide them with lucrative profits.

Six years later the state extended the charter for another thirty years. The proprietors almost immediately realized their anticipated profits, and then some; by 1814, stock in the corporation sold for over $2,000 per share, up more than 600 percent from the original price.

But in December 1828 there was new cause for rejoicing among some of the townspeople and businessmen, but certainly not among the proprietors and their friends. It was then that a second Charlestown bridge was completed. Overriding the proprietors' claims for exclusive privileges, the Massachusetts legislature had chartered the Warren Bridge Corporation in March 1828 to construct a new bridge nearly adjacent to the existing facility, terminating on the Charlestown side less than ninety yards from the Charles River Bridge. The new company could charge the same tolls as the old, but with a six-year time limit, after which its bridge was to revert to the Commonwealth and become a free avenue.

Constitutional rhetoric and considerations of public policy dominated the controversy over a new bridge. The advocates of a free bridge insisted that the state had never bartered away its right to charter competing franchises, and that the state retained the power to provide improvements for public necessities. In response, the proprietors argued that their charter guaranteed them a vested and exclusive right that could be abrogated only upon the payment of proper compensation. Constitutional principles aside, the antagonists pitched their battle lines around competing views of the state's public policy role. The proponents of a free bridge contended that charter rights should be strictly construed so that privilege would not hamper opportunity or the pressing needs of the community. The Charles River Bridge supporters maintained that the state must scrupulously respect existing titles and interpret their rights liberally in order to ensure a favorable investment climate for future private enterprises.

Defeated in the legislature, the proprietors turned to the courts in defense of their rights. First, in 1828, they sought an injunction from the state supreme court to prevent the completion of the bridge. Daniel Webster and Lemuel Shaw, their distinguished counsel, argued that the Charles River Bridge charter granted exclusive privileges to the corporation, and therefore the legislative act of 1828 impaired the obligation of the contract and was repugnant to the federal constitution. They further contended that the chartering of a new bridge destroyed the tolls—in effect, the property—of the old structure and thus constituted the taking of private property for public use without compensation, in violation of the Massachusetts constitution. The court refused to grant the injunction, however, primarily because of the proprietors' ambiguous claims to exclusive rights. The state court subsequently heard the case on its merits, but in January 1830 dismissed the complainants' bill. The proprietors immediately appealed to the United States Supreme Court.

The Charles River Bridge case was first argued in Washington in 1831, with John Marshall presiding. Despite a determined effort by Justice Joseph Story to secure a judgment for the Charles River Bridge proprietors, the Supreme Court divided on the issue. Subsequent absences and vacancies prevented a decision by the Marshall Court before the Chief Justice's death in 1835. After the appointment of his successor; Roger B. Taney, and before a fully constituted bench, the case was reargued in January 1837. The Court's opinion followed the next month. A clear majority of the Court sustained the state's action and denied the appeal of the proprietors. For Justice Story it was a sad occasion, symbolizing in his mind the evil days that had come upon the court and the law he revered. "With a pained heart, and subdued confidence," Story found himself almost alone as "the last of the old race of judges." . . . .

The Charles River Bridge case had much more at stake than a relatively petty local dispute over a new, free bridge. The Warren Bridge was a symbol for the rapid technological developments competing for public acceptance against existing, privileged property forms. The destruction of vested interest in favor of beneficial change reflected a creative process vital to ongoing development and progress. Within its contemporary setting, and for its historical significance, the case assumes greater meaning if railroads and the development of a new and improved transportation infrastructure—or even the benefits the community could derive from all inventions and scientific knowledge—are substituted for bridges. The competing principles of the parties in the bridge case fundamentally involved the state's role and power of encouraging or implementing innovations for the advantage of the community. . . . ■

NOTES AND COMMENTS

1. One distinguished legal historian summarizes the Charles River Bridge case in the following way: "On one side of the case were the old-money Federalists, who owned many monopoly franchises and argued that private construction of public improvements required monopoly protection for the investors. On the other side was a new group of entrepreneurs, poised to enter American markets. They believed that all markets should be competitive." Herbert Hovenkamp, Enterprise and American Law 1836–1937 (Harv. U. Press 1991) at 110. Who won?

2. Stanley Kulter discusses how corruption may have been present in the initial grant to the proprietors of Charles River Bridge over the alternative charter proposal:

> That the legislature chose to grant a charter to the Russell group for purposes of profit, rather than to the Cabot brothers who had proposed a schedule of tolls that merely would recoup their investment and development costs raises obvious questions of economic ideology and legislative behavior. Beginning in 1792, and in recurring years afterward, critics of the Charles River Bridge company charged that the proprietors had gained their charter under fraudulent conditions, an allegation never proved. But what motivated the legislature to select the group that frankly sought a long-standing profit arrangement? There may have been some vague, but conscious, perception that the pursuit of profit, even at the public's expense, was a desirable good, one that would regularly attract further investments in behalf of the community. But, more practically, the legislature's decision probably stemmed from the intensive lobbying activities of the Charleston community which was involved most directly, and whose need was clearly greater than that of its neighbors who would have benefited most from the Cabot's proposal.

Stanley I. Kutler, Privilege and Creative Destruction: The Charles River Bridge Case 11 (1971).

3. In a concurrence to the Supreme Court's opinion, Justice John McLean characterized the relationship between the state of Massachusetts and the proprietors of the Charles River Bridge as a contract:

> Where the Legislature, with a view of advancing the public interest by the construction of a bridge, a turnpike road, or any other work of public utility, grants a charter, no reason is perceived why such a charter should not be construed by the same rule that governs contracts between individuals. . . .

36 U.S. at 557 (McLean, J., concurring). This regulatory contract rationale for regulation contains an appealing logic. The utility agrees to serve

customers and, in return, the state provides the utility protection against new entrants and guarantees recovery of its costs through regulated rates. Judge Kenneth Starr, when sitting on U.S. Court of Appeals for the D.C. Circuit, also endorsed this view of regulation:

> The utility business represents a compact of sorts: a monopoly on service in a particular geographic area (coupled with state conferred rights of eminent domain or condemnation) is granted to the utility in exchange for a regime of intensive regulation, including price regulation, quite alien to the free market. Each party to the contract gets something in the bargain.

Jersey Central Power & Light v. FERC, 810 F.2d 1168, 1189 (D.C. Cir. 1987) (Starr, J., concurring). Should the same rules regarding construction of contracts between individuals apply where one of the contracting parties is the government? What incentives do these rules create for the private sector? What approach does the Supreme Court appear to take in the Charles River Bridge case?

4.   The Charles River bridge case is of considerable importance to issues in energy regulation today, as natural gas and electric utilities undergo deregulation and a new infusion of competition. These issues are discussed further in Chapters 8 and 11–12.

Munn v. Illinois

94 U.S. 113 (1877).

■ WAITE, C.J. The question to be determined in this case is whether the general assembly of Illinois can, under the limitations upon the legislative power of the States imposed by the Constitution of the United States, fix by law the maximum of charges for the storage of grain in warehouses at Chicago and other places in the State having not less than one hundred thousand inhabitants, "in which grain is stored in bulk, and in which the grain of different owners is mixed together, or in which grain is stored in such a manner that the identity of different lots or parcels cannot be accurately preserved."

It is claimed that such a law is repugnant ... to that part of amendment 14 which ordains that no State shall "deprive any person of life, liberty, or property, without due process of law, nor deny to any person within its jurisdiction the equal protection of the laws."

While this provision of the amendment is new in the Constitution of the United States, as a limitation upon the powers of the States, it is old as a principle of civilized government. It is found in Magna Carta, and, in substance if not in form, in nearly or quite all the constitutions that have been from time to time adopted by the several States of the Union. By the Fifth Amendment, it was introduced into the Constitution of the United States as a limitation upon the powers of the national government, and by the Fourteenth, as a guaranty against any encroachment upon an acknowledged right of citizenship by the legislatures of the States.

When one becomes a member of society, he necessarily parts with some rights or privileges which, as an individual not affected by his relations to others, he might retain. "A body politic," as aptly defined in the preamble of the Constitution of Massachusetts, "is a social compact by which the whole people covenants with each citizen, and each citizen with the whole people, that all shall be governed by certain laws for the common good." This does not confer power upon the whole people to control rights which are purely and exclusively private, *Thorpe v. Rutland and Burlington Railroad Co.*, 27 Vt. 140; but it does authorize the establishment of laws requiring each citizen to so conduct himself, and so use his own property, as not unnecessarily to injure another.

This is the very essence of government, and has found expression in the *maxim sic utere tuo ut alienum non laedas.* From this source come the police powers, which, as was said by Mr. Chief Justice Taney in the *License Cases*, 5 How. 583, "are nothing more or less than the powers of government inherent in every sovereignty, . . . that is to say, . . . the power to govern men and things." Under these powers the government regulates the conduct of its citizens one towards another, and the manner in which each shall use his own property, when such regulation becomes necessary for the public good. In their exercise it has been customary in England from time immemorial, and in this country from its first colonization, to regulate ferries, common carriers, hackmen, bakers, millers, wharfingers, innkeepers, &c., and in so doing to fix a maximum of charge to be made for services rendered, accommodations furnished, and articles sold.

To this day, statutes are to be found in many of the States on some or all these subjects; and we think it has never yet been successfully contended that such legislation came within any of the constitutional prohibitions against interference with private property. With the Fifth Amendment in force, Congress, in 1820, conferred power upon the city of Washington "to regulate . . . the rates of wharfage at private wharves, . . . the sweeping of chimneys, and to fix the rates of fees therefore, . . . and the weight and quality of bread," 3 Stat. 587, sect. 7; and, in 1848, "to make all necessary regulations respecting hackney carriages and the rates of fare of the same, and the rates of hauling by cartmen, wagoners, carmen, and draymen, and the rates of commission of auctioneers," 9 *id.* 224, sect. 2.

. . . Looking, then, to the common law, from whence came the right which the Constitution protects, we find that when private property is "affected with a public interest, it ceases to be juris privati only." This was said by Lord Chief Justice Hale more than two hundred years ago, in his treatise De Portibus Maris, 1 Harg. Law Tracts, 78, and has been accepted without objection as an essential element in the law of property ever since. Property does become clothed with a public interest when used in a manner to make it of public consequence, and affect the community at large. . . .

Thus, as to ferries, Lord Hale says, in his treatise De Jure Maris, 1 Harg. Law Tracts, 6, the king has "a right of franchise or privilege, that no man may set up a common ferry for all passengers, without a prescription time out of mind, or a charter from the king. He may make a ferry for his own use or the use of his family, but not for the common use of all the king's subjects passing that way; because it doth in consequence tend to a common charge, and is become a thing of public interest and use, and every man for his passage pays a toll, which is a common charge, and every ferry ought to be under a public regulation, viz., that it give attendance at due times, keep a boat in due order, and take but reasonable toll; for if he fail in these he is finable.'' So if one owns the soil and landing places on both banks of a stream, he cannot use them for the purposes of a public ferry, except upon such terms and conditions as the body politic may from time to time impose; and this because the common good requires that all public ways shall be under the control of the public authorities. This privilege or prerogative of the king, who in this connection only represents and gives another name to the body politic, is not primarily for his profit, but for the protection of the people and the promotion of the general welfare.

And the same has been held as to warehouses and warehousemen. In *Aldnutt v. Inglis*, 12 East, 527, decided in 1810, it appeared that the London Dock Company had built warehouses in which wines were taken in store at such rates of charge as the company and the owners might agree upon. Afterwards the company obtained authority, under the general warehousing act, to receive wines from importers before the duties upon the importation were paid; and the question was, whether they could charge arbitrary rates for such storage, or must be content with a reasonable compensation....

But we need not go further. Enough has already been said to show that, when private property is devoted to a public use, it is subject to public regulation. It remains only to ascertain whether the warehouses of these plaintiffs in error, and the business which is carried on there, come within the operation of this principle.

From [a brief filed by plaintiffs] it appears that ''the great producing region of the West and Northwest sends its grain by water and rail to Chicago, where the greater part of it is shipped by vessel for transportation to the seaboard by the Great Lakes, and some of it is forwarded by railway to the Eastern ports. ... Vessels, to some extent, are loaded in the Chicago harbor, and sailed through the St. Lawrence directly to Europe. ... The quantity [of grain] received in Chicago has made it the greatest grain market in the world. This business has created a demand for means by which the immense quantity of grain can be handled or stored, and these have been found in grain warehouses, which are commonly called elevators, because the grain is elevated from the boat or car, by machinery operated by steam, into the bins prepared for its reception, and elevated from the bins, by a like process, into the vessel or car which is to carry it on. ... In this way the largest traffic between the citizens of the country north and west of Chicago and the citizens of the country lying on the Atlantic coast north of Washington is in grain which passes through the elevators of Chicago. In this way the trade in grain is carried on by the inhabitants of seven or eight of the great States of the West with four or five of the States lying on the sea-shore, and forms the largest part of interstate commerce in these States.... It has been found impossible to preserve each owner's grain separate, and this has given rise to a system of inspection and grading, by which the grain of different owners is mixed, and receipts issued for the number of bushels which are negotiable, and redeemable in like kind, upon demand. This mode of conducting the business was inaugurated more than twenty years ago, and has grown to immense proportions. The railways have found it impracticable to own such elevators, and public policy forbids the transaction of such business by the carrier; the ownership has, therefore, been by private individuals, who have embarked their capital and devoted their industry to such business as a private pursuit."

In this connection it must also be borne in mind that, although in 1874 there were in Chicago fourteen warehouses adapted to this particular business, and owned by about thirty persons, nine business firms controlled them, and that the prices charged and received for storage were such "as have been from year to year agreed upon and established by the different elevators or warehouses in the city of Chicago, and which rates have been annually published in one or more newspapers printed in said city, in the month of January in each year, as the established rates for the year then next ensuing such publication." Thus it is apparent that all the elevating facilities through which these vast productions "of seven or eight great States of the West" must pass on the way "to four or five of the States on the seashore" may be a "virtual" monopoly.

Under such circumstances it is difficult to see why, if the common carrier, or the miller, or the ferryman, or the innkeeper, or the wharfinger, or the baker, or the cartman, or the hackney coachman, pursues a public employment and exercises "a sort of public office," these plaintiffs in error do not. They stand, to use again the language of their counsel, in the very "gateway of commerce," and take toll from all who pass. Their business most certainly "tends to a common charge, and is become a thing of public interest and use." Every bushel of grain for its passage "pays a toll, which is a common charge," and, therefore, according to Lord Hale, every such warehouseman "ought to be under public regulation, viz., that he ... take but reasonable toll." Certainly, if any business can be clothed "with a public interest, and cease to be juris privati only," this has been. It may not be made so by the operation of the Constitution of Illinois or this statute, but it is by the facts.

In matters not in this case that these plaintiffs in error had built their warehouses and established their business before the regulations complained of were adopted. What they did was from the beginning subject to the power of the body politic to require them to conform to such regulations as might be established by the proper authorities for the common good. They entered upon their business and provided themselves with the means to carry it on subject to this condition. If they did not wish to submit themselves to such interference, they should not have clothed the public with an interest in their concerns. The same principle applies to them that does to a proprietor of a hackney-carriage, and as to him it has never been supposed that he was exempt from regulating statutes or ordinances because he had purchased his horses and carriage and established his business before the statute or the ordinance was adopted.

It is insisted, however, that the owner of property is entitled to a reasonable compensation for its use, even though it be clothed with a public interest, and that what is reasonable is a judicial and not a legislative question.

As has already been shown, the practice has been otherwise. In countries where the common law prevails, it has been customary from time immemorial for the legislature to declare what shall be a reasonable compensation under such circumstances, or, perhaps more properly speaking, to fix a maximum beyond which any charge made would be unreasonable. Undoubtedly, in mere private contracts, relating to matters in which the public has no interest, what is reasonable must be ascertained judicially. But this is because the legislature has no control over such a contract. So, too, in matters which do affect the public interest, and as to which legislative control may be exercised, if there are no statutory regulations upon the subject, the courts must determine what is reasonable. The controlling fact is the power to regulate at all. If that exists, the right to establish the maximum of charge, as one of the means of regulation, is implied. In fact, the common-law rule, which requires the charge to be reasonable, is itself a regulation as to price. Without it the owner could make his rates at will, and compel the public to yield to his terms, or forego the use.

We conclude, therefore, that the statute in question is not repugnant to the Constitution of the United States, and that there is no error in the judgment. In passing upon this case we have not been unmindful of the vast importance of the questions involved. This and cases of a kindred character were argued before us more than a year ago by most eminent counsel, and in a manner worthy of their well earned reputations. We have kept the cases long under advisement, in order that their decision might be the result of our mature deliberations.

Judgment affirmed.

■ **Field, J., with whom Strong J., concurs, dissenting:** I am compelled to dissent from the decision of the court in this case, and from the reasons upon which that decision is founded. The principle upon which the opinion of the majority proceeds is, in my judgment, subversive of the rights of private property, heretofore believed to be protected by constitutional guaranties against legislative interference, and is in conflict with the authorities cited in its support. . . .

The declaration of the Constitution of 1870, that private buildings used for private purposes shall be deemed public institutions, does not make them so. The receipt and storage of grain in a building erected by private means for that purpose does not constitute the building a public warehouse. There is no magic in the language, though used by a constitutional convention, which can change a private business into a public one, or alter the character of the building in which the business is transacted. A tailor's or a shoemaker's shop would still retain its private character, even though the assembled wisdom of the State should declare, by organic act or legislative ordinance, that such a place was a public workshop, and that the workmen were public tailors or public shoemakers. One might as well attempt to change the nature of colors, by giving them a new designation. The defendants were no more public warehousemen, as justly observed by counsel, than the merchant who sells his merchandise to the public is a public merchant, or the blacksmith who shoes horses for the public is a public blacksmith; and it was a strange notion that by calling them so they would be brought under legislative control.

If [the majority's approach] be sound law, if there be no protection, either in the principles upon which our republican government is founded, or in the prohibitions of the Constitution against such invasion of private rights, all property and all business in the State are held at the mercy of a majority of its legislature. The public has no greater interest in the use of buildings for the storage of grain than it has in the use of buildings for the residences of families, nor, indeed, any thing like so great an interest; and, according to the doctrine announced, the legislature may fix the rent of all tenements used for residences, without reference to the cost of their erection. If the owner does not like the rates prescribed, he may cease renting his houses. He has granted to the public, says the court, an interest in the use of the buildings, and "he may withdraw his grant by discontinuing the use; but, so long as he maintains the use, he must submit to the control." . . .

The power of the State over the property of the citizen under the constitutional guaranty is well defined. The State may take his property for public uses, upon just compensation being made therefore. It may take a portion of his property by way of taxation for the support of the government. It may control the use and possession of his property, so far as may be necessary for the protection of the rights of others, and to secure to them the equal use and enjoyment of their property. The doctrine that each one must so use his own as not to injure his neighbor sic utere tuo ut alienum non laedas is the rule by which every member or society must possess and enjoy his property; and all legislation essential to secure this common and equal enjoyment is a legitimate exercise of State authority. Except in cases where property may be destroyed to arrest a conflagration or the ravages of pestilence, or be taken under the pressure of an immediate and overwhelming necessity to prevent a public calamity, the power of the State over the property of the citizen does not extend beyond such limits.

It is only where some right or privilege is conferred by the government or municipality upon the owner, which he can use in connection with his property, or by means of which the use of his property is rendered more valuable to him, or he thereby enjoys an advantage over others, that the compensation to be received by him becomes a legitimate matter of regulation. Submission to the regulation of compensation in such cases is an implied condition of the grant, and the State, in exercising its power of prescribing the compensation, only determines the conditions upon which its concession shall be enjoyed. When the privilege ends, the power of regulation ceases.■

* * *

The *Munn* decision arose out of a long and bitter political battle between farmers and food processors in the Midwest. The context of the dispute is analyzed in William Cronon's book, excerpts from which follow:

William Cronon, Nature's Metropolis
(W.W. Norton 1991).

The *Chicago Tribune* led the way in arguing for government intervention against corrupt elevator practices. The *Tribune*, for instance, reported that among farmers in the city's hinterland, "the name of a Chicago warehouseman has become a synonym with that of a pirate.... It may be safely affirmed that no man voluntarily sends his grain to Chicago who can send it elsewhere." Negative perceptions of this sort could only hurt the city in general, so booster editors who wished to protect Chicago took it upon themselves to ferret out corruption and hold it up for public condemnation. Because such newspapers were widely read throughout the state, they helped shape public thinking about the issue. Much of the most damaging information that farmers knew about Chicago's markets came to them via the Chicago newspapers, which had in turn learned insider stories from grain traders at the Chicago Board of Trade. If, as many farmers believed, Chicago was the font of corruption in the grain trade, the city also pointed the way to its own redemption.

The constitution's proposed article for regulating grain warehouses had in fact been drafted by none other than a committee of the Board of Trade. This led at least one rural delegate to oppose elevator regulation as "a grain gamblers' article, and not a farmers' article." Another rural delegate thereupon leapt to the measure's defense by declaring that although "this report came from the city of Chicago" and "had its manliness and all its garments laid on there," he was still "willing to receive anything good, that may come out of evil." The *Tribune's* reform editor, Joseph Medill, was himself a delegate and delivered what was probably the convention's most grandiloquent indictment of the elevators:

> The fifty million bushels of grain that pass into and out of the city of Chicago per annum, are controlled absolutely by a few warehouse men and the officers of railways. They form the grand ring, that wrings the sweat and blood out of the producers of Illinois. There is no provision in the fundamental law standing between the unrestricted avarice of monopoly and the common rights of the people; but the great, laborious, patient ox, the farmer, is bitten and bled, harassed and tortured, by these rapacious, blood sucking insects.

With the republican body politic so infested with vermin, Medill argued, only the law could "step between these voracious monopolies and the producers." The new constitution should attack the elevator plague, save the farmer, and redeem Chicago at the same time. . . .

Article 13 as it finally appeared in the 1870 constitution remained largely as Board members had written it. It designated all warehouses in Illinois to be "public," thereby asserting the state's power to regulate their activities and confirming a grain owner's right to inspect the goods stored in such places. Despite the statewide definition of public warehouses, convention delegates understood their real target and did not wish to subject rural warehouse owners to needless cost and regulations. The most important requirements of the article therefore applied only to elevators in cities with over 100,000 inhabitants—and there was only one such city in Illinois. Elevators in Chicago were to post weekly notices of how much grain of each grade they had in store. To prevent them from issuing fraudulent receipts, they were to keep a public registry of all outstanding receipts they had issued. And they were forbidden to mix different grades without permission. Furthermore, all railroads in the state were required to deliver grain to any elevator a shipper desired—and, if necessary, permit new track construction to accomplish this.

The Illinois legislature supplemented Article 13 in 1871 with a series of laws assigning the task of grain inspection to a new Railroad and Warehouse Commission that would henceforth regulate all grain movement and storage in the state. . . . Elevator operators initially contested the legality of the new laws by refusing to take out licenses for themselves, thereby denying that Illinois had a right to regulate their activities. When the state prosecuted them, public outcry about the case was so strong that voters changed the composition of the Illinois supreme court to make sure that the Warehouse Act and other new "Granger laws" would be declared constitutional.

Finally, in 1877, the U.S. Supreme Court issued its famous ruling in *Munn v. Illinois*, establishing forever the principle that grain elevators and other such facilities were "clothed with a public interest" and could not escape state regulation. The name of Ira Munn, Chicago's leading elevator operator, would henceforth be associated with the legal ruling which enabled state governments to regulate the boundary between private interest and public good in economic matters. . . .

Wheat and corn came to Chicago from farms that were themselves radical simplifications of the grassland ecosystem. Farm facilities had destroyed the habitats of dozens of native species to make room for the much smaller bundle of plants that filled the Euroamerican breadbasket. As a result, the vast productive powers of the prairie soil came to concentrate upon a handful of exotic grasses, and the resulting deluge of wheat, corn, and other grains flowed via the railroads into Chicago. And there another simplification occurred. In their raw physical forms, wheat and corn were difficult substances: bulky to store, hard to handle, difficult to value properly. Their minute and endless diversity embodied the equal diversity of the prairie landscape and of the families who toiled to turn that landscape into farms. An older grain-marketing system had preserved the fine distinctions among these natural and human diversities by maintaining the legal connection between physical grain and its owner. But as the production of western grain exploded, and as the ability to move it came to depend on capital investments in railroads and elevators, the linkage between a farm's products and its property rights came to seem worse than useless to the grain traders of Chicago. Moving and trading grain in individual lots was slow, labor-intensive, and costly. By severing physical grain from its ownership rights, one could make it abstract, homogeneous, *liquid*. If the chief symbol of the earlier marketing system was the sack, whose enclosure drew boundaries around crop and property alike, then the symbol of Chicago's abandonment of those boundaries was the golden torrent of the elevator chute. . . .

To understand wheat or corn in the vocabulary of bulls, bears, corners, grades, and futures meant seeing grain as a commodity, not as a living organism planted and harvested by farmers as a crop for people to mill into flour, bake into bread, and eat. As one bewildered delegate to the Illinois Constitutional Convention remarked after trying to read a Chicago market report, "this buying short" and "buying long" and the "last bulge" is perfect Greek to the grain producer of the State.

By imposing their own order and vocabulary on the world of first nature, the city's traders invented a world of second nature in which they could buy and sell grain as commodity almost independently from grain as crop. "In the business centre of Chicago," wrote a bemused visitor in 1880, "you see not even one 'original package' of the great cereals." In Chicago, the market turned inward upon itself to trade within its own categories and boundaries.■

* * *

Summary: The Common Law Rules for Public Utilities:

1. Service to public. It operates a business that is thought to provide a service to the public.

2. Monopoly power. It has the legal or *de facto* authority to prevent other businesses from competing with it.

3. Fixed territory. A geographical boundary is defined, within which the business is required to provide service.

4. Technological limits. As technology changes, the nature of the businesses' monopoly may be narrowly construed.

5. Duty to serve. The business has a duty to serve all members of the public, but only for the specific service for which it has a monopoly.

6. Reasonable prices. Rates charged by public utilities, which the common law had required be reasonable, could be regulated by the legislative branch. We will consider at some length later what "reasonable" means.

* * *

The Supreme Court's increasing willingness to allow government to regulate a wider range of businesses occurred at the point in history when a wide range of new technologies for the generation and distribution of energy (and other services) were being developed, as pointed out in the following excerpt.

Charles M. Haar & Daniel W. Fessler, The Wrong Side of the Tracks 142–49

(Simon & Schuster 1986).

In 1865 the first natural gas utility was opened in Fredonia, New York; in 1892 a 120–mile pipeline from wells in Indiana to Chicago made the long distance transmission of natural gas possible for the first time. Americans in 1878 first saw the electric arc for street and home lighting, followed in 1882 by the first central electric station, with 5500 lamps, at Pearl Street Station, New York. Shortly thereafter, central stations were constructed in Boston, Brooklyn, and Chicago. By 1886, there were forty seven Edison illuminating companies; more than 1,000 central stations were listed in 1890. The proliferation of waterworks was also impressive from 136 in 1860 (when fewer than 400 cities had populations over 2500) to over 3000 systems by the end of the century (when there were over 1737 such cities). In 1852, 23,000 miles of telegraph lines were in operation. The Western Union Telegraph Company completed the first telegraph line to the Pacific Coast in 1861, and in 1866 it merged with the two other large telegraph companies. After Alexander Graham Bell constructed the initial pair of magneto telephones in 1875, it was but three years until first New Haven, then San Francisco, Albany, Chicago, St. Louis, Detroit, and Philadelphia had local service. By 1880 there were over 34,000 miles of wire for the nation's 50,000 telephones; the American Telephone and Telegraph Company was organized in 1885 to develop long distance service. The modern, mechanized American city had been born.

The new utility networks possessed many of the characteristics of common carriers: they provided what were more and more commonly perceived as essential services; they were usually natural or legal monopolies, or both; they exercised the power of eminent domain; and they operated under a franchise from the state or municipality.... [But the view that this new type of business] was not a public enterprise that concerned the courts ... remained the prevailing judicial stance until the United States Supreme Court spoke in *Munn v. Illinois* in 1876.

The *Munn* decision, written by Chief Justice Waite, upheld the Illinois statutes that regulated and set maximum rates for warehouses, grain elevators, and railroads. The decision became most memorable for its now famous delineation of property that becomes "clothed with a public interest when used in a manner to make it of public consequence, and affect the community at large." Waite consulted Lord Hale's famous treatise to support his assertions: "Every bushel of grain for its passage 'pays a toll, which is a common charge,' and, therefore, according to Lord Hale, every such warehouseman 'ought to be under public regulation, viz., that he . . . take but reasonable toll.' Certainly, if any business can be clothed 'with a public interest, and cease to be *juris privati* only,' this has been."

Yet beneath the constitutional catchwords "affected with a public interest," the *Munn* case was more fundamentally grounded in the Court's awareness of the shifting social, political, and economic patterns of the post-Civil War period. . . . In blessing the validity of some governmental control (state regulation by commission) the highest federal judges served as priests of a juridical reformation. The orthodoxy of private competition handed down in the Charles River Bridge decision forty years before had been weakened by the public outcry over abuses and panic attributed to the railroad juggernaut and other malefactors of great power.

By the close of the nineteenth century, courts generally recognized that the common law requirement to proffer equal service should apply to the increasing variety of business affected with a public interest whether they were common carriers or not. . . .

Courts have used four different rationales in imposing the obligation to furnish adequate supply or service without discrimination:

(1) The imposition of a common right to access drawn from the doctrine of services as *a public calling, essential to individual survival within the community;*

(2) The duty to serve all equally, inferred from and recognized as an essential part of *natural monopoly power;*

(3) The duty to serve all parties alike, as a consequence of the *grant of the privileged power of eminent domain; and, finally,*

(4) The duty to serve all equally, *flowing from consent, expressed or (more frequently) implied.*

A notion of reciprocity informs each of the judge-made justifications of the duty to serve. In each case, the court is presenting the elements of a multifaceted *quid pro quo:* if one wants the power to take private property against the wishes of the owner, one has to assume the responsibility of making the land (or the services that spring forth from the land) available to all members of the society; if one claims an exclusive franchise, one has to abide by the rules of the game and provide equal access; if one were going to act like a government, then one assumes the obligations of the sovereign to act in the common interest of all its citizens.

Whichever the rationale proffered, the courts in a pinch could always rest their argument upon "consent." Consent, to them, meant accepting the responsibilities along with the rest of the bargain: if a company has freely chosen to engage in providing a service to the public, then it has voluntarily assented to the appropriate requirements of a public service. Deducing a sufficient incentive for this free choice was easy, for a corporation "has, or must be supposed to have, an equivalent for its consent." Hence, the corporation, it was reasoned, had sought out and willingly assumed the very burdens it was now seeking to negate or avoid.■

NOTES AND COMMENTS

1. In deciding whether the Chicago grain warehouses were devoted to a public use, the court relied on the warehouse companies' own brief in which they bragged about how important they were to the entire Western United States because they served as the shipping point for all of the area's grain. In the nineteenth century, Chicagoans had the reputation of being insufferable braggarts about their great city. It was this trait, not the climate, that gave Chicago the nickname "the Windy City." Emmett Dedmon, Fabulous Chicago 221 (2d ed. 1981).

2. While today the *Munn* decision may appear obvious, historically it is of great significance. After the Civil War, American States that long had promoted and encouraged railroads and utilities began to regulate them. The *Munn* decision grew out of the varied legislative responses states were taking to the "railroad problem"—a problem associated with large railroad companies that could charge different prices to different customers and control access to transportation markets. It was one of seven cases known as the "Granger cases," historical rulings that tested the constitutional authority of state police power, through legislation, to regulate private businesses.

3. The decision in *Munn* shed some light on the recently enacted Fourteenth Amendment. Justice Stephen J. Field, in a dissent joined by William Strong, made an early plea for substantive due process limitations on regulation. This view would later be endorsed by the court in *Lochner v. New York*, 198 U.S. 45 (1905), a case which made the Supreme Court the overseer of all kinds of regulatory activity until the mid–1930's.

4. With the growth of regulation, states set up commissions to regulate public utilities. The states usually adopted a series of statutes, one for each type of common public service. Thus there would be a gas act, an electric act and a telephone act, which might eventually be consolidated. But the states usually assigned the power to administer all of these acts to a single board or commission called the "Public Utilities Commission," "Public Service Commission," "Railroad Commission," or "Commerce Commission." The terminology still varies from state to state, but such commissions are commonly referred to generically as "public utility commissions."

5. The Supreme Court's definition of "business affected with a public interest" was further expanded in *Nebbia v. New York*, 291 U.S. 502 (1934). After dairy prices in New York collapsed as a result of oversupply, the legislature commanded a milk control board to fix both maximum and minimum retail milk prices. After Nebbia, a grocer, was convicted for selling milk too cheaply, he contested the conviction under the due process and equal protection clauses, arguing that neither the milk business nor retail grocery sales were monopolies or traditional regulated industries. In affirming Nebbia's conviction, the Court said that "affected with a public interest" means "no more than that an industry, for adequate reason, is subject to control for the public good." 291 U.S. at 536. The Court said that "price control, like any other form of regulation, is unconstitutional only if

arbitrary, discriminatory, or demonstrably irrelevant to the policy the legislature is free to adopt." 291 U.S. at 539. The *Nebbia* case was seen as an indication that the Court would no longer actively question the extent to which particular businesses could be subjected to regulation. *Lochner*'s reasoning, of course, was expressly overruled only a few years later, in *West Coast Hotel v. Parrish*, 300 U.S. 379 (1937).

6. Following *Munn*, most states interpreted the case as granting them broad authority to set up programs to regulate public utilities. The Court had said that states were free to substitute more detailed statutory rules for the common law principles. Originally, many of the states adopted a series of statutes, one for each type of common public service (e.g., a gas act, an electric act and a telephone act). But the states usually assigned the power to administer all of these acts to a single board or commission called the "Public Utilities Commission" or something similar.

Today, in many states the statutory responsibilities of the commission may all be consolidated in a Public Utilities Act. Typically, these commissions had, and still have, the following five basic powers:

    1. Assign territory. To assign territories through "certificates of public convenience and necessity."

    2. Set service standards. To enforce the duty to serve by establishing standards of service.

    3. Regulate rates. To review the utility's rates and reject those that are not "just and reasonable."

    4. Approve spending. To review the utility's major capital expenditures, including borrowings, against a standard of "prudent investment."

    5. Control abandonment. To prevent the utility from abandoning service without its approval.

Note that these powers generally track the common law rules, but over time the statutes and the rules of the commissions usually provide a lot more detail in the way of guidance to the utility than was obtained from the common law rules.

B. REGULATORY OBJECTIVES

As the previous cases suggest, although American jurisdictions often reject public ownership as the norm, they certainly do not eschew active regulation of privately-owned resources. Why should the government regulate the activities of private energy resource property owners?

1. THEORIES OF REGULATION

The history of enterprise in the U.S. suggests a variety of rationales for regulation. A variety of political, economic, and legal considerations are involved.

Extreme political skeptics of governmental regulation (as well as many public choice economists) may describe regulation as the result of strong political forces—whether industry, environmental groups, or consumers—mustering the support to protect their interests.[1] By contrast, many neoclassical economists may explain regulation as a response to the market failures introduced by natural monopoly, ensuring that prices and quantities in naturally monopolistic markets approximate those of a competitive market. Still another theory of regulation is based on deliberative democracy—that some enterprises are inextricably linked to the public good and the process of government regulation is most likely to promote the public interest, rather than purely private gain.[2]

While all of these theories provide a useful and relevant lens through which to view public utility regulation, perhaps the most powerful analytical tool—indeed, the tool most widely accepted by regulators in market economies—comes from the neoclassical economists. We live in a market economy, one in which competition is valued both for its process and its outcomes.

The neoclassical economic model attempts to approximate the behavior of a firm in a perfectly competitive market. A perfectly competitive market assumes certain conditions: a firm faces many buyers and sellers in the market, all firms and buyers have equal access to information, the costs of transaction between any seller and buyer are extremely low, and there are no significant impediments to market entry and exit. Given such conditions, the neoclassical economic model shows that perfectly competitive firms will price their products or services at marginal cost—the cost to the firm of producing one additional unit of output. If a firm prices above marginal cost, the lure of economic profits will result in new firms entering the market and, as supply increases, driving price downward towards marginal cost. By contrast, if a firm was to price below marginal cost, the cost of each new unit of production or sales would exceed the revenue from the additional unit; since firms cannot stay in operation for long if their costs exceed their revenues, some firms would be likely to exit such a market and, as supply decreases, drive price upward towards marginal cost.

However, most markets which are price regulated are not perfectly competitive. While a perfectly competitive market marks one extreme of the neoclassical market spectrum (indeed, its ideal), at the other end of the spectrum is natural monopoly: a market that can be served at a lower average cost by a single firm than by two or more firms. A market is a natural monopoly if it faces decreasing average costs over its entire range of production; a single firm in such a market could increase its production

---

1. A good summary of this literature is included in George Priest, The Origins of Regulation and the "Theories of Regulation" Debate, 36 J. L. Econ. & Org. 289 (1993). For early works arguing this general thesis *see* Sam Peltzman, Towards a More General Theory of Regulation, 19 J. L. & Econ. 211 (1976); George Stigler, The Theory of Economic Regulation, 2 Bell J. Econ. & Mgmt. Sci. 3 (1971).

2. *See* Paul L. Joskow & Roger Noll, Regulation in Theory and Practice: An Overview, in Studies in Public Utility Regulation (Gary Fromm, ed., MIT Press 1981).

or sales at a lower average cost than if a new entrant were to also compete in the market.

Consider, for example, electricity transmission. Assume that one firm serves the entire city of Chicago by building a transmission network to reach all customers and by centralizing its power generation and distribution decisions. Once a firm has built a transmission network to serve a fraction of the customers throughout this densely populated urban area (say the largest customers, such as factories, hotels, and large retail establishments), it will be cheaper for that same firm to increase its customer base incrementally than for a new firm to begin a network from scratch to serve additional customers (such as smaller residential customers). Indeed, we could imagine the unnecessary duplication that would result if multiple utilities were required to build transmission lines to the same neighborhoods to provide electricity to different customers. Electricity transmission is characterized by economies of scale: the cost of transmitting electricity decreases over the entire range of production for the market. Thus, it is cheaper for a single firm to expand its operations than for additional firms to enter the market.

For this reason, governments grant certain utilities and common carriers a monopoly franchise to provide service to a specified geographic area. A monopoly is able to provide more reliable and economic service in markets that face significant economies of scale.

However, once a utility has been granted a monopoly franchise, this raises a new problem: the specter of monopoly pricing. It is well established that the monopolist faces strong incentives to charge a price higher and produce less of a good or service than a perfectly competitive market would yield. For this reason, monopoly franchises are typically subject to some sort of price regulation.[3]

Several economic rationales lie at the heart of traditional public utility regulation.

2.   NATURAL MONOPOLY

The extraction, conversion, and distribution of many energy resources, such as natural gas and electricity, have historically been price regulated to protect against abuses by their owners. Since *Munn v. Illinois*, it has been recognized that certain industries are "clothed with the public interest" and subject to an obligation to provide equal service to all. Firms providing natural gas or electricity to end-use customers have traditionally been regulated as "public utilities"—firms granted a monopoly franchise in a geographic area in return for a duty to serve the public.

---

3.   Some argue that the presence of a single firm need not necessarily lead to monopolistic pricing. *See* Harold Demsetz, Why Regulate Utilities?, 9 J. L. & Econ. 55 (1968). In addition, more modern work in contestable market theory calls into question monopoly pricing. *See* Elizabeth E. Bailey and William J. Baumol, Deregulation and the Theory of Contestable Markets, 1 Yale J. on Reg. 111 (1984).

For example, Florida Power & Light (FP&L), an investor-owned utility, has been granted an exclusive service territory in Florida in exchange for its promise to provide power to any customer within its service territory at a reasonable rate. This protection against competition within a geographic area is often called a "horizontal monopoly." There are two distinct economic reasons that FP&L is granted this type of a monopoly franchise.

First, FP&L possesses many characteristics of what economists call a classic "natural monopoly"—a single firm that is able to provide a good or service to a market at a lower average cost than two or more firms because of economies of scale or other network economies.[4] Economies of scale occur when the average cost of production declines over the entire range of production for the industry. In addition to simple production efficiency, recent developments in economics focus on network efficiencies. Network economies, a type of economy of scale, may occur when a single firm is able to more efficiently operate than multiple firms, because it is better able to coordinate interdependent aspects of an industry's operations or because it is able to process information more efficiently. For example, it may be considered more efficient for a single firm to operate a nationwide distribution network for a product. A single firm may be able to coordinate its operations, such as times for delivery, more efficiently than multiple firms. In addition, the single firm may be able to gather and process information about market supply and demand more efficiently than multiple firms.

Second, it may be advantageous to allow a single firm to provide power service because there are efficiencies to be gained by integrating different market services. This is often called "vertical integration," and its rationales are discussed further in Chapter 3. In the computer industry, for example, it may be efficient for a manufacturer to bundle computer hardware with basic operating system software. A classic example in the energy industry is the electric utility: often, a single firm can more efficiently transport and distribute energy if it serves other market functions, such as power generation, as well.[5]

NOTE ON THE ECONOMICS OF NATURAL MONOPOLY

The economic phenomenon of economies of scale can be illustrated by comparing the general cost functions of different types of firms. A firm's costs can be divided into fixed and variable costs. Fixed costs are the costs associated with the firm's plant; assuming the firm remains in business with a constant plant size, they do not vary with the level of production. Variable costs, however, change with the firm's output level. For example, in making a decision to operate a plant 24 hours a day, as opposed to 12 hours a day, a manufacturing firm raises its variable costs significantly. Total costs represent the sum of fixed and variable costs.

---

4. *See* William W. Sharkey, The Economic Theory of Natural Monopoly (1983).

5. Harold L. Platt, The Electric City 74–82 (University of Chicago Press; 1991); Paul L. Joskow & Richard Schamalensee, Markets for Power: An Analysis of Electric Utility Deregulation (MIT Press 1983).

Figure 2–1 illustrates the relationship between total costs and a hypothetical firm's output level. Imagine, for example, that the firm in

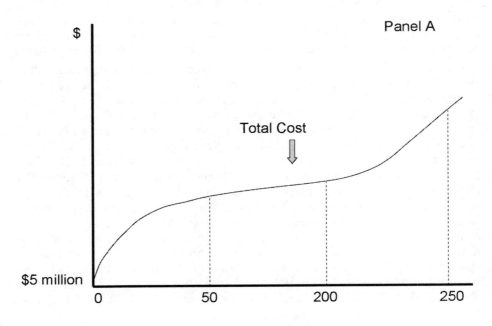

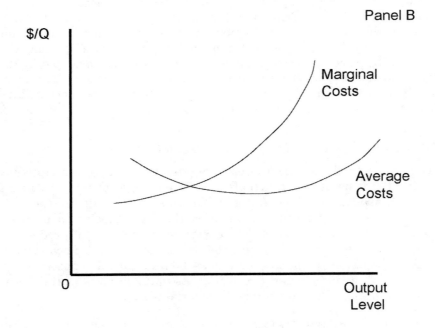

Figure 2–1

panel A is a power plant with 250 megawatts (MW) capacity. The horizontal axis represents the firm's operation level, in MW. The vertical axis represents the total costs of production, in dollars. Assume that the fixed costs of the plant are $5 million. Since the firm will have to pay these costs even if it chooses not to operate the plant, the vertical axis begins at $5 million. The graph in panel A is drawn to reflect a cost phenomenon observed in most production processes, including power generation. At low levels of operation, such as those below 50 MWs, variable costs rise rapidly, although at a decreasing rate. Initially, it may take a lot of fuel to fire up the power plant's turbines, just as it takes a lot of fuel to quickly accelerate a car from zero to forty miles per hour. Between the 50 and 200 MW level, variable costs rise more slowly with increased operation levels and output. Once the power plant's turbines are running, additional operation levels are more efficient than the initial startup, for reasons similar to an automobile's improved gas mileage in highway driving. Above the 200 MW level, however, the plant may lose some of its earlier efficiencies. Here costs may climb at a greater rate with each additional unit of output. The shape of this curve suggests that the plant operates most efficiently in the 50 to 200 MW range of output.

The graph in panel B illustrates how this cost phenomenon translates into a relationship between marginal and average costs for the hypothetical firm. Average costs are calculated by dividing total costs by the output level. The average cost curve in panel B is derived from the curve in panel A; each point in the average cost curve represents total costs divided by the corresponding output level, or the slope of the total cost curve. Marginal (or incremental) costs, by contrast, refer to the costs associated with each additional unit of output. When marginal costs are below average costs average costs fall, and when marginal costs are above average costs average costs rise. Of course, every law student is familiar with this concept: if a law student's average is 75, her GPA will rise if she receives an 80 in torts but will fall if she receives a 70.

Over the long run, nearly all costs are variable. For example, a firm must eventually replace even the plant itself. Cost considerations come into play in determining the optimal size of a firm's plant. These decisions, as well as many regulatory decisions, will depend on the shape of an industry's long run average cost curve. Consider **Figure 2–2**, which represents an entire industry rather than a single firm. A plant of size A has average production costs C1, while a plant of size B has average production costs C2. In the range between A and B, this industry experiences economies of scale: the larger plant produces lower average costs. However, a plant of size C has greater average production costs than size B. Between B and C, the industry experiences diseconomies of scale. The curve connecting these various plant average cost curves corresponds to the industry's long run average cost curve.

What does this long run average cost curve tell us about regulatory policy? A lot depends on the level of demand for an industry's products or services. In an industry with a demand curve similar to that in **Figure 2–3**, firm B would be able to compete more effectively than firm A because firm

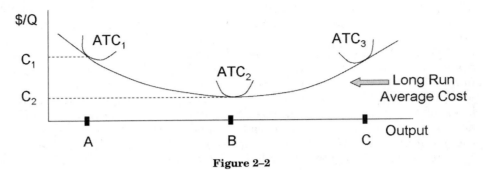

Figure 2–2

B's larger size and production scale give it lower average costs. Over time, firm B would drive firm A out of business. In this industry, a single firm is more efficient than two or more firms. If two or more firms operated in this market, prices would be higher and output would be lower, since the quantity demanded would decrease with higher prices. Such a market is called a *natural monopoly*.

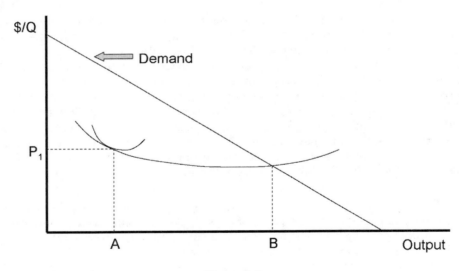

Figure 2–3

Contrast a natural monopoly market with a competitive market. **Figure 2–4** illustrates a very different relationship between market demand and long run average costs. At price P1, this industry could support five firms. The cost characteristics of various industries are determined primarily by technological issues and transactions costs. Some industries, such as agriculture, have cost curves more like **Figure 2–4** than **Figure 2–3**. These industries will be able to support a larger number of firms. The relationship between long run average costs and demand is the major economic factor in determining the optimal number of firms serving a given market. For further discussion of industry cost characteristics, *see* F.M. Scherer & David Ross, Industrial Market Structure and Economic Performance (Houghton Mifflin Co., 3d ed. 1990); W. Kip Viscusi, John M. Vernon & Joseph E. Harrington, Jr., Economics of Regulation and Antitrust (Heath 1992).

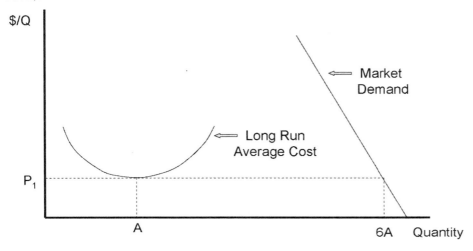

Figure 2–4

3. PRICE REGULATION

The establishment of a monopoly franchise also raises the specter of monopoly pricing, at potential harm to consumers. According to Stephen Breyer, who wrote an important book on the topic of regulation prior to his elevation to Justice of the U.S. Supreme Court,

> In a perfectly competitive market, firms expand output to the point where price equals incremental cost—the cost of producing an additional unit of their product. A monopolist, if unregulated, curtails production in order to raise prices. Higher prices mean less demand, but the monopolist willingly forgoes sales—to the extent that he can more than compensate for the lost revenue (from fewer sales) by gaining revenue through increased price on the units that are still sold.

Stephen Breyer, Regulation and Its Reform 15–16 (Harv. U. Press 1982). It is well established that the monopolist faces incentives to charge a price above the competitive level, produce less output than a competitive market, and transfer wealth from consumers to itself.

Price regulation is designed to yield the mix of price, output, and profits approximating that which would be produced by a competitive market. Price regulation began with the local railroad and gas boards of the late nineteenth century. Today, most state public service commissions ("PSCs"), as well as the Federal Energy Regulatory Commission ("FERC"), FPC's successor agency, continue to regulate the prices public utilities charge their end-use or wholesale customers on the basis of the cost incurred to provide service. This cost of service regulation is subject to the requirement, under the Takings Clause to the Fifth Amendment of the

Constitution, that a utility's investors be allowed to return an adequate rate of return on their investments.[6]

The essence of the traditional formula for calculating utility rates is simple. First, regulators determine a utility's aggregate "revenue requirements"—the amount a utility must earn in a given year to cover its variable and fixed costs,[7] including its cost of capital. The fixed costs of providing service, such as power plants and transmission lines, are included in what is called rate base. Revenue requirements (R) are determined through application of the following formula: $R = O + B(r)$, where O is the utility's annual operating expenses (i.e., its costs that vary with its level of production, such a fuel costs, maintenance, and non-union wages), B is the firm's rate base (i.e., its fixed costs, such as its capital resources), and r is the rate of return allowed on the utility's rate base. Next, a utility's rate per unit of energy consumed is calculated by dividing its revenue requirement by the number of energy units consumed by a class of customers.

As a much-simplified example, consider the following: Assume that FP&L incurs $10,000,000 in operating expenses, such as coal or natural gas, and builds its power plant and transmission lines at a cost of $250,000,000 in order to provide 28,000,000 kwh of service to a single class of residential customers in a given year. Further assume that the average cost of FP&L's various sources of capital − the interest it pays on its debt and the rate of return on its equity − is 10%. FP&L's revenue requirement is $10,000,000 + ($250,000,000 × .10), or $35,000,000. The Florida PSC will set its residential rates at $35,000,000/28,000,000, or $1.25 a kwh. Price regulation and its flaws are discussed in more detail in Chapter 3, on rate regulation.

NOTE ON THE ECONOMICS OF PRICE REGULATION

Where a monopoly is present, a single firm serves the entire market. Often, in such markets regulators protect monopoly markets, including public utilities, against competitive entrants. The monopolist faces a type of competition in that it cannot charge an infinite price for its products. However, it will be able to charge more than a competitive price without losing so many sales that its price increase is unprofitable.

To illustrate this phenomenon, consider **Figure 2–5**. Assume that the monopolist seeks to maximize its profits and that it charges all consumers the same price. Since the monopolist is the only firm serving the market, the firm's demand curve is the industry demand curve; it is downward sloping, reflecting that consumers will buy more of a product if the price is lower. The monopolist, like any other firm, must choose the level of output to produce and the price to charge. Like any other firm, it will produce to the point where marginal revenues equal marginal costs. A competitive

---

6. *Bluefield Waterworks and Improvement Co. v. Public Service Commission*, 262 U.S. 679 (1923); *Federal Power Comm'n v. Hope Natural Gas Co.*, 320 U.S. 591 (1944).

7. Variable costs change with an increase in a utility's level of production (say, with an extremely hot Summer or cool Winter), while fixed costs do not.

firm would also produce up to the point where marginal revenue (including a rate of return) equals marginal costs, although a competitive firm would face a very different demand curve; if a market is competitive the demand curve is relatively flat, since the competitive firm will be unable to increase its price significantly without losing all or most of its customers to its competitors. By contrast, the monopolist faces a downward sloping demand curve, indicating its degree of market power over price. It can increase its prices through output restrictions.

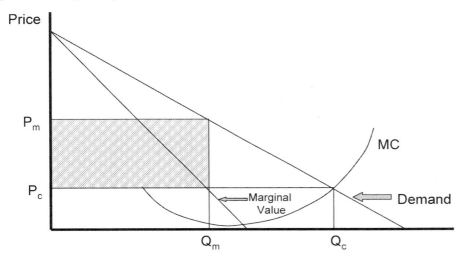

Figure 2–5

Although the monopolist will follow a basic decision-making process very similar to the competitive firm—producing at an output level up to the point additional revenues (including a rate of return) equal additional costs—characteristics of monopolist markets make the outcomes of this process very different. A competitive market would produce QC and charge price PC. The monopolist will produce less and charge a higher price than a competitive market would yield. It will produce QM and charge price PM. In so doing it maximizes its profits.

There are some losses produced by such monopoly pricing that may make government regulation desirable. Once such loss is reduced access to products and higher prices, as is reflected in the shaded box of **Figure 2–5**. This shaded box may represent monopoly profits, or money spent by the monopolist to exclude potential rivals. Government might regulate monopoly pricing for a variety of purposes, including protection of consumers against pricing abuses, ensuring monopoly rents are spent on socially valuable items, protecting against the risks of political influence, and limiting size and encourage small business. The economics of price regulation and its failures are discussed further in Chapter 3, on rate regulation. For further discussion of the basics, *see* Mark Seidenfeld, Microeconomic Predicates to Law and Economics 61–62 (Anderson 1996); Richard A.

Posner, Economic Analysis of Law 343–66 (Little Brown, 4th ed. 1992); W. Kip Viscusi, John M. Vernon & Joseph E. Harrington, Jr., Economics of Regulation and Antitrust (Heath 1992).

C. THE ROLE OF THE PUBLIC UTILITY COMMISSION

Public utility regulation is largely controlled by state agencies. Insofar as federal regulation is concerned, in the early part of the twentieth century most public utilities couldn't have been effectively regulated by the federal government because at that time the Supreme Court had a fairly restrictive view of the extent of federal power under the commerce clause. As a result, the more local aspects of public utility operation would have been constitutionally exempt from federal regulation. (This would not necessarily be true today since the companies are more integrated into national networks and the Court takes a more expansive view of federal power under the Commerce Clause.)

Local regulation, on the other hand, was widely seen as ineffective. Originally, it was the cities that tried to regulate public utilities: "Transit, gas and electric companies had extensive, and corrupt, influence in . . . city councils," but business consumers and employee unions were also influential. And the interests of neighboring municipalities and rival utilities "generated intense legal and political controversy." Morton Keller, Regulating a New Economy: Public policy and Economic Change in America, 1900–1933 58–59 (Harvard Univ. Press, 1990). Many municipal governments offered franchises to private utility operators, subject to a competitive process of franchise review and renewal. Alternatively, the municipal government itself sometime entered into the utility business, which often left regulatory decisions to big city political machines. The result was a decentralized, piecemeal regulatory process, one that provided little uniformity and made many of the private utilities unhappy with the uncertainty of their franchises. State legislatures were sometimes involved in regulatory decisions, but their ability to address serious regulatory problems was seriously limited. So, at the state level the growth of regulation by agency officials can be attributed in large part to the failures of municipal regulation of energy utilities. The creation of state public utility commissions was intended to supersede a pattern of municipal regulation that had proved to be controversial.

"The initiation and development of public service regulation by state commissions owed much to the forces of political reform—under the leadership of men like Charles Evans Hughes of New York and Robert LaFollette of Wisconsin . . . [in] response to the excesses of the public service companies and the inadequacies of other methods of control." But many of the companies themselves "encouraged the movement to vest regulatory powers in state commissions—at the expense of municipal authorities [believing that] their operations and investments would be more secure if insulated from politically motivated interference from uninformed (and often corrupt) state and local political factions." William K. Jones,

Origins of the Certificate of Public convenience and Necessity: Developments in the States, 1870–1920, 79 Colum. L. Rev. 426, 432 (1979). Following the leadership of New York and Wisconsin (whose state Public Service Commission legislation was drafted by the University of Wisconsin economist John Commons), many states established state-wide regulatory commissions for public utilities in the early twentieth century. *See* Robert L. Bradley, Jr., The Origins of Political Electricity: Market Failure or Political Optimism, 17 Energy L.J. 59 (1996).

Although initially skeptical, many electric and gas and telephone companies actively began to seek state regulation. They were being bedeviled by all sorts of inconsistent demands by local governments and they saw state regulation as a way to preempt them. Consequently, most public utilities acts preempted local regulation.

Although the concept of a public utility has common law roots, today most utility regulation begins with a provision of a statute or state constitution that designates the enterprises to be regulated and the type of regulatory powers that may be exercised over them.

At the national level, public utility regulation is implemented by the Federal Energy Regulatory Commission ("FERC"), formerly the Federal Power Commission ("FPC"). FERC derives its regulatory powers from three primary statutes: the Natural Gas Act ("NGA"), which regulates natural gas sales; the Federal Power Act ("FPA"), which regulates sales of electricity for resale (i.e., wholesale sales) in interstate commerce; and the Interstate Commerce Act ("ICA"), which gives FERC jurisdiction over the shipment of oil by pipeline. FERC is composed of five commissioners appointed by the President and confirmed by the Senate. Commissioners are appointed for a term of four years, but no more than three members of FERC can be from the same political party. FERC, like the Interstate Commerce Commission and Federal Communications Commission, is an "independent" agency: it performs legislative functions and the President's removal power is limited. In addition to limitations on the number of FERC members from a single political party, the President may only remove FERC commissioners for "inefficiency, neglect of duty, or malfeasance in office," not for simple disagreement with policies. 42 U.S.C. § 7171. In addition to its five commissioners, FERC employs a staff of approximately 1500, which includes lawyers, accountants, engineers, and economists as well as "street level" bureaucrats.

State regulatory control is exercised by a specialized agency of government called the Public Service Commission, Public Utility Commission, Railroad Commission, or Corporation Commission. (These state agencies, discussed in Chapter 3, will be referred to generically as "PSCs.") The practice for selecting PSC members varies from state to state: some are elected, while others are appointed by the state governor. Similar to the FERC, most PSCs have a staff of lawyers, accountants, engineers, and economists, although the training and experience of the staff members varies widely from state to state.

While both FERC and state PSCs have the power to initiate actions on their own, they are generally reactive regulatory bodies. A regulated utility will come to the agency to increase its rates or change its existing structure. Alternatively, a prospective entrant may seek to provide service in a regulated market, drawing complaints from customers or competitors. Agencies will often be asked to resolve such matters.

Although the process varies from state to state and in different contexts at the federal level, most public utility regulation imposes the following general requirements:

1) **Certificate of Convenience and Necessity:** The business must obtain permission to enter into and operate within the regulated market. This is achieved by securing a "certificate of convenience and necessity."

2) **Monopoly Franchise:** As part of this licensing process, the government often creates a monopoly by establishing an exclusive geographic franchise. Within this service area, the utility has the right to serve the market without competition.

3) **Duty to Serve:** In return for this exclusive service territory, the government often requires the utility to provide a certain level of service to all customers within the service territory. The utility has a duty to serve customers and cannot selectively choose its customer base for its own private gain.

4) **Price Regulation:** The regulatory body will allow the utility to charge only "just and reasonable" rates to customers. This is normally done on the basis of the cost of providing service to each class of customers (see Chapter 3).

For example, consider two separate industries: food packaging and electricity distribution. A new entrant to the food packaging business (Packco) need not seek government permission to build and operate its plant. However, before building a power transmission line, a power generator (Genco) must obtain a certificate of convenience and necessity from the relevant state authority, usually a PSC. Packco will likely compete with numerous other food packaging companies within the same geographic market. By contrast, Genco may seek an exclusive service territory and may ask the PSC to grant a monopoly franchise. If the PSC has approved Genco's franchise, Genco will no longer face competition in this geographic area. If granted a franchise, the PSC will require Genco to serve all customers within its territory and will ensure that it charges these customers just and reasonable rates. Packco, however, will continue to face competition from other food packaging companies, as well as potential new entrants to the food packaging business. Although certain aspects of the food packaging business may be regulated, such as the information that may be presented on certain products and the materials that may be used, Packco will charge the price that the market yields, not a price set by regulators.

Today every state has some sort of commission or agency charged with regulating different types of public utilities in the energy sector. A utilities commission will typically monitor market power utility companies charge for natural gas, electricity and telephone service within the state. Visit your state utilities commission web site. Does it set rates for energy companies? Does it otherwise regulate how they price and offer service? How does it do so?

* * *

The California Energy Commission has offered the following reasons for no government intervention in the setting of gasoline prices. The debate has been revived following outage of gasoline refining due to Hurricane Katrina in 2005. Are you convinced?

Questions and Answers: California Gasoline Price Increase

http://www.energy.ca.gov/gasoline/gasoline_q-and-a.html

Where does our oil and gasoline come from?

California consumes substantial amounts of gasoline—about 16 billion gallons per year! Crude oil is made into gasoline, and the crude comes from within-state oil wells (42%), Alaska (22%) and foreign sources (36%).

Most (about 90%) of our gasoline is refined in-state, but additional quantities of gasoline and blending components are imported because refining capacity cannot keep pace with growing demand.

California is also isolated from other refining centers in the United States. Because most of California is designated by the federal government as an air quality "non-attainment" area, our gasoline must meet stringent air quality requirements to burn cleanly to protect public health and the environment.

What happened to oil and gasoline prices this year?

Retail regular-grade California gasoline prices increased to $2.29 per gallon on March 14, 2005, up from $1.98 at the beginning of the year.

Statewide spot wholesale gasoline prices in California were $1.65 per gallon on March 14, 2005; up from $1.23 at the first of the year.

California retail diesel prices have also increased, rising to $2.42 on March 14, 2005, up from $2.06 at the beginning of the year.

What factors influenced these price increases?

The answer is two-fold: demand and supply.

Demand

In California, gasoline refinery production is not keeping pace with demand, which causes the state to rely on more imported gasoline. California currently imports more than 10 percent of its gasoline, and those imports are expected to grow to about 20 percent by 2010. Over the past several years, gasoline demand has grown between two to three percent per year, primarily as a result of our state's growing population. However, consumers are also choosing less fuel-efficient vehicles. Of the new vehicles purchased in 2003, one-half were minivans, SUVs or light duty trucks. The supply/demand imbalance becomes even greater in the summer months when gasoline consumption typically rises by nearly 10 percent during the "summer driving season."

If a refinery problem occurs in California, the state relies on tankers to ship gasoline to California from the half dozen refineries around the world that can produce the state's clean-burning gasoline. Even the closest refinery, in the state of Washington, is 7 to 10 days away, and gasoline from Texas must come across Panama. In other states, there is a system of pipelines that move gasoline and diesel products throughout the mid-West and eastern states, especially, if there is a refinery problem.

Supply Problems

Gasoline consumption typically rises during the summer because more people are on the road during the "summer driving season." For example, in 2003 and 2004, daily gasoline demand rose 9 percent and 7 percent, respectively, when you compare consumption in January to August.

Refineries prepare for this increased summertime demand by doing their routine maintenance during January and February. Refineries reduce their gasoline production to perform maintenance and change over to summer blend gasoline during what are called "turn-arounds." Refiners typically build inventories to take them through this turn-around period when production at the refinery fluctuates.

At the start of this year's refinery maintenance season, inventories of gasoline were at high levels. But above normal refinery turn-arounds this year, combined with unexpected problems with restarts and other difficulties, cut deeply into production and stocks, causing sharp price increases.

Six refineries began turn-arounds in January, one in February, and another in March. One other refinery had unexpected problems in late February. While restarting, three of these refineries experienced difficulties that, combined, caused unplanned purchases of about a million barrels of gasoline to meet requirements.

High world crude oil prices have contributed to raising the price of all petroleum products. However, in the most recent California gasoline price spike, oil prices are secondary to lost refinery production and resulting product shortages.

What are the various costs associated with producing gasoline?

There are four main areas associated with the costs of gasoline:

1. Crude oil cost
2. Taxes
3. Refinery costs and profit margin
4. Dealer costs and profit margin

About the only area that doesn't change much are taxes.

Crude oil cost is the price paid for a barrel of crude oil on the international market divided by 42 gallons in a barrel. This will give the price of crude oil per each gallon of gasoline. This is often the most volatile price of the fuel. Crude oil is traded as a commodity, and as the price goes up, prices for gasoline can change very quickly. When prices for crude come down, the price for gasoline typically comes down—but very slowly. This is typical for most commodities.

For every one dollar increase of the cost of a barrel of crude oil, there is an average increase of about 2.5–cents per gallon of gasoline. So, a $10 increase per barrel in crude prices means a 25–cent increase at the pump. A $15 increase in crude oil means a 37.5–cent a gallon increase in gasoline prices. This additional cost will not go away until crude oil prices start to come down.

Taxes for gasoline in California are: 18.4 cents/gallon for federal excise taxes; 18 cents/gallon for state excise taxes; and local and state sales taxes. Sales taxes vary depending on the city and county you may be in ... but on average the sales tax adds between 9 and 12 cents to a gallon of gasoline, depending on final price.

Dealer costs and profit margin (or the amount that the dealer charges for the fuel) includes all costs associated with the distribution and retailing of motor fuel, including but not limited to: franchise fees and/or rents, wages, utilities, supplies, equipment maintenance, environmental fees, licenses, permitting fees, credit card fees, insurance, depreciation, advertising and profit. Dealer margin normally lags changes in the wholesale price of gasoline.

Refinery costs and profit margin (or the prices charged by the oil companies) must cover all costs associated with production, distribution, and acquisition of gasoline. The refinery costs and profit margin covers all costs associated with refining and terminal operation: crude oil processing, oxygenate/ethanol, product shipment and storage, oil spill fees, depreciation, brand advertising, purchases of gasoline to cover refinery shortages and profits.

Why not just tell the oil companies to lower their prices? Why can't government do something about the prices?

Ronald Reagan removed regulations on oil companies and petroleum prices when he was President. Since then, gasoline prices have been dictated by supply and demand and free market economics. There are no government controls on the price of oil or gasoline. So, government cannot tell gasoline companies to hold their prices at one level or to decrease them.

Does a free market really exist with gasoline? It seems all the gasoline stations sell at the same price.

This is untrue. There are differences between stations and prices. Some stations have lower prices because they typically do not take credit cards— they take only cash or ATM cards. Credit cards can add about two to three percent to the cost of the transaction. This extra cost is passed on to the customer in higher prices at the pump for the convenience of using a credit card. Other stations, such as independents and so-called "Mom and Pop" stations usually have lower prices because they do not have multi-million dollar advertising campaigns to convince you to buy their product. So, their prices usually are lower than the "name brand" stations.

The independents and non-branded stations buy gasoline usually on what's called the unbranded "spot" market. This is the wholesale market that is most vulnerable to refinery problems and the fluctuating cost of crude oil. The price is normally lower than the branded wholesale prices. But we can have unbranded prices soar higher than branded prices when the supplies get tight. So, the independents and "Mom and Pop" stations sometimes will have to price their gasoline higher than branded stations.

Aren't the oil companies all in collusion to set their prices at the same level? Aren't they all price fixing?

Rumors and charges of collusion among the oil companies have been raised for decades with nothing ever proven. Investigations have been undertaken by California Attorney General and by federal authorities looking into these allegations.

Why do the gasoline stations raise their prices almost daily, and it seems like they sometimes do it hourly?

Prices are set by what the station owner will have to pay for the NEXT delivery of gasoline. If prices are going up on the wholesale level, The station operator has to pay for what the next shipment will cost when it's delivered. If the delivery is going to cost more than what the dealer is charging at the pump now, they are going to lose money on the higher-priced new gasoline. So, the dealer has to increase his price whenever there is an increase in the wholesale price of the fuel to pay for that more expensive gasoline in the future.

But sometimes, station owners will hold down their price increases in order to remain more competitive with other stations, temporarily costing them money. This can be especially true for independent service station owners during period of rapid wholesale price increases.

What is going to happen this spring and summer?

It's hard to predict the future, especially with a commodity like gasoline, whose price is extremely volatile.

As refineries come back into normal production, upward pressure on gasoline prices will ease once inventories return to normal. However, unplanned refinery outages can occur at any time. Depending on their extent and duration, and prevailing market conditions at the time, these events could sharply increase gasoline and diesel prices.

The transition to summer-grade gasoline could also make gasoline prices increase. As of January 1, 2004, most of California's gasoline uses ethanol instead of MTBE (methyl-tertiary butyl ether) as an oxygenate to help burn the gas more cleanly. Other states are also changing and not using MTBE because of the problems with that additive. As the U.S. East Coast makes this transition to MTBE-free gasoline for the first time, competition for valuable gasoline blend stocks could raise the cost of making California gasoline.

Wholesale ethanol prices generally declined during the gasoline price spike. Short-term changes in ethanol prices are a relatively small factor directly affecting gasoline prices.

Strong demand for gasoline and diesel in California and the U.S. would increase the pressure on prices.

If worldwide crude oil demand stays high, the dollar remains weak against other currencies, and crude oil inventories do not build, gasoline prices will be higher than normal, even if no California refinery problems arise.■

D. LIMITATIONS ON REGULATION

1. CONSTITUTIONAL LIMITATIONS

The constitutional issues raised by regulation are hardly settled, and discussion of them will reappear throughout this book. Even in the post-New Deal era, the Constitution is often invoked to invalidate energy statutes and regulations. Regulation raises the specter of constitutional challenges on the basis of a variety of doctrinal and textual theories.

First, how much judicial deference is appropriate to a Congressional determination that an activity is within its commerce power? In *U.S. v. Lopez*, discussed in Chapter 5, the Supreme Court, in a 5–4 decision in 1995, held invalid a federal statute that criminalized the possession of a gun in a local school zone as beyond Congress' power under the Commerce Clause of the Constitution. The Court reasoned that the statute did not regulate an economic activity that had a "substantial effect" on interstate commerce. After *Lopez*, can the federal government require states to consider certain conservation criteria in approving power plant expansion plans for municipal utilities selling power locally? Regardless of *Lopez's* significance, the Tenth Amendment, which reserves to the states those powers not given to the federal government, remains an important mechanism for challenging energy regulation. *See, e.g., New York v. United States*, 505 U.S. 144 (1992); *FERC v. Mississippi*, 456 U.S. 742 (1982).

Second, a state regulatory program may favor one state's economic interests at the expense of the citizens of another state. Such action may violate the "dormant" commerce clause—a judicially created doctrine that has been inferred from the textual language of the commerce clause. *See, e.g., New England Power Co. v. New Hampshire*, 455 U.S. 331 (1982) (state prohibition on the export of locally generated hydropower unconstitutional because it favors New Hampshire citizens at the expense of out-of-state citizens).

Third, a state regulatory program may be preempted by a federal law or program. *See, e.g., Pacific Gas & Elec. Co. v. Energy Res. & Dev.*

Comm'n, 461 U.S. 190 (1983). Under the Supremacy Clause of the U.S. Constitution, the federal law takes precedence over state regulation.

Fourth, regulation must comply with the due process clause of the Constitution: due process challenges to regulatory procedures are quite common in the energy context. Such challenges often focus on whether agency decision-making processes provided for adequate procedural protections pursuant to the Due Process Clause of the Constitution or the Administrative Procedure Act. *See, e.g., Cajun Elec. Power Coop. Inc. v. FERC*, 28 F.3d 173 (D.C. Cir. 1994) (per curiam).

Finally, although regulation of a utility is not per se subject to Takings Clause challenges, the Takings Clause does place many constraints on rate regulation. *See, e.g., Duquesne Light Co. v. Barasch*, 488 U.S. 299 (1989). Such limitations may also be invoked in condemnation and siting proceedings.

2.   STATUTORY AND OTHER JURISDICTIONAL LIMITATIONS

The concept that the government may regulate the prices or rates charged by an enterprise if it is "clothed with the public interest" remains the basic rule today—any such business is called a "public utility." However, regulation of public utilities is not exclusively a common law issue. Modern public utilities are legally controlled largely by statutes or regulations. For example, section 205 of the Federal Power Act, 16 U.S.C. § 824d provides for rate regulation of "any public utility" selling electricity to consumers where the transaction is subject to the Federal Energy Regulatory Commission's jurisdiction. Many state statutes provide for similar regulation of electric and natural gas "utilities." Many state statutes also provide for regulation of electric and natural gas "utilities."

Although the common law is useful in interpreting such language, the definition of a public utility remains a contentious issue of statutory interpretation which often makes its way to court. Drawing the line between those businesses that are "clothed" with the public interest and those that are "unclothed" is no less contentious today than it was when *Munn v. Illinois* was decided. For example, should a gas distribution company (a regulated public utility) be allowed to recover from its ratepayers expenses for oil exploration and production (which is unregulated)? *See Committee of Consumer Servs. v. Pub. Serv. Comm'n*, 595 P.2d 871 (Utah 1979). Or, should a company selling energy conservation and efficiency services have an duty to serve? As competition has grown in the electrical utility industry, many electric utilities now own power marketing or supply companies, which are unregulated. Regulators have been required to police carefully to make sure that ratepayers do not bear the risks of these non-public utility activities.

Before an agency can resolve a matter affecting enterprise, it must have jurisdiction over the enterprise's activities. The initial step for determining an agency's jurisdiction is to look to the common law or the words of the regulatory statute the agency is applying. But the words themselves often will not answer a jurisdictional issue before a court: courts will often be asked to interpret words in light of legislative intent, policy, and the common law. As discussed in Chapter 3, the FERC and most state PSCs have jurisdiction over enterprise deemed to be a "public utility" within the meaning of a regulatory statute. The case that follows raises a more perplexing issue, but a similar exercise in statutory interpretation applies.

California v. Lo–Vaca Gathering Co.

379 U.S. 366 (1965).

■ DOUGLAS, J. El Paso Natural Gas Co. is an interstate natural gas pipeline company that delivers gas at the Arizona–California border to three California distribution companies. The present controversy concerns gas to be purchased by it in Texas from Lo–Vaca Gathering Co. and Houston Pipe Line Co. Under Lo–Vaca's contract gas produced in Texas is to be delivered to a subsidiary of El Paso's at a Texas point for delivery into its pipeline. The contract contains the following two clauses:

> "All of the gas to be purchased by El Paso from Gatherer [Lo–Vaca] under this agreement shall be used by El Paso solely as fuel in El Paso's compressors, treating plants, boilers, camps and other facilities located outside of the State of Texas. It is understood, however, that said gas will be commingled with other gas being transported in El Paso's pipe line system."

> "It is the intent and understanding of the parties hereto that the sale of natural gas hereof is not subject to the jurisdiction of the Federal Power Commission because this sale is not for resale."

This "restricted use" agreement provides for a separate metering of the contract volumes prior to their delivery into El Paso's system. El Paso will meter the gas used for fuel purposes in its New Mexico and Arizona facilities to make certain this amount invariably exceeds the volumes of gas taken from Lo–Vaca under this agreement. . . .

In spite of these "restricted use" covenants it is conceded that the gas sold by Lo–Vaca and Houston to El Paso will flow in a commingled stream with gas from other sources and that at least a portion of the gas will in fact be resold out of Texas.

The Federal Power Commission asserted jurisdiction over these sales as sales in interstate commerce "for resale," as that term is used in § 1(b) of the Natural Gas Act, 52 Stat. 821, 15 U.S.C. § 717 (1958 ed.) [1][1]

---

1. Section 1(b) of the Act provides:

"The provisions of this Act shall apply to the transportation of natural gas in interstate commerce, to the sale in interstate commerce of natural gas for resale for ultimate public consumption for domestic, commercial, industrial, or any other use, and to natural-gas companies engaged in such transportation or sale, but shall not apply to any other transportation or sale of natural gas or to the local distribution of natural gas or to the facilities used for such distribution or to the production or gathering of natural gas."

Section 2(7) of the Act reads as follows:

We said in *Connecticut Co. v. Federal Power Comm'n*, 324 U.S. 515, 529, "Federal jurisdiction was to follow the flow of electric energy, an engineering and scientific, rather than a legalistic or governmental, test." And that is the test we have followed under both the Federal Power Act and the Natural Gas Act, except as Congress itself has substituted a so-called legal standard for the technological one. *Id.*, at 530–531. In *Interstate Natural Gas Co. v. Federal Power Comm'n*, 331 U.S. 682, 687, we considered the anatomy of the pipeline system to discover the channel of the constant flow; again in *Federal Power Comm'n v. East Ohio Gas Co.*, 338 U.S. 464, 467; and most recently in *Federal Power Comm'n v. Southern California Edison Co.*, 376 U.S. 205, 209, n. 5. The result of our decisions is to make the sale of gas which crosses a state line at any stage of its movement from wellhead to ultimate consumption "in interstate commerce" within the meaning of the Act.

Attempts have been made by one convention or another to convert a local transaction into one of interstate commerce (*Sprout v. South Bend*, 277 U.S. 163; *Superior Oil Co. v. Mississippi*, 280 U.S. 390) or to make a segment of interstate commerce appear to be only intrastate (*Baltimore & O.S.W.R. Co. v. Settle*, 260 U.S. 166). But those attempts have failed. Similarly, we conclude that when it comes to the question what gas is for "resale" the present contracts should not be able to change the jurisdictional result.

The fact that a substantial part of the gas will be resold, in our view, invokes federal jurisdiction at the outset over the entire transaction. Were suppliers of gas and pipeline companies free to allocate by contract gas from a particular source to a particular use, havoc would be raised with the federal regulatory scheme, as it was construed and applied in *Phillips Petroleum Co. v. Wisconsin*, 347 U.S. 672. A pipeline would then be able to discriminate in favor of its "non-jurisdictional" customers. Moreover, a pipeline company by a contract clause could immunize a particular supplier from the reach of federal regulation as defined by *Phillips Petroleum Co. v. Wisconsin, supra.* There would be created in those and in other ways an "attractive gap" in the federal regulatory scheme (*Federal Power Comm'n v. Transcon. Gas Pipe Line Corp.*, 365 U.S. 1, 28) which the producing States might have little incentive to close, since the gap would often involve either lower costs to intrastate customers or else merely higher pipeline costs which ultimately would be reflected in rates paid by consumers in other States. Whether cases could be conjured up where in spite of original commingling there might be a separate so-called non-jurisdictional transaction of a precise amount of gas not-for-resale within the meaning of the Act is a question we need not reach. . . .

"When used in this Act, unless the context otherwise requires—

. . . .

"(7) 'Interstate commerce' means commerce between any point in a State and any point outside thereof, or between points within the same State but through any place outside thereof, but only insofar as such commerce takes place within the United States."

Reversed.■

* * *

If a statute uses the words "public utility," or instructs regulators to regulated "in the public interest," what does this include? In *National Association For The Advancement of Colored People v. Federal Power Commission*, 425 U.S. 662 (1976), the Court held that the Federal Power Commission, in the performance of its functions under the Federal Power Act and the Natural Gas, did not have the authority to prohibit discriminatory employment practices on the part of its regulatees. The Court noted, "The use of the words 'public interest' in the Gas and Power Acts is not a directive to the Commission to seek to eradicate discrimination, but, rather, is a charge to promote the orderly production of plentiful supplies of electric energy and natural gas at just and reasonable rates."

What about the environment? Beginning in the 1960s, many states began to be concerned about air and water pollution. Public utilities were one of the major contributors to air pollution. They hoped that the regulatory role of the public utilities commissions could insulate them from the new environmental agencies that were springing up.

Orange County Air Pollution Control District v. Public Utilities Commission

484 P.2d 1361 (1971).

■ PETERS, J. We are presented in this case with an issue of some importance to urban California: Whether the authority conferred upon the Public Utilities Commission to grant permission to construct and operate privately owned electric generating units supersedes, in cases of conflict, the authority conferred upon an air pollution control district to condition construction of such units upon compliance with district emission controls.

We conclude that neither the commission nor the district has exclusive or paramount authority. Subject to judicial review provided by law, a utility must comply with the rules and regulations of both the commission and the district. Both the commission and the various districts have jurisdiction over the construction of electric generating units. This jurisdiction is set forth in the statutory schemes governing each agency.

The commission has historically been the agency charged by the Legislature with regulation of privately owned public utilities. Some of the commission's powers are derived by direct grant from the Constitution; others may be conferred by the Legislature, which is given plenary power to confer additional powers upon the commission.

The Legislature has used its authority to confer broad powers upon the commission. The commission "may supervise and regulate every public utility in the State", may order construction or modification of facilities or equipment, and may fix standards of service to be furnished. No privately owned utility may construct an electric generating unit or plant without first obtaining a certificate of public convenience and necessity from the commission. Finally, public utilities are directed to obey and comply with all commission orders as to any matter affecting its business as a public utility.

Air pollution control districts were created by the Legislature in 1947 to protect the state's "primary interest in atmospheric purity". The air pollution control district is The agency charged with enforcing both state-wide and district emission controls. The districts may also require that a permit be obtained before any building is constructed or equipment is erected or operated, and may condition the permit upon a showing that the proposed facility will comply with applicable emission controls. The district is empowered to make and enforce emission controls tailored to the peculiar pollution conditions of the district.

The district's enforcement powers are broad. The district air pollution control officer may enter any building or premises to ascertain compliance with emission controls. He may require an applicant for or holder of any permit to provide information disclosing the nature, extent, quantity, or degree of air contaminants which are or may be discharged. A permit may be denied or suspended for refusal to furnish information or failure to comply with applicable emission standards. Failure to obtain a permit, operate a facility in accord with the terms of a permit, or otherwise obey Any order, rule, or regulation of an air pollution control district constitutes a misdemeanor. Any violation of statewide or district regulations by any state or local governmental agency or public district may also be enjoined in a civil action.

Southern California Edison Company, real party in interest herein, sought permission to construct and operate two new steam electric generating units (utilizing fossil fuels) at its Huntington Beach generating station. On August 1, 1969, Edison applied to the commission for a certificate of public convenience and necessity covering its proposed construction. On September 30, 1969, Edison similarly applied to the Orange County Air Pollution Control District for a permit covering the proposed new units.

The district took action on Edison's application first. On October 13, 1969, its control officer requested that Edison furnish further information regarding the new units. The information was submitted by letter on November 14. On November 18, 1969, the control officer denied the application, stating that the information submitted was not adequate to show that the units would not violate Health and Safety Code, section 24243.

On December 23, 1969, the district's governing board adopted rule 67, which sets forth specific emission control requirements applicable to all nonmobile fuel burning equipment. The emission requirements of rule 67 are identical to those previously adopted by the Los Angeles district. Petitioners allege in their briefs that identical rules have now been adopted by all other air pollution control districts in the South Coast Air Basin, of which Orange County is a part. This allegation is not denied. On December 29, 1969, the control officer denied Edison's original application on the independent ground that the proposed facility would not comply with rule 67.

The district hearing board continued to hold hearings on Edison's application on December 29 and 30, 1969. On June 17, 1970, the hearing board issued its decision sustaining the control officer's denial of the requested permit "under authority of Rule 20, and, independently and separately thereof . . . under the authority of Rule 67." No judicial review of this decision was requested, although such review is provided for pursuant to sections 24322 and 24323.

The commission held hearings on Edison's application on 19 days between December 17, 1969, and March 9, 1970. The district participated in these hearings, presenting evidence and argument in opposition to the application. The commission was aware that Edison's application had been denied by the district based on rules 20 and 67. Nevertheless, on June 23, 1970, a week after the hearing board's final decision, the commission granted Edison's application and further directed Edison to begin construction immediately.

In its decision the commission did not contradict the district's finding that Edison would not comply with rule 67. The commission recognized, as it must, that sections 24224, 24260, 24263, and 24264, on their face give the district jurisdiction to condition permission to construct a power plant facility upon compliance with district rules and regulations. Without discussion or citation, however, the commission characterized this statutory authority as that of a "local agency."

Having made this assumption, the commission then asserted that its jurisdiction was paramount: "The cases are clear that in matters involving more than strictly local interest the broader regulatory authority, in this case the State through its Public Utilities Commission, should prevail. (*California Water and Tel. Co. v. Los Angeles County*, 16 Cal. Rptr. 618 (2d Cal. Ct. App. 1967); *Los Angeles Ry. Corp. v. Los Angeles*, 16 Cal.2d 779, 108 P.2d 430 (1940) As to concurrent jurisdiction, it may well exist as to some matters but . . . if . . . there is a direct confrontation with the jurisdiction exercised by this Commission . . . the jurisdiction of this Commission in the matter is either exclusive or paramount. That was essentially the determination made in the California Water and Telephone Company and the Los Angeles Railway Corp. cases."

The commission correctly stated that local ordinances are controlled by and subject to general state laws and the regulations of statewide agencies regarding matters of statewide concern. Accordingly, the commission has been held to have paramount jurisdiction in cases where it has exercised its authority, and its authority is pitted against that of a local government involving a matter of statewide concern.

Where its jurisdiction conflicts with other than a local agency, commission directives have not been given such controlling effect. The commission, for example, has broad authority to promote the safe operation of utilities. Yet compliance with commission directives does not preclude a jury's finding that the commission's standards did not constitute a minimum standard of reasonable care.

Perhaps an even more relevant issue is jurisdiction to regulate the health and sanitation of common carrier employees. While the commission has been said to have such jurisdiction (37 Ops.Cal.Atty.Gen. (1961) 31, 33), the Industrial Welfare Commission and the Division of Industrial Safety have been held to have Concurrent jurisdiction over such matters. The Attorney General's opinion makes it clear that a common carrier must not only obtain an operating permit from the commission and comply with commission orders, but must Also comply with pertinent orders of the Industrial Welfare Commission or the Division of Industrial Safety. "(O)wners of common carriers must comply with the orders of Each of the agencies so empowered." (37 Ops.Cal.Atty.Gen. at p. 36; italics added.)

When the Legislature considered the problem of air pollution control in 1947, it was no doubt aware of the jurisdictional limitations of local city and county governments. It is obvious that air is not a matter of purely local concern, and that the effective control of air pollution therefore should be undertaken on a nonlocal basis. . . .

Edison contends that districts have only local powers because they function only with the consent of the county board of supervisors, have boundaries coextensive with that of the county, and have as officers the entire board of supervisors sitting ex officio. What is most significant, however, is the care with which the Legislature separated the legal status of the air pollution control district from that of the county. One prime reason that the board of supervisors must give in its resolution declaring that a district is needed is that "it is not practical to rely upon the enactment or enforcement of local county and city ordinances to prevent or control . . . such pollution. . . ." The board must appropriate separate funds for the operation of the district, deposit such funds in a separate treasury, and record the appropriation as a legal charge against the county. The district is a separate corporate and political body from the county, with powers (inter alia) to sue and be sued, hold or dispose of real property, and contract with the county or city to perform services. Since any contract between a district and a county would be made by two distinct political bodies composed of identical individuals, the Legislature must have intended the district to have a separate existence from that of the county.

The Legislature did not, it is true, intend to occupy the field completely in delegating powers over pollution to air pollution control districts. Aware that some local ordinances of cities and counties might be valid but for the Legislature's intervention, and not wishing to abrogate any power that local governments might have, the Legislature declared that it did not mean to prohibit the "enactment or enforcement by any county or city of any local ordinance stricter than the provisions of this article and stricter than the rules and regulations adopted (by a district). . . ." The possible validity of local pollution controls, however, obviously has no effect on the validity of district regulation of nonlocal matters.

It might be contended that the Legislature did not consider the possibility that air pollution control districts might regulate the emissions of public utilities. The possibility of such legislative inadvertence is unlikely. In upholding the Los Angeles County district's rule 67 as reasonable against the attack of a municipally owned utility, the Los Angeles Superior Court noted that 44 percent of the nitrogen oxides discharged from nonvehicular sources in the county came from power plants. (*Department of Water and Power v. Hearing Bd. of the Air Pollution Control Dist. of the County of Los Angeles*, Los Angeles Superior Court No. 971991, judgment entered July 9, 1970).

In the instant case it was estimated that 63 percent of the nitrogen oxides from nonvehicular sources in Orange County come from Edison's power plants. It is extremely doubtful that the Legislature, in considering the need for districts with broad powers over private and public "persons," did not contemplate district regulation of power plants. There is also no evidence that the Legislature contemplated a patchwork structure in which districts might regulate the emissions of municipally owned utilities but not those of privately owned utilities, and in the absence of such evidence we are unwilling to reach such a result.

We conclude that the Legislature has established one statutory scheme for the general regulation of public utilities, another for the general regulation of air pollution. As in the field of industrial health and sanitation (37 Ops.Cal.Atty.Gen. 31), the commission must share its jurisdiction over utilities regulation where that jurisdiction is made concurrent by another (especially a later) legislative enactment. Here the Legislature has itself enacted specific emission control standards and has erected a comprehensive statutory structure for the adoption of further controls. These controls without doubt apply to public utilities. The Legislature has delegated enforcement of these emission controls to air pollution control districts. Where the district has found that a proposed or existing facility does not comply with applicable regulations, the commission may not order a utility to violate district rulings.

Rather, the Legislature has clearly provided a means by which the utility may challenge a district ruling. "Any person deeming himself aggrieved ... may maintain a special proceeding in the superior court, to determine the reasonableness and legality of any action of the hearing board." The superior court, pursuant to Code of Civil Procedure section 1094.5, may then determine the validity of such action. If a court for any reason finds that a discharge in excess of that permitted by district rules and regulations is necessary, it may so order. There is thus little likelihood that the horrific nightmare envisioned by the commission—inadequate electrical service will become a reality.

The commission has acted in excess of its jurisdiction in purporting to overrule the Orange County Air Pollution Control District's denial of Edison's application. The order of the commission is annulled, without prejudice to Edison's right to seek judicial review of the district's order pursuant to section 24322.■

NOTES AND COMMENTS

1. As the California example illustrates, environmental regulation and economic regulation of public utilities often overlap significantly. Not only do they overlap, but different regulators may be charged with implementing environmental and economic goals. What is the effect of this on regulatory objectives? On the industry? On consumers? On the environment?

2. In *Grand Central Council of the Crees (of Quebec) v. Federal Energy Regulatory Commission*, 198 F.3d 950 (D.C. Cir. 2000), a panel for the U.S. Court of Appeals for the D.C. Circuit addressed a similar issue under federal economic regulation. The Federal Power Act charges the Federal Energy Regulatory Commission (FERC) to set rates for electric utilities within its jurisdiction at a "just and reasonable" level. *See* 16 U.S.C. § 824d(a). Groups appealing FERC's rate decisions based their standing on allegations that the agency's decision, by impacting the uses of electricity, will "devastate the lives, environment, culture and economy of the Crees" and "will destroy fish and wildlife upon which Cree fisherman, trappers and hunters depend." 198 F.3d at 954. The D.C. Circuit, however, denied standing to these groups, holding that the environmental concerns they raised are outside of the zone of interests of FERC's statutory mandate to set "just and reasonable" rates. The panel reasoned that "[T]he fixing of 'just and reasonable' rates[] involves a balancing of the investor and consumer interests," but that "[b]oth interests are economic and tied directly to the transaction regulated." *Id.* at 956. The D.C. Circuit also noted that, "The Supreme Court has never indicated that the discretion of an agency setting 'just and reasonable' rates for sale of a simple, fungible product or service should, or even could, encompass considerations of environmental impact (except, of course, as the need to meet environmental requirements may affect the firm's costs)." *Id.* at 957. The court also gave weight to the fact that FERC had affirmatively forsworn environmental considerations in adjudicating rates.

3. Peter Huber argues that the multiple agencies regulating the utility industry result in "only a cycle of ecstasy and agony" in the electricity industry. According to him, "Utilities may be pleased with regulatory inertia when the issue is emissions from older, coal-fired power plants, but they are dismayed when regulatory paralysis smother a half-built nuclear power station." Environmentalists fare no better: "Those who favor more electricity production are pleased that it is enormously difficult to shut down older power plants, regardless of how unsafe or dirty those plants may be." Huber concludes "There is something in the system for everyone, but always something negative. Where can any of the contending parties turn for affirmative regulatory leadership?" *See* Peter Huber, Electricity and the Environment: In Search of Regulatory Authority, 100 Harv. L. Rev. 1002, 1054 (1987). Is there a better way to regulate a utility industry? Do other activities that are subject to regulation, such as product safety, suffer the same problem?

3. THE INTERSECTION OF REGULATION AND ANTITRUST LAW

Generally, private firms exercising market power are subject to enforcement under the antitrust laws, which are intended to protect against abuses or market power. Regulation of public utilities may implicate legal concerns under sections 1 and 2 of the Sherman Act, which address agreements in restraint of trade and illegal monopolization, respectively. For example, utility rate cases may raise concerns of price fixing (a section 1 problem) and price squeeze (a section 2 problem). *See, e.g.*, Lawrence J. Spiwak, Is the Price Squeeze Doctrine Still Viable in Fully Regulated Energy Markets?, 14 Energy L.J. 75 (1993).

Two doctrines work to allow rate regulation under the antitrust laws, but an agency's regulatory approach must be carefully assessed before concluding that regulation will not run into conflicts with federal antitrust law.

The filed rate doctrine has historically worked to protect firms with a "filed rate" (approved by a federal or state agency) from antitrust suits. This doctrine serves to protect consumers against discrimination in the setting of rates, by not allowing a firm to provide some customer discounts due to a legal judgment. In addition, the doctrine serves to advance goals such as deference to agency regulators and federalism. *See* Jim Rossi, Lowering the Filed Tariff Shield: Judicial Enforcement for a Deregulatory Era, 56 Vand. L. Rev. 1591 (2003). However, the doctrine does not apply automatically, but only if a regulator carefully evaluate and sets prices. In addition, there are recognized exceptions to the doctrine in the contexts of claims for injunctive relief and in price squeeze cases.

Under the doctrine of primary jurisdiction—along with a doctrine called the "state action doctrine"—agencies responsible for enforcing state and federal antitrust laws often defer to the price regulation schemes applied by state PSCs and FERC where the agency is engaged in a pervasive scheme of regulation. However, if an agency's approval of activity initiated by a firm is only pro forma or if the agency failed to evaluate fully the effects of the firm's activities on competition, there is some room for antitrust enforcement. *See Hughes Tool Co. v. Trans World Airlines,* 409 U.S. 363 (1973). If the costs of pervasive agency regulation are higher than the costs of competition as enforced through antitrust litigation, what is the most efficient regulatory scheme? See discussion of competition in Chapter 11 and Chapter 12, below.

CHAPTER 3

PRICE REGULATION AND ITS ALTERNATIVES

A. Principles of Rate Regulation
    1. Regulation of Rates Based on Cost of Service
        a. Rate Base and Rate of Return
        b. Rate Setting Objectives
        c. Common Rate Case Issues
        d. "Used and Useful" Property
        e. Operating Expenses
        f. Intergenerational Allocation
        g. Rate Design
    2. Regulation Based on Non-Cost Factors
B. Problems with Rate Regulation and Alternatives
    1. Critiques
    2. Price–Cap Regulation
    3. Market–Based Rates and Market Monitoring

A. PRINCIPLES OF RATE REGULATION

1. REGULATION OF RATES BASED ON COST OF SERVICE

As is discussed in Chapter 2, rate regulation is one way of limiting losses, in higher price and reduced output, associated with granting a monopoly. At the same time, rate regulation is designed to assure that a regulated firm earns what it needs to remain in business. Regulators achieve these goals by attempting price at a level that would approximate a competitive market. Since no comparable competitive market for natural monopoly services exists, regulators set rates based on the cost of service, including a fair rate of return on investment.

Cost of service regulation begins with calculation of a firm's revenue requirements—i.e., the total amount a utility needs to recover from its customers to cover its costs. Revenue requirements (R) can be stated as the following formula:

$$R = B*r + O$$

The variables to this formula include:

R the utility's revenue requirement—the total amount the firm needs to recover from its customers to cover its costs.

B the utility's rate base, representing its capital investment in plant and other assets.

78

r the rate of return regulators allow the utility to earn on its rate base.

O the utility's operating expenses, or expenses such as fuel and labor that may vary with its level of production.

This formula may be deceptive, since the calculation of R is rarely simple, but it expresses the basic components and the details are discussed further below. Once R has been calculated, rates can be set for customers. For example, if rates are set on a per unit basis for customers, $P = R/V$ where P is the price per unit the firm is permitted to charge, R is the firm's allowed revenue requirements, and V is the number of units of volume of the product the firm expects to sell.

a. RATE BASE AND RATE OF RETURN

Rate base, B, and rate of return, r, are often treated as distinct issues in rate cases before regulatory commissions. Each of these elements has been the subject of litigation. What legal protections constrain application of this formula for the protection of consumers? For investors and utilities? The following case, decided by the Supreme Court in an era where it was beginning to recognize stronger constitutional protections of private property under a doctrine known as "substantive due process," illustrates some of the legal limitations on the setting of utility rates.

Smyth v. Ames

169 U.S. 466 (1898).

[Railroads argued that a Nebraska statute establishing maximum rates applicable to rail service within the state violated the constitutional prohibition on taking private property without just compensation. After comparing the revenues each railroad would have earned by charging the prescribed rate with each railroad's operating costs for each of several years, the Court addressed the issue of rate base.]

■ HARLAN, J. A corporation maintaining a public highway, although it owns the property it employs for accomplishing public objects, must be held to have accepted its rights, privileges and franchises subject to the condition that the government creating it, or the government within whose limits it conducts its business, may by legislation protect the people against unreasonable charges for the services rendered by it. It cannot be assumed that any railroad corporation, accepting franchises, rights and privileges at the hands of the public, ever supposed that it acquired, or that it was intended to grant to it, the power to construct and maintain a public highway simply for its benefit, without regard to the rights of the public. But it is equally true that the corporation performing such public services and the people financially interested in its business and affairs have rights that may not be invaded by legislative enactment in disregard of the fundamental guarantees for the protection of property. The corporation may not be required to use its property for the benefit of the public without receiving just compensation for the services rendered by it. How such compensation may be ascertained, and what are the necessary elements in such an inquiry, will always be an embarrassing question. As said in the case last cited:

Each case must depend upon its special facts; and when a court, without assuming itself to prescribe rates, is required to determine whether the rates prescribed by the legislature for a corporation controlling a public highway are, as an entirety, so unjust as to destroy the value of its property for all the purposes for which it was acquired, its duty is to take into consideration the interests both of the public and of the owner of the property, together with all other circumstances that are fairly to be considered in determining whether the legislature has, under the guise of regulating rates, exceeded its constitutional authority, and practically deprived the owner of property without due process of law.... The utmost that any corporation operating a public highway can rightfully demand at the hands of the legislature, when exerting its general powers, is that it receive what, under all the circumstances, is such compensation for the use of its property as will be just both to it and to the public.

We hold, however, that the basis of all calculations as to the reasonableness of rates to be charged by a corporation maintaining a highway under legislative sanction must be the fair value of the property being used by it for the convenience of the public. And in order to ascertain that value, the original cost of construction, the amount expended in permanent improvements, the amount and market value of its bonds and stock, the present as compared with the original cost of construction, the probable earning capacity of the property under particular rates prescribed by statute, and the sum required to meet operating expenses, are all matters for consideration, and are to be given such weight as may be just and right in each case. We do not say that there may not be other matters to be regarded in estimating the value of the property. What the company is entitled to ask is a fair return upon the value of that which it employs for the public convenience. On the other hand, what the public is entitled to demand is that no more be exacted from it for the use of a public highway than the services rendered by it are reasonably worth. But even upon this basis, and determining the probable effect of the act of 1893 by ascertaining what could have been its effect if it had been in operation during the three years immediately preceding its passage, we perceive no ground on the record for reversing the decree of the Circuit Court. On the contrary, we are of opinion that as to most of the companies in question there would have been, under such rates as were established by the act of 1893, an actual loss in each of the years ending June 30, 1891, 1892 and 1893; and that, in the exceptional cases above stated, when two of the companies would have earned something above operating expenses, in particular years, the receipts or gains, above operating expenses, would have been too small to affect the general conclusion that the act, if enforced, would have deprived each of the railroad companies involved in these suits of the just compensation secured to them by the Constitution. Under the evidence there is no ground for saying that the operating expenses of any of the companies were greater than necessary.■

NOTES AND COMMENTS

1. Does this case concern rate base or rate of return? Because *Smyth v. Ames* is generally concerned with the "fair value of the property being used," it is more concerned with a utility's assets, or rate base, than its rate of return, or the cost the utility must pay to attract investors.

2. How helpful is the term "fair value" as a substantive legal requirement? The Court suggests that four criteria are relevant in the determination of "fair value": 1) "original cost of construction"; 2) "the amount and market values of [the utility's] bonds and stocks"; 3) "the present as compared with the original cost of construction"; 4) "the probable earning capacity of the property under particular rates prescribed." Does this give PSCs and subsequent courts a meaningful standard to apply? Is there any difference between 2) and 4)? Are these really concerns in calculating rate base?

3. As is discussed below, later cases repudiate the "fair value" doctrine. The doctrine did, however, reign during the *Lochner* era. *See* Stephen A, Siegel, Understanding the *Lochner* Era: Lessons from the Controversy Over Railroad and Utility Rate Regulation, 70 Va. L. Rev. 187 (1984).

* * *

With the end of the *Lochner* era, *Smyth v. Ames* is now only history, but the following cases both remain good law:

Bluefield Water Works & Improvement Co. v. Public Service Commission

262 U.S. 679 (1923).

■ BUTLER, J. The company contends that the rate of return is too low and confiscatory. What annual rate will constitute just compensation depends upon many circumstances and must be determined by the exercise of a fair and enlightened judgment, having regard to all relevant facts. A public utility is entitled to such rates as will permit it to earn a return on the value of the property which it employs for the convenience of the public equal to that generally being made at the same time and in the same general part of the country on investments in other business undertakings which are attended by corresponding risks and uncertainties; but it has no constitutional right to profits such as are realized or anticipated in highly profitable enterprises or speculative ventures. The return should be reasonably sufficient to assure confidence in the financial soundness of the utility and should be adequate, under efficient and economical management, to maintain and support its credit and enable it to raise the money necessary for the proper discharge of its public duties. A rate of return may be reasonable at one time and become too high or too low by changes affecting opportunities for investment, the money market and business conditions generally.■

Federal Power Commission v. Hope Natural Gas Co.

320 U.S. 591 (1944).

■ DOUGLAS, J. The primary issue in these cases concerns the validity under the Natural Gas Act of 1938 (52 Stat. 821, 15 U.S.C. § 717) of a rate order issued by the Federal Power Commission reducing the rates chargeable by Hope Natural Gas Co....

The Commission established an interstate rate base of $33,712,526 which, it found, represented the "actual legitimate cost" of the company's interstate property less depletion and depreciation and plus unoperated acreage, working capital and future net capital additions. The Commission, beginning with book cost, made certain adjustments not necessary to relate here and found the "actual legitimate cost" of the plant in interstate service to be $51,957,416, as of December 31, 1940. It deducted accrued depletion and depreciation, which it found to be $22,328,016 on an "economic-service-life" basis....

Hope introduced evidence from which it estimated reproduction cost of the property at $97,000,000. It also presented a so-called trended "original cost" estimate which exceeded $105,000,000. The latter was designed "to indicate what the original cost of the property would have been if 1938 material and labor prices had prevailed throughout the whole period of the piecemeal construction of the company's property since 1898." 44 PUR. (N. S.), pp. 8–9. Hope estimated by the "per cent condition" method accrued depreciation at about 35% of reproduction cost new. On that basis Hope contended for a rate base of $66,000,000. The Commission refused to place any reliance on reproduction cost new, saying that it was "not predicated upon facts" and was "too conjectural and illusory to be given any weight in these proceedings." *Id.*, p. 8. It likewise refused to give any "probative value" to trended "original cost" since it was "not founded in fact" but was "basically erroneous" and produced "irrational results." ...

The fixing of prices, like other applications of the police power, may reduce the value of the property which is being regulated. But the fact that the value is reduced does not mean that the regulation is invalid. *Block v. Hirsh*, 256 U.S. 135, 155–157; *Nebbia v. New York*, 291 U.S. 502, 523–539 and cases cited. It does, however, indicate that "fair value" is the end product of the process of rate-making not the starting point as the Circuit Court of Appeals held. The heart of the matter is that rates cannot be made to depend upon "fair value" when the value of the going enterprise depends on earnings under whatever rates may be anticipated.

We held in *Federal Power Comm'n v. Natural Gas Pipeline Co.*, *supra*, that the Commission was not bound to the use of any single formula or combination of formulae in determining rates. Its rate-making function, moreover, involves the making of "pragmatic adjustments." p. 586. And when the Commission's order is challenged in the courts, the question is whether that order "viewed in its entirety" meets the requirements of the Act. *Id.*, p. 586. Under the statutory standard of "just and reasonable" it is the result reached not the method employed which is controlling. *Cf. Los*

Angeles Gas & Elec. Corp. v. R.R. Comm'n, 289 U.S. 287, 304–305, 314; *West Ohio Gas Co. v. Public Utilities Commission (No. 1),* 294 U.S. 63, 70; *West v. Chesapeake & Potomac Tel. Co.,* 295 U.S. 662, 692–693 (dissenting opinion). It is not theory but the impact of the rate order which counts. If the total effect of the rate order cannot be said to be unjust and unreasonable, judicial inquiry under the Act is at an end. The fact that the method employed to reach that result may contain infirmities is not then important. Moreover, the Commission's order does not become suspect by reason of the fact that it is challenged. It is the product of expert judgment which carries a presumption of validity. And he who would upset the rate order under the Act carries the heavy burden of making a convincing showing that it is invalid because it is unjust and unreasonable in its consequences....

The rate-making process under the Act, i.e., the fixing of "just and reasonable" rates, involves a balancing of the investor and the consumer interests. Thus we stated in the *Natural Gas Pipeline Co.* case that "regulation does not insure that the business shall produce net revenues." 315 U.S. p. 590. But such considerations aside, the investor interest has a legitimate concern with the financial integrity of the company whose rates are being regulated. From the investor or company point of view it is important that there be enough revenue not only for operating expenses but also for the capital costs of the business. These include service on the debt and dividends on the stock. *Cf. Chicago & Grand Trunk Ry. Co. v. Wellman,* 143 U.S. 339, 345–346. By that standard the return to the equity owner should be commensurate with returns on investments in other enterprises having corresponding risks. That return, moreover, should be sufficient to assure confidence in the financial integrity of the enterprise, so as to maintain its credit and to attract capital. *See Missouri ex rel. Southwestern Bell Tel. Co. v. Pub. Serv. Comm'n of Mo.,* 262 U.S. 276, 291 (Mr. Justice Brandeis concurring). The conditions under which more or less might be allowed are not important here. Nor is it important to this case to determine the various permissible ways in which any rate base on which the return is computed might be arrived at. For we are of the view that the end result in this case cannot be condemned under the Act as unjust and unreasonable from the investor or company viewpoint....

As we have noted, the Commission fixed a rate of return which permits Hope to earn $2,191,314 annually. In determining that amount it stressed the importance of maintaining the financial integrity of the company. It considered the financial history of Hope and a vast array of data bearing on the natural gas industry, related businesses, and general economic conditions....

In view of these various considerations we cannot say that an annual return of $2,191,314 is not "just and reasonable" within the meaning of the Act. Rates which enable the company to operate successfully, to maintain its financial integrity, to attract capital, and to compensate its investors for the risks assumed certainly cannot be condemned as invalid, even though they might produce only a meager return on the so-called fair value rate base.■

* * *

Market Street Railway Co. v. Railroad Commission of California

324 U.S. 548 (1945).

■ JACKSON, J. The Market Street Railway Company at the commencement of these proceedings operated a system of passenger transportation by street car and by bus in San Francisco and its environs. The Railroad Commission of California instituted on its own motion an inquiry into the Company's rates and service. After hearings, an order was promulgated reducing the fare from seven to six cents. The Company obtained review by the Supreme Court of California. It also obtained a stay of the Commission's order, conditioned upon impounding the disputed one cent per passenger to abide settlement of the issues upon which its ownership would depend. The Supreme Court of California affirmed the order and appeal is taken to this Court.

Meanwhile the Company sold its operative properties to the City of San Francisco. The case is saved from being moot only because its decision is necessary to determine whether the Company is entitled to the impounded portion of the fares or whether the money shall be refunded to passengers making claims and unclaimed amounts thereof be paid over to the state, as required by conditions of the stay order.

The appeal raises constitutional issues only. The contention is that the order [is] a taking of its property [since] it would force the Company to operate at a loss because the Commission used a rate base of $7,950,000, the price at which appellant had offered to sell its operative properties to the City, and did not consider reproduction cost, historical cost, prudent investment, or capitalization bases, on any of which under conventional accounting the six-cent fare would produce no return on its property and would force a substantial operating deficit upon the Company.

The appellant ... invokes many decisions of this Court in which statements have been made that seem to support its contentions. But it should be noted at the outset that most of our cases deal with utilities which had earning opportunities, and public regulation curtailed earnings otherwise possible. But if there were no public regulation at all, this appellant would be a particularly ailing unit of a generally sick industry. The problem of reconciling the patrons' needs and the investors' rights in an enterprise that has passed its zenith of opportunity and usefulness, whose investment already is impaired by economic forces, and whose earning possibilities are already invaded by competition from other forms of transportation, is quite a different problem. The Company's practical situation throws important light on the question of whether the rate reduction has taken its property.

Transportation history of San Francisco follows a pattern not unfamiliar. This property has passed through cycles of competition, consolidation and monopoly, and new forms of competition; it has seen days of prosperity, decline, and salvage. In the 1850's an omnibus service began to operate in San Francisco. In the 1860's came the horse car. The 1870's saw the beginning of the cable car, for which the contour of the city was peculiarly adapted. The Market Street Railway Company was incorporated in 1893 and took over 11 of the 17 street car lines then independently operated in the city. In 1902, United Railroads of San Francisco was organized. This consolidated under one operating control properties of the Market Street Company and five other lines, comprising 229 miles of track, much of which was cable-operated. It suffered greatly from the earthquake and fire of 1906, but carried out a considerable program of reconstruction between 1906 and 1910. In 1921 it failed to pay interest on outstanding bonds. Bondholders acquired the properties and revived the Market Street Railway Company, which had been a dormant subsidiary of United, to operate them.

In 1912 the City and County of San Francisco began operation of a municipal street railway line. This line is not and never has been under the Railroad Commission's jurisdiction. It expanded rapidly, its routes in some instances parallel those of appellant, and its competition has been serious. Throughout the period of competition the municipal lines have operated on a five-cent fare. The Market Street Line also operated on a five-cent fare until July 6, 1937. In that year it applied to the Commission for an increase to a seven-cent fare. This was denied, but a two-cent transfer charge and other adjustments were authorized. In March 1938 the Company again petitioned for a seven-cent fare, with reduction for school children. The Commission authorized a seven-cent fare, but required some concession to token buyers. A few months later the Company again asked a straight seven-cent fare and relief from the token rate. The Commission directed the Company to apply to the City for permission to abandon certain lines and to protect it against "jitney competition," stipulating that the seven-cent fare could be made effective if the City failed to respond. The City did not act, and the seven-cent fare became effective January 1, 1939.

But the increase of fare brought no increase of revenue. Both traffic and revenue continued to decline, and in 1941 reached the lowest point in twenty years. Then came war, bringing accelerated activity, increase of population of the city, rubber and gas shortage, restrictions on purchase of new and retirement of many old automobiles. Traffic and revenues showed a sudden increase. The Commission found, however, that the service had constantly deteriorated and was worse under the seven-cent fare than under the former five-cent rate. It recognized that some of the causes were beyond the Company's control. But after allowance for those causes, it also found evidence of long-time neglect, mismanagement, and indifference to urgent public need. It found the Company's service inferior to the service of the municipal lines, although appellant charged a 40 per cent higher fare. Defects in service consisted of failure to operate on schedule, long intervals between cars, followed by several cars operating with little headway, overloading, inadequate inspection, and inadequately maintained rolling stock. The Company had some 70 cars out of operation and in storage because of shortage of manpower. Its street car rolling stock was obsolete, 73 electric cars and 12 cable cars being out of service. None of the cars was modern....

Reviewing the financial results of fare increases, the Commission concluded that the Company would reap no lasting benefit from rates in excess of five cents, due to the tendency of a higher rate to discourage patronage. The war traffic the Commission thought temporary. But it concluded that a six-cent fare would sufficiently stimulate traffic to leave after operating expenses approximately a six per cent return on a rate base of $7,950,000. This was the figure at which the Company had offered to sell its operative properties to the City. Accordingly the Commission found the six cents to be a reasonable rate to the Company and to be all or more than the reasonable value of the services being rendered to patrons. It considered this rate to be experimental and kept the proceeding open for such further orders as might be just and reasonable. The Company applied for rehearing on substantially the grounds it urges here. Its arguments were considered at length in an opinion which denied rehearing. The Supreme Court of California overruled all of the Company's objections and affirmed the Commission's order.

The reduced rate never took effect. The Company obtained delay from the Commission and a stay order from the Court. It then sold its properties to the City, which took over and continued the seven-cent fare. So the anticipations of the Commission as to increased patronage from the rate reduction never have been put to the test of experience. Our review considers only whether the order was valid when and as made.

The order is asserted to be invalid because it is said to be confiscatory and to compel appellant to operate at a loss. The Commission used a rate base of $7,950,000, the price at which the property had been offered to the City, and the six-cent rate is not calculated to permit any return on a greater valuation. Before we consider the validity of this rate base, we may well consider what alternatives the case presents. No study of the present cost of reproduction is shown, no present fair value is suggested. Nor do we think it important. Apart from familiar objections to the reproduction-cost method, no responsible person would think of reproducing the present plant, consisting in substantial part of cable cars and obsolete equipment. There is no basis for assuming that anyone, in the light of conditions which prevail in the street-surface railroad industry generally, would consider reproducing any street railway system. It was no constitutional error to proceed to fix a rate in disregard of theoretical reproduction costs.

The Commission in 1920 made a valuation study of appellant's properties and found an historical reproduction cost of road and equipment to be $29,715,147. This valuation, brought forward by adding additions and betterments and deducting retirements, shows a total amount for road and equipment as of December 31, 1942 of $25,343,543.

Actual investment is not disclosed by the record. It does disclose that the book value of appellant's properties as of December 31, 1942 was $41,768,505.20.

The Company's outstanding securities at the end of 1942, issued with the approval of the Commission, totaled $37,921,323.96 at face value. They consisted of common stock of over $10,000,000; 3 different classes of preferred stock of $21,000,000; first mortgage bonds of $4,217,500; equipment notes of $735,748.28; and additional long-term debt of $1,041,625.68.

Not one of these, nor any combination of them affords a practical or possible rate base, nor does the Company suggest that allowance of any rate will earn it a return upon any of these. It has not itself ventured to ask a rate higher than seven cents, although the inadequacy of its yield to take care of the financial requirements of the Company has for some time been apparent. This company obviously is up against a sort of law of diminishing returns; the greater amount it collects per ride, the less it collects per car mile. It has long been recognized that this form of transportation could be preserved only by the most complete cooperation between management and public and the most enlightened efforts to make the service attractive to patrons.[8][1] It is obvious that, for whatever cause, the appellant has not succeeded in maintaining its service on a paying basis.

It is idle to discuss holdings of cases or to distinguish quotations in decisions of this or other courts which have dealt with utilities whose economic situation would yield a permanent profit, denied or limited only by public regulation. While the Company does not assert that it would be economically practicable to obtain a return on its investment, it strongly contends that the order is confiscatory by the tests of *Federal Power Comm'n v. Hope Natural Gas Co.*, 320 U.S. 591, 603, 605, from which it claims to be entitled to a return "sufficient to assure confidence in the financial integrity of the enterprise, so as to maintain its credit and to attract capital" and to "enable the company to operate successfully, to maintain its financial integrity, to attract capital, and to compensate its investors for the risks assumed." Those considerations, advanced in that case (which was reviewed pursuant to statute rather than under the Fourteenth Amendment), concerned a company which had advantage of an

---

1. In May of 1919 the Secretary of Commerce and the Secretary of Labor joined in a letter to President Wilson, advising him that 50 or more urban street railway systems representing a considerable percentage of the electric railway mileage was in the hands of receivers, affecting some of the largest cities of the country, and that other systems were on the verge of insolvency and the industry as a whole was virtually bankrupt. They urged the appointment of a commission to study and report upon the problem. President Wilson on June 1, 1919 named a commission which held extensive public hearings. The first witness was ex-President William Howard Taft, speaking for the National War Labor Board, and others, including leading municipal and railway officials and such experienced persons in the problem of regulation as Newton D. Baker, Milo R. Maltbie, Morris L. Cook, Joseph B. Eastman, and many others. Proceedings of the Federal Electric Railways Commission, v. 1. An exhaustive report with many recommendations was made. *See* Analysis of the Electric Railway Problem prepared for the Federal Electric Railways Commission by De Los F. Wilcox, New York City, 1921. Its recommendations were extensive, including certain changes both by the municipalities and by the companies affected. The recommendations were not generally heeded by either.

economic position which promised to yield what was held to be an excessive return on its investment and on its securities. They obviously are inapplicable to a company whose financial integrity already is hopelessly undermined, which could not attract capital on any possible rate, and where investors recognize as lost a part of what they have put in. It was noted in the *Hope Natural Gas* case that regulation does not assure that the regulated business make a profit. 320 U.S. at 603; *see Federal Power Comm'n v. Natural Gas Pipeline Co.*, 315 U.S. 575, 590. All that was held was that a company could not complain if the return which was allowed made it possible for the company to operate successfully. There was no suggestion that less might not be allowed when the amount allowed was all that the company could earn. Without analyzing rate cases in detail, it may be safely generalized that the due process clause never has been held by this Court to require a commission to fix rates on the present reproduction value of something no one would presently want to reproduce, or on the historical valuation of a property whose history and current financial statements showed the value no longer to exist, or on an investment after it has vanished, even if once prudently made, or to maintain the credit of a concern whose securities already are impaired. The due process clause has been applied to prevent governmental destruction of existing economic values. It has not and cannot be applied to insure values or to restore values that have been lost by the operation of economic forces.

The owners of a property dedicated to the public service cannot be said to suffer injury if a rate is fixed for an experimental period, which probably will produce a fair return on the present fair value of their property. If it has lost all value except salvage, they suffer no loss if they earn a return on salvage value. If the property has no prospect of salvage except through dismantling and sale for scrap, the scrap value for such of it as is to be scrapped may represent its present worth. In this case the owners were fortunate in having a potential buyer. Negotiations had long been under way. The operative properties were twice offered to the City of San Francisco for $7,950,000 and twice the voters rejected the proposition. Ultimately the properties were sold for $7,500,000. The evidence shows that the president of the Company reported to the directors "that the price mentioned is the amount that has been agreed upon for the purchase by the City and County of San Francisco of the operative properties of the Company after negotiations in respect thereto which covered a considerable period of time and, as previously mentioned, is the best price obtainable therefor." Upon this understanding the Board of Directors ratified the offer and directed the officers to consummate it.

It is now contended that this offer was calculated by a capitalization of earning power and that this Court condemned such a basis of valuation in *Federal Power Comm'n v. Hope Natural Gas Co.*, 320 U.S. 591, 601, when it said, "The heart of the matter is that rates cannot be made to depend upon 'fair value' when the value of the going enterprise depends on earnings under whatever rates may be anticipated." The pronouncement in the *Hope* case was directed to a situation where the demand for the service permitted such a range of choice in rates as would greatly affect the value of the property. No such choice appears open to the appellant. Apart from a little brief war-time prosperity, it seems doubtful whether any rate would yield appellant's operating expenses.

Under these circumstances we do not find that anything has been taken from the appellant by the impact of public regulation. If the expectations of the Commission as to traffic increase were well founded, it would earn under this rate on the salvage value of its property, which is the only value it is shown to have. If expectations of increased traffic were unfounded, it could probably not earn a return from any rate that could be devised. We are unable to find that the order in this case is in violation of constitutional prohibitions, however unfortunate the plight of the appellant.

We have considered appellant's complaints in considerable detail because the case in so many ways departs from the usual rate case. We find no constitutional infirmity in the result or in the procedure by which it is reached. The judgment of the Supreme Court of California is therefore

Affirmed.■

NOTES

1. This case addresses the liability of government for changes in technological and economic conditions in an industry. During the early twentieth century, the streetcar industry faced enormous pressures from the growth of subway, bus, and other transportation systems (including roads and parking for the ordinary automobile). Many of these other modes of transportation became possible because of technological innovations and changes in economic conditions. What case from earlier in the book does this scenario remind you of?

2. Today, cable cars in San Francisco charge $2.00, are overflowing with customers, and are seen as an asset to the city. Some of this continued viability in the industry may be due to public ownership of the resource. Notice that the company alleging damages in *Market Street Railway* sold their properties to the City of San Francisco, which continues to operate the cable car system. Would the cable car have survived without public ownership?

* * *

Rate of return, like most ratemaking issues, raises complex accounting, economics, and forecasting matters. It is an extremely important issue, since its calculation reflects the time value of the investors' money and utility investments are often financed over long periods of time.

At its most basic level, a rate of return represents the utility's cost of capital—i.e., the opportunity it forgoes by using its capital to provide utility services rather than engage in some other profitable activity. Cost of capital can be broken into two main components: 1) the cost of money that is borrowed on both a long-and short-term basis, also known as "debt"; and 2) money received by the utility in exchange for its stock, or "equity."

The equity capital of a public utility is generally of two types: (1) preferred and (2) common. The former is essentially the same as long-term debt capital as regards specified and agreed rates of return or dividends and times of payment. While the consequences of nonpayment are not as onerous, dividends on or the cost of the preferred stock capital of a public utility nevertheless must be paid before any dividends may be paid on common stock.

The common equity capital of a public utility is that which incurs the highest risk. Unlike most debt capital, its ultimate recovery by those who furnished the funds is not secured by liens against the property of the utility, and, unlike both debt capital and preferred stock investors, those who hold common stock are not entitled to any agreed or assured rate of return on their investment. In short, their earnings consist of the net remaining from revenues after all other creditors of the public utility, including long-term debt and preferred stock investors, have been paid. While the return on this type of capital is actually measured by the amount of net income from gross receipts so remaining, this actual return is not necessarily synonymous with the cost of this category of capital. The cost or rate of return a public utility must pay or be able to pay in order to obtain common equity funds from the private capital markets is set for the company by the market, not by this commission or the company. It is particularly important to stress and recognize that the cost of a public utility's common equity capital is simply another cost of furnishing service, which is not generically different from any of its other costs. Those who furnish common equity capital to a utility, whether by purchasing new stock of the company or by permitting the company to retain and invest their earnings in new plant and equipment, expect and are entitled to a return or earnings for the use of their money by the utility. In an economic sense, this return represents the company's cost of the common equity capital employed, just as rent on an office building leased by the company or wages to those who work for the company constitute costs to it.

Re Public Service Company of New Mexico, 8 P.U.R.4th 113 (1975).

Equity is the more difficult cost for regulators to determine. Since there is rarely a fixed commitment to a dividend rate, the actual cost of floating a stock issue is uncertain. "Investors' decisions are largely based on a utility's expected earnings and upon their stability, as well as upon alternative uses of investment funds. Yet, since the allowable amount of earnings is the object of a rate case, a commission's decision, in turn, will affect investors' decisions." Charles F. Phillips, Jr., The Regulation of Public Utilities 394 (3d ed. 1993). Two principle methods are used to estimate the cost of equity capital: the "market-determined" standard, which focuses on investor expectations in terms of the utility's earnings, dividends and market prices; and a "comparable earnings" standard, which focuses on what capital can earn in various alternative investments with comparable risks. Id.

A related issue in measuring cost of capital is determining the appropriate capital structure. Since the interest rate on debt is normally lower than the cost of equity capital (why?), the overall cost of capital will be lower when the debt-equity ratio is high. Some argue that regulators should look to the ideal rather than actual capital structure, in order to minimize the possibility that utility capitalization decisions are made based on rate regulation decisions. As the utility industries moves towards competition, as is discussed in Chapters 9, 11, and 12, debt-equity ratios have moved upward.

As the United States Supreme Court acknowledged in *Bluefield Water Works & Improvement Co. v. Public Service Commission,* 262 U.S. 679 (1923), there are constitutional limits on the setting of cost of common equity capital:

> A public utility is entitled to such rates as will permit it to earn a return on the value of the property which it employs for the convenience of the public equal to that generally being made at the same time and in the same general part of the country on investments in other business undertakings which are attended by corresponding risks and uncertainties; but it has no constitutional right to profits such as are realized or anticipated in highly profitable enterprises or speculative ventures. The return should be reasonably sufficient to assure confidence in the financial soundness of the utility, and should be adequate under efficient and economical management, to maintain and support its credit and to enable it to raise the money necessary for the proper discharge of its public duty. A rate of return may be reasonable at one time, and become too high or too low by change affecting opportunities for investment, the money market and business conditions generally.

In *Federal Power Comm'n v. Hope Natural Gas Co.,* 320 U.S. 591 (1944), where the court endorsed an "end result" test, it also specified three conditions of a fair return on the invested capital of a public utility: (1) it should be sufficient to maintain the financial integrity of the utility; (2) it should be sufficient to compensate the utility's investors for the risks assumed; (3) it should be sufficient to enable the utility to attract needed new capital.

NOTES AND COMMENTS

1. Regulated firms use a two-step strategy to maximize their returns to shareholders. First, they attempt to obtain a rate of return, r, that exceeds the actual cost of capital. Second, they may overinvest in capital, producing a product of B and r that is greater than the actual cost of capital used. *See* Harvey Averch & Leland L. Johnson, Behavior of the Firm Under Regulatory Constraint, 52 Am. Econ. Rev. 1052 (1962).

2.   What are the capital sources available to a firm? Like any other business enterprise, an energy utility needs to attract investors. Generally a firm has two options in raising capital: debt (bond obligations) and equity (stock). Capital structure refers to a firm's mix of debt and equity. Would an unregulated firm ever intentionally choose a suboptimal mix of capital? No. Because it competes in markets as a buyer of capital, the unregulated firm faces strong economic incentives to choose the debt-equity ratio that minimizes its risk-adjusted cost of capital. Cost of service regulation, by guaranteeing a utility a minimum rate of return, reduces the strength of this incentive. How likely are regulators to determine a firm's correct capital structure—.e., the mix of debt and equity the regulated firm would face in a competitive market?

3.   *Smyth* required regulators to use "fair value" in determining rate base. Generally the choice for determining "fair value" comes down to two alternatives: original cost (or historical cost) and reproduction cost (or present cost). Early on, the Court read *Smyth* to require a regulator to consider both. In several cases decided between 1898 and 1944, the Supreme Court held rate decisions unconstitutionally confiscatory where an agency gave undue consideration to original cost and insufficient consideration to reproductive cost. *See, e.g., Missouri ex rel. Southwestern Bell Tel. Co. v. Pub. Serv. Comm'n of Mo.*, 262 U.S. 276 (1923). Holmes and Brandeis, in a concurrence to that case, dissented from the majority's reliance on the indeterminate "fair value" standard of Smyth.

In the 1944 *Hope* case, a majority agreed with Holmes and Brandeis' 1923 concurrence: "If the total effect of the rate order cannot be said to be unjust and unreasonable, judicial inquiry under the Act is at an end.... Rates which enable the company to operate successfully ... cannot be condemned as invalid, even though they might produce only a meager return on the so-called 'fair value' rate base." 320 U.S. at 602–05. *Hope* marks a departure from Smyth's "fair value" standard—a standard first enunciated during the rise of the substantive due process era of the late nineteenth and early twentieth centuries. See Basil L. Copeland, Jr. & Walter W. Nixon, III, *Procedural Versus Substantive Economic Due Process for Public Utilities*, 12 ENERGY L.J. 81 (1991).

4.   In *In re Permian Basin Area Rate Cases*, 390 U.S. 747 (1968), the Court reviewed Commission orders setting area-wide rates for gas producers. Writing for the majority, Justice Harlan affirmed *Hope*, stating that a court reviewing rate orders must assure itself both that "each of the order's essential elements is supported by substantial evidence" and that "the order may reasonably be expected to maintain financial integrity, attract necessary capital, and fairly compensate investors for the risks they have assumed, and yet provide appropriate protection to the relevant public interests, both existing and foreseeable." *Id.* at 792. In examining the end result of the rate order, a court cannot affirm simply because each subpart of that order, taken in isolation, was permissible; it must be the case "that they do not together produce arbitrary or unreasonable consequences." The reviewing court, according to Harlan, must determine that "the record

before the Commission contained evidence sufficient to establish that these rates, as adjusted, will maintain the industry's credit and continue to attract capital." *Id.* at 812.

5. The most recent case addressing rate base and rate of return decided by the Supreme Court is *Duquesne Light Co. v. Barasch*, 488 U.S. 299 (1989), which is discussed further below.

b. RATE-SETTING OBJECTIVES

What interests should a regulator take into account in determining whether rates are just and reasonable? Certainly, as the above excerpt suggests, regulators are concerned with ensuring that the utility and its investors are provided with sufficient revenue to keep the utility operational. However, utility rate filings are often subject to challenge by a myriad of non-utility interest groups with a stake in the outcome: consumers, who seek the lowest possible rates; environmental groups who may seek to increase rates to discourage wasteful consumption, or have regulators force the utility to adopt conservation-enhancing mechanisms; and public advocates, such as state attorneys general or consumer protection offices, who may advocate some version of the public interest. The preferences of these interest groups often clash.

So what objectives should regulators consider when setting rates? First, as the readings have suggested, regulators should attempt to ensure that the utility meets its revenue requirement. This includes not only the payment of operating expenses, but the cost of capital as well. Cost of capital is not pure profit or gain for the utility and its shareholders; maintenance of a minimum cost of capital is in the public interest as well. As the New Mexico PSC suggests, if a utility does not receive a competitive rate of return, existing investors may find alternative investments. While consumers are justifiably concerned with paying high rates to subsidize utility profits, they certainly would not want to see their local utility struggling to stay one-step away from bankruptcy.

A second objective of rate-setting is economic efficiency. Rates should encourage the regulated enterprise to provide service at the lowest social cost and explore ways to further reduce costs through better management and the adoption of newer, more efficient technological processes.

A third objective is environmental. Approved rates should not encourage waste or encourage uses that are threatening to the environment or energy resource base. This is certainly related to the second objective: if all social costs (including environmental costs) are fully internalized in the rate making process, then efficient rates will reflect environmental costs as well as the financial costs necessary for a utility to continue to provide service. However, environmental costs are often not fully internalized for two reasons. As a practical matter, it is difficult to quantify the actual impact of a certain energy conversion or distribution process on the environment. In addition, many environmental costs affect parties or deplete resources outside of a regulatory body's jurisdiction.

A final regulatory objective is social and distributional. Should some customers—say wealthy or middle-class suburban customers—pay higher rates to subsidize other customers—say low income urban customers—or to build a distribution network to serve rural customers? Should a state that has adopted a policy of encouraging manufacturing set rates for industrial customers low?

c.   COMMON RATE CASE ISSUES

There are several classic treatises on rate regulation. *See, e.g.*, James C. Bonbright, Albert L. Danielson & David R. Kamerschien, Principles of Public Utility Rates (2d ed. 1988); Paul J. Garfield & Wallace F. Lovejoy, Public Utility Economics (1964); Charles Phillips, The Regulation of Public Utilities (3d ed. 1993). Some common issues raised in utility rate cases include the following:

The Test Year. The purpose of a rate case is to set utility rates for the future. A utility is seeking approval for the rate it will charge its customers for months or years to come—at least until another rate increase is approved. However, it is impossible to obtain exact financial information for a future year. For this reason, regulators use what is known as a "test year" in setting rates. This is a hypothetical future period into which regulators attempt to forecast a utility's revenue requirements: its operating expenses (O), rate base (B) and rate of return (r). Like any forecast, use of a test year depends upon certain assumptions about consumer demand, input prices, and the state of the economy in general. In actuality, some years may provide for over recovery of costs and other years may provide for under recovery.

Determining Rate Base. Recall the two alternatives presented in *Smyth v. Ames*: reproduction cost or original (historical) cost. In *Union Electric Co. v. Commerce Commission*, the Illinois Supreme Court adopted an original cost approach. 77 Ill.2d 364, 396 N.E.2d 510 (1979). The Court noted: "... [A] cost based rate reflects the amount of capital whereas a value rate base reflects the value of assets which the utility has devoted to serving the public." *Id.* at 516. FERC bases property valuations on original cost, as do the vast majority of state PSCs.

Does the calculation of rate base on reproduction cost give utility shareholders a windfall? Or does it encourage an efficient allocation of resources? During a period of inflation, the rates of regulated utilities may be lower than the rates of non-regulated enterprises with which they compete (which would reflect reproduction cost). This could increase the demand for the services of a regulated utility and lead to an uneconomical expansion of capacity. For discussion of the merits of reproduction cost versus original cost, *see* Charles F. Phillips, Jr., The Regulation of Public Utilities 299–307 (1984).

Appeals. An interested party aggrieved by the procedural consideration or end result of a utility rate case may appeal. The Johnston Act, 28 U.S.C. § 1342, prohibits a U.S. District Court from exercising jurisdiction over a rate appeal from a state PSC where there is an adequate remedy in state court. The proper avenue for appeal of a state PSC rate determination is through the state court system and then to the U.S. Supreme court. Under the FPA and NGA, FERC rate cases are appealed to the U.S. Court of Appeals for the D.C. Circuit or the circuit within which the utility or aggrieved party sits.

On appeal, challenges to rate proceedings may focus not only on the substance of public utility law, but also on the procedures by which agencies make their factual, policy, and legal determinations. Rate cases often involve hearings before the decision-making body, during which the utility and intervening parties are given an opportunity to present expert testimony in support of their positions in both oral and written form and are given an opportunity to seek discovery of and cross-exam the testimony of other parties. Hearings can last from a period of days to months. Normally, uncontested factual findings do not require a hearing before an agency. However, a hearing is required where an agency is making a factual determination under contest by a party or where the agency is making a new policy or legal decision. *See Cajun Elec. Power Coop. v. FERC*, 28 F.3d 173 (D.C. Cir. 1994). Often, an agency will make generic policy and legal decisions through a process called notice and comment rulemaking.

d. "USED AND USEFUL" PROPERTY

Recall that *Smyth v. Ames* refers to "the fair value of the property being used" in its definition of rate base. In *Denver Union Stock Yard Co. v. United States*, 304 U.S. 470, 475 (1938) the Court held that property not used or useful in providing regulated services does not have to be included in rate base. What has come to be known as the "used and useful" doctrine prohibits the inclusion of rate base of assets used exclusively to provide unregulated goods or services, or assets that are technologically or economically obsolete. How does a regulator determine whether property is used and useful? The clearest example is where a utility has placed the most economical plant into operation to meet a specific customer demand. It is beyond dispute that such a facility is used and useful. Beyond this, regulators have been flexible in applying the used and useful doctrine on an ad hoc basis. As the following two cases address, however, there is some constitutional limitation on regulators' decisions to deem property used and useful.

Jersey Central Power & Light Co. v. FERC

810 F.2d 1168 (D.C. Cir. 1987).

[The Federal Energy Regulatory Commission allowed Jersey Central Power and Light Co. to amortize a $397 million investment in a canceled nuclear plant over a fifteen-year period. Jersey Central was not allowed, however, ti include the unamortized balance in its rate base, because FERC determined the plant was not "used and useful." The effect of this treatment meant that the interest costs of the $397 million were charged to shareholders while the principal costs were charged to ratepayers over a fifteen-year period.]

■ BORK, J. Jersey Central Power and Light Company petitions for review of Federal Energy Regulatory Commission orders modifying the electric utility's proposed rate schedules and requiring the company to file reduced rates. Jersey Central charges that it alleged facts which, if proven, show that the reduced rates are confiscatory and violate its statutory and constitutional rights as defined by the Supreme Court in *Federal Power Comm'n v. Hope Natural Gas Co.*, 320 U.S. 591 (1944). Though it is probable that the facts alleged, if true, would establish an invasion of the company's rights, the Commission refused the company a hearing and reduced its rates summarily.

The decision of the Commission is vacated and the case remanded for a hearing at which Jersey Central may finally have its claim addressed. . . .

The teaching of [*Hope* and *Permian Basin*] is straightforward. In reviewing a rate order courts must determine whether or not the end result of that order constitutes a reasonable balancing, based on factual findings, of the investor interest in maintaining financial integrity and access to capital markets and the consumer interest in being charged non-exploitative rates. Moreover, an order cannot be justified simply by a showing that each of the choices underlying it was reasonable; those choices must still add up to a reasonable result. . . .

The allegations made by Jersey Central and the testimony it offered track the standards of *Hope* and *Permian Basin* exactly. The *Hope* Court stated that the return ought to be "sufficient to ensure confidence in the financial integrity of the enterprise, so as to maintain its credit and to attract capital," and that "it is important that there be enough revenue not only for operating expenses but also for the capital costs of the business. These include service on the debt and dividends on the stock." 320 U.S. at 603. *Permian Basin* reaffirmed that the reviewing court "must determine" whether the Commission's rate order may reasonably be expected to "maintain financial integrity" and "attract necessary capital." 390 U.S. at 792. Jersey Central alleged that it had paid no dividends on its common stock for four years and faced a further prolonged inability to pay such dividends. [It also alleged] that the company was unable to sell senior securities; that its only source of external capital was the Revolving Credit Agreement, which was subject to termination and which placed the outstanding bank loans the company was allowed to maintain below the level necessary for the upcoming year; that the need to pay interest on the company's debt and dividends on its preferred stock meant that common equity investors not only were earning a zero return, but were also forced to pay these interest costs and dividends and that "continued confiscation of earnings from the common equity holder . . . will prolong the Company's inability to restore itself to a recognized level of credit worthiness"; that its "inability to realize fully its operating and capital costs so as to provide a fair rate of return on its invested capital has pushed its financial capability to the limits"; that "adequate and prompt relief is necessary in order to maintain the past high quality of service"; and that the rate increase requested was "the minimum necessary to restore the financial integrity of the Company."

The Commission maintains that because excluding the unamortized portion of a canceled plant investment from the rate base had previously been upheld as permissible, any rate order that rests on such a decision is unimpeachable. But that would turn our focus from the end result to the methodology, and evade the question whether the component decisions together produce just and reasonable consequences. We would be back with the assertion made in *Jersey Central I* that "the end result test is to be applied . . . only to those assets which valid Commission rules permit to be included in the rate base." 730 F.2d at 823. That statement was one which neither party endorsed. It was incorrect. The fact that a particular rate-making standard is generally permissible does not per se legitimate the end result of the rate orders it produces. . . .

In addition to prohibiting rates so low as to be confiscatory, the holding of Hope Natural Gas makes clear that exploitative rates are illegal as well. If the inclusion of property not currently used and useful in the rate base automatically constituted exploitation of consumers, as one of the amici maintains, then the commission would be justified in excluding such property summarily even in cases where the utility pleads acute financial distress. A regulated utility has no constitutional right to a profit, *see Federal Power Comm'n v. Natural Gas Pipeline Co.*, 315 U.S. at 590, and a company that is unable to survive without charging exploitative rates has no entitlement to such rates. *Market St. Ry. Co. v. R.R. Comm'n of Cal.*, 324 U.S. 548 (1945). But we have already held that including prudent investments in the rate base is not in and of itself exploitative, and no party has denied that the Forked River investment was prudent. Indeed, when the regulated company is permitted to earn a return not on the market value of the property used by the public, *see Smyth v. Ames*, but rather on the original cost of the investment, placing prudent investments in the rate base would seem a more sensible policy than a strict application of "used and useful," for under this approach it is the investment, and not the property used, which is viewed as having been taken by the public. The investor interest described in *Hope*, after all, is an interest in return on investment. *Hope*, 320 U.S. at 603.

The central point, however, is this: it is impossible for us to say at this juncture whether including the unamortized portion of Forked River in the rate base would exploit consumers in this case, or whether its exclusion, on the facts of this case, constitutes confiscation, for no findings of fact have been made concerning the consequences of the rate order. Nor, for the same reason, can we make a judgment about the higher rate of return the utility sought as an alternative to inclusion in the rate base of its unamortized investment. Jersey Central has presented allegations which, if true, suggest that the rate order almost certainly does not meet the requirements of *Hope Natural Gas*, for the company has been shut off from long-term capital, is wholly dependent for short-term capital on a revolving credit arrangement that can be canceled at any time, and has been unable to pay dividends for four years. In addition, Jersey Central points out that the rates proposed in its filing would remain lower than those of neighboring utilities, which at least suggests, though it does not demonstrate, that the proposed rates would not exploit consumers. The Commission treated those allegations as irrelevant and hence has presented us with no basis on which to affirm its rate order. The necessary findings are simply not there for us to review. When the Commission conducts the requisite balancing of consumer and investor interests, based upon factual findings, that balancing will be judicially reviewable and will be affirmed if supported by substantial evidence. That is the point at which deference to agency expertise will be appropriate and necessary. But where, as here, the Commission has reached its determination by flatly refusing to consider a factor to which it is undeniably required to give some weight, its decision cannot stand. *Citizens to Preserve Overton Park, Inc. v. Volpe*, 401 U.S. 402, 416 (1971). The case should therefore be remanded to the Commission for a hearing at which the Commission can determine whether the rate order it issued constituted a reasonable balancing of the interests the Supreme Court has designated as relevant to the setting of a just and reasonable rate.

■ STARR, J., concurring: The Commission's stated justification for summarily dismissing these allegations was the weight of its prior used and useful precedent. But as the court's opinion shows, that body of precedent did not constitute as iron-clad a rule as the Commission would have us believe. It is certainly not evident from those precedents that the rule could be summarily applied in the face of the financial demise of the regulated entity.

Indeed, the Commission as a matter of policy has departed over the years from the strictures of the "used and useful" rule. This is illustrated by its treatment of "construction work in progress" (CWIP), part of which, the Commission recently determined, can be included in a utility's rate base. *See Mid–Tex Electric Coop v. FERC*, 773 F.2d 327 (D.C. Cir. 1985), *aff'd*, 864 F.2d 156 (D.C.Cir.1988). In that proceeding, the Commission recognized that its own practice admits of "widely recognized exceptions and departures" from the "used and useful" rule, "particularly when there are countervailing public interest considerations." *See* 48 Fed. Reg. 24,323, 24,335 (June 1, 1983) (CWIP final rule). In that setting, financial difficulties in the electric utility industry played a significant role in the Commission's decision to bend the rule. *See id.* at 24,332; 773 F.2d at 332–34. *See also, e.g., Tenn. Gas Pipeline Co. v. FERC*, 606 F.2d 1094, 1109–10 (D.C. Cir. 1979) (departure from "used and useful" to permit rate base treatment of natural gas prepayment is justified as means of encouraging development of additional gas reserves), *cert. denied*, 445 U.S. 920 (1980).

This policy of flexibility, it seems to me, reflects the practical reality of the electric utility industry, namely that investments in plant and equipment are enormously costly. Rigid adherence to "used and useful" doctrines would doubtless imperil the viability of some utilities; thus, while not articulating its results in *Hope* or "takings" terms, the Commission—

whether as a matter of policy or perceived constitutional obligation—has in the past taken these realities into account and provided relief for utilities in various forms.

The utility business represents a compact of sorts; a monopoly on service in a particular geographical area (coupled with state-conferred rights of eminent domain or condemnation) is granted to the utility in exchange for a regime of intensive regulation, including price regulation, quite alien to the free market. *Cf. In re Permian Basin*, 390 U.S. 747, 756–57 (1967) (unlike public utilities, producers of natural gas "enjoy no franchises or guaranteed areas of service" and are "intensely competitive"). Each party to the compact gets something in the bargain. As a general rule, utility investors are provided a level of stability in earnings and value less likely to be attained in the unregulated or moderately regulated sector; in turn, ratepayers are afforded universal, non-discriminatory service and protection from monopolistic profits through political control over an economic enterprise. Whether this regime is wise or not is, needless to say, not before us.

In the setting of rate regulation, when does a taking from the investors occur? It seems to me that it occurs only when a regulated rate is confiscatory, which is a short-hand way of saying that an unreasonable balance has been struck in the regulation process so as unreasonably to favor ratepayer interests at the substantial expense of investor interests. Thus, in my view, a taking does not occur when financial resources are committed to the enterprise. That is especially so since a utility's capital investment is made not simply in satisfaction of legal obligations to provide service to the public but in anticipation of profits on the investment. The utility is not a servant to the state; it is a for-profit enterprise which incurs legal obligations in exchange for state-conferred benefits. A profit-seeking capital investment is scarcely the sort of deprivation of possession, use, enjoyment, and ownership of property which can conceptually be deemed a taking. *See generally* R. Epstein, Takings 63–92 (1985). Indeed, it would seem odd to consider as a taking government's disavowal of any interest in property which remains unregulated and which reflects a profit-seeking investment.

For me, the prudent investment rule is, taken alone, too weighted for constitutional analysis in favor of the utility. It lacks balance. But so too, the "used and useful" rule, taken alone, is skewed heavily in favor of ratepayers. It also lacks balance. In the modern setting, neither regime, mechanically applied with full rigor, will likely achieve justice among the competing interests of investor and ratepayers so as to avoid confiscation of the utility's property or a taking of the property of ratepayers through unjustifiably exorbitant rates. Each approach, however, provides important insights about the ultimate object of the regulatory process, which is to achieve a just result in rate regulation. And that is the mission commanded by the Fifth Amendment. Unlike garden-variety takings, the requirements of the Takings Clause are satisfied in the rate regulatory setting when justice is done, that is to say the striking of a reasonable balance between competing interests.

Thus it is that a taking occurs not when an investment is made (even one under legal obligation), but when the balance between investor and ratepayer interests—the very function of utility regulation—is struck unjustly. Although the agency has broad latitude in striking the balance, the Constitution nonetheless requires that the end result reflect a reasonable balancing of the interests of investors and ratepayers. As we have seen, both investors and ratepayers were the intended beneficiaries of the Forked River investment; both should presumptively have to share in the loss. Filling in the gaps, the making of the specific judgments that constitutes the difficult part of this enterprise, belongs in the first instance to the politically accountable branches, specifically to the experts in the agency, not to generalist judges.

■ MIKVA, J., with whom CHIEF JUDGE WALD, and JUDGES ROBINSON and EDWARDS join, dissenting: The real mischief of today's decision lies not in the majority's belief that the utility has raised an issue of fact necessitating a hearing, but in its determination that Jersey Central has actually made out a case of constitutional confiscation. As Justice Douglas remarked, "he who would upset the rate order under the Act carries the heavy burden of making a convincing showing that it is invalid because it is unjust and unreasonable in its consequences." *Hope*, 320 U.S. at 602. The majority believes that Jersey Central can meet this burden. We simply cannot swallow the majority's assertion that "it is probable that the facts alleged [by Jersey Central], if true, would establish an invasion of the company's rights." In our view, it is beyond cavil that Jersey Central has not presented allegations which, if true, would establish that the Commission's orders result in unjust and unreasonable rates.

Permian Basin teaches that if the Commission reasonably balances consumer and investor interests, then the resulting rate is not confiscatory. The separate opinion ably translates this into a working definition of a confiscatory rate: it exists when "an unreasonable balance has been struck in the regulation process so as unreasonably to favor ratepayer interests at the substantial expense of investor interests." The majority appears to agree with the teaching of *Permian Basin*. The lesson it gleans, however, is incongruous. According to the majority, balancing competing interests is not enough; a rate is confiscatory if it does not satisfy the "legitimate investor interest" outlined by the Court in *Hope*. This interpretation of *Hope* and *Permian Basin* is implausible.

. . . The *Hope* court did not define "unjust or unreasonable"; nor did it articulate when a rate would be confiscatory. It certainly did not hold that the end result could be condemned if the investor criteria defined in the case were not fulfilled. Indeed, it expressly noted that its holding made no suggestion that more or less might not be allowed. 320 U.S. at 603; *see Market Street*, 324 U.S. at 566.

This understanding of *Hope* is the only way to reconcile the Court's recitation of investor interests with its avowal that "regulation does not insure that the business shall produce net revenues." *See Hope*, 320 U.S. at 603 (*quoting Natural Gas Pipeline*, 315 U.S. at 590). Investor interests are only one factor in the assessment of constitutionally reasonable, therefore non-confiscatory, rates. *Permian Basin*, 390 U.S. at 769. In any instance, the rate must also "provide appropriate protection to the relevant public interests, both existing and foreseeable." *Id.* at 792. A just and reasonable rate which results from balancing these conflicting interests might not provide "enough revenue not only for operating expenses but also for the capital costs of the business ... includ[ing] service on the debt and dividends on the stock." *See Hope*, 320 U.S. at 603.

The Court made this abundantly clear in *Market Street.* . . . Neither the regulatory process nor the fifth amendment shelter a utility from market forces. Thus, contrary to the majority's intimations, rates do not fall outside the zone of reasonableness merely because they do not enable the company to operate at a profit or do not permit investors to recover all their losses. . . .

Application of this principle is readily apparent in the Commission's current treatment of electric utility plants, investments prudent when made but sometimes frustrated in fruition. If the investment is successful, the customer benefits from controlled rates for the service provided. But the ratepayer also shares the costs if the investment fails; he must pay for the expenditure made on an unproductive facility from which he obtains no service. From the investor's viewpoint, price regulation cabins both his upside and downside risk. He cannot collect the windfall benefits if the project is a boon; he does not bear all costs if the project is a bust. Electric utility stockholders do not lose equity in the non-serviceable facility, as they might in the marketplace. They simply do not procure a return on the investment.

The majority quibbles with this risk allocation; it would prefer a world in which the investor is guaranteed a return on his investment, if prudent when made. Its resultant holding today is directly at odds with fundamental principles laid out in *Hope* and its progeny. Adherence to the majority's insistence on the inclusion of prudent investments in the rate base would virtually insulate investors in public utilities from the risks involved in free market business. This would drastically diminish protection of the public interest by thrusting the entire risk of a failed investment onto the ratepayers. . . . ■

Duquesne Light Co. v. Barasch

488 U.S. 299 (1989).

■ REHNQUIST, C. J. Pennsylvania law required that rates for electricity be fixed without consideration of a utility's expenditures for electrical generating facilities which were planned but never built, even though the expenditures were prudent and reasonable when made. The Supreme Court of Pennsylvania held that such a law did not take the utilities' property in violation of the Fifth Amendment to the United States Constitution. We agree with that conclusion, and hold that a state scheme of utility regulation does not "take" property simply because it disallows recovery of capital investments that are not "used and useful in service to the public." 66 Pa. Const. Stat. § 1315 (Supp.1988).

I

In response to predictions of increased demand for electricity, Duquesne Light Company (Duquesne) and Pennsylvania Power Company (Penn Power) joined a venture in 1967 to build more generating capacity. The project, known as the Central Area Power Coordination Group (CAPCO), involved three other electric utilities and had as its objective the construction of seven large nuclear generating units. In 1980 the participants canceled plans for construction of four of the plants. Intervening events, including the Arab oil embargo and the accident at Three Mile Island, had radically changed the outlook both for growth in the demand for electricity and for nuclear energy as a desirable way of meeting that demand. At the time of the cancellation, Duquesne's share of the preliminary construction costs associated with the four halted plants was $34,697,389. Penn Power had invested $9,569,665.

In 1980, and again in 1981, Duquesne sought permission from the Pennsylvania Public Utility Commission (PSC) to recoup its expenditures for the unbuilt plants over a 10–year period. The Commission deferred ruling on the request until it received the report from its investigation of the CAPCO construction. That report was issued in late 1982. The report found that Duquesne and Penn Power could not be faulted for initiating the construction of more nuclear generating capacity at the time they joined the CAPCO project in 1967. The projections at that time indicated a growing demand for electricity and a cost advantage to nuclear capacity. It also found that the intervening events which ultimately confounded the predictions could not have been predicted, and that work on the four nuclear plants was stopped at the proper time. In summing up, the Administrative Law Judge found "that the CAPCO decisions in regard to the [canceled plants] at every stage to their cancellation, were reasonable and prudent." He recommended that Duquesne and Penn Power be allowed to amortize their sunk costs in the project over a 10–year period. The PSC adopted the conclusions of the report.

In 1982, Duquesne again came before the PSC to obtain a rate increase. Again, it sought to amortize its expenditures on the canceled plants over 10 years. In January 1983, the PSC issued a final order which granted Duquesne the authority to increase its revenues $105.8 million to a total yearly revenue in excess of $800 million. The rate increase included $3.5 million in revenue representing the first payment of the 10–year amortization of Duquesne's $35 million loss in the CAPCO plants.

The Pennsylvania Office of the Consumer Advocate (Consumer Advocate) moved the PSC for reconsideration in light of a state law enacted about a month before the close of the 1982 Duquesne rate proceeding. The Act amended the Pennsylvania Utility Code by limiting "the consideration of certain costs in the rate base." It provided that "the cost of construction or expansion of a facility undertaken by a public utility producing ... electricity shall not be made a part of the rate base nor otherwise included in the rates charged by the electric utility until such time as the facility is used and useful in service to the public." On reconsideration, the PSC affirmed its original rate order. It read the new law as excluding the costs of canceled plants (obviously not used and useful) from the rate base, but not as preventing their recovery through amortization.... [The Pennsylvania Supreme Court affirmed, holding that exclusion from rate base was not a taking in violation of the Fifth Amendment of the U.S. Constitution.]

III

As public utilities, both Duquesne and Penn Power are under a state statutory duty to serve the public. A Pennsylvania statute provides that "[e]very public utility shall furnish and maintain adequate, efficient, safe, and reasonable service and facilities" and that "[s]uch service also shall be reasonably continuous and without unreasonable interruptions or delay." 66 Pa. Const. Stat. § 1501 (1986). Although their assets are employed in the public interest to provide consumers of the State with electric power, they are owned and operated by private investors. This partly public, partly private status of utility property creates its own set of questions under the Takings Clause of the Fifth Amendment.

The guiding principle has been that the Constitution protects utilities from being limited to a charge for their property serving the public which is so "unjust" as to be confiscatory. If the rate does not afford sufficient compensation, the State has taken the use of utility property without paying just compensation and so violated the Fifth and Fourteenth Amendments. As has been observed, however, "[h]ow such compensation may be ascertained, and what are the necessary elements in such an inquiry, will always be an embarrassing question." *Smyth v. Ames*, 169 U.S. 466, 546 (1898). *See also Permian Basin Area Rate Cases*, 390 U.S. 747, 790 (1968) ("'[N]either law nor economics has yet devised generally accepted standards for the evaluation of rate-making orders'").

At one time, it was thought that the Constitution required rates to be set according to the actual present value of the assets employed in the public service. This method, known as the "fair value" rule, is exemplified by the decision in *Smyth v. Ames, supra*. Under the fair value approach, a "company is entitled to ask ... a fair return upon the value of that which it employs for the public convenience," while on the other hand, "the public is entitled to demand ... that no more be exacted from it for the use of [utility property] than the services rendered by it are reasonably worth." 169 U.S., at 547. In theory the *Smyth v. Ames* fair value standard mimics the operation of the competitive market. To the extent utilities' investments in plants are good ones (because their benefits exceed their costs) they are rewarded with an opportunity to earn an "above-cost" return, that is, a fair return on the current "market value" of the plant. To the extent utilities' investments turn out to be bad ones (such as plants that are canceled and so never used and useful to the public), the utilities suffer because the investments have no fair value and so justify no return.

Although the fair value rule gives utilities strong incentive to manage their affairs well and to provide efficient service to the public, it suffered from practical difficulties which ultimately led to its abandonment as a constitutional requirement.[5][2] In response to these problems, Justice Brandeis had advocated an alternative approach as the constitutional minimum, what has become known as the "prudent investment" or "historical cost" rule. He accepted the *Smyth v. Ames* eminent domain analogy, but concluded that what was "taken" by public utility regulation is not specific physical assets that are to be individually valued, but the capital prudently devoted to the public utility enterprise by the utilities' owners. *Missouri ex rel. Southwestern Bell Tel. Co. v. Pub. Serv. Comm'n of Mo.*, 262 U.S. 276, 291 (1923) (dissenting opinion). Under the prudent investment rule, the utility is compensated for all prudent investments at their actual cost when made (their "historical" cost), irrespective of whether individual investments are deemed necessary or beneficial in hindsight. The utilities incur fewer risks, but are limited to a standard rate of return on the actual amount of money reasonably invested.[6][3]

Forty-five years ago in the landmark case of *Federal Power Comm'n v. Hope Natural Gas Co.*, 320 U.S. 591 (1944), this Court abandoned the rule of *Smyth v. Ames*, and held that the "fair value" rule is not the only constitutionally acceptable method of fixing utility rates. In *Hope* we ruled that historical cost was a valid basis on which to calculate utility compensation. 320 U.S., at 605 ("Rates which enable [a] company to operate successfully, to maintain its financial integrity, to attract capital, and to compensate its investors for the risk assumed certainly cannot be condemned as invalid, even though they might produce only a meager return on the so called 'fair value' rate base"). We also acknowledged in that case that all of the subsidiary aspects of valuation for ratemaking purposes could not properly be characterized as having a constitutional dimension, despite the fact that they might affect property rights to some degree. Today we reaffirm these teachings of *Hope Natural Gas*: "[I]t is not theory but the impact of the rate order which counts. If the total effect of the rate order cannot be said to be unreasonable, judicial inquiry ... is at an end. The fact that the method employed to reach that result may contain

---

2. Perhaps the most serious problem associated with the fair value rule was the "laborious and baffling task of finding the present value of the utility." The exchange value of a utility's assets, such as powerplants, could not be set by a market price because such assets were rarely bought and sold. Nor could the capital assets be valued by the stream of income they produced because setting that stream of income was the very object of the rate proceeding. According to Brandeis, the *Smyth v. Ames* test usually degenerated to proofs about how much it would cost to reconstruct the asset in question, a hopelessly hypothetical, complex, and inexact process.

3. The system avoids the difficult valuation problems encountered under the *Smyth v. Ames* test because it relies on the actual historical cost of investments as the basis for setting the rate. The amount of a utility's actual outlays for assets in the public service is more easily ascertained by a ratemaking body because less judgment is required than in valuing an asset.

infirmities is not then important." *Id.*, at 602. This language, of course, does not dispense with all of the constitutional difficulties when a utility raises a claim that the rate which it is permitted to charge is so low as to be confiscatory: whether a particular rate is "unjust" or "unreasonable" will depend to some extent on what is a fair rate of return given the risks under a particular rate-setting system, and on the amount of capital upon which the investors are entitled to earn that return. At the margins, these questions have constitutional overtones.

Pennsylvania determines rates under a slightly modified form of the historical cost/prudent investment system. Neither Duquesne nor Penn Power alleges that the total effect of the rate order arrived at within this system is unjust or unreasonable. In fact the overall effect is well within the bounds of *Hope*, even with total exclusion of the CAPCO costs. Duquesne was authorized to earn a 16.14% return on common equity and an 11.64% overall return on a rate base of nearly $1.8 billion. Its $35 million investment in the canceled plants comprises roughly 1.9% of its total base. The denial of plant amortization will reduce its annual allowance by 0.4%. Similarly, Penn Power was allowed a charge of 15.72% return on common equity and a 12.02% overall return. Its investment in the CAPCO plants comprises only 2.4% of its $401.8 million rate base. The denial of amortized recovery of its $9.6 million investment in CAPCO will reduce its annual revenue allowance by only 0.5%.

Given these numbers, it appears that the PSC would have acted within the constitutional range of reasonableness if it had allowed amortization of the CAPCO costs but set a lower rate of return on equity with the result that Duquesne and Penn Power received the same revenue they will under the instant orders on remand. The overall impact of the rate orders, then, is not constitutionally objectionable. No argument has been made that these slightly reduced rates jeopardize the financial integrity of the companies, either by leaving them insufficient operating capital or by impeding their ability to raise future capital. Nor has it been demonstrated that these rates are inadequate to compensate current equity holders for the risk associated with their investments under a modified prudent investment scheme.

Instead, appellants argue that the Constitution requires that subsidiary aspects of Pennsylvania's ratemaking methodology be examined piecemeal. One aspect which they find objectionable is the constraint Act 335 places on the PSC's decisions. They urge that such legislative direction to the PSC impermissibly interferes with the PSC's duty to balance consumer and investor interest under *Permian Basin*, 390 U.S., at 792. Appellants also note the theoretical inconsistency of Act 335, suddenly and selectively applying the used and useful requirement, normally associated with the fair value approach, in the context of Pennsylvania's system based on historical cost. Neither of the errors appellants perceive in this case is of constitutional magnitude.

It cannot seriously be contended that the Constitution prevents state legislatures from giving specific instructions to their utility commissions.

We have never doubted that state legislatures are competent bodies to set utility rates. And the Pennsylvania PSC is essentially an administrative arm of the legislature. This is not to say that any system of ratemaking applied by a utilities commission, including the specific instructions it has received from its legislature, will necessarily be constitutional. But if the system fails to pass muster, it will not be because the legislature has performed part of the work.

Similarly, an otherwise reasonable rate is not subject to constitutional attack by questioning the theoretical consistency of the method that produced it. "It is not theory, but the impact of the rate order which counts." *Hope*, 320 U.S., at 602. The economic judgments required in rate proceedings are often hopelessly complex and do not admit of a single correct result. The Constitution is not designed to arbitrate these economic niceties. Errors to the detriment of one party may well be canceled out by countervailing errors or allowances in another part of the rate proceeding. The Constitution protects the utility from the net effect of the rate order on its property. Inconsistencies in one aspect of the methodology have no constitutional effect on the utility's property if they are compensated by countervailing factors in some other aspect.

Admittedly, the impact of certain rates can only be evaluated in the context of the system under which they are imposed. One of the elements always relevant to setting the rate under Hope is the return investors expect given the risk of the enterprise. *Id.*, at 603 ("[R]eturn to the equity owner should be commensurate with returns on investments in other enterprises having corresponding risks"); *Bluefield Water Works & Improvement Co. v. Public Service Comm'n of West Virginia*, 262 U.S. 679, 692–693 (1923) ("A public utility is entitled to such rates as will permit it to earn a return ... equal to that generally being made at the same time and in the same general part of the country on investments in other business undertakings which are attended by corresponding risks and uncertainties"). The risks a utility faces are in large part defined by the rate methodology because utilities are virtually always public monopolies dealing in an essential service, and so relatively immune to the usual market risks. Consequently, a State's decision to arbitrarily switch back and forth between methodologies in a way which required investors to bear the risk of bad investments at some times while denying them the benefit of good investments at others would raise serious constitutional questions. But the instant case does not present this question. At all relevant times, Pennsylvania's rate system has been predominantly but not entirely based on historical cost and it has not been shown that the rate orders as modified by Act 335 fail to give a reasonable rate of return on equity given the risks under such a regime. We therefore hold that Act 335's limited effect on the rate order at issue does not result in a constitutionally impermissible rate. Finally we address the suggestion of the Pennsylvania Electric Association as amicus that the prudent investment rule should be adopted as the constitutional standard. We think that the adoption of any such rule would signal a retreat from 45 years of decisional law in this area which would be as unwarranted as it would be unsettling. Hope clearly held that the Commission was not bound to the use of any single formula or combination of formulae in determining rates. 320 U.S., at 602.■

NOTES AND COMMENTS

1.   On rehearing in *Jersey Central III*, the Commission sustained the amortization scheme after holding a hearing. *See Jersey Central Power & Light*, 49 F.E.R.C. ¶ 63,004 (1989).

2.   Does *Duquesne* resolve the differences between the majority and dissent in *Jersey Central III*? Would the Supreme Court have sided with the majority, the dissent, or Judge Starr's concurrence? The *Duquesne* case raises the relationship between regulatory takings and takings in the ratemaking context. Should utility regulation that is found to satisfy the *Hope* "end results" test be subjected to additional tests to determine whether or not the regulation results in "confiscation" and is a "regulatory taking"? *See* Richard Goldsmith, Utility Rates and "Takings," 10 Energy L.J. 241 (1989). Judge Starr, in his concurrence to *Jersey Central III*, suggests that the Hope test operates independent of the takings tests that might apply in other contexts, and the dissent appears to agree.

   Duquesne purports to reaffirm *Hope*, but there is considerable disagreement over whether the Court opened the door to second-guessing regulators' choices of measures for rate base. According to some commentators, "a wolf in sheep's clothing, the *Duquesne* opinion has resurrected the language of substantive economic due process, and has the potential for undoing everything for which *Hope* stood." Basil M. Copeland, Jr. & Walter W. Nixon, III, Procedural Versus Substantive Economic Due Process for Public Utilities, 12 Energy L.J. 81, 89 (1991). Does the language of *Duquesne* support Copeland and Nixon's argument? Others disagree with this reading, maintaining that *Hope* and *Duquesne* effectively remove the judiciary from constitutional review of ratemaking. *See* Richard J. Pierce, Jr., Public Utility Regulatory Takings: Should the Judiciary Attempt to Police the Political Institutions?, 77 Geo. L.J. 2031, 2062 (1989). The approach of lower courts in adjudicating recent takings challenges in the ratemaking context seem to lend more support for Pierce's views on the issue. *See* discussion of stranded costs in Chapter 12.

3.   **Depreciation Expenses**. Even if original cost is chosen as the method for valuing rate base, there is still a significant question as to how original cost should be determined. As an accounting matter, rate base, B, does not remain constant from year-to-year; rather, a utility's investments in capital assets depreciate over their useful lives and are eventually retired, scrapped, or sold. Assets are capitalized over their useful years, not expensed in a single year. By contrast, variable expenses are expensed during the periods in which they are consumed.

   For example, many modern consumers finance automobiles over a 4–5 year period; in doing this, the consumer spreads the cost of the automobile over its most useful years. By contrast, in buying a hamburger, the cost is incurred immediately. If the hamburger is bought on a on credit card, it is charged simultaneous with consumption of the hamburger. Only an unwise or financially irresponsible consumer would pay for hamburger over a 4 or 5 year period. When assets are paid for over time, their original value needs to be adjusted to take into account what has already been paid and used. Depreciation, d, represents the cumulative amount of assets that have been retired for accounting purposes. Rate base, B, is typically adjusted by d, by subtracting d from V, the gross value of the utility's capital investment.

In *Jersey Central III*, briefly excerpted above, Jersey City's investment of $397 million in the canceled Forked River nuclear plant was at issue. FERC allowed Jersey City to amortize its $397 million investment over a fifteen-year period. (Amortization is the functional equivalent of depreciation; it expenses a portion of an intangible asset's value over its useful life.) It did not, however, allow Jersey City to put the unamortized balance in rate base, because the plant was not "used and useful." As a result, interest costs are charged to shareholders while principal costs are charged to ratepayers over the fifteen year period. In other words, the firm loses the time value of its money by only recovering a portion of the $397 million as an operating expense. To the utility, failure to include depreciation in rate base can make a large difference in revenue requirements, as it may deny the utility (and its investors) the ability to earn a rate of return on the entire capital investment.

4. **Depreciated v. Trended Original Costs**. If depreciation is included in rate base, there are basically two approaches available to regulators in applying d to B: depreciated original cost (DOC) and trended original cost (TOC). Both measure the amount of fixed investment for the provision of utility service in actual dollars, as adjusted, not only for depreciation, but also for some complicated accounting concepts—e.g., allowance for funds used during construction and normalized taxes—which are beyond the scope of our discussion.

Under DOC, assets are depreciated on what accountants call a "straight-line" basis—i.e., rate base declines at a steady rate over the useful life of the asset as d increases at a steady rate. Under DOC a front-end asset load is created: investors in early years pay higher rates on the new assets, while investors in later years pay lower rates on the depreciated plant. (As rate base is depreciated, smaller and smaller portions of rate base are left to which apply cost of capital.)

With TOC, rate base is increased by an inflation factor at the same time that the facilities are depreciated over their remaining useful life of the asset. FERC has give the following example to illustrate the TOC method:

> Assume a new pipeline with an original equity investment of $1,000. Also assume that a just and reasonable overall rate of return on equity would be 16 percent and that 7 percent of that represents inflation. That leaves 9 percent as a so-called "real" rate of return. In its first year of service, the pipeline would be entitled to earn $90 (9 percent times $1,000) and $70 (7 percent times $1,000) would be capitalized into its equity rate base to be amortized over the life of the

property starting with the first year, along with the depreciation on the $1,000. If that life were twenty years, in addition to the return of $90, the pipeline would be entitled to recover, in the first year, $3.50 as amortization ($70 divided by 20), $50 as depreciation ($1,000 divided by 20), its embedded debt cost, and depreciation associated with debt investment. This process would continue over the life of the property until the rate base (assuming no salvage value) hit zero. Unless changed in a rate case, the real rate, which should be relatively stable, would be 9 percent each year. The inflation rate would vary as the chosen inflation index varies.

Williams Pipe Line Company, 31 F.E.R.C. ¶ 61,377 at 61,834 (1985).

Unlike DOC, application of TOC results in a rate base that increases in the initial year of operation and then turns downward until the facilities are fully depreciated. TOC and DOC are essentially the same except for their treatment of inflation. TOC has been advanced as a mechanism that will more nearly replicate competitive markets, by avoiding the front-loading problem of DOC. For criticism, *see* Henry E. Kilpatrick, Jr. & Dennis H. Melvin, The Trended Vs. Depreciated Original Cost Controversy: How Real Are the Real Returns?, 12 Energy L. J. 323 (1991).

5. **CWIP.** Application of the used and useful doctrine is controversial in instances where a utility has invested in plants that are never completed or when a utility builds plants beyond its needs to serve customers. Are power plants under construction "used and useful"? On one hand, the electric generating plant that is not yet producing electricity is not "used and useful" to customers. On the other hand, the construction expense and length of time required to create the new generating facility suggests the utility should get at least some recovery for its expenses from the commission.

As Judge Starr notes in his concurrence to *Jersey Central III*, FERC has departed from the used and useful rule to allow utilities to include a portion of the costs of construction work in progress in rate base. Utilities in every state are allowed to include at least a portion of CWIP in rate base. FERC allows utilities to include in rate base up to 50 percent of CWIP allocable to electric power sales and 100 percent of CWIP associated with pollution control and fuel conversion facilities. 48 Fed. Reg. 24,323; 18 C.F.R. §§ 35.12, 35.13, 35.26, *remanded in Mid–Tex Electric Coop v. FERC*, 773 F.2d 327 (D.C. Cir. 1985), *aff'd*, 864 F.2d 156 (D.C. Cir. 1988).

In *Legislative Utility Consumers' Council v. Public Service Commission*, 119 N.H. 332, 402 A.2d 626 (1979), the New Hampshire Supreme Court upheld the state PSC's inclusion in rate base of construction work in progress (CWIP) of $111,258,428 to finance construction of the Seabrook nuclear generating plant. The Legislative Utility Consumer's Council, a legislative agency comprised of state legislators statutorily authorized to intervene in rate proceedings on behalf of consumers, contested the commission's inclusion of in the company's rate base as contravening the "used and useful" requirement, which was codified in New Hampshire. The court noted:

. . . The commission should consider whether the CWIP asked to be included in the rate base represents the cost of money expended for raising capital to finance construction that is undertaken upon sound business judgment and in accordance with a definite plan to meet the needs of future utility consumers. . . .

The factual determination that the commission had to make in its used and useful analysis was whether the company's CWIP represents an expenditure incurred in raising capital to finance a reasonable construction program that will inure to the benefit of energy consumers by assuring a future supply of electricity. . . .

We next consider the LUCC's argument that inclusion of CWIP in the company's rate base violates the basic "just and reasonable" principle of RSA ch. 378. The thrust of the LUCC's position is that including CWIP in the rate base forces present ratepayers to pay costs that should fall on future ratepayers who will actually benefit from the plant under construction when it comes on line. The LUCC argues that the traditional AFUDC treatment of CWIP, whereby it is capitalized and collected from future ratepayers via inclusion in the rate base over the period of the useful life of the plant when it comes on line, is required by the "just and reasonable" principle. The LUCC suggests that "the inclusion of CWIP [in the current rate base] is detrimental to present consumers while providing a windfall to future consumers."

We reject the LUCC's contention that AFUDC treatment of CWIP is mandated by law. The commission's decision to include CWIP in the rate base instead of capitalizing it in an AFUDC account is a factual one to be made on a case-by-case basis. Incorporating the burden of proof standard of RSA 378:8, we hold that "the burden of proving the necessity" of including CWIP in the rate base instead of employing traditional AFUDC treatment is upon the public utility. In the present case, we cannot say that "a clear preponderance of the evidence before [us]," demonstrates that the commission erroneously decided that the company has met its burden. RSA 541:13.

. . . The building of a nuclear powered generating facility requires very substantial lines of bank credit for the early construction stages. Immediate financing must be available. If credit is not forthcoming, the construction program will be jeopardized. *Amyot, supra* at 281. Because it is fundamental that rate making must take into account the need for the utility to maintain the confidence of investors, *Bluefield Water Works & Improvement Co. v. Pub. Serv. Comm'n*, 262 U.S. 679, 693 (1923); *accord, Federal Power Comm'n v. Hope Natural Gas Co.*, 320 U.S. 591, 603 (1944), the commission properly exercised its regulatory function by allowing the company to prove the necessity of including its CWIP in the rate base. . . .

Ratepayers like taxpayers come and go but ratepayers like taxpayers cannot expect to be charged solely on the basis of their individual benefit. Schools and other public buildings are benefitting the taxpayers today but were fully paid for by taxpayers of yesterday. . . .

If CWIP is not allowed in rate base, a firm cannot earn a current rate of return on its investment. However, it is permitted to use an alternative method of recovering the cost of capital invested in CWIP during the period before new plant is placed into service through an account known as Allowance for Funds Used During Construction (AFUDC); the firm accumulates in AFUDC an amount each year that represents the annual cost of capital in its CWIP account. Once a plant is completed and placed in service, all costs of the plant, including the accumulated AFUDC, are transferred to the firm's rate base. This allows the firm to earn a return on its CWIP, but the receipt of that money is deferred until after the plant is in service. In the above case, the New Hampshire Supreme Court rejected this approach:

> The commission also evaluated alternative ratemaking approaches to that of including CWIP in the rate base. It considered full normalization of tax benefits of accelerated depreciation and allowing a higher return on equity capital. It found that these methods were "disadvantageous and undesirable in many respects." The commission relied on witness Trawicki's testimony to reject the alternative of allowing a higher return on equity capital. Trawicki stated "that such an alternative would result in an inflated return which is unrealistic when compared to other utilities and it could have the effect of establishing an inappropriate precedent." In rejecting the option of full normalization of tax benefits from accelerated depreciation, the commission found that this method would not generate enough funds to remedy the company's revenue deficiency and also that this procedure is imprecise and not readily controllable. The commission's report elaborated on the reasoning favoring CWIP in the rate base as the most desirable ratemaking approach.

> We find that setting a rate of return higher than normal [on equity capital] would impose the same burdens on customers, that is, the rates would be the same while providing none of the advantages of the CWIP method, that is, a future reduction in rates because of a smaller future rate base. In other words, if the interest on the CWIP component is paid for today, it will not be included in the rate tomorrow. If CWIP were not allowed and the needed cash revenue were generated through a rate of return, the Company would continue to accumulate AFUDC along conventional accounting principles and eventually add this total amount to the total capitalization of plant. Thus, there would be no future reduction in rates stemming from discontinuance of AFUDC. . . .

6. Used and useful, as a criteria for including costs in rate base, serves to protect current generations from bearing the burden of paying for the capital necessary to generate energy for future generations. Does this create the right incentives for energy consumption? What are the effects of the doctrine on technological innovation? Does allowing recovery of CWIP serve any useful distributive or economic purpose?

7. The used and useful doctrine has been most controversial in the nuclear context, where many expensive plants took longer to build than was initially planned and were never fully utilized to the benefit of consumers. Consider the following excerpt:

James A. Throgmorton, Planning as Persuasive Storytelling: The Rhetorical Construction of Chicago's Electric Future

70–72, 244–45 (1997).

In 1956, [Commonwealth] Edison obtained the ICC's permission to build Dresden 1, the nation's first full-scale, privately financed nuclear power plant. Almost one decade later, with its forecasts showing the demand for electric power growing at 7 percent per year, and believing that nuclear power would be the best way of providing adequate and reliable power in the future, Edison announced a major expansion of what has become the nation's largest program to construct nuclear power plants. Between 1965 and 1973, the company announced its intention to build twelve or more large nuclear units at its Dresden, Quad Cities, Zion, LaSalle, Byron, and Braidwood stations. More specifically, in 1970, 1972, and 1973, Edison applied to the ICC for "certificates of public convenience and necessity" to authorize and direct construction of six nuclear generating units totaling approximately 6,600 MW at its LaSalle, Byron, and Braidwood stations. According to material submitted with those applications, the units would be completed by 1980 at a cost of $2.5 billion (ICC 1980a; ICC 1985b; BPI and CUB 1989b). They would extend the modernist story of a regulated natural monopoly building larger power plants that increased earnings and reduced consumer rates.

This was an ambitious plan. As time passed, it also proved to be highly controversial and difficult to carry out completely or on time. The plan assumed that the economic stability of the 1960s would continue. It also assumed that nuclear power plants, which heretofore had been designed as 300 MW units, could easily be modified to operate equally efficiently at the 1,000 MW scale. Consequently this plan was shaken by the energy price shocks of the 1970s, by price inflation, by the 1979 nuclear accident at Three Mile Island. Moreover, it was assaulted by the rise of consumer, environmental, and antinuclear movements.

Edison's plants took longer to build, and they cost much more than expected. The last of the six nuclear units was not completed until 1988, and the final construction cost turned out to be approximately $13.7 billion (see table 4.1). Thus Edison's nuclear plan was completed eight years behind schedule and $11.2 billion over budget!

To pay for its increasingly expensive plants, the company had to apply for a series of large rate increases. As the price of electricity increased, the rate of growth in demand for electric power declined. Edison's capacity and load factors decreased, while its reserve margin increased. Faced with steadily increasing electricity prices, consumers looked for alternative ways of obtaining needed power and energy services. . . .

And the commissioners—ah, the commissioners they struggled to "balance the interests" of characters who were beginning to bewilder them by telling very different stories about planning and ratemaking in Illinois, stories that implied fundamental changes in the very notion of balancing interests through regulatory action. . . .

The data said that demand for electric power in Edison's service area had been growing at an average annual rate of 7.8 percent from 1961 through 1973. The data said that peak load—which stood at 10,943 megawatts in 1970—would grow to 17,850 megawatts in 1977 and that the company would need to add almost 7,000 megawatts of additional generating capacity to meet that demand. The data showed that nuclear power would provide the least costly way of generating the additional power. Consequently, the one best solution to the problem (or opportunity) of rapidly increasing demand was for Edison to build six new nuclear power generating units, each with a capacity of 1,100 megawatts, at its LaSalle, Byron, and Braidwood stations. Cost estimates showed that construction of those units would be completed by 1980 at a cost of $2.506 billion. Net present value revenue projections showed that the rates (prices) consumers pay for electric power would decline as the plants began generating useful power.

Confident in its forecasts and plan, Edison began building its six nuclear units in the early 1970s. However, the company soon encountered a series of difficulties (all due, of course, to factors beyond its control) which endangered that plan. Rather than growing at 7.8 percent, peak demand grew at an average annual rate of 2.3 percent from 1974 through 1988. Rather than growing by 6,900 megawatts between 1970 and 1977, peak load grew by 2,990 megawatts. (As of 1990 it still had not reached the load Edison projected for 1977.) Rather than costing approximately $400 per kilowatt, Edison's last six nuclear units turned out to cost almost $2,100. Rather than declining, the average rates that Edison charged its customers (measured in terms of gross operating revenues divided by kilowatt-hour sales) increased from 4.51¢/kWh to 7.35¢/kWh in constant 1982 dollars. Despite these difficulties, the company did finish building its six nuclear units. But it did not finish them until 1988 at a total cost of $13.7 billion, and along the way it had to increase its rates by 63 percent (in constant 1982 dollars), saw its earnings drop from $4.75 per common share in 1987 to $0.08 in 1991, and had to cut its dividends from $3 per common share in 1987 to $1.60 per share in 1991.

Rigidly focused on completing the company's troubled expansion plan, on cutting a clear path through the wilderness below, Edison's managers found that they could no longer simply contemplate and control the future from their central plateau. To their dismay, the plan and its tidal wave of rate increases motivated consumer, environmental, antinuclear, community groups, and sympathetic elected officials to coalesce in opposition. Instead of simply presenting evidence that justified the plan, Edison's planners and managers had to descend from their plateau and then try to persuade specific audiences at specific times in specific contexts, in the face of determined opposition.

e. OPERATING EXPENSES

The day-to-day operational decisions of a regulated utility remain largely in the hands of its management. Operating and maintenance expenses are often recorded in the utility's actual books and records, so their identification and measurement does not pose the same challenge as other aspects of the ratemaking formula. FERC and state PSCs generally defer to private management regarding the utility's decisions as to what type of fuel to purchase, the need for more service workers, or a salary increase for management.

Depreciation and taxes are operating expenses for most utilities. Although, as is noted above, depreciation is typically deducted from capital investment to determine rate base, depreciation for the relevant period is also included as an operating expense. So, although the utility's rate base may be declining with time, the utility is able to recover the value of the reduction in value from customers.

Although operating expenses generally comprise around 75% of a utility's revenue requirements, in practice operating expenses may be the least controversial of the costs in the ratemaking formula. Deference is the standard with respect to operating expenses, but not every expense item is rubber-stamped for rate inclusion by FERC or state PSCs. In dictum, *Smyth v. Ames* qualified its description of the operating costs, O, a utility must be allowed to recover: "Under the evidence there is no ground for saying that the operating expenses of any companies were greater than necessary." This has come to be known as the "prudent expenditure" and "prudent investment" doctrines. Regulators will disallow operating expenses or investments that do not meet the prudence standards. These two standards are distinct. A decision to build (prudent investment) is evaluated separately from the reasonableness of costs once that decision has been made (prudent expenditure). In evacuating prudence, regulators apply a general presumption of managerial competence. *See Missouri ex rel. Southwestern Bell Tel. Co. v. Pub. Serv. Comm'n of Mo.*, 262 U.S. 276 (1923).

While the prudent investment doctrine is primarily a rate base issue, FERC and state PSCs have disallowed many operating expenses under the prudent expenditure standard. For example, state commissions have also disallowed from rate recovery portions of wages they deem to be excessive. *See, e.g., Southwestern Bell Tel. Co. v. Arkansas Pub. Serv. Comm'n*, 715 S.W.2d 451 (Ark. App.1986); *S. Cal. Edison Co. v. Pub. Utils. Comm'n*, 20 Cal. 3d 813 (1978). In addition, the costs of unnecessary advertising[4] and charitable contributions have regularly been disallowed. *See, e.g., Central*

---

4. The U.S. Supreme Court has recognized that utility advertising may raise First Amendment concerns. *Consolidated Edison Co. v. Public Serv. Comm'n*, 447 U.S. 530 (1980); *Central Hudson Gas & Elec. Co. v. Pub. Serv. Comm'n of N.Y.*, 447 U.S. 557 (1980).

Maine Power Co., 26 P.U.R.4th 407 (Maine PSC 1978) (disallowing advertisements designed to influence pending rate proceedings as "political"); *Cleveland v. Public Utilities Commission of Ohio*, 406 N.E.2d 1370 (Ohio 1980) (disallowing charitable contributions "not reasonably necessary to produce safe, reliable service to utility customers").

Should the prudence of each of a utility's charitable contributions be evaluated, or is it the overall amount of the contribution that should be subject to a reasonableness standard? In *Business & Prof'l People v. Illinois Commerce Comm'n*, 585 N.E.2d 1032 (Ill. 1991), the Illinois Supreme Court held that is the overall amount of expenses that are important to the assessment of just and reasonable rates. Commonwealth Edison argued that the Commission arbitrarily disallowed $1.269 million of charitable contributions from Edison's operating expenses. The Court reasoned:

> Edison is correct that the Act prohibits the Commission from "disallowing by rule, as an operating expense, any portion of a reasonable donation for public welfare or charitable purposes." (Ill. Rev. Stat. 1987, ch. 111 2/3, par. 9–227.) However, section 9–227 does not provide that every donation Edison makes to a qualified organization is presumed reasonable. Edison still has the burden of showing that a donation is reasonable in amount. When this burden of proof is considered, the Act merely states that the Commission shall not disallow any portion of that amount which Edison has shown to be reasonable in amount. Contrary to Edison's position, we believe that the Commission must determine the reasonableness of the amount of contributions based on the total contributions rather than on an individualized basis. There are numerous charitable organizations worthy of Edison's support. If Edison were to make a reasonable donation to each of these organizations, the aggregate total of the donations could very easily exceed a reasonable amount.

The Court refused to substitute its judgment for the Commission on which requested charitable expenses to exclude from an overall reasonable amount.

Another prevalent operational expense is fuel costs or the costs of purchased power (i.e., wholesale power bought by a utility for resale to its customers). Since its is costly to evaluate rates on a continuing basis, many regulators have provided for automatic adjustments in the price and quantity of fuel used through a Fuel Adjustment Clause (F.A.C.). The Illinois Supreme Court has commented:

> Perhaps the most significant operating expenses utilities incur are fuel costs. In 1973, a four-fold increase in petroleum prices and the escalation of coal and natural gas prices left utilities with far higher rates than those based on test year projections. Thus, utilities faced a revenue shortfall. A response to this development was the fuel adjustment clause. The fuel adjustment clause (FAC) is a statutory or regulatory rule that allows a utility to automatically pass through to rates increased fuel costs, without the need for a formal rate proceeding. From the utility's perspective, this allows a closer matching of

actual expenses and the revenues received from consumer rates. Consumers may also benefit if fuel costs decrease between rate filings. However, FACs also reduce incentives for utilities to negotiate low fuel costs.

Business & Prof'l People v. Illinois Commerce Comm'n, 585 N.E.2d 1032 (Ill. 1991). The Illinois Supreme Court noted, however, that usage of a F.A.C. on the basis of entirely forecasted data can lead to over collection of revenues by utilities:

> Not surprisingly, at the hearings below Edison's witness was extremely reluctant to admit that the company in fact treated such overcollections as earnings; rather, he took refuge in the repeated assertion that the funds could not be "isolated" from Edison's overall revenues. It clearly appears from published figures, however, that Edison's overcollections pursuant to the fuel clause were not only large in the absolute sense, they amounted to a very significant proportion of the company's general revenue picture. For example, for the year 1974 Edison reported a total net income from all sources of $218.3 million; yet during the same 12–month period, according to Edison's own figures filed with the commission in compliance with the decision under review, Edison's net fuel clause overcollections were $122.5 million—in other words, they constituted more than 56 percent of the company's system-wide net income for the entire year. Moreover, that net income was itself 47.8 percent higher than in the previous year, even though sales were lower; Edison's reported earnings per share were $4.10 for 1974, as compared with $2.70 for 1973; and the company's board of directors voted to increase the common stock dividend in 1974, the first such raise in three years. (Annual Rep., p. 4.) In announcing all these benefits to the shareholders, Edison acknowledged that the fuel clause adjustments, together with a general rate increase in late 1973, "contributed substantially to higher revenues."

> These continuing overcollections by Edison and other electric utility companies did not pass unnoticed. On the contrary, they triggered a sequence of public complaints, investigations, and proposals for reform or abolition of the entire fuel clause procedure. Among the most vocal critics were consumer groups (e.g., The Fuel–Adjustment Caper (Nov. 1974) 39 Consumer Rep. 836) and organs of the Congress (*see* Rep. of Subcom. on Oversight and Investigations of House Com. on Interstate and Foreign Commerce on Electric Utility Automatic Fuel Adjustment Clauses (Oct. 1975) passim).

> While sharing many of the concerns voiced by critics of the clause, the commission determined that the cost adjustment concept should be preserved but the clause should be modified to eliminate the defects revealed by experience. The principal such defect, as we have seen, was the provision authorizing Edison to base its calculations on a prediction of its fossil fuel needs for the 12–month period following each application for a billing adjustment, premised on the assumption that "average" weather conditions would prevail throughout that time. The

commission abandoned this procedure, and in lieu thereof adopted a clause which operates on a "recorded data" basis, i.e., on the actual fuel expenses incurred by the utility during the period preceding its application for a billing adjustment. The utility is now required to maintain a monthly "balancing account," into which it will enter the amount by which its actual energy cost for the month was greater or less than the revenue generated by the clause; and on each occasion hereafter that the clause is invoked, the billing factor will be adjusted so as to bring the balance of this account back to zero. By this device the possibility of large over-or under-collections accumulating in the future is eliminated. And because the commission expanded the clause to include all sources of purchased energy—e.g., nuclear and geothermal, in addition to fossil fuels—it renamed the device the energy cost adjustment clause.

Id. The Court held that adjustment clause did not result in retroactive ratemaking. *Id.*

NOTES AND COMMENTS

1.   Operating expenses may also be disallowed if they are underrepresentative (or nonrecurring). Generally non-recurring expenses, such as repair expenses attributable to a hurricane or excess fuel costs incurred during an excessively hot summer, will not be used as a basis for test year recovery of expenses, but will be allowed one-time recovery as extraordinary expenses. In addition, some operating expenses simply may not qualify for agency regulation. *See Sandstone Resources, Inc. v. FERC*, 973 F.2d 956 (D.C. Cir. 1992) (costs incurred in removing liquid brine from natural gas held to be nonrecoverable production costs).

2.   How would you oppose or defend the inclusion of the following as legitimate utility operating expenses? Are all of these operating expenses, or should some of them be included in rate base?

> — A contribution to an industry-wide Gas Research Institute. *See Pub. Utils. of Colo. v. FERC*, 660 F.2d 821 (D.C. Cir. 1981).

> — Research programs in solar energy and nuclear reactor technology standards. *See Caldwell v. Public Utilities Comm'n of State of Colorado*, 613 P.2d 328 (Colo. 1980).

> — A discount on electric charges for company employees. *See Central Maine Power Co. v. Pub. Utils. Comm'n*, 405 A.2d 153 (Maine 1979).

> — A commercial scale plant demonstrating a new coal gasification technique. *See Transwestern Pipeline Co. v. FERC*, 626 F.2d 1266 (5th Cir. 1980).

> — Expenses incurred when a plant under construction is abandoned. *See Office of Consumers' Council v. Pub. Utils. Comm'n*, 67 Ohio St.2d 153, 423 N.E.2d 820 (1981).

— Advertising expenses encouraging the conservation of electricity.

— Flyers included with utility bills responding to allegations that a utility's nuclear facilities are unsafe.

— A utility-sponsored research lab to investigate the effects of electro-magnetic fields from power lines.

— The medical costs for future retired employees.

Should a utility be allowed to recover attorneys fees incurred defending claims of environmental harm during construction of a new gas or power transmission line? The following case illustrates the skepticism with which regulators have treated such claims for recovery. Why was the agency reversed?

Iroquois Gas Transmission System v. FERC

145 F.3d 398 (D.C. Cir. 1998).

◼ WILLIAMS, J. Iroquois Gas Transmission System, L.P., ran up substantial legal defense costs as a result of federal investigations into environmental violations committed in its construction of a natural gas pipeline. The Federal Energy Regulatory Commission issued orders excluding these legal costs from the rate base used to calculate Iroquois's permissible charges, explaining that Iroquois had failed to carry the burden of proving that the costs were prudently incurred. Iroquois says the orders were grounded in an impermissible presumption of non-recoverability and asks us to set them aside, relying primarily on our decisions in *Mountain States Telephone and Telegraph Co. v. FCC*, 939 F.2d 1021 (D.C.Cir.1991) ("Mountain States I") and *Mountain States Telephone and Telegraph Co. v. FCC*, 939 F.2d 1035 (D.C.Cir.1991) ("Mountain States II"). Because the Commission has failed to come to grips with the questions that Mountain States II said must be answered when addressing a utility's recovery of legal expenses, we remand the case for a more reasoned decision.

* * *

In November 1990 the Commission granted Iroquois a certificate of public convenience and necessity under Section 7 of the Natural Gas Act (the "Act"), authorizing the company to build and operate a new pipeline stretching from the Canadian border to Long Island. The pipeline went into full service in January 1992. Before long, however, Iroquois found itself in trouble for environmental violations. Around November 1991 the U.S. Attorney's Office for the Northern District of New York, in conjunction with the FBI and the Environmental Protection Agency, began an investigation into whether Iroquois's construction activities violated the Clean Water Act. The record suggests that the investigation focused on points where the pipeline crossed creeks and streams in upstate New York, allegedly discharging silt and sediment in violation of Iroquois's Clean Water Act permit, and on Iroquois's alleged failure to build so-called trench breakers, which control soil erosion and pipeline corrosion. An Army Corps of Engineers inspection report from early 1992 cited a potential overall penalty of more than $115,000,000. Civil investigations, presumably closely related, were also undertaken by the U.S. Attorney's offices for the Northern, Eastern, and Southern Districts of New York. In addition, FERC's own enforcement staff launched a separate investigation to determine whether Iroquois had violated the environment-related conditions of its Section 7 certificate. Ultimately an Iroquois affiliate and four of its employees entered into guilty pleas and a civil settlement costing $22 million in fines and penalties, and Iroquois consented to a settlement with the Commission admitting violations of environmental conditions in its certificate and agreeing not to pass the fines and penalties on to its ratepayers. *Iroquois Gas Transmission System, L.P.*, 75 F.E.R.C. ¶ 61,205 (1996).

In the course of resolving these disputes Iroquois ran up a legal bill of more than $15,000,000. While the various investigations were still under way, Iroquois filed with the Commission for a general rate increase to recover its pipeline construction costs. The rate proceeding culminated in a settlement between Iroquois and its customers resolving all issues except the rate and accounting treatment of the legal defense costs. Hearings on these reserved issues were held before an administrative law judge, who determined that the legal costs were not unrecoverable per se, and observed that "[t]he participants have presented nothing to rebut Iroquois's position that the legal costs were incurred as an appropriate and normal response to investigatory activities arising from the construction undertaken to provide service to the ratepayers." *Iroquois Gas Transmission System, L.P.*, 72 F.E.R.C. ¶ 63,004, at 65,027 (1995).

The Commission reversed the ALJ's initial decision and held that Iroquois's legal defense costs could not be included in its rate base. *Iroquois Gas Transmission System, L.P.*, 77 F.E.R.C. ¶ 61,288 (1996). "Allowing recovery of Iroquois' litigation expenses," the Commission concluded,

> would fail to recognize the interests of Iroquois' ratepayers, shared by the Commission, that emanate from Section 7 of the NGA. These interests are to ensure that the pipeline is built in compliance with all applicable federal environmental and safety laws so as to prevent any future personal injuries or environmental damage.

Id. at 62,280. The Commission based its disallowance of recovery on Iroquois's failure to demonstrate any countervailing economic or non-economic benefit to ratepayers from the activities that gave rise to the investigations. The Commission denied Iroquois's request for rehearing, *Iroquois Gas Transmission System, L.P.*, 78 F.E.R.C. ¶ 61,216 (1997), and later rejected similar claims in a second rate case filed by Iroquois. *Iroquois Gas Transmission System, L.P.*, 77 F.E.R.C. ¶ 61,352, at 62,538 (1996), rehearing denied, 80 F.E.R.C. ¶ 61,199, at 61,797–98 (1997). Iroquois petitioned for review in this court.

At the outset the Commission concedes two propositions, one general and one specific to this case. First, the Commission admits that although the Act gives the natural gas company the burden of showing that a proposed rate increase is just and reasonable, 15 U.S.C. § 717c(e), as a matter of FERC practice "a natural gas company is ordinarily not required to show that all of its expenditures were prudent unless serious doubts are raised regarding the prudence of those costs." FERC Br. at 24. *See, e.g., Trans World Airlines, Inc. v. Civil Aeronautics Bd.*, 385 F.2d 648, 657 (D.C.Cir.1967); *Minnesota Power & Light Co.*, 11 F.E.R.C. ¶ 61,312, at 61,645 (1980). Second, the Commission does not seriously contest that it effectively raised a presumption against recovery in this case, putting the burden on Iroquois to demonstrate that its expenditures were prudently incurred. *See* 78 FERC at 61,927 ("[S]ince [Iroquois] was seeking to recover the legal defense costs in its rates, it had the burden of proving that the costs were just and reasonable."). Indeed, at times the Commission seemed to erect something close to an irrebuttable presumption against recovery. See id. ("Iroquois placed itself in the untenable position of arguing that its illegal activities, supposedly taken to save time and money during construction, were in the interests of its ratepayers, and, therefore, just and reasonable.") (emphasis added).

The Commission contends, however, that it adequately justified its decision to invert the normal presumption in this case, because Iroquois's legal costs by their very nature raised a serious doubt as to prudence (i.e., because they grew out of civil and criminal violations). *See* FERC Br. at 24. One immediate problem with this approach is that as of the time the hearing was held before the ALJ no violations had been proven or admitted; the investigations were still ongoing and the precise contours of any eventual charges were still uncertain. But even if that problem is put aside, the Commission runs into another barrier: our decisions in the Mountain States cases.

In Mountain States I we held that the Federal Communications Commission had failed to provide a reasoned justification for its presumption that antitrust litigation expenses incurred by AT&T could not be recovered from ratepayers. 939 F.2d at 1029–35. "Illegality of carrier conduct from which an antitrust litigation expense stems," we concluded, "does not inexorably compel or warrant either rejection or stigmatization of the expense as a factor in rate calculations." *Id.* at 1031. We noted that in two tax decisions the Supreme Court had described litigation expenses—even those incurred in a losing cause—as ordinary and legitimate costs of doing business. *Id.* at 1031–32 (*citing Commissioner v. Heininger*, 320 U.S. 467, 64 S.Ct. 249, 88 L.Ed. 171 (1943), and *Commissioner v. Tellier*, 383 U.S. 687, 86 S.Ct. 1118, 16 L.Ed.2d 185 (1966)).

In Mountain States II, issued the same day as Mountain States I, we reviewed a new FCC regulation governing the accounting treatment of litigation expenses generally. The new rule attached a presumption of non-recoverability to all litigation expenses that resulted in an adverse final judgment or post-judgment settlement in any federal statutory case, unless the regulated company could show that ratepayers benefitted from the underlying activity. 939 F.2d at 1039. Holding that "the FCC may disallow any expense incurred as a result of carrier conduct that cannot reasonably be expected to benefit ratepayers," id. at 1043, we found the new rule quite sensible in the context of antitrust violations, since the effect of such violations is typically to injure consumers. But we went on to say that the FCC had inadequately justified its application of the new rule to statutory violations beyond antitrust, where an absence of ratepayer benefit "is neither self-evident, as it is in the antitrust context, nor bolstered by either analytical or empirical support." Id. at 1044. By the same token we rejected the FCC's "terse assertion" that violations of federal statutory law "raise public policy implications" sufficient to justify presumptive disallowance of associated litigation costs. Id. at 1045.

We emphasized in Mountain States II that the FCC had not taken sufficient account of the perverse incentive effects set in motion by a presumption against recovery of litigation expenses. Such a presumption, we observed, was likely to induce excessive caution in carriers, causing them to shun activities that might conceivably be found to violate federal law, even when those activities promise benefits to ratepayers. Id. at 1046. We illustrated the point in a passage whose uncanny relevance to the instant case calls for full quotation:

> Consider the following example: A carrier has to choose between instituting a strict pollution monitoring policy or a lax policy that is arguably sufficient under the law and would cost $50,000 less than the strict policy. The carrier will surely be sued under a federal statute if it adopts the lax policy, and there is a 10% chance that it will lose; if it does, the plaintiff would recover $100,000, making the expected or ex ante cost of the lawsuit ($100,000 × .10 =) $10,000. Thus the carrier reasonably determines that adopting the lax policy will produce a net benefit of $40,000 to the ratepayers, who would otherwise have to pay the cost of the strict monitoring policy. It would be misleading to say that requiring ratepayers to bear the cost of the resulting judgment, if any, causes them to subsidize the carrier's illegal activity. The carrier made the "right" decision, i.e., what the ratepayers would have decided in their own economic self-interest; it just turned out to be the "wrong" decision as a matter of how the law was finally interpreted. Perhaps the agency has a more capacious notion of ratepayer benefit than merely paying lower rates. If it does, however, it has neither said as much nor indicated why ratepayers are generally harmed in some non-economic way by the violation of federal statutes.

Id. at 1044–45.

The Commission quoted this passage in its initial order, see 77 FERC at 62,279–80, acknowledging its relevance but claiming to find refuge in its final two sentences. While the FCC in Mountain States II had failed to articulate any noneconomic harm flowing from violations of federal statute law, the Commission said, here Iroquois's ratepayers have a general interest in compliance with federal environmental and safety laws, and thus are harmed whenever those laws are violated. 77 FERC at 62,280. The inclusion of environmental compliance requirements in Iroquois's Section 7 certificate, according to the Commission, represented an "implicit recognition that it would be appropriate for ratepayers to pay costs that may be incurred to build a pipeline in an environmentally responsible manner. It is not reasonable then to elevate the ratepayer interest in saving time and money to such a preeminent position in the interests to be considered when deciding whether costs are recoverable in the rates." *Id.*

We pause here to note that the Commission correctly placed its initial focus on the prospect of ratepayer benefits from the underlying activity rather than from the litigation. Even though it is commonly prudent (in the conventional sense of the term) to incur legal expenses in defending conduct that turns out to have been illegal, there appears no reason why ratepayers should bear the expense of defending conduct that had no ex ante prospect of benefitting them. *See* Mountain States II, 939 F.2d at 1043.

Nonetheless, we find the Commission's treatment of Mountain States II unconvincing. The asserted ratepayer interest in compliance with environmental and safety laws is virtually as generic as the amorphous "public policy implications" we found inadequate to justify the presumption of nonrecoverability in Mountain States II, 939 F.2d at 1045. Because all citizens share an interest in widespread compliance, not just with environmental or safety laws but with laws of any kind, the Commission's approach would result in the presumptive disallowance of all litigation expenses leading to anything short of outright triumph for the regulated entity.

More important, the Commission's approach utterly fails to respond to the problem of incentives posed in Mountain States II. Iroquois's ratepayers, in common with the general population of upstate New York, undoubtedly share an interest in maintaining the purity of the region's creeks and streams. But the same ratepayers have a unique and concentrated interest in timely and efficient pipeline construction. Although our concurring colleague asserts that some ratepayers would willingly pay higher rates in exchange for assurances of environmental compliance, see Concurring Op. at 276–77, laws obligating firms to satisfy environmental standards are necessary precisely because most consumers, if given a choice, appear unwilling to pay the full cost of satisfying higher standards. If consumer demand were actually enough to cause ordinary firms in competitive industries to incur the costs of protecting the environment, there would be little need for environmental regulation.

Indeed, because of the limitation of the utility's rates to recovery of cost under the statute's "just and reasonable" formula, the ratepayers have the same interest in optimizing environmental compliance costs as they would if they built the pipeline themselves through a cooperative or a partnership. As our opinion in Mountain States II made clear, a firm incurring optimal environmental compliance costs will on occasion take measures that are ultimately found illegal. In Mountain States II's example, where a saving of $50,000 runs a 10% risk of triggering $100,000 in additional costs, the ex ante expected benefit for the ratepayers is $40,000. Contrary to our concurring colleague's suggestion, see Concurring Op. at 277, Mountain States II does not establish a ratemaking principle that affirmatively encourages regulated companies to violate environment-related certificate conditions. It does, however, recognize that ratepayers often benefit from activities that tack reasonably close to the wind, and that policies inducing management to pursue absolutely risk-free environmental compliance measures are therefore not, on their face, in the ratepayers' interest.

Yet the Commission's approach seems sure to chill some lawful activity beneficial to ratepayers; indeed, it would seem calculated to encourage regulated firms to avoid any and all litigation risks. "[L]awsuits are a recurring fact of life in operating a business," Mountain States I, 939 F.2d at 1034, and in the area of federal environmental regulation the line between permissible and impermissible conduct is often drawn in (muddy) water. Compare United States v. Mango, 997 F.Supp. 264, 285 (N.D.N.Y. 1998) (holding that CWA authorized Army Corps of Engineers to regulate Iroquois's "backfilling of trenches excavated in waterways and wetland areas") with id. at 283–87, 295–98 (holding that CWA does not authorize Corps to impose permit conditions not related to discharge of dredged or fill material, such as those designed to prevent wetland drainage).[4] Thus the Commission must do a better job of explaining why all activities that turn out to violate environmental laws should be presumed unlikely "to benefit ratepayers," as required for presumptive disallowance under Mountain States II, 939 F.2d at 1043.

The Commission's attempted distinction of Appalachian Elec. Power Co. v. Fed. Power Comm'n, 218 F.2d 773 (4th Cir.1955), is also insubstantial. There the Fourth Circuit held that legal costs incurred by a regulated utility in an unsuccessful challenge to the Commission's jurisdiction over a proposed power plant were recoverable from ratepayers as expenses necessary to the development of the project. According to the Commission, the costs of the jurisdictional challenge in Appalachian were an example of "normal civil litigation" costs; other examples given by the Commission were the "cost of attorneys hired to secure any state or federal permits, or litigation to perfect eminent domain rights or to establish property values." 77 FERC at 62,281. Iroquois's case is different, the Commission said, because it "is not the type of case where a regulated company, interpreting the law in a manner most favorable to the company, loses a court case." Id. In fact that description seems, at least at first glance, to fit Iroquois's case quite snugly. Beyond offering a few conclusory statements ("there is no punitive aspect associated with the loss of a challenge [to] the agency's regulatory jurisdiction," id.), the Commission never explains why action based on a legal interpretation "most favorable to the company" should have been presumptively beneficial to ratepayers in Appalachian but presumptively harmful here.

In short, the Commission has not made clear which types of legal defense costs are presumed recoverable for ratemaking purposes and which

---

4. [Editors note: On appeal, the district court decision cited here was reversed and the Second Circuit held that the conditions attached by the Corps. were proper. United States v. Mango, 199 F.3d 85 (2d Cir. 1999).]

not, or why the costs here belong on the nonrecoverable side of the line. Particularly in light of the explicit discussion of pollution laws in Mountain States II, the Commission's burden here requires more than the making of general allusions to the public interest in compliance with environmental statutes or with Section 7 certificate requirements. Of course, we do not reach the ultimate question whether Iroquois's legal defense costs were in fact prudently or imprudently incurred, and thus whether they may or may not be borne by the ratepayers. We hold only that the Commission has not adequately justified its apparent decision to impose upon Iroquois the burden of proving that its activities benefitted ratepayers.

The case is remanded to the Commission for further proceedings consistent with this opinion.

So ordered.

■ WALD, J., concurring in the judgment: Although I agree that this case must be remanded for further consideration, I write separately to emphasize the breadth of the analysis FERC should undertake on remand. Although the ultimate issue in this case is who is to bear Iroquois's litigation costs, not whether Iroquois's conduct was legal or illegal, the latter consideration is certainly relevant, in my view. It is worth noting, therefore, that Iroquois admitted violating several environmental-related conditions of its section 7 certificate, and our discussion of whether it is "just and reasonable" for the company to then shift the litigation costs related to those violations to its ratepayers should in no way be read as directing FERC to ignore the harm to the environment that has been suffered as a result of those violations. Rather, I think it important that the calculus of whether a rate is reasonable take into consideration noneconomic benefit as well as economic benefit. It may well be true that a thoroughly informed ratepayer will prefer a cheaper product obtained by way of environmental violations over a more expensive product produced legally. But I'm not sure that this can be presumed to be the case, as the majority opinion appears to assume. In an antitrust case, as Mountain States II recognized, the analysis is easier: A presumption that litigation expenses associated with a violation of the antitrust laws are disallowed is reasonable because we can assume that consumers would prefer to buy products in a competitive market, since competition is presumed to make products both cheaper and better. Thus, it would be difficult to show that anticompetitive conduct would be beneficial to ratepayers in any way. Here, however, the equation is not so simple: We cannot presume that noncompliance with environmental regulations would be a benefit to ratepayers if the economic costs of compliance outweigh the economic costs of noncompliance, since the noneconomic benefit of compliance must also enter the calculus. It may well be the case, for example, that a ratepayer would prefer to pay higher rates in exchange for the assurance that the pipeline from which it obtains its gas is in compliance with environmental laws. (I can imagine several reasons for this preference: for the goodwill benefits compliance confers, to aid in thwarting litigation, or even because the ratepayer lives in the geographic area for which noncompliance is proposed and will suffer as a citizen.) I agree that under our precedent FERC's simple assertion that ratepayers have an interest in compliance with the law is insufficient to disallow recovery of Iroquois's litigation costs. As Mountain States II holds, FERC must also take into consideration the economic benefits noncompliance may confer, though I must admit I have a good deal of trouble with the proposition that FERC can validly attach an environmental condition on a section 7 permit, but the company is simultaneously encouraged by ratemaking principles to violate it if it can build the pipeline cheaper or faster by doing so. That kind of law makes no sense to me. But I also believe that even the Mountain States II calculus is far more expansive than the majority opinion suggests. By seeming to give priority to economic over noneconomic considerations, I fear that the majority will dissuade FERC from adequately considering the environmental costs of Iroquois's conduct, costs that may well affect the decision about whether forcing ratepayers to bear its litigation costs is indeed "just and reasonable."■

f. INTERGENERATIONAL ALLOCATION

The most controversial expense issue regulators currently face is the intergenerational allocation of costs in utility rates. The general principle of cost of service ratemaking is that customers should pay for the costs of the services they consume. However, as issues such as CWIP, depreciation, and the FAC illustrate, it is much simpler to state the principle than make it work in practice. Consumers today, through items such as CWIP, may pay for services that benefit future generations. Although commissions generally frown upon "retroactive ratemaking," there is no hard and fast rule that commissions or courts use to match costs and benefits across generations. It generally comes down to balancing the various interests before the regulator.

In this balancing of interests, since future generations are not represented it might be expected that often the costs associated with benefits to today's ratepayers are passed on to future generations. Ratepayers today are paying for services that may have unanticipated costs for future generations. As a result, future generations may pay greater rates to benefit today's consumers.

As an example, billions of dollars are at stake in the recovery of nuclear "decommissioning" costs—the costs utilities must incur when nuclear plants producing power today are retired 10, 20, or 30 years into the future to seal off radioactive waste and return nuclear facilities to a low-risk status. Regulators failed to account for these costs in determining the prudence of nuclear construction. Because it would be unfair to impose these costs on future ratepayers, utilities have been required to seek recovery in current rates.

Commonwealth Edison Company: Proposed General Increase In Electric Rates

158 P.U.R.4th 458 (Ill. Commerce Comm. 1995).

On February 10, 1994, Commonwealth Edison Company ("Edison" or "Company") filed with the Illinois Commerce Commission (the "Commission'') certain revised tariff schedules and amendments (collectively "the Filed Tariffs'') by which it proposed to increase annual revenues by about 7.9%, or $460.3, which includes a base rate increase of $461.7 million, decreased meter lease revenues of $2.2 million and increased fuel adjustment revenues of $.8 million. . . .

Edison requests approval of $170.3 million annually to be paid directly into its external decommissioning trust funds. This amount, which represents an increase over the currently authorized level of $127.1 million, as allowed in Docket 90–0169, is attributable to: (1) site-specific or generic regional decommissioning cost estimates in 1993 dollars prepared by Edison witness Mingst; (2) Edison's intention to use the immediate dismantlement or "DECON" method; (3) its plan to return the sites of its nuclear plants to "greenfield" status, i.e., to demolish both radioactive and nonradioactive structures rather than leave the nonradioactive structures standing; (4) a 5.3% annual escalation rate derived from the Nuclear Regulatory Commission ("NRC") formula; (5) estimated rates of return on investments in the external decommissioning trust funds; and (6) a 25% contingency factor. Edison contends that these assumptions are consistent with state and federal laws requiring owners of nuclear generating facilities to provide reasonable assurance that adequate funds will be available to decommission those facilities at the end of their operating lives.

Edison claims that it has no incentive to overestimate its decommissioning costs because all funds will be deposited in trusts beyond its control. Thus, overestimating such costs would raise the Company's rates, making it less competitive, without providing any additional funds to the Company itself. Moreover, Edison maintains that since the Company is required by law to pay its decommissioning collections directly into external trust funds outside its control, and ultimately would be required to refund any unneeded funds to ratepayers, it does not benefit at all from these collections. . . .

Edison intends to demolish both radioactive and nonradioactive structures on the sites of its nuclear units and thereby return these sites to greenfield status. As Mr. Mingst stated, "non-radioactive plant structures are demolished for safety and environmental reasons," and "[a]ll responsible organizations plan for the eventual demolition" of such structures. Therefore, "[i]t is a standard industry practice to include the costs of demolishing the nonradioactive structures as a necessary component of total decommissioning costs." Also, the 1978 Battelle/Pacific Northwest Laboratories ("Battelle") site-specific decommissioning cost studies of the reference Trojan and WNP–2 nuclear plants, which have served as the bases for NRC rules, included the costs of nonradioactive demolition as normal decommissioning costs. . . .

Based upon the evidence in the record, the Commission denies any funds to return sites to greenfield status. The burden is on the Company to prove that it will not reuse old structures. The Company has failed to convince the Commission that nonradioactive structures will not be used in the future. The Commission cannot allow ratepayers to pay for returning facilities to greenfield status when, in fact, some facilities may be reused.

In addition, this Commission does not have a statutory obligation to return sites to greenfield status. Illinois law mandates that decommissioning trusts be established to fund the costs of decommissioning. However, it does not require that sites be returned to greenfield status. It is also clear from the evidence in the record that the NRC does not mandate greenfield status.

From a technical perspective, it is not clear from the evidence in the record that greenfield status is a commonly accepted decommissioning practice. The Commission was persuaded by the evidence that potential changes in regulations may encourage use of nonradioactive portions of facilities. Given the technical changes that will occur, it would be unwise for the Commission to allow funds for greenfield status without being certain that nonradioactive facilities will be returned to greenfield status....■

g. RATE DESIGN

The intergenerational problem illustrates the issue of rate design. Even once revenue requirements are determined, regulators must decide who, among the various customer classes, should pay the costs of service. Several rate design issues may arise, among them demand and energy charges, marginal cost pricing, or seasonal or peak load pricing.

In terms of the cost of service rate formula, distinct costs of service can be allocated to distinct customer classes. For example, it may be more costly for a utility to build the distribution infrastructure to serve the hundreds of residential customers in a development than to serve one or two very large industrials customers, even though the two classes—residential and industrial—may consume similar total amounts of energy.

In allocating costs to classes of customers, including residential, industrial, and small business customers, regulators use two billing components: demand and energy charges. Demand charges generally refer to the portion of utility costs allocated to a customer group to meet the aggregate demand of that group. In other words, these costs represent the amount of plant and other fixed assets allocated to a customer group through a utility rate base ($B*r$). Energy charges generally refer to the cost of providing a certain amount of kWh to a class of customers. These costs vary with the amount of power consumed (e.g., fuel) and thus represent the amount of a utilities operating expenses allocated to a class of customers (O). On a customer's bill, distinct charges for demand and energy will appear. Depending on how "firm" the customer's service is—i.e., the level of reliability the utility has guaranteed—the appropriate charges will be assessed. Because many industrial customers take service on an "interruptible" basis, their bills have small demand components relative to the portion of their bill attributed to energy charges (given the large number of units that they consume). By contrast, residential customers generally have high demand components (given that they need "firm" power) relative to the energy charges on their bills.

Fuels Research Council, Inc. v. Federal Power Commission

374 F.2d 842 (7th Cir. 1967).

[Three coal associations and the mineworkers union challenged the FPC's approval of the rate design of two interstate pipelines, Natural Gas Pipeline Company of America and Midwestern Gas Trans mission Company. The Commission upheld a two-part rate structure, in which most of the capital cost of the pipeline facilities was charged to firm customers based on the maximum amount of gas to which they were entitled (the "demand" component) while the rates for industrial customers who bought gas on an interruptible basis were largely based on the volume of gas that they actually used (the "commodity" component). The coal associations appealed the Commission's decision to the Seventh Circuit Court of Appeals.]

■ SWYGERT, J. The first step in setting the rates to be charged by a regulated pipeline is the determination of the pipeline's "cost of service," that is, the total revenues required to cover the pipeline's cost of operation plus a fair return on its investment. Once the cost of service has been ascertained, rates are "designed" to recover it. For reasons allegedly related to different types of services desired by different customers but more realistically attributable to the basic economic laws of supply and demand as they concern natural gas, the "designing" operation is not reducible to a simple mathematical exercise.

One "demand" for gas, the demand by those consumers who can be made to pay for both the pipeline and the gas flowing through it, is highly seasonal in the midwestern states. The desirability of gas for domestic and commercial space heating purposes in the winter, the "peak" period, is such that the demand for gas during that period by this type of consumer far exceeds the demand by the same consumer at other times of the year. This economic fact creates a "valley" period, a capacity in the pipeline to supply other potential users during the "non-peak" season, including many whose "demand" is constant but so low that they would never become users if they were compelled to pay a proportionate share of the pipeline's cost of service. The valley periods might well go unfilled were it not for the principle, widely accepted by rate-makers, that a more complete utilization of existing facilities spreads the costs of the entire system to whatever extent the additional utilization contributes to the fixed costs of the facilities over and above the payment of variable costs.

The rate-making theory urged upon us blends a concept of "peak cost-responsibility" with a desire to take advantage of the above principle in the following manner. First, the proposition that a pipeline is built to serve the peak period demand is accepted as a fact.[5] Stated another way, the pipeline

---

5.   See generally, Bonbright, Principles of Public Utility Rates (1961). But see the view expressed by Mr. Justice Jackson in *Colorado Interstate Gas Co. v. Fed. Power Comm'n, 324*

capacity provided to take care of the demand on peak days of the system is viewed as creating the bulk of the fixed costs of the pipeline company. These costs do not depend upon the amount of gas flowing through the pipeline. The variable or "volumetric" costs of pipeline operation are essentially related to the amount of gas transported and sold; they are incurred in proportion to the gas actually used. It follows that those responsible for the creation of the peak demand would bear the entire cost of pipeline operation were it not for the opportunity provided by "valley filling" or "off peak" sales. Sales during valley periods (sales to those who will take gas if the price is right), since they do not require the construction of additional facilities, may and should be made at variable cost plus (as the Commission puts it) "such amounts in addition thereto as may be determined to be a proper contribution to the fixed charges," so that the fixed costs can be spread over more sales units, thus reducing the per unit costs.

The theory just described and the recognition that a pipeline's cost of service encompasses both fixed costs and variable costs have been reflected by ratemakers in the form of two-part rates. The rates are split into "demand" and "commodity" components. The demand component is a charge intended to reflect the fact that a customer has contracted for the right to take a given quantity of gas during the peak period. The demand charge is imposed whether the gas is actually taken from the system or not. The commodity component is a charge based upon the volume of gas consumed by each customer. The combination of these charges, multiplied by the anticipated units of the demand component to be contracted for plus the anticipated units of gas to be actually sold is expected to generate revenues equal to the cost of service. The significant problem posed by the two-part formula concerns the allocation of the costs of pipeline operation to the demand and commodity components, more specifically, to the determination of what contribution to the fixed costs of the system is to be recovered by the commodity charge. In the instant case the problem is accentuated, not because the customers of the pipeline, the distribution companies, have different peak demands, but due to the fact that the price of gas to certain customers of the distribution companies during the "valley" periods is based upon the commodity component of the pipelines' rate design.

At the hearing before the examiner, the coal associations argued that two-part rates for Midwestern and Natural were invalid, that the proper rate was a straight one-part rate representing the average cost of each unit of gas sold to the distributors. They introduced expert testimony to indicate the one-part rate which would be necessary to recover Midwestern's cost of service. In their brief on this petition for review, the coal associations do not directly attack the validity of two-part rates, but they do argue inferentially that the only permissible rates are those which reflect average unit costs.

U.S. 581, 615, 65 S. Ct. 829, 845, 89 L. Ed. 1206 (1945) (concurring opinion), that "I do not think it can be accepted as a principle of public regulation that industrial gas may have a free ride because the pipe line and compressor have to operate anyway * * *."

We agree with the Commission that it may approve the formulation of a two-part rate structure. The demand-commodity formula has long been a rate device of regulatory agencies and there can be no objection to the use of it (or any other formula) in designing the recovery of a pipeline's cost of service, absent some indication that the results of its application may be in violation of the Natural Gas Act. Demand-commodity methods producing different rates for different types of services have been justified both because it is thought that the costs necessitated by the various services differ, *Mississippi River Fuel Corp. v. Federal Power Commission,* 163 F.2d 433, 437–438 (D.C. Cir. 1947), and because of the principle that fuller use of closed utility systems involving fixed costs results in lower unit costs. *National Coal Ass'n v. Fed. Power Comm'n,* 247 F.2d 86, 87 (D.C. Cir. 1957). . . .

At the hearing before the examiner the coal associations offered evidence to show the impact of pipeline rates on the consumption of coal in the Chicago area. The examiner excluded the evidence as improper for consideration in a section 5(a) proceeding. The coal associations do not challenge the examiner's ruling directly but seek to avoid it by other means. Thus they alternately argue competitive injury to coal and assert that they are "persons" within that portion of section 4(b)(1) of the act, *15 U.S.C. § 717c*(b)(1), which states that "no natural-gas company shall * * * make or grant any undue preference or advantage to any person or subject any person to any undue prejudice or disadvantage * * *." The coal associations say that the rate designs approved by the Commission grant an "undue advantage" to the distributors and subject coal producers to "undue prejudice," and that therefore their effect upon the coal industry should be considered in a section 5(a) proceeding to determine whether rates are "unjust, unreasonable, unduly discriminatory, or preferential." The examiner answered this contention by saying that section 4(b)(1) deals with discriminations and preferences between different gas customers and does not apply to the effect of gas rates upon competing fuels. In view of the congressional purpose of the act to protect consumers against exploitation, we think that this is the proper construction. The interpretation urged by the coal associations would produce a result contrary to the authority of *Federal Power Comm'n v. Hope Natural Gas Co.,* 320 U.S. 591, 602 (1944) and *Alston Coal Co. v. Fed. Power Comm'n,* 137 F.2d 740 (10th Cir. 1943), which held that the economic effect of pipeline rates upon competing fuels is not open for consideration in a section 5(a) proceeding. In Hope, the Court stated:

> It is also pointed out that West Virginia has a large interest in coal and oil as well as in gas and that these forms of fuel are competitive. When the price of gas is materially cheapened, consumers turn to that fuel in preference to the others. As a result this lowering of the price of natural gas will have the effect of depreciating the price of West Virginia coal and oil.

* * *

We have considered these contentions at length in view of the earnestness with which they have been urged upon us. We have searched the legislative history of the Natural Gas Act for any indication that Congress entrusted to the Commission the various considerations which West Virginia has advanced here. And our conclusion is that Congress did not. 320 U.S. at 609, 64 S. Ct. at 291.

The Commission takes the position that although a competitor may not intervene in rate proceedings under sections 4 and 5 of the act to argue his own injury, a competitor may participate in such proceedings to insure the protection of the public interest by offering evidence and argument relating to the factors pertinent to the Commission's determination. In this proceeding the coal associations are free to challenge the rates of Natural and Midwestern as "unjust, unreasonable, unduly discriminatory, or preferential," but only as the rates affect the distributors and their customers. Thus, even though the Commission considers competitive fuel prices in approving rate designs, competitors of the distributors may not urge competitive injury in design proceedings. This situation may seem anomalous, but for the reasons expressed in *Federal Power Comm'n v. Hope Natural Gas Co., supra,* the matter is not open to question. . . .

The record supports the findings of the Commission and warrants the conclusion that the rate designs of Natural and Midwestern are just and reasonable. The order is affirmed.■

NOTES AND COMMENTS

1. Economists have long argued that all of a firm's capital costs, such as pipelines and compressor stations, should be included entirely in the demand charge of a two-part rate because a company's decision to invest in capital facilities is based on the maximum demand for the firm's product. Therefore, these "capacity" costs should be allocated to those customers who require service in periods of peak demand, in proportion to the maximum number of units of service that they are entitled to demand.

For many years, however, the FPC and its successor, FERC, used a compromise formula in which roughly half the capacity costs were included in the demand charge and the other half in the commodity charge. In 1992, however, the FERC in Order 636, discussed in Chapter 8, switched to a rate design in which all capacity costs are included in the demand charge and are thus paid only by the firm customers. See Richard J. Pierce, Jr., and Ernest Gellhorn, Regulated Industries in a Nutshell 202–203 (West Group, 3d ed., 1994).

2. Gas and electricity distribution companies often use a three part rate structure. In addition to a demand and commodity component, they include a "customer" component, which is a fixed amount per customer to cover such charges as meter reading and billing, which do not vary either with total amount used or with maximum demand.

* * *

While, as is discussed in Chapter 2, we entertain the myth that natural monopoly prices should approximate marginal costs, the rate formula suggests a different pricing criterion. Because utility rates are set based on the cost of service, regulated utility prices more closely approximate average costs—not marginal costs, as a competitive market would yield. Yet, the disparity between average and marginal costs for some customer classes have led to some problems in the industry. For example, if average costs exceed marginal costs, utilities are more than compensated at a rate adequate to stay in business. In contrast, if marginal costs exceed average costs, utilities may find themselves in a profitability squeeze. Pricing at average cost makes economic sense. Yet it is extremely difficult for regulators to adopt marginal cost pricing, given the lack of a complete and accurate system for evaluating utility marginal cost information. At the same time, pricing solely on the basis of marginal costs might have a disproportionate impact on some customers, particularly smaller ones.

For a long time, utilities were encouraged to build capacity and sell as much energy as possible to customers. Through the 1960s and early 1970s, technological improvements and growing economies of scale led electric utilities to build new and more efficient power plants. New power plant projects were very large—typically in the 1000 MW range. Once a power plant project was under construction, sales and marketing experts attempted to sell the excess capacity by encouraging large industrial users to abandon their in-house generating facilities, adding new customers to their geographic service areas, and encouraging greater electric usage by existing customers (e.g., the "all electric home" in the 1960s). A rate structure arose that favored the large industrial customer, recognizing that some customers could easily shift to alternative fuel sources or self-generation.[6] However, even advocates of small consumers were unabashed in their goal of settings rates as low as possible for all customers. During this period of capacity expansion, electric utilities were more concerned with increasing consumer demand and covering capacity costs, not with having insufficient capacity to serve their customers.

About twenty-five years ago, attitudes toward rate design began to change. With the dawn of a grass-roots inspired environmental movement and the establishment of environmental interest groups at the state, local and national levels, conservation—not increased consumption—became an important concern for regulators. The oil crisis of the mid–1970s magnified the importance of conservation as one means of bringing about U.S. energy independence. New environmental legislation required the installation of pollution control equipment and added regulatory delay to the licensing of new power plants, thus making new power plant construction very expensive. Moreover, in the 1970s, utilities incurred construction and fuel cost overruns and, with improvements to the efficiency of power plants as small

---

6. The phenomenon known as "Ramsey Pricing," borrowed from taxation, advises regulators to set price higher for consumers with price-inelastic demand if they wish to maximize revenues. *See* Frank P. Ramsey, A Contribution to the Theory of Taxation, 37 Econ. J. 47 (1927).

as 250 MW, an end to economies of scale in power generation; soon it was not only environmental groups and progressive regulators who were concerned with the traditional rate structure, but utilities as well.

In the early 1970s, conservation—which avoided the need to build new power plants—replaced merchandising of kilowatt hours at the lowest possible cost as a regulatory objective. This forced a rethinking of the rates that different customer groups must pay to cover utility expenses and capital costs. Remember that a utility has an obligation to meet consumer demand, whatever that might be. However, electricity poses a unique problem because, unlike natural gas and oil, it cannot be stored. This raises an issue that utilities often face: short-term mismatches between supply and demand. When the temperature reaches 105 degrees, everyone wants their air conditioning to work at full power, without interruption. To help encourage conservation, many regulars approved inclining block rates—rates that increase with additional units of use—or adopted "peak load" pricing—cost of service principles that charge higher rates during those "peak periods when the utility is operating at or near capacity." Like limited supply urban taxi cabs that charge higher rates during rush hours to encourage cab-pooling or alternatives, such as walking or taking a train, many utilities charge higher rates during peak periods to discourage use. During nonpeak periods, their rates may go down again to encourage more customer use.

By the mid–1980s, excess supply was again a concern of many electric utilities. This led to the re-emergence of many utilities offering low rates to maintain industrial customers. Many utilities with excess capacity also stand to benefit from the recent efforts to introduce competition into the electric utility industry, as discussed in Chapter 11.

Re Central Maine Power Company
150 P.U.R.4th 229 (Me. P.U.C. 1994).

When we review an electric utility's request for an increase in its base or fuel rates, our perspective is largely historic; we look in fine detail at all the ways the utility has spent its money during a recent actual year, to determine whether its overall revenues in the year ahead could suffice to pay the costs of the service needed. Although inevitably requiring much judgment about the likely levels of future costs and revenues and about the prudence of the utility's management of its operations, such "revenue requirement" cases are rooted in historic accounting data.

When, instead, we review a utility's long-term resource plans, projected cost structures, and rate design proposals, our perspective is largely forward-looking and uncertain. We ask how a utility can best meet its customers' needs over the long-term planning period? What are the most likely costs? How should those costs be assigned to each class of customer? How should the costs be reflected in the pricing details of the specific rate structures offered? To answer these questions, we must look into an uncertain future, choose among competing planning strategies on the basis of educated judgments about future supply and demand conditions, and decide how those choices can best be reflected in the design of rates. Thus, this case leads us neither to specify the annual revenue amount that rates should be designed to allow the utility to collect, nor to say how much revenue should be collected from each rate class, and with what rate structure. Instead, our tasks here are to find the general utility planning strategy that best comports with the public interest, and to develop a set of general guidelines that can be used by CMP in a subsequent case to translate that strategy and its underlying costs into a specific rate design proposal. . . .

B. Declining block rates

. . . [W]e turn first to the single, key question on which much of the argument in the case has centered: Should public policy allow or encourage CMP to promote load growth through a broad adoption of a rate structure known as "declining block" rates? In electric utility parlance, a rate structure in which the average price paid per kilowatt-hour remains the same at different levels of monthly usage is known as a "flat rate." If the average price per kilowatt-hour changes with usage, the rate is either "declining" or "inclining," according to whether it falls or rises with usage; because declining rates were once very common, an inclining rate has at times been known as an "inverted" rate. When the rate is flat within broad ranges or "blocks" of usage, but changes between blocks, it is either an "inclining block" or "declining block" rate. Since 1986, CMP's rate for most of its residential customers, known as Rate A, has had an "inclining block" structure, in which the price per kWh for the first 400 kWh per month is 20 percent lower than the price for usage above 400 kWh per month. Other customers, including high-use residential customers who are on time-of-use rates, and commercial and industrial customers, have a more complicated bill that includes a fixed monthly customer charge. For the higher-use rate classes, the bill includes a demand charge as well. Both of these can cause the overall average rate per kilowatt-hour paid to vary considerably with usage. However, the energy charge component of these rates is currently a flat rate per kWh used.

In this case, CMP has asked us to approve the concept of replacing the inclining block structure of residential Rate A, and the flat rate energy charge of other residential and many commercial customers, with a declining block rate, so that the "tail block" monthly consumption above certain thresholds would be priced at a much lower rate. According to CMP, the purpose of this proposal is to improve economic efficiency, to make the price of electricity more competitive with oil for space or water heating, and, implicitly, to encourage a general increase in usage of electricity. In reviewing the evidence and argument developed in this case over the past year, we find that CMP has not made a convincing case for such a substantial revision to our long-standing rate design policies. The record lacks evidence on the likely extent of customer response to CMP's proposed changes in rate structure; we have no basis to say with any confidence that CMP's overall revenue would be higher than otherwise as a result of such changes. Given the normal expectations about demand elasticity, revenue would probably fall. Consistent with the virtual consensus among the other parties to the case, we are persuaded that the pursuit of economic efficiency through declining block rates, as the AARP put it, "does not ensure any additional revenue contribution and, indeed, gives rise to a substantial risk of revenue erosion, especially in the short run."

We do know, however, that a major rate design change such as a broad move to declining block rates would be likely to cause large increases in the bills paid by many customers, in order to offset the large decreases to high-use customers; simply changing the current inclining block structure of Rate A to a flat rate would cause the bills of the many customers using less than 400 kWh per month to go up by 12 percent, on average. (In January of 1992, the number of these customers was nearly 150,000; in August, more than 200,000.) Thus, the uncertain benefits of increased economic efficiency from the imposition of declining block rates would be bought at the certain expense of large rate changes for many customers. We find CMP's proposal especially unwise at this time of unusually high customer sensitivity to further changes in electric rates and low public confidence in the utility's ability to control its costs and charge reasonable rates.

Even if it could be shown that a change to declining block rates would be likely to yield at least a short-run revenue increase, we are not persuaded that such a move would be in the public interest. CMP argues that its current cost situation, in which marginal costs are well below average costs, will persist indefinitely, as a result of future cost-saving technologies and competitive pressures, and that rates should therefore be designed to encourage load growth. The record provides little support for such untempered optimism. Instead, the evidence shows that current cost relationships result to a significant degree from a temporary excess of "base-loaded" resources and expensive long-term power purchases. A strategy of encouraging marginal usage through broad adoption of declining rates would run a substantial risk of higher costs and rates, as current excesses diminish and new resources are needed....

We find that rates should continue to reflect the long-run marginal costs of service and the differences in costs between seasons and among times of day. As a general matter, making cost-based rate elements (such as variation with time of use) optional is likely to create adverse selection problems for other ratepayers, and thus would be inequitable, as customers with higher-cost usage patterns select the more beneficial rate and ultimately cause class rates to rise. In designing rates, the customer charge, if any, should reflect marginal customer costs; the demand charge, if any, should reflect the marginal capacity costs of generation, transmission, and distribution. For rate classes without a demand charge, we have seen no evidence that demand costs are disproportionately driven by usage in the lower usage blocks. If, for any rate class without a separately stated demand charge, a utility wishes to structure rates in blocks according to total energy used, then the rates for each block should reflect the total long-term cost of capacity associated with that usage.

As a general matter, promotional pricing should be "risk-averse" by requiring that discounted rates be set high enough to have a high probability of exceeding the relevant marginal costs. We will separately review the Conservation Group proposal to allow special promotion of certain electric end uses. CMP also should offer cost-based rates for backup and maintenance service. In calculating long-run avoided costs, transmission and distribution costs should be included.

Methods. To estimate the long-term marginal cost of generation, utilities should use the cost of the least capital-intensive capacity option. Marginal energy costs should be estimated using a forward-looking average of annual marginal energy costs, with the average calculated using estimated costs for a period beginning with the rate-effective period and extending six years.

C. Legal context

The Legislature and Congress have provided statutory guidance to the Commission in deciding the questions presented in this proceeding, but as we will explain, this statutory guidance is not determinative of any issue before us in this investigation.

This investigation is concerned with CMP's resource planning, rate structures and long-term avoided and marginal costs. Our regulatory policies in these areas have been shaped first and foremost by the enactment of the Federal Public Utilities Regulatory Policies Act of 1978, Pub. L. No. 95–617, 92 Stat. 3117 (PURPA). The relevant provisions of PURPA are designed to encourage the adoption of certain regulatory practices. The goals as stated by Congress are:

... to encourage—

1. conservation of energy supplied by electric utilities;

2. the optimization of the efficiency of the use of facilities and resources by electric utilities; and

3. equitable rates to electric consumers.

Section 101, 92 Stat. 3120, enacting 16 U.S.C.A. § 2611 (1985). To achieve these goals, Congress directed state utility regulatory commissions to consider the adoption and implementation of specific rate design and regulatory standards.

PURPA sets forth six primary rate design standards, which we summarized in an earlier rate design proceeding:

1. **Cost of Service**—Rates charged to each class of electric consumers should, to the extent practicable, reflect the cost of providing service.

Methods used to determine cost of service should identify differences in cost due to variations in daily or seasonal time of use and due to variations in customer demand in energy components of cost. [16 U.S.C.A. § 1621(d)(1)]

2. **Declining Block Rates**—The energy component of a rate should not decrease as consumption increases, except to the extent that such a rate reflects decreases in cost to the utility in providing the service. [16 U.S.C.A. § 1621(d)(2)]

3. **Time of Day Rates**—Rates should be based on the cost of providing service at different times of the day if the long run benefits are likely to exceed the metering and other costs associated with such rates. [16 U.S.C.A. § 1621(d)(3)]

4. **Seasonal Rates**—Rates should vary by seasons of the year to the extent that costs vary seasonably. [16 U.S.C.A. § 1621(d)(4)]

5. **Interruptible Rates**—Industrial and commercial consumers should be offered interruptible rates which reflect the cost of providing such service. [16 U.S.C.A. § 1621(d)(5)]

6. **Load Management Techniques**—Consumers should be offered nonpricing techniques designed to provide useful energy or capacity management advantages to the extent they are practicable, cost effective, and reliable. [16 U.S.C.A. § 1621(d)(6)] *Re: Bangor Hydro–Electric Company*, Docket No. 80–108, slip op. at 2 (Me. PSC, 1985)

In 1979, the Maine Legislature enacted the Electric Rate Reform Act (ERRA), 35–A M.R.S.A. §§ 3151–55. As part of the ERRA, the Legislature required the Commission, to the extent feasible, to consider and adopt the federal rate design standards established by PURPA and, for any standard or standards not adopted, to provide the facts and rationales supporting the rejection of the standard.

The ERRA also provides a policy basis that governs rate design, coinciding in most major respects with PURPA. For instance, the purpose of the ERRA is to "require the Commission to relate electric rates more closely to the costs of providing electric service." 35–A M.R.S.A. § 3152(1)(A) (supp. 1992). There are broad policy statements in both PURPA and ERRA that rate design should promote conservation, efficient use of resources and equity. The ERRA also directs the Commission, when ordering rate design improvements, to "consider rate design stability" and to "assure the revenue requirement of the utility." 35–A M.R.S.A. § 3154(1).

The Commission adopted the six federal standards contained in PURPA in the so-called PURPA investigation for CMP, *Re: Central Maine Power Company* (Cost of Service and Rate Design), Docket No. 80–66 (Me. PSC, Sep. 11, 1985). The Commission did not adopt specific rate designs in the CMP PURPA investigation but did establish several overriding principles relevant to designing rates. Among these was the policy that rates should reflect the marginal costs of service, including daily and seasonal cost differences. While the Commission found that flat rates for residential customers were proper, the Commission also stated that time-of-use and inclining block rates would be implemented if future cost studies supported such results. *Id.*

The Commission established new rate designs for CMP and Bangor Hydro–Electric Company during 1985 and 1986. *Re: Bangor Hydro–Electric Company, Investigation of Cost of Service and Rate Design*, Docket No. 85–209 (Me. PSC, Oct. 1, 1986); *Re: Central Maine Power Company, Investigation Into Cost of Service and Rate Design*, Docket No. 86–002 (Me. PSC, Oct. 3 and Oct. 17, 1986). In the BHE proceeding, the Commission adopted what became known as a "hybrid" approach, wherein customer class revenue responsibility would be based on embedded costs, while the design of rates within classes would reflect marginal costs and time-of-use cost differentials. BHE Docket No. 85–209 at 4, 8. The same approach was adopted for CMP in Docket No. 86–002. In the BHE docket, the Commission expressed the preference, where cost differences were shown, to implement seasonal and time-of-day rates. . . .

Despite the "hybrid" approach, the increased importance of marginal cost information was emphasized in nearly every rate design case throughout the 1980s. For instance, in *Re: Bangor Hydro–Electric Company*, Docket No. 86–242 (Me. PSC, Dec. 22, 1987), we said that as a general policy matter, the Commission is moving toward greater reliance on long-run marginal costs as the basis for setting prices. This policy also means that customer class revenue requirements will be set on a long-run marginal cost basis. *Id*. at 90.

In that docket, the Commission for the first time stated a policy preference for using marginal cost studies for allocating costs to customer class, as well as for rate design within the classes.

Our most recent rate design case for CMP occurred during 1989 and 1990. *Re: Central Maine Power Company*, Docket No. 89–068 (Me. PSC, Mar. 29, 1991). The Commission decided to replace the "hybrid" approach, so that both customer class revenue responsibilities and rate design within classes would be based on marginal cost. Equity would then be best achieved, "because each customer and class will pay on the basis of what it would cost if service to that customer or class were expanded." *Id*. at 26. The Commission found that embedded cost allocation methods sent distorted price signals because such methods allocate costs to rate classes on the basis of historic average total cost calculations, which may have only a coincidental connection to current, forward-looking estimates of marginal cost. Furthermore, because the hybrid approach mixed class revenue allocations based on embedded cost with marginal cost rate design within classes, large anomalies among rate elements occurred in implementing Docket No. 86–002.

In addressing the problem of reconciling the marginal cost approach to the Company's total revenue requirement, we adopted the equiproportional marginal cost (EPMC) method, under which the difference between total revenue requirement and marginal costs incurred to serve each class is allocated in proportion to the marginal costs. We stated that:

> The Commission recognizes that full pursuit of its efficiency goals would suggest the use of an inverse elasticity (Ramsey) rule to reconcile the total cost arrived at under the marginal cost approach to the

Company's overall revenue requirement. However, in the absence of reliable customer elasticity information, equity dictates that the EPMC reconciliation method be used at least for the present time. This is because it is fair for each class to be responsible for the embedded revenue requirement in proportion to its share of total marginal cost.

Id. at 26–27.

In the most recent legislative session, sections 3152 and 3153–A were both amended to add the consideration of reduced electric rates, along with reduced electric costs, in the setting of electric rates and in developing conservation programs. P.L. 1993, c. 402 (An Act to Minimize Electric Rates). In fact, the Commission "shall give equivalent consideration to the goals of minimizing cost and minimizing rates of electricity to consumers." The following language was also contained in P.L. 1993, c. 402, although not included in Title 35–A: Sec.

> 3. Construction. Nothing in this Act is intended or may be construed to discourage energy conservation and demand management programs or to encourage continued or additional use of electric baseboard resistance heating systems. Nothing in this Act may be construed to encourage or discourage the development or implementation of any particular rate design.

> As a result of giving equal consideration to the goals of minimizing costs and minimizing rates pursuant to this Act, the Public Utilities Commission may not adopt any rate design that results in increased rates for residential customers with usage or less than 750 kilowatt hours per month. Nothing in the preceding sentence may be construed to prohibit the Public Utilities Commission from increasing rates for residential customers with usage of less than 750 kilowatt hours per month to the extent justified by other legitimate rational principles or legislative mandates.

There is no real disagreement as to the legal principles explained above or their interpretation. The disagreements among the parties, as explained below, are about factual issues or the relevance of various facts in determining the proper costs of service that should be reflected in CMP's rates at this time. Still, these legal principles and the regulatory "common law" developed in implementing them will guide us in resolving the factual and policy disputes....

In planning, building, and operating an electric power system, a utility can choose among various types of generating plant. For some, like nuclear power plants, the fixed (capital) costs are high and the variable (fuel) costs are low. In other words, they are relatively expensive to build and cheap to run. For others, like diesel units or combustion turbines, the opposite conditions hold; with low capital costs per kilowatt of capacity and high fuel costs per kilowatt-hour of energy, they are relatively cheap to build but expensive to run. Because the total power demanded by its customers varies widely, and not always predictably, with the hour, day, and season, a utility needs a balanced mix of generation types if it is to produce power at the lowest overall cost per kilowatt-hour generated.

The "base load" portion of the power demand, comes from uses that are in constant operation, such as refrigerators, hospitals, and three-shifts-per-day factories. The base load has the highest "load factor," or ratio of total energy (kilowatt-hours) used over the course of the year to maximum demand (kilowatts) placed on the system at one time. For this reason, it can be served most economically with "base-load" generation that has relatively low energy costs (and relatively high capital cost). Conversely, the "peak load" portion of the power demand, that occurs in only a few hours of the year, such as in the late afternoon on a very cold winter weekday, can be served most economically with "peaking" generation that has relatively low capital costs (but high energy costs). At intermediate points on the load curve, "cycling" units with an intermediate balance of costs, such as CMP's Wyman 4 oil burner, may be the most economical choice. On the customer's side of the meter, there are DSM measures analogous to base-load generation, such as water heater insulation, and to peaking units, such as interruptible power contracts and water heater control programs.

Given a range of energy resource options, one can find the optimum mix to serve a utility's load pattern at lowest overall cost. In CMP's case, the current resource mix is out of balance. Additions to its own base-load plant, combined during the last decade with large blocks of power purchased from qualifying facilities (QF) under "must-run" contract terms, have produced an uneconomic resource mix under today's cost and load conditions.

Excess must-run/baseload generation has driven CMP's average costs and rates up. It has also driven CMP's marginal costs down; excess baseload, although not the optimal mix, nevertheless means that dispatchable peaking capacity, with its higher energy cost, is needed less. CMP, through its witness Peaco, estimates that its system is about 400 megawatts out of balance; that is, to achieve the optimum resource mix under today's planning assumptions, CMP would need to replace some 400 MW of existing base-load capacity with more readily dispatchable resources. If CMP's system were in balance, Staff witness Huntington found, marginal energy costs would increase by some 38 percent on a weighted average basis, with the increases ranging from 15 percent in the winter on-peak period to as much as 63 percent in the non-winter, off-peak period. CMP's total marginal costs would increase by more than 20 percent relative to current levels, if its generation system were in balance. Much of CMP's must-run capacity is from QF purchased power contracts that are themselves very expensive, averaging over 9 cents/kWh. . . .

We agree with Staff and OPA that marginal energy costs matter, and are sensitive to the supply mix, especially when (as now) that mix is out of balance. This result suggests, as discussed below, that marginal cost projections will be less reliable when significant swings in the supply mix are likely. . . .

Clearly, the widespread connection of non-utility generation to the power grid during the last decade has made the power industry more competitive, putting a lid on generation costs. During the same period, and as an intended result of the same public policies that opened the grid to competition, innovative technologies to capture waste heat through cogeneration and achieve other efficiencies with smaller units and renewable fuels has added new fuels and diversity to power generation and reduced the demand for and price of oil. Although these innovations initially cost almost as much as the projected cost of the utility plants they displaced, the technologies have resulted in lower costs as they have matured.

Arguably, the electric utility industry may have a "flatter" cost structure today than it had in 1991, when we were last designing CMP's rates. In the interim, avoided costs have continued to drop. General inflation rates have declined and interest rates are sharply lower, both of which tend to reduce the construction costs of new generating capacity. The design of natural gas-fired electric generation, whether with combustion turbines or combined-cycle units, has continued to improve, and wind generators may have become increasingly cost-effective. The potential addition of significant gas pipeline capacity in New England, combined with changes in federal regulation of gas pipelines, make gas-fired electric units an increasingly viable source of generation in the NEPOOL region, especially considering their suitability as peaking and cycling facilities. With more excess capacity at CMP and in New England today than we anticipated in 1991, the cost of serving new load is less today than we expected it to be. All of these observations tend to support the inference that the long-run average cost curve for the generation of electricity may have shifted downward since 1991, and also may have today less of an upward slope than it appeared to have in 1991. . . .

VI. Rate structure policies

Our investigation in this proceeding of CMP's long-term costs has been designed to provide the basis for decisions about CMP's general rate structure policies, such as the relative desirability of inclining block rates, flat rates, and declining block rates; the desirability of time-of-use rates; and the desirability of rates designed to encourage increases in the use of electricity over the long term. In this section, we review the record evidence on fifteen such rate policy issues raised in this case, working from the general to the specific.

A. Should rates in general reflect the long-run marginal cost of service?

Uncertainty is inherent in planning scenarios for the optimal power supply 25 years or more into the future. Trying to make current rates reflect true long-run costs, over the period in which the system can be substantially rebuilt and thus "reoptimized," may sound like a fool's errand, but we do not agree that today's prices can completely ignore such costs. CMP, like most utility companies, continues to invest in very long-lived assets. Much of its new T&D plant, for example, will still be in service a decade or more beyond the 25–year horizon that it alleges "it makes no sense" to consider in pricing. When making long-term investment decisions, utilities reduce future costs and returns to a present value using some appropriate discount rate. Long-term avoided costs of competing resource options are similarly discounted. This technique properly places greater weight on the near-term and less on the more distant future.

Logically, the costs underlying rate design should be viewed from a similar perspective. CMP must already use long-term cost projections as the basis for a great many of the utility's planning decisions, many of which we will have to live with for decades. We, therefore, reject both CMP's claim that the proper planning horizon for pricing purposes is five years or less, and the CCUC position that all such projections, short or long, are too uncertain to serve as the basis for rate design. We agree with the general principle that we should not pursue short-run efficiency at the expense of long-run efficiency....

Reliance on CMP's short-run marginal costs for rate design purposes also raises serious questions of fairness.... [W]hen the resource mix is seriously out of balance on the side of excess base-load capacity, as it is today, the system will display unusually low marginal energy costs, particularly in off-peak periods. If these low marginal costs were used to allocate revenue among customer classes (the EPMC method) and to design rate components (energy and demand charges), customers with high load factors would receive, in effect, a windfall. Other customers, especially those with low load factors or with usage concentrated in peak and shoulder hours, would pay disproportionately for the cost of the system imbalances. Since no one has suggested any causal link between the usage patterns of the customers so affected and the costs imposed by the suboptimal planning, and we find it hard even to imagine such a linkage, the end result of short-run cost approach is clearly inequitable.

Overall, we see no reason to abandon our long-standing policy of taking a long view of costs when designing rates.... Over the past decade, as more diverse and flexible resource options and strategies have become available, CMP's investment horizon has contracted. Therefore, we instruct the parties to develop marginal costs for the six-year period, 1995 through 2000. To the extent that the planning horizon affects the calculation of marginal capacity costs, the same time frame should be used.■

NOTES AND COMMENTS

1. Marginal cost and peak load pricing are discussed in *In re Rate Design for Electric Corps.*, 15 P.U.R.4th 434 (N.Y. 1976); *In Re Madison Gas & Electric Co.*, 5 P.U.R.4th 28 (Wis. 1974). For an examination of the background and impact of peak-load pricing by a former Wisconsin PSC commissioner (Richard Cudahy, now a judge on the U.S. Court of Appeals for the Seventh Circuit), *see* Cudahy & Malko, Electric Peak–Load Pricing: Madison Gas & Beyond, 1976 Wis. L. Rev. 47. For a good examination of electric pricing issues, *see* Hunington, The Rapid Emergence of Marginal

Cost Pricing and the Regulation of Electric Utility Rate Structures, 55 Boston U. L. Rev. 689 (1975).

2. The same conservation principles apply outside of the energy context as well. For example, in *Bryden v. East Bay Mun. Util. Dist.*, 24 Cal. App. 4th 178 (1st Cal. Ct. App. 1994), a California water utility adopted an inclining block rate for water conservation as a part of its comprehensive Drought Management Program. The inclining block structure imposes higher charges per unit of water as the level of customer consumption increases. The court held that the inclining block rates did not violate California Proposition 13 prohibition on "special taxes" absent approval of 2/3 of the voters. "Special taxes" are fees that "exceed the reasonable cost of providing the service or regulatory activity for which the fee is charged and which is not levied for general revenue purposes." *Id.* at 187. The court concluded that the District, by acting prospectively to create incentives for conservation through water rates rather than waiting for apocalyptic drought circumstances to develop, had developed a "well-conceived and eminently reasonable" Drought Management Program. *Id.* at 204.

3. A useful exercise on ratemaking has been written by William Anderson and is available in the Computer–Assisted Legal Instruction (CALI) administrative law library. Now would be a good time to work parts A–E of this exercise, which should be available through your law library.

2. RATE REGULATION BASED ON NON-COST FACTORS

a. "LIFE-LINE" RATES

One of the more controversial issues in rate design involves special rates to benefit low-income groups. An issue that has been the subject of some debate is whether low-income rates are undertaken not on the basis of cost considerations, but distributional fairness. Some have suggested that, with low-income programs, like "lifeline" rates, service for some customers is subsidized at a cost well below marginal or average costs, a subsidy borne by other ratepayers. *Mountain States* examines this argument.

Mountain States Legal Foundation v. Public Utilities Commission

590 P.2d 495 (Colo. 1979).

■ HODGES, J. Plaintiffs-appellees, Mountain States Legal Foundation and Colorado Association of Commerce and Industry, commenced separate actions in the trial court challenging Public Utilities Commission (PSC) decisions which established a reduced gas rate for low-income elderly and low-income disabled persons. The trial court entered a judgment which set aside these decisions. It held that the adoption of this special reduced rate exceeded the PSC's authority under Article XXV of the Colorado Constitution and violated section 40–3–106(1), C.R.S. 1973. The appellant PSC and intervener-appellant Mountain Plains Congress of Senior Organizations urge reversal. We affirm the trial court's judgment.

On November 8, 1977, the PSC, in two decisions, ordered gas utilities under its regulatory authority to implement a discount gas rate plan for low-income elderly and low-income disabled persons. The low-income customers who would be eligible for the discounted gas rate are "identified" through a procedure utilized by the Department of Revenue to administer the Colorado property and rent credit program.

In order to qualify for the discounted rate, a customer must have been a full year resident of Colorado; the customer must be 65 years of age or older or be the surviving spouse, 58 years old or older, of a deceased spouse who met the age requirement, or the customer must be receiving full disability benefits from a bona fide public or private insurance plan; and if the discounted gas rate plan were to go into effect during the 1978–1979 heating season, a customer would have to have an income of $7,300 or less if single, and $8,300 or less if married. These income standards are different from those which were in effect during the 1977–1978 heating season because of a legislative change in the standards for the Colorado property tax and rent credit.

The resulting revenue loss for the discounted services would be recovered by higher rates on all other customers.

We give full recognition to the fact that many of our state's elderly live on fixed incomes which are severely strained by today's inflationary economy, as are low-income disabled persons who are often shut out of the employment market. While efforts to provide economic relief to such needy persons are laudatory, the PSC has limited authority to implement a rate structure which is designed to provide financial assistance as a social policy to a narrow group of utility customers, especially where that low rate is financed by its remaining customers.

In *Mountain States Telephone and Telegraph Co. v. Public Utilities Commission*, 576 P.2d 544 (Colo. 1978), we held that Article XXV of the Colorado Constitution gives the PSC full legislative authority to regulate public utilities. We noted in that case, however, that the legislative authority in public utility matters delegated by Article XXV to the PSC could be restricted by statute. *Id.* at 547. It is clear in the case before us that the PSC's authority to order preferential utility rates to effect social policy has, in fact, been restricted by the legislature's enactment of section 40–3–106(1), C.R.S. 1973 and section 40–3–102, C.R.S. 1973.

Section 40–3–106(1), C.R.S. 1973, prohibits public utilities from granting preferential rates to any person, and section 40–3–102, C.R.S. 1973, requires the PSC to prevent unjust discriminatory rates. When the PSC ordered the utility companies to provide a lower rate to selected customers unrelated to the cost or type of the service provided, it violated section 40–3–106(1)'s prohibition against preferential rates. In this instance, the discount rate benefits an unquestionably deserving group, the low-income elderly and the low-income disabled. This, unfortunately, does not make the rate less preferential. To find otherwise would empower the PSC, an appointed, non-elected body, to create a special rate for any group it determined to be deserving. The legislature clearly provided against such discretionary power when it prohibited public utilities from granting "any preference." In addition, section 40–3–102, C.R.S. 1973, directs the PSC to prevent unjust discriminatory rates. Establishing a discount gas rate plan which differentiates between economically needy individuals who receive the same service is unjustly discriminatory.... affirm the judgment of the trial court.

■ CARRIGAN, J., dissenting: The majority opinion depends entirely on characterization of the special rate classification here involved as a "preference" forbidden by section 40–3–106(1). Thus the decisive issue is whether the instant rate classification is so clearly of the type that the legislature intended to forbid when it enacted that section that it must be held to be a "preference" as a matter of law. The majority opinion cites no precedent or other authority for its holding and we have found no case law from any state dealing with the issue. Moreover the majority opinion fails to define the term "preference" for guidance of the P.U.C. in future cases. In effect the majority opinion has condemned the rate scheme here involved by saying, "We can't define a 'preference' but we know one when we see one." Such an ad hoc determination does not provide needed rational standards as precedent for future cases....

Apparently, the purpose of section 40–3–106(1) was to prevent the public utilities' then-common practice of favoring certain customers with lower utility rates to the competitive disadvantage of others in the same class of customers similarly situated. *Columbia Gas of N.Y., Inc. v. New York State Elec. & Gas Co.*, 28 N.Y.2d 117, 268 N.E.2d 790 (1971); *Hays v. Pennsylvania Co.*, 12 Fed. 309 (N.D. Ohio 1882).

The issue, therefore, becomes whether the statutory language so clearly forbids the P.U.C.'s rate classification plan that this Court, as a matter of law, must outlaw it rather than leaving the decision whether to overrule it to the General Assembly as a matter of state policy.

In the law the word "preference" denotes giving an advantage or priority to one or more claimants in a manner which discriminates unjustly or unreasonably against other claimants in the same class. This connotation of the term clearly was intended by section 40–3–106(1), for in the sentence immediately following the use of the term "preference" in that section, public utilities are forbidden to "establish or maintain any unreasonable difference as to rates...." If only unreasonable rate differentials are forbidden, it is plainly implied that reasonable differences in rates are not forbidden. It follows that a classification for rate purposes should not be considered a "preference" if the classification is reasonable.

This rationale is further buttressed by section 40–3–102, C.R.S. 1973, which empowers the P.U.C. "to prevent unjust discriminations ... in the rates, charges and tariffs of ... public utilities...." The clear implication is that just discrimination in rates may be tolerated.

Whether a particular classification among ratepayers is "unreasonable" or "unjust" is a question on which this court has no more expertise than the P.U.C. or the General Assembly. Indeed we probably have less. Such questions are at bottom fact issues, or at best mixed law-fact issues. They involve social policy determinations rather than legal decisionmaking.

The P.U.C. as a specialized, quasi-legislative agency is a particularly appropriate body to effectuate—at least in the first instance—the legislative factfinding and policymaking function incident to setting rates. It possesses unique expertise and the capacity to analyze the complex technical, economic, and social information necessary to set public utility rates intelligently and fairly. The constitution, as well as the statute governing P.U.C. rate regulation, wisely leave to the P.U.C. the initial authority to determine policy. Colo. Const., Art. XXV; Section 40–3–101, C.R.S. 1973. . . . ■

NOTES AND COMMENTS

1. Does the "lifeline" principle make sense? The Madison Gas case suggests that sound economics would price energy resources at marginal cost to ensure the most efficient allocation of resources. "Lifeline rates," which encourage pricing below marginal cost, seem to run counter to this proposition.

2. As the *Mountain States* case suggests, any rate that creates an unjustified preference for one class of customers seems inconsistent with well-accepted principles of public utility law. Several states, however, have recognized "lifeline" rates. Is this inconsistent with the goals of public utility law, as we have studied them to this point?

3. Is there any sound economic rationale for subsidizing low-income customers? Is this an instance of market failure for which some regulatory solution may be justified? Or is this a pure redistributive program that serves non-cost goals?

Charging and collecting rates are two different actions. Many customers who are charged rates may never pay them, and utilities are often required to undergo costly collection efforts, sometimes at a cost to all customers. One way to conceptualize of low-income rates is as based upon cost. As Roger Colton describes:

> The National Consumer Law Center has developed the energy assurance program (EAP) to address these dual problems [charging as opposed to collecting rates]. The EAP recognizes that some households simply do not have sufficient income to pay for the basic necessities of life, including energy. There is no question but that this inability to pay is a social problem. There is no question, however, that this inability to pay also represents a business problem for utilities. For these households, regardless of the number of disconnect notices sent, regardless of the number of times service is disconnected, regardless of the type of payment plan that is offered, there will be insufficient household funds available to pay utility bills. A utility can recognize

this fact and seek to collect what it can, while minimizing collection expenses, or a utility can deny this fact and devote its time, energy, and attention to what will prove to be fruitless and expensive collection attempts. . . .

The EAP is not simply sound social policy. It is based on sound regulatory principles as well. A utility is required to operate with all reasonable efficiency. This is part and parcel of the obligation to provide least-cost service. Accordingly, utilities should pursue all reasonable means of minimizing the total revenue requirement, including the adoption of innovative credit and collection techniques.

Roger D. Colton, "A Cost-based Response to Low-income Energy Problems," Public Utilities Fortnightly, March 1, 1991. As Colton see it, this type of a program "is not designed to serve as a social program providing rate discounts to low-income households." Instead, it "is intended to be a collection device. It is a means of collection that will maximize the receipt of revenue from customers who cannot afford to pay their bills, while at the same time minimizing all of the expenses associated with delinquent payments." This makes some sense in a rate-regulated system: since fixed costs do not vary with the amount of service consumed, if a customer can cover at least the variable costs attributed to that customer, in the short-run other customers are not made any worse off. Colton states:

The concept behind this statement is simple: It is better to collect 95 percent of a $70 bill than it is to collect 50 percent of a $100 bill. . . .

Removing a nonpaying customer from the utility system does not necessarily result in the least-cost provision of service to all remaining ratepayers. Whenever a customer's service is disconnected, two things happen. The company does avoid the variable cost of delivering that unit of energy to the household. However, the company also foregoes the revenue that would have been collected from the household but for the disconnection of service.

To the extent that the revenue would have exceeded the variable cost of delivering the energy (whether it be gas or electricity), other ratepayers lose a contribution toward the payment of the fixed charges of the company. In this instance, the disconnection of service leaves remaining, paying customers worse off than had the disconnection not occurred.

In general, there is an advantage to all ratepayers from keeping as many households on the system as possible. So long as households pay the variable costs of delivering the energy they consume, other ratepayers are no worse off. To the extent that households pay anything beyond the variable cost of the energy they consume, they are making a contribution toward the fixed costs of the system and all ratepayers are better off than they would have been had those households been disconnected. It is thus cost-effective for the utility, and for all remaining ratepayers, to provide payment-troubled customers with an incentive to make reduced payments (even when full payment cannot be made) by deciding not to disconnect so long as these customers continue to pay more than the variable cost of providing service. In essence, this proposal is no different than the treatment that many states accord their large natural gas and telecommunications customers who have the ability and inclination to engage in bypass. In effect, these residential customers who, because of their inability to pay their utility bill, would be disconnected from the utility system and forced to move to alternative sources of home energy, would be treated as opportunity sales by the utility.

Id. Roger Colton's article was written in response to Howard M. Spinner's article, "Choosing an Efficient Energy Assistance Program," which appeared in the December 20, 1990 issue of the Public Utilities Fortnightly. For further development of the concept, *see* Roger D. Colton, The Duty of a Public Utility to Mitigate "Damages" from Nonpayment Through the Offer of Conservation Programs, 3 B.U. Pub. Interest L.J. 239 (1993); Roger D. Colton & Mike Sheehan, A New Basis for Conservation Programs for the Poor: Expanding the Concept of Avoided Costs, 21 Clearinghouse Review 135 (1987).

4. Subsidies for low-income energy consumers have received congressional attention. PURPA supported low income rate concepts. 16 U.S.C. § 2624. In addition, federal agencies, such as the formerly-named Department of Housing and Urban Development, provide assistance (approximately one billion dollars annually) to the poor in meeting their energy needs through a number of federal programs. *See* Steven Ferry, In from the Cold: Energy Efficiency and the Reform of HUD's Utility Allowance System, 32 Harv. J. on Legis. 145 (1995); Steven Ferry, Cold Power: Energy and Public Housing, 23 Harv. J. on Legis. 33 (1986).

5. *Mountain States* is out-of-date in its analysis of the issue of low-income rates and possibly inconsistent with the approach of most utility commissions today. Although states today rarely even consider "lifeline" rates, low-income rate discounts are now prevalent, for reasons similar to those articulated by Roger Colton. According to Peter Fox–Penner:

> In recent years [] state utility commissions have begun to use discount rates as a more cost-effective alternative than other low-income programs. Utility regulators reason that it is less expensive to provide affordable utility rates to low-income households in the first place, than to provide service at higher rates, incur the costs of providing working capital to cover unpaid arrears, spend money on credit and collection, and still write-off a substantial part of the unbilled revenue to certain customers as uncollectible. By offering such affordable rates, utilities have found that they actually can increase the revenues they collect and decrease the expenses they incur in the process of collection, to the benefit of all involved, including nonparticipating customers.

Peter Fox–Penner, Electric Utility Restructuring: A Guide to the Competitive Era 325 (1997).

6. Do the benefits of administering any low income rate program exceed the potential costs? For example, how will a PSC distinguish between low-income and middle-income and wealthy residential customers? Can it establish an eligibility test? What is the best way to do this?

B. Problems With Rate Regulation and Alternatives

1. Critiques

In recent years, dissatisfaction with cost-based regulation has been expressed by many observers. Both in this country and abroad, legislatures and regulatory agencies have been exploring completely different approaches to the subject of utility pricing.

There are several critiques to the traditional cost-based approach to rate regulation.

Rate regulation relied on case-by-case determinations which are firm specific, rather than on evaluation of industry-wide conditions. The process is information intensive and is very costly to both firms and to regulators.

There is also a likelihood of mistakes in the calculation of rates. If a regulator or a firm makes a mistake in estimating costs, this could be frozen into utility rates until the next rate determination. While many the ratemaking process may be self-correcting if firms face regular rate evaluation, in many jurisdictions a decade or more will pass between rate adjustments. Regulated rates may not be sensitive to adjustments in fuel costs and other economic variables, such as interest rates or the rate of inflation.

Rate proceedings also create incentives for firms to exaggerate costs and to engage in strategic manipulation of the types of information presented to regulators. Even if manipulation of the system is not intentional, there is evidence to suggest that rate regulation has lead to a higher than optimal capital to labor ratio in the industry. *See* Harvey Averch & Leland L. Johnson, Behavior of the Firm Under Regulatory Constraint, 52 Am. Econ. Rev. 1052 (1962).

As a result, there may be overinvestment in certain infrastructure or technology, a cost that is born by consumers in higher rates, shareholders in reduced returns, or both.

Finally, to the extent that regulated rates are tied to specific capital decisions, such as a specific power plant or transmission line, rate regulation disfavors new investment and may work to thwart innovation. While this is a potential cost to rate regulation, regulated utilities also may have been more likely to invest in newer, higher risk technologies to the extent that they are guaranteed cost recovery in their rates.

2. Price Cap Regulation

One of the most popular non-cost methods of pricing is price ceilings or caps. To counteract the effects of inflation and save the regulatory costs associated with calculate revenue requirements, regulators will limit the charges utilities can pass on to certain customers. For instance, the British government, adopted price ceilings when it privatized its telecommunications industry in 1984, and several federal state regulators in the U.S. have experimented with price level regulation as well. In some instances, utilities may favor price caps since they give utilities the ability to make their own decisions about expenditures without regulatory oversight. And, if a utility can find ways to decrease its costs, it may keep some or all of the additional revenue it generates as profit. Regulators may find price caps attractive too, since they may create incentives for utilities to become productive.

Nevertheless, price level regulation has not been widespread in the U.S. Regulators are unable to accurately set ceiling prices: when utilities make excess profits public pressure leads regulators to return to cost of service regulation, yet if utilities are making little or no profits they will pressure regulators to raise ceiling prices.

A price cap limits the retail or wholesale price that a supplier can charge. Many price caps are benchmarked to inflation, allowing some flexibility in their implementation. Regulators have experimented with price caps in the context of nearly every energy resource, from gasoline to natural gas and electricity. In nearly every context in the energy sector, they have failed to achieve their overall policy goal, yet they are often embraced by federal and state regulators as a way of keeping energy prices low. Consider the following critique:

Richard J. Pierce, Price Level Regulation Based on Inflation is Not an Attractive Alternative to Profit Level Regulation

84 Nw. U. L. Rev. 665 (1990).

When the British government privatized its telecommunications industry in 1984, it was forced to confront for the first time the issue of how, if at all, to regulate that industry. It rejected traditional cost-of-service regulation in favor of a system of price level regulation. Price level regulation relies entirely on a price cap that changes automatically over time in accordance with a formula that incorporates expected future changes in costs and in productivity. The changes in regulated price are unrelated to actual changes in firm costs or profits. British Telecommunication's ceiling price at any time is determined through application of a simple formula: present price equals initial price, plus inflation, minus a three percent productivity adjustment factor (CPI–3)....

In their 1989 book, Price Level Regulation for Diversified Public Utilities, Professors Jordan Jay Hillman and Ronald Braeutigam of Northwestern University urge serious consideration of price level regulation as a substitute for profit level regulation of all natural monopolies.... I conclude that price level regulation based on the CPI–3 formula holds little realistic promise of yielding acceptable results.

Proponents of price level regulation refer to the British Telecom experience to demonstrate the viability of the concept. I doubt the predictive value of this experience for three reasons: (1) it is limited to a single context; (2) we have only four years of experience; and (3) it may constitute de facto profit level regulation disguised as price level regulation.

Recent experience with real price level regulation has much greater predictive power. The United States adopted price level regulation for important purposes in the Natural Gas Policy Act ("NGPA"), Crude Oil Windfall Profits Tax Act ("COWPT"), and the Public Utility Regulatory Policies Act ("PURPA"). The experience under each of those statutes is not encouraging.

In the NGPA Congress imposed price ceilings at varying levels on each of several categories of natural gas. Each price ceiling consisted of an initial price and an automatic price adjustment mechanism designed to further several goals simultaneously. The price ceiling applicable to "new natural gas' " illustrates the NGPA approach. In 1978, Congress chose an initial price ceiling slightly higher than the pre-existing price ceiling derived from profit level regulation and somewhat lower than what Congress perceived to be the price that would exist in a competitive market. Congress then selected a price adjustment mechanism based on its desire to achieve parity between the "new gas' " ceiling price and the market-clearing price of gas by 1985. To accomplish this purpose the price adjustment clause was designed to reflect simultaneously four factors: (1) expected increases in nominal costs; (2) expected increases in real costs attributable to the depleting resource effect; (3) expected productivity increases; and (4) the need to close the perceived gap between the initial ceiling price and the efficient price. Based on extensive testimony, Congress ultimately selected a price adjustment mechanism that consisted of the Gross National Product implicit price deflator minus 0.2%, plus 3.5%. The first term in the adjustment mechanism was intended to reflect changes in nominal costs, while the second term was intended to reflect the net effect of the other three factors.

Even with perfect hindsight, it is difficult to determine the relationship between the initial price level Congress chose and the "efficient price' " in 1978. It is easy, however, to assess the performance of the automatic price adjustment mechanism Congress chose. That mechanism performed miserably, largely because it was incapable of reflecting major changes in demand factors. The quantity of gas demanded at the new gas ceiling price soared in 1979 in response to changes in the closely related oil market in the wake of the Iranian Revolution. For two years, it appeared that Congress had seriously underestimated the rate of change in the "new gas' " ceiling price necessary to yield an efficient price.

That concern was replaced quickly in 1981 with the opposite concern. The world price of oil began to decline, yielding a rapid decrease in the quantity of gas demanded at the "new gas' " ceiling price. In the meantime, that ceiling price continued its inexorable climb as a function of the operation of the automatic adjustment mechanism. The costs of the factors of production later declined in response to the change in demand factors. The automatic adjustment mechanism was incapable of reflecting either the downward changes in demand or the ensuing reductions in factor costs. The ceiling price kept increasing as the efficient price decreased rapidly. Eventually, the ceiling price was more than double the efficient price.

This experiment with price level regulation in the gas industry had devastating effects on all market participants. Gas consumers were particularly hard hit, faring far worse than they would have if the government had withdrawn completely from any attempt to regulate even those components of the gas industry that possess some degree of natural monopoly power. Regulation through the use of price ceilings yielded prices higher than would have resulted from the unconstrained exercise of natural monopoly power by pipelines and distributors. Ineffective price regulation was combined with the typical anticompetitive features of economic regulation to minimize both regulatory and market constraints on prices and output. The regulated market intermediaries, pipelines and distributors, enjoyed considerable insulation from competitive pressures through the usual array of tariff provisions, regulatory barriers to entry, and regulatory barriers to exit that create barriers to entry.

This experience suggests the possibility that adoption of price level regulation in other contexts also has the potential to create allocative inefficiencies worse than those resulting from unconstrained monopoly if the typical anticompetitive features of economic regulation are retained. This raises an important issue—if we move from profit level regulation to price level regulation, do we simultaneously discard all of the constraints on competition that usually accompany regulation based on perceived natural monopoly? If we do not, the NGPA experience suggests the existence of one set of significant risks. Yet, if we abandon those aspects of economic regulation, we risk the very problems that originally caused us to impose regulatory barriers to entry, exit, and competition in natural monopoly markets.

It is tempting to dismiss the NGPA experience with price level regulation as attributable merely to a one-time error in selecting an appropriate price adjustment formula. Yet, it is not so easy to suggest ways in which Congress could have avoided its error. Congress assumed that the real costs of exploration and production attributable to the depleting resource effect would increase at a level sufficient to offset any productivity gains and to yield a net real cost increase of 3.5% per year. That assumption seemed plausible at the time. Congress can be criticized for failing to incorporate changes in demand factors in the automatic adjustment mechanism. It is difficult even today, however, to conceive of any method of accomplishing that important goal through a price adjustment mechanism designed to further the primary goal of tracking expected changes in costs.

Congress was not alone in making enormous errors in the process of implementing price level regulation under NGPA. Congress delegated authority to the Federal Energy Regulatory Commission (FERC) to identify new categories of gas produced under conditions that justified a price ceiling at or near the market price. FERC exercised this authority in 1980. It determined that gas produced from "tight sands' " merited a special price ceiling. FERC decided that the incentive price applicable to this new category should be based on FERC's approximation of the present and expected future market price of gas—the "efficient price' " in the parlance of price level regulation. It chose for this purpose an initial price level of $4.50 per million Btus, subject to an automatic price adjustment of twice the level of inflation. Ex post, it is easy to conclude that both the initial price and the automatic adjustment mechanism chosen by FERC were wrong. The ceiling price rose to $7.00, while the efficient price declined to less than $2.00. In this case it is also easy to criticize FERC's decision ex ante. Its estimates were naive even in 1980. It is much more difficult, however, to suggest a price adjustment mechanism that would have performed acceptably. Any of the mechanisms used or proposed for use in the new systems of price level regulation would have produced a ceiling price far higher than the efficient price.

The federal government tried a different version of price level regulation in COWPT. The "windfall profit' " subject to tax was based on the difference between the market price at which a barrel of oil was sold and the "adjusted base price' " applicable to that barrel. Each of three "tiers" of oil was subject to a different adjusted base price. The initial base prices selected in 1979 were $16.55, $15.20, and $12.81 per barrel. In the case of the lower two base prices, the automatic price adjustment mechanism was the level of inflation. For the higher base price category, the adjustment mechanism was inflation plus two percent, again reflecting the expected net effect of real cost increases and expected productivity increases.

The adjusted base price in this system was not intended to be the "efficient price' "; Congress relied on the market for that purpose. The adjusted base price applicable to the high base price category—$16.55 plus inflation plus two percent—was intended, however, to parallel the market price, thereby yielding a steady flow of tax revenue each year. Thus, the automatic price adjustment mechanism applicable to Tier Three Oil in COWPT was designed to perform a function analogous to the automatic price adjustment mechanism in a system of price level regulation. The government expected to raise revenues of $227.3 billion through COWPT between 1979 and 1991. Its total revenues to date are a tiny fraction of that amount. The large disparity between expected and actual tax revenues is attributable entirely to one feature of COWPT. The automatic price adjustment mechanism Congress chose as a surrogate for expected future changes in the costs of finding and producing crude oil was incapable of reflecting changes in demand factors. Demand for domestically produced crude oil plummeted, while the adjusted base price increased. Eventually, finding costs also fell significantly, but the price adjustment mechanism was incapable of reflecting that change either. The adjusted base price applicable to Tier Three Oil, which was intended always to lie below the market price, has been well above the market price since 1981.

The final recent experience with a version of price level regulation arose under PURPA. Section 210 of PURPA requires state utility commissions to compel electric utilities to purchase power from qualified cogenerators and small power producers at a price that represents each utility's "full avoided cost' " of generating electricity. Since cogeneration and small power production projects depend for their financial viability on continuity of markets at predictable prices, the statute required each state agency to reflect in long-term contracts the agency's projection of the utility's "full avoided cost' " of generation for the next several decades. The pricing provisions of the mandated contracts typically included an initial price and an automatic price adjustment mechanism based on the agency's best estimate of expected future changes in the utility's costs. In a high proportion of cases, the price adjustment mechanism chosen by the agency produced a mandatory price to the utility far above the utility's actual avoided cost. Again, the adjustment mechanism was incapable of reflecting either major changes in demand factors or the resulting major changes in firm costs.

All of these descriptions of recent disastrous experiences with inflation-based price level regulation are drawn from the energy context. Based on these experiences, I feel confident in urging complete rejection of any inflation-based form of price level regulation for potential application to electric and gas utilities. This experience also explains in part my extreme skepticism that the CPI–3 version of price level regulation represents an alternative to profit level regulation worthy of serious consideration in any context. . . .

Having acknowledged the high social costs of profit leve regulation and criticized the theoretically promising alternative of CPI–3 price level regulation, I feel obligated to identify other alternatives that offer greater promise. The approach that offers the highest probability of improving allocative and productive efficiency depends critically on the present and expected future characteristics of a market that is now subject to profit level regulation. The alternatives to price level regulation that are likely to enhance social welfare in some contexts include: (1) plain vanilla deregulation; (2) deregulation of sales markets combined with mandatory equal access to significant sunk cost facilities; (3) deregulation combined with reliance on relational contracts; and (4) flexible pricing within boundaries. . . . ■

NOTES AND COMMENTS

1. Price caps have effectively been integrated into many state retail restructuring plans, to the extent they limit the prices that can be charged for power. Many of the state retail electric plans discussed in Chapter 12 guarantee residential consumers a rate decrease or set limits on future rates. Do you think that price caps in this context will pose some of the problems Pierce discusses? Why or why not?

2. Jordan Jay Hillman and Ronald Braeutigam responded to Professor Pierce:

> Our position can be described more fully as follows: Given the serious deficiencies of profit level regulation and the potential efficiency benefits of price level regulation, especially in the case of diversified public utilities serving both natural monopolies and other markets with varying price elasticities, we should continue efforts to minimize certain impediments to the success of price level regulation in the natural monopoly markets.
>
> Pierce initially seems to agree with us about the serious deficiencies of profit level regulation and the substantial potential benefits of price level regulation. In the end, however, his views and ours on the potential comparative efficacy of the two systems diverge in two major respects: (1) we attach greater weight to the identified deficiencies of profit level regulation, and (2) we are more hopeful that credible economic standards and decisional processes important to the success of a price level regime can be established. . . .
>
> We do not differ from Pierce in finding substantial impediments to the success of price level regulation. In the case of our shared concerns, however, we sense a greater possibility of workable solutions. Other of his concerns to us seem inapposite. In particular, we find little predictive value in the notable failures he cites in the regulation or taxation of energy commodities by rigid price formula. As Pierce notes, these prices were subject to unusual volatility. These energy commodities involve competitive markets in which the price of any single commodity is greatly affected by changes in alternative fuel prices. In the case of natural gas, the question is whether any regulation was warranted in 1978, when Congress imposed a rigid, wholly formulaic price adjustment mechanism on a commodity whose market price was driven by the price of oil. We find no analogy in this experience to the more flexible price adjustment mechanisms proposed for the retail markets of regulated public utilities with relatively stable demand. . . .

Jordan Jay Hillman & Ronald Braeutigam, The Potential Benefits and Problems of Price Level Regulation: A More Hopeful Perspective, 84 N.W. U. L. Rev. 695 (1990). But, if competition is presented as an alternative to cost-of-service regulation, do Hillman and Braeutigam's proposals still have relevance for regulators?

3. MARKET-BASED RATES, MARKET POWER AND MARKET MONITORING

Other non-cost methods of pricing include incentive regulation and economic development regulation. These theories will be discussed in the context of the regulation of electricity prices in Chapter 11.

As competition has been introduced into various energy industries, FERC and many states have experimented with market-based rates. These rates are not based on cost-of-service, but are negotiated by supplier firms and purchasers. Section 205 of the Federal Power Act, 16 U.S.C. § 824d, states:

(a) Just and reasonable rates

All rates and charges made, demanded, or received by any public utility for or in connection with the transmission or sale of electric energy subject to the jurisdiction of the Commission, and all rules and regulations affecting or pertaining to such rates or charges shall be just and reasonable, and any such rate or charge that is not just and reasonable is hereby declared to be unlawful.

(b) Preference or advantage unlawful

No public utility shall, with respect to any transmission or sale subject to the jurisdiction of the Commission, (1) make or grant any undue preference or advantage to any person or subject any person to any undue prejudice or disadvantage, or (2) maintain any unreasonable difference in rates, charges, service, facilities, or in any other respect, either as between localities or as between classes of service.

Notwithstanding this language, courts have allowed FERC is to set market based rates so long as FERC engages in sufficient oversight to ensure that rates are not unjust, discriminatory, or otherwise preferential. *See Lockyer v. FERC*, 383 F.3d 1006 (9th Cir. 2004).

For example, electric power marketers can qualify for market-based rates if they demonstrate a lack of market power in generation or transmission and file quarterly reports with FERC that disclose ownership and affilation with other facilities. FERC's guidelines on how to receive market-based rate authority are available online at http://www.ferc.gov/industries/electric/gen-info/how-to-pm.pdf.

Market power is the ability of a firm to to set prices above competitive rates. FERC has reduced this process to reliance on a market screening test. In April 2004, FERC adopted two interim screens to indicate which market based rate applicants would require more detail scrutiny of market power.

The first screen, the pivotal-supplier screen, looks at whether a supplier is pivotal to the market. Will supplies (including imports) from other entities be sufficient to meet wholesale demand in the market? The second screen, the market-share screen, calculates an applicant's share of uncommitted generation capacity in the wholesale market. If the applicant's share exceeds 20 percent, the applicant fails the screen. As has been pointed out, the market-share screen is designed to fail for most traditionally vertically-integrated utilities. Few vertically-integrated utilities have a sufficiently low share of generation within their own control area to pass the test (those most likely to pass tend to have a high share of hydro power). See John R. Morris, FERC's Market Test: The Good, The Bad and the Ugly, Public Utilities FoRtnightly, July 2005 at 37.

Failing one or both of the screens creates a rebuttable presumption of market power. The commission then initiates a Section 206 hearing, where applicants can provide evidence that they do not posses market power. For those who cannot, they then either can accept the commission's default cost-based rates, or they can propose a mitigation plan that would address the commission's market-power concerns.

Once market-based rates are approved, FERC's monitoring of market power typically occurs through the disclosure of information in quarterly reports. In addition, every three years firms qualifying for market-based rates are required to file a market analysis. If FERC finds that a firm charging market-based rates has exercised market power, FERC has the authority to require the refunding of prices charged above the competitively set prices.

In 2002, FERC recognized how the traditional rate hearing was no longer the primary mechanism for evaluating the firms it regulates. It established the Office of Market Oversight and Investigations to assess market performance, assure conformance with Commission rules and report on its findings to the Commission and the public. The office is made up of economists, engineers, attorneys, auditors, data management specialists, financial analysts, and regulatory and energy policy analysts. The Office analyzes overall energy markets to identify and remedy energy market problems, remedy improper behavior and maintain just and reasonable rates.

CHAPTER 4

WATER POWER

A.   WATER AS A SOURCE OF ENERGY

If water is located at any place higher than the level of the area towards which it seeks to flow, it has potential gravitational energy. From the dawn of recorded history, humans have experimented with ways to turn that potential energy into useful kinetic energy.

1.   THE WATER MILL

One of the first devices to utilize the force of falling water as a source of energy was the simple water mill. Flowing water in a river turned some sort of paddle wheel attached to a drive shaft that connected it to some type of machinery. The earliest examples were mills to grind grain, as described in the excerpt from Woolrych in Chapter 2. Both windmills and watermills were common in the medieval world, but watermills were far more abundant; in the Domesday Book count of 1086, there were 5624 mills in southern and eastern England, or one for every 350 people.

By the eighteenth century, water mills were widely used in England to run factories that created textiles, tools and other commodities. To the English settlers of North America, the search for water power was the obvious way to control one of the most important sources of energy. After the revolutionary war, Americans wanted to establish their economic independence from England by manufacturing their own goods, such as clothing and tools, which had traditionally been imported from England. To do so, they needed to utilize the water power potential of the rivers flowing into the Atlantic Ocean, which proved to easiest in the rolling terrain of New England.

This New England regional complex had an interdependence and an inner dynamic that shaped the role of the textile industry in the national economy. Geographically, the industry spread inward along the rivers of New England, eventually studding the great waterpower sites with clusters of large mills and housing for workers. Mill towns were connected by river, canal, turnpike, and eventually railroad to major mercantile centers, which imported the raw cotton, shipped the finished goods, and served as general supply centers and managerial and financial headquarters. D.W. Meinig, II The Shaping of America 377 (1993).

Most of America's first important industrial facilities were located along Northeastern rivers at locations where dams could be built to run mills powered by water wheels. Even after coal-fired steam engines were common in New England in the mid 1850s, steam was still about three times more expensive than water as a prime mover. Vaclav Smil, Energy in World History 108 (1994).

Effective use of water power usually required the construction of a dam that would store large quantities of water. As the needs of industry grew, higher and higher dams were needed to provide the power. The difference in the height of the water above and below the dam is called the "head" of the dam. As the height of the head increased, flooding of lands behind the dam increased, which often created conflict between mill owners and farmers whose land was flooded.

When a mill dam is built and the reservoir filled, the water is then released in a steady flow so that the water mill will run continuously and evenly. Because the construction of a dam affected the landowners both above and below the dam, legal rules were needed for determining the rights of the various landowners. These rules set precedents that influenced the development of energy law as new and more powerful sources of potential energy came into operation later in the century.

The ability to capture a "higher head" of water by building a dam was a rearrangement of the natural flows of energy. Water that naturally would have flowed freely downstream was captured and held by the dam so that its potential energy could be used to turn the mill's machinery. The dam reduced the amount of water (and potential energy) that would otherwise be available to downstream landowners and also caused flooding of the land adjacent to the river upstream from the dam.

American courts wrestled with the legal issues arising out of these energy transfers. As you consider the ways in which the lawmakers attempted to resolve this conflict, think about the similarities and differences between the capture of the potential energy in water and the capture of the potential energy in sunlight.

2. Impact on Property Rights

Fiske v. Framingham Manufacturing Co.
29 Mass. (12 Pick.) 68 (1831).

Action on the case. The plaintiff alleges that he is owner of a tract of meadow land situate in Natick, on one side of and near a pond, called

Wansemog Pond, and that the defendants, by drawing water from the pond, overflowed his land, whereby his hay was injured.

■ SHAW C. J. The statutes in regard to mills, and the rights and liabilities of mill-owners in relation to flowing the lands of others, are to be regarded as statutes in pari materia and to be construed together as one system of regulations.

By the Statute 1824, c. 153, § 1, it is provided, that when any person shall complain that he sustains damage in his lands, by their being flowed, whether situated above or below any mill dam, the court may order, &c. It is well settled, that in all these cases, where the party is entitled to his damage upon complaint, under the statute, his common law remedy by an action on the case is taken away.

In the case of *Wolcott Woollen Manufacturing Co. v. Upham*, 22 Mass. (5 Pick.) 292 (1827), a construction was put upon this statute, and it was there held, as under the former one, that where the statute remedy by complaint applies, the common law remedy by action on the case is taken away. It was further held, in that case, that a dam erected several miles above a mill for the purpose of raising a head of water, and creating a reservoir, for the use of such mill, is a mill dam within the meaning of the act, and a remedy for damage done by the water flowing away from the dam of such reservoir, must be sought under the statute. Were the plaintiff's meadow situated on a natural stream, and the defendants' dam erected above it, on a natural stream, there would be nothing to distinguish this from the case cited, and the question is, whether the statute can apply to an artificial stream created by means of a canal.

The statute of 1824 makes no distinction in terms or by implication, between a natural stream, and a canal or artificial stream. But, as already suggested, this statute is to be construed with the other statutes in pari materia, and regarded not as establishing a new principle, but as enlarging and extending a beneficial remedy, before given in certain cases, to other analogous cases. The statute of 1796 is but a revision of a former law, and the origin of these regulations is to be found in the provincial statute of 1714. They are somewhat at variance with that absolute right of dominion and enjoyment which every proprietor is supposed by law to have in his own soil; and in ascertaining their extent, it will be useful to inquire into the principle upon which they are founded. We think they will be found to rest for their justification, partly upon the interest which the community at large has in the use and employment of mills, and partly upon the nature of the property, which is often so situated, that it could not be beneficially used without the aid of this power. A stream of water often runs through the lands of several proprietors. One may have a sufficient mill-site on his own land, with ample space on his own land for a mill pond or reservoir, but yet, from the operation of the well known physical law, that fluids will seek and find a level, he cannot use his own property without flowing the water back more or less on the lands of some other proprietor. We think the power given by statute was intended to apply to such cases, and that the legislature meant to provide, that as the public interest in such case coincides with that of the mill-owner, and as the mill-owner and the owner of lands to be flowed cannot both enjoy their full rights, without some interference, the latter shall yield to the former, so far that the former may keep up his mill and head of water, notwithstanding the damage done to the latter, upon payment of an equitable compensation for the real damage sustained, to be ascertained in the mode provided by the statute.

From this view of the object and purpose of the statute, we think it quite manifest, that it was designed to provide for the most useful and beneficial occupation and enjoyment of natural streams and water-courses, where the absolute right of each proprietor to use his own land and water privileges, at his own pleasure, cannot be fully enjoyed, and one must of necessity, in some degree, yield to the other. But we think it would be an extension of the principle not warranted by the statute, if it were so construed as to authorize one person to make a canal or artificial stream in such manner as to lead the water into the lands of another; and in such case, therefore, the right of the party whose lands are flowed, to recover damages by an action at common law, is not taken away or impaired.

It appears by the facts reported, that the sluice and gate, through which the water was drawn which flooded the plaintiff's meadow, were not placed upon any natural stream, but upon a canal or artificial cut, by means of which the water flowed through the plaintiff's meadow, where it did not flow before; and therefore the Court are of opinion, for the reasons before given, that the statute does not apply, and that the plaintiff is not barred by it from his remedy at common law.

Nonsuit taken off and the cause to stand for trial.■

Morton J. Horwitz

The Transformation of American Law, 1780–1860 (1977).

The various acts to encourage the construction of mills offer some of the earliest illustrations of American willingness to sacrifice the sanctity of private property in the interest of promoting economic development. The first such statute, enacted by the Massachusetts colonial legislature in 1713, envisioned a procedure for compensating landowners when a "small quantity" of their property was flooded by the raising of waters for mill dams. The statutory procedure was rarely used, however, since the Massachusetts courts refused to construe the act to eliminate the traditional common law remedies for trespass or nuisance. After the act was amended in 1795 and 1798, mill owners began to argue that it provided an exclusive remedy for the flooding of lands. As a result, the mill acts adopted in a large number of states and territories on the model of the Massachusetts law were, more than any other legal measure, crucial in dethroning landed property from the supreme position it had occupied in the eighteenth century world view, and ultimately, in transforming real estate into just another cash-valued commodity. The history of the acts is a major source of information on the relationship of law to economic change. For reasons of convenience the discussion that follows concentrates on the Massachusetts experience which, though particularly rich, is not atypical.

Under the 1795 Massachusetts statute, Act of Feb. 27, 1795, ch. 74, [1794–96] Mass. Acts & Resolves 443, an owner of a mill situated on any nonnavigable stream was permitted to raise a dam and flood the land of his neighbor, so long as he compensated him according to the procedures established by the act. The injured party was limited to yearly damages, instead of a lump sum payment, even if the land was permanently flooded, and the initial estimate of annual damages continued from year to year unless one of the parties came into court and showed that circumstances had changed. The act conferred extensive discretion on the jury, which, in addition to determining damages, could prescribe the height to which a dam could be raised as well as the time of year that lands could be flooded. Unlike the statutes in some states, such as Virginia, *See Wrote v. Harris,* 2 Va. (2 Wash.) 126 (1795), the Massachusetts law authorized the mill owner to flood neighboring lands without seeking prior court permission. Thus, except for the power of the jury to regulate their future actions, there was no procedure for determining in advance the utility of allowing mill owners to overflow particular lands.

The exclusive remedial procedures of the mill acts foreclosed four important alternative avenues to relief:

First, they cut off the traditional action for trespass to land, in which a plaintiff was not required to prove actual injury in order to recover. In a mill act proceeding a defendant could escape all liability by showing that, on balance, flooding actually benefitted the plaintiff.

Second, the statutory damage formula removed the possibility of imposing punitive damages in trespass or nuisance. The common law view had been that unless punitive damages could be imposed, it might pay the wrongdoer to "keep it up forever; and thus one individual will be enabled to take from another his property against his consent, and detain it from him as long as he pleases."

A third form of relief at common law allowed an affected landowner to resort to self-help to abate a nuisance. Indeed, there are a number of reported cases in which mill dams not covered by the protection of the mill acts were torn down by neighbors claiming to enforce their common law rights.

Finally, the acts foreclosed the possibility of permanently enjoining a mill owner for having created a nuisance.

In the early nineteenth century the need to provide a doctrinal rationale for the extraordinary power that the mill acts delegated to a few individuals was acute. Not only had the use of water power vastly expanded in the century since the original Massachusetts act, but there was also a major difference between the eighteenth century grist mill, which was understood to be open to the public, and the more recently established saw, paper, and cotton mills, many of which served only the proprietor.

By 1814, the significance of the growing separation between public and private enterprise was only beginning to penetrate the judicial mind. Some still conceived of mills as a form of public enterprise in which competition was impermissible. Business corporations were only beginning to upset the old corporate model, in which the raison d'etre of chartered associations was their service to the public. Nor is there any evidence that the increasingly private nature of mills, which was painfully evident to everyone fifteen years later, had as yet caused judges the slightest conceptual difficulty. At this time in Virginia, for example, where the old corporate model still prevailed, judges were also clear that the state's mill act could be defended on the ground that "the property of another is, as it were, seized on, or subjected to injury, to a certain extent, it being considered in fact for the public use." *Skipwith v. Young*, 19 Va. (5 Munf.) 276, 278 (1816).

The dramatic growth of cotton mills after 1815 provided the greatest incentive for mill owners to flood adjoining land and, in turn, brought to a head a heated controversy over the nature of property rights. The original mill dams were relatively small operations that caused some upstream flooding when proprietors held back water in order to generate power. With the growth of large integrated cotton mills, however, the flooding of more lands became necessary not only because larger dams held back greater quantities of water but also because of the need to generate power by releasing an enormous flow of water downstream. In light of this fact, the Massachusetts legislature amended the mill act in 1825 to allow the flooding of "lands ... situated either above or below any mill dam." Act of Feb. 26, 1825, ch. 153, § 1 [1822–25] Mass. Laws 658.

Extension of the mill act to manufacturing establishments brought forth a storm of bitter opposition. One theme—that manufacturing establishments were private institutions—appeared over and over again.... The nearly unanimous denunciation of the mill acts soon brought forth a degree of change. From 1830, when Lemuel Shaw began his thirty year tenure as chief justice, the Massachusetts court began a marked retreat away from its earlier reluctant, but expansive, interpretation of the act. Conceding that the mill acts "are somewhat at variance with that absolute right of dominion and enjoyment which every proprietor is supposed by law to have in his own soil," *Fiske v. Framingham Mfg. Co.*, 29 Mass. (12 Pick.) 68, 70 (1832). Shaw nevertheless proceeded to offer a dual justification for the acts. The legislation could be defended, he wrote, "partly upon the interest which the community at large has, in the use and employment of mills"—a theory of eminent domain—"and partly upon the nature of the property, which is often so situated, that it could not be beneficially used without the aid of this power." *Id.* at 70–71. However artificial it may have been in the existing context, Shaw argued that the mill act "was designed to provide for the most useful and beneficial occupation and enjoyment of natural streams and water-courses, where the absolute right of each proprietor, to use his own land and water privileges, at his own pleasure, cannot be fully enjoyed, and one must of necessity, in some degree, yield to the other." *Id.* at 71–72.

The main contribution of Shaw's formulation was to force courts to see that a conception of absolute and exclusive dominion over property was incompatible with the needs of industrial development. Whether the rationale for state intervention was eminent domain or a more explicit recognition of the relativity of property rights, under the influence of the mill acts men had come to regard property as an instrumental value in the service of the paramount goal of promoting economic growth.■

NOTES AND COMMENTS

1. When the mill owner's dam flooded the farmer's land, a natural resource (i.e., agricultural land) was lost that could have converted the sun's energy into crops. On the other hand, the stored water in the dam was potential energy that could be converted to kinetic energy that would grind corn or convert cotton into textiles. Was the dam's conversion of energy more efficient (i.e., did it create less entropy) than the farmer's conversion of solar energy into corn or cotton? How would such efficiency be measured? Did the rules of law created in Massachusetts to resolve the conflicts between the mill owner and the farmer take into account any differences in relative efficiency of energy conversion?

2. If the mill owner were required to pay the farmer the value of her land, would the relative market values of the respective parcels of land automatically take into account the relative efficiency of the mill owner's and the farmer's conversion of energy?

3. "The Virginia Mill Act provided significant protection for landowners against incursions by the mills and was interpreted in a way that made it quite difficult to construct a mill.... First, the Act protected landowners directly by requiring millers to obtain permission from a court before flooding nearby land and by ensuring that the millers paid adequate damages. Second, judges added extra protection for landowners by construing the act very strictly, often finding technical reasons to forbid construction of a mill. Thus, the Virginia Mill Act did allow for some industrial development, but without enriching 'men of commerce and industry' at the expense of less powerful groups or running roughshod over other interests." Note: Water Law and Economic Power: A Reinterpretation of Morton Horwitz's Subsidy Thesis 77 Va. L.Rev. 397 (1991). What differences between the conditions in Massachusetts and Virginia might have contributed to the development of different laws governing the balance of power between millowners and farmers?

4. The Mill Acts effectively gave mill owners a power of private eminent domain to flood their neighbors' land as long as they paid damages. In 1991, Peter Dorey, who had purchased an old mill near Foster Pond in Bridgton Maine, sought a declaratory judgment that he was entitled to increase the height of the dam under the Maine Mill Act, which was similar to the Massachusetts Act. His action would cause flooding for forty-four owners of waterfront property on the pond. How should the court decide the case? *See Dorey v. Estate of Spicer*, 715 A.2d 182 (Me. 1998).

B. PUBLIC VS. PRIVATE POWER

Early in the twentieth century, the technology for the use and distribution of electricity became readily available (see Chapter 10), leading to a search for the most efficient way of generating electricity. One of the earliest technologies to be developed was a relatively simple one; the rotating movement of the traditional water mill was transferred to a turbine, which generated electric current. Such electricity became known as hydroelectric power (also called hydropower or simply hydro).

Considerable hydropower development had occurred by the time Congress passed a series of statutes to govern hydroelectric development, culminating in the Federal Power Act of 1935, 16 U.S.C. § 792 et seq., which created the modern federal hydropower licensing program. In the Federal Power Act, Congress delegated licensing responsibility to the Federal Power Commission ("FPC"), predecessor to the modern Federal Energy Regulatory Commission ("FERC"), and authorized the FPC to grant licenses for the development of hydroelectric facilities that are "best adapted to a comprehensive plan for development of the waterway," consistent with "the public interest." The FPC set out to license a tremendous variety of new and existing hydro facilities, including large dams with hundreds of megawatts of generating capacity and very small dams with only a few kilowatts of capacity, old facilities that generated power for paper and textile mills, utility generators, municipal power facilities and more.

While the FPC was granted broad authority to manage the licensing of privately-and municipally-owned hydroelectric facilities, Congress sometimes directly authorized the construction of federally-owned hydroelectric facilities outside the Federal Power Act licensing process. Indeed, the builders of some of the largest dams were two federal agencies, the Bureau of Reclamation and the U.S. Army Corps of Engineers. Projects such as the Colorado River's Boulder Dam (later renamed Hoover Dam after the President who was one of its strongest backers) and the Columbia River's Grand Coulee Dam were triumphs of engineering that still awe people by their size. These agencies also built hundreds of smaller dams as Congressional delegations sought to bring federal money into their districts.

With the election of President Franklin Roosevelt and the "New Deal" policies he espoused, the role of the federal government in hydroelectric power was intensified. The Congress created the Tennessee Valley Authority as a federal agency with a monopoly on electric generation in the valley of the Tennessee River and its tributaries, and it began the construction of a whole series of dams to produce power. In the northwest, another federal agency, the Bonneville Power Authority, was created to harness the power potential of the Columbia River. The reservoirs created by these dams displaced thousands of people, but the promised economic benefits of the new technology were so great that the minor hardship (Congress provided fairly generous compensation) was widely seen as simply the price of progress.

Robert L. Bradley, Jr., The Origins of Political Electricity: Market Failure or Political Opportunism

17 Energy L.J. 59 (1996).

As governor of New York in the 1920s, Franklin Roosevelt endorsed municipal provision of electric power to ensure that more Americans gained access to power and to use as a "yardstick" enterprise to compete against investor-owned utilities. Power provision to FDR was "a national problem," and in his first term as president he formulated a National Power Policy not only to bring interstate electricity under federal public utility regulation but also to make electricity "more broadly available at cheaper rates to industry, to domestic and to agricultural consumers." Hydropower as a federal public works program and rural subsidy program was key.

Three major laws ... would follow as part of FDR's public works program to promote economic recovery during the Great Depression.

1.   Tennessee Valley Authority. On April 10, 1933, FDR proposed a major hydro project to Congress to rectify "the continued idleness of a great national investment in the Tennessee Valley." The next month, Congress approved the Tennessee Valley Act (TVA) "in the interest of national defense and for agricultural and industrial development, and to improve navigation in the Tennessee River and to control the destructive flood waters." The Act established a three-member board with eminent domain powers to "construct dams, reservoirs, power houses, power structures, transmission lines ... and to unite the various power installations into one or more systems by transmission lines." The agency was empowered to "produce, distribute, and sell electric power" with preference to "States, counties, municipalities, and cooperative organizations of citizens and farmers, not organized or doing business for profit, but primarily for the purpose of supplying electricity to its own citizens or members." Contracts could be for up to twenty years, and agreements with for-profit entities could be voided with five years' notice if the power was needed on the non-profit side.... The fateful decision made by Congress was to construct and operate the facilities as a public project. Numerous applications for private development languished before Congress between 1903 and 1933 without approval. Two Tennessee utilities applied for federal permits to invest between $60 and $100 million to develop eleven waterpower sites only to encounter years of inaction. The result of government provision was a competitive antagonism between TVA and neighboring private systems who were discriminated against under the preference system and feared taxpayer-funded raiding that led to litigation and obstructionism that retarded rural electrification. Facilities were also duplicated.

2.   Rural Electrification Act of 1936. In early 1935, FDR endorsed a program to subsidize rural electrification to which Congress responded with a $100 million appropriation. On May 11, 1935, FDR issued an executive order creating a new agency to transmit electricity "to as many farms as possible in the shortest possible time, and to have it used in quantities sufficient to affect rural life." The Rural Electrification Administration (REA) was empowered to make loans to private and public parties to finance connections with farms. As a public works program, 90% of involved workers had to originate from the relief rolls unless an exemption was granted by the REA. The next year the program was put on a more permanent basis with the passage of the Rural Electrification Act. The REA was instructed to "make loans in the several States and Territories of the United States for rural electrification and the furnishing of electric energy to persons in rural areas [defined as residing in population centers under 1,500 persons] who are not receiving central station service." The REA was appropriated $50 million for fiscal year 1937 and $40 million for each of the next eight years to finance generation, transmission, and distribution facilities. Loans for such assets could not exceed 85% of the principal amount and had to be fully amortized over a twenty-five-year period (with a maximum five-year extension) at an interest rate paid by the government on long term debt. Financing preference was given to governmental bodies and private cooperatives and nonprofits....

3.   Bonneville Power Administration Act of 1937. Federal monies to develop the water resources of the Pacific Northwest were first allocated by Congress in 1933 as part of the employment program of the Public Works Administration. An additional allocation followed two years later in the Rivers and Harbors Improvement Act. The final push was the Bonneville Power Administration Act of 1937 (BPA), which authorized the Secretary of War to "provide, construct, operate, maintain, and improve at [the dam projects under construction at Bonneville, Oregon and North Bonneville, Washington] such machines, equipment, and facilities for the generation of electric energy ... to develop such electricity as rapidly as markets may be found therefor." To "encourage the widest possible use of all electricity," the Bonneville Power Administrator was authorized to construct transmission facilities to interconnect with other markets. Eminent domain rights were granted to facilitate land requisition associated with the above....

FDR's policy of "direct and indirect competition in reducing electricity prices ... including yardstick federal power projects, birch rod potential competition from municipalities and rural cooperatives, [and] well-publicized annual rate surveys" has been found by one business historian to be "quite sound." This analysis adds the caveats, however, that (1) rates could have fallen further still without FDR's activism, and (2) the "administrative costs, rent-seeking costs, price discrimination practices, government subsidies, and other factors" related to his activism would have to be assessed. While the first point can probably be discounted—more generation and distribution investment would surely increase supply to lower prices compared to its absence—the second point raises a very obvious issue: a large dedication of taxpayer resources amid Depression scarcity was not a free lunch. But the foregone opportunity of FDR's action was not so much his inaction. It was the deregulation of electric utilities and privatized electric provision to let market forces guide the industry where, by definition, no taxpayer or regulatory costs would be incurred.■

The Federal Power Act was enacted at a time of national ambivalence over the question of whether the private sector or the public sector should take the lead in the development and control of electric power. This conflict was heightened in the context of hydroelectric development because many viewed the nation's waterways as a public resource the flows of which ought not to be subjected to private control, irrespective of riparian property rights regimes. Beyond the general requirement that licensing decisions be made "in the public interest," the Federal Power Act favored governmental influence over hydropower development in several ways. First, Section 4 of the Act gives federal agencies directly affected by a proposed project the authority to specify conditions to be included in any license granted to that project. Thus, for example, if a private applicant seeks a license to build a hydroelectric project at a dam owned by the U.S. Army Corps of Engineers or on land owned by the U.S. Forest Service or Bureau of Land Management, the Commission must include in the license conditions specified by those agencies. (However, this power has been weakened somewhat by the passage of the Energy Policy Act of 2005. *See infra* § D.1.). Second, Section 7(a) established the so-called "municipal preference" at licensing, which acted as a tie-breaker in favor of municipal license applicants in any competitive licensing proceeding between municipal and private sector applicants. Third, Section 7(b) established a mechanism by which the FPC might deny license applications and recommend development of the site by the federal government.

Udall v. Federal Power Commission

387 U.S. 428 (1967).

■ DOUGLAS, J. The Federal Power Commission has awarded Pacific Northwest Power Company (a joint venture of four private power companies) a license to construct a hydroelectric power project at High Mountain Sheep, a site on the Snake River, a mile upstream from its confluence with the Salmon. 31 F.P.C. 247, 1051. The Court of Appeals approved the action, 358 F.2d 840 (D.C. Cir.); and we granted the petitions for certiorari. 385 U.S. 926, 927.

The primary question in the cases involves an interpretation of § 7(b) of the Federal Water Power Act of 1920, as amended by the Federal Power Act, 49 Stat. 842, 16 U.S.C. § 800(b), which provides:

"Whenever, in the judgment of the Commission, the development of any water resources for public purposes should be undertaken by the United States itself, the Commission shall not approve any application for any project affecting such development, but shall cause to be made such examinations, surveys, reports, plans, and estimates of the cost of the proposed development as it may find necessary, and shall submit its findings to Congress with such recommendations as it may find appropriate concerning such development.''

The question turns on whether § 7(b) requires a showing that licensing of a private, state, or municipal agency[1] is a satisfactory alternative to federal development. We put the question that way because the present record is largely silent on the relative merits of federal and nonfederal development. What transpired is as follows:

Both Pacific Northwest and Washington Public Power Supply System, allegedly a ''municipality'' under § 4(e) and under § 7(a) of the Act,[2] filed applications for licenses on mutually exclusive sites; and they were consolidated for hearing. Before the hearing the Commission solicited the views of the Secretary of the Interior. The Secretary urged postponement of the licensing of either project while means of protecting the salmon and other fisheries were studied. That was on March 15, 1961. But the hearings went forward and on June 28, 1962, after the record before the Examiner was closed, but before he rendered his decision, the Secretary wrote the Commission urging it to recommend to Congress the consideration of federal construction of High Mountain Sheep. The Commission reopened the record to allow the Secretary's letter to be incorporated and invited the parties to file supplemental briefs in response to it. On October 8, 1962, the

---

1. Section 4 of the Act provides in part:

''The Commission is hereby authorized and empowered—

(a) To make investigations and to collect and record data concerning the utilization of the water resources of any region to be developed, the water-power industry and its relation to other industries and to interstate or foreign commerce, and concerning the location, capacity, development costs, and relation to markets of power sites, and whether the power from Government dams can be advantageously used by the United States for its public purposes, and what is a fair value of such power, to the extent the Commission may deem necessary or useful for the purposes of this Act

. . . .

(e) To issue licenses to citizens of the United States, or to any association of such citizens, or to any corporation organized under the laws of the United States or any State thereof, or to any State or municipality for the purpose of constructing, operating, and maintaining dams, water conduits, reservoirs, power houses, transmission lines, or other project works necessary or convenient for the development and improvement of navigation and for the development, transmission, and utilization of power across, along, from, or in any of the streams or other bodies of water over which Congress has jurisdiction under its authority to regulate commerce with foreign nations and among the several States, or upon any part of the public lands and reservations of the United States (including the Territories), or for the purpose of utilizing the surplus water or water power from any Government dam, except as herein provided. . . .'' 49 Stat. 839, 840, 16 U.S.C. §§ 797(a), (e).

2. *See* n. 1, *supra*, for § 4(e). Section 7(a) of the Act provides: ''In issuing preliminary permits hereunder or licenses where no preliminary permit has been issued and in issuing licenses to new licensees under section 15 hereof the Commission shall give preference to applications therefor by States and municipalities, provided the plans for the same are deemed by the Commission equally well adapted, or shall within a reasonable time to be fixed by the Commission be made equally well adapted, to conserve and utilize in the public interest the water resources of the region. . . .'' 49 Stat. 842, 16 U.S.C. § 800(a).

Examiner rendered his decision, recommending that Pacific Northwest receive the license. He disposed of the issue of federal development on the ground that there "is no evidence in this record that Federal development will provide greater flood control, power benefits, fish passage, navigation or recreation; and there is substantial evidence to the contrary."

The Secretary asked for leave to intervene and to file exceptions to the Examiner's decision.[3] The Commission allowed intervention "limited to filing of exceptions to the Presiding Examiner's decision and participation in such oral argument as might subsequently be ordered."

The Secretary filed exceptions and participated in oral argument. The Commission on February 5, 1964, affirmed the Examiner saying that it agreed with him "that the record supports no reason why federal development should be superior," observing that "[while] we have extensive material before us on the position of the Secretary of the Interior, there is no evidence in the record presented by him to support his position." 31 F.P.C., at 275.

It went on to say that it found "nothing in this record to indicate" that the public purposes of the dam (flood control, etc.) would not be served as adequately by Pacific Northwest as they would under federal development. And it added, "We agree that the Secretary (or any single operator) normally would have a superior ability to co-ordinate the operations of HMS with the other affected projects on the river. But there is no evidence upon which we can determine the scope or the seriousness of this matter in the context of a river system which already has a number of different project operators and an existing co-ordination system, i.e., the Northwest Power Pool." *Id.* at 276–277.

The Secretary petitioned for a rehearing, asking that the record be opened to permit him to supply the evidentiary deficiencies. A rehearing, but not a reopening of the record, was granted; and the Commission shortly reaffirmed its original decision with modifications not material here.

The issue of federal development has never been explored in this record. The applicants introduced no evidence addressed to that question; and the Commission denied the Secretary an opportunity to do so though his application was timely. The issue was of course briefed and argued; yet

---

3. The Secretary argued that federal development of High Mountain Sheep is necessary because (1) hydraulic and electrical coordination with other Columbia River Basin projects, particularly the federal dams already or to be constructed on the downstream sites, could be more effectively achieved if High Mountain Sheep is a part of the federal system; (2) federal development will assure maximum use of the federal northwest transmission grid, thus contributing to maximum repayment of the federal investment in transmission, which will, in turn, redound to the benefit of the power consumers; (3) federal development would provide greater flexibility and protection in the management of fish resources; (4) flood control could better be effected by flexible federal operation; (5) storage releases for navigation requirements could be made under federal ownership and supervision with less effect on power supply; (6) federal development can better provide recreational facilities for an expanding population. The Secretary noted, however, that immediate construction of the project would produce an excess of power in the Pacific Northwest which would cause large losses to Bonneville Power Administration and severe harm to the region's economy.

no factual inquiry was undertaken. Section 7(b) says "Whenever, in the judgment of the Commission, the development of any water resources for public purposes should be undertaken by the United States itself," the Commission shall not approve other applications. Yet the Commission by its rulings on the applications of the Secretary to intervene and to reopen precluded it from having the informed judgment that § 7(b) commands.

We indicate no judgment on the merits. We do know that on the Snake–Columbia waterway between High Mountain Sheep and the ocean, eight hydroelectric dams have been built and another authorized. These are federal projects; and if another dam is to be built, the question whether it should be under federal auspices looms large. Timed releases of stored water at High Mountain Sheep may affect navigability; they may affect hydroelectric production of the downstream dams when the river level is too low for the generators to be operated at maximum capacity; they may affect irrigation; and they may protect salmon runs when the water downstream is too hot or insufficiently oxygenated. Federal versus private or municipal control may conceivably make a vast difference in the functioning of the vast river complex.

Beyond that is the question whether any dam should be constructed. As to this the Secretary in his letter to the Commission dated November 21, 1960, in pleading for a deferment of consideration of applications stated:

> "In carrying out this Department's responsibility for the protection and conservation of the vital Northwest anadromous fishery resource and in light of the fact that the power to be available as a result of ratification of the proposed Columbia River treaty with Canada will provide needed time which can be devoted to further efforts to resolve the fishery problems presently posed by these applications, we believe that it is unnecessary at this time and for some years to come to undertake any project in this area.
>
> You may be assured that the Fish and Wildlife Service of this Department will continue, with renewed emphasis, the engineering and research studies that must be done before we can be assured that the passage of anadromous fish can be provided for at these proposed projects."

Since the cases must be remanded to the Commission, it is appropriate to refer to that aspect of the cases.

Section 10(a) of the Act provides that "the project adopted" shall be such "as in the judgment of the Commission will be best adapted to a comprehensive plan for improving or developing a waterway ... and for other beneficial public uses, including recreational purposes."

The objective of protecting "recreational purposes" means more than that the reservoir created by the dam will be the best one possible or practical from a recreational viewpoint. There are already eight lower dams on this Columbia River system and a ninth one authorized; and if the Secretary is right in fearing that this additional dam would destroy the waterway as spawning grounds for anadromous fish (salmon and steelhead) or seriously impair that function, the project is put in an entirely different light. The importance of salmon and steelhead in our outdoor life as well as in commerce is so great that there certainly comes a time when their destruction might necessitate a halt in so-called "improvement" or "development" of waterways. The destruction of anadromous fish in our western waters is so notorious that we cannot believe that Congress through the present Act authorized their ultimate demise.

Mr. Justice Holmes once wrote that "A river is more than an amenity, it is a treasure." *New Jersey v. New York*, 283 U.S. 336, 342. That dictum is relevant here for the Commission under § 10 of the 1920 Act, as amended, must take into consideration not only hydroelectric power, navigation, and flood control, but also the "recreational purposes" served by the river. And, as we have noted, the Secretary of the Interior has a mandate under the 1965 Act to study recommendations concerning water development programs for the purpose of the conservation of anadromous fish. Thus apart from § 7(b) of the 1920 Act, as amended, the Secretary by reason of § 2 of the 1965 Act comes to the Federal Power Commission with a special mandate from Congress, a mandate that gives him special standing to appear, to intervene, to introduce evidence on the proposed river development program, and to participate fully in the administrative proceedings.

In his letter of November 21, 1960, the Secretary noted that, due to increased power resources, the projects could be safely deferred. "These projects could extend the time still further, as could also be the case in the event nuclear power materialized at Hanford in the 1960–1970 period. This possibility, as you know, has been under intensive study by your staff for the Atomic Energy Commission...."

By 1980 nuclear energy "should represent a significant proportion of world power production." *Id.* at 109. By the end of the century "nuclear energy may account for about one-third of our total energy consumption." Ibid. "By the middle of the next century it seems likely that most of our energy needs will be satisfied by nuclear energy." *Id.* at 110.

Some of these time schedules are within the period of the 50–year licenses granted by the Commission.

Nuclear energy is coming to the Columbia River basin by 1975. For plans are afoot to build a plant on the Trogan site, 14 miles north of St. Helens. This one plant will have a capacity of 1,000,000 kws. This emphasizes the relevancy of the Secretary's reference to production and distribution of nuclear energy at the Hanford Thermal Project which he called "most important of all" and which Congress has authorized. 76 Stat. 604.

The need to destroy the river as a waterway, the desirability of its demise, the choices available to satisfy future demands for energy—these are all relevant to a decision under § 7 and § 10 but they were largely untouched by the Commission.

On our remand there should be an exploration of these neglected phases of the cases, as well as the other points raised by the Secretary.

We express no opinion on the merits. It is not our task to determine whether any dam at all should be built or whether if one is authorized it should be private or public. If the ultimate ruling under § 7(b) is that the decision concerning the High Mountain Sheep site should be made by the Congress, the factors we have mentioned will be among the many considerations it doubtless will appraise. If the ultimate decision under § 7(b) is the other way, the Commission will not have discharged its functions under the Act unless it makes an informed judgment on these phases of the cases. We reverse the judgment and remand the case to the Court of Appeals with instructions to remand to the Commission.

Each remand is for further proceedings consistent with this opinion.

[Justice Harlan, with whom Justice Stewart joined, dissented on the ground that the Commission's decision was supported by substantial evidence.]■

NOTES AND COMMENTS

1. The opinion of the Supreme Court in the *Udall* case came at the beginning of a decade of heightened environmental sensitivity that produced much federal environmental legislation. The case is often cited as one of the earliest examples of the "hard look" doctrine, which was used extensively by federal courts in the 1970s to force federal agencies to examine the environmental implications of their decisions. See James Oakes, The Judicial Role in Environmental Law, 52 N.Y.U. L. Rev. 498 (1977).

2. The Court's citation to predictions that nuclear power would replace the need for traditional sources of power generation now seems rather ironic. Not only has such power proven to be more expensive than was then anticipated, but the environmental opposition to it has been even more intense than to hydroelectric projects. Nuclear power is discussed in Chapter 14. This is not the last example you will see of a confidently voiced energy prediction that proves widely off the mark.

3. The history of hydropower development reflects a theme that will be seen again and again in the history of technology, and particularly energy technology. A new and more efficient way of producing energy is discovered and the public is willing to sacrifice other objectives in order to bring it about. Some years later, when the technology is no longer at the forefront, the public often has difficulty remembering why it was willing to make such sacrifices. *See* Richard White, The Organic Machine: The Remaking of the Columbia River, Hill & Wang, 1995. The dilemma of the *Charles River Bridge* case (*see* Chapter 2) is repeated over and over in the history of energy law.

4. The High Mountain Sheep Dam was never built. Eight years after the Udall decision, Congress included the proposed dam site in the Hells Canyon National Recreation Area, thereby prohibiting the construction of dams and preserving the area's free-flowing rivers and salmon habitat.

However, the "designation did nothing to restore the spring fish flows that young Idaho salmon needed to survive the eight federal dams that now obstructed their journey from their spawning grounds to the ocean." Michael C. Blumm and F. Lorraine Bodi, in The Northwest Salmon Crisis: A Documentary History, Joseph Cone and Sandy Ridlington, eds., Oregon State University Press, 1996.

5.   Snake River politics is just as volatile today as it was in the 1960s. The Snake River is home to many species of fish, including several species listed as "endangered," including steelhead and chinook salmon. It is estimated that millions of salmon returned to the Snake and Columbia Rivers each year to spawn, and now only a few hundred thousand make the journey. Many things have contributed to the decline in fish stock in the Snake River, such as over-harvesting, and effects on the habitat from farming, grazing, mining, logging, etc. But most people agree that dams significantly contributed to the salmons' decline, especially those dams that eliminate access to fresh water for spawning purposes. Scientists believe that the salmon need more natural river conditions-cold, clean, free-flowing water-to remain a viable species.

There are many dams in the Columbia and Snake River basin, eight of which are operated by the United States Army Corps of Engineers ("USACE"). The USACE implemented several mechanisms in efforts to preserve the existing fish population. Adult fish ladders are used to assist the adult salmon in forging their way upstream to places to spawn. Juvenile fish bypass systems are also in place, to allow juvenile fish to make their way to the ocean. However, these bypass systems involve the fish going through a turbine or over a dam spillway, which can be detrimental to the fish. Another measure being used to aid in the preservation of fish species is the trap and haul method. Fish are caught and transported by truck around the hydropower projects and then released back into the river. For a discussion of how these issues are being addressed in proceedings governing the relicensing of Snake River dams, see infra § D.2.

C.   HYDROELECTRIC LICENSING AND THE PUBLIC INTEREST

In addition to the question of *who* should develop hydroelectric sites, the Commission also faced the question of *whether* and *how* such sites should be developed. The Federal Power Act gave the Commission precious little guidance on the question of how to answer these questions. Section 4 of the FPA authorized the Commission to issue licenses "in the public interest." 49 Stat. 840, 16 U.S.C. § 797(a), 16 U.S.C.A. § 797(e). Section 10 of the FPA directed the Commission to license projects which are "best adapted to a comprehensive plan for improving or developing a waterway," which might included hydropower development or "other beneficial public uses, including recreational purposes ..." 49 Stat. 842, 16 U.S.C. § 803(a), 16 U.S.C.A. § 803(a). The task of balancing these various values was left entirely to the Commission. In order to fulfill this mission, the Commission faced the question of whether and how to license not only new proposed projects, but already-built hydroelectric facilities as well.

1. JURISDICTION

A hydroelectric project does not need the approval of the FERC unless it is located on a river over which the FERC has jurisdiction. A publicly-owned water authority in Fairfax County, Virginia, had built two dams on the Occuquan River to store water for public water supply. It included hydroelectric power generating facilities to supplement its own need for electricity to run its water pumping operations. The Authority did not think it needed to get a license from the FERC, but the FERC's Director of Hydropower Licensing disagreed. The Authority appealed his decision to the full Commission:

Fairfax County Water Authority

43 F.E.R.C. P 61,062 (1988).

By orders issued January 21, 1987 and March 16, 1987, the Director, Office of Hydropower Licensing (Director), determined that the Fairfax County Water Authority's (Authority) Upper and Lower Occoquan Projects, located on the Occoquan River in Fairfax County, Virginia, are required to be licensed pursuant to Section 23(b)(1) of the Federal Power Act, 16 U.S.C. § 817(1) (1982) (FPA). The Director concluded that the projects are located on a stretch of the Occoquan River that is navigable within the meaning of Section 3(8) of the FPA, 16 U.S.C. § 796(8). Accordingly, the orders required the Authority to file license applications for the Occoquan projects.

The Authority filed timely appeals of the January 21 and March 16 orders, arguing that the Director erred in concluding that the stretch of the Occoquan River where the projects are located is navigable. The Authority also claims that the projects do not affect the interests of interstate or foreign commerce. . . .

Section 23(b)(1) of the FPA would require licensing of the Occoquan projects if: (1) they are located on a navigable water of the United States; (2) they occupy lands of the United States; (3) they utilize surplus water or water power from a government dam; or (4) they are located on a body of water over which Congress has Commerce Clause jurisdiction, project construction occurred on or after August 26, 1935, and the projects affect the interests of interstate commerce. Since the Authority's projects do not occupy lands of the United States or utilize surplus water or water power from a government dam, whether the projects are required to be licensed depends on whether they are located on a navigable water or come within the scope of (4) above.

Navigability. Under Section 3(8) of the FPA[4], navigable waters are generally those streams which in their natural or improved condition are

---

4. Section 3(8) provides: "navigable waters" means those parts of streams or other bodies of water over which Congress has jurisdiction under its authority to regulate commerce used or suitable for use for the transportation of persons or property in interstate or foreign commerce, including any interrupting falls, shallows, or rapids compelling land carriage. *See United States v. Appalachian Elec. Power Co.*, 311 U.S. 377 (1940).

The Occoquan River rises in Loudoun, Fairfax, and Fauquier Counties and drains the upper part of Prince William County. It is formed by the junction, about a mile south of Brentsville, Virginia, of Broad Run and Cedar Run, and thence flows northeast to where it is joined by Bull Run and continues in a generally southeast direction for approximately 14 miles to the Potomac River. The Occoquan River crosses the fall-line[5] just before it reaches the town of Occoquan, which is the head of tidewater, and up to which there is a navigable depth of five feet at low tide and seven feet at high tide. A fall, now partially inundated by the dams of the Occoquan projects, begins approximately three miles above the head of tidewater and continues down to tide, falling about 80 feet in that distance. At its mouth, the Occoquan River is five miles wide. At the head of tide, approximately six to seven miles above, it narrows to 75 yards.

The Director relied on a 1938 Federal Power Commission Report on the Potomac River Basin to conclude that the Occoquan projects are located on a stretch of the Occoquan River that is navigable. The 1938 Report indicates, and the Authority agrees, that for six miles above its mouth the river is navigable. However, the Authority claims that the projects are located above the navigable tidal reach, which extends to the town of Occoquan just below the falls.

Staff inspection reveals that the upper project is located where the falls once existed, approximately one and one-half miles above the head of tidewater. Nevertheless, the falls are navigable waters if the river above the falls is navigable. *See Rochester Gas Elec. Corp. v. Fed. Power Comm'n*, 344 F.2d 594, 595 (2d Cir. 1965). However, the 1938 Report does not indicate any use of the river above the town of Occoquan for transportation of commerce, and additional research regarding this stretch has uncovered no substantial evidence to support a finding that the river, in the vicinity of the upper project, is navigable.

Effect on Interstate Commerce. The Occoquan River is a body of water that Congress has authority to regulate under the Commerce

---

with foreign nations and among the several States, and which either in their natural or improved condition notwithstanding interruptions between the navigable parts of such streams or waters by falls, shallows, or rapids compelling land carriage, are used or suitable for use for the transportation of persons or property in interstate or foreign commerce, including therein all such interrupting falls, shallows, or rapids, together with such other parts of streams as shall have been authorized by Congress for improvement by the United States or shall have been recommended to Congress for such improvement after investigation under its authority.

5.   The fall-line is an imaginary boundary line separating the middle and western watershed divisions from the eastern division, which extends from the coast to the head of tidewater and navigation. It marks the last considerable fall on the rivers. *See* United States Department of the Interior, Report on the Water Power of the United States, Middle–Atlantic Water–Shed 520 (1885).

Clause,[6] and project construction at the site occurred after 1935. Accordingly, a license is required to operate the Occoquan projects if they affect the interests of interstate or foreign commerce.

The Authority states that all of the energy from the Occoquan projects is used to serve its own power needs and that therefore the projects do not affect the interests of interstate commerce. The Authority claims in the alternative that, while it admittedly purchases less power from its supplier, Virginia Electric and Power Company ("VEPCO"), because of the projects' generation, any resultant effect on interstate commerce is too minimal to meet the "real and substantial" standard used in *City of Centralia v. FERC*, 661 F.2d 787 (9th Cir. 1981).

In *Federal Power Comm'n v. Union Elec. Co.*, 381 U.S. 90, 96 (1965), the Supreme Court interpreted Section 23(b)'s reference to "affecting the interests of interstate commerce," finding that Congress had invoked "its full authority over commerce, without qualification, to define what projects on non-navigable streams are required to be licensed." The Court held that the central purpose of the FPA to provide comprehensive control over uses of the nation's water resources would be more fully served if the Commission "considers the impact of the project on the full spectrum of commerce interests." *Id.* at 98, 101. Since Part I of the FPA thus embodies the full reach of the Commerce Clause, whether projects generate to transmit energy across state lines or feed into an interstate power system for distribution is not dispositive of the effect on interstate commerce issue. Rather, the relevant point of inquiry is the relationship between the activity to be regulated and interstate commerce. Thus, if a project on a Commerce Clause water with post–1935 construction affects any of the broad range of commerce clause interests, it is required to be licensed under Section 23(b)(1) of the FPA. Moreover, as noted by the Centralia court, *supra*, 661 F.2d at 789, even if the project itself does not substantially affect the interests of commerce, it can nevertheless be reached if it belongs to a class of projects whose activities affect interstate commerce, [and] a substantial effect can be measured by the cumulative effect of a class of activities. *See Wickard v. Filburn*, 317 U.S. 111 (1942).

The Authority operates the Occoquan projects to provide power generation for its water supply pumping station located in the town of Occoquan. The upper project contains two 500–kW synchronous generating units, and the lower project contains a single 350–kW synchronous generating unit. The generators' 4.16–kV terminals are continuously paralleled with the 4.16–kV incoming utility circuit from VEPCO's 34.5/4.16–kV, 16.2–MVA Aqua Substation. Direction of power flow over this utility circuit is always toward the project, since the project load always exceeds its generating capability. The magnitude of this flow varies, depending upon the relative levels of project generation and load. The respective estimated average annual output of the upper and lower projects is 4,320,000 kwh and

---

6. The Occoquan River is a tributary of the Potomac, a navigable river, and thus comes within the scope of the Commerce Clause. See *FPC v. Union Electric Co.*, 381 U.S. 90, 97 (1965).

1,296,000 kwh. The projects supply an estimated 24.29 percent of the Authority's needs on an annual basis. The remainder of the Authority's energy needs is met with purchases from VEPCO. VEPCO's system serves load in Virginia, North Carolina, and West Virginia, and is directly connected with Allegheny Power, Appalachian Power Company, Carolina Power and Light Company, and Potomac Electric Power Company.

The units within this interstate system are interlocked electromagnetically, and thus the actions of one unit within the system affect every other generating unit in the system. *See Federal Power Comm'n v. Florida Power & Light Co.,* 404 U.S. 453 (1972). . . . To the extent the projects do or do not generate, they affect the functioning of the interstate energy and thus interstate commerce, because they increase or decrease the amount of power that other resources must produce to keep the system balanced.

An interconnected project that generates to supply its own power needs, thereby displacing power that would otherwise be purchased from the interstate system, affects the operation of the system as does the project that generates to directly sell energy, because both affect the supply of and the demand for energy.

The foregoing demonstrates the effect of the Occoquan projects on electricity as a basic element of interstate commerce.

Since the projects are located on Commerce Clause waters, involve post–1935 construction, and affect the interests of interstate or foreign commerce, they are required to be licensed pursuant to Section 23(b)(1) of the FPA.

The Commission orders: (A)The appeals filed by the Fairfax County Water Authority on February 9, 1987, in Docket No. UL87–3–001, and on April 10, 1987, in Docket No. UL87–9–001, are denied. (B) Fairfax County Water Authority must file with the Secretary of the Commission, within 45 days of the date of this order, an expeditious schedule for submitting a license. . . . ■

NOTES AND COMMENTS

1. The definition of navigable water in the Federal Power Act is specific to that act only. The various statutory and judge-made definitions of navigability have created a long history of legal puzzles. *See generally* A. Dan Tarlock, Law of Water Rights and Resources § 9.03 (1995).

Federal jurisdiction over navigable waterways has evolved since the formation of our country. The distinction between navigable and non-navigable waterways first arose in a commerce clause context. The Commerce Clause "comprehends navigation, within the limits of every state in the Union; so far as that navigation may be, in any manner, connected with 'commerce with foreign nations, or among the several states, or with the Indian Tribes.'" *Gibbons v. Ogden,* 22 U.S. (19 Wheat.) 1, 197 (1824). For some time after this decision, federal policies dealt only with protection and enhancement of navigation, a power that was exercised often, usually to improve the navigable capacity of water bodies. The Report of the President's Water Resources Policy Commission, Vol. 3 Water Resources Law 87–91 (1950).

The first challenge to the definition of navigable waterways came with the effects that tidal movements had on navigability. Until 1851, inland lake and river systems were not considered navigable waterways. In 1851, the Supreme Court adopted "suitability for commercial navigation" as the test for federal jurisdiction. *The Propeller Genesee Chief v. Fitzhugh,* 53 U.S. (12 How.) 443 (1851). This test worked well for the larger bodies of water, but did not include smaller rivers and lakes. Several years later, the test changed to include rivers which are "navigable in fact. And they are in their ordinary condition as highways of commerce, over which trade and travel are or may be conducted in the customary modes of trade and travel over water." *The Daniel Ball,* 77 U.S. (10 Wall.) 557, 563 (1871).

The "navigation in fact" test is still used today, however it has been expanded by the Supreme Court. Federal jurisdiction was first extended to obstructions and diversions on non-navigable portions of navigable rivers. *United States v. Rio Grande Dam & Irrigation Co.,* 174 U.S. 690 (1899). Federal jurisdiction then extended to rivers that could be made navigable by "reasonable improvement." *United States v. Appalachian Elec. Power Co.,* 311 U.S. 377 (1940). Currently, courts must consider whether a river (1) is presently in use or suitable for use, or (2) was used or suitable for use in the past, or (3) could be made usable by reasonable improvements. *Rochester Gas and Elec. Corp. v. Fed. Power Comm'n,* 344 F.2d 594, 596 (2d Cir.), *cert. denied,* 382 U.S. 832 (1965). This is the controlling test for FERC jurisdiction.

The environmental movement of the 1960's created confusion in the definition of navigable waters. Environmentalists exerted pressure on the federal government to regulate the protection of shallow water bodies and wetlands. During this period, courts were split as to whether small streams were navigable or not. Those that denied federal jurisdiction did so if the parties could not produce substantial evidence of past commercial navigation or that navigation is possible by reasonable improvements. *United States v. Crow, Pope & Land Enters., Inc.,* 340 F. Supp. 25 (N.D. Ga. 1972). Other courts allowed federal jurisdiction if the river served commercial recreational purposes. *United States v. Underwood,* 344 F. Supp. 486 (M.D. Fla. 1972). Commerce Clause opinions were cited by courts for support that federal jurisdiction did not hinge upon a water body being navigable in fact. *Id.*

The definition of navigable water in the Clean Water Act codified the most recent of the courts' definitions. Navigable waters, as defined in the Clean Water Act, are "the Waters of the United States, including the territorial seas." Federal jurisdiction has been extended to small tributaries and associated groundwater, lagoons separated from the ocean, to land-locked lakes and associated wetlands. *See Quivera Mining Co. v. EPA,* 765 F.2d 126 (10th Cir. 1985); *Boone v. United States,* 944 F.2d 1489 (9th Cir. 1991); *United States v. Byrd,* 609 F.2d 1204 (7th Cir. 1979); *Slagle v.*

United States, 809 F. Supp. 704 (D. Minn. 1992). However, the United States Supreme Court placed new limits on the reach of federal jurisdiction in 2001 when it adopted a more restricted interpretation of the Clean Air Act definition, in *Solid Waste Agency of Cook County v. U.S. Army Corps of Engineers*, 531 U.S. 159 (2001), concluding that the definition did not cover isolated wetlands.

2. In *Federal Power Comm'n v. Florida Power & Light Co.*, cited by the FERC in the above opinion, the Supreme Court held that any electric system that is connected to a network of power lines that crosses state lines is subject to federal regulation pursuant to the interstate commerce clause. The power flow within state lines is subject to federal regulation if a utility is connected to an interstate grid, even if the utility does not transmit energy beyond the state's borders because the power has the potential to be in interstate commerce. *Id.* This ruling was reaffirmed in *New England Power Co. v. New Hampshire*, 455 U.S. 331 (1982), where the court held that FERC has regulatory jurisdiction over transmission service performed by a utility connected to the interstate network. Virtually all electric systems are so connected, other than those in Hawaii, Alaska and arguably Texas. Congress, however, has never chosen to exercise fully the federal regulatory power, so by far the largest share of the regulation of the electric industry remains with the state governments. See Chapter 10.

2. DEVELOPMENT VS. THE ENVIRONMENT

Since the beginning of the hydro licensing program, the licensing process has provoked disputes over environmental issues. Conservation organizations, Indian tribes, governmental agencies, and others raised concerns about the impacts of hydro projects on fisheries and recreation long before the advent of the modern environmental movement, and the FERC imposed conditions on project licenses in response to these concerns. As early as 1953, the Commission rejected a license application for a proposed project on environmental grounds. *In the Matter of Namekagon Hydro Company*, 12 F.P.C. 203 (1953), *aff'd* 216 F.2d 509 (7th Cir. 1954). The Commission denied Namekagon's application for a license because its project would be located on a river with special and unique scenic and recreational values and explicitly acknowledged that environmental amenities can sometimes trump development interests in the licensing process.

However, application denials have been the exception rather than the rule, and by the 1960s environmental groups were lamenting the Commission's apparent lack of attention to environmental values. In 1963 one commissioner took his colleagues to task in an order issuing a license for an existing project:

> "We should not lose sight of our obligation to properly utilize and conserve our natural resources.... For an agency merely to say we have no objection ... is not the searching type of review I consider necessary or appropriate. Would recreation be increased, would stream flow regulation be improved, would stream pollution be lessened, would fish runs [*sic*] be restored, would fish and wildlife be benefited by

either the removal of the project or conversion to nonpower uses? These questions and similar ones should be asked each time an applicant for a constructed project comes before us.''

See *S.C. Electric & Gas Co.*, 30 F.P.C. 1338, at 1342–43 (1963) (dissenting opinion of Commissioner Ross).

Of course, hydroelectric projects have a wide variety of environmental impacts on project sites in addition to aesthetic and recreational impacts. The construction of dams disrupts migratory fish patterns: fish cannot survive downstream migration either over a dam or through a turbine, and the dam completely blocks upstream migration. Fish passage facilities like fish ladders or so-called "trap and truck" methods restore only a fraction of the unimpeded migration. The replacement of moving water with a warmer, still water reservoir behind the dam and a dewatered or reduced flow stretch of river between the dam and the tailrace also disrupts and changes fisheries. Unless the project is operated in "run of river" mode, such that the reservoir height stays constant and downstream flows (through the generators and over the dam) always equal natural inflows from upstream, shifts in reservoir height can damage wetland habitats adjacent to the reservoir. The creation and operation of a hydro project can affect dissolved oxygen levels and other indices of water quality in the river. By the 1960s advances in the science of ecology and the embryonic national environmental movement had heightened concerns about impacts like these, prompting Commissioner's Ross's objections.

Environmental groups were particularly unhappy with a special category of hydroelectric project called "pumped storage" projects. These projects did not require falling water to generate head to produce power; rather, pumped storage projects created new reservoirs at uphill locations near a body of water, so that power could be pumped up to the reservoir when electricity demand was low (and so electricity was plentiful and cheap), and released back downhill through the turbines to the river or lake when electricity demand was high (and so electricity was scarce and valuable). These pumped storage projects were energy inefficient in that they consumed more power (pumping water uphill to the reservoir) than they generated, but they made economic sense because the price difference between peak power and nonpeak power more than compensated for this energy inefficiency. Environmentalists' dissatisfaction with one such pumped storage project led to the D.C. Circuit's landmark *Scenic Hudson* decision.

Scenic Hudson Preservation Conference v. Federal Power Commission

354 F.2d 608 (D.C. Cir. 1965).

■ HAYS, CIRCUIT JUDGE. In this proceeding the petitioners . . . Scenic Hudson Preservation Conference, an unincorporated association consisting of a number of non-profit, conservationist organizations . . . ask us . . . to set aside ... an order of March 9, 1965 granting a license to the intervener, the Consolidated Edison Company of New York, Inc., to construct a pumped storage hydroelectric project on the west side of the Hudson River at Storm King Mountain in Cornwall, New York ...

A pumped storage plant generates electric energy for use during peak load periods, using hydroelectric units driven by water from a headwater pool or reservoir. The contemplated Storm King project would be the largest of its kind in the world. Consolidated Edison has estimated its cost, including transmission facilities, at $162,000,000. The project would consist of three major components, a storage reservoir, a powerhouse, and transmission lines. The storage reservoir, located over a thousand feet above the powerhouse, is to be connected to the powerhouse, located on the river front, by a tunnel 40 feet in diameter. The powerhouse, which is both a pumping and generating station, would be 800 feet long and contain eight pump generators.

Transmission lines would run under the Hudson to the east bank and then underground for 1.6 miles to a switching station which Consolidated Edison would build at Nelsonville in the Town of Philipstown. Thereafter, overhead transmission lines would be placed on towers 100 to 150 feet high and these would require a path up to 125 feet wide through Westchester and Putnam Counties for a distance of some 25 miles until they reached Consolidated Edison's main connections with New York City.

During slack periods Consolidated Edison's conventional steam plants in New York City would provide electric power for the pumps at Storm King to force water up the mountain, through the tunnel, and into the upper reservoir. In peak periods water would be released to rush down the mountain and power the generators. Three kilowatts of power generated in New York City would be necessary to obtain two kilowatts from the Cornwall installation. ...

The Storm King project has aroused grave concern among conservationist groups, adversely affected municipalities and various state and federal legislative units and administrative agencies.

To be licensed by the Commission a prospective project must meet the statutory test of being "best adapted to a comprehensive plan for improving or developing a waterway," Federal Power Act § 10(a), 16 U.S.C. § 803(a). ...

Section 10(a) of the Federal Power Act, 16 U.S.C. § 803(a), reads:

"§ 803. Conditions of license generally.

All licenses issued under sections 792, 793, 795–818, and 820–823 of this title shall be on the following conditions:

... (a) That the project adopted, * * * shall be such as in the judgment of the Commission *will be best adapted to a comprehensive plan for improving or developing a waterway or waterways for the use or benefit of interstate or foreign commerce, for the improvement and utilization* [**12] *of water-power development, and for other beneficial* *public uses, including recreational purposes*; and if necessary in order to secure such plan the Commission shall have authority to require the modification of any project and of the plans and specifications of the project works before approval." (Emphasis added.)

"Recreational purposes" are expressly included among the beneficial public uses to which the statute refers. The phrase undoubtedly encompasses the conservation of natural resources, the maintenance of natural beauty, and the preservation of historic sites. n10 *See Namekagon Hydro Co. v. Fed. Power Comm'n*, 216 F.2d 509, 511–512 (7th Cir. 1954). All of these "beneficial uses," the Supreme Court has observed, "while unregulated, might well be contradictory rather than harmonious." In licensing a project, it is the duty of the Federal Power Commission properly to weigh each factor. . . .

The Commission in its opinion recognized that in connection with granting a license to Consolidated Edison it "must compare the Cornwall project with any alternatives that are available." There is no doubt that the Commission is under a statutory duty to give full consideration to alternative plans. . . .

On January 7, 1965 the testimony of Mr. Alexander Lurkis, as to the feasibility of an alternative to the project, the use of gas turbines, was offered to the Commission by Hilltop Cooperative of Queens, a taxpayer and consumer group. The petition to intervene and present this new evidence was rejected on January 13, 1965 as not "timely." It was more than two months after the offer of this testimony, on March 9, 1965, that the Commission issued a license to Consolidated Edison. When Mr. Lurkis's testimony was subsequently reoffered by the petitioners on April 8, 1965, it was rejected because it represented "at best" a "disagreement between experts." On the other hand, we have found in the record no meaningful evidence which contradicts the proffered testimony supporting the gas turbine alternative. . . .

Mr. Lurkis's analysis was based on an intensive study of the Consolidated Edison system, and of its peaking needs projected year by year over a fifteen year period. He was prepared to make an economic comparison of a gas turbine system (including capital and fuel operating costs) and the Storm King pumped storage plant. Moreover, he was prepared to answer Consolidated Edison's objections to gas turbines . . .

Aside from self-serving general statements by officials of Consolidated Edison, the only testimony in the record bearing on the gas turbine alternative was offered by Ellery R. Fosdick. Fosdick's hastily prepared presentation considered turbines driven by steam and liquid fuel as well as gas; his direct testimony occupied less than ten pages of the record. n18 Fosdick's testimony was too scanty to meet the requirement of a full consideration of alternatives. Indeed, under the circumstances, we must conclude that there was no significant attempt to develop evidence as to the gas turbine alternative; at least, there is no such evidence in the record. . . .

It is not our present function to evaluate this evidence. Our focus is upon the action of the Commission. The fact that Lurkis's testimony was originally offered by a non-petitioner, Hilltop Cooperative, is irrelevant. A party acting as a "private attorney general" can raise issues that are not personal to it. Especially in a case of this type, where public interest and concern is so great, the Commission's refusal to receive the Lurkis testimony, as well as proffered information on fish protection devices and underground transmission facilities, a disregard of the statute and of judicial mandates instructing the Commission to probe all feasible alternatives. . . . .

The Federal Power Commission argues that having intervened "petitioners cannot impose an affirmative burden on the Commission." But, as we have pointed out, Congress gave the Federal Power Commission a specific planning responsibility. See Federal Power Act § 10(a), 16 U.S.C. § 803(a). The totality of a project's immediate and long-range effects, and not merely the engineering and navigation aspects, are to be considered in a licensing proceeding. . . .

In this case, as in many others, the Commission has claimed to be the representative of the public interest. This role does not permit it to act as an umpire blandly calling balls and strikes for adversaries appearing before it; the right of the public must receive active and affirmative protection at the hands of the Commission.

This court cannot and should not attempt to substitute its judgment for that of the Commission. But we must decide whether the Commission has correctly discharged its duties, including the proper fulfillment of its planning function in deciding that the "licensing of the project would be in the overall public interest." The Commission must see to it that the record is complete. The Commission has an affirmative duty to inquire into and consider all relevant facts. . . .

In addition to the Commission's failure to receive or develop evidence concerning the gas turbine alternative, there are other instances where the Commission should have acted affirmatively in order to make a complete record. . . .

[The court found that the Commission had ignored or excluded evidence on fisheries impacts and the availability of power for purchase from other utilities as well.]

On remand, the Commission should take the whole fisheries question into consideration before deciding whether the Storm King project is to be licensed.

The Commission should reexamine all questions on which we have found the record insufficient and all related matters. The Commission's renewed proceedings must include as a basic concern the preservation of natural beauty and of national historic shrines, keeping in mind that, in our affluent society, the cost of a project is only one of several factors to be considered. The record as it comes to us fails markedly to make out a case for the Storm King project on, among other matters, costs, public convenience and necessity, and absence of reasonable alternatives. Of course, the Commission should make every effort to expedite the new proceedings.

Petitioners' application, pursuant to Federal Power Act § 313(b), 16 U.S.C. § 825l(b), to adduce additional evidence concerning alternatives to the Storm King project and the cost and practicality of underground transmission facilities is granted.■

NOTES AND COMMENT

1. Does the *Scenic Hudson* decision force the Commission to accede to the demands of environmental groups? Does it require the Commission to strike the balance between development and environment in favor of the environment? The subsequent history of the case offers some insight into these questions. After the court remanded the case back to the FPC, it issued a license to Consolidated Edison once again. However, changes in project economics killed the project before it was ever built. While the Commission did license of number of pumped storage projects prior to the 1980s, pumped storage projects have fallen out of favor with the Commission and developers alike.

2. The *Scenic Hudson* case provided a template for the National Environmental Policy Act ("NEPA"), 42 U.S.C. § 4331 *et seq.*, which imposed on all federal agencies, including the FERC, the obligation to review the environmental impacts of actions they propose to undertake or approve before undertaking or approving such actions. NEPA requires the preparation of an Environmental Impact Statement ("EIS") for any "major federal action significantly affecting the quality of the human environment." NEPA § 102(c); 42 U.S.C. § 4332(c) (1998). If the agency determines that an EIS is unnecessary, a "Finding of No Significant Impact" ("FONSI") is prepared giving reasons for this conclusion. At this point, no further action is taken under NEPA. The great majority of agency decisions on NEPA compliance conclude that an EIS is not necessary.[7] In practice, the FERC

---

7. If an EIS is necessary, the agency will publish a "notice of intent" to prepare and EIS. The agency will also note the scope of the EIS and the important issues that will be addressed. A draft EIS is then prepared, giving complete analysis of the project, alternatives, actions to mitigate adverse effects, and possible environmental consequences. Upon completion, a draft EIS must be made available for public comment. Public comments must be included in the record of the final agency decision. The agency must respond to public comments and modify the draft if necessary, and the final EIS is then prepared. Final agency actions are subject to judicial review, usually to review the decision not to prepare an EIS or whether the procedural requirements of NEPA have been met. An EIS must contain several key components. Alternatives to the proposed action must be considered. § 102(2)(C)(iii), 42 U.S.C. § 4332(2)(C)(iii); § 102(2)(E), 42 U.S.C. § 4332(2)(E). Only reasonable alternatives need be identified. These must include a discussion of the "no action" alternative, reasonable alternatives that would eliminate or lessen the need for the proposed action, and alternatives that would mitigate the environmental impacts of the proposed action. Sometimes, there is inadequate scientific information about the environmental effects of a proposed action. At the very least, the agency must disclose what information is lacking. An agency may choose to prepare a "worst case analysis" (EA), as a way of dealing with the unknown. An agency may

prepares EISs in connection with very few hydroelectric licensing proceedings. See David B. Spence, Agency Discretion and the Dynamics of Procedural Reform, 59 Pub. Admin. Rev.425 (1999). However, the FERC routinely prepares "environmental assessments" a shorter and less procedurally cumbersome analysis of environmental impacts for proposed hydro projects. Nevertheless, NEPA, like the *Scenic Hudson* decision, merely requires the FERC to analyze environmental impacts, not to avoid them.

3.   In the *Fairfax Water Authority* case, discussed *supra* in section C.1 of this chapter, the FERC followed its determination of jurisdiction over the project with a licensing order that included the requisite NEPA review. *Fairfax County Water Authority,* 54 F.E.R.C. ¶ 62,142 (1991). The Water Authority hired a consultant to prepare a draft EA which was submitted to the FERC in the hope that the FERC would adopt it and make a Finding of No Significant Impact (FONSI). The great majority of NEPA compliance actions are handled in this way. *See* Rodgers, *supra,* at 893–896. Nowadays, the FERC routinely publishes the EA as an appendix to its licensing orders, and the EA often contains a fairly lengthy and systematic analysis of environmental issues, though not nearly as lengthy as an EIS.

4.   One reason why environmental issues have proven so contentious in the hydropower licensing process for so long is that the FERC has an unusual amount of decision-making autonomy over environmental issues, and groups opposing hydro development have unusually little legal recourse outside of the FERC licensing process. This is due in part to U.S. Supreme Court's conclusion that the Federal Power Act's broad grant of authority to the FERC preempts of state and local environmental laws (by operation of the Supremacy Clause). See *First Iowa Hydro–Elec. Coop. v. Florida Power Comm'n,* 328 U.S. 152 (1946); and *California v. FERC,* 495 U.S. 490 (1990). While state and local environmental agencies routinely participate in the licensing process (and private interests may intervene as well), they cannot force the FERC to adopt their point of view.[8]

5.   This unique concentration of environmental policy-making authority in the hands of a single agency has made for persistent conflict over environmental issues in the licensing process. After the 1965 *Scenic Hudson* decision, politicians (particularly those in Congress) attempted to influence the FERC's resolution of environmental issues in a variety of ways. Statutes like NEPA in 1970, the 1968 Wild and Scenic Rivers Act, 16 U.S.C. § 1271 *et seq.,* and the 1972 Clean Water Act, 33 U.S.C. § 1251 *et seq.,* were aimed at least partly at the FERC and were intended to create more environmentally protective agency decisions and policies. The Wild and Scenic Rivers Act of 1968 prohibited hydroelectric development at waterways designated by Congress as "wild or scenic" under the statute. That is,

---

also be required to prepare a supplemental EIS in the event that new information becomes available or the design of the proposal changes.

   8. As noted, federal agencies have more leverage by way of Section 4 of the Federal Power Act, but that section grants no such leverage to state and local agencies. State environmental agencies have one source of leverage on water quality issues in Section 401 of the Clean Water Act, discussed *infra.*

the statute established a system for removing the FERC's decision-making authority over projects on river segments designated by Congress as environmentally sensitive. However, designation of river segments as "wild" or "scenic" required Congressional action, and could not be accomplished by agencies or environmental groups without this legislative help.

6. The previously-mentioned Public Utility Regulatory Policies Act of 1978 ("PURPA"), 16 U.S.C. § 2601 *et seq.* sparked an explosion of hydroelectric licensing activity in the 1980s by providing financial incentives for the development of alternative sources of energy, including hydro power, by nonutility developers. Specifically, the statute required electric utilities to purchase power from independently owned hydroelectric (and other) power producers at full "avoided cost" rates. As a result of this statute, the FERC began to process hundreds of license applications for much smaller hydroelectric projects from a new class of applicants. Prior to the 1980s, most FERC licensees used hydroelectric power either to service retail customers or for on-site industrial operations. The former category included investor-owned and state or municipal utilities; the latter category comprised mostly paper and textile mills. The passage of PURPA introduced independent entrepreneurs into the licensing mix. Now many small hydroelectric projects are owned and operated by merchant generating companies who neither use the power they generate, nor sell it at retail.

D. THE CHANGING LANDSCAPE OF HYDROELECTRIC DEVELOPMENT

1. THE ENVIRONMENT VS. DEVELOPMENT BALANCE TODAY

If anything, the increased licensing activity spurred by PURPA's passage only accelerated conflict over environmental issues. To environmental groups, the *Namekagon* and *Scenic Hudson* decisions were the exceptions that proved the rule: namely, that the FERC was insufficiently attentive to environmental concerns in its licensing decisions. They pressed Congress to require FERC to give more weight to environmental concerns in its licensing decisions. Meanwhile, during the 1990s hundreds of existing hydroelectric licenses were set to expire, which would require relicensing proceedings. Existing licensees urged Congress to abolish the municipal preference at relicensing, fearing that the municipal preference would force licenses (and projects) to change hands as municipalities simply copied licensees'project plans and submitted those plans as their own license applications during the relicensing proceedings. These twin desires set the stage for the legislative bargain that produced the Electric Consumers Protection Act of 1986 ("ECPA"), Pub. L. 99–495, amending 16 U.S.C. § 791 *et seq.* (1986).

ECPA. ECPA abolished the municipal preference at relicensing, ensuring that competing proposals would have to be superior to the incumbent's proposal in order to secure the new license. At the same time, ECPA added teeth to the environmental provisions of the FPA's previously-vague licensing standards, admonishing the FERC to "give equal consideration" not only to "power and development purposes" but "energy conservation, ... fish and wildlife ... recreational opportunities, and the preservation of other aspects of environmental quality." 16 U.S.C. § 797(e). ECPA also added two important procedural requirements to the licensing process, both of which were designed to benefit environmental interests. One sought to force FERC to consider the impacts of multiple dams on a single river basin by requiring the use of a "cumulative impact assessment procedure" (CIAP) in such situations. See FERC's Cluster Impact Assessment Procedure (CIAP), 18 C.F.R. § 2.23 (1998), and 50 Fed. Reg. 3385 (1985). The other requirement, found in section 10(j) of the statute, required FERC to accept and include in hydroelectric licenses any conditions recommended by state or federal "resource agencies" (including environmental regulatory agencies) or to explain in writing why it was rejecting the recommended conditions. That section states, in pertinent part:

> All licenses issued under this subchapter shall be on the following conditions: ... (j) ... *each license issued under this subchapter shall include conditions for protection, mitigation, and enhancement [of fish and wildlife].... Such conditions shall be based on recommendations received ... from the National Marine Fisheries Service, the United States Fish and Wildlife Service, and State fish and wildlife agencies.* Whenever the Commission believes that any [such] recommendation ... may be inconsistent with the purposes and requirements of ... applicable law, the Commission and the agencies shall attempt to resolve any such inconsistency, giving due weight to the recommendations, expertise, and statutory responsibilities of such agencies. If, after such attempt, the commission does not adopt in whole or in part a recommendation of any such agency, the commission shall publish each of the following findings (together with a statement of the basis for each of the findings): (A) A finding that adoption of such recommendation is inconsistent with the purposes and requirements of this subchapter or with other applicable provisions of law. (B) A finding that the conditions selected by the commission comply with the requirements of [the statute].

16 U.S.C. § 803(j) (1998) (emphasis added). Note that while Section 10(j) does not impose a mandatory requirement of the kind found in Section 4 of the statute, it does increase the transaction costs of ignoring the wishes of environmental agencies in the licensing process. It is not clear whether Section 10(j) has made the FERC any more receptive to environmental concerns. One study of the FERC's licensing decisions concludes that the passage of ECPA did not produce any durable change in the FERC's decision-making on environmental issues. See David B. Spence, Managing Delegation Ex Ante: Using Law to Steer Administrative Agencies, 28 J. Legal Stud. 413 (1999). On the other hand, it may have had an impact on relicensing decisions. See discussion of relicensing issues, infra, at § D.2. As for the ECPA-added requirement that the FERC consider "not only" development concerns but environmental concerns as well, both the FERC and the courts have interpreted the language as merely procedural,

rejecting the notion that environmental concerns be accorded any particular weight. *See, e.g.,* U.S. Dept. of the Interior v. FERC, 952 F.2d 538 (D.C. Cir. 1992).

The "Integrated" Licensing Process. As a practical matter, applicants for hydroelectric licenses are required by the FERC to put a great deal of effort into addressing potential environmental concerns prior to filing their license applications. The primary mechanisms by which this occurs are the FERC's pre-filing consultation requirements and NEPA. Under the pre-filing consultation process, prospective license applicants are required to seek input on their project plans from local, state and federal resource agencies, and to incorporate responses to those agencies' concerns in their project proposals. Indeed, failure to do so can result in the FERC's refusal to accept the license application for processing. Once the application is accepted, federal resource agencies retain significant leverage over the FERC's consideration of environmental issues by virtue of Section 4 of the FPA (described above). Furthermore, NEPA requires the FERC to prepare an EA or EIS for each project proposal, guaranteeing that, at a minimum, the FERC must do as the *Scenic Hudson* court directed it to do, namely, consider the environmental impacts of the proposed project.

In response to concerns about the large transaction costs associated with these review processes, the FERC issued in July of 2003 a rule establishing its so-called "Integrated Licensing Process" ("ILP"). See Federal Energy Regulatory Commission, Hydroelectric Licensing Under the Federal Power Act, 104 FERC ¶ 61,109 (July 23, 2003), 68 Fed. Reg. 51069 (August 25, 2003). After July 25, 2005, ILP becomes the default licensing process under the FERC's rules. The ILP tries to streamline the licensing process by permitting the pre-filing consultation process, and the early stages of NEPA review (called the "scoping" process) to occur concurrently rather than sequentially. The ILP applies to both licensing and relicensing applications, and is outlines at 18 C.F.R. Part 5. At the heart of the process are (a) the required pre-application notification of all parties potentially affected by the proposed project, including federal resource agencies, described at 18 C.F.R. § 5.5, and (b) the circulation of the "pre-application document," described at 18 C.F.R. § 5.6:

§ 5.5   Notification of intent.

(b) *Requirement to Notify.* . . . a potential license applicant must file with the Commission . . . an original and eight copies of a letter that contains the following information:

(1) The potential applicant or existing licensee's name and address.

(2) The project number, if any.

(3) The license expiration date, if any.

(4) An unequivocal statement of the potential applicant's intention to file an application for an original license, or, in the case of an existing licensee, to file or not to file an application for a new or subsequent license.

(5) The type of principal project works licensed, if any, such as dam and reservoir, powerhouse, or transmission lines.

(6) The location of the project by state, county, and stream, and, when appropriate, by city or nearby city.

(7) The installed plant capacity, if any.

(8) The names and mailing addresses of:

(i) Every county in which any part of the project is located, and in which any Federal facility that is used or to be used by the project is located;

(ii) Every city, town, or similar political subdivision;

(A) In which any part of the project is or is to be located and any Federal facility that is or is to be used by the project is located, or

(B) That has a population of 5,000 or more people and is located within 15 miles of the existing or proposed project dam;

(iii) Every irrigation district, drainage district, or similar special purpose political subdivision:

(A) In which any part of the project is or is proposed to be located and any Federal facility that is or is proposed to be used by the project is located; or

(B) That owns, operates, maintains, or uses any project facility or any Federal facility that is or is proposed to be used by the project;

(iv) Every other political subdivision in the general area of the project or proposed project that there is reason to believe would be likely to be interested in, or affected by, the notification; and

(v) Affected Indian tribes.

§ 5.6   Pre–Application document.

(a) *Pre-Application Document.* (1) Simultaneously with the filing of its notification of intent to seek a license as provided for in § 5.5, ... a potential applicant for a license ... must file with the Commission and original and eight copies and distribute to the appropriate Federal, state, and interstate resource agencies, Indian tribes, local governments, and members of the public likely to be interested in the proceeding, the Pre–Application Document provided for in this section. . . .

(b) *Purpose of Pre–Application Document.*

(1) The Pre–Application document provides the Commission and the entities identified in paragraph (a) of this section with existing information relevant to the project proposal. . . . ■

The notice and circulation of the pre-application document set in motion a process of give and take between the applicant, the FERC staff, and the commenting agencies. The recipients of the pre-application document must submit comments on the document within a specified period of time. These comments, in turn, are used by the FERC staff uses to initiate the environmental assessment (scoping) process and by the applicant to construct a "study plan" according to which it will provide more detailed information about the environmental impacts of its proposal. The product of these efforts is a "preliminary licensing proposal" which, if satisfactory, will lead, finally, to the submission of the license application to the FERC. Once the application has been accepted, interested parties may intervene before the FERC to contest environmental or other issues. The FERC will then resolve those disputes before making its final decision whether to issue a license, and if so, under what conditions.

401 Certification. While the *First Iowa* principle reserves for the FERC the lion's share of authority to balance development interests against the environmental concerns raised by states, municipalities and interest groups, states do have one source of leverage in the process: namely, Section 401 of the Clean Water Act. Section 401 requires "any applicant for a Federal license or permit" to secure from the appropriate state environmental agency a "certification ... that any ... discharge [from the project] will comply with the [the Clean Water Act]." 33 U.S.C. § 1341(a). Hydroelectric projects are not required to secure permits under the Clean Water Act because they do not "add" pollutants to waterways. *See infra* Chapter 5. One might suspect, then, that securing a so-called "401 certification" under this section might be a relatively straightforward matter. However, over the years state environmental agencies lacking any other means of exerting influence in the hydroelectric licensing process have used the 401 certification process to attempt to extract concessions from license applicants. Throughout the 1980s and early 1990s these attempts were unsuccessful. Courts interpreted the 401 certification requirement as one aimed only at ensuring that the hydroelectric project in question would not impair water quality, narrowly defined, and overturned attempts by state environmental agencies to impose broader environmental protection conditions in 401 certificates. *See e.g.*, In the Matter of Niagara Mohawk Power Corp. v. New York State Dep't of Environmental Conservation, *82 N.Y.2d 191, 624 N.E.2d 146, 604 N.Y.S.2d 18 (1993). However, in 1994 the Supreme Court broadened the meaning of the 401 certification process in* PUD No. 1 of Jefferson County v. Washington Department of Ecology, *114 S.Ct. 1900, 1909 (1994).*

Petitioners in *PUD No. 1,* applicants for a license to build a hydroelectric project, sought a 401 certificate from the Washington Department of Ecology ("DEQ"). The DEQ issued a certification requiring that the petitioners maintain a minimum stream flow in order to protect fisheries in the areas to be affected by the dam. Petitioners argued that under the CWA the state only had the authority to regulate discharges, not stream flow. The Court disagreed with this position, quoting 401(d) of the CWA, which provides "any certification shall set forth 'any effluent limitations and

other limitations ... necessary to assure that any applicant' will comply
with various provisions of the Act and appropriate state law requirements."
The Court found that this section of the CWA applies to the applicant, not
to the particular discharge, which allows the state to impose other limitations as needed. *PUD No. 1 v. Washington Department of Ecology,* 114 S.Ct.
1900, 1909 (1994). Said the Court:

> "In many cases, water quantity is closely related to water quality; a
> sufficient lowering of the water quantity in a body of water could
> destroy all of its designated uses, be it for drinking water, recreation,
> navigation or, as here, as a fishery. In any event, there is recognition in
> the Clean Water Act itself that reduced stream flow, *i.e.*, diminishment
> of water quantity, can constitute water pollution. First, the Act's
> definition of pollution as 'the man-made or man induced alteration of
> the chemical, physical, biological, and radiological integrity of the
> water' encompasses the effects of reduced water quantity. 33 U.S.C.
> § 1362(19). This broad conception of pollution—one which expressly
> evinces Congress' concern with the physical and biological integrity of
> water—refutes petitioners' assertion that the Act draws a sharp dis-
> tinction between the regulation of water 'quantity' and water 'quality.'
> Moreover, § 304 of the Act expressly recognizes that water 'pollution'
> may result from 'changes in the movement, flow, or circulation of any
> navigable waters ..., including changes caused by the construction of
> dams.' 33 U.S.C. § 1314(f). This concern with the flowage effects of
> dams and other diversions is also embodied in EPA regulations, which
> expressly require existing dams to be operated to attain designated
> uses. 40 C.F.R. § 131.10(g)(4) (1992)."

The Court concluded that minimum stream flow requirements were acceptable state water quality standards. The result was to substantially increase
the power of the states in hydropower licensing.

Following that decision, the Second Circuit Court of Appeals had
occasion to consider some limits imposed in a 401 certificate by the State of
Vermont on certain hydropower projects in that state that were on FERC's
licensing agenda.

American Rivers, Inc. v. FERC

129 F.3d 99 (2d Cir. 1997).

■ WALKER, J. Petitioners, the State of Vermont and American Rivers, Inc.,
seek review of several orders issued by the Federal Energy Regulatory
Commission ("FERC" or "Commission") licensing six hydropower projects
located on rivers within the State of Vermont. The dispute surrounds (1)
the authority of the State under § 401 of the Clean Water Act ("CWA"), 33
U.S.C. § 1341, to certify—prior to the issuance of a federal license—that
such projects will comply with federal and state water quality standards
and (2) the appropriate route for review of a state's certification decisions.
The Commission argues that, when it determines that a state has exceeded
the scope of its authority under § 401 in imposing certain pre-license

conditions, it may refuse to include the ultra vires conditions in its license as it did in each of the proceedings at issue.

Petitioners contend that the Commission is bound by the language of § 401 to incorporate all state-imposed certification conditions into hydropower licenses and that the legality of such conditions can only be challenged by the licensee in a court of appropriate jurisdiction. We agree with petitioners and, thus, grant the petition for review, vacate the Commission's orders, and remand.

The principal order under review in this proceeding arises from the efforts of the Tunbridge Mill Corporation ("Tunbridge") to obtain a license from FERC for the operation of a small hydroelectric facility on the First Branch of the White River in Orange County, Vermont, restoring an historic mill site in Tunbridge Village. Pursuant to § 401(a)(1) of the CWA, 33 U.S.C. § 1341(a)(1), an applicant for a federal license for any activity that may result in a discharge into the navigable waters of the United States must apply for a certification from the state in which the discharge originates (or will originate) that the licensed activity will comply with state and federal water quality standards. *See P.U.D. No. 1 of Jefferson County v. Washington Dep't of Ecology*, 511 U.S. 700 (1994). Such certifications, in accordance with § 401(d), 33 U.S.C. § 1341(d), shall

> set forth any effluent limitations and other limitations, and monitoring requirements necessary to assure that any applicant for a Federal license or permit will comply with any applicable effluent limitations and other limitations, under section 1311 or 1312 of this title, standard of performance under section 1316 of this title, or prohibition, effluent standard, or pretreatment standard under section 1317 of this title, and with any other appropriate requirement of State law set forth in such certification. . . .

The CWA further provides that the state certification "shall become a condition on any Federal license or permit subject to the provisions of this section." *Id.*

The [Vermont natural resources agency] issued a draft certification on September 18, 1991, for public notice and comment in compliance with § 401(a)(1), 33 U.S.C. § 1341(a)(1), and Vermont law. A week later, on September 25, 1991, the certification was issued. No one challenged the ruling through the state's process of administrative and judicial review, and thus the certification became final fifteen days later. *See* 10 Vt. Stat. Ann. § 1024(a).

As issued, the certification contained eighteen conditions (designated by letters "A" through "R"), three of which, P, J, and L, are relevant for our purposes. Condition P reserves the right in Vermont to amend (or "reopen") the certification when appropriate. Condition J requires Tunbridge to submit to the state for review and approval any plans for significant changes to the project. Finally, condition L requires Tunbridge to seek clearance from the state before commencing construction so that the state may ensure that plans are in place to control erosion and manage water flows.

Certificate in hand, Tunbridge sought a license from FERC, which is vested with authority under 4(e) of the Federal Power Act ("FPA"), 16 U.S.C. § 797(e), to issue licenses for "the development, transmission, and utilization of power across, along, from, or in any of the streams or other bodies of water over which Congress has jurisdiction...." FERC may issue such licenses "whenever the contemplated improvement is, in the judgment of the Commission, desirable and justified in the public interest," *id.*, and "best adapted to a comprehensive plan ... for the improvement and utilization of water-power development, for the adequate protection, mitigation, and enhancement of fish and wildlife ..., and for other beneficial public uses," 16 U.S.C. § 803(a)(1).

On July 15, 1994, FERC ... granted Tunbridge a 40–year license "to construct, operate, and maintain the Tunbridge Mill Project." However, ... FERC found that conditions P, J, and L were beyond the scope of Vermont's authority under the CWA. Accordingly, FERC refused to incorporate them into the Tunbridge license. Vermont and American Rivers now seek review in this court of the Commission's determination.

Prior to Tunbridge Mill, FERC had held that it was required by § 401 to include in its licenses all conditions imposed by a state in its certifications notwithstanding the Commission's view that the conditions were beyond a state's authority under § 401.

In Tunbridge Mill, however, the Commission reversed field, finding that "to the extent that states include conditions that are unrelated to water quality, these conditions are beyond the scope of Section 401 and are thus unlawful." "We conclude that we have the authority to determine that such conditions do not become terms and conditions of the licenses we issue." *Id.* The Commission reasoned, in part: "We believe that, in light of Congress' determination that the Commission should have the paramount role in hydropower licensing process, whether certain state conditions are outside the scope of Section 401(d) is a federal question to be answered by the Commission."

The principal dispute between petitioners and the Commission in this case surrounds the relative scope of authority of the states and the Commission under the CWA and the FPA. Petitioners' contention is straightforward, resting on statutory language. In their view, the plain language of § 401(d) indicates that FERC has no authority to review and reject the substance of a state certification or the conditions contained therein and must incorporate into its licenses the conditions as they appear in state certifications. FERC disagrees, arguing that the language of § 401(d) is not as clear as petitioners would have it. Rather, FERC contends, it is bound to accede only to those conditions that are within a state's authority under § 401, that is, conditions that are reasonably related to water quality and that otherwise conform to the dictates of § 401. The Commission also argues that without the authority to reject state-imposed § 401 conditions its Congressionally mandated role under the FPA of ensuring comprehensive planning and development of hydro-power would be undermined.

The Clean Water Act. Before considering the Commission's conten-tions regarding the CWA, we note that FERC's interpretation of § 401, or any other provision of the CWA, receives no judicial deference under the doctrine of Chevron USA, Inc. v. Natural Resources Defense Council, 467 U.S. 837 (1984), because the Commission is not Congressionally authorized to administer the CWA. *See* 33 U.S.C. § 1251(d) ("Except as otherwise expressly provided in this chapter, the Administrator of the Environmental Protection Agency ... shall administer this chapter."); *see also* West v. Bowen, 879 F.2d 1122, 1137 (3d Cir. 1989) (holding that "no deference is owed an agency's interpretation of another agency's statute"). Thus, we review de novo the Commission's construction of the CWA.

We begin, as we must, with the statute itself. In this case, the statutory language is clear. Section 401(a), which is directed both to prospective licensees and to the federal licensing agency (in this case, the Commission), provides, in relevant part:

> Any applicant for a Federal license or permit to conduct any activity ... which may result in any discharge into the navigable waters, shall provide the licensing or permitting agency a certification from the State in which the discharge originates or will originate.... No license or permit shall be granted until the certification required by this section has been obtained or has been waived.... No license or permit shall be granted if certification has been denied by the State....

33 U.S.C. § 1341(a). More important, § 401(d), reads, in pertinent part:

> Any certification provided under this section ... shall become a condi-tion on any Federal license or permit subject to the provisions of this section.

33 U.S.C. § 1341(d).

This language is unequivocal, leaving little room for FERC to argue that it has authority to reject state conditions it finds to be ultra vires. Rather, in this case, to the extent that the Commission contends that Congress intended to vest it with authority to reject "unlawful" state conditions, the Commission faces a difficult task since it is generally assumed—absent a clearly expressed legislative intention to the contrary—"that Congress expresses its purposes through the ordinary meaning of the words it uses...." *Escondido Mutual Water Co. v. La Jolla Band of Mission Indians*, 466 U.S. 765, 772 (1984).

The Commission argues that, notwithstanding the mandatory language of the provision, § 401(d) itself restricts the substantive authority of states to impose conditions: "Section 401 authorizes states to impose only condi-tions that relate to water quality." This is plainly true. Section 401(d), reasonably read in light of its purpose, restricts conditions that states can impose to those affecting water quality in one manner or another. *See P.U.D. No. 1 of Jefferson County*, 114 S. Ct. at 1909 (holding that a state's authority to impose conditions under § 401(d) "is not unbounded"). However, this is not tantamount to a delegation to FERC of the authority to decide which conditions are within the confines of § 401(d) and which are not. And this is the crux of the dispute in this case.

In *Escondido Mutual Water Co. v. La Jolla Band of Mission Indians*, 466 U.S. 765 (1984)—a case which the Commission goes to great lengths to distinguish—the Supreme Court was called upon to consider a strikingly analogous factual and legal scenario. At issue was a pre-license certification scheme within the FPA itself, permitting (in this instance) the Secretary of the Interior to impose requirements on licenses issued "within" any Native American "reservation." In particular, this certification scheme, § 4(e) of the FPA, 16 U.S.C. § 797(e), provides that licenses issued under this provision "shall be subject to and contain such conditions as the Secretary of the department under whose supervision such reservation falls shall deem necessary for the adequate protection and utilization of such reservation." 16 U.S.C. § 797(e). FERC, however, refused to accept the Secretary's conditions, and an aggrieved party sought review. In construing § 4(e), the Supreme Court focused closely on the provision's plain language, remarking that "the mandatory nature of the language chosen by Congress appears to require that the Commission include the Secretary's conditions in the license even if it disagrees with them." *Escondido*, 466 U.S. at 772. Consistent with this view, the Court gave effect to the plain language of 4(e), 16 U.S.C. § 797(e), finding no "clear expressions of legislative intent to the contrary." *Id.*

Although Escondido arose in a different context, it is instructive in this case for several reasons. In both contexts, FERC is required in clear statutory language to incorporate conditions imposed by an independent governmental agency with special expertise, in Escondido, the Department of the Interior, 16 U.S.C. § 797(e), and in this instance, the states, *see* 33 U.S.C. § 1251(b) ("It is the policy of the Congress to recognize, preserve, and protect the primary responsibilities and rights of States to prevent, reduce, and eliminate pollution. . . ."); *see also United States v. Puerto Rico*, 721 F.2d 832, 838 (1st Cir. 1983) ("states are the prime bulwark in the effort to abate water pollution"). In both cases, the Commission attempted to ignore this command and substitute its own judgment for that of the certifying agency. In both cases, the real issue in dispute is not whether there are limits on the certifying agency's authority to impose conditions on federal licenses, but "whether the Commission is empowered to decide when the . . . conditions exceed the permissible limits." *Escondido*, 466 U.S. at 777. In neither case do the underlying statutes or their schemes for administrative and judicial review suggest that Congress wanted the Commission to second-guess the imposition of conditions.

Finally, and most persuasively, in both cases the Commission argued that without the authority to review conditions imposed by the certifying agency its ability to carry out its statutory mission would be compromised. In *Escondido*, notwithstanding this contention, the Supreme Court found that absent a challenge by the applicant-licensee, the Interior Secretary's conditions must either be incorporated in full into any license that it issues or the Commission must deny the license altogether. 466 U.S. at 778 n.20. In reaching this conclusion, the Court expressly addressed difficulties inherent in such a statutory scheme, difficulties the Commission decries in this case:

> We note that in the unlikely event that none of the parties to the licensing proceeding seeks review, the conditions will go into effect notwithstanding the Commission's objection to them since the Commission is not authorized to seek review of its own decisions. The possibility that this might occur does not, however, dissuade us from interpreting the statute in accordance with its plain meaning. Congress apparently decided that if no party was interested in the differences between the Commission and the Secretary, the dispute would best be resolved in a nonjudicial forum. *Id.*

The Commission's efforts to distinguish Escondido are unavailing.

The Federal Power Act. Independent of FERC's concerns that Vermont's 401 conditions violate the terms of the CWA, the Commission contends that the 401 conditions run afoul of the FPA. The Commission primarily fears that "to accept the conditions proposed would give the state the kind of governance and enforcement authority that is critical and exclusive to the Commission's responsibility to administer a license under the Federal Power Act, a power the Courts have repeatedly concluded belongs exclusively to the Commission." Brief of the Fed. Energy Regulatory Comm'n at 16. In particular, FERC argues (1) that the conditions that impose deadlines on construction conflict with § 13 of the FPA, 16 U.S.C. § 806, which places construction deadlines largely within the discretion of the Commission and generally contemplates that construction will be commenced within two years of the date of the license, *see First Iowa Hydro–Elec. Coop. v. Federal Power Comm'n*, 328 U.S. 152, 168 n.13 (1946); (2) that the reopener conditions and pre-approval conditions violate § 6 of the FPA, 16 U.S.C. § 799, which provides that a license, once issued, "may be revoked only for the reasons and in the manner prescribed under the provisions of this chapter, and may be altered or surrendered only upon mutual agreement between the licensee and the Commission," as well as other provisions of the FPA, see 16 U.S.C. § § 803(b), 820, 823b; and, (3) more generally, that the conditions "eviscerate[] the carefully balanced approach" to environmental concerns expressed in the Electric Consumers Protection Act ("ECPA"), Pub.L. No. 99–495, 100 Stat. 1243 (1986), amending the FPA, *see, e.g.*, 16 U.S.C. §§ 797(e), 803(a), 803(j).

We have no quarrel with the Commission's assertion that the FPA represents a congressional intention to establish "a broad federal role in the development and licensing of hydroelectric power." *California v. FERC*, 495 U.S. 490, 496 (1990). Nor do we dispute that the FPA has a wide preemptive reach. *Id.* The CWA, however, has diminished this preemptive reach by expressly requiring the Commission to incorporate into its licenses state-imposed water-quality conditions. *See* 33 U.S.C. § 1341(a)(1). Although we are sympathetic to the Commission's suggestion that without the authority to reject states' conditions that are beyond the scope of § 401, the preemptive reach of the FPA may be narrowed at the will of the states, *see, e.g.,* Brief of Amici Curiae Edison Elec. Inst. at 14, the Commission's concerns are overblown.

The Commission fails to acknowledge appropriately its ability to protect its mandate from incursion by exercising the authority to refuse to issue a hydropower license altogether if the Commission concludes that a license, as conditioned, sufficiently impairs its authority under the FPA. *See, e.g., Escondido,* 466 U.S. at 778 n.20. If the Commission is concerned that the conditions imposed by a state "intrude[] upon the Commission's exclusive authority under the FPA," Brief of the Fed. Energy Regulatory Comm'n at 44, nothing in the CWA prevents it from protecting its field of authority by simply refusing to issue the license as so conditioned.

The Commission, however, has chosen to forgo this route, arguing that refusing to issue a license is not a "practical option" in relicensing cases. *Id.* at 20 n.10. Although we understand that refusing to relicense a hydroelectric project would result in the disassembly of the project, presenting "serious practical and economic problems" and affecting all manner of local interests, id., the Commission's dissatisfaction with the remedy of license denial is not reason enough to turn a blind eye to FERC's assumption of authority to review and reject a state's 401 conditions. Rather, the Commission must establish that the authority it proposes is rooted in a Congressional mandate. And this they have failed to do.

Finally, with respect to the ECPA amendments to the FPA, the Commission is mistaken. Under these provisions, the Commission must "give equal consideration to . . . the protection, mitigation of damage to, and enhancement of, fish and wildlife . . . and the preservation of other aspects of environmental quality," 16 U.S.C. § 797(e), and must impose conditions, based on recommendations of relevant federal agencies and affected states, to "protect, mitigate damages to, and enhance, fish and wildlife . . . affected by the development, operation, and management of the project . . . ," 16 U.S.C. § 803(j)(1). *See U.S. Dep't of Interior v. FERC,* 952 F.2d 538, 543 (D.C. Cir. 1992) (describing environmental aspects of the ECPA amendments). The Commission argues that absent the authority to reject state-imposed conditions beyond the scope of § 401 of the CWA, the carefully balanced approach of the ECPA amendments, in general, and § 10(j), 16 U.S.C. § 803(j), in particular, would be "eviscerated . . . through the simple expedient of [states'] labeling . . . recommendations 'conditions' to the Section 401 certification." Brief of the Fed. Energy Regulatory Comm'n at 39. In short, the Commission is concerned that it would be "held hostage" to every state imposed condition, compromising its role under the ECPA amendments of reconciling competing interests. *Id.* Such a result, the Commission contends, is impermissible under § 511(a) of the CWA, 33 U.S.C. § 1371(a), which provides, in part, that the Act "shall not be construed as . . . limiting the authority or functions of any officer or agency of the United States under any other law or regulation not inconsistent with this chapter. . . ."

The Commission's claim that the CWA—as we construe it—and the ECPA amendments are incompatible must be rejected. The Commission's concern that states will hold the Commission hostage through the § 401 process is misplaced because states' authority under § 401 is circumscribed in notable respects. First, applicants for state certification may challenge in courts of appropriate jurisdiction any state-imposed condition that exceeds a state's authority under § 401. In so doing, licensees will surely protect themselves against state-imposed ultra vires conditions. Second, even assuming that certification applicants will not always challenge ultra vires state conditions, the Commission may protect its mandate by refusing to issue a license which, as conditioned, conflicts with the FPA. In so doing, the Commission will not only protect its mandate but also signal to states and licensees the limits of its tolerance. Third, and most important, to the extent that the existence of states' authority to impose 401 conditions may otherwise conflict with the ECPA amendments, the ECPA is inconsistent with the terms of the CWA, thus, making inapplicable § 511(a) of the CWA. *See* 33 U.S.C. § 1371(a) (the Act "shall not be construed as . . . limiting the authority or functions of any officer or agency of the United States under any other law or regulation not inconsistent with this chapter . . .").

We have considered the Commission's remaining arguments and find them to be without merit. For the foregoing reasons, we grant the petition for review, vacate the orders of the Commission, and remand for proceedings consistent with this opinion.■

NOTES AND COMMENTS

1. Upon remand, the FERC issued the license subject to the state's conditions. *Tunbridge Mill Corporation*, 82 F.E.R.C. P61,265 (1998). For a discussion of the impact of the *American Rivers* case, *see* Comment: Who's in Charge Here? The Shrinking Role of the Federal Energy Regulatory Commission in Hydropower Licensing, 70 U. Of Colo. L. Rev. 603 (1999).

2. American Indian Tribes share with the States the power to set conditions on water usage within reservations. Tribes have been active participants in the negotiations on many of the contested hydropower licensing proceedings. *See* Jane Marz, *et. al.*, Tribal Jurisdiction over Reservation Water Quality and Quantity, 43 S. D. L. Rev. 315 (1998).

3. Just exactly which environmental issues fall within the state's 401 certification authority after *P.U.D. No. 1 of Jefferson County v. Washington Dep't of Ecology*? It is easy to see the connection between water quantity in the river below the dam and water quality issues. Of the litany of environmental concerns raised by hydroelectric projects, which affect water quality and which do not, in your view? Given our growing understanding of the interdependent relationships between flora and fauna within ecosystems, do you expect a growing number of issues to fall within the states' jurisdiction under section 401? *See* Michael C. Blumm and Viki A. Nadol, The Decline of the Hydropower Czar and the Rise of Agency Pluralism in Hydroelectric Licensing, 26 Colum. J. Envtl. L. 81 (2001) (arguing that

FERC's dominance over the licensing process has been eroded by decisions like this one).

3. Certain small hydroelectric projects that are otherwise subject to the FERC's jurisdiction are "exempt" from licensing under the Federal Power Act and the FERC's regulations. These exempt facilities are narrowly defined, and most require that the applicant already own all the property rights necessary to build and operate the project. The project owner files a notice with the FERC, who then issues an "exemption" for the project. These projects are exempt from many of the licensing standards contained within the Federal Power Act, but the term "exemption" is a bit of a misnomer, since the FERC-issued exemptions usually contain conditions that are very like those contained in hydroelectric licenses. See 18 C.F.R. §§ 4.31 and 4.106.

4. The Energy Policy Act of 2005, signed into law by President Bush in August of 2005, runs counter to the recent historical trend toward increasing leverage for environmental interests in the FERC licensing process. The Act adds procedural protections against (and increases the transaction costs associated with) decisions imposing environmental conditions in hydroelectric licenses. For example, section 231 of the 2005 Act provides project owners with a right to a "trial type hearing" to challenge license conditions imposed by resource agencies under Section 4(e) of the Federal Power Act, as well as FERC-imposed license conditions requiring the construction of fish passage facilities. The Act further weakens the leverage of federal resource agencies under Section 4(e) by authorizing the FERC to select "alternate" license conditions over conditions proposed by resource agencies when it finds that such alternate conditions would provide "adequate protection" and be less costly or more efficient. It remains to be seen whether (or to what extent) Congress' attempt to increase the procedural costs associated with imposing environmental protection conditions in hydroelectric licenses will lead FERC to impose fewer, or weaker, environmental protection conditions in future licenses.

2. RELICENSING AND THE ENVIRONMENT

After the passage of ECPA in 1986, environmental interests argued that many of the hundreds of hydro projects up for relicensing in the 1990s and early 21st century ought to be decommissioned rather than relicensed, and their dams removed in order to restore historic fish runs and the dam sites to their "natural" condition. As described in the *Udall* decision, dams had destroyed historic fish runs on both the east and west coasts. For decades the Commission responded to this problem by requiring hydroelectric project owners to install fish passage facilities, which was insufficient to restore historic fish migration patterns. By the 1980s state environmental agencies and Indian tribes had established programs for restoring salmon migration routes by restocking salmon rivers, and had begun to bring pressure on the FERC to do more to help. Environmental groups like American Rivers supported this effort by intervening in hydroelectric relicensing proceedings urging the FERC to deny relicensing applications and order the decommissioning of existing dams.

This cause received a boost from the FERC in December of 1994 in the form of a policy statement declaring that the FERC had the power to order complete removal of existing hydroelectric power generating dams. F.E.R.C. Project Decommissioning at Relicensing; Policy Statement, 60 Fed. Reg. 339 (1994). Only three years after its 1994 policy statement, the FERC exercised this authority by ordering the removal of the Edwards Dam, a dam across the Kennebec River near Augusta, Maine. The site had been dammed since the early 1800s, and when Edwards Manufacturing filed its relicensing application in 1991, the application brought resistance from various environmental groups, sporting organizations, state and federal agencies, and other businesses. Several of the intervenors sought to have the dam removed in order to restore migration for anadromous fish. After a lengthy proceeding involving two EISs, the FERC concluded "that the project's negative impact on fishery resources could not be mitigated except by removal of the dam," and ordered the dam removed at the owner's expense. *Edward's Mfg. Co. and City of Augusta, Me.*; Order Denying New License and Requiring Dam Removal, 81 F.E.R.C. ¶ 61,255 (1997).

While the courts were considering the appeal of the FERC's Edwards Dam decision, the case was settled pursuant to a larger agreement among dam owners and resource agencies on the lower Kennebec River in Maine. The State of Maine had established spawning programs that were already making progress reintroducing anadromous species to the river, and sought a global settlement of the problem of dams and fish migration on the Kennebec. Meanwhile, the Edwards Dam decision raised the prospect that other dams blocking other historic salmon runs—like those on Columbia River basin in the Pacific Northwest—might be ordered removed at relicensing. Environmental groups and others urged the removal of several dams on the Klamath and Snake Rivers in the Pacific Northwest, and relicensing proceedings in the northwest became even more contentious, pitting developers, fishermen and Indian tribes, irrigation districts, farmers, environmental groups and resource agencies against one another in a Hobbesian war of all against all. *See* Holly Doremus and A. Dan Tarlock, Fish, Farms, and the Clash of Cultures in the Klamath Basin, *30 Ecology L.Q. 279 (2003)*(detailing the role played by the ESA in fights over relicensing projects on the Klamath River); Michael C. Blumm, *et. al.*, Symposium on Water Law: Saving Snake River Water and Salmon Simultaneously, 28 Envtl. L. 997 (1998); and *Studies: PacifiCorp could remove Klamath dams cheaply, safely,* Tuesday, July 20, 2004, at the American Rivers web site <http://www.americanrivers.org/site/News2?JServSession-Idr005=4hgertiso1.app6b&page=NewsArticle&id=6658&news_iv_ctrl=_1129>. Some environmental organizations have their eyes on even larger dams. The Glen Canyon dam in the Colorado River is one of the largest dams in the country. In 1996, the Sierra Club voted to support the decommissioning of the dam in order to protect various endangered species of fish in the Colorado River. Scott K. Miller, Undamming Glen Canyon: Lunacy, Rationality, or Prophecy?, 19 Stan. Envtl. L. J. 121 (2000).

These contests are complicated further by the listing of several species of salmon as endangered under the Endangered Species Act, 16 U.S.C. § 1531 et. seq. Once a particular fish population has been listed as an endangered or threatened species under the Endangered Species Act, the powerful sanctions of the Act begin to play a dominant role in the management of the river. Federal wildlife agencies need to sign off on federal projects or federal permits that affect the river. 16 U.S.C. § 1536. It becomes unlawful to "take" any such fish, 16 U.S.C. § 1538, including taking through habitat destruction. *Palila v. Hawaii Dep't of Land & Natural Res.*, 639 F.2d 495 (9th Cir. 1981). The management of the Columbia and Snake Rivers is now subject to very different legal rules than it was at the time the *Udall* case was decided. "The Columbia Basin is now awash with ESA listings of salmonids. No fewer than twelve Columbia Basin salmonid species are currently under ESA protection. [In 1990,] there were no salmonid listings at all. The ESA has assumed a dominant role in salmon law and policy in the basin." Michael C. Blumm & Greg D. Corbin, Salmon and the Endangered Species Act: Lessons from the Columbia Basin, 74 Washington L. Rev. 519, 586 (1999). *See also* John M. Volkman, How Do You Learn From a River? Managing Uncertainty in Species Conservation Policy, 74 Wash. L. Rev. 719 (1999). Given the impact of dams on salmon migration routes, the National Wildlife Federation and other groups seek to use the ESA to compel removal of existing dams in the Pacific northwest. *See National Wildlife Fed'n et al. v. Nat'l Marine Fisheries Serv. et al.*, 422 F.3d 782 (9th Cir.2005) (affirming a federal district court injunction holding that the National Marine Fisheries Service had violated the Endangered Species Act when it issued a 2004 "biological opinion" that had formed the basis of the operating plans for the Federal Columbia River Power System.)

While environmental groups' hopes for compelling dam removal remain high, the following decision is fairly typical of recent relicensing cases. In this case, the FERC considers and rejects dam removal to restore fish runs in the context of another relicensing application concerning the Kennebec River in Maine.

Merimil Limited Partnership, Project No. 2574–032, Order Issuing New License

110 F.E.R.C. ¶ 61,240 (2005).

On April 29, 2002, Merimil Limited Partnership (Merimil) filed an application for a new license, pursuant to sections 4(e) and 15 of the Federal Power Act (FPA), 16 U.S.C. §§ 797(e) and 808, respectively, for the continued operation and maintenance of the existing 6.915–megawatt (MW) Lockwood Project No. 2574, located on the Kennebec River, a navigable waterway, in Kennebec County, Maine.

The Lockwood Project, located at river mile 63, is now the first dam on the mainstem of the Kennebec River. The Lockwood Project includes an 81.5–acre reservoir, an 875–foot-long and 17–foot-high dam with two spillway sections and a 160–foot-long forebay headworks section, a 450–foot-long forebay canal, two powerhouses, and two transmission lines. The dam and forebay headworks span the Kennebec River immediately upstream of the U.S. Route 201 bridge along a site originally known as Ticonic Falls.
. . .

The Kennebec River in the vicinity of the Lockwood Project supports a varied fish population. The impoundment supports a warm water fish community, including naturally reproducing smallmouth bass. Migratory species in the impoundment include American shad, alewife, and American eel. The fish communities in the river below the project consist of both warm water and cold water species typical in the region, including small-mouth bass, largemouth bass, perch, black crappie and a variety of forage species. Anadromous species that could move up to the project tailwaters include striped bass, rainbow smelt, Atlantic sturgeon, shortnose sturgeon, Atlantic salmon, American shad, and alewife. Only American shad, alewife, and Atlantic salmon have historically migrated upstream of the project area. American eel have unobstructed access to the base of the dam. Large numbers of eels observed in the bypassed reach, in the impoundment, and at the Hydro–Kennebec Project (the next upstream dam) confirm that eels are successfully passing the Lockwood Project. Efforts are underway to restore American shad, alewife, Atlantic salmon, and American eel to the Kennebec River Basin.

In 1989, the license for the project was amended to include the terms of a January 1987 agreement (known as the Kennebec Hydro Developer Group [KHDG]) agreement . . . to facilitate the restoration of American shad, alewife, and Atlantic salmon in the Kennebec River Basin. The licensees agreed to provide funding to the state fishery agencies for interim trap and truck operations at the projects, to install and operate permanent downstream and upstream fish passage facilities according to a schedule, and to conduct studies related to the restoration efforts. Permanent upstream and downstream fish passage facilities were to be installed and operational at the Lockwood Project by May 1, 1999. This schedule was based on the assumption that fish passage would be provided at the Edwards Project by the late 1980s.

In April 1997, the licensees of the KHDG agreement projects requested the Commission to amend the licenses to delay installation of the permanent fishways at the projects (including Lockwood) until fish passage was available at the Edwards Project or the dam removed and restoration of salmon, shad, and alewives in the Kennebec River had proved successful. . . . On May 28, 1998, an offer of settlement, now known as the Lower Kennebec River Comprehensive Settlement Accord (1998 Accord), was filed by state and federal fisheries agencies, environmental groups, and the licensees of the Edwards Project and seven upstream projects. The 1998 Accord modified the KHDG agreement and included provisions for removing the Edwards dam and, upon the occurrence of certain triggering events, installing fish passage at the upstream projects, including the Lockwood Project. The Lockwood license was amended in September 1998 to incorporate the terms of the 1998 Accord. Merimil's relicense proposal includes these measures . . .

Friends of the Kennebec Salmon intervened in opposition to the relicensing of the project, contending that the goals of the fishery restoration programs in the Kennebec River Basin cannot be achieved using fish passage facilities at the Lockwood Project, and thus the license should be denied and the project removed.

On October 3, 2003, the Commission issued a draft environmental assessment (EA) that analyzed the impacts of relicensing the project under the terms of the 1998 Accord (Merimil's proposal), as proposed by Merimil with additional staff-recommended measures (staff alternative), and without interim and permanent upstream fishways (no-action alternative). . . .

Water Quality Certification

On April 25, 2002, Merimil applied to the Maine DEP for water quality certification. Merimil twice withdrew and refiled the application for certification (April 18, 2003, and April 16, 2004). Maine DEP issued water quality certification for the project on August 24, 2004. Ordering Paragraph (D) incorporates into the license the conditions of the certification, which is attached as Appendix A.

In summary, Merimil must: (1) operate in a run-of-river mode; (2) minimize impoundment level fluctuations (within six inches of full pond when all flashboards are in place and above the spillway crest when flashboard failure has occurred); (3) maintain minimum leakage flows of 30 to 50 cfs from the dam; (4) implement fish rescue measures during flashboard replacement or impoundment drawdown; (5) maintain the existing shoreline angler access site in the project's tailwater; and (6) comply with the requirements of the 1998 Accord. . . .

Threatened and Endangered Species

Section 7(a) of the Endangered Species Act of 1973 (ESA), 16 U.S.C. § 1536(a), requires federal agencies to ensure that their actions are not likely to jeopardize the continued existence of federally listed threatened and endangered species, or result in the destruction or adverse modification of designated critical habitat. . . . Federally listed species that occur in the project area are the threatened bald eagle and endangered shortnose sturgeon. In the final EA, staff found that relicensing the project would not be likely to adversely affect the bald eagle, but would be likely to adversely affect the shortnose sturgeon. Adverse effects on the shortnose sturgeon result from handling during the rescue of shortnose sturgeon that may become entrapped in isolated pools in the bypassed reach during flashboard repair, and during sorting and returning to the river any sturgeon caught in the fish lift that is to be constructed. . . .

On October 16, 2003, Commission staff requested formal consultation with NOAA Fisheries under section 7(a)(2) of the ESA on the shortnose sturgeon. NOAA Fisheries requested additional information, which was provided in the final EA along with a recommendation that Merimil prepare a sturgeon rescue plan that defines handling protocols and notification procedures. ... The plan defines procedures for handling and returning shortnose sturgeon to the Kennebec River below the project during operation of the fish lift and during fish rescue efforts associated with flashboard replacement.

On January 14, 2005, NOAA Fisheries filed its biological opinion on relicensing the Lockwood Project, which found that relicensing the project with staff's recommended measures would not jeopardize the continued existence of the Kennebec River population of the shortnose sturgeon.

Recommendations of Federal and State Fish and Wildlife Agencies

Pursuant to section 10(j) of the FPA, 16 U.S.C. § 803(j)(1), the Commission, when issuing a license, includes conditions based on the recommendations of federal and state fish and wildlife agencies submitted pursuant to the Fish and Wildlife Coordination Act, 16 U.S.C. § 661 *et seq.*, for the protection and enhancement of fish and wildlife and their habitat affected by the project. ... For the Lockwood Project, Interior and the Maine SPO on behalf of Maine Department of Marine Resources, Maine Department of Inland Fisheries and Wildlife, and the Maine Atlantic Salmon Commission submitted a total of 15 recommendations (some of which are duplicative) that fall within the scope of section 10(j). The license contains conditions consistent with all of these recommendations.

Other Issues

Friends of the Kennebec Salmon argue that relicensing the project will prevent the restoration of Atlantic salmon, American shad, and alewives to the Kennebec River Basin. The group contends that fish passage inefficiencies at the Lockwood Project, and at other upstream dams, will reduce the number of fish that reach the upstream spawning habitat to the point that a self-sustaining population cannot be achieved. As a result, it argues that the application for a new license should be denied and that the project should be decommissioned and the dam removed.

As noted above, in 1987, Merimil, together with the other members of KHDG, entered into an agreement with fisheries resource agencies to facilitate the restoration of Atlantic salmon, American shad, and alewives to the lower Kennebec River Basin. KHDG provided funds to the agencies to help pay for acquiring and stocking fish to restore populations and studying restoration efforts. The KHDG licensees also agreed to construct and operate fish passage facilities according to a schedule that called for sequential construction of the facilities, beginning with the downstream projects and moving upstream. The licenses for the KHDG projects were amended to reflect the fish passage provisions of the agreement. In 1998, the agreement was modified (the 1998 Accord) to provide for the removal of the Edwards Dam and link the construction of fish passage facilities to biological triggers instead of to specific dates. The 1998 Accord continued the requirement for financial support by the licensees of the restoration activities.

Fishery restoration activities in the lower Kennebec River Basin have made significant progress. In 2003, the latest year for which data are available, over 135,000 alewives were trapped at the Ft. Halifax project. This provided enough fish for the resource agencies to meet all their stocking goals and have additional fish available for stocking outside the Kennebec River Basin. The alewife spawning run is now large enough to meet the stocking needs and support a commercial fishery; reports from 48 percent of the commercial fisherman showed a catch of over 128,000 alewives from the Sebasticook River at Ft. Halifax. Earlier estimates of the size of the alewife run were 1 to 2 million fish and biologists reported that there seemed to be more alewives in 2003 than in previous years.

The number of shad fry stocked above Lockwood increased from 1.75 million in 2002 to 2.54 million in 2003, and the interim downstream fish passage measures at Lockwood, Hydro Kennebec, and Shawmut appear to be allowing juvenile shad and alewife to migrate downstream without significant injury or mortality. The existing license for the Lockwood Project requires Merimil to install and operate interim upstream fish passage facilities by May 1, 2006.

The Maine Atlantic Salmon Commission does not currently have an active salmon restoration program in the Kennebec River. No Atlantic salmon are stocked in the Kennebec above Lockwood and any adult salmon returning to the river are either strays from other rivers or the result of natural reproduction in the Kennebec or its tributaries below Lockwood.

We believe that the 1998 Accord has created an effective, comprehensive, and coordinated program for achieving the fishery restoration goals for the lower Kennebec River Basin. The Accord provides for continuing restoration activities and installation of fish passage facilities as required by the growth of the fish populations and their expansion into upstream habitat. Friends of the Kennebec Salmon argue that dam removal is needed to guarantee success of the restoration efforts. The evidence to date shows that the restoration plans are making significant progress. We believe it is too early in the restoration efforts to conclude that the plan will ultimately succeed or fail. Therefore we do not agree that we should abandon the plan embodied in the 1998 Accord.

Coastal Zone Consistency Certification

Under section 307(c)(3)(A) of the Coastal Zone Management Act, 16 U.S.C. § 1456(c)(3)(A), the Commission cannot issue a license for a project within or affecting a state's coastal zone unless the state CZMA agency concurs with the license applicant's certification of consistency with the state's CZMA program, or the agency's concurrence is conclusively presumed by its failure to act within 180 days of its receipt of the applicant's certification. . . .

The Commission orders:

(A) This license is issued to Merimil Limited Partnership (licensee) to operate and maintain the Lockwood Project, for a period of 31 years and 8 months, effective the first day of the month in which this order is issued. The license is subject to the terms and conditions of the Federal Power Act (FPA), which is incorporated by reference as part of this license, and subject to the regulations the Commission issues under the provisions of the FPA. . . .■

NOTES AND COMMENTS

1. Is it possible for an agency to quantify and weigh the competing values of wild fish and electric power? Can environmental values be stated in dollars? Consider the following quote from the noted ecologist, Eugene P. Odum: "Money is related to energy, since it takes energy to make money. Money is a counterflow to energy in that money flows out of cities and farms to pay for the energy and materials that flow in. The trouble is that money tracks human-made goods and services but not the equally important natural goods and services. At the ecosystem level, money enters the picture only when a natural resource is converted into marketable goods and services, leaving unpriced (and therefore not appreciated) all the work of the natural system that sustains this resource." Eugene P. Odum, Ecology and Our Endangered Life Support Systems 105 (2d ed. 1993). As the quote from Odum indicates, our present systems of accounting assume that when we use a natural resource we are creating an asset, even though we are depleting the long term supply of the resource. Many economists and accountants are debating ways in which our systems of cost accounting could be changed to take into account depletion of natural resources.

2. Hundreds of the early project licenses have now expired, and applications are pending before FERC to reissue many of these licenses. "Between 1993 and 2010, the licenses for 419 projects have expired or will expire. Many of the largest projects will expire between 2005 and 2010. . . . Some re-licenses have been granted and some projects are operating on annual permits pending decision." Marla E. Mansfield, Hydroelectric Power, in James E. Hickey, Jr., Energy Law and Policy for the 21st Century 11–19 (Rocky Mountain Mineral Law Foundation, 2000). In many cases, these applications have produced political controversy and have raised difficult legal issues.

3. The FERC's 1994 policy statement on dam decommissioning indicated that dam removal would be an unusual remedy, and that prediction has proven correct. In practice, the Edwards Dam decision is proving to be the *Namekagon* of its time—namely the exception that proves the rule. While the FERC has endorsed voluntary agreements to remove dams that were part of hydroelectric projects originally slated for relicensing, it has not ordered decommissioning and dam removal against the wishes of relicensing applicant since the Edwards Dam decision. It appears that far more

dams are being removed as the result of negotiation (with the aid of state resource agencies) than intervention in relicensing proceedings.

4.   The nature and extent of FERC's authority to require dam removal upon decommissioning has yet to be decided by the courts. Some dam operators have suggested that dam decommissioning may amount to a regulatory taking for which the licensees should be compensated. There is speculation as to how this exception applies to dam decommissioning. Licensees assert they have an interest in the hydro project lands, the physical structures, water use rights, and even the FERC license and should therefore be compensated if ordered to decommission a dam. However, it is difficult to say that there is property interest in an expired license. A FERC license may be considered a "regulatory contract" between the licensee and the federal government. Existing FERC licenses may be regarded as property rights. But, once the license expires, the contract ends and the property right no longer exists. *See U.S. v. Fuller*, 409 U.S. 488 (1973) (taking of grazing land required no compensation for any value added to the lands by the permits.) One court has held that the *Fuller* case is the relevant precedent if the federal government condemns a licensed hydroelectric project, so that the project is to be appraised as if its license will not be renewed. *United States v. 42.13 Acres of Land*, 73 F.3d 953 (1996).

Hydropower project owners also do not have a property interest in the value of water power or the value of the land as a hydropower site. *See United States v. Chandler–Dunbar Water Power Co.*, 229 U.S. 53 (1913) (compensation not required for lost water use for power production when federal government condemned land in order to take navigable river flow for interstate commerce and revoked a hydropower license); and *Lewis Blue Point Oyster v. Briggs*, 229 U.S. 82 (1913)(despite a lessee's contrary interest, the United States Congress may pursuant to the commerce clause order dam removal without paying compensation); *see also United States v. Grand River Dam Authority*, 363 U.S. 229 (1960) (the U.S. has a superior navigation easement which precludes private ownership of the water or its flow). But compensation for the condemnation of private riparian land was required in *United States v. Kelley*, 243 U.S. 316 (1917). *See* Katharine Costenbader, Damning Dams: Bearing the Cost of Restoring America's Rivers, 6 Geo. Mason L. Rev. 635 (1998); Comment, FERC's Dam Decommissioning Authority under the Federal Power Act, 74 Wash. L. Rev. 95 (1999).

5.   American Rivers claims that more than 100 dams have been removed in the last half decade, most through a series of voluntary agreements and commercial decisions. The Federal Power Act has always provided a mechanism for surrender of a hydroelectric license and several licenses are surrendered each year. Some are for projects that are no longer economical or technically feasible to run. Sometimes the FERC will order dam removal as part of the surrender process. See e.g., *FPL Energy Maine Hydro, LLC*, 107 F.E.R.C. ¶ 61,120 (May 6, 2004), an order issued by the FERC to further the objectives of the 1998 KHDG agreement, ordering the surrender of an existing license and a partial dam removal, with the licensee's agreement.

CHAPTER 5

COAL

A. THE EVOLUTION OF THE MODERN COAL INDUSTRY

The coal industry has evolved from a highly labor intensive industry plagued by health and safety problems to a highly mechanized industry heavily dependent on huge strip mining operations that are plagued by environmental problems. Many of its traditional markets have disappeared, yet it still supplies the majority of the fuel that produces electricity in the United States.

The coal industry is one of the most heavily regulated industries in the United States. Various constitutional challenges to federal and state regulations of the coal industry have produced some of the most important decisions in American constitutional history. However, before addressing the regulatory environment of the coal industry, it is important to understand the important role that coal has played in the development of the United States, and the changing nature of the coal industry in today's environment.

1. FROM WOOD TO COAL

Ever since prehistoric humans discovered how to make fire they have been cutting down trees to obtain wood as a fuel. Wood, along with muscles, water and wind, continued to be the dominant source of energy until the mid-nineteenth century. In the United States today, wood is still used as a fuel in fireplaces and wood stoves, but it accounts for only a minute fraction of our energy usage.

Human beings also have a long history of using peat for fuel. Peat is the remains of wetland vegetation that has formed a coherent mass. For centuries it has been dug and used as fireplace fuel in many parts of the world. But peat's heating efficiency is very low, and it produces lots of smoke. When geological changes cause peat to be buried under layers of rock, the peat becomes compressed and turns into coal. This compression packs a lot of potential energy into a small space, with the result that coal is a much more efficient fuel than peat.

Coal varies greatly in heat content and in sulfur content. The relative efficiency of different types and grades of coal can vary significantly depending on differences in original vegetation and, more importantly, in the magnitude and duration of transforming temperatures and pressures.

Anthracites and the best bituminous coals—ancient fuels derived primarily from the wood of large, scaly-barked trees laid down in immense coastal swamps more than two hundred million years ago— break up to reveal hard, jet-black facets of virtually pure carbon. These fuels contain hardly any water and very little ash, and their heat values are near 30 MJ/kg [megajoules per kilogram] In contrast, the youngest lignites are soft, often crumbly, clayish, fairly wet chunks of brownish hues. They contain large shares of ash and water, often a great deal of sulfur, and their energy density is as low as 10 MJ/kg, inferior to air-dried wood.

Not surprisingly, all large lignite-producing nations call them brown coals. As with their drawbacks, the redeeming qualities of brown coals spring from their relative immaturity: their deposits are often very thick, quite level and close to the surface, conditions making a large-scale extraction in huge open-cast mines very economical.

Vaclav Smil, Energies: An Illustrated Guide to the Biosphere and Civilization 136–137, The MIT Press, 1999.

But a switch to coal is not just a simple matter of replacing one energy base with another. Coal is more difficult to extract and process than wood or peat because it takes a great deal more energy to transform it into a usable state. Jeremy Rifkin suggests that this may reflect a universal principle: the second law of thermodynamics. "The available energy in the world is constantly being dissipated. The more available sources of energy are always the first to be used. Each succeeding environment relies on a less available form of energy than the one preceding it. It is more difficult to mine coal and process it than it is to cut down trees. It's still more difficult to drill and process oil, and even harder to split atoms for nuclear energy" Jeremy Rifkin with Ted Howard, Entropy: A New World View 85 (1985).

2. THE INDUSTRIAL REVOLUTION

Coal not only provided a more efficient source of heat than wood, it was a sufficiently concentrated form of energy that it became practical to convert it to motion through the use of the steam engine. The development of the steam engine was the foundation of the dramatic change in living conditions that became known as the Industrial Revolution. Early steam engines burned coal (to produce steam to drive a piston), and were first put to industrial uses, exploiting the mechanical energy they produced in mills, and later, on trains. While these great engines powered the industrial revolution, they could deliver power only on-site:

> Once you pare away the fancy additions, all the bells and whistles, all steam engines share one central property—they deliver energy mechanically, by making a shaft move or a wheel spin. This is a serious limitation on the steam engine's usefulness, because it means that the power must be developed close to the place where it will be used. Whatever is to be moved by the engine has to be connected to it. The great puffs of smoke issuing from a steam locomotive are a reminder of the fact that you have to carry both the coal and the engine along with you if you expect the wheels to turn. You can see the same thing in photos and etchings of turn-of-the-century factories, where long lines of lathes or other machines are run by belts connected to rotating overhead shafts near the factory ceiling. This meant that when the great manufacturing cities of the nineteenth century were built, every factory with power-driven machinery had to have its own steam engine (or engines) and supply of coal.

James Trefil, A Scientist in the City (Doubleday 1994).

3. COAL RESERVES IN THE UNITED STATES

Coal remains one of the major sources of energy in the United States and throughout much of the world today. The conversion of coal to energy requires four steps: mining, processing, transportation, and combustion. The big coal companies typically operate large mines that often ship their entire output to a few major users such as power plants or large factories, but some coal is mined by smaller companies that sell to wholesalers.

In the United States, coal was initially found primarily in the Appalachian Mountains, particularly in Pennsylvania and West Virginia. As the nation expanded westward, coal mines were opened first in the Midwestern states and, more recently, in the Rocky Mountain area. Today, nearly one-fourth of the nation's coal reserves are in Montana, with another 14% in neighboring Wyoming.

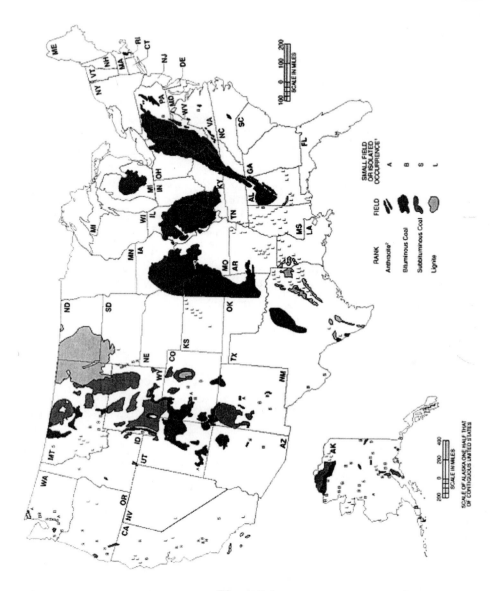

Figure 5–1

(Source: Environmental Protection Agency)

It is difficult to estimate the exact amount of coal buried underground, but there is no question that the United States has enormous coal reserves, probably in the neighborhood of five hundred billion tons of readily extractable coal. Almost half of this coal is in the Rocky Mountain area, but significant coal reserves remain in Illinois, West Virginia, Kentucky, Pennsylvania and Ohio. However, the increasing abandonment of small mines in these states has contributed to a significant loss of potential coal reserves.[1]

---

1. Small blocks of coal are not amenable to the larger-scale, higher-technology mining that can boost average productivity rates. The closing of these small mines has left significant

The predominant type of coal in the eastern United States has a high heat content but usually has a high sulfur content as well, which means that it will create high volumes of sulfur dioxide when burned. Typical western coal, on the other hand, has less sulfur but also has a lower heat content, which means that more tons of coal must be mined and shipped to produce the same energy. Historically, these regional differences have had a major impact on the politics of coal in the United States. Congressional representatives from the Eastern states have tended to support requirements for the installation of power plant scrubbers, which would remove sulfur compounds from the emitted stack gas and thus allow the plants to continue to burn high-sulfur coal. Representatives from the Rocky Mountain states have tended to promote laws that would promote shipment of low-sulfur Western coal to power plants in the East and Midwest. *See* Bruce A. Ackerman and William T. Hassler, Clean Coal/Dirty Air, Yale University Press, 1981.

4.   Changing Markets for Coal

Iron and steel used to be big consumers of coal in the form of coke. Now, much of our steel is imported, and what is made here doesn't use much coke any more. Today less than 5% of American coal goes to the steel industry.

It is the electric utilities that now consume about 92 percent of the coal mined in the United States. The remainder is used for industrial purposes, such as cement plants and foundries. The heaviest use of coal tends to be in the eastern-central part of the country, from Pennsylvania to Missouri. Less coal is used on the East and West Coasts. But the state that burns the most coal is Texas, mostly lignite that is used for power generation.

U.S. coal exports have fallen sharply in the last decade. In 2004, the United States exported only about 48 million tons of coal to countries around the world, a reduction of almost 50 percent since 1992. Fred Freme, U.S. Coal Supply and Demand: 2004 Review, Energy Information Administration, April, 2005. The widespread availability of coal resources in other countries means that the export market will probably be limited to particular grades of high-quality coal.

B.   Coal Mining

Mines are thriving in the West, but they are closing in many coal-mining areas east of the Mississippi. Although coal production in the

---

coal reserves permanently unmineable. Some operators choose to extract only the quickest-or easiest-to-mine parts of a coal deposit or only the highest-grade coal that will fetch a premium price, leaving the rest, which will probably be spoiled by caving and weathering. With prices low and competition keen, coal deposits once regarded as reserves at producing properties were found to be no longer marketable. If reserve blocks contain coal of moderate to high sulfur content, for which markets are shrinking, the changes of permanent closure are high. *See* Bonskowksi, *supra* at 8–9.

Coal Production by Region, 1970-2025 with
Long-Term Projections (million short tons)

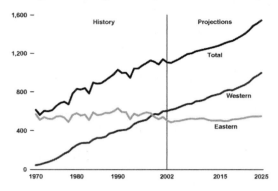

Coal Production by Sulfur Content, 2002, 2010, and
2025 (million short tons)

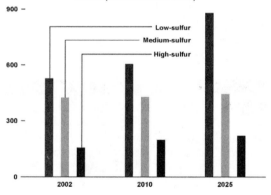

Coal Consumption for Electricity and Other,
1970-2025 (million short tons)

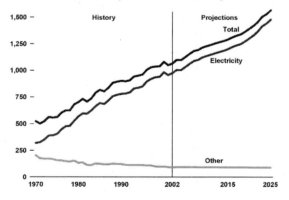

Figure 5–2

Source: Annual Energy Outlook 2004, January 2004

United States increased from 890 million tons in 1986 to 1111 million tons in 2004, thousands of small mines have closed as the total number of mines has declined over that same period. This gradual switch to larger-scale, higher-technology mining has cut the number of jobs in the industry almost by half between 1986 and 1997, from about 155,000 to about 82,000.

The jobs have also been moving west, particularly into the Powder River Basin of Wyoming, where huge new surface mines have become the primary source of fuel for electric generation. In eastern underground mines, productivity per miner has also increased through the use of larger-scale longwall mining techniques and improved cutting technology.

The decline in underground mining and the growth of surface mining has aggravated the legal problems of the industry in two key respects: (1) the declining number of companies engaged in underground mining has depleted a potential source of financial support for remedying the health and environmental problems created by these mines, and (2) the increasing number of surface mines has aroused significant opposition to the transformation of the landscape that they create.

1. HEALTH AND SAFETY IN UNDERGROUND MINING

Originally, most coal was mined through underground methods—the digging of shafts and tunnels spreading out underground from a single minehead. Although this creates highly intensive activity on the surface around the minehead, it does not necessarily appear to have a substantial impact on the surface of most of the land under which the coal lies because most of the work takes place underground.

Underground coal mines pose significant health and safety problems for the mine workers: (1) Methane gas, which is commonly found in association with coal, is potentially explosive and can also cause asphyxiation, so underground mines must be carefully ventilated. (2) As the coal is removed from an underground seam there is always a danger that the mine shaft will collapse, crushing anyone who happens to be in it; engineering plans to prevent mine collapse are not always successful. (3) Coal miners inhale large amounts of coal dust which, over a period of years, can cause black lung disease, a progressive loss of lung capacity that can be fatal unless the miner retires promptly after the initial diagnosis. Alan Derickson, Black Lung: Anatomy of a Public Health Disaster (Cornell University Press, 1998).

Public attention focused on the hazards of coal mining in the 1960s. Congress passed the Federal Coal Mine Health and Safety Act of 1969, 30 U.S.C. § 801 *et seq.*, and the Black Lung Benefits Act of 1972, 30 U.S.C. § 900 *et seq.* The latter statute required coal companies to pay benefits both to miners who had contracted the disease, including some who had left the companies' employ long ago. *Usery v. Turner Elkhorn Mining Co.*, 428 U.S. 1 (1976) (upholding retroactive application of Act).

Because the onset of black lung disease and other work-related illnesses may arise long after the miner quits working, the attribution of the injury to a particular employer has proven to be a problem, especially because many mining companies have gone out of business in the interim. The Coal Industry Retiree Health Benefit Act of 1992, 26 U.S.C. § 9701 *et seq.*, increased the responsibility of mining companies to pay lifetime medical benefits to miners. It adopted the policy that coal mining companies were retroactively liable for these health benefits if they had been in the coal business after the point in time when there was a "general understanding" between the industry and the United Mine Workers that lifetime health benefits would be paid. The retroactive elements of the Act were challenged by Eastern Enterprises, a company that had gotten out of the coal business many years ago[2], but now found itself responsible for the medical costs of some retired miners.

Eastern Enterprises alleged that it had been in the coal business only until 1966, at which time it spun off its coal business to a subsidiary that it later sold. The Act assigned Eastern the responsibility for paying the medical benefits of certain miners if the miners had worked for Eastern prior to 1966 and had not worked for any other currently existing mine operator since that time. In 1998, the case reached the Supreme Court, which held the Act unconstitutional as applied to Eastern in one of the most confusing opinions in recent Court history. The Court considered three potential Constitutional defects in the Coal Act and its application to Eastern Enterprises. One option was the Ex Post Facto Clause, but since *Calder v. Bull*, 3 U.S. 386 (1798) the Court had limited the application of that clause primarily to criminal statutes. A second option was the Due Process Clause, and the use of the once-popular notion of "substantive due process" to address the Act's unfairness. The third option was the Takings Clause, which had been more commonly applied to statutes that impose burdens on real property. Although the Court held the application of the Act to Eastern to be unconstitutional, there was no majority agreement on which clause of the Constitution had been violated. Four justices found that the Act constituted a taking of property without just compensation, but refused to consider the issue of substantive due process. One justice, Justice Kennedy, found that there was no taking, but held that the Act violated substantive due process as applied to Eastern Enterprises. Four dissenters would have upheld the Act. They agreed with Justice Kennedy that there was no taking, and they agreed that the Act should be tested on grounds of substantive due process, but they said that the statute did <u>not</u> violate substantive due process. *Eastern Enterprises v. Apfel,* 524 U.S. 498 (1998).

In the course of his opinion, Justice Kennedy interpreted the taking clause in a new way; he said that a liability to make a monetary payment, such as a tax or a fee, could never be the subject of a taking because it did not involve an "identified property interest" that was protected by the taking clause. The four dissenting justices all announced their agreement

---

2. Eastern Enterprises is the parent corporation of Boston Gas Company, the largest distributor of natural gas in New England, and of Midland Enterprises, Inc., the leading barge carrier of coal. See Note, Nontraditional Takings and the Coal Act, 20 Energy L. J. 117, 123 (1999).

with Justice Kennedy on this issue. As a result, a majority of the Court now supports an interpretation of the taking clause that would appear to make it completely inapplicable to statutes such as the Coal Industry Retiree Health Benefit Act.

Therefore the *Eastern Enterprises* case produced the highly unusual result of a part of a statute being found invalid but with no majority agreeing on the reason for the invalidity. The lack of any consistent rationale for the Court's result has posed difficult problems for the lower courts, as the following case illustrates. The case arose because the *Eastern Enterprises* decision struck down the Act as applied to a coal company that had left the business in 1966, but it left open the issue of the Act's validity to other companies who had continued in business after that time. The companies in the following case stayed in the coal business through the 1970s, but they argued that the precedent of *Eastern Enterprises* should protect them as well.

Unity Real Estate Co. v. Hudson

178 F.3d 649 (3d Cir.), cert. denied 528 U.S. 963 (1999).

■ BECKER, C.J. In *Eastern Enterprises v. Apfel,* 524 U.S. 498 (1998), the Supreme Court held unconstitutional the portion of the 1992 Coal Industry Retiree Health Benefit Act (Coal Act), 26 U.S.C. §§ 9701–9722 (1994 & Supp. II), that required former coal mine operators to pay for health benefits for retired miners and their dependents, as applied to a former operator who last signed a coal industry benefit agreement [an "NBCWA"] in 1964. In this case, we are asked to apply *Eastern* to former coal mine operators who were signatories to coal industry agreements in 1978 and thereafter. *Eastern* was decided by a sharply divided Court, and the parties disagree as to what, if any, principles commanded a majority.

The plaintiffs, Unity Real Estate ("Unity") and Barnes & Tucker Co. ("B&T"), challenge the Coal Act as applied to them as both a violation of substantive due process and an unconstitutional uncompensated taking. Although it is an exceedingly close question, and we are highly sympathetic to plaintiffs' unfortunate situation, in which retroactively imposed liability operates to bind them to commitments they had thought satisfied when they left the coal industry, we conclude that the Act is constitutional as applied to these plaintiffs. Accordingly, their recourse must be to Congress rather than to the courts.

First, we conclude, albeit with substantial hesitation, that the Coal Act does not violate due process. Our due process inquiry proceeds in two parts. We acknowledge at the outset that there is a gap between what the contracts between the union and the mining companies required and what the Coal Act now mandates from those former mining companies. Because this is a substantive due process challenge, we accord deference to Congress's judgments, based on the report and recommendations of the Coal Commission. While reasonable minds could differ on the point, we are satisfied that the agreements signed by the plaintiffs in 1978 and thereafter promised that miners and their dependents would receive lifetime benefits from the benefit funds, and that, at all events, these agreements informed reasonable expectations that the benefits would continue for life. Similarly, we conclude that it was reasonable for Congress to conclude that the plaintiffs' withdrawal from the funds contributed to the funds' financial instability, though the agreements themselves permitted withdrawal. The history of coal mining in this country also supports Congress's decision to step in when the funds that provided health benefits to retired miners began to falter.

The question we must then answer is whether those congressional judgments provide enough of a rationale for closing the gap between the contracts and the needs of the benefit funds through the mechanism of the Coal Act. Consistent with our due process jurisprudence, we ask whether the Coal Act was a rational response to the problems Congress identified, taking into account the Act's retroactivity, which is highly disfavored in our legal culture. In light of Congress's findings and in the context of extensive government regulation of the coal industry, we hold that it was not fundamentally unfair or unjust for Congress to conclude that the former coal companies should be responsible for paying for such benefits, even if they were no longer contractually obligated to pay into the benefit funds. The retroactive scope of this enactment, especially as applied to plaintiff Unity (eleven years), approaches the edge of permissible legislative action, but we cannot say that the law is beyond the legislative power.

We also decline to find a compensable taking on the ground that the Coal Act will put the plaintiffs out of business, because it is contrary to the reasoning of a majority of the Supreme Court in *Eastern*. Moreover, granting relief whenever a plaintiff could credibly argue that it would be driven out of business by a regulation would create major difficulties in evaluating the constitutionality of much modern legislation. We therefore decline to construe this regulatory burden as a "categorical taking" analogous to the total destruction of the value of a specific piece of real property.

[The court then analyzed the Supreme Court's *Eastern Enterprises* opinion:] Eastern Enterprises was involved in coal mining until 1965, and signed every NBCWA from 1947 until 1964. It was assigned liability for over 1000 miners, based on Eastern's status as the pre–1978 signatory for whom the miners had worked for the longest period of time; its total liability was estimated to be between $50 and $100 million. Eastern sued, claiming that the Coal Act was unconstitutional.

Four Justices concluded that the Act was a compensable taking as to Eastern. The plurality looked to three factors of particular significance in determining whether a taking had occurred: the economic impact of the regulation, its interference with reasonable investment-backed expectations, and the retroactive character of the government action. The plurality examined several previous cases to set the stage for its analysis [and] summarized this line of cases as follows:

> Our opinions make clear that Congress has considerable leeway to fashion economic legislation, including the power to affect contractual

commitments between private parties. Congress also may impose retroactive liability to some degree, particularly where it is "confined to
short and limited periods required by the practicalities of producing
national legislation." Our decisions, however, have left open the possibility that legislation might be unconstitutional if it imposes severe
retroactive liability on a limited class of parties that could not have
anticipated the liability, and the extent of that liability is substantially
disproportionate to the parties' experience.

Eastern, 118 S. Ct. at 2149 (plurality). The plurality held that the Coal Act,
as applied to Eastern, presented such an extreme case. On the economic
impact factor of the takings test, the plurality found "no doubt that the
Coal Act has forced a considerable financial burden upon Eastern," between $50 and $100 million. *Id.* (plurality). The plurality referred to
previous cases requiring that liability be proportional to a party's experience with the object of the challenged legislation. In the pension plan cases,
the parties had voluntarily negotiated and maintained pension plans, at
least for a while, and consequently their statutorily imposed liability was
linked to their own conduct. *See id.* at 2149–50 (plurality). Eastern did not
participate in the negotiations for the 1974 or subsequent NBCWAs, nor
did it agree to make contributions thereunder. "[The 1974, 1978, and
subsequent agreements] first suggest an industry commitment to the
funding of lifetime health benefits for both retirees and their family
members." *Id.* at 2150 (plurality).

The plurality then concluded that the Coal Act substantially interfered
with Eastern's reasonable investment-backed expectations. *See id.* at 2151
(plurality). It reasoned that retroactivity is generally disfavored in the law,
and that the length of the period of retroactivity and the extent of
Eastern's liability raised substantial questions of fairness. *See id.* at 2152
(plurality). Finally, the plurality found the nature of the government action
to be quite unusual, because the liability imposed was substantial, based on
conduct thirty to fifty years in the past, and unrelated to any commitment
Eastern made or injury it caused. *See id.* at 2153 (plurality).

The plurality declined to reach Eastern's substantive due process
argument, although it noted that takings and due process analyses are
often correlated. *See id.* (plurality). The plurality reiterated the Court's
past concerns about using the "vague contours" of the due process clause
to nullify laws. *Eastern,* 118 S. Ct. at 2153 (plurality) (citation omitted).
Justice Thomas agreed with the plurality's Takings Clause analysis but
wrote separately to reaffirm his belief that the Ex Post Facto Clause would
also apply to Eastern's predicament. *See id.* at 2154 (Thomas, J., concurring).

Justice Kennedy concurred in the judgment, providing the critical fifth
vote to strike the law down as applied to Eastern. He found takings
analysis inapplicable: "The Coal Act imposes a staggering financial burden
on the petitioner ... but it regulates the former mine owner without
regard to property. It does not operate upon or alter an identified property
interest, and it is not applicable to or measured by a property interest." *Id.*

at 2154 (Kennedy, J., concurring). Instead, he emphasized the law's distaste for retroactivity and found that the Coal Act's extreme retroactivity violated due process as applied to Eastern. *See id.* at 2158–59 (Kennedy, J., concurring). When the Court upheld retroactive legislation in the past, he noted, the statutes at issue were "remedial, designed to impose an actual, measurable cost of [the employer's] business which the employer had been able to avoid in the past." *Id.* at 2159 (Kennedy, J., concurring) (citation and internal quotation marks omitted) (alteration in original). Justice Kennedy concluded that "statutes may be invalidated on due process grounds only under the most egregious of circumstances. This case represents one of the rare instances in which even such a permissive standard has been violated." *Id.* (Kennedy, J., concurring).

Four Justices dissented, finding neither a taking nor a due process violation.

[The Court of Appeals then concluded that the key issue in the case then pending before it was whether companies that had stayed in the coal business through 1981, like the present plaintiffs, were distinguishable from Eastern because the bargaining agreements entered into during the time period between 1978 and 1981 implicitly promised the miners that they would receive lifetime health benefits.]

Unlike Eastern, Unity and B&T, as members of the Bituminous Coal Operators' Association (BCOA), participated in the negotiations that created the post–1978 funding structure. They benefitted from the NBCWAs by obtaining labor peace. Although the contract allowed the companies to unload their obligations to the retirees onto the Trustees, they should reasonably have anticipated that such a strategy would threaten the Funds and might well prompt a congressional response.... The question is what reasonable expectations the coal companies' actions created. While an expectation cannot be reasonable without some foundation in the real world, an explicit representation that the companies would provide lifetime benefits is not required, since reasonable expectations may arise from a consistent course of conduct as well.

Plaintiffs and amici argue that the coal companies never made any promises, implicit or explicit, or raised any expectations of lifetime benefits. They first point to the text of the NBCWAs, which did not themselves require the coal companies to provide lifetime benefits under all circumstances.... It is true that the funding contribution requirements were limited to the life of the agreement, "ending when this Agreement is terminated," in 1978 and subsequent NBCWAs. Yet all of these arguments have the same fundamental weakness, which is that they go to the contract and not to the reasonable expectations that might have been created by the contract. The United Mine Workers Association ("UMWA") negotiator's testimony is a particularly strong example of this: the parties could have agreed to eliminate benefits in any given negotiation, but there was no realistic chance that they would....

Ultimately, although the issue is close, we conclude that the Coal Act is targeted to address the problem of insufficient resources in the benefit funds and that it puts the burden on those who, in Congress's reasonable judgment, should bear it. The law's retroactivity is troubling, yet given the nature of the commitments at issue and the relationship of Coal Act liabilities to past acts in the industry, we cannot say that the Act violates due process.

■ ALDISERT, J., concurring: As a native of Carnegie, Pennsylvania—a coal mining and steel mill town near Pittsburgh—who is old enough to remember the organizational efforts of John L. Lewis in the coal fields in the 1930s and the 1947 Krug–Lewis Agreement, I no doubt have a unique perspective. I know first-hand the mantra of every coal miner through decades of strikes and picketing: "No Contract, No Work."

To the miner, the actual contract controlled, not the expectation of future agreements. Without the contract in hand, the miners would not pick up their lamps at the lamp house and descend into the shafts. They worked under the precise language in a given contract and under no other representations. The sordid history of the coal company towns that surrounded Carnegie, and the inhumane treatment of the miners and their families prior to effective unionization in the mines, impelled the miners to require thereafter that every representation of working conditions and benefits be set forth in clear language in a hard-fought written collective bargaining agreement.

The foregoing discussion is but my gratuitous interpretation of some of the history and contents of the Wage Agreements, and admittedly, it may be contrary to that expressed in most other judicial opinions. My views and those of judges with contrary interpretations are important in one respect only: My views and those of other judges are totally irrelevant. What is relevant is only that on the basis of evidence before it, Congress concluded that a promise of lifetime benefits had been made. This furnished the rational basis for enacting the controversial provisions of the Coal Act.

This, too, must be said. I am conscious that in light of the view that we take here, the handwriting is on the wall that a kind of hydraulic pressure will generate economic disasters in companies whose financial circumstances are similar to Unity and Barnes and Tucker. Without additional and more realistic Congressional intervention, we may see a phenomenon of the "last man standing," as companies disappear from the economic scene and responsibility for paying benefits shifts to surviving companies. If this case is any example and a forerunner of things to come, the operation of the present statutory solution to the vexing health benefit problem of retirees and their dependents may serve as a full employment program for bankruptcy lawyers of companies unable to make prescribed payments. Sadly, I do not believe that this statement is an argumentum ad terrorem.

I join in the judgment of the court.■

NOTES AND COMMENTS

1. Professor Jan Laitos of the University of Denver Law School has been suggesting for some years that retroactivity is one of the Court's half-

hidden concerns in all property rights cases, not just takings cases. See Jan G. Laitos, Legislative Retroactivity, 52 Wash. U. J. Urb. & Contemp. L. 81 (1997). In his 1999 treatise on property rights, he cites the *Eastern Enterprises* opinion as a vindication of his position. For his extended discussion of the history of the Supreme Court's retroactivity decisions and their modern relevance, see Jan Laitos, The Law of Property Rights Protection, Chs. 13–16 (1999).

2.   On the other hand, the Supreme Court in *Eastern Enterprises* is certainly not saying that all retroactive legislation is invalid on its face.[3] Both the plurality opinion by Justice O'Connor[4] and Justice Kennedy's concurrence carefully limit their discussion to the specific facts of that particular company's situation. Professor Mark Tushnet refers to such narrowly limited opinions as "judicial minimalism," and calls *Eastern Enterprises* the best recent example because "it used so many standards and made each important to the conclusion." Mark Tushnet, The New Constitutional Order and the Chastening of Constitutional Aspiration, 113 Harv. L. Rev. 29, 92–93 (1999). Is the most that we can discern from the *Eastern Enterprises* opinions that the Court may be telling us that it will employ some higher level of scrutiny in reviewing laws that have "severe retroactive" effect? Will the Court ever be able to come up with a bright line rule that alerts us to the degree of retroactivity that would be permitted?

3.   There have been no successful challenges to the Act's constitutionality since the *Unity* opinion. The standard set forth in *Unity* has been applied several times, and no plaintiff has succeeded in meeting the standard. The courts have tended to apply the substantive due process test, concluding that the plaintiff fails to meet that test. *See, e.g., Anker Energy Co. v. Consolidation Coal Co.*, 177 F.3d 161 (3d Cir.1999); *Berwind Corp. v. Comm'r of Soc. Sec.*, 307 F.3d 222 (3d Cir.2002); *Coltec Indus., Inc. v. Hobgood*, 280 F.3d 262 (3d Cir.2002); *Pittston Co. v. United States*, 368 F.3d 385 (4th Cir.2004); *A.T. Massey Coal Co., Inc. v. Massanari*, 305 F.3d 226 (4th Cir.2002); and *Apogee Coal Co. v. Holland*, 296 F.3d 1294 (11th Cir.2002).

4.   The Coal Act does not involve the acquisition of any property or money by the government, but requires the coal companies to pay money directly to a fund for the coal miners. Does the fact that the government is transferring wealth from one group to another, rather than acquiring a property interest itself, suggest the need for an analysis under the due process clause rather than the taking clause? *See* John V. Orth, Taking

---

3.   It should be noted, however, that a brief concurrence by Justice Thomas suggests that he may be willing to go that far (118 S. Ct. at 2154, Thomas J., concurring).

4.   "[L]egislation might be unconstitutional if it imposes severe retroactive liability on a limited class of parties that could not have anticipated the liability, and the extent of that liability is substantially disproportionate to the parties' experience." 118 S.Ct. at 2149. Legislation that "singles out certain employers to bear a burden that is substantial in amount, based on the employers' conduct far in the past, and unrelated to any commitment that the employers made or to any injury they caused, the governmental action implicates fundamental principles of fairness underlying the Taking Clause." 118 S.Ct. at 2153.

from A and Giving to B: Substantive Due Process and the Case of the Shifting Paradigm, 14 Constitutional Commentary 337 (1997).

5.   Today, surface mining (called strip mining by its critics) is the most efficient way of mining coal if the coal is relatively near the surface. About three-fifths of the coal mined in the United States is currently mined by surface mining using huge shovels the size of a multistory building. Surface mining does not create the same health and safety issues for the mine workers as underground mining. Moreover, surface mining is much less labor-intensive, so the productivity of each employee is far higher than in underground mines. On the other hand, the impact of surface mining on the use of the surface of the land is more extensive than the impact of underground mining (see § 2b of this chapter).

2.   EXTERNALITIES OF COAL MINING

In addition to the health and safety problems of mining workers, coal mining often has serious adverse impacts on other people who are not associated with the coal industry. These impacts have led to extensive legislation designed to regulate these impacts.

a.   UNDERGROUND MINING EXTERNALITIES

Underground mining was the only method of coal mining used in the 19th century and it still accounts for at least a third of the coal produced in the United States. A mine shaft is drilled down to the coal seam. Then tunnels are excavated through the seam. Two specific problems associated with underground mining have posed major regulatory issues: (1) Mines cause subsidence of the surface; either intentional, in the case of longwall mining[5], or accidental after the mine is abandoned and the support system collapses; and (2) Mines tap into seams of minerals and heavy metals that then leak out of the mines into streams or aquifers where they become water pollutants.

i.   Subsidence

Coal mine subsidence is the lowering of strata overlying a coal mine, including the land surface, caused by the extraction of underground coal. This lowering of the strata can have devastating effects. It often causes substantial damage to foundations, walls, other structural members, and the integrity of houses and buildings. Subsidence frequently causes sink-holes or troughs in land which make the land difficult or impossible to develop. Its effect on farming has been well documented: many subsided areas cannot be plowed or properly prepared. Subsidence can also cause the

---

5.   Longwall mining is a modern system of underground mining that uses highly automated coal cutting machines that excavate the entire coal seam and allow the earth above the seam to subside after excavation is complete. J. Thomas Lane II, Fire in the Hole to Longwall Shears: Old Law Applied to New Technology and other Longwall Mining Issues, 96 W.Va. L. Rev. 577 (1994).

loss of groundwater and surface ponds. *Keystone Bituminous Coal Ass'n v. DeBenedictis,* 480 U.S. 470 (1987).

In the famous case of *Pennsylvania Coal Co. v. Mahon,* 260 U.S. 393 (1922), the Supreme Court held that the Kohler Act, a Pennsylvania statute that prevented coal companies from mining coal in a way that caused subsidence to the owner of a surface estate, was invalid as a taking of property without just compensation. Justice Holmes, writing for the majority, acknowledged that while "there is a public interest ... in every purchase and sale and in all that happens within the commonwealth ...," that interest "does not warrant ... this kind of interference." Balancing the "extent of the public interest" (which Holmes characterized as largely private and "limited") against "the extent of the taking" (which Holmes characterized as "great" in that it rendered commercial mining impracticable), the Court concluded that the statute effected a taking requiring compensation. The *Pennsylvania Coal* decision represented the first time that the Supreme Court had held that a regulation could be "tantamount to a taking." In recent years, the Court has devoted increased attention to the issue of regulatory takings.

Sixty-five years after the initial *Pennsylvania Coal* decision, The Court returned to the issue of coal mine subsidence. In *Keystone Bituminous Coal Ass'n v. DeBenedictis,* 480 U.S. 470 (1987), this time upholding another Pennsylvania statute preventing coal companies from mining coal in a way that caused subsidence to roads, schools and other public facilities. The Court distinguished the earlier case on the ground that it was designed only to rearrange the rights among private parties, while the later statute was designed to protect public safety.

The holdings and assumptions of the Court in *Pennsylvania Coal* provide obvious and necessary reasons for distinguishing *Pennsylvania Coal* from the case before us today.... First, unlike the Kohler Act, the character of the governmental action involved here leans heavily against finding a taking; the Commonwealth of Pennsylvania has acted to arrest what it perceives to be a significant threat to the common welfare. Second, there is no record in this case to support a finding, similar to the one the Court made in *Pennsylvania Coal,* that the Subsidence Act makes it impossible for petitioners to profitably engage in their business, or that there has been undue interference with their investment-backed expectations.

Unlike the Kohler Act, which was passed upon in *Pennsylvania Coal,* the Subsidence Act does not merely involve a balancing of the private economic interests of coal companies against the private interests of the surface owners. The Pennsylvania Legislature specifically found that important public interests are served by enforcing a policy that is designed to minimize subsidence in certain areas.

After Keystone, the courts have had difficulty deciding whether to award damages to coal companies that have been denied permits. Where the federal government refused to issue a permit to mine coal to a company on the ground of a risk of public injury because of large cracks in the ground, collapsing structures, and breaks in gas, water and electrical lines, the federal circuit found that the mining company was not deprived of all beneficial use because "the nature of the owner's estate shows that the prescribed use interests were not part of the title to begin with." *M&J Coal Company v. United States*, 47 F.3d 1148 (Fed. Cir. 1995). But see *Machipongo Land and Coal Company, Inc. v. Commonwealth*, 719 A.2d 19 (Pa. Commw. Ct. 1998) (discussing various theories for measuring the extent to which the regulation diminishes the company's interest) and *Eastern Minerals International, Inc. v. U.S.*, 36 Fed. Cl. 541 (1996) (holding that an inexcusable delay in issuing a mining permit may constitute a taking).

Congress entered the dispute in 1992 by adding a new § 720 to the Mining Act, see Energy Policy Act of 1992, Pub. L. No. 102–486, § 2504(a)(1), § 720, 106 Stat. 2776, 3104 (1992), which provides:

(a) Requirements. Underground coal mining operations conducted after October 24, 1992, shall comply with each of the following requirements:

(1) Promptly repair, or compensate for, material damage resulting from subsidence caused to any occupied residential dwelling and structures related thereto, or non-commercial building due to underground coal mining operations. Repair of damage shall include rehabilitation, restoration, or replacement of the damaged occupied residential dwelling and structures related thereto, or non-commercial building. Compensation shall be provided to the owner of the damaged occupied residential dwelling and structures related thereto or non-commercial building and shall be in the full amount of the diminution in value resulting from the subsidence. Compensation may be accomplished by the purchase, prior to mining, of a noncancellable premium-prepaid insurance policy.

(2) Promptly replace any drinking, domestic, or residential water supply from a well or spring in existence prior to the application for a surface coal mining and reclamation permit, which has been affected by contamination, diminution, or interruption resulting from underground coal mining operations. Nothing in this section shall be construed to prohibit or interrupt underground coal mining operations.

The D.C. Circuit Court of Appeals upheld regulations promulgated under the Energy Policy Act requiring coal companies to repair or fully compensate homeowners for property damage caused by subsidence, even if a waiver agreement was in place. *National Mining Ass'n v. Babbitt*, 172 F.3d 906 (D.C. Cir. 1999). The National Mining Association ("NMA") had challenged the regulation as unreasonable "to the extent it purports to nullify prior agreements between owners of eligible structures and underground mine operators." The NMA argued that if the statute authorizes the annulment of waiver agreements, landowners would receive a windfall, and coal mining companies could suffer an unconstitutional taking of contract rights through a "double recovery" scheme, in which the mining company first pays a landowner for subsidence damage by buying waiver rights and then has to pay again for post-mining damage through the Energy Policy Act.

The government argued in response that there would be no "double recovery" because the cost of the waiver would be subtracted from the post-mining damage amount. The court agreed with the government's position.

NMA also argued that interference with contract rights is a per se taking. The court disagreed, citing the rule from *Connolly v. Pension Benefit Guar. Corp.*, 475 U.S. 211, 244 (1986): "legislation [that] disregards or destroys existing contractual rights does not always transform the regulation into an illegal taking." NMA should have been prepared to demonstrate why "(1) the economic impact of the regulation on the claimant; (2) the extent to which the regulation has interfered with investment-backed expectations; and (3) the character of the governmental action" show that an unconstitutional taking would result. (quoting *Penn Cent. Transp. Co. v. City of New York*, 438 U.S. 104, 124 (1978)).

At the present time, therefore, coal mining companies are responsible for most significant damages caused by subsidence. Although Justice Holmes' famous opinion in *Pennsylvania Coal* is still widely cited, the factual context on which it was based now appears to be obsolete.

ii. Acid Mine Drainage

Acid mine drainage can be associated with either surface mining or underground mining, and often results in water polluted with not only with high acidity but with toxic substances. The purpose of the Clean Water Act ("CWA") "is to restore and maintain the chemical, physical, and biological integrity of the nation's waters." 33 U.S.C. § 1251. The idea is to use technology-based effluent limitations and water quality-based ambient standards to achieve swimmable and fishable water throughout the United States. These standards are implemented through the national pollutant discharge elimination system ("NPDES") permit. The NPDES permit applies to discharges from point sources. 33 U.S.C. § 1342. Individual states are responsible for administering the CWA. The EPA may administer a program only if the state's program is found to be inappropriate.

The CWA makes the discharge of any pollutant into navigable waters by any person unlawful, except when in compliance with designated sections of the statute. 33 U.S.C. § 362. A pollutant is basically anything other than sewage from vessels or fluids used to facilitate the production from an oil or gas well.[6] Discharge of a pollutant is the addition of any pollutant to navigable waters from a point source. Navigable waters are the waters of the United States including the territorial seas. 40 C.F.R. § 122.2 (1998). "Point source" is broadly defined, and includes pipes, tunnels and animal feed lots. 33 U.S.C. § 1362(14).

In the following case, the Fourth Circuit attempted to apply the statutory language to acid mine drainage from a West Virginia mine.

---

6. Pollution from oil and gas wells is dealt with under other statutes. See Chapter 6.

United States v. Law

979 F.2d 977 (4th Cir.), cert. denied 507 U.S. 1030 (1993).

■ Per curiam Lewis R. Law and Mine Management, Inc. appeal their felony convictions for violating the Clean Water Act, 33 U.S.C. § 1319(c)(2) ("CWA") by knowingly discharging polluted water into Wolf and Arbuckle Creeks in Fayette County, West Virginia without a National Pollution Discharge Elimination System ("NPDES") permit. Finding no reversible error, we affirm.

In 1977 Lewis R. Law formed Mine Management, Inc. ("MMI"), a West Virginia corporation, to engage in various coal-related business activities. From MMI's inception, Law was its sole officer and stockholder. In 1980, MMI purchased 241 acres from the New River Company ("New River"). The conveyance included an aged coal preparation plant, masses of coal refuse ("gob piles"), and a water treatment system. New River installed this system in the late 1970s to collect, divert, treat, and discharge runoff and leachate from a gob pile that covered a large portion of the subject property.

The water treatment system was designed to reduce the acidity and metal content of drainage from the gob pile. The system comprised a collection pond near Wolf Creek, a pump, and piping that channeled the collected water over a ridge and through a hopper, which dispensed soda ash briquettes to raise the pH of the water. Iron and manganese then precipitated out as the water flowed through two settling ponds before its discharge into Arbuckle Creek.

The water treatment system was subject to an NPDES permit when MMI purchased the site. Despite repeated notice, however, neither MMI nor Law ever applied for, or was granted, an NPDES permit authorizing discharges into Wolf or Arbuckle Creeks. Due to MMI's failure to operate the water treatment system effectively, acid mine drainage discharged from the collection pond into Wolf Creek, or from the second settling pond into Arbuckle Creek, on at least 16 occasions between March, 1987 and November 15, 1991. Law and MMI were indicted for violating the CWA, 33 U.S.C. § 1319(c)(2), tried to a jury, and found guilty. Law was sentenced to two years in prison and Law and MMI were fined $80,000.00 each.

Law and MMI challenge their convictions on two grounds. They argue, first, that the trial court instructed the jury erroneously on the law governing their case and, second, that the court abused its discretion in barring evidence regarding New River's alleged policy of concealing preexisting environmental problems from prospective purchasers of its property. We reject both grounds of appeal.

Under the CWA, it is a felony to (a) knowingly (b) discharge 8 a pollutant (d) from a point source (e) into a navigable water of the United States (f) without, or in violation of, an NPDES permit. See 33 U.S.C. §§ 1311(a), 1319(c)(2), 1342(a); *Arkansas v. Oklahoma*, 112 S. Ct. 1046, 1054 (1992); see also 33 U.S.C. § 1362(12) (defining "discharge" as "any addition of any pollutant to navigable waters from any point source") (emphases added). Appellants do not contest that they added untreated acid mine drainage to Wolf and Arbuckle Creeks from the collection pond and the settling pond, respectively, knowing that they lacked the requisite NPDES permit.

In challenging the trial court's jury instructions, however, appellants contend that the CWA imposes liability only upon the generators of pollutants discharged into navigable waters of the United States, and not upon persons over whose property preexisting pollutants are passed along to flow finally into navigable waters. They contend that the trial court erred by refusing to instruct the jury that no responsibility lies for discharging pollutants that originate beyond one's own property, and by instructing the jury instead that

> . . . it is not a defense to the charge that the water discharged from the point source came from some other place or places before its discharge from the point source. It is not a defense to this action that some, or all, of the pollutants discharged from a point source originated at places not on the defendants' property. This is because the offense consists of the knowing discharge of a pollutant from a point source into a water of the United States [without, or in violation of, an NPDES permit]. J App 489–90

Appellants rely for this contention upon decisions in *National Wildlife Federation v. Consumers Power Co.,* 862 F.2d 580 (6th Cir. 1988), *National Wildlife Federation v. Gorsuch,* 224 U.S. App. D.C. 41, 693 F.2d 156 (D.C. Cir. 1982), and *Appalachian Power Co. v. Train,* 545 F.2d 1351 (4th Cir. 1976). In these cases, operators of power plants and dams diverted, then released, navigable waters of the United States. The appellate courts held that where "pollutants" existed in the waters of the United States before contact with these facilities, the mere diversion in the flow of the waters did not constitute "additions" of pollutants to the waters. *Consumers Power,* 862 F.2d at 585–86; *Gorsuch,* 693 F.2d at 174–75; *Train,* 545 F.2d at 1377–78. Appellants sought to square their case with these decisions by showing that the headwaters of Wolf and Arbuckle Creeks originated, and were polluted, before entering their water treatment system, so that, like the power plant and dam operators, they had no duty to remove preexisting pollutants.

With respect to pollutants preexisting in the waters of the United States, where the flow of the waters is merely diverted, the trial court's jury instructions did not state the law with strict accuracy ("it is not a defense . . . that some, or all, of the pollutants . . . originated at places not on the defendants' property"). The error was harmless, however, because, as a matter of law, appellants' water treatment system was not part of the waters of the United States; to the contrary, the system constituted a point source.

Unlike the river and lake waters diverted in *Consumers Power, Gorsuch,* and *Train,* appellants' water treatment system collected runoff and leachate subject to an NPDES permit under the CWA, and therefore was not part of the "waters of the United States." *See* 40 C.F.R. § 122.2(g)

("Waste treatment systems, including treatment ponds and lagoons designed to meet the requirements of CWA ... are not waters of the United States."). The origin of pollutants in the treatment and collection ponds is therefore irrelevant. The proper focus is upon the discharge from the ponds into Wolf and Arbuckle Creeks.

Appellants' treatment system is also unlike the power plants and dams at issue in *Consumers Power, Gorsuch*, and *Train* because it clearly satisfies the statutory definition of "point source." *See* 40 C.F.R. § 122.2 (a "point source" is "any discernible, confined and discrete conveyance, including but not limited to any pipe, ditch, channel, ... conduit, ... discrete fissure, ... [or] landfill leachate collection system ... from which pollutants are or may be discharged" (emphasis added); "discharge" includes "surface runoff which is collected or channeled by man"); see also *Sierra Club v. Abston Constr. Co.*, 620 F.2d 41, 47 (5th Cir. 1980) (collection and channeling of runoff constitutes a point source). Because appellants' treatment system was, as a matter of law, not part of the waters of the United States but instead a point source, the trial court's instructions to the jury were without prejudicial error.

Appellants also claim that the trial court abused its discretion in excluding evidence concerning New River's alleged policy of concealing existing environmental problems from prospective purchasers. Under the foregoing analysis of the CWA, the relevant *mens rea* issue was Law's knowledge as of March, 1987, that the ponds were discharging pollutants into the creeks without, or in violation of, an NPDES permit. Appellants' attempts to cross-examine former New River employees Louis Briguglio and Don Reedy regarding the alleged policy were therefore properly excluded as irrelevant. Law's testimony regarding his conversations with Briguglio were properly excluded as hearsay.

For the foregoing reasons, we affirm the convictions of Lewis R. Law and Mine Management, Inc. on all counts.▪

NOTES AND COMMENTS

1.   There are two main categories of criteria with which compliance is required under the Clean Water Act. (A) Technology-based effluent limits establish discharge requirements from coal mining point sources based on control technology. The regulations require compliance with numerical limits based on the capacities of technologies examined, but do not prescribe the use of a particular technology. Technology-based limits are used to ensure the uniform adoption of advanced effluent standards across entire industry groups without considering the discharge locations or water quality in the receiving water body. 40 C.F.R. § 434. (B) Water quality standards are based on the physical qualities of the water body and are designed to protect the designated uses of that water body. Individual states set their own water quality standards, subject to EPA approval. These standards must "protect the public health or welfare, enhance the quality of the water, and serve the purposes of the CWA." 33 U.S.C.

§ 1313(c)(2)(A). NPDES permit limitations are then established regardless of the availability or effectiveness of treatment technologies. If the existing water quality is above what is necessary to support designated activities, the water quality standards cannot be set lower than what currently exists. Waters that have been designated "special national resources" may not be degraded at all. 40 C.F.R. §§ 131.10, 131.12.

The EPA has published regulations governing discharge of acid mine drainage from mines. These so-called "new source performance standards" establish different sets of rules for different subcategories of mines, and specify the procedures mine owners should use to control discharges of stormwater runoff that contain acids. See 40 C.F.R. Part 434. The NPDES permit program would require a permit for a mine even after the close of operations if a discharge occurs, but there is little incentive to comply with a permit once mining is finished. Often coal companies become insolvent or the responsible owner no longer exists. Caroline Henrich, Acid Mine Drainage: Common Law, SMCRA, and the Clean Water Act, 10 J. Nat. Resources & Envtl. L. 235 (1994–95). For these reasons, CWA compliance is usually applied only to active mining sites. Mary J. Hackett, Remining and the Water Quality Act of 1987: Operators Beware!, 13 Colum. J. Envtl. L. 79, 115–17 (1987). The EPA and state environmental agencies seek to prevent the development and release of acid mine drainage by requiring either active or passive treatment systems. An active system may be manual or mechanical and requires the periodic addition of reagents, ongoing support, and maintenance; for example, adding lime to a treatment pool to raise the pH of an acidic discharge. Passive systems are designed to be self-sustaining and use chemical or biological processes that rely on no external support. For example, constructed wetlands are sometimes used to treat mine drainage because many of the plant species that comprise wetlands thrive on acidic material.

Drainage from abandoned underground coal mines is often a major water pollution problem in those areas where coal has been mined for many years, and many such mines have been placed on the National Priority List under the Comprehensive Environmental Response, Compensation, and Liability Act ("CERCLA"), 42 U.S.C. § 9601 et seq. This problem is often aggravated in the East because of the high sulfur content of the coal. See William H. Rodgers, Jr., Environmental Law 724 (West Publishing, 2d ed. 1994).

2.   Does U.S. v. Law mean that if anyone owns a point source that is discharging pollutants into water of the United States without a permit, that person is in violation of the CWA, regardless of where the pollutants originated? A review of the joint appendix in the record of the case shows the complexity of the situation faced by Law and MMI.[7]

---

7.   See generally Phillip B. Scott, S. Benjamin Bryant, Criminal Enforcement of the Clean Water Act in the Coal Fields: United States v. Law and Beyond, 95 W.Va. L. Rev. 663 (Spring, 1993).

Law formed Mine Management Company in 1977 to engage in various business activities related to the coal industry. MMI leased the right to recover coal from the property owned by New River Company. Prior to this, New River Company operated the Lochgelly mine on the site. Coal mining activities also took place on the property adjacent to the site. Refuse from New River's coal processing was dumped at the site, resulting in a gob pile that covered approximately 100 acres of the surface, and approximately 100 feet deep. The head waters of the Wolf and Arbuckle Creeks are located near the foot of this gob pile. New River installed a series of collection ponds on the Wolf and Arbuckle Creeks to treat acid mine drainage in 1979. New River acquired an NPDES permit, which was in place when MMI purchased the property.

MMI purchased 241 acres of the surface of the property owned by New River, including the various treatment ponds, in 1980. Between 1980 and 1991, Law was informed on numerous occasions that an NPDES permit was required for the treatment ponds on his property. Law failed to comply.

Conflicting evidence was presented at trial as to how acid mine drainage entered the Wolf Creek collection pond. Prosecution experts testified that acid mine drainage ("AMD") leached from the surface of the gob pile as a result of rain and the migration of water through the pile. Defense experts testified that the AMD came from underground springs contaminated as a result of mining activities on other properties adjacent to MMI's site. Law argued that he had no duty to treat the AMD because he was the surface owner and could not be required to treat pollutants generated below the surface. However, Law's argument was unpersuasive because the statute does not require that the defendant create the pollutants. The CWA does not regulate the generation of pollutants, but the addition of pollutants to navigable waters. See *Natural Resources Defense Council v. EPA,* 859 F.2d 156, 170 (D.C. Cir. 1988) (CWA jurisdiction limited to regulation of discharge of pollutants).

If Law's argument were accepted, could a mining company discharge pollutants as long as the pollutants were generated by someone else? In the coal fields, could the CWA be circumvented by severing (1) the AMD producing estate, (2) the subsurface from the AMD discharging estate, and (3) the surface? Should there be special treatment of environmental criminal defendants, sometimes called "green collar" criminals, in regard to the criminal intent requirement? *See* Lawrence Friedman & H. Hamilton Hackney III, Questions of Intent: Environmental Crimes and "Public Welfare" Offenses, 10 Villanova Envtl L. J. 1 (1999).

3. Another one of Law's challenges was that the Wolf and Arbuckle Creeks were polluted before entering the collection ponds. He claimed that the ponds added no additional pollutants and therefore were not regulated by the CWA. This argument was based on evidence that the original headwaters of the stream extended to the area now covered by the gob pile and that the ponds lay in the original stream beds. This argument rested on an analogy to the reservoirs created by power plants and dams. Law relied on a long line of cases holding that power plants and dams, which

merely divert or accumulate waters of the United States and then release those waters, do not require an NPDES permits if they do not physically add pollutants from the outside world into those waters, and they are not required to remove pollutants from the waters that were already there. The *Law* court rejected this analogy. The court held that the treatment ponds were a part of Law's water treatment system and the waters in them were not waters of the United States, unlike the reservoir behind the dam in a river. Thus when water was discharged from the treatment pond into a river, it was a discharge into the waters of the United States and therefore subject to the CWA. *See Rayle Coal Co. v. Chief, Division of Natural Resources,* 401 S.E.2d 682 (W.Va. 1990).

4. Is criminal prosecution the appropriate way to deter environmental crimes? Some contend that its complexity and reliance on detailed prescriptive and proscriptive rules makes application of traditional criminal liability standards frequently unfair in the context of environmental law. This unfairness may be exacerbated by the fact that federal environmental laws typically provide that any responsible officer of a corporation can be held criminally responsible for violations if they knew or should have known that the corporation was violating environmental regulations. For contrasting views on this fairness issues see Richard Lazarus, Meeting the Demands of Integration in the Evolution of Environmental Law: Reforming Environmental Criminal Law, 83 Geo. L.J. 2407 (1995); and Kathleen Brickey, Environmental Crime at the Crossroads: The Intersection of Environmental and Criminal Law Theory, 71 *Tulane L. Rev.* 487 (1997). For a challenge to the traditional deterrence-based theory of enforcement in environmental law, see David B. Spence, The Shadow of the Rational Polluter, 89 Calif. L. Rev. 917 (2001).

b.   SURFACE MINING EXTERNALITIES

Although surface mining lacks the pervasive health and safety problems of underground mining, it has a massive impact on the landscape. As the mining equipment has grown in size and efficiency, its ability to reach deep into the earth and permanently transform its surface has greatly exceeded the expectations of people familiar only with early forms of strip mining.

Since 1977, the Federal Surface Mining Control and Reclamation Act ("SMCRA", 30 U.S.C. § 1201 *et seq.*) has imposed regulations on strip mining to mitigate the adverse effects on the use of the surface of the land. In general, where the land is capable of being farmed, mining companies must restore the original surface; in other cases, they must leave it in a way that retards erosion. Land that is classified as prime farmland is not supposed to be mined at all. Agricultural interests were among the strong proponents of tough legislation designed to protect farmland.

Mining companies must get approval of reclamation plans before proceeding to mine. Under these plans the company must: (1) restore the land to a condition capable of supporting uses as good as existed before; (2) restore the approximate original contour of the land; (3) stabilize the soil; (4) spread the topsoil back over the area; and (5) revegetate the site.

i.   *Federalism Issues*

From the beginning, questions were raised about whether a national program was the appropriate way to deal with surface mining. First, surface mining for coal was concentrated in a relatively small number of states, and was not on the radar screen of many people outside these areas. Second, the issues associated with surface mining differ greatly depending on the terrain and climate of the particular region; the Appalachian ridges, the Illinois prairies, and the high plains of Montana vary so greatly in terms of geomorphology and climate that the ability to generalize on national standards was in question.

Despite these doubts, Congress passed SMCRA to "establish a nationwide program to protect society and the environment from the adverse effects of surface coal mining operations" while assuring that there is an adequate supply of coal to meet the nation's energy needs. 30 U.S.C. § 1202(a), (f). Like the CAA and CWA, SMCRA is a cooperative effort between the federal and state governments to control surface mining. The federal role is administered by the Office of Surface mining (OSM) in the Department of the Interior.

Congress did provide for a great deal of state participation in the program. States may get federal approval to administer the Act themselves. Under SMCRA, a state may obtain jurisdiction for regulating surface mining on non-federal lands within the state by submitting a program proposal to the Secretary of the Interior. 30 U.S.C. § 1253. Once a state achieves "primacy," the federal Office of Surface Mining acts only as an overseer and its authority is limited.

States may submit any proposed changes in the surface mining program to the Director of the Office of Surface Mining. 30 C.F.R. § 732.17. The director may approve the changes upon a finding that the amendment is consistent with SMCRA, 30 U.S.C. § 1253(a)(7), and consistent with the implementation of SMCRA 30 C.F.R. § 730.5. These amendments must also comply with other federal environmental laws, such as the Clean Water Act. 30 U.S.C. § 1292(a)(3). *Fincastle Mining, Inc. v. Babbitt*, 842 F. Supp. 204 (W.D. Va. 1993).

The adoption of SMCRA was challenged by a number of states that thought the federal government was infringing on states' traditional responsibilities. SMCRA was one of a number of federal environmental statutes passed in the 1970s pursuant to the authority of Congress under the interstate commerce power. Little doubt was expressed about the basic constitutional authority of the federal government to regulate most of the problems addressed by this environmental legislation. It was obvious that air and water moved across state lines, so legislation designed to control the pollution of these media was clearly within the scope of the federal government's power under the interstate commerce clause of the Constitution. SMCRA, on the other hand, posed a more complex constitutional issue. The primary externality of surface mining might be characterized as "land pollution," and land is more localized than air or water.

The coal industry initially challenged SMCRA as an overreaching of federal power under the commerce clause, and district judges in Indiana and Virginia initially held the statute invalid. A district judge in Indiana, in *Indiana v. Andrus*, 501 F. Supp. 452 (1980), held (1) that the sections of SMCRA designed to protect prime farmland are directed at facets of surface coal mining which have no substantial and adverse effects on interstate commerce; (2) that the prime farmland provisions are not related to the removal of air and water pollution and are, therefore, not reasonably and plainly adapted to the legitimate end of removing any substantial adverse effect on interstate commerce; and (3) that all of these sections are not within powers delegated to Congress and are unlawful as being contrary to the Tenth Amendment to the Constitution. He also held unconstitutional the "approximate original contour provisions, the topsoiling requirements, the areas unsuitable for surface mining provisions, [and those provisions] which combine to require a commitment by an operator to a certain postmining land use" because they "are not directed at the alleviation of water or air pollution, to the extent there are such effects, and are not means reasonably and plainly adapted to removing any substantial and adverse effect on interstate commerce. These sections are outside the enumerated powers of Congress and are, therefore, unconstitutional and unlawful."

The district judge went on to hold that these provisions of the statute also violated the Tenth Amendment, which reserves to the states those powers not delegated to the federal government, because (a) A[l]and use control and planning is a traditional or integral governmental function or area of State sovereignty, and (b) the statute constituted "displacement, regulation and altering of the management structure and operation of the traditional area of State sovereignty or integral governmental function of land use planning and control" in violation of the Tenth Amendment. The federal government appealed to the United States Supreme Court from both the Indiana and Virginia decisions. The Court reversed and upheld the validity of the statute in two separate opinions, *Hodel v. Virginia Surface Mining & Reclamation Ass'n, Inc.*, 452 U.S. 264 (1981) and *Hodel v. Indiana*, 452 U.S. 314 (1981). In the latter case the Court said "In our view, Congress was entitled to find that the protection of prime farmland is a federal interest that may be addressed through Commerce Clause legislation. ... The court incorrectly assumed that the Act's goals are limited to preventing air and water pollution.... Congress was also concerned about preserving the productive capacity of mined lands and protecting the public from health and safety hazards that may result from surface coal mining. All the provisions invalidated by the court below are reasonably calculated to further these legitimate goals."

The Supreme Court also rejected summarily the district court's Tenth Amendment analysis:

> The District Court ruled that the real purpose and effect of the Act is land-use regulation, which, in the court's view, is a traditional state governmental function. ...We hold that the District Court erred in

concluding that the challenged provisions of the Act contravene the Tenth Amendment. The sections of the Act under attack in this case regulate only the activities of surface mine operators who are private individuals and businesses, and the District Court's conclusion that the Act directly regulates the States as States is untenable.

The Court also reversed the district court on the issues of the takings and due process clauses.

The Court's analysis of the interstate commerce clause in the two *Hodel* opinions was almost routine. Between 1937 and 1995, the Court never held a federal statute invalid for exceeding federal power under the commerce clause. That string was broken by the Court's decision in *United States v. Lopez*, 115 S. Ct. 1624 (1995) in which the Court struck down a federal statute making it a crime to carry a gun within a certain distance of a school. The crucial votes in the 5–4 decision were provided by Justice Kennedy and Justice O'Connor, who joined in a concurring opinion written by Justice Kennedy, which noted that earlier decisions upholding "the exercise of federal power where commercial transactions were the subject of regulation [is] within the fair ambit of the Court's practical conception of commercial regulation and are not called in question by our decision today...."

[U]nlike the earlier cases to come before the Court here neither the actors nor their conduct have a commercial character, and neither the purposes nor the design of the statute have an evident commercial nexus. The statute makes the simple possession of a gun within 1,000 feet of the grounds of the school a criminal offense. In a sense any conduct in this interdependent world of ours has an ultimate commercial origin or consequence, but we have not yet said the commerce power may reach so far. If Congress attempts that extension, then at the least we must inquire whether the exercise of national power seeks to intrude upon an area of traditional state concern.

An interference of these dimensions occurs here, for it is well established that education is a traditional concern of the States.... The proximity to schools, including of course schools owned and operated by the States or their subdivisions, is the very premise for making the conduct criminal. In these circumstances, we have a particular duty to insure that the federal-state balance is not destroyed.

Does the standard set forth in Justice Kennedy's opinion threaten SMCRA's continuing validity?[8] Can you think of any federal laws regulating energy that might not have "an evident commercial nexus?"

ii. *Enforcement Issues*

The regulations adopted by the Secretary of Interior under SMCRA were also subjected to numerous challenges in the courts. Final rules

---

8. Prior to 1937, when the Supreme Court reversed its earlier narrow readings of the commerce clause, it was well accepted that "mining" was a local activity that was not within federal control under the commerce power. Federal authority began only when the mined

setting out the responsibilities of the Office of Surface Mining ("OSM") were adopted near the end of President Carter's term. These were challenged by the coal industry, but in 1981 a new Secretary of the Interior took office in the Reagan administration, with the result that the regulations were significantly relaxed, which in turn led to litigation by environmental groups.

On paper, SMCRA is one of the toughest environmental statutes on the books. In practice, there is often little support for enforcing the act to the letter. The cost of restoring the site to permit agricultural use is often much greater than the cost of simply keeping it safe and forested.

The permitting requirements of SMCRA say that a permit is necessary before any person may engage in surface mining operations. 30 U.S.C. § 1256(a). The permit application requires the mine operators to plan the mining operation in detail, identify adverse effects on the environment, and devise a reclamation plan. The permit application must be denied if the owner has unabated violations of SMCRA or other environmental laws.

The permit must contain details regarding timing of the operation, and engineering and design provisions that will ensure field performance. The permit must be revoked or suspended if the operation is in non-compliance.

Reclamation requirements are often the most controversial issues in a SMCRA permit. SMCRA is designed to assure "complete reclamation of mine sites." *Cat Run Coal Co. v. Babbitt,* 932 F. Supp. 772, 774–5 (S.D. W.Va. 1996). Every operator of a mining operation must post a bond which is calculated to ensure that the commitments set forth in the permit are carried out. 30 U.S.C. § 1259(a). The bond requirement ensures that funds are available to reclaim mined lands if an operator defaults and to give incentive to comply with the reclamation requirements. See Barlow Burke, Reclaiming the Law of Suretyship, 21 So. Ill. U. L. J. 449 (1997).

To be released from liability under SMCRA, an operator must apply to the appropriate agency and demonstrate performance of the reclamation work required under SMCRA and the bond. 30 U.S.C. § 1269(c). The appropriate agency inspects the reclamation work. First, the operator must complete backfilling, grading, and drainage control in accordance with the reclamation plan. Then the operator must revegetate the regraded mine lands. Finally, if the agency finds that all reclamation requirements have been met, it will release the reclamation bond.

National Wildlife Federation v. Lujan

950 F.2d 765 (D.C. Cir. 1991).

■ RANDOLPH, J. Surface coal mining is a temporary use of the land. When mining ends the land must be restored. After revegetation is complete, and

products moved into the stream of commerce. In *Lopez*, Justices Kennedy and O'Connor make it clear that they would not reopen the Court's 1937 reversal of those decisions. In a separate concurrence, Justice Thomas suggested a willingness to do so.

sufficient time has passed to ensure its success—5 years in the east, 10 years in the arid west—a mine operator who has fulfilled all legal requirements is entitled to have his performance bond released. The principal question in this case is whether under the Surface Mining Control and Reclamation Act of 1977, 30 U.S.C. §§ 1201–1328 (1988), regulatory jurisdiction may then be terminated. The Secretary of the Interior issued regulations so providing. *See* 52 Fed. Reg. 24,092 (1987) (Notice of Proposed Rulemaking); 53 Fed. Reg. 44,356 (1988) (Final Rule). The district court, at the behest of the National Wildlife Federation and others ("NWF"), struck them down. *National Wildlife Fed'n v. Interior Dep't,* 31 Env't Rep. Cas. (BNA) 2034, 2040–41 (D.D.C. 1990). Because we find the Act silent on the issue presented and the Secretary's interpretation permissible, we reverse.

As night follows day, litigation follows rulemaking under this statute. Since the Act's passage in 1977, in cases challenging regulations, our opinions have described in considerable detail the Act's structure and operation. We shall assume familiarity with those opinions. In brief, the Act is intended to protect the environment from the adverse effects of surface coal mining while ensuring an adequate supply of coal to meet the nation's energy requirements. 30 U.S.C. § 1202(a), (f). Section 501(b) directs the Secretary to promulgate regulations establishing regulatory procedures and performance standards "conforming to the provisions of" the Act (30 U.S.C. § 1251(b)). Section 515 contains detailed "environmental protection performance standards" applicable to "all surface coal mining and reclamation operations." 30 U.S.C. § 1265. Through the Office of Surface Mining Reclamation and Enforcement ("OSMRE"), the Secretary is to take steps "necessary to insure compliance with" the Act. 30 U.S.C. § 1211(a), (c)(1). The states too have a significant role to play. After an interim period of federal regulation, states had the option of proposing plans for implementing the Act consistent with federal standards on non-federal lands. When the Secretary approved the programs submitted by the states, those states became primarily responsible for regulating surface coal mining and reclamation in the non-federal areas within their borders. 30 U.S.C. § 1253. In states not having an approved program, the Secretary implemented a federal program. 30 U.S.C. § 1254(a), (b). The "permanent program" regulations issued under section 501(b) set standards for federally-approved state programs and for the federal program that takes effect when a State fails to "implement, enforce, or maintain" its program. 30 U.S.C. § 1254(a). Enforcement is carried out by the "regulatory authority," that is, the state agency administering the federally-approved program, the Secretary administering a federal program, or OSMRE conducting oversight of state programs. *See* 30 C.F.R. § 700.5.

The primary means of ensuring compliance is the permit system established in sections 506 through 514 and section 515(a). 30 U.S.C. §§ 1256–1264, 1265(a). A permit is required for "any surface coal mining operations." 30 U.S.C. § 1256. Summaries of applications for permits must be published, and objections may be submitted by local agencies or by "any person having an interest which ... may be adversely affected" by a proposed operation. 30 U.S.C. § 1263. Each application must include a reclamation plan. Section 507(d), 30 U.S.C. § 1257(d). A reclamation plan describes the present use of the land, proposed and possible post-mining uses of the land, and what steps the operator will take to ensure the viability of the latter. Among other things, the plan must show how the operator will achieve soil reconstruction and revegetation of the mined area. Section 508, 30 U.S.C. § 1258. A permit application can only be approved if it demonstrates that "all requirements" of the Act have been satisfied and that "reclamation as required by [the Act] . . . can be accomplished." 30 U.S.C. § 1260.

Section 509 requires the operator to post a performance bond in an amount sufficient to secure completion of reclamation. The operator and the surety remain liable under the bond for the duration of the surface mining and reclamation operation and until the end of the "revegetation period" (5 or 10 years) prescribed by section 515(20). 30 U.S.C. § 1259(b). At that time, the operator may petition the regulatory authority for release of the bond. The petition must be published, and is subject to the same opportunities for comment and hearing as the permit application. 30 C.F.R. § 800.40(a)(2), (b)(2). Further, "no bond shall be fully released . . . until reclamation requirements of the Act and the permit are fully met." *Id.* § 800.40(c)(3).

Prior to this rulemaking, the relationship between bond release and continuing regulatory jurisdiction was unclear. 53 Fed. Reg. 44,356 (1988). State authorities would decline to act on violations reported after bond release, even when the allegation was that the bond had been released improperly. In some such cases, OSMRE would re-assert jurisdiction directly. *Id.* This led to confusion about whether a site was or was not subject to the Act. In order to end this confusion, the Secretary promulgated the rules at issue, which specify when regulatory jurisdiction over a site terminates. *Id.* Thus, 30 C.F.R. § 700.11(d)(1) provides that "a regulatory authority may terminate its jurisdiction . . . over [a] reclaimed site" when (and only when) the authority determines (either independently or pursuant to a bond release) that "all requirements imposed" have been completed. *Id.* By tying termination of jurisdiction to bond release, the Secretary sought to resolve doubts about the former, while imposing minimum standards for the latter on the state authorities.

In the district court NWF claimed that it was "premature" to terminate regulatory jurisdiction at the time of bond release. Complaint of National Wildlife Federation at 14, Civ. No. 88–3345 (D.D.C. filed Nov. 17, 1988). The district court interpreted NWF's complaint not simply as an objection to timing, but as an attack on "the concept of terminating jurisdiction." *National Wildlife Federation v. Interior Dept.,* 31 Env't Rep. Cas. (BNA) at 2039. Seizing on language found in section 521 of the Act, 30 U.S.C. § 1271, the court noted that the Secretary was under "an ongoing duty . . . to correct violations . . . without limitation." 31 Env't Rep. Cas. (BNA) at 2040. The court also believed that allowing termination of jurisdiction would "hinder" the Act's goal of "protecting the environment."

Id. at 2041. In view of these considerations, the court believed it proper to interpret Congress' silence on the precise question of termination of jurisdiction as a call for perpetual regulation. *Id.*

The district court's opinion and NWF's claim of prematurity suffer from the same flaw. Section 521 cannot be read to express or assume that regulatory jurisdiction over a surface coal mining and reclamation operation must continue forever. It is true that section 521 requires the regulatory authority to "take ... action" "whenever" a violation occurs, 30 U.S.C. § 1271(a)(1) (emphasis added). But by "action," section 521 means primarily the issuance of an order requiring "cessation of surface coal mining and reclamation operations." 30 U.S.C. § 1271(a)(2). Section 521(a)(2) also empowers the Secretary to impose other "affirmative obligations" on the operator; these, however, are to be exacted "in addition to the cessation order," 30 U.S.C. § 1271(a)(2). It thus appears that Congress contemplated enforcement actions only during mining and reclamation operations. If the site were no longer the scene of a "surface coal mining and reclamation operation," and it could not be by the time the bond is released, it would be difficult to see how section 521 could nevertheless continue to apply. The regulation, then, cannot be upheld or struck down solely by reference to Congress' intent, at least not as that intent was expressed in section 521. . . .

NWF apparently believes that because, under the regulations, it is possible for some operators to avoid liability for violations of the Act that are undiscovered or undiscoverable at the time of bond release, the regulations improperly fail to promote the Act's purpose: protection of the environment. The Act, however, was a compromise, designed both to protect the environment and to ensure an adequate supply of coal to meet the nation's energy requirements. *See* 30 U.S.C. § 1202(a), (f). The Secretary struck a reasonable balance between these competing interests in his interpretation of the Act (and, as noted above, responded to NWF's concerns about unabated environmental harm by adding 30 C.F.R. § 700.11(d)(2)).

The regulation also strikes a reasonable balance between the gradual increase, due to improving technology, in what legitimately may be demanded of an operator, and an operator's need for certainty regarding closed sites. "It would not be appropriate ... to require operators who had ... met the standards of their permits and the applicable regulatory program to ... reclaim [closed sites] in accordance with new technology." 53 Fed. Reg. 44,361 (1988).

In short, we find the regulation consistent with the goals of the Act and a reasonable interpretation of it. Furthermore, the factors supporting "the concept of terminating jurisdiction," 31 Env't Rep. Cas. (BNA) at 2039, buttress the Secretary's decision to use bond release as the point at which termination occurs. Until bond release the operator is still liable, and an attempt to terminate jurisdiction sooner would violate the terms of the Act. Nothing in the statute speaks in fixed temporal terms of regulation after bond release. Under the regulation that is the point at which the regulatory authority must "sign off" on the reclamation project. Bond release also has the advantage of being an independently identifiable point in time. For these reasons the Secretary's choice was not arbitrary or capricious. Accordingly, we reverse the district court's judgment insofar as it invalidated 30 C.F.R. § 700.11(d).■

NOTES AND COMMENTS

1.   The coal industry estimates that more than two million acres of mined lands have been reclaimed in the past twenty years. This represents an area larger than the state of Delaware. Reclamation involves the following steps: leveling off fill soil by bulldozers, placing topsoil or approved substitute over graded area, reseeding with native vegetation, crops and/or trees, and monitoring the area for many years to ensure success of reclamation. National Coal Mining Association, Fast Facts About Coal, www.nma.org.

Coal mining lands have been restored to a variety of uses. Farming is one of the most common post-mining land uses. Housing development is often used for mined lands located near urban centers. Often, special uses arise out of reclamation projects. For example, the OSM coordinates the use of trees grown on reclaimed coal mine lands in Maryland for the National Christmas Pageant of Peace tree-lighting ceremony in Washington, D.C. A former coal mine in West Virginia now includes a little league baseball field. Post mining land uses, www.osmre.gove.

2.   Depending on the nature of the soils and terrain and on the desired end use, the time that it takes to determine with some confidence whether reclamation has been successfully accomplished can range from a few years to many decades. In most instances, the mining companies are not enthusiastic about retaining responsibility for sites that are no longer producing income, but once the company's deep pocket disappears, conditions on the site may deteriorate. Can you think of other solutions for the long-term maintenance of reclaimed mining sites?

3.   Definition of the relative powers of the federal and state agencies under SMCRA remains a source of controversy. *See* Robert E. Beck, Water and Coal Mining in Appalachia: Applying the Surface Mining Control and Reclamation Act of 1977 and the Clean Water Act, 106 W. Va L. Rev. 629 (2204). The D.C. Circuit upheld the regulations of the federal Office of Surface Mining under which it retains backup authority to issue a notice of violation even though it has delegated to a state agency primary enforcement authority. *National Mining Ass'n v. U.S. Dep't of the Interior*, 70 F.3d 1345 (D.C. Cir. 1995).

c. MOUNTAIN-TOP MINING

The most controversial form of surface mining has been the so-called "mountain-top mining" that has become prevalent in southern Appalachia, particularly West Virginia. In the southern part of the state, the terrain consists primarily of ridges and valleys. The mine operators use surface mining equipment to take off the tops of the ridges to expose coal seams. The overburden is dumped into the adjacent valleys.

The deposit of overburden is governed by both the permitting and reclamation provisions of SMCRA and the discharge permit provisions of the Clean Water Act. 30 CFR Parts 773–780 address requirements for obtaining a Surface Mining Control and Reclamation Act of 1977 permit for all methods of coal mining. 30 CFR § 785.14 specifically addresses permits for the mountaintop removal mining method. In situations in which the overburden is deposited into a "navigable water" or adjacent wetland, the Clean Water Act prohibition against "discharges" of pollutants without a permit would appear to apply, because the Act defines "dirt" as a pollutant, and (as in *U.S. v. Law*) its addition to navigable waters and adjacent wetland constitutes a "discharge" requiring a permit under the Act.

However, the Army Corps of Engineers, which exercises permitting jurisdiction over the deposit of fill into wetlands, has traditionally permitted this activity under one of its so-called "nationwide permits," granting general approval for certain kinds of fill activities, including deposit of overburden from mountaintop mining operations. This practice has long proved controversial and prompted litigation alleging that it is inconsistent with the Clean Water Act. In 2002, in *Kentuckians for the Commonwealth v. Rivenburgh*, 204 F. Supp. 2d 927 (S.D. W.V. 2002), a citizens group challenged the Corps' nationwide permit as ultra vires under the Clean Water Act. Judge Charles H. Haden agreed:

> The [Corps attempts] to legalize filling the waters of the United States under the CWA solely for waste disposal. The obvious perversity of this proposal forced the agencies to suggest baseless distinctions among wastes: "trash" and "garbage" are out; plastic, construction debris and wood chips are in. The final rule for "discharge of fill material" highlights that the rule change was designed simply for the benefit of the mining industry and its employees. Only one type of waste is added to the otherwise constructive list: "overburden, slurry, or tailings or similar mining-related" waste are now permissible fill in the nation's waters.

> The agencies' attempt to legalize their longstanding illegal regulatory practice must fail. The practice is contrary to law, not because the agencies said so, although their longstanding regulations correctly forbade it. The regulators' practice is illegal because it is contrary to the spirit and the letter of the Clean Water Act.

> Accordingly, the Court FINDS and CONCLUDES § 404 fills may not be permitted solely to dispose of waste.

Just a few days before Judge Haden's decision, the Corps and EPA finalized a rule (the "new rule") "clarifying" and broadening the nationwide permit authorizing the deposit of overburden from mountaintop mining. See 40 C.F.R. § 232.2. Judge Haden criticized the new rule in his opinion, finding it "fundamentally inconsistent with the CWA, its history, predecessor statutes, longstanding regulations, and companion statutes."

However, on appeal the Fourth Circuit overturned the District Court's decision and upheld the new rule, concluding that:

> the Corps' interpretation of "fill material" as used in § 404 of the Clean Water Act to mean all material that displaces water or changes the bottom elevation of a water body except for "waste"—meaning garbage, sewage, and effluent that could be regulated by ongoing effluent limitations as described in § 402—is a permissible construction of § 404. . . . [I]t is neither plainly erroneous nor inconsistent with the text of the regulation.

> The Corps' issuance of the permit to Martin Coal on June 20, 2000, therefore, was not arbitrary, capricious, an abuse of discretion, or otherwise contrary to law insofar as Kentuckians alleged in Count I of the complaint. On this issue, we reverse the judgment of the district court.

Kentuckians for the Commonwealth v. Rivenburgh, 317 F.3d 425 (4th Cir. 2003). Meanwhile, the Office of Surface Mining Reclamation and Enforcement issued a controversial proposed rule in 2003 that critics say would loosen historical restrictions against mining within 100 feet of a stream. See Office of Surface Mining, Surface Coal Mining and Reclamation Operations; Excess Spoil; Stream Buffer Zones; Diversions, 69 Fed. Reg. 1036 (January 7, 2004).

3. MINERAL RIGHTS

The English common law, which was incorporated into American law, gave the owner of the surface of the land the right to all minerals underneath it, but it allowed the "mineral rights" to land to be separated from the right to use the surface of the land because lawyers needed to develop a vehicle for allowing a mining company to control the mining without having to assume all of the responsibility for the uses on the surface. Indeed, it was this mineral estate that the Court determined to have been "taken" by the State of Pennsylvania in *Pennsylvania Coal v. Mahon*.

The terms defining the mineral rights vary with the needs of the parties. For example, the rights might be to all minerals, just coal, coal in a particular seam, or coal of a particular grade. The landowner and the mining company may define the rights conveyed in any manner they choose. Once the mineral rights are divided as a separate interest, they can be transferred independently from the surface. Often, the mineral rights are leased rather than purchased from the surface owner.

The modern mineral rights deed or lease will spell out the obligations of each party in regard to, among other things, (1) the extent to which a mineral owner has a right to use the surface for mine openings, roads, etc.; (2) the extent to which the mine operator is liable for subsidence of the land; and (3) whether the mineral rights owner has an obligation to explore and develop the minerals within a particular time.

Where underground mining is contemplated, coal mining companies typically purchase only the mineral rights from the landowner rather than purchasing a fee simple interest in the land on which the coal was located. Because the surface owner could continue to farm or develop the land for a profit while the mining was taking place underneath it, she would normally ask a lower price for the mineral rights than for the property as a whole.

Surface mining has become prevalent only since the 1950s. If a coal company purchased the mineral rights from a landowner at a time when the only known method of mining was underground mining, does the coal company now have the right to remove the coal by surface mining, thus effectively destroying the value of the surface owner's interest? This contentious issue has been a source of both legal and political battles in the coal mining states. For example, mineral rights owners in Kentucky acquired rights to mineral estates from surface owners through so-called "broad form" deeds, most of which were created prior to the advent of surface mining. Typically, the deeds granted the mineral owner rights to use the surface to the extent necessary or convenient to gain access to the minerals. In 1956, in *Buchanan v. Watson*, 290 S.W.2d 40 (1956), the Kentucky Supreme Court ruled that surface owners could not prevent mineral rights holders from using strip mining to mine coal pursuant to these broad form deeds. When the Kentucky legislature attempted to overturn this rule by limiting mineral estate holders to the use of techniques common at the time of execution of the deed, the Kentucky Supreme Court invalidated the critical portion of the statute (KRS § 381.940) in *Akers v. Baldwin*, 736 S.W.2d 294 (Ky. 1987). In response, the Kentucky legislature in 1988 ratified an amendment to the Kentucky Constitution, denoted Section 19(2), which stated that:

> In any instrument heretofore or hereafter executed purporting to sever the surface and mineral estates or to grant a mineral estate or to grant a right to extract minerals, which fails to state or describe in express and specific terms the method of coal extraction to be employed, or where said instrument contains language subordinating the surface estate to the mineral estate, it shall be held, in the absence of clear and convincing evidence to the contrary, that the intention of the parties to the instrument was that the coal be extracted only by the method or methods of commercial coal extraction commonly known to be in use in Kentucky in the area affected at the time the instrument was executed, and that the mineral estate be dominant to the surface estate for the purposes of coal extraction by only the method or methods of commercial coal extraction commonly known to be in use in Kentucky in the area affected at the time the instrument was executed.

The Kentucky Supreme Court reviewed that amendment in the case of *Ward v. Harding*, 860 S.W.2d 280 (Ky. 1993). Reasoning that it is "neither fair nor just to permit surface mining contrary to the wishes of the surface owner and beyond the contemplation of the original parties to [the instrument]," the court upheld the amendment's conclusion that broad form deeds do not authorize strip mining, and expressly overruled all contrary precedent. In so doing, the court rejected arguments that the Amendment 19(2) contravened both the Contracts Clause of the U.S. Constitution:

> As we have said hereinabove, at the time of the original mineral conveyance, the parties could not have intended any substantial disturbance of the surface. The original contract did not create a right to surface mine; this right, such as it was, arose by court decision half a century after the conveyance. While appellees acquired their mineral ownership after our decision in Buchanan and with an expectation of the right to strip mine, they acquired no greater right than their vendors possessed.

The court also rejected a claim that the amendment amounts to a regulatory taking of the mineral estate.

The longwall method of underground mining is another mining technique that was unknown at the time many mineral rights were granted. This method often produces a great deal of surface subsidence. With the longwall method, entries into the coal seam are made and supported by pillars. The mining equipment is moved to the furthest point on the panel and begins cutting toward the front. As the machine moves forward, the supports collapse, along with the overburden. Extraction is around 90%, but subsidence is usually immediate. S. Peng & H. Chaing, Longwall Mining (1984).

In *Smerdell v. Consolidation Coal Co.*, 806 F. Supp. 1278 (N.D.W.Va. 1992) the owners of the surface had waived all claims for damages from subsidence in 1905. The current owners of the surface claimed that their predecessors' waiver was no longer valid because the coal company had switched to the longwall mining method. The district court held that the effect of changed circumstances, such as the development of new mining techniques, on an unambiguous written instrument was not subject to judicial interpretation, and that the right to subjacent support was waived no matter what method of coal extraction is used. *See also* Lane, *supra* at 611–615.

Today, it is most common for the surface owner to lease the mineral rights to the mining company for a modest cash rental plus a significant percentage of the minerals that are found—this is known as a royalty interest. For example, the surface owner might retain a 1/8 royalty interest in all coal discovered and produced from under the land. The mining company will want the lease to set out its right to erect structures and build roads on the land, if underground mining is contemplated. Whether underground or surface mining is contemplated, the lease should expressly set out the methods of mining that are anticipated. The owner will also want to know what type of land reclamation the mining company contemplates when the mining operation has been completed.

The broad form deeds at issue in *Ward*, and the court's construction of them prior to that decision, reflected the attitude prevalent in the nineteenth century—that because coal was dramatically increasing peoples' ability to produce goods and raise their standard of living, the law ought to construe instruments in a way that encouraged the production of this valuable commodity. *See generally* Morton J. Horwitz, The Transformation of American Law, 1780–1860 (Harvard University Press, 1977). Only much later did people fully realize some of the adverse impacts of coal mining.

A large part of the remaining coal reserves underlie federal lands in the western states, so companies seeking to mine this coal must comply with the complex laws relating to federal public lands. Coal on federal lands is under the jurisdiction of the Department of the Interior, where different aspects of coal production are handled by different agencies, including the Bureau of Land Management and the Minerals Management Service. For an analysis of these federal regulations, *see* Marla E. Mansfield, Coal, in James E. Hickey et. al., Energy Law & Policy in the 21st Century, Ch. 9 (Rocky Mountain Mineral Law Foundation, 2000).

Texas has extensive deposits of brown coal known as lignite, much of which can be mined by surface mining methods. Under Texas law, a landowner's conveyance of the rights to "oil, gas and other minerals" has been construed not to convey the rights to any lignite that is near the surface. *Reed v. Wylie*, 597 S.W.2d 743 (Tex. 1980).

PROBLEM

The Rith Energy Company was denied a mining permit under SMCRA and brought suit in the United States Court of Federal Claims. The government sought to dismiss the complaint, arguing as follows:

> Plaintiff's just compensation claim fails because plaintiff does not possess the compensable expectancy it presumes. First, one of plaintiff's two leases, the Eagle/Boylan lease, allows the mining of coal only by underground methods. As to that lease, plaintiff's "bundle of rights" never included the expectancy to surface mine at all. *Lucas v. South Carolina Coastal Council,* 505 U.S. 1003, 1027 (1992).

> Second, plaintiff's claim in essence presumes it possesses a constitutionally protected right to mine in a particular manner. However, the property interests under which plaintiff has mined, and seeks to mine further, were created after the enactment of SMCRA. Accordingly, when plaintiff received those interests, its expectancies were already affected by the restrictions of the Act. Thus, it could have acquired no right to mine in a manner which was in violation of the Act. *M&J Coal Co. v. United States,* 30 Fed. Cl. 360, 369 (1994), *aff'd,* 47 F.3d 1148 (1995), *cert. denied,* 116 S. Ct. 53 (1995). In other words, before plaintiff's interests were created, SMCRA required that a permit be denied if the operator would not be able to reclaim the site or if mining operations would cause offsite hydrologic impacts. Plaintiff could have acquired no right to mine in a manner which was already prohibited by the Act. For that reason alone, Rith's just compensation claim must fail . . .

Finally, the governmental action challenged here is itself reactive to plaintiff's seeking to engage in a mining method with nuisance-like impacts. Measured against a variety of factors, including longstanding federal regulation under SMCRA and the risk that the mining practices in which plaintiff sought to engage would have nuisance-like consequences under state law, plaintiff could have acquired no "historically rooted" expectancy—no "property" for purposes of Fifth Amendment compensation—to mine in a manner which would cause nuisance-like impacts. The "background principles" analysis articulated in *Lucas v. South Carolina Coastal Council* confirms that, when acquired, Rith's right to mine could not have included an expectation of being allowed to mine if to do so would cause a nuisance.

Are the government's arguments persuasive? How would you respond on behalf of the plaintiff? What additional facts would you like to know? *See Rith Energy, Inc. v. United States,* 44 Fed. Cl. 108 (1999), *aff'd Rith Energy v. United States,* 247 F.3d 1355 (Fed Cir. 2001).

C.   COAL TRANSPORTATION

As a relatively heavy fuel, coal has always cost a lot to ship to markets. Seventy-five percent of all coal shipments are handled by railroads and barge lines. Trucks and conveyor systems are also used to move coal, but primarily over short distances. The price of coal to the consumer is thus heavily affected by the distance from its markets and the relative efficiency of the transportation routes between the mine and the market. Eastern coal tends to be more expensive at the mine, but for power plants in the East its transportation costs are lower due to shorter hauls. Eastern coal is often shipped by barge, which makes transportation costs even lower. Western coal is less expensive at the mine. However, it is usually shipped great distances by rail, making transportation expense higher. Energy Information Administration, Challenges of Electric Power Industry Restructuring for Fuel Suppliers, Sept. 1998, at 21.

As deregulated railroads consolidated in the late 1980's and the 1990's, they increasingly used large unit trains with lighter-weight, high-capacity cars, and added new sections of track, to help move coal from Wyoming's Powder River Basin to the Midwest. They also offered lower ton-per-mile rates and coordinated efforts with barge line operators to improve rail-barge transloading facilities, incorporating coal-blending capabilities. This served the need of new customers of Western coal whose boilers often required some ratio of bituminous coal to be blended with the new low-sulfur subbituminous coal for proper combustion.

The relationship between the coal industry and the railroads has had its ups and downs. They have joined forces on many lobbying projects. Coal shipping is beneficial to the railroads, which receive almost one-fourth of their gross revenue from coal shipments. Coal transportation costs have decreased even though the average distance coal must travel has increased.

This has contributed to the competitiveness between the western coal sources in the eastern markets. But the competitiveness of the different markets is sensitive to rail rates and small differences can make one regional market much more favorable than another.

Recently there is an increasing tension between the two industries because the major railroads are merging, often over the objections of the coal companies. *See, e.g., Western Coal Traffic League v. Surface Transp. Bd.*, 169 F.3d 775 (D.C. Cir. 1999). In 1970, there were 71 Class I railroad companies. By 2004, there were only seven Class I railroad companies. Mergers over the past sixteen years have made it possible for the railroads to raise rates over segments of track on which coal needs to be moved. The coal shippers are concerned that the railroads will charge discriminatory rates, favoring coal producers and power plants that create the most profitable traffic. Shippers argue that they will have fewer choices for coal deliveries. "Captive shippers," those that only have one transportation option, are particularly concerned. *See* Salvatore Massa, Injecting Competition in the Railroad Industry Through Access, 26 Transp. L.J. 283 (1999).

The railroads insist that competition will be adequate and longer operations will result in lower costs to the coal shippers. They argue that in order for coal shippers to compete with each other, they should "take advantage of economies of scale through mergers and acquisitions." Rail companies also believe that the larger geographic scope of operations will broaden markets for coal producers and offer more coal supply choices for electricity generators. *See* Energy Information Agency, Challenge of Electric Power Industry Restructuring for Fuel Suppliers (Sept. 1998).

MidAmerican Energy Co. v. Surface Transportation Board

169 F.3d 1099 (8th Cir. 1999).

■ WOLLMAN, J. Petition for Review of an Order of the Surface Transportation Board. This is a consolidated action involving MidAmerican Energy Company ("MidAmerican"), Central Power & Light Company ("CP&L"), and Pennsylvania Power & Light Company ("PP&L") (collectively the utilities). They petition for review of two orders of the Surface Transportation Board ("the Board") dismissing their complaints against rail carriers. The carriers cross-appeal from the portion of the Board's decisions regarding reasonableness review of contractual shipping rates, arguing that the issue was not ripe for adjudication. We affirm the dismissal of the utilities' complaints. We dismiss the cross-appeal for lack of jurisdiction.

I.

MidAmerican ships coal approximately 750 miles from the Powder River Basin in Wyoming to its generating facility near Sergeant Bluff, Iowa. At the time it filed its complaint, MidAmerican was shipping the coal from origin to destination under contract with the Union Pacific Railroad ("UP"). This contract was scheduled to expire at the end of 1997. Anticipating the contract's expiration, MidAmerican began to compare UP's rates with those of other carriers to obtain the most favorable shipping rates. The only other carrier offering rail service originating in the Powder River Basin is the Burlington Northern Railroad ("BN").

BN does not service the final 90 miles of the route, a stretch from Council Bluffs, Iowa, to the generating station. Such a rail segment is commonly termed a "bottleneck," because it is serviced by only one carrier. Thus, MidAmerican could not directly compare the rates of BN and UP, as UP is the only carrier capable of shipping all the way to the generating station. To obtain a competitive rate for the 660–mile stretch from Wyoming to Council Bluffs, MidAmerican requested that UP provide a rate for its service over the bottleneck.

UP refused to provide the rate. Instead, it provided a rate for the entire route from the Powder River Basin to the generating station. This precluded MidAmerican from using BN as a carrier from Wyoming to Council Bluffs, essentially extending the bottleneck over the entire 750–mile route. Consequently, MidAmerican brought an action before the Board requesting a rate prescription over the 90–mile bottleneck segment. Although MidAmerican could not challenge a local "unit-train" rate for the bottleneck service, it asked the Board to prescribe a reasonable rate for the bottleneck if it found the published "class" rate for the 90–mile stretch unreasonable.[9]

CP&L transports coal from the Powder River Basin in Wyoming to its Coleto Creek generating station in Texas. Although both BN and UP offer rail service originating at the coal mines, the Southern Pacific Railroad ("SP") is the only carrier from an interchange point in Victoria, Texas, to Coleto Creek. UP's lines run from Wyoming to Victoria; BN's lines run from Wyoming to Fort Worth, Texas, where SP's service to Victoria and Coleto Creek begins. Therefore, UP and BN directly compete on the portion of the route from Wyoming to Fort Worth. SP and UP directly compete on the portion from Fort Worth to Victoria. After both BN and UP indicated a willingness to offer competitive rates for their service, CP&L requested that SP provide it a local unit-train rate for the segment from Fort Worth to Coleto Creek, which represented SP's longest haul, or for the bottleneck from Victoria to Coleto Creek.

---

9. A local unit-train rate is a published rate applicable to transport of a trainload of a specific good between two points on a carrier's line. A local class rate, on the other hand, is a published rate applicable to transport of a certain type of good in smaller quantities between two points on a carrier's line. Railroads must maintain class rates because of their common carrier obligation to transport goods to any point on their lines upon request by a shipper. *See Thompson v. United States,* 343 U.S. 549, 558, 96 L. Ed. 1134, 72 S. Ct. 978 (1952); *Westinghouse Elec. Corp. v. United States,* 388 F. Supp. 1309, 1311 (W.D. Pa. 1975) (*citing New York v. United States,* 331 U.S. 284, 289–90, 91 L. Ed. 1492, 67 S. Ct. 1207 (1947)). Because it is more costly for carriers to offer service for unspecified quantities of goods, however, class rates are seldom used and are generally significantly higher over the same stretch of rail. See Routing Restrictions over *Seatrain Lines, Inc.,* 296 I.C.C. 767, 773 (1955); *Burlington Northern, Inc. v. United States,* 555 F.2d 637, 639 (8th Cir. 1977) (noting that a class rate for coal shipment was more than double the unit-train rate).

SP refused to provide either rate, offering instead to provide a joint rate with UP. CP&L chose to obtain a unit-train rate from UP for service from Wyoming to Victoria, and to ship from Victoria to Coleto Creek under SP's class rate. It could thus take advantage of neither the competition between UP and BN from Wyoming to Fort Worth, nor the competition between SP and UP from Fort Worth to Victoria. Subsequently, CP&L brought a complaint before the Board challenging the class rate as unreasonable and requesting a rate prescription for the bottleneck segment.

SP's class rate for the coal shipment from Victoria to Coleto Creek was $19.95 per ton. At the Board's hearing, CP&L offered the testimony of eight expert witnesses that the highest reasonable rate for this stretch was $0.63 per ton, less than one-thirtieth of the actual class rate charged. [The court also described the facts of two similar cases that had been consolidated]

In considering the utilities' requests, the Board grappled with the tension between two competing policies expressed in the Interstate Commerce Act (the Act). Under 49 U.S.C. § 10701a(a) (1995) (now § 10701(c)), rail carriers possess broad discretion in setting rates and routes. This reflects Congress's goal of deregulating the railroad industry and allowing railroads to achieve revenue adequacy by competing on a free-market basis. Under sections 10101a(6) and 10701a(b) (now §§ 10101(6) and 10701(d)), however, some rate regulation is required when carriers possess monopoly power over a section of rail. These provisions codify railroads' common carrier obligations, which require them to provide service at reasonable rates to all shippers upon request.

The Board resolved this tension in favor of the "rate freedom" of bottleneck carriers. Specifically, it held that bottleneck carriers satisfy their common carrier duties and thus comply with the Act by providing origin-to-destination service that includes the bottleneck, as in MidAmerican's case, or by providing joint or proportional service with other carriers that includes transportation over the bottleneck. In addition, the Board held that shippers may not challenge class rates as an "indirect basis for obtaining prescription of a local unit-train rate" for bottleneck segments. Subsequently, the utilities moved for clarification and reconsideration of the decision. The Board responded by issuing a second decision, granting in part the motion for clarification and denying the motion for reconsideration. *See Central Power & Light Co. v. Southern Pac. Transp. Co.*, No. 41242, at (Surface Transp. Bd. Apr. 28, 1997) (Bottleneck II). The utilities appeal from both rulings.

II.

Before we address the specific issues raised in these cases, we briefly review the relevant history of railroad regulation. From its passage in 1887 until the mid–1970s, the Interstate Commerce Act provided for a strict regulatory framework to govern the federal railroad industry. This legislative approach resulted in an industry chronically plagued by capital shortfalls and service inefficiencies. *See* H.R. Rep. No. 96–1035, at 33 (1980), *reprinted in* 1980 U.S.C.C.A.N. 3978, 3978; *Coal Exporters Ass'n of United States v. United States,* 240 U.S. App. D.C. 256, 745 F.2d 76, 81 (D.C. Cir. 1984).

To assure railroads greater freedom in establishing routes and rates, Congress modified the Act with the Railroad Revitalization and Regulatory Reform Act (4R Act), Pub. L. No. 94–210, 90 Stat. 31 (1976), and the Staggers Rail Act (Staggers Act), Pub. L. No. 96–448, 94 Stat. 1895 (1980). *See* H.R. Conf. Rep. No. 96–1430, at 79 (1980), *reprinted* in 1980 U.S.C.C.A.N. 3978, 4110. These acts were intended to end "decades of ICC control over maximum rates and to permit carriers not having market dominance to set rates in response to their perception of market conditions." *Midtec Paper Corp. v. United States,* 857 F.2d 1487, 1506 (D.C. Cir. 1988).

Underlying these reform efforts was the notion that market forces would operate in the rail industry as they do in other spheres. Congress believed that free competition for rail services would ensure that consumer demand dictated the optimal rate level, while facilitating enough long-term capital investment to maintain adequate service. Congress was also mindful, however, that the free market would protect consumers only if there was "effective" competition. Therefore, the new enactments included provisions allowing regulatory intervention where competition would not control prices. *See* 4R Act § 101(b), 90 Stat. 31, 33; Staggers Act § 101(a), 49 U.S.C. § 10101a(6) (now § 10101(6)); *Coal Exporters,* 745 F.2d at 81 n.6.

Indeed, in bottleneck situations the Staggers Act actually "increased the ICC's regulatory power—by authorizing the agency to require railroads to enter into agreements to 'switch' other railroads' cars to and from shippers located along each other's lines. . . ." *Baltimore Gas & Elec. Co. v. United States,* 260 U.S. App. D.C. 1, 817 F.2d 108, 113 (D.C. Cir. 1987);*see* 49 U.S.C. § 11103 (now 11102). After the 4R and Staggers Acts, the agency (previously the ICC, now the Surface Transportation Board) is still required to use rate prescription and other remedies such as reciprocal switching arrangements to ensure reasonable shipping rates on bottlenecks. It is also responsible for ensuring that free competition is preserved to the greatest extent possible on non-bottleneck segments.

Congress's decision to deregulate the railroad industry has been largely successful. Experts for both sides in these cases have acknowledged that competition has led to more efficient routes, increased profits, better service, and an enhanced ability to attract capital investment. *See, e.g.,* Verified Statement of William J. Baumol & Robert D. Willig at 6–7, J.A. at 1111–12; Verified Statement of Alfred E. Kahn at 15–16, J.A. at 2931–32. However, the experts dispute the role of bottleneck rail segments in increasing profits and facilitating the overall revenue adequacy of the railroad industry.

III.

We have jurisdiction under 28 U.S.C. §§ 2321 and 2341 (Supp. 1998), which provide for review of the Board's decisions. Because Congress has entrusted the Board with interpreting and administering the Act, in reviewing its decisions we ask only whether they are " 'based on a permissible construction of the statute.' "

As the utilities and shipper organizations assert, carriers are bound both at common law and under the Act to "provide . . . transportation or service on reasonable request" to any shipper. *GS Roofing*, 143 F.3d at 391. This duty not only requires carriers to provide service on their lines, but also requires rates for such service to be reasonable. *See Thompson*, 343 U.S. at 554; 49 U.S.C. § 10701a(b) (now § 10701(d)).

As the Board and the railroads assert, however, there are significant limitations to the common carrier duties. It is usually at the discretion of the carrier how it wishes to satisfy its duty to provide rates and service. *See* 49 U.S.C. § 10701a(a) (now § 10701(c)). Further, a carrier generally may provide common carrier service in a manner that protects its "long hauls." *See* 49 U.S.C. § 10705(a) (now § 10705(a)). The Board may order a carrier to provide service over a shorter haul than it wishes only if the Board first makes specific findings under the Act. *See Id.* § 10705(a)(2). Thus, a carrier such as UP may normally choose to provide service to a shipper such as MidAmerican over a route longer than the 90 miles from Council Bluffs to Sergeant Bluff, unless the longer route would be "unreasonably long" or inefficient.

Therefore, the Act protects both shippers and carriers. It guarantees that shippers will receive rail service at reasonable rates, and it allows carriers to provide such service in a manner that achieves revenue adequacy.

The Board has recognized that an important part of achieving revenue adequacy is differential pricing. *See Consolidated Rail Corp. v. United States*, 812 F.2d 1444, 1453–54 (3d Cir. 1987) (*citing* Coal Rate Guidelines, Nationwide, 1 I.C.C. 2d 520 (1985)). This is a practice by which carriers charge a higher mark-up on rail segments where demand elasticity is low, such as bottlenecks, to compensate for low mark-ups on competitive segments. *See Coal Rate Guidelines*, 1 I.C.C. 2d at 526–27. Therefore, "services may be priced above their attributable costs according to observable market demand, but only to the extent necessary to cover total costs, including return on investment of an efficient carrier." *Id.* at 533–34. Accordingly, in reviewing the reasonableness of bottleneck rates, the Board allows bottleneck carriers to charge up to stand-alone cost (SAC), a level that is significantly higher than marginal cost[10].

In the present case, the Board determined that exploiting bottlenecks by refusing to provide separately challengeable bottleneck rates also assists carriers in achieving revenue adequacy. Specifically, in the MidAmerican

---

10. Stand-alone cost represents the minimum amount that a hypothetical carrier, or the shipper itself, would have to spend to build a new rail line to compete over the bottleneck segment. *See Coal Rate Guidelines,* 1 I.C.C. 2d at 528–29. This measure better allows railroads to achieve true revenue adequacy, because it takes into account profits and the cost of long-term capital investment, while marginal cost does not. *See id.* at 526.

case, allowing UP to provide only an origin-to-destination rate enables it to charge up to SAC over the entire 750–mile route, rather than just over the 90–mile section from Council Bluffs to Sergeant Bluff. Were UP required to provide a separate bottleneck rate, it would be forced to charge lower competitive rates from the mine to Council Bluffs. Based on these economic factors and extensive expert testimony, the Board concluded that the Act did not require carriers to provide separate bottleneck rates.

Regardless of how we would resolve the tension in the Act if we were to independently rule on the utilities' claims, we cannot say that the Board's interpretation was incorrect. The Board's considerable expertise in the economic underpinnings of the railroad industry is entitled to a great degree of deference, and its decision to allow carriers to determine how they wish to fulfill their duties under the Act is consistent with the current national railroad policy of maximizing carrier discretion in setting routes and rates. Because the utilities have not demonstrated that the Board's rulings were incorrect, we affirm the Board's dismissal of the utilities' complaints.■

NOTES AND COMMENTS

1. What policy reasons justify a system in which the railroads can charge monopolistic prices to captive customers in order to be able to reduce rates to other customers? Are the railroads engaged in a business in which they cannot be expected to make a profit in the free market? Compare the *Market Street Railway* case, discussed in Chapter 3, *infra*. Is the Staggers Act simply a well-hidden redistributional subsidy by which some of the costs of operating a railroad system are shifted to the consumers of electric power?

2. In many instances, the electric utilities entered into contracts to purchase the output of a coal mine and transport it by a particular railroad at a time when the electric utility was subject to traditional rate regulation, which allowed the utility to pass its costs on to the consumers. Today, many of these utilities are facing increasing competition (see Chapter 11, *infra*) and are much more concerned about their costs.

3. The Surface Transportation Board has modified its regulations to reduce the evidentiary requirements for shipper seeking to prove that a railroad has "market dominance" over a particular route. Shippers now need to show only that the railroad dominated the transportation market; they no longer need to present evidence on the broader issues of product and geographic competition. Surface Transportation Board, Market Dominance Determinations, Ex Parte No. 627 (Dec. 21, 1998).

4. The District of Columbia Court of Appeals, in a case that it held in abeyance until the Eighth Circuit decided the *MidAmerican* case, upheld the STB's bottleneck policy against an argument by the railroads that the policy was too favorable to shippers. "We think the Board adequately reconciled the particular statutory tensions raised by the Bottleneck cases; confronting the unenviable task of balancing the rail carriers' rate and

route prerogatives and the shippers' contract rights, the Board produced what is, on balance, a reasonable policy." *Union Pac. R.R. Co. v. Surface Transp. Bd.*, 202 F.3d 337, 344–45 (D.C. Cir. 2000).

5.   In 2003, the Eighth Circuit issued another decision affecting the STB rate review process, this one exploring the role of the National Environmental Policy Act (NEPA, discussed *supra* in Chapter 4) in that process. Recall that NEPA requires federal agencies to examine beforehand the environmental affects of actions they plan to undertake *or approve*. In *Mid States Coalition for Progress v. Surface Transportation Board*, 345 F.3d 520 (8th Cir. 2003), the court considered an application to the STB by the Dakota, Minnesota & Eastern Railroad ("DM&E") for authority to upgrade and expand a rail line for transport of coal out of the Powder River Basin in Wyoming, and through South Dakota and Minnesota. In the case, the STB had approved the proposal, even though it would have imposed new environmental impacts in downtown Rochester, Minnesota, including the introduction of noise and other impacts near the Mayo Clinic. Recalling the discussion in Chapter 4 indicating that NEPA does not require federal agencies to minimize environmental impacts (only to recognize them), the Eighth Circuit did not overturn the STB's decision that these effects were acceptable. Is this the way NEPA should work, in your opinion? The court also held, however, that NEPA requires the STB to consider not only the environmental effects of the actions by the railroad for which STB approval is required (construction and operation of the rail line), but also the environmental effects on air quality that may be expected from the burning of the coal to be transported by the railroad's customers. Since the STB had not considered these impacts, the court remanded the decision back to the STB. Was the Eighth Circuit's reading of NEPA a correct one, in your view?

D.   COAL COMBUSTION

The only economically productive function of coal is to be burned. Coal-fired power plants use combustion to produce steam to drive a turbine, which in turn produces electricity. Coal combustion produces an impressive list of potentially-harmful pollutants, and has always been a high-profile source of air pollution. Particulate matter (fine dust) is a source of respiratory problems, heart and lung disease, and haze. Particulates from coal combustion can also contain mercury, a toxic metal that can enter the food chain through deposition of combustion particulates into waterways. Sulfur dioxide ("SO_2") mixes with moisture in the upper atmosphere to form sulfuric acid, which falls as acid rain, damaging vegetation and changing the pH of aquatic environments. Nitrogen oxides ("NOx") are a precursor to both acid rain and ground-level ozone (smog), which triggers respiratory problems in some humans. Carbon dioxide ("CO_2"), another byproduct of coal combustion, is the earth's most plentiful greenhouse gas, and human contributions of carbon dioxide into the atmosphere are widely believed to be hastening global warming. Furthermore, the link between coal combustion and pollution problems has long been understood.

Barbara Freese, Coal: A Human History (2003)

pp. 98–100, 166–73.

London had long been known for its fogs, including occasional "Great Stinking Fogs," as one seventeenth-century astronomer called them in his weather records. There was, though, a marked increase in the frequency of London fogs between 1750 and 1890. Natural climate fluctuations could have contributed to the increase, but inevitably so did the smoke. The city could barely be seen from above, such as the top of St. Paul's Cathedral. Lord Byron described the London skyline as a "wilderness of steeples peeping on tiptoe through their sea-coal canopy." Smoke was such a quintessential part of London that for a long time the city held the nickname "The Big Smoke."

While the fogs were unnatural, they could also be beautiful. * * * [However, w]ith all its potential for aesthetic appeal, it's quite clear that the pollution of Victorian London could bring confusion and death, particularly when a dense fog planted itself over the city for three or more days. On a Wednesday in December 1873, for example, a thick cold fog settled in and stayed until the following Saturday, at one point stretching fifty miles from the city. Visibility was reduced to a few yards, and according to the brief articles printed in the weather section of the *Times*, "all locomotion, especially to people on foot a the crossings of great thoroughfares, became extremely dangerous." The fog was blamed for a sad and chaotic parade of sometimes fatal accidents that left the hospitals straining to care for the injured: Carriages crashed into light posts and other obstacles, people were run over by omnibuses and Hanson cabs (one poor fellow was run over by both), horses tripped and crushed their riders, and a train struck a man who was putting fog lights along the track. The police were kept busy trying to handle the multitudes of lost children. The most common reported fog-related deaths were the twenty drownings that took place over the four-day period, caused when people simply stumbled into the Thames or the canals of the city, or when barge collisions threw them into the water. The paper failed to report that several cattle, in the city for an exhibition, dropped dead in the fog, and many others were in such distress that they had to be immediately slaughtered.

Amidst the various locomotion related deaths, the *Times* also noted the deaths of two gentlemen who in separate incidents fell into the street and shortly died from "inhaling the fog." In reporting just these two deaths by inhalation, the *Times* was off by two orders of magnitude. An analysis of the city's death statistics performed decades later shoed that the 1873 fog quietly killed from 270 to 700 Londoners. Another foggy week in 1880 would kill from 700 to 1,100 people, and one in 1892 would kill about 1,000.

These deaths went largely unreported, while people worried instead about the far less deadly but more dramatic confusion in the streets.

* * *

Following coal's emissions through nature is an ongoing scientific odyssey. Already it has forced us to increase our understanding of how the wind blows, how the rain falls, how light scatters, and how chemicals cycle through the air and soil and water. It has also taught us things about our own lungs and hearts and brains, and about the subtle and sometimes not-so-subtle ways that things we release into the world can come back to haunt us. All in all, tracking the smoke has given us ample proof that we're intimately linked, through our economic decisions and through large-scale natural processes, to the broader web of life on Earth and to each other.

The first great wave of environmental sentiment swept through the nation in 1970, marked by the celebration of the first Earth Day. In the wake of this new awareness came the formation of the Environmental Protection Agency ("EPA") and passage of a string of new laws, the most ambitions and far-reaching of which was the 1970 Clean Air Act. The act established the straightforward requirement that the nation's air be cleaned up to healthy levels by 1975. To a nation that had just landed men on the Moon, such a lofty goal must have seemed entirely possible. Three decades later it looks hopelessly naïve, a reflection of how little we knew about air pollution, health and environmental politics.

When the Clean Air Act was passed, the nation's primary concern was the effect of urban air pollution levels on health. The potentially deadly nature of the urban smoke had been demonstrated some years earlier during London's historic "Black Fog" on December 5–9, 1952. A temperature inversion trapped the city's smoke close to the ground. On the first day it was still a white fog, but so extraordinarily dense that cars and buses moved slower than a walk, and the opera had to cancelled when fog seeped into the theater and made it impossible for the singers to see the conductor. By the last day, the fog had turned black, visibility was limited to a mere eleven inches, and the hospitals were full of Londoners perishing from the smoke. Many of the 4,000 or so people killed by this episode never made it to the hospital but died on the streets; fifty bodies were removed from one small city park. In 1956, after nearly seven hundred years of complains about the coal smoke in London, Parliament finally banned the burning of soft coal in the central city, and the air immediately improved.

The primary culprit in the deaths was a gas called sulfur dioxide. Sulfur dioxide, or SO_2, is not some exotic chemical contrived in a laboratory. Nature spews it out through volcanic eruptions, but we spew out more with our coal fires, our own slow-motion, domesticated little volcanoes. This old-fashioned and surprisingly dangerous pollutant results, quite literally, from mixing fire and brimstone, or, in other words from bruning the sulfur that contaminates coal.

In 1970, total SO_2 emissions in the United States were reaching an all-time high. The greatest sources by far were the coal-fired power plant, which doubled their SO_2 emissions eery decade between 1940 and 1970. Despite these increasing SO_2 emissions, in most city centers the air probably held much less SO_2 than it had earlier in the century because taller smoke stacks were spewing it farther. Some of the Clean Air Act regulations promoted the continuation of this trend. A common saying among environmental regulators was "the solution to pollution is dilution." Of course, this is only true if your fires are small enough and your planet is big enough, and neither turned out to be the case. In time, the dirtiest air got cleaner but downwind some of the cleanest air got dirtier. Health concerns persisted, but they were soon overshadowed by the other issues, like the mystery of the missing fish.

In the late 1960s, scientists were perplexed over the disappearance of fish that had formerly thrived in certain pristine lakes in southern Sweden and Norway and the Adirondack Mountains of New York. The lakes looked more beautiful than ever because the microorganisms that used to cloud the water were also gone. There were other mysteries, too: High-elevation stands of trees were dying of unknown causes, and, oddly enough, in parts of Sweden people were surprised to find their hair turning green. Researchers finally linked all these problems back to acid-forming pollution, and particularly to SO_2 emissions from the enormous coal fires in Britain and Germany (causing pollution in Scandinavia) and in the industrial Midwest (causing pollution in the northeastern United States and Canada).

Acid rain not only raises the acidity of distant lakes and streams, which directly harms fish, but as it passes through the soils it also leaches out toxic minerals like aluminum and mercury, causing more damage to the ecosystems. By the 1970s the acid had seeped into thousands of shallow wells in southern Sweden, corroding the copper pipes and contaminating the tap water with copper sulfate. The fair-haired Swedes who washed in the contaminated water found that it tinted their hair green, sometimes as "green as a birch in spring," as a Swedish researcher described it in 1981. It was an ironic choice of words, because the same pollutants were causing the certain trees to lose their green needles and turn brown.

. . . Finally, in 1990, Congress adopted an Acid Rain Program requiring power plants to cut their SO_2 emissions nearly in half by 2010.

* * *

Even before the evidence of the continuing acid rain problems emerged, coal-burning was being increasingly blamed for a surprising proportion of our other long-standing pollution problems. For example, we know now that SO_2, invisible when it comes out of the smokestack, is the primary reason people can't see great distances in the eastern United states. On an average day in the East, you can see about fourteen miles. If not for human-made air pollution, you could see from forty-five to ninety miles. The main cause of the vista-destroying haze that covers virtually everything east of the Mississippi are tiny sulfate particles that scatter sunlight; the particles are formed from SO_2 emissions, which come mostly from coal fires. In the West, even though SO_2 emissions are much less, there is still enough coal pollution to obscure views: The EPA found that a significant part of the haze problem at the Grand Canyon has been due to SO$_2$ emissions from a coal plant seventy-five miles away. One economic study found that the Acid Rain Program's improvement of visibility—a benefit barely considered when the law was passed—is alone worth the substantial cost of pollution controls, quite apart from the many other environmental and health benefits.

Of course, vistas are also impaired by what we call "smog." Smog is mainly ozone—a gas we have too little of up in the stratosphere, where it shields us from radiation, but too much of down here. Ozone is a big problem both in rural areas, where it harms the growth of forests and crops, and in urban areas. . . .

Ozone does not come out of smoke stacks. Rather, it forms when gases called nitrogen oxides (NOx) combine with other air pollutants in the presence of sunshine and heat. Although smog is mainly blamed on road traffic, coal contributes nearly a quarter of the nation's NOx emissions, which is more than all cars, vans and sport utility vehicles combined. NOx emissions are also a secondary cause of acid rain, and, because nitrogen is a fertilizer, they contribute to excessive algae growth and the depletion of oxygen in coastal waters such as the Chesapeake Bay.

And then there is the slippery problem of mercury. Many thousands of lakes in the United States contain fish so tainted with mercury that pregnant women and children are warned not to eat them because mercury can damage the developing brain. Most mercury in lakes rains down from the air, and perhaps as much as a third of mercury emissions to the air comes from coal plants, making them the largest source. The public health threat posed by mercury is not trivial: A recent report by the National Academy of Sciences warns that 60,000 babies born in the United States each year may have been exposed to enough mercury in utero to cause poor school performance later in life. Once mercury is introduced into the environment, it is impossible to clean up because it keeps reevaporating and raining down again indefinitely, ping-ponging its way mercurially around the world, posing new risks wherever it lands.■

Today coal is the fuel source for roughly 50 percent of total net power generation in the United States, and an even higher percentage of power generated from utility-owned power plants. One aim of the Clean Air Act of 1970, and of its major amendments in 1977 and 1990, was to force plant owners to internalize some of the external costs of coal combustion by requiring new plants to install pollution controls to limit their emissions. While the Act has significantly reduced emissions of some pollutants into the atmosphere, it has not so much resolved the problem of pollution from coal-fired power plants as it has provided a structured backdrop for a three decade-long process of conflict over the issue.

The Act requires new, stationary sources of pollution, like power plants, to secure a permit from state regulators before emitting convention-al pollutants, like sulfur dioxide, particulates and nitrogen oxides into the air. The permit must contain emissions limitations for these pollutants that reflect certain technology-based standards which are described and defined in the Act itself. The stringency of these standards, in turn, depend upon whether the source is located in area that is in attainment with national ambient air quality standards ("NAAQS") for the pollutant in question. If the plant is located in an attainment area, the emissions limitation must reflect the "best available control technology" ("BACT") 42 U.S.C. § 7475(a)(4). In nonattainment areas, the limitation must reflect the "lowest achievable emissions rate" ("LAER"). 42 U.S.C. § 7503(a)(2). In either case, the emissions limits must be relatively more stringent than levels of pollution control achieved by most other similar sources. Thus, as new permits are issued and old permits expire and are renewed, and as pollution control technology grows more efficient and effective, the statutory technology-based standards—the levels of pollution control that are available, achievable, and better than the industry norm—grow more stringent over time.

This Clean Air Act permitting regime has resulted in significant reductions in pollution levels and in emissions of six conventional pollutants (which include sulfur dioxide, particulates and nitrogen oxides) since its passage, as **Figure 5–3** indicates.

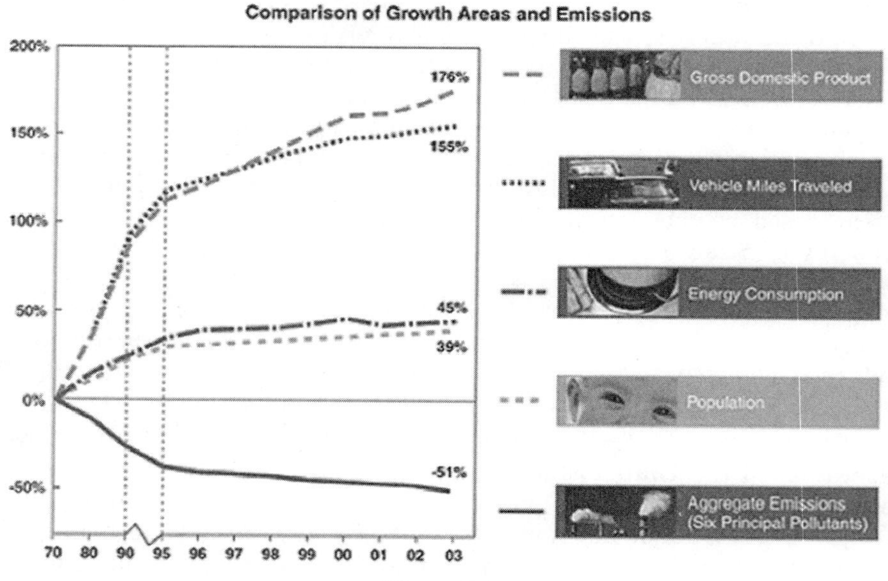

Comparison of Growth Areas and Emissions

Figure 5–3

(Source: Environmental Protection Agency)

Even without controlling for economic and population growth, emissions of sulfur dioxide in 2003 were just over half of what they were in 1970, while particulate emissions in 2003 were approximately one tenth of their 1970 levels. Reductions in nitrogen oxides emissions have been much more gradual, but only because steep reductions in stationary source emissions of nitrogen oxides were offset by increases in emissions from automobiles. Despite this progress, critics contend that coal combustion continues to do harm by emitting pollution that slips through the cracks of the Clean Air Act regulatory regime. One such crack, say critics, is the new source review program.

1. NEW SOURCE REVIEW

Since the Act's tough permitting provisions applied only to "new" sources of air pollution, coal fired power plants that were in existence at the time the permitting requirements took effect—"grandfathered" plants—fall outside the scope of their coverage. The Act calls for application of a "new source" permitting standards to "stationary source[s] the construction or modification of which is commenced after" the effective date of the Act's new source permitting requirements. Congress may have intended that this provision operate gradually to widen the scope of coverage of the new source permitting provisions as old plants were replaced or modified, so that over time the number of exempted plants would dwindle to zero. In any case, older coal-fired power plants, many of them in the Midwest, continued to pollute at essentially unregulated rates long after the passage of the Act, depositing acid rain on, and contributing to violations of NAAQS in, downwind (eastern) states. These unregulated power plants have been the source of long-running disputes between eastern and midwestern states, and between industry and environmental groups.

During the 1990s, the transformation of the electric utility industry from price regulation to price competition stoked fears that sellers of electricity would rely more heavily than ever on cheap, reliable power from grandfathered coal-fired plants. Consequently, the Clinton EPA stepped up its efforts to bring those plants within the ambit of new source review. The language of Section 111 of the Clean Air Act authorizes the EPA to apply new source review to any plant that had been "modified"—that is, any plant that has undergone a "physical change" resulting in an increase in emissions. However, in 1978, the EPA promulgated a rule defining the term "physical change" to exclude "routine maintenance, repair and replacement," apparently signaling its intention to exempt repairs that increase emissions from new source review. The apparent conflict between the statute and the rule was addressed by the following case.

Wisconsin Electric Power Co. v. Reilly

893 F.2d 901 (7th Cir. 1990).

■ CUDAHY, J. The Petitioner, Wisconsin Electric Power Company (WEPCO), challenges two final determinations issued by the Environmental Protection Agency (the EPA). In these determinations, the EPA concluded that WEPCO's proposed renovations to its Port Washington power plant would subject the plant to certain pollution control provisions of the Clean Air Act. . . .

In section 111 of the 1970 Amendments, Congress required the EPA to promulgate New Source Performance Standards ("NSPS") in order to regulate the emission of air pollutants from new sources. These standards addressed hourly rates of emission and, in addition to new sources, applied to modifications of existing facilities that created new or increased pollution. Indeed, section 111(a)(2) of the Act stated that NSPS would apply to

> any stationary source, the construction *or modification* of which is commenced after the publication of regulations (or, if earlier, proposed regulations) prescribing a standard of performance under this section which will be applicable to such source.

42 U.S.C. § 7411(a)(2) (emphasis supplied).

Congress then defined "modification" as

> *any physical change* in, or change in the method of operation of, a stationary source *which increases the amount of any air pollutant emitted* by such source or which results in the emission of any air pollutant not previously emitted. . . .

From this statutory framework, the EPA promulgated regulations for both the NSPS and PSD programs. In this case, its regulations concerning modifications are central. The EPA defines "modification" in substantially the same terms used by Congress . . . [However,] . . . the EPA promulgated specific exceptions to the modification provisions:

> The following shall not, by themselves, be considered modifications under this part:
>
> (1) Maintenance, repair, and replacement which the Administrator determines to be routine for a source category . . .
>
> (2) An increase in production rate of an existing facility, if that increase can be accomplished without a capital expenditure on that facility.
>
> (3) An increase in the hours of operation. . . .

40 C.F.R. § 60.14(e) (1988). These regulations (and the statutes from which they derive) are the focal point of this case.

WEPCO's Port Washington electric power plant is located on Lake Michigan north of Milwaukee, Wisconsin. The plant consists of five coal-fired steam generating units that were placed in operation between 1935 and 1950. Each generating unit has a design capacity of 80 megawatts, but the recent performance of some of the units has declined due to age-related deterioration of the physical plant.

WEPCO and its consultant, Bechtel Eastern Power Corporation, conducted a Plant Availability Study in 1983 to examine and assess the condition of the power plant. As a result of the Study, WEPCO concluded "that *extensive renovation* of the five units and the plant common facilities is needed if operation of the plant is to be continued." The Study noted that the air heaters on the first four units had deteriorated severely, while the rear steam drums in units 2 through 5 had experienced serious cracking. Air heater deterioration prevented units 1 and 4 from operating at full capacity, while the potential for steam drum blowout required a reduction in pressure (and output) in units 2 and 3. The possibility of catastrophic failure (steam drum blowout) in unit 5 was so great that WEPCO shut down the unit completely.

As a result of this Study, WEPCO submitted a proposed replacement program (which it termed a "life extension" project) to the Wisconsin Public Service Commission for its approval, as required by state law. WEPCO explained in its proposal that "renovation is necessary to allow the Port Washington units to operate beyond their currently planned retirement dates of 1992 (units 1 and 2) and 1999 (units 3, 4 and 5) . . . [and that renovation would render the plant] capable of generating at its designed capability until year 2010. . . ." Among the renovations required were repair and replacement of the turbine-generators, boilers, mechanical and electrical auxiliaries and the common plant support facilities. After preliminary review of the program, the Public Service Commission consulted the Wisconsin Department of Natural Resources (which then consulted EPA Region V) to determine whether WEPCO needed to obtain a [new source] permit before commencing the repair and replacement program. . . .

[The EPA determined] that the project would constitute a "physical change" resulting in an increase of production and emissions, which would therefore subject the plant to the relevant strictures of the Clean Air Act. YAlleging that the EPA has misconstrued both the Clean Air Act and its own regulations, WEPCO appeals the EPA's final determination. . . .

* * *

[W]e find [no] support in the relevant case law for the narrow constructions of "modification" and "physical change" offered by WEPCO. . . . Senator Muskie, one of the principal supporters of the Clean Air Act, remarked: "A source . . . is subject to all the nonattainment requirements as a modified source if it makes *any physical change* which increases the amount of any air pollutant. . . ." And other courts considering the modification provisions of NSPS and PSD have assumed that "any physical change" means precisely that. *See, e.g., National–Southwire Aluminum Co. v. EPA, 838 F.2d 835 (6th Cir.1988), cert. denied, 488 U.S. 955, 109 S.Ct. 390, 102 L.Ed.2d 379 (1988)* (turning off pollution control equipment constitutes "physical change" and modification); *Alabama Power Co. v. Costle, 204 U.S. App. D.C. 51, 636 F.2d 323, 400 (D.C.Cir. 1979)* ("The term 'modification' is nowhere limited to physical changes exceeding a certain magnitude."); *ASARCO Inc. v. EPA, 188 U.S. App. D.C. 77, 578 F.2d 319, 322 (D.C.Cir. 1978)* (NSPS applies to any stationary source that is "physically or operationally changed in such a way that its emission of any air pollutant increases.") (emphasis removed). *Cf. United States v. Narragansett Improvement Co., 571 F. Supp. 688, 694–95 (D.R.I. 1983)* (replacement program not modification because, despite physical change, no increase in emissions).

Further, to adopt WEPCO's definition of "physical change" would open vistas of indefinite immunity from the provisions of NSPS and PSD. Were we to hold that the replacement of major generating station systems—including steam drums and air heaters—does not constitute a physical change (and is therefore not a modification), the application of NSPS and PSD to important facilities might be postponed into the indefinite future. There is no reason to believe that such a result was intended by Congress. The Clean Air Act Amendments were enacted to "speed up, expand, and intensify the war against air pollution in the United States" with a view to assuring that the air we breathe throughout the Nation is wholesome once again." In particular, the permit program established by the 1977 Amendments to the Clean Air Act represented a balance between "the economic interests in permitting capital improvements to continue and the environmental interest in improving air quality." (Citation omitted.). A too restrictive interpretation of "modification" might upset the economic-environmental balance in unintended ways.

* * *

Our reading of the phrase "any physical change" is also consistent with another of the basic goals of the 1977 Amendments: technology-forcing. The legislative history suggests and courts have recognized that in passing the Clean Air Act Amendments, Congress intended to stimulate the advancement of pollution control technology. The development of emissions control systems is not furthered if operators could, without exposure to the standards of the 1977 Amendments, increase production (and pollution) through the extensive replacement of deteriorated generating systems.

* * *

In an era of increasing environmental concern, Congress enacted the Clean Air Act to "speed up, expand, and intensify the war against air pollution in the United States" with a view to assuring that the air we breathe throughout the Nation is wholesome once again. The EPA is entitled to substantial deference in interpreting the technical provisions of the Act and its own regulations. We cannot grant deference, however, where the EPA has attempted to implement the Act's lofty goals in contravention of its own statutory regime. We therefore affirm in part and vacate in part, remanding the cause to the EPA for further proceedings not inconsistent with this opinion.■

NOTES AND COMMENTS

1. The other core idea in the statutory definition of "modification," besides the concept of a physical change, is the requirement that the work *increase* emissions. Deciding whether an emissions increase has taken place, or will take place, as the result of any physical change in the plant, is not always straightforward. Consider an old coal-fired power plant that has operated at less than full capacity for many years, either because of lack of demand for its output or because it's old equipment cannot run at full capacity without repairs. At full capacity it emits X tons of pollutant per year, representing y pounds of pollutant per unit of energy generated. But in fact it has emitted less than $X2$ tons of pollutant per year. After repairs and replacement of equipment, the plant is more efficient and durable. It

now emits z pounds of pollutant per unit of energy generated ($z<y$), but will certainly operate at closer to full capacity in the future, emitting up to W tons of pollutant next year ($W>X/2$). Is the work producing these changes a "modification" triggering new source review? Should an "increase" in emissions be measured by an increase in pollutant output per year, output of pollutant per hour, or output of pollutant per unit of energy generated?

2. In *WEPCO*, the court disapproved the EPA's practice of deciding whether emissions have increased by comparing a plant's pre-modification *actual* emissions with the plant's post-modification *potential* emissions. Industry complained that the use of this "potential-to-emit" approach compares apples to oranges, since the post-modification emission estimate assumes that the plant will operate at a higher capacity after the modification than it did beforehand. EPA responds that that is in fact often the case. The Seventh Circuit noted that even if one compares actual pre-work emissions with actual post-work emissions, the modifications at issue in that case increased plant emissions. After *WEPCO*, the EPA decided to use an "actual-to-projected actual" emissions standard. In June of 2005, however, the Fourth Circuit rejected the EPA's comparison of pre-and post-modification levels of actual *annual* emissions in *United States v. Duke Energy Corp.*, 411 F.3d 539 (4th Cir. 2005). Duke Energy had replaced boilers and other major parts of several coal-fired power plants, thereby increasing annual but not *hourly* emissions. The court interpreted EPA's own regulations governing modifications to limit "modifications" to those that produce an increase in hourly emissions rates.

3. The Clinton Administration used precedents like the *WEPCO* case to dramatically step up its enforcement of new source review, contending that past repairs at many coal-fired power plants triggered new source permitting standards. The Administration initiated judicial enforcement actions against approximately 30 such plants (including the *Duke Energy* case, *supra*), and took administrative action against the Tennessee Valley Authority with respect to nine additional coal-fired plants. Most of these cases were still pending by the time the Bush Administration took power in early 2001. After the transition, the Bush Administration immediately signaled its concerns about the Clinton new source review policy by calling for a review of the policy in its National Energy Policy ("NEP"), which contended that aggressive application of new source review to old coal-fired power plants was confusing and unwieldy and could jeopardize energy security. The Bush Administration ultimately replaced the Clinton Administration's new source review policy with a new, less aggressive policy in 2002, one that permits plant owners to perform many physical plant changes without triggering new source review. Specifically, in December 2002 the EPA modified its new source review rules by, among other things, adding "plantwide applicability limits" ("PALs"). 67 Fed. Reg. 80186 (December 31, 2002). The creation of PALs allows sources to lump together emissions of different pollutants in determining when there has been a emissions increase that could trigger new source review. The December 2002 rule has

been challenged by a variety of state attorneys general and environmental organizations and a decision on that litigation is pending as of this writing.

4.   In 2003 EPA added a new version of the routine maintenance, repair and replacement exemption to its new source review rules. 68 Fed. Reg. 61248 (October 27, 2003). The 2003 rule excludes from the definition of "modification" any work for which "the fixed capital cost of the replaced component" plus other costs "does not exceed 20 percent of the replacement value of the entire process unit," and for which "the replacement does not cause the unit to exceed any emissions limits." How do these standards differ from the standards articulated by the *WEPCO* and *Duke Energy* courts? The D.C. Circuit Court of Appeals has stayed the 2003 rule pending resolution of litigation challenging the rule filed by 14 states and a variety of other interest groups and governmental entities.

5.   The Bush Administration coupled its gentler approach to new source review with a legislative proposal to reduce emissions from old coal-fired power plants, called the Clear Skies Act, which has not been enacted into law. Meanwhile, the Justice Department continues to prosecute some of the pending Clinton-era new source review enforcement actions, and has even filed a few additional enforcement suits. Several state attorneys general and environmental groups have initiated parallel negotiations with, and suits against, coal-fired power plants seeking to apply new source standards to older plants. These negotiations and suits are continuing as of this writing.

2.   POLLUTANT TRANSPORT—SO_2

The Clean Air Act contemplates the problem of the transport of pollution across state boundaries, and Sections 110 and 126 of the Act, 42 U.S.C. § 7410 and § 7426, require states to prohibit emissions that "contribute significantly" to NAAQS violations in other states. For a state to permit such emissions is a violation of the Act enforceable by the EPA or by citizen suit, and downwind states may petition the EPA under section 126 of the Act for a finding that that prohibition has been violated. Northeastern states have attempted to use these provisions to persuade EPA to curb emissions from largely unregulated Midwestern power plants, but prior to the 1990s these provisions were narrowly read by EPA and the courts, and were therefore relatively ineffective remedies for downwind states. Furthermore, these provisions offered no help with the problem of acid rain, which does much of its damage without triggering violations of NAAQS. However, downwind states received some help with the acid rain problem from Congress in the form of the Clean Air Act amendments of 1990, which mandated a sharp, staged decrease in sulfur dioxide emissions from coal-fired power plants, including existing sources left unregulated by the Act's new source permitting requirements.

The acid rain program, 42 U.S.C. §§ 7401–7642, took a new approach to pollution reduction by creating a market for acid rain "allowances" (rights to pollute), which owners may freely trade, buy or sell. The total number of allowances distributed to owners of coal-fired power plants each year is based upon a historical baseline of plant emissions, and is gradually reduced over time to achieve the more than 50 percent total emissions reduction called for by the 1990 Clean Air Act amendments. Allowance holders face a combination of the following choices: (1) to simply reduce emissions to match the number of allowances they receive, (2) to buy additional allowances from other allowance holders in order to pollute more, or (3) to reduce their pollution further than required and sell their "excess" allowances to others. In this way, those who can reduce their pollution most cheaply will tend to bear the lion's share of the pollution reduction burden, while those for whom reducing pollution is most expensive, will engage in less pollution control. This creates the potential for pollution "hot spots," or at least an uneven distribution of the pollution reduction burden (measured in tons of pollution reduced). The danger of hot spots is mediated somewhat by the requirement that any applicable preexisting permit or other limits applicable to plants' SO_2 emissions continue to act as a ceiling on individual plant emissions covered by the acid rain program, and by the fact that acid rain allowances grow more scarce over time.

Since the mid–1990s acid rain allowances have been traded on the Chicago Board of Trade and elsewhere, and the EPA tracks the market. The price of allowances, estimated to be in the low thousands of dollars per ton before the creation of the program, have hovered in the low hundreds of dollars per ton since the creation of the market. This overestimation has been attributed to reductions in the cost of pollution control and of shipping (cleaner) western coal to eastern plants, overstatement of compliance costs by utilities and the coal industry prior to creation of the program, or some combination of the two. The early years of the program saw relatively little trading activity. The Environmental Law Institute attributed this in part to state laws that constrained trading. In states that continue to rely on traditional cost-of-service ratemaking, utility owners of coal-fired power plants were sometimes unsure of how acid rain allowance transactions might be treated in rate cases. State public utility commissions were slow to develop rules governing allowance transactions, which created uncertainty and presented a significant barrier to risk-averse utilities. In addition, in most states the standard rules governing the allowed rate of return, the depreciation rate, and the risk that expenses, such as allowance purchases, may not be recoverable in electricity rates are all less favorable to allowance transactions. Furthermore, prohibitions against shareholder earnings on capital gains (but not capital losses) impose one-sided risks on utilities that purchase allowances. Douglas R. Bohi, Utilities and State Regulators Are Failing to Take Advantage of Emission Allowance Trading, Elec.J., Mar. 1994, at 20.

The big losers in the compromise that produced the 1990 Clean Air Act Amendments were the states in which high-sulfur coal was mined. A number of these states sought to adopt laws or regulations that would discourage their local electric companies from switching from local high-sulfur coal to low-sulfur coal from out of state. But it proved difficult to enact such rules without violating the dormant Commerce Clause of the

Constitution. The term "dormant" commerce clause refers to the fact that the Supreme Court has used the interstate commerce clause of the Constitution as a limitation on the power of the states to regulate businesses that are involved in interstate commerce. When used in this manner, the clause is often referred to as the "dormant" commerce clause, a reference to the fact that although the Constitution does not specifically say that the states may not regulate interstate commerce, the Court has held that such a limitation is implicit (i.e., dormant) in the grant of power to Congress to regulate interstate commerce. In the last fifty years, cases arising under the dormant commerce clause that contest the validity of state regulation have been far more frequent than cases challenging federal power under the direct application of the commerce clause. *See* Dan T. Coenen, Business Subsidies and the Dormant Commerce Clause, 107 Yale L. J. 965 (1998).

Alliance for Clean Coal v. Miller

44 F.3d 591 (7th Cir. 1995).

■ CUMMINGS, J. Plaintiff Alliance for Clean Coal ("Alliance") is a Virginia trade association whose members include Colorado and Oregon coal companies and three railroads that transport coal. The defendants are the chairman and six commissioners of the Illinois Commerce Commission in charge of the administration and enforcement of the Illinois Public Utilities Act.

Coal has long been and continues to be the most important source of fuel for the generation of electric power in this country, accounting for 56 percent of all electricity generated in 1992. Electric utilities, the primary consumers of domestic coal, burned 78 percent of the 998 million tons of coal produced in the United States in 1992. Coal is produced in over half the states and is sold in a highly competitive national market. *See* Alliance Ex. 10.

Coal's sulfur content varies greatly depending on its geographical origin. Western coal, mined west of the Rocky Mountains, generally has the lowest sulfur content of any coal produced in the country. Coal mined in the "Illinois Basin," which includes most of Illinois and parts of Indiana and western Kentucky, is relatively high in sulfur. Burning coal emits sulfur dioxide in an amount proportional to the coal's sulfur content. *See generally* Bruce A. Ackerman & William T. Hassler, Clean Coal/Dirty Air (1981).

In the 1970 Amendment to the Clean Air Act, Congress authorized the Environmental Protection Agency ("EPA") to set new standards to regulate various emissions, including sulfur dioxide. See 42 U.S.C. § 7411 (1970) (amended 1977). The EPA provided for two methods to control sulfur dioxide emissions: (1) the use of low sulfur coal; and (2) the use of pollution control devices ("scrubbers").

In 1977 Congress again amended the Clean Air Act, requiring new electric plants to build scrubbers. By requiring scrubbers regardless of the sulfur content of the coal burned, Congress essentially eliminated for new facilities the low-sulfur coal compliance option that had been available under the 1970 Amendment.

In 1990 Congress once again amended the Act, this time requiring a drastic two-stage reduction in industrial sulfur dioxide emissions in an attempt to combat acid rain. The 1990 Act implements a market-driven approach to emissions regulation, allowing for the free transfer of emission "allowances." The Act is aimed at reducing sulfur dioxide emissions in the most efficient manner and, like the 1970 Act, allows electric generating plants to meet the emission standards in the cheapest way possible. The principal methods of compliance now include installing new scrubbers, using low-sulfur coal, switching to another fuel source, or buying additional emission allowances.

The 1990 amendments meant the end of the salad days for high-sulfur coal-producing states such as Illinois. Low-sulfur western coal once again offered a viable alternative to the continued burning of high-sulfur coal combined with the installation of expensive new scrubbers. Faced with potentially damaging competition for the local coal industry, in 1991 the Illinois General Assembly passed the Coal Act, an addition to the Utilities Act, concerning implementation and compliance with the 1990 Clean Air Act amendments. *See* 220 ILCS 5/8–402.1. Under the Coal Act, utilities must formulate Clean Air Act compliance plans which must be approved by the Illinois Commerce Commission. In preparing and approving these compliance plans, the utilities and the Commerce Commission are required to:

> Take into account the need for utilities to comply in a manner which minimizes to the extent consistent with the other goals and objectives of this Section the impact of compliance on rates for service, the need to use coal mined in Illinois in an environmentally responsible manner in the production of electricity and the need to maintain and preserve as a valuable State resource the mining of coal in Illinois. 220 ILCS 5/8–402.1(a).

The Act encourages the installation of scrubbers to allow the continued burning of Illinois coal, stating that the combination can be an environmentally responsible and cost effective means of compliance when the impact on personal income in this State of changing the fuel used at such generating plants so as to displace coal mined in Illinois is taken into account. *Id.*

The four largest generating plants in Illinois currently burning Illinois coal are required to include the installation of scrubbers in their compliance plans so that they will be able to continue their use of Illinois coal. The cost of these scrubbers will be deemed "used and useful" when placed in operation and the utilities are guaranteed that they will be able to include the costs in their rate base. The Act further provides that the Commerce Commission must approve any 10 percent or greater decrease in the use of Illinois coal by a utility.

Plaintiff asked the district court to declare the Illinois Coal Act repugnant to the Commerce Clause of the federal Constitution and to enjoin its enforcement. In December 1993, District Judge Conlon handed down a memorandum opinion and order granting such relief. *Alliance for Clean Coal v. Craig,* 840 F. Supp. 554 (N.D. Ill. 1993). The court enjoined the Illinois Commerce Commission from enforcing the Illinois Coal Act and voided federal Clean Air Act compliance plans approved in reliance on the Illinois Coal Act.

On appeal, the defendant commissioners request that we dismiss the case for want of jurisdiction or, if we reach the merits, reverse the judgment below....

Alliance attacks the constitutionality of the Illinois Coal Act under the Commerce Clause of the Constitution. That clause provides that "the Congress shall have power ... to regulate commerce ... among the several states." Article I, Section 8, Clause 3. It has long been interpreted to have a "negative" aspect that denies the states the power to discriminate against or burden the interstate flow of articles of commerce.... "If a statute discriminates against interstate commerce either on its face or in its practical effect, it is subject to the strictest scrutiny ... 'Where simple economic protectionism is effected by state legislation, a virtual per se rule of invalidity has been erected.' " *DeHart v. Town of Austin,* 39 F.3d 718, 723 (7th Cir.1994), *quoting Philadelphia v. New Jersey,* 437 U.S. 617, 624.

Two recent Supreme Court cases interpreting the negative Commerce Clause are controlling here. In *Oregon Waste Systems v. Department of Environmental Quality,* 128 L. Ed. 2d 13, 114 S. Ct. 1345, the Court held that the negative Commerce Clause prohibited a state surcharge on the disposal of solid waste generated out of state. In *West Lynn Creamery, Inc. v. Healy,* 129 L. Ed. 2d 157, 114 S. Ct. 2205, the Court struck down a Massachusetts milk-pricing order which employed a tax on all milk sold to fund a subsidy to in-state producers. Because the Illinois Coal Act, like the milk-pricing order in West Lynn, has the same effect as a "tariff or customs duty—neutralizing the advantage possessed by lower cost out of state producers," it too is repugnant to the Commerce Clause and the principle of a unitary national economy which that clause was intended to establish. *West Lynn,* 114 S. Ct. at 2212.

The Illinois Coal Act is a none-too-subtle attempt to prevent Illinois electric utilities from switching to low-sulfur western coal as a Clean Air Act compliance option. Indeed, the statute itself states that the Illinois General Assembly determined that there was "the need to use coal mined in Illinois" and "the need to maintain and preserve as a valuable State resource the mining of coal in Illinois." 220 ILCS 5/8–402.1(a). The Act implements this protectionist policy in four ways. First, it tilts the overall playing field by requiring that commissioners take account of the effect on the local coal industry when considering compliance plans. *Id.* Second, the Act requires that certain large generating units install scrubbers "to enable them to continue to burn Illinois coal." 220 ILCS 5/8–402.1(e). Third, the Act guarantees that the cost of these scrubbers can be included in the utility's rate base and passed through to consumers, even where the use of low-sulfur western coal would be a cheaper compliance option. 220 ILCS 5/8–402.1(e) and 220 ILCS 5/9–212. Finally, the Act requires Commerce Commission approval before a utility can make a change in fuel that would result in a 10 percent or greater decrease in the utility's use of Illinois coal. In determining whether to grant approval, the Commerce Commission "shall consider the impact on employment related to the production of coal in Illinois." 220 ILCS 5/8–508. The intended effect of these provisions is to foreclose the use of low-sulfur western coal by Illinois utilities as a means of complying with the Clean Air Act. This of course amounts to discriminatory state action forbidden by the Commerce Clause.

Illinois seeks to save the Act by claiming that it merely "encourages" the local coal industry and does not in fact discriminate. This argument rings hollow. The Illinois Coal Act cannot continue to exist merely because it does not facially compel the use of Illinois coal or forbid the use of out-of-state coal. As recognized in *West Lynn Creamery*, even ingenious discrimination is forbidden by the Commerce Clause. 114 S. Ct. at 2215. By "encouraging" the use of Illinois coal, the Act discriminates against western coal by making it a less viable compliance option for Illinois generating plants. Moreover, the requirement that certain generators be equipped with scrubbers essentially mandates that these generators burn Illinois coal: that is the purpose of the scrubber requirement, and the Commerce Commission would likely not allow the pass-through of the then-unnecessary additional cost of low-sulfur western coal. Such a mandate runs directly afoul of *Wyoming v. Oklahoma,* 502 U.S. 437 (requirement that Oklahoma generating plants burn 10 percent Oklahoma coal held to violate the Commerce Clause). Similarly, the guaranteed pass-through of the scrubber cost to rate-payers is equivalent to the minimum price fixing for the benefit of local producers held unconstitutional in *Baldwin v. G.A.F. Seelig, Inc.*, 294 U.S. 511.

Illinois argues that it has merely "agreed to 'subsidize' the cost of generating electricity through the use of Illinois coal by requiring its own citizens to bear the cost of pollution control devices." First, the fact that Illinois rate-payers are footing the bill does not cure the discriminatory impact on western coal producers. As the Supreme Court noted in rejecting an identical argument in West Lynn, "the cost of a tariff is also borne primarily by local consumers yet a tariff is the paradigmatic Commerce Clause violation." *West Lynn*, 114 S. Ct. at 2216–2217. Second, Illinois' characterization of the Act as an "agreement to subsidize" does not suffice to fit this case into the "market participant" exception to the negative Commerce Clause created in *Hughes v. Alexandria Scrap Corp.,* 426 U.S. 794. Illinois is not acting as a purchaser of either coal or electricity but as a regulator of utilities. The fact that its regulatory action "has the purpose and effect of subsidizing a particular industry ... does not transform it into a form of state participation in the free market." *New Energy Co. of Indiana v. Limbach,* 486 U.S. 269, 277 (state tax credit for the use of Ohio-produced ethanol violated the Commerce Clause).

Finally, defendants champion the Illinois Coal Act as a means of protecting Illinois and its citizens from economic harm that would result from a decline in the local coal industry. Such concerns do not justify discrimination against out-of-state producers. "Preservation of local industry by protecting it from the rigors of interstate competition is the hallmark of economic protection that the Commerce Clause prohibit." *West Lynn,* 114 S. Ct. at 2217.

The purpose of the Illinois Coal Act was "to maintain and preserve . . . the mining of coal in Illinois" and to continue "to use Illinois coal as a fuel source." 220 ILCS 5/8–402.1(a). The Illinois Commerce Commission was required to take into account "the need to use coal mined in Illinois." *Id.* The obvious intent was to eliminate western coal use by Illinois generating plants, thus effectively discriminating against western coal. The Commerce Clause compels us to invalidate this statute, and consequently the compliance plans thereunder.

Judgment affirmed.

■ CUDAHY, J., concurring: Although the framework provided by the majority opinion is supportable, I believe that it is incomplete and, at the same time, may overstate the case. When all the conflicting considerations are weighed, there is some basis for concluding that Illinois has crossed the constitutional line, but its actions are probably only the first in a series of efforts to accommodate conflicting but important and legitimate public policies. . . .

The State's most effective argument is that we are dealing with a local (retail) ratemaking and electric operations problem over which the states have plenary authority. Appellants Br. at 33; *see Arkansas Elec. Coop. v. Arkansas Public Serv. Comm'n,* 461 U.S. 375, 395 (1983) (replacing the bright line distinction between state regulation of retail versus wholesale electricity sales with the balancing test of modern Commerce Clause jurisprudence, but reaffirming the general premise of "leaving regulation of retail utility rates largely to the States.") The basic principle under the Coal Act (as elsewhere) for the conduct of electric operations is to arrive at the "least cost" solution. The State argues, in accordance with unimpeachable economic theory, that "cost" means "social cost" and should include the cost of providing compensation for the sectors of society suffering injury from the lost Illinois coal business (such as the cost of unemployment compensation and loss of tax revenue). This is an "externality" not incorporated in ordinary commercial calculations but is a real cost to society nonetheless.

The answer to this argument seems to be that this is an externality that the states may not recognize since the Commerce Clause effectively precludes consideration of local economic damage as a legitimate reason to handicap interstate commerce. *Wyoming,* 112 S. Ct. at 800 ("When the state statute amounts to simple economic protectionism, a virtually per se rule of invalidity has applied."). Another way of handling this problem would be to offset the externality of damage to the Illinois coal industry with the additional externality of the long-term benefit accruing to Illinois from the free trade bias of the Constitution. In any event, the external cost of damage to the Illinois coal industry is something that presumably may not be recognized in computation of "least cost" for present purposes.

Nonetheless, the assurance of rate base treatment for scrubbers (which provide a capability for using Illinois coal) seems a tenuous basis for finding a violation of the Commerce Clause. I believe no Supreme Court case goes so far as clearly to support the conclusion that this is a violation although the trend of the Court's decisions may point this far. (*See* discussion above of *Wyoming*, 502 U.S. 437; *New Energy*, 486 U.S. 269; *Bacchus Imports*, 468 U.S. 263.) It is difficult to perceive the realities here since, as discussed above, we do not know the price and cost relationships involved and, in addition, it is hard to know how far this statute takes us beyond the already existing commercial and regulatory biases.

In this connection, I assume that both the utilities and the Illinois Commerce Commission may have reason to favor Illinois coal even without this legislation. The utilities are pervasively state regulated and simply as a matter of political prudence one would expect them to be more sensitive to major Illinois political and economic interests—like the coal industry and the labor it employs—than to the needs of the same interests in Wyoming or Montana. Similarly, the members of the Illinois Commerce Commission are appointed by a Governor dependent for votes on Illinois' coal-producing areas. One would not expect them to be hard at work furthering the aims of out-of-state mines or railroads. The mandates of the Coal Act may bring a local bias into more focus, but I doubt that they bring about a fundamental shift in preference.

I am also inclined to consider this legislation as possibly vulnerable under the Supremacy Clause. In contrast to the 1978 law, when Congress ordered scrubbers for all new coal plants, in 1990 . . . there seems to have been a disposition to leave the matter to the markets. It might be argued that Congress intended to "occupy the field" with a market-based approach, eschewing any mandatory measures. If this were the case, any "putting of thumbs on the scale" by the states might be preempted by the prescribed market-oriented methodology. The relevant Court cases, however, seem to make much easier the striking down of state legislation on Commerce Clause grounds, where relatively little burden or interstate commerce need be shown, than on grounds of preemption, where the requirements seem quite exacting. *See English v. General Electric Co.,* 496 U.S. 72 (1990); *Pacific Gas and Electric,* 461 U.S. 190.

These somewhat inconsistent considerations seem to create a conundrum in the case before us, whatever the standard for striking down state "encouragement" to local industry. In the end, I join, but with significant reservations, in the result reached by the majority opinion. ■

NOTES AND COMMENTS

1. The 1990 Clean Air Act Amendments (CAAA90) subjected several hundred existing coal-fired electric generating units to stricter regulation,

but gave all power producers greater discretion to create least cost overall strategies to achieve national pollution control targets. The most likely compliance option for the 435, mostly older, electric power units affected by Phase I of the CAAA90 was to switch to low-sulfur coal, and Powder River Basin (PRB) coal was potentially a less expensive source for many of them. During the 2 to 3 years following CAAA90, legislatures and other authorities in Oklahoma, Illinois, Indiana, and Kentucky passed legislation or took other steps to protect in-State coal mining jobs through legal requirements or economic incentives designed to persuade in-State utilities to burn local high-sulfur coals and to install flue gas scrubbers. By 1995 these challenges had been overcome as a result of decisions such as the preceding case finding that the laws violated the interstate commerce clause *See also Alliance for Clean Coal v. Bayh*, 72 F.3d 556 (7th Cir. 1995).

2. As **Figure 5–4** shows, trading activity in the acid rain program has grown steadily over time.

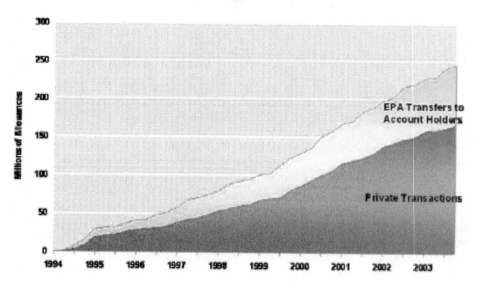

Figure 5–4

3. Is it immoral to trade pollution rights? Some scholars contend that the commodification of pollution rights in programs like the acid rain program remove the stigma that should properly be attached to polluting behavior. See Michael J. Sandel, It's Immoral to Buy the Right to Pollute, New York Times, Op–Ed, p. A29 (December 15, 1997); and Stephen Kelman, Cost–Benefit Analysis: An Ethical Critique, 5 Regulation 33 (1981). Do you agree with this view? Is pollution immoral? Should there be a moral stigma attached to polluting behavior, legal or illegal?

3. POLLUTANT TRANSPORT—NOx

Throughout the 1990s, many communities struggled to comply with the EPA's standards (NAAQS) for ground-level ozone. While the lion's share of the problem was attributable to local vehicle emissions, the problem was exacerbated in the eastern United States by the downwind (mostly eastward) transport of ozone and its precursors, including nitrogen oxides (NOx). In response to pressure from northeastern states and Congress, EPA began to study the problem of ozone transport with an eye toward imposing further limits on the emission of ozone precursors in the eastern half of the United States. After concluding that the existing ozone NAAQS was insufficient to protect human health, the Clinton Administration promulgated a new, more stringent ozone standard in 1997,[1] which further exacerbated the ozone compliance problem for the states. The Clinton EPA also issued a rule in 1998 requiring 22 states in the eastern half of the country to further reduce their emissions of ozone precursors, specifically mandating that electric generating units share a significant portion of the burden of those reductions. This rule is known as the "NOx SIP Call," because it required states to submit revised "state implementation plans," or "SIPs" to describe how they planned to implement these additional restrictions on emissions of ozone precursors. Finding of Significant Contribution and Rulemaking for Certain States in the Ozone Transport Assessment Group Region for Purposes of Reducing Regional Transport of Ozone, 63 Fed. Reg. 57356 (October 27, 1998). The rule required states to submit specific plans for achieving these reductions, which the states have done. The Bush EPA has left these two rules substantially intact, and has not deviated much from the plans laid out by the Clinton EPA for ozone pollution. However, Section 1443 of the Energy Policy Act of 2005 amends the Clean Air Act to require the EPA Administrator to extend NAAQS compliance deadlines for ozone for communities whose compliance is hindered by upwind sources of ozone precursors, like NOx and volatile organic chemicals.

4. MERCURY

Sulfur dioxide and Nitrogen Oxides are regulated as *conventional* pollutants under the Clean Air Act. However, the Act reserves its most stringent technology-based permitting standards for emissions of *toxic* pollutants. Permits for toxic pollutants must reflect "maximum achievable control technology," or "MACT." The Act defines MACT as:

> Emission standards promulgated under this subsection *for existing sources* in a category or subcategory may be less stringent than standards for new sources in the same category or subcategory but shall not be less stringent, and may be more stringent than (A) the

---

1. The existing standard was expressed in terms of a one-hour average limit. That standard was replaced by an 8–hour standard at a level of 0.08 parts per million (ppm), which was generally considered to be a more stringent standard. See National Ambient Air Quality Standards for Ozone; Final Rule, 62 Fed. Reg. 2 (July 18, 1997).

average emission limitation achieved by the best performing 12 percent of the existing sources (for which the Administrator has emissions information), excluding those sources that have, within 18 months before the emission standard is proposed or within 30 months before such standard is promulgated, whichever is later, first achieved a level of emission rate or emission reduction which complies, or would comply if the source is not subject to such standard, with the lowest achievable emission rate ... or (B) the average emission limitation achieved by the best performing 5 sources (for which the Administrator has or could reasonably obtain emissions information) in the category or subcategory for categories or subcategories with fewer than 30 sources.

Clean Air Act 112(d)(3), 42 U.S.C. § 7412(d)(3) (emphasis added). Note that for toxic pollutants, unlike conventional pollutants like SO_2 and NOx, the Act's stringent permitting standards apply to new and existing sources of emissions alike.

Despite growing a concern that the accumulation of mercury in the food chain might be responsible for an increased incidence of birth defects and neurological damage in humans, by the 1990s the EPA had not yet regulated mercury emissions from coal-fired power plants. The 1990 Amendments to the Clean Air Act directed EPA to study, and report to Congress on, the risks associated with toxic emissions from coal-fired power plants. The Sierra Club and Natural Resources Defense Council sued EPA for missing the statutory deadline for submitting its mercury report to Congress, and for failing to include coal-fired power plants on its list of sources of toxic pollution to be regulated under Section 112 of the Act. The EPA subsequently submitted two reports to Congress on this issue in the late 1990s: a study of the effects of mercury required by section 112(n)(1)(B) of the Act, and a second study focusing specifically on power plant emissions, required by section 112(n)(1)(A). See U.S. EPA, Mercury Study: Report to Congress, (EPA–452/R–97–003, December 1997); and U.S. EPA, Study of Hazardous Air Pollutant Emissions from Electric Steam Generating Units: Final Report to Congress (EPA–453/R–98–004a, February, 1998).

The EPA's 1998 report to Congress on toxics emissions from coal-fired power plants concluded that regulating these emissions was both "appropriate and necessary." That conclusion, in turn, led to a December, 2000 proposal by the Clinton EPA to regulate mercury emissions from coal-fired power plants as a toxic pollutant under Section 112 of the Clean Air Act, and to create a MACT standard for mercury emissions from coal-fired power plants. However, the Bush Administration has reversed the finding that regulating mercury emissions under Section 112 is appropriate and necessary, and has abandoned the Clinton EPA's proposal in favor of a less stringent "cap and trade" system for mercury emissions, one which did not include establishment of a MACT standard for mercury emissions from coal-fired power plants. The EPA finalized the rule on March 15, 2005. Modeled after the acid rain program, the rule would establish state budgets for mercury emissions, and a system of graduated total emission reductions. 70 Fed. Reg. 15,994 (March 29, 2005). In May of 2005 various environmental groups filed suit in federal court to challenge the legality of the EPA's new approach to regulating mercury emissions from coal-fired power plants. The rule has not been stayed pending those challenges. However, on October 28, 2005, the EPA announced that it had granted petitions to reconsider portions of the rule, including the size of the mercury budgets allocated to each state under the newly-established cap and trade system. Standards of Performance for New and Existing Stationary Sources: Electric Utility Steam Generating Units: Reconsideration, 70 Fed. Reg. 62213) October 28, 2005).

NOTES

1. *Carbon Dioxide.* Even though most climatologists had concluded by the mid–1990s that greenhouse gas emissions were contributing the global warming, the EPA has declined to use its regulatory authority under the Clean Air Act to regulate those emissions. However, throughout the first Clinton Administration, the United States participated actively in negotiations on this issue and signed the Kyoto Protocol in 1997. Carbon Dioxide emissions from coal-fired power plants remain unregulated under the Clean Air Act, though the Bush and Clinton Administrations disagreed over the question of whether the Act authorizes such regulation. For a fuller discussion of this issue, see Chapter 16.

2. *Legislation.* Several bills before the last several Congresses have reflected these disputes between Democrats and environmental interests, on the one hand, and Republicans and industry, on the other, over air pollution from coal-fired power plants. A bill sponsored by Senator Jim Jeffords, designated S.366, the Clean Power Act of 2003, would require reductions in emissions of sulfur dioxide, nitrogen oxides, mercury and carbon dioxide from coal-fired power plants. The President's Clear Skies Act, designated S.1844, would address emissions of the first three pollutants only, and would achieve smaller reductions at a slower pace. These were two of several bills proposing further regulation of coal-fired power emissions during the 108th Congress, none of which progressed beyond committee consideration.

E. THE FUTURE OF COAL

Coal has major advantages and disadvantages as an energy source. Its biggest advantage is the sheer volume of it that is available; we will not need to worry about worldwide coal shortages for many generations. Second, the reserves of coal within the United States are sufficiently great that we need not be concerned about interruptions caused by international conflict, which gives coal a major advantage over oil.

Coal has the disadvantage of being a relatively dirty fuel, which means that much more money must be spent on pollution control equipment if one burns burn coal rather than oil or especially natural gas. Second, the externalities caused by the mining of coal, as described above, are quite significant. Third, and perhaps most important, coal has the big disadvantage of being relatively inflexible in the way it can be used. While it can be conveniently burned under boilers, the cost of transforming it into a liquid or gas that can be more easily transported remains prohibitive, and in our increasingly mobile society this limitation is increasingly serious.

Coal mining has changed much in the last half of the twentieth century. There are several emerging trends: Air pollution problems have led to a heavy emphasis on the quality of coal, particularly in regard to sulfur content. Western mines are accounting for an increased share in total production. Electric utilities have come to dominate the market for coal, typically buying in large quantities. There are fewer total active mines, but the active mines are larger in size. The overall production is increasing in surface mines, as well as underground production from longwall mining.

The market for electric generation, on which coal is heavily dependent, is undergoing major structural changes (see Chapters 11–13, *infra*). Will restructuring in the electricity industry be a boon for coal? Certainly, the prospect of deregulation of the utility industry intensified the fight over pollution from coal combustion in the 1990s. Why? Because traditional rate regulation can act as a kind of indirect check on pollution from coal combustion. The power to set utilities' rates, and the *way* in which those rates are set, gives governments leverage over electric utilities, leverage that can be used to favor cleaner rather than dirtier sources of electricity generation. Many public service commissions encourage electric utilities to diversify their generation portfolios as a way to ensure service reliability. Furthermore, some public service commissions have used their leverage over utilities to favor alternatives to coal in another way—namely, by compelling utilities to invest in conservation and cleaner sources of power. Since the energy crises of the 1970s, state and federal governments have encouraged conservation and renewable power sources using a combination of federal and state statutes, and public service commission orders. The restructuring of the electricity industry that began in the mid–1990s threatened to change these incentives. As competition replaced administratively set rates, some worried that generation owners would no longer have an incentive to invest in cleaner, more expensive sources of power and that the demand for cheap, coal-fired power and the production of air pollution from coal-fired power, would increase. These 1996 remarks of an energy industry consultant were typically skeptical about the environmental effects of restructuring:

> the lowest-cost producers of power, by far, are the older, Midwest power plants that have the fewest environmental controls. These plants, which are also incidentally upwind of the Northeast and Midwest population centers of the eastern half of the United States, with

no further governmental intervention, will benefit from the greatest consumer demand and will significantly increase production in turn increasing emissions. If a purely free market selling price is the only issue, rather than utilizing clean burning nuclear or gas power or building a new clean generator, customers across the country will favor the cheapest power (typically a coal-based generator) instead of local production—even if the local producer offers cleaner energy.

William G. Rosenberg, Restructuring the Electric Utility Industry and Its Effect on the Environment, 14 Pace Envtl. L. Rev. 69 (1996). On the other hand, governments retain significant leverage over the power generation mix even within restructured electricity markets, and many are already using that leverage to try to ensure that price competition in electricity markets will not squeeze out cleaner sources of power in favor of dirtier ones. Restructuring states have created or strengthened laws and rules favoring the use of cleaner generation sources. New York, California, Texas and several other states that have opened retail electricity markets to competition in the last decade have instituted renewable portfolio standards requiring that retail service providers purchase a specified percentage of their power from renewable sources. What about the non-renewable portion of the electric generation mix: will coal-fired power comprise an increasing portion that remainder? According to the U.S. Energy Information Administration ("USEIA"), coal-fired generation has grown in the last few years, but no more quickly than total generation. Indeed, projected additions of coal-fired generating capacity to the grid will be dwarfed by additions of capacity from other sources, primarily natural gas. USEIA projects that just under 1000 megawatts of coal-fired plant capacity will be added to the grid between 2003 and 2007, representing about one half of one percent of the roughly 200,000 megawatt total.

Thus, the growth in coal-fired power production has not kept pace with growth in other sources, particularly natural gas. Coal plants require a larger investment than gas plants and other alternatives. Investors eyeing volatile electricity prices in some newly restructured markets may be wary of making such a large investment until these markets mature. The regulatory environment of coal-fired power generation, particularly environmental rules, is very uncertain. The Energy Policy Act of 2005 provides for federal financial assistance for research and development of a wide variety of so-called "clean coal" technologies, including new gasification technologies like IGCC as well as new pollution control technologies for coal emissions. See Energy Policy Act, Title IV. Some of these technologies appear to hold the promise of much cleaner coal combustion. However, these technologies have not yet solved the problem of carbon dioxide emissions from coal combustion. Indeed, perhaps the biggest unknown in coal's future is how the United States and the world will ultimately respond to the problem of the greenhouse effect and its potential warming of the atmosphere. The issue is discussed in Chapter 16.

CHAPTER 6

DOMESTIC PETROLEUM

A. SOME BASICS

1. THE LONG-TERM PRICE OF OIL

Fluctuations in the price of oil have driven much of the legislation enacted by both state and federal governments in the United States. Here is a long-term view of this key determinant of our energy policies:

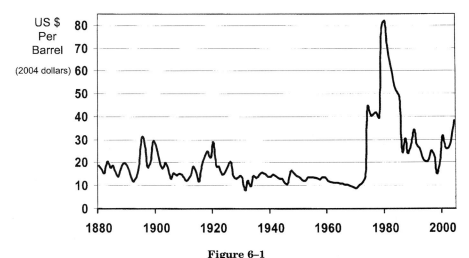

Figure 6–1
Real Price of Crude Oil, 1880–2004

Source: BP Statistical Review of World Energy 2005, www.bp.com, "Table of spot crude oil prices."

2. TERMINOLOGY

"Petroleum" is found in certain geological formations under the surface of the earth. In place, it typically consists of a mixture of liquid hydrocarbons called "crude oil," and various gaseous hydrocarbons, primarily methane, known as "natural gas."[1] Like coal, petroleum is considered a fossil fuel because it is the byproduct of millennia of decay and compression of organic material. About 62% of the energy used in the United States today is from oil and gas, from both domestic and imported sources.

For many purposes, the law treats petroleum as a single commodity regardless of whether it consists of crude oil, natural gas or a mixture. For example, standard leases between landowners and oil companies apply to both oil and gas. For other purposes, however, oil and gas[2] have separate legal characteristics; *e.g.*, the federal regulation of oil pipelines has been quite different from that of gas pipelines.

Petroleum is found underground in locations where impervious rock forms some sort of dome or trap that prevents the petroleum, which is located in the pore spaces of rock such as sandstone or limestone, from migrating to the surface. If the quantities of discovered petroleum are large enough to be produced profitably, the location is given a specific name, such as "the Seminole field." Such fields are often referred to as pools or

---

1. The line between liquid and gas will vary depending on pressure and temperature. For example, condensate is a liquid recovered at the surface from hydrocarbons that were initially in a gaseous phase in the reservoir and in the well bore. The gas condenses into a liquid at the lower temperatures and pressures of the surface.

2. The term "gas" is commonly used as a shorthand term for "gasoline," a liquid derivative of crude oil. In this book, the term "gas" refers to natural gas unless the context makes it obvious that gasoline is intended.

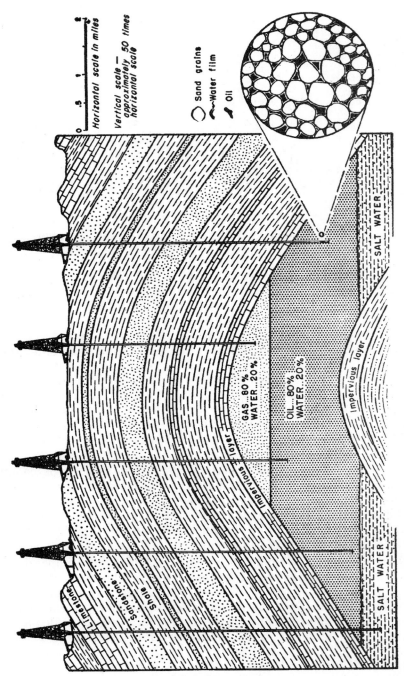

Figure 6–2
Distribution of Fluids Within a Reservoir

At right is a magnified view of sand grains, with film of water around each grain and oil in remainder of pore space.

Source: Richard C. Maxwell, Stephen F. Williams, Patrick H. Martin, Bruce M. Kramer, Oil and Gas: Cases and Materials 9 (6th ed. 1992, Foundation Press).

reservoirs, but these "pools" are not huge holes or caves in the ground. The pools are sedimentary rocks which look and feel like concrete. If you spill gasoline or motor oil onto a concrete pavement, much of the liquid will seep into the tiny pore spaces of the concrete rather than remain in a puddle on the surface. Similarly, in reservoirs, oil and gas are stored in the tiny pore spaces of sedimentary rocks, but they are under pressure caused by the weight of hundreds of feet of overlying silt and rock.

Some fields produce only gas (often with accompanying condensate liquids dripped out at the surface), and some produce mainly oil, inevitably accompanied by gas called "casinghead gas." This gas was originally dissolved in the oil underground, but when the pressure is lowered, the gas comes out of solution, much like bubbles of carbon dioxide in a soda drink are released when you pop the top off a soda can.

The oil in some fields is so fully saturated with natural gas that the gas forms a separate layer of lighter hydrocarbons sitting on top of the oil called a "gas cap." Often, the oil and gas layers sit on top of a layer of salt water which is also trapped in the porous rock as pictured in **Figure 6–2** above.

The largest oil field in the United States is the Prudhoe Bay field in northern Alaska. It is a gas-cap field containing billions of barrels of oil and trillions of cubic feet of natural gas. To date, only the oil is being produced because it can be shipped 770 miles south through the Trans–Alaskan pipeline to tankers and markets in the lower 48 states. The increasingly large quantity of gas which comes up with the oil has been reinjected back into the reservoir for many years, awaiting market conditions that justify either building a gas pipeline from the Arctic North Slope through Canada to the United States or cooling gas to a liquid (called liquefied natural gas or LNG) and shipping it by tanker.

The prospects for Alaskan gas development were slim in the year 2000 when the first edition of this casebook was launched. However, the surge in oil and gas prices since 2001 (to over $60 per barrel of oil and $6 per thousand cubic feet of gas in July 2005) and the inauguration of George W. Bush as president, whose national energy policy calls for developing domestic sources, led to the passage of the Alaska Natural Gas Pipeline Act in 2004 (15 U.S.C.A. § 720) after more than twenty years of debate. The bill authorizes a federal loan guarantee to private investors to construct the pipeline, which would take about ten years to permit and build and would be the largest privately financed construction project ever undertaken. The bill streamlines the regulatory process for pipeline construction by providing for a single environmental impact study, expedited judicial review, and a Federal Coordinator position within the executive branch to facilitate communications between the many agencies with jurisdiction over at least some aspect of the pipeline. The loan amount is capped at 80 percent of the capital costs of the project, not to exceed $18 billion, and pledges the full faith and credit of the U.S. government to pay all of the principal and interest on any debt obligations of the private investors building the pipeline. The construction route is still undecided.

3.   THE OIL AND GAS LEASE

The United States is unique in that private landowners can own oil and gas and other minerals in the ground as real property. In virtually all other countries of the world, the state owns the mineral resources. In these countries, oil and gas are typically developed by national oil companies, such as Pemex in Mexico or the China National Offshore Oil Corporation (which announced a bid to buy Unocal, a U.S company in June 2005), often in joint ventures with multinational corporations such as ExxonMobil and British Petroleum (BP) or Royal Dutch Shell. The relationship between the host country and the corporation is discussed in Chapter 7 on International Petroleum.

In the United States, private ownership of oil and gas has created a body of oil and gas law governed by the common law of property, contract, and tort. This common law operates within a complex framework of state conservation legislation and federal statutes. In addition to this system of private ownership, our federal government owns substantial mineral resources on public lands through its ownership of about 30 percent of the total land area in the United States, located mostly in the western states and Alaska. *E.g.,* 83 percent of Nevada and 68 percent of Alaska are federal land. The federal government also owns the outer continental shelf which produces much oil and gas from offshore wells drilled in the Gulf of Mexico and other coastal areas. The coastal states usually own the first three miles of offshore lands, at which point federal jurisdiction begins. (See Section 6(E) of this chapter).

Despite this diverse system of private, state, and federal ownership of minerals in the U.S., the exploration and production of oil and gas are typically done pursuant to an "oil and gas lease" between the landowner as lessor (whether private or public) and an oil company (the "operator") as lessee. This core contract is designed to meet the unique needs of an industry exploring for and producing a substance hidden thousands of feet underground. The lessee wants the right, but not the duty, to develop a leasehold for a certain time. If promising deposits are found, the lessee wants the right to hold the lease for as long as profitable production continues.

The typical lessor does not have the capital or technical expertise to develop the oil and gas himself and does not want to bear the costs and risks of drilling and producing wells. Therefore, the lessor transfers the exclusive right to develop the oil and gas to the lessee in return for a cost-free share of production, called a royalty. In addition, the lessor will bargain with the lessee for a bonus—a one-time cash payment to the lessor for signing the lease. In "hot" territory where discoveries have been found on nearby acreage, the bonus may amount to thousands of dollars an acre.

In "wildcat" territory where no operators have yet drilled, the bonus may be a few dollars an acre. If a lessee never drills, or drills only dry holes, the lessor's royalty payments are zero because there is no production, but the lessor has at least received the bonus payment. When the lessor is the state or federal government, leases are usually awarded through competitive auctions to the company that submits the highest bonus bid for a particular tract.

The relationship between the lessor and lessee is the mainstay of courses in oil and gas law, but it is premised on these straightforward economic goals of the two parties to the lease. Briefly, a typical oil and gas lease includes three basic clauses:

1. A granting clause that transfers the mineral estate under the described land to the lessee from the lessor.

2. The habendum clause which reads: "This lease shall be for a primary term of ___ years and as long thereafter as oil or gas is produced from said land."

3. The royalty clause which typically grants the lessor a 1/8 royalty on all the oil and gas produced from the lease.

NOTES AND COMMENTS

1. Test your knowledge of the lessor/lessee relationship:

(a) If you are the lessee, will you bargain for a three-year or a ten-year primary term in the blank in the habendum clause? If you are the lessor, which will you prefer?

(b) The lessee usually hands the lessor a printed lease form with a 1/8 royalty printed in the royalty clause and hopes that the lessor will not bargain for a higher royalty. However, when oil and gas prices are high and leases are valuable, lessors may be able to secure a 1/6 or greater royalty share. The larger the cost-free royalty, the less money remains for the lessee to pay for all the costs of producing the oil and gas. Conversely, when oil prices dip to record lows, why might a lessor grant temporary royalty relief to a lessee and lower royalties until prices rise to an agreed level? (*See, e.g.,* the Deepwater Royalty Relief Act, which provides incentives to develop domestic deepwater resources by providing royalty holidays for initial production increments.)

(c) If a lessee signs a lease on January 1, 1995 containing a three-year primary term, and has no production on January 1, 1998, what happens to the lease? What if the lessee has no production but is drilling a well on that day? What if the lessee has drilled a number of good wells and discovered a large gas field, but is not yet producing gas because no pipeline connection exists?

(d) The giant East Texas oil field was discovered on October 9, 1930. Many leases in this field were signed in the 1930s "for 10 years and as long thereafter as oil and gas are produced." The wells on the western part of this field have now "watered out" as the oil has migrated from west to east due to the natural reservoir drive in the field. The western wells produce only salt water and have been shut in. Are the leases still alive on the western acreage? On the eastern acreage? Is it "fair" to allow the lessees and lessors of eastern wells to produce the oil which originated from someone else's land to the west?

(e) You are the employee for Bigg Oil Company responsible for submitting bids on tracts offered for lease on the outer continental shelf by the Minerals Management Service (the federal agency within the Department of Interior). Would your supervisors or shareholders be happy with you if you won the bid for Tract 91 by offering $1.1 billion when the second highest bidder offered $500,000? What does this difference tell you about the risks of exploration?

2. The lessee under a typical lease never promises to drill even a single well. If the lessee never drills and never secures production, the lease will terminate automatically at the end of the primary term because of the wording of the habendum clause. Lessors often seek to encourage drilling by contracting for the lessee's payment of annual delay rentals in exchange for the privilege of delaying the commencement of a well. Thus, if a lease has a primary term of 10 years and the lessee does not drill by the end of the first year, the lessee will have to pay delay rentals if it wants to extend the lease for another year. Nonetheless, it is still the lessee's option to either drill or pay delay rentals; there is no contractual obligation to drill.

4. THE OIL BUSINESS

Between the wellhead and an enduser's gasoline tank, stove top, boiler or blast furnace, oil and gas are transported and processed from lower-valued hydrocarbons, often produced in remote areas of the country, to higher-valued products used in populated centers of industrial activity. The largest companies in the industry are often vertically integrated and operate in all five stages of the value chain: 1. exploration; 2. production; 3. refining; 4. distribution; and 5. marketing. However, a significant number of small-, medium-, and large-size companies also operate as "independent" producers, refiners, transporters and marketers, active in just one or two of the stages. Natural gas is treated like oil for purposes of exploration and production, but it is distributed and marketed through different networks than those used for oil. Crude oil usually flows to a refinery for processing into gasoline, jet fuel, diesel and other products, while gas is often processed in the field to recover hydrocarbon liquids and to eliminate undesirable elements like sulfur and water. The gas then needs no further refining and is transported by pipeline to markets.

a. EXPLORATION

The exploration staff is led by petroleum geologists who use tools such as seismographs, magnetic surveys from NASA satellites, gravimeters and infrared remote sensors to unlock the earth's buried secrets. Geologists look for underground formations of porous, permeable rock which have trapped oil and gas as illustrated in **Figure 6–2**.

Despite technological improvements, any exploratory "wildcat" well remains a gamble. In 1975, only three out of 100 exploratory wells drilled were commercially successful. Technological progress in supercomputers in the 1990s now allows the processing of enormous amounts of data from geological surveys. Computers can produce brightly colored 3–D seismic images which virtually shout "drill here" and this can greatly increase the probability of successful drilling. Still, even promising locations can result in "dusters" or dry holes rather than the "gushers" depicted in movies like "Giant."[3] For example, Conoco took a $19 million charge against earnings in early 1999 to write off an unsuccessful deepwater wildcat well drilled in 4,800 feet of water off New Zealand.

Today, most of the easy places to find petroleum in the United States have been explored. The most promising areas for discoveries are in deep offshore waters and in the remote Arctic where the challenges and costs of drilling are great. Many of the major oil companies have reallocated their exploration budgets to overseas ventures in places like Russia, South America and Nigeria, where large political risks are added to geological risk and the financial risk of highly fluctuating oil prices. See Chapter 7 on International Petroleum.

b. PRODUCTION

The efficient recovery of crude oil from the tiny pore spaces of the reservoir rock is technically rather complicated. When a well bore penetrates a formation holding oil under high pressure, the well bore creates an area of low pressure, and the pressure differential causes oil to flow into the well. Yet crude oil cannot expel itself from the rock. It is the compressed gas or water trapped in the reservoir with the oil that expands in response to the lower pressure at the well bore. The expanding gas or water forces the oil up and out of the well in a displacement process and provides the continuing pressure essential for producing oil without the use of pumps. If the original field pressure is low or has decreased over time as oil is withdrawn, wells will need to be put "on the pump."

Three types of oil displacement mechanisms exist either alone or in combination. They are the dissolved-gas drive, the gas-cap drive, and the water drive.

In the ***dissolved gas drive***, oil in the reservoir contains gas in solution. This dissolved gas expands as a result of the pressure gradient around the well bore and comes out of solution. This free gas fills the void spaces once occupied by the oil flowing out of the well. As oil production proceeds, pressure is reduced throughout the reservoir and more and more

---

3. No driller today would want to dance in a fountain of black crude erupting from a discovery well like James Dean (playing Jett Rink) does in the movie "Giant." Blowout preventers and proper drilling techniques are used today to prevent such spectacular, but environmentally disastrous, scenes.

gas is freed from solution everywhere. Eventually, the free gas begins to flow into the well along with the oil. The gas-oil ratio of the well increases and reservoir pressure declines continuously until all of the gas originally contained in the reservoir has been withdrawn. At this point there is no more pressure to expel the oil, and oil production ceases. Unfortunately, only 10 to 30 percent of the oil in the reservoir can be recovered in a dissolved gas drive.

In the **gas-cap drive**, the upper part of the reservoir is filled with gas, and oil with dissolved gas lies beneath the gas cap. When a well is drilled into the lower oil zone, the pressure differential causes the compressed gas in the gas cap to expand. The gas cannot expand upward through the impervious rock that traps the hydrocarbons, so it expands into the lower oil zone, driving the oil toward the low-pressure area at the well bore. This oil migration continues as the gas cap expands to fill the space voided by withdrawn oil, until the gas invades the lower part of the formation and enters the well. Then, the gas-oil ratio rises sharply, reservoir pressure declines rapidly, and when the gas completely fills the original oil zone, oil production ceases. However, a properly controlled gas-cap drive can result in recovery rates of 25 to 50 percent of the oil. If gas production is prohibited from the gas cap, and oil wells are located to produce only from the lower parts of the reservoir, the gas in the gas cap can be retained in the formation for a longer period of time. This maintains pressure in the reservoir and allows more oil to be flushed out. The same effects can be had if any gas produced from the gas cap is returned continuously to the formation.

In a **water-drive** field, the oil lies atop a layer of compressed water which expands upward slightly when the pressure reduction from the well bore spreads outward. Water is a more effective pushing agent than gas and can "scrub" the reservoir rock more thoroughly as it migrates through the pore spaces. The water drives the oil in front of it toward the well bore. Eventually, as the water invades the oil zone, more water and less oil are produced from the wells. Oil production ceases when the cost of operating the uppermost wells exceeds the value of the oil withdrawn from them. It is not loss of pressure that causes abandonment of the reservoir but the fact that the oil content of the rock has been depleted. Recovery rates of 75 to 85 percent are possible if the reservoir is operated to preserve the flushing action of the water. This requires that the oil be produced largely from wells located in the upper part of the reservoir having low water-oil ratios. Wells bottomed in the lower zone will produce large amounts of water with the oil and will dissipate the reservoir's source of pressure unless the withdrawn water is continually reinjected into the formation.

Thus, two factors must be controlled to produce a reservoir efficiently: (1) the rate of production; and (2) the location of wells. A controlled rate of production maintains reservoir pressure by preventing the rapid release of dissolved gas from solution. It also assures that the boundary between the migrating oil and the advancing gas or water front is fairly uniform so that the entire reservoir is effectively flushed without bypassing areas of oil-saturated rock.

The proper location of wells also increases recovery rates. No wells should be allowed to produce gas from the gas cap until all of the oil is flushed out; and oil wells in a water-drive field should be located high on the structure where they will not prematurely produce large amounts of water and dissipate the water drive.

Thus, for each reservoir there is generally a dominant displacement mechanism, an optimal pattern of well locations, and a maximum efficient rate of production (called the MER) which, if exceeded, will lead to an avoidable loss of ultimate oil recovery. The MER of a field is determined technically through engineering studies. The use of the MER to control production rates is probably the single most important conservation measure for assuring efficient oil recovery.

Further improvements in production efficiency can result from artificial pressure-maintenance activities such as injecting water or gas into the reservoir. The injected gas or water may be recycled from the reservoir or brought in from extraneous sources. Many of the older fields in West Texas are being repressured with carbon dioxide (CO_2) delivered through a 400–mile pipeline from natural deposits of this gas in Colorado.

The recovery of natural gas is much less complicated than recovery of crude oil because gas is highly expansible. It can be recovered from porous rock simply by allowing it to migrate by expansion into the low-pressure area around the well bore. This process commonly can recover 90 percent or more of the original gas in place. Recovery rates less than this occur only when the permeability of the reservoir rock is so low that gas cannot flow freely into the well bore. This is called a "tight sand" formation. Operators will often use hydraulic fracturing to create cracks in the formation so that the gas can flow freely. Fluids are forced under high pressure down the well bore to crack the tight formation. In "Project Gas Buggy," one of the more spectacular efforts to promote the peaceful use of atomic energy after World War II, the federal government exploded a nuclear bomb underground in New Mexico to fracture the formation and stimulate the flow of gas. Although a technical success, the gas was too radioactive to market.

c. REFINING

Crude oil in its natural state is of little practical value. It is a complex chemical compound consisting of a mixture of hundreds of hydrocarbon compounds, each having its own boiling point. Refining separates these compounds into desired products such as gasoline, jet fuel, kerosene, diesel fuel, heating oil, and asphalt. Petroleum hydrocarbons are also the source of many feedstocks for chemical plants producing everything from nylons to insecticides.

Refining first separates the hydrocarbons in crude oil by heating them and distilling the different vapor streams which result at different temperatures. Heated crude oil is sent to a fractionation tower which may be a hundred feet high.

The hydrocarbons with the lowest boiling points, such as gasoline, will vaporize first. As other hydrocarbons rise and then cool, they condense at different heights in the tower and are withdrawn as separate products, as shown in **Figure 6–3**.

FRACTIONATION

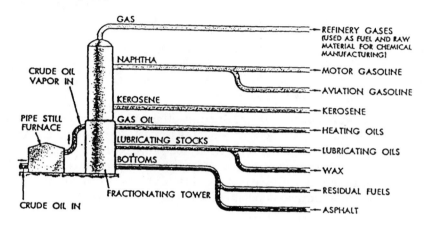

Figure 6–3
Science Service, Petroleum at 35 (undated)

Distillation of crude oil into its fractions does not produce the correct proportion of products demanded by the marketplace. For example, it produces relatively small amounts of gasoline. Therefore, refineries use thermal cracking and catalytic cracking to break larger hydrocarbon molecules into smaller ones that will rise to the top of the fractionation tower.

Oil refineries pose major problems of air and water pollution. Many refineries are located in sensitive coastal areas because they are designed to receive and ship products by tanker. In addition, refineries process tremendous quantities of liquids and vapors at high temperatures and high pressures. Explosions and blasts, while rare, can kill and injure workers and seriously affect the health and property of people living in surrounding neighborhoods.

As noted earlier, natural gas is not refined in the way that crude oil is. The gas that comes out of the well may require some treatment, such as removal of sulfur, but this is a much simpler operation than the refining of petroleum.

d. TRANSPORTATION AND DISTRIBUTION

In general, the method of distributing petroleum compounds varies with their relative weight. Heavy compounds, like asphalt, usually go by truck, rail or barge. Liquids can vary from heavy crude, which is like molasses, to gasoline, which evaporates readily. Heavy crude usually goes by tanker or barge, although it may go by pipeline if it is not too heavy to flow. Refined products are typically distributed by pipeline to a terminal and then by truck or train to the ultimate user. Natural gas can be liquefied and shipped by LNG tankers, but it is far more commonly transported by pipeline. Crude oil is a "niche" fuel. Its refined products are used mainly in only one sector of the economy—transportation. This sector uses almost 80 percent of the oil consumed in the United States.

A "spaghetti bowl" of pipes underlies cities like Houston located near producing fields and refinery complexes. A large network of interstate pipelines moves oil and gas from the producing states to consuming centers. Pipelines are specialized for natural gas and different types of petroleum products. In 1906, oil pipelines were regulated as common carriers by federal law. *See* the Hepburn Act Amendment of 1906, Pub. L. No. 357, 34 Stat. 584 (1906). At that time, the major pipeline companies attempted to circumvent this Act by transporting only oil produced from their own leases or purchased at the wellhead, thereby refusing to hold themselves out as public pipelines for hire. In *The Pipeline Cases*, 234 U.S. 548 (1914), the U.S. Supreme Court held that the 1906 law applied to interstate pipelines, even if the pipeline owned the oil being transported. Justices Holmes wrote: "Availing itself of its monopoly of the means of transportation the Standard Oil Company refused through its subordinates to carry any oil unless the same was sold to it or to them and through them to it on terms more or less dictated by itself. In this way it made itself master of the fields without the necessity of owning them and carried . . . a great subject of international commerce coming from many owners but, by the duress of which the Standard Oil Company was master, carrying it all as its own." *Id.* at 559. *See* George S. Wolbert, Jr., The Pipe Line Story, 4 Okla. L. Rev. 305–36 (1951); Edwin I. Malet, Oil Pipelines as Common Carriers: Issues of Form and Substance, 20 Hous. L. Rev. 801 (1983).

The technology for gas pipelines did not exist in 1906. Gas pipelines were regulated in 1938 when the Natural Gas Act was passed in recognition of the monopoly power of interstate gas pipelines. Gas pipelines were not originally regulated as common carriers; the pipeline owners carried only their own gas, purchased directly from producers in the fields. The effort to convert these pipelines to "open access" pipelines that would carry gas owned by many other market participants, including competitors' gas, was the primary mission of the Federal Energy Regulatory Commission during the 1980s and 1990s. This story of natural gas restructuring is told in Chapter 8 on Natural Gas.

B.   THE EARLY HISTORY OF PETROLEUM

1.   OIL BEFORE PETROLEUM

a.   OF WHALES AND WAX

In the newly formed United States, the primary source of power for mills and other growing industries was water power. Water could turn wheels, but it could not produce light. For illumination, most people still relied on candles and fireplaces. Wealthier people were able to light their homes with oil lamps, which produced a brighter and more reliable flame, but the animal and vegetable fats used to fuel such lamps were expensive. The premium fuel, whale oil, became increasingly expensive as the whalers wiped out the whale populations of the Atlantic and had to travel to the Antarctic to obtain supplies.

Until the end of the eighteenth century, artificial indoor light came only in units of one candle. Bright illumination was possible only through massive multiplication of these tiny sources. Candles convert only about 0.01 percent of their chemical energy into light. The bright spot in a candle flame has an average irradiance (rate of energy falling on a unit area) just 20 percent higher than clear sky. The first eighteenth-century lighting innovations doubled and tripled this low performance. In 1794, Aime Argand introduced lamps that could be regulated for maximum luminosity by using wick holders with a central air supply and chimneys to draw in the air. Soon afterward came "town gas," gas made from coal and piped into street lamps and the homes of middle- and upper-class families in urban areas. Town gas was too expensive for many households, however. For more than half of the nineteenth century, tens of millions of rural households around the world continued to fill their lamps with an exotic biomass fuel—the oil rendered from the blubber of sperm whales.

Whaling, a poorly paid and dangerous way of life—portrayed so unforgettably in 1851 in Melville's "Moby Dick"—reached its peak just before 1850. The American whaling fleet, by far the largest in the world, had a record total of more than 7,900 vessels in 1846. As the number of sperm whales dwindled and competition from coal gas and kerosene increased, whaling rapidly declined. This was the first Tragedy of the Commons to affect America's energy supplies.

b. KEROSENE

In the 1850s, a Canadian inventor discovered a way to extract a liquid from natural deposits of tar and asphalt. He called this liquid, which could be burned in existing oil lamps, kerosene. Although expensive, it produced higher quality illumination than vegetable or animal oils, and a number of firms began to produce it. The kerosene lamp then became a common fixture in the homes and offices of the wealthy.

The growing market for kerosene increased the interest in learning more about the still mysterious properties of oil. This interest "arose from pure necessity," writes Daniel Yergin, because "[b]urgeoning populations and the spreading economic development of the industrial revolution had increased the demand for artificial illumination beyond the simple wick dipped into some animal grease or vegetable fat, which was the best that most could afford over the ages, if they could afford anything at all."[4]

---

4. Daniel Yergin, The Prize: The Epic Quest for Oil, Money and Power 22–23 (1991). Yergin's book is the classic history of the oil industry. A documentary, based on the book, is periodically aired by public television stations and is available in videocassette form.

c. THE FIRST OIL WELL

As storm clouds were gathering for the Civil War, the discovery of oil in Pennsylvania foretold a breakthrough in energy utilization that would rank with the great technological advances of all time. The tar-like substances that provided the source material for kerosene were scarce and difficult to process, so kerosene remained a luxury. Until 1859, petroleum was gathered from natural seeps and springs or skimmed off ponds. Then, in 1859, the Pennsylvania Rock Oil Company hired Edwin Drake to drill a well near an old oil spring, using a rig made from an old steam engine and an iron bit attached by a rope to a wooden windlass. The drill bit hit oil at 69 feet below the surface. "Drake's Folly" had proved the practicality of a new technique for tapping liquid petroleum from the earth.

The discovery that oil could be found by drilling sparked a "gold rush" into the northwestern Pennsylvania region. Wild speculation in land followed as prospectors rushed into the area to try their luck. No one knew why oil could be found in one place but not another, so whenever someone struck oil, everyone else scurried to buy up the rights to nearby land. "Close-ology" was the geology of the day. In 1861, the first refinery went into operation in this region, producing mostly kerosene. To supply more distant refineries, railroads built spurs into the region, and in 1865 a railroad tank car was developed especially for carrying crude in two large wooden tanks. As large quantities of Pennsylvania oil reached the market, the price of kerosene dropped dramatically and the kerosene lamp became the basic source of lighting for homes and businesses all over the eastern United States.

2. THE RULE OF CAPTURE: THE TRAGEDY OF THE COMMONS I

The discovery of oil, and then natural gas, from wells tapping underground reservoirs, posed a novel legal question: Who owned the oil and gas? The courts' resolution of this issue had a major impact on the way that the oil business was conducted.

Barnard v. Monangahela Natural Gas Co.

216 Pa. 362, 65 A. 801 (1907).

[Daniel and Elizabeth Barnard brought a bill in equity against the Monangahela Natural Gas Company for an injunction and an accounting. The plaintiffs owned a 66–acre farm adjoining the 156–acre farm owned by James Barnard. The gas company held leases on both farms. James' farm joined the other Barnards' farm in such a way that one corner of his farm formed an angle of about 12 degrees less than a right angle. A circle large enough to include ten acres with its center at this corner would enclose 2 1/2 acres of James' land and 7 1/2 acres of Daniel and Elizabeth's land. The gas company drilled a well on James' farm near the corner of this angle, only 35 feet from the line dividing the two farms.

On appeal, the supreme court dismissed the bill in equity, quoting the opinion of the court below as follows:]

The first question stated broadly is this: "Can a landowner in gas territory drill a well on his farm close to the line of his adjoining landowner and draw from the land of the latter three-fourths of the gas that his well may produce without so invading the property rights of the adjoining landowner as to be legally accountable therefore?" There is no doubt that the oil and gas confined in the oil and gas-bearing sands of a farm belong to the one who holds title to the farm, but it is also recognized, both as a question of fact and law, that oil and gas are fugitive in their nature, and will by reason of inherent pressure seek any opening from the earth's surface that may reach the sand where they are confined. . . .

The right of every landowner to drill a well on his own land at whatever spot he may see fit certainly must be conceded. If, then, the landowner drills on his own land at such a spot as best subserves his purposes, what is the standing of the adjoining landowner whose oil or gas may be drained by this well? He certainly ought not to be allowed to stop his neighbor from developing his own farm. There is no certain way of ascertaining how much of the oil and gas that comes out of the well was when in situ under this farm and how much under that. What then has been held to be the law? It is this: . . . every landowner or his lessee may locate his wells wherever he pleases, regardless of the interests of others. He may distribute them over the whole farm or locate them only on one part of it. He may crowd the adjoining farms so as to enable him to draw the oil and gas from them. What then can the neighbor do? Nothing; only go and do likewise. He must protect his own oil and gas. He knows it is wild and will run away if it finds an opening and it is his business to keep it at home. This may not be the best rule; but neither the Legislature nor our highest court has given us any better. No doubt many thousands of dollars have been expended "in protecting lines" in oil and gas territory that would not have been expended if some rule had existed by which it could have been avoided. Injunction certainly is not the remedy. If so, just how far must the landowner be from the line of his neighbor to avoid the blow of "this strong arm of the law"?■

NOTES AND COMMENTS

1. The rule of capture adopted for oil and gas was based, perhaps surprisingly, on the principle expressed in the famous case of *Pierson v. Post*, 3 Caines 175 (N.Y. Sup. 1805), involving ownership of a wild fox. In *Westmoreland & Cambria Natural Gas Co. v. De Witt*, 130 Pa. 235, 18 A. 724 (1889), the court wrote:

> Water and oil, and still more strongly gas, may be classed by themselves, if the analogy be not too fanciful, as minerals ferae naturae. In common with animals, and unlike other minerals, they have the power and the tendency to escape without the volition of the owner. Their "fugitive and wandering existence within the limits of a particular tract was uncertain." . . . They belong to the owner of the land, and are part of it, so long as they are on or in it, and are subject to his control; but when they escape, and go into other land . . . the title of

the former owner is gone. Possession of the land, therefore is not necessarily possession of the gas. . . .

2.   The rule of capture has been adopted in all oil and gas producing states. On January 10, 1901, the greatest gusher the world had ever seen erupted in Spindletop, Texas, spewing over 75,000 barrels of oil a day over the coastal plain. Does it surprise you that Spindletop's Boiler Avenue looked like **Figure 6–3** in 1903?

Figure 6–4
Boiler Avenue at Spindletop

Photo courtesy of American Petroleum Institute. This photo and many others, just as picturesque, appear in Walter Rundell, Jr., Early Texas Oil: A Photographic History 1866–1936 (Texas A&M Press 1977).

Land that had once been pig pastures sold for as much as $900,000 an acre. A glut of oil dropped the price to as little as three cents a barrel, while a cup of water cost five cents. The boom, however, was short-lived. Rapid and uncontrolled production depleted the field's pressure so quickly that by 1903 the field had begun to decline and within ten years, Spindletop was a virtual ghost town. Less than five percent of the field's oil was produced.

3.   Many natural gas reservoirs have produced all of the native gas originally in the pore spaces of the reservoir formation. These depleted reservoirs are valuable "pieces of rock," especially when they are located near cities or industry, because they can be used to store gas which has been produced and transported from other distant fields. The gas is pumped into the pore spaces of the depleted reservoir and then can be quickly extracted when, for instance, a cold snap hits and homeowners all turn up the thermostats on their gas furnaces. Underground storage is usually the only feasible and safe method of storing large quantities of natural gas.

In *Lone Star Gas Co. v. Murchison*, 353 S.W.2d 870 (Tex. App. 1962), the plaintiff, Lone Star, was a public utility engaged in the business of distributing natural gas to a large number of customers. Because the demand for gas, especially for residential use, fluctuates widely, Lone Star stored gas during periods of low demand and withdrew it to meet periods of peak demand. Lone Star had acquired the rights to all of the underground formation except for a small amount of acreage underlying the Jackson land. The Jacksons leased this land to Murchison and he drilled a well into the gas formation and started extracting large quantities of gas. Lone Star sought an injunction to prevent the Murchison well from producing gas, and also sued for damages for conversion of its gas.

Should the rule of capture apply to stored gas? The Texas courts said no, holding that stored gas is the personal property of the storer.

Could Murchison then claim that Lone Star was trespassing on his property? Lone Star's gas molecules were invading his mineral estate without his permission. The court ducked this question, writing that "[t]he status of this record is such . . . that we must, as Ulysses 'lash ourselves to the mast and resist Siren's songs' of trespass." *Id.* at 875. How would you be tempted to rule on the trespass issue? If you find a trespass, would you grant Murchison an injunction against the gas storer? What if it is impossible for Lone Star to "fence off" its part of the reservoir? Unlike wild animals, Lone Star cannot corral its molecules into a holding pen to prevent them from escaping on to Murchison's tract. Yet an injunction will destroy the value of the reservoir as a storage device. Lone Star could offer to lease Murchison's subsurface estate. If other landowners had leased for a dollar an acre, do you think Murchison will accept this amount? Or will he demand, say,$1,000 an acre, to buy out his trespass cause of action? Is this "extortion" to allow Murchison to extract monopoly rents from Lonestar?

If you were a Texas legislator, would you vote for a statute which authorized public utility companies to exercise the right of eminent domain over depleted gas reservoirs which can be used for storage? Why would such a law operate in the public interest? If one person owns the surface of the tract and another owns the mineral estate underlying that tract, which person owns the depleted gas reservoir that has been emptied of its native gas? The ownership of depleted reservoirs on such "split estates" is discussed in Chapter 8, Section B.

4.   An early Kentucky case held that the rule of capture applied to stored gas. *See Hammonds v. Central Kentucky Natural Gas Co.*, 75 S.W.2d 204 (Ky. 1934). In 1987, the Kentucky Supreme Court was asked to render a declaratory judgment by joint petition of a bank and a gas storer. The bank wanted to loan the gas company $24 million to finance the purchase of gas to be stored in a Kentucky field. The question arose: Should the bank secure its loan with a lien against the gas as personal property under Article 9 of the Uniform Commercial Code, or with a real estate mortgage? In *Texas American Energy Corp. v. Citizens Fidelity Bank & Trust Co.*, 736 S.W.2d 25 (Ky. 1987), the court distinguished the earlier *Hammonds* case as follows:

> In *Hammonds* there was a known "leak" in the gas storage reservoir inasmuch as Mrs. Hammonds' land was, in fact, a part of the natural reservoir, though not controlled by the storage company. In the case at hand, however, it has been stipulated that the gas reservoir has total integrity, and the gas cannot escape nor can it be extracted by anyone other than [Texas American Energy]. Using the *ferae naturae* analogy, [Texas American] has captured the wild fox, hence reducing it to personal property. The fox has not been released in another forest, permitting it to revert to the common property of mankind; but rather, the fox has only been released in a private confinement zoo. The fox is no less under the control of [Texas American] than if it were on a leash.

Id. at 28.

5.   Are there any other limits to the rule of capture under the common law in addition to the exception for stored gas? Suppose the driller next door to you negligently blows out a well, creating an enormous low-pressure area to which your gas rapidly flows and erupts in a fiery inferno that can be seen for miles around. Is the driller shielded from liability for draining all of your gas because of the rule of capture?

Elliff v. Texon Drilling Co.

210 S.W.2d 558 (Tex. 1948).

[Plaintiff owned land overlying a gas field. Defendant was engaged in drilling a well on the neighboring tract only 466 feet east of plaintiff's property line. The well struck gas under high pressure and exploded and burned, resulting in the waste of a large part of the petroleum in the reservoir. Plaintiff sought to recover damages for the hydrocarbons lost from underneath plaintiff's land. The jury found that the drilling company had been negligent in blowing out the well.]

■ FOLLEY, J.... In our state the landowner is regarded as having absolute title in severalty to the oil and gas in place beneath his land. The only qualification of that rule of ownership is that it must be considered in connection with the law of capture and is subject to police regulations. The oil and gas beneath the soil are considered a part of the realty. Each owner of land owns separately, distinctly and exclusively all the oil and gas under his land and is accorded the usual remedies against trespassers who appropriate the minerals or destroy their market value.

The conflict in the decisions of the various states with reference to the character of ownership is traceable to some extent to the divergent views entertained by the courts, particularly in the earlier cases, as to the nature and migratory character of oil and gas in the soil. 31A Tex. Jur. 24, Sec. 5. In the absence of common law precedent, and owing to the lack of scientific information as to the movement of these minerals, some of the courts have sought by analogy to compare oil and gas to other types of property such as wild animals, birds, subterranean waters, and other migratory things, with reference to which the common law had established rules denying any character of ownership prior to capture. However, as was said by Professor A. W. Walker, Jr., of the School of Law of the University of Texas: "There is no oil or gas producing state today which follows the wild-animal analogy to its logical conclusion that the landowner has no property interest in the oil and gas in place." 16 Tex. L.R. 370, 371. In the light of modern scientific knowledge these early analogies have been disproved, and courts generally have come to recognize that oil and gas, as commonly found in underground reservoirs, are securely entrapped in a static condition in the original pool, and, ordinarily, so remain until disturbed by penetrations from the surface. It is further established, nevertheless, that these minerals will migrate across property lines towards any low pressure area created by production from the common pool. This migratory character of oil and gas has given rise to the so-called rule or law of capture. That rule simply is that the owner of a tract of land acquires title to the oil or gas which he produces from wells on his land, though part of the oil or gas may have migrated from adjoining lands. He may thus appropriate the oil and gas that have flowed from adjacent lands without the consent of the owner of those lands, and without incurring liability to him for drainage. The nonliability is based upon the theory that after the drainage the title or property interest of the former owned is gone. This rule, at first blush, would seem to conflict with the view of absolute ownership of the minerals in place, but it was otherwise decided in the early case of *Stephens County v. Mid–Kansas Oil & Gas Co.*, 254 S.W. 290, 292 (1923). Mr. Justice Greenwood there stated:

> "The objection lacks substantial foundation that gas or oil in a certain tract of land cannot be owned in place, because subject to appropriation, without the consent of the owner of the tract, through

drainage from wells on adjacent lands. If the owners of adjacent lands have the right to appropriate, without liability, the gas and oil underlying their neighbor's land, then their neighbor has the correlative right to appropriate, through like methods of drainage, the gas and oil underlying the tracts adjacent to his own."

Thus it is seen that, notwithstanding the fact that oil and gas beneath the surface are subject both to capture and administrative regulation, the fundamental rule of absolute ownership of the minerals in place is not affected in our state. In recognition of such ownership, our courts, in decisions involving well-spacing regulations of our Railroad Commission, have frequently announced the sound view that each landowner should be afforded the opportunity to produce his fair share of the recoverable oil and gas beneath his land, which is but another way of recognizing the existence of correlative rights between the various landowners over a common reservoir of oil or gas.

It must be conceded that under the law of capture there is no liability for reasonable and legitimate drainage from the common pool. The landowner is privileged to sink as many wells as he desires upon his tract of land and extract therefrom and appropriate all the oil and gas that he may produce, so long as he operates within the spirit and purpose of conservation statutes and orders of the Railroad Commission. These laws and regulations are designed to afford each owner a reasonable opportunity to produce his proportionate part of the oil and gas from the entire pool and to prevent operating practices injurious to the common reservoir. In this manner, if all operators exercise the same degree of skill and diligence, each owner will recover in most instances his fair share of the oil and gas. This reasonable opportunity to produce his fair share of the oil and gas is the landowner's common law right under our theory of absolute ownership of the minerals in place. But from the very nature of this theory the right of each land holder is qualified, and is limited to legitimate operations. Each owner whose land overlies the basin has a like interest, and each must of necessity exercise his right with some regard to the rights of others. No owner should be permitted to carry on his operations in reckless or lawless irresponsibility, but must submit to such limitations as are necessary to enable each to get his own.

In Summers, Oil and Gas, Permanent Edition, Volume 1, page 142, correlative rights of owners of land in a common source of supply of oil and gas are discussed and described in the following language:

"These existing property relations, called the correlative rights of the owners of land in the common source of supply, were not created by the statute, but held to exist because of the peculiar physical facts of oil and gas. The term 'correlative rights' is merely a convenient method of indicating that each owner of land in a common source of supply of oil and gas has legal privileges as against other owners of land therein to take oil or gas therefrom by lawful operations conducted on his own land; that each such owner has duties to the other owners not to exercise his privilege of taking so as to injure the common source of supply; and that each such owner has rights that other owners not exercise their privileges of taking so as to injure the common source of supply...."

In like manner, the negligent waste and destruction of petitioners' gas and distillate was neither a legitimate drainage of the minerals from beneath their lands nor a lawful or reasonable appropriation of them. Consequently, the petitioners did not lose their right, title and interest in them under the law of capture. At the time of their removal they belonged to petitioner, and their wrongful dissipation deprived these owners of the right and opportunity to produce them. That right is forever lost, the same cannot be restored, and petitioners are without an adequate legal remedy unless we allow a recovery under the same common law which governs other actions for damages and under which the property rights in oil and gas are vested.... The fact that the major portion of the gas and distillate[5] escaped from the well on respondents' premises is immaterial. Irrespective of the opening from which the minerals escaped, they belonged to the petitioners and the loss was the same. They would not have been dissipated at any opening except for the wrongful conduct of the respondents. Being responsible for the loss they are in no position to deny liability because the gas and distillate did not escape through the surface of petitioners' lands.■

C. STATE CONSERVATION REGULATION

1. PREVENTING PHYSICAL WASTE

The rule of capture resulted in pell-mell development that wasted large amounts of petroleum both above and below ground. States sought to regulate the chaotic, dangerous and wasteful conditions. Not surprisingly, operators whose production was crimped by such laws sought refuge in the Takings Clause of the Constitution. A few years after Spindletop, a takings case reached the highest court of the land. The state of Indiana had adopted a statute in 1893, requiring the operator of any oil or gas well to confine the flow of oil or gas into a pipeline or other safe receptacle within two days of discovery.

The state attorney general sued the Ohio Oil Company to enjoin it from allowing gas to escape. Ohio Oil had drilled five wells which produced gas along with the oil. From the court's description, the field appeared to have a gas-cap drive and a water drive. Ohio Oil's oil wells were producing large amounts of casinghead gas, *i.e.,* gas dissolved in oil which separates from the oil when it reaches the reduced pressure at the top of the well, called the casing head. Until the late 1950s, casinghead gas was often an undesirable byproduct of oil production. Operators burned it at the well-head, which is called "flaring." However, in this case, nearby cities were using some gas from the field as fuel. The state's complaint alleged that Ohio Oil's flaring was destroying the "back pressure" in the field that

---

5. Editors note: Distillate is condensate, *i.e.,* the liquids dripped out of "wet" gas.

prevented the salt water from encroaching into the oil wells. Ohio Oil contended that it was impossible to produce the oil without producing the gas; that the gas had no value to the defendant; and that enforcing the statute deprived it of the right to produce oil in violation of its due process rights. The Supreme Court responded:

Ohio Oil Co. v. Indiana

177 U.S. 190 (1900).

■ WHITE, J. . . . [I]t is apparent, from the admitted facts, that the oil and gas are commingled and contained in a natural reservoir which lies beneath an extensive area of country, and that as thus situated the gas and oil are capable of flowing from place to place, and are hence susceptible of being drawn off by wells from any point, provided they penetrate into the reservoir. . . . From this it must necessarily come to pass that the entire volume of gas and oil is in some measure liable to be decreased by the act of any one who bores wells from the surface and strikes the reservoir containing the oil and gas. And hence, of course, it is certain, . . . that unless laws can prevent it, a single owner could use the unrestrained license to waste the entire contents of the reservoir by allowing the gas to be drawn off and to be dispersed in the atmospheric air, and by permitting the oil to flow without use or benefit to any one. These things being lawful, as they must be if the acts stated cannot be controlled by law, it follows that no particular individual having a right to make borings can complain, and thus the entire product of oil and gas can be destroyed by any one of the surface owners. . . . But it cannot be that property as to a specified thing vests in one who has no right to prevent any other person from taking or destroying the object which is asserted to be the subject of the right of property. . . .

Hence it is that the legislative power, from the peculiar nature of the right and the objects upon which it is to be exerted, can be manifested for the purpose of protecting all the collective owners by preventing waste. This necessarily implied legislative authority is borne out by the analogy suggested by things *ferae naturae* which it is unquestioned the legislature has the authority to forbid all from taking, in order to protect them from undue destruction, so that the right of the common owners, the public, to reduce to possession, may be ultimately efficaciously enjoyed. Viewed, then, as a statute to protect or to prevent the waste of the common property . . . [the law at issue here] is a statute protecting private property and preventing it from being taken by one of the common owners without regard to the enjoyment of the others. . . . ■

NOTES AND COMMENTS

1. *Ohio Oil Co. v. Indiana* was one of the earliest cases to recognize the doctrine of correlative rights, which appeared in the *Elliff v. Texon Drilling Co.* case *supra* involving negligent drainage. The doctrine holds that each

owner of a common source of supply has both legal rights and legal duties toward the other owners. The strongest right continues to be the rule of capture if exercised properly under common law tort principles and in compliance with a broad range of state conservation laws which were enacted after 1900. Does the doctrine of correlative rights guarantee that each owner of a common reservoir receives a fair share of the oil and gas in the reservoir, even if that owner never drills a well? Or does it guarantee only the opportunity to produce a fair share, which if unexercised, allows one owner to drain another without liability?

2.   Does this Indiana statute ensure that this reservoir will be produced at its Maximum Efficient Rate of Recovery (MER)? Should any wells be producing gas from the gas cap? Should Ohio Oil be allowed to market its gas rather than reinject it into the gas cap if reinjection would increase the ultimate recovery of oil? Why wasn't Ohio Oil marketing its gas to the cities nearby?

2.   PREVENTING ECONOMIC WASTE WITH MARKET DEMAND PRORATIONING

With the discovery of oil at Spindletop in 1901, the mad rush was on to explore for oil in Texas and the neighboring states of Oklahoma and Louisiana. Many large fields were discovered in the next few decades, leading to a sharp increase in oil production in the familiar "boom and bust" pattern caused by the rule of capture. Fortuitously, the invention of the gasoline-powered engine sparked an enormous increase in the demand for gasoline. In the 19th century, the primary use for petroleum had been for kerosene. In the 20th century, the primary use soon became gasoline for the "horseless carriage." Kerosene sales shrank to negligible levels after Thomas Edison's invention of the incandescent light bulb.

The excessive well drilling and wasteful production engendered by the rule of capture were difficult to ignore. States began to enact conservation legislation like that in *Ohio Oil,* and created regulatory agencies to implement the new laws. Many states enacted well spacing rules which provided that no well could be drilled on less than a certain number of acres or closer than so many feet from an existing well. However, these regulations were often not enforced in situations where small tracts of land, often town lots, already existed. Moreover, well spacing alone did not address the most important factor affecting the ultimate percentage of oil recovered from a field: the field's production rate.

In addition, producers were battered by the widely fluctuating swings in the price of oil. Flush production from the Seminole field in Oklahoma and the great East Texas field caused the price to drop from three dollars a barrel in 1920 to as low as ten cents a barrel in the early 1930s. Some operators imposed voluntary controls on themselves, such as a moratorium on new drilling until pipeline capacity and storage facilities were enlarged to handle the increased flow. However, most voluntary efforts to conserve were doomed to failure under the inexorable logic of the Tragedy of the

Commons. Many operators pressed their state legislators to enact pro-rationing statutes which would authorize a state agency to restrict production in a field by establishing a maximum "allowable" that each well could produce. Inevitably, such a statute was challenged by other operators and ultimately reached the highest court of the land.

The plaintiff in the case, Champlin Refining Co., was a vertically integrated oil company that produced and refined crude oil and transported and marketed the crude and its products in interstate commerce. Its refinery had a daily capacity of 15,000 barrels of crude. It owned 735 tank cars, operated 470 miles of pipeline, and had 256 wholesale and 263 retail gasoline stations supplied from its refinery. At the refinery it had gas-tight steel storage tanks which could hold 645,000 barrels of petroleum and its products. It did not use earthen storage and the court acknowledged that it utilized all the crude oil that it could produce for commercial purposes without letting any crude "run at large." Yet, Oklahoma's statute forced Champlin to cut back production from its wells quite drastically so that it only took a "proportional share" of production from the field.

Champlin Refining Co. v. Corporation Commission of Oklahoma

286 U.S. 210 (1932).

The refining company by this suit seeks to enjoin the commission, attorney general and other state officers from enforcing certain provisions of c. 25 of the laws of Oklahoma enacted February 11, 1915, [C. O. S. 1921, §§ 7954–7963] and certain orders of the commission on the ground that they are repugnant to the due process and equal protection clauses of the Fourteenth Amendment and the commerce clause.

The Act prohibits the production of petroleum in such a manner or under such conditions as constitute waste. Section 3 defines waste to include—in addition to its ordinary meaning—economic, underground and surface waste, and waste incident to production in excess of transportation or marketing facilities or reasonable market demands, and empowers the commission to make rules and regulations for the prevention of such wastes. Whenever full production from any common source can only be obtained under conditions constituting waste, one having the right to produce oil from such source may take only such proportion of all that may be produced therefrom without waste as the production of his wells bears to the total. The commission is authorized to regulate the taking of oil from common sources so as to prevent unreasonable discrimination in favor of one source as against others.

The [plaintiff has nine wells in the] Greater Seminole [field which] covers a territory fifteen to twenty by eight to ten miles and has eight or more distinct pools in formations which do not overlie each other. The first pool was discovered in 1925 and by June 15, 1931, there were 2141 producing wells having potential production of 564,908 barrels per day. The wells are separately owned and operated by 80 lessees. About three-fourths of them, owning wells with 40 per cent of the total potential capacity of the field, have no pipelines or refineries and are entirely dependent for an outlet for their crude upon others who purchase and transport oil. Five companies, owning wells with about 13 per cent of the potential production, have pipelines or refinery connections affording a partial outlet for their production. Nineteen other companies own or control pipelines extending into this area having a daily capacity of 468,200 barrels, and most of them from time to time purchase oil from other producers in the field.

Crude oil and natural gas occur together or in close proximity to each other, and the gas in a pool moves the contents toward the point of least resistance. When wells are drilled into a pool, the oil and gas move from place to place. If some of the wells are permitted to produce a greater proportion of their capacity than others, drainage occurs from the less active to the more active.... Where proportional taking from the wells in flush pools is not enforced, operators who do not have physical or market outlets are forced to produce to capacity in order to prevent drainage to others having adequate outlets. In Oklahoma prior to the passage of the Act, large quantities of oil produced in excess of transportation facilities or demand therefor were stored in surface tanks, and by reason of seepage, rain, fire and evaporation enormous waste occurred. Uncontrolled flow of flush or semi-flush wells for any considerable period exhausts an excessive amount of pressure, wastefully uses the gas and greatly lessens ultimate recovery....

The first of the present series of proration orders took effect August 1, 1927, and applied to the then flush and semi-flush pools in the Seminole.... In order No. 5189, June 30, 1930, [the Corporation Commission] found that the potential production in the United States was approximately 4,730,000 barrels per day and that imports amounted to about 300,000 barrels, creating a supply of over 5,000,000 barrels as against an estimated domestic and export demand of 2,800,000 barrels.... The orders ... operated to restrict plaintiff to much less than the potential production of its nine wells in the Seminole pools.

The court found that at all times covered by orders involved there was a serious potential overproduction throughout the United States and particularly in the flush and semi-flush pools in the Seminole and Oklahoma City fields; that, if no curtailment were applied, crude oil for lack of market demand and adequate storage tanks would inevitably go into earthen storage and be wasted; that the full potential production exceeded all transportation and marketing facilities and market demands; that accordingly it was necessary, in order to prevent waste, that production of flush and semi-flush pools should be restricted as directed by the proration orders, and that to enforce such curtailment, with equity and justice to the several producers in each pool, it was necessary to enforce proportional taking from each well and lease therein and that, upon the testimony of operators and others, a comprehensive plan of curtailment and proration conforming to the rules prescribed in the Act was adopted by the commission and was set forth in its orders.

[The district court also found that none] of the commission's orders has been made for the purpose of fixing the price of crude oil or has had that effect. When the first order was made the price was more than two dollars per barrel, but it declined until at the time of the trial it was only thirty-five cents. In each case the commission has allowed to be produced the full amount of the market demand for each pool. It has never entered any order under § 2 of the Act [which expressly allowed the commission to set a wellhead price for crude if lack of market demand resulted in a price that did not equal the "actual value" of crude]. It was not shown that the commission intended to limit the amount of oil entering interstate commerce for the purpose of controlling the price of crude oil or its products or of eliminating plaintiff or any producer or refiner from competition, or that there was any combination among plaintiff's competitors for the purpose of restricting interstate commerce in crude oil or its products, or that any operators' committee made up of plaintiff's competitors formulated the proration orders.

. . . . .

1. Plaintiff here insists that the Act is repugnant to the due process and equal protection clauses of the Fourteenth Amendment.

Plaintiff insists that it has a vested right to drill wells upon the lands covered by its leases and to take all the natural flow of oil and gas therefrom so long as it does so without physical waste and devotes the production to commercial uses. But if plaintiff should take all the flow of its wells, there would inevitably result great physical waste, even if its entire production should be devoted to useful purposes. The improvident use of natural gas pressure inevitably attending such operations would cause great diminution in the quantity of crude oil ultimately to be recovered from the pool. Other lessees and owners of land above the pool would be compelled, for self-protection against plaintiff's taking, also to draw from the common source and so to add to the wasteful use of lifting pressure. And because of the lack, especially on the part of the non-integrated operators, of means of transportation or appropriate storage and of market demand, the contest would, as is made plain by the evidence and findings, result in surface waste of large quantities of crude oil. . . .

We put aside plaintiff's contentions resting upon the claim that § 2 or § 3 authorizes or contemplates directly or indirectly regulation of prices of crude oil. The commission has never made an order under § 2. The court found that none of the proration orders here involved were made for the purpose of fixing prices. The fact that the commission never limited production below market demand, and the great and long continued downward trend of prices contemporaneously with the enforcement of proration, strongly support the finding that the orders assailed have not had that effect. . . . As plaintiff has failed to prove that any order in force at the time of the trial was not in accordance with the rule prescribed by § 4 [granting plaintiff a proportional share of the limited production from the field] or otherwise invalid, the part of the decree from which it appealed will be affirmed . . . . ■

NOTES AND COMMENTS

1.   How was Champlin wasting oil? Did the court uphold the prorationing statute because it prevented waste by restricting the field's output to its MER? Or because it protected correlative rights by assuring fair shares of production to all operators? Or, because it raised the price of oil (coincidently providing tax revenues to the state treasury) by restricting output far below the field's MER?

2.   What is the relationship between restricting a field's production to its MER to prevent physical waste, and restricting production to meet market demand and prevent economic waste? Suppose that the MER of a field would allow 500,000 barrels per day of production under good reservoir engineering practices, but the market "demands" only 30 percent of this amount. With market-demand prorationing, the wells in this field will be allowed to produce a total of 150,000 barrels per day. Return to **Figure 6–1**. Does market-demand prorationing explain the remarkable stability in the price of crude oil from the mid–1930s until about 1973?

Here is a chart of the market demand factor (MDF) applied to Texas fields from 1950 through 1975:

Year	% MDF	Year	% MDF	Year	% MDF
1950	63	1960	28	1970	72
1951	76	1961	28	1971	73
1952	71	1962	27	1972	94
1953	65	1963	28	1973	100
1954	53	1964	28	1974	100
1955	53	1965	29	1975	100
1956	52	1966	34		
1957	47	1967	41		
1958	33	1968	45		
1959	34	1969	52		

The data show that wells were prorated to 28 percent of their capacity in 1960, *i.e.,* a well that could produce 100 barrels a day was restricted to 28 barrels. If the nation demanded more crude oil to satisfy its hunger for gasoline in the post-war years, the Texas Railroad Commission could simply raise the MDF to 41 percent. Producers would turn the valves on their wells, and more oil would flow.

Over these same years, the domestic cost of drilling rose because new fields were generally smaller and deeper than the large discoveries of old. As costs rose, fewer producers drilled new wells. The United States imported increasing quantities of crude oil from supergiant fields developed abroad, especially in Saudi Arabia.[6] In what year was the U.S. first

---

6. In 1996, the average production per well in the U.S. was 11.2 barrels of oil per day. Wells in Saudi Arabia averaged 6,000 barrels per day. 2 Energy Law and Transactions (David J. Muchow and William A. Mogel, eds.) Appendix 10, at 51–82 (1999).

vulnerable to an Arab embargo of imports to our shores? Since 1973, market-demand prorationing has been meaningless for oil production in the United States. Virtually all domestic oil wells produce at their capacity, restricted only by the field's MER. However, as explained in the chapter on International Petroleum, OPEC (the Organization of Petroleum Exporting Countries, many of whom are Mideastern nations) has its own form of market-demand prorationing on an international scale. As a cartel, OPEC is often able to control the price of oil on the international market, and this price ultimately sets the domestic price that U.S. producers receive for their oil.

3. If Texas severely prorated its wells to market demand, but other producing states like Oklahoma or Louisiana did not, Texas producers would lose market share to their competitors in other states, a clearly unacceptable result. So how was market demand prorationing to be coordinated among all the major producing states? In 1934, Secretary of the Interior Harold Ickes was pushing for federal control of the petroleum industry to prevent the rampant waste of oil and gas. His plan used a public utility model to regulate the industry. To forestall federal intervention, the governors of Oklahoma, Texas, and other producing states met to devise an interstate oil compact as an alternative. The governor of Oklahoma pressed for a compact which would allocate the federal Bureau of Mines' monthly estimates of national market demand to the states as binding quotas, resulting in a clear and direct mechanism for price-fixing. Texas resisted this degree of interference in its affairs. In the end, Texas prevailed. In 1935, the Interstate Compact to Conserve Oil and Gas was created and approved by the President and Congress. The compact now has 30 member states and 6 associate members. It relies on voluntary agreements to accomplish its objectives. *See* Erich W. Zimmermann, Conservation in the Production of Petroleum 201–236 (1957). Given this history, what do you think was Oklahoma's objective in restricting production so severely in the *Champlin* case?

4. Support for proration was not universal in the industry. Some smaller companies viewed prorationing as a conspiracy by the major oil companies to bankrupt the independent producer by depriving him of the cash flow from flush production. Some believed that by appealing to state agencies for production controls, the oil industry was drifting toward governmental control. Chief Justice Fletcher Riley of the Supreme Court of Oklahoma, in a dissenting opinion, expressed this viewpoint: "In my opinion, proration of oil was born of monopoly, sired by arbitrary power, and its progeny (such as these orders) is the deformed child whose playmates are graft, theft, bribery and corruption." H.F. Wilcox Oil & Gas Co. v. State, 162 Okla. 89 (1933).

In the East Texas field, producers regularly ignored Railroad Commission prorationing orders. In July 1931, 1,300 wells were producing 1.4 million barrels of oil per day. The price dropped below ten cents a barrel. Finally, in August, the Texas Governor declared martial law and sent the National Guard into the field to shut down every well. Troops patrolled the field. Military officers ran a prorationing office and re-opened the wells with a maximum allowable of 225 barrels of oil per day per well. *See* James H. Keahy, Jr., The Texas Mineral Interest Pooling Act: End of an Era, 4 Natural Resources Lawyer 359, at 360–61. The shutdown was effective in raising the price of oil, and this considerably tamed the opposition to market-demand prorationing.

5.   How is the state conservation agency to determine each producer's "fair share" of the total field allowable? Should every well be allowed to produce the same amount, regardless of how much acreage it drains? (This is the "per well" allowable system which the National Guard used.) Is it fair that the owner of one well on a town lot no bigger than 1/10 of an acre be allowed to produce the same amount of oil as the owner of a well on a ten-acre tract? Should the owner of the ten-acre tract be granted additional wells as exceptions to the field's well-spacing rule requiring at least ten acres for a well permit? If so, won't this encourage unnecessary well drilling, just like occurred under the rule of capture?

6.   As the science of petroleum engineering progressed, state conservation agencies adopted larger and larger spacing units. As a rule of thumb, one well can drain oil from about 40 acres. A gas well can drain gas from about 640 acres. Assume you own a one-acre tract in the Excalibur oil field. The 40–acre spacing rule prohibits you from getting a well permit to drill. Your neighbor owns a 40–acre tract and drills a well close to your boundary in a field that is determined to be 4,000 acres large. The conservation commission sets the total field allowable equal to a market demand of 4,000 barrels a day for the field. The commission allocates this total using a prorationing formula based on acreage. Under this formula your neighbor can produce 40 of these barrels because she owns 40/4000 (or one percent) of the acreage in the field. While your neighbor is selling the 40 barrels for $3 per barrel, (or $120 a day in revenues), you are producing nothing. Are your correlative rights protected in this scenario?

Suppose the commission grants you an exception to the spacing rule so that your oil will not be confiscated through drainage to your neighbor's well. If you drill and produce your own well, you will be granted an allowable of 1/4000, or one barrel of oil per day. If oil is selling for $3 dollars a barrel, you will have revenues of $3 a day. This amount does not cover the costs of drilling and producing the well on your one acre. You will lose money. Are your correlative rights protected in this scenario?

Suppose the commission grants every well in the field the same allowable of 40 barrels of oil per day, whether it drains from 40 acres or from one acre. Now your well on one acre is profitable to drill and produce. Does this prorationing formula protect the correlative rights of your larger neighbor?

Can you think of a better way to run an oil field? Many states enacted compulsory pooling laws. These statutes allow the conservation commission to pool small tracts into acreage large enough to secure a well permit under the spacing rules. All the owners with interests in the pooled acreage share in the production from the one well, usually on a surface-acreage basis.

Thus, four owners, owning 1, 5, 10, and 24 acres respectively, could be pooled into a 40–acre unit on which one well would be drilled. The owners would receive 1/40, 5/40, 10/40 and 24/40, respectively, of the production from the single well. Does pooling protect correlative rights and prevent the waste of unnecessary well drilling? Why is compulsory process usually needed to coerce operators into pooling and sharing the production from one well? If you were the owner of the drillsite well, would you voluntarily agree to pool with others?

3.   SECONDARY RECOVERY: THE TRAGEDY OF THE COMMONS II

Because many U.S. fields were produced so inefficiently under the rule of capture, much oil remained in the reservoirs after the natural reservoir drive was depleted. Secondary recovery can sweep this oil up. In 1979, secondary recovery accounted for about 60 percent of Texas's total oil production and about 38 percent of Oklahoma's. In a typical secondary recovery operation, powerful machines on the surface of a tract inject gas or water down into the pore spaces of the reservoir rock. These high-pressured substances drive oil away from the injection wells toward producing wells. A waterflood operation commonly uses a five-spot pattern which places injection wells at the corners of a square and a producing well at the center. The injected water pushes a bank of oil toward the producing well. In recent years, advanced forms of secondary recovery—called enhanced oil recovery—have been devised. For example, carbon dioxide is piped from a large natural reservoir of CO_2 in Colorado some 400 miles to large oil fields in West Texas. There it is injected and miscibly displaces oil from the pore spaces of the rock. Sometimes chemical surfactants and polymers are added to waterflooding to better "scrub" the rock clean of the clinging oil.

Do conservation laws and the common law maximize the efficiency of these "second chance" operations? Imagine a field comprised of 1000 acres, 900 leased by Big Oil and 100 leased by Little Oil. Big Oil wants to conduct a secondary recovery operation using salt water as an injectant at a cost of several million dollars, but Little Oil refuses to join in the project. If Big Oil conducts the recovery by itself, its 900 acres of leasehold will have higher reservoir pressure than Little's 100 acres. All fluids flow to the area of lowest pressure, and it is virtually impossible for Big Oil to prevent either the oil under its tract or the injected salt water from crossing the lease line and invading Little's lease. In fact, the salt water may "drown out" some of Little's producing oil wells located near the lease line. These wells will begin to produce salt water, not oil.

Can Little bring a cause of action in trespass against Big for injuring Little's underground estate and Little's ability to produce oil? This issue arose in *Railroad Commission of Texas v. Manziel*, 361 S.W.2d 560 (Tex. 1962). Whelan and Manziel were competitive operators in the Vickie Lynn Field. Only 15% of the original oil in place in the field had been recovered because the operators had failed to maintain adequate pressure in the dissolved-gas drive reservoir. Pressures had fallen from 2650 pounds per square inch (psi) to 371 psi. The remaining oil in the field was essentially "dead" without repressuring.

Whelan applied to the Railroad Commission for approval of waterflooding in its part of the field; Manziel refused to join in the operation. The commission approved the secondary recovery because it was expected to significantly increase oil production from the field. For several years, Manziel benefited from this arrangement as oil flowed slowly under the ground toward the lower-pressure tract. To stop this flow to its rival, Whelan asked the Railroad Commission to allow Whelan to place an injection well very close to the lease line. Since salt water spreads out radially from the injection well, two effects are inevitable: First, the injection well will cause salt water to invade the Manziel tract and drown out Manziel's nearby oil well; second, it will stop the flow of Whelan's oil onto the Manziel tract by pushing oil back towards the Whelan tract.

The injection well location that Whelan sought was only 206 feet from the lease line, necessitating a commission exception to the standard distance of 660 feet. Manziel strongly objected to the Railroad Commission about the placement of the proposed injection well so near the lease line because it spelled an early death to the nearby Manziel well. The commission nonetheless approved the exception location. The commission found that the same amount of oil would ultimately be recovered from the field, whether the injection well was placed 206 feet from the lease line or the standard distance of 660 feet. The issue before the commission was not one of preventing waste, but of protecting correlative rights: What constituted "fair shares" of oil between the two owners of this common reservoir?

The commission estimated that four times as much of the oil beneath the Whelans' lease would be pushed to the Manziel lease if the injection well was located 660 feet from the lease line as opposed to a 206–foot location. On the other hand, the Manziel's nearby well would have an estimated life of 32 months if the injection well were placed 660 feet from lease line, but its life would be reduced to 3 1/2 to 8 months if placed closer.

The Railroad Commission approved the closer location, and the Texas Supreme Court ultimately upheld this decision on the basis that it protected correlative rights and was not arbitrary or capricious. The Manziel tract had originally had no more than 2.4% of the original oil in place in the field, yet it had recovered more than 5.8% of the field's total production to date. Clearly, the Manziel tract had been draining oil from the Whelan tract for several years, and it was now fair to allow the Whelan tract to place an injection well advantageously to secure its fair share of the original oil in place in the field.

The Texas Supreme Court then squarely addressed the issue of trespass raised by Manziel. In the most famous, oft-quoted part of the case, the court wrote:

> Secondary recovery operations are carried on to increase the ultimate recovery of oil and gas, and it is established that pressure maintenance projects will result in more recovery than was obtained by

primary methods. It cannot be disputed that such operations should be encouraged, for as the pressure behind the primary production dissipates, the greater is the public necessity for applying secondary recovery forces. It is obvious that secondary recovery programs could not and would not be conducted if any adjoining operator could stop the project on the ground of subsurface trespass.... The orthodox rules and principles applied by the courts as regards surface invasions of land may not be appropriately applied to subsurface invasions as arise out of the secondary recovery of natural resources. If the intrusions of salt water are to be regarded as trespassory in character, then under common notions of surface invasions, the justifying public policy considerations behind secondary recovery operations could not be reached in considering the validity and reasonableness of such operations.

Certainly, it is relevant to consider and weigh the interests of society and the oil and gas industry as a whole against the interests of the individual operator who is damaged; and if the authorized activities in an adjoining secondary recovery unit are found to be based on some substantial, justifying occasion, then this court should sustain their validity.

We conclude that if, in the valid exercise of its authority to prevent waste, protect correlative rights, or in the exercise of other powers within its jurisdiction, the Commission authorizes secondary recovery projects, a trespass does not occur when the injected, secondary recovery forces move across lease lines, and the operations are not subject to an injunction on that basis. The technical rules of trespass have no place in the consideration of the validity of the orders of the Commission.

NOTES AND COMMENTS

1. The deliberate invasion of injurious salt water onto another's property sure looks like a trespass. Why does the court refuse to find that orthodox rules of trespass apply? Would the holding be different if Whelan had not secured the Railroad Commission's approval of the waterflooding as being in the public interest of increasing production from the field? The courts in many states have adopted the reasoning in *Manziel* in order to encourage secondary recovery operations.

2. Is there then no liability whatsoever when one operator floods out another? Does commission approval of waterflooding immunize an operator from all liability? The court specifically stated that no injunction would issue in this case. Are damages possible in a *Manziel*-type situation? Or has the court adopted a "negative rule of capture" which allows a waterflooder to damage an adjoining owner without liability, much as the "positive rule of capture" allows one owner to drain a neighbor without liability.

Most states, including Texas, have recognized that damages are still possible as a remedy for waterflooding that may unreasonably injure an adjoining operation. The language quoted from *Manziel supra* about weighing "the interests of society and the oil and gas industry as a whole against the interests of the individual operator who is damaged" mimics the law of nuisance. Thus, tort damages are still possible against a neighboring waterflooder, although very few complaining operators have ever been able to prove the unreasonableness of a waterflooding operation that has been approved by the state's conservation commission. For one interesting case in which damages were awarded against a waterflooding operator, see *Tidewater Oil Co. v. Jackson*, 320 F.2d 157 (10th Cir.), *cert. denied*, 375 U.S. 942 (1963) (adjacent oil well still in primary recovery drowned out within hours of a waterflooding operation conducted by a rival operator using a commission-approved injection well only 12 feet from the lease line).

3.   The high oil prices of the past three years have spurred secondary recovery in many old oil fields with the help of new supercomputer systems that can read seismics and well data and find new pockets of untapped oil in old fields. Generally, only 30 percent of the oil in a field is recovered using traditional secondary recovery methods such as waterflooding. However, engineers are now exploiting new "tertiary" recovery methods, using carbon dioxide (CO_2), chemicals and even colonies of specially grown microbes that generate CO_2 and detergent-like chemicals biologically. One oilfield specialist projects that some of these methods will lead to recovery rates of 60 percent or more, doubling the known reserves of oil. Anadarko, for one, is reinjecting CO_2 that was once vented from a gas processing plant operated by Exxon about 125 miles away. By 2008, all of the Exxon plant's CO_2 will be pumped into the earth and permanently disposed of after Anadarko extracts an additional 150 million barrels from the field. Otis Port, Tapping Gushers Beneath the Gushers, Business Week, July 5, 2005.

4.   Unitization: Overcoming the Tragedy of the Commons

A leading treatise in oil and gas law concludes, after surveying the *Manziel*-type cases in several jurisdictions:

> It is extremely hazardous . . . to engage in a secondary recovery program in the absence of unitization (voluntary or compulsory) of all premises which may be adversely affected by injection of fluids.

Patrick H. Martin and Bruce M. Kramer, 6 Williams and Meyers Oil and Gas Law, § 204.5 (1998).

How then are conservation commissions to both prevent waste and protect correlative rights of all owners of oil and gas in a common field; and how is the operator of a repressuring project to avoid tort liability and yet prevent a holdout or "free rider" from being unjustly enriched by the repressuring operation of other hard-working producers on adjoining acreage?

The answer lies in securing a unitization agreement from all the owners in a common field. Such an agreement binds all the parties to develop the field cooperatively for the good of all. One operator, usually the one with the largest share of the field, becomes the unit operator and produces the field in a manner which minimizes the number of wells drilled and maximizes efficient recovery from the field. All owners then receive a fair share of the production from the entire field, regardless of where the wells are located. A unitization agreement substitutes cooperative development for the competitive rule of capture.

However, all owners in the field are unlikely to be able to agree on the unitization agreement's formula for allocating fair shares among the owners. For example, why didn't Manziel agree to cooperate with Whelan, each operator paying a fair share of the waterflooding operation and each reaping a fair share of the profits from production? With cooperation, the total size of the "pie" would be larger because the two operators would save the costs of drilling unnecessary injection wells along lease lines as barriers to the flow of oil. Did Manziel prefer to be a "free rider" and benefit from the repressuring without paying for it?

Determining the formula to measure each operator's fair share is the same contentious issue that arose under prorationing. A large-tract owner will want shares based on acreage. A small-tract owner will want almost any other factor than acreage in the formula since he has very little acreage. Because securing 100% agreement among all the owners is so difficult, almost all oil and gas producing states have enacted compulsory unitization statutes which allow the state conservation commission to force a minority of owners into a unit agreed to by a supra-majority of owners. The following case illustrates the need for compulsory process.

Gilmore v. Oil and Gas Conservation Commission

642 P.2d 773 (Wyo. 1982).

■ BROWN, JUSTICE. On July 1, 1980, the Wyoming Oil and Gas Conservation Commission (hereinafter referred to as Commission) entered its order approving a plan of unitization of the Hartzog draw field. Appellant appeals the unitization plan approved by the Commission and its affirmance by the district court [alleging that the order does not protect his correlative rights].

We will affirm.

The Hartzog draw field is located in Campbell and Johnson Counties, Wyoming. The field is about 18 miles long and from one to three miles wide, embracing approximately 31,065 acres. At the time of the hearing before the Commission on the application to unitize the field, there were 177 producing wells with working interest ownership held by more than 80 individuals or entities.

The Commission took an interest in the field in April 1977, initiated numerous hearings and required the operators to keep the Commission advised of progress in development, production and the nature of the reservoir in the field. Technical committees and subcommittees of operators and their representatives met numerous times. Hearings were held before the Commission pursuant to s 30–5–104(b), W.S.1977. This provision of the law makes it the Commission's duty to investigate and determine whether waste exists or is imminent, or whether other facts justify or require action by the Commission. It eventually became apparent that reservoir pressure was falling to the bubble point. The lower the pressure the more difficult it becomes to recover additional oil. The further the pressure falls below the bubble point, the less likely a successful secondary recovery operation can be accomplished.

A technical committee of operators and their representatives concluded that reservoir pressure had fallen from an original pressure of 5,000 PSIG [pounds per square inch gauge] to slightly below the bubble point of 1,500 PSIG as of January 1979. This committee recommended that the field be unitized as soon as possible. It was estimated that the contemplated secondary recovery operation would recover 30,525,000 barrels of oil. Evidence before the Commission was that 1,800,000 barrels of oil would be wasted by a one-year delay in unitization and secondary recovery and 4,000,200 barrels by a two-year delay. In other words, 5,753.5 barrels of oil would be wasted each day that unitization and secondary recovery was [sic] delayed.

The Commission found that waste was occurring and would continue to occur by delaying secondary recovery, and as a result, after a November 13, 1979, hearing, ordered a curtailment of production pending unitization.

The operators held various meetings at which they voted on formulae to be used in allocating production under unitization. The 81 working interest owners considered a total of 71 formulae. Naturally, each of the owners wanted parameters favorable to them and wanted more weight to be given these parameters. After voting on almost 60 formulae, the owners were frustrated in their attempt to find one that would receive the statutory approval. As a result, they examined their voting records and used a computer to arrive at an equitable compromise formula that could receive the required approval. The resulting formula number 67 at issue here, received 75.89 percent approval. It appeared that no greater percentage would approve any formula proposed.

Section 30–5–110(f), W.S.1977, as amended, provides in pertinent part:

[The court quoted the Wyoming compulsory unitization statute which requires the approval of 80% of the lessees and royalty interest owners in the field before the commission can use compulsory process to force the other 20% of the owners into the unit against their will. In certain circumstances, the statute allows the commission to reduce the minimum percentage approval to 75%.]

... On July 1, 1980, the Commission approved a unitization plan based on formula 67 and reduced the required approval from 80 to 75 percent.... Formula 67 allocated appellant about 1.2 percent of unitized production. Formula 67, which was approved by the Commission, allocated unitization production based on eleven parameters or factors of varying weight [including the number of usable wells, the remaining primary oil under each tract, the porosity of each acre-foot of reservoir rock, and the last six months production ending March 31, 1979].

Appellant complains that some parameters of this formula are unfair, specifically, the last three months and last six months production ending March 31, 1979. He further complains that he receives a net acreage shortage of 33.66 acres. Acreages used in the unitization plan were based on an 1880 survey of the General Land Office (GLO). All parties agree that there were some inaccuracies in this survey. The Commission made extensive findings, together with ultimate findings of fact and conclusions of law. The final finding of fact and conclusion of law states:

"10. The approval of the proposed unit is in the public interest, will substantially increase the ultimate recovery of hydrocarbons from the Shannon Sandstone Formation in the Hartzog Draw Unit, will assist in the prevention of waste, and will protect the correlative rights of all parties in interest within the Unit Area."

Appellant generally objects to the latter portion of Finding and Conclusion No. 10 that the unitization plan "will protect the correlative rights of all parties in interest within the unit area." More specifically, he objects to the Commission's finding that inaccuracies in the General Land Office survey would affect all working interests indiscriminately, and that the unitization formula gave appellant his fair, just and equitable share of the unit production. He also alleges that no findings were made with respect to his objection before the Commission that the last six months and last three months production parameters were not fair to him [because his wells had suffered undue downtime during the selected periods].

... When asked the nature of his objection, appellant stated:

"A. Well, two of our three tracts are larger than depicted on the GLO maps which were made back in, I believe, 1870. This map is highly inaccurate. And therefore, we do have more acreage than is shown in the parameters that are developed, that are used using the GLO maps. We take a pretty good beating there."

. . . .

All operators experience some downtime. All operators are naturally going to want their periods of peak production as parameters in the allocation formula or other favorable parameters. They will want more weight to be given to these parameters. Though appellant does not complain that these parameters inaccurately reflect his production for the periods in question, he claims they should be updated. If this were done, the operators would probably never have achieved unitization. Some cutoff date had to be used. With over eighty working interest owners and 177 wells in the field, it would have been difficult, if not impossible, to find a period when someone would not have had excessive downtime.

... Regardless of when the downtime occurred, appellant presented no evidence to show how much downtime his wells experienced or how much production suffered because of it. Appellant's Exhibits 2–A, 2–B, and 2–C generally reflect an erratic production history for his three wells. The causes of the fluctuation are unknown.... As to the last six and last three months parameters, even if they understated the potential of his wells, these parameters are weighted to account for a total of 3.25 percent of the total allocation. Their effect is insubstantial.

... Appellant's Exhibit 1 is a comparison of nonunitized against unitized production. It tends to indicate that he would be better off by not unitizing. The same is shown by appellant's Exhibit 3, except that it does show a projected figure for the remaining primary oil that is higher than the projections of the unit engineer committee.

. . . .

Appellant concedes that unit operation "was probably the most effective which the Commission had available to it," to prevent waste. He contends that in preventing waste his correlative rights cannot be ignored. We agree, but hold that substantial waste cannot be countenanced by a slavish devotion to correlative rights. We are faced with a delicate balancing problem between prevention of waste and correlative rights, but prevention of waste is of primary importance.

. . . .

Here the Commission strived mightily to strike an equitable balance between correlative rights and prevention of waste. We agree with the Commission's acting Chairman, "And when that public interest conflicts with the private interest, the public interest has to come first."

. . . .

The eleven factor formula used here is fairer because it diminishes the loss caused by coming up a little short on one factor.... Coming up short on one of eleven parameters is much less drastic than coming up short on one if there are only two or three parameters.

There is no indication that a more equitable formula could be devised. After three years, formula number 67 appeared to be the fairest that could receive the necessary approval. The operator's technical committee and the Commission, both having experience and expertise at unitization, settled the formula 67 as the fairest and most feasible. Appellant did not suggest a better formula to the Commission, the district court, or to us. It would appear, therefore, that there is little chance that anyone involved could devise a better formula, nor is it likely that a different formula could receive the necessary approval.

. . . .

Appellant acknowledges he will receive 321,622 barrels of the additional oil from secondary recovery, which is 321,622 barrels more than he would receive if the field were not unitized.

Appellant's position has not been consistent throughout the history of this unitization plan. Appellant, by offering to lease the lands or by participating in a competitive bid, in effect relied on the survey of the lands by the United States 1880 GLO survey. He accepted the leases, which were subject to the regulations and requirements which might be imposed by the United States Geological Survey. When the unitization plan was proposed, however, appellant tried to avoid the survey. . . .

We do not understand what appellant expects to accomplish by his lawsuit except perhaps force a settlement advantageous to him someplace along the line. A reversal here would not give appellant a larger share of the allocation, but would send the case back to the Commission with a mandate to come up with another formula. We do not believe that even appellant has any real expectation of a different formula that would receive the required approval. If a new formula were found and agreed upon, it could spawn new lawsuits. . . .

The owners and technical committees worked for three years, trying to develop a formula that would get the necessary approval. As appellant says, "All operators worked long and hard, in good faith, to attempt to get a satisfactory unit agreement." The matter became so complicated that a computer was used to attempt a solution. Further, the Commission used its expertise in an effort to arrive at a satisfactory formula, and the owners and operators used their expertise. The group effort at compromise should not be discarded because of appellant's general disagreement with the plan. Appellant seems to expect perfection. Justice was accomplished here, as much as could be under the circumstances. This litigation should end.

Affirmed.■

NOTES AND COMMENTS

1. Does compulsory unitization solve the Tragedy of the Commons problem by subjecting some operators to the tyranny of the majority of other operators in the field? To the tyranny of government bureaucrats?

2. Unitization is the joint, coordinated operation of all, or a substantial part, of a reservoir as a single unit by all the different operators holding leases in the field. This term is distinguished from "pooling" which is the process of combining small tracts of land into acreage large enough to secure a drilling permit to meet the spacing rules of the conservation commission. Pooling prevents the drilling of unnecessary wells and protects the correlative rights of all the owners being drained by the one well on the spacing unit and usually occurs during primary production. Unitization combines many spacing units into a fieldwide unit, usually to conduct secondary recovery operations. A fieldwide unit may have hundreds of different owners. The more owners, the more difficult it is to reach an agreement voluntarily.

3. Most states have compulsory unitization statutes like that in *Gilmore* which allow the conservation agency to force holdouts into a unit that is expected to increase the total recovery from the field. Texas, the largest oil producing state, does not. Compulsory unitization was castigated by the

Texas independent producers for years as a "substitution of force for persuasion ... another fetter on the step of Freedom, another move down the road towards confiscation, tyranny, and unmorality" whose advocates were "socialists, bureaucrats, self-seeking politicians [and] fuzzy thinkers of the left." Comment, Prospects for Compulsory Fieldwide Unitization in Texas, 44 Tex. L. Rev. 510 at 524 (1966). Independent operators generally received more than their fair share of a reservoir's bounty under the peculiar (and very inefficient) prorationing and drilling permit system used in Texas for decades. These operators felt threatened by a compulsory unitization statute that would give them only fair shares. In 1998, the lack of such a statute was retarding secondary recovery in West Texas fields to such an extent that TIPRO, the Texas Independent Producers and Royalty Association, drafted and supported a compulsory unitization bill. However, it never reached the floor of the legislature, largely because an ideology of private property rights held sway. A substantial number of the largest fields in Texas have been unitized because the Railroad Commission arm-twisted the operators to unitize "voluntarily" by shutting in the fields or prorating them severely under the agency's broad authority to prevent waste. *See* Jacqueline L. Weaver, Unitization of Oil and Gas Fields in Texas: A Study of Legislative, Administrative and Judicial Policies 137–166 (1986).

4.   Despite secondary recovery efforts and the discovery of new (but relatively smaller) oil fields in the U.S., domestic production peaked in 1970 and has followed a downward trend since then (with a slight increase after 1974 when Alaskan crude from Prudhoe Bay entered the market as shown in **Figure 6–5**).

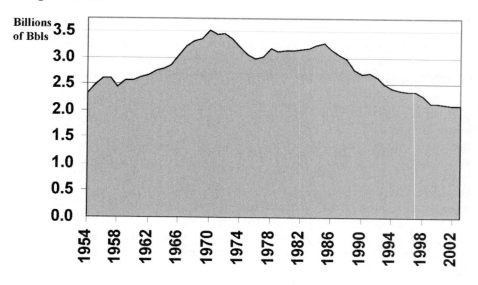

Figure 6–5
U.S. Oil Production 1954–2003

Source: EIA

The sustained rise in oil and gas prices since 2001 has led to a torrent of commentary and conferences on the subject of "Peak Oil," asking whether the world is running out of oil. Chapter 7, Section B(1)(i) addresses the Peak Oil issue. While the global answer to this question inspires much debate, there is no doubt that conventional U.S. oil production will continue its downward trend. The U.S. does have vast Western reserves of a resource called oil shale. Oil in the form of kerogen is locked into the reservoir rock so tightly that the shale, when brought up, looks like lumps of shiny coal. The oil does not flow; it is like a hard mineral. It is estimated that the nation has more than 2 trillion barrels of shale oil reserves (about 60% of the world's known deposits) located largely in Colorado, Utah and Wyoming. This amount, if converted to commercially recoverable reserves, would give the U.S. reserve totals that rival Saudi Arabia's conventional proven oil reserves. In fact, in 2004, with oil prices in the $40 to $60 per barrel range, Canada added 174 billion barrels of recoverable reserves to its total recoverable oil reserves. The addition represented oil from Canadian tar sands. Tar sands are like asphalt and must be dug up with enormous bulldozers and then heated to separate the thick oil from the sand. Canada has an estimated reserve base of 1.7 trillion barrels of tar sands. Both tar sands and oil shale are far more expensive to produce than conventional oil from wells. Moving barrels of oil from the reserve base to the category of commercially recoverable oil reserves is purely a function on the price of oil compared to the costs of production. To attract investment in tar sands of its lands, the Canadian government set a royalty rate of only one percent until developers recovered their costs.

Should the United States pursue similar policies to foster oil shale and tar sands development in the United States? The oil shale boom of the 1970s in Colorado resulted in $5 billion in losses to investors and producers when oil prices, projected to rise above $100 a barrel, fell in the 1980s. In June 2005, the House Subcommittee on Energy and Mineral Resources heard testimony from Shell Exploration and Production Company about its new technology to heat oil shale underground to separate the hydrocarbons from the rock, a process that would be far less destructive of the surface of the tracts. Shell is seeking favorable royalty and tax treatment to commercialize oil shale. The Bureau of Land Management has solicited nominations for tracts of land to be offered for research and demonstration leases. Ben Geman, Shell Calls for Streamlined Shale Process, Greenwire, June 24, 2005. In mid–2005, Congress authorized a Programmatic Environmental Impact Statement for a commercial leasing program for oil shale and tar sands on public lands in Section 369 of the National Energy Act of 2005.

If oil shale becomes a commercial resource, then oil and gas lawyers will need to become more familiar with the General Mining Law of 1872 than merely watching Humphrey Bogart in the movie titled *The Treasure of the Sierra Madre*. The 1872 mining law allows developers to prospect on federal lands for hard minerals like gold and copper. If the prospector "strikes gold" at a particular location by making a "valuable discovery," the 1872 law allows the developer to acquire a patent (a deed from the federal government) to the tract as long as he continuously does assessment work on the claim. The developer with a successful claim can produce without paying any royalties. Before 1920, oil shale was a locatable mineral under the 1872 law. The Mineral Leasing Act of 1920 moved oil shale into a leasing procedure like that used for oil and gas. However, valid existing rights to pre–1920 oil shale claims linger on. When oil prices soared in the 1970s after the OPEC oil embargo, litigation over oil shale claims also surged. The incredible litigation over these claims, which may resume if oil prices stay around $60 a barrel, is succinctly described in George C. Coggins & Robert Glicksman, 3 Public Natural Resources Law § 24 (2005). The most recent case disfavors claimants, although the history of the judicial treatment of oil shale claims is best described as "aberrational." *Id.* at § 24:4. In 2002, in *Cliffs Synfuel Corp. v. Norton*, 291 F.3d 1250 (10th Cir. 2002), *cert. denied*, 123 S.Ct. 884 (2003), an oil shale claim, originally located in 1917, but neglected for 46 years until assessment work resumed in 1977, was declared invalid because the work was "too little, too late." Meanwhile, watch the movie.

5.   The rule of capture and the absence of pooling and unitization statutes in the early decades of the oil and gas development in the U.S., coupled with private ownership of small tracts of land, have left an enduring legacy. We are a nation of marginal wells, many of which have become idle and orphaned. Abandoned wells that are not properly plugged pose serious hazards, such as escaping gases and salt water migrating into freshwater reservoirs. Of the 550,000 producing oil wells in the U.S. in 1998, some 419,000 (or 76%) produced an average of two barrels per well per day. An astounding number of additional wells, about 343,000, were idle—not producing at all. Of these, only about half are idle with state approval. At least 57,000 orphan wells existed—idle wells with no known operator and which had not been properly plugged and sealed under state conservation laws. See Jacqueline Lang Weaver, The Federal Government as a Useful Enemy: Perspectives on the Bush Energy/Environmental Agenda from the Texas Oilfields, 19 Pace Envtl. L. Rev. 1 (2001). In the past decade, states like Texas have instituted oilfield clean-up funds from permit fees and taxes on operators and have required higher well-plugging bonds as security against future orphaned wells. On average, it costs about $5,000 to plug an onshore well and $60,000 to plug a well in bay water.

6.   Because minerals in the United States can be privately owned, mineral estates are often subdivided into fractional interests owned by many cotenants when deeds, wills or intestacy laws transfer the property from one generation to another or to unrelated buyers. The mineral estates also often become subdivided into smaller and smaller physical tracts over time, particularly as ranches and large urban tracts are broken up into residential subdivisions. The subdivision and fractionalization of privately owned interests cause serious problems for lessees. For example, as early as 1928, a cotenant who owned an undivided 1/768 interest in a tract of land in West Virginia prevented its development; the 131–acre tract would have to be partitioned into separately owned tracts before a lessee could drill. *Law v. Heck*, 106 W.Va. 296, 145 S.E. 601 (1928). Even though the common law in most states today would allow one cotenant to lease or drill without the

consent of all the others, the developing cotenant must still account to the nondeveloping cotenants for their share of profits from any producing operations. Over time, many owners end up being paid a percentage interest that begins in the sixth decimal place to the right of zero. This owner will receive less than $10 a month from a well's oil production worth $1 million a month. Few wells produce that much revenue in one month, so thousands of royalty owners are due only a few pennies. The administrative costs to lessees of accounting to so many owners for their rightful shares of a well's revenues are very high. *See* Owen L. Anderson & Ernest E. Smith, The Use of Law to Promote Domestic Exploration and Production, 50 Inst. of Oil & Gas L. & Tax'n 2–1 (1999). This fractionated ownership is one reason that oil companies have sought to explore in areas where large tracts of land are available owned by a single lessor—the government. Such lands exist offshore the United States on the outer continental shelf, on federal-or state-owned land in the western United States and Alaska, and throughout the rest of the world where private ownership of minerals is not recognized. Here, the government owns all the oil and gas. The next two sections look at these areas of the world, although producing in foreign countries also merits its own Chapter 7.

D.   THE GEOPOLITICS OF OIL

American oil exports fueled the victorious Allied forces in both World Wars I and II. However, after the second World War, U.S dominance in crude oil production quickly faded as the enormous oil fields of the Mideast came on stream. The United States moved from oil exporter to importer. While the world was soon awash with crude oil for the two decades following the end of the war, excess reserves in the United States dwindled as fewer new fields were discovered at home and consumer demand for oil and its products zoomed. This nation was becoming ever more dependent on imports of crude oil from foreign countries that were increasingly nationalistic and anti-American. The stage was set for the massive oil shocks of the 1970s, precipitated by the Arab countries' embargo of oil to the West and Japan in late 1973.

A more detailed account of the rise of OPEC, the Organization of Petroleum Exporting Countries, and its Arab counterpart (OAPEC) appears at the start of Chapter 7 on International Petroleum. This account is also useful reading as background to the current chapter, because it explains the roller coaster rise and fall of the price of oil in **Figure 6–1** from 1973 to 1985. In brief, the dramatic price increases of the 1970s ultimately led to massive conservation efforts by importing countries and to the rapid development of diversified sources of new crude supplies in many new parts of the world. The price of oil plummeted in the early 1980s. Market forces seemed triumphant.

Today, crude oil is traded as a commodity, much like grain and pork bellies. However, the market for crude is by no means free of the geopolitical forces which have dominated its production since the early 1900s when

Great Britain (through British Petroleum), the Netherlands (through Royal Dutch Shell) and the United States (through Standard Oil) battled for spheres of influence over global oil supplies. Today, many more players compete on the international scene: state-run oil companies, majors, independents, organizations of producer and consumer nations, and the nations themselves. Geopolitics rather than free market forces of supply and demand play a major role in the international price of oil. International oil diplomacy remains an important part of the foreign policy of the United States, as witnessed by Project Desert Storm in 1990–91 when U.S. troops were sent to the Persian Gulf to defend Kuwait against Iraqi invasion. And many commentators, especially from other countries, doubt that the U.S. would have invaded Iraq in 2003 if that country did not possess massive oil reserves. However colorful and political the history of the domestic oil industry in the U.S., it pales in comparison to the international scene.

The relationship between private, multinational companies and host governments, often acting through their own national oil companies is far more complicated than the leasing transaction between a government lessor in the United States and private operators. Chapter 7 and some of Chapter 9 explore this relationship and other issues unique to international operations. Multinational companies abroad face political risks which are magnitudes greater than those in the United States. Here are some examples:

Venezuela

In 2001, President Hugo Chavez decreed a new Hydrocarbons Law which more than doubled the royalty rates on projects negotiated with international oil companies in the 1990s and which requires that these projects become joint ventures with a majority 51% ownership by the Venezuelan state oil company. President Chavez has portrayed the 1990s agreements as giveaways of the nation's patrimony to foreign imperialists. In 2005, with oil prices at record highs, several U.S. companies renegotiated their agreements to accord with the 2001 decree. Brian Ellsworth, Harvest Accepts Oil Deal, Houston Chronicle, Aug. 6, 2005, at D1. Meanwhile, Chavez renamed several large oil projects that are jointly operated with Western companies after famous Venezuelan battles for independence. David Luhnow and Jose de Cordoba, With Oil, Chavez Plays It Safe, Wall St. J., Aug. 29, 2005, at A7. Venezuelan tax authorities are now pursuing millions of dollars of back tax payments allegedly owed under these agreements.

Ecuador

In August 2005, violent protests in Ecuador suspended exports of state oil while protest leaders pressed for a greater percentage of oil revenues for domestic uses, especially direct payments to local governments. The protestors also sought to rescind U.S.-based Occidental's contract to produce oil as a "vindication for so much maltreatment, humiliation, exclusion, poverty and misery . . . in comparison to the riches that the oil companies take away." Gonzalo Solano, Ecuador Oil Negotiations Remain Tense, Houston Chronicle (AP), Aug. 24, 2005, at D8. An executive of a foreign oil company responded: "This is an extremely dysfunctional place. You want some measure of stability, some measure of predictability, some sense that when you wake up tomorrow, that things will not be dramatically different." Carla D'Nan Bass and Juan Forero, New York Times, Aug. 24, 2005, at C6.

Nigeria

Activists captured and shut down 61 oil wells and a pipeline flow station operated by Shell Co. in an effort to pressure the government for development funds, a common occurrence in the Niger Delta which is a large producing area that was long neglected by a succession of corrupt military leaders who robbed most of the country's oil wealth. Houston Chronicle, July 9, 1999, at. 24A.

Under circumstances like these, what expected rate of return would be required to attract foreign investors to develop petroleum resources abroad? Perhaps drilling "at home" on the outer continental shelf is more attractive. This is the most promising area of development in the U.S. today.

E.   OFFSHORE OIL AND GAS

1.   INTRODUCTION

In 2004, about 29 percent of U.S. oil production and 21 percent of gas production came from wells on the federal offshore outer continental shelf (OCS). It is estimated that over half of our nation's undiscovered oil and gas reserves lie on the OCS, particularly in the Gulf of Mexico. The late 1990s saw a resurgence of drilling offshore in the Gulf of Mexico due to a number of factors: (1) new knowledge of how sands were deposited far from shore (as far as 130 miles) in the Gulf of Mexico millions of years ago in flood-related currents from the Mississippi River; (2) 3–D seismic technology; (3) the 1995 Deep Water Royalty Relief Act which exempts up to 87.5 million barrels of oil from royalty payments from each newly discovered field; and (4) advances in the evolution of offshore oil platforms from towers that rest on the sea bottom to floating or guyed structures, some of which are taller than the Sears Tower in Chicago. Peter Wilson, Science and Technology in the Offshore Oil Industry, Natural Res. & Env't, Spring 1990, at 552.

Little political opposition exists to drilling in the Gulf of Mexico. However, other coastal states, notably California, Massachusetts, and Florida have not been so welcoming. And Alaska presents its own unique set of environmental and political challenges as the following material demonstrates.

2.   THE STATUTORY FRAMEWORK

One event, above all, was the catalyst for the wave of environmental legislation enacted from 1969 onwards: the Santa Barbara oil spill of January 28, 1969. In 1966 the first federal leases on the Pacific offshore were issued in the Santa Barbara Channel. As Union Oil drilled the fifth well on its Platform A in the channel, the well blew out. Eleven days passed before the well was plugged and some 24,000 to 71,000 barrels of oil spilled into the channel and onto nearby beaches. **Figure 6–6,** infra, depicts the ensuing tsunami of environmental legislation.

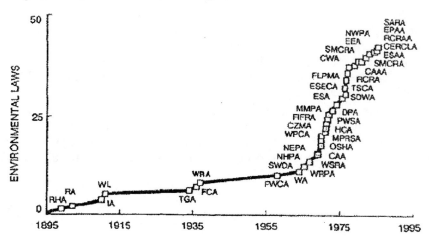

1899 - River and Harbors Act (RHA)
1902 - Reclamation Act (RA)
1910 - Insecticide Act (IA)
1911 - Weeks Law (WL)
1934 - Taylor Grazing Act (TGA)
1937 - Flood Control Act (FCA)
1937 - Wildlife Restoration Act (WRA)
1958 - Fish and Wildlife Coordination Act (FWCA)
1964 - Wilderness Act (WA)
1965 - Solid Waste Disposal Act (SWDA)
1965 - Water Resources Planning Act (WRPA)
1966 - National Historic Preservation Act (NHPA)
1968 - Wild and Scenic Rivers Act (WSRA)
1969 - National Environmental Policy Act (NEPA)
1970 - Clean Air Act (CAA)
1970 - Occupational Safety and Health Act (OSHA)
1972 - Water Pollution Control Act (WPCA)
1972 - Marine Protection, Research and
       Sanctuaries Act (MPRSA)
1972 - Coastal Zone Management Act (CZMA)
1972 - Home Control Act (HCA)
1972 - Federal Insecticide, Fungicide and
       Rodenticide Act (FIFRA)
1972 - Parks and Waterways Safety Act (PWSA)
1972 - Marine Mammal Protection Act (MMPA)

1973 - Endangered Species Act (ESA)
1974 - Deepwater Port Act (DPA)
1974 - Safe Drinking Water Act (SDWA)
1974 - Energy Supply and Environmental
       Coordination Act (ESECA)
1976 - Toxic Substances Control Act (TSCA)
1976 - Federal Land Policy and Management Act (FLPMA)
1976 - Resource Conservation and Recovery Act (RCRA)
1977 - Clean Air Act Amendments (CAAA)
1977 - Clean Water Act (CWA)
1977 - Surface Mining Control and Reclamation Act
       (SMCRA)
1977 - Soil and Water Resources Conservation Act
       (SWRCA)
1978 - Endangered Species Act Amendments (ESAA)
1978 - Environmental Education Act (EEA)
1980 - Comprehensive Environmental Response
       Compensation and Liability Act (CERCLA)
1982 - Nuclear Waste Policy Act (NWPA)
1984 - Resource Conservation and Recovery Act
       Amendments (RCRAA)
1984 - Environmental Programs and Assistance Act (EPAA)
1986 - Safe Drinking Water Act Amendments (SDWAA)
1986 - Superfund Amendments and Reorganization Act
       (SARA)

Figure 6–6

Source: National Academy of Engineering, Energy, Production, Consumption and Consequences 185 (National Academy Press 1990).

When **Figure 6–6** is superimposed on **Figure 6–1**, the wave of environmental protection closely coincides with the rocketing price of crude oil following the 1973 embargo and its ensuing decade of energy shocks and crisis. Energy competed with the environment for national attention. Could a balance be struck? Nowhere was this question more sharply framed than on the outer continental shelf and Alaska, the two areas of highest potential to provide a staggering nation with the domestic crude oil so essential to the transportation sector.

After the Santa Barbara spill, Congress enacted in rapid succession the National Environmental Policy Act of 1969 (NEPA), the Marine Protection, Research and Sanctuaries Act of 1972, the Coastal Zone Management Act (CZMA) of 1972, the Marine Mammal Protection Act of 1972, and the Endangered Species Act of 1973, followed by the massive Clean Water and Clean Air Acts of 1977. In 1978, Congress significantly revised the Outer Continental Shelf Lands Act (OCSLA) of 1953, reflecting widespread dissatisfaction with the Department of Interior's administration of the earlier law. The 1978 amendments expanded the role of state and local government officials in the federal OCS leasing process in the hopes that this action would quell the unrelenting litigation between many coastal states and the Department of the Interior, so that OCS oil could be expeditiously developed in the wake of the 1970s price shocks. However, opposition to OCS leasing continued unabated in states like California, except that the states now had additional legal mechanisms to fight the federal government in its attempts to develop domestic oil and gas. The "cooperative federalism" scheme championed in the CZMA was failing miserably.

In 1977, the Interior Department prepared another lease sale off the Santa Barbara coast. In the following case, the U.S. Supreme Court was called upon to interpret the CZMA of 1972 and the OCSLA Amendments of 1978 in the context of this leasing decision. The case provides a good history of the 1972 and 1978 acts and a nice description of the potential adverse impacts of offshore leasing on coastal states. Better yet, the strong dissenting opinion of four justices sharply illuminates the policy choice which Congress confronted when it later amended the CZMA in 1990 and deleted the word "directly" in the phrase "directly affecting" at issue in this case.

Secretary of Interior v. California

464 U.S. 312 (1984).

■ O'CONNOR, J. This case arises out of the Department of Interior's sale of oil and gas leases on the outer continental shelf off the coast of California. We must determine whether the sale is an activity "directly affecting" the coastal zone under § 307(c)(1) of the Coastal Zone Management Act (CZMA). That section provides in its entirety:

> "Each Federal agency conducting or supporting activities directly affecting the coastal zone shall conduct or support those activities in a manner which is, to the maximum extent practicable, consistent with approved state management programs." 16 U.S.C. § 1456(c)(1).

We conclude that the Secretary of the Interior's sale of outer continental shelf oil and gas leases is not an activity "directly affecting" the coastal zone within the meaning of the statute.

I

CZMA defines the "coastal zone" to include state but not federal land near the shorelines of the several coastal states, as well as coastal waters extending "seaward to the outer limit of the United States territorial sea." 16 U.S.C. § 1453(1). The territorial sea for states bordering on the Pacific or Atlantic Oceans extends three geographical miles seaward from the coastline. *See* 43 U.S.C. § 1301; United States v. California, 381 U.S. 139, (1965). Submerged lands subject to the jurisdiction of the United States that lie beyond the territorial sea constitute the "outer continental shelf" (OCS). *See* 43 U.S.C. § 1331(a). By virtue of the Submerged Lands Act, passed in 1953, the coastal zone belongs to the states, while the OCS belongs to the federal government.[7] 43 U.S.C. §§ 1302, 1311.

CZMA was enacted in 1972 to encourage the prudent management and conservation of natural resources in the coastal zone. Congress found that the "increasing and competing demands upon the lands and waters of our coastal zone" had "resulted in the loss of living marine resources, wildlife, nutrient-rich areas, permanent and adverse changes to ecological systems, decreasing open space for public use, and shoreline erosion." 16 U.S.C. § 1451(c). Accordingly, Congress declared a national policy to protect the coastal zone, to encourage the states to develop coastal zone management programs, to promote cooperation between federal and state agencies engaged in programs affecting the coastal zone, and to encourage broad participation in the development of coastal zone management programs. 16 U.S.C. § 1452.

Through a system of grants and other incentives, CZMA encourages each coastal state to develop a coastal management plan. Further grants and other benefits are made available to a coastal state after its management plan receives federal approval from the Secretary of Commerce. To obtain such approval a state plan must adequately consider the "national interest" and "the views of the Federal agencies principally affected by such program." 16 U.S.C. §§ 1455(c)(8), 1456(b).

Once a state plan has been approved, CZMA § 307(c)(1) requires federal activities "conducting or supporting activities directly affecting the coastal zone" to be "consistent" with the state plan "to the maximum extent practicable." 16 U.S.C. § 1456(c)(1). The Commerce Department has promulgated regulations implementing that provision. Those regulations require federal agencies to prepare a "consistency determination" document in support of any activity that will "directly affect" the coastal zone

---

7. Editors' note: In 1950, the Supreme Court ruled that the entire continental shelf was under federal control (*United States v. Texas*, 339 U.S. 707 (1950) and cases cited therein), but in 1953 Congress passed the Submerged Lands Act which gave the states the rights to certain offshore waters, typically three miles seaward of the shore. Texas and Florida prevailed in their historical claims to extend their territorial sea jurisdiction to three marine leagues, or about ten miles seaward. This jurisdictional "wrinkle" has enriched Texas state coffers by millions of dollars. *See* Francis J. Gaynor, Beyond All Boundaries—A Study of Marine Jurisdiction of the State of Texas—Past History and Current Issues, 17 Hous. J. Int'l L. 253 (1994).

of a state with an approved management plan. The document must identify the "direct effects" of the activity and inform state agencies how the activity has been tailored to achieve consistency with the state program. 15 C.F.R. § 930.34, 930.39 (1983).

II

OCS lease sales are conducted by the Department of the Interior (Interior). Oil and gas companies submit bids and the high bidders receive priority in the eventual exploration and development of oil and gas resources situated in the submerged lands on the OCS. A lessee does not, however, acquire an immediate or absolute right to explore for, develop, or produce oil or gas on the OCS; those activities require separate, subsequent federal authorization.

In 1977, the Department of Commerce approved the California Coastal Management Plan. The same year, Interior began preparing Lease Sale No. 53—a sale of OCS leases off the California coast near Santa Barbara. Interior first asked several state and federal agencies to report on potential oil and gas resources in this area. The Agency then requested bidders, federal and state agencies, environmental organizations, and the public, to identify which of 2036 tracts in the area should be offered for lease. In October 1978, Interior announced the tentative selection of 243 tracts, including 115 tracts situated in the Santa Maria Basin located off western Santa Barbara. Various meetings were then held with state agencies. Consultations with other federal agencies were also initiated. Interior issued a Draft Environmental Impact Statement in April, 1980.

On July 8, 1980 the California Coastal Commission informed Interior that it had determined Lease Sale No. 53 to be an activity "directly affecting" the California coastal zone. The state commission therefore demanded a consistency determination—a showing by Interior that the lease sale would be "consistent" to the "maximum extent practicable" with the state coastal zone management program. Interior responded that the Lease Sale would not "directly affect" the California coastal zone. Nevertheless, Interior decided to remove 128 tracts, located in four northern basins, from the proposed lease sale, leaving only the 115 tracts in the Santa Maria Basin. In September 1980, Interior issued a final Environmental Impact Statement. On October 27, 1980, it published a proposed notice of sale, limiting bidding to the remaining 115 blocks in the Santa Maria Basin. 45 Fed. Reg. 71140 (1980).

On December 16, 1980, the state commission reiterated its view that the sale of the remaining tracts in the Santa Maria Basin "directly affected" the California coastal zone. The commission expressed its concern that oil spills on the OCS could threaten the southern sea otter, whose range was within 12 miles of the 31 challenged tracts. The commission explained that it "has been consistent in objecting to proposed offshore oil development within specific buffer zones around special sensitive marine mammal and seabird breeding areas...." App. 77. The commission concluded that 31 more tracts should be removed from the sale because "leasing within 12 miles of the Sea Otter Range in Santa Maria Basin would not be consistent" with the California Coastal Management Program.

Interior rejected the State's demands. In the Secretary's view, no consistency review was required because the lease sale did not engage CZMA § 307(c)(1), and the Governor's request was not binding because it failed to strike a reasonable balance between the national and local interests. On April 10, 1981, Interior announced that the lease sale of the 115 tracts would go forward, and on April 27 issued a final notice of sale. 46 Fed. Reg. 23674 (1981).

Respondents filed two substantially similar suits in federal district court to enjoin the sale of 29 tracts situated within 12 miles of the Sea Otter range. Both complaints alleged, inter alia, Interior's violation of § 307(c)(1) of CZMA. They argued that leasing sets in motion a chain of events that culminates in oil and gas development, and that leasing therefore "directly affects" the coastal zone within the meaning of § 307(c)(1).

The district court entered a summary judgment for respondents on the CZMA claim. The Court of Appeals for the Ninth Circuit affirmed that portion of the district court judgment that required a consistency determination before the sale. We granted certiorari, and we now reverse.

III

Whether the sale of leases on the OCS is an activity "directly affecting" the coastal zone is not self-evident. As already noted, OCS leases involve submerged lands outside the coastal zone, and as we shall discuss, an OCS lease authorizes the holder to engage only in preliminary exploration; further administrative approval is required before full exploration or development may begin. Both sides concede that the preliminary exploration itself has no significant effect on the coastal zone. Both also agree that a lease sale is one ... in a series of decisions that may culminate in activities directly affecting that zone.

A

We are urged to focus first on the plain language of § 307(c)(1). Interior contends that "directly affecting" means "[h]av[ing] a [d]irect, [i]dentifiable [i]mpact on [t]he [c]oastal [z]one." Brief for Federal Petitioners 20. Respondents insist that the phrase means "[i]nitiat[ing] a [s]eries of [e]vents of [c]oastal [m]anagement [c]onsequence." Brief for Respondents State of California, et al. 10. But CZMA nowhere defines or explains which federal activities should be viewed as "directly affecting" the coastal zone, and the alternative verbal formulations proposed by the parties, both of which are superficially plausible, find no support in the Act itself.

B

OCSLA was enacted in 1953 to authorize federal leasing of the OCS for oil and gas development. The Act was amended in 1978 to provide for the "expeditious and orderly development, subject to environmental safeguards," of resources on the OCS. 43 U.S.C. § 1332(3) (1976 ed., Supp. III). As amended, OCSLA confirms that at least since 1978 the sale of a lease has been a distinct stage of the OCS administrative process, carefully separated from the issuance of a federal license or permit to explore, develop, or produce gas or oil on the OCS.

The leases in dispute here, however, were sold in 1981. By then it was quite clear that a lease sale by Interior did not involve the submission or approval of "any plan for the exploration or development of, or production from" the leased tract. Under the amended OCSLA, the purchase of a lease entitles the purchaser only to priority over other interested parties in submitting for federal approval a plan for exploration, production, or development. Actual submission and approval or disapproval of such plans occurs separately and later.

Since 1978 there have been four distinct statutory stages to developing an offshore oil well: (1) formulation of a five year leasing plan by the Department of the Interior; (2) lease sales; (3) exploration by the lessees; (4) development and production. Each stage involves separate regulatory review that may, but need not, conclude in the transfer to lease purchasers of rights to conduct additional activities on the OCS. And each stage includes specific requirements for consultation with Congress, between federal agencies, or with the States. Formal review of consistency with state coastal management plans is expressly reserved for the last two stages.

(1) Preparation of a leasing program. The first stage of OCS planning is the creation of a leasing program. Interior is required to prepare a 5–year schedule of proposed OCS lease sales. During the preparation of that program Interior must solicit comments from interested federal agencies and the governors of affected states, and must respond in writing to all comments or requests received from the state governors. The proposed leasing program is then submitted to the President and Congress, together with comments received by the Secretary from the governor of the affected state. [43 U.S.C. § 1344 (1976 ed., Supp. III)].

Plainly, prospective lease purchasers acquire no rights to explore, produce, or develop at this first stage of OCSLA planning, and consistency review provisions of CZMA § 307(c)(3)(B) are therefore not engaged. There is also no suggestion that CZMA § 307(c)(1) consistency requirements operate here, though we note that preparation and submission to Congress of the leasing program could readily be characterized as "initiat[ing] a [s]eries of [e]vents of [c]oastal [m]anagement [c]onsequence." Brief for Respondents State of California, et al. 10.

(2) Lease sales. The second stage of OCS planning—the stage in dispute here—involves the solicitation of bids and the issuance of offshore leases. 43 U.S.C. § 1337(a) (1976 ed., Supp. III). Requirements of the National Environmental Policy Act and the Endangered Species Act must be met first. The governor of any affected state is given a formal opportunity to submit recommendations regarding the "size, timing, or location" of a

proposed lease sale. 43 U.S.C. § 1345 (1976 ed., Supp. III). Interior is required to accept these recommendations if it determines they strike a reasonable balance between the national interest and the well-being of the citizens of the affected state. Local governments are also permitted to submit recommendations, and the Secretary "may" accept these. The Secretary may then proceed with the actual lease sale. Lease purchasers acquire the right to conduct only limited "preliminary" activities on the OCS—geophysical and other surveys that do not involve seabed penetrations greater than 300 feet and that do not result in any significant environmental impacts. 30 C.F.R § 250.34–1 (1982).

Again, there is no suggestion that these activities in themselves "directly affect" the coastal zone. But by purchasing a lease, lessees acquire no right to do anything more. Under the plain language of OCSLA, the purchase of a lease entails no right to proceed with full exploration, development, or production that might trigger CZMA § 307(c)(3)(B); the lessee acquires only a priority in submitting plans to conduct those activities. If these plans, when ultimately submitted, are disapproved, no further exploration or development is permitted.

(3) Exploration. The third stage of OCS planning involves review of more extensive exploration plans submitted to Interior by lessees. 43 U.S.C. § 1340 (1976 ed., Supp. III). Exploration may not proceed until an exploration plan has been approved. A lessee's plan must include a certification that the proposed activities comply with any applicable state management program developed under CZMA. OCSLA expressly provides for federal disapproval of a plan that is not consistent with an applicable state management plan unless the Secretary of Commerce finds that the plan is consistent with CZMA goals or in the interest of national security. 43 U.S.C. § 1340(c)(2) (1976 ed., Supp. III). The plan must also be disapproved if it would "probably cause serious harm or damage ... to the marine, coastal, or human environment...." 43 U.S.C. §§ 1334(a)(2)(A)(I), 1340(c)(1) (1976 ed., Supp. III). If a plan is disapproved for the latter reason, the Secretary may "cancel such lease and the lessee shall be entitled to compensation...." 43 U.S.C. § 1340(c)(1) (1976 ed., Supp. III).

There is, of course, no question that CZMA consistency review requirements operate here. CZMA § 307(c)(3)(B) expressly applies, and as noted, OCSLA itself refers to the applicable CZMA provision.

(4) Development and production. The fourth and final stage is development and production. 43 U.S.C. § 1351 (1976 ed., Supp. III). The lessee must submit another plan to Interior. The Secretary must forward the plan to the governor of any affected state and, on request, to the local governments of affected states, for comment and review. Again, the governor's recommendations must be accepted, and the local governments' may be accepted, if they strike a reasonable balance between local and national interests. Reasons for accepting or rejecting a governor's recommendations must be communicated in writing to the governor. In addition, the development and production plan must be consistent with the applicable state coastal management program. The State can veto the plan as "inconsis-

tent," and the veto can be overridden only by the Secretary of Commerce. 43 U.S.C. § 1351(d) (1976 ed., Supp. III). A plan may also be disapproved if it would "probably cause serious harm or damage . . . to the marine, coastal or human environments." 43 U.S.C. § 1351(h)(1)(D)(I) (1976 ed., Supp. III). If a plan is disapproved for the latter reason, the lease may again be canceled and the lessee is entitled to compensation. 43 U.S.C. § 1351(h)(2)(C) (1976 ed., Supp. III).

Once again, the applicability of CZMA to this fourth stage of OCS planning is not in doubt. CZMA § 307(c)(3)(B) applies by its own terms, and is also expressly invoked by OCSLA.

Congress has thus taken pains to separate the various federal decisions involved in formulating a leasing program, conducting lease sales, authorizing exploration, and allowing development and production. Since 1978, the purchase of an OCS lease, standing alone, entails no right to explore, develop, or produce oil and gas resources on the OCS. The first two stages are not subject to consistency review; instead input from State governors and local governments is solicited by the Secretary of Interior. The last two stages invite further input for governors or local governments, but also require formal consistency review. States with approved CZMA plans retain considerable authority to veto inconsistent exploration or development and production plans put forward in those latter stages. The stated reason for this four part division was to forestall premature litigation regarding adverse environmental effects that all agree will flow, if at all, only from the latter stages of OCS exploration and production. . . .

It is argued, nonetheless, that a lease sale is a crucial step. Large sums of money change hands, and the sale may therefore generate momentum that makes eventual exploration, development, and production inevitable. On the other side, it is argued that consistency review at the lease sale stage is at best inefficient, and at worst impossible: Leases are sold before it is certain if, where, or how exploration will actually occur.

The choice between these two policy arguments is not ours to make; it has already been made by Congress. In the 1978 OCSLA amendments Congress decided that the better course is to postpone consistency review until the two later stages of OCS planning, and to rely on less formal input from State governors and local governments in the two earlier ones. It is not for us to negate the lengthy, detailed, and coordinated provisions of CZMA § 307(c)(3)(B), and OCSLA §§ 1344–1346 and 1351, by a superficially plausible but ultimately unsupportable construction of two words in CZMA § 307(c)(1).

V

Collaboration among state and federal agencies is certainly preferable to confrontation in or out of the courts. In view of the substantial consistency requirements imposed at the exploration, development, and production stages of OCS planning, the Department of the Interior, as well as private bidders on OCS leases, might be well advised to ensure in advance that anticipated OCS operations can be conducted harmoniously with state coastal management programs. But our review of the history of CZMA § 307(c)(1), and the coordinated structures of the amended CZMA and OCSLA, persuades us that Congress did not intend § 307(c)(1) to mandate consistency review at the lease sale stage.

Accordingly, the decision of the Court of Appeals for the Ninth Circuit is reversed insofar as it requires petitioners to conduct consistency review pursuant to CZMA § 307(c)(1) before proceeding with Lease Sale No. 53.

It is so ordered.

■ JUSTICE STEVENS, with whom JUSTICE BRENNAN, JUSTICE MARSHALL, and JUSTICE BLACKMUN join, dissenting In this case, the State of California is attempting to enforce a federal statutory right. Its coastal zone management program was approved by the Federal Government pursuant to a statute enacted in 1972. In § 307(c)(1) of that statute, the Coastal Zone Management Act (CZMA), the Federal Government made a promise to California:

> "Each Federal agency conducting or supporting activities directly affecting the coastal zone shall conduct or support those activities in a manner which is, to the maximum extent practicable, consistent with approved state management programs." 86 Stat. 1285, 16 U.S.C. § 1456(c)(1) (1982).

The question in this case is whether the Secretary of the Interior was conducting an activity directly affecting the California Coastal Zone when he sold oil and gas leases in the Pacific ocean area immediately adjacent to that zone. One would think that this question could be easily answered simply by reference to a question of fact—does this sale of leases directly affect the coastal zone? The District Court made a finding that it did, which the Court of Appeals affirmed, and which is not disturbed by the Court. Based on a straightforward reading of the statute, one would think that that would be the end of the case. [The dissent then conducted its own review of the plain language and legislative history of the CZMA] . . . .

The majority's construction of § 307(c)(1) is squarely at odds with [the purpose of the CZMA]. Orderly, long-range, cooperative planning dictates that the consistency requirement must apply to OCS leasing decisions. The sale of OCS leases involves the expenditure of millions of dollars.[8] If exploration and development of the leased tracts cannot be squared with the requirements of the CZMA, it would be in everyone's interest to determine that as early as possible. On the other hand, if exploration and development of the tracts would be consistent with the state management plan, a pre-leasing consistency determination would provide assurances to prospective purchasers and hence enhance the value of the tracts to the Federal Government and, concomitantly, the public. Advance planning can only minimize the risk of either loss or inconsistency that may ultimately confront all interested parties. It is directly contrary to the legislative

---

8. [FN15] In the lease sale at issue in this case, $220 million was bid on the disputed tracts.

scheme not to make a consistency determination at the earliest possible point. Such a construction must be rejected.

There is no dispute about the fact that the Secretary's selection of lease tracts and lease terms constituted decisions of major importance to the coastal zone. The District Court described some of the effects of those decisions:

. . .

"The Secretarial Issue Document ("SID"), prepared in October 1980 by the Department of Interior to aid the Secretary in his decision, contains voluminous information indicative of the direct effects of this project on the coastal zone. For instance, the SID contains a table showing the overall probability of an oil spill impacting a point within the sea otter range during the life of the project in the northern portion of the Santa Maria Basin to be 52%. Both the SID and the EIS [Environmental Impact Statement] contain statistics showing the likelihood of oil spills during the life of the leases; based on the unrevised USGS estimates, 1.65 spills are expected during the project conducted in the Santa Maria subarea. According to the SID, the probability of an oil spill is even higher when the revised USGS figures are utilized.

. . . Both documents refer to impacts upon air and water quality, marine and coastal ecosystems, commercial fisheries, recreation and sportfishing, navigation, cultural resources, and socio-economic factors. For instance, the EIS states that "[n]ormal offshore operations would have unavoidable effects . . . on the quality of the surrounding water." Pipelaying, drilling, and construction, chronic spills from platforms, and the discharge of treated sewage contribute to the degradation of water quality in the area. As to commercial fisheries, drilling muds and cuttings "could significantly affect fish and invertebrate populations"; the spot prawn fishery in the Santa Maria Basin is particularly vulnerable to this physical disruption. In reference to recreation and sportfishing, the EIS indicates the possibility of adverse impacts as a result of the competition for land between recreation and OCS/related onshore facilities as a result of the temporary disruption of recreation areas caused by pipeline burial. There are the additional risks of "the degradation of the aesthetic environment conducive to recreation and the damage to recreational sites as a result of an oil spill." Another impact on the coastal zone will occur as a result of the migration of labor into the area during the early years of the oil and gas operations. Impacts on the level of employment and the size of the population in the coastal region are also predicted.

"The SID notes that there are artifacts of history interest as well as aboriginal archaeological sites reported in the area of the Santa Maria tracts. The FWS and NMFS biological opinions, appended to the SID, indicate the likelihood that development and production activities may jeopardize the existence of the southern sea otter and the gray whale.

"These effects constitute only a partial list. Further enumeration is unnecessary. The threshold test under § 307(c)(1) would in fact be satisfied by a finding of a single direct effect upon the coastal zone. Although the evidence of direct effects is substantial, such a showing is not required by the CZMA."

520 F.Supp. 1359, 1380–1382 (C.D.Cal.1981). . . .

I therefore respectfully dissent.■

NOTES AND COMMENTS

1. In an omitted footnote in this case, the majority opinion noted that the California Coastal Commission had warned: "Any attempt to explore or develop these tracts will face the strong possibility of an objection to a consistency certification of the Plan of Exploration or Development." What projected rate of return would warrant the political risks of leasing in the Santa Barbara Channel? What property right have lessees bought in exchange for the $221 million spent in bids? Do you agree that "[t]he price of confirming federal supremacy was destruction of the protectible property aspects of the offshore leasehold"? *See* George C. Coggins and Doris K. Nagel, "Nothing Beside Remains": The Legal Legacy of James G. Watt's Tenure as Secretary of the Interior on Federal Land Law and Policy, 17 Envt'l Affairs 474 at 527 (1990). Keep these questions in mind as you read the material on OCS leasing moratoria in Subsection 4 below.

In mid–1999, Chevron sold its interests in offshore California fields, ending 41 years of production along the state's coast. Instead, it will focus on exploration projects in Kazakhstan, West Africa and the Gulf of Mexico. Houston Chronicle, Business Briefs, July 3, 1999, at 2C.

2. Section 307(c)(1)(A) of the CZMA currently reads: "Each Federal agency activity within or outside the coastal zone that affects any land or water use or natural resource of the coastal zone shall be carried out in a manner which is consistent to the maximum extent practicable with the enforceable policies of approved State management programs." 16 U.S.C.A. § 1456(c)(1)(A) (1999 Supp.). How does this amendment affect the balance between federal and state power over control of vital OCS resources? Does it give states a veto power over OCS leasing?

Section 307(c)(1)(B) allows the President, under certain conditions, to exempt a specific federal agency activity from compliance with the new consistency requirements if the President determines such a waiver is "in the paramount interest of the United States." Would the existing political instability in the Mideast justify a presidential waiver against a state like Florida that continues to oppose drilling off its shores?

3. Walter Mead, a professor of economics at the University of California at Santa Barbara, testified on March 11, 1969 before the Senate Subcommittee on Antitrust and Monopoly which was investigating government intervention in petroleum markets. After analyzing the numerous government programs (such as market-demand prorationing by the states and the

federal percentage depletion allowance) which resulted in subsidizing the domestic oil industry and shielding it from international price competition, he stated: "The oil spillage case in the Santa Barbara Channel is directly related to the subsidy system. Leases were purchased and drilling occurred in the California offshore area because operations were made profitable by the subsidy legislation. Under free market conditions, oil prices would be substantially lower, tax costs substantially higher, and the profit inducement to buy leases in the Channel would probably be lacking.... In addition, we have the external cost (aptly called 'spillover costs' even before this oil spillage case) of environmental pollution." Walter Mead, The System of Government Subsidies in the Oil Industry, 10 Nat. Res. J. 113, at 123–24 (1970). Professor Mead recommended that the subsidies be phased out so that "the massive burden of resource misallocation in this industry be removed as a drag on this nation's strength." In light of subsequent events, notably the OPEC oil embargo in 1973 and post–9/11 terrorism, do you agree with Professor Mead's advice?

4. The staged structure of offshore oil development explicated in *Secretary of Interior v. California* has ramifications for the Environmental Impact Statement process required for any major federal activity significantly affecting the human environment under NEPA.

In *Village of False Pass v. Clark,* 733 F.2d 605 (9th Cir. 1984), the court explained the interaction among OCSLA, NEPA, and the Endangered Species Act (ESA), in a case involving "an important marine environment, rare whales, large sums of money, [and] a search for increasingly scarce energy resources." *Id.* at 607.

In this case, the Secretary of Interior had approved federal leasing in the St. George Basin, located off the west coast of Alaska in the Bering Sea, "the gateway to virtually every marine mammal, fish, and bird species moving between the North Pacific and the Bering Sea." The Basin potentially held oil reserves of 1.12 billion barrels for which oil companies were willing to spend almost half a billion dollars for the right to investigate the chance (rated at 28 to 37 percent) of discovering such commercial quantities.

The Village of False Pass and other interveners argued that the Secretary had abused his discretion under NEPA by failing to perform a worst-case analysis in the EIS of an oil spill of 100,000 barrels or larger occurring while whales migrated nearby. In response, the court wrote:

> The village would have a better argument for the importance of a worst case analysis at the lease sale stage of a 100,000 barrel oil spill if that were the only time the Secretary could review the potential environmental impacts of those leases.... As our earlier discussion of OCSLA's three stage process made clear, however, NEPA may require an environmental impact statement at each stage: leasing, exploration, and production and development. Furthermore, each stage remains separate. The completion of one stage does not entitle a lessee to begin the next [citing *Secretary of Interior v. California*].

A strong dissent in *False Pass* argued that the *California* case should not affect the interpretation of NEPA's requirements. The earlier case held that the OCSLA lease sale stage did not "directly affect" the coastal zone so as to require a consistency review under the CZMA. But the purposes of NEPA are different, explained the dissent:

> Prior to sale, the Secretary has absolute discretion to decline to lease an OCS tract. *See* 43 U.S.C. § 1344(a). He can therefore decline to lease on the ground that exploration or development will run a small but real risk of immense environmental harm. Once the Secretary leases a tract, however, he loses that freedom, and consequently commits himself to incur such a risk. The reasons why the Secretary loses his freedom upon sale of the leases are both legal and practical.

> As a legal matter, the Secretary is allowed to cancel an existing lease for environmental reasons only if he determines that:

>> (I) continued activity . . . *would probably cause* serious harm or damage to . . . [the] environment; (ii) the threat of harm or damage will not disappear or decrease to an acceptable extent within a reasonable period of time; and (iii) the advantages of cancellation outweigh the advantages of continuing such lease or permit in force.

43 U.S.C. § 1334(a)(2)(A) (emphasis added); 43 U.S.C. § 1351(h)(1)(D).

> The requirement of a determination that continued activity "would *probably* cause serious harm to the environment" is a forceful restriction on the Secretary's authority. At least under ordinary circumstances, it prohibits cancellation because of the possibility of a major oil spill; . . . a major oil spill is not a *probable* occurrence, but rather is "an event of low probability but catastrophic effects." The effect of the statute, therefore is that sale of the leases ends the Secretary's right to call a total halt to exploration and development out of concern over remote environmental catastrophes. . . .

> It is true that the Secretary's power to *suspend* operations remains broad, but we have held that the power to suspend is exceeded when the suspension is so open-ended as to amount to a cancellation of a lease. *Union Oil Co. of Cal. v. Morton,* 512 F.2d 743, 750–51 (9th Cir. 1975). Suspension is therefore a temporary remedy, and being temporary, cannot eliminate the possibility of a major oil spill. Only cancellation can do that.

Id. at 617–18.

5. The *Village of False Pass* case also involved the Endangered Species Act (ESA) and whales. Section 7(a)(2) of this Act requires that every federal agency "insure that any action authorized, funded, or carried out by such agency . . . is not likely to jeopardize the continued existence of any endangered species or threatened species" or adversely modify its critical habitat. 16 U.S.C.A. § 1536(a)(2) (1985). The majority opinion states that "ESA appears to apply equally to each stage [of offshore activity] of its own force and effect." *Id.* at 609. The court found no violation of the ESA

because the Secretary had placed special disclaimers in the Notice of Lease Sale, stating that the Secretary retained authority to regulate seismic testing and to suspend drilling whenever migrating whales came close enough to be subject to the risk of spilled oil. The opinion continues:

> The Village characterizes these [disclaimers] as "only a plan for later action." We conclude that, given the Fisheries Service's general recommendations about oil spills and exploration stage seismic testing, the Secretary could properly limit his action at the lease sale stage to a plan for later implementation. The ESA applies to every federal action. . . . The lease sale decision itself could not directly place gray or right whales in jeopardy, and the plan insures that the many agency actions that may follow indirectly from the sale will not either.
>
> By choosing this plan, however, the Secretary recognizes his obligation under ESA to implement it. *See generally Conservation Law Found. of New England, Inc. v. Andrus*, 623 F. 2d at 715. With each exploration plan, development and production plan, or permit to drill, the Secretary must: implicitly conclude that any approval does not affect an endangered species, *see* 50 C.F.R. § 402.04(a)(2) (1982); take appropriate steps to insure, on the basis of his previous consultation with the Fisheries Service, the absence of jeopardy to an endangered species; or reinitiate formal consultation, *see*, e.g., *Village of False Pass v. Watt*, 565 F. Supp. at 1161 & n.28 (strong suggestion that formal consultation about oil spill risks on whales will be required at the exploration stage); 50 C.F.R. § 402.04(h) (1982).
>
> The monitoring agreement with the Fisheries Service will help the Secretary take these steps and diligently pursue ESA compliance after the lease sale, *see Village of False Pass v. Watt*, 565 F. Supp. at 1161. The Secretary's own regulations require an environmental report from each lessee for each exploration plan, . . . and development and production plan. . . . Approval of these plans may even require a full environmental impact statement. *See* 30 C.F.R. § 250.34–4(a) (1982); *see also* 43 U.S.C. § 1351(e) (OCSLA); 42 U.S.C. § 4332(2)(C) (NEPA). Even if not a full environmental impact statement, these reports and plans must include information about marine mammal use of the area. *See* 30 C.F.R. § 250.34–3(a)(1)(I)(G)(4) (1982). . . . This means that the Secretary will have precise, site-specific information in each case to insure the best compliance with ESA.
>
> These regulations, promulgated in part under OCSLA, help make the Secretary's plan a real safeguard. Neither the regulations, nor OCSLA itself, dilute the full application of ESA to actions by the Secretary. . . .

Could the Secretary of Interior cancel a lease permanently because she found that exploration on the tract would jeopardize an endangered species and no temporary suspension could "unjeopardize" it? Would the lessee be entitled to compensation for lease cancellation?

Continue to keep these questions in mind as you approach the material on OCS leasing moratoria.

6.   Can the best-made plans either predict or adjust to the disequilibrium of Mother Nature's own cycles? Consider the ecological crisis threatening the entire coastal ecosystem of the Aleutian islands in western Alaska, as reported in 282 Science 390–91 and 473–76 (Oct. 16, 1998). In the late 1980s, the sea lion and seal populations of this region fell to about 1/10 their usual size. Killer whales that usually feed on seals then turned to eating sea otters. The sea otter population quickly dropped by 90 percent. This rapid drop in otters led to a population explosion of sea urchins, the otters' favorite food, and the urchins in turn began stripping the undersea kelp forest, turning lush marine areas into barren wastelands. As one marine ecologist stated: "[This] research demonstrates how disrupting just one link in a food chain can threaten an entire ecological system." He estimated that a single killer whale required 1,825 otters a year to stay nourished and that only four killer whales could cause the entire sea otter population in the Aleutian island chain to crash. As one ecologist said, "It's just mindblowing that as few as four whales could cause an ecosystem effect over such a huge part of the Earth." *Id.* at 390. *See also* Houston Chronicle, Killer whales' search for new food source blamed for ecological crisis, Oct. 16, 1998, at 9A.

The researchers suspect that the seal and sea lion populations have declined because of intensified trawler fishing in the Bering Sea, although warmer ocean temperatures or the local extinction of baleen whales may also be the cause. The extinction of the baleen whale has allowed one fish, the pollack, which is low in fat, to flourish.

7.   In a study of oil and gas leasing on federal onshore lands, the National Research Council was informed by the federal agencies that, as a rule of thumb, about 10 percent of all oil and gas leases issued are ever drilled on, and about 10 percent of those drilled on ever produce oil and gas. Does this rule of thumb bolster the views of the majority? Should NEPA generate paperwork evaluating speculative possibilities that are a long shot? *See Park County Res. Council, Inc. v. U.S. Dep't of Agriculture*, 817 F.2d 609 (10th Cir. 1987) (lease issuance not a major federal action significantly affecting the human environment in a national forest because, among other factors, future drilling was "nebulous").

Until 1987, federal onshore leasing was conducted under the Mineral Leasing Act of 1920. In 1987, Congress enacted FOOGLRA, the Federal Onshore Oil and Gas Leasing Reform Act, to amend serious deficiencies in the 1920 Act. Onshore production of oil and gas from federal lands is small compared to OCS production, although the production of coalbed methane on federal lands in the west is growing rapidly, as discussed in Chapter 8 on Natural Gas. For a full discussion of onshore leasing, *see* George C. Coggins and Robert L. Glicksman, 3 Public Natural Resources Law § 23 (2005).

3. Alaska

a. ABORIGINAL RIGHTS TO SUBSISTENCE HUNTING AND FISHING

Prudhoe Bay on Alaska's North Slope is the largest oil field in North America. It was discovered in late 1967 on land which the state of Alaska had selected (with some foresight) under the Alaskan Statehood Act of 1958. This Act gave Alaska the right to select over 100 million acres from the vacant and unreserved lands which had once been federal territory. Natives objected to many of the state's selections and by 1968 had filed land claims over 80 percent of Alaska. Congress stepped in to resolve the competing state, federal, and Native ownership claims. In the Alaskan Native Claims Settlement Act (ANCSA) of 1971, Congress allowed Native Alaskans to select 44 million acres of land, but in return, the Native Alaskans were required to relinquish all aboriginal rights to the exclusive use of the lands and waters in Alaska. These aboriginal rights were based on the immemorial custom and practice of the natives and their ancestors dating from long before the United States asserted sovereignty over Alaska. The rights of Indians to hunt and fish for subsistence had long been recognized as "not much less necessary to [their] existence . . . than the atmosphere they breathed." *United States v. Winans*, 198 U.S. 371, 381 (1905). The Settlement Act vested land titles in native Villages and Regional Corporations, but did not specifically address Native subsistence hunting and fishing. Much of Alaska remained in federal hands as national parks, forests, wilderness, and wildlife refuges.

The Settlement Act's inadequate protection of Native subsistence rights resulted in the passage of the Alaska National Interest Lands Conservation Act (ANILCA) nine years later. At that time, much of Alaska's rural population lived a subsistence life style based on harvesting wild resources such as salmon, seals, caribou, bear, and berries. Subsistence living is more than a matter of providing food and shelter to households hundreds of miles from markets. It is a cultural way of life involving special skills, communal attitudes, and spiritual ceremony passed down from generation to generation. Title VIII of ANILCA established a priority for nonwasteful subsistence fishing and hunting on federal lands.

Inevitably, perhaps, OCS leasing came into conflict with the subsistence rights of some Native Alaskan Eskimo tribes living in small villages along the coasts, and the court was called upon to resolve this dispute between an endangered lifestyle and OCS leasing.

Amoco Production Co. v. Village of Gambell

480 U.S. 531 (1987).

■ White, J. Petitioner Secretary of the Interior granted oil and gas leases to petitioner oil companies in the Norton Sound (Lease Sale 57) and Navarin Basin (Lease Sale 83) areas of the Bering Sea under the Outer Continental Shelf Lands Act (OCSLA), 67 Stat. 462, as amended, 43 U.S.C. § 1331 *et seq.* (1982 ed. and Supp. III). The Court of Appeals for the Ninth Circuit directed the entry of a preliminary injunction against all activity in connection with the leases because it concluded that it was likely that the Secretary had failed to comply with § 810 of the Alaska National Interest Lands Conservation Act (ANILCA), 94 Stat. 2371, 16 U.S.C. § 3120, prior to issuing the leases. We granted certiorari, . . . and we now reverse.

I

When the Secretary of the Interior proposed Outer Continental Shelf (OCS) Lease Sale 57, the Alaska Native villages of Gambell and Stebbins sought to enjoin him from proceeding with the sale, claiming that it would adversely affect their aboriginal rights to hunt and fish on the OCS and that the Secretary had failed to comply with ANILCA § 810(a), 16 U.S.C. § 3120(a), which provides protection for natural resources used for subsistence in Alaska.[9] The District Court denied their motion for a preliminary injunction and thereafter granted summary judgment in favor of the Secretary and oil company intervenors, holding that the villagers had no aboriginal rights on the OCS and that ANILCA did not apply to the OCS.[10]

The Court of Appeals for the Ninth Circuit affirmed the District Court's ruling on aboriginal rights, although on different grounds, and reversed the ruling on the scope of ANILCA § 810. *People of Gambell v. Clark*, 746 F.2d 572 (1984) (Gambell I). With respect to the claim of aboriginal rights, the court assumed without deciding that the villagers once had aboriginal rights to hunt and fish in the Norton Sound, but concluded that these rights had been extinguished by § 4(b) of the Alaska

9. [FN2] Section 810(a), 16 U.S.C. § 3120(a), provides: "In determining whether to withdraw, reserve, lease, or otherwise permit the use, occupancy, or disposition of public lands under any provision of law authorizing such actions, the head of the Federal agency having primary jurisdiction over such lands or his designee shall evaluate the effect of such use, occupancy, or disposition on subsistence uses and needs, the availability of other lands for the purposes sought to be achieved, and other alternatives which would reduce or eliminate the use, occupancy, or disposition of public lands needed for subsistence purposes. No such withdrawal, reservation, lease, permit, or other use, occupancy or disposition of such lands which would significantly restrict subsistence uses shall be effected until the head of such Federal agency—

"(1) gives notice to the appropriate State agency and the appropriate local committees and regional councils established pursuant to section 3115 of this title;

"(2) gives notice of, and holds, a hearing in the vicinity of the area involved; and

"(3) determines that (A) such a significant restriction of subsistence uses is necessary, consistent with sound management principles for the utilization of the public lands, (B) the proposed activity will involve the minimal amount of public lands necessary to accomplish the purposes of such use, occupancy or other disposition, and (C) reasonable steps will be taken to minimize adverse impacts upon subsistence uses and resources resulting from such actions."

10. [Editors' note: While the villages appealed and moved to enjoin the issuance of the leases pending appeal, 59 tracts were leased for bonus payments totaling over $300 million, and the Secretary approved exploration plans submitted by the lessees. Exploration proceeded in 1984 and the Secretary leased an additional 163 tracts in 1984 for total bonus payments of over $500 million.]

Native Claims Settlement Act (ANCSA), 85 Stat. 690, 43 U.S.C. § 1603(b). That section provides:

> "All aboriginal titles, if any, and claims of aboriginal title in Alaska based on use and occupancy, including submerged land underneath all water areas, both inland and offshore, and including any aboriginal hunting or fishing rights that may exist, are hereby extinguished."

The Court of Appeals construed the phrase "in Alaska" to mean "the geographic region, including the contiguous continental shelf and the waters above it, and not merely the area within the strict legal boundaries of the State of Alaska." 746 F.2d, at 575. Finding the phrase ambiguous, the court examined the legislative history and concluded that Congress wrote the extinguishment provision broadly "to accomplish a complete and final settlement of aboriginal claims and avoid further litigation of such claims." Ibid. The court then concluded that ANILCA § 810 had the same geographical scope as ANCSA § 4(b):

> "[The villages] make a compelling argument that the provisions of Title VIII of [ANILCA] protecting subsistence uses were intended to have the same territorial scope as provisions of the earlier Claims Settlement Act extinguishing Native hunting and fishing rights. The two statutory provisions are clearly related. When Congress adopted the Claims Settlement Act it was aware that extinguishing Native rights might threaten subsistence hunting and fishing by Alaska Natives.... It is a reasonable assumption that Congress intended the preference and procedural protections for subsistence uses mandated by Title VIII of [ANILCA] to be co-extensive with the extinguishment of aboriginal rights that made those measures necessary." 746 F.2d, at 579–580.

The court found support for this view in ANILCA's legislative history. But, according to the Court of Appeals, "[t]he most compelling reason for resolving the ambiguous language of Title VIII in favor of coverage of outer continental shelf lands and waters is that Title VIII was adopted to benefit the Natives." Id. at 581. The court acknowledged the familiar rule of statutory construction that doubtful expressions must be resolved in favor of Indians. See *Alaska Pac. Fisheries v. United States*, 248 U.S. 78, 89 (1918). It then remanded to the District Court the questions whether the Secretary had substantially complied with ANILCA § 810 in the course of complying with other environmental statutes,[11] and if not, whether the leases should be voided.

---

11. [FN5] The Coastal Zone Management Act, Marine Protection, Research, and Sanctuaries Act, Marine Mammal Protection Act, Fishery Conservation and Management Act, Endangered Species Act, and National Environmental Policy Act all apply to activities on the OCS. Pursuant to the National Environmental Policy Act (NEPA), the Department of the Interior drafted in 1982 a 332-page Final Environmental Impact Statement (EIS) on proposed Lease Sale 57. Interior analyzed in the EIS the effects that the lease sale, and subsequent exploration, development, and production, could conceivably have on "subsistence uses," as defined by ANILCA § 803, 16 U.S.C. § 3113. The EIS documented the fish and shellfish, sea

In compliance with the Court of Appeals' decision, the Secretary prepared a postsale evaluation of possible impacts on subsistence uses from Lease Sale 57.[12] The Secretary found that the execution of the leases, which permitted lessees to conduct only limited preliminary activities on the OCS, had not and would not significantly restrict subsistence uses. He further found that the exploration stage activities, including seismic activities and exploratory drilling, that had occurred in Norton Sound had not significantly restricted subsistence uses and were not likely to do so in the future. Finally, he found that, if development and production activities were ever conducted, which was not likely, they might, in the event of a major oil spill, significantly restrict subsistence uses for limited periods in limited areas.

In April 1985, the villages sought a preliminary injunction in the District Court against exploratory activities in Norton Sound. At the same time, the village of Gambell, joined by Nunam Kitlutsisti, an organization of Yukon Delta Natives, filed a complaint seeking to void Lease Sale 83 and to enjoin imminent exploratory drilling in the Navarin Basin. The District Court consolidated the motions for preliminary injunctions and denied them. . . . [W]ith respect to the post-sale evaluation for Lease Sale 57, the District Court concluded that because development and production activities, if they ever occurred, could significantly restrict subsistence uses in certain areas, the Secretary was required to conduct the hearing and make the findings required by §§ 810(a)(1)–(3) prior to conducting the lease sale. Nevertheless, the court concluded that injunctive relief was not appropriate based on the following findings:

> "(1) That delay in the exploration of the OCS may cause irreparable harm to this nation's quest for new oil resources and energy independence. Expedited exploration as a policy is stated in OCSLA. See 43 U.S.C. § 1332(3);

> "(2) That exploration will not significantly restrict subsistence resources; and

mammal, bird, and land animal resources utilized by the villages in the region, including Gambell and Stebbins, and analyzed the sensitivity of these resources to oil spills, other exploration and development impacts, and harvest pressure. EIS 47–53, 136–148. The EIS also considered the sociocultural impact of changes in the availability of subsistence resources. Interior concluded as follows:

"While some changes in local subsistence use and take may occur with this proposal, the probability of significant disturbance, in the form of long-term reduction of subsistence take, large-scale disruption of subsistence harvesting activities, or significant reductions in primary resources utilized for subsistence is unlikely for the region as a whole. For Savoonga, and to a lesser extent other 'big sea mammal hunting' villages (Diomede, Gambell, King Island, Wales) due to a relatively greater vulnerability to oil spill events, the short-term disturbance is more likely, particularly during the peak development period." EIS 142. . . .

12. [FN6] . . . The Secretary examined the effects on subsistence uses of Lease Sale 57 itself, present and future exploratory activities, and development and production activities, which the Secretary estimated had a 13% probability of being undertaken. . . . The Secretary stressed that a definite evaluation with respect to the latter stage could only be made if and when plans for development and production were submitted and that a separate § 810 evaluation would be prepared at that time.

"(3) That the Secretary continues to possess power to control and shape the off-shore leasing process. Therefore, if the ANILCA subsistence studies require alteration of the leasing conditions or configuration the Secretary will be able to remedy any harm caused by the violation." *Id.*, at 62a–63a.

Accordingly, applying the traditional test for a preliminary injunction, the court concluded that the balance of irreparable harm did not favor the movants; in addition, the public interest favored continued oil exploration and such exploration in this case would not cause the type of harm that ANILCA was designed to prevent.

Respondents appealed from the District Court's denial of a preliminary injunction. The Ninth Circuit reversed. People of Gambell v. Hodel, 774 F.2d 1414 (1985) (Gambell II). The court, agreeing that the villages had established a strong likelihood of success on the merits, concluded that the District Court had not properly balanced irreparable harm and had not properly evaluated the public interest. Relying on its earlier decision in *Save Our Ecosystems v. Clark*, 747 F.2d 1240, 1250 (1984), the court stated: " 'Irreparable damage is presumed when an agency fails to evaluate thoroughly the environmental impact of a proposed action.' " 774 F.2d, at 1423. It ruled that "injunctive relief is the appropriate remedy for a violation of an environmental statute absent rare or unusual circumstances." Ibid. . . . The court found no such circumstances in the instant case. The Ninth Circuit also concluded that the policy declared in OCSLA to expedite exploration of the OCS had been superseded by ANILCA's policy to preserve the subsistence culture of Alaska Natives. . . .

II

[In this part of the opinion, the Court held that the Ninth Circuit had erred in issuing a preliminary injunction. Because the District Court had found that exploration would not significantly affect subsistence uses and the Secretary continued to possess the power to control later stages of the offshore leasing process, there was little probability of irreparable injury to the Native Alaskans. The Court continued. "[O]n the other side of the balance of harms was the fact that the oil company petitioners had committed approximately $70 million to exploration to be conducted during the summer of 1985 which they would have lost without chance of recovery had exploration been enjoined."]

III

Petitioners also contend that the Court of Appeals erred in holding that ANILCA § 810 applies to the OCS. We agree. By its plain language, that provision imposes obligations on federal agencies with respect to decisions affecting use of federal lands *within the boundaries of the State of Alaska*. Section 810 applies to "public lands." Section 102 of ANILCA, 16 U.S.C. § 3102, defines "public lands," and included terms, for purposes of the Act as follows:

"(1) The term 'land' means lands, waters, and interests therein.

"(2) The term 'Federal land' means lands the title to which is in the United States after December 2, 1980.

"(3) The term 'public lands' means land situated *in Alaska* which, after December 2, 1980, are Federal lands, except [land selected by the State of Alaska or granted to the State under the Alaska Statehood Act, 72 Stat. 339, or any other provision of federal law, land selected by a Native Corporation under ANCSA, and lands referred to in ANCSA § 19(b), 43 U.S.C. § 1618(b)]." (*Emphasis in the original.*)

The phrase "in Alaska" has a precise geographic/political meaning. The boundaries of the State of Alaska can be delineated with exactitude. The State of Alaska was "admitted into the Union on an equal footing with the other States," and its boundaries were defined as "all the territory, together with the territorial waters appurtenant thereto, now included in the Territory of Alaska." Alaska Statehood Act (Statehood Act) §§ 1, 2, 72 Stat. 339. Under § 4 of the Submerged Lands Act, 43 U.S.C. § 1312, the seaward boundary of a coastal State extends to a line three miles from its coastline. At that line, the OCS commences. OCSLA § 2(a), 43 U.S.C. § 1331(a). By definition, the OCS is not situated in the State of Alaska. Nevertheless, the Ninth Circuit concluded that "in Alaska" should be construed in a general, "nontechnical" sense to mean the geographic region of Alaska, including the Outer Continental Shelf. 746 F.2d at 579. We reject the notion that Congress was merely waving its hand in the general direction of northwest North America when it defined the scope of ANILCA as "Federal lands" "situated in Alaska." Although language seldom attains the precision of a mathematical symbol, where an expression is capable of precise definition, we will give effect to that meaning absent strong evidence that Congress actually intended another meaning. . . .

■ Justice Stevens, with whom Justice Scalia joins, concurring in part and concurring in the judgment Given the Court's holding that § 810 of the Alaska National Interest Lands Conservation Act (ANILCA), 94 Stat. 2371, 16 U.S.C. § 3120, does not apply to the Outer Continental Shelf, it is unnecessary to decide whether the Court of Appeals applied the proper standard in determining the availability of injunctive relief. Accordingly, I join only Parts I and III of the Court's opinion.■

NOTES AND COMMENTS

1. Is there stronger protection for endangered species or for endangered people in the network of laws governing OCS leasing?

2. A similar conflict between endangered species and endangered people has arisen over the Inuit right to hunt the bowhead whale. Inuits are Eskimo natives of the Arctic, often referred to as "the People of the Whale" because their culture and values are rooted in whale hunting and sharing of the harvest. Whale hunting provides them with food, clothing, light, and heat, and is the central ritual of their community life. Archeological evidence suggests that their ancestors have hunted the bowhead whale for 2,500 years. Yet commercial overhunting of the bowhead has led the

international community, through the International Whaling Commission, to establish a moratorium on bowhead hunting. The moratorium spells death for the Inuit culture. Rupa Gupta argues that Inuits should have a formal role on the Whaling Commission so that their views and their extensive traditional knowledge of the bowhead whales' life cycle can be heard in the regulatory forum. Rupa Gupta, Indigenous Peoples and the International Environmental Community, 74 N.Y.U.L.Rev. 1741 (1999). Any international regime based on principles of sustainable development should integrate indigenous knowledge and practices into a regime of co-management of resources rather than relying only on scientific experts from the Western communities. Only with a heightened sensitivity to the interdependence of Inuit cultural and physical survival will the international community solve the problems posed by the global commons. Historically, indigenous populations have been marginalized and viewed by the international community through a narrow lens of assimilation. A member of one indigenous community expresses the danger inherent in such a perspective:

> "The surest way to kill us is to separate us from our part of the Earth. Once separated, we will either perish in body or our minds and spirits will be altered so that we end up mimicking foreign ways, adopt foreign languages, accept foreign thoughts and build a foreign prison around our indigenous spirits which suffocates [us].... Over time, we lose our identity and eventually die or are cripples as we suffer under the name of 'assimilation' into another society." *Id.* at 784–85.

Chapter 9 considers in more detail the rights of indigenous peoples, particularly in the context of drilling for oil and gas in tropical rainforests. Chapter 9 also discusses oil and gas operations on Arctic permafrost.

3. Why did the majority of the Supreme Court decide the injunction issue? If preliminary injunctions against federal lease sales are automatically granted, it is easier for opponents to block federal programs that are found to be in "probable" conflict with environmental laws. Faced with the real prospect of delays due to preliminary injunctions issued under a vague "public interest" standard, oil companies may withdraw from participating in bids for leases.

In *Sierra Club v. Georgia Power Co.*, 180 F.3d 1309 (11th Cir.1999), the court of appeals upheld the district court's finding that a preliminary injunction requested by the Sierra Club would be adverse to the public interest. The Sierra Club sought the injunction to require Georgia Power to meet the temperature discharge limits in its Clean Water Act permit. Hot water discharges from the plant had resulted in fish kills. The Sierra Club contended that the company could meet its permitted discharge temperatures by reducing the amount of power generated in the plant. The company contended that it could not do so without seriously impacting the power generated throughout its entire electrical grid. Noting that the fish kills were "temporary, not significant and limited to a small percentage of the lake," the court found that the potential harm of reduced electrical power during summer heat waves outweighed the potential injury to the lake.

4. A moratorium is essentially an "injunction" issued by either the Executive or Congressional branch prohibiting leasing. Frustrated with the results of litigation, the coastal states used their political clout, quite successfully, to press for moratoria on OCS leasing off the Pacific and Atlantic coasts, as discussed in the next section.

4.   MORATORIA AND WITHDRAWALS OF LAND FROM LEASING

a.   OFFSHORE

The moratorium movement gained momentum when James Watt became Secretary of the Interior under Ronald Reagan in 1981 and proposed to lease virtually the entire federal offshore area. Almost one billion acres were to be offered for lease during the five-year period from 1982–1987. This amounted to 25 times as much land as was offered during the entire period from 1954 to 1980. In 1982, Congress responded by writing into the Interior's 1982 appropriations bill a prohibition against offering certain areas for lease in California. By 1989, succeeding appropriation bills had extended the moratoria to more than 181 million acres off the coasts of California, the North Atlantic, and the eastern Gulf of Mexico (near Florida). This "off limits" acreage equaled more than twice the acreage that had been leased in the entire history of the OCS program. The reasons for the Congressional moratoria have been summarized as follows:

> They were partly a political response to the intractable approach of former Secretary Watt toward placing one billion acres of OCS for lease sale. The rapid pace and magnitude of leasing proposed under this program undermined the ability of state and local governments to adequately assess the environmental impact of leasing and to plan for OCS development. The Reagan administration's continued support for the areawide leasing concept and its refusal to delete areas of environmental sensitivity and economic importance from lease sales was perceived by coastal states and environmental groups as a resource program weighted heavily toward energy production, irrespective of legitimate state concerns for balanced OCS development. The administration's opposition to continued funding for state coastal management programs, OCS revenue sharing, and consistency requirements lead [sic] states and local citizens to conclude that they were taking all the risks of OCS activity but receiving none of the benefits in return.

G. Kevin Jones, Understanding the Debate over Congressionally Imposed Moratoria on Outer Continental Shelf Leasing, 9 Temp. Envtl L. & Tech. J. 117 at 144 (1990).

The domestic oil industry characterized the moratoria thusly: "If a foreign power had managed to do to us what we have done to ourselves, to shape our energy policy so disastrously, we would call it an act of war." *Id.* at 147. In the first two years of the Watt program, eight of the 15 scheduled lease sales were challenged in court, resulting in major delays and uncertainties in the program rather than Watt's hoped-for acceleration. ARCO forfeited a $30 million investment by abandoning a high potential area off California because of the litigation. *Id.* at 163.

The leasing fiasco and Secretary Watt's other controversial efforts to privatize and develop America's public lands ultimately led to his resignation in 1983 (sparked by his refusal to allow the Beach Boys to perform at a free outdoor concert on the Washington D.C. mall), and to the following ditty:

"Buy the shores of Gitche Gumee
Buy the shining offshore leases
Buy the shining mining leases
Giving me the credit due me,
And you'll be as rich as Croesus
* * *

Thus spake Watt in his ascendence,
Pillar of Conservatism,
Glowing with a great resplendence
Til he brewed a mess of pottage
That created massive schism.
* * *

Even in the Great White Cottage
* * *

Thereupon Watt drew dismissal,
Drew dismissal unexpected
When the Wise Men blew the whistle:
Reagan must be re-elected."

Felicia Lamport, The Song of High Watt (1983), N.Y. Times, Oct. 28 1983, Sec 4 at 19 (copyright Felicia Lamport) as reprinted in George C. Coggins and Doris K. Nagel, "Nothing Beside Remains": The Legal Legacy of James G. Watt's Tenure as Secretary of the Interior on Federal Land Law and Policy, 17 Envt'l Affairs 473 (1990).

President Reagan's subsequent five-year leasing programs were also amply litigated. *See* Edward A. Fitzgerald, Natural Resources Defense Council v. Hodel: The Evolution of Interior's Five Year Outer Continental Shelf Oil and Gas Leasing, 12 Temple Envtl. L. & Tech. J. 1 (1993). Subsequent presidents took the ditty to heart, undoubtedly also influenced by the sharp drop in oil prices in 1981 that crimped demand for federal leases. In 1990, the first President Bush canceled all lease sales pending off California, Washington, Oregon, Florida, and the Georges Bank area off New England (one of the richest fishing areas in the world). *Id.* at 44–45. Further, he issued a moratorium on leasing in these areas until the year 2002. President Clinton's OCS leasing plan for 1997 to 2002 expressly weighted the goals and policies of affected States as a primary factor to consider in federal leasing plans. Information on OCS leasing programs is available at the Minerals Management Services website at http://www.mms.gov.

In 1998, President Clinton extended through the year 2012 the Bush moratoria against drilling off most of the U.S. coastline, except in the Central and Western Gulf of Mexico (excluding the Eastern Gulf of Mexico off Florida) and parts of Alaska. The American Petroleum Institute responded: "The extension is unfortunate because it ignores the near-perfect performance of the American petroleum industry in operating offshore in a safe and environmentally sensitive manner. U.S. government statistics show that natural seeps from the ocean floor introduce 100 times more crude oil into U.S. marine waters than do the petroleum industry's offshore activities." In turn, the Natural Gas Supply Association said cleaner air and increased use of affordable, clean-burning natural gas depended on access to the large gas fields off the nation's coasts. The moratoria made projections of a 35 percent growth in U.S. gas consumption by 2010 or 2015 "virtually untenable." Oil and Gas J., June 22, 1999 at 32.

Even the second President Bush has trod lightly in the political arena surrounding OCS development off the East and West coasts. While strongly advocating the development of increased domestic oil and gas sources, the administration's implementation has focused on opening the federal National Petroleum Reserve in Alaska (situated to the west of the Prudhoe Bay field), spurring more deepwater drilling in the Gulf of Mexico, and providing speedier access to federal lands in the Rockies, Wyoming and Montana. The OCS moratoria on the populated East and West coasts (and opening up the Arctic National Wildlife Refuge) are simply too hot to handle.

However, record-high oil and gas prices in summer 2005 led Congress to authorize, in Section 357 of the National Energy Act of 2005, a controversial inventory of OCS oil and gas resources to be completed in six months which would identify and explain all laws, regulations, moratoria, lease stipulations, programs and processes (federal, state or local) that restrict or impede development of identified OCS resources. Some non-coastal state senators had called for such an inventory so that policymakers could more accurately assess the costs and benefits of lifting the moratoria. Even this information-gathering proposal had drawn the ire of Florida's senators who threatened a filibuster (but did not follow through in light of gasoline prices close to $3.00/gallon) if such an inventory were included in any energy bill.

Public opinion research shows that even Californians (especially lower-income Californians) will strongly increase their support for drilling off their own coast when gasoline prices rise substantially. See Eric R.A.N. Smith, Support for Offshore Oil and Gas Drilling Among the California Public, University of California Energy Inst. Working Paper, available at www.ucei.org. Smith traces the following pattern of support for drilling off the California coast: Support grew at the end of the 1970s, following the OPEC oil embargo; then peaked in 1980; fell gradually during the 1980s as gasoline prices fell; dropped sharply in 1989 when the *Exxon Valdez* oil spill occurred; continued to decline; and then turned sharply upwards in the period from 1998 to 2001 when gasoline prices rose significantly (to about $1.50 per gallon).

Some senators have proposed legislation that would allow the citizens of coastal states to decide if they want to waive the federal moratoria off their coasts, but the leasing would be restricted to allow only gas wells (thus avoiding potential oil spills) drilled many miles from shore. The bill's sponsors estimate that 70 trillion cubic feet (TCF) of natural gas reserves exist in moratoria areas, and 16 billion barrels of oil. (The U.S. uses about 23 TCF of gas a year.) The massive Gulf Coast petrochemical industries in Louisiana, Texas, and Alabama have been seriously impacted by the recent extraordinarily high prices of natural gas. Republican Senator Mel Martinez from Florida responded that he was "dead set" against any OCS-related laws that would weaken any moratoria and allow drilling off neighboring states that could "affect" Florida. Ben Geman, New Offshore Access Language in Doubt as Energy Debate Begins, Environment & Energy Daily, June 14, 2005. Senate Energy Committee leaders agreed to continue the ban on drilling off Florida in any energy bill. Florida Governor Jeb Bush, the president's brother, has been an outspoken opponent of drilling off Florida, although he has stated that he would be satisfied with a ban limited to the first 100 miles off Florida's coasts. *See generally*, Edward A. Fitzgerald, The Seaweed Rebellion: Florida's Experience with Offshore Energy Development, 18 J. Land Use & Envtl. L. 1 (2002).

Can recalcitrant coastal states be lured into accepting oil and gas development through a revenue-sharing mechanism that gives them more of the OCS bounty? States currently receive 50 percent of federal onshore oil and gas revenues, but such largesse does not extend to the OCS. Six states with OCS production began to receive 27 percent of OCS revenues in 1986 under section 1337(g) of OCSLA, but only from federal leases directly bordering their submerged lands, *i.e.*, within 3 miles of the border of the state-owned coastal waters. However, much OCS production is now located much further out on the continental shelf, and until 2005, there was no revenue-sharing with the states from these OCS leases.

Senator Mary Landrieu of Louisiana has been especially active in promoting increased shares to the states. Louisiana's coastline has been severely impacted by a network of canals dredged by pipeline companies for their transportation facilities or by oil companies to float drilling equipment to state-owned coastal lands. These canals have contributed to erosion of Louisiana's coastal wetlands; in short, Louisiana is sinking and shrinking. *See, e.g.,* Terrebonne Parish School Board v. Columbia Gulf Transmission Co., 290 F.3d 303 (5th Cir. 2002); and *see generally,* Edward A. Fitzgerald, The Conservation and Reinvestment Act of 1999: Outer Continental Shelf Revenue Sharing, 30 ELR 10165 (Mar. 2000).

The National Energy Act of 2005, section 384, authorized payments of $1 billion (over four years) to coastal states and their political subdivisions to be used for coastal restoration and preservation, planning assistance, and mitigation of the impacts of OCS activities through onshore infrastructure and public service needs. Some OCS lease revenues are already earmarked for the Land and Water Conservation Fund, created in 1965, to finance new recreational areas and improve existing national parks, refuges, and forests. LWCF grants to states have added two million acres to state and local government recreational lands. However, actual spending from this fund has been far below the amounts authorized. *See* Robert E. Glicksman & George C. Coggins, Federal Recreation Land Policy: The Rise and Decline of the Land and Water Conservation Fund, 9 Colum. J. Envt'l L. 125 (1984).

If states cannot be "bought off" to accept OCS leasing activities off their coastlines, will oil companies that have paid millions of dollars in bonus money for leases that cannot be explored or developed be entitled to compensation? In *Marathon Oil Co. v. United States,* 158 F.3d 1253 (Fed. Cir. 1998), *reversed sub. nom., Mobil Oil Exploration & Producing Southeast, Inc.,* 530 U.S. 604 (2000), the Court of Appeals for the Federal Circuit refused to order restitution of $156 million in bonuses paid by Marathon and Mobil for leases 45 miles off the coast of North Carolina. This court held that the two oil companies were sophisticated lessees who bargained "with their legal eyes wide open" for nothing more than a lottery ticket (citing the precedent of *Secretary of Interior v. California,* 464 U.S. 312 (1984), excerpted in the text *supra*). The leases were a gamble: They gave the companies the right to explore *if* they could secure a state consistency certificate under the CZMA or a federal override of a state's refusal to find that the federal leasing was consistent with its approved coastal plan. Recall the clear description of "Stage 3, Exploration Plans," of the federal leasing process in *SOI v. California, supra.*

The U.S. Supreme Court, with a lone dissent by Justice Stevens, reversed and ordered the restitution of the $156 million in the following opinion which reads like a treatise in first-year Contracts.

Mobil Oil Exploration & Producing Southeast, Inc. v. United States

530 U.S. 604 (2000).

■ BREYER, J. Two oil companies, petitioners here, seek restitution of $156 million they paid the Government in return for lease contracts giving them rights to explore for and develop oil off the North Carolina coast. The rights were not absolute, but were conditioned on the companies' obtaining a set of further governmental permissions. The companies claim that the Government repudiated the contracts when it denied them certain elements of the permission-seeking opportunities that the contracts had promised. We agree that the Government broke its promise; it repudiated the contracts; and it must give the companies their money back.

I A

A description at the outset of the few basic contract law principles applicable to this case will help the reader understand the significance of the complex factual circumstances that follow. "When the United States enters into contract relations, its rights and duties therein are governed generally by the law applicable to contracts between private individuals." *United States v. Winstar Corp.*, 518 U.S. 839, 895, 116 S.Ct. 2432, 135 L.Ed.2d 964 (1996) (plurality opinion). The Restatement of Contracts reflects many of the principles of contract law that are applicable to this case.... [T]he relevant principles specify that, when one party to a contract repudiates that contract, the other party "is entitled to restitution for any benefit that he has conferred on" the repudiating party "by way of part performance or reliance." Restatement (Second) of Contracts § 373 (1979) (hereinafter Restatement). The Restatement explains that "repudiation" is a "statement by the obligor to the obligee indicating that the obligor will commit a breach that would of itself give the obligee a claim for damages for total breach." *Id.*, § 250. And "total breach" is a breach that "so substantially impairs the value of the contract to the injured party at the time of the breach that it is just in the circumstances to allow him to recover damages based on all his remaining rights to performance." *Id.*, § 243.

As applied to this case, these principles amount to the following: If the Government said it would break, or did break, an important contractual promise, thereby "substantially impair[ing] the value of the contract[s]" to the companies, *ibid.*, then (unless the companies waived their rights to restitution) the Government must give the companies their money back. And it must do so whether the contracts would, or would not, ultimately have proved financially beneficial to the companies. The Restatement illustrates this point as follows:

> "A contracts to sell a tract of land to B for $100,000. After B has made a part payment of $20,000, A wrongfully refuses to transfer title. B can recover the $20,000 in restitution. The result is the same even if the market price of the land is only $70,000, so that performance would have been disadvantageous to B." *Id.*, § 373, Comment a, Illustration 1.

B

In 1981, in return for up-front "bonus" payments to the United States of about $158 million (plus annual rental payments), the companies received 10-year renewable lease contracts with the United States. In these contracts, the United States promised the companies, among other things, that they could explore for oil off the North Carolina coast and develop any oil that they found (subject to further royalty payments) provided that the companies received exploration and development permissions in accordance with various statutes and regulations to which the lease contracts were made "subject."

The statutes and regulations, the terms of which in effect were incorporated into the contracts, made clear that obtaining the necessary permissions might not be an easy matter. In particular, the Outer Continental Shelf Lands Act (OCSLA), 67 Stat. 462, as amended, 43 U.S.C. § 1331 et seq. (1994 ed. and Supp. III), and the Coastal Zone Management

Act of 1972 (CZMA), 16 U.S.C. § 1451 *et seq.*, specify that leaseholding companies wishing to explore and drill must successfully complete the following four procedures.

First, a company must prepare and obtain Department of the Interior approval for a Plan of Exploration. 43 U.S.C. § 1340(c). Interior must approve a submitted Exploration Plan unless it finds, after "consider[ing] available relevant environmental information," § 1346(d), that the proposed exploration

> "would probably cause serious harm or damage to life (including fish and other aquatic life), to property, to any mineral . . ., to the national security or defense, or to the marine, coastal, or human environment." § 1334(a)(2)(A)(i) [in which event the statute provides that the Secretary may "cancel such lease and the lessee shall be entitled to compensation. . . ."]

Where approval is warranted, Interior must act quickly—within "thirty days" of the company's submission of a proposed Plan. § 1340(c)(1).

Second, the company must obtain an exploratory well drilling permit. To do so, it must certify (under CZMA) that its Exploration Plan is consistent with the coastal zone management program of each affected State. 16 U.S.C. § 1456(c)(3). If a State objects, the certification fails, unless the Secretary of Commerce overrides the State's objection. If Commerce rules against the State, then Interior may grant the permit. § 1456(c)(3)(A).

Third, where waste discharge into ocean waters is at issue, the company must obtain a National Pollutant Discharge Elimination System permit from the Environmental Protection Agency. 33 U.S.C. §§ 1311(a), 1342(a). It can obtain this permit only if affected States agree that its Exploration Plan is consistent with the state coastal zone management programs or (as just explained) the Secretary of Commerce overrides the state objections. 16 U.S.C. § 1456.

Fourth, if exploration is successful, the company must prepare, and obtain Interior approval for, a Development and Production Plan—a Plan that describes the proposed drilling and related environmental safeguards. 43 U.S.C. § 1351. Again, Interior's approval is conditioned upon certification that the Plan is consistent with state coastal zone management plans—a certification to which States can object, subject to Commerce Department override. § 1351(a)(3).

C

The events at issue here concern the first two steps of the process just described—Interior's consideration of a submitted Exploration Plan and the companies' submission of the CZMA "consistency certification" necessary to obtain an exploratory well drilling permit. The relevant circumstances are the following:

1. In 1981, the companies and the Government entered into the lease contracts. The companies paid the Government $158 million in up-front cash "bonus" payments.

2. In 1989, the companies, Interior, and North Carolina entered into a memorandum of understanding. In that memorandum, the companies promised that they would submit an initial draft Exploration Plan to North Carolina before they submitted their final Exploration Plan to Interior. Interior promised that it would prepare an environmental report on the initial draft. It also agreed to suspend the companies' annual lease payments (about $250,000 per year) while the companies prepared the initial draft and while any state objections to the companies' CZMA consistency certifications were being worked out, with the life of each lease being extended accordingly.

3. In September 1989, the companies submitted their initial draft Exploration Plan to North Carolina. Ten months later, Interior issued the promised ("informal" pre-submission) environmental report, after a review which all parties concede was "extensive and intensive." App. 179 (deposition of David Courtland O'Neal, former Assistant Secretary of the Interior) (agreeing that the review was "the most extensive and intensive" ever "afforded an exploration well in the outer continental shelf (OCS) program"). Interior concluded that the proposed exploration would not "significantly affec[t]" the marine environment or "the quality of the human environment."

4. On August 20, 1990, the companies submitted both their final Exploration Plan and their CZMA "consistency certification" to Interior.

5. Just two days earlier, on August 18, 1990, a new law, the Outer Banks Protection Act (OBPA), § 6003, 104 Stat. 555, had come into effect. That law prohibited the Secretary of the Interior from approving any Exploration Plan or Development and Production Plan or to award any drilling permit until (a) a new OBPA-created Environmental Sciences Review Panel had reported to the Secretary, (b) the Secretary had certified to Congress that he had sufficient information to make these OCSLA-required approval decisions, and (c) Congress had been in session an additional 45 days, but (d) in no event could he issue an approval or permit for the next 13 months (until October 1991). § 6003(c)(3). OBPA also required the Secretary, in his certification, to explain and justify in detail any differences between his own certified conclusions and the new Panel's recommendations. § 6003(c)(3)(A)(ii)(II).

6. About five weeks later, and in light of the new statute, Interior wrote a letter to the Governor of North Carolina with a copy to petitioner Mobil. It said that the final submitted Exploration Plan "is deemed to be approvable in all respects." It added:

> "[W]e are required to approve an Exploration Plan unless it is inconsistent with applicable law or because it would result in serious harm to the environment. Because we have found that Mobil's Plan fully complies with the law and will have only negligible effect on the

environment, we are not authorized to disapprove the Plan or require its modification." App. to Pet. for Cert. in No. 99–253, at 194a (letter from Regional Director Bruce Weetman to the Honorable James G. Martin, Governor of North Carolina, dated Sept. 28, 1996).

But, it noted, the new law, the "Outer Banks Protection Act (OBPA) of 1990 . . . prohibits the approval of any Exploration Plan at this time." It concluded, "because we are currently prohibited from approving it, the Plan will remain on file until the requirements of the OBPA are met." In the meantime a "suspension has been granted to all leases offshore the State of North Carolina."

About 18 months later, the Secretary of the Interior, after receiving the new Panel's report, certified to Congress that he had enough information to consider the companies' Exploration Plan. He added, however, that he would not consider the Plan until he received certain further studies that the new Panel had recommended.

7. In November 1990, North Carolina objected to the companies' CZMA consistency certification on the ground that Mobil had not provided sufficient information about possible environmental impact. A month later, the companies asked the Secretary of Commerce to override North Carolina's objection.

8. In 1994, the Secretary of Commerce rejected the companies' override request, relying in large part on the fact that the new Panel had found a lack of adequate information in respect to certain environmental issues.

9. In 1996, Congress repealed OBPA. § 109, 110 Stat. 1321–177.

D

In October 1992, after all but the two last-mentioned events had taken place, petitioners joined a breach-of-contract lawsuit brought in the Court of Federal Claims. On motions for summary judgment, the court found that the United States had broken its contractual promise to follow OCSLA's provisions, in particular the provision requiring Interior to approve an Exploration Plan that satisfied OCSLA's requirements within 30 days of its submission to Interior. The United States thereby repudiated the contracts. And that repudiation entitled the companies to restitution of the up-front cash "bonus" payments it had made. *Conoco Inc. v. United States*, 35 Fed. Cl. 309 (1996).

A panel of the Court of Appeals for the Federal Circuit reversed, one judge dissenting. The panel held that the Government's refusal to consider the companies' final Exploration Plan was not the "operative cause" of any failure to carry out the contracts' terms because the State's objection to the companies' CZMA "consistency statement" would have prevented the companies from exploring regardless. 177 F.3d 1331 (C.A.Fed.1999).

We granted certiorari to review the Federal Circuit's decision.

II

The record makes clear (1) that OCSLA required Interior to approve "within thirty days" a submitted Exploration Plan that satisfies OCSLA's requirements, (2) that Interior told Mobil the companies' submitted Plan met those requirements, (3) that Interior told Mobil it would not approve the companies' submitted Plan for at least 13 months, and likely longer, and (4) that Interior did not approve (or disapprove) the Plan, ever. The Government does not deny that the contracts, made "pursuant to" and "subject to" OCSLA, incorporated OCSLA provisions as promises. The Government further concedes, as it must, that relevant contract law entitles a contracting party to restitution if the other party "substantially" breached a contract or communicated its intent to do so.... Yet the Government denies that it must refund the companies' money.

This is because, in the Government's view, it did not breach the contracts or communicate its intent to do so; any breach was not "substantial"; and the companies waived their rights to restitution regardless. We shall consider each of these arguments in turn.

A

The Government's "no breach" arguments depend upon the contract provisions that "subject" the contracts to various statutes and regulations. Those provisions state that the contracts are "subject to" (1) OCSLA, (2) "Sections 302 and 303 of the Department of Energy Organization Act," (3) "all regulations issued pursuant to such statutes and in existence upon the effective date of" the contracts, (4) "all regulations issued pursuant to such statutes in the future which provide for the prevention of waste and the conservation" of Outer Continental Shelf resources, and (5) "all other applicable statutes and regulations." The Government says that these provisions incorporate into the contracts, not only the OCSLA provisions we have mentioned, but also certain other statutory provisions and regulations that, in the Government's view, granted Interior the legal authority to refuse to approve the submitted Exploration Plan, while suspending the leases instead.

. . . .

... [T]he Government refers to 30 C.F.R. § 250.110(b)(4) (1999), formerly codified at 30 C.F.R. § 250.10(b)(4) (1997), a regulation stating that "[t]he Regional Supervisor may ... direct a suspension of any operation or activity ... [when the] suspension is necessary for the implementation of the requirements of the National Environmental Policy Act or to conduct an environmental analysis." The Government says that this regulation permitted the Secretary of the Interior to suspend the companies' leases because that suspension was "necessary ... to conduct an environmental analysis," namely, the analysis demanded by the new statute, OBPA.

The "environmental analysis" referred to, however, is an analysis the need for which was created by OBPA, a later enacted statute. The lease contracts say that they are subject to then-existing regulations and to certain future regulations, those issued pursuant to OCSLA and §§ 302 and 303 of the Department of Energy Organization Act. This explicit reference to future regulations makes it clear that the catchall provision that references "all other applicable . . . regulations," must include only statutes and regulations already existing at the time of the contract, a conclusion not questioned here by the Government. Hence, these provisions mean that the contracts are not subject to future regulations promulgated under other statutes, such as new statutes like OBPA. Without some such contractual provision limiting the Government's power to impose new and different requirements, the companies would have spent $158 million to buy next to nothing. In any event, the Court of Claims so interpreted the lease; the Federal Circuit did not disagree with that interpretation; nor does the Government here dispute it.

. . . .

Third, the Government refers to OCSLA, 43 U.S.C. § 1334(a)(1), which, after granting Interior rulemaking authority, says that Interior's

"regulations . . . shall include . . . provisions . . . for the suspension of any operation . . . pursuant to any lease . . . if there is a threat of serious, irreparable, or immediate harm or damage to life . . ., to property, to any mineral deposits . . ., or to the marine, coastal, or human environment."

The Government points to the OBPA Conference Report, which says that any OBPA-caused delay is "related to . . . environmental protection" and to the need "for the collection and analysis of crucial oceanographic, ecological, and socioeconomic data," to "prevent a public harm." H.R. Conf. Rep. No. 101–653, p. 163 (1990). At oral argument, the Government noted that the OBPA mentions "tourism" in North Carolina as a "major industry which is subject to potentially significant disruption by offshore oil or gas development." § 6003(b)(3). From this, the Government infers that the pre-existing OCSLA provision authorized the suspension in light of a "threat of . . . serious harm" to a "human environment."

The fatal flaw in this argument, however, arises out of the Interior Department's own statement—a statement made when citing OBPA to explain its approval delay. Interior then said that the Exploration Plan "fully complies" with current legal requirements. And the OCSLA statutory provision quoted above was the most pertinent of those current requirements. The Government did not deny the accuracy of Interior's statement, either in its brief filed here or its brief filed in the Court of Appeals. Insofar as the Government means to suggest that the new statute, OBPA, changed the relevant OCSLA standard (or that OBPA language and history somehow constitute findings Interior must incorporate by reference), it must mean that OBPA in effect created a new requirement. For the reasons set out however, any such new requirement would not be incorporated into the contracts.

. . . .

We conclude, for these reasons, that the Government violated the contracts. Indeed, as Interior pointed out in its letter to North Carolina, the new statute, OBPA, required Interior to impose the contract-violating delay. ("The [OBPA] contains provisions that specifically prohibit the Minerals Management Service from approving any Exploration Plan, approving any Application for Permit to Drill, or permitting any drilling offshore the State of North Carolina until at least October 1, 1991"). It therefore made clear to Interior and to the companies that the United States had to violate the contracts' terms and would continue to do so.

. . . .

We do not say that the changes made by the statute were unjustified. We say only that they were changes of a kind that the contracts did not foresee. . . . Hence, in communicating to the companies its intent to follow OBPA, the United States was communicating its intent to violate the contracts.

B

The Government next argues that any violation of the contracts' terms was not significant; hence there was no "substantial" or "material" breach that could have amounted to a "repudiation." In particular, it says that OCSLA's 30–day approval period "does not function as the 'essence' of these agreements." The Court of Claims concluded, however, that timely and fair consideration of a submitted Exploration Plan was a "necessary reciprocal obligation," indeed, that any "contrary interpretation would render the bargain illusory." 35 Fed. Cl., at 327. We agree.

We recognize that the lease contracts gave the companies more than rights to obtain approvals. They also gave the companies rights to explore for, and to develop, oil. But the need to obtain Government approvals so qualified the likely future enjoyment of the exploration and development rights that the contract, in practice, amounted primarily to an opportunity to try to obtain exploration and development rights in accordance with the procedures and under the standards specified in the cross-referenced statutes and regulations. Under these circumstances, if the companies did not at least buy a promise that the Government would not deviate significantly from those procedures and standards, then what did they buy?

The Government's modification of the contract-incorporated processes was not technical or insubstantial. It did not announce an (OBPA-required) approval delay of a few days or weeks, but of 13 months minimum, and likely much longer. The delay turned out to be at least four years. And lengthy delays matter, particularly where several successive agency approvals are at stake. Whether an applicant approaches Commerce with an Interior Department approval already in hand can make a difference (as can failure to have obtained that earlier approval). Moreover, as we have pointed out, OBPA changed the contract-referenced procedures in several other ways as well. . . .

D

Finally, the Government argues that repudiation could not have hurt the companies. Since the companies could not have met the CZMA consistency requirements, they could not have explored (or ultimately drilled) for oil in any event. Hence, OBPA caused them no damage. As the Government puts it, the companies have already received "such damages as were actually caused by the [Exploration Plan approval] delay," namely, none. This argument, however, misses the basic legal point. The oil companies do not seek damages for breach of contract. They seek restitution of their initial payments. Because the Government repudiated the lease contracts, the law entitles the companies to that restitution whether the contracts would, or would not, ultimately have produced a financial gain or led them to obtain a definite right to explore. If a lottery operator fails to deliver a purchased ticket, the purchaser can get his money back—whether or not he eventually would have won the lottery. And if one party to a contract, whether oil company or ordinary citizen, advances the other party money, principles of restitution normally require the latter, upon repudiation, to refund that money. Restatement § 373.

III

Contract law expresses no view about the wisdom of OBPA. We have examined only that statute's consistency with the promises that the earlier contracts contained. We find that the oil companies gave the United States $158 million in return for a contractual promise to follow the terms of pre-existing statutes and regulations. The new statute prevented the Government from keeping that promise. The breach substantially impair[ed] the value of the contract[s]. *Id.*, § 243. And therefore the Government must give the companies their money back.

■ JUSTICE STEVENS, dissenting. Since the 1953 passage of the Outer Continental Shelf Lands Act (OCSLA), 43 U.S.C. § 1331 et seq., the United States Government has conducted more than a hundred lease sales of the type at stake today, and bidders have paid the United States more than $55 billion for the opportunity to develop the mineral resources made available under those leases. The United States, as lessor, and petitioners, as lessees, clearly had a mutual interest in the successful exploration, development, and production of oil in the Manteo Unit pursuant to the leases executed in 1981. If production were achieved, the United States would benefit both from the substantial royalties it would receive and from the significant addition to the Nation's energy supply. Self-interest, as well as its duties under the leases, thus led the Government to expend substantial resources over the course of 19 years in the hope of seeing this project realized.

From the outset, however, it was apparent that the Outer Banks project might not succeed for a variety of reasons. Among those was the risk that the State of North Carolina would exercise its right to object to the completion of the project. That was a risk that the parties knowingly assumed. They did not, however, assume the risk that Congress would enact additional legislation that would delay the completion of what would obviously be a lengthy project in any event. I therefore agree with the Court that the Government did breach its contract with petitioners in failing to approve, within 30 days of its receipt, the plan of exploration petitioners submitted.

I do not, however, believe that the appropriate remedy for the Government's breach is for petitioners to recover their full initial investment.... [T]he remedy ordered by the Court is excessive.■

NOTES AND COMMENTS

1. Justice Stevens, in lone dissent, obviously agreed that the federal government had breached its contract. However, he viewed the context quite differently. Justice Stevens found that the DOI made every effort to advance the leasing. It worked with the lessees and the recalcitrant state through drafts and final versions of the exploration plan and environmental impact statements. Even after the OBPA was passed, the DOI pursued additional studies and research. The lessees also treated the leases as if they were continuing in effect, thereby, in Stevens' view, waiving their right to assert repudiation and rescission damages. Here are the time sequence and events of importance to Justice Stevens:

- Aug. 18, 1990—Congress passes OBPA.

- Aug. 20, 1990—Despite OBPA, lessees submit final exploration plan, triggering DOI's duty to review within 30 days. The DOI transmits the exploration plan to the state, receives the state's comments, and prepares on environmental assessment. Both DOI and the lessees continue to act as if the lease has not been repudiated.

- Sept. 19, 1990—DOI misses the review deadline.

- Sept. 21, 1990—DOI sends letter to lessees explaining the lack of any review due to OBPA and leases are suspended (not cancelled).

- Nov. 19, 1999—North Carolina files its formal CZMA objections.

- December 1990—Lessees seek to have Secretary of Commerce override the objections. The Secretary of Commerce and the DOI spend much time and money soliciting comments and reports to evaluate the lessee's request to override the state.

- Sept. 12, 1994—Commerce declines to override the state.

- The lessees seek additional lease suspensions while appealing the Commerce decision.

In Stevens' view the question was whether the government's actions entitled the lessees to restitution rather than the usual remedy of damages for a breach of contract. He quoted the relevant blackletter rules for repudiation and restitution: An injured party may obtain restitution only if the action "so substantially impairs the value of the contract to the injured party ... that it is just in the circumstances to allow him to recover damages based on all his remaining rights to performance." Such a standard required the Court to look at the equities of the situation as a whole.

Using these rules and his view of the facts, Stevens did not think that the actions by the government amounted either to a repudiation (anticipatory or otherwise) of the contracts or to a total breach by way of neglecting an "essential" contractual provision. First, the government continued to perform under the contractual terms as best it could, even after the OBPA's passage. Second, the breach-by-delay acknowledged by MMS in its September 21 letter was not "of sufficient gravity that, if the breach actually occurred, it would of itself give the obligee a claim for damages for total breach." Indeed, the lessees' own conduct showed that they did not consider the MMS/DOI to have fully repudiated the leases; they requested that the lease suspensions remain in effect, even after the adverse decision from Commerce.

Absent repudiation, Justice Stevens asked whether "the nature of the Government's breach was so 'essential' or 'total' in the scope of the parties' contractual relationship as to justify the remedy of restitution." The blackletter rule from Farnsworth on Contracts stated that a breach justified restitution if it "deprive[d] the injured party of the benefit that it justifiably expected."

Based on the time sequence and events outlined above, Justice Stevens found that the impact of the government's breach was "close to none"—a mere 60 days of delay. His opinion concludes:

> Sixty days after the Government entered into breach—from September 19, 1990, to November 19, 1990—the State of North Carolina filed its formal objection to CZMA certification. . . . While this objection remained in effect, the project could not go forward unless the objection was set aside by the Secretary of Commerce. Thus, the Government's breach effectively delayed matters during the period between September 19, 1990, and November 19, 1990. Thereafter, implementation was contractually precluded by North Carolina.

While Justice Stevens agreed with the majority that "lengthy delays matter" and could form the basis of substantial breach of contract, in this case, the lessees knew that their venture was "rife with possibilities" for long delays. While the lessees could not foresee that the OBPA would be enacted, nonetheless, Stevens concluded:

> Any long-term venture of this complexity and significance is bound to be a gamble. The fact that North Carolina was holding all the aces should not give petitioners the right now to play with an entirely new deck of cards. . . . A breach that itself caused at most a delay of two months in a protracted enterprise of this magnitude does not justify the $156 million draconian remedy that the Court delivers.

2.   Does it surprise you that the Supreme Court granted writ on a case which revolves around basic principles of private contract law? Do the major differences between the majority and the dissent involve interpretations of law or of the underlying facts in the case and how to apply them to an agreed-upon body of law? How can an OCS lessee be reasonably justified in expecting quick approval of a controversial leasing decision?

3. Should the Secretary of Interior, despite the OBPA, have issued approval to the POE? If so, and the state of North Carolina had secured a judicial decree enjoining the Secretary's actions, would the Secretary then have been authorized to suspend the leases? One of the OCSLA regulations reads as follows:

> The Regional Supervisor may also direct . . . suspension of any operation or activity, including production, because . . . (7) [t]he suspension is necessary to comply with judicial decrees prohibiting production or any other operation or activity, or the permitting of those activities. . . . 30 C.F.R. § 250.10(b)(7) (1990).

Would this sequence of events have affected the majority's opinion?

4. Why was the Outer Banks Protection Act passed in 1990? As you will soon learn, the *Exxon Valdez* oil spill occurred on March 23, 1989, reviving memories of the Santa Barbara platform spill.

5. Should one state be allowed to deprive U.S. citizens of the bounty of the OCS? Are these federal lands your land? Our land? North Carolina's or Florida's land (because OCS drilling off North Carolina could "affect" Florida)?

6. *Review problem.* There are 36 federal oil and gas leases still extant off the coast of California, the legacy of *SOI v. California*'s holding that the CZMA, as originally passed, did not allow California to challenge the federal government's decision to conduct a lease sale. (The leases were granted between 1968 and 1986, before Congress amended the Coastal Zone Management Act in 1990 to override the holding in *SOI v. California*.) The leases have never produced any oil or gas; without production, they would expire. Over the years, and again in 1999 (under President Clinton), the Department of Interior granted suspensions to these leases, keeping them in effect. The state of California asserted that it had the authority to review these lease suspensions for consistency with its coastal management plan. The United States argued that the suspensions did not have the potential to affect the coastal environment and so did not require a state's consistency review. California brought sought alleging that the federal government was violating both the CZMA and NEPA (no EIS was prepared).

Based on your readings in this section, which sovereign is likely to win this suit, and why? Is your opinion influenced by the "brief recollection" of the 1968 blowout and oil spill which forms the introductory section of the Ninth Circuit Court of Appeals' answer to the question?

> Five miles off the shore of the small beach town of Summerland, California, at 10:45 a.m. on Tuesday, January 28, 1969, crews on Union Oil Company offshore Platform Alpha were pulling the drilling tube out of well A–21 in order to assess their progress. Mud began to ooze up from the depths through the well shaft. . . . Within minutes, tons of mud spewed out of the top of the well propelled by a blast of natural gas. . . . The unlined walls of the well shaft gave way and oil poured into the surrounding geological formation under the sea floor. As the pressure continued to build, the oil burst upward through the

roof of the Venture Anticline, ripped five long gashes in the ocean floor, and rose 188 feet through the blue-green waters of the Santa Barbara channel [spreading a tar-black patch seaward over 800 square miles of ocean for a week, after which the wind shifted and drove the oil onto 30 miles of coastal beaches where an "acrid stench" clung to the shoreline for weeks on end].

* * *

The nation was confronted with an environmental disaster of unprecedented proportions that might have been avoided but for a failure of federal oversight. A federal regulator had approved Union Oil's request to waive safety requirements that called for well shafts to be lined with hardened casing to prevent just the type of accident that occurred.

See *California v. Norton*, 311 F.3d 1162 (9th Cir. 2002).

7.   Can a FERC license for a hydroelectric power plant located 30 miles inland from the ocean trigger the need for a consistency review under the Coastal Zone Management Act? What if the National Oceanic and Atmospheric Administration (NOAA, the office within the Department of Commerce that administers the consistency reviews) has approved a map of the "coastal zone" which extends inland this distance based on a county's borders? See Mountain Rhythm Resources v. FERC, 302 F. 3d 958 (9th Cir. 2002).

8.   California is currently seeking to prohibit permanently all drilling off California and have the federal government buy back the leases. In May 2002, President George W. Bush promised to buy back the OCS leases off the Florida Panhandle for $115 million after Florida rejected Chevron's development plan for the geologically promising Destin Dome area of the Gulf. Chevron had promptly sued the DOI under the *Mobil v. U.S.* precedent. Chevron settled the suit after the buyback payment. The oil companies in the Santa Barbara Channel have brought suit against the federal government for breach of contract. The Bush administration does not seem inclined to buy back the California leases, as of July 2005, despite the election of a new Republican governor of California, Arnold Schwarzenegger, who opposes federal leasing activity off California's shores.

9.   Because of the extensive moratoria, there has been almost no opportunity for agencies, state officials, or courts to test the difference between "directly affecting" and "affecting" in post–1990 consistency certifications.

10.   The Federal Consistency Coordinator of NOAA stated in 2003 that "the CZMA is compatible with and indeed supports, the viability of the offshore oil and gas industry." David W. Kaiser, The Coastal Zone Management Act Furthers Offshore Oil and Gas Development and Supports a National Energy Policy, 54 Inst. on Oil & Gas, Chapter 13 at 13–8 (2003). In support of his statement, he presented data showing that, since 1978, MMS has approved over 10,600 Exploration Plans and over 6,000 Development Plans. During this time, only 14 instances occurred where a lessee appealed a state's consistency objection to the Secretary of Commerce

resulting in a decision at that level. In 7 of the 14 cases, the Secretary overrode the state objection, in the other 7, he did not.

Perhaps this attitude explains why the CZMA survived, largely unscathed, in the National Energy Act of 2005. Section 381 of the 2005 Act expedites appeals of state consistency objections by allowing the Secretary of Interior to close the record in any such appeal within 160 days of publishing notice of the objection in the Federal Register. Within 60 days of the period after closure of the record, the Secretary must issue a decision, with no extension allowed past 75 days. What effect do you think this provision will have? Section 382 also provides for a consolidated record of all agencies' actions in CZMA consistency appeals.

More importantly, Section 311 of the 2005 Act, which gives exclusive jurisdiction to FERC over the siting of onshore LNG terminals, specifically provides that nothing in the section will affect the rights of the states under the CZMA. LNG siting issues are discussed in Chapter 9, Section C.

b.   ONSHORE

Withdrawals of federal onshore land from oil and gas and other resource development have also occurred throughout our nation's history. For example, the Congressional branch has often acted to create national parks and wilderness areas in which development is forbidden. When Congress has refused to act quickly to protect areas against commercial activity, presidents have acted unilaterally under the Antiquities Act of 1906. This Act authorizes the President "in his discretion to declare by public proclamation historic landmarks, historic and prehistoric structures and other objects of historic or scientific interest that are situated upon the lands owned or controlled by the Government of the United States to be national monuments." 16 U.S.C.A. § 431. President Roosevelt withdrew 270,000 acres of the Grand Canyon from mining claims under this Act in 1920.

More recently, President Clinton used the 1906 Act to set aside 1.8 million acres in southeast Utah's canyonlands as the Grand Staircase Escalante National Monument. The President's move blocked plans by a Dutch company, Andalex Resources, to develop a coal reserve twice the size of Manhattan located in the middle of the set-aside area. The state of Utah owns about 180,000 acres of scattered tracts in the monument areas. Income from these state lands supports public education in Utah. Senator Frank Murkowski (R–Alaska), chair of the Senate Energy and Natural Resources Committee, issued a statement claiming that the president's decision would cost the Utah education system as much as $1 billion in lost revenues from coal and other mineral development. He also claimed that the monument might be locking up as much as 62 billion tons of clean, low-sulfur coal, which would force utilities to burn dirtier coal and exacerbate air pollution. Daily Executive Report, Sept. 19, 1996, at A–31.

The new National Monument also contains 59 federal oil and gas leases owned by Conoco covering 108,000 acres. In September 1997, the Interior Department's Bureau of Land Management approved exploratory drilling of a single well by Conoco on an existing lease to test for the existence of millions of barrels of oil suspected to lie underneath the red rocks. Secretary Bruce Babbitt viewed a fight over this permit as unwarranted because the odds of striking oil were so slight and President Clinton's proclamation creating the monument recognized valid existing rights. Other federal agencies and environmentalists warned that the precedent could lead to "widespread development, marking the area for decades to come with tall rigs, networks of roads and pipelines, bright lights blotting out the stars above ballfield-size drilling pads, and impoundments of toxic drilling mud despoiling pristine habitats." John H. Cushman, Jr., U.S. Approves Test Oil Drilling On National Parkland in Utah, New York Times, Sept. 9, 1997, at A1.

The Southern Utah Wilderness Alliance (SUWA) and the Sierra Club challenged the BLM's decision, but the Interior Board of Land Appeals (IBLA) held that the BLM had made a convincing case that no significant impact would result. *See* Southern Utah Wilderness Alliance, 141 I.B.L.A. 85 (1997). As of 2003, Conoco's exploratory drilling appears not to have been successful. Environmentalists and oil drillers are battling in three other others of picturesque Utah recreational lands: the Canyonlands National Park, the Arches National Park, and the Nine Mile Canyon area. See Stephen H. M. Block & Heidi J. McIntosh, A View from the Front Lines: The Fate of Utah's Redrock Wilderness under the George W. Bush Administration, 33 Golden Gate U. L. Rev. 473 (2003).

Loosening constraints on industry access to oil and gas resources on public lands has been at the top of the petroleum industry's wish list for years. Within two weeks of taking office, President George W. Bush directed Vice President Dick Cheney to develop a national energy policy. A few months later, in May 2001, the National Energy Policy Development Group had completed its report. The National Energy Policy report recommended that the administration expedite an ongoing study of the land status and lease impediments to federal oil and gas leasing. After the terrorist attacks of September 11, 2001, Congress also prioritized the completion of this study. In January 2003, the study's report appeared, jointly prepared by the Departments of Interior, Agriculture, and Energy and titled "Scientific Inventory of Onshore Federal Lands' Oil and Gas Resources and Reserves and the Extent and Nature of Restrictions or Impediments to their Development."

This report inventoried the resources and constraints in the five basins of the western lands containing most of the onshore natural gas and much of the oil under federal ownership in the lower 48 states. These five basins cover almost 104 million acres of land, of which 59 million acres are under ʹ___ʹral management. Only five states—Montana, Wyoming, Colorado, and New Mexico—contain the bulk of the lands. The report docu-ʹ whether the federal lands were "open" or "closed" to leasing, and ʹiewed more than 1,000 lease stipulations to determine how tightly ʹwas controlled on the lands open to leasing. Here are the results:

About 39% of the federal land is available for leasing with standard ʹerms that contain no special stipulations limiting normal oil and gas operations. These lands contain 57% of the technically recoverable oil and 63% of such gas in the 5 basins.

   2.   About 25% of the federal land is available for leasing with more stringent stipulations on how oil and gas operations can be conducted. These lands contain 28% of the recoverable oil and 25% of such gas in the basins. The lease stipulations usually affect the number of months in the year when drilling is allowed (e.g., to protect migratory wildlife or mating seasons) or they control surface use of the tract.

   3.   About 36% of the federal land in the basins is closed to leasing. These lands contain an estimated 15% of the recoverable oil and 12% of the gas in the basins. (Fortunately, oil and gas "run downhill" and are not found at high elevations in the spectacular mountain regions of the Rockies where national parks would block development. The higher elevations harbor other minerals, like gold).

   Based on this data, do you think our federal land policy has generally balanced development with preservation? A full accounting of the many laws and policies for resource use and management of our federal lands, such as national forests, grazing lands, wildlife refuges and parks, demands its own course. An excellent case book, Federal Public Land and Resources Law by George Coggins, Charles Wilkinson and John Leshy awaits the eager student.

   The Utah National Monument withdrawal was wrathfully denounced by the entire Utah delegation to Congress. Such withdrawals create many of the same state/federal conflicts over the use of the public lands as the OCS has engendered, except that the roles are usually reversed. The Western states have generally taken a pro-development stance against the use of executive or congressional powers to withdraw land from resource use. However, as hundreds of new oil and gas wells, particularly coalbed methane wells, are drilled on or near ranchlands and recreational sites in Wyoming and Montana or drilled close to residential areas of major cities like Denver, Colorado and Fort Worth, Texas, many pro-development citizens are reassessing their stance. This is particularly so when the owners of private lands learn that they own only the surface estate and that the mineral estate is dominant and can use their surface to develop oil and gas. The externalities of drilling and producing are discussed in the following section of this chapter in the context of both offshore and onshore wells. Chapter 8 on Natural Gas looks in more detail (in Section B) at the effects of coalbed methane development and Chapter 9 looks at development in the Amazon rainforest and in the Arctic.

F.   THE ENVIRONMENTAL IMPACT OF OIL

1.   SUMMARY OVERVIEW OF IMPACTS

   The production, transport, refining, and consumption of oil and petroleum products have significant environmental impacts, briefly summarized in this excerpt:

Margriat F. Carswell, Balancing Energy and the Environment 179, 182–85

in the Environment of Oil (Richard J. Gilbert, ed. 1993).

Air Quality. Energy development and use can affect air quality in many ways. Both onshore and offshore production pollute the air with emissions from drilling equipment, escaping hydrocarbons, flaring of natural gas, and emissions form support vehicles. Pipelines contribute very little to air pollution during normal operations although there may be some emissions produced during transfer from wells or to refineries or tankers. Tankers and barge tugs emit hydrocarbons when under power and may have fugitive vapors escape during cargo transfer. However, the consumption of oil and gas contributes most greatly to air quality degradation. The incomplete combustion of petroleum products yields carbon monoxide, hydrocarbons, oxidation products, and particulates. The principal stationary-source contributors are inorganic and organic chemical plants, iron and steel mills, petroleum refiners, pulp and paper mills, electric-power plants, and nonferrous-metal smelters. By weight alone, motor vehicles contribute nearly half of the total pollutants, attributable to the fact that carbon monoxide constitutes such a large proportion of emissions.

Water Quality. Degradation of water quality can occur in the marine environment or in surface or ground freshwater supplies. Both onshore and offshore production require the proper disposal of produced water.[13] Produced water is the largest source of contaminants from offshore oil and gas development, where up to 1 barrel of produced water is obtained for each barrel of crude oil that is recovered. Improper disposal can contaminate the marine environment or freshwater supplies. The disposal of drilling muds can also present problems, especially during offshore production.[14]

Oil spills from offshore production and discharges from tankers and barges have added many polluting constituents to water environments, ... From all sources, about 6 million tons of oil pollutants get to the ocean each year. Consumption of petroleum products contributes to some water pollution indirectly through the deposition of airborne contaminants. In addition, individuals disposing of engine oil have unknowingly jeopardized their own water sources, since one quart of crankcase oil that reaches a source of clean water will cause 250,000 gallons to be unusable for a drinking water supply. Leaking gasoline storage tanks also can constitute a severe problem for fresh groundwater supplies, and many service stations have been required to replace tanks and remove contaminated soil.

13. Produced water is the aqueous waste that has existed in the interstitial spaces of fossil fuel-bearing formations for thousands of years. Produced water may contain elevated concentrations of metals, hydrocarbons, and other organic substances.

14. Drilling muds are used to remove cuttings from under the drill bit, to control well pressure, to cool and lubricate the drill string, and to seal the well. They can contain clay minerals, barite, trace metals, sodium hydroxide, biocides, diesel fuel, and other minor constituents.

Biological Resources. Both plants and animals can be affected directly by petroleum development activities or indirectly through the air and water quality changes discussed above. The integrity of an ecosystem can be destroyed if only one link in the food chain is eliminated. Therefore, environmentalists tend to focus on an indicator species such as the caribou in Alaska when protesting energy development projects. Such a focus can be misleading if the species chosen is not the most predictive indicator of ecosystem health. The species is often chosen because it is easily identified and tracked. Public opinion is often swayed by the careful choice of an indicator species—popularly known as a "charismatic megafauna." Land-based production and transport can affect large territories during construction and by blocking migratory patterns with pipelines....

Unfortunately, scientific knowledge of the complex interactions and dynamic nature of ecosystems is not adequate to accurately determine the effects of petroleum development on biological resources. Therefore, many environmentalists recommend erring on the side of caution (precluding development) until more is known. The relative benefits and costs of gaining more knowledge are seldom considered, however, ... [L]ittle is known about the chronic exposure of marine resources to drilling muds and produced water that are the byproducts of offshore production. Neither refining nor consumption affect biological resources directly, although there is a possible secondary impact from degraded water and air.■

NOTES AND COMMENTS

1.   Does it appear that oil and gas production or its consumption has the most deleterious effects on the environment? What would cause you to reduce your consumption of gasoline by 10% this semester?

2.   New research shows that the wide open spaces of West Texas and rural Oklahoma and Kansas have "urban smog," from the formation of ozone. The precursors of this bad air are the hydrocarbons released from oil and gas wells and processing plants located in these rural areas. Certain hydrocarbon compounds (alkyl nitrates) existed in larger quantities in rural Kansas than in New York, Houston, or Karachi, Pakistan. The study suggests that the emissions of methane and other hydrocarbons from field operations are larger than currently estimated. Aaron S. Katzenstein, Lambert A. Doezema *et al.*, Extensive Regional Atmospheric Hydrocarbon Pollution in the Southwestern United States, 100 Proceedings of the National Academy of Sciences 11,975–979 (Oct. 14, 2003). An EPA National Methane Emissions Inventory estimated that gas processing plants in the U.S. emitted 37 billion cubic feet of methane in 2000, most of which (70%) resulted from fugitive emissions from equipment leaks and the remainder (25%) from venting and combustion during normal operations. Methane is a greenhouse gas, 21 times more potent than CO_2 in contributing to global warming. Such simple "best management practices" as closing valves more tightly could cost-effectively save significant amounts of methane from escaping into the air. Roger Fernandez, Donald Robinson, and Vineet

Aggarwal, Study Comparison Reveals Methane–Emissions Reduction Opportunities in Gas Processing, Oil & Gas J. (June 13, 2005) at 53–59.

2.   OFFSHORE WASTES AND THE CLEAN WATER ACT

All too frequently, regulations designed to improve one environmental condition create an environmental problem elsewhere. Pollutants removed from the air end up in the water, and vice versa. This phenomenon is nowhere more evident than in the problem of disposing of wastes from offshore oil platforms. Such a platform is a world in microcosm. As waste products are generated, they can be deposited in the ocean, burned at the platform, or shipped back to shore for burial.

The EPA, after long study and debate, issued regulations governing offshore disposal. The regulations were challenged by both industry and environmentalists (the Natural Resources Defense Council). In a voluminous decision, the Sixth Circuit addressed the complaints of both sides. For those students who have not had a course in Environmental Law, the Clean Water Act presents a maze of almost impenetrable acronyms, largely defining the severity of technological controls required by industry. Yet the legal issues can be clearly grasped in the excerpted version of this case, which illustrates both the workings of the Clean Water Act and the working of judges tackling complex technical issues.

As a preface to this case, consider Professor Oliver Houck's ode to BAT—the Best Available Technology standard at issue in the case:

> [I]t is easy to see why science-based approaches fare so poorly [in environmental law and practice]. One lesson in this regard can be drawn from the Federal Water Pollution Control Act, aimed at the attainment of water quality standards. Scientists would establish concentration limits for every pollutant, and when waters exceeded these limits, scientists would determine the cause and require abatement. But concentration limits for what use: swimming, drinking water, or fishing? If for fishing, would the target be catfish or trout? . . . States lowered their standards to attract industry, which then held them hostage under the threat of moving away.

> The "scientific" part of the act . . . involved extrapolating "acceptable" concentration limits from laboratory experiments to natural surroundings; from single pollutants to cocktails of multiple pollutants; and then from rapid, observable, lethal effects to long-term, sublethal, and reproductive effects. . . . When it came next to enforcement, someone had to prove who and what were causing the exceedance of the standards. . . . [W]as it the cattle farming, the shoe tannery, the local sewage system, or Mother Nature?

> . . . .

> In 1972, after 15 years of futility with the water quality standards program, during which the Cuyahoga River and the Houston Ship Canal caught fire, . . . Congress changed the rules of the clean water game and adopted a new standard: best available technology (BAT).

The theory of BAT was very simple: If emissions could be reduced, just do it. It did not matter what the impacts were. . . . It didn't matter what scientists said the harm was or where it came from. Just do it.

Oliver Houck, Tales from a Troubled Marriage: Science and Law in Environmental Policy, 302 Science 1926–1929, Dec. 12, 2003.

BP Exploration & Oil, Inc. v. United States EPA

66 F.3d 784 (6th Cir. 1995).

■ BATCHELDER, J. In these consolidated cases, petitioners BP Exploration & Oil, Inc., American Petroleum Institute, Conoco Inc., Marathon Oil Co., Natural Resources Defense Council, Inc., and Svedala Industries, Inc., challenge the effluent limitations promulgated for the offshore oil and gas industry by the United States Environmental Protection Agency [EPA]under the Clean Water Act. For the reasons that follow, we affirm the effluent limitations promulgated by the Environmental Protection Agency (EPA) for the offshore oil and gas industry.

I.

The disputed effluent limitations guidelines are the final regulations and standards of performance for the "Offshore Subcategory of the Oil and Gas Extraction Point Source Category," published pursuant to sections 301, 304, and 306 of the Clean Water Act (CWA or "Act"). 33 U.S.C.A. §§ 1311, 1314, 1316 (West 1986). . . . These regulations (the "Final Rule") were also formulated in response to a Consent Decree entered on April 5, 1990, in *NRDC v. Reilly*, C.A. No. 79–3442 (D.D.C.) (subsequently modified on May 28, 1992). The Final Rule became effective on April 5, 1993, ending a process that began in 1975 with EPA's publication of interim guidelines for the offshore oil and gas industry.

Petitioners BP Exploration & Oil, Inc., American Petroleum Institute, Conoco Inc., Marathon Oil Co., and Svedala, Inc. (hereinafter referred to as "Industry petitioners"), contend that the effluent standards are too stringent. Generally, Industry petitioners allege that the EPA violated the CWA by (1) setting an unreasonable standard for the discharge of oil and grease in effluent discharges, (2) prohibiting the discharge of certain drilling wastes within three miles of shore, and (3) banning the discharge of contaminated sand. At the other end of the spectrum, petitioner Natural Resources Defense Council, Inc. (NRDC), representing environmental interests, contends that EPA violated the CWA by promulgating effluent standards that are generally too lenient. In short, NRDC alleges that EPA (1) illegally rejected zero discharge of drilling wastes, (2) violated the Act by failing to regulate radioactive pollutants in discharged water, and (3) should have required reinjection of polluted water.

A.   The Clean Water Act

The objective of the CWA "is to restore and maintain the chemical, physical, and biological integrity of the Nation's waters." § 1251. Congress' original goal was for the discharge of all pollutants into navigable waters to be eliminated by the year 1985. § 1251(a)(1). Consequently, the discharge of any pollutant is illegal unless made in compliance with the provisions of the CWA. Because numerous other courts have fully described the CWA, *see E.I. du Pont de Nemours & Co. v. Train*, 430 U.S. 112 (1977), it is unnecessary here to include more than an outline of the statutory structure for promulgating effluent limitations.

The CWA directs EPA to formulate national effluent limitation guidelines for those entities that discharge pollutants into the navigable waters of the United States. In formulating these guidelines, the CWA directs EPA to institute progressively more stringent effluent discharge guidelines in stages. Congress intended EPA to consider numerous factors in addition to pollution reduction: "The Committee believes that there must be a reasonable relationship between costs and benefits if there is to be an effective and workable program." Clean Water Act of 1972, Pub. L. No. 92–500, 1972 U.S.C.C.A.N. (86 Stat.) 3713.

At the first stage of pollutant reduction, EPA is to determine the level of effluent reduction achievable within an industry with the implementation of the "best practicable control technology currently available" (BPT). § 314(b)(1)(A). In general, BPT is the average of the best existing performances by industrial plants of various sizes, ages, and unit processes within the point source category or subcategory. In arriving at BPT for an industry, EPA is to consider several factors, including the total cost of the application of the technology in relation to the effluent reduction benefits to be achieved from such application.[15] For the offshore oil and gas subcategory, BPT was to be achieved by July 1, 1977. § 1311(b)(1)(A).

At the second stage, EPA is to set generally more stringent standards for toxic and conventional pollutants. For toxic pollutants, EPA is to set the standard for the "best available technology economically achievable" (BAT). BAT represents, at a minimum, the best economically achievable performance in the industrial category or subcategory. *NRDC, Inc. v. EPA*, 863 F.2d 1420, 1426 (9th Cir. 1988) (*citing EPA v. National Crushed Stone Ass'n*, 449 U.S. 64, 74 (1980)). Compared to BPT, BAT calls for more stringent control technology that is both technically available and economically achievable. Among the factors that EPA must consider and take into account when setting BAT are the cost of achieving such effluent reduction and the non-water quality environmental impact including the energy requirements of the technology. § 1314(b)(2)(B). For the offshore oil and gas subcategory, BAT was to be achieved by July 1, 1987. § 1311(b)(2)(A).

Conventional pollutants[16] are treated differently from toxics under the CWA. Pursuant to 1977 amendments to the Act, a new standard was

---

15. [FN4] Other factors EPA must consider are the age of equipment and facilities involved, the process employed, the engineering aspects of the application of various types of control techniques, process changes, non-water quality environmental impacts, and such other factors as the Administrator deems appropriate. § 1314(b)(1)(B); *see also Environmental Prot. Agency v. Nat'l Crushed Stone Ass'n*, 449 U.S. 64, 71 n.10 (1980).

16. [FN8] Conventional pollutants include biochemical oxygen demand (BOD), total suspended solids (TSS) (nonfilterable), pH, fecal coliform, oil and grease. 40 C.F.R. § 401.16 (1994).

conceived for conventional pollutants entitled "best conventional pollutant control technology" (BCT). This standard is designed to control conventional pollutants about which much is known but for which stringent BAT standards might require unnecessary treatment. Congress intended for BCT to prevent the implementation of technology for technology's sake. BCT is not an additional level of control, but replaces BAT for conventional pollutants.

Consequently, the technology chosen as BCT must pass a two-part "cost reasonableness" test. *American Paper Inst. v. EPA*, 660 F.2d 954 (4th Cir. 1981). According to the Act, the Administrator shall include in the determination of BCT

> [a] consideration of the reasonableness of the relationship between the costs of attaining a reduction in effluents and the effluent reduction benefits derived, and the comparison of the cost and level of reduction of such pollutants from the discharge from publicly owned treatment works [POTWs] to the cost and level of reduction of such pollutants from a class or category of industrial sources.... § 1314(b)(4)(B). The first part of the BCT cost test is referred to as the "industry cost-effectiveness test"; the second part is known as the "POTW test."

Finally, the CWA directs EPA to establish a separate standard for new sources of pollutants. These "new source performance standards" (NSPS) require application of the technology chosen as BAT to remove all types of pollutants from new sources within each category. § 1316. Factors to be considered in formulating NSPS include the cost of achieving such effluent reduction and any non-water quality environmental impact and energy requirements. § 1316 (b) (1) (B).

C.   The Industry

EPA identified a total of 2,550 offshore structures that will be affected by the Final Rule. Of these structures, 2,517 are located in the Gulf of Mexico, 32 are located off the coast of California, and one is located off the coast of Alaska. Petitioners challenge those portions of EPA's Final Rule relating to (1) produced water, (2) drilling fluids and drill cuttings, and (3) produced sand. Although wastewater originates both from the exploration and development process and from the production phase of the oil and gas industry's offshore operations, drilling fluids make up the majority of the effluent produced from exploration and development, and produced water represents a majority of the effluent from production. Produced sand is a minimal component of the effluent from production.

D.   The Standard of Review

[The court reiterated the standard principles of judicial review of agency action. If Congressional intent is clear, it must be given effect. *Chevron, U.S.A., Inc. v. Natural Resources Defense Council, Inc.*, 467 U.S. 837, 842 (1984). If the statute is silent or ambiguous, the question for the court is whether the agency's answer is based on a permissible construction of the statute. Much deference must be given to an agency's construction of a statutory scheme that it is entrusted to administer. A court must set aside agency action, findings, and conclusions if they are found to be "arbitrary, capricious, an abuse of discretion, or otherwise not in accordance with law" 5 U.S.C. § 706(2)(A).]

In the present case, neither EPA's statutory authority nor the procedural steps taken has been challenged. Only substantive aspects of the Final Rule are being challenged. Consequently, this Court must determine "whether the agency 'abuse[d its] discretion' (or was 'arbitrary' or 'capricious') in exercising the quasi-legislative authority delegated to it by Congress, or, on the other hand, whether its 'decision was based on a consideration of the relevant factors and [was not the product of] a clear error of judgment.' " *Weyerhaeuser*, 590 F.2d at 1025 (*quoting Citizens to Preserve Overton Park*, 401 U.S. at 416).

Finally, this Court will defer in large part to EPA's scientific findings. . . . In *Baltimore Gas & Elec. Co.*, "the Supreme Court recognized that a reviewing court should be at its most deferential in reviewing an agency's scientific determinations in an area within the agency's expertise." *Natural Resources Defense Council v. EPA*, 863 F.2d at 1430.

II.

A.   Produced Water

The bulk of produced water is water trapped in underground reservoirs along with oil and gas that eventually rises to the surface with the produced oil and gas. Most of the oil and gas in the produced water is separated as part of the oil and gas extraction process. The remaining produced water, still containing some oil and grease, is then discharged overboard or otherwise disposed of. Produced water also includes the injection water used for secondary oil recovery and various well treatment chemicals added during production and oil and gas extraction. Produced water is the highest volume waste source in the offshore oil and gas industry.

Under the Final Rule, EPA determined that BAT and NSPS would be set to limit the discharge of oil and grease[17] in produced water to a daily maximum of 42 mg/l and a monthly average of 29 mg/l, based on the improved operating performance of gas flotation technology (otherwise referred to as improved gas flotation). BCT for produced water was set by the Final Rule to equal current BPT limitations (72 mg/l daily maximum, 48 mg/l 30–day average) [measured using EPA Method 413.1].

Gas flotation is a technology that forces small gas bubbles into the wastewater to be treated. As the bubbles rise through the produced water, they attach themselves to any oil droplets in their paths. As the gas and oil are separated from the wastewater, they rise to the surface, where they are

---

17. Although oil and grease are conventional pollutants rather than toxics, oil and grease are limited under BAT and NSPS as an "indicator" pollutant to measure discharge of toxic and nonconventional pollutants.

skimmed away. EPA characterizes "improved performance" gas flotation as the gas flotation technology enhanced through improved operation and maintenance, more operator attention to treatment systems operations, chemical pretreatment to enhance system effectiveness, and possible resizing of certain treatment system components for increased treatment efficiency.... In setting the limits, EPA used the "median" platform from the 83 Platform Composite Study. In other words, 50 percent of the platforms in the study discharged higher levels of pollutant, and 50 percent of the platforms discharged lower levels of pollutant. The daily maximum limitation was set so that there would be a 99 percent likelihood that a physical composite sample taken from the median platform would have a total oil and grease measurement less than or equal to that limitation. The monthly average was set so that there would be a 95 percent probability that a monthly average taken from the median platform would also be less than or equal to that limitation. EPA estimates that 60 percent of the platforms in the composite of 83 platforms already meet the new BAT limitations. For those platforms that do not already meet the new BAT standard, chemical coagulants can be used to improve the removal of dissolved or soluble oil.

In light of the deference due the EPA, especially concerning scientific and technical data, Industry petitioners have not proven their claim that improved gas flotation does not remove "dissolved" oil or that EPA violated either the CWA or the APA by using Method 413.1 to measure oil and grease in produced water.

2. Radioactive Pollutants in Produced Water

Also in relation to produced water, petitioner NRDC argues that EPA illegally refused to regulate radioactive pollutants in produced water, despite NRDC's contention that ample record evidence proves the presence and negative impacts of radionuclides. In contrast, EPA maintains that the agency was justified in its decision not to regulate radionuclides in produced water because inadequate information existed to issue rules regarding the radionuclides, Radium 226 and Radium 228 (referred to as NORM). According to the EPA, the CWA does not require the promulgation or implementation of regulations if there is not sufficient evidence on which to base those regulations. As EPA argues, the agency is continuing to gather information on radionuclides and could issue regulations in the future if the compiled information shows a need for such regulation. See § 1314(e). In fact, EPA has stated its intent to require radium monitoring as part of the permitting process for offshore oil and gas producers....

The present case is unlike *NRDC v. EPA*, in which the Ninth Circuit concluded that EPA should not delay requiring such technologically feasible limitations as BAT in order to wait for precise cost figures. *NRDC v. EPA*, 863 F.2d at 1426. In this case, EPA has legitimately declined to regulate radionuclides in produced water due to the lack of data on radionuclides in produced water—particularly information on the environmental and health harms presented by NORM. In light of EPA's discretion to promulgate this

Final Rule, we agree that EPA reasonably decided that insufficient evidence existed to regulate this pollutant in produced water at this time.

3.   Reinjection of Produced Water

The NRDC also contends that EPA illegally refused to require zero discharge of produced waters through reinjection because record evidence shows that reinjection is technologically and economically feasible. . . .

EPA admits that reinjection may be technologically feasible.[18] The only evidence that reinjection may not be feasible is the possibility that geographic formations in some areas may preclude reinjection. However, EPA's rejection of reinjection as a BAT, while based in part on concerns regarding feasibility, was, more importantly, based on several relevant factors, such as unacceptably high economic and nonwater quality environmental impacts.

EPA estimates the cost of implementing reinjection as BAT and NSPS would exceed several billion dollars. The extraordinary cost was one basis for rejecting reinjection, although NRDC is correct that EPA did not conclusively determine that reinjection was not economically attainable. In addition to the high expense of reinjection, the negative impact reinjection would have on air emissions and the loss of production resulting from reinjection combined to cause EPA to reject reinjection for BAT and NSPS.

EPA estimates that the implementation of reinjection at existing platforms in the Gulf and Alaska alone would increase the emission of air pollutants by 1,041 tons/year for BAT and 849 tons/year for NSPS. The existing air quality of Southern California is so bad that reinjection was not considered an option at all. Reinjection was also rejected based on the increased energy required to run the reinjection pumps. According to EPA, reinjection would result in additional energy requirements of 977,000 barrels of oil equivalent (BOE)/year for BAT and 785,000 BOE/year for NSPS. Finally, EPA projected that reinjection would result in a one percent loss in production. (It is worth noting that one percent of oil and gas production from the Gulf of Mexico amounts to several million BOE/year.) The accumulation of these factors led EPA to reject reinjection as BAT and NSPS for produced water.

We think that EPA acted within its statutory authority in rejecting zero discharge based on reinjection. As EPA correctly points out, NRDC's contention that economic, energy, and nonwater quality environmental impacts are less important than achieving zero discharge merely reflects NRDC's disagreement on a policy level. This Court may not substitute NRDC's judgment, any more than our own, for that of the EPA.

---

18. [FN14] A majority of the platforms in California already reinject their produced water to enable recovery of the heavy crude oil that is typically produced in that part of the country. The only offshore rig in Alaska also reinjects its produced water in order to comply with state regulation. Reinjection of produced water is much less common in the Gulf of Mexico, although some studies have shown it to be feasible there as well. It is important to remember, however, that of 2,500 offshore platforms, only 33 platforms are located off the coast of California and Alaska.

B. Drilling Fluids and Drill Cuttings

Drilling fluid (also called drilling mud) is any fluid sent down the drillhole to aid the drilling process. This includes fluid used to maintain hydrostatic pressure in the well, lubricate and cool the drill bit, remove drill cuttings from the well, and stabilize the walls of the well during drilling or work over operations. The fluid is pumped down the drill pipe and through the drill bit. At the bottom of the hole, it sweeps crushed rock drill cuttings from beneath the bit, carries them back to the surface, is separated from drill cuttings and is discharged or is returned to the mud tank for recirculation.

Under the Final Rule, EPA prohibits all discharge of drilling fluids and drill cuttings from wells located within three nautical miles from shore for the Gulf and California regions. The BAT, NSPS, and BCT all require any dischargers within the three-mile limit to transport drilling fluids and drill cuttings to shore by barge and to dispose of the discharge in landfills. Beyond the three-mile limit, drilling fluids and drill cuttings may be discharged under BCT after meeting the limitation for no discharge of free oil measured by the static sheen test.[19] BAT and NSPS for dischargers beyond the three-mile limit are more stringent, requiring compliance with four basic requirements.[20]

Industry petitioners challenge the EPA's decision to impose the zero discharge limitation on drilling fluids and drill cuttings discharged within three miles of shore in the Gulf and California regions. The BAT, NSPS, and BCT chosen for these dischargers is to barge the drilling fluids and cuttings to shore to be disposed of in landfills. Industry petitioners assert that EPA acted arbitrarily and violated the CWA by (1) improperly calculating the BCT cost test, (2) regulating drill cuttings as Total Suspended Solids (TSS), and (3) failing adequately to consider the cost factor in its BAT and NSPS determination.

1. BCT Cost Test

The portion of the BCT cost test at issue here, the industry cost-effectiveness test, has been translated into the following mathematical formula [which divides the difference in costs between the BCT and BPT technologies in the numerator of the fraction with the difference in costs between using or not using BPT technology in the denominator, and then requires that the resulting ratio be less than 1.29]:

BCT cost/lb. − BPT cost/lb./< 1.29 BPT cost/lb. − pre BPT cost/lb.

19. [FN17] Fluids fail the static sheen test if a "sheen, iridescence, gloss, or increased reflectance" appears on the surface of test seawater after drilling fluid samples are introduced into ambient seawater in a container having an air-to-liquid interface area of 1,000 cm. 50 Fed. Reg. 34,592, 34,627 (1985).

20. [FN18] These requirements are: (1) a toxicity limitation set at 30,000 ppm in the suspended particulate phase; (2) a prohibition on the discharge of diesel oil; (3) no discharge of free oil based on the static sheen test; and (4) a limitation on cadmium and mercury in barite of 3 mg/kg and 1 mg/kg, respectively.

Based on this formula, EPA's first step was to calculate the existing cost of BPT under which some drilling muds were hauled to shore when they did not meet the "no free oil" test. EPA then calculated the BCT cost of hauling all drilling muds and cuttings within the Final Rule's three-mile limit.

Industry petitioners allege that EPA made two mistakes in calculating the cost of BPT. First, Industry petitioners contend that EPA mistakenly classified the costs of substituting mineral oil for diesel oil as a BPT cost. EPA candidly admits that it did commit this error. EPA contends, however, that this mistake was harmless error because, even with a substitution cost of zero (which EPA does not concede), the BCT level chosen still passes the BCT cost test once Industry petitioners' second contention is rejected.

Industry petitioners' second contention is that EPA exaggerated BPT onshore disposal costs for oil-based muds. According to Industry petitioners, no cost should be attributed to the onshore disposal of oil-based muds because dischargers actually sell the muds to mud companies who recondition the mud for reuse as drilling fluids. Industry petitioners assert that a correct calculation of the BPT cost should include only the transportation of oil-based muds to shore. As Industry petitioners view it, a recalculation of the industry cost-effectiveness test, omitting the cost attributed to product substitution and the cost attributed to the disposal of oil-based muds, causes EPA's zero discharge BCT level to fail the BCT cost test. EPA counters that Industry petitioners are not permitted to raise their claim relating to the disposal cost of oil-based muds, because the issue was not raised during the rulemaking process. The requirement that a party raise its concerns to an agency prior to the publication of the final rule promotes agency autonomy and judicial efficiency. *Ohio v. EPA*, 997 F.2d 1520, 1528–29 (D.C. Cir. 1993). Industry petitioners counter that they could not have raised this issue earlier because EPA's calculations were not available until the Rule was published. Industry petitioners' claim is not persuasive, however, because although the exact calculations may have been unavailable, we find ample record evidence that Industry petitioners had sufficient notice that disposal costs of oil-based muds were being considered by EPA as part of the BCT cost test.

Even if Industry petitioners had the right to raise this issue, EPA persuasively argues that some cost must be associated with disposal of oil-based muds. For example, EPA suggests that there will be some solids in the process that still require disposal because they will not pass the no free oil test; that reconditioning all of the drilling fluid may not be feasible; and that for those fluids that are reused, there is probably some limit to the number of times such reuse can occur. Logically, there must be some cost associated with the reconditioning operation itself. EPA claims that all of these factors make the Industry petitioners' argument for zero disposal cost an unreasonable one. We are persuaded by EPA that its revised BPT calculation passes the BCT cost test. When EPA drops the mistaken amount included for product substitution, and leaves the rest of the numbers the same, the result of the equation is 1.239. This figure is still lower than the permissible threshold of 1.29.

2. Regulating Drill Cuttings as TSS

Industry petitioners also argue that EPA improperly classified, and then regulated, drill cuttings as Total Suspended Solids (TSS). According to Industry petitioners, it is arbitrary to ban an entire waste stream (such as all drill cuttings) as TSS when only a small portion of the waste is actually suspended. In Industry petitioners' opinion, a large percentage of the drill cuttings are heavy bits of rock that sink immediately to the ocean floor and should therefore not be classified as TSS.

EPA counters that drill cuttings are classified as TSS because they fit within the definition of TSS. According to EPA, TSS is defined as "nonfilterable residue." This definition requires only that the substance will not pass through a glass filter. Consequently, EPA uses Method 160.2[21] to measure the amount of solid retained by a fiber filter. Because the drill cuttings discharged by oil and gas producers will not pass through such a filter, drill cuttings are, by EPA's definition, TSS. Industry petitioners maintain that it is illogical to include drill cuttings in a test method that is intended to filter much smaller particles. According to Method 160.2, the practical range of material to be measured is 4 mg/l to 20,000 mg/l. However, as Industry petitioners point out, a representative drill cutting sample is over 1.1 million mg/l. We are persuaded by Industry's argument that EPA has arbitrarily classified drill cuttings as TSS. It is error for EPA to classify drill cuttings, typically on the magnitude of 1.1 million mg/l, by measuring TSS using a test designed to include only particles smaller than 20,000 mg/l. Despite the deference due to EPA in its choice of analytical methodology and testing procedures, it is apparent to this Court that most drill cuttings may not qualify as TSS because they are not "suspended." Our view is further bolstered by another of EPA's own tests, Method 160.5, which measures residue classified as "settleable." 40 C.F.R. § 136.3, Table 1B (1994). The drill cuttings discharged from the oil and gas development and production phases should not be measured by Method 160.2 unless they fit within that test's practical guidelines.

Despite our belief that EPA may have erred in classifying drill cuttings as TSS, it appears senseless here to remand this portion of the Final Rule. Because BAT and NSPS for drill cuttings require the same technological control on drill cuttings as BCT, that is, zero discharge within three nautical miles of shore and no discharge of free oil beyond three miles, altering BCT in this case would not change the result. Furthermore, even if EPA improperly classified drill cuttings as TSS, the agency is not precluded from regulating drill cuttings as an indicator for oil and grease. It is well documented that once drill cuttings are separated from the reusable drilling mud, they continue to carry drilling fluid residues of conventional and toxic pollutants. It is apparent in this specific situation that altering

---

21. [FN20] EPA's Method 160.2 entails filtering a sample of the industrial waste through a glass fiber filter and then weighing the retained residue after it has dried.

BCT would not in any way change the treatment of drill cuttings in the Gulf of Mexico, California, or Alaska. In this case, therefore, we will not disturb the EPA's treatment of drill cuttings as TSS in the Final Rule although we find some merit in Industry petitioners' allegation.

3. BAT and NSPS Cost Calculation

Finally, Industry petitioners challenge the BAT and NSPS levels set by EPA for drilling fluids and cuttings. The BAT and NSPS for dischargers within three miles of shore (excluding Alaska) require zero discharge of the pollutant by barging the mud and cuttings to shore for onshore disposal. Industry petitioners contend that EPA failed to consider adequately the relevant factors required, specifically the cost of barging. Phrased another way, Industry petitioners claim that the BAT and NSPS levels were improperly promulgated because the environmental benefits of the limitations are negligible.

EPA counters that it has discretion whether or not to use cost considerations under BAT and NSPS, and that EPA need only find that the technology is technically and economically achievable and that the cost of the technology is "reasonable." *Natural Res. Def. Council v. EPA*, 863 F.2d at 1426; *see also CPC Int'l, Inc. v. Train*, 540 F.2d 1329, 1341–42 (8th Cir. 1976) (setting NSPS does not require cost-benefit analysis, "what is required . . . is a thorough study of initial and annual costs and an affirmative conclusion that these costs can be reasonably borne by the industry"), cert. denied, 430 U.S. 966 (1977). The CWA does not require a precise calculation of BAT and NSPS costs. *Natural Resources Defense Council v. EPA*, 863 F.2d at 1426. Congress intended that EPA have discretion "to decide how to account for the consideration factors, and how much weight to give each factor." *Weyerhaeuser*, 590 F.2d at 1045.

Industry petitioners maintain that when environmental benefits are de minimis, the regulation is not valid. However, EPA points to several environmental benefits of the zero discharge rule, primarily, the decrease in pollutants ingested by fish and shellfish and passed along the food chain. Among the non-monetary benefits of zero discharge is the reduction in recreation degradation. Industry petitioners maintain that zero discharge is not necessary because simply meeting the four basic requirements under BAT for dischargers outside the three mile limit reduces virtually any pollution harm. However, Industry petitioners have not carried their burden of showing that zero discharge does not achieve any additional environmental benefit.

We are persuaded that EPA acted within its discretion in setting BAT and NSPS for drilling muds and drill cuttings.

4. Nonwater Quality Environmental Impacts

In promulgating the permissible discharge of drilling fluids and cuttings in this part of the Final Rule, EPA determined that zero discharge for all offshore platforms in the Gulf, California and Alaska was technologically available (through barging to shore) and economically achievable ($12.3 million for drilling fluids, $6.6 million for drill cuttings). However, unacceptably high nonwater quality environmental impacts led EPA to establish the three-mile zero discharge limit for the Gulf and California. In the Gulf of Mexico, EPA rejected zero discharge beyond three miles from shore because of a lack of landfill capacity in the region. In California, zero discharge beyond three miles was rejected because of its serious impact on air pollution. NRDC challenges each of these decisions.

a. Volume of Waste and Landfill Capacity in Gulf

NRDC contends (1) that EPA overestimated the volume of waste that would be generated by platforms outside the three-mile limit, and (2) underestimated land disposal capacity. According to NRDC, correcting these errors clears the way for a zero discharge requirement for drilling fluids and drill cuttings from all oil and gas rigs in the Gulf of Mexico.

EPA estimated the landfill capacity in the Gulf region over the next 15 years and determined that 8.5 million barrels of waste could be disposed each year. Because the landfills in that area are already receiving 3 million barrels of waste each year from other sources, EPA calculated that only an additional 5.5 million barrels of waste from offshore sources could be accommodated. EPA then examined the amount of waste that would be generated offshore if a zero discharge limitation were in place for all platforms. It was estimated that offshore platforms would generate 6.6 million barrels/year. In addition to the 1.1 million barrels/year already being produced by coastal drilling operations, the total amount of drilling wastes generated totals 7.7 million barrels of waste per year. Because EPA estimated landfill capacity at only 5.5 million barrels each year, EPA devised its three-mile mark, beyond which platforms are not required to comply with zero discharge.

NRDC first contends that EPA overestimated the amount of waste that would require disposal by use of the zero discharge limit. NRDC claims that EPA used poor solids control technology in its calculations. Solids control technology removes drill cuttings from the drilling fluid system and reduces the total amount of drilling wastes that cannot be reused. As EPA points out, however, improved solids control technology only increases the volume of drill cuttings separated from reusable drilling fluid. Consequently, EPA found that the additional waste reduction that might be achieved is minimal. NRDC also raised the oil-based muds issue, contending that such muds are reused and that EPA did not take this into consideration. EPA maintains that reconditioning oil-based muds cannot eliminate all drilling fluids from the waste stream and that, therefore, any reuse does not drastically change its calculations.

NRDC also contends that EPA underestimated the landfill capacity of the Gulf region. NRDC believes that EPA ruled out acceptable landfills for insufficient reasons. For example, in its estimation of landfill capacity, EPA did not include landfills that are not now in operation. NRDC contends that those landfills currently are not operating because of a lack of demand. If it were more economically productive for those landfills to operate, NRDC presumes that more space would open up for drilling wastes. Nor did EPA consider landfills whose licenses are currently suspended. NRDC asserts that those sites might regain their licenses. Despite NRDC's contentions, however, this Court would have to engage in pure speculation to determine whether landfill operators would reopen or regain their licenses. Furthermore, the confusion cited by NRDC over the names of several of the landfills in the EPA estimate is adequately explained by the fact that several landfills are known by more than one name.

Finally, NRDC criticizes EPA for failing to include in its estimate of landfill capacity any sites equipped to accept hazardous wastes. However, EPA purposely omitted hazardous landfill sites due to the high demand for such hazardous sites. According to EPA, the decision to exclude hazardous sites from its estimation of total landfill capacity is consistent with its 1988 decision not to regulate oil and gas under the hazardous waste portion of the Resource Conservation and Recovery Act (RCRA), 42 U.S.C. §§ 6901–6987. It is EPA's position that hazardous waste sites must be reserved for disposing of those substances that are more hazardous and dangerous than drilling fluids and drill cuttings.

This Court believes that EPA has both the discretion and the expertise to make the decisions and value judgments behind its rejection of the zero discharge option beyond three miles off the shore of the Gulf of Mexico. Furthermore, EPA continuously reevaluated data and collected comments on the estimated volume of drilling fluids and cuttings, revising its information as recently as 1993. It is clear from the record that EPA made the decisions NRDC challenges after considering all of the options raised by the NRDC and after weighing the benefits and drawbacks of those options. We find that EPA's decisions are not arbitrary or capricious, nor are they the result of an abuse of the agency's discretion.

b.   Air Quality Impact in California

NRDC also alleges that EPA illegally rejected zero discharge of drilling wastes in California beyond the three-mile limit. Having found zero discharge to be achievable in the California region, EPA nevertheless rejected zero discharge beyond the three-mile limit, based on the severity of the air pollution in Southern California. In EPA's opinion, the increased air emissions that would result from barging all drilling wastes from offshore platforms to the coast of California vastly outweighed the benefit of a zero discharge limitation beyond three miles from shore.

NRDC generally charges that EPA cannot reject zero discharge on the basis of possible increased air emissions. According to NRDC, EPA cannot reject a limit based on nonwater quality environmental impacts unless the impacts are "wholly disproportionate" to the possible pollution reduction. NRDC also argues that the estimated addition of 54 tons/year of air pollution off the coast of California is small compared to the present degree of air pollution in California, and that offshore platforms that increase air emissions would be able to purchase pollution offsets to compensate for the increased air pollution. We find each of NRDC's arguments unpersuasive.

The overriding principle in our review of the Final Rule is that the agency has broad discretion to weigh all relevant factors during rulemaking. The CWA does not state what weight should be accorded to the relevant factors; rather, the Act gives EPA the discretion to make those determinations. *Natural Res. Def. Council v. EPA*, 863 F.2d at 1426. Compared to the benefit of a zero discharge requirement for all California offshore platforms, EPA views this increase in air pollution to be unjustified.

Furthermore, Southern California is a severe nonattainment area under the measurements of the Clean Air Act (CAA).[22] There is some doubt that emissions offsets are available at any cost. Even if offsets could be purchased by offshore oil producers, they would cost approximately $15,000 per ton of nitrogen dioxide and $5,000 per ton of hydrocarbons.

If any entity has the ability to weigh the relative impact of two different environmental harms, it is the EPA. Here, EPA has weighed all the factors and has decided to compromise by requiring zero discharge within a three-mile limit. In the absence of a showing of clear error or abuse of discretion, this Court will not overturn EPA's determination....

For the foregoing reasons, we AFFIRM the Final Rule for the offshore oil and gas subcategory promulgated by EPA pursuant to the CWA.■

NOTES AND COMMENTS

1.   Do you feel confident in either the EPA's or the judge's ability to understand the technical or economic aspects of an industrial activity? Is there a better way to formulate control standards than through the rulemaking procedures under the Administrative Procedure Act? Regulatory negotiations, or "reg-negs" are a form of alternative dispute resolution designed to bring together potential litigants to resolve differences before a proposed rule is published. In 1985, Santa Barbara County sued Exxon to force better air pollution controls on its offshore platforms. The MMS held three years of reg-negs with five different caucuses (the oil industry, environmentalists, federal, state, and local governments), but to no avail. The reg-neg process failed because of disputes about factual issues, the complexity of technical issues, and whipsawing national politics. *See* William Fulton, *Reg–Neg: How California's First Regulatory Negotiations Fell Victim to the Politics of Offshore Drilling*, 9 Calif. Lawyer 65 (Nov. 1989). Exxon did agree, however, to fully electrify its Santa Ynez project (in lieu of using diesel fuel) at a cost of millions of dollars. *Id.* at 136. Does this victory for Santa Barbara simply move pollution around, perhaps to the coal-fired power plants near the Grand Canyon?

2.   Do you agree with Professor Houck's positive assessment of BAT and a technology-based approach to cleaning up pollution? Suppose industry "just does it" and all firms adopt the requisite technologies to reduce water

---

22. It is convenient in this case for NRDC to make its argument for zero discharge beyond EPA's three-mile limit at the expense of compliance with the Clean Air Act. We reject the temptation to speculate about NRDC's seeming willingness to sacrifice clean air for a more stringent discharge regulation.

pollution. Yet the Cuyahoga River is still unsafe for human contact or fishing. The Clean Water Act has a second-stage system of pollution control based on water quality standards. States must classify each body of water for particular uses every three years, and then set a Total Daily Maximum Load (TDML) of discharges into that water body by all the parties using that water to dispose of wastes under authorized permits. The goal is to ultimately achieve a fishable/swimmable classification. If the discharges exceed the total maximum load, then some users have to either shut down or adopt better technology to reduce the total discharges. Does this approach remind you of the difficulties of agreeing to "fair shares" in unitizing a common reservoir? Relative to the TDML process, perhaps setting BCT, BAT and NSPS technology standards is a piece of cake. For an overview of the Clean Water Act, see Parthena B. Evans (ed.), The Clean Water Act Handbook (ABA Section of Natural Resources, Energy and Environmental Law, now renamed the Section of Environment, Energy and Resources, 1994).

3.   Note that new platforms are subject to more stringent technological standards than existing sources under the Clean Water Act. A similar statutory framework has been a source of contentious litigation under the New Source Review provisions of the Clean Air Act, discussed in the Coal chapter.

4.   Virtually all produced water from conventional wells onshore is reinjected. (The disposal of produced water from coalbed methane wells is discussed in Chapter 8 on Natural Gas.) The San Juan power plant in New Mexico uses 22,000 acre-feet of water annually to cool steam to reuse as water in electricity generation. The plant received a $440,000 grant to study how to transport and use 6,000 acre-feet of produced saline water from oil and gas drilling that would otherwise be reinjected. An extended drought in the Southwest has spurred this effort. Rosalie Rayburn, New Mexico Utility to Use Drilling Byproduct for Power Plant, Albuquerque J, Nov. 10, 2003

5.   The General Permit at issue in the *BP Exploration* case applies to all operators in a particular industry sector that are similarly situated in a particular geographic area. Use of a General Permit standardizes the permit-granting process and provides industry with stable guidelines. A General Permit is issued for a set number of years and then reviewed. What if an operator has unique circumstances which differ from the general? The CWA makes provisions for the grant of variances for "fundamentally different factors" See Evans, The Clean Water Handbook, *supra* at 24.

6.   *Review problem.* The State of Alaska certified that the installation and operation of a new offshore drilling platform (called the Osprey) in Cook Inlet, near Anchorage (on state, not federal lands), was consistent with its Coastal Zone Management Plan. The EPA had issued a general permit covering exploratory drilling discharges in the area and the platform would meet these standards. The state excluded from its consistency review the platform's proposed waste discharges because the state had already re-

viewed the EPA general permit and found it to be consistent with the CZMA plan. An environmental group, Cook Inlet Keeper, brought suit, arguing that the state impermissibly failed to conduct a specific consistency review in the particularized context of the Osprey project. The court reviewed two regulatory provisions of Alaska's coastal act. The first read that "each state agency shall grant [consistency] authorization if, in addition to finding that the use or activity compiles with the agency's statutes and regulations, the agency finds that the use or activity is consistent with [the coastal plan]." The second read that the Governor's Office must make a consistency determination "when a project requires a permit, lease, or authorization" from one or more state agencies.

Wouldn't it be inefficient and duplicative to require Osprey's discharge activities to undergo two separate consistency reviews? Should a project get two "hard looks?" See *Cook Inlet Keeper v. Alaska*, 46 P.3d 957 (Alaska 2002).

7. In 2003, an EPA report found that 25% of major industrial facilities are in significant noncompliance with their Clean Water Act discharge permits, but few were penalized by the agency. "Significant noncompliance" is an automatic designation in the software compliance system used by EPA. It may involve discharges above permitted levels or paperwork violations, such as late filing of monitoring reports. In 2001, nearly half of the facilities that violated their permit limits for toxic pollutants had exceedances that were twice the allowable levels. Thirteen percent of exceedances were 1,000 percent above permitted levels for toxic pollutants. The report said that some EPA staff believe some of these exceedances may be the result of unachievable water quality based limits due to technical limitations or cost. The report recommended that EPA officials discuss the issue of unachievable permit limits. Susan Bruninga, Most Large Industrial Sites Not Penalized for Violations of their Discharge Permits, Daily Report for Executives, June 9, 2003 at A–29.

Are our environmental laws just too complicated for even the best-intentioned firms to ever be in compliance? *See* David B. Spence, The Shadow of the Rational Polluter: Rethinking the Role of Rational Actor Models in Environmental Law, 89 Cal. L. Rev. 917 (2001) (yes); and J.B. Ruhl & James Salzman, Mozart and the Red Queen: The Problem of Regulatory Accretion in the Administrative State, 91 Georgetown L.J. 757 (2003) (yes).

8. If the EPA determines that a state has failed to impose the best available technology in a permit approving a developer's project (perhaps because the state is more disposed to welcome industry for the jobs and taxes that it brings), can the federal agency overrule the state? In a sharply divided opinion, the U.S. Supreme Court, in *Alaska Dep't of Environmental Conservation v. EPA*, 540 U.S. 461 (2004), upheld an EPA determination that Alaska had not required BAT to control air pollution in a permit issued for expansion of the world's largest zinc mine. The Red Dog mine, 100 miles north of the Arctic Circle, is the largest private employer in northwest Alaska. Alaskan officials had selected a "logistically and econom-

ically less onerous" technology as BAT, but the EPA ruled that the state had not justified its refusal to adopt a cleaner technology. The dissent characterized the holding as "relegating states to the role of mere provinces or political corporations, instead of coequal sovereigns." *Id.* at 518.

9.   Most high-volume wastes from oil and gas drilling are exempt from the mandates of the Resource Conservation and Recovery Act (RCRA) of 1976. This act creates a cradle-to-grave program for managing solid hazardous wastes in landfills. Produced water, drilling fluids, and other wastes uniquely associated with oil and gas drilling and production were exempted from the act because Congress feared the economic impact on the energy industry of subjecting these huge quantities of wastes to the strict requirements of Subtitle C of RCRA. An EPA report, required under RCRA, determined that this impact would cost the industry from $1 billion to $6.5 billion and result in oil production declines that would raise the price of oil by as much as 76 cents per barrel, costing consumers $4.5 billion per year. The EPA decided that removal of the exemption was not justified based on a further finding that current disposal methods for such wastes were not causing significant damage to human health or the environment. This exemption is controversial and is periodically attacked by environmental groups. *See generally,* Daniel L. McKay, RCRA's Oil Field Wastes Exemption and CERCLA's Petroleum Exclusion: Are They Justified?, 15 J. Energy, Nat. Resources, & Envtl. L. 41 (1995).

10.   Two other environmental laws threatened to impose additional costs on drilling and production, but passage of the National Energy Act of 2005 preempted these threats. In late 1999, EPA had issued a final rule expanding its stormwater permitting program to encompass construction sites of one- to five-acres in size. The EPA assumed that few oil and gas drill sites, processing plants or other facilities would be affected by the rule, which requires operators to obtain an NPDES permit to mitigate sediment and contaminated stormwater runoff from construction sites. However, the EPA later learned from the Department of Energy that 30,000 oil and gas sites might be affected by the rule. Section 323 of the 2005 Energy Act removes oil and gas field facilities from the definition of "construction site" under the Clean Water Act's permitting system. In light of the EPA rulemaking, the industry had developed "Reasonable and Prudent Practices for Stabilization (RAPPS)" to control runoff and guide the EPA's rulemaking. The RAPPS document is at www.ipaa.org/govtrelations /RAPPS.asp.

Hydraulic fracturing of wells had also come under review by the EPA Inspector General. Fracturing forces a mix of sand, water and sometimes diesel oil (containing benzene) into a reservoir at high pressure to crack the rock open and allow gas to pass more easily into the well bore. The practice is regulated under the Safe Drinking Water Act's underground injection control rules. A 2004 EPA report concluded that the practice posed minimal risk of contaminating ground water. An EPA whistleblower said EPA had done limited research and five of the seven members of the panel that peer-reviewed the study had conflicts of interest. Hydraulic fracturing is especially important in coalbed methane (CBM) production in western states. While contamination is quite unlikely when wells are drilled to deep reservoirs, CBM wells are often shallow and closer to groundwater aquifers. See April Reese, Enviros Urge Regulation of Hydraulic Fracturing, Greenwire, Apr. 15, 2005. Section 322 of the 2005 Energy Act removes the underground injection of fluids or proppants used in fracturing, other than diesel fuels, from the permit requirements of the Safe Drinking Water Act.

11.   The expedited onshore permitting provisions of the National Energy Act of 2005 are discussed in Chapter 8, Section B(4).

G.   OIL TRANSPORTATION

1.   OIL SPILLS

Tanker accidents have created some of the most telegenic of environmental disasters. We have all seen the television pictures of oil-soaked birds and dead otters which demonstrate the destructiveness of major oil spills.

The safety of oil tanker shipments requires a system in which the people who operate the system remain in a continual state of sharp awareness and preparedness. Think about this human element as you read about the famous 1989 Alaskan oil spill and Congress's reaction to it.

In the Wake of the Exxon Valdez: The Story of American's Most Devastating Oil Spill

by Art Davidson. Excerpts from pp. 10–18.
Copyright 1990 by Art Davidson, reprinted with permission of Sierra Club Books.

By 9:00 p.m., [on March 23, 1989] the Exxon Valdez was ready to depart. Earlier, Third Mate Gregory Cousins had tested the vessel's navigation equipment: radar, gyro compass, automatic pilot, course indicator, rudder control, and other sophisticated instrumentation. At 9:12 p.m., the tanker's last mooring line was detached from the pier and two tugs nudged the Exxon Valdez from its berth. On the bridge were harbor pilot Ed Murphy and Captain Hazelwood. Coast Guard regulations require that harbor pilots—who are trained to know about navigational hazards in local waters—be contracted to guide tankers from port to open water. Earlier, when they were boarding, Murphy had smelled alcohol on Hazelwood's breath but had said nothing about it.

At 9:21 p.m., Murphy, directing the vessel's speed and course settings, began to steer the Exxon Valdez out of the harbor toward Valdez Narrows, 7 miles from port. The Narrows, a channel that forms the entrance to Valdez Bay, is 1,700 yards wide. Middle Rock, a rock in the channel sometimes called "the can opener," reduces the minimum usable width to 900 yards. In computer simulations before the route was sanctioned, pilots repeatedly wrecked their imaginary tankers on Middle Rock. However, with the help of escort tugs and harbor pilots, tankers three football fields long had successfully negotiated the Narrows for eleven years. "We all know what the stakes are," said one longtime Valdez harbor pilot. "You've always got to be on your toes. I see these ships as eggs that are a quarter of a mile long. You can't make mistakes with them. A mistake ends your career."

The Exxon Valdez steamed through the Narrows in relatively calm weather: a 10–mph breeze from the north, with 4–mile visibility through low clouds and some snow and fog. With Murphy at the helm of the vessel, Hazelwood left the bridge, which was highly unusual and against company policy. But the two men had known each other for years and had eaten together that afternoon. Murphy mentioned nothing; he knew Hazelwood well and respected his seamanship. On a previous passage through the Narrows, when Murphy was piloting the ship, Hazelwood had helped avert disaster. "It was a winter night with very limited visibility. I was making a course change on Potato Point, and we were accelerating," Murphy recalled later. "The quartermaster applied the helm the wrong way.... The loaded vessel was rapidly swinging toward the beach. Captain Hazelwood picked up that mistake even before I did."

On this March 23 evening, the Exxon Valdez passed through the Narrows without mishap. Fourteen miles out of port, the tanker reached Rocky Point, where harbor pilots normally transfer command of a ship back to the captain. Murphy had to order Hazelwood called back to the bridge. When Hazelwood returned to the control room, Murphy again noticed the smell of alcohol on the captain's breath. However, a Valdez harbor pilot had never challenged a captain's command of his vessel. A pilot's continued employment by a given vessel can depend on the captain's good will. Murphy decided that Hazelwood looked fit and focused enough to assume command. At 11:20 p.m., Captain Joseph Hazelwood took control of the Exxon Valdez.

In the dimly lit radar room atop the three-story Coast Guard station in Valdez, civilian radar man Gordon Taylor watched a bright orange ring on the radar scope. The ring represented the Exxon Valdez as it moved from the terminal out through the Narrows. At Rocky Point, radar coverage became fainter and Taylor found it difficult to read. "You can pick up vessels off Bligh Island if there are no squalls, no heavy seas, no wind, and the radar is tuned up and working well," Taylor explained later. He added that it's easy to lose track of a tanker. "The vessel is there one sweep; the next, no vessel."

In 1981, James Woodle, then the Valdez Coast Guard commander, had recommended that the Coast Guard radar system be improved. He had wanted to ensure sharp vessel coverage between Bligh Island and the leading edge of the Columbia Glacier. The U.S. Geological Survey had predicted even more extensive glacial ice floes over the next ten to thirty years, and Woodle had argued that "placement of a radar site on either Glacier Island or Bligh Island could prove to be an invaluable tool.... Expanded radar coverage in this area is strongly recommended."

The Coast Guard had not acted on Woodle's recommendation, because it deemed the additional radar sites, at $100,000 a year, "cost prohibitive." In fact, budget cuts and the transfer of personnel to President Reagan's war on drugs had continually drained money from the Valdez Coast Guard budget and had whittled its staff from thirty-seven to twenty-four since the pipeline's completion in 1977.

Far from pushing for the recommended additions, Commander Steve McCall, who took over as the Coast Guard's ranking officer in Valdez in 1986, favored a downgraded system. "It's been twelve years since the tankers began operating, and nothing major has gone wrong," McCall had commented regarding the recommended radar upgrade. "So a lot of things have changed from what people thought was necessary in 1977. . . . We started downgrading in 1984. . . . We changed the radars in § 82, and made manpower cuts. . . . How much do you really need to watch a ship that is going in and out, all by itself, with nobody around it?"

As the Exxon Valdez approached the edge of radar coverage, Hazelwood radioed the Coast Guard that he was "heading outbound and increasing speed."

At 11:24 p.m., harbor pilot Ed Murphy, who had already turned over command to Hazelwood, left the tanker and boarded a pilot boat that would speed him back to the port of Valdez. Hazelwood radioed Traffic Valdez, the Coast Guard's radio monitoring station:

Hazelwood: We've departed a pilot. At this time hooking up to sea speed. And ETA [estimated time of arrival] to make it out [past Naked Island] on 0 100 [1:00 a.m.]. Over.

Traffic Valdez: Roger, Request an updated ice report when you go down through there. Over.

Hazelwood: Okay. Was just about to tell you that judging by our radar I will probably divert from TSS [Traffic Separation Scheme] and end up in an inbound lane. Over.

Traffic Valdez: No reported traffic. I got the Chevron California one hour out and the ARCO Alaska is right behind him. But they are an hour out from Hinchinbrook.

Hazelwood: That'd be fine, yeah. We may end up over in the inbound lane, outbound track. We'll notify you when we . . . cross over the separation zone. Over.

Shortly after Hazelwood notified the Coast Guard that he was going to divert from the Traffic Separation Scheme (designated one-way inbound and outbound tanker lanes), he radioed that he was going to angle left and reduce speed in order to work through some floating ice: "At the present time I am going to alter my course to 200 [degrees] and reduce speed about 12 knots to wind my way through the ice. And Naked Island ETA may be a little out of whack. But once we're clear of the ice, out of Columbia Bay, we'll give you another shout. Over." However, despite Hazelwood's assurance to the Coast Guard, the ship's speed was not reduced.

At 11:40 p.m., the night shift took over at the Coast Guard station back in Valdez. Radar man Taylor had seen the Exxon Valdez "blinking on and off the screen" but had lost the vessel by this time. Before heading home, Taylor told his replacement, Bruce Blanford, that the Exxon Valdez was crossing into the separation zone—possibly into the northbound land to avoid the ice.

However, Hazelwood did not notify the Coast Guard when he left the traffic separation zone. And instead of ending up in the inbound lane, he went on through the inbound lane, taking the tanker farther off course. In one transmission, he mistakenly identified his vessel as the Exxon Baton Rouge, and his speech was slurred.

At the Coast Guard station, it was now Blanford's responsibility to track tankers and warn of impending danger. Instead of trying to locate the Exxon Valdez on radar or trying to monitor its movements by radio, Blanford began to rearrange the tanker traffic data sheets. To track the progress of the tankers traveling in and out of Valdez, he moved stacks of paper, each representing a different vessel, around the room.

"As soon as [Taylor] left and I got everything sorted out in my mind, I checked all of the vessel data sheets," Blanford would report. "We each have our little way of keeping things straight in our heads and keeping our watches flowing smoothly. I'm left-handed. The rest of them are right-handed, so they all set their sheets up [one] way and I set mine up this way. And so I go through and get them where I can understand them. And I generally lay [the sheets for each tanker] from left to right.... When their sheets end up all the way on the right-hand side, a tanker would be in Valdez."

By the time Blanford had arranged his stacks of paper to represent vessels going to and from the port, the Exxon Valdez was nearing the ice. "After I got things squared away, so to speak, I went down and got a cup of coffee," Blanford said. "I may have been gone a couple of minutes. I really couldn't say how long."

Meanwhile, on the Exxon Valdez, Third Mate Gregory Cousins had joined Hazelwood on the bridge to make a navigational fix on the vessel's position in the sound. The night was too dark for the seaman on watch to see any bergs, but ice was silhouetted on the radar screen. It was an extensive floe—thousands of chunks of ice had broken from the Columbia Glacier and were being massed together by the current. Cousins and Hazelwood discussed skirting the ice. Some of the ice, broken into pieces the size of a car and smaller, were of little consequence to a tanker. But the massive bergs—those the size of a house and larger, the ones they called growlers—caused concern. However, Cousins couldn't tell from the radar screen whether there were any growlers out there in the night.

The northern edge of the floe appeared to be two miles dead ahead. At their current course setting, they would run into it. The ice was backed up to Columbia Glacier, so they couldn't pass it to the right. To the left of the ice was a gap of nine-tenths of a mile between the edge of the ice and Bligh

Reef. They could wait until the ice moved, or reduce speed and work their way through the ice. Captain Hazelwood chose another option: turn and enter the gap between the ice and the reef. The ship was still accelerating.

Hazelwood ordered the helmsman to alter their course "180 degrees to port"—to turn left across the 2,000–yard-wide zone separating inbound and outbound traffic and continue across the 1,500–yard-wide inbound lane. A well-timed right turn would be necessary to avoid Bligh Reef, which lay six miles ahead in the darkness. There would be little room for error. The vessel needed at least six-tenths of a mile to make the turn, and the gap between the ice and Bligh Reef was only nine-tenths of a mile wide. The tanker itself was nearly two-tenths of a mile long. The tanker would have to start its turn well before the gap between the ice and the reef if it was to make it through.

At 11:46 p.m., Maureen Jones left her cabin to go on duty. Captain Hazelwood relayed an order to her to stand on the bridge wing instead of standing her watch from the bow. Although 800 feet farther from the front of the boat, she would have the advantage of watching for hazards and buoy lights from a high position. She went to the bridge as requested.

As Jones came on duty, Helmsman Harry Claar's shift was coming to an end. Claar's job as helmsman was to physically move the steering wheel at the direction of the captain or qualified mates. Hazelwood gave him two last orders: to accelerate to sea speed and to put the ship on automatic pilot. Both commands were highly unusual. Speed was normally reduced when ice was encountered, both to minimize impact with bergs and to allow the crew more time to plot vessel position, make course adjustments, and react to an emergency. The automatic pilot—almost never used in the sound—would have to be released if any course changes had to be made.

Though puzzled by Hazelwood's orders, Claar increased speed and locked the controls on automatic pilot. He was then replaced at the helm by Robert Kagan.

On the bridge, Hazelwood told Cousins he was going below and asked if he felt comfortable navigating alone. Cousins had made only a few voyages with Hazelwood, and he had never maneuvered the Exxon Valdez in tight quarters. Nevertheless, he replied, "Yes, I feel I can manage the situation."

Standard Coast Guard procedure dictates that in the presence of danger, two officers must be on the bridge. The junior of the two is responsible for fixing the location of the vessel. The senior officer is responsible for directing the vessel's course based on this navigational information. Before leaving Cousins alone on the bridge, Hazelwood told him to make a right turn when the ship was across from the Busby Island light and to skirt the edge of the ice—but he neither gave Cousins an exact course to follow nor plotted a line on the chart. If he had, Hazelwood might have noticed that it was virtually impossible to turn abeam the Busby light and also miss the ice.

Hazelwood left the bridge at 11:53 p.m. "to send a few messages from [my] cabin." Cousins was now the only officer on the bridge. The chief mate and second mate were off duty, resting. Moments after the captain left, Cousins, who had not heard Hazelwood's orders to Claar, discovered that the vessel was on automatic pilot, and he shifted it back into manual mode. The ship was still headed on a 180–degree course toward Bligh Reef, and Cousins faced a critical maneuver: he had to avoid the ice but couldn't wait too long before turning. The vessel was increasing speed.

At 11:55 p.m., Cousins called Hazelwood to say, "I think there's a chance that we may get into the edge of this ice."

Hazelwood said, "Okay," and asked if the second mate had made it to the bridge yet. Cousins replied that the second mate hadn't arrived. They talked for less than a minute and neither mentioned slowing the vessel down.

Once more, Cousins assured the captain that he could handle things and then told the helmsman to make a 10–degree right turn. Cousins turned again to the radar, trying to locate the leading edge of ice. As he concentrated on the ice, Cousins may have lost track of time for a few minutes. He was peering at the radar screen when the tanker slipped past the Busby Island light without beginning to turn.

It was nearly midnight, the beginning of Good Friday, March 24, when Maureen Jones, now on watch, noticed that the red light on the Bligh Reef buoy was to the ship's right. Red navigational lights are placed to the right of ships returning to port, and almost every seaman knows the adage "red, right, returning." Since the Exxon Valdez was leaving port, the light should have been on the left side, to port. Jones alerted Cousins that "a red light was flashing every four seconds to starboard."

At virtually the same moment, though the ship was turning slowly, Cousins concluded that the tanker had not responded to his 10–degree right-turn command. He immediately ordered a 20–degree right turn, and this time he noticed the vessel responding.

Jones called Cousins a second time. She had a more accurate count on the red light; it was flashing every five seconds. It was still on the wrong side of the ship.

Cousins ordered a hard right and called Hazelwood, saying, "I think we are in serious trouble."

At 12:04 a.m., the Exxon Valdez shuddered. Hazelwood raced to the bridge. After first impact, the tanker advanced 600 feet before it ground to a halt on Bligh Reef.

Hazelwood didn't try to back off the reef. With the engines running full speed forward, he ordered a hard right, then a hard left. In the engine room, the chief engineer did not know they had grounded; he couldn't figure out why the system was overloading.

Chief Mate James Kunkel had been sleeping in his quarters, but awoke at first impact. "The vessel began to shudder and I heard a clang, clang,

clang. I feared for my life. I thought I would never see my wife again. I knew my world would never be the same," Kunkel recalled.■

2. REMEDIAL LEGISLATION: OPA 90

The Exxon Valdez spill was to the Oil Pollution Act of 1990 (often called OPA 90) as the Santa Barbara spill was to NEPA and the Coastal Zone Management Act. OPA 90 passed the Senate without a single dissenting vote, even though attempts to strengthen oil spill laws had foundered for years until then. Perhaps the following figure, showing the extent of the Exxon Valdez spill juxtaposed against the west and east coasts, explains the unanimity:

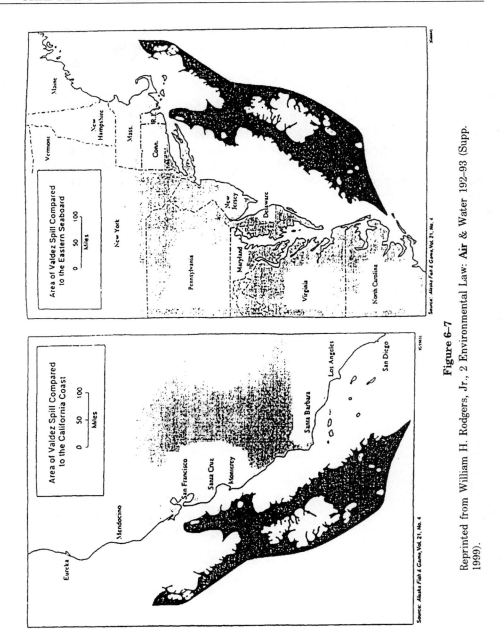

Figure 6-7

Reprinted from William H. Rodgers, Jr., 2 Environmental Law: **Air & Water** 192–93 (Supp. 1999).

Professor Rodgers, a leading authority on environmental law and an avid student of evolutionary biology and its interface with law, has written an interesting commentary on the likely success of certain sections of OPA:

William H. Rodgers, Jr., Where Environmental Law and Biology Meet: Of Panda's Thumbs, Statutory Sleepers, and Effective Law

65 U. COLO. L. REV. 25, 66–74 (1993).

One is tempted to condemn without further inquiry false behavioral assumptions whenever they appear in law. Delusions of compliance are an unlikely ingredient of an effective rule of law.[23] To gain further enlightenment on this subject, though, we will examine the Oil Pollution Act of 1990, which became law on August 18th of that year. The 1990 Act marked the initial Congressional response to the Exxon Valdez oil spill of March 1989. In an approximate way, the Exxon Valdez accident was the product of a combination of failures that included erratic navigation by an incapacitated captain in a vulnerable vessel under poorly planned conditions.[24] In a long (ninety-one pages), comprehensive (amendments were made to nine different statutes), and detailed response, Congress spread solutions across this spectrum of navigation, operations, vessel condition, and planning. Behind the Oil Pollution Act of 1990 are a wide variety of human behavioral assumptions about bad-weather observations, upstart second-officers, clever programmers, casual use of the auto-pilot, aggressive engineers, and careful planners. But it is the specter of the drunken captain, personified as Joseph Hazelwood, that drove this legislative engine. Our discussion will be limited to the legalized mutiny and the planning provisions. The central question is whether these measures represent effective law.

a. Legalized Mutiny and the Myth of Compliance

Section 4104 of the 1990 Act tackles the problem of the drunken captain by obliging the second-in-command to take over the vessel temporarily "when the [two] next most senior licensed officers on a vessel reasonably believe that the master or individual in charge of the vessel is under the influence of alcohol or a dangerous drug and is incapable of commanding the vessel." Assuming for the moment that this law is meant to serve a functional and not merely an aesthetic purpose, namely, the elimination of the risk of accident due to captain drunkenness, can we say anything useful about the effectiveness of this law as adjudged from a behavioral perspective? Borrowing from ethology, we will attempt to construct for this law a compliancegram, which can be defined as a description of the range and probability of behaviors that must coincide in order to

23. [FN257] Margaret Gruter, Law and The Mind: Biological Origins Of Human Behavior 21 (1991). "The effectiveness of law will be proportional to the degree to which the function of a particular law complements the function of the behavior that the law intends to regulate." *Id.*

24. [FN259] ... The findings of the Alaska Oil Spill Commission make clear that whatever the captain's shortcomings, the Exxon Valdez oil spill was an accident that was bound to happen: the combination of regulatory and corporate complacency, crew fatigue, insufficient personnel, insufficient radar, and insufficiently rigorous loading practices, as well as insufficient response preparations, created the preconditions for predictable spill disasters in the oil transport system. Alaska Oil Spill Comm'n, Spill: The Wreck of the Exxon Valdez, Implications for Safe Transportation of Oil iv (1990).

achieve the professed objective of the law. So viewed, this legalized mutiny can be expected to happen if one of the junior officers knows of the law (K), recognizes the risk (R), overcomes (O) his hesitation to initiate a takeover, persuades (P) his colleague to join in the endeavor, and defeats (D) other practical barriers to the takeover.

What are the probabilities that all conditions (K, R, O, P, D) will be satisfied to bring the vessel under safe command? Knowledge (K) of the law is usually assumed for legal purposes, and for good reason since the assumption is unlikely to be established as an empirical matter. One is left to speculation as to whether and how junior officers will be advised of their mutiny rights. The option to take over the vessel may well be spelled out in various directives, commands, manuals, and rules known best by the novitiates and least by the veterans. The possibility may be mentioned (featured?) in a mandatory (optional?) meeting on compliance with the oil spill rules. Each officer might be given the full text (all 91 pages?) of the Oil Pollution Act of 1990, which makes it a theoretical possibility that Section 4104 could be read and understood by at least a tiny fraction of the licensed merchant mariners. One suspects that years of education would be necessary to elevate the mutiny-option rule to the status of plausible hypothesis among working junior officers. There is no ship's lawyer, and if there were, he would be working for the captain. There is no report either of any captain posting a notice on a bulkhead spelling out the "Mutiny Option." A conservative estimate of the probability of the (K) requirement being satisfied is 1:5.

Risk recognition (R) is not a serious barrier to compliance, but a knowledge of human behavior could help in the analysis. Surely the mate can recognize a drunken captain when he sees one (and avoid the risk of confusing inebriation with, say, a stroke) although the use of "drugs" other than alcohol might give rise to odd behavior creating some ambiguities in interpretation. The big problem with risk recognition (R) is in appreciating that the drunken captain is "incapable" of commanding the vessel. The situation is bound to be ambiguous (the captain might be only slightly drunk, or indisposed to interfere, or soon to be so drunk that he can't interfere, or waters could be calm, or the automatic-pilot dependable, etc.), and ambiguity can be resolved as non-threatening in the mind of a junior officer. There is evidence also that self-deception may be at work to convince both the captain and the junior officers that the risks are non-emergent.[25] We will assign a probability of 1:2 that a junior officer will recognize (R) the captain-drunkenness risk when it appears on the scene.

Having recognized the risk, will the mate overcome (O) hesitation to put in motion the machinery of this legalized mutiny? Even with personal safety at stake, the behavioral constraints against this sort of challenge to authority are formidable. Within primate bands the very idea of a "temporary" takeover of leadership is implausible because of small rewards and high risks of subsequent retaliation. Sociological studies of modern bureau-

---

25.   [FN265] *See* Robert Trivers & Huey P. Newton, The Crash of Flight 90: Doomed By Self–Deception? Sci. Dig., Nov. 1982, at 66.

cracies underscore the difficulties of encouraging communication contrary to established norms,[26] much less direct challenges to the authority of the leadership. In the maritime world, of course, centuries of tradition have accorded the captain a role of unquestioned authority, and those in the business are entirely familiar with the career-threatening consequences of challenging these traditions. Junior officers who will rock this boat will be made of stern and unusual stuff. We will fix the probabilities of O being satisfied as 1:12.

Having convinced himself, will junior officer A be able to persuade (P) junior officer B to go along with the takeover? There are a number of variables here we can not account for: is this a case of a subordinate attempting to persuade a superior, or a superior a subordinate? Are the junior officers friends or rivals? Or long-term acquaintances or relative strangers? Was the decision to take over the vessel jointly arrived at, or did one overcome hesitation and make a commitment to action before seeking to persuade the other? The severity of the emergency obviously will influence the resolution of K and P by both actors. With this said, the second officer, like the first, will be contemplating a course of action under highly ambiguous and stressful conditions that will be of some considerable risk to her career. Even with the support of a colleague, the probability of the P barrier being overcome is not high—1:10 is the choice.

Even with the juniors committed to overthrowing the captain's authority, we must add a factor (D) to account for other miscellaneous obstacles that might stand in the way of a successful shift of power. What if the captain resists, and resists with force? Will the crew cooperate? Systems of formal approval (e.g., radio communication) might be superimposed on the process to constrain the choices otherwise open to the junior officers. Or what if the ship's doctor announces an interpretation of "under the influence" that deviates from the conclusion of the juniors? Or the turmoil of the moment may lend itself to a "nobody in charge" solution where the junior officers can take some steps to combat the pollution risk while protecting themselves from the career risks that might attend a complete takeover. These D obstacles will be assigned a probability of 1:2 of preventing the shift in command envisaged by the law.

Our compliancegram for the legalized mutiny rule tells us, then, that a limited knowledge of the law compounded with difficulties of recognizing the risk and of conforming to the legal mandates will lead to a low rate of compliance. The combined probabilities of K (1:5), R (1:2), O (1:12), P (1:10), and D (1:2) amount to 1:2400. Put another way, this law can be expected to repair one of every 2,400 drunken-captain, oil-spill-risk en-

---

26. [FN266] *See* Presidential Comm'n On The Space Shuttle Challenger Accident, Report to the President chs. 4–5, 95–96, 99, 101, 107 (1986) (the contractors (Morton Thiokol) recommended against the launch because of concerns regarding O-ring temperatures, ran into opposition from middle-level NASA managers and Morton Thiokol's superiors (one key person was told to "take off his engineering hat and put on his management hat,") took another "perspective" under this pressure, identified an "ambiguity" in the data, and caved in by withdrawing the no-launch recommendation; NASA upper-level management responsible for the launch were never informed about the safety concerns or the engineers' opposition).

hancements. This is not an effective law. A legislator might vote for the measure on symbolic grounds or because it does not hurt but not because it materially reduces the risks of oil spills from the navigation of tankers.

b. Planning and the Attrition of Time

Oil spill contingency plans have been a primary exhibit in the law of water pollution since the 1960s, and the concept received a thorough empirical test in the wake of the Exxon Valdez disaster:

> The fishermen of Prince William Sound watched in the hours after the wreck on Bligh Reef as eleven million gallons poured out into their waters. On Friday morning, some of them hired a small airplane to fly out from Cordova to survey the wreck. "It was eerie," said Riki Ott. "On the radio, the whole world was talking about the disaster. People in the lower forty-eight were busily planning volunteer cleanup and animal rescue units to support the official response forces, but here in Prince William Sound lay the Exxon Valdez completely quiet, surrounded by a pool of oil a mile across, with blue fog vapors rising from it, just a few people standing on the deck, shaking their heads, looking at this catastrophe, and no one out there doing anything on the water." That morning, nine hours after the spill, the fishermen could fly around the oil slick in only eight minutes. And they waited, watching, expecting the official governmental and corporate mechanisms to jump into action, as so often promised in contingency plans, political representations, and courtroom proceedings. For almost forty hours the weather of Prince William Sound was uncharacteristically generous. The normal winds of March were nowhere to be seen; the seas were calm and the oil stayed in a compact floating mass near the Exxon Valdez. But no one showed up with the necessary skimming barges, the containment booms, the storage materials and clean-up equipment so confidently promised earlier. And then at the end of the second day, the winds came back with a vengeance. One fisherman looked up from Valdez Sunday afternoon and saw a ribbon of snow blowing off the shoulder of one of the mountain peaks. "Uh-oh," he said, "there it goes," and within 24 hours the oil had blown forty miles southeastward, out of control forevermore, as the official players still continued to try to figure out what to do.[27]

The reasons for this contingency nonresponse are not much in doubt: confusion of authority (all looked to Alyeska), lack of preparedness (Exxon took over command of the response operation within twenty-four hours but was untrained for the job), staff limitations (supervision of all operations at the Valdez terminal was assigned to one-half the time of one full-time Alaska Department of Environmental Conservation field person), shortages of equipment (skimming barges, containment booms), lack of expertise (not enough people to operate the equipment, interpret the tides, etc.). It is another question, of course, and not a trivial one, to ask whether any

---

27. [FN270] Zygmunt J.B. Plater, Essay, "A Modern Political Tribalism in Natural Resource Management," 11 Pub. Land L. Rev. 1, at 1–9 (1990).

response would have sufficed to contain the 10.8 million gallons of crude oil that found its way into the waters of Prince William Sound on March 22, 1989.

How did Congress respond to this demonstrated failure of contingency planning? By adding to the Act "an extremely elaborate system of contingency planning, consisting of a national response unit ("NRU"), Coast Guard strike teams, Coast Guard district response groups, area committees, area contingency plans, and individual vessel and facility response plans." The facility and vessel response plans, which have their own histories going back to 1973, must be written to combat a "worst case discharge" and are expected to cover topics such as training, equipment testing, unannounced drills, and planned responses. They are supposed to dovetail in unspecified ways with similar legal requirements under the Emergency Planning and Community—Right-to-Know Act.

[Professor Rodgers then develops a compliancegram for OPA's mandated contingency plans, and concludes]:

To complete the calculations, then, our compliancegram for the contingency planning requirements advises us that even if the plans are written, they are unlikely to be adequate, and if adequate they are unlikely to be implemented, and if implemented they are unlikely to be successful. The combined probabilities of [each of these events] are 1:12,000. Rephrased, a Las Vegas gambler would fix the odds of the next million-gallon spill being stopped by a contingency plan as 12,000:1. The contingency plan requirements of the 1990 Act are not an effective tool for stopping major spills. A legislator might vote for the measure on symbolic grounds or because it is packaged with other effective provisions or because a plan might be helpful for dealing with small spills in confined waters.■

NOTES AND COMMENTS

1. How do you prevent people working in areas of safety hazard from growing complacent after years of no trouble? The same problem affects any business in which the risk of failure is small but the cost of failure is catastrophic, such as the nuclear power industry, petrochemical facilities or LNG plants. Boredom is apparently another problem. In March 2000, workers at a British company that makes plutonium fuel for nuclear reactors reportedly were bored counting fuel pellets for shipment and instead falsified numbers. New York Times, C1, Mar. 22, 2000.

Does the saga of the Exxon Valdez affect your opinion about whether a "worst case analysis" of a 100,000 barrel oil spill should have been included in the challenged EIS in *Village of False Pass*, discussed in note 4 on p. 333 *See* Edward A. Fitzgerald, The Rise and Fall of Worst Case Analysis, 18 Dayton L. Rev. 1 (1992). OPA now requires a "worst case" response plan, defined as a spill of a vessel's entire cargo in adverse weather, as part of the national contingency plan, area contingency plans, and the facility response plans. Are plans likely to work in the event of a worst case disaster?

From the Houston Chronicle, Feb. 22, 1999, at 7A:

> Public health infrastructures in the United States and Canada, in their current states, would be devastated by a "high-impact" bioterrorism event in which an attacker uses modern germ technology, officials say.

> A tell-tale scenario—role-played by public health experts using smallpox as the biological agent involved and epidemic response plans similar to those in many American cities—left 15,000 people dead over two months and 80 million dead within a year, primarily because of insufficient global vaccine supplies.

> "We blew it," said Dr. Michael Ascher, ... one of a number of experts asked to make decisions as the scenario played out. "It clearly got out of control. Whatever planning we had ... didn't work. I think this is the harsh reality, what would happen."

(by Laurie Garrett, Smallpox Bioterrorism Exercise Proves Disaster in Preparedness).

2.   Are Rodgers' statistics convincing? Or would this methodology make almost anything seem improbable? The Chairman of the Flight Safety Foundation commented as follows on the cause of the cargo fire that led a Valujet to crash in the Everglades in 1998: "Who would ever have thought somebody would one day mislabel the package [of oxygen generators], never put the safety caps on them, throw them into a rough box and put them into a hold full of things that would burn? ... There are so many minute probabilities there." New York Times, A16, Feb. 6, 2000.

An analysis of ship accidents from 1991–2002 found that human error continues to dominate as the cause of maritime accidents. Intertanko: Tanker Incidents Level Off since 2001, Oil & Gas J., Aug. 9. 2004, at 58–59.

3.   Are there other ways to deal with the problem of the drunken captain? Of human error? The U.S. Coast Guard reports that since 1990, the number of spills of more than 10,000 gallons in the U.S. decreased by about 50 percent. Perhaps the legislation has had a positive effect, despite Prof. Rodgers' pessimism, or because of other sections of the law. As you read the following summary of other provisions of the act, ask how they might affect the compliancegram for preventing oil spills:

(A) Owners and operators of vessels or facilities are strictly liable for cleanup costs and damages caused by discharges of oil. Sec. 1002, 33 U.S.C. § 2702.

(B) The federal liability limit was raised to $1,200 per gross ton, eight times the liability cap under the Clean Water Act. Sec. 1004.

(C) A new $1 billion Oil Spill Liability Trust fund is available to pay for cleanup costs in excess of the liability limit, funded by a five-cent-per-barrel tax on oil. The entire amount can be used for one spill, with up to $500 million for payments for damage to natural resources

(D) OPA 90 requires more drug and alcohol reporting, testing and retesting of merchant mariners., and limits the number of hours worked to prevent exhaustion.

(E) All newly constructed tankers must have double hulls, and existing tankers must be retrofitted for double hulls under a phased in schedule over 20 years. 33 U.S.C. § 4115.

(F) Civil penalties were dramatically increased, as were criminal sanctions for failure to report discharges.

(G) OPA 90 expressly denies any intent to preempt more stringent state laws regarding oil spills, such as laws imposing unlimited liability. Sec. 1018, 33 U.S.C. § 2718.

Many states have enacted their own oil spill laws. *See, e.g.,* Gary V. Pesko, Comment: Spillover from the *Exxon Valdez*: North Carolina's New Offshore Oil Spill Statute, 68 Envtl L. 1214 (1990). Following the *Valdez* spill, the state of Washington enacted laws that require tanker operators to comply with the state's "best achievable protection (BAP)" regulations. These regulations consisted of many operating and personnel rules, such as requirements that all deck officers be proficient in English and able to speak a language understood by the crew, that the crew have completed a comprehensive state training program; and that the navigation watch be composed of at least two licensed deck officers, a helmsman, and a lookout. The International Association of Independent Tanker Owners (Intertanko) brought suit, alleging that 16 of the BAP regulations were federally preempted. The lower courts upheld almost all of the 16 rules, relying on OPA's expression of non-preemption.

However, in *United States v. Locke,* 120 S.Ct. 1135 (2000), the Supreme Court held that reliance on OPA's savings clause was misplaced. OPA's non-preemption effect was limited to state laws involving oil spill liability, similar to the Florida law which the Court had upheld in *Askew v. American Waterways Operators, Inc.*, 411 U.S. 325 (1973). OPA's passage did not affect the preemptive powers of another federal statute, the Ports and Waterways Safety Act of 1972 (as amended in 1978). The Supreme Court had ruled in 1978, in *Ray v. Atlantic Richfield Co.*, 435 U.S. 151 (1978), that this Ports Safety Act preempted many of Washington state's earlier attempts to regulate tanker traffic in Puget Sound (much of it carrying crude oil from the Alaskan North Slope) by restricting tanker size, tanker design, and pilotage requirements. OPA's saving clause reads that "nothing in this Act" shall "affect, or be construed or interpreted as preempting, the authority of any State" to impose "any additional liability or requirements with respect to (A) the discharge of oil...." The Court found that these savings clauses applied only to Title I of OPA, captioned Oil Pollution and Compensation, and not to the whole Act, because the clause was placed in Title I. Title I does not regulate vessel operation, design, or manning, which were the subject of Washington's 16 BAP rules. In short, maritime commerce is largely a matter for federal and international regulation, unless "peculiarities of local waters" call for special, local regulations (such as requiring a local tug escort or local pilot in Puget Sound). Many of

Washington's requirements applied at all times in all waters and so could not survive the *Ray* preemption test.

The Court concluded: "When one contemplates the weight and immense mass of oil ever in transit by tankers, the oil's proximity to coastal life, and its destructive power even if a spill occurs far upon the open sea, international, federal, and state regulation may be insufficient protection. Sufficiency, however, is not the question before us. The issue is not adequate regulation but political responsibility; and it is, in large measure, for Congress and the Coast Guard to confront whether their regulatory scheme, which demands a high degree of uniformity, is adequate." 120 S.Ct. at 1152.

The Coast Guard is the lead agency for assuring the safety of LNG tankers as they reach our shores and ports. The sufficiency of protection against explosions from terrorist attacks on these vessels is certainly a question before many citizens and policymakers today.

4. Retrospective analyses of the first ten years of OPA are generally favorable, although Swanson assails the lack of uniformity resulting from OPA 90 because of its failure to preempt state law. See Steven R. Swanson, OPA 90 + 10: The Oil Pollution Act of 1990 after Ten Years, 32 J. Mar. & Com. 135 (2001); Lawrence I. Kiern, Liability, Compensation, and Financial Responsibility under the Oil Pollution Act of 1990: A Review of the First Decade, 24 Tul. Mar. L. J. 481 (2000).

5. The reach of OPA's strict liability provisions was tested in *Rice v. Harken Exploration Co.*, 250 F.3d 264 (5th Cir. 2001) when owners of the Big Creek Ranch in the Panhandle of Texas sued Harken, seeking $38 million in damages and remediation for discharging pollutants from drilling operations onto ranch land and into a small seasonal creek. The creek flowed into the Canadian River, which flows into the Arkansas River, which flows into the Mississippi River, which flows into the Gulf of Mexico, some 500 miles distant. Under OPA, a person operating an onshore facility is liable if the facility has discharged oil, or poses a substantial threat of discharging oil into the nation's navigable waters. 33 U.S.C. §§ 2701(32), 2702(a). Under OPA, the ranchers had to prove two elements: (1) that a discharge of oil occurred, and (2) that it threatened navigable waters.

The Clean Water Act and OPA define "navigable waters" very broadly, as "waters of the United States." Some courts had interpreted the Clean Water Act expansively to mean any natural surface water in the U.S., including sloughs, wetlands, and prairie potholes that have some connection to interstate commerce. However, in *Solid Waste Agency of Northern Cook County (SWANCC) v. U.S. Army Corps of Engineers*, 531 U.S. 159 (2001), the Supreme Court held that a Corps regulation defining "waters of the United States" as including isolated intrastate waters such as sandflats, mudflats and playa lakes exceeded the Corps' jurisdiction under the CWA. Applying *SWANCC*, the Fifth Circuit in *Harken* wrote that "it appears that a body of water is subject to regulation under the CWA if the body is actually navigable or is adjacent to an open body of navigable water."

Should "navigable waters" under OPA 90 be interpreted identically to the phrase as used in the CWA? The ranch owners alleged that the navigable Canadian River was threatened by Harken's discharges onto dry land because contaminants passed by subsurface flow to groundwater under the ranch and then into the river. The Fifth Circuit ruled against the ranchers' "unwarranted expansion" of OPA to gradual natural seepage from a discharge onto dry land.

Would Harken be liable if, instead of discharging oilfield wastes onto the ground, it discharged the wastes directly into the intermittent Big Creek or into a trench that carried wastes into a nearby county drainage ditch which then flowed into other waterways and ultimately into the Gulf of Mexico? *See Watts v. State*, 140 S.W.3d 860 (Tex. App. 2004) (Texas statutory definition of "water in the state" includes "beds and banks of all watercourses, artificial or natural"); *In re Needham*, 354 F.3d 340 (5th Cir. 2003) (landowners liable for oil spill clean up costs when oil traveled from a containment basin on their land to a drainage ditch to an unnavigable bayou which flowed into another unnavigable bayou that was adjacent to a navigable canal); and *United States v. Gerke Excavating*, 412 F.3d 804 (7th Cir. 2005) (whether wetlands are 100 miles from a navigable waterway or 6 feet, if water from the wetlands enters a stream that flows into a navigable waterway, the wetlands are "waters of the United States").

In March 1998, the EPA and the Department of Justice filed a lawsuit against ExxonMobil claiming that between 1991 and 1999, about 83 oil spills at Mobil's fields on Navaho land in Utah reached tributaries of the San Juan River. The suit settled in 2004 when the oil company agreed to pay $5.5 million as a penalty and to spend about $44.7 million to improve field operations to reduce spills. Daily Report for Executives, Aug. 4, 2004, at A–26.

6. Note that cargo owners are not liable for spills under OPA. If Exxon had chartered a tanker owned by someone else, would Exxon have any liability for a spill of its cargo? What prevents cargo owners from chartering old, poorly maintained, low-cost tankers sailing under foreign "flags of convenience"?

7. How would you create the incentives to ensure that plans for responding to oil spills are understood and implemented? The techniques for cleaning up after an oil spill are themselves controversial. For example, should dispersants be used to break the oil into smaller particles which will sink to the bottom? The pros and cons of dispersants are discussed in International Maritime Organization, Manual on Oil Pollution, sec. 4, pp. 123–51 (1988). For a description of the program for cleaning up Prince William Sound after the Exxon Valdez wreck, *see* Jeff Wheelwright, Degrees of Disaster (1994).

Has the decrease in oil spills after passage of OPA 90 led to complacency and lack of real situational experience by OSROs, the Oil Spill Response Organizations that must be able to arrive on scene within one hour of spill detection? A chief of port operations in the Coast Guard worries about these effects of OPA's success. Sharon Grau, Oil Spill Preparedness: Is the Focus Shifting, Oil & Gas J., May 23, 2005, at 20–25.

8.   The tenth anniversary of the spill in March 1999 spawned assessments of the Sound's recovery. Bald eagles and river otters are fully recovered; three bird species, Pacific herring, sea otters, clams, mussels, and pink and sockeye salmon are recovering; killer whales, harbor seals, and four bird species are not recovering. *See* 195 National Geographic (March 1999) at 98. The Dec. 19, 2003 issue of *Science* reports a study that the effects of the spill have lasted much longer than expected and that low levels of residual pollution have caused chronic harm to biota. The National Oceanic and Atmospheric Administration, which was heavily involved in the *Exxon Valdez* clean-up, has a website devoted to the spill, with many photos. Visit http://response.restoration.noaa/gov/spotlight/spotlight.html.

A volunteer who organized citizens to hand-scrub the oil off hundreds of otters and birds now looks back on this effort: "Exxon spent $80,000 per otter that survived the cleaning, but at least half of those are thought to have died soon after they were released. So it was closer to $160,000 per animal. I think that money would have been better spent restoring and protecting habitat." Sierra, Sea of Crude, Legacy of Hope, Mar/April 1999, at 81. Nearly $700 million of Exxon's settlement with the state and federal governments has been used to purchase over half a million acres of spectacular Alaskan coastline to preserve as parks and wildlife refuges.

9.   On November 18, 1997, the D.C. Circuit upheld most of the regulations implementing the natural resources damages sections of the Oil Pollution Act of 1990. *General Elec. Co. v. U.S. Dep't of Commerce*, 128 F.3d 767 (D.C. Cir. 1997). Natural resource damages compensate for injury to or loss of natural resources. Exxon paid a total of $900 million to the state and federal governments for such damages. (Exxon also incurred expenses of $2.2 billion in cleanup costs.) Natural resource damages must be placed in a fund administered by a trustee and can be spent only to restore, replace or acquire the equivalent of the damaged resource. Such damages include compensation for "nonuse values," such as the value of knowing that you or your children might be able to visit Alaska in the future and see a pristine Prince William Sound with otters and seals playing in the water. Economists measure such nonuse values using "contingent valuation" surveys that ask people how much they are willing to pay to experience a resource in a particular environmental condition. Contingent valuation has been attacked as speculative nonsense *(see, e.g.,* Note, Ask a Silly Question. . . . Contingent Valuation of Natural Resource Damages, 105 Harv. L. Rev. 1981 (1992)); and supported as consistent with economists' concept of option values. *See, e.g.,* Miriam Montesinos, It May Be Silly, but It's an Answer: The Need to Accept Contingent Valuation Methodology in Natural Resource Damage Assessments, 26 Ecology L.Q. 48 (1999). Several state attorney generals opposed the sale of Unocal to the Chinese National Offshore Oil Co. (CNOOC) because: "Were the owner of the company to be outside the United States, it might make it more difficult for states to be compensated for damage to natural resources." Greenwire, July 6, 2005.

10.   Litigation arising out of the *Exxon Valdez* spill lingers on, especially over punitive damages. The federal district court had certified a Commercial Fishing Class, a Native Class, and a Landowner Class for compensatory damages. The district court also certified a mandatory punitive damages class, so the award would not be duplicated in other litigation and would include all punitive damages the jury thought appropriate. For purposes of this litigation, Exxon stipulated that its negligence caused the oil spill. In 1996, a jury awarded $287 million in compensatory damages and, in what was then the largest punitive damages award in American history, $5 billion in punitive damages against Exxon, as well as $5,000 in punitive damages against Hazelwood. In 2001, in *In re The Exxon Valdez,* 270 F.3d 1215 (9th Cir. 2001), the court remanded the case to the district court to reduce the punitive damages award based on factors set forth in *BMW of North America, Inc. v. Gore,* 116 S. Ct. 1589 (1996). In upholding punitive damages in some amount, the Ninth Circuit wrote

> Exxon argues that there was insufficient evidence for the jury to award punitive damages against Hazelwood or against itself for Hazelwood's conduct. Its theory is that the evidence, which it concedes established negligence, can establish no more. As Exxon portrays it, Hazelwood left the vessel in the hands of an experienced mate, with a clear instruction to turn right at the Busby Island light, and the mate unaccountably failed to carry out this simple instruction.
>
> A jury could have interpreted the evidence as Exxon suggests, but it plainly did not. A far more damning account was well supported by testimony, exhibits, and reasonable inferences from them. The jury reasonably could have concluded that Hazelwood took command of the ship so drunk that a non-alcoholic would have passed out, made it harder to avoid the reef by taking the course east of the ice, made it harder to maneuver between the ice and the reef by putting the ship on an autopilot program that sped the vessel up, then left the ship in the hands of an overtired third mate just two minutes before the critical maneuver, barely enough time to calculate what to do and conduct the maneuver. Hazelwood's instructions were vague, and turning a supertanker right at the light is not like turning a car right at the light on dry pavement, more like turning right on glare ice. In so doing, Hazelwood violated numerous legal regulations as well as common sense in caring for his vessel. 270 F.3d 1215, at 1236.

On remand, the District Court reevaluated the size of the award and determined that $5 billion did not violate due process as described in *BMW v. Gore* because Exxon's conduct was highly reprehensible and the ratio of punitive harm to quantifiable damages was 9.85 to 1, in line with precedent. The district court determined quantifiable damages by adding up 21 awards, payments and settlements made by Exxon to get an amount of "actual harm" of $507,509,094. Nonetheless, to comply with the Ninth Circuit's remand, the court lowered the award to $4 billion. After final judgment was entered on a $4 billion award (in *In re The Exxon Valdez,* 236 F. Supp. 2d 1043 (D. Alaska 2002)), both Exxon and plaintiffs appealed.

Meanwhile in April 2003, the U.S. Supreme Court altered the case law on punitive damages in *State Farm v. Campbell*, 123 S. Ct. 1513 (2003), with respect to the substantive due process aspects of such awards. When the Ninth Circuit again took up the appeal, it applied the new precedent, again vacated the punitive damages judgment and remanded the case to Judge Holland in the district court with instructions to reconsider the award in light of *State Farm*. See *Sea Hawk Seafoods, Inc. v. Exxon Corp.*, Nos. 30–35166 and 03–32519 (9th Cir., Aug. 18, 2003).

On January 28, 2004, having reviewed *State Farm* on remand, Judge Holland increased the award and ordered Exxon to pay $4.5 billion in punitive damages plus more than $2.3 billion in interest that has been accumulating since September 24, 1996. *In re The Exxon Valdez*, 296 F. Supp.2d 1071 (D. Alaska 2004). Exxon is again appealing.

Footnote 12 of the 2001 case in the Ninth Circuit briefly describes almost 30 cases spawned by the spill, including *In re Exxon Valdez, Alaska Native Class* v. *Exxon Corp.*, 104 F.3d 1196 (9th Cir. 1997), a class action based on public nuisance brought by Alaskan Natives for injury to their subsistence way of life which was dismissed for failure to prove "special injury" because the damage suffered by the Natives varied only in magnitude, not in kind, from that suffered by all Alaskans. The conviction of Captain Hazelwood of the criminal charge of negligent discharge of oil was upheld by the Alaska Supreme Court in *State of Alaska v. Hazelwood*, 946 P.2d 875 (1997).

Clearly, the nightmare spill has been a litigator's dream.

11. Almost ten times as much oil is released into the environment from used engine oil dumped into storm sewers and from road runoff as from major tanker spills. *See* National Research Council, Oil in the Sea: Inputs, Fates and Effects 82 (1985). What laws can change the behavior of the weekend "do it yourselfer" who dumps used engine oil down sewers?

12. Outside the jurisdiction of the United States, a complex series of international treaties governs claims for compensation for damage from oil spills. These treaties are administered by the International Maritime Organization, based in London, and claims are paid out of the International Fund for Compensation for Oil Pollution Damage. In general, the types of damage for which compensation is available are more limited than in the United States, and the amount of damages is determined through administrative procedures rather than by a jury, which tends to result in smaller awards, but the time for processing awards is usually quite expeditious. *See generally* Gordon L. Becker, Acronyms and Compensation for Damages from Tankers, 18 Tex. Intl'l L. J. 475 (1983).

13. Does the double hull requirement of OPA 90 effect a regulatory taking of single hull tank barges that, if not retrofitted, must be phased out of operation within 20 years? Maritrans claimed that its large barge fleet was of no commercially viable use if it could not carry oil; that the barges had negligible scrap value; and that its reasonable investment-backed expectations of a 60–year life for its barges had been destroyed by OPA 90. As

proof of its expectations, Maritrans presented testimony from Coast Guard officials that the Guard had proposed a double hull requirement in 1980; however, a National Academy of Sciences study in 1981 ended all discussion of imposing it. *See* Maritrans, Inc. v. U.S., 342 F.3d 1344 (Fed. Cir. 2003).

3. Pipeline Safety

In August 2000, twelve members of an extended family were camping on the banks of the Pecos River in a rural part of New Mexico when an El Paso gas pipeline ruptured 675 feet away, instantly burning six members alive and ultimately killing all of them. The gas was being transported under high pressure in a major transmission line to California which was in the throes of an energy crisis now best known for its ultimate expose of market manipulation by Enron and other parties involved in the state's newly opened retail electricity markets. The year before, in 1999, in an urban area of Bellingham, Washington, a pipeline released 250,000 gallons of gasoline which exploded, sent a fireball more than 1 1/2 miles long through the city, and killed three children. In 2002, Congress enacted the Pipeline Safety Improvement Act of 2002 [Pub. L. No. 107–355, codified at 49 U.S.C. §§ 6103–6107 and 60104–60133], following years of industry inertia and agency incompetence. Like the Santa Barbara blowout and the Exxon Valdez spill, a catastrophe led to lawmaking.

In "The Pipeline Industry Meets Grief Unimaginable: Congress Reacts with the Pipeline Safety Improvement Act of 2002," Carol M. Parker documents in detail the nature of pipelines, their safety issues, the pre–2002 legislative framework for regulating pipeline safety, and agency action (largely inaction) in implementing pipeline safety. *See* Parker, 44 Natural Res. J. 243 (2004). The U.S. has more than 161,000 miles of liquid pipelines and 307,000 miles of natural gas pipelines. This section of the chapter briefly summarizes key aspects of her article.

Understanding pipelines. Pipelines are controlled by continuous, remote sensing units which monitor flows and pressures, but usually detect releases only after they have occurred. Prevention is the key to pipeline safety, but the best integrity testing measures (such as the use of "smart pigs" which are instruments placed inside the pipe to detect corrosion) are difficult to use in older lines and require highly skilled engineers to interpret the data. Often, operators inspect a small sample of pipe by excavating in suspect places and examining the pipe directly. Large transmission lines for liquids or natural gas most commonly rupture because of corrosion; smaller gas distribution lines (usually near customers in urban areas) most often rupture because an outside force damages the pipe.

The legal framework. In 1968, Congress created the Office of Pipeline Safety (OPS) within the Department of Transportation to implement the first pipeline safety act for interstate pipelines. (States oversee intrastate pipelines.) Both in 1978 and in 2000, the General Accounting Office produced reports highly critical of the OPS as a regulator or enforcer. Indeed, in 2001, OPS still did not have a map of the pipelines under its control because it relied on voluntary submission of maps from operators. A third tragedy propelled a slow-moving Congress (which failed to pass tougher safety laws in 2000 or 2001) to act—the terrorist attack of 9/11, 2001. (Also, a month after 9/11, a drunk Alaskan fired a rifle shot into the Trans–Alaskan Pipeline, causing a leak and shutting down 20% of U.S. oil production). The possible consequences of pipeline ruptures became a homeland security issue. In late 2002, the new Pipeline Safety Improvement Act became law.

Parker summarizes its provisions in five sections:

1.   *Reforms in the OPS.* For the first time, the OPS has the power to order immediate corrective action for potential safety conditions so that ruptures can be prevented rather than detected only after they have occurred. The Act increased penalties; strengthened judicial enforcement; rewrote the prior OPS mandate of providing "minimum safety standards" to now mandate "adequate protection against risks to life and property"; and gave the public five of the 15 seats on the OPS technical safety committee, also dictating that the five government members and five industry members cannot have a significant financial interest in the pipeline or petroleum or gas industries.

2.   *More state power.* The 2002 Act allows a state to take over inspection authority for interstate pipelines, although the Secretary of Transportation retains all enforcement authority. The Secretary must respond within 60 days to state notices of alleged safety standards.

3.   *More public information.* Cities, school districts, businesses and residents near a pipeline must receive educational material about how to recognize a leak and what to do about it, with grants to local groups and nonprofits to provide technical assistance, such as paying for engineering analysis of pipeline safety issues or promoting public participation in meetings. A Community–Right-to-Know section which would alert citizens to the location of pipelines near them was omitted because of security concerns that such information would help terrorists.

4.   *Mandates to industry.* Companies are now required to assist the government in accident investigations. Pipeline company employees must be well-trained and, rather than trust OPS to develop a training program, Congress itself provided specific employee qualifications to be tested with written results.

The Act's Risk Analysis and Integrity Management Program requires inspection of all natural gas pipelines in high-density population areas to be completed within ten years, with the highest risk areas being assessed first, and all facilities reassessed every seven years. Even though Congress had mandated a national inventory of pipelines in 1992, companies were not required to submit mapping data; in 2002, data for only 64% of the U.S. pipeline mileage had been submitted. The new Act requires that all pipeline operators provide geospatial data to the National Pipeline Mapping System within six months of passage.

The Act added whistleblower protection to employees that provide information about safety concerns to their employer or to the government. [In 1994, Alyeska, the operator of the Trans–Alaskan Pipeline, settled several whistleblower suits charging it with intimidation of employees who pointed out safety and other problems with the operations during a government-ordered audit in 1993. In 1999, Alyeska presented a 225–page report to Congress which found that retaliation against whistleblowers was still a problem and was retarding quality control and the updating of technical work. The new manager of Alyeska vowed to change the company's old culture of resistance to criticism and change. New York Times, B4, Sept. 22, 1999. Alyeska is largely owned by Exxon, BPAmoco, and Arco].

5. *Making industry compliance easier.* The Act creates an Interagency Committee, chaired by the Council on Environmental Quality, not by the Department of Transportation, to coordinate environmental reviews of pipelines and to set "best practice" standards for access, excavation and repair of pipelines. No federal, state, or local environmental laws are preempted by this review process. The Act also requires pipeline operators, excavators, and contractors to participate in the One–Call program which requires a centralized system of locating pipelines and utilities using a single phone call before excavation begins.

Recommendations for improving the Act, including imposing financial responsibility on the parent corporation of often-undercapitalized pipeline subsidiaries, conclude the article.

NOTES AND COMMENTS

1. Might the new pipeline safety act have prevented the "grief unimaginable" of the twelve family members who died while camping in rural New Mexico? What is a "high-density population area?" Would the camping site qualify? Would it have been better to draft the Act to require inspections for all areas of "high consequence," such as rural camping and picnicking sites that are frequently visited by small numbers of people? Note that the Act does not require that all pipelines be inspected. Only 22,000 miles of the 300,000 miles of gas transmission lines will be subject to pipeline integrity management inspections.

2. In January 2000, Koch Industries, one of the largest pipeline operators in the U.S., agreed to pay a $30 million fine, the largest civil environmental penalty ever collected to date. The EPA had found that Koch had failed to inspect its lines for cracks or corrosion, resulting in leaks of 3 million gallons of crude oil, gasoline, and other oil products in 300 separate incidents in the past 9 years. Instead of doing inspections, it apparently was cheaper for Koch to find pipeline flaws by waiting for them to break. New York Times, Jan. 14, 2000, at A21. Does the new Act change the company's incentives? The executive in charge of the Bellingham pipeline was given a six-month prison sentence for willful safety violations. Is criminal liability a more effective deterrent?

3.   Can best technology and eternal vigilance prevent the kind of disaster which occurred in October 1994 near Houston, Texas after several days of rainstorms resulting in swollen rivers? Thirty pipelines under the San Jacinto River were shut off after a large pipeline carrying gasoline ruptured and caused a fire that sent 120 people to the hospital, most with throat or lung irritation. Three more pipelines carrying diesel, heating oil and crude oil also ruptured. Nearby homes and buildings caught fire and the black mixture of fuels washed 20 miles downstream into Galveston Bay. Many officials and citizens were surprised that the distance between shut-off valves on some pipelines was so far. The valves were ten miles apart on the gasoline pipeline, but the flooding prevented reaching the closest shut-off to the rupture and at one point 30 miles of pipeline product were feeding the fire. The ruptures affected the availability of oil and raised its market price on the East coast substantially. Gaynell Terrell, Emergency Alert Issued on Pipelines, Houston Post, Oct. 26, 1994, at A1.

In September 2004, Hurricane Ivan swept through the Gulf of Mexico, destroying seven platforms, injuring 24 others, and damaging 102 pipelines, many of which lay deep under water on the bed of the Gulf, but were nonetheless tossed around by wave action that surprised observers with its force. Numerous oil spills occurred, and the price of crude oil rose again. The 2004 season of hurricanes caused $20 billion in damages to offshore facilities in the Gulf.

4.   Note that the industry received help securing environmental reviews for pipeline projects in the 2002 Act. Legislators feared that the two accidents would stoke even further citizen opposition to pipeline construction. Are all environmental groups what they appear to be? Florida receives all of its oil by tanker, even that coming from Texas and Louisiana. For years the oil companies have sought authority to build an oil pipeline from those states into Florida. Their efforts have consistently been frustrated by opposition from local Florida "environmental" groups, but some of these groups are funded by the maritime community that is threatened by a pipeline. See Campion Walsh, Shipping Companies Lead Florida Effort to Block Oil Pipeline, Oil Daily, Aug. 26, 1994, at 165.

5.   The "best available technology" for field leak detection appears to be trained dogs whose acute sense of smell lets them find pinhole-size gas leaks in pipe buried eight feet under frozen clay. Judy Clar, Going to the Dogs, Oil & Gas J., Dec. 6, 2004, at 17.

CHAPTER 7

INTERNATIONAL PETROLEUM

A. INTRODUCTION AND SCOPE

No single chapter can do justice to the legal, political, and socio-economic complexity of international energy transactions. Yet no study of energy law and policy is complete without at least a dip into the wider world of international petroleum. Most of the major American oil companies have shifted their attention and their budgets to international exploration and development. This is where the "elephants"—fields containing over one billion barrels of oil—are to be found. Even large-sized independents have been bitten by the international bug. Many domestic oil and gas

407

lawyers have retooled themselves in international law to work this new frontier.

This chapter is designed to introduce the student to some of the major principles and problems involved when oil companies go abroad to explore for and produce oil and gas, such as:

State ownership of minerals. The United States and Canada are virtually the only countries on earth where minerals can be owned privately. Chapter 6 on Domestic Oil analyzed many of the problems which arise under private ownership: the wastefulness of the rule of capture; the need for state conservation legislation; the conflicts between state and federal regulation; the tension between government regulation and unconstitutional takings. Which of these problems disappear and which new ones arise when the state owns all the minerals?

The major forms of international concession agreements between host governments and multinational oil companies. The early concessions are compared to the oil and gas lease used in the United States and to modern agreements used today. Corruption has plagued the negotiating and implementing stages of petroleum contracts in many developing countries; can anti-corruption laws change behavior?

The legal doctrines encountered in litigation under these concession agreements. Which nation's law will govern the dispute? Can a private company overcome legal barriers to suing a government or a state oil company, such as sovereign immunity and the act of state doctrine? Can a company be sued in the United States for violations of foreign laws committed abroad?

The constraints of human rights laws on companies that choose to develop in countries led by oppressive and brutal regimes. Through the lens of the Alien Tort Claims Act, the last section surveys the suits which foreign plaintiffs have brought in U.S. courts alleging human rights abuses by multinational companies in their native countries.

The overarching theme of this chapter is the interplay of national sovereignty with private rights and, then, their combined interaction with the international public law of human rights. Chapter 9 contains related material on the legal framework, particularly industry-developed codes of conduct, that are used in drilling and development in the Amazon rainforest to protect indigenous communities and promote sustainable development.

Before setting out on this tour of international petroleum transactions, this chapter begins with a summary history of the geopolitics and statistical background of world oil markets. Students should use **Figure 6–1** in Chapter 6, showing the price of crude oil from 1880 to 2004 as a road map to this next section.

B.   THE HISTORY AND CURRENT STRUCTURE OF INTERNATIONAL OIL

1.   THE GEOPOLITICS OF OIL

a.   THE UNITED STATES: FROM EXPORTER TO IMPORTER

For almost half a century after oil was discovered in Pennsylvania, the United States was the primary source of petroleum and exported its products throughout the world. With little oil production abroad, American oil companies competed only with themselves.

Boom and bust conditions characterized the oil business in the 1860s and early 1870s, but by the 1880s prices began to stabilize when the Standard Oil Company, headed by John D. Rockefeller, obtained control of some 85 to 90 percent of the oil refineries in the United States and was able to establish monopoly prices. The Standard Oil Trust agreement allowed the company to control the production of refined petroleum. In 1889, Congress enacted the Sherman Anti–Trust Act, aimed directly at protecting consumers from the predatory practices of monopolists, especially the Standard Oil Trust. The Standard Oil Trust was ''busted'' in 1911, and Standard Oil was dissolved into separate entities which ultimately became Exxon, Mobil, Chevron, Sohio/BP, Amoco, Conoco, and ARCO/Sun. Some of the smaller progeny have now merged with their larger siblings or with other oil companies; witness today's ExxonMobil, ConocoPhillips, Chevron (which dropped Texaco's name), and BP, which took both Amoco and Arco under its roof.

In the 1890s, oil from Russia and Sumatra began to provide competitive sources of kerosene. Standard Oil was forced to compete internationally with various European enterprises, such as the Nobel brothers, the Rothschilds and the newly-formed Royal Dutch Company.

In 1901, oil was first discovered in the region known as the Middle East by British companies in Persia (now Iran). This stimulated the search that located the extensive fields of Iraq, Kuwait, Saudi Arabia and neighboring states. The American dominance in oil production ended after World War II when it became clear that other parts of the world had oil reserves that would far outlast American supplies.

b.   FROM THE 1930s TO 1970s

The following excerpts from Daniel Yergin's history of the oil industry highlight some of the key events leading to creation of an international market in oil.

Daniel Yergin, The Prize: The Epic Quest for Oil, Money and Power

(Simon & Schuster 1991) at 395–396, 531–32, 544, 567, and 569.

"We're Running Out of Oil!"

The late 1920s and early 1930s had seen an explosive growth in the United States in discoveries and in additions to known reserves. But from the middle 1930s onward, while significant "revisions and additions" were made to existing oil fields, the discovery rate of new fields had fallen off very sharply, leading to the view that additions in the future would be more difficult, more expensive, and more limited. The precipitous decline in new discoveries transfixed and frightened those responsible for fueling a global war. "The law of diminishing returns is becoming operative," said the director of reserves for the Petroleum Administration for War in 1943. "As new oil fields are not being formed and as the number is ultimately finite, the time will come sooner or later when the supply is exhausted." For the United States, he added, "the bonanza days of oil discovery, for the most part, belong to history."

Such gloomy analyses could lead to only one conclusion. Although oil was then flowing out from American ports to all the war fronts, the United States was destined to become a net importer of oil, a transformation of historic dimensions, and one with potentially grave security implications. The wartime gloom about America's recoverable oil resources gave rise to what became known as the "conservation theory" that the United States, and particularly the United States government, had to control and develop "extraterritorial" (foreign) oil reserves in order to reduce the drain on domestic supplies, conserve them for the future, and thus guarantee America's security.... And where were these foreign reserves to be found? There was only one answer. "In all surveys of the situation," Herbert Feis, the State Department's Economic Adviser, was to say, "the pencil came to an awed pause at one point and place: the Middle East."

The New Competitors

The proliferation of players in the oil game was remarkable, especially in the Middle East. In 1946, 9 oil companies operated in the region; by 1956, 19; and by 1970, the number reached 81. Yet even this was only part of a larger expansion. Between 1953 and 1972, by one estimate, more than 350 companies either entered the foreign (that is, non-U.S.) oil industry or significantly expanded their participation. Among these "new internationals" were 15 large American oil companies; 20 medium-sized American oil companies; 10 large American natural gas, chemical, and steel companies; and 25 non-American firms. How different this was from the situation at the beginning of the postwar period, when only six American firms, in addition to the five acknowledged American majors, had any active exploration interests anywhere overseas at all. In 1953, no private oil company anywhere in the world, other than the seven largest, had as much as 200 million barrels of proven foreign reserves; by 1972, at least thirteen of the "new internationals" each owned more than 2 billion barrels of foreign reserves. Altogether, the new entrants owned 112 billion barrels, of proven reserves a quarter of the free world total. By 1972, the "new internationals" had a total daily output among them of 5.2 million barrels per day.

One of the most obvious results of such a crowded arena was a decline in profitability. The industry had earned high rates of return on its foreign investment until the mid–1950s—the rewards, some would say, for the risks taken in distant, inaccessible regions in the turbulent postwar days, or, others would say, the result of an oligopoly, an industry dominated by a handful of major players. The series of crises in Mossadegh and Iran, the Korean War, and Suez all continued to buoy the profit rate above 20 percent. But with the reopening of the Suez Canal in 1957, the intense competition to sell supplies started to force both prices and profits down. Thereafter, and continuing through the sixties, investment in foreign oil yielded 11 to 13 percent returns, which were pretty much the same as for manufacturing industries. While the exporting countries were counting more money than they had ever seen before, the oil industry itself was no longer being as well rewarded as in the past.

The Conversion of Europe

Part of the reason for oil's victory over coal was environmental, especially in Britain. London had long suffered from "Killer Fogs" as the result of pollution from coal burning, particularly the open fires in houses. So thick were those fogs that confused motorists literally could not find their way home to their own streets and instead would drive their cars onto lawns blocks away from their own houses. Whenever the fogs descended, London's hospitals would fill with people suffering from acute respiratory ailments. In response, "smokeless zones" were established where the burning of coal for home heating was banned, and in 1957 Parliament passed the Clean Air Act, which favored oil. Still, the biggest force promoting the switch was cost; oil prices were going down, and coal prices were not. From 1958 onward, oil was a cheaper industrial fuel than coal.

The End of the Twenty–Year Surplus: To a Seller's Market

The 1970s also saw a dramatic shift in world oil. Demand was catching up with available supply, and the twenty-year surplus was over. As a result, the world was rapidly becoming more dependent on the Middle East and North Africa for its petroleum. * * *

In the period 1957 to 1963, surplus capacity in the United States had totaled about 4 million barrels per day. By 1970, only a million barrels per day remained, and even that number may have been overstated. That was the year, too, that American oil production reached 11.3 million barrels per day. That was the peak, the highest level it would ever reach. From then on, it began its decline. In March 1971, for the first time in a quarter century, the Texas Railroad Commission allowed all-out production at 100 percent of capacity.... With consumption continuing to rise, the United States had to turn to the world oil market to satisfy the demand.... Imports as a share of total oil consumption [from 1967 to 1973]rose from 19 percent to 36 percent.

Environmental Impact

Another significant shift was taking place in the industrial countries. Man's view of the environment and his relationship to it were also changing.... Beginning in the mid–1960s, environmental issues began to compete successfully for their place in the political process, in the United States and elsewhere. Air pollution prompted utilities around the world to shift from coal to less-polluting oil....

The retreat from coal was accelerated, and reliance on cleaner-burning oil grew. Nuclear power was bruited as an environmental improvement over the combustion of hydrocarbons. Efforts were accelerated to search for new sources of oil, and toward the end of the 1960s, hopes grew for major production offshore of California. There, after all, before the end of the nineteenth century, the very first drilling in water had taken place from piers near Santa Barbara. Now, more than seventy years later, rigs were being positioned along the scenic Southern California coastline. But then, in January 1969, the drilling of an offshore well in the Santa Barbara channel encountered an unexpected geological anomaly, and as a result, an estimated six thousand barrels of oil seeped out of an uncharted fissure and bubbled to the surface. A gooey slick of heavy crude oil flowed unchecked into the coastal waters and washed up on thirty miles of beaches. The public outcry was nationwide and reached right across the political spectrum. The Nixon Administration imposed a moratorium on California offshore development, in effect shutting it down. However great the need for oil, the leak increased opposition to energy development in other environmentally sensitive areas, including the most promising area in all of North America, ... Alaska.■

c. NATIONALIZATION, WAR, AND EMBARGO: THE FIRST OIL SHOCK

The relative stability of oil prices ended with a bang at about two o'clock in the afternoon on October 6, 1973. In the middle of the Jewish holiday of Yom Kippur, Syria and Egypt launched a surprise attack on Israel. The United States, fearful that Israel might be overrun by the combined attack, rushed supplies to the Israeli armed forces. Israel counterattacked, and regained the territory it had lost. In return, Arab nations that had supported Syria and Egypt declared an embargo on the shipment of oil to the United States, the Netherlands, and other countries friendly to Israel. As certain Arab producers cut back production, U.S. refineries scrambled for oil, and shortages sent crude prices soaring. (See **Figure 6–1** in the Oil chapter).

The events of the 1970s unsheathed the power of the "oil weapon" and led to a radical transformation in the international oil industry. In 1970, large, vertically integrated companies dominated the industry. They owned 94 percent of oil production in the non-Communist world and sold 91 percent of all refined products. By 1984, the companies' share of crude oil ownership had been reduced to less than 40 percent as most African and

Middle East countries nationalized their oil reserves and production. The excerpt below provides a brief summary of this transformation.

The Center for Strategic and International Studies, The Critical Link: Energy and National Security in the 1980s

pp. 126–27 (Ballinger, pub. rev. ed. 1982).

Nationalization of Production

Up to 1970 the Seven Sisters [Royal Dutch Shell, Exxon, Gulf, Texaco, BP, Mobil and Standard Oil of California (Chevron)] dominated world petroleum trade. They produced the oil, shipped it to major markets in Europe and Japan, refined it and sold the products to the final user. Vertical integration gave the companies extraordinary logistical flexibility. As the main suppliers of crude oil to most refiners worldwide and as distributors of refined products, they could readily adjust supply and demand in most markets. Furthermore, even when a few countries nationalized production—notably Mexico and Iran in the 1930s and 1950s—power over the downstream end of the industry allowed the companies to maintain considerable control over the market for those nations' crude oil. As one historian of the oil industry has noted,

> However successful host governments were in finding technicians to help the oil flowing, they were lost without customers on world markets. These were difficult to find as long as the bulk of the world's refineries have either been owned by the majors or tied to them by long-term supply contracts, and this difficulty was exacerbated by the general world glut of oil in the 1960s.

Thus, with the ability to restrict markets for the producing nations for their crude oil, the major companies could preserve their preeminence in both the upstream and downstream aspects of the industry.

Originally the major oil companies received concessions from the oil-bearing countries of Latin America and the Persian Gulf, under which the companies developed oil fields in certain areas for a given length of time (fifty years, for example). In return the companies paid royalties or excise taxes to their "host" governments. This system gave the companies complete control over the rate of oil production, pricing, and exports. In short, the companies took all the risks of failure and all the financial rewards of success. The countries by contrast received an income from production with little investment of capital or labor.

"The concession system", as one expert has noted, "by its very nature could not satisfy the desire of producing country governments for more influence on the rate at which their oil was produced or on other decisions concerning the exploitation of their resources." Any reduction in prices for crude oil because of market conditions automatically cut revenues to the producing government. Moreover, the gradual depletion of reserves eroded the base for future revenues, especially for the Persian Gulf states, since oil is virtually their sole source of income.

Concerned about the exploitation of their resources, some of the Middle Eastern oil producers—Saudi Arabia, Iran, Iraq, and Kuwait—joined Venezuela in forming the Organization of Petroleum Exporting Countries (OPEC) in 1960. OPEC set out to coordinate long-term policies on production rates, pricing, and taxation of the companies. During the 1960s OPEC wielded little power, largely because of a world oil glut and constant price-cutting as older companies battled with newer companies to preserve or increase markets. The price wars eventually led to a confrontation between the oil companies and the producing countries that would mark the end of oil company control over world oil production.■

d. THE ERA OF PRICE CONTROLS

The sharp rise in oil prices following the 1973 embargo caused anguished cries of pain from millions of American consumers. The reaction of the various members of Congress was heavily influenced by the particular part of the country they represented. Regional politics had always permeated national oil policy. When foreign oil was cheap, consumers on the east coast sought to import as much as possible. Producers from Texas and other states, however, argued that cheap foreign oil was driving them out of business. Representatives of the producing states demanded limits on oil imports, arguing that national security required a strong domestic industry. Early in the Eisenhower Administration, voluntary quotas on imported oil were tried and failed. Then in 1957, Eisenhower instituted the Mandatory Oil Import Program (MOIP), which limited the amount of foreign oil that could be brought into the country. Despite this program, imports continued to climb because of exemptions in the program that fed America's hunger for inexpensive crude oil and refined products. With the 1973 embargo, foreign oil prices rose to such an extent that MOIP became obsolete. Federal attention instead turned to protecting the consumer from this first oil shock.

Between 1970 and 1981, the federal government maintained a complex system of oil price controls, first as an anti-inflationary measure and then to prevent "windfall profits" to domestic producers whose $3 per barrel oil could sell for $30 a barrel in 1980. Oil prices were regulated at each stage of production, refining, wholesaling, and retailing. These controls were first administered through the President's Cost of Living Council, the now defunct Federal Energy Administration, and finally through the Department of Energy ("DOE"). The Emergency Petroleum Allocation Act, 15 U.S.C.A. § 751 *et seq.*, authorized the President to allocate petroleum products because of the national oil shortage.

The regulations resulted in an intricate price and allocation structure, involving such complex concepts as "two-tier pricing, entitlements, exception relief, small refiner bias, and the stripper well exemption, to name a few of the arcane terms that have become associated with the regulation of petroleum at the federal level during the 1970s."[1] The general policy of the program was to encourage producers to explore for "new oil" by allowing them to sell such oil at a higher price, while preventing them from raising the price of "old oil" and reaping windfall profits. Thus the legal question of whether any particular crude oil was new or old had great economic significance to the producer. Old oil prices were determined by reference to both historical and current levels of production from a given property (the "base production control level"). Oil produced at or below that level was "old" oil, while oil produced in excess of that level was "new" oil. If producers invested capital in new production, the cost was passed through to the refiners of the new oil and then to consumers, and the price of new oil rose to market levels.

The disparity between the price of controlled oil and uncontrolled new oil had an unequal impact on different groups of refiners. With a dual pricing system, the major integrated oil companies, which as a class had greater access to old oil, had significantly lower refining costs than did small independent refiners. The government's response was the Entitlements Program Regulations under the Energy Policy and Conservation Act, 42 U.S.C.A. § 6201 *et seq.*, which tried to equalize the impact of the two-tier pricing system. Each refiner was required to have an "entitlement" for each barrel of old oil it refined. Refiners were issued monthly entitlements equal to their proportionate share of the national ratio of old oil to new oil. A refiner that used more old oil than the national average had to buy additional entitlements from refiners that were below the national average. Small refiners received special entitlements to cheaper old oil so that they could stay competitive.

The price and allocation controls pitted the majors against the independents, importers against domestic producers, and states with new oil against states with old oil. Virtually no one was happy with the program, and its expiration in 1981 was greeted joyfully by almost everyone.

e.   THE AYATOLLAH AND THE SECOND OIL SHOCK

The sharp price increases that followed the Yom Kippur war of 1973 became known as the first oil shock. A second shock hit in 1979, when the Shah of Iran was ousted and replaced by a theocratic government headed by the Ayatollah Khomeini. On November 12, 1979, in response to the taking of hostages by Iran, President Carter banned the importation into the United States of oil produced in Iran. The Iranian government then placed an embargo on the export of its oil to the United States. Oil prices skyrocketed again.

The price increases were fueled by a wave of panic buying at all levels. Industrial users and utilities furiously built inventories as insurance against rising prices and possible shortages. Consumers did the same:

---

1.   Jan G. Laitos and Joseph P. Tomain, Energy and Natural Resources Law 443 (West 1992).

Before 1979, the typical motorist in the Western world drove around with his tank only one-quarter full. Suddenly worried about gasoline shortages, he too started building inventories, which is another way of saying that he now kept his gas tank three-quarters full. And suddenly, almost overnight, upwards of a billion gallons of motor fuel were sucked out of gasoline station tanks by America's frightened motorists. Yergin, *supra* at 687.

With supply down by about 2,000,000 barrels a day, and demand increased by 3,000,000 barrels of panic buying, the United States suddenly had a five million barrel shortfall. This drove the price of oil from about $13.00 to $34.00 a barrel.

In an effort to alleviate the hardships caused by the shortage, the Department of Energy imposed quotas on the sale of oil products and implemented a new system of mandatory allocations that allowed those domestic refiners most injured by the embargo to receive cheaper oil from other domestic refiners. A program to ration gasoline was readied, but it was never needed because of the third (and even less expected) oil shock which hit in early 1981. This third shock requires some knowledge about OPEC.

f. THE ROLE OF OPEC

In 1960, Venezuela had persuaded Saudi Arabia, Kuwait, Iraq and Iran to join together as the Organization of Petroleum Exporting Countries (OPEC) with the goal of increasing their oil revenues.[2] During the 1960s, OPEC was relatively ineffective, but Egypt's seizure of the Suez Canal in 1969 provided a rallying point for the producing nations. When oil production in the U.S. peaked and the Mideast conflicts erupted, OPEC's solidarity made it appear invincible. More nations joined the cartel, and petrodollars filled the coffers of their national treasuries. The following excerpt describes OPEC more fully.

Alfred A. Marcus, The Organization of Petroleum Exporting Countries *in* Controversial Issues in Energy Policy 57–61

(Sage 1992).

The Organization of Petroleum Exporting Countries (OPEC) is a cartel that was formed in 1960 by Iran, Iraq, Kuwait, Saudi Arabia, and Venezuela. OPEC now includes 13 countries—Algeria, Ecuador, Gabon, Indonesia, Libya, Nigeria, Qatar, and the United Arab Emirates in addition to the 5 founding members. Of these 13 nations, 6 are Arab—Iraq, Kuwait, Saudi

---

2. Ironically, the birth of OPEC was brought about by a Venezuelan oil minister, Perez Alfonzo, who had studied the oil industry while living in the United States. He proposed to model a global alliance on the Texas Railroad Commission's system of market demand prorationing which would restrict production and prevent Venezuela's high-cost oil industry from being swamped by cheap oil from the Mideast. *See* Yergin, *supra* at 512.

Arabia, the United Arab Emirates, Libya, and Algeria. Although Iran is not an Arab nation, it is Islamic and borders Arab nations. In 1967–1968, the Arab members of OPEC formed an exclusively Arab organization, the Organization of Arab Petroleum Exporting Countries (OAPEC). Syria and Egypt subsequently joined OAPEC. On October 17, 1973, 11 days after the armies of Syria and Egypt launched a surprise attack on Israel, OAPEC announced a cutoff of oil to Western countries and Japan. The 1973 oil embargo was one of the most dramatic actions taken by a cartel in history, catching nearly all observers by surprise and altering the course of post-World War II history.

On January 1, 1979, oil production in another OPEC nation, Iran, was almost entirely shut down because of the strikes and political disturbances that led to the overthrow of the Shah and the establishment of a fundamentalist Islamic republic. Iraq then invaded Iran, and on September 25, 1980, both countries started to bomb each other's oil facilities. The Iraqis damaged the Iranian refinery at Abadan—the world's largest—and the Iranians retaliated against Iraqi refineries at Basra. Oil tankers and freighters, trapped in the Shatt al-Arab waterway, had nowhere to go. Oil tanker traffic through the Strait of Hormuz was delayed because shipowners feared they would be caught in the conflict. With supplies reduced, the world again faced a major petroleum price hike.

No matter what the effects of the 1973 Arab boycott were, the impetus for the boycott was political. The Iranian Revolution and Iran–Iraq War were not pursued for economic reasons. Indeed, by contributing to a worldwide recession, they weakened the hold of oil on the world economy. The collapse in world oil prices then devastated the economies of the OPEC countries.... The economic theory of cartel behavior misses the deep-seated political passions that affect the behavior of Persian Gulf nations. Thus, along with economics, it is necessary to consider political explanations for what OPEC does.

Conditions vary considerably among the OPEC countries. Some are democracies; some are dictatorships. Some are ruled by military juntas and some are governed by traditional monarchies.... Population, per capita income, and oil wealth divide the OPEC nations. There are over 150 million Indonesians and almost 100 million Nigerians, but only about 1 million people living in the United Arab Emirates, and only 200,000 in Qatar. Indonesia is a very poor country with GDP per capita under $500, whereas the United Arab Emirates and Qatar are very rich countries with GDP per capita above $20,000. Saudi Arabia, Kuwait, Iraq, and Iran have the largest crude oil reserves in the world. Indonesia possesses less than 6% of the proven Saudi reserves, and Nigeria less than 10%. Some OPEC countries have sufficient production capacity to generate oil revenues to meet their economic development needs, but others cannot meet their economic development requirements with oil revenues alone. Saudi Arabia, Qatar, the United Arab Emirates, and Kuwait belong in the former category; their oil revenues provide all they need for economic development. Indonesia, Nigeria, Algeria, and Venezuela belong in the latter category, with oil revenues insufficient to provide for their economic development needs.

OPEC nations that are able to finance their economic growth with their oil revenues have different economic interests than OPEC nations that cannot.... Nations like Saudi Arabia, which are rich in crude oil reserves, do not want prices rising to the point where alternatives to OPEC oil become feasible. They are likely to remain oil exporters for a very long time and therefore have an interest in preserving a healthy oil market over the long term. OPEC nations unable to finance their economic growth with their oil revenues have a different outlook: Their need is to generate revenues as quickly as possible. Their oil reserves are limited and their potential for future oil discoveries slim, so they do not care if prices rise to the point where it becomes feasible to develop alternatives....

Because the nations with small reserves are not likely to be major producers in the future, they have no reason to consider Saudi Arabia's long-term interests. But the price increases they favor can be achieved only if such countries as Saudi Arabia keep oil from the market. The countries with small reserves are not in a position to achieve price increases on their own to help them maximize short-term earnings; thus, it has to be the nations rich in crude oil reserves that withhold the oil. For these nations to withhold oil depends on whether they can earn more money from doing so than from investing abroad. From 1973 to 1979, when oil prices went up more rapidly than the rate of return from investments abroad, it was in their interest not to produce oil. The rate of return on their investments did not match the rate of return from keeping oil in the ground. This situation reversed itself in the 1980s, however. When oil prices declined and interest rates on investments abroad increased, it was no longer profitable for these countries to withhold oil from the market. From a purely economic point of view, OPEC's cohesion diminished in the later period.

For economic reasons, Saudi Arabia, the United Arab Emirates, Kuwait, and Qatar can be expected to pursue a policy of moderation. These countries have extensive investments in the West and do not want to see Western economies hurt or the power of Western governments undermined. The political reasons for a policy of moderation are to maintain the support of the United States and other Western governments. These nations also rely on the United States and the West for military protection. Without weapons and other assistance, the survival of these regimes is in jeopardy. The threat comes from Arab extremists. Politically, however, association with the West is a liability because extremists in the Arab and Islamic world attack them because of it.

For some OPEC countries, economic calculations are not paramount. Iraq, Iran, and Libya are ruled by cliques hostile to Western pragmatism and materialism. (They would say western exploitation and power.) For them, economic prosperity is incidental to political ambitions. Oil can finance terrorism and be exchanged for weapons to fight the West. The ruling cliques of the oil-rich nations also are sympathetic to many of the causes of the extremists (e.g., Palestinian nationalism), supporting them monetarily and in other ways. Without hesitation in 1973, they used oil as a political weapon in a campaign against Western interests, and they remain vulnerable to political blackmail from the extremists. The premise of economic theory is that cartel members are rational, calculating economic actors that seek to maximize their material gain, but the reality of OPEC is that oil is used not only for the purposes of economic development but also for redressing political grievances.■

OPEC functioned rather well as long as Saudi Arabia was willing to produce far less than its capacity in order to maintain high prices. As a country with a small population and huge oil reserves, Saudi Arabia had more flexibility to control production without causing internal hardship than did many other OPEC countries. However, in 1979, with the price of oil exceeding $30.00 per barrel, the Saudis began to worry that oil might be priced out of the market, or that the consuming countries might "destabilize" the situation by fomenting revolutions or engaging in military activity. They became increasingly reluctant to hold down their production as a means of maintaining such high prices.

g. THE THIRD OIL SHOCK: PRICES DROP

The Saudis' worries proved to be accurate. The third oil shock came when consumers began to switch from expensive oil to other fuels in a big way. Economists had generally assumed that the demand for oil would not vary even if the price went up because oil was a necessity. This theory was tested in the early 1980s and found to be wrong. Although it took a few years, consumers and endusers responded to the high price of oil by implementing conservation practices. Oil consumption began to drop off. The third oil shock was the shock of seeing prices plunge in the early 1980s. (Again, see Fig. 6–1 in Chapter 6.)

Energy conservation was largely the result of fuel switching and technological innovation. Responding to 1975 legislation that mandated a doubling of the average fuel efficiency of new automobiles, automobile companies created cars that reduced oil consumption by 2 million barrels per day. By 1985, the United States was 25 percent more energy efficient and 32 percent more oil efficient than it had been in 1973. Similarly, Japan became 31 percent more energy efficient and 51 percent more oil efficient. By 1983, oil consumption in the entire non-Communist world was 45.7 million barrels per day, about 6 million barrels less than daily consumption had been at its peak in 1979. Yergin, *supra* at 718. The effects of conservation and fuel substitution on the demand for oil in the United States are depicted in **Figure 7–1**.

Although OPEC tried to stabilize prices by cutting output, its members could not agree on how to share the painful burden. (Recall in Chapter 6 how difficult it was to establish fair prorationing and unitization allocations in U.S. oil fields.) Some members produced more than their assigned

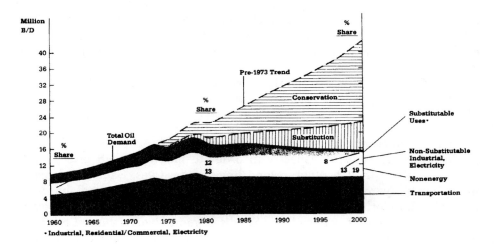

Figure 7-1

U.S. Oil Demand, Actual (1960–79) & Projected (1980–2000), from Exxon Co. USA, Energy Outlook 1980–2000 (1981) as printed in Government Institutes, Inc., Energy Reference Handbook (3rd ed. 1981) p. 296.

quotas, and oil prices started to decline in 1981. In 1985, with growing tensions between Iran and Saudi Arabia, the two largest producers, the Saudi government opened its taps. Oil prices plummeted, reaching $10 a barrel in Texas. As Yergin writes: "This was the Third Oil Shock, but all the consequences ran in the opposite direction. Now, the exporters were scrambling for markets, rather than buyers for supplies. And buyers rather than sellers were playing leapfrog, each jumping over the other in pursuit of the lowest price." Yergin, *supra* at 750.

Today, America's oil imports come from more corners of the globe, as multinational companies sought to diversify and secure new supplies from Latin America, Canada, the North Sea—and most recently, Africa—rather than rely on oil from the Mideast. In the first half of 2005, Mexico, Canada and Venezuela each supplied from 13 to 15 percent of U.S. oil imports, roughly the same percentage as Saudi Arabia. Nigeria supplied almost 10 percent, and Angola almost 5 percent of our crude imports. Midyear Forecast, Oil & Gas J., July 4, 2005, at 32. In 1998, the U.S. imported more than half of its oil demand; this percentage surged to 60 percent in 2001, and the Energy Information Administration projected a rise to 68 percent by 2025 under current policies. Daily Report for Executives, June 16, 2005, at A–38. Only the Mideast has the oil reserves to fuel the projected growth in total world demand for oil over the next decades. The national security implications of our growing dependence on imports, and on Mideast imports in particular, are discussed in the last section of this chapter.

h. OIL ON THE COMMODITY EXCHANGE

After the price plunge to ten-dollar oil in 1986, prices stayed relatively stable in the range of $15 to $19 a barrel through the end of 1999. This price range represented a consensus of both OPEC nations and non-OPEC producing nations (such as Norway and Mexico) after the Third Oil Shock. The 1986 price collapse had transferred $50 billion from oil producers to oil consumers. As both an importer and a large domestic producer, U.S. policy also favored such a range. Ten-dollar oil could cripple the U.S. domestic oil industry, with its high-cost wells. Vice President (and later President) George Bush, a former independent oil man from West Texas, is reported to have warned the Saudis on a visit in 1986 that the United States would impose a tariff on imported oil if prices remained so low. A tariff would transfer petrodollars from oil exporters to the U.S. Treasury. Whether this warning was real or not, the December 1986 meeting of OPEC ministers adopted a "reference price" of $18 a barrel, and members agreed to quotas that succeeded in raising prices. Yergin, *supra* at 750–64.

The relative stability of average prices over these 15 years masks the shorter term volatility that is now a feature of oil markets. Oil prices are set on the commodity markets, such as the New York Mercantile Exchange (NYMEX), which trades oil futures daily. Spot markets (short-term buying and selling) dominate industry pricing. A handful of vertically integrated, multinational oil companies can no longer control prices nor can state conservation agencies like the Railroad Commission (see Chapter 6) through prorationing controls; and even OPEC countries sometimes have had only limited success in maintaining fixed prices when market forces shift. **Figure 7–2** shows monthly prices from January 1997 to September 2004. Note that oil prices dipped again to $10 a barrel for a few brief months in early 1999. However, by January 2000, prices had risen well

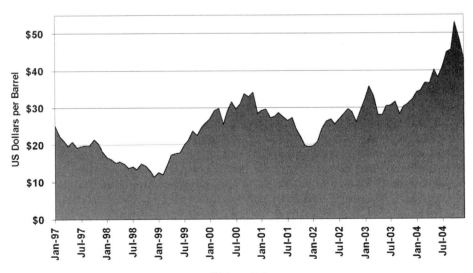

Figure 7–2
Crude Oil Prices (January 1997–December 2004)

Source: Reuters: The crude oil price is calculated as the monthly average of the daily settlement price for the front month NYMEX crude oil futures price for West Texas Intermediate crude oil delivered at Cushing, OK.

beyond the consensus range. From January 2001 to January 2002, prices fell back to $20 a barrel, at the high end of what importing countries considered the "comfort zone." But, from 2002 onwards, prices have climbed relentlessly, reaching $50 a barrel in 2004—and then upwards to $60 a barrel in 2005. What world events explain the rollercoaster ride depicted below?

NOTES AND COMMENTS

1.   Iraq invaded Kuwait in August 1990, launching Project Desert Storm which sent U.S. troops to defend Kuwait and other friendly Arab countries against Saddam Hussein's aggression. Iraq set virtually all of Kuwait's 1000 wells on fire. One correspondent described the scene as follows: "Dante would have felt right at home in Kuwait, a desert paradise that has suddenly been transformed into an environmental inferno. Across the land hundreds of orange fireballs roar like dragons, blasting sulfurous clouds high into the air. Soot falls like gritty snowflakes.... From overcast skies drips a greasy black rain, while sheets of gooey oil slap against a polluted shore." Time, March 18, 1991 at p.36.[3]

No fourth oil shock occurred during Desert Storm. Why not?

2.   What explains the sharp fall and then rise in crude prices in 1998–2000 in **Figure 7–2**? With weakened demand in 1998 due to the Asian financial crisis, oil prices fell throughout the year. But when they plummeted to $10 a barrel in December 1998, a twelve-year low, OPEC ministers resolved to act. OPEC oil export revenues had fallen by 35 percent in just one year, to the lowest point since 1972 on an inflation-adjusted basis. The sharp decline sent OPEC members' budgets into steep deficits. At their March 1999 meeting, both OPEC and non-OPEC countries agreed to cut output by 2.1 million barrels a day. The non-OPEC members, Mexico, Norway, Russia, and Oman, agreed to trim 400,000 barrels and ten of the 11 members of OPEC pledged to cut output by 1.7 million barrels. By July, compliance with their pledges boosted prices to almost $20 a barrel. Nigeria, one of the group's weaker members in compliance, saw output fall by 30,000 barrels a day because of civil unrest. However, Iraq boosted output in July to take advantage of newly approved exports of oil-for-food by the United Nations. A U.N. release reported that Iraq was producing its fields so quickly that reservoir damage and lower ultimate yields were inevitable.

With prices heading above $20 a barrel in the second half of 1999, Qatar said the cartel would be forced to abandon its supply cutbacks if skyrocketing prices started to reduce demand. In July 1999, the president of Venezuela's national oil company declared that OPEC should increase supplies if prices climbed to $22. The price of crude oil immediately fell 5 percent, the biggest drop in seven months. However, by March 2000, the

---

3.   The "Fires of Kuwait" is a stunning documentary of the heroic feats of oil well firefighters from around the world, but especially from Texas, to bring the wells under control. It is often shown in IMAX theaters connected to science museums and is a "must see."

price of a barrel of crude oil was over $30, and high gasoline prices had become part of the presidential primary debates and election-year politics. President Clinton's Secretary of Energy, Bill Richardson, was dispatched on a whirlwind tour to convince the major OPEC players that they should increase output to moderate the impact on importing countries' economies. In March 2000, the House of Representatives passed legislation requiring the President to consider restrictions on military aid to oil-producing countries engaged in price-fixing. Still, prices continued to rise.

i.   ARE WE RUNNING OUT OF OIL? THE PEAK OIL DEBATE

By 2003, only a short four years after the National Petroleum Council and many other groups released reports that were quite optimistic about the prospects of increased domestic natural gas supplies, many forecasters reversed themselves: the U.S. was running out of natural gas and urgently needed to begin importing LNG (liquefied natural gas, cooled and shipped by tankers from oversea ports). Moreover, the world as a whole was running out of oil. We urgently needed to boost renewables like wind energy, turn domestic coal into gas, revive nuclear, and prepare ultimately for a hydrogen-based economy. The future prospects for imported oil supplies seemed particularly alarming because so many of the countries which exported crude oil to the U.S. showed signs of increased instability or hostility to the West. In December 2004, Osama Bin Laden's tape-recorded message to followers commanded them to take the jihad (holy war) to the Mideast oil fields[4] to stop Americans from getting the oil. Oil & Gas J., Jan. 10, 2005, at 27. And as insurgent attacks strengthened in Iraq, the once-bright prospects of rebuilding that country's large producing potential dimmed. Oil prices hit $50 a barrel, and then $60; a Goldman Sachs energy analyst warned that "super spikes" could shoot oil prices to $100 a barrel (Wall St. J., Apr. 1, 2005, at C10). Discussions of "peak oil" flooded the media waves, industry conferences, and the trade press.

While often blended together, the "peak oil" discussions are better thought of as reflecting three different, although related, concerns:

1.   The "true" peak oil debate is about when world-wide, long-term oil production will follow the famous "Hubbert curve" and thereafter inevitably decline, as has already occurred in the United States and the North Sea. This debate is independent of short-term spikes in prices due to geopolitical events (*e.g.*, the London subway bombings in July 2005) or natural disasters.

2.   A related discussion involves why short-term prices in 2004–2005 have shot up to such near-record levels, not forecast as late as 2003, and expected to continue in the near-term.

3.   The third track focuses largely on the long-term national security implications of the Western world's dependence on oil from hostile and

---

4.   In May, 2004, al-Qaeda terrorists attacked oil contractors in Saudi Arabia, killing six Westerners and a Saudi; a second terrorist shooting spree at an oil company's residential compound in Saudi Arabia killed 22 people, 19 of them foreigners.

unstable countries, regardless of when Hubbert's peak might occur globally.

Considerable consensus seems to exist on why crude oil prices are so high in 2005. The reasons given are: soaring demand for oil from China, coupled with an economic upturn in India, the United States and other countries; lack of any spare capacity in the Mideast to meet this demand (global spare capacity decreased from 8.7 million barrels per day (bpd) to a razor-thin 1 million bpd, being held by Saudi Arabia as its own strategic petroleum reserve); the four hurricanes in the Gulf of Mexico in 2004 which shut down much OCS production; a "fear factor" or "terror premium" of $7 to $15 a barrel due to global insecurity; and (with less consensus) hedge fund speculation in oil futures. The first two factors are clearly the most important and reflect the basic market fundamentals—strong demand and limited supply equals rising prices.

The terror premium which market analysts say is reflected in recent prices clearly relates to the third discussion track and its implications for national energy policy and national security. The last section of this chapter discusses oil security options for the U.S., especially the Strategic Petroleum Reserve. Good background reading (in addition to the daily newspaper) includes Michael T. Klare's book on *Blood and Oil: The Dangers and Consequences of America's Growing Dependency on Imported Petroleum* (2004) which explores our "lethal embrace" of Saudi Arabia as we lie trapped in that region, struggling over access to the Caspian and Persian Gulf resources against Russia and China. A second book, *Winning the Oil Endgame: Innovations for Profits, Jobs and Security* by Amory B. Lovins *et al* (Rocky Mountain Institute 2004), was partly sponsored by the Pentagon and propounds the development of ultra-light metallurgy that can substantially decrease the weight of military and civilian vehicles. When coupled with the increased use of home-grown biofuels, the U.S. could curtail all oil imports from the Persian Gulf by 2015. The ultimate checkmate in the "oil endgame" is the move to hydrogen as a transportation fuel.

The true "peak oil" debate involves the application of Hubbert's curve to global oil production. In 1956, geologist M. King Hubbert forecast that oil production would peak in the U.S. in 1970—and it did. The Peak Oil proponents apply Hubbert's model, or variants of it, to global oil production today. Hubbert's model is based on the following pattern: Oil discoveries will peak at some point because oil is a finite resource and the big fields that are easy to find are found first. Once discoveries peak, oil production will peak some years later as these new discoveries are exploited and depleted over time. In short, when discoveries start falling, production will ultimately fall too, around 40 years later. At that point, we will not have "run out of oil," but we will be on an irreversible decline curve. (Picture a bell curve that first rises, peaks at the top of the bell, and then declines).

Here is where geological pessimism confronts economic and technological optimism, as best shown by juxtaposing two sets of competing books whose titles are self-explanatory:

- David Goodstein (a physicist and vice provost at the California Institute of Technology), *Out of Gas: The End of the Age of Oil* (2003); Paul Roberts, *The End of Oil: On the Edge of a Perilous New World* (2004); and Matthew Simmons, *Twilight in the Desert: The Coming Saudi Oil Shock and the World Economy* (2005).

- Peter W. Huber and Mark P. Mills, *The Bottomless Well: The Twilight of Fuel, the Virtue of Waste, and Why We Will Never Run Out of Energy* (2005); and Peter R. Odell, *Why Carbon Fuels Will Dominate the 21st Century's Global Energy Economy* (2004).

Geological pessimism is best displayed in the Simmons' book which focuses in detail on the Saudi oil fields. After surveying more than 200 technical papers on these fields, Mr. Simmons, a respected investment banker in the energy industry, disputes the Saudi claim that it has enough oil to fuel the world for 70 more years. About 90% of its oil output comes from seven huge fields, including three that have pumped for more than 50 years. When U.S. output peaked in 1970, Saudi Arabia ramped up production from its fields—from 3 million bpd in 1970 to an astounding 8 million bpd just four years later. Simmons, *supra* at 47–52. However, this surge had a big downside: some wells were produced above the Maximum Efficient Recovery rate (see Chapter 6(A)) so pressures dropped in parts of the field, creating "water cuts" which allowed saltwater to invade the wells prematurely. From 1974 onward, the Saudis have struggled with unsustainable water injection programs that will ultimately result in rapid declines in these giant fields within the next 5 to 10 years. When Saudi production peaks, the age of oil ends.[5]

The anti-Peak Oil proponents argue that energy comes from human ingenuity—a bottomless well. Anything is possible—surely bacteria will be invented to ferment tar sands. The cost of extracting oil will go up slowly, but we will always find more. Prices are so high today because the current costs of producing Saudi oil are so low that the Saudis could wipe out any private investments in tar sands, shales, and alternate energy sources, using oil as a weapon. Thus, private capital will not develop unconventional oil and gas sources or other fuels unless their price is very high, offsetting the high market risk. Also, the Peak Oil theorists do not properly account for the often-negative role of government policies in restricting access to petroleum reserves, both in the U.S. and around the world. Governments, not Mother Nature, create the "geological" shortages.

The two camps see very different oil scenarios in our future. One foresees the possibility of Oil War III, abrupt recessions in oil-consuming countries, and continuous global conflicts between the U.S., Europe, China, and Japan to secure oil supplies unless consumers adapt to a more frugal lifestyle. The other camp says "keep the lights on" and enjoy the use of

---

5. Saudi Arabia's rebuttal to the Simmons' analysis appears in Sadad al-Husseni, Rebutting the Critics: Saudi Arabia's Oil Reserves and Production Practices Ensure its Cornerstone Role in Future Oil Supply, Oil & Gas J., May 17, 2004. As Simmons and many others have noted, the Saudis, like many foreign nations, treat reserve data as a state secret, making it difficult to assess the future of oil globally compared to the U.S.

energy as technology, human intelligence and markets bring good things to life.

Any reader might be confused by the jarring dissonance between the competing brainpower on both sides of the Peak Oil issue. However, the "disconnect" may not be quite so large when framed as follows: The real Peak Oil debate is about conventional oil, although this is not always clear from the material. And the debate is not about living without oil completely; it is about living with oil when global supplies are declining, not increasing. All players seem to recognize that the world has large supplies of unconventional oil locked in tar sands and shales, and even larger amounts of unconventional natural gas (see Chapter 8). The world also has hundreds of years of coal and ample uranium for nuclear power (although air pollution, global climate change, and nuclear security issues make these sources less than ideal; and neither coal nor nuclear can be used directly in the transportation sector). The heart of the debate reflects two basic questions: (1) What will be the pattern of oil prices as we transition to new sources of oil and substitute fuels; and (2) When will the peak in conventional global oil (and particularly in Saudi output) occur as a definitive stage in this transition? If you want to "bet on the future," here are the dates when oil production will peak and then begin an inexorable decline, according to some leading experts:[6]:

- Kenneth Deffeyes (geologist and author of *Beyond Oil: The View from Hubbert's Peak*)—late 2005 or 2006.

- Richard Heinberg (author of *The Party's Over: Oil, War, and the Fate of Industrial Societies*)—2007–08.

- Matthew Simmons (author noted *supra*)—2007–2009.

- Colin Campbell (author of *The Essence of Oil and Gas Depletion (2003)* [7])—between now and 2010.

- Petroleum Review (a trade publication)—2007.

- David Goodstein (author noted *supra*)—2010.

- Daniel Yergin (Cambridge Energy Research Associates)—not before 2010.

- Francis Harper (oil company consultant)—between 2010 and 2020.

- PFC Energy (a well-known energy consulting firm)—2010 to 2015.

---

6. The listed dates appears in various publications, notably Jeffrey Ball, As Prices Soar, Doomsayers Provoke Debate on Oil's Future, Wall St. J., Sept. 21, 2004 at A1; Matt Creson, Experts Ponder Oil's Peak, Houston Chronicle, May 29, 2005; Lynn J. Cook, No Consensus on Future of Oil, Houston Chronicle, June 23, 2005, at D1. The Oil and Gas Journal has run many articles devoted to Peak Oil and "Hubbert Revisited," starting in July 2003.

7. This is a collection of articles by members of the Association for the Study of Peak Oil (ASPO) and the Oil Depletion Analysis Center. It has a good bibliography of both sides of the debate. Campbell's data shows that oil production is reaching a plateau or declining in 33 of 48 major oil producing countries, including 6 of the 11 OPEC countries. He states that since the early 1980s, the world has been pumping more oil out than finding oil. By 2005, the world will have produced half of the total that exists—the peak of Hubbert's curve. We would have oil for another century, but we will never again have cheap oil.

The Peak Oil debunkers include Michael Lynch and Peter Odell who dispute that Hubbert's curve can be applied globally. They think that oil supplies may ultimately peak in 2025 or 2030—giving the world plenty of time to adapt slowly to other sources of supply. So scenarios of doom and gloom featuring $5/gallon gasoline and crashing economies are unwarranted.[8] Our own Department of Energy projects a possible peak in 2037,[9] although the EIA says that a more probable peak year is 2026. The U.S. Geological Service (USGS) puts the peak around 2040, but says that the timing depends on users' moves to conserve, the development of unconventional sources, actions of OPEC, and political and environmental constraints.[10] (Is the USGS date a "forecast" or pure conjecture, given the number of qualifying assumptions? Aren't such assumptions built into any forecast?)

NOTES AND COMMENTS

1. After picking a peak year, consider what national energy policies to recommend to the U.S. Congress and administration, recognizing that implementation of almost any policy often takes years. Explain what environmental trade-offs will be necessary in adopting your recommendations.

Would you bet real money in the stock market on particular companies based on your prediction?

2. Now predict the future price of crude oil over the next 3 years, 7 years, and 20 years. In 2002, OPEC kept its index of crude oil at about $25 a barrel, significantly higher than the average of $19 a barrel that prevailed throughout the 1990s. In January 2002, OPEC reduced its production targets to the lowest level in 11 years. In early 2005, OPEC suspended its price band of $22–28 a barrel, stating that higher oil prices did not appear to be harming world economic growth (or U.S. drivers' addiction to gasoline). Sheikh Ahmad of Kuwait said that he considered $32 to $35 as a plausible new range. Nigeria argued for $45 to $55 per barrel as the new target range. PFC Energy stated that there is a new floor price of $40 a barrel today. OPEC Suspends Price Band System, Greenwire, Jan. 31, 2005.

Analysts assert that many energy companies are still basing their investment decisions on a long-term crude price in the low 20–dollar range and therefore are not investing much of their 2005 record profits in finding new reserves. The companies' investments have a 7–to 10–year lead time, and they seem unconvinced that the current high prices will stick. If given

---

8. The price of gasoline in Europe has been $5 to $6 per gallon for years due to high taxes imposed on it.

9. The EIA (the U.S. Energy Information Administration) and the IEA (the International Energy Agency of oil-importing countries) project that Saudi capacity will double in the next 15 to 20 years, a forecast that Simmons says is based on unsubstantiated data.

10. The USGS report can be accessed at: http://www.eia.doe.gov/pub/oil_gas/petroleum /feature_articles/2004/worldoilsupply/oilsupply04.html

a credible assurance that prices would stabilize in the range of $28–$34 a barrel, they would boost investment. John Gault, Remarks at European Union Inst. for Security Studies, Oct. 15, 2004.

Why should OPEC be expected to bear the burden of maintaining idle capacity for the world? What is the incentive to do so? Will private investors do so? State-owned oil companies own 80% of the world's reserves and produce almost two-thirds of the world's oil today. Lynn J. Cook, Big Oil Hashes Out Issues with State–Run Firms, Houston Chronicle, Sept. 17, 2004.

3.   Will Canada's wilderness continue to be America's gas tank? Or will China pull up first? Today, most Canadian oil and gas flows to the U.S. However, in 2005, China and Canada signed 13 agreements and memoranda of understanding focused on oil and gas and energy projects as priority areas of long-term mutual cooperation, including Chinese investment in Canadian tar sands. People's Daily Online, China, Canada Sign Energy Agreements, Jan. 25, 2005; Daniel K. Berman & Mark Heinzl, Canada Welcomes China's Cash, Wall St. J., July 13, 2005, at C1; Nelson D. Schwartz, Why China Scares Big Oil, Fortune, July 25, 2005 at 89.

China's bid for Unocal, a U.S. company with production in Asia and the Gulf of Mexico, caused a considerable stir in Congress and the media in mid–2005. *See, e.g*, Ben Geman, Defense Bill Latest Target for CNOOC Review in Senate, Greenwire, July 25, 2005.

China and Japan are in an "undeclared oil war" for access to the big Siberian oil fields in Russia. Japan wants to construct a 2,300–mile pipeline from Siberia to coastal Japan; China is pushing for a 1,400 mile pipeline south to Daqqing. Paul Roberts, The Undeclared Oil War, Washington Post Online, June 28, 2004. In 2003, China surpassed Japan as the second largest consumer of petroleum in the world.

2.   STATISTICAL BACKGROUND TO INTERNATIONAL OIL

Between 1953 and 1972, over 300 private companies and more than 50 different state-owned companies either entered or expanded into the international oil business. See Neil H. Jacoby, Multinational Oil: A Study in Industrial Dynamics 120 (1974). Today, the Western international oil majors control less than 10% of the world's oil and gas reserves. The top ten oil companies in 2003 in terms of reserves are state monopolies: Saudi Aramco, National Iranian Oil Co., Gazprom (Russia), Iraqi National Oil Council, Qatar Petroleum, Kuwait Petroleum, Petroleos de Venezuela, Adnoc (United Arab Emirates), Nigerian National Petroleum Co., and Sonatrach (Algeria). ExxonMobil is a distant 14th and BP, Shell, and Chevron follow at 17th, 20th and 22d. Here are some snapshot profiles of the international petroleum industry.

Figure 7–3 below shows how the percentage shares of total industry profits reflect the changing structure of the industry. National Oil Companies (NOCs) and governments now take almost 80% of industry profits:

	1970	1977	1983	1990	1995
NOCs & Government	50%	60%	90%	80%	78%
Oil companies	50%	40%	10%	20%	22%

Figure 7–3
Global Oil Industry Upstream Profit Shares
Source: McKinsey & Co. data, in George E. Kronman *et al.* (eds.), International Oil and Gas
Ventures: A Business Perspective 36 (2000).

Figure 7–4 below shows that return on investment (ROI) for both
U.S. and foreign projects has declined significantly since 1980–81. In recent
years, the ROI for foreign projects has converged with the domestic rate:

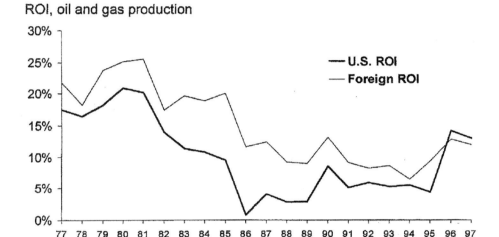

Figure 7–4
Rate on Investment
Source: U.S. Energy Information Administration (EIA) data, as presented in International Oil
and Gas Ventures, *supra* Table 7–3, at 15.

This fall in rates of return drove the industry to restructure through
mergers and acquisitions and to adopt new technologies like 3–D seismic to
lower costs. Finding costs for oil fell significantly, accompanied by large-
scale employment reductions as multinationals slimmed down to compete
more agilely against a host of new competitors in a world of sharply lower
oil prices:

- Exploration & Production expenditures per barrel of reserve additions (a common measure of the costs of finding oil) fell from about
  $12 per barrel in 1980 to $5–$6 per barrel in the mid–1990s. *Id.* at
  15.
- Employment in the industry dropped from a high of almost 1.4
  million employees in 1980 to half that number by 1996. *Id.*

During the 1980s, employee parking lots of major oil companies in Houston
were only half-full; personal bankruptcies rose, and small businesses failed

as the local economy cratered in the energy capital of the world. The restructuring of the petroleum industry had high transition costs, but the marketplace is a relentless force for change.

From 1978 to 1998, OPEC and the countries of the former Soviet Union (FSU) continued to dominate world oil reserves, even though South America and Africa showed some growth in reserves while North America and Europe lost ground, as seen in **Figure 7–5**:

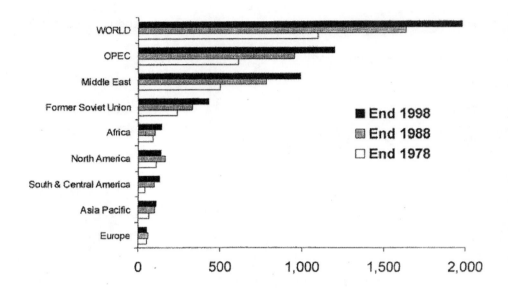

Figure 7–5
Worldwide Reserves of Oil and Gas

Source: BP Statistical Review of World Energy 1999, as appearing in International Oil and Gas Ventures, *supra* Table 7–3, at 18.

OPEC's share of world oil production, both past and forecast, is depicted in **Figure 7–6** below:

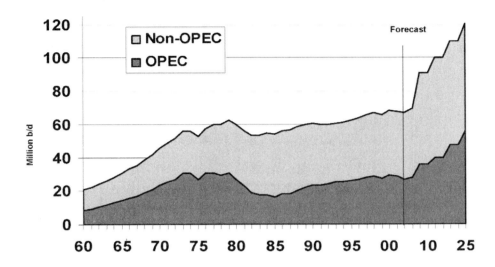

Figure 7–6
Total World Oil Production

Source: EIA, International Energy Outlook 2004.

A telling depiction of the distribution of the world's oil potential is in **Figure 7–7** adapted from a book by Daniel Johnston. The United States is a "super mature" area with more than 600,000 wells producing an average of 12 barrels of oil a day. By comparison, the Middle East has barely been tapped.

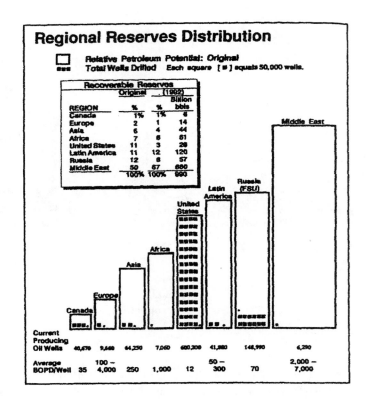

Figure 7–7
Regional Reserves Distribution

Source: Daniel Johnston, International Petroleum Fiscal Systems and Production Sharing Contracts 205 (1994).

Our dependence on petroleum imports continues to rise, as shown in **Figure 7–8** below:

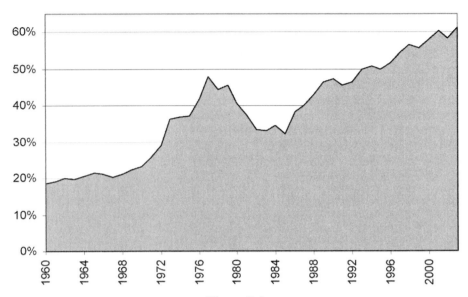

Figure 7–8
Petroleum Imports as Percentage of U.S. Petroleum Consumption

C. Concessions Through the Ages

1. The Earliest Concessions

The following article by Professors Smith and Dzienkowski examines the early history of oil and gas leases executed by private landowners to oil companies in the U.S. and compares these with the early Middle Eastern and Mexican concessions. (The private oil and gas lease is discussed in Chapter 6, Section B). It offers an interesting perspective on the role of the courts in interpreting private contracts in common law countries like the United States.

Ernest E. Smith and John S. Dzienkowski, A Fifty–Year Perspective on World Petroleum Arrangements
24 Texas Int'l L. J. 13 at 17–23 (1989).

The archetypal Middle Eastern concession was obtained by William D'Arcy from the Shah of Persia in 1901. For a $100,000 "bonus," another $100,000 in stock in his oil company, and a 16% royalty, D'Arcy received exclusive oil rights to 500,000 square miles of Persia for the next sixty years. Other concessions in the region generally followed this format; they were granted for very long terms and covered immense areas. The 1933 concession that the King of Saudi Arabia granted to Standard Oil Company of California for, 50,000 was for a sixty-six-year term and ultimately covered almost as much territory as the D'Arcy grant. Six years later, the Ruler of Abu Dhabi granted a seventy-five year concession covering the entire country to a consortium composed of five major oil companies. The Kuwait concession was also for a seventy-five-year term and covered the entire country.

These concessions did not specifically obligate the companies to drill on any of the lands granted or to release territory if exploration and drilling were not undertaken. Moreover, the host countries had no right to participate in managerial decisions, including decisions on drilling and development. After the initial consideration and, occasionally, other agreed-upon payments had been made, the sole financial benefit received by the countries or their rulers was the right to royalties. Many early concessions even freed the companies from all tax obligations other than those specifically provided for in the agreement.

The royalty provisions in the Middle Eastern concessions granted in the 1930s were generally less favorable to rulers than those in the original grant to D'Arcy. These later concessions typically provided for a royalty calculated as a flat rate per ton of oil rather than as a percentage of the value of the sale price of production. Thus, both the Ruler of Abu Dhabi and the Sultan of Muscat and Oman received three rupees per English ton of oil produced from their respective concessions; the Arabian concession set the royalty at four gold shillings per ton.

The Middle Eastern concessions were strikingly similar to the oil and gas leases granted in the United States in the first three decades of this century. By 1900, the conditions that had characterized mid-nineteenth century development in Pennsylvania—shallow, inexpensive wells drilled by operators willing to take oil leases on tracts of an acre or less—had largely disappeared in the United States. Lessees, faced with more costly drilling and the need to have greater established reserves for expanding markets, insisted on leasing larger tracts. Although United States oil and gas leases rarely, if ever, covered tracts as immense as those in the Middle East, this difference was attributable to the size of the farms and ranches owned by lessors, rather than to a greater skill in bargaining. Like the Ruler of Abu Dhabi, a landowner in Texas or Oklahoma typically entered into a single oil and gas lease covering all the property he owned, whether it was a forty-acre farm or an 85,000–acre ranch. Moreover, many fixed-term leases, some for as long as ninety-nine years, were still in effect, and new ones were occasionally executed. Other leases, as written, might in theory last forever, even though production was never obtained. These no-term leases permitted the lessee to maintain the lease in effect indefinitely by paying an annual rental. If oil production was obtained, however, royalty clauses in United States leases generally entitled the landowner to a fraction of the oil produced rather than a fixed payment per ton, although the percentages varied considerably from lease to lease. In the case of natural gas, some leases did not base the payment on the volume of production, but merely provided for an annual payment of a fixed amount per gas well.

By the 1930s, however, a standard United States oil and gas lease had emerged that differed significantly from its Middle Eastern counterparts of the same period. Leases covering all property owned by the lessor were still the rule, but fixed-term and no-term leases had disappeared. The lease term had assumed its modern form, providing that the lessee's interest would last for a specified time period, usually five or ten years, and so long thereafter as oil or gas might be produced. Unless drilling and production occurred by the end of the primary term, the lease terminated. Additionally, the royalty clause for both oil and gas had become standardized at one-eighth of production for oil and one-eighth of the sale price or market value for gas.

Rather curiously, the midwestern farmer who leased his land to an oil company was in a better contractual position than the Middle Eastern sheik. Under the typical Middle Eastern concession, the oil company did not risk losing its concession if it failed to drill. The opposite was true under the United States oil and gas lease; the lease format, although it did not guarantee drilling, at least assured the landowner that his land would not be tied up indefinitely by the payment of a small annual rental. If oil was discovered, neither the Middle Eastern concession nor the United States lease imposed upon the oil company any express contractual duty to produce from the well. Under the concession, the company could safely shut in the well if it wanted to do so. The lessee in the United States, however, risked losing the lease for lack of production at the end of the primary term, at least if the shut-in well was the initial discovery well. Finally, if production was obtained, the lessor was not limited to a flat sum per ton, but received one eighth of the production or its sale price.

The lessor in the United States had not only the benefit of the lease format, but also the more significant benefit of the United States courts. The most widely used printed oil and gas leases were drafted for use by oil companies and contained relatively few provisions favorable to the lessor. The courts, however, had long shown their willingness to redress egregious imbalances in contractual rights between the oil companies and their lessors. Judicial hostility to the patent unfairness of the no-term lease was the principal factor leading to its discontinuance. Judicial suggestions that the no-term lease lacked consideration brought into question its enforceability, and the emergence of the implied covenants doctrine assured its demise. Indeed, the judicial doctrine that the lessee impliedly covenants to perform as a reasonably prudent operator and to undertake the various obligations imposed by such a standard provided the lessor with his greatest protection.

By the turn of the century, United States courts had concluded that an oil and gas lessee impliedly covenants to explore, develop, and produce from the leased premises for the mutual benefit of both itself and the landowner. In 1905, the Eighth Circuit commented in *Brewster v. Lanyon Zinc Co.* that "a covenant arising by necessary implication is as much a part of the contract—is as effectually one of its terms—as if [it] had been plainly expressed." Although different rationales were suggested for implying covenants in oil and gas leases, and disagreement existed over the obligations imposed by the implied covenants, the existence of the implied covenants doctrine itself was not open to serious challenge. By the early years of this century, courts had held that a lessee had an implied duty to drill offset wells to protect the leased premises from drainage by wells on adjacent tracts. The courts had also construed the no-term lease to contain an implied covenant to drill an initial exploratory well.

The basic format of the modern lease reflected a direct reaction to these rulings. By providing for a fixed, relatively short primary term, a payment for the privilege of deferring drilling during each year of that term, and automatic termination if no drilling or production occurred before the end of the primary term, the lease obviated the need for an implied duty to drill an initial exploratory well. The other implied covenants, however, were unaffected and remained intact under the modern oil and gas lease. In 1934, the United States Supreme Court had no difficulty in stating that the lessee's implied covenant to develop was a generally accepted rule.

The implied covenants gave a lessor in the United States significant legal advantages not available to his Middle Eastern counterparts. Whether the lessor was a Texas rancher or an Arabian sheik, the principal consideration for granting the lease was the right to royalties on production. But neither the concession nor the printed form lease contained express production or developmental obligations. In the Middle East, where some wells might produce over 40,000 barrels of oil a day, low-producing wells, including those producing "only" 10,000 or fewer barrels a day, were commonly shut in as a matter of course. The country (or its ruler) was thus deprived of the income from those wells until the company holding the concession chose to begin production. The Texas rancher, if faced with such a situation, could invoke the implied covenant to operate a well capable of producing oil in paying quantities.

* * *

The more common problem that lessors faced was a lessee's failure to develop a field after initial drilling discovered a reservoir capable of production. As the leases and concessions were written, a company desiring to hold its proven reserves indefinitely, in hopes of a larger demand at a higher price, was free to do so. Indeed, this strategy was the rule. The Middle Eastern concessions were almost invariably held by consortia with partially overlapping memberships. This interrelationship of the major oil companies resulted in joint offtake agreements limiting the total amount of production from virtually all of the major concessions. Because these agreements limited each company to production of a fixed amount of oil for market, the incentive to drill new wells into an established and proven reservoir was slight. Nothing in the early concessions prohibited these abusive practices by the companies.

In the United States, however, the oil companies were faced with a much different legal environment. The antitrust laws made domestic offtake agreements illegal, and the implied covenant of reasonable development gave the lessor a remedy against a company that had failed to drill additional wells into a proven reservoir. As a general rule, the lessor was required to show that his lessee had delayed unreasonably in drilling additional wells, that the lessee had a reasonable expectation that such wells would be profitable, and that the lessor had given the lessee notice of breach and had demanded compliance. A landowner who successfully met this burden of proof might be entitled to a variety of remedies, ranging from damages to outright cancellation of the undeveloped portions of the lease. Alternatively, the lessor might obtain a conditional decree requiring the lessee to drill a specified number of wells within a specified period of time in order to maintain all or part of the lease. No similar rights or remedies were found in contemporaneously executed Middle Eastern concessions.

[The authors then proceed to contrast the early Mideast concessions with the concession rights asserted by companies in Mexico. In Mexico, the companies claimed fee simple ownership of mineral rights under Mexican mining laws which provided that petroleum was the "exclusive property of the owner of the soil" and that such ownership was both "irrevocable" and "perpetual." Using these laws, foreign companies bought huge areas of Mexican land. By the time of the Mexican Revolution in 1911, much of the subsoil was claimed by foreign companies as perpetual and exclusive grants of the right to the petroleum].

III. Changes in the Concession System

In the United States, the doctrine of implied covenants helped to balance the rights of the oil companies and the lessors. Lacking such judicial redress, foreign sovereigns inevitably turned to other methods to establish more equitable arrangements. Two principal options appeared available to accomplish this result: expropriation or renegotiation. In some instances no bright line existed between these two methods. Renegotiation under political duress may appear to a company as differing only marginally from outright nationalization; expropriation can take place so gradually that the process may not seem significantly different from ongoing renegotiation. Typically, however, both the changes in petroleum arrangements and the methods used to change them differed markedly. In many ways, the methods of change in Mexico and in the Middle East were at opposite ends of the spectrum of options that sovereigns could use to obtain control over the exploitation of their natural resources.■

NOTES AND COMMENTS

1. One cause of the Mexican Revolution of 1911 was the extraordinary concentration of Mexico's wealth in foreign hands. Article 27 of the 1917 Constitution vested ownership of all natural resources such as hydrocarbons in the state of Mexico. The oil companies protested that the post-revolutionary laws were illegal because they were retroactive and deprived the companies of their fee simple ownership by requiring them to transfer

their holdings to a concession system. For 20 years, the two sides argued about the transfer to a new concession system until, in 1938, the government simply expropriated the assets of the multinational oil companies and banished them. The companies, in turn, boycotted the purchase of Mexican oil and attempted to deny Mexico access to virtually all foreign oil markets. The Mexican government created Pemex (Petroleos Mexicanos) to take over the assets of the foreign companies and to operate the oil fields without any foreign assistance.

Professors Smith and Dzienkowski assert that Mexico (and Pemex) still suffer from this long history of isolation from joint participation in development with profit-driven multinational oil companies. By contrast, those countries which undertook more gradual expropriation of foreign interests and which allowed foreign companies to continue to participate in the oil and gas industry acquired expertise and knowledge from their working relationship with their multinational partners. This expertise then allowed their state oil companies to move into the profitable downstream end of the oil and gas industry. For example, Saudi Arabia formed a joint venture with Texaco to operate refineries and gas stations in the United States. By investing in transportation, refining and marketing activities, these countries have secured outlets for their reserves, and have obtained a greater share of profits from the value chain between production and the end use sale. Pemex remains largely a crude oil exporter. *Id.* at 42–46.

2.   The implied covenants imposed on lessees by the courts in oil and gas cases are similar to the implied promise found to exist in the famous case of *Wood v. Lucy, Lady Duff–Gordon*, 222 N.Y, 88, 118 N.E. 214 (1917), read by virtually all students in first-year contracts. In this case, the court inferred a promise on the part of plaintiff Wood to use reasonable efforts to market Lucy's fashionable dresses, thereby rescuing the plaintiff's exclusive agency arrangement with Lucy from the claim that the agency contract lacked consideration or mutuality of obligation. The reasoning of *Wood v. Lucy* has been adopted by the Uniform Commercial Code which requires that both buyers and sellers in exclusive deals use "best efforts" to supply and promote the goods subject to the contract. John D. Calamari and Joseph M. Perillo, The Law of Contracts, § 4.12 (4th ed.1998).

Professor Walter Pratt views *Wood v. Lucy* as epitomizing the transformation of contract doctrine from the needs of a rural society in 1870 to the needs of a modern manufacturing society marked by accelerated change, national markets, and large enterprises. He writes:

> Recognizing that the doctrines of the past were not adequate for the needs of a changing commercial world, the judges modified the doctrines to embrace the greater uncertainty that characterized the new agreements.... In the language of the courts, the central concept for both enforcement and performance came to be that of "good faith." Through the use of that concept courts strove to preserve some of the moral decency of the rural past [with its localism and face-to-face communication] while allowing the development of commercial practices for the urban future, with as yet undefined morals. Walter F.

Pratt, Jr., American Contract Law at the Turn of the Century, 39 S.C. L. Rev. 415 at 418–19 (1988).

Why did the moral decency of "good faith" and "best efforts" not develop in international petroleum contracting?

2.   NATIONALIZATION IN THE 1970S

The "creeping nationalization" model often used by Middle Eastern countries is described in the following arbitration between Libya and LIAMCO, an American oil company owned by Arco/Sinclair. The Libyan concession at issue was "modern" and advanced compared to D'Arcy's concession. As you read the excerpt, note the provisions that protected the lessor and provided more balance in the bargain between private investors and the state. Also note that many oil companies "caved in" to the inevitable and accepted the new demands of the host government. LIAMCO did not, and this arbitration ensued. Libya was one of the first countries to assert control over the oil companies. Its position was enhanced in 1970 when the Trans–Arabian pipeline, which carried 500,000 barrels of crude oil per day from Saudi Arabia to the Mediterranean, was shut down for many months because a tractor ruptured the line.[11] This made Libyan oil much more valuable to Europe.

Most disputes between oil companies and host countries are resolved thorough arbitration rather than litigation. This excerpted version of the 173–page award contains many principles of property and contract law used internationally in the settlement of disputes.

Arbitral Tribunal: Award in Dispute Between Libyan American Oil Company (LIAMCO) and the Government of the Libyan Arab Republic Relating to Petroleum Concessions

[Reproduced from the text filed originally with the U.S. District Court for the District of Columbia in Misc. No. 79–57. April 12, 1977].
20 International Legal Materials (I.L.M.) 1 (1981).

(Sole Arbitrator: Dr. Sobhi Mahmassani)

ARBITRATION PROCEEDINGS

1.   By its letter dated 2 July 1974 addressed to the President of the International Court of Justice, the Hague, the Claimant Libyan American Oil Company (hereinafter called "LIAMCO") stated: that under date of 12 December 1955, the United Kingdom of Libya, now the Libyan Arab Republic (the Respondent herein), pursuant to provisions of its Petroleum Law 1955, adopted 21 April 1955, entered with the Claimant into three Petroleum Concessions Nos. 16, 17 and 20, all of which were in the same form (as prescribed by the Law) as to substantive clauses, relating, inter

---

11.   The "Libyan squeeze" is colorfully described in Yergin, *supra* at 574–87.

alia, to the extraction of Petroleum from certain land areas in Libya over a period of fifty years, renewable for an additional ten years.

. . . . That by a so-called Nationalization Decree, made public 1 September 1973, the Revolutionary Command Council of the Respondent issued Law Number 66 expressed to provide for the nationalization and transfer to the Respondent of fifty one percent of all properties, privileges, assets, rights, shares, activities and interests of the Claimant under its said Petroleum Concessions.

That this premature and unilateral repudiation in part of the Concession Agreements some thirty-two years before the expiry of the period of the concessions and some forty-two years before the time to which such period could be extended, is a fundamental breach of the Concession Agreements, thereby occasioning a claim by Claimant for restitution in integrum and damages and giving rise to an arbitral dispute within the meaning of Clause 28 of the Concession Agreements.

[A second nationalization decree seized the remaining 49 percent of the interests of the Claimant under the concessions. Liamco exercised the arbitration provision in Clause 28 of the Concession Agreements. The state of Libya refused to respond, and the arbitration proceeded without its participation, as authorized in Clause 28. The President of the International Court of Justice appointed a Sole Arbitrator, Dr. Sobhi Mahmassani, Counselor-at-Law of Beirut].

* * *

FACTS AND EVIDENCE

As the Respondent did not appear, the Arbitral Tribunal had to admit the best evidence available and to rely chiefly on the basic facts as supported by copies of the various official documents and by conclusive technical reports or expert testimony presented by the Claimant.

I.   LIBYAN LAW ON CONCESSIONS

1.   Petroleum Law of 1955

Libya, a federation of three provinces of Tripolitania, Cyrenaica and Fezzan, was recognized as an independent sovereign State by the United Nations in 1949, effective 2 January 1952. Its form of government was monarchical under King Idriss I.

In order to improve its economic conditions, to encourage foreign capital investment, and to insure the exploitation and protection of its natural resources, Libya enacted Petroleum Law No. 25 of 21 April 1955 (28 Sha'ban 1374 h.), effective 18 August 1955, i.e. 30 days after publication in the Official Gazette.

This Law is a modern enactment which established a framework for the exploration and production of petroleum within the Libyan Kingdom. In its Article 1, it laid down the basic rule that:

"(1) All petroleum in Libya in its natural state, in strata, is the property of the Libyan State;

(2) No person shall explore or prospect for, mine or produce petroleum, unless authorized by a permit or concession issued under this Law".

This Law provided a concessionary system for the exploitation of petroleum products, and established an autonomous Petroleum Commission responsible for the implementation of the provisions of the Law under the supervision of the appropriate Minister (Article 2.3). The Commission was empowered to "grant concessions in the form set out in the Second Schedule to this Law and not otherwise, provided that they may contain such minor non-discriminatory variations as may be required to meet the circumstances of any particular case". [Concessions terms were limited to a maximum of 50 years with a possible extension not to exceed 60 years.] Under the "working obligations" of the concessionnaire, Article 11 provided for an obligation to make certain minimum capital expenditures and that:

"The holder of any concession granted under this Law shall, within eight months of the grant of such concession, commence operations to explore for petroleum within the concession area. He shall diligently prosecute all his operations under the concession in a workmanlike manner and by appropriate scientific methods. . . ."

The Law provided for the surrender by the concessionnaire of parts of the concession granted, within a period of five years under conditions detailed in Article 10. The Law provided also for pipeline facilities, exemption from certain import and export duties, payments to the State as taxes, fees, rents, royalties and division of profits (Articles 12–16). It laid down the conditions for the assignment and revocation of permits and concessions, defined the rights and obligations of the parties in the event of force majeure and laid down provisions for penalties, definitions and other regulations (Articles 17–25).

Article 20 also provided that "any disputes between the Commission and the concession holder arising from any concession granted under this Law shall be settled by arbitration in the manner set out in the Second Schedule hereto", i.e. Clause 28 of said Schedule which will be analyzed in its amended form in a later section.

* * *

3. Royal Decree of 20 November 1965

This legislation was intended to amend the Petroleum Law of 1955 in such a manner as to significantly increase the State's income from the concessionaires, and to secure their consent to such increase. The amendments included the following economic advantages:

a) The royalty of 12 1/2 percent was to be paid no longer on the value of exported oil determined according to the "free competitive market price" at a Libyan port as provided in the original concession, but according to the "posted price," to be determined according to procedures set forth in the

Amended Law. (Claimant contends that while the Law called for mutual consultancy prior to setting the "posted price," it is a fact that thereafter the posted price was set at levels higher than the free market price).

b) The amounts of marketing and quality allowances and discounts to be made in determining the "value" for the determination of royalties and taxes was to be fixed by the law and regulations, and not by the concession-aires.

c) The Ministry of Petroleum was to have the right to purchase, at the same price upon which royalties were to be calculated, a substantial amount of the concession oil.

d) Clause 8 of the Concession Agreements was to be amended to provide that the 12 1/2 percent royalty was no longer to be considered as a credit against the 50% income tax, but simply as an expense in determining taxable profits. The effect was to increase taxes payable to the State in the amount of one-half of the royalties.

On 22 November 1965, an official Explanatory memorandum was issued by the Ministry of Petroleum. It explained that the amended Law was enacted in consistency with the OPEC (Organization of the Petroleum Exporting Countries) settlement reached in 1964 with the major oil companies. It underscored the abovementioned advantages which Libya should enjoy from its oil in a way similar to that enjoyed by other oil producing countries. The Memorandum stated that the new regime should be applied to all companies without exception, and that this application was to be made retroactive to January 1, 1965. It showed by a schedule of Figures that due to the resulting increase the government oil revenues for that year would rise from 87.5 to 135.5 in million Libyan pounds.

* * *

The original 1955 law contained a Clause 16 entitled "security of company's rights," whereby the government of Libya assured that it would "take steps necessary to ensure Company's enjoyment of all the rights conferred under this Concession." The 1965 Law amended Article 16 to read:

"(2) This Concession shall throughout the period of its validity be construed in accordance with the Petroleum Law and the Regulations in force on the date of the execution of the agreement of amendment by which this paragraph (2) was incorporated into this concession agreement. Any amendment to and repeal of such Regulations shall not affect the contractual rights of the Company without its consent."

II. LIAMCO'S CONCESSION AGREEMENTS

* * *

2. LIAMCO's concession grants and partial assignments

After adopting its Petroleum Law of 1955, the Libyan Government, in the late summer of 1955, invited applications for exploration permits and concessions from companies which could meet the requirements of the Law, esp.Article 5 thereof. Among the invitees were Texas Gulf and its subsidiary LIAMCO, Sinclair and ARCO, all of which complied with the statutory requirements and belonged to the group called "independents." This group were actively solicited to participate by the Libyan Government, because (according to Claimant) they were noted for their aggressive exploration for oil and offered a counter-weight to the large integrated oil producers, called the "Seven Sisters." Within the framework of the Libyan Petroleum Law, approximately 133 concessions were granted to American, British, German, Italian and French companies prior to the end of 1971. Among the first applicants, LIAMCO was granted, as of December 10, 1955, Concessions 16, 17, 18, 19, 20, 21 and 22.... [LIAMCO, with the consent of the proper Ministers, assigned parts of its concessions to W.R. Grace and to a subsidiary of Exxon. LIAMCO's concessions covered 8,000 square kilometers].

LIAMCO continued to own that 25.5% undivided interest in said Concessions. It is this interest which was expropriated by the Libyan Government, and has constituted the subject matter of the present arbitration.

3. The Concession Deeds

Concessions were granted to LIAMCO in the form of "Deeds of Concession," each representing a bilateral agreement concluded between the Petroleum Commission and LIAMCO, and approved by the Minister of Petroleum. All these concessions were dated 12 December 1955, and were executed in contractual form by a member of the Petroleum Commission, by two members of the Council of Ministers and by a representative of LIAMCO....

* * *

5. Principal provisions of the Concession Agreements

The LIAMCO Concession agreements of 1955 provided for the payment of rents, royalties and taxes. These were to be calculated as follows:

a) An annual rent, under Clause 6, was to be paid for each 100 square kilometers of concession territory, in the amount of:

—Ten Libyan pounds yearly for the first eight years;

—Twenty Libyan pounds for each of the next seven years, or until the petroleum is discovered in commercial quantities, whichever date shall come first;

—2500 Libyan pounds for each year thereafter.

b) Royalties, under Clauses 7 and 9, were to be paid quarterly in the amount of 12 1/2% of the value of field production of petroleum during the previous quarter....

c) Annual taxes, under Clause 8, were payable under the Laws of Libya, provided that if the total amount of taxes added to fees, rents and royalties falls short of 50 percent of the Company's profits, the Company shall pay to the Government such sum by way of surtax as will make the total of the Company's payments equal to 50 percent of such profits.

In addition to the above economic obligations, LIAMCO undertook a number of contractual obligations pursuant to the terms of its Concession Agreements. Among the principal of such obligations are the following:

a) Clause 4 of the Agreements imposed upon the concessionnaire the obligation to "work" the concession in conformity with Article 11 of the Petroleum Law, whose provisions are set forth above. This obligation entails the necessity to engage the minimum amounts of investment and expenses necessary to actively explore the concession area and to prosecute diligently all operations required thereby.

b) Pursuant to Clause 5 of the Agreements, the Company was required to perform all operations consistent with the exercise of proper field practice prevailing in the industry.

c) In Clause 18, the concessionnaire undertook an obligation to train Libyan national employees and, within ten years of operations, to employ nationals to constitute at least 75% of its total number of employees, as well as to found special training programs for Libyans as soon as exports should be undertaken from the concession area.

d) The concessionnaire likewise undertook to render both technical and economic reports to the Petroleum Commission (Clause 20), and to permit inspection by the Commission of the project and of the Company's books and records (Clause 21).

As a counterpart to the numerous obligations undertaken, the concessionnaire received, pursuant to the terms of the Concessions as initially granted, the following protections:

a) "Security of Company's Rights" (Clause 16). This provided, as above set forth, that the contractual rights expressly created by the concession shall not be altered except by mutual consent....

c) "Cancellation of the Concession" (Clause 27). The Petroleum Commission was given the right to terminate the contract for several grounds of non-performance by the concessionnaire and, in particular, failure to pay rents and royalties overdue for at least six months or failure to pay amounts as required by the decision of an arbitral tribunal rendered against it. The Clause particularly provided that: "Whenever the Company disputes the grounds under which cancellation is based and requests arbitration under Clause 28 of this contract, the cancellation shall only become effective subject to and in accordance with the result of the arbitration."

d) "Arbitration" (Clause 28). The Concession Agreements provided that all disputes arising out of or in connection with the concession shall be finally settled by arbitration as will be explained hereafter. They provided also that the concession shall be governed by and interpreted in accordance with the Laws of Libya and such principles and rules of international law as may be relevant.

6. Modifications of the Concession Agreements

[LIAMCO agreed to amend its Concession Agreements to conform to the Royal Decree of 1965].

III. NATIONALIZATION DECREES

1. Measures prior to LIAMCO's nationalizations

On September 1, 1969, a Revolutionary Command Council, headed by Colonel Muammar el Qadhafi, overthrew the Government of King Idriss, and announced the formation of the Libyan Arab Republic. The new regime, from the outset, assured foreign interests that there would be no specific changes in policy and that the obligations of the State would be respected. Later on, it took gradual measures which were proclaimed as a protection against imperialism and in harmony with the nationalistic aims of the Revolution.

The first measure was the demand that British and American forces evacuate the military bases established by them. Then followed the confiscation of all land, establishments and interests of Italian colonists established in Libya.

At the end of January 1970, the Libyan Government summoned local oil representatives and demanded substantial modifications in the "posted price" of petroleum. During the ensuing negotiations, the Government, acting under the authority of the "conservation" provisions of the above-mentioned Regulation 8 of 1968, took measures to cut back production and increase pressure on the oil companies. In September 1970, LIAMCO agreed to a $0.30 increase in posting and a 55% tax rate. Shortly after the agreement to terms, the production rates which had been cut back as "conservation measures" were restored to their pre-existing levels. Similar arrangements were made with other oil producers.

The September 1970 settlement forced up posted prices to approximately $2.53 per barrel. In January 1971, local representatives of oil companies in Libya were again summoned to the Ministry of Petroleum to agree to even higher posted prices, plus additional increases arising from the then pending Teheran negotiations between Gulf States' governments and petroleum concessionaires. This demand was backed up by threats of complete stoppage of production. Finally, on April 2, 1971, fifteen oil companies, including LIAMCO, signed the Tripoli Agreement, increasing posted prices to $3.44 with assorted other new financial obligations on the companies.

On December 7, 1971, the Arab Government of Libya passed a law nationalizing the entire [50%] interest of British Petroleum (BP) in Concession No. 65. As stated by the Libyan representative in his speech before the United Nations Security Council on 9 December 1971, the motive of this nationalization was in retaliation to the British non-intervention with regard to the Iranian occupation of three islands in the Arabian Persian

Gulf.... [Bunker Hunt, an American "independent" company, owned the other 50% of Concession 65; Libya nationalized it in 1973].

* * *

In July of 1973, the Libyan Government announced a general plan for participation in the oil industry. Under pressure pursuant to that plan, Occidental and three of the four members of the Oasis Group (Amerada, Continental and Marathon, but not Shell) agreed to accept the nationalization of 51% of their concession interests on the terms set forth in Nationalization Laws Nos. 44 and 51 of August 1973. In exchange, they received separate agreements with the Minister of Petroleum giving them certain assurances as to continuing sources of supply in the future, and entailing for them additional financial obligations, constituting very important modifications of their rights in the remaining 49% of the Concession.

2. Nationalization of 51% of LIAMCO's concession rights

In summer of 1973, the Libyan Government asked the oil producers to accept a 51% participation by the State in the oil concessions. It set the end of August as a deadline for their acceptance, under threat of taking "appropriate measures."

As no acceptance was made, the appropriate measures were the issuance by the Libyan Revolutionary Command Council on September 1, 1973 of Law No. 66, nationalizing 51% of the concession rights of the following companies (Article 1): Esso Standard Libya Inc., Libyan American Oil Company (LIAMCO), Grace Petroleum Corporation, Esso Sirte Inc., Shell Libya, Mobil and Gelsenberg Libya, Texaco Overseas Petroleum Company and California Oil Company.

The relevant articles for said nationalization were the following:

Article I

"The ownership of 51% of all property, rights, assets, portions, shares, activities and interests in any form ... as regards petroleum concession deeds ... shall be nationalized and transferred to the State...."

Article 6

"All property, rights and assets of the Companies, the ownership of which has reverted to the State in accordance with the provisions of Article 1, shall be transferred to the National Oil Corporation."

Article 7

"The nationalized concession areas shall be invested through the National Oil Corporation in association with the Companies referred to in Article 1. The Corporation's share in the participation shall be 51% and the share of these Companies in the participation shall be 49%."

"The operation shall be made through the operating company which was actually operating before the execution of the provisions of this Law. A committee for the management of the operating company shall be appointed by a decision from the Minister of Petroleum. The committee shall consist of three members, two of whom shall represent the government and the other member shall represent the nationalized companies.''

The nationalization measures were immediately implemented. The operator of LIAMCO's concessions, Esso Sirte, LIAMCO's co-concessionnaire, was put under control of a management committee as provided in said Article 7. The National Oil Corporation appropriated 51% of all benefits accruing from those concessions, and LIAMCO was deprived of its rights thereunder.

As to compensation, Article 2 of said Nationalization Law provided as follows:

"The State shall compensate people concerned for the property, rights and assets that have reverted to it under Article 1. [Compensation was to be assessed by a committee selected by the Minister of Petroleum, consisting of a Libyan judge, a representative of the National Oil Corporation, and a representative of the Ministry of Treasury].''

* * *

4. Reactions to said nationalizations

Explaining the principles of the Nationalization Decree of 1973, the Libyan Prime Minister, in a statement of 2 September 1973, defined the basic principles for conducting negotiations with oil companies. The first principle is that Libya cannot buy its own oil which is underground, and consequently, compensation for nationalization should be based on the net book value of the concession. This means the balance of the funds a company brought into Libya and spent on the concession (for studies, exploration, pipe, reports), after deducting the funds it recovered from it.

LIAMCO immediately reacted to the September 1, 1973 Decree. Together with five other oil companies it filed a protest to the 51% nationalization measures, refusing to give its agreement to them.

By note dated September 14, 1973, the State Department of the U.S.A. duly protested through diplomatic channels. It recalled the statement of the Revolutionary Command Council, made on September 1, 1969 to the diplomatic corps, that the new regime would fulfill all its international obligations and would respect the rights of the petroleum companies operating in Libya, and recalled the provisions of the concession agreements that the contractual rights of the concessionaires should not be altered except by mutual consent of the parties. The note stated that the "net book value" formula for compensation did not meet the minimum standards for prompt, adequate and effective compensation required by international law. It further stated that it expected Libya to respond positively to any requests for arbitration under the agreements.

* * *

By a circular letter to all oil companies dated 8 December 1973, the Minister of Petroleum advised that Libya, handling a matter at the heart of its sovereignty, did not accept therein any dispute which would be arbitrable under Clause 28 of the Concession Deeds; and that compensation being guaranteed according to procedures of the Nationalization Law, all arbitration applications should be rejected.

Under these circumstances, some concessionaires finally did agree to compensation terms for the 51% taking and, after agreeing to drop any requests for arbitration, entered into supplemental agreements in respect to the remaining 49% interest.

Moreover, the Libyan Government proceeded to the total liquidation of LIAMCO's interests in Libya by the second nationalization in February 1974.

No compensation was paid or offered to LIAMCO for either the first or the second nationalization measures. . . .

* * *

Meanwhile, by another diplomatic note addressed to the Libyan Government on June, 1974, the State Department of the U.S.A. stated that it was clear that the reason for the nationalization of 1974 was political retaliation. It noted that "under the principles of international law, measures taken by a State against the interests of foreign nationals, which are motivated not by reason of public utility, but of political retaliation against the State of which those nationals are citizens, are invalid and are not entitled to recognition by other States". . . .

That position of the U.S. State Department was reaffirmed on 30 December 1975 in a press release No. 630 on foreign investment and nationalization. In that Statement it was repeated that:

"Under international law, the United States has a right to expect:

—That any taking of American private property will be nondiscriminatory;

—That it will be for a public purpose; and

—That its citizens will receive prompt, adequate and effective compensation from the expropriating country."

". . . The State Department wishes to place on record its view that foreign investors are entitled to the fair market value of their interests. Acceptance by U.S. nationals of less than fair market value does not constitute acceptance of any other standard by the United States Government."

5.   Summary of LIAMCO's activities

* * *

When LIAMCO entered into its concession agreements in December 1955, it acted as a pioneer in a desert land where no extensive exploration had been undertaken by any company. It faced exceptional difficulties with regard to any facilities that might be utilized in connection with supplies of any kind. There were no machine or repair shops, no roads, no adequate ports, no personnel nor labor, no water, no communications, no fuel and no experienced governmental departments to handle the required formalities and enterprise. LIAMCO was even confronted with the unusual and costly task of clearing abandoned World War II mines.

Under such circumstances, LIAMCO had to operate, and had, moreover, to agree to an expedited discovery program which required it to accept an obligation to commence the drilling of an exploration well by April 30, 1956, i.e. four and one-half months only after the grant of the concessions, subject to forfeiture of all its seven concessions in case of failure to meet that deadline. This was an obligation that the major petroleum companies would not accept.

LIAMCO struggled hard and overcame all those difficulties. Experienced personnel were brought from abroad, including a great number of Egyptians. Water supply was drilled and provided in sufficient quantities, even for Libyan tribes. LIAMCO pioneered these efforts which other companies followed, and even shared with them all its knowledge and experience.

Thus, by very intense day and night toil, the works of the initial operation well were completed on 19 April 1956, and next day the drilling operation began on schedule as agreed with the Petroleum Commission.

* * *

Claimant has summarized the status of Concessions 16, 17 and 20, on the eve of said nationalization measures, as follows: LIAMCO had performed all its obligations to "work" the concessions accorded to it as required by the concessionnaire acting alone and in concert with its co-concessionaires; it had performed extensive scientific survey work, drilled numerous exploratory wells, drilled and completed 79 development or producing wells, constructed a 54–mile crude oil pipeline, and an accompanying gas transmission line and road, drilled two water supply wells and one water injection well; it constructed a 105 million cubic foot per day gas processing plant, and constructed all required supporting facilities necessary to the proper development of the petroleum reserves discovered in the concession area.

As a result of these exploratory and operational activities, LIAMCO and its co-concessionaires discovered and defined a petroleum field containing substantial petroleum reserves, which on the dates of 1973 and 1974 was capable of producing up to 133,000 barrels of crude oil and liquids per day, plus 150 million cubic feet of gas per day.

6. Claimant's characterization of the facts of the case

On the basis of the above facts, the Claimant contends that the Libyan nationalization measures of 1973 and 1974 concerning LIAMCO's 25.5% undivided interest in Concessions Nos. 16, 17 and 20 of 1955 as amended in 1966, were politically motivated, discriminatory and confiscatory in nature, and constituted a denial of justice, a wrongful taking and an unlawful breach of contract, and are illegal as contrary to the principles of the law of Libya common to the principles of international law.

In consequence, Claimant requests the issue of an award ordering: as a principal relief the restoration of its concession rights together with all the benefits accruing from such restoration, and as an alternative relief the payment of adequate damages plus interest as will be detailed later.

PART THREE. CONSIDERATIONS OF LAW AND REMEDIES

I. GENERAL NATURE AND PROTECTION OF CONCESSIONS

The petroleum concession agreements entered into between LIAMCO and the Libyan Government constitute the subject matter of the dispute. These agreements, as other similar agreements, are classified by some international jurists under the type of the so-called "international development contracts."

A contract of this type is a semi-public agreement made between a State and a private individual, whose object covers a project of public utility or the exploitation of certain natural resources, and in which are defined the rights and obligations of the parties in their mutual relationship.

Such a contract has special characteristics of which the most common are the following: The contracting parties are not ordinary private persons, one of them being the State or a Government organ, the other very commonly being a foreign corporation. The object of the contract is usually a long-term exploitation of natural resources, involving expensive plants and installations. . . .

Although a concession contract partakes of mixed public and private legal character, it retains a predominant contractual nature. According to the general rules of the law of concessions, widely accepted by modern jurists, the concessionnaire's activities in mining, petroleum and similar concessions, do not have the character of public service, but are considered as private projects and enterprises, and as such are generally governed by the principles of the private law of contracts (V. Duez et Debeyre, Traite de droit administratif, No. 803 p. 606; et Andre de Laubadere, Traite elementaire de droit administratif, No. 49 p. 45).

* * *

To strengthen this contractual character in LIAMCO's and similar other concession agreements as a precaution against the fact that one of the parties is the State, it was deemed necessary to ensure a certain protection for the contractual rights of the concessionnaire. Usually, foreign investors before taking the risk of investing substantial amounts of money and labor for "working" their concessions, are anxious to seek sufficient assurance for the respect of the principle of the sanctity of contracts. In other words, they seek to be guaranteed against the possibility of arbitrary exercise by the State of its sovereignty power either to alter or to abrogate unilaterally their contractual rights. Any such alteration or abrogation of concession agreements should be made by mutual consent of the parties.

To ensure such protection in LIAMCO's Concessions, a specific provision has been inserted to that effect in Clause 16 of its Agreements.... [as modeled on the same standard clause authorized in the Petroleum Laws of 1955 and 1965 reading as follows]:

"(1) The Government of Libya, the Commission and the appropriate provincial authorities will take all steps necessary to ensure that the Company enjoys all the rights conferred by this Concession. The contractual rights expressly created by this Concession shall not be altered except by mutual consent of the parties."

"(2) This Concession shall throughout the period of its validity be construed in accordance with the Petroleum Law and the Regulations in force on the date of execution of the Agreement of Amendment by which this paragraph (2) was incorporated into this Concession Agreement. Any amendment to or repeal of such Regulations shall not affect the contractual rights of the Company without its consent."

The above Clause comes under what has been termed "stabilization" and "intangibility" clauses, which have been considered as legally binding under international law.

Moreover, Clause 16 is justified not only by the said Libyan Petroleum legislation, but also by the general principle of the sanctity of contracts recognized also in municipal and international law, as will be analyzed at a later stage hereof. It is likewise consistent with the principle of non-retroactivity of laws, which denies retrospective effect to a new legislation and asserts the respect of vested rights (droits acquis) acquired under a previous legislation. The principle of non-retroactivity of laws is also admitted by Islamic law, and is based on the following Koranic verse:

"We never punish until We have sent a messenger." (XVII, 15) (Islamic script)

* * *

II. PRINCIPLES OF LAW APPLICABLE IN THE DISPUTE

1. Validity of the choice of law clause

In a concession agreement, an important question arises regarding the choice of the proper law to be applied for its interpretation and enforcement and for governing any details that are not explicitly provided for in it.

The legal systems of the two contracting parties are usually dissimilar. It is not fair to rely on one of them to the exclusion of the other without infringing the principle of the equality of the parties, unless expressly agreed to by mutual consent either in the original contract or in a later document. Moreover, the two or one of these systems might be vague or insufficient on the various concession issues.

Hence, in a case involving a foreign litigant, the tribunal to which it is submitted has to refer for guidance to the general principles governing the conflict of laws in private international law.

According to said principles, the proper law of a contract is that "by which the parties to a contract intended, or may fairly be presumed to have intended, the contract to be governed; or ... to submit themselves "(Dicey's Digest of the Conflict of Laws, Rule 155; and Lord McNair's article "The General Principles of Law Recognized by Civilized Nations", in British Yearbook of International Law, 1957, p. 69–98).

Pursuant to that established rule on the solution of the conflict laws in contracts in general, concession agreements usually contain an explicit provision stating the intention of the parties as to the choice of the proper law to which they submit their contract.

In accordance with that practice, Clause 28, para. 7, of the original LIAMCO Concession Agreements Nos. 16, 17 and 20 of 12 December 1955 [as amended in 1966] provided that:

"This Concession shall be governed by and interpreted in accordance with the principles of law of Libya common to the principles of international law, and in the absence of such common principles then by and in accordance with the general principles of law as may have been applied by international tribunals."

* * *

Moreover, Libyan municipal public law has explicitly authorized the said choice of law clause by Clause 28, para. 7, of the Schedule II annexed to Petroleum Laws of 1955 and 1965. [Eds. note: "municipal" means "domestic" in international law].

The two laws were duly promulgated by the appropriate Libyan legislature. They have continued in force after the Libyan Revolution, according to the legal international public rule that the change of government does not, per se, affect the validity of the existing legal system and the rights and liabilities derived from it.

* * *

2. Analysis of the choice of law clause

* * *

Hence, the principal proper law of the contract in said Concessions is Libyan domestic law. But it is specified in the Agreements that this covers only "the principles of law of Libya common to the principles of international law." Thus, it excludes any part of Libyan law which is in conflict with the principles of international law.

To determine the meaning of "the principles of international law", it is useful to refer to those of its sources that are accepted by the International Court of Justice. Article 38 of its Statute provides as follows:

"1. The Court, whose function is to decide in accordance with international law such disputes as are submitted to it, shall apply:

"a. international conventions, whether general or particular, establishing rules expressly recognized by the contesting states;

"b. international custom, as evidence of a general practice accepted as law;

"c. the general principles of law recognized by civilized nations;

"d. subject to the provisions of Article 59 (concerning the relative effects of judgments), judicial decisions and the teachings of the most highly qualified publicists of the various nations, as subsidiary means for the determination of rules of law."

* * *

As to the meaning of "the principles of the law of Libya" in this connection, it is relevant to point out that this comprises any legislative enactment consistent with international legal principles. It includes, inter alia, all Petroleum concessions laws, all consistent relevant sections of any private or public Libyan legislation, including the Civil Code.

In particular, Article 1, para. 2, of the Libyan Civil Code, promulgated on 28 November 1953, provides that:

"(2) If there is no legal text to be applied the judge will adjudicate in accordance with the principles of Islamic law, failing which in accordance with custom, and failing that in accordance with natural law and the rules of equity."

* * *

Moreover, the Revolutionary Government underscored the importance of this source of law in its new legislation. Pursuant to this policy, the Revolutionary Command Council, by Decree dated 28 October 1971 (9 Ramadan 1391 H.), provided that Islamic law shall be the principal source of Libyan legislation, and appointed special commissions to review existing laws and to amend them according to dictates of Islamic Shari'a. Typical examples of such amended laws are the Statute on Wakfs No. 124 of 1972, the Larceny Statute No. 148 of 1972, and the Adultery Statute No. 70 of 1973.

It is relevant to note that the other subsidiary legal sources mentioned in said Article 1 of the Libyan Civil Code, namely custom and natural law and equity, are also in harmony with the Islamic legal system itself. As a matter of fact, in the absence of a contrary legal text based on the Holy Koran or the Traditions of the Prophet, Islamic law considers custom as a source of law and as complementary to and explanatory of the contents of contracts, especially in commercial transactions. This is illustrated by many Islamic legal maxims, of which the following may be quoted:

—"Custom is authoritative."

* * *

—"What is customary amongst merchants is deemed as if agreed upon between them."

—"A matter established by custom is like a matter established by law." (Articles 36, 37, 43–45 of the Ottoman Majallah Code. V . . . .

Similarly, equity (Istihsan) is considered as an auxiliary source of law, especially by the Maliki and Hanafi Schools. Further, all Islamic rules of law are based on and influenced by religious and moral precepts of Islam (V. Ibid).

* * *

Thus, it has been pointed out that Libyan law in general and Islamic law in particular have common rules and principles with international law, and provide for the application of custom and equity as subsidiary sources. Consequently, these provisions are, in general, consistent and in harmony with the contents of the proper law of the contract chosen and agreed upon in Clause 28, para. 7, of LIAMCO's Concession Agreements, . . .

Moreover, in the absence of that primary law of the contract, the same Paragraph provides as a secondary choice to apply subsidiarily "the general principles of law as may have been applied by international tribunals."

These general principles are usually embodied in most recognized legal systems, and particularly in Libyan legislation, including its modern codes and Islamic law. They are applied by municipal courts and are mainly referred to in international and arbitral case-law. They, thus, form a compendium of legal precepts and maxims, universally accepted in theory and practice. Instances of such precepts are, inter alia, the principle of the sanctity of property and contracts, the respect of acquired vested rights, the prohibition of unjust enrichment, the obligation of compensation in cases of expropriation and wrongful damage, etc.

III. LEGALITY OF THE ARBITRATION

* * *

The arbitration Clause 28, in its final modified version, reads as follows:

"(1) If at any time during or after the currency of this contract any difference or dispute shall arise between the Government and the Company concerning the interpretation or performance of the provisions of this contract, or its annexes, or in connection with the rights and liabilities of either of the contracting parties hereunder, and if the parties should fail to settle such difference or dispute by agreement, the same shall, failing any agreement to settle it in any other way, be referred to [arbitration]."

* * *

It is widely accepted in international law and practice that an arbitration clause survives the unilateral termination by the State of the contract in which it is inserted and continues in force even after that termination. This is a logical consequence of the interpretation of the intention of the contracting parties, and appears to be one of the basic conditions for creating a favorable climate for foreign investment.

* * *

It has been contended by the Libyan Government, in its Circular letter of 8 December 1973, addressed to all oil companies and referred to above, that it rejects arbitration as contrary to the heart of its sovereignty. Such argument cannot be retained against said international practice, which was also confirmed in many international conventions and resolutions. For instance, the Convention of 1966 on the Settlement of Investment Disputes between States and Nationals of other States provides, in its Article 25, that whenever the parties have agreed to arbitrate no party may withdraw its consent unilaterally. More generally, Resolution No. 1803 (XV11) of the United Nations General Assembly, dated 21 December 1952, while proclaiming the permanent sovereignty of peoples and nations over their natural resources, confirms the obligation of the State to respect arbitration agreements (Section I, para. I and 4).

Therefore, a State may always validly waive its so-called sovereign rights by signing an arbitration agreement and then by staying bound by it.

Moreover, that ruling is in harmony with Islamic law and practice, which is officially adopted by Libya. This is evidenced by many historical precedents. For instance, Prophet Muhammad was appointed as an arbitrator before Islam by the Meccans, and after Islam by the Treaty of Medina. He was confirmed by the Holy Koran (S IV, 65) as the natural arbitrator in all disputes relating to Muslims. He himself resorted to arbitration in his conflict with the Tribe of Banu Qurayza. Muslim rulers followed this practice in many instances, the most famous of which was the arbitration agreement concluded in the year 657 A.D. (37 H.) between Caliph 'Ali and Mu'awiya after the battle of Siffin.

* * *

IV. CLAIMANT'S DEMANDS AND LEGAL ARGUMENTS

[LIAMCO requested the Arbitral Tribunal to issue an award ordering the restoration to LIAMCO of its concession rights; the transfer to LIAMCO of the benefits of the exercise of its concession rights by the National Oil Company of Libya from the time of the purported transfer of such concession rights until the time of effective restoration to LIAMCO of its concession rights; or, as an alternative to the above relief, the payment of $250 million by the Government of Libya to LIAMCO as damages for the irremediable breach and termination of its concession agreements].

* * *

The legal arguments presented in support of these claimed remedies may be classified under two groups: unlawful taking of property by unlawful nationalization, and breach of contract.

* * *

V. LAWFULNESS OF THE LIBYAN NATIONALIZATION MEASURES AND THE RESULTANT TAKING OF PROPERTY

* * *

This expose will treat successively the following topics, namely: the classical concept of property, evolution of that concept and the right of nationalization, United Nations Resolutions on the subject, concession rights as property, the sanctity of contracts, and the examination of LIAMCO's nationalizations in the light of said legal considerations.

1. The classical concept of property

One of the fundamental rights universally recognized is the right of private ownership or property (Dominium).

The Classical concept of this right defines it as the right to the use, exploitation and disposal (usus, fructus, abusus) of the object owned.

Although this classical definition has been tempered and limited sometimes by reason of public interest, nonetheless the inviolability of the right of property has remained throughout history as a sacred proposition confirmed and reaffirmed by a succession of constitutional and international declarations and charters. The most famous instances of such basic documents are: the English Magna Charta of 1215, the French "Declaration des droits de l'homme et du citoyen" of 1789 which was recently incorporated in the Preamble to the French constitution of 1958, the Fifth amendment to the American constitution of 1789, the two Hague Conventions of 1890 and 1907, the Declarations of the International Law Association of Vienna in 1926 and of Oxford in 1932, and last but not least the United Nations Bill of Human Rights of 1948, the Pan–American Bill of the same name and date, and the Protocol of 1952 annexed to the Convention of Rome on Human Rights of 1950.

The same concept of this absolute right of property was adopted in private law, in particular Roman law, the European civil codes influenced by it, and many other modern codes. For instance, Article 811 of the Libyan Civil Code provides as follows:

"The owner of a thing has alone, within the limits of the law, the right to use it, to exploit it and to dispose of it."

Applied to land (immovable property) the contents of this absolute right extended in theory to the air space above it and to things lying underground, as was often expressed in the Latin maxim: "Cujus est solum ejus est usque ad coelum, et ad inferos" (Whose is the soil, his is also that which is above and below it). Article 812 para. 2, of the Libyan Civil Code incorporates the same rule with the limitations imposed by the special legislation on quarries and mines.

* * *

In comparison with these views on property, it is relevant to record that Islamic law recognized the inviolable character of the right of property, on the basis of the Holy Koranic Verse.

"And do not appropriate unlawfully each other's property" (S II, 188).

Muslim jurists moulded the meaning of this Verse in a general maxim which provides that:

"One is not allowed to take another's property without legal cause." (Article 97 of the Ottoman Majallah Code).

But they limited the generality of that rule by the requirements of public necessity in order to prevent public nuisance [hence the legal maxim: "Private damage has to be suffered in order to fend off public damage." (Article 26 of the Ottoman Majallah Code, V.)].

2. Evolution of the concept of property and the emergence of the right of nationalization

From the outset of this century and especially after World War I, new political and economic trends have tempered the absolute character of the aforementioned classical meaning of property.

Gradually, property came to be viewed as having a dominant "social function or role," and has as such to be subservient to the public interest of the Community represented by the State. The old sacred character of property has become subject to the influence of social objectives. Its protection has thus been attenuated in domestic as well as in international law.

Moreover, natural resources, in general, do not belong anymore to the owner of the land, but to the Community represented by the State as a privilege of its sovereignty. This view has been adopted in Libya and expressly laid down in its legislation on mines and petroleum....

* * *

Likewise, nationalization by the State of private property began to be practiced on a larger scale than in the past. As differentiated from individual expropriation acts based on administrative law and public necessity, nationalization has taken, in general, the feature of a collective legislative measure motivated by the public social policy of the State. It became thus characterized as a sovereign act, immune from judicial control and subject to international law whenever foreign elements were at issue.

According to the definition formulated in 1952 by the "Institut de droit international":

"Nationalization is the transfer to the State, by a legislative act and in the public interest, of property or private rights of a designated character, with a view to their exploitation or control by the State, or their direction to a new objective by the State." (Annuaire 1952, II p. 279).

The objectives of nationalization vary according to the general political and economic policies of various States.

In communist States, all land and means of production and capital, whether or not foreign-owned, were nationalized on a general scale, often with no compensation. This was done, for instance, by the Soviet State, following the Russian Revolution at the end of World War I.

Nationalization was also frequent in the period between the two world wars, and was even enhanced in some European and American States by express constitutional provisions. As an instance thereof, may be cited the

Mexican nationalizations which were effected since 1936 on seventeen oil companies and on foreign-owned land in a program of agrarian reform.

After World War II, more nationalizations were executed on a very wide level by Eastern European nations, covering land and means of production, and in which only partial indemnities were paid. Even in England and France nationalization of many companies and enterprises was effected, in which the principle of prior, full compensation was not strictly respected (V. Konst. Katzarov, Theorie de la nationalisation, Neuchatel, 1960, p. 412 et s.)

Moreover, during that period and afterwards, many new nations, in particular those forming the so-called "Third World", have emerged and attained their independence. Motivated by a nationalistic spirit to stress their prestige and to control their national economy, many of these new States as well as some other old ones had recourse, especially since 1950, to general measures of nationalization covering chiefly oil concessions and other natural resources and public utilities.

Among such measures were those taken by: Iran in 1951, Egypt in 1956, Indonesia in 1957, Iraq, Ceylon and Cuba in 1961, Algeria from 1963, Syria in 1964, Peru in 1968, Bolivia and Zambia in 1969, Chile in 1970, Libya from 1970, Saudi Arabia in 1972, and Kuwait since 1973. Some of these nationalizations will be discussed hereafter.

This overreaching tendency was implemented and aided by national organizations, such as the Algerian Sonatrach and the National Oil Company of Libya. Further, it was encouraged and systematized after the founding in 1960 of OPEC (Organization of the Petroleum Exporting Countries), in which most oil producing States were regrouped and are still represented. OPEC's tremendous influence is largely felt in the global oil business and consequently in the economic and financial situation all over the world.

On the basis of such frequent precedents, mostly uncontested as to their principle, most publicists today uphold the sovereign right of a State to nationalize foreign property, in the sense that a State possesses as an attribute of its sovereignty and supreme power the right to nationalize all things belonging to any person within its jurisdiction. They stress that States possess that right to nationalize in "the manner and form they consider best," and that they "enjoy complete freedom in this field ... Neither international judicial decisions, nor international treaty practice, nor legal principles provide any evidence of a restrictive rule." (V. S. Friedman, Expropriation in International Law, London, 1953, p. 134, 140–142; and Gillian White, Nationalisation of Foreign Property, New York, 1961, p. 35 et seq.).

* * *

3.   United Nations Resolutions on Nationalization

The frequency of the above mentioned general measures of nationalization has evoked international attention. Since 1952, the United Nations General Assembly has delivered a series of successive resolutions, in which the sovereign right of States to nationalize and to control their natural resources, as being the pro-property of the Community, has been confirmed and reaffirmed. Hereunder are recalled the provisions of the principal resolutions relevant to the points at issue.

(I) Resolution No. 626 (VII) of 21 December 1952 [omitted].

(II) Resolution No. 1803 (XVII) of 14 December 1962; ...

"1. The right of peoples and nations to permanent sovereignty over their wealth and resources must be exercised in the interest of their national development and of the well-being of the people of the State concerned.

"2. The exploration, development and disposition of such resources, as well as the import of the foreign capital required for these purposes, should be in conformity with the rules and conditions which the peoples and nations freely consider to be necessary or desirable with regard to the authorization, restriction or prohibition of such activities."

(III) Resolution of 25 November 1966, which recommends increased participation of developing nations in the operation of projects exploited by foreign companies.

(IV) Resolution No. 3281 (XXIX) of 12 December 1974, in which it was provided, in its Chapter II, Article 2, as follows:

"1. Every State has and shall freely exercise full permanent sovereignty, including possession, use and disposal, over all its wealth, natural resources and economic activities.

"2. Each State has the right:

"(a) To regulate and exercise authority over foreign investment within its national jurisdiction in accordance with its laws and regulations and in conformity with its national objectives and priorities. No State shall be compelled to grant preferential treatment to foreign investment;

"(b) To regulate and supervise the activities of transnational corporations within its national jurisdiction and take measures to ensure that such activities comply with its laws, rules and regulations and conform with its economic and social policies. Transnational corporations shall not intervene in the internal affairs of a host State. Every State should, with full regard to its sovereign rights, co-operate with other States in the exercise of the right set forth in this subparagraph;

"(c) To nationalize, expropriate or transfer ownership of foreign property in which case appropriate compensation should be paid by the State adopting such measures, taking into account its relevant laws and regulations and all circumstances that the State considers pertinent. In any case where the question of compensation gives rise to a controversy, it shall be settled under the domestic law of the nationalizing State and by its tribunals, unless it is freely and mutually agreed by all States concerned that other peaceful means be sought on the basis of the sovereign equality of States and in accordance with the principle of free choice of means."

In response to the invitation proffered by the Arbitral Tribunal, the Claimant commented on the resolutions of the U.N. General Assembly bearing on the subject matter in a Memorial which it submitted to the Tribunal at its meeting of 11 January 1977. Referring to Resolution No. 1803 of 1962, the Memorial concluded that it specifically provided for the respect of foreign investment agreements, and was in contemplation of the Parties when they entered into their Agreements of 1965. As to the Economic Charter contained in Resolution No. 3281 of 1974, it does not represent a consensus of nations and cannot be invoked as a source of international law.

In this connection, the Arbitral Tribunal has reached the conclusion that the said Resolutions, if not a unanimous source of law, are evidence of the recent dominant trend of international opinion concerning the sovereign right of States over their natural resources, and that the said right is always subject to the respect for contractual agreements and to the obligation of compensation, as will be explained in a later section.

4.   Concession Rights as Property

[The arbitrator classified concession rights as incorporeal property, similar to the usufruct recognized by Islamic law.]

5.   Sanctity of contracts

The right to conclude contracts is one of the primordial civil rights acknowledged since olden times. It was the essence of "commercium" or "jus commercii" of the Roman "jus civile" whose scope was enlarged and extended by "jus gentium". Then it was always and constantly considered as security for economic transactions, and was even extended to the field of international relations.

This fundamental right is protected and characterized by two important propositions couched respectively in the expression that "the contract is the law of the parties", and in the Latin maxim that "Pacta sunt servanda" (pacts are to be observed).

* * *

In fact, the principle of the sanctity of contracts, in its two characteristic propositions, has always constituted an integral part of most legal systems. These include those systems that are based on Roman law, the Napoleonic Code (e.g. Article 1134) and other European civil codes, as well as Anglo–Saxon Common Law and Islamic Jurisprudence (Shari'a).

Libya adopted and incorporated this legal principle in its Article 147 of the Civil Code (Same in Article 147 of the Egyptian code, Article 146 of the Iraki and Kuweiti codes, Article 148 of the Syrian code, and Article 221 of the Lebanese Code of Obligations and Contracts), whose paragraph 1 reads as follows:

"The contract is the law of the parties. It cannot be canceled or amended except by their mutual consent or for reasons admitted by the law."

The binding force of the contract is expressed in Article 148, para. 1, of the same Code:

"A contract shall be performed according to its contents and in the manner which accords with good faith."

* * *

This maxim is corroborated by the various sources of Islamic law. For instance, a Koranic Verse ordains:

"Oh, you who believe, perform the contracts" (S V, 1). (Al–Jami' As–Sagheer, II, No. 9213).

* * *

Consequently, one of the parties cannot unilaterally cancel or modify the contents of the agreement, unless it is so authorized by the law, by a special provision of the agreement, or by its nature which implies such presumed intention of the parties.

* * *

6. Legal qualification and implications of LIAMCO's nationalizations

Having laid down the views generally held in municipal law which are common to international legal principles on the right of nationalization versus the right of property and the respect for contracts, it is necessary to examine the legal qualification of LIAMCO's nationalization measures in the light of those views.

LIAMCO contends that such measures are wrongful, because they are politically motivated, discriminatory and confiscatory.

As to the contention that the said measures were politically motivated and not in pursuance of a legitimate public purpose, it is the general opinion in international theory that the public utility principle is not a necessary requisite for the legality of a nationalization. This principle was mentioned by Grotius and other later publicists, but now there is no international authority, from a judicial or any other source, to support its application to nationalization. Motives are indifferent to international law, each State being free "to judge for itself what it considers useful or necessary for the public good ... The object pursued by it is of no concern to third parties ..."

This assertion is easily comprehensible, because nationalization in itself usually presupposes a general policy or political plan in support of which it is executed.

However, ... [i]t is clear and undisputed that non-discrimination is a requisite for the validity of a lawful nationalization. This is a rule well established in international legal theory and practice. Therefore, a purely discriminatory nationalization is illegal and wrongful.

In support of its contention of discrimination in its case, LIAMCO maintains that the nationalizations complained of were "specifically aimed at LIAMCO, an American company, because of its American corporate nationality and due to its insistence, amongst other things, on certain rights guaranteed to it under the concession agreements including the right to have all disputes determined by arbitration. . . ." And they were "part of an overall program of political retaliation against these nations whose politics were contrary to those of the new Libyan regime." In particular, "they were timed to coincide with the opening of the Washington Conference on energy."

[The arbitrator found that, while Libya first nationalized only British Petroleum (BP) and the Bunker Hunt Company in 1973, subsequent nationalization acts covered 51% of LIAMCO's concessions as well as those of Shell, Esso, Grace, Mobil, Texaco and California Oil Company. All these other companies later made arrangements with Libya, and continued to operate in Libya at the time of the arbitration. Some companies, like the American Murphy Oil Co., were not nationalized. In 1974 the second LIAMCO nationalization act took the remaining 49% of LIAMCO's concession interests, apparently motivated by the failure of LIAMCO to agree with the Government as other companies had done].

From the above facts, it appears, that LIAMCO was not the first company to be nationalized, nor was it the only oil company nor the only American company to be nationalized by the first nationalization Act, nor was it nationalized alone on the date of the second nationalization Act. Other companies were nationalized before it, other American and Non–American companies were nationalized with it and after it, and other American companies are still operating in Libya.

Thus, it may be concluded from the above that the political motive was not the predominant motive for nationalization, and that such motive per se does not constitute a sufficient proof of a purely discriminatory measure.

* * *

VI.   REMEDIES FOR PREMATURE TERMINATION OF CONTRACT

[Having found that Libya was obligated to LIAMCO, the arbitrator addressed LIAMCO's requested remedies. LIAMCO preferred restoration of the concession, called "restitutio in integrum," to the alternative award of damages. The arbitrator found that under general principles of both international law and of Libyan law, obligations are to be performed in kind, if such performance is possible].

[However], impossibility is in fact most usual in the international field. For this reason, it has been asserted that "it is impossible to compel a State to make restitution, this would constitute in fact an intolerable interference in the internal sovereignty of States."

Restitution has thus been considered in international law as against the respect due for the sovereignty of the nationalizing State. . . .

Further, restitution presupposes the cancellation of the nationalization measures at issue, and such cancellation violates also the sovereignty of the nationalizing State. Moreover, nationalization is sometimes qualified as an "Act of State," which is immune from control, judicial or otherwise.

* * *

[For similar reasons, the arbitrator rejected LIAMCO's call for a declaratory judgment that Libya did not have lawful title to oil extracted from LIAMCO's concession until effective payment was made. International precedents from courts in Tokyo, Italy and Britain confirmed the unenforceability of any decree to seize nationalized oil in tankers at various ports.]

NOTES AND COMMENTS

1. The remainder of the arbitration decree discusses whether LIAMCO could claim damages for lost profits. Libya was clearly obligated to compensate LIAMCO for the value of the physical assets seized. Had the nationalization been an unlawful taking, international law would also allow the grant of lost profits. However, in cases of lawful nationalization, international precedent was decidedly mixed. Few settlements seemed to have adopted the U.S. position that adequate compensation had to include full compensation for lost profits. Instead, a legal doctrine was developing which allowed courts to revise contracts or treaties which had become onerous due to "unforeseen events" by providing "equitable" compensation.

Juxtaposed to the U.S. position was that of Libya's Prime Minister who explained his country's view that compensation should be based on "net book value," as follows:

> The first principle is that I cannot buy my own oil which is underground because this would be like a person who buys his house twice.... The net estimated book value is, for example, when the Occidental Company came and obtained a concession in Libya paying for example 100 million Libyan dinars.... [Assume] that this particular company ... had recovered something like 60 million dinars. The book value at the time of nationalization or participation is 40 million dinars ...
>
> The second principle is that anyone who would like to be among us and cooperate with us must realize that the Libyan Arab Republic is not a milk cow.... [and] that part of the profits should be utilized in the interest of the Libyan Arab people. 20 I.L.M. at 75.

In light of the opposite positions of the U.S. and Libya, and confusion in international standards, the arbitrator resorted to the principle of Equity, recognized as a supplementary source of law in Libyan law, Islamic law, and international law. The arbitrator decreed that "equitable compensation" for LIAMCO consisted of: $13.8 million for physical plant and equipment, $66 million for lost profits, and interest at the 5% standard set in the Libyan Civil Code. LIAMCO had requested $194 million in lost profits and interest at 12%.

2.   The dispute between Kuwait and Aminoil (the American Independent Oil Company) over nationalization of that company's rich concession is reported in 66 I.L.R 519, 21 I.L.M. 976 (1982). Aminoil unsuccessfully tried to use contract principles of duress to invalidate its consent to bow to some of Kuwait's increased demands. The arbitral award reads at paragraph 44: "In truth, the Company made a choice; disagreeable as certain demands might be, it considered that it was better to accede to them because it was still possible to live with them." In determining damages, the arbitrators used as a guide the "legitimate expectations" of both parties to the contract. Because of the many years of negotiations with Kuwait in which Aminoil had reluctantly consented to many Kuwaiti demands, the arbitrators found that "Aminoil had come to accept the principle of a moderate estimate of profits, and that it was this that constituted its legitimate expectation." (Para. 160).

In a separate opinion, one of the three appointed arbitrators, Sir Fitzmaurice wrote (Para. 26):

> It is an illusion to suppose that monetary compensation alone, even on a generous scale, necessarily removes the confiscatory element from a take-over.... It is like paying compensation to a man who has lost his leg. Unfortunately it does not restore the leg.... What the company wants is to be able to go on operating its Concession for the agreed term, not to be compensated for having to cease doing so against its will. In being deprived of the right to go on, all sorts of factors enter in that are not simply financial. In this respect, businesses are very like human beings, who do not relish being compulsorily retired and relegated to the side-lines ... even though it may be accompanied by a "golden handshake" ... Nationalizations may be lawful or unlawful, but the test can never be "whether they are confiscatory or not" because by virtue of their inherent character, they always are.

3.   Did the succession of United Nations resolutions quoted in the Libyan award invite host countries to institute creeping expropriation of foreign interests? Note that LIAMCO tried to eliminate the 1974 U.N. Resolution 3281 from the accepted principles of international law to be used in its arbitration. Why? Did the arbitrator ultimately adopt this Resolution's method of determining compensation?

4.   While the United States continues to propound a standard of "prompt, adequate and effective" compensation for expropriation, the international community has more often used the standards of "appropriate" and "just" compensation. (The Aminoil–Kuwait arbitration discussed in Note 2 *supra* used the "appropriate" standard of U.N. Resolution 1803). In the Chilean expropriation of Kennecott Copper, Chile offered to pay compensation after deducting excess profits earned by the company in Chile for several years. The profits exceeded the value of the property, so Chile argued that it owed nothing. Is this "appropriate" or "just"? *See generally*, Ralph H. Folsom,

Michael Wallace Gordon, John A. Spanogle, Jr., International Business Transactions in a Nutshell 411–35 (1992). U.S. companies may be able to buy insurance against expropriation from OPIC, the Overseas Private Investment Corporation or the Export–Import Bank. *Id.* at 436–52.

Some commentators see a recent trend toward "full" compensation as the appropriate international standard as a result of "the now widely accepted need to encourage investment in the Third World [which has] eroded the rationale for a partial compensation standard that appeared so compelling to many observers just a short time ago." Patrick M. Norton, A Law of the Future or a Law of the Past? Modern Tribunals and the International Law of Expropriation, 85 American J. Int'l L. 474 (1991). *See also* Paul D. Friedland and Eleanor Wong, Measuring Damages for the Deprivation of Income–Producing Assets: ICSID Case Studies, ICSID Review—Foreign Investment L. J. 400 (1991).

5. Compare the principles of property law used in these arbitrations to the analysis used by U.S. courts under the Takings Clause of the U.S. Constitution that private property shall not "be taken for public use without just compensation." How do the principles announced differ from those used by public utility regulators in the U.S. to determine fair rates of return for utility companies?

Outright expropriations by government takeovers reached a modern high in the mid–1970s, but have diminished greatly in recent years. Investors today more commonly face the risk that a government will seek to void or renegotiate a contract because it results in unconscionably high profits or was the result of a corrupt payoff made by a now-ousted political party. *See* Susan Rose–Ackerman & Jim Rossi, Disentangling Regulatory Takings, 86 Va. L. Rev. 1435 (2000).

6. How are arbitration awards enforced? The United States is one of more than 80 parties to the 1958 U.N. Convention on the Recognition and Enforcement of Foreign Arbitral Awards, 21 U.S.T. 2517, T.I.A.S. No. 6997 (June 10, 1958), as implemented in the U.S. through 9 U.S.C. §§ 201–208. *See also* 28 U.S.C. §§ 1605(a)(1) and (a)(6) on arbitral agreements with foreign states. The U.N. Convention commits the courts of each signatory nation to recognize and enforce arbitration clauses and agreements in international commercial disputes. The U.S. is also a party to several other bilateral and investment treaties that include provisions recognizing and enforcing arbitral agreements and awards. Some of these bilateral treaties may also contain compensation standards for nationalization that accord better with the U.S. standard of "prompt, adequate and effective."

7. Arbitration rather than litigation is the major dispute resolution device used in international agreements. The arbitration clause is extremely important to the parties, especially its choice of law provision. Would the result in LIAMCO have been different if the dispute was to be governed by Libyan law only, without reference to international law? *See generally* John P. Bowman, Dispute Resolution Planning and Pitfalls for Energy and Natural Resources Disputes, 50 Rocky Mtn. Min. L. Inst., ch. 8 (2004).

8. In the decades after the Libyan nationalizations in the 1970s and the imposition of U.S. sanctions against it, starting in 1986, Libya's oil industry declined from the fourth largest producer in the world in 1970 (at about 3 million barrels per day) to 13th (about 1.3 million b/d). Libya holds some of the most promising, largely untapped deposits of oil and gas in the world today. In April 2004, after Muammar al-Qaddafi took responsibility for the downing of a jetliner over Lockerbie, Scotland in 1988, President Bush lifted many trade sanctions, even though Libya is still designated as a state sponsor of terrorism. Libya opened its industry to foreign investors, offering 15 exploratory blocks per year. U.S and U.K. companies were allowed to bid for these blocks. Libya hopes to return to the 3 million b/d production level by 2010. More than 120 companies participated in the first bidding round. Muammar al-Qaddafi still heads the country. Sam Fletcher, Libya is "exploration buzz" among IOCs for 2005, Oil & Gas J., Nov. 8, 2004, at 24.

3. Modern Forms of Petroleum Agreements

a. OVERVIEW

How do governments today grant rights to develop their oil and gas resources? Professor Gary Conine describes and contrasts the major types of systems used today to grant rights to companies:

Gary B. Conine, International Oil and Gas Transactions: Basic Contracts and Dispute Resolution

State Bar of Texas, Advanced Oil, Gas & Mineral Law Course.
pp. J–1 to J–2 (1994).

In general, three legal mechanisms are used by states in granting operating rights to private investors. One involves detailed and rigid legal codes which may go so far as to prescribe not only the conditions under which these rights will be granted but also the form of any agreement between the host government and the oil company. The government is free to negotiate very few terms with the firm. Such legislation is employed in the United States, Canada, Australia, Latin America and most West European countries.

A second regime authorizes a state commission or a national oil company to negotiate and execute *ad hoc* agreements with individual foreign oil companies. For example, the petroleum laws of some countries entrust all petroleum development to a national oil company which, in turn, negotiates contracts with foreign companies to explore for and develop the resource.

An increasing number of countries hive adopted a third system that represents a combined, or hybrid, approach that permits a degree of flexibility in formulating each transaction within broad legislative constraints designed to assure adherence to public policies.

There are various advantages and disadvantages to each form of legal system used for issuing petroleum investment agreements. Detailed legislative systems have been credited with affording an opportunity to include general policy objectives in the law and with imposing a standardized system that makes government oversight and enforcement easier and more effective. It reduces the scope of bargaining, which strengthens the government's negotiating position and ensures public policies will be satisfied, while it produces some assurance that all potential operators will be treated alike.

The disadvantage of a detailed code lies in its lack of flexibility. In order to entice companies to invest in a country, the government often must be able to adjust the terms of its agreements to make its offers as attractive as those of other countries....

On the other hand, the *ad hoc* approach gives the state agency considerable latitude in negotiations, enhancing the country's ability to structure attractive proposals. But it often creates uncertainty among investors and bureaucrats over the terms that will be acceptable to the government, complicates the evaluation of competing offers due to the lack of uniformity in terms, and results in highly complex agreements that may be difficult to formulate and monitor or which invite opportunities for corruption and discrimination.

* * *

The [third] hybrid system uses a code that delegates authority over mineral resources to a specific agency of the government, establishes the procedures for offering development contracts, and prescribes minimum standards and conditions that are non-negotiable, such as provisions on environmental, safety, labor and tax matters. Factors important to the financial evaluation of a project, such as the allocation of risk and revenues, are assigned to the discretion of the licensing agency to allow it the flexibility to attract companies to specific projects.

* * *

B.   Selecting the Licensee of Contractor

World petroleum laws have used, again, one of three procedures for the award of investment agreements. One procedure vests the government with complete discretion over the selection of a licensee or contractor, and the negotiation of contract terms.... As with the *ad hoc* approach, the primary advantage of the discretionary award of licenses lies in the ability to adjust license terms to attract investment at various times to different projects. It also allows the government to select the investor that it believes will be best qualified technically and financially to undertake the operations that will be required in specific situations.

A second procedure relies on public auctions to select the licensee. If there is to be any screening of potential bidders, it must be accomplished prior to the auction. Moreover, all terms of the license, with the exception of the one that is the subject of the bid, must be determined in advance.

The auction is compatible with detailed legislation that prescribes most terms in the license or requires the use of a prescribed license form. . . . The applicant submitting the highest bid on the open term is awarded the license.

A variant of the auction is the open competition. Here the government may announce the general terms it is seeking for a license in a designated area and permit each applicant to construct its own offer. There is usually more than one open term, so that each proposal must be separately evaluated on the basis of the criteria announced for the competition. While a competition suggests that all proposals are to be submitted on a certain date and evaluated against one another, common practice more often results in a series of proposals from each applicant as the government discloses deficiencies in the offers in an effort to get the applicants to bid against one another.

The auction offers two advantages. First, it minimizes the need for the application of non-quantifiable criteria that permit discretionary decisions, reducing the need for bureaucratic judgment. The most meritorious proposal can be determined by any party based on the stated criterion without explanation or justification. Second, the auction provides greater assurance that the winning bid maximizes the financial benefits that can be extracted by the government for a license under the circumstances. Assuming a sufficient number of participants, competition will force the bidders to offer the best terms that the economics of the project will allow. Where expertise in evaluating competing proposals is unavailable to the government, the auction simplifies the process while providing some assurance that the winning proposal is the best deal for the country.

Yet auctions have also been criticized as a licensing procedure. Like the detailed legislation with which it is often associated, the auction is inherently inflexible. To achieve the benefits of the auction, most terms must be prescribed in advance, leaving only a few terms open for bidding. This precludes the use of more complex selection criteria that could be used to attain public objectives other than enhanced revenues. At the same time, it requires the state licensing agency to have considerable experience in formulating licenses as investment packages and to use that experience wisely to assure widespread interest among potential investors.

It is also charged that the auction does not assure that the highest bidder will be the most competent. Indeed, some assert that it tends to favor major companies that have the resources necessary to make large bonus payments upon the issuance of a license and forgo recovery of that investment for years until the license area can be explored and developed. This factor discourages bidding by independent companies and dilutes the competitive forces relied on to maximize bids. While this makes sense, it does not explain the clear preference among major companies for the award of licenses based on direct negotiations. One can only assume that this preference is related again to the greater resources of the major companies and their resulting ability to compete more effectively in negotiations. Their ability to commit experts from various fields for prolonged periods and to devise numerous financial scenarios to accommodate specific concerns and needs of the host country seem to give them a negotiating advantage. This form of competitive advantage is against other companies and does not necessarily assure the government that it is getting the best possible deal. Contemporary surveys have indicated that auctions are employed by a minority of countries.■

NOTES AND COMMENTS

1. Which method of bidding and selection best guards against bribery and corruption?

2. Four types of petroleum investment contracts are in common use today. First is the modern *concession or license*. This contract grants exclusive rights to explore, produce and sell petroleum to the licensee, but with extensive provisions governing work commitments and a development program. Revenues to the state generally accrue through royalties, bonus, rentals, and taxes, but the fiscal terms are far more sophisticated than in an oil and gas lease or the early concessions.

The second common contract is a *production sharing agreement (PSA)* whereby the host country grants a company the right to explore and develop a particular area in exchange for the opportunity to recover its costs and a specific profit share from any production obtained under the contract. The company takes the risk that production revenues will cover costs. The country usually maintains control over the producing properties by creating a state-owned oil company which enters into the contract with the foreign company. The foreign company serves as a "contractor" for the state. The state receives revenues as a share of the "profit oil" remaining after part of the oil, the "cost oil," is used to reimburse the contractor for expenses.

The third type of contract is the *joint venture* whereby the state oil company (or government) and the foreign company form a new entity to develop the oil and gas reserves. A management committee composed of representatives from both parents operates the joint venture. Many concession and production sharing agreements give the government the option of electing to participate in the agreement without creating an entirely new joint venture. Such a provision in the concession or PSA is called a *participation agreement*.

The final type of agreement is a *service contract*, under which a company agrees to provide certain services or technical assistance to the host country or its state oil company in return for a fixed fee or a share of production.

Why don't U.S. landowners, including the federal government, adopt some of these forms of international petroleum agreements in lieu of the oil and gas lease?

3. Do you agree with the following observations of one scholar of petroleum agreements?:

The modern mineral agreement negotiated with host governments ... is an anomaly. It is nominally a contract to conduct certain activities under host government supervision, but since the risk and financing are borne by the contractor, it is a foreign equity investment. The foreign investment is basically the contract itself, since in most agreements title to the resources in the ground and even to the equipment and installations is held by the host government or reverts to the government at the termination of the contract. Moreover, the contracts have not been regarded by most host governments as covenants to be honored throughout their term, but rather as a framework for more or less continuous negotiation as the relative bargaining power and opportunities created by new conditions change in favor of the government.

In the major OPEC countries, such as Saudi Arabia and Kuwait, the position of the original Contractor has diminished to that of a technician and buyer of the oil produced, with little or no control over the amount of oil produced or received, or over the price that must be paid to the host government for the oil. The position of petroleum companies operating in non-OPEC countries, as well as in some of the smaller OPEC producers such as Ecuador and Indonesia, is much stronger since most of these countries need substantial exploration and development to expand their reserves and output, and the governments lack the financial and technical resources to undertake investments on an adequate scale....

Raymond F. Mikesell, Petroleum Company Operations and Agreements in the Developing Countries 135 (Resources for the Future 1984).

4. "Contractor take" is the measure of a contractor's share of profits (gross revenues minus total costs) after royalties and taxes are paid to the government. Contractor take is about 10% in Abu Dhabi and Indonesia; between 30% to 40% in China, Colombia, Papua New Guinea; and 40% or more in Australia, the U.S., and the Philippines. Daniel Johnston, International Petroleum Fiscal Systems and Production Sharing Contracts 14 (1994). The expected contractor's take necessary to attract investors will vary with perceptions of many kinds of risk: the geological risk of finding reserves, development risks of getting production to a market; political risks; and risks relating to the future price of oil or gas. The book by Johnston provides a good overview of the business side of petroleum contracting. Countries which impose onerous fiscal terms will find few multinational companies bidding to assist them in exploiting their reserves. Many developing countries initially tried to imitate OPEC countries' fiscal terms. In the absence of OPEC-size fields, these countries attracted little foreign investment until they revised their petroleum contracts and laws. Professor Mikesell concludes that many countries lost years of potential production, at an enormous cost to the countries.

The Energy Information Administration of the U.S. Department of Energy writes excellent country reports on the petroleum industry in every producing nation. Visit www.eia.doe.gov/emeu/cabs/

5. A nine-page legal checklist of at least 200 items to research before venturing abroad with accompanying commentary appears in Michael P. Darden, Legal Research Checklist for International Petroleum Operations, Monograph No. 20 (Section of Natural Resources, Energy and Environmental Law, American Bar Ass'n, 1994).

A casebook on "International Petroleum Transactions" by Professors Smith, Dzienkowski, et al. (Rocky Mountain Mineral Law Foundation 2000) awaits the intrepid student. Would you expect to find discussions of the rule of capture and unitization in this casebook, as compared to a casebook on U.S. oil and gas law? Why or why not?

6. Many countries that created state oil companies in the 1970s when oil prices were high have had second thoughts. The 1990s saw a strong trend toward greater privatization and participation by private companies in many countries. Falling oil prices exposed the inefficiency and bloated costs of many state-run operations. Government revenues fell drastically as oil prices dropped, and many states could no longer provide the capital needed to invest in their own oil and gas resources. Private lenders were equally wary of investing in wasteful operations run by state governments.

Privatization can be accomplished in several ways: by selling company stock to private investors; by selling the company's assets; by downsizing and reorganizing the company into subsidiaries, some of which are sold and some retained; by joint venturing with foreign companies; or by "privatizing" the management of the company by entering into service contracts with private firms who will provide the skills and technology necessary for efficient development. *See, e.g.,* Carlos E. Martinez, Early Lessons of Latin American Privatizations, 15 Suffolk Transnat'l L. J. 468 (1992). Argentina has transformed its once state-controlled energy sector. In 1993, it privatized its national oil company, YPF; shortly thereafter, YPF acquired Dallas-based Maxum Petroleum and now operates in many Latin American countries. *See* Jay G. Martin, Privatization of Latin American Energy, 14 Nat. Resources & Env't 103 (1999). Privatization of industrial enterprises in Russia and the countries of the former Soviet Union has not been nearly as successful. *See, e.g.,* Anne E. Peck, Foreign Investment in Kazakhstan's Mineral Industries, 40 Post–Soviet Geography and Economics 471 (1999).

Privatization often results in high unemployment and social unrest as workers in inefficient industries or in bloated bureaucracies are laid off so that the newly privatized firm can compete in the world market against its agile rivals. In 1998 and 1999, the Chinese government laid off 10 million workers from money-losing state-owned enterprises. Only some of these workers were absorbed into the growing private sector. Daily Report for Executives, A–1 (Jan. 18. 2000). (Review **Figure 7–4** for employment trends in the U.S. oil industry as market forces worked their will.)

7. Internationally, the abandonment and decommissioning of oil and gas facilities in depleted fields has legacy costs, just as in the United States. Decommissioning about 1600 offshore platforms in the North Sea is estimated to cost at least $22 billion.

b. CORRUPTION

Increasingly, corruption has come to be recognized as one of the most serious current barriers to investment and growth especially in natural resource industries in developing countries. It is also a serious impediment to democratic institutions. *See generally* Susan Rose–Ackerman, Corruption and Government: Causes, Consequences and Reform (1999); and George Moody–Stuart, Grand Corruption: How Business Bribes Damage Developing Countries (1997); 14 Conn. J. Int'l L., Issue No. 2 (1999) (entire issue devoted to corruption). Russia's economic failure after the fall of Communism has been partly attributed to the vast corruption, bordering on kleptocracy, that appears to have accompanied many efforts to privatize its state industries. The management of Russia's giant oil companies are often former Soviet ministers and ranking Communist Party officials. By 1999, five chief executives of Russia's privatized oil companies made it onto the *Forbes* list of the world's 200 wealthiest people. *See* Tina Obut, Avik Sarkar & Sankar Sudner, Roots of Systemic Woes in Russian Oil Sector Traceable to Industry Evolution, Oil & Gas J. 27 (Jan. 25, 1999). Ostensibly to recoup some of the ill-gotten gains, the Russian government arrested Mikhail Khodorkovsky, the CEO of Yukos, Russia's top oil producer, in October 2003 and tried him on charges of fraud and tax evasion. To recoup the cost of some of the allegedly questionable tax schemes used by Yukos, the government auctioned off 77% of the company's prime asset, Yuganskneftegaz, in late 2004. (This subsidiary produces about 1% of the world's oil supply and 11% of Russia's oil supply). An unknown company called Baikal Finans Group (BFG) won the bidding auction; a few days later Rosneft, the state oil company, announced it would buy BFG for $9.35 billion with a loan partly financed by the Chinese National Petroleum Corporation, far less than the unit's fair market value. See www.eia.doe.gov/emeu/cabs/, the EIA's website for country analysis briefs (cabs, for short) and select Russia.

Corruption has not been a stranger to resource acquisition in the United States. The Teapot Dome scandal involved the award of leases to two oil companies in 1922 on the Navy's oil reserves at Teapot Dome in Wyoming and Elk Hill in California. The leases were awarded after executives of the oil companies made payments (in the guise of loans or investments) to Albert Fall, the Secretary of the Interior. The Supreme Court canceled the leases and the Secretary was jailed. This scandal notwithstanding, the United States has been a global leader in the fight against corruption since 1977 with the passage of the Foreign Corrupt Practices Act (FCPA), 15 U.S.C.A. §§ 78dd–1, 78dd–2, 78dd–3 and 78m (West 1997 & West Supp. 1999).

This act owes its birth to the Watergate scandal that ultimately led to the impeachment of President Nixon. The Watergate burglary of the Democratic National Committee's headquarters in 1972 led to a Senate investigation of contributions to Richard Nixon's reelection campaign. The Senate investigating committee found that 15 major corporations had violated the campaign contribution laws by making illegal payments. A report from one of these corporations, Gulf Oil, described an elaborate system of overseas bribes, totaling more than $5 million. A subsequent investigation by the Securities and Exchange Commission (SEC) found that more than 400 U.S. companies had made "questionable payments" of more than $300 million abroad. No specific law expressly prohibited Americans from paying a bribe to a foreign official. The FCPA was passed to fill the void. The U.S. became the first country in the world to make payments of bribes to foreign officials illegal. The Act also requires that corporations keep accounting records to prevent bribes from being hidden. Individual officers, directors and employees of companies are subject to fines and imprisonment for violating the Act.

The Act left America standing alone in the world, with its corporations at a serious disadvantage against foreign competitors who could continue to use bribes to secure valuable contracts. The Department of Commerce reported that U.S. businesses lost 100 foreign contracts valued at $45 billion to overseas competitors during 1994 and 1995. Kari Diersen, Foreign Corrupt Practices Act, 36 Am. Crim. L. Rev. 753 at 764 n. 88 (1999). The United States undertook a foreign policy campaign to level the playing field by exhorting other countries and international organizations to join the anti-bribery bandwagon. Years of lobbying the Organization for Economic Cooperation and Development (the OECD is a group of leading industrialized countries) finally bore fruit in 1997 when all 29 member countries signed the Convention on Combating Bribery of Foreign Public Officials in International Business Transactions (37 I.L.M. 1 (1998). The Convention entered into force in 1999 and makes it a criminal offense to give a bribe to a foreign public official. The OECD's Centre for Anti–Corruption Compliance has an extensive website on foreign corruption at www.oecd.org/daf /nocorruption/ In addition, the U.N. General Assembly approved a resolution against corruption in 1997 and an African Union Convention on Preventing and Combating Corruption was signed in July 2003.

Transparency International (TI) is a nongovernmental organization founded to stop international bribery. It publishes a Corruption Perception Index that lists the most and least corrupt countries in the world in terms of taking bribes. It recently added a Bribe Payers Index ranking 19 leading industrialized countries in terms of their paying bribes. TI's homepage is at www.transparency.de. The index is quite useful to firms venturing abroad. Where do you think U.S. officials and companies rank on the respective list—as bribe takers and bribe payers—using a scale of 1 to 10 with 10 being negligible corruption?

The World Bank, the International Monetary Fund, the World Trade Organization, the International Chamber of Commerce and the Organization of American States have also undertaken significant anti-corruption initiatives. The World Bank has refused to fund projects in countries with corruption. For example, it suspended a $76 million load to Kenya for energy development because it could not ensure that the contracts would be awarded fairly and openly. *See* A. Timothy Martin, The Development of International Bribery Law, 14 Nat. Resources & Env't 95 (Fall 1999).

China ranks quite poorly on the indexes. In a speech to the Chinese parliament in March 2000, the Chinese Prime Minister repeatedly cited corruption as one of China's most pressing problems. A few days later, China executed a former provincial vice governor for taking bribes worth $600,000. New York Times, Mar. 9, 2000, at A10.

Some key prosecutions in the United States under the FCPA have involved oil companies. In 1986, Ashland Oil was prosecuted for its actions in securing offshore petroleum rights from the Sultanate of Oman. The SEC settled a civil action against Triton Energy in 1997 involving petroleum operations in Indonesia. The FCPA poses special challenges to U.S. companies developing natural resource projects abroad with state-owned oil companies as their joint venturers. *See* Lucinda A. Low and John E. Davis, Coping with the Foreign Corrupt Practices Act: A Primer for Energy and Natural Resource Sectors, 16 J. Energy & Nat. Resources L. 286 (1998); and Christopher F. Corr & Judd Lawler, Damned If You Do, Damned If You Don't? The OECD Convention and the Globalization of Anti–Bribery Measures, 32 Vanderbilt J. Transnat'l L. 1249 (1999).

Under the FCPA it is not illegal to pay gratuities to foreign officials who perform "routine governmental action", *i.e.,* "grease" payments for processing permits, visas, providing phone service, etc. Is it easy to draw a line between legal and illegal payments? Steven R. Salbu argues that the "world is not ready to agree about what comprises corruption" and that the FCPA and its progeny unwisely promote the extraterritorial criminalization of bribery when "[t]he world is not sufficiently homogenized to embrace one conceptualization of morality in gray areas." Is the FCPA a "culturally arrogant encroachment" on the international law principle of national sovereignty? *See* Salbu, The Foreign Corrupt Practices Act as a Threat to Global Harmony, 20 Mich. J. of Int'l L. 419 (1999). Is Transparency International's approach a better way to reduce bribery than the FCPA's use of legal fiat?

The FCPA prohibits payments to foreign officials for purposes of:

(i) influencing any act or decision of such foreign official in his official capacity, (ii) inducing such foreign official to do or omit to do any act in violation of the lawful duty of such official, or (iii) securing any improper advantage ... in order to assist [the company making the payment] in obtaining or retaining business for or with, or directing business to, any person. 15 U.S.C. § 78dd–1(a)(1).

Clearly this language prohibits bribes paid to win approval of a bid for a new government contract or to renew an existing contract. Does it apply to bribes paid to Haitian government officials to reduce an American company's customs duties and taxes on rice imported into Haiti? Do such payments "assist" the company to indirectly "obtain or retain business" by securing an "improper advantage?" After extensive resort to legislative history, the Fifth Circuit Court of Appeals wrote in *United States v. Kay,* 359 F.3d 738, at 749, 761 (5th Cir. 2004):

Congress was obviously distraught not only about high profile bribes to high-ranking foreign officials, but also by the pervasiveness of foreign bribery by United States businesses and businessmen.

* * *

[T]he concern of Congress with the immorality, inefficiency, and unethical character of bribery presumably does not vanish simply because the tainted payments are intended to secure a favorable decision less significant than winning a contract bid ... [T]here is little difference between this example [of bribing to win a contract bid] and that of a corporation's lawfully obtaining a contract from an honest official or agency by submitting the lowest bid, and—either before or after doing so—bribing a different government official to reduce taxes and thereby ensure that the under-bid venture is nevertheless profitable. Avoiding or lowering taxes reduces operating costs and thus increases profit margins, thereby freeing up funds that the business is otherwise legally obligated to expend. And this, in turn, enables it to take any number of actions to the disadvantage of competitors.

* * *

When the FCPA is read as a whole, its core of criminality is seen to be bribery of a foreign official to induce him to perform an official duty in a corrupt manner.

NOTES AND COMMENTS

1. Bribery and corruption may be immoral, but how are they inefficient, *i.e.*, how do they distort a free market economy? Several studies show a link between high levels of corruption and retarded economic development. Can't some bribes substitute as salaries to underpaid civil servants who live in poverty? Is there a difference between "petty" corruption where "greed is based on need," and the "grand" corruption in the millions of dollars that has accompanied multinational bidding for contracts? See Nikolay A. Ouzounov, Facing the Challenge: Corruption, State Capture and the Role of Multinational Business, 37 John Marshall L. Rev. 1181 (2004).

c. SANCTIONS

U.S. oil companies venturing abroad are also subject to federal laws and Executive Orders which may impose trade sanctions against repressive regimes which violate human rights. For example, Congress enacted a law authorizing the President to prohibit U.S. persons from making new investments in Burma if the President certifies that the Government of Burma has maltreated or exiled Daw Aung San Suu Kyi (winner of the Nobel peace prize in 1991) or committed repression or violence against its democratic opposition. In May, 1997, the President found that Burma had committed large-scale repression of the democratic opposition, and issued an order imposing trade sanctions on Burma.

Several states of the United States, such as Massachusetts, passed laws prohibiting the state or its agencies from purchasing goods or services from companies that do business with Burma. In signing the bill into law, the Lieutenant Governor of Massachusetts stated that a steady flow of foreign investment into Burma was allowing the brutal military regime to supply itself with weapons and portray itself as the legitimate government. In *Crosby v. Nat'l Foreign Trade Council*, 120 S.Ct. 2288 (2000), the Court held that Massachusetts' Burma Law unconstitutionally encroached on the federal government's exclusive power over foreign relations and also was preempted by federal law.

Do trade sanctions like this create another "unlevel" playing field for U.S. companies operating abroad, as did the Foreign Corrupt Practices Act? In an opinion ad on the OpEd pages of the New York Times, ExxonMobil wrote: "Unless broadly adopted by many countries, sanctions do little more than damage U.S. businesses that are unable to compete with foreign companies not similarly constrained. Moreover, government entities in the U.S. have been on a sanctions binge since the 1980s, so that now some form of U.S. sanctions applies to countries with over two-thirds of the world's population. And this leads to more than simply an economic loss for Americans—it can also deprive developing nations of a positive force for change that is often associated with the participation of private U.S. enterprise in their national economies." New York Times, Mar. 9, 2000, at A29. In 1996, Conoco was awarded a contract worth $1 billion by the National Iranian Oil Co to develop a large offshore field. After the contract was signed, President Clinton issued an executive order imposing trade sanctions on Iran, and Conoco was forced to withdraw from the project, which later was awarded to Total, the French oil company. Daily Report for Executives, Sept. 29, 1999, at A–46.

D.   BARRIERS TO LITIGATING DISPUTES IN U.S. COURTS

One reason for the prevalence of arbitration as a dispute resolution mechanism in international petroleum agreements is that substantial barriers exist to litigating claims against host governments or their national oil companies. By resorting to arbitration, many of these barriers disappear and private investors are better assured of a forum in which disputes can be resolved. The nationalization of oil company interests by OPEC countries in the 1970s provided a cornucopia of law on the issues of sovereign immunity, political question, and the act of state doctrine. Under these three doctrines, a court will dismiss a cause of action, even though the court has personal jurisdiction and subject matter jurisdiction over the defendant under the principles advanced in *International Shoe* and other cases studied in Civil Procedure or International Law.

1.   SOVEREIGN IMMUNITY

The doctrine of sovereign immunity derives from the common law principle of international law that sovereigns are equal and should not be subject to suit in the courts of another nation. Application of the doctrine in the United States was codified in the Foreign Sovereign Immunities Act of 1976, 28 U.S.C. §§ 1330, 1602–1611, after court decisions began restricting the doctrine so that immunity did not apply to commercial activities of states. As state oil companies proliferated and expanded their commercial reach, the Act's usefulness as a tool to bring these companies to court was often tested. *See generally* Jordan J. Paust, Joan M. Fitzpatrick, & Jon M. Van Dyke, International Law and Litigation in the U.S. 567–638 (West 2000). The Act grants to federal district courts jurisdiction over any civil action against a foreign state which falls into one of several exceptions to sovereign immunity. These exceptions include:

1. Waiver of immunity by the foreign state. § 1605(a)(1).

2. Action based on commercial activity conducted in the U.S. by the foreign state, or conducted outside the U.S. "in connection with a commercial activity of the foreign state elsewhere . . . [which] causes a direct effect in the United States." § 1605(a)(2).

3. Claims that rights in property were taken in violation of international law, and that property is present in the U.S. in connection with a commercial activity carried on by the foreign state in the U.S.; or that the property is "owned or operated by an agency or instrumentality of the foreign state" which is engaged in commercial activity in the United.States. § 1605(a)(3).

4. A claim for money damages against a foreign state for personal injury or death, or for damage to property occurring in the U.S. and caused by the tortious act of the foreign state or its officials and employees, as long as the tortious act is not the exercise of a discretionary function by the foreign state. § 1605(a)(5).

Which of these exceptions are likely to be at issue under the following claims? What do you think is the likely result?

- Libya nationalized its oil concessions and then embargoed exports of crude oil to the U.S. To obtain crude oil supplies, a Bahamian refiner entered into new contracts with the Libyan National Oil Corporation at prices triple the previous price. The refiner was a subsidiary of a New England merchant who sold fuel oil in that area. The New England merchant sued the Libyan National Oil company for $1.6 billion in damages for breach of contract and other overcharges. Carey v. National Oil Corp., 592 F.2d 673 (2d Cir. 1979).

- LIAMCO (the Libyan American Oil Company) sought to confirm and enforce an arbitration award against Libya for nationalizing its concession rights. LIAMCO had entered into the concession agreement in 1955 and negotiated arbitration and choice of law provisions with Libya in amendments to the original contract in 1966 and 1967. Libyan American Oil Company v. Socialist People's Libyan Arab Jamahirya (Libya), 482 F. Supp. 1175 (D.D.C. 1980).

- PEMEX was engaged in drilling a well, the Ixtoc I, in the Bay of Campeche. The well blew out, leading to a massive oil spill which reached the lower Texas beaches, entailing huge cleanup efforts and losses of recreational business. Private plaintiffs and the state of Texas brought suit against PEMEX. In re Sedco, 543 F. Supp. 561 (S.D. Tex. 1982).

- The owner of a shrimp trawler sought damages against a tug owned by PEMEX, which collided with the trawler. S.T. Tringali Co. v. The Tug Pemex XV, 274 F. Supp. 227 (S.D. Tex. 1967).

2. Political Question

If an action in a U.S. court survives analysis under the Foreign Sovereign Immunities Act, it might still be dismissed because it is best left to another branch of government. The Persian Gulf again provides a good example of the "political question" doctrine. In *Occidental of Umm Al Qaywayn, Inc. v. A Certain Cargo of Petroleum*, 577 F.2d 1196 (5th Cir. 1978), Occidental brought an action for conversion of tankers full of crude oil brought to the United States by rival oil companies. Occidental traced its right to the oil from a concession it had signed with the sheikhdom of Umm. Rival Buttes Oil Company entered into a concession agreement with the neighboring sheikhdom of Sharjah. The rulers of the two sheikdoms then each claimed title to the same tiny island of Abu Musa in the Gulf as part of their territorial waters. Iran also claimed ownership of the island. Iran teamed up with Sharjah and these two states confirmed Buttes' concession. Then Iran invaded the island, leaving Occidental and Umm without any protection. The rulers of Umm and Sharjah ultimately resolved to share royalties, but Occidental was left out in the cold. Umm terminated its concession. After reciting this history, the court wrote:

> A political question clearly emerges under the proper analysis.... Shorn of its factual complexity, appellants claim a tortious conversion of oil.... [W]e find that to successfully maintain its tortious conversion action, appellant would have to establish its right to possess the oil at the time of conversion. Appellant apparently contends that the conversion occurred when appellant was supplanted by Buttes through the intervention of Iran, sometime after November 30, 1971. Because, as a matter of international law, one who receives an interest in land which is in dispute between sovereigns takes subject to the dispute, ... appellant must necessarily develop Umm's right to undisputed possession of the portion of the continental shelf where the oil was extracted.... Therefore, in order to resolve appellant's right to possess the oil, we would have to resolve the dispute over Abu Musa. The resolution of a territorial dispute between sovereigns, however, is a political question which we are powerless to decide.

Throughout the history of the federal judiciary, political questions have been held to be nonjusticiable and therefore not a "case or controversy" as defined by Article III.... In *Marbury v. Madison*, 1 Cranch 137, 164–66, 2 L.Ed. 60 (1803), Chief Justice Marshall acknowledged the existence of a class of cases which involve a "mere political act of the executive" and which were placed by the Constitution in the hands of the executive. The Supreme Court therefore appreciated that the genesis of the political question is the constitutional separation and disbursement of powers among the branches of government. *Id.* at 1201–03.

3. THE ACT OF STATE DOCTRINE

More common than the political question is the judicially created act of state doctrine. In 1897, the Supreme Court formulated the doctrine when it held that "the courts of one country will not sit in judgment on the acts of the government of another, done within its own territory." *Underhill v. Hernandez*, 168 U.S. 250, 252 (1897). The doctrine requires, first, that public acts occurred, and second, that the acts took place in the foreign country.

In the following case, again arising from the Persian Gulf, the court distinguishes the defense of sovereign immunity from the act of state doctrine. The International Association of Machinists and Aerospace Workers (IAM) sued OPEC for violating the U.S. antitrust laws by price-fixing. (Recall that the OPEC embargo and huge run-up in crude oil price caused high unemployment as well as inflation).

International Association of Machinists and Aerospace Workers (IAM) v. OPEC

649 F.2d 1354 (9th Cir. 1981), *cert. denied*, 454 U.S. 1163 (1982).

■ CHOY, CIRCUIT JUDGE:

* * *

The OPEC nations produce and export oil either through government-owned companies or through government participation in private companies. Prior to the formation of OPEC, these diverse and sometimes antagonistic countries were plagued with fluctuating oil prices. Without coordination among them, oil was often in oversupply on the world market resulting in low prices. The OPEC nations realized that self-interest dictated that they "formulate a system to ensure the stabilisation (sic) of prices by, among other means, the regulation of production, with due regard to the interests of the producing and of the consuming nations, and to the necessity of securing a steady income to the producing countries, an efficient economic and regular supply of this source of energy to consuming nations" OPEC Resolution of the First Conference, Resolution 1.1(3), September 1960.

OPEC achieves its goals by a system of production limits and royalties which its members unanimously adopt. There is no enforcement arm of OPEC. The force behind OPEC decrees is the collective self-interest of the 13 nations.

After formation of OPEC, it is alleged, the price of crude oil increased tenfold and more. Whether or not a causal relation exists, there is no doubt that the price of oil has risen dramatically in recent years, and that this has become of international concern.

* * *

In December 1978, IAM brought suit against OPEC and its member nations. IAM's complaint alleged price fixing in violation of the Sherman Act, 15 U.S.C. § 1, and requested treble damages and injunctive relief under the Clayton Act, 15 U.S.C. §§ 15, 16. IAM claimed a deliberate targeting and victimization of the United States market, directly resulting in higher prices for Americans.

The defendants refused to recognize the jurisdiction of the district court, and they did not appear in the proceedings below. Their cause was argued by various amici, with additional information provided by court-appointed experts. The district court ordered a full hearing, noting that the Foreign Sovereign Immunities Act ("FSIA") prohibits the entry of a default judgment against a foreign sovereignty "unless the claimant establishes his claim or right to relief by evidence satisfactory to the court." 28 U.S.C. § 1608(e).

* * *

At the close of the trial, the district judge granted judgment in favor of the defendants. The court held, first, that it lacked jurisdiction over the defendant nations under the Foreign Sovereign Immunities Act. * * *

A. Sovereign Immunity

In the international sphere each state is viewed as an independent sovereign, equal in sovereignty to all other states. It is said that an equal holds no power of sovereignty over an equal. Thus the doctrine of sovereign immunity: the courts of one state generally have no jurisdiction to entertain suits against another state. This rule of international law developed by custom among nations. Also by custom, an exception developed for the commercial activities of a state. The former concept of absolute sovereign immunity gave way to a restrictive view. Under the restrictive theory of sovereign immunity, immunity did not exist for commercial activities since they were seen as non-sovereign.

In 1976, Congress enacted the FSIA and declared that the federal courts will apply an objective nature-of-the-act test in determining whether activity is commercial and thus not immune: "The commercial character of an activity shall be determined by reference to the nature of the course of conduct or particular transaction or act, rather than by reference to its purpose." 28 U.S.C. § 1603(d).

A critical step in characterizing the nature of a given activity is defining exactly what that activity is. The immunity question may be determined by how broadly or narrowly that activity is defined. In this case, IAM insists on a very narrow focus on the specific activity of "price fixing." IAM argues that the FSIA does not give immunity to this activity. Under the FSIA a commercial activity is one which an individual might "customarily carr(y) on for profit." H.R.Rep. No.94–1487, 94th Cong., 2d

Sess. 16, reprinted in (1976) U.S. Code Cong. & Ad. News 6604, 6615. OPEC's activity, characterized by IAM as making agreements to fix prices, is one which is presumably done for profit; it is thus commercial and immunity does not apply.

The court below defined OPEC's activity in a different way: "(I)t is clear that the nature of the activity engaged in by each of these OPEC member countries is the establishment by a sovereign state of the terms and conditions for the removal of a prime natural resource to wit, crude oil from its territory." 477 F. Supp. at 567. The trial judge reasoned that, according to international law, the development and control of natural resources is a prime governmental function. *Id.* at 567–78. The opinion cites several resolutions of the United Nations' General Assembly, which the United States supported, and the United States Constitution, Art. 4, § 3, cl. 2, which treat the control of natural resources as governmental acts.

IAM argues that the district court's analysis strays from the path set forth in the FSIA. The control of natural resources is the purpose behind OPEC's actions, but the act complained of here is a conspiracy to fix prices. The FSIA instructs us to look upon the act itself rather than underlying sovereign motivations.

The district court was understandably troubled by the broader implications of an anti-trust action against the OPEC nations. The importance of the alleged price-fixing activity to the OPEC nations cannot be ignored. Oil revenues represent their only significant source of income. Consideration of their sovereignty cannot be separated from their near total dependence upon oil. We find that these concerns are appropriately addressed by application of the act of state doctrine. While we do not apply the doctrine of sovereign immunity, its elements remain relevant to our discussion of the act of state doctrine.

B. The Act of State Doctrine

The act of state doctrine declares that a United States court will not adjudicate a politically sensitive dispute which would require the court to judge the legality of the sovereign act of a foreign state....

The doctrine recognizes the institutional limitations of the courts and the peculiar requirements of successful foreign relations. To participate adeptly in the global community, the United States must speak with one voice and pursue a careful and deliberate foreign policy. The political branches of our government are able to consider the competing economic and political considerations and respond to the public will in order to carry on foreign relations in accordance with the best interests of the country as a whole. The courts, in contrast, focus on single disputes and make decisions on the basis of legal principles. The timing of our decisions is largely a result of our caseload and of the random tactical considerations which motivate parties to bring lawsuits and to seek delay or expedition. When the courts engage in piecemeal adjudication of the legality of the sovereign acts of states, they risk disruption of our country's international diplomacy. The executive may utilize protocol, economic sanction, compromise, delay, and persuasion to achieve international objectives. Ill-timed judicial decisions challenging the acts of foreign states could nullify these tools and embarrass the United States in the eyes of the world.

* * *

While the act of state doctrine has no explicit source in our Constitution or statutes, it does have "constitutional underpinnings." *Banco Nacional de Cuba v. Sabbatino*, 376 U.S. 398, 423, 84 S.Ct. 923, 937, 11 L.Ed.2d 804 (1964). The Supreme Court has stated that the act of state doctrine

> arises out of the basic relationships between branches of government in a system of separation of powers The doctrine as formulated in past decisions expresses the strong sense of the Judicial Branch that its engagement in the task of passing on the validity of foreign acts of state may hinder rather than further this country's pursuit of goals both for itself and for the community of nations as a whole in the international sphere. *Id.*

* * *

The doctrine of sovereign immunity is similar to the act of state doctrine in that it also represents the need to respect the sovereignty of foreign states. The two doctrines differ, however, in significant respects. The law of sovereign immunity goes to the jurisdiction of the court. The act of state doctrine is not jurisdictional. *Ricaud v. American Metal Co.*, 246 U.S. 304, 309, 38 S.Ct. 312, 313, 62 L.Ed. 733 (1918). Rather, it is a prudential doctrine designed to avoid judicial action in sensitive areas. Sovereign immunity is a principle of international law, recognized in the United States by statute. It is the states themselves, as defendants, who may claim sovereign immunity. The act of state doctrine is a domestic legal principle, arising from the peculiar role of American courts. It recognizes not only the sovereignty of foreign states, but also the spheres of power of the co-equal branches of our government. Thus a private litigant may raise the act of state doctrine, even when no sovereign state is a party to the action. *See, e. g., Timberlane Lumber Co. v. Bank of Am.*, 549 F.2d 597, 606 (9th Cir. 1976). The act of state doctrine is apposite whenever the federal courts must question the legality of the sovereign acts of foreign states.

It has been suggested that the FSIA supersedes the act of state doctrine, or that the amorphous doctrine is limited by modern jurisprudence. We disagree.

Congress in enacting the FSIA recognized the distinction between sovereign immunity and the act of state doctrine [citing legislative history of the FSIA]. . . .

The act of state doctrine is not diluted by the commercial activity exception which limits the doctrine of sovereign immunity. While purely commercial activity may not rise to the level of an act of state, certain seemingly commercial activity will trigger act of state considerations. As the district court noted, OPEC's "price-fixing" activity has a significant sovereign component. While the FSIA ignores the underlying purpose of a state's action, the act of state doctrine does not. This court has stated that the motivations of the sovereign must be examined for a public interest basis. *Timberlane*, 549 F.2d at 607. When the state qua state acts in the public interest, its sovereignty is asserted. The courts must proceed cautiously to avoid an affront to that sovereignty. Because the act of state doctrine and the doctrine of sovereign immunity address different concerns and apply in different circumstances, we find that the act of state doctrine remains available when such caution is appropriate, regardless of any commercial component of the activity involved.

* * *

The record in this case contains extensive documentation of the involvement of our executive and legislative branches with the oil question. IAM does not dispute that the United States has a grave interest in the petro-politics of the Middle East, or that the foreign policy arms of the executive and legislative branches are intimately involved in this sensitive area. It is clear that OPEC and its activities are carefully considered in the formulation of American foreign policy.

The remedy IAM seeks is an injunction against the OPEC nations. The possibility of insult to the OPEC states and of interference with the efforts of the political branches to seek favorable relations with them is apparent from the very nature of this action and the remedy sought. While the case is formulated as an anti-trust action, the granting of any relief would in effect amount to an order from a domestic court instructing a foreign sovereign to alter its chosen means of allocating and profiting from its own valuable natural resources. On the other hand, should the court hold that OPEC's actions are legal, this "would greatly strengthen the bargaining hand" of the OPEC nations in the event that Congress or the executive chooses to condemn OPEC's actions. *Sabbatino*, 376 U.S. at 432, 84 S.Ct. at 942.

A further consideration is the availability of internationally-accepted legal principles which would render the issues appropriate for judicial disposition. As the Supreme Court stated in *Sabbatino*,

> It should be apparent that the greater the degree of codification or consensus concerning a particular area of international law, the more appropriate it is for the judiciary to render decisions regarding it, since the courts can then focus on the application of an agreed principle to circumstances of fact rather than on the sensitive task of establishing a principle not inconsistent with the national interest or with international justice. 376 U.S. at 428, 84 S.Ct. at 940.

While conspiracies in restraint of trade are clearly illegal under domestic law, the record reveals no international consensus condemning cartels, royalties, and production agreements.[12] The United States and other na-

---

12. [FN9] The amici suggest that production quotas and royalties are accepted sovereign practices, citing, inter alia, the Connally Hot Oil Act, 15 U.S.C. § 715; United States' payment

tions have supported the principle of supreme state sovereignty over natural resources. The OPEC nations themselves obviously will not agree that their actions are illegal. We are reluctant to allow judicial interference in an area so void of international consensus. . . .

IV. Conclusion

The act of state doctrine is applicable in this case. . . . The issue of whether the FSIA allows jurisdiction in this case need not be decided, . . .

The decision of the district court dismissing this action is affirmed.■

NOTES AND COMMENTS

1. Both Bunker Hunt and LIAMCO were thwarted by the act of state doctrine in their quest to be compensated for the loss of their Libyan concessions. Both sought to avoid the doctrine by resort to the Hickenlooper Amendment to the Foreign Assistance Act of 1964. The Hickenlooper Amendment was passed by an angry Congress after the U.S. Supreme Court held that the act of state doctrine precluded the judiciary from examining the legality of the Cuban expropriation of foreign assets in *Banco Nacional de Cuba v. Sabbatino*, 376 U.S. 398 (1964). The Amendment and its application were construed in *Libyan American Oil Company v. Socialist People's Libyan Arab Jamahirya*, 482 F. Supp. 1175, at 1179 (1980), as follows:

> Since the ruling in *Underhill*, courts have consistently found a foreign state's act of nationalization to be the classic example of an act of state. "Expropriations of the property of an alien within the boundaries of the sovereign state are traditionally considered to be public acts of the sovereign removed from judicial scrutiny by application of the act of state rubric." Hunt v. Mobil Oil Corp., 550 F.2d 68, 73 (2d Cir. 1977), *cert. denied*, 434 U.S. 984, 98 S.Ct. 608, 54 L.Ed.2d 477.

> Petitioner argues that even if the act of state doctrine should be applied in this case, the exception embodied in the Hickenlooper Amendment to the Foreign Assistance Act of 1964 would still require this Court to decide this case. The amendment provides that unless the President, for foreign policy reasons, suggests otherwise, courts must not decline on the ground of the act of state doctrine to decide the merits of a claim of title or other right to property . . . based upon (or traced though) a confiscation or other taking after January 1, 1959, by an act of that state in violation of the principles of international law. 22 U.S.C. § 2370(e)(2).

> The President has made no suggestion in this matter, but petitioner has failed to show that the amendment's requirements have been met.

to farmers not to produce wheat; and Japan's voluntary reduction of TV and automobile production to maintain prices.

The contract rights that lie at the heart of petitioner's claim do not constitute property for purposes of the amendment, *Menendez v. Saks & Co.*, 485 F.2d 1355, 1372 (2d Cir. 1973), *rev'd on other grounds, sub nom.* Alfred Dunhill of London, Inc. v. Republic of Cuba, 425 U.S. 682, 96 S.Ct. 1854, 48 L.Ed.2d 301 (1976), nor have courts found that the repudiation of contractual obligations amounts to a "confiscation or other taking," as those terms are employed in the statute. *Occidental of Umm al Qaywayn, Inc. v. Cities Service Oil Co.*, 396 F. Supp. 461, 472 (W.D. La.1975). Finally, petitioner has failed to show that the taking was in violation of international law. The nationalization provisions of Libyan law established means for LIAMCO to recover its investment. Because LIAMCO may not have been satisfied with the rate at which Libya was prepared to recompense the company does not render the original nationalization in violation of international law.

For the reasons set forth above, the Court declines to recognize or enforce the arbitral award.

How does the result in this case—based on a rationale that a contract right is not property—accord with the arbitrator's opinion reproduced in *LIAMCO v. Libya supra*?

2.   Nelson Bunker Hunt tried to circumvent the act of state doctrine in a suit for conversion against Coastal States, a company which had purchased "hot" oil from Libya after the expropriation of Hunt's concession. In *Hunt v. Coastal States Gas Producing Co.*, 583 S.W.2d 322 (Tex. 1979), six judges of the Texas Supreme Court adopted the same narrow reading of the Hickenlooper Amendment. Since Libya was the place of the contract's execution and performance, as well as the location of the subject matter, Libyan substantive law governed the interpretation of Hunt's rights by the Texas court. Under Libyan law, all petroleum belonged to the state, and Hunt had only a contractual right to explore for and produce it. Hunt had no property right to protect under the Hickenlooper Amendment.

A strong dissent argued that "[i]t has long been recognized that contract rights are a form of property protected by the Fifth Amendment" (citing United States Trust Co. v. New Jersey, 431 U.S. 1 (1977)), and that the legislative history of the Hickenlooper Amendment showed that Congress contemplated precisely this sort of claim. Furthermore, the Department of State had indicated its belief that the Amendment was passed precisely to allow American courts to entertain such suits; that Libya's expropriation violated international law (because it was discriminatory and offered inadequate compensation); and that Hunt should be supported in his pursuit of remedies. *Id.* at 326–336. *See also Hunt v. Mobil Oil Corp.*, 550 F.2d 68 (2d Cir. 1977), *cert. denied*, 434 U.S. 984, 98 S.Ct. 608 (1978) (act of state doctrine precluded Hunt's claim that Mobil, BP, Exxon and the other "Seven Sisters" violated the antitrust laws by conspiring to preserve the competitive advantage of Persian Gulf crude over Libyan crude; their conspiracy allegedly prevented Hunt from reaching any settlement with Libya, thus resulting in nationalization).

It seems clear that the courts are reluctant to intervene in cases involving expropriation of natural resource industries in developing countries.

3. These cases should give the reader a greater appreciation of the importance of an arbitration clause in an international petroleum agreement. Such a clause allows the parties to choose a forum for arbitration, to select the law which will govern the dispute, and to agree that the arbitration award will be final, without appeal to a court. The parties' agreement on these matters will be upheld in almost all circumstances. *See generally*, Henry P. De Vries, International Commercial Arbitration: A Contractual Substitute for National Courts, 57 Tul. L. Rev. 42 (1982); and David J. Branson & Richard E. Wallace, Jr., Choosing the Substantive Law to Apply in International Commercial Arbitration, 27 Va. J. Int'l L. 39 (1986).

4. Does the Foreign Corrupt Practices Act abrogate the act of state doctrine? In *Clayco Petroleum Corp. v. Occidental Petroleum Corp.*, 712 F.2d 404 (9th Cir. 1983), *cert. denied,* 464 U.S. 1040 (1984), Clayco filed a private antitrust suit against Occidental Petroleum, its subsidiary and its chief executive, Armand Hammer, charging them with making bribes to the rulers of Umm Al Qaywayn. The rulers had allegedly agreed to grant Clayco an oil concession in September 1969, but two months later the concession was granted to Occidental. Clayco first learned of the reasons for losing the concession when the Oakland Tribune published an article reporting that Occidental had made questionable payments of $30 million. The SEC commenced an action against Occidental for violating the reporting requirements of the Security Exchange Act and a subsequent report prepared for the SEC confirmed that bribes were paid.

The *Clayco* court held that the act of state doctrine prohibited a private suit which would embarrass the political branches of the U.S. in its conduct of foreign policy and which would "impugn or question the nobility of a foreign nation's motivation." 712 F.2d at 407. Clayco then argued that the Foreign Corrupt Practices Act created an exception to the act of state doctrine. The court responded:

> The FCPA was intended to stop bribery of foreign officials and political parties by domestic corporations. Bribery abroad was considered a "severe" United States foreign policy problem; it embarrasses friendly governments, causes a decline of foreign esteem for the United States and casts suspicion on the activities of our enterprises, giving credence to our foreign opponents [citing legislative history, with a footnote that it may be "the revelation of bribery, more than bribery itself" which causes these problems]. The FCPA thus represents a legislative judgment that our foreign relations will be bettered by a strict anti-bribery statute. There is also no question, however, that any prosecution under the Act entails risks to our relations with the foreign governments involved. . . .
>
> The Justice Department and the SEC share enforcement responsibilities under the FCPA. They coordinate enforcement of the Act with

the State Department, recognizing the potential foreign policy problems of these actions. Therefore, any governmental enforcement represents a judgment on the wisdom of bringing a proceeding, in the light of the exigencies of foreign affairs. Act of state concerns are thus inapplicable. . . .

Here, however, we are faced with a private lawsuit, rather than a public enforcement action. It is the screening of governmental proceedings, with State Department consultation, which distinguishes FCPA enforcement from private suits. . . . Hence, in private suits, the act of state doctrine remains necessary to protect the proper conduct of national foreign policy. *Id.* at 408–09.

Does this decision make the work of Transparency International more important to private investors? To U.S. officials who do not want the blame for embarrassing corrupt foreign officials?

4. The Doctrine of Forum Non Conveniens

Increasingly, multinational oil companies are the defendants, not plaintiffs, in U.S. courts in lawsuits brought by citizens claiming injuries from the company's operations in their homeland. As defendants, the companies often raise a threshold question as to whether the U.S. court is the proper forum for such disputes. Forum non conveniens is a judicially created doctrine designed to prevent plaintiffs from harassing defendants by filing suit in an inconvenient forum, even though personal jurisdiction and subject matter jurisdiction exist in that forum. Why might a U.S. corporation "prefer" to be sued in a foreign court?

In the well-known *Bhopal* case of *In re Union Carbide Gas Plant Disaster*, 809 F.2d 195 (2d Cir. 1987), the court affirmed the dismissal of personal injury and wrongful death suits brought by Indian plaintiffs in U.S. district court on the grounds of forum non conveniens, conditioned on Union Carbide's consent to personal jurisdiction in India. Over 2000 persons were killed and 200,000 injured by a lethal gas released from a chemical plant in Bhopal, operated by Union Carbide India Limited, a company incorporated under India's laws whose stock was traded on the Bombay Stock Exchange. The plant was managed and operated entirely by Indians in India. The U.S. district court found that the Indian judicial system was competent to handle complex technological issues and that the tort law of India was similarly suitable; the appellate court affirmed this decision.

In 1989, Union Carbide Corp. entered into a $470 million settlement with the Indian government for claims arising from the Bhopal tragedy. Most claimants received about $600 for injuries and $3000 for death.

Could these amounts explain why Texaco vigorously pursued a forum non conveniens argument in a class action lawsuit brought by Ecuadorans in a New York district court (where Texaco was headquartered), alleging environmental damages? The case was bought by indigenous tribes of the Oriente region of Ecuador and by residents of Peru who lived downstream.

Both groups of plaintiffs alleged that Texaco polluted the rain forests and rivers in Ecuador and Peru during oil exploitation activities between 1964 and 1992. In particular, they alleged that Texaco improperly dumped large quantities of toxic by-products into local rivers and landfills or spread them on local dirt roads, contrary to prevailing industry practice of reinjecting such substances back into the wells. They also alleged that the Trans–Ecuadoran Pipeline, constructed by Texaco, had leaked large quantities of petroleum into the environment, all such pollution resulting in physical injuries, including poisoning and the development of pre-cancerous growths.

The plaintiffs sought damages under theories of negligence, public nuisance, private nuisance, strict liability, trespass, and civil conspiracy and also sought equitable relief including undertaking environmental cleanup, renovating or closing the Trans–Ecuadoran Pipeline, creation of an environmental monitoring fund, formulating standards to govern future Texaco oil development, creation of a medical monitoring fund, an injunction restraining Texaco from entering into activities that run a high risk of environmental or human injuries, and restitution.

Texaco responded with a motion to dismiss on the grounds of (1) forum non conveniens; (2) international comity; and (3) failure to join the Republic of Ecuador as an indispensable party. Inherent in all three defenses was the close participation of the Ecuadoran government in the activities for which Texaco which was being sued. Texaco submitted an affidavit averring that Texaco had operated in Ecuador only through a fourth-level subsidiary, Texaco Petroleum Company ("TexPet"). Beginning in 1965, TexPet operated the concession for a consortium owned in equal shares by TexPet and Gulf Oil. In 1974, the Ecuadoran government, through its state-owned oil agency, PetroEcuador, obtained a 25 percent share of the consortium. By 1976, PetroEcuador owned a majority stake, and by 1992, it had become the sole owner of the consortium. TexPet continued to operate the consortium's production and pipeline operations until 1989–1990, when PetroEcuador took over. In 1992, TexPet surrendered all its interests in the consortium, leaving it wholly owned by PetroEcuador.

Texaco also submitted a copy of a letter from Ecuador's ambassador to the U. S. State Department, asserting that the Republic considered the lawsuit as an affront to Ecuador's national sovereignty; Ecuador had a paramount interest in formulating its own environmental and industrial policies, and Ecuador's courts were open to adjudicate such disputes. The plaintiffs countered with documents signed by representatives of the Ecuadoran National Congress, in support of the plaintiffs' action. In the course of lengthy, pre-trial maneuverings, elections in Ecuador resulted in a change in administration and the new president of Ecuador supported the plaintiffs' suit in New York. However, the Attorney General of Ecuador, while seeking to intervene in the lawsuit in New York, refused to waive Ecuador's sovereign immunity.

The federal district court dismissed the suit on several grounds: (1) forum non conveniens; (2) comity; and (3) failure to join an indispensable party. This appeal followed:

Jota v. Texaco Inc.

157 F.3d 153 (2d Cir. 1998).

■ JON O. NEWMAN, CIRCUIT JUDGE:

* * *

1. Forum Non Conveniens

The forum non conveniens doctrine allows dismissal only where the court determines that "an alternative forum is available, because application of the doctrine 'presupposes at least two forums in which the defendant is amenable to process.' " (quoting *Gulf Oil Corp. v. Gilbert*, 330 U.S. 501, 506–07, 67 S.Ct. 839, 91 L.Ed. 1055 (1947)). "Through a discretionary inquiry, the court determines where litigation will be most convenient and will serve the ends of justice." *PT United Can Co. v. Crown Cork & Seal Co.*, 138 F.3d 65, 73 (2d Cir.1998). "[I]n order to grant a motion to dismiss for forum non conveniens, a court must satisfy itself [among other things] that the litigation may be conducted elsewhere against all defendants." *Id.*

... [T]he appellants argue that the only defendant in the present case, Texaco, is not subject to suit in Ecuador. Texaco's only response is that TexPet is subject to suit in Ecuadoran courts, and is both a defendant and a plaintiff in various actions currently pending in that jurisdiction. But Texaco does not dispute that Texaco itself is not amenable to suit in Ecuador.

Accordingly, dismissal for forum non conveniens is not appropriate, at least absent a commitment by Texaco to submit to the jurisdiction of the Ecuadoran courts for purposes of this action. *Cf.* In re Union Carbide Corp. Gas Plant Disaster, 809 F.2d 195, 203–04 (2d Cir.1987) (affirming dismissal for forum non conveniens that was conditioned upon defendant's consent to personal jurisdiction in India); ...

On remand, in addition to requiring Texaco's consent to Ecuadoran jurisdiction, the District Court should independently reweigh the factors relevant to a forum non conveniens dismissal, ...

2. Comity

International comity is "the recognition which one nation allows within its territory to the legislative, executive or judicial acts of another nation." (quoting *Hilton v. Guyot*, 159 U.S. 113, 164, 16 S.Ct. 139, 40 L.Ed. 95 (1895)). Under the principles of comity, United States courts "ordinarily refuse to review acts of foreign governments and defer to proceedings taking place in foreign countries, allowing those acts and proceedings to have extraterritorial effect in the United States." *Id.* This doctrine "is best understood as a guide where the issues to be resolved are entangled in international relations." The District Court's dismissal on the ground of international comity is reviewed for abuse of discretion.

In dismissing the complaints in this litigation on the ground of comity, the District Court . . . [applied] the factors set forth in Restatement (3d) of Foreign Relations § 403 (1986), . . . and concluded that "the challenged activity and the alleged harm occurred entirely in Ecuador"; that the conduct at issue was regulated by the Republic and "exercise of jurisdiction by this Court would interfere with Ecuador's sovereign right to control its own environment and resources"; and that "the Republic of Ecuador has expressed its strenuous objections to the exercise of jurisdiction by this Court." *Id.*

When a court dismisses on the ground of comity, it should normally consider whether an adequate forum exists in the objecting nation and whether the defendant sought to be sued in the United States forum is subject to or has consented to the assertion of jurisdiction against it in the foreign forum. . . . Though extreme cases might be imagined where a foreign sovereign's interests were so legitimately affronted by the conduct of litigation in a United States forum that dismissal is warranted without regard to the defendant's amenability to suit in an adequate foreign forum, this case presents no such circumstances.

With the comity issue remanded for lack of conditioning dismissal on Texaco's consent to jurisdiction in Ecuador, it will then be appropriate for the District Court to reconsider the merits of the comity issue in light of Ecuador's changed litigating position. . . .

* * *

3.   Failure to Join Indispensable Party

* * *

The District Court dismissed the complaint under Rule 19(b) on the ground that the Republic's participation was necessary to afford the plaintiffs the full scope of the equitable relief they sought. . . .

* * *

In this case, the District Court reasoned that in the absence of the Republic, the plaintiffs would not be able to obtain "complete relief," since their desired equitable relief would require enjoining the Republic (the current owner and operator of the oil drilling equipment). The Court then explained that dismissal was appropriate under Rule 19(b) because, in the absence of the Republic, "any order of this Court granting any material part of the Ecuador-directed equitable relief sought by the plaintiffs would be unenforceable on its face, prejudicial to both present and absent parties, and an open invitation to an international political debacle." Aquinda, 945 F. Supp. at 628. . . .

Rule 19(a) requires the Court to join any person who is necessary to effect "complete relief," where such joinder is feasible. But Rule 19(b) does not authorize dismissal simply because such a party cannot be joined.

Instead, the Court is to determine "whether in equity and good conscience the action should proceed among the parties before it, or should be dismissed, the absent person thus being regarded as indispensable." Fed. R.Civ.P. 19(b). And in making this determination, the Court is to consider, among other things, "the extent to which, by protective provisions in the judgment, by the shaping of relief, or other measures, the prejudice can be lessened or avoided." *Id.* Among the Court's options is to "order a pleading amended . . . when by restructuring the relief requested plaintiff is able to change the status of an 'indispensable' party to that of merely a Rule 19(a) party or otherwise prevent the ill effects of nonjoinder." 7 Charles A. Wright, Arthur R. Miller & Mary Kay Kane, Federal Practice and Procedure § 1609, at 132–33 (2d ed.1986).

Since some aspects of the equitable relief sought by the plaintiffs would have required substantial participation by the Ecuadoran government, which at an earlier stage had resisted joinder, the District Court had discretion to dismiss some portions of the plaintiffs' complaint. But since much of the relief sought could be fully provided by Texaco without any participation by Ecuador, dismissal of the entire complaint on Rule 19 grounds exceeds that discretion. For example, an injunction might require Texaco to make good faith efforts to institute all, or at least portions, of the relief that the plaintiffs seek, an obligation the performance of which might not encounter any obstruction from Ecuador. A remand to reconsider the dismissal on Rule 19 grounds is required.

[The court then discussed Ecuador's post-judgment motion to intervene and held that the district court on remand should reassess this motion to determine whether granting it would prejudice Texaco and to give Ecuador the opportunity to promptly advise the court of its role and any sovereign immunity claims it intended to retain].

* * *

For the above stated reasons, we vacate the judgment of the District Court and remand for proceedings not inconsistent with this decision.■

NOTES AND QUESTIONS

1.   The factors to be used in a forum non conveniens analysis are barely discussed in the *Jota* case. One important factor is whether the plaintiff has a fair and adequate forum in the foreign country. On remand, the district court should also look at the following types of factors, enunciated in the seminal case of *Gulf Oil Corp. v. Gilbert*, 330 U.S. 501, 67 S.Ct. 839 (1947):

> Important considerations [of the private interest of the litigant] are the relative ease of access to sources of proof; availability of compulsory process for attendance of unwilling, and the cost of obtaining attendance of willing, witnesses; possibility of view of premises, if view would be appropriate to the action; and all other practical problems that make trial of a case easy, expeditious and inexpensive.

There may also be questions as to the enforceability of a judgment if one is obtained. The court will weigh relative advantages and obstacles to fair trial. . . .

Factors of public interest also have place in applying the doctrine. Administrative difficulties follow for courts when litigation is piled up in congested centers instead of being handled at its origin. Jury duty is a burden that ought not to be imposed upon the people of a community which has no relation to the litigation. In cases which touch the affairs of many persons, there is reason for holding the trial in their view and reach rather than in remote parts of the country where they can learn of it by report only. There is a local interest in having localized controversies decided at home. There is an appropriateness, too, in having the trial of a diversity case in a forum that is at home with the state law that must govern the case, rather than having a court in some other forum untangle problems in conflict of laws, and in law foreign to itself. *Id.* at 508–09.

How would you apply these factors to the *Jota* facts?[13]

2.   Does forum non conveniens make any sense in today's world of widespread jet travel, photocopiers, videographers, and internet access?

The doctrine's international application has been the subject of much commentary. Supporters of the doctrine's usefulness in dismissing claims and sending plaintiffs back to their home courts typically cite Lord Denning in *Smith Kline & French Lab. Ltd. v. Bloch*, [1983] 1 W.L.R. 730, 733 (C.A. 1982): "As a moth is drawn to the light, so is a litigant drawn to the United States. If he can only get his case into their courts, he stands to win a fortune." The United States judicial system offers the following advantages to a foreign plaintiff: attorneys who will work for contingency fees; no liability for defendants' attorney costs; the world's most extensive pretrial discovery; strict liability laws; the award of damages for many more types of harms, including punitive damages; and the right to a jury. See Russell J. Weintraub, International Litigation and Forum Non Conveniens, 29 Texas Int'l L. J. 321, 323–24 (1994).

On the other hand, critics of dismissals on the grounds of forum non conveniens often quote Justice Doggett's concurring opinion in *Dow Chemical Co. v. Castro Alfaro*, 786 S.W.2d 674, 680–90 (Tex. 1990) that the doctrine is used to shield alleged wrongdoers: "The refusal of a Texas corporation to confront a Texas judge and jury is to be labeled 'inconvenient' when what is really involved is not convenience but connivance to avoid corporate accountability." *Id.* at 680. In this case, Costa Rican farmworkers sued Dow and Shell Oil Company in a Texas court for personal injuries allegedly sustained as a result of exposure to a pesticide

---

13.   In fact, Texaco agreed to submit to the jurisdiction of an Ecuadoran court and, as of July 2005, the trial was ongoing in Lago Agria, Ecuador, where ChevronTexaco has presented arguments in support of its motion to dismiss. For the company's legal arguments, visit www.texaco.com/sitelets/equador/en. A PBS documentary called "Extreme Oil" shows the trial and visits nearby sites which are undeniably polluted with crude oil.

("DBCP") made in Texas plants. The EPA had banned the pesticide's use in the United States, but Dow and Shell had allegedly shipped DBCP to Costa Rica for use in the banana plantations there. In a 5–4 decision, a majority of the court held that the Texas legislature had statutorily abolished the doctrine of forum non conveniens in personal injury cases arising out of events in a foreign country. [The Texas legislature subsequently amended the law and revived the doctrine].

Justice Doggett further commented on the doctrine of judicial comity that was designed to show deference to the foreign forum: "There is a sense of outrage on the part of many poor countries where citizens are the most vulnerable to exports of hazardous drugs, pesticides and food products." *Id.* at 688. In an accompanying footnote, Justice Doggett cited a senior vice president of Monsanto who acknowledged that "[t]he realization at corporate headquarters that liability for any [industrial] disaster would be decided in the U.S. courts, more than pressure from Third World governments, has forced companies to tighten safety procedures, upgrade plants, supervise maintenance more closely and educate workers and communities." *Id.* at 687, note 10.

And finally, Justice Doggett addressed the public policy concerns of the dissent that Texas citizens would bear an undue burden of jury duty as foreign plaintiffs flooded into Texas courts:

> The doctrine of forum non conveniens is obsolete in a world in which markets are global and in which ecologists have documented the delicate balance of all life on this planet. . . . [The doctrine's parochial] perspective ignores the reality that actions of our corporations affecting those abroad will also affect Texans. Although DBCP is banned from use within the United States, it and other similarly banned chemicals have been consumed by Texans eating foods imported from Costa Rica and elsewhere. *Id.* at 689.

3. Dismissal of a suit by a U.S. court is usually outcome-determinative. One study showed that fewer than four percent of cases dismissed ever reached trial in a foreign court. David W. Robertson, Forum Non Conveniens in America and England: "A Rather Fantastic Fiction," 103 L.Q. Rev. 398, 409 (1987)

4. Complex questions of comity and the appropriate judicial forum also arise in the United States on Indian lands. *See, e.g.,* El Paso Natural Gas Co. v. Neztsosie, 119 S.Ct. 1430 (1999), holding that comity did not require the defendant companies to first submit to the jurisdiction of Navajo tribal court in a suit bought by the tribe for water pollution and exposure to radioactivity from the operation of uranium mines on Navajo land. The Supreme Court held that the Price–Anderson Act gave the district court original jurisdiction over claims arising out of a nuclear incident.

A course in American Indian Law is good background for attorneys seeking to practice international energy law. Aboriginal land titles can be a major impediment to investment in natural resources in many countries of the world, including Canada and Australia. *See, e.g.,* G.P.J. McGinley,

Natural Resource Companies and Aboriginal Title to Land: The Australian Experience—Mabo and its Aftermath, 28 Int'l Lawyer 695 (1994); and D.E. Fisher, Indigenous Interests and Infrastructure Development, 18 J. Energy & Nat. Res. L 67 (2000). In December 1999, the National Energy Board of Canada approved the operation of a $560 million gas pipeline from offshore Nova Scotia to the northeastern United States, but only after settling legal battles with the Mi'kmaq Indians over environmental monitoring and promotion of aboriginal participation in the project's workforce.

E.   HUMAN RIGHTS AND THE OIL COMPANIES

1.   THE SCENARIO

Your client is an American oil company doing business in Myanmar (formerly Burma) as a joint venturer with the Burmese national oil company in the construction of a gas pipeline. Your client has been served with a complaint filed in a U.S. district court in the district where your client is headquartered, naming your client, its chief executive, the State Oil Company (called Myanmar Oil and Gas Enterprise, or "MOGE") and the Myanmar military junta (called the State Law and Order Restoration Council, or "SLORC") as defendants. The complaint alleges that the State Oil Company is controlled by the junta that seized control of Myanmar in 1988. The junta arrested all the democratic leaders of the nation who had captured 82 percent of parliamentary seats in an election in 1991. Plaintiffs seek to represent a class of hundreds of Burmese who want injunctive, declaratory and compensatory relief for international human rights violations perpetrated by the joint venturers. Plaintiffs allege that the junta's military and police forces use violence, intimidation, and torture to relocate villages, seize private property and enslave farmers as forced laborers on the pipeline project, in violation of state, federal and customary international law. The complaint asserts jurisdiction in the federal district court under the Alien Tort Claims Act of 1789, which reads in its entirety:

> The district courts shall have original jurisdiction of any civil action by an alien for a tort only, committed in violation of the law of nations or a treaty of the United States.
>
> 28 U.S.C. § 1350.

The complaint further contends that your client negotiated a production-sharing contract with the junta's Council on State Law and Order Restoration in 1991, resulting in a joint venture with the State Oil Company. The Council, acting as an agent for the joint venture, cleared land and provided forced labor for the pipeline. Your client company has allegedly subsidized these activities with monetary payments, and its executives continue to make major decisions involving the project at its U.S. headquarter offices, knowing that serious human rights abuses are occurring. Plaintiffs seek an order directing your client to cease paying money to the Council and to cease its joint venture with State Oil Company until the human rights violations cease. There is no functioning judiciary in Burma and any suits filed in Burma would result in terrible reprisals against the plaintiffs.

REVIEW QUESTIONS

Based on material presented in the preceding section of this chapter, you should be able to offer a preliminary assessment of the probability that a U.S. court has proper jurisdiction over this case. Of course, you will do far more research later, but your client's management committee would like your preliminary thoughts immediately about ways to dismiss the lawsuit— and then, if not dismissed, they want to know what risks their company faces under the substantive law which the plaintiffs claim that the company has violated. You should draft quick notes for an oral presentation on the first four items below. Then, after reading the *Sosa* case, assess the risks to the company of being found liable for having violated international human rights law under the Alien Tort Claims Act.

1.   Under the Foreign Sovereign Immunities Act are the junta's Council and the State Oil Company immune from suit? Is their American partner (your client)?

2.   If the Council (SLORC) and State Oil Company (MOGE) are immune, will the court necessarily dismiss the suit for failure to join an indispensable party?

3.   Does the act of state doctrine apply to dismiss the suit in part or in whole?

   (a) Does the act of state doctrine prohibit plaintiffs' claims based on expropriation of property?

   (b) Of what import are the federal law and the executive orders and sanctions which prohibit only "new investment" in Burma?

   (c) Is there more likely to be an international consensus condemning torture (but not cartels, as in *IAM v. OPEC supra*)?

4.   Can the doctrine of forum non conveniens help your client company remove the case to a court in Myanmar?

5.   What substantive law has been violated?

2.   The Alien Tort Claims Act

Until your client received this complaint, you had never heard of the Alien Tort Claims Act (ATCA). Your research discovers that this Act was passed more than 200 years ago in 1789 and lay virtually dormant until the last fifteen years. Incredibly, you discover that the U.S. Supreme Court has just issued a lengthy decision about the meaning of this once-obscure, one-sentence-long statute, quoted *supra* in the scenario. The statute seems simple and direct in application. The plaintiffs need prove only three things to trigger the jurisdiction of the federal district courts in the United States:

   1.   the plaintiff is an alien;

2. a tort has allegedly been committed against him or her;

3. the tort violates "the law of nations" (or a treaty of the U.S., but you quickly discover that the U.S. has no treaties with Myanmar).

It seems clear that the first two conditions have been met, but you need to research and understand whether the alleged acts of forced labor, torture, forced removal, and murder are considered to violate the law of nations. The 2004 decision by the U.S. Supreme Court in the *Sosa* case *infra* arose in a rather unique context. In 1985, an agent of the Drug Enforcement Administration (DEA) was captured while on assignment in Mexico and taken to a house in Guadalajara, where he was tortured for two days and then murdered. Based in part on eyewitness testimony, DEA officials in the United States came to believe that Humberto Alvarez–Machain (Alvarez), a Mexican physician, was present at the house and acted to prolong the agent's life in order to extend the interrogation and torture. The DEA approved using Sosa, a Mexican national, to abduct Alvarez–Machain (Alvarez), also a Mexican national, from Mexico to stand trial in the United States for the agent's torture and murder. Sosa and other Mexicans abducted Alvarez from his house in Mexico, held him overnight in a motel, and brought him by private plane to El Paso, Texas, where he was arrested by federal officers.

After his acquittal on these charges, Alvarez sued the United States for false arrest under the Federal Tort Claims Act (FTCA), and sued Sosa for violating the law of nations under the Alien Tort statute (ATS). The District Court granted the government's motion to dismiss the FTCA claim, but awarded summary judgment and $25,000 in damages to Alvarez on the Alien Tort claim. The Ninth Circuit, in a divided *en banc* opinion, at 331 F.3d 604 (2003), affirmed the Alien Tort judgment (but reversed the FTCA claim's dismissal). The court relied on its own precedent, "that [the ATS] not only provides federal courts with subject matter jurisdiction, but also creates a cause of action for an alleged violation of the law of nations." *Id.*, at 612. The 9th Circuit then held that there was a "clear and universally recognized norm prohibiting arbitrary arrest and detention," *id.*, at 620, to support the conclusion that Alvarez's arrest amounted to a tort in violation of international law.

The U.S. Supreme Court disagreed. Justice Souter delivered the opinion of the Court. All justices agreed with Part III of the opinion interpreting the Alien Tort Claims Act, abbreviated as "ATS" (Alien Tort Statute) in the case. Part IV also interpreted the ATS, but Scalia, Rehnquist and Thomas disagreed with its analysis and Justice Scalia wrote a strong concurring opinion on the meaning of the ATS.

Sosa v. Alvarez–Machain

124 S.Ct. 2739 (2004).

■ JUSTICE SOUTER * * *

[Part] III

Alvarez has brought an action under the ATS against petitioner, Sosa, who argues (as does the United States supporting him) that there is no relief under the ATS because the statute does no more than vest federal courts with jurisdiction, neither creating nor authorizing the courts to recognize any particular right of action without further congressional action. Although we agree the statute is in terms only jurisdictional, we think that at the time of enactment the jurisdiction enabled federal courts to hear claims in a very limited category defined by the law of nations and recognized at common law. We do not believe, however, that the limited, implicit sanction to entertain the handful of international law *cum* common law claims understood in 1789 should be taken as authority to recognize the right of action asserted by Alvarez here.

A.

Judge Friendly called the ATS a "legal Lohengrin," *IIT v. Vencap, Ltd.*, *519 F.2d 1001, 1015 (2d Cir. 1975)*; "no one seems to know whence it came," *ibid.*, and for over 170 years after its enactment it provided jurisdiction in only one case. The first Congress passed it as part of the Judiciary Act of 1789, in providing that the new federal district courts "shall also have cognizance, concurrent with the courts of the several States, or the circuit courts, as the case may be, of all causes where an alien sues for a tort only in violation of the law of nations or a treaty of the United States." Act of Sept. 24, 1789, ch. 20, § 9(b), 1 Stat. 79.

The parties and *amici* here advance radically different historical interpretations of this terse provision. Alvarez says that the ATS was intended not simply as a jurisdictional grant, but as authority for the creation of a new cause of action for torts in violation of international law. We think that reading is implausible. As enacted in 1789, the ATS gave the district courts "cognizance" of certain causes of action, and the term bespoke a grant of jurisdiction, not power to mold substantive law. See, *e.g.*, The Federalist No. 81, pp. 447, 451 (J. Cooke ed. 1961) (A. Hamilton) (using "jurisdiction" interchangeably with "cognizance"). The fact that the ATS was placed in § 9 of the Judiciary Act, a statute otherwise exclusively concerned with federal-court jurisdiction, is itself support for its strictly jurisdictional nature. . . .

But holding the ATS jurisdictional raises a new question, this one about the interaction between the ATS at the time of its enactment and the ambient law of the era. Sosa would have it that the ATS was stillborn because there could be no claim for relief without a further statute expressly authorizing adoption of causes of action. *Amici* professors of federal jurisdiction and legal history take a different tack: that federal courts could entertain claims once the jurisdictional grant was on the books, because torts in violation of the law of nations would have been recognized within the common law of the time. We think history and practice give the edge to this latter position.

[The Court then conducts a survey of 18th and 19th century commentary on the law of nations, and concludes:]

There was, finally, a sphere in which these rules binding individuals for the benefit of other individuals overlapped with the norms of state relationships. Blackstone referred to it when he mentioned three specific offenses against the law of nations addressed by the criminal law of England: violation of safe conduct, infringement of the rights of ambassadors, and piracy. 4 Commentaries on the Laws of England 68 (1769). An assault against an ambassador, for example, impinged upon the sovereignty of the foreign nation and if not adequately redressed could rise to an issue of war. It was this narrow set of violations of the law of nations, admitting of a judicial remedy and at the same time threatening serious consequences in international affairs, that was probably on minds of the men who drafted the ATS with its reference to tort.

* * * [The Court laments the paucity of drafting history for the ATS].

Still, the history does tend to support two propositions. First, there is every reason to suppose that the First Congress did not pass the ATS as a jurisdictional convenience to be placed on the shelf for use by a future Congress or state legislature that might, some day, authorize the creation of causes of action or itself decide to make some element of the law of nations actionable for the benefit of foreigners. The anxieties of the preconstitutional period cannot be ignored easily enough to think that the statute was not meant to have a practical effect. . . . Consider, too, that the First Congress was attentive enough to the law of nations to recognize certain offenses expressly as criminal, including the three mentioned by Blackstone. See An Act for the Punishment of Certain Crimes Against the United States, § 8, 1 Stat. 113–114 (murder or robbery, or other capital crimes, punishable as piracy if committed on the high seas), and § 28, *id.*, at 118 (violation of safe conducts and assaults against ambassadors punished by imprisonment and fines described as "infract[ions of] the law of nations"). It would have been passing strange for . . . this very Congress to vest federal courts expressly with jurisdiction to entertain civil causes brought by aliens alleging violations of the law of nations, but to no effect whatever until the Congress should take further action. There is too much in the historical record to believe that Congress would have enacted the ATS only to leave it lying fallow indefinitely.

The second inference to be drawn from the history is that Congress intended the ATS to furnish jurisdiction for a relatively modest set of actions alleging violations of the law of nations. Uppermost in the legislative mind appears to have been offenses against ambassadors, see *id.*, at 118; violations of safe conduct were probably understood to be actionable, *ibid.*, and individual actions arising out of prize captures and piracy may well have also been contemplated. *Id.*, at 113–114. But the common law appears to have understood only those three of the hybrid variety as definite and actionable, or at any rate, to have assumed only a very limited set of claims. As Blackstone had put it, "offences against this law [of nations] are principally incident to whole states or nations," and not individuals seeking relief in court. 4 Commentaries 68.

* * *

In sum, although the ATS is a jurisdictional statute creating no new causes of action, the reasonable inference from the historical materials is that the statute was intended to have practical effect the moment it became law. The jurisdictional grant is best read as having been enacted on the understanding that the common law would provide a cause of action for the modest number of international law violations with a potential for personal liability at the time.

[Part] IV [Scalia, Rehnquist and Thomas not joining]:

We think it is correct, then, to assume that the First Congress understood that the district courts would recognize private causes of action for certain torts in violation of the law of nations.... We assume, too, that no development in the two centuries from the enactment of § 1350 to the birth of the modern line of cases beginning with *Filartiga v. Pena–Irala*, 630 F.2d 876 (CA2 1980), has categorically precluded federal courts from recognizing a claim under the law of nations as an element of common law; Congress has not in any relevant way amended § 1350 or limited civil common law power by another statute. Still, there are good reasons for a restrained conception of the discretion a federal court should exercise in considering a new cause of action of this kind. Accordingly, we think courts should require any claim based on the present-day law of nations to rest on a norm of international character accepted by the civilized world and defined with a specificity comparable to the features of the 18th-century paradigms we have recognized. This requirement is fatal to Alvarez's claim.

A.

A series of reasons argue for judicial caution when considering the kinds of individual claims that might implement the jurisdiction conferred by the early statute. First, the prevailing conception of the common law has changed since 1789 in a way that counsels restraint in judicially applying internationally generated norms. When § 1350 was enacted, the accepted conception was of the common law as "a transcendental body of law outside of any particular State but obligatory within it unless and until changed by statute." *Black and White Taxicab & Transfer Co. v. Brown and Yellow Taxicab & Transfer Co., 276 U.S. 518, 533, 72 L. Ed. 681, 48 S. Ct. 404 (1928)* (Holmes, J., dissenting). Now, however, in most cases where a court is asked to state or formulate a common law principle in a new context, there is a general understanding that the law is not so much found or discovered as it is either made or created [as explained by Holmes in 1881 that "in substance the growth of the law is legislative"].

One need not accept the Holmesian view as far as its ultimate implications to acknowledge that a judge deciding in reliance on an international norm will find a substantial element of discretionary judgment in the decision.

Second, along with, and in part driven by, that conceptual development in understanding common law has come an equally significant rethinking of the role of the federal courts in making it. *Erie R.R. Co. v. Tompkins, 304 U.S. 64, 82 L. Ed. 1188, 58 S. Ct. 817 (1938)*, was the watershed in which we denied the existence of any federal "general" common law, *id., at 78, 82 L. Ed. 1188, 58 S. Ct. 817*, which largely withdrew to havens of specialty, some of them defined by express congressional authorization to devise a body of law directly, *e.g., Textile Workers v. Lincoln Mills of Ala., 353 U.S. 448, 1 L. Ed. 2d 972, 77 S. Ct. 912 (1957)* (interpretation of collective-bargaining agreements); Fed. Rule Evid. 501 (evidentiary privileges in federal-question cases). Elsewhere, this Court has thought it was in order to create federal common law rules in interstitial areas of particular federal interest. *E.g., United States v. Kimbell Foods, Inc.*, 440 U.S. 715, 726–727, 59 L. Ed. 2d 711, 99 S. Ct. 1448 (1979). And although we have even assumed competence to make judicial rules of decision of particular importance to foreign relations, such as the act of state doctrine, see *Banco Nacional de Cuba v. Sabbatino, 376 U.S. 398, 427, 11 L. Ed. 2d 804, 84 S. Ct. 923 (1964)*, the general practice has been to look for legislative guidance before exercising innovative authority over substantive law. It would be remarkable to take a more aggressive role in exercising a jurisdiction that remained largely in shadow for much of the prior two centuries. Third, this Court has recently and repeatedly said that a decision to create a private right of action is one better left to legislative judgment in the great majority of cases. [citations omitted]. The creation of a private right of action raises issues beyond the mere consideration whether underlying primary conduct should be allowed or not, entailing, for example, a decision to permit enforcement without the check imposed by prosecutorial discretion. . . .

Fourth, the subject of those collateral consequences is itself a reason for a high bar to new private causes of action for violating international law, for the potential implications for the foreign relations of the United States of recognizing such causes should make courts particularly wary of impinging on the discretion of the Legislative and Executive Branches in managing foreign affairs. . . . Since many attempts by federal courts to craft remedies for the violation of new norms of international law would raise risks of adverse foreign policy consequences, they should be undertaken, if at all, with great caution. Cf. *Tel-Oren v. Libyan Arab Republic*, 233 U.S. App. D.C. 384, 726 F.2d 774, 813 (D.C. Cir. 1984).

The fifth reason is particularly important in light of the first four. We have no congressional mandate to seek out and define new and debatable violations of the law of nations, and modern indications of congressional understanding of the judicial role in the field have not affirmatively encouraged greater judicial creativity. It is true that a clear mandate appears in the Torture Victim Protection Act of 1991, 106 Stat. 73, providing authority that "establish[es] an unambiguous and modern basis for" federal claims of torture and extrajudicial killing, H. R. Rep. No. 102–367, pt. 1, p. 3 (1991). But that affirmative authority is confined to specific subject matter, and although the legislative history includes the remark that § 1350 should "remain intact to permit suits based on other norms that already exist or may ripen in the future into rules of customary international law," *id.*, at 4, Congress as a body has done nothing to promote such suits. Several times, indeed, the Senate has expressly declined to give the federal courts the task of interpreting and applying international human rights law, as when its ratification of the International Covenant on Civil and Political Rights declared that the substantive provisions of the document were not self-executing. 138 Cong. Rec. 8071 (1992).

B.

These reasons argue for great caution in adapting the law of nations to private rights. Justice Scalia [in his concurrence] concludes that caution is too hospitable, and a word is in order to . . . focus our difference with him on whether some norms of today's law of nations may ever be recognized legitimately by federal courts in the absence of congressional action beyond § 1350. All Members of the Court agree that § 1350 is only jurisdictional. We also agree, or at least Justice Scalia does not dispute, that the jurisdiction was originally understood to be available to enforce a small number of international norms that a federal court could properly recognize as within the common law enforceable without further statutory authority. Justice Scalia concludes, however, that two subsequent developments should be understood to preclude federal courts from recognizing any further international norms as judicially enforceable today, absent further congressional action. As described before, we now tend to understand common law not as a discoverable reflection of universal reason but, in a positivistic way, as a product of human choice. And we now adhere to a conception of limited judicial power first expressed in reorienting federal diversity jurisdiction, see *Erie R.R. Co. v. Tompkins,* 304 U.S. 64, 82 L. Ed. 1188, 58 S. Ct. 817 (1938), that federal courts have no authority to derive "general" common law.

Whereas Justice Scalia sees these developments as sufficient to close the door to further independent judicial recognition of actionable international norms, other considerations persuade us that the judicial power should be exercised on the understanding that the door is still ajar subject to vigilant doorkeeping, and thus open to a narrow class of international norms today. *Erie* did not in terms bar any judicial recognition of new substantive rules, no matter what the circumstances, and post-*Erie* understanding has identified limited enclaves in which federal courts may derive some substantive law in a common law way. For two centuries we have affirmed that the domestic law of the United States recognizes the law of nations. See, *e.g., Sabbatino,* 376 U.S., at 423, 11 L. Ed. 2d 804, 84 S. Ct. 923 ("[I]t is, of course, true that United States courts apply international law as a part of our own in appropriate circumstances"); *The Paquete Habana,* 175 U.S., at 700, 44 L. Ed. 320, 20 S. Ct. 290 ("International law is part of our law, and must be ascertained and administered by the courts of justice of appropriate jurisdiction, as often as questions of right depending upon it are duly presented for their determination"); *The Nereide,* 13

U.S. 388, 9 Cranch 388, 423, 3 L. Ed. 769 (1815) (Marshall, C. J.) ("[T]he Court is bound by the law of nations which is a part of the law of the land"); see also *Tex. Indus., Inc. v. Radcliff Materials, Inc.,* 451 U.S. 630, 641, 68 L. Ed. 2d 500, 101 S. Ct. 2061 (1981) (recognizing that "international disputes implicating . . . our relations with foreign nations" are one of the "narrow areas" in which "federal common law" continues to exist). It would take some explaining to say now that federal courts must avert their gaze entirely from any international norm intended to protect individuals.

. . . We think it would be unreasonable to assume that the First Congress would have expected federal courts to lose all capacity to recognize enforceable international norms simply because the common law might lose some metaphysical cachet on the road to modern realism. Later Congresses seem to have shared our view. The position we take today has been assumed by some federal courts for 24 years, . . . Congress . . . has not only expressed no disagreement with our view of the proper exercise of the judicial power, but has responded to its most notable instance by enacting legislation supplementing the judicial determination in some detail [notably in passing the Torture Victim Protection Act].

While we agree with Justice Scalia to the point that we would welcome any congressional guidance in exercising jurisdiction with such obvious potential to affect foreign relations, nothing Congress has done is a reason for us to shut the door to the law of nations entirely. It is enough to say that Congress may do that at any time (explicitly, or implicitly by treaties or statutes that occupy the field) just as it may modify or cancel any judicial decision so far as it rests on recognizing an international norm as such.

C.

We must still, however, derive a standard or set of standards for assessing the particular claim Alvarez raises, and for this case it suffices to look to the historical antecedents. Whatever the ultimate criteria for accepting a cause of action subject to jurisdiction under § 1350, we are persuaded that federal courts should not recognize private claims under federal common law for violations of any international law norm with less definite content and acceptance among civilized nations than the historical paradigms familiar when § 1350 was enacted. See, *e.g., United States v. Smith,* 18 U.S. 153, 5 Wheat. 153, 163–180, 5 L. Ed. 57 (1820) (illustrating the specificity with which the law of nations defined piracy). This limit upon judicial recognition is generally consistent with the reasoning of many of the courts and judges who faced the issue before it reached this Court. See *Filartiga, supra,* at 890 ("[F]or purposes of civil liability, the torturer has become—like the pirate and slave trader before him—*hostis humani generis,* an enemy of all mankind"); *Tel-Oren, supra, at 781* (Edwards, J., concurring) (suggesting that the "limits of section 1350's reach" be defined by "a handful of heinous actions—each of which violates definable, universal and obligatory norms"); see also *In re Estate of Marcos Human Rights Litigation,* 25 F.3d 1467, 1475 (CA9 1994) ("Actionable violations of international law must be of a norm that is specific, universal, and obligatory"). And the determination whether a norm is sufficiently definite to support a cause of action should (and, indeed, inevitably must) involve an element of judgment about the practical consequences of making that cause available to litigants in the federal courts.

Thus, Alvarez's detention claim must be gauged against the current state of international law, looking to those sources we have long, albeit cautiously, recognized.

"[W]here there is no treaty, and no controlling executive or legislative act or judicial decision, resort must be had to the customs and usages of civilized nations; and, as evidence of these, to the works of jurists and commentators, who by years of labor, research and experience, have made themselves peculiarly well acquainted with the subjects of which they treat. Such works are resorted to by judicial tribunals, not for the speculations of their authors concerning what the law ought to be, but for trustworthy evidence of what the law really is." *The Paquete Habana,* 175 U.S., at 700, 44 L. Ed. 320, 20 S. Ct. 290.

To begin with, Alvarez cites two well-known international agreements that, despite their moral authority, have little utility under the standard set out in this opinion. [Alvarez claimed that his abduction by Sosa was an "arbitrary arrest" within the meaning of the U. N. Universal Declaration of Human Rights and Article 9 of the International Covenant on Civil and Political Rights. However, the Court found that neither document created binding, self-executing obligations enforceable in federal courts]. Accordingly, Alvarez cannot say that the Declaration and Covenant themselves establish the relevant and applicable rule of international law. He instead attempts to show that prohibition of arbitrary arrest has attained the status of binding customary international law.

* * *

Alvarez invokes a general prohibition of "arbitrary" detention defined as officially sanctioned action exceeding positive authorization to detain under the domestic law of some government, regardless of the circumstances.... Alvarez cites little authority that a rule so broad has the status of a binding customary norm today.[14] He certainly cites nothing to justify the federal courts in taking his broad rule as the predicate for a federal lawsuit, for its implications would be breathtaking.... It would create an action in federal court for arrests by state officers who simply exceed their authority; and for the violation of any limit that the law of any country might place on the authority of its own officers to arrest....

Alvarez's failure to marshal support for his proposed rule is underscored by the Restatement (Third) of Foreign Relations Law of the United States (1987), which says in its discussion of customary international

---

14. Alvarez relied on a law review article surveying national constitutions, a case from the International Court of Justice involving Iran's holding hostage members of the American consular staff for several months; and some lower court authority that had interpreted the ATS in a broader way than the Court approved.

human rights law that a "state violates international law if, as a matter of state policy, it practices, encourages, or condones ... prolonged arbitrary detention." *Id.,* § 702.... Any credible invocation of a principle against arbitrary detention that the civilized world accepts as binding customary international law requires a factual basis beyond relatively brief detention in excess of positive authority. Even the Restatement's limits are only the beginning of the enquiry, because although it is easy to say that some policies of prolonged arbitrary detentions are so bad that those who enforce them become enemies of the human race, it may be harder to say which policies cross that line with the certainty afforded by Blackstone's three common law offenses. In any event, the label would never fit the reckless policeman who botches his warrant, even though that same officer might pay damages under municipal law. *E.g., Groh v. Ramirez,* 540 U.S. 551, 157 L. Ed. 2d 1068, 124 S. Ct. 1284 (2004).

Whatever may be said for the broad principle Alvarez advances, in the present, imperfect world, it expresses an aspiration that exceeds any binding customary rule having the specificity we require....[15] It is enough to hold that a single illegal detention of less than a day, followed by the transfer of custody to lawful authorities and a prompt arraignment, violates no norm of customary international law so well defined as to support the creation of a federal remedy.

* * *

The judgment of the Court of Appeals is reversed.

■ CONCUR: JUSTICE SCALIA, with whom the CHIEF JUSTICE and JUSTICE THOMAS join, concurring in part and concurring in the judgment.

There is not much that I would add to the Court's detailed opinion, and only one thing that I would subtract: its reservation of a discretionary power in the Federal Judiciary to create causes of action for the enforcement of international-law-based norms....

[Justice Scalia's opinion then argued the following points:

1.   The ATS provides a federal forum for aliens to bring suit for torts committed in violation of the law of nations, which in 1789, was the general common law. This general common law did not rise to the level of supreme federal law like the Constitution, statutes or treaties.

2.   The Court's later decision in *Erie v. Tompkins* announced that "there is no federal general common law."

3.   After *Erie,* came the birth of a new and different common law pronounced by federal courts for a few, restricted areas, necessary to

---

15.   [FN29] It is not that violations of a rule logically foreclose the existence of that rule as international law. Cf. *Filartiga v. Pena–Irala,* 630 F.2d 876, 884, n. 15 (2d Cir. 1980) ("The fact that the prohibition of torture is often honored in the breach does not diminish its binding effect as a norm of international law"). Nevertheless, that a rule as stated is as far from full realization as the one Alvarez urges is evidence against its status as binding law; and an even clearer point against the creation by judges of a private cause of action to enforce the aspiration behind the rule claimed.

protect uniquely federal interests or authorized by Congress (such as admiralty law). The new federal common law was deliberately "made," not transcendentally "discovered." Vesting jurisdiction in the federal courts does not in and of itself give rise to authority to create federal common law either by displacing a state rule or creating a private cause of action under a federal statute.

4. The question is not what case or congressional action prevents federal courts from applying the law of nations as part of the general common law; it is what authorizes that peculiar exception from *Erie*'s fundamental holding that a general common law does not exist.]

* * *

■ J. SCALIA concluded:

Because today's federal common law is not our Framers' general common law, the question presented by the suggestion of discretionary authority to enforce the law of nations is not whether to extend old-school general-common-law adjudication. Rather, it is whether to create new federal common law. The Court masks the novelty of its approach when it suggests that the difference between us is that we would "close the door to further independent judicial recognition of actionable international norms," whereas the Court would permit the exercise of judicial power "on the understanding that the door is still ajar subject to vigilant doorkeeping." The general common law was the old door. We do not close that door today, for the deed was done in *Erie*. Federal common law is a *new* door. The question is not whether that door will be left ajar, but whether this Court will open it.

* * *

The Ninth Circuit brought us the judgment that the Court reverses today. Perhaps its decision in this particular case, like the decisions of other lower federal courts that receive passing attention in the Court's opinion, "reflects a more assertive view of federal judicial discretion over claims based on customary international law than the position we take today." But the verbal formula it applied is the same verbal formula that the Court explicitly endorses [that an actionable claim under the [ATS] requires the showing of a violation of the law of nations that is "specific, universal, and obligatory."] Endorsing the very formula that led the Ninth Circuit to its result in this case hardly seems to be a recipe for restraint in the future.

* * *

. . . [T]he Framers who included reference to "the Law of Nations" in Article I, § 8, cl. 10, of the Constitution would be entirely content with the post-*Erie* system I have described, and quite terrified by the "discretion" endorsed by the Court. That portion of the general common law known as the law of nations was understood to refer to the accepted practices of nations in their dealings with one another (treatment of ambassadors, immunity of foreign sovereigns from suit, etc.) and with actors on the high seas hostile to all nations and beyond all their territorial jurisdictions (pirates).... The notion that a law of nations, redefined to mean the consensus of states on *any* subject, can be used by a private citizen to control a sovereign's treatment of *its own citizens* within *its own territory* is a 20th-century invention of internationalist law professors and human-rights advocates. The Framers would, I am confident, be appalled by the proposition that, for example, the American peoples' democratic adoption of the death penalty, see, *e.g.*, *Tex. Penal Code Ann. § 12.31* (2003), could be judicially nullified because of the disapproving views of foreigners.

* * *

We Americans have a method for making the laws that are over us. We elect representatives to two Houses of Congress, each of which must enact the new law and present it for the approval of a President, whom we also elect. For over two decades now, unelected federal judges have been usurping this lawmaking power by converting what they regard as norms of international law into American law. Today's opinion approves that process in principle, though urging the lower courts to be more restrained.

* * *

American law—the law made by the people's democratically elected representatives—does not recognize a category of activity that is so universally disapproved by other nations that it is automatically unlawful here, and automatically gives rise to a private action for money damages in federal court. That simple principle is what today's decision should have announced.■

NOTES AND COMMENTS

1. Does the *Sosa* case help you advise your oil company client whether the federal court has jurisdiction over their claims of forced labor (slavery), torture, murder, rape, forced removal from their villages, extortion and expropriation?

- Is the law of nations a part of federal common law? Where do you find the norms of the law of nations?

- Assume that one such customary norm is a prohibition against official torture. Can your client be deemed to have participated in state acts of torture as a joint venturer? Can your client be liable for violations of international law even absent any direct participation in state action? Suppose your research shows that forced labor, piracy and slave trading are included in the handful of crimes for which the law of nations attributes individual responsibility. And that your client did know that SLORC's security forces were committing abuses, yet continued to finance them in order to protect the pipeline.

- Does international law extend the scope of liability for a violation of an international norm to a defendant who is a private actor, like a corporation or individual? Compare *Tel-Oren v. Libyan Arab Republic,* 726 F.2d 774, 791–795 (D.C. Cir. 1984) (Edwards, J., concurring) (insufficient consensus in 1984 that torture by private actors violates international law), with *Kadic v. Karadzic,* 70 F.3d 232, 239–241 (2d Cir. 1995) (sufficient consensus in 1995 that genocide by private actors violates international law).

2. The Souter opinion noted another reason for deference to other political branches in specific cases. Several class actions were pending in federal district courts seeking damages from corporations that participated in or abetted apartheid in South Africa. The Government of South Africa asserted that these cases interfered with the policy of its Truth and Reconciliation Commission, which "deliberately avoided a 'victors' justice' approach to the crimes of apartheid and chose instead one based on confession and absolution, informed by the principles of reconciliation, reconstruction, reparation and goodwill." The U.S. Department of State had agreed with South Africa's position and the federal courts should give "serious weight" to such views in all ATCA cases.

3. After reading *Sosa,* would you advise your client to settle with plaintiffs? In the real world of *Doe v. Unocal,* Unocal settled on the eve of the Ninth Circuit's *en banc* hearing of the case upon which this scenario is realistically modeled. The terms of the settlement are confidential, but include compensation to the plaintiffs and funds to develop programs to improve health care and education and protect the rights of people. Unocal also agreed to enhance its company's training programs in human rights. Unocal Settles Four Lawsuits over Alleged Myanmar Abuses, Wall St. J. Online, Mar. 21, 2005. The evidence presented by plaintiffs in the lower courts of Unocal executives' knowledge of abuses of SLORC offers a devastating picture of what it is like to be a joint venturer with one of the world's most oppressive regimes. A 1996 State Department cable noted that "when foreigners come on daily helicopter trips to inspect work sites, involuntary laborers are forced into the bush outside camera range." *Doe I v. Unocal Corp.,* 100 F. Supp.2d 1294, 1302 (C.D. Cal. 1999).

On June 13, 2005, the U.S. District Court for the Southern District of New York refused to dismiss a suit brought against Talisman Energy, a Canadian company, for its role in human rights abuses in the Sudan. Residents of Sudan alleged they were victims of genocide and other crimes against humanity. In *Presbyterian Church of Sudan v. Talisman Energy, Inc.,* 374 F. Supp.2d 331 (S.D.N.Y. 2005), the court held that (1) corporations can be held liable under international law for violations of *jus cogens* norms (these are norms of international law that are binding on nations even if not agreed to); (2) international law recognizes theories of secondary liability such as conspiracy and aiding and abetting, citing decisions from the Nuremberg trials, from international criminal statutes and treaties, and from international criminal tribunals in Rwanda and the former Yugoslavia.

Talisman claimed that secondary, corporate liability for aiding and abetting other parties in their violation of international norms was not of such definite content and acceptance as the historical paradigms recognized in *Sosa*. The court responded that liability for aiding and abetting falls under "a settled, core notion of aider and abettor liability in international law 'for knowing practical assistance or encouragement which has a substantial effect on the perpetuation of the crime'." *Id.* at 340. Therefore Talisman's motion for judgment on the pleadings was denied.

Because of an onslaught of negative media reports, Talisman had already sold its small share of the Sudanese oil project to an Indian oil company. According to the 2003 Human Rights Watch report titled "Sudan, Oil and Human Rights," 60% of the oil revenues to the Sudanese government in Khartoum went to the military to purchase weapons to use against Sudanese rebels. The Janjaweed, an Arab militia armed by the government, have carried out ethnic cleansing in the Darfur regions of Sudan. Frida Berrigan, Peace in Sudan: Good News for People or Oil Companies?, Sudan Tribune, Jan. 15, 2005. A Chinese oil company now has majority control of the oil consortium in the Sudan, which once harbored Osama bin Laden.

4.   Many multinational oil companies operate in areas where dictatorships and ethnic and military conflicts are a way of life. Shell has extensive investments in Nigeria, the world's sixth largest oil exporter. When members of the Ogoni tribe attacked its oil field facilities to protest environmental damage to their land in 1996, Shell requested protection from Nigeria's military government. The government sent the notoriously brutal mobile police to the area. Shell paid for the transportation and salary bonuses of some troops who acted as "oil field guards." The police laid waste to whole villages and the government of General Abacha executed the most prominent Ogoni, a political activist and writer named Ken Saro–Wiwa, after a rigged secret trial. Paul Lewis, Nigeria's Deadly Oil War: Shell Defends its Record, New York Times, Feb. 13, 1996, at A1. After being accused of complicity in the murder of Ken Saro–Wiwa, Shell turned to Amnesty International for help in drafting a code of conduct regarding human rights. *See* Armin Rosenkranz & Richard Campbell, Foreign Environmental and Human Rights Suits Against U.S. Corporations in U.S. Courts, 18 Stanford Envtl. L. J. 145, 207 (1999). In March 2000, Nigeria's newly elected government announced a crackdown on sabotage of oil facilities. It is creating a new police unit that is authorized to shoot vandals on sight. The unit will be subsidized by the Nigerian National Petroleum Corp. Houston Chronicle, 24A, Mar. 23, 2000.

Shell's involvement in the Ogoni region of Nigeria is also the subject of an ATCA suit. In *Wiwa v. Royal Dutch Shell Petroleum Co.*, 226 F.3d 88 (2d Cir. 2000), the court reversed and remanded a decision by the district court which had dismissed the case on forum non conveniens grounds. The Second Circuit held that the lower court had failed to give proper consideration to the choice of a U.S. forum by a U.S. resident plaintiff and to the interests of the U.S. in providing a forum for adjudicating claims of human rights abuses. One of the plaintiffs is the brother of the murdered Ken Saro–Wiwa. The suit alleged that Shell had provided money, weapons and support to the Nigerian military which committed murder and torture. The alternate forum was a court in Britain, which the Second Circuit acknowledged as "exemplary in their fairness," but nonetheless found that the U.S. resident-plaintiff's choice of forum was entitled to substantial deference, especially in cases involving the ATCA and the Torture Victim Protection Act, enacted in 1991. The court held that "[t]he new formulations of the Torture Victim Protection Act convey the message that torture committed under color of law of a foreign nation in violation of international law is 'our business.'" Because the plaintiffs were impecunious and Shell was so wealthy, the lower court, on remand, should consider the inconvenience, to the plaintiffs of having to re-file suit in England, as well as considering the U.S. interest in adjudicating human rights abuses in the U.S.

In 2001, the U.S. Supreme Court denied a petition to review the Second Circuit's opinion in *Royal Dutch Petroleum Co. v. Wiwa*, 532 U.S. 941 (2001). In March 2001, the plaintiffs added Brian Anderson, the former Managing Director of the Shell Nigeria subsidiary, as a defendant. In 2002, the federal district court refused to dismiss the ATCA claims, finding that the complaint sufficiently alleged specific violations of five international norms: (1) crimes against humanity, (2) torture, (3) cruel, inhuman or degrading treatment, (4) violation of the rights to life, liberty and security of person, and (5) violation of the right to peaceful assembly. *Wiwa v. Royal Dutch Petroleum Co.*, 2002 WL 319887 (S.D.N.Y. 2002).

While plaintiffs in ATCA suits have won many jurisdictional battles, no oil company has yet been found to have violated international human rights norms. Most of the major oil companies have ATCA suits filed against them, and unless these settle, a trial on the substantive merits of plaintiffs' human rights claims should occur within the near future. Which of the five norms listed above seem likely to meet the standards of *Sosa*? The 1980 *Filitarga* decision, often quoted in *Sosa*, started the modern law of ATCA. It held that an offense violated the law of nations if it was "definable, obligatory (rather than hortatory), and *universally* condemned." 630 F.2d at 881. Does ATCA then apply only to "shockingly egregious" violations of universal norms? *Zapata v. Quinn*, 707 F.2d 691, 692 (2d Cir. 1983) (*per curiam*).

5. In December 2000, five leading oil companies—Chevron, Texaco (now merged with Chevron), Conoco, Royal Dutch Shell, and BP—were prodded by the U.S. and British governments to sign a new code of conduct, pledging to discourage police and private security forces from abusing people who live near oil projects. The Voluntary Principles on Security and Human Rights can be found at www.state.gov/g/drl/rls/2931.htm. One principle states that: "Companies should record and report any credible allegations of human rights abuses by public security in their areas of operation to appropriate host government authorities. Where appropriate, Companies should urge investigation and that action be taken to prevent any recurrence. Companies should actively monitor the status of investigations and press for their proper resolution." Do such principles place private enterprise in an untenable position? What is the alternative? To withdraw and

allow state oil companies from nations with less regard for human rights to develop oil and gas areas with repressive or lawless states?

6.   Is it a violation of international norms to pollute the environment, leaving dangerous and toxic by-products of oil and gas drilling and production in the rainforests used by indigenous tribes for subsistence living and cultural identity? Does this amount to a form of genocide? In *Beanal v. Freeport–McMoran, Inc.*, 197 F.3d 161 (5th Cir.1999), the court held that an Indonesian citizen failed to state claims under ATCA for international human rights violations and genocide because treaties and agreements did not contain articulable environmental standards as a basis of international law claim. *E.g.*, the Rio Declaration on Environment and Development "merely refer[s] to a general sense of environmental responsibility and state[s] abstract rights." *Id.* at 167. Although the U.S. has articulated standards in statutory law that apply to discharges of mine tailings and to endangered species, the federal courts should not override the environmental policies of other governments on their own lands with U.S. standards. The plaintiff alleged that Freeport's mining had displaced him and destroyed his tribe's habitat, but the court held that cultural genocide was not recognized as a violation of international law.

See also *Flores v. Southern Peru Copper Corp.*, 343 F.3d 140 (2d Cir. 2003) (personal injury and death claims brought under ATCA against mining company for severe lung disease dismissed because rights to health and life were not sufficiently definite to be a binding rule of customary international law nor did such customary law prohibit pollution that did not cross national borders).

7.   The World Bank, under enormous pressure from the international NGO community, conducted a review of its role in financing oil and gas and mining projects in developing countries. Too often, such projects had resulted in long-lasting environmental harm to the local communities that received no share of the oil revenues. The revenues flowed to corrupt dictators who lavished money on themselves and their compatriots while the population became poorer. (Sani Abachi, the dictator of Nigeria from 1993–1998 looted between $2-to $5-billion; Suharto's 32–year reign in Indonesia reportedly netted him between $15 and $35 billion. Transparency International has a list of the ten top embezzlers.) The lengthy report called the Extractive Industries Review is available at www.worldbank.org /ogmc. It is the end result of a consultative process that engaged all stakeholders—governments, NGOs, indigenous people, local communities, labor unions, industry, academia and the Bank itself. The Review was to determine whether resource extraction could be compatible with sustainable development and poverty reduction. The report concluded that the Bank had too often supported projects that had neither effect, and recommended that the Bank phase out its investments in oil and coal by the year 2008. The Bank rejected the phase-out, but pledged that it would no longer fund projects without safeguards in place to assure more effective social and environmental policies and respect for human rights, especially in the use of security forces to guard production sites. The Bank pledged to focus

on the need for good governance to wisely spend the revenues from resource extraction. However, the Bank rejected the recommendation to support only projects where local communities had given their informed, voluntary consent. Instead, the Bank will require informed consultation, greater disclosure of project effects, and mechanisms to assure direct benefits to local communities, such as revenue sharing. The lead author of the report, the former environment minister of Indonesia, called the Bank's response "business as usual with marginal change." Jim Butler, The World Bank Responds to the Extractive Industries Review, 36 Trends (ABA Section of Env't, Energy & Resources, at 10–11 (Jan./Feb. 2005)). In its financing of the Chad–Cameroon pipeline, the Bank instituted a Revenue Management Plan to assure that 80% of the governments' oil revenues go to basic infrastructure and social needs; 10% be held in trust for future generations (for when the oil revenues dry up); and 5% flow to local, affected communities. ExxonMobil's role as project operator makes it, in Fortune magazine's words: "a multinational as missionary," serving as "development agency, human-rights promoter, de facto local government, and even (don't laugh) environmental watchdog." Jerry Useem, Exxon's African Adventure, Fortune at 102, April 15, 2002. Information on the project is available at www.essochad.com and on the World Bank's website. Shell declined to participate in the project, fearful that Chad would become another Nigeria.

8.   Even if lawsuits brought by foreign nationals in U.S. courts are dismissed on their pleadings, the bad publicity accompanying claims of human rights abuses has a serious impact on many companies' behavior. NGO groups focus primary attention on multinational companies, especially American companies and natural resource companies. Their many websites are visited by the media and many citizens of the globe:

> Earthrights International [http://www.earthrights.org]
>
> Corporate Watch [http://www.corpwatch.org]
>
> Friends of the Earth [http://foe.org/camps/intl/index.html]
>
> Rainforest Action Network [http://www.ran.org]
>
> Third World Network (Malaysia) [http://www.twnside.org.sg]
>
> Oil Watch (Equador) [http://www.oilwatch.org]

9.   For an account of a modern oil and gas development project in the heart of the rainforests of Peru, see Chapter 9. The Camisea project developers, notably Shell Oil, promised a "best efforts" policy that would avoid the mistakes of the past and assure benefits to the local indigenous tribes.

10.   The *Sosa* opinion and the Alien Tort Claims Act in general have been the subject of extensive commentary in the law reviews. The reader is invited to sample a few of the dozens of articles offering different perspectives on liability for human rights abuses. One interesting article is Emeka Duruigbo, The Economic Cost of Alien Tort Litigation: A Response to "Awakening Monster," 14 Minn. J. Global Trade 1 (2004), reviewing a

book by Hufbauer and Mitrokostas who approach ATCA litigation from the business perspective of an "awakening monster."

F.   NATIONAL ENERGY SECURITY

1.   POLICY OPTIONS

The 1973 OPEC oil embargo caused profound social and economic dislocation in the United States and other Western nations. In the U.S., unemployment rose from 4.7 percent in the fall of 1973 to over 8.5 percent by the end of 1974. Inflation jumped from an annual rate of 6.1 percent to 11.4 percent over the same period. One econometric study estimated that 53 percent of the loss in national output and 29 percent of the inflation was due to the embargo. A new term was coined to name the combination of high unemployment and high inflation: stagnation. The Second Oil Shock of 1979 led most forecasters to believe that world oil prices would be at the mercy of the Mideast oil exporters for decades to come.

How could the nation be weaned from this dependence on insecure oil imported from unfriendly nations? Presidents Nixon and Ford launched Project Independence; President Carter called the energy crisis the "Moral Equivalent of War" (unfortunately acronymed as MEOW) and pushed for major energy initiatives in Congress; and the nation actually did go to war in the Persian Gulf in 1991 to counter Saddam Hussein's invasion of Kuwait with Operation Desert Storm. Imports started to fall as a percentage of U.S. consumption in 1977, but by 1983, the percentage had turned sharply upwards again. In 1999, the U.S. was more than 50 percent dependent on foreign oil compared to 32 percent on the eve of the embargo. In 2004, over 60% of our oil consumption came from imports, and this is projected to rise to 68% by 2025. See **Figures 7–6** and **7–8**.

No American, or citizen of any oil-importing nation for that matter, wants to live through the serious macroeconomic impacts of another energy shortage, yet the geopolitical vagaries of world oil supplies are hard to miss—or dismiss—especially since the attacks of 9/11 and terrorism. Should our nation do anything to protect its national security against supply disruptions in imported oil? Two economists discuss whether there is a rationale for government intervention in energy markets and then discuss the various options available and which ones are optimal:

James M. Griffin and Henry B. Steele, Energy Economics and Policy 216–17, 229–38

(2d ed. Academic Press 1986).

The Rationale for Government Intervention

The fact that the industrialized nations are highly susceptible to future supply disruptions does not automatically prove that a market failure exists and that government intervention is called for. After all, the vagaries inflicted by the weather on many agricultural crops are neither less severe nor more predictable than supply disruptions for oil. There is no public outcry for strategic orange juice or wheat reserves. What is so special about oil? Is it that oil is essential for life while wheat for bread is merely a want? No, obviously not, as we shall soon see.

A close look at a wide variety of commodity markets such as wheat shows active futures markets and numerous speculators who maintain substantial speculative inventories. Speculators acquire buffer inventories, which they hope to sell later at much higher prices. Is there any evidence that the levels of such speculative inventory holdings for these commodities are too small? After all, private investors can assess the probability of a shortage, weighing the probable gain against the inventory holding costs, just as accurately as the government can.

In contrast, a look at U.S. private inventories of crude oil and petroleum products reveals an inventory level just sufficient to enable the smooth day-to-day operations of the oil industry. The absence of large speculative inventories seems at first bizarre given the instability of the world oil market. But is there an explanation? The experience of domestic producers in the 1970s with oil price controls, and before that with natural gas price controls, suggests that price controls would likely be imposed in response to a supply disruption, preventing one from reaping large speculative profits.

Paradoxically, the primary argument favoring government intervention to increase emergency supplies is that private investors under-invest because they assume that price controls would likely be imposed to prevent their earning "obscene" profits. There is another prominent explanation given for the tendency to underinvest in inventories. The social value of emergency supplies during a disruption may well exceed the private value, which is the basis for the private firm's inventory level decision. For example, private demand schedules for oil may not include the external effects brought about by macroeconomic linkages. Put another way, providers of emergency supplies may not be able to appropriate the full social benefits of their inventories. They may receive only a $20 per barrel profit due to the crude price increase, but the full social benefit of that incremental oil in an emergency situation may be $30 or $40 when the macroeconomic effects are factored in . . . . ■

Having discovered a source of market failure, the economists discuss the selection of an optimal set of national security programs. Their list includes:

- Conservation—reducing demand as a market response to higher prices or through government actions such as rationing supplies, reducing the speed limit, and mandatory thermostat settings and lighting restrictions.
- Oil import tariffs or quotas
- Self-sufficiency in domestic oil production: draining America first
- Drain OPEC first

- Long-term contracts with secure oil exporters
- International sharing agreements among major consuming nations
- Maintaining reserve stand-by capacity in U.S. reservoirs
- Oil storage in vast underground caverns for emergency use

What are the relative advantages and disadvantages of each of these approaches? For example, import tariffs or quotas would raise the domestic price of oil such that it reflects a security premium which more accurately represents its market value. *See id.* at 238–42. Domestic self-sufficiency would entail large investments in oil shale and tar sands at significantly higher costs than conventional oil supplies. Draining OPEC first and saving our reserves for future generations leaves us even more vulnerable to an embargo in the interim because we would not have the infrastructure of domestic wells and pipelines available to make up import shortages. (And wouldn't such a policy virtually invite OPEC to use embargos as a weapon against the West?) Should we pay domestic producers not to produce, but to maintain idle wells and facilities to transport crude to refineries in an emergency? What fields are suitable as stand-by reserves, and how much would we have to pay producers to provide this service?

Long-term contracts with secure suppliers (who might they be, other than Canada?) would appear to be a sound solution to national security concerns. Griffin and Steele offer this caution based on two realities:

> First, the world's existing oil production can be seen as coming from the same bathtub. Even though one country can establish the right to purchase some portion of the secure oil present in the bathtub, the total amount of secure oil is not increased. Consequently, from a world perspective, security is not enhanced.

> Second, it is unrealistic for a country to assume that it can remain unaffected by a worldwide supply disruption. . . . Even if a country chose to hoard its oil, the severe macroeconomic dislocations affecting its trading partners would ultimately spread to it.

> There are situations where long-term contracts with secure producers can actually enhance world security. Continuing the analogy of the bathtub, if the long-term contract puts more water (oil) in the tub, security is enhanced. Suppose the long-term contract leads to the development of additional productive capacity in secure areas. The existence of such contracts could provide funds necessary for the development of additional productive capacity earmarked for purposes of fulfilling a long-term contract.

One way of dealing with the "we're all in the same global oil bathtub" problem is to develop an international sharing agreement among the major consuming countries. The International Energy Agency was formed as the importing nations' response to the 1973 Arab oil embargo. IEA members have agreed that they will share oil if an embargo is directed against any one or more member countries, so that the effect of the embargo is spread evenly over the various members. Each IEA member has also agreed to invest in oil storage for emergency supplies equal to 90 days of imports. This stored oil reduces the probability of an embargo against any one country because OPEC would realize that it could not cripple a single embargoed nation. However, Griffin and Steele observe that "agreements among sovereign nations are frequently violated with complete impunity." If Country A, a non-embargoed IEA member, were threatened with an embargo if it shared oil with Country B, the object of the embargo, would Country A share oil or withdraw from the IEA? Also, how would the price of the shared oil be set?

2. THE STRATEGIC PETROLEUM RESERVE

In 1976, Congress created the Strategic Petroleum Reserve to store 90 days of crude oil in enormous salt domes located along the Gulf Coast near existing refineries and pipelines. Salt domes are huge sealed underground caverns, artificially created by dissolving natural salt deposits to create voids of space that can store oil at one-tenth the cost of above-ground steel storage tanks. Originally, the Strategic Petroleum Reserve was to hold one billion barrels by 1980, but by 1983, it held only 325 million barrels, and the total goal was reduced to 750 million barrels. Griffin and Steele discuss the two key questions about the SPR as the major factor in our energy security:

> First, what is the optimal size of the SPR? Second, what is or should be the trigger mechanism to initiate withdrawals from the SPR? The answer to the question of the optimal SPR size requires a complicated analytical framework employing dynamic programming techniques together with a host of assumptions regarding the frequency, intensity, and duration of likely future embargos. Almost all studies recommend a reserve greater than 750 million barrels and most recommend a reserve greater than 1 billion barrels.

> The trigger mechanism to initiate withdrawals from the SPR currently rests with the President. On the face of it, it would appear to be a simple matter to know when to begin selling oil from the SPR and at what rate, but imagine yourself as President of the U.S. facing the following situation: The Iran–Iraq war spreads as routed Iraqi troops pour into Kuwait and Iranian forces pursue, cutting off all oil shipments from Iran, Iraq, and Kuwait. The loss of 3 million barrels per day of oil supply from world markets sends spot prices up by $10 per barrel. Your economic advisors argue that since in the very short run supply and demand are most inelastic, SPR shipments should begin immediately in volumes of at least 1.5 million barrels per day, offsetting at least half of the shortfall. They argue that such a move would stabilize spot prices and bring about orderly supply and demand adjustments. But your National Security Advisor and Secretary of Defense argue that the SPR should be saved for potentially worse days to come. They fear the conflict will spread into Saudi Arabia, resulting in the loss of another 5 million barrels per day of production. In such event, they argue, war damage and sabotage of these fields will prevent

any flow of oil from the Persian Gulf for at least two years. They argue that SPR reserves should be saved until the war picture is more certain. As President you opted for the "wait and see" strategy. The war is then confined to Kuwait and, by the time this becomes apparent, spot prices have risen by $30 above predisruption levels. By the time you begin production from the SPR four months later at a rate of .5 million barrels per day, the economic damage has been done

Due to the inherent tendency to underutilize the SPR, observers have attempted to formulate a simple set of rules regarding when and how much to withdraw from the SPR. It is extremely difficult to specify the full set of rules that would apply for a large number of situations. The most appealing plan uses the options market as a signaling device for the intensity and duration of supply disruption. [The authors then describe how to use the options market as the trigger. The options system allows the aggregate expectations of the private sector about future market conditions to control rather than the expectations of government officials. The oil is sold to the highest bidder so that it goes to the highest valued uses].■

NOTES AND COMMENTS

1.   Shortly after the 9/11 attacks, President Bush ordered the SPR filled to its maximum capacity of 700 million barrels. In mid–2005, this level was reached. A few weeks later in the National Energy Act of 2005, Congress mandated that other storage sites be developed so that the SPR could be expanded to one billion barrels, as originally authorized in 1976. Crude oil can be extracted from the SPR at a maximum rate of 4.1 million barrels per day; the 700 million barrels in storage now can cover about two months of U.S. oil imports. The SPR has been used for domestic purposes other than a national security crisis induced by an embargo. *E.g.,* crude oil was sold from the SPR in 1996 to help balance the federal budget. In September 2004, several Gulf Coast refiners received oil from the SPR on a short-term loan basis after Hurricane Ivan caused delays in crude imports. In 2004–2005, when crude oil prices soared to $50–$60 per barrel and gasoline prices were well above $2 per gallon, President Bush was often exhorted to release oil from the SPR to put downward pressure on prices. As of July 2005, he had resisted all such pressure.

2.   The SPR has also been caught up in the geopolitics of the United States' efforts to sustain a good relationship with Saudi Arabia, the largest of the Mideast producers, and a country ruled by a royal family that is relatively pro-Western. In the late 1970s, the U.S. was importing Saudi oil which helped to replace domestic oil supplies that were then going to fill the reserve. With the world oil market in growing surplus by 1979, the U.S. stopped buying oil for the SPR for a time. When the General Accounting Office recommended the resumption and faster filling of the SPR, the U.S. refused to do so without prior Saudi approval. Morris Adelman, a noted authority on world oil markets, describes the following events in his book,

"The Genie Out of the Bottle: World Oil Since 1970" (MIT Press 1995) at 181–82 [citations omitted]:

> The Saudis urged delay, which they said was "necessary to help bolster the power of pro-American Saudi officials and offset the efforts of militant pro-Arab groups seeking to gain control of the kingdom." It was said in the United States that many Saudi "senior officials are anxious to cut exports as soon as possible to placate conservative Moslems, who regard high oil production as an unsound concession to the U.S."

3. For a recent survey of energy security policies in many nations, see Barry Barton *et al.* (eds.), Energy Security: Managing Risk in a Dynamic Legal and Regulatory Environment (Oxford Univ. Press 2004) (often asking whether liberalizing energy markets conflicts with energy security).

CHAPTER 8

NATURAL GAS: PRODUCTION, PRICES AND PIPELINES—FROM REGULATION TO MARKETS

A. SOME BASICS

Methane, which is largely natural gas, is the world's most common hydrocarbon (CH_4). It forms whenever organic material mixes with water in an airtight space. Anaerobic bacteria digest the organic material and produce methane. Swamps, rice fields and landfills release huge amounts of methane every day and billions of living creatures belch it or exhale it in other ways. Indeed, emissions from dairy cows are now a larger contributor to smog than cars in the San Joaquin Air Control District of Southern California. (The cows release volatile organic compounds, or VOCs.) Greenwire, Aug. 2, 2005. Yet, to be useful, methane gas must be trapped in sufficient volumes to allow it to be easily tapped and used as a fuel. Mother Nature, fortunately, has stored large amounts of natural gas underground.

This chapter on Natural Gas complements Chapter 6 on Domestic Oil. The oil and gas lease contract, state conservation regulations, rule of capture, and leasing moratoria all affect natural gas production in the same way as oil production, and this Gas chapter will not repeat that discussion. The Gas chapter instead focuses on property and ownership issues unique to natural gas, in particular to coalbed methane extraction on "split estate" lands, and then addresses federal regulatory policies in the sale and transportation of gas. Natural gas prices, unlike crude oil prices, were heavily controlled by the federal government for many years, with profound effects on the industry. Also, natural gas pipelines were regulated in 1938 quite differently from the oil pipeline act of 1906. Oil pipelines were treated as common carrier, open-access pipelines from the very start, whereas gas pipelines had to be restructured in the 1970s and 1980s to achieve this result and allow more competitive gas markets. Thus, this Gas chapter has many sections on pipeline regulation that have no counterpoint in the oil chapter. The problems of pipeline safety appear in the Oil chapter because they are linked to the discussion of externalities and oil spills; however, protecting the public from devastating explosions is largely an issue for gas pipelines, as explained in the prior chapter. Readers will find various cross-references to the Oil chapter as they traverse this Gas chapter.

1. THE PHYSICAL FLOW THROUGH FOUR ENTITIES

Natural gas, as used today, flows through a continuous chain of links between four types of entities:

Producers. These are the operators of the wells in oil and gas fields. For the most part, they are the same companies that produce oil because the two hydrocarbons are so often found together and are leased together in the same oil and gas lease discussed in the Oil chapter. Gas comes from two types of fields: Associated gas (also called casinghead gas) is gas that is produced along with oil from oil wells, separated from the oil, and then sent into gas pipelines. Other gas wells produce from gas-only fields that have no accompanying oil production. Gas is gathered in small-diameter pipelines (called gathering lines) from all the wells in a field; run through processing facilities in the field to remove water and impurities; compressed to boost its pressure so that it will flow into a large transmission pipeline; and transported to storage or marketing centers as depicted in **Figure 8–1**:

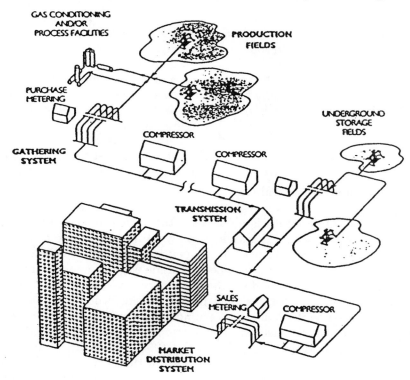

Figure 8–1
Typical Natural Gas Pipeline System

Source: 2 Energy Law and Transactions, p. 50–108 (David J. Muchow & William A. Mogel eds., 1999) (Matthew Bender).

Transmission Pipelines. These large pipelines of high-strength steel (20 inches to 42 inches in diameter) form an "interstate highway" system of 280,000 miles for natural gas to travel. The interstate pipeline companies have, for antitrust reasons, been independent from the gas producing companies. Interstate pipelines are regulated by the Federal Energy Regulatory Commission (FERC) using many of the principles of utility rate regulation discussed in Chapter 2, such as conditioning new pipeline construction on certificates of public convenience and regulating rates. In large producing and consuming states like Texas, many intrastate pipelines also exist. These are regulated by a state agency, often the public utility commission. State agencies, often the oil and gas conservation commissions, also regulate the smaller gathering lines.

Distributors or LDCs. In each urban area there is usually a "gas company" that distributes gas through gas mains under the streets to homes for heating and cooking and to commercial and industrial businesses. These local distribution companies are known as LDCs or distributors. They are usually investor-owned utilities regulated by the state public utility commission, but in some cases municipalities operate the gas distribution business.

Industrial Users and Power Plants. Gas is used as fuel in many industrial processes like boilers and blast furnaces. During the 1990s, it became the fuel of choice for most new electricity generation plants and the fate of both gas and electricity restructuring became intertwined. Industrial users often use very large volumes of gas and are quite sensitive to its price. Unlike residential and commercial users who buy gas from the area's LDC, industrial users may take gas directly from the pipeline, in a practice known as "industrial bypass" (bypassing the LDC as an intermediary). Most power plants also take gas directly from a pipeline or a spur off the pipeline.

In 2003, the industrial sector used about 37% of all natural gas consumed in the U.S., electric utilities used about 23%, and the residential and commercial sectors used about 38%, leaving a little sliver of 2% to 3% for the transportation sector.

2. BASIC PIPELINE OPERATIONS AND RATES

The market for natural gas has wide seasonal variations. In the Northern states, gas is commonly used for space heating; residential gas usage is seven times as high in the winter as in the summer. The electricity sector's demand for gas as a generation fuel for residential electricity use is 50% higher in the summer than in the fall and spring because air conditioning has become so prevalent. Thus, different pipelines face differing seasonal demand patterns. The laws of physics limit how much gas can be pushed through a pipe, depending on the size and strength of the pipe. Compressor stations posted about every 70 miles along a transmission line keep the gas under considerable pressure, but there are limits on the extent to which it can be compressed without risking a rupture which can be disastrous. (See the section on pipeline safety in Chapter 6.) A pipeline system must be designed to have enough capacity to meet the demands of customers on the most extreme cold- or hot-weather day, known as the "peak." On off-peak days, there will be room in the pipeline for other users.

To address this variability in demand, two different methods are often employed. First, depleted reservoirs nearer to consuming areas are converted into gas storage units by injecting gas into the reservoir during off-peak days, and drawing it out during peak days. (The ownership of stored gas was discussed in Chapter 6(B)(2) in the context of the rule of capture.) Especially in the last decade as gas has become the premier fuel for power plants, gas storage facilities have greatly expanded and this alleviates, but does not eliminate, the problem of supplying peak demand.

Second, many industrial users, such as petrochemical plants or steel mills that use very large quantities of gas on a year-round basis, are large enough to maintain alternative coal or fuel oil facilities to which they can switch if gas is not available or becomes relatively expensive compared to substitute fuels. These large, flexible customers are quite desirable for a pipeline company which is always seeking to maximize the use of its facilities every day of the year.[1] To attract such customers, pipeline companies designed "interruptible" rates which allow industrial users to buy gas at low rates on condition that they can be cut off if the pipeline space is needed, say, for residential gas heating on very cold days.

This interruptible customer pays a rate based primarily on the amount of gas it actually transports through the pipeline, called the "usage" or "commodity" charge. A commodity charge is defined as the charge per unit of gas (measured by volume or heat content), delivered to the buyer.[2] This customer pays little of the fixed cost of the pipeline because the pipeline serves the user only when spare capacity exists.

The "firm" customer (like the residential consumer) pays a two-part rate. The first part is based on the actual amount of gas used, *i.e.,* the usage or commodity rate. In addition, the firm customer pays for the right to demand service even on the coldest day. This second part of the rate is called a "reservation" or "demand" charge because the pipeline reserves space to meet this customer's demand at all times. The customer pays this charge whether they use the service or not. The charge is often based on the actual or estimated peak usage of the customer over a certain time period. (Review Chapter 3(A)(1)(g) on rate design.)

---

1. An industrial user with a steady demand has a "high load factor." Load factors are the ratio of average demand to peak demand. Thus, if a firm has an average demand of 8 units and a peak demand of 10 units, the load factor is 80%. Residential space heating customers have low load factors, *i.e.,* volatile demand swings due to weather.

2. Websites for terms glossaries of energy terms and natural gas in particular include:

http://www.eia.doe.gov/pub/oil_gas/natural_gas/analysis_publications/energy_policy_act_transportation_ study/pdf/epactgls.pdf

http://www.aga.org/Content/NavigationMenu/About_Natural_Gas/Natural_Gas_Glossary/Natural_Gas_ Glossary_(L)htm

http://www.nrel.gov/vehiclesandfuels/ngvtf/pdfs/glossary_ng_purchasing.pdf

http://www.platts.com/Oil/Resources/Glossaries/

If the weather becomes so extreme that even a cutoff of the industrial customers is inadequate to free up enough gas to serve the firm customers, LDCs typically establish priority lists to allocate gas among the firm customers. Usually the customers that will suffer the least damage from a shutdown are the first to be cut off, but any such action is an emergency situation to be avoided if at all possible.

3. CHANGING INDUSTRY LANDSCAPES

The business relationships among these companies were well-established until the energy shocks of the 1970s forced a radical restructuring of the industry. Historically, the pipelines bought gas from producers, transported it to markets, and sold it to distributors and industrial users. Because financing to construct a pipeline was not available unless the company could show that it had an assured source of supply and demand for twenty years or so, pipeline companies entered into long-term contracts to buy gas from producers, usually at relatively fixed prices. Similarly, distributors entered into long-term agreements to buy gas from the pipelines at rates approved by the state public utility commission.

The physical flow of gas and the straightforward buy/sell arrangements in the gas chain from the "upstream" wells to the "downstream" consumer before the restructuring are depicted in **Figure 8–2 above**. The pipeline was both a merchant—buying gas from the producer on one end and then selling it to the LDC at the other—and the sole provider of the transportation service to move the gas. All the gas in the pipeline belonged to the pipeline company.

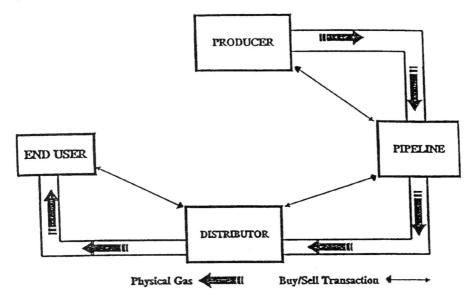

Figure 8–2
Historical Marketplace for Gas

Today, gas still flows in pipelines from the wellhead to the users, but the buy/sell financial transactions involve new players and new risk management tools created in response to fast-moving market forces. The new landscape is depicted in **Figure 8–3 below**. This chapter covers the evolution of the natural gas production and pipeline business from the "merchant pipeline" model of public utility control over monopolistic pipelines in **Figure 8–2** to the "open access," market-oriented model of **Figure 8–3**.

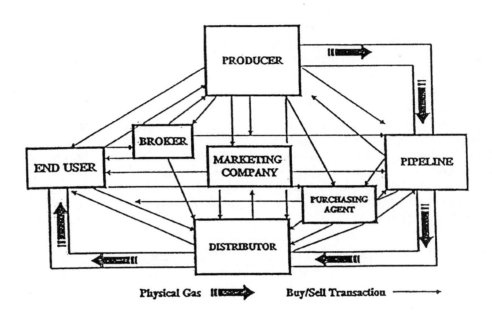

Figure 8–3
Today's Marketplace for Gas

4.   GAS PRICES OVER THE YEARS

As with oil, the long-term price of natural gas explains much about natural gas law and policy. Here is the price of gas from 1949–2003:

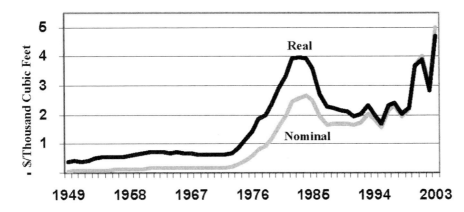

Figure 8–4
Natural Gas Wellhead Prices (1949–2003)

Source: Energy Information Administration.

A comparison of gas prices with the prices of the other two fossil fuels—crude oil and coal—during the key decades of 1960–2000 shows the following pattern:

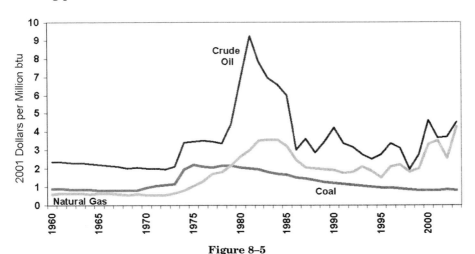

Figure 8–5
Fossil Fuel Production Prices Prices (1960–2003)

Source: EIA Data.

Four price stages are evident. First, natural gas prices stayed very low (less than 50 cents per thousand cubic feet ("MCF")) until 1973. Second, gas prices turned sharply upwards in 1973 until 1981, corresponding to the embargo-induced shortage in oil supplies and oil's even sharper price rise (see Chapter 6 on Oil). However, unlike oil, gas prices resisted the 1981 price plunge. Indeed, from 1981 through 1985, gas prices stayed on a high plateau. This aberrant behavior is due largely to the perverse legal framework created to regulate natural gas, as discussed in Section C of this chapter. After 1985, the volatility of natural gas prices increased, with more ups and downs, but the price stayed largely in the $1.50 to $2.00 range until about 2000. Then, in the fourth, most recent stage, gas prices have risen to unimagined highs: We were running out of domestic gas supplies and needed to move quickly to import LNG (liquefied natural gas) from other countries, as discussed in the last section of this chapter.

Both policy-driven factors and the fundamentals of demand and supply explain these stages.

5.   THE RESOURCE BASE OVER THE YEARS

a.   1900–1978: FROM BY-PRODUCT TO REGULATION

For many years, gas was an unwanted by-product of the hunt for oil. Finding a gas field rather than an oil field was a serious disappointment. For years, operators simply flared casinghead gas at the wellhead, burning it off rather than collecting it to sell or use. Many Houstonians can still remember driving at night to Galveston beach, 30 miles away, through oil fields so brightly illuminated by the gas flares that they could read a newspaper in the car.

In the 1920s and 1930s, huge gas fields covering millions of acres were discovered in the Texas Panhandle and in Oklahoma, but the gas was in the wrong place—far from the populated East coast. The excess supply of gas was reflected in its price. From 1935 to 1951, the average price of gas on a BTU basis was about 6 cents per million BTUs, while the price of crude oil rose from 18 cents to 43 cents on the same BTU basis.[3] Thus, gas sold for 1/3 to 1/7 of the equivalent heating value of oil. Gas was the "Cinderella" of fuels, the forgotten stepchild of oil.

After World War II, during which crude oil was in very short supply, natural gas began to come into its own as a clean and useful fuel. The interstate gas transmission system expanded and provided new and more distant markets. Gas is about 30 times more expensive to transport than oil (on an energy equivalent basis), so its markets are crucially dependent on development of this infrastructure. The passage of the Clean Air Act in 1970 elevated gas to a premium fuel. Unfortunately, by this time, federal price controls on gas had begun to create shortages in gas supplies. When the OPEC oil embargo hit in 1973, natural gas was already in short supply and the U.S. had a full-blown energy crisis on its hands. In 1978, interstate pipelines were forced to curtail and ration gas to end users along the East coast, and Congress was finally prompted to pass a huge National Energy Policy Act, a good part of which involved policies to solve natural gas shortages.

---

3.   Erich W. Zimmermann, Conservation in the Production of Petroleum 237–51 (1957). Natural gas is measured either by volume (such as thousands of cubic feet or MCFs) or by its heat value in BTUs (British Thermal Units). One BTU is roughly the amount of energy produced by a match tip. One million BTUs of energy is about one million MCFs of gas (which is the same as one billion cubic feet of gas).

While little could be done policy-wise to stop the decline in domestic oil production in the United States after its peak year of 1970, the natural gas shortages of the 1970s stemmed in some significant degree from bad regulatory policies. The U.S. had a significant amount of conventional natural gas reserves still sitting underground in the same types of oil and gas fields that had been discovered since the early 1900s. In addition, we had large reserves of "unconventional" natural gas that could be tapped if the price was right. On the eve of passage of the Natural Gas Policy Act of 1978, an issue of the *National Geographic* featured the many new technologies that could be used to access huge reserves of natural gas, once considered too difficult or costly to exploit. At that time, both industry and government experts estimated that the U.S. had about 208 trillion cubic feet ("TCF") of gas reserves, about a ten-year supply at then-current consumption rates. Gas supplied 41 percent of the nation's non-transportation energy, serving 41 million homes and providing 40 percent of industrial needs. Would the featured new sources rescue the nation from what looked like a permanent shortage?

The potential supply from unconventional sources described in Bryan Hodgson, Natural Gas: The Search Goes On, 154 Nat'l Geographic 632–51 (Nov. 1978) included:[4]

- **Deep reservoir gas**. Gas found at depths between 15,000 and 30,000 feet where drilling is technically difficult because of high pressures and temperatures.

- **Tight sands gas.** Located largely in the Rockies, concrete-hard sandstones could contain some 800 TCF of gas.

- **Coal seams**. At least 850 TCF of gas existed in the nation's coalbed seams.

- **Devonian shales**. More than 1,000 TCF could be trapped in dense rock underlying 90,000 square miles of Appalachia.

- **Geopressurized methane.** Located largely in the Gulf Coast region, this is gas dissolved at high temperatures in deep aquifers of saline water that may contain 60,000 TCF of natural gas.

- **Methane hydrates**. Methane and water form a lattice-like, solid substance beneath permafrost and in deep-ocean bottoms. Discovered only in the late 1960s, hydrates may have trapped almost unlimited quantities of gas thought to have dissipated millennia ago.

The *National Geographic* article ends with "barnyard gas" produced by a plant which was then converting cow manure into more than a million cubic feet of methane a day; and with a scientist breeding algae in a lab to study how to simulate photosynthesis, the process by which green plants convert sunlight into energy. Some day, the scientist promised, we will harness that chemistry and make our fuel this way.

---

4. For comparison, the U.S. currently uses about 23 TCF of gas per year.

b.   1978–2000: NATURAL GAS MARKETS DEVELOP

As price controls were gradually lifted on natural gas production after 1978, the optimism expressed in the article proved accurate. At higher prices, producers drilled more wells, invested in newer technologies, and discovered and produced more gas. Between 1978 and 1987, the Powerplant and Industrial Fuel Use Act (PIFUA) prohibited the use of natural gas or oil as a fuel for power plants or large industrial boilers. Congress reserved these two fuels which were in scarce supply for use in the transportation and space heating sectors. New power plants could use coal or "go nuclear." The Fuel Use Act was mostly repealed in 1987 because its restrictions on natural gas demand led to a surplus of natural gas (called the natural gas "bubble"); gas producers urgently pleaded for new markets for the gas they discovered in response to higher prices. The repeal of PIFUA led to a surge in the construction of gas-fired power plants. By the decade of the 1990s, natural gas prices had settled at about $2.00 per MCF, a relatively low price considering the clean air benefits of burning gas versus coal. Gas became the "golden fuel," eagerly sought by the new generation of merchant power plants built to compete in deregulated electricity markets and also by traditional utilities that found siting or operating coal-fired power plants increasingly difficult. For example, a Florida utility charged by the EPA with violating the Clean Air Act agreed to switch a coal-fired power plant to gas, a move that was expected to produce electricity for about the same price while reducing emissions of sulfur dioxide by 60 tons a year, particulates by 2,000 tons per year, and nitrogen oxide by 30 tons per year. New York Times, Mar. 1, 2000, at A21. Between 2000 and 2004, in just five years, 200,000 megawatts of gas-fired power plants were added to the electricity sector in the U.S.—the functional equivalent of 245 nuclear units (of the size built at Calvert Cliffs). Frank Clemente, The Problem with Natural Gas, July 14, 2005, at 2 (EnergyPulse ECP Online). These new plants were not just peaking units, but also served baseload customers at times.

Gas also has a big advantage over coal combustion in reduced emissions of carbon dioxide ("CO_2"), one of the primary greenhouse gases contributing to global warming. The carbon content per BTU of natural gas is only 55 percent of that for coal and 70 percent of that for oil. (Climate Change is discussed in Chapter 16.) If the Kyoto Protocol on climate change were to become an effective treaty to reduce greenhouse gases, it could further increase the demand for gas as a substitute for coal. Global climate change and clean air benefits could also increase the demand for natural gas-powered automotive engines. While experimentation with gas-powered trucks and buses is still in the early stages, today's prototype vehicles are far more efficient and safe than those of a decade ago. If natural gas replaced even a small share of the market for gasoline, this would bring a big increase in the demand for natural gas nationwide. (Chapter 15 looks at Energy in Transportation.)

Moreover, extensive research and development has been ongoing for fuel cells powered by natural gas. Fuel cells are electrochemical devices in which electric current is created directly by the combination of oxygen and hydrogen ions without the need for a mechanical generator. The development of cost-effective fuel cells on a large scale may be one of the byproducts of the space program, which has been using small fuel cells to provide power for spacecraft for decades. If restructured energy markets lead to many small, distributed generation sources that are independent of the electric grid (such as fuel cells or mini-gas turbines small enough to power, say, a single McDonalds outlet) natural gas would again lead the way as a premium fuel.

The new gas-powered generating plants of the 1990s often used a new, sleek technology: the combined-cycle gas turbine, or CCGT, to convert natural gas into electricity. Gas turbine generators have been used to produce electricity for many years. The mechanics are simple: Gas is burned in the functional equivalent of an airplane's jet engine which turns the wheels of an electric generator. Both small- and large-scale turbine models are equally feasible, and they can be turned on and off quickly. Power companies have used gas turbine plants as sources of "peaking" power, turning them on when temperatures rise and air conditioners hum, and turning them off when the weather cools. The combined-cycle power plant includes both a gas turbine and a steam turbine; the latter utilizes the excess heat thrown off by the gas turbine to create steam which also turns an electric generator. This improved plant design and the low gas prices of the 1990s reduced the price of electricity derived from gas to levels below that of coal, oil and sometimes even hydropower sources. Gas-fired plants were built for more than peaking purposes. In February 2000, the Department of Energy and GE Power Systems unveiled a new-generation "H System" with turbines two percentage points more efficient than the most efficient combined-cycle power plants in existence (60% versus 58%). Breaking the 60–percent efficiency threshold was tantamount to the first runner breaking the four-minute mile. The increased efficiency could translate into savings of $30 to $40 million over the lifetime of a plant, in addition to reducing pollution from less fuel use. (The new system was developed by a public-private R and D effort to which the DOE contributed about $100 million and GE Power about $500 million).

Of the new power plants built between 2000 and 2004, 90% were powered with natural gas and many had no alternative fuel capability. Clemente, *supra*, at 3.

Thus, at the beginning of a new century, gas seemed poised for a bright and sunny future, both from the demand and supply side. Environmental think-tanks and the industry's own National Petroleum Council (a federally chartered and privately funded advisory committee to the executive branch) conducted large studies of the long-term outlook for natural gas and found no major problems ahead for the increased use of gas. For example, in 1999, the Environmental Law Institute (ELI) studied government and industry gas supply forecasts to assess the nation's ability to switch from dirty coal to clean gas as a response to global climate change and nonattainment of air pollution goals. Official estimates of recoverable gas reserves, based on current prices and little technological growth, then totaled 1,331 trillion cubic feet (TCF) or about 60 years of supply. Technical progress measured by the historical trend would add another 100 years to future gas supplies. If technological progress instead advanced at the rapid rate of the 1990s, this would unlock even greater gas resources considered economically unrecoverable at the price of $2 per thousand cubic feet (MCF), such as coal bed methane (300 TCF), tight sands (6,600 TCF), deep gas deposits (3,200 TCF), and geopressurized aquifers (5,700 TCF). The potential gas stored in methane hydrates could add an astounding 200,000 TCF of gas to the resource base.

The ELI concluded, based on its survey of many other studies, that gas could be used as an abundant energy source for centuries, depending on technology and one other key factor: price. If the price of gas dropped significantly below $2 per MCF, technology advances would be slow and supply would fall below even the official reserve estimate of 1,331 TCF. On the other hand, a price of $4 per MCF would trigger major new supplies around the world and would allow liquefied natural gas (LNG) from large foreign reserves to enter U.S. coastal markets. This price would also make large Alaskan gas reserves, now trapped at Prudhoe Bay, marketable via a gas pipeline to the lower 48 states. ELI Research Report, How Abundant? Assessing the Estimates of Natural Gas Supply, accessed at http://www. elistore.org/reports_detail.asp?ID'471.

The National Petroleum Council's December 1999 study shared the same basic conclusions as the ELI report. As its title proclaimed, the industry was capable of "Meeting the Challenges of the Nation's Growing Natural Gas Demand." Gas demand could climb from about 23 trillion cubic feet a year to 30 TCF a year by 2010 because supplies were amply available at about $3/MCF. "30 at $3" was a catchphrase often heard.

c.   2000–2005: PRICE SHOCKS AND SHORTAGE

No sooner had the ink dried on the reports described above, then the price of natural gas began a steep, almost relentless climb to heights unanticipated by anyone. In April 2000, the price was already at $3/MCF and it soared to $8 in a cold snap in late 2000. (See Section E(2) of this chapter for the problems of gas price manipulation in the Western markets at this time.)

At this price, industrial users with switching capability turned off the gas taps. Between 2000 and 2002, industrial demand for gas dropped from 17.1 billion cubic feet per day to 10.3 bcf/day and many ammonia and methanol plants that produced fertilizers along the Gulf Coast closed. Gas-fired power plants took the gas released from the industrial sector. Mild weather moderated prices in 2002, although $4 gas was becoming the norm by fall 2002. Then, in an abnormally cold period in late February 2003, gas prices on one day rose to an astounding $22/MCF, although they dropped again fairly quickly.

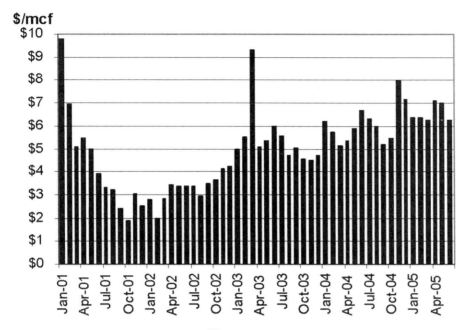

Figure 8–6
NYMEX Monthly Futures Prices (January 2001–June 2005)

Source: Reuters—Average of the settlement prices for the last 3 days of trading for the nearby NYMEX Natural Gas futures contract.

Gas users and suppliers built up storage capacity during the summer of 2003 such that the Secretary of Energy announced in November 12, 2003 that the supply of natural gas was "healthy." Associated Press, Nov. 12, 2003. One month later headlines screamed "Natural Gas Run-up Stuns Analysts: Senator Says Probe Ahead." Houston Chronicle, Dec. 13, 2003 at C1. Below-normal cold weather had hit New England and the Midwest, and prices surged 50% into the $7 to $8 range. Several energy analysts asserted that the levels and volatility were not consistent with market fundamentals. Senator Orrin Hatch (R–Utah), chair of the Judiciary Committee, called for hearings into whether improper manipulation of gas markets was occurring. *Id.* Some gas traders suggested that hedge funds were running up the price in a "speculative froth." Simon Romero, Natural Gas Prices Surge and Fingers Are Pointing, New York Times, Dec. 13, 2003, at B1. The White House invited 24 ministers and officials from OPEC and other major energy-producing countries to meet to discuss the growing U.S. thirst for imports of LNG. Reuters, Dec. 16, 2003 (ECP Online). Trying to look on the bright side, the Energy Department reported that growth in natural gas demand would moderate in the U.S. as our industries moved overseas, taking jobs with them. Editorial, Volatile, Houston Chronicle, Dec. 19, 2003, at 46A.

Since the end of 2003, natural gas prices have stayed high in a range of $6.50 to $7 per MCF and rising (as of mid–2005 when this casebook went to print). What happened?

Beneath the sunny outlooks of late 1999 lay some disturbing trends. The production of natural gas from conventional domestic sources in the U.S. had peaked in 1973, just two years after the peak in domestic oil (see Chapter 7(B)(1) on Peak Oil). The increased domestic production of natural gas in response to deregulated prices during the 1980s had never increased the total amount of gas produced above its 1973 peak. (For example, 23,500 gas wells in Texas produced 9.5 billion cubic feet of gas in 1970; by 2004, about 70,000 gas wells produced only 5.8 BCF, a significant drop in well productivity. Clemente, *supra* at 5). Domestic gas production has basically been flat for the past 10 years. In fact, the gas wells in existing fields had experienced accelerated and rapid rates of decline in production. Production from new fields discovered on the Outer Continental Shelf and in the Rockies could not offset the declines in the old fields nor could increased production from tight sands or coal seams. Throughout the 1990s, the United States increased its imports of natural gas from Canada to meet the growing gap between domestic supply and demand. Successful exploration in both western Canada around Alberta and in eastern Canada (onshore and offshore) had made Canada eager to export gas to the U.S. market. New pipelines were built into the U.S. market, and by 2000, Canadian gas supplied about 20 percent of the U.S. market. But such pipelines were constrained by their capacity levels, and when bitter cold hit New England, there was no more natural gas to route to the region quickly.

In 2003, the National Petroleum Council issued a gloomy report stating that a "fundamental shift" in gas supply and demand had occurred in just three years. An energy analyst summarized the new report's major findings. Matthew R. Simmons, U.S. Natural Gas Crisis: Is It Real?, National Research Council Workshop, Apr. 21, 2003. Washington DC:

- The 1999 NPC study greatly underestimated the explosion in construction of gas-fired power plants.

- Access to leasing areas became further restricted as OCS moratoria continued and new areas were classified as national monuments and closed to future leasing. The OCS held 80 TCF of technically recoverable reserves subject to leasing moratoria. Another 56 TCF in the Rockies was suffering added costs and development delays because of access-related restrictions.

- The drilling boom simply could not replace rapidly depleting supplies from existing wells, especially when technological advances in drilling slowed. In 1999, 10,877 gas wells were completed in U.S.; by 2001, the drilling boom resulted in 22,083 completed gas wells. Still, the U.S. could not drill itself out of the shortage because supplies were depleting about 29% a year and, in the NPC's words, there was "a lower average production response to higher prices from new wells."

The NPC 2003 Report presented Americans with a choice: the "Reactive Path" or a "Balanced Future." The Reactive Path assumed continued conflict between policies that encouraged gas use but discouraged supply development. It would result in long-term gas prices of $5 to $7 per MCF through 2025. The Balanced Future scenario, built on policies such as phased lifting of moratoria and better demand-response technologies, projected long-term prices in the $3 to $5 range. The NPC Report estimated that if restrictions were lifted on access to domestic gas resources, gas consumers would save $300 billion over the next 20 years. Even this "balanced" future path set aggressive production goals. It requires that deepwater OCS gas and Rocky Mountain supplies (largely coalbed methane) offset decline rates of 25% in existing wells. And even the Reactive Path would require overcoming obstacles to building an Alaskan gas pipeline, siting LNG terminals and leasing federal lands. If these obstacles were not hurdled, long-term prices would average 18% more. Simmons warned that the industrial sector has made all of the easy demand reductions it could make. We had "bet the ranch" on natural gas at a time when about 55% of current global gas production was in terminal decline and when Arctic gas supplies were at least 10 years away.

In April 2004, Dupont, a large chemical company, announced it was laying off 3,500 workers in order to reduce costs and stay competitive against companies with much lower gas prices abroad. Thaddeus Herrick, Dupont to Eliminate 3, 500 Jobs As High Gas Prices Take a Toll, Wall St. J., Apr. 15, 2004, at A16. The New England grid operator reported that in January 2004, many gas-fired power generators shut down to avoid paying high prices for natural gas on the spot market during the cold snap, cutting deeply into the region's power reserves.[5] Connecticut Post, May 13, 2004 (Energy Central Professional (ECP) Online). Because of the Enron scandal, many energy traders and middleman no longer were creditworthy, making it more difficult for gas users to find middlemen who would take the risk of price volatility by contracting with users for long-term, fixed-price deals. Pipeline & Gas J., Jan. 7, 2004 (ECP Online).

In short, deregulated gas markets (and electricity markets on the West Coast), especially during the California energy crisis discussed in Chapter 11, hardly reflected the sunny optimism that had been voiced at the start of the new century. With domestic natural gas prices now perpetually above $3/MCF, importing LNG from abroad was the quickest "bridge" supply

---

5. The FERC Staff's 2004 State of the Markets Report (June 2005), discussed in Section E(1) of this chapter, describes this event as follows in its section titled "Markets Under Stress: New England Reacts to Record Cold," at 14:

> Much of New England's natural gas-fired capacity relies on the spot market for supply. When heating demand increased with the extreme cold, spot natural gas availability dropped and prices spiked. On January 14, 7,073 MW of natural-gas fired generation (53%) was out of service, largely because of a lack of fuel. These outages resulted, in part, from electric price signals that failed to attract spot natural gas to electric generation.
>
> As a consequence, some generators with firm natural gas contracts sold their supplies on the spot market rather than produce power. Resulting high outage levels caused an electric reserve deficiency, prompting ISO–NE to urge conservation and issue a potential blackout warning. System stability was restored when several natural gas units returned to service at ISO direction.

Warmer weather ultimately ended the crisis. [NE–ISO is the New England Independent Power Organization which coordinates electricity flows in that area].

source, although the liquefaction plants, special LNG tankers, and regasification terminals needed were multi-billion dollar ventures with 3– to 4–year lead times. Utilities have started building coal-fired plants rather than natural-gas generating units.

President Bush had long pushed for a national energy act that would provide incentives to oil and gas operators to spur more drilling; reduce restrictions on access to public lands for leasing; and diversify the nation's energy portfolio by encouraging nuclear and clean coal. Just before its 2005 summer recess, Congress passed such an act and the President signed it into law. (The act also includes incentives for energy efficiency. A loan guarantee for an Alaskan Natural Gas Pipeline to bring gas from Prudhoe Bay to the lower 48 had already been enacted in 2004.) Within days, the Energy Information Administration released an analysis of the House version of the sweeping energy bill: It would have only a "modest impact" on energy production, imports, oil prices, overall energy consumption and economic growth. In particular, it would provide no improvement in lower–48 natural gas production through 2025. EIA, Impacts of Modeled Provisions of H.R. 6 (the Energy Policy Act of 2005) at vii (Aug. 2005). Because the act neither opens ANWR to development nor lifts the OCS moratoria on drilling, little additional domestic supplies of oil and gas would result from the bill's passage.

Query: Are you now wary of anyone's forecasts of oil and gas demand, supply and prices, whether long-term or short-term?

d.   THE FUTURE GAS RESOURCE BASE

This section surveys the latest developments in other sources of natural gas that we may be using in the future. LNG, which is already at our doorstep, is discussed in the last section of this chapter.

Stranded gas and GTL. Many companies have launched major R&D projects that aim at other sources of natural gas from conventional, but "stranded," gas fields. For example, Conoco has identified 1,200 stranded fields which have no pipeline access that would allow gas to be produced and transported to markets. In 2000, Conoco announced plans to build a $35– to $50–million plant to test its technology for converting gas to synthetic petroleum which could then be economically shipped by pipeline, tanker, barge, or truck. It estimated that its "gas-to-liquids" ("GTL") technology would be profitable at oil prices of about $25 a barrel. Monica Perin, Is it Gas? Is It Liquids? It's Both and It's Big, Houston Bus. J., Feb. 18–24, 2000, at 1A.

About half of the world's proven gas reserves of about 6,200 TCF are considered stranded. Oil & Gas J., Mar. 14, 2005, at 20. GTL technology will obviously compete with LNG, which brings stranded gas supplies to distant markets by cooling the gas to a liquid shipped in tankers and then regasifying it. The virtue of GTL technology is that the synthetic liquid can be used as clean-burning transportation fuels. Syntroleum Corporation in Tulsa, Oklahoma has a GTL technology that produces ultra-clean synthetic gasoline and diesel fuels (which can also be used in fuel cells). Syntroleum is working with partners in Nigeria to build a floating GTL plant 10 miles from shore mounted on a barge (and relatively inaccessible to onshore civil unrest that often erupts in Nigeria). Lynn J. Cook, Plan To Convert Gas to Diesel Advances, Houston Chronicle, Sept. 3, 2004, at D4. Many energy giants, like BP, are testing new GTL technologies that promise to bring down costs.

The small Mideast nation of Qatar has launched an enormous GTL industry to turn its large reserves of natural gas into clean diesel fuel that will be priced competitively with crude oil on the export market. ExxonMobil, Shell and Chevron have pledged $20 billion to build GTL facilities in an industrial park in Qatar that is twice the size of Manhattan. Russell Gold, In Qatar, Oil Firms Make Huge Bet on Alternative Fuel, Wall St. J., Feb. 15, 2005, at A1. In Bolivia, a company is working on a smaller project that will produce 10,000 barrels per day of diesel from Bolivia's large gas reserves, allowing the country to reduce its imports of this expensive fuel. Brian A. Toal, Gas–To–Liquids, Oil & Gas Investor, July 2002 (available at www.oilandgasinvestor.com).

Hydrates and global warming. R&D continues on methane hydrates also. An enormous source of methane lies at the outer edges of the ocean's continental shelf, just beneath the ocean floor. It may contain more carbon than all the world's fossil fuels combined. These hydrates form naturally when organic matter accumulates on the deep-sea floor and bacteria invade the muddy sediments, digest the organic material, and release methane gas. Under certain conditions of pressure, temperature and high concentrations of gas, the methane molecules get trapped inside an ice-like lattice of water crystals. Hydrates dissolve when exposed to seawater without gas and can melt rapidly, releasing methane when temperatures rise or pressure falls. Research shows that significant amounts of carbon are added to and removed from hydrates all the time.

The instability of the carbon-hydrate cycle poses many issues. If even minor changes in ocean temperatures and currents can trigger massive release of methane from the oceans, this has profound implications for global climate change. Methane is a greenhouse gas, 21 times more potent as a greenhouse gas than carbon dioxide in the atmosphere. Over the last 200 years, methane concentrations in the atmosphere have more than doubled, largely due to human-related activities. China is the biggest methane emitter from both coal and rice production. India is a major emitter because of rice and livestock production. In the U.S., landfills are the largest source of methane emissions.[6]

Hydrates are also trapped onshore in the Arctic. (Chapter 9 discusses petroleum development in the Arctic.) The DOE is working with energy companies to map, quantify and assess the feasibility of producing gas from North Slope gas hydrates, and an international consortium including the

---

6. An EPA report on greenhouse gases is available at http://yosemite.epa.gov/OAR/global warming.nsf/content/ResourceCenterPublicationsGHGEmissionsUSEmissionsInventory2005. html.

U.S. Geological Survey, the DOE, Canada, Japan, India, Germany and the energy industry conducted test drilling into hydrates in the Canadian Arctic. As deeper wells are drilled offshore in the search for conventional gas fields, industry is concerned that the ice-like hydrates on the sea floor will melt, causing the seabed and the well bores that passed through the hydrate layer to collapse. As a member of Environmental Defense stated: "We ought to do the science first so [we] don't have any big mistakes." *Greenwire*, Apr. 20, 2005. *See generally*, Henry R. Linden, Reversing the Gas Crisis: The Methane Hydrate Solution, Public Utilities Fortnightly, Jan 2005, at 35.

For futurists or science fiction fans, scientists from several national and university labs used a diamond anvil and squeezed common materials in the earth's surface—iron oxide, calcite and water—at pressures similar to those found deep in the earth (12 miles deep; the deepest gas wells drilled to date are about 6 miles deep). Methane was formed by combining the carbon in calcite with the hydrogen in water. Virtually inexhaustible supplies may be found in a "journey to the center of the earth," but this awaits the invention of tools that can operate in ferocious heat and pressure. UPI, Deep Methane Possible Huge Energy Source, Sept. 13, 2004 (ECP Online). The Colorado School of Mines has adapted laser technology from the Reagan "Star Wars" military defense program and is testing the use of lasers which can "slice through rock like a hot knife through butter," to allow cheaper, faster and more environmentally benign drilling for oil and gas. Alexander's Gas & Oil Connections, Vol. 9, No. 2, Jan. 29, 2004, at www.gasandoil.com/goc/features/fex40407.htm

Coal gasification and carbon sequestration. One other source of gas competes with unconventional or imported gas supplies: the integrated gasification combined-cycle ("IGCC") power plant. The technology exists to turn coal into a gas that can be used to generate electricity. Capturing CO_2 emissions from the plant and sequestering the CO_2 in depleted reservoirs creates a "zero-emissions" power plant. Because the U.S. has very large reserves of coal (about 1/4 of the world's total reserves), this source of energy diminishes our dependence on unstable imports of either oil or gas.

William Rosenberg (an engineering professor at Carnegie Mellon, a fellow at the Harvard Kennedy School of Government and a previous state public utility commissioner) has proposed that the federal government launch a robust program to build 50 IGCC power plants that use coal, biomass and petroleum refinery wastes to produce enough synthetic gas to reduce natural gas prices, alleviate our dependence on imports of LNG, achieve greater national energy security, and create many commercial platforms to demonstrate carbon capture, sequestration and hydrogen-fueled technologies. The federal government should grant loan guarantees (as it did for the Alaskan gas pipeline in 2004) or other credit financing support to create a "3Party Covenant" to deploy this fleet of IGCC plants. The three parties are the federal government, utility companies, and state public utility commissions which, without the federal aid, probably would not approve utility proposals to build IGCC plants rather than conventional coal plants because of the additional expense (capital costs are about 20% higher than conventional coal) and operating risks of being the first such project. American Electric Power has announced that it will build a commercial, full-sized IGCC plant if the proper regulatory environment is created. William G. Rosenberg *et al.*, A National Gasification Strategy, 143 Pub. Util. Fortnightly 66 (2005). The Energy Policy Act of 2005 (in Section 413) authorizes one demonstration IGCC plant capable of removing and sequestering CO_2.

B.   OWNERSHIP AND EXTERNALITIES: FOCUS ON COALBED METHANE AND SPLIT ESTATES

This section discusses the fiercely contentious issues of ownership and externalities in the context of "split estates" and coalbed methane ("CBM") development in the West. Split estates are common in the United States: One owner owns the surface of the land and a second owner owns the minerals on the same tract. Which estate is dominant? Can the mineral estate owner start drilling in the middle of someone's cow pasture or backyard? How will the externalities of development be controlled to mitigate injury to the surface owners' uses of the land? More fundamentally, which estate owns minerals which are not the traditional oil and gas resource? These issues are discussed in terms of the fastest growing source of domestic gas today—coalbed methane. The third issue discussed is who owns depleted gas reservoirs which are valuable pieces of rock for storing sources of natural gas near markets and for sequestering carbon dioxide to mitigate global climate change.

1.   SPLIT ESTATES AND MINERAL DOMINANCE

Split estates, where the surface of a tract has been severed from the minerals, are a source of eternal conflict between the surface owner and the oil and gas or mineral developer. The surface owner may be an Alabama cotton farmer, a West Texas rancher, a Utah retiree in a small town near a national park, a hedge-fund manager from New York with a palatial second home in Wyoming, or entire suburban communities outside Fort Worth, Houston, and Denver. The mineral estate owner is most often someone entirely unrelated and often unknown to the surface owner. When an area becomes "hot" for an oil and gas play, operators will search county title records for the owners of the mineral estate, not the surface estate. The mineral estate owner is often happy to grant an oil and gas lease for a healthy bonus in the hundreds of dollars per acre, and for the opportunity to receive royalty checks in the mail every quarter should the lessee find and produce oil or gas beneath the tract. The surface owner, of course, will often be devastated by the news that a drilling rig will soon be placed in the middle of his cotton crop, grasslands, backyard, or scenic view. The surface owner will not receive any of the bonus money or royalties from the leasing transaction; he or she does not own the severed oil and gas.

Sometimes, the original owner of both estates may have placed restrictions governing oil and gas development or other surface uses into the deed which severed the minerals. In this case, assuming the covenants are found to run with the land, the surface owner and subsequent assignees will have some protection from later development. Deed restrictions in residential subdivisions often prohibit commercial uses of the surface. More often than not, though, the severance documents contain no surface-use restrictions, especially in rural areas.

When split-estate conflicts arose in the United States, the British common law of the monarchies of yore was readily adopted to govern the dispute. After all "royalty" itself meant the payment owed the king or sovereign. The monarchy had once owned all valuable minerals like gold and silver in the kingdom and the common law had early developed the rule that the mineral estate was dominant. If the king no longer owned the surface estate because, *e.g.,* he had granted it to a lord in return for military service, the king nonetheless retained the minerals and had an easement of necessity across the surface to access his mines and assure that he would receive "royalty" payments from those to whom he leased the mines. In short, the mineral estate was dominant and could use the surface freely, without negotiating access rights or payments for damages to crops or other surface uses.

The early Texas case of *Grimes v. Goodman Drilling Co.*, 216 S.W. 202 (1919) illustrates this dominance. The owner of a small, town lot sought an injunction to abate a nuisance against the lessee drilling a well on the tract. Plaintiff had bought the surface of the lot, subject to a prior oil and gas lease, at a time when no well was located thereon, but many wells had already been drilled in and around the town. Goodman Drilling erected a derrick in the front yard without asking permission or compensating the plaintiff. The court continued:

> The slush pit connected with the well is near to and runs along the side of plaintiff's house, and slush spatters onto the sides of the house, the doors, and windows, and necessitates that side of the house being closed up. The running of the engine is very objectionable to the plaintiff's family and often prevents their sleeping at nights, and is so loud as to require them in ordinary conversation to speak in very loud tones. *Id.* at 204.

The court ruled against the plaintiff: He had purchased the lot on the severed estate burdened with the lease and was presumed to know that drilling a well would make the use of the home "disagreeable, inconvenient, and perhaps dangerous." There was no evidence that the driller was negligent in placing the boiler or slush pit near the house; that is where they could fit.

Over the years, the implied rights of the dominant mineral estate to use the surface have been held to cover a wide range of activities: seismic tests, storage tanks, roads, and use of the surface owners' freshwater (which might be quite scarce in the arid West) for drilling or secondary recovery operations. (Drilling operations do not use much water, but secondary operations like waterflooding can use millions of gallons of water a month to repressure an oil field.) In Texas, the mineral owner does not have an obligation to protect the surface owner's cattle by fencing the well site or any obligation to restore the surface, absent provisions in the lease requiring such acts.

Over the years, courts and legislatures have acted to reduce the dominance of the mineral estate in several ways. As you read through these measures, ask yourself if a mineral estate owner could successfully argue that his property rights have suffered an unconstitutional taking.

1. *City zoning ordinances*. Even though the earliest boom towns in Texas seemed to embrace rigs and wells in backyards, many municipalities later enacted zoning ordinances to protect public health and safety. The courts have had little difficulty upholding the power of towns to restrict drilling by passing well-density and pooling ordinances. *E.g.*, in *Tysco Oil Co. v. Railroad Commission*, 12 F. Supp. 195 (S.D. Tex. 1935); 12 F. Supp. 202 (S.D. Tex. 1935), the plaintiffs sought an injunction against the city of South Houston which had passed a 1935 ordinance subdividing the city into drilling districts of 16 acres each. Only one well could be drilled in each district and only after a permit was obtained from the city. The permit was conditioned on the permittee's sharing the production from the well proportionately (based on surface acreage) with other landowners in the district. (See Chapter 6(C) on pooling and unitization.) The city reserved the right to refuse a permit where the location of the proposed well posed a serious problem to the city or its citizens—a wise move given that 18 of the 64 existing businesses in the city manufactured and stored explosive fireworks. Could the city absolutely prohibit drilling without incurring liability for inverse condemnation from a taking? Could the city absolutely prohibit fireworks manufacturing within the city limits? Why might one be different from the other? Some cities' drilling regulations are quite detailed and restrict noise levels and truck deliveries to the well site; require watchmen and security fencing; and provide details on allocating the costs and proceeds of production among what may be dozens of owners.

In a later case under a similar ordinance as that in *Tysco, supra,* the plaintiffs had obtained a drilling permit from the state oil and gas conservation commission. However, the city of Tomball had passed an ordinance which conflicted with the state permit. The plaintiffs alleged that the commission had the exclusive authority to regulate well drilling in Texas, but the court held that the city retained its fundamental police power to regulate drilling and production within city limits to protect citizens and property. The basic functions of the conservation commission are to prevent the waste of oil and gas and protect correlative rights; municipalities regulate drilling to protect health and safety. Sometimes the line is hard to draw. Bruce M. Kramer, Local Regulation of Oil and Gas Operations: Don't All Homeowners Want a Pumpjack in Their Backyard, 41 Rocky Mtn. Min. L. Fd. J. 213 (2004) (also containing a discussion of takings issues); Smith & Weaver, *supra,* at § 9.1(B) (2004).

   2. ***The accommodation doctrine***. The courts have also whittled the
common law dominance of the mineral estate to uses of the surface that are
"reasonably necessary" to develop the oil and gas and to non-negligent
uses. Thus, if a reasonable operator would have used 2 acres as a drill site,
but an operator strews equipment or spills oil over 5 acres of a corn field,
then damages are due the surface owner for use of the additional 3 acres.
In addition, the lessee must make efforts to reasonably accommodate
existing surface uses. The best-known case on the accommodation doctrine
involved a surface farmer growing a crop in the nearly rainless Panhandle
area of Texas, the "dust bowl." Farming was possible only by using large
sprinkler systems that took groundwater from wells through pipes and
hoses linked to wheeled sprinklers that moved across the surface of the
farm to reach all corners. For many years, farmer Jones had co-existed
peacefully with Getty Oil's operations. The sprinklers could roll over the 4–
foot high wellheads. However, when pressure in the field decreased, Getty
Oil put some of the wells on pumpjacks, mechanical pumping units over 20
feet high. The wheeled sprinkler system was doomed and with it, the
farmer's livelihood. The court in *Getty Oil Co. v. Jones*, 470 S.W.2d 618
(Tex. 1971) held:

> [W]here there is an existing use by the surface owner which will
> otherwise be precluded or impaired, and where under the established
> practices in the industry there are alternatives available to the lessee
> whereby the minerals can be recovered, the rules of reasonable usage
> of the surface may require the adoption of the alternative by the lessee.
> *Id.* at 622.

   Because other operators in the area were putting their pumping units
in underground pits or were using smaller electric pumps at an additional
cost of just $12,000 per well, the lessee was required to accommodate the
farmer's pre-existing use. Both crops and oil would continue to be produced. *See also, Gerrity Oil & Gas Corp. v. Magness*, 946 P.2d 913 (Colo.
1997) (adopting accommodation doctrine as gas wells proliferated in populous counties).

   Query: If no such reasonable alternative existed, who would win this
case?

   In later cases, the court narrowed the surface owner's protection under
the accommodation doctrine: the lessee could never be forced to go off the
leased premises to develop an alternative that would mitigate damage to
the surface estate overlying the lease, regardless of how reasonable this
alternative was. *Sun Oil v. Whitaker*, 483 S.W.2d 808 (Tex. 1972). Directional drilling from off-lease surfaces is widely practiced in offshore
production and onshore in the Arctic. Several wells are clustered in a
central spot and then the wells, rather than being drilled straight down, are
directionally drilled to radiate out to distant parts of the reservoir, often a
mile and sometimes 5 miles from the central platform. This type of drilling
significantly decreases surface impacts and reduces the number of expensive offshore platforms required in deep water. However, under Texas law,
the accommodation doctrine cannot stretch so far as to force a lessee to

seek a surface location adjacent to a leased farm from which the lessee could drill directionally and bottom the well under the farm. Many leases on federal and state lands do have "no surface occupancy" restrictions in environmentally sensitive or scenic areas and these lease stipulations require directional drilling from nonrestricted surface sites.

Query: If the town where Grimes owned his small house did not have a drilling ordinance, who would win in the facts in *Grimes v. Goodman Drilling supra* under the accommodation doctrine?

3. ***Surface damages acts***. Many farming and ranching states (but not Texas) have passed surface damages acts that require the mineral operator to pay for the loss of use of the surface. While the common law has no such compensation requirement, operators almost always offer surface owners a pre-set schedule of payments for each well site or rod of pipeline laid on the land; the payments are minimal compared to the cost of drilling. If the surface owner refuses to accept the payments, the common law allows the operator to proceed without paying anything. Surface damages acts require the operator to give the surface owner adequate notice of the commencement of drilling operations and compensation for actual damages from the drilling regardless of fault. The types of damages are often listed, such as loss of crops, lost land value, and lost use of the surface or any surface improvements. Some acts require the operator to pay damages for groundwater contamination from drilling. *See generally*, Andrew Miller, Comment: A Journey Through Mineral Estate Dominance, the Accommodation Doctrine and Beyond, 40 Hous. L. Rev. 461 (2003). These statutes have been sustained against challenges that they are an unconstitutional taking of the mineral estate owner's rights.

4. ***Surface development statutes.*** Some states, particularly those with growing populations of both people and well sites near major cities (like Houston and Dallas), have enacted statutes that offer some protection from backyard wells to housing developments. *E.g.,* in Texas, the surface developer in certain populated counties can bind the mineral owner to plats designed by the surface owner to accommodate the residential community. Tex. Nat. Res. Code §§ 92.001–92.007 (Vernon 2003). The purpose of the statute is "to assure proper and orderly development of both the mineral and land resources of this state." The surface owner of a tract of land (no more than 640 acres in size) can create a "qualified subdivision" by securing conservation commission approval of a plat of the subdivision and filing the plat with the county clerk. The plat must contain an oil and gas operations site for each separate 80 acres in the subdivision, with access roads and pipeline easements located for these sites. The operations site is an area of two or more acres, large enough to fit a drilling rig and its accompanying facilities. If the commission approves the plat, the mineral interest owners may use only the surface areas designated as operations sites and access easements. The commission will not approve the plat unless it finds that the application ensures that the mineral resources of the subdivisions can be "fully and effectively exploited." Thus, the commission may approve more than one well site for each 80 acres.

This type of statute requires mineral owners on undeveloped land to have considerable foresight in judging what drillsites and easements might be necessary in the future. Two drillsites on 160 acres might be enough for the development of gas, but not for oil. Two acres per site may be adequate for shallow drilling but not for deep drilling. If the mineral owner has not yet leased the land to an operator, the mineral owner is unlikely to be knowledgeable about the requirements for effective exploitation of the oil and gas in the future. If these owners do not obtain experts to testify at the commission hearing on the plat, the commission may approve a plat that makes mineral development difficult and costly. 2 Smith & Weaver, *supra*, § 9.2.

The city of Fort Worth, Texas is a metropolis of 1.6 million people overlying the Barnett Shale formation holding 27 TCF of gas. Centurion, a residential developer planning an 8,900–home community on a severed surface near Fort Worth, negotiated with Devon Energy for 18 months over ways to accommodate the oil and gas development. Centurion originally wanted to build baseball diamonds where the planned 4–acre well sites would be located, but switched to soccer fields which can more easily be disassembled and reconstructed during the drilling operations. Centurion will also plant trees with roots in metal baskets that can be pulled up and moved and then put back. Russell Gold, Drilling for Gas Faces a Sizable Hurdle: Fort Worth, Wall St. J. Apr. 29, 2005, at A1.

5. ***Other statutes.*** Because of the boom in drilling in recent years in response to high oil and gas prices, affected states have enacted a variety of statutes. For example, in Colorado in January 2005, a statute gave authority to surface owners to request that the Colorado Oil and Gas Conservation Commission conduct an onsite inspection where a proposed well had been applied for. The statute requires that the surface owner and operator conduct good faith consultations, but if they are unable to agree, the surface owner can trigger a request for inspection to determine if the proposed drill site is reasonably located, given the surface uses on the tract. The inspection does not address surface owner compensation or property value diminution. The purpose of the inspection is to determine if technical or operational conditions of approval should be attached to the drilling permit to mitigate environmental, health, safety or welfare concerns, including: visual or aesthetic impacts, moving the access road, controlling noxious weeds, muffling motors or installing sound barriers, watering roads to reduce dust, analyzing water samples and monitoring wells, sampling for gas that might be collecting in residential crawl spaces, installing fences, and limiting drilling to seasonal periods when wildlife impacts are minimized. Any conditions must be cost-effective, technically feasible and prevent waste, but the commission cannot require an operator to use directional drilling or "otherwise compromise its reasonable geologic and petroleum engineering considerations." Colorado Oil & Gas Conservation Commission, Policy for Onsite Inspection (2005), implementing 2 Colo. Code Regs. 401–1, Sec. 201 (2005). In earlier legislation, Colorado required that mineral estate owners be given 30 days notice of impending applications for surface plats or similar land use classification. See Jean Feriancek,

Competing Mineral and Surface Development—One State's Struggle, 17 Natural Res. & Env't 36 (Summer 2002). A thorough survey of surface use issues, with a useful bibliography of cases on point, appears in Donald N. Zillman, The Common Law of Access and Surface Use in Oil, Gas and Mining, 42 Rocky Mtn. Min. L. J. 117 (2005).

It is not clear under principles of federalism and the Commerce Clause whether surface-protective state acts such as these apply to federal lease-holders whose operations are located on privately owned surface land. Perhaps this explains some of the problems discussed in the next sections.

2. Split Estates: Who Owns Coalbed Methane?

a. ON PUBLIC LANDS

As noted in the Oil Chapter, much of the land in the Western states is owned by the federal government. The U.S. Forest Service ("USFS") in the Department of Agriculture and the Bureau of Land Management ("BLM") in the Department of Interior have the authority to manage millions of acres of land for multiple uses: recreation, grazing, timber, wildlife conservation, mining, and oil and gas development. The BLM and USFS manage their lands though resource management plans that classify which areas of land in a particular region can be used for which of the multiple purposes authorized by the Federal Land Policy and Management Act or the National Forest Management Act. The land use planning task is daunting: the BLM has 162 resource management plans to review, implement and update, governing 262 million acres of land and 700 million acres of subsurface minerals. The plans are updated every 15 years or so. Much of this land is split-estate land. Federal minerals underlie private surface lands on 57 million acres. Many land acts passed by Congress granted the surface to farmers and ranchers, but reserved the minerals to the federal government, as you will see in the upcoming *Southern Ute* case. Thus, the surface owner is subject to the government's dominant mineral estate, and a federal lessee acquires this same dominance, absent any other laws or contractual stipulations in the federal leases. James J. O'Malley & Kendor P. Jones, Chained Gates and No Trespassing Signs: Dealing with Landowners in a Brave New World, 51 Rocky Mtn. Min. L. Inst., ch. 7 (forthcoming 2005).

In other instances, the reverse situation occurs: the government owns the surface, but private parties own the underlying minerals. The Padre Island National Seashore in Texas is one such example. If the government completely forbids access to or development of the underlying privately owned oil and gas, would this be a taking? *See* Miller Bros. v. Department of Natural Resources, 513 N.W.2d 217 (Mich. App. 994) (finding a taking); *Cane Tennessee, Inc. v. United States*, 60 Fed. Cl. 694 (2004) (royalty owners in a tract designated as unsuitable for mining who had no other interests in nearby lands from which they could derive payments must be compensated for a taking). Would there be a taking if the government required drillers to do directional drilling from barges near the shore rather than on the public beach where vacation-goers relax? On Padre Island, several wells have been drilled on the seashore. The drivers of the operators' heavy equipment trucks are given "turtle awareness training" to avoid injury to endangered sea turtles and their eggs. Many other conditions also apply to the operation. Blaine Harden, They Brake for Turtles in Padre Island Park, New York Times, Dec. 1, 2002, at 25.

Disputes seldom arise over the ownership of conventional oil and gas. These two resources belong to the mineral estate owner, usually as a matter of law. However, the courts in many states have had to settle major litigation over the ownership of other resources which completely destroy the surface during the extraction process. Oil and gas wells can co-exist, albeit not often peacefully, with other surface uses, but a stripmining operation for coal or an open pit mine for copper cannot. Many states, like Texas, developed a rule to determine ownership of these hard minerals that greatly favored the surface owner. If the deed which severed the two estates was silent about which minerals were included in the mineral severance, then the courts applied the "surface destruction" test to determine the ownership of the resource. If extracting the resource (coal, uranium, iron ore, etc.) would destroy the surface, then the courts assumed that the parties could not have intended the mineral estate owner to own it. No surface owner would have bargained for a worthless estate. Therefore, the surface owners of East Texas own vast amounts of low-grade coal called lignite which is stripmined and used in power plants, even though everyone may think of coal as a "mineral." Smith & Weaver, 1 Texas Law of Oil & Gas § 3.6 (2004). (Of course, if the parties expressly granted lignite or coal as a defined mineral in the deed, the courts follow the intent of the parties.)

Coalbed methane production has soared so much in the United States (with a boost from very significant tax credits) that it is no longer unconventional to produce it. Its ownership in a split-estate situation has been much litigated, however, even in the U.S. Supreme Court, as the following case illustrates. [Most citations have been deleted from the case.]

Amoco Production Co. v. Southern Ute Indian Tribe

526 U.S. 865 (1999).

■ KENNEDY, J. Land patents issued pursuant to the Coal Lands Acts of 1909 and 1910 conveyed to the patentee the land and everything in it, except the coal, which was reserved to the United States. Coal Lands Act of 1909 (1909 Act), 35 Stat. 844, 30 U.S.C. § 81; Coal Lands Act of 1910 (1910 Act), ch. 318, 36 Stat. 583, 30 U.S.C. §§ 83–85. The United States Court of Appeals for the Tenth Circuit determined that the reservation of "coal" includes gas found within the coal formation, commonly referred to as coalbed methane gas (CBM gas). *See* 151 F.3d 1251, 1256 (1998) (en banc). We granted certiorari, 119 S.Ct. 921 (1999), and now reverse.

I

During the second half of the nineteenth century, Congress sought to encourage the settlement of the West by providing land in fee simple absolute to homesteaders who entered and cultivated tracts of a designated size for a period of years. *See, e.g.*, 1862 Homestead Act, 12 Stat. 392; 1877 Desert Land Act, ch. 107, 19 Stat. 377, as amended, 43 U.S.C. §§ 321–323. Public lands classified as valuable for coal were exempted from entry under the general land-grant statutes and instead were made available for purchase under the 1864 [and 1873] Coal Lands Act[s], which set a maximum limit of 160 acres on individual entry and minimum prices of $10 to $20 an acre. Lands purchased under these early Coal Lands Acts—like lands patented under the Homestead Acts—were conveyed to the entryman in fee simple absolute, with no reservation of any part of the coal or mineral estate to the United States. The coal mined from the lands purchased under the Coal Lands Acts and from other reserves fueled the Industrial Revolution.

At the turn of the twentieth century, however, a coal famine struck the West. *See* Hearings on Coal Lands and Coal–Land Laws of the United States before the House Committee on Public Lands, 59th Cong., 2d Sess., 11–13 (1906) (testimony of Edgar E. Clark, Interstate Commerce Commissioner). At the same time, evidence of widespread fraud in the administration of federal coal lands came to light. Lacking the resources to make an independent assessment of the coal content of each individual land tract, the Department of the Interior in classifying public lands had relied for the most part on the affidavits of entrymen. *Watt v. Western Nuclear, Inc.*, 462 U.S. 36, 48, and n. 9 (1983). Railroads and other coal interests had exploited the system to avoid paying for coal lands and to evade acreage restrictions by convincing individuals to falsify affidavits, acquire lands for homesteading, and then turn the land over to them. C. Mayer & G. Riley, Public Domain, Private Dominion 117–118 (1985).

In 1906, President Theodore Roosevelt responded to the perceived crisis by withdrawing 64 million acres of public land thought to contain coal from disposition under the public land laws. *Western Nuclear*, 462 U.S., at 48–49. As a result, even homesteaders who had entered and worked the land in good faith lost the opportunity to make it their own unless they could prove to the land office that the land was not valuable for coal.

President Roosevelt's order outraged homesteaders and western interests, and Congress struggled for the next three years to construct a compromise that would reconcile the competing interests of protecting settlers and managing federal coal lands for the public good. President Roosevelt and others urged Congress to begin issuing limited patents that would sever the surface and mineral estates and allow for separate disposal of each. Although various bills were introduced in Congress that would have severed the estates—some of which would have reserved "natural gas" as well as "coal" to the United States—none was enacted. . . .

Finally, Congress passed the Coal Lands Act of 1909, which authorized the Federal Government, for the first time, to issue limited land patents. In contrast to the broad reservations of mineral rights proposed in the failed bills, however, the 1909 Act provided for only a narrow reservation. The Act authorized issuance of patents to individuals who had already made good-faith agricultural entries onto tracts later identified as coal lands, but the issuance was to be subject to "a reservation to the United States of all coal in said lands, and the right to prospect for, mine, and remove the same." 30 U.S.C. § 81. The Act also permitted the patentee to "mine coal for use on the land for domestic purposes prior to the disposal by the United States of the coal deposit." *Ibid.* A similar Act in 1910 opened the remaining coal lands to new entry under the homestead laws, subject to the same reservation of coal to the United States. 30 U.S.C. §§ 83–85.

Among the lands patented to settlers under the 1909 and 1910 Acts were former reservation lands of the Southern Ute Indian Tribe, which the Tribe had ceded to the United States in 1880 in return for certain allotted lands provided for their settlement. In 1938, the United States restored to the Tribe, in trust, title to the ceded reservation lands still owned by the United States, including the reserved coal in lands patented under the 1909 and 1910 Acts. As a result, the Tribe now has equitable title to the coal in lands within its reservation settled by homesteaders under the 1909 and 1910 Acts.

We are advised that over 20 million acres of land were patented under the 1909 and 1910 Acts and that the lands—including those lands in which the Tribe owns the coal—contain large quantities of CBM gas. At the time the Acts were passed, CBM gas had long been considered a dangerous waste product of coal mining. By the 1970's, however, it was apparent that CBM gas could be a significant energy resource, *see* Duel & Kimm, Coalbed Gas: A Source of Natural Gas, Oil & Gas J., June 16, 1975, p. 47, and, in the shadow of the Arab oil embargo, the Federal Government began to encourage the immediate production of CBM gas through grants, *see* 42 U.S.C. §§ 5901–5915 (1994 ed. and Supp. III), and substantial tax credits, *see* 26 U.S.C. § 29 (1994 ed. and Supp. III).

Commercial development of CBM gas was hampered, however, by uncertainty over its ownership. "In order to expedite the development of this energy source," the Solicitor of the Department of the Interior issued a 1981 opinion concluding that the reservation of coal to the United States in the 1909 and 1910 Acts did not encompass CBM gas. *See* Ownership of and Right to Extract Coalbed Gas in Federal Coal Deposits, 88 Interior Dec. 538, 539. In reliance on the Solicitor's 1981 opinion, oil and gas companies entered into leases to produce CBM gas with individual landowners holding title under 1909 and 1910 Act patents to some 200,000 acres in which the Tribe owns the coal.

In 1991, the Tribe brought suit in Federal District Court against petitioners, the royalty owners and producers under the oil and gas leases covering that land, and the federal agencies and officials responsible for the administration of lands held in trust for the Tribe. The Tribe sought, inter alia, a declaration that Congress' reservation of coal in the 1909 and 1910 Acts extended to CBM gas, so that the Tribe—not the successors in interest of the land patentees—owned the CBM gas.

The District Court granted summary judgment for the defendants, holding that the plain meaning of "coal" is the "solid rock substance" used as fuel, which does not include CBM gas. 874 F. Supp. 1142, 1154 (D.Colo.1995). On appeal, a panel of the Court of Appeals reversed. 119 F.3d 816, 819 (C.A.10 1997). The court then granted rehearing en banc on the question whether the term "coal" in the 1909 and 1910 Acts "unambiguously excludes or includes CBM." 151 F.3d, at 1256. Over a dissenting opinion by Judge Tacha, joined by two other judges, the en banc court agreed with the panel. *Ibid.* The court held that the term "coal" was ambiguous. It invoked the interpretive canon that ambiguities in land grants should be resolved in favor of the sovereign and concluded that the coal reservation encompassed CBM gas.

The United States did not petition for, or participate in, the rehearing en banc. Instead, it filed a supplemental brief explaining that the Solicitor of the Interior was reconsidering the 1981 Solicitor's opinion in light of the panel's decision. On the day the Government's response to petitioners' certiorari petition was due, the Solicitor of the Interior withdrew the 1981 opinion in a one-line order. The United States now supports the Tribe's position that CBM gas is coal reserved by the 1909 and 1910 Acts.

II

We begin our discussion as the parties did, with a brief overview of the chemistry and composition of coal. Coal is a heterogeneous, noncrystalline sedimentary rock composed primarily of carbonaceous materials. *See, e.g.,* Gorbaty & Larsen, Coal Structure and Reactivity, in 3 Encyclopedia of Physical Science and Technology 437 (R. Meyers ed., 2d ed.1992). It is formed over millions of years from decaying plant material that settles on the bottom of swamps and is converted by microbiological processes into peat. Van Krevelen, Coal 90 (3d ed.1993). Over time, the resulting peat beds are buried by sedimentary deposits. As the beds sink deeper and deeper into the earth's crust, the peat is transformed by chemical reactions which increase the carbon content of the fossilized plant material. The process in which peat transforms into coal is referred to as coalification.

The coalification process generates methane and other gases. Because coal is porous, some of that gas is retained in the coal. CBM gas exists in the coal in three basic states: as free gas; as gas dissolved in the water in coal; and as gas "adsorbed" on the solid surface of the coal, that is, held to the surface by weak forces called van der Waals forces. These are the same three states or conditions in which gas is stored in other rock formations. Because of the large surface area of coal pores, however, a much higher proportion of the gas is adsorbed on the surface of coal than is adsorbed in other rock. When pressure on the coalbed is decreased, the gas in the coal formation escapes. As a result, CBM gas is released from coal as the coal is mined and brought to the surface.

III

While the modern science of coal provides a useful backdrop for our discussion and is consistent with our ultimate disposition, it does not answer the question presented to us. The question is not whether, given what scientists know today, it makes sense to regard CBM gas as a constituent of coal but whether Congress so regarded it in 1909 and 1910. In interpreting statutory mineral reservations like the one at issue here, we have emphasized that Congress "was dealing with a practical subject in a practical way" and that it intended the terms of the reservation to be understood in "their ordinary and popular sense." *Burke v. Southern Pac. R.R. Co.*, 234 U.S. 669 (1914) (rejecting "scientific test" for determining whether a reservation of "mineral lands" included "petroleum lands"); *see also Perrin v. United States* 444 U.S. 37, 42 (1979) ("[U]nless otherwise defined, words will be interpreted as taking their ordinary, contemporary, common meaning" at the time Congress enacted the statute). We are persuaded that the common conception of coal at the time Congress passed the 1909 and 1910 Acts was the solid rock substance that was the country's primary energy resource.

A

At the time the Acts were passed, most dictionaries defined coal as the solid fuel resource. For example, one contemporary dictionary defined coal as a "solid and more or less distinctly stratified mineral, varying in color from dark-brown to black, brittle, combustible, and used as fuel, not fusible without decomposition and very insoluble." 2 Century Dictionary and Cyclopedia 1067 (1906). *See also* American Dictionary of the English Language 244 (N. Webster 1889) (defining "coal" as a "black, or brownish black, solid, combustible substance, consisting, like charcoal, mainly of carbon, but more compact"); 2 New English Dictionary on Historical Principles 549 (J. Murray ed. 1893) (defining coal as a "mineral, solid, hard, opaque, black, or blackish, found in seams or strata in the earth, and largely used as fuel"); Webster's New International Dictionary of the English Language 424 (W. Harris & F. Allen eds.1916) (defining coal as a "black, or brownish black, solid, combustible mineral substance").

In contrast, dictionaries of the day defined CBM gas—then called "marsh gas," "methane," or "fire-damp"—as a distinct substance, a gas "contained in" or "given off by" coal, but not as coal itself. *See, e.g.,* 3 Century Dictionary and Cyclopedia 2229 (1906) (defining "fire-damp" as "[t]he gas contained in coal, often given off by it in large quantities, and exploding, on ignition, when mixed with atmospheric air"; noting that "[f]ire-damp is a source of great danger to life in coal-mines") As these dictionary definitions suggest, the common understanding of coal in 1909 and 1910 would not have encompassed CBM gas, both because it is a gas rather than a solid mineral and because it was understood as a distinct substance that escaped from coal as the coal was mined, rather than as a part of the coal itself.

B

As a practical matter, moreover, it is clear that, by reserving coal in the 1909 and 1910 Act patents, Congress intended to reserve only the solid rock fuel that was mined, shipped throughout the country, and then burned to power the Nation's railroads, ships, and factories. In contrast to natural gas, which was not yet an important source of fuel at the turn of the century, coal was the primary energy for the Industrial Revolution. *See, e.g.,* D. Yergin, The Prize 543 (1991).

As the history recounted in Part I, *supra,* establishes, Congress passed the 1909 and 1910 Acts to address concerns over the short supply, mismanagement, and fraudulent acquisition of this solid rock fuel resource. Rejecting broader proposals, Congress chose a narrow reservation of the resource that would address the exigencies of the crisis at hand without unduly burdening the rights of homesteaders or impeding the settlement of the West.

It is evident that Congress viewed CBM gas not as part of the solid fuel resource it was attempting to conserve and manage but as a dangerous waste product, which escaped from coal as the coal was mined. Congress was well aware by 1909 that the natural gas found in coal formations was released during coal mining and posed a serious threat to mine safety. Explosions in coal mines sparked by CBM gas occurred with distressing frequency in the late nineteenth and early twentieth centuries. Congress was also well aware that the CBM gas needed to be vented to the greatest extent possible. Almost 20 years prior to the passage of the 1909 and 1910 Acts, Congress had enacted the first federal coal-mine-safety law which, among other provisions, prescribed specific ventilation standards for coal mines of a certain depth "so as to dilute and render harmless ... the noxious or poisonous gases." 1891 Territorial Mine Inspection Act, § 6, 26 Stat. 1105

That CBM gas was considered a dangerous waste product which escaped from coal, rather than part of the valuable coal fuel itself, is also confirmed by the fact that coal companies venting the gas to prevent its accumulation in the mines made no attempt to capture or preserve it. The more gas that escaped from the coal once it was brought to the surface, the better it was for the mining companies because it decreased the risk of a dangerous gas buildup during transport and storage.

* * *

There is some evidence of limited and sporadic exploitation of CBM gas as a fuel prior to the passage of the 1909 and 1910 Acts. *See, e.g.,* E. Craig & M. Myers, Ownership of Methane Gas in Coalbeds, 24 Rocky Mt. Min. L. Inst. 767, 768 (1978) ("As early as 1746, methane was being drained from an English coal mine through pipes and used for heating"); *see also U.S. Steel Corp. v. Hoge,* 503 Pa. 140, 146, 468 A.2d 1380, 1383 (1983) (noting that as early as 1900, "certain wells were drilled [into coalbeds in Pennsylvania, which] produced coalbed gas"). It seems unlikely, though, that Congress considered this limited drilling for CBM gas. To the extent Congress had an awareness of it, there is every reason to think it viewed the extraction of CBM gas as drilling for natural gas, not mining coal.

That distinction is significant because the question before us is not whether Congress would have thought that CBM gas had some fuel value, but whether Congress considered it part of the coal fuel. When it enacted the 1909 and 1910 Acts, Congress did not reserve all minerals or energy resources in the lands. It reserved only coal, and then only in lands that were specifically identified as valuable for coal. It chose not to reserve oil, natural gas, or any other known or potential energy resources.

The limited nature of the 1909 and 1910 Act reservations is confirmed by subsequent congressional enactments. When Congress wanted to reserve gas rights that might yield valuable fuel, it did so in explicit terms. In 1912, for example, Congress enacted a statute that reserved "oil and gas" in Utah lands. Act of Aug. 24, 1912, 37 Stat. 496. . . .

C

Respondents contend that Congress did not reserve the solid coal but convey the CBM gas because the resulting split estate would be impractical and would make mining the coal difficult because the miners would have to capture and preserve the CBM gas that escaped during mining. We doubt Congress would have given much consideration to these problems, however, because—as noted above—it does not appear to have given consideration to the possibility that CBM gas would one day be a profitable energy source developed on a large scale.

It may be true, nonetheless, that the right to mine the coal implies the right to release gas incident to coal mining where it is necessary and reasonable to do so. The right to dissipate the CBM gas where reasonable and necessary to mine the coal does not, however, imply the ownership of the gas in the first instance. Rather, it simply reflects the established common-law right of the owner of one mineral estate to use, and even damage, a neighboring estate as necessary and reasonable to the extraction of his own minerals. *See, e.g., Williams v. Gibson*, 84 Ala. 228, 4 So. 350 (1888); Rocky Mountain Mineral Foundation, 6 American Law of Mining § 200.04 (2d ed.1997). Given that split estates were already common at the time the 1909 and 1910 Acts were passed, *see, e.g., Chartiers Block Coal Co. v. Mellon*, 152 Pa. 286, 25 A. 597 (1893), and that the common law has proved adequate to the task of resolving the resulting conflicts between estates, there is no reason to think that the prospect of a split estate would have deterred Congress from reserving only the coal.

Were a case to arise in which there are two commercially valuable estates and one is to be damaged in the course of extracting the other, a dispute might result, but it could be resolved in the ordinary course of negotiation or adjudication. That is not the issue before us, however. The question is one of ownership, not of damage or injury.

In all events, even were we to construe the coal reservation to encompass CBM gas, a split estate would result. The United States concedes (and the Tribe does not dispute) that once the gas originating in the coal formation migrates to surrounding rock formations it belongs to the natural gas, rather than the coal, estate. Natural gas from other sources may also exist in the lands at issue. Including the CBM gas in the coal reservation would, therefore, create a split gas estate that would be at least as difficult to administer as a split coal/CBM gas estate. If CBM gas were reserved with the coal estate, those developing the natural gas resources in the land would have to allocate the gas between the natural gas and coal estates based on some assessment of how much had migrated outside the coal itself. There is no reason to think Congress would have been more concerned about the creation of a split coal/CBM gas estate than the creation of a split gas estate.

Because we conclude that the most natural interpretation of "coal" as used in the 1909 and 1910 Acts does not encompass CBM gas, we need not consider the applicability of the canon that ambiguities in land grants are construed in favor of the sovereign or the competing canons relied on by petitioners.

The judgment of the Court of Appeals is reversed.

It is so ordered.

■ JUSTICE BREYER took no part in the consideration or decision of this case.

■ GINSBURG, J. I would affirm the judgment below substantially for the reasons stated by the Court of Appeals and the federal respondents. As the Court recognizes, in 1909 and 1910 coalbed methane gas (CBM) was a liability. Congress did not contemplate that the surface owner would be responsible for it. More likely, Congress would have assumed that the coal owner had dominion over, and attendant responsibility for, CBM. I do not find it clear that Congress understood dominion would shift if and when the liability became an asset. I would therefore apply the canon that ambiguities in land grants are construed in favor of the sovereign. *See Watt v. Western Nuclear, Inc.*, 462 U.S. 36, 59 (1983) (noting established rule that land grants are construed favorably to the Government, that nothing passes except what is conveyed in clear language, and that if there are doubts they are resolved for the Government, not against it).■

NOTES AND COMMENTS

1. An estimated $200 million of coalbed methane was located underneath the Ute land (valued in the $2/MCF price range of the 1990s). The holding of this case will apply to another 16 million acres of land with similar split ownership.

b. ON PRIVATE LANDS

CBM can exist as free gas in the macropores (the fractures) of a coal seam, but most CBM adheres to the micropores within the internal structure of the coal itself. The pressure exerted on the CBM trapped in the coal is greater than atmospheric pressure. Mining of the coal releases CBM in a two-step process: CBM is released from the coal micropores and into the surrounding macropores; the CBM then proceeds from the macropores to the mine surface following a decrease in pressure. Deeper coal beds are subject to higher pressure and temperature, and will therefore have a higher CBM content. There are several techniques for CBM production. One method simply employs traditional drilling technology to extract CBM from the coal bed through vertical wells independent from any mining of the coal itself. Other methods for CBM production have been developed to extract the gas in conjunction with the coal mining operation. Where the gas yield is insufficient, hydrofracturing is used. This process involves injection of pressurized fluid into the coalbed to enhance the fracture system, which in turn allows the release of more CBM into the borehole.

Another method is used with the longwall mining of coal. CBM can be extracted from vertical holes called "gob wells," which drain CBM from the "gob zone" (the area of fractured rock created when the overburden caves into the unsupported, mined-out area). Large quantities of CBM are often released from the collapse and fracture of the overburden into the resulting rubble creating the gob zone. To ventilate these gob areas, vertical boreholes are drilled in advance of mining. Production of gob gases therefore begins shortly after the overburden collapses. Gob gases often contain methane released from several different sources: (1) CBM released from residual coal in the primary seam, from thin and unmineable coal seams in the roof and floor, or from separate mine workings nearby; (2) strata gases that escaped from the coal seams and became trapped in non-coal strata; and (3) natural gas that originated in non-coal strata.

While *Amoco v. Southern Ute Indian Tribe supra* decided the ownership of CBM under federal land patents, the courts have often had to decide the same issue under common law rules governing private deeds. The common law offers a number of choices:

i.   CBM is Gas. Under this rule, CBM is defined as a gas within the ordinary meaning of the term as used in standard mineral conveyances. *See, e.g.,* In re Hillsborough Holdings Corp., 207 Bankr. 299 (1997). One objection to this approach is that coal owners must vent the CBM for safety reasons when mining, and they fear suits by gas owners will prevent them from this venting. How did the justices in the *Amoco v. Ute* case envision these types of problems to be solved?

ii. CBM is Coal. Because CBM is physically intermixed with the coal itself, it is included within any grant or reservation of coal rights. *See, e.g.,* U.S. Steel Corp. v. Hoge, 503 Pa. 140, 468 A.2d 1380 (1983) (coalbed owner owns the CBM intermixed in the coal but loses ownership once the CBM migrates out of the coal bed into adjoining strata). This practical problem with the rule arises: Much of the CBM released during coal mining does not come from the actual coal seam being mined, but instead comes from the overburden or other strata that fracture and collapse as a result of the mining operation. Ownership of CBM based on ownership of the coal would not extend to any CBM that migrated from other non-coal strata, so gob gas would have to be apportioned between the coalbed owner and the owner of the surrounding strata.

iii. Priority at Severance. Some commentators suggest that competing claims between coal and gas owners should be resolved under a "first in time" theory, whereby rights accrue in the order in which the competing deeds or leases were created. Others argue that priority of severance leads to arbitrary results.

iv. Analysis of the Parties' Intent. This reasoning rejects strict and simple rules such as "CBM is gas" and looks to other factors beyond priority at severance. The focus is on the specific language of the deed or lease, the state of knowledge or opinion regarding CBM at the time of drafting, and any other evidence of intent at the time of drafting. The court looks only at the instant transaction between the parties, a labor-intensive approach for both lawyers and judges, but perhaps one which best respects contract principles. *See e.g, Newman v. RAG Wyoming Land Co.*, 53 P.3d 540 (Wyo.2002); *McGee v. Caballo Coal Co.*, 69 P.3d 908 (Wyo. 2003); *Hickman v. Groves*, 71 P.3d 256 (Wyo. 2003); and *Caballo Coal Co. v. Fidelity E&P Co.*, 84 P.3d 311 (Wyo. 2004). Do you understand why the court had to decide four cases within a two-year period under this fourth approach?

v. Successive Ownership. Under this rule, coal owners have title to the CBM absorbed within the coal, but would not retain title to any CBM that escapes into other strata or that enters the gob zone as a result of longwall mining (since the CBM is no longer intermixed with the coal). In *Hoge, supra*, the Pennsylvania Supreme Court may have implicitly approved this rule. Would coal owners or gas owners be happy with this rule if gob gas is a major portion of the CBM released during longwall mining?

vi. Mutual Simultaneous Rights. Under this rule, gas owners have title to CBM, but coal owners have the right to capture it during the coal mining process as an exercise of the coal owner's "incidental mining rights," *i.e.*, those rights that are reasonably necessary to facilitate extraction of coal. The coal owner's right of capture is based on his need to ventilate the mines for safety purposes.

A survey of coalbed methane issues focused in the Appalachian area is contained in Elizabeth A. McClanahan, Coalbed Methane: Myths, Facts, and the Legends of Its History and the Legislative and Regulatory Climate Into the 21st Century, 48 Okla. L. Rev. 471 (1995). A Western focus on CBM issues appears in Kurt M. Petersen, Coalbed Gas Development in the Western United States: Legal Issues and Operational Concerns, 7th Ann. Rocky Mtn Min. L. Inst., ch. 13 (1991). Legislation at both the federal and state level has been enacted to create a temporary bypass of ownership issues while the courts resolve the dispute. The acts allow CBM production via "forced pooling." See 42 U.S.C. § 13368; Va. Code Ann. §§ 45.1–361–ff; W.Va. Code §§ 22–21–ff; and Jeff L. Lewin, Coalbed Methane: Recent Court Decisions Leave Ownership "Up in the Air," But New Federal and State Legislation Should Facilitate Production, 96 W.Va. L. Rev. 577 (1994).

c. WHO OWNS DEPLETED RESERVOIRS?

Depleted oil and gas reservoirs are very valuable pieces of rock, even though little native gas is left in them. They are the least expensive way of storing natural gas closer to population centers to meet the peak demand for gas during winter cold snaps (for space heating) or summer heat waves (for electricity generation to power air conditioners). There are over 400 underground gas storage reservoirs in the U.S.—a big business indeed, and one crucial to deregulated electricity markets as you will see later.

In addition, these reservoirs are now being viewed as storage containers for the permanent sequestration of carbon dioxide (CO_2), the main greenhouse gas. In mid–2005, four energy companies, led by BP announced a plan to build the world's largest carbon-free power plant near the North Sea in Scotland. The 350–megawatt power plant would ship CO_2 to a depleted North Sea oil field. See also, Intergovernmental Panel of Climate Change, Special Report on Carbon Dioxide Capture and Storage (2005), available at www.climatescience.gov. The Carbon Sequestration Leadership Forum is an international effort of many nations to cooperate in CO_2 capture and storage projects. See www.fossil.energy.gov/programs/sequestration/.

When the land containing the depleted reservoir is a split estate, does the surface owner or mineral estate owner own this valuable storage space? To obtain the right to produce the original gas, the developer bargained with the mineral owner. Once production of the native gas has ceased, does this lessee have any rights to continue to use the reservoir in a new way as a storage vessel? What happens to an oil and gas lease when production ends? (See Chapter 6(A)(3)). If a new developer wants to lease the space for storage, with whom should he or she negotiate? Where states have passed eminent domain statutes allowing utilities to condemn underground reservoirs for gas storage, which split-estate owner should receive the payments?

If the analogy to depleted underground coal mines is apt, the surface owner will probably win. The empty tunnels and shafts left by the mining operation typically will revert back to the surface owner, perhaps to rent for mushroom growing, tourism, or secure data storage. However, the tiny pore spaces in a depleted gas reservoir are hardly like the tunnels left in coal mining. Since the pore spaces are so closely related to the enjoyment and exploitation of the mineral estate, should ownership go to the mineral owner? Should the depleted reservoir rock be considered a unique "mineral" in and of itself? See John Lyckman, Comment, The Underground Natural Gas Storage and Conservation Act of 1977: A Threshold Issue, 29 Baylor L. Rev. 1066 (1977) (yes, especially since it would not destroy or seriously impair the surface estate to so hold). Surprisingly little case law exists on this point, but most commentators appear to think that the surface owner is the proper owner, under the following reasoning:

> Unlike pressure maintenance ..., underground injections for storage purposes are not directly related to production. Indeed, they are usually not even associated with initial marketing [of the native gas], but with downstream activities more closely connected to final retail sales. From this perspective, it would seem that the right to store [nonnative] gas ... is roughly analogous to the right to open a service station, a right that belongs more properly to the surface estate than the mineral estate.

Smith & Weaver, 1 Texas Law of Oil and Gas § 2.1(B)(3) (2003).

3. COALBED METHANE EXTERNALITIES AND MINERAL DOMINANCE

Since 1989, CBM production has grown more than 1,700 percent in the United States. In Colorado alone, production went from 12 billion cubic feet in 1989 to about 500 BCF in 2003, more than a 40–fold increase (EIA data). CBM gas now makes up about 7% of U.S. gas production. Litigation over CBM on split estates has amounted to a virtual western World War III in the ferocity of the combatants: On the one side, the federal government as mineral owner, armed with a national energy policy aimed at more gas production from the Rockies. On the other side: ranchers, recreationists, homeowners and environmentalists, armed with an undying love for the blue skies and landscapes of rural areas of Montana, Wyoming, Utah and Colorado which is understandable to any visitor who has traveled there. Why has CBM development proved so much more contentious than conventional natural gas development which existed in some of these areas, relatively quietly for decades?

The environmental impacts of gas production are very similar to those for oil, except that gas does not spill. When a gas well blows out, the gas vents into the air or else burns. Gas mishaps mostly pose safety hazards to persons rather than pollution hazards to the environment. Many externalities of CBM production are similar to conventional oil and gas production including: road construction, drill pads, noisy pumps and compressors, air pollution, habitat disruption, and impaired vistas and solitude. However, CBM wells are not spaced at the center of 640–acre sections, as many gas wells are in conventional gas reservoirs. CBM wells are usually quite shallow—drilled to coal beds that are only 3,000 feet below the surface. (Drinking water wells are typically 200 to 400 feet deep.) The drilling takes only a few days to complete. The wells are often more closely spaced (on 40– or 80–acre spacing), so the surface impacts are more dense. For example, the 40,000 CBM wells planned in the draft 2002 EIS in Wyoming's Powder River Basin were accompanied by 17,000 miles of roads, 20,000 miles of pipelines and 5,300 miles of utility lines. Julie Ziegler, Gas Field Runs Afoul of EPA, Houston Chronicle, May 19, 2002, at 7D. Recently, operators in the Jonah field in Wyoming requested that the BLM approve "infill" drilling among existing wells spaced at 40–acres so that well density would increase to one well pad on 10 acres; a total of 3,100 more wells. Greenwire, Feb. 17, 2005. The draft EIS for the project noted that significant effects on wildlife habitat have already occurred from the 40–acre spacing. The BLM office said sage grouse have been declining in the Jonah field and elsewhere at least in part because of oil and gas activity, but the BLM was "doing what we can." The Biodiversity Conservation Alliance argued that the BLM should impose directional drilling from the 500 existing well pads, but the BLM office said this alternative would not save much land from human disturbance and impacts, so it would not be worth imposing. The operators have committed to various mitigation measures, including a fund to pay for off-site mitigation and are willing to consider other methods of "compensatory mitigation." *Id.* EnCana's operations will disturb 16,200 more acres; it has proposed to contribute $20 million for mitigation (such as revegetation and raptor nest enhancement) on 70,000 off-site acres. Greenwire, April 28, 2005.

Water production is the key, unique externality involved in CBM production in the semi-arid West, where water is more critical to the local economies than any other resource. Professor Gary Bryner has written an excellent article summarizing the externalities of CBM development in the Rockies, with accompanying recommendations for improved policies. Gary Bryner, Coalbed Methane Development: The Costs and Benefits of an Emerging Energy Resource, 43 Natural Res. J. 519 (2003). The following information comes from this article:

> CBM is not released from coal until the water pressure that traps it there is released. Thus, CBM drillers must first dewater the coal seams by producing large amounts of water from the coal bed, raising serious issues about groundwater depletion, contamination, and disposal of the produced water when it is separated from the methane. The following disposal methods are possible, from least costly to most costly:
>
> - Surface discharge that travels downstream and evaporates or sinks into the soil
> - Use for irrigation without treatment
> - Treatment for irrigation, livestock watering, drinking supplies, etc.
> - Containment in surface impoundments, some of which may be used by livestock
> - Atomizing the water and spraying it in the air for quick evaporation
> - Injection of good quality water into shallow fresh water aquifers
> - Deep injection of salty water
>
> Differences in water quality explain the very different disposal methods used in different regions. In the San Juan basin along the Colorado/New Mexico border, 99.9% of the briny water is injected back into the ground, as is typical with conventional wells. However, in the Powder River Basin in Wyoming, 99.9% of the water is discharged to the surface. The water from this basin is often useable for many purposes, such as dust control from construction and road traffic, irrigation, fish and wildlife, recreation, and freshwater aquifer recharge. Indeed, the quality of some produced water rivals that of your favorite store-bought bottled brand. But the tremendous quantities of it pose a challenge. Put simply, there are not enough cows, sheep, or people in Wyoming to drink or use the millions of gallons of released water. When the projected 51,000 CBM wells in this basin are all operating, about 700 million gallons of water a day will be produced

(enough for 45 million cows or 325 million sheep; the basin currently has only 500,000 of these animals).

The release of so much water into streams and rivers can cause erosion of ditches and banks and inundate the native vegetation. Salts may concentrate in the soil over time with evaporation and harm the soil. Stock ponds for livestock are useful, but the space they use takes land out of production. Water withdrawals from CBM development are so large that aquifer replenishment is a real concern. Some studies warn that by 2010, surface discharges of water will reach 1 billion gallons a day and recharging the aquifers will take more than 800 years, threatening the region's long-term water supply and growth prospects. The Final EIS for one round of development in the Powder River Basin more optimistically projected that by the year 2060, aquifer water levels would recover to within 10 to 50 feet of pre-CBM levels.■

NOTES AND COMMENTS

1. So many containment ponds have been built in some semi-arid, CBM areas that mosquitoes bearing the West Nile virus (a potentially fatal disease that can sicken and kill both people and animals) have become a health problem. Unlike irrigation ditches and seeps, the CBM ponds contain standing water all year round and are ideal breeding grounds for vast numbers of mosquitoes. The mosquitoes have spread the virus to the sage grouse which has been declining in such numbers that it is a candidate for the endangered species list. A BLM study found that about 90% of the sage grouse nesting near CBM ponds in one Wyoming County had died of West Nile, while none of the hens nesting away from them had the virus. The BLM's coalbed methane coordinator said that "It's something that we probably didn't consider as well as we should have." Julie Cart, Amid a Natural Gas Boom, West Nile Cases on the Rise, Los Angeles Times, June 6, 2004. If the sage grouse is put on the endangered species list, will this stop or slow CBM development? How are species "listed"? Most of the current CBM wells will be depleted in 20 years and plugged and abandoned. Will the sage grouse then come back?

2. The water quality regulations governing produced water from CBM wells are the same as discussed in other parts of this casebook, such as Chapter 6(F). The Clean Water Act requires NPDES permits to discharge the water into surface waters and these discharges must meet water quality standards. If reinjected, a Safe Drinking Water Act permit is required to assure that poor quality water does not contaminate drinking water aquifers. Methane migration into water supplies and to surface seeps that may spontaneously combust when exposed to air is more of a worry in CBM extraction than in conventional gas reservoirs because the CBM wells are so shallow.

3. The Western water law governing the rights to produce and use water is an entirely different body of law than that for water quality (rightly

meriting a full course of its own in many law schools). In many (but not all) Western states, the state allocates and prorates water among users, much like the oil and gas conservation commissions allocate oil and gas production among owners in a common field. (See Chapter 6(C)). The large amounts of produced water from CBM do not fit very well into either the groundwater or the surface water laws of the Western states. Prof. Bryner's article summarizes the major problems and makes recommendations. One recommendation addresses a basic issue: States should clarify who owns the produced water. This water does not come from a typical groundwater aquifer and so may not fit into the groundwater ownership laws. If developers are deemed to own it, he suggests that this will encourage them to invest in the large-scale collection, marketing and interstate transportation of clean CBM water to burgeoning cities (like Denver? as far as Phoenix?) whose populations are growing because of their access to sun, mountains, and unparalleled vistas. In August 2005, Anadarko announced that it was now producing enough CBM water to consider a large system of transporting it to another part of Wyoming to recharge an aquifer. The water is too clean to put into the Powder River, a muddy stream that is a rare example of a prairie river system harboring native species well-adapted to the murk. To date, most of the water has been impounded on the surface. Coalbed Methane Water Reinjection Gets New Look, AP, Aug. 7, 2005 (ECP Online).

4. Air pollution from hundreds of generators and compressors at drill sites, from increased road traffic due to an influx of workers in the area, and from heavy construction equipment and gas processing plants will impair the visibility in several national parks and on the Cheyenne Indian reservation when combined with emissions from already existing power plants and surface coal mines. The BLM moved forward with CBM development in Wyoming and Montana even though it had concluded that air pollution would cloud views at more than a dozen national parks and monuments, exceed federal air quality standards in several communities and cause acid rain to fall on mountain lakes. The EPA, National Park Service and Forest Service all expressed their concerns to BLM about the air quality in a "new industrial zone" of gas wells and service facilities.

Wyoming air quality officials have planned a large network of monitoring sensors to measure the air pollution in the CBM fields, but are not sure how the state will pay for it. The air pollution from the gas project, when combined with emissions from cars, coal mines and power plants is expected to diminish visibility at Mt. Rushmore for 26 days a year, at Yellowstone for 13 days a year, and on the Northern Cheyenne Indian Reservation for 92 days a year. BLM officials admitted they were under orders from Washington to approve the project quickly. Miguel Bustillo, It's Not All Blue Skies for Drilling Project, Los Angeles Times, Jan. 29, 2005. For the applicability of the Clean Air Act's Prevention of Significant Deterioration rules and the new rules to reduce haze in areas near national parks, see Mary A. Thomas, Air Quality Issues in Coalbed Methane Development, 4 Wyo. L. Rev. 643 (2004). The author warns that the potential impact of regional haze rules should not be underestimated because most resource development occurs in areas with the potential to impact Class I [national park] areas. These areas are to achieve natural visibility conditions by 2064 and will require regulations on all industry sectors, even one composed of mostly minor, but numerous, sources.

5. For a very critical view of CBM development, written by two lawyers with the Wyoming Outdoor Council, see Thomas F. Darin & Amy W. Beatie, Debunking the Natural Gas "Clean Energy" Myth: Coalbed Methane in Wyoming's Powder River Basin, 31 ELR 10566 (May 2001).

6. How well has CBM development been regulated to date in these key basins by the federal and state agencies in charge? NGO groups, particularly the Northern Plains Resources Council comprised of farmers, ranchers, and conservationists and the Wyoming Outdoor Council, have won a number of significant cases involving the failure of the BLM or other agencies to obey the requirements of various statutes, notably the CWA and NEPA:

- *Northern Plains Res. Council v. Fid. Exploration & Dev. Co.*, 325 F.3d 1155 (9th Cir. (2003), *cert. denied*, 540 U.S. 967 (2003). The Ninth Circuit held that produced water from CBM wells, no matter how clean or naturally occurring, was a pollutant under the CWA; the states could not exempt this source from the NPDES discharge permits on the rationale that the water was unaltered groundwater. The court found that the water was "industrial waste" because it was a useless byproduct of gas extraction.

- *Wyoming Outdoor Council v. U.S. Army Corps of Eng'rs*, 351 F. Supp. 2d 1232 (D. Wyo. 2005). Environmental groups challenged the decision by the U.S. Army Corps of Engineers to issue a general permit under the Clean Water Act (CWA) to streamline the increased demand for permits to discharge dredge and fill materials associated with the release of produced water in the Powder River Basin. The court found that the Corps had acted arbitrarily and capriciously by failing to consider the cumulative impacts on resources other than wetlands, by failing to disclose impacts on private ranch lands, and by relying on the efficacy of unmonitored and unsupported mitigation measures to conclude there would be no significant impact.

- On June 9, 2005, a federal district court magistrate in Wyoming found for a second time that the BLM's full-field EIS for CBM in Montana was inadequate for failing to consider a phased development alternative for CBM production. *American Lands Alliance v. BLM*, CV 03–71–BLG–RWA. The first case is *Northern Plains Resource Council v. U.S. Bureau of Land Management*, No. CV 03–69–BLG–RWA (D. Mont. Feb. 25, 2005). In April 2005, the court issued an injunction limiting the scale of CBM development to 500 new wells while the BLM prepared supplemental NEPA analysis.

- In a fourth case, a BLM action was thwarted by the Interior's own Board of Land Appeals ("IBLA"). In *Pennaco Energy, Inc. v. U.S. Dep't of Interior*, 377 F.3d 1147 (10th Cir. 2004), the Interior Board of Land Appeals (IBLA) reversed the BLM's issuance of leases because of NEPA violations. IBLA determined that the proposed use of the leases for extraction of coalbed methane raised significant new environmental concerns, especially regarding water discharges and air quality, which had not been addressed by existing NEPA documents relating to conventional oil and gas leasing. Pennaco appealed to the U.S. District Court in Wyoming which reinstated the BLM's approval of CBM leasing. The Tenth Circuit reversed and remanded to the district court with instructions to reinstate the IBLA's decision.

Additional decisions of the IBLA on CBM leasing in the Rockies appear in Robert C. Mathes, Continuing Controversy: The Courts' and the IBLA's Challenges to Coalbed Natural Gas Development, 42 Rocky Mtn. Min. L. J. 45 (2005).

7.   Wyoming leads the nation in producing low-sulfur coal through surface mining, over 90% of which comes from the Powder River Basin. The conflicts between CBM developers and surface coal developers are discussed in Jeanine Feriancik, Coal and Coalbed Methane Development Conflicts: No Easy Solution, 14 Nat. Res. & Env't 260 (Spring 2000).

8.   The Western Governors' Association produced a Coal Bed Methane Best Management Practices Handbook in April 2004, available at www.westgov.org with the help of an Advisory Committee of members from state and federal governments, industry, and many respected conservation and environmental groups

9.   Denver-based Luca Technologies is conducting lab experiments to allow "methane farming," the use of colonies of naturally occurring microorganisms called "methanogens" or "geobioreactors" which can be placed underground in oil, shale or coal strata. The bacteria will break down organic matter and produce methane. Ben Geman, Denver Company Eyes Commercial "Methane Farming," Land Letter, June 2, 2005. If commercialized, will natural gas move into the category of a renewable fuel?

CBM development is occurring round the world in Botswana, Australia, Germany, Canada and China.

10.   The July 2005 issue of *National Geographic* has a narrative and many accompanying photos of the CBM development in Wyoming. It illustrates many of the issues discussed in this text quite vividly, especially the size and density of the CBM ponds and pads in the Jonah field. Good photos also appear at www.rmmlf.org/AI51/PPTindex.htm, in the article by O'Malley and Jones on "Chained Gates and No Trespassing Signs."

11.   Is it good national energy policy to extend billions of dollars in tax credits to the CBM industry? What market failure is being corrected by such a subsidy? What market failure is the tax credit causing?

4.   USE AND MANAGEMENT OF FEDERAL LANDS FOR ENERGY DEVELOPMENT

The furious debate over CBM development in the West can be framed within a wider debate over how our federal lands—which belong to all of us—should be managed. What is the "public" interest in these "public lands" that are managed by the "public servants" employed in Washington DC and in the BLM and Forest Service offices in these Western communities? Are they doing their job of balancing the multiple goals which the federal lands are to serve? The success of much litigation opposing their decisions suggests not. Even ranchers and environmentalists, one-time enemies (the latter believe that cattle have ruined the West), have become allies in the fight to keep CBM from destroying their grasslands, ecology, and landscapes. Jim Carlton, Green Groups, Ranchers Bury Hatchet to Curb Oil Drilling, Wall. St. J., Mar. 23, 2005, at B4. And rifle-toting hunters, a mainstay of the Republican voter base, are deserting their party because of its policies to spur drilling on BLM lands where deer and elk graze. Timothy Egan, Drilling in West Pits Republican Policy Against Republican Base, New York Times, June 22, 2005. Is this discord built into the political structure of our federalist form of government or is it caused by lax enforcement of environmental laws or by the impossibly conflicting multiple goals of federal land use statutes?

While detailed study of public land management must be left to its own course, the beginning of an article by two professors vividly frames the current status of federal land management:

Jan G. Laitos & Elizabeth Getches, Multi-Layered and Sequential: State and Local Barriers to Extractive Resource Development

23 Va. Envtl. L. J. 1, at 1–2 (2004).

Natural resources developers throughout America, and particularly in the West, seek to extract valuable energy resources (oil, gas, coal, and coalbed methane), as well as precious minerals (gold and copper) and building materials (stone, sand, and gravel). Even though these developers may have a perfectly valid legal ownership right to remove resources, state and local regulatory barriers interfere with, and in some cases prevent, the developers' exercise of that right. These barriers arise in ways that may be characterized as both "vertical" and "horizontal." Vertically, layer after layer of state and local regulatory uncertainty and confusion force the developer to spend time, money, and effort attempting to understand whether, and how, state and local law applies to the development project. Horizontally, over the entire life cycle of the development, from permitting to reclamation, state and local regulations and restrictions operate, sometimes with maddening predictability, to deter, retard, or stop the extraction of resources.

These governmental limits are usually imposed for environmental, land use, or jurisdictional dominance purposes. Unfortunately, no matter how worthy their motive, the sheer quantity of these multi-layered and sequential state and local barriers makes resource development very time-consuming and expensive. The relentless nature of these non-federal regulations sometimes discourages or halts otherwise useful and legally valid resource extractive operations. This consequence benefits neither the local governments imposing the regulations nor the frustrated developer. The American resource market is a victim as well because such barriers slow or even halt the movement of needed commodities to demanding consumers. . . .

In this article, we will make the case that the law, especially local regulations and state rules, has become antithetical to rational resource development. First, we consider the many layers of regulatory confusion that resource developers face. We focus on the issue of whose right prevails. This question arises between (1) surface and mineral estate owners, (2) coal developers and coalbed methane gas developers, and (3) oil and gas developers and CBM developers, when the former has a dormant estate and the latter is in the process of mineral extraction. Next, we discuss the confusion developers must face when they attempt to determine whose law applies. Choice of law questions occur when developers (1) confront competing state and local regulations, or (2) encounter the two entirely different and contradictory water regulatory regimes that potentially apply to the immense quantity of water produced during CBM extraction. Then, we consider another baffling layer of legal conflict facing resource developers: the battle between private property resource rights protected by the Takings Clause of the U.S. Constitution and the police power of government that regulates this property.

After describing the layers of conflict that work to choke off even thoughtful and measured development activity, we address the discouraging and relentless pattern of regulatory obstacles that are endemic at every critical stage of a resource extractive operation. . . . These barriers range from changing zoning regulations to heavy-handed conditional use permits, unexpected moratoria, and even stringent post-mining reclamation requirements.

We then suggest, by way of conclusion, that it is in the interest of both developers and state and local governments to impose a more rational and unified set of regulatory rules on resource extractive operations. Increasing predictability would help to avoid the delays, confusion, and litigation that the current system encourages.■

Compare this article with the views of one of its authors in a 1998 article which traced a fundamental shift in America's public land uses in the past century. The "twin" uses of recreation and preservation now dominate the declining commodity uses of timber harvesting, mining, and grazing:

Jan G. Laitos & Thomas A. Carr, The New Dominant Use Reality on Multiple Lands

44 Rocky Mtn. Min. L. Inst. 1–1. at 1–4, 1–22, 1–27 (1998).

The emergence of twin dominant uses on public lands is a startling development that necessitates a new land management strategy. As this century comes to a close, so too does a lengthy history of federal multiple use lands chiefly valuable to commodity interests. The value of public lands now lies in recreation and preservation. Since these twin dominant uses will characterize the new era of public land use, the continued viability of multiple use as a management policy is questionable. The problem of applying a multiple use strategy to only two dominant uses is aggravated by the reality that multiple use was historically grounded in commodity exploitation, the complete opposite of recreation and preservation. *Id.* at 1–4.

[In a series of telling graphs, the authors document the steep long-term declines in the number of livestock grazing on national forest land; the number of mineral patents and mining claims for hard minerals; and the amount of oil and gas acreage leased (showing a steep decline after 1981); the 1996 leasing level was 71% below the peak 1960 level. Juxtaposed against these silhouettes of decline, are graphs that head in one basic direction—up. Recreational visits to national forests, BLM lands, and national parks soar from the 1950s onwards, and acreage devoted to wilderness areas and wildlife refuges climbs steadily with no downward path in sight. *Id.* at 1–34 to 1–47. The authors then comment on reasons for the declining commercial role of resource exploitation on the public lands]:

The more dependent a community is on a resource extractive industry, the more economically depressed it is likely to be. Specialization in, and reliance on, a traditional commodity use of public lands risks long-term economic decline for local communities if relative prices of extractive commodities fall over time. . . . [W]hen an extractive industry leaves a local community, that community may suffer initially, but in the long run, the local economy benefits because the community has ended its dependence on the exploitation of one natural resource. Indeed, in many western communities, the loss of a mining or timber harvesting operation on adjacent public lands has resulted in improved employment and real income levels.

In fact, while extractive industries have been in relative decline, there has been a vigorous expansion in economic sectors that do not need to remove and develop raw materials on public lands. Localities that are economically vital include those that are linked to environmental and recreational amenities, and that have a diversified economic base. *Id.* at 1–22.

In virtually all population centers near public lands, recreational activities and tourism provide many times as much employment as commodity resource extraction. Most western states now count on recreation and tourism as the first or second largest part of their economies. *Id.* at 1–27.■

NOTES AND COMMENTS

1. The authors then suggest that management of the public lands shift from a multiple use approach to one using economic principles to allocate

land to its highest and best use. An efficient allocation would maximize the total value of goods and services derived from the public lands. Economists can use new methodologies, such as contingent valuation, to assess the economic value of non-marketed commodities such as recreation, amenity and landscape values and the value of being able to appreciate nature. The authors call upon policymakers to adopt the principle of economic efficiency for managing our public lands and allocating uses between traditional commodity extraction and non-extractive, service uses. *Id.* at 1–31 to 1–33.

2.   In 1998, would a federal land manager using economic efficiency principles allocate multiple-use land differently than in 2005? Why or why not? Would an efficient decision be based on judgments about the future prices of oil and gas and other resources?

Gary Bryner suggested that the states adopt a law that produced water from CBM belongs to the CBM developer, who will then have market incentives to collect and transport the water in large volumes to those areas that need the water. Would sales of such water to thirsty cities fit into the economic calculus that Laitos and Carr assert should be used to manage our federal lands today? How would the destruction of the quiet solitude of nature, the pristine air of a mountain valley or the breathtaking scenery of a wide vista fit into this market-oriented approach to public land management? Could a Four Seasons resort developer outbid a CBM developer for access to the scenic value of a tract of federal land in Wyoming?

3.   What can be done to keep the vistas intact when 51,000 wells and many acres of access roads and compression equipment have transformed the landscape in a CBM basin area? The Western Governors' Association Handbook on best practices for CBM recommends reducing visual impacts by painting facilities to blend with the background. One operator does more: It builds small ridge lines and plants trees on them to hide the wells. Bryner, *supra* at 547–48.

4.   Low drilling costs and high well densities for CBM extraction have contributed to a rapid influx of people in a short time frame that the infrastructure and services of small towns cannot readily accommodate, even though local property tax collections or impact fees may soar. Bryner, *supra*, at 532, 534, 543–44. Booms are often as hard to handle as busts. Recall that a district court in Montana limited CBM development because the BLM had failed to analyze the alternative of slower, phased development versus full-field development in the Powder River Basin. Does NEPA require the choice of phased development or only that the BLM properly consider this as an alternative? The court noted in *Northern Plains Resource Council v. U.S. Bureau of Land Management*, No. CV 03–69–BLG–RWA (D. Mont. Feb. 25, 2005) that the EPA had recommended phased development to mitigate the "boom and bust" nature of CBM development. By avoiding the construction of infrastructure useful only during a peak, the number of workers, drilling rigs, and amount of equipment needed to build containment ponds, well pads, etc. could be staged over a longer period of time which would also allow the agencies more time to conduct the necessary studies and monitor the impacts. Do

you think the BLM will ultimately adopt such an alternative after studying it? Why or why not?

The BLM advanced two reasons for its decision to not consider phased development: (1) its duty to prevent drainage of leased federal minerals to private leases nearby; and (2) the "investment-backed rights" of the federal lessees under the 1994 Resource Management Plan which authorized the right to undertake exploratory drilling and small-scale development of CBM in the Powder River Basin. The BLM cited *Mobil Oil Exploration and Producing Southeast, Inc. v. United States*, 530 U.S. 604 (2000), appearing in Chapter 6(E)(4) of this casebook, in support of its position. Is this good precedent? Is the rule of capture a good reason? Does "haste make waste?"

As Western towns are transformed to serve cappuccino-sipping tourists, hikers, skiers, and retirees from the big city, what becomes of the local communities' cultural heritage built up over decades of farming, ranching, mining or timber harvesting? Professor Dan Tarlock evaluates whether such communities, stressed with rapid growth from the new service economy, deserve protection as an "endangered remnant culture," even though the communities' status is not based on religion (like some Amish or Mormon communities) or aboriginal rights such as Native Americans. A. Dan Tarlock, Can Cowboys Become Indians? Protecting Western Communities as Endangered Cultural Remnants, 31 Ariz. State L. J. 539 (1999).

5. Landmen, who may or may not be lawyers, are the personnel who deal with landowners on the ground, negotiating oil and gas leases, pipeline easements and other development documents. Their lament and frustration is voiced in Access to Public Lands: Its Effect on Natural Gas Supply in the United States, Landmen 45–62 (Jan./Feb. 2004) complete with lists of the laws and policies which block access and estimates of the amount of gas unrecovered as a result.

Another study estimates the extra costs of drilling for oil and gas on federal land as compared to private land in Wyoming in a checkerboarded 40–mile strip of land where the Union Pacific Railroad was granted off-numbered square-mile sections as private land, surrounded by alternating even-numbered sections of federal land. The study estimated that drilling costs per well were about $200,000 higher on federal land, attributable to more environmental and land use regulations. Mitch Kunce *et al.*, Effects of Environmental and Land Use Regulation in the Oil and Gas Industry Using the Wyoming Checkerboard as an Experimental Design, 92 Amer. Econ. Rev. 1588 (2002). How would you assess whether the increased costs were greater than the benefits?

6. With record-high oil and gas prices, the local BLM offices in the areas of most intense drilling cannot handle the Resource Management Plans that are required under federal law to cover the multiple uses of large land regions, the hundreds of Applications for Permits to Drill ("APDs") filed with them, and the monitoring of species and habitat necessary to do environmental impact statements. *See generally*, Ezekiel J. Williams & Carolyn McIntosh, The Growing Phenomenon of Challenges to Federal Land Use Plans in Natural Resources Litigation, 51 Rocky Mtn. Min. L.

Inst., Ch. 11 (forthcoming 2005); and Denise Dragoo, Federal Land Use Planning Primer under FLMPA and NFMA, 49 Rocky Mtn. Min. L. Inst. Ch. 16 (2003). Energy policy studies have recommended that the BLM be given more staffing and funding to effectively perform their duties and enable them to plan oil and gas development with appropriate mitigation measures, thus avoiding lengthy court delays from injunctions issued for failure to obey all the protective measures in federal statutes such as the Endangered Species Act. *See, e.g.,* National Commission on Energy Policy, Ending the Energy Stalemate, at 49–50 (Dec. 2004).

In June 2005, the General Accountability Office released a report documenting its title: "Oil and Gas Development: Increased Permitting Activity Has Lessened BLM's Ability to Meet Its Environmental Protection Responsibilities" (GAO–05–418). The number of drilling permits approved by BLM nationwide had tripled from 1999 to 2004; the staff time spent processing permits left less time for environmental inspections and mitigation activities; and then increased staff time was needed to handle the numerous appeals and litigation over BLM actions. The environmental lapses ranged from excessive removal of a few acres of vegetation at drill sites to fragmenting thousands of acres of winter range used by wildlife. The GAO recommended that BLM implement a fee structure to recover the cost of processing permits from the applicants. Another GAO report, issued earlier in January 2005 highlighted the BLM's failure to keep track of public challenges of agency decisions and the delays caused to oil and gas drilling. GAO, Oil & Gas Development Challenges to Agency Decisions and Opportunities for BLM to Standardize Data Collection, GAO–05–124 (Nov. 2004).

In July 2005, BLM drew up plans to phase in drilling permit fees of $4,000 per application, allowing the BLM to recover $23 million more to meet its workload. Various state oil and gas associations complained loudly that small producers and marginal projects would be hurt by the fees (a rather skeptical assertion when most marginal wells are old, already-permitted and producing wells and gas prices are at historic highs). The National Energy Act of 2005, passed a few weeks later, blocked the BLM's proposed fee plan. Instead, Sections 361 to 366 and Section 390 of the new Act provide for:

- An internal review of all onshore oil and gas leasing practices by the Interior Department and Department of Agriculture, including time frames for processing applications, identification of lease stipulations, and improvements made to expedite the processes, with a report to Congress due within 180 days. (Sec. 361).

- Expeditious compliance with NEPA and all other environmental and cultural resource laws, improved consultation with the states and the public, and improved information collection to ensure timely action on oil and gas leases. In 18 months, the two Departments shall have developed and implemented best management practices ("BMPs") to this end. Within 180 days of the BMP phase, the Secretaries must publish proposed regulations, including deadlines for application processing. They must also improve inspection and enforcement of oil and gas activities and compliance with lease stipulations. The Act appropriates $70 million to carry out this Section 362.

- A memorandum of understanding on the coordinated leasing of Forest Service and BLM lands to ensure timely processing of surface use plans, drilling permits and lease applications, including a joint data base to track the status of applications. (Sec. 363).

- An inventory of onshore federal oil and gas resources. (Sec. 364).

- A Federal Permit Streamlining Pilot Project, staffed within 90 days by field office employees who are expert in endangered species law, air and water permitting and planning under the federal land management acts and NEPA. The Pilot Project will have offices in 7 "hot" drilling spots in Wyoming, Montana, New Mexico, Colorado, and Utah. The results of the pilots must be reported to Congress within three years. (Sec. 365)

More substantively, the Act provides for two immediate changes in agency practices:

i. Within 10 days of receiving an application for a permit to drill (APD), the applicant must be notified that the APD is complete or told what information is missing to be complete. Once complete, the federal office must issue the permit within 30 days if all NEPA requirements and other applicable law are met, or defer the APD, specifying what steps the applicant and the agency must take to complete compliance. The applicant then has 2 years to complete all requirements specified. If completed, the permit is granted. If not, the permit is denied. (Sec. 366).

ii. NEPA compliance will be easier because Section 390 of the Act creates a rebuttable presumption that certain oil and gas activities may be categorically excluded from NEPA. The activities include: surface disturbances of less than 5 acres so long as the total surface disturbance on a lease is not greater than 150 acres and the site-specific analysis in a NEPA document has been previously completed; and drilling a well in a developed field which has an approved NEPA document "analyzing such activity as a reasonably foreseeable activity," if the NEPA document was approved within 5 years before the date the well was started.

What effect are these last two provisions likely to have on CBM leasing in the Rockies?

No sooner had the 2005 Act passed than the Interior Department made public a review of the past years' permit processing in one active BLM office in Wyoming. Approvals of the APDs took an average of 117 days rather than the 30 days provided in the laws. And what was the biggest contributor to the delay? Applicants' deficiencies in filling out the APD forms. Of the 117 days, BLM took 31 days to process the APD; 86 days were due to industry's deficient responses. The Assistant Secretary of DOI called for the BLM and industry to have facilitated discussions on the implications of these findings. Greenwire, Aug. 4, 2005. What do you think the implications are?

A BLM spokesman said that because most well pads are less than 5 acres, new wells and "infill" wells in developed fields will be NEPA-exempt, but the new bill may have little effect because other environmental laws still apply. Tom Kenworthy, Oil Projects May Get Less Scrutiny, USA Today, May 4, 2005. Does this mean that no environmental studies will be done of the produced water from these wells? Who is paying for the additional information and studies during the two-year deferral process?

If the field office misses the new APD deadlines, has the government breached its contract with the applicant? Compare *Mobil Oil Exploration & Producing Southeast, Inc. v. United States*, 530 U.S. 604 (2000) in Chapter 6(E)(4).

7.   Shortly after the January 2003 release of the report on the extent of leasing restrictions in major producing basins in the U.S. (see Chapter 6(E)(4)(b)), the BLM directed that field offices in these basins review all the environmental stipulations in current leases and reduce mitigation measures to "the least restrictive necessary to accomplish the desired protection" or grant waivers to them. For example, if a lease area restricted drilling activity because of winter wildlife grazing, but elk no longer used the area or a mild winter had changed their grazing pattern, then waivers should be granted. Mike Ferullo, Interior Directs Officials to Remove Obstacles to Oil, Gas Projects, Daily Report for Executives, Aug. 11, 2003, at A–16. What effect will this directive have on BLM workloads?

On July 27, 2005, the BLM and the Forest Service issued proposed rules to improve oil and gas permit processing while protecting surface owners and public lands. 70 Fed. Reg. 43349–43364, July 27, 2005. The proposal would require developers to make good-faith efforts to reach an access agreement with surface owners. If none is reached, developers must then post a bond that ensures compensation for certain defined economic losses. The proposal would allow a Master Development Plan to approve several related drilling permits in a single environmental analysis. It also encourages operators to use Best Management Practices such as reducing surface or visual impacts, clustering wells on a single well pad, establishing buffer zones to protect wildlife habitat, painting structures to match vegetation, and burying pipelines under access roads. These offsite mitigation measures are voluntary and optional. The BLM stated that its shift to voluntary mitigation measures was a "subtle change" because the measures were never officially mandatory, although a few BLM offices had required them. BLM officials said they could still withhold drilling permits if companies balked at doing the mitigation work. EnCana, one of the largest gas producers in Wyoming and Colorado, said it will consider offsite mitigation even though it is voluntary. Judith Kohler, Drilling Compensation Voluntary, AP Release, Aug. 5, 2005. What does it cost EnCana to "consider" mitigation? Does this mean EnCana will implement mitigation? Why would it do so voluntarily? As a shareholder of EnCana, would you want to know how much additional money it spent clustering wells and drilling directionally to reduce surface impacts? As a non-shareholder, would you care? Why? Chapter 9 discusses corporate social responsibility for socio-economic and environmental impacts.

C. FEDERAL FRAMEWORK OF NATURAL GAS REGULATION

1. OVERVIEW

The Natural Gas Act of 1938 still operates today, largely unchanged, as the primary federal statute regulating interstate transportation of gas. It is now clothed in six decades of case law interpretation, including the famous, or rather infamous, case of *Phillips v. Wisconsin* that has been blamed for creating the serious gas shortages of the 1960s and 1970s. A second statute, the Natural Gas Policy Act ("NGPA") of 1978, was enacted to overrule the *Phillips* case and undo the gas shortages. This Act died a well-deserved death (in the opinion of most observers) when Congress passed the Well-head Decontrol Act of 1989, decreeing the end of federal price controls on all gas as of 1993.

The foremost scholar of natural gas regulation has summarized these two acts and previewed the revolution to come in the following article, which provides a whirlwind tour of the past and present structure of the industry as it moved from Figure 8–2 to Figure 8–3.

Richard J. Pierce, Jr., The Evolution of Natural Gas Regulatory Policy

Natural Resources and Environment 53–85 (Summer 1995).

Deregulation of the market for natural gas surely ranks as one of the most significant accomplishments in natural resources law over the past decade. During the period 1985 to 1995, the Federal Energy Regulatory Commission (FERC) accomplished this massive task by, in effect, reversing through regulatory decisionmaking a pair of unfortunate public policy errors made by Congress in 1938 and by the U.S. Supreme Court in 1954. The results of FERC's carefully constructed deregulatory program are impressive. They include at least a $5 billion annual improvement in aggregate social welfare and significant air quality improvements attributable to use of natural gas to displace dirtier fuels.

The history of regulation and deregulation of the natural gas industry is worth recounting because it provides insights that can be useful in identifying potential ways of attaining socially beneficial results in many analogous contexts. The ongoing effort to create a competitive electricity market is an obvious case in point. *See* Richard Pierce, The State of the Transition to Competitive Markets in Natural Gas and Electricity, 15 Energy L.J. 323 (1994); Richard J. Pierce, Using the Gas Industry as a Guide to Reconstituting the Electricity Industry, 13 J. Res. in L. & Econ. 7 (1991).

The story begins in the 1920s. The development of high-tensile steel and electric welding permitted the construction of high-pressure steel pipelines that allowed gas to be transported long distances at relatively low costs. State public utility commissions (PUCs) attempted to regulate the then newly emerging business of transporting natural gas across state lines for resale in states other than the state in which the gas was produced. It made sense to regulate interstate pipelines because interstate transportation of gas, like distribution of gas by local distribution companies (LDCs), was a natural monopoly function, characterized by large economies of scale and high barriers to entry. State regulation of interstate transportation of gas created intolerable problems, however. The firms that engaged in this new activity were subjected both to conflicting regulatory orders from different states and to regulatory policies that were designed to help the residents of one state at the expense of residents of other states.

The Supreme Court responded to these problems with a trilogy of opinions in which it held that the dormant Commerce Clause prohibited any state from regulating interstate transportation or wholesales of gas. *Pub. Utils. Comm'n of R.I. v. Attleboro Steam & Elec. Co.,* 273 U.S. 83 (1927); *Missouri v. Kansas Gas Co.,* 265 U.S. 298 (1924); *Pennsylvania v. West Virginia,* 262 U.S. 553 (1923).

The Supreme Court performed a constructive function by redefining the geographic scope of the problem and by prohibiting an attempted solution that could only exacerbate the problem. The basic problem remained, however: interstate transportation of gas was a natural monopoly function that required regulation by someone. In response to numerous complaints from consumers and producers about alleged abuses of monopoly power by interstate pipelines, Congress assigned the Federal Trade Commission ("FTC") the duty to study the gas industry to determine whether there was a need for federal regulation of the industry. In 1935, the FTC submitted a comprehensive, high quality report in which it concluded that interstate transportation of gas was a natural monopoly that should be regulated by a federal agency. The FTC found that pipelines were exercising their monopoly power by extracting high prices from LDCs.

Up to this point, there is no basis to criticize the performance of any of the institutions that played roles in the policymaking process. Each institution performed its role in an exemplary manner. In 1938, however, Congress made a decision that ultimately produced a series of unfortunate results. The FTC found a justification to regulate only interstate transportation of gas. This could have been accomplished easily by subjecting interstate gas pipelines to federal regulation as common carriers; the method of regulation Congress had imposed on interstate oil pipelines decades earlier. Gas pipelines objected to this treatment, however. They sought to preserve their monopoly relationship with LDCs and their monopsony relationship with producers. Common carrier status would strip them of their monopoly and monopsony power by forcing them to transport gas owned by third parties.

Pipelines successfully urged Congress to impose a different form of regulation. In the Natural Gas Act of 1938 ("NGA"), Congress instructed the Federal Power Commission ("FPC") to regulate interstate pipelines as if they were utilities. Congress prohibited the FPC from requiring any pipeline to transport gas for a third party. This policy decision enabled interstate pipelines to use their monopoly power over gas transportation to create and to maintain monopsony power in the market for the purchase of gas at the wellhead and monopoly power in the market for the sale of gas to LDCs. The available evidence suggests that FPC regulation of pipelines as utilities was not effective. *See* Breyer & MacAvoy, Energy Regulation By The Federal Commission (1974). The FPC was able to perform the difficult task assigned it with no serious adverse effects, however, for sixteen years.

In 1954, a five-Justice majority of the Supreme Court made the second major public policy error. In *Phillips Petroleum Co. v. Wisconsin*, 347 U.S. 672 (1954), the Court held that NGA required the FPC to regulate the price of natural gas sold by independent gas producers in interstate commerce. The five-Justice majority focused exclusively on the words Congress used to describe the scope of the FPC's regulatory jurisdiction. The majority ignored both the long-standing contrary interpretation of the statute by the agency responsible for its implementation and the effects of the alternative interpretations of the statute that were consistent with the ambiguous language of the statute. . . .

Unlike transportation of gas, production of gas is not a natural monopoly. It is an activity characterized by low economies of scale and low barriers to entry. Thousands of firms compete to produce gas and to make wellhead sales. The FTC had not detected any problem of monopoly power in producing gas and selling it at the wellhead in the comprehensive investigation of the gas industry it conducted during the 1930s, and the FPC saw no justification to regulate producer prices. Indeed, producers were among the victims of interstate pipelines—pipelines used their monopsony power in the producing fields to depress the wellhead price of gas, just as they used their monopoly power to sell gas to LDCs at excessive prices.

The Supreme Court assigned the FPC an impossible task in *Phillips*. No agency can impose price controls on a structurally competitive market without creating a shortage of the regulated product or service. Between 1954 and 1960 the FPC attempted to implement the Court's mandate in *Phillips* in a manner that had little effect. The FPC attempted to set a maximum rate applicable to sales made by each producer by determining the costs incurred by each of the thousands of producers. By 1960, it had completed ten rate cases and had developed a backlog of 2,900 pending cases. At this point, the Supreme Court issued an opinion in which it chastised the FPC for the slow rate at which it was implementing the mandate of *Phillips* and held that the FPC could not authorize any new sales to the interstate market unless and until it established price ceilings applicable to the gas that the producer proposed to sell. *Atlantic Refining Co. v. Pub. Serv. Comm'n of N.Y.*, 360 U.S. 378 (1959). In 1961, the FPC responded to the Court's decision in *Atlantic Refining* by switching to a new method of implementing the *Phillips* decision. The FPC established rates applicable to all gas produced in each producing area based on the agency's estimate of the average historical cost of finding and producing a unit of gas in each area.

The new method was effective; its effect was to create a gas shortage. The gas shortage began to manifest itself initially in forms that were invisible to the public. Price controls reduced the rate of exploration for new supplies of gas. That in turn, reduced the inventory of gas supplies available to the interstate market. Eventually, the available inventory declined to the point at which deliverability could not be sustained at levels sufficient to meet demand. In 1969, fifteen years after the *Phillips* decision, the effects of that decision emerged in a publicly visible form. Interstate pipelines began to reduce their deliveries to LDCs. The deliverability shortage grew rapidly during the early 1970s. By the unusually cold winter of 1976–1977, the shortage had reached the point at which gas service was no longer available to most prospective new customers; thousands of manufacturing plants and schools were closed by service curtailments; and, over 1 million workers were laid off because of their employer's inability to obtain gas.

Congress had debated the wisdom of the Court's decision in *Phillips* nearly continuously between 1954 and 1977. It came close to reversing that decision legislatively in 1955 and again in 1976, but ignorance with respect to basic principles of microeconomics induced many legislators to believe that price controls benefitted consumers. The severe shortages of 1976–1977 finally forced Congress to act. Congress enacted the Natural Gas Policy Act of 1978 (NGPA), in which it instructed the FPC, then recently renamed the Federal Energy Regulatory Commission (FERC), to implement a new regulatory regime applicable to the gas industry. The NGPA regulatory regime was extraordinarily complicated: it divided gas supplies into over a score of different categories, each subject to different rules and statutory price ceilings. *See* Richard J. Pierce, Reconsidering the Roles of Regulation and Competition in the Natural Gas Industry, 97 Harv. L. Rev. 345 (1983).

In one sense, NGPA was a major breakthrough. It was designed ultimately to deregulate the wellhead gas market, and it did create the conditions in which FERC ultimately was able to accomplish that task. In another sense however, NGPA was a catastrophe. Congress drafted NGPA based on the assumption that market forces are relatively weak and require many years to yield beneficial results. Congress assumed that the quantity of gas demanded and supplied would change slowly in response to changes in the price of gas. Thus, for instance, Congress scheduled deregulation to take place gradually over a period of many years, with most gas subject to constantly increasing statutory price ceilings for a decade or more. Congress expected the statutory ceiling prices to remain below the market price of gas for the entire period in which the NGPA authorized gradual replacement of ceiling prices with prices determined by market forces.

Congress also expected the shortage to persist for many years. Instead, as the price of gas increased, the quantity of gas demanded fell rapidly, the quantity of gas supplied rose rapidly, and the market price of gas plummeted to well below the statutory ceiling prices.

In the meantime, however, pipelines had entered into thousands of long-term contracts to purchase large volumes of gas at the ceiling prices established by NGPA. Because the NGA insulated pipelines from competition for the sale of gas, they were not particularly concerned about the risk that they would lose sales to competitors if they committed to buy gas at prices well above the price at which gas would sell in a competitive market. Within a few years after enactment of NGPA, the flawed assumptions on which the statute was based became apparent to all market participants and observers. The NGA and the NGPA combined to create market conditions attainable only through regulation—a large surplus of gas that coexisted with consumer prices far in excess of the price that would exist in an unregulated market.

By the mid–1980s, FERC confronted a daunting task. It had to change the regulatory rules applicable to the gas market in ways that would eliminate the severe adverse effects of decades of misguided policy decisions made with respect to that market. FERC proved to be up to that challenge, however, Between 1985 and 1992, FERC took a series of regulatory actions that had the effect of reversing the many disastrous policy decisions that were made between 1938 and 1978. The details of FERC's successful strategy are too intricate to recount in this summary, but two regulatory actions formed the core of that strategy. The first took place in 1985 when FERC issued Order 436. That order used regulatory sticks and carrots to coerce interstate pipelines into agreeing to become "equal access" carriers; pipelines obligated themselves to transport gas owned by third parties on terms equivalent to the terms on which the pipelines transported their own gas. A year later, in Order 451, FERC changed the rules with respect to ceiling prices in ways that allowed producers and pipelines to adjust their prices to be compatible with the new relationship between gas supply and demand. The Order 436 equal access policy and the Order 451 flexible pricing policy went a long way toward eliminating pipelines' monopoly power in the wholesale gas market and toward forcing producers and pipelines to sell gas at market-based prices. With pipelines operating under equal access tariffs, LDCs and industrial consumers were free to buy gas directly from thousands of producers and independent marketers. That access to competing suppliers forced pipelines and producers to lower their prices significantly. Consumer prices plummeted; the quantity of gas consumed increased; and, the gas surplus began to dissipate.

FERC encountered one major impediment to implementation of its critical initial step toward reforming the gas market. By allowing third-party sellers to compete with pipelines in the wholesale gas market, FERC's new policies had the effect of forcing pipelines to lower the prices they charged LDCs to a level consistent with market forces. That, in turn. exposed pipelines to the risk of losing approximately $20 billion attributable to the long-term contracts in which they had committed to buy large quantities of gas at above-market prices. Pipelines were understandably reluctant to absorb such enormous losses. Pipelines pursued a multifaceted litigation strategy that was designed to stall the process of implementing the new market-based regulatory strategy and to reallocate to other market participants the bulk of the cost of their problem contracts. Eventually, the costs of the problem contracts were allocated among pipelines, producers, LDCs, and consumers. The legal disputes over the appropriate allocation of those costs delayed the transition process, however, and made the process painful for all market participants. That complicated litigation took place over the period 1985 to 1995 at FERC, at state PUCs, and in hundreds of state and federal courts. . . .

By 1989, Congress was sufficiently impressed with the results of FERC's regulatory restructuring that it enacted the Natural Gas Wellhead Decontrol Act. That statute ratified FERC's de facto deregulation of the gas sales market, formally eliminated all wellhead price ceilings effective on January 1, 1993, and encouraged FERC to take such further actions as it deemed appropriate to create a fully competitive gas sales market. FERC responded to the admonition in the 1989 Wellhead Decontrol Act with its second major policy initiative. In 1992 FERC issued Order 636. That order completed the process of deregulating the gas sales market. It required interstate pipelines to provide fully unbundled services; henceforth, pipelines were required to sell separately transportation services, storage services, and natural gas. After Order 636, LDCs and industrial consumers were free to purchase gas, storage services, and even transportation services from scores of potential suppliers.

The participants in the gas market have responded to the spur of competition by implementing numerous efficiency-enhancing commercial and technological innovations. Gas is being found, produced, stored, and transported at much lower cost than was the case a decade ago. Gas is traded constantly at dozens of market hubs at constantly changing spot prices. Hundreds of new pipeline interconnections have transformed the previously fragmented transportation system into a closely integrated network that links all North American supplies with all markets in the United States and Canada. Electronic bulletin boards allow market participants to engage in continuous trade with respect to transportation capacity so that all gas can move from supply areas to market areas over the least expensive route. Market participants have changed their methods of using storage in a variety of ways that have simultaneously reduced costs and increased service reliability

The deregulated gas market performed extremely well during the unusually cold 1993–1994 winter. That performance was in sharp contrast both to the miserable performance of the then-regulated gas industry during the severe 1976–1977 winter and to the disappointing performance of the still-regulated electricity industry during the 1993–1994 winter. The gas industry continued to provide reliable service even in extreme conditions, while all industrial, commercial, and governmental activities in the middle Atlantic states had to be halted for a day in January 1994 to avoid a complete electricity blackout of that region.

Some work remains to be done to ensure that all consumers reap the full benefits of FERC's deregulatory restructuring of the gas industry. State PUCs are in the process of discovering that their traditional methods of regulating LDCs are incompatible with the dynamic, robustly competitive wholesale gas market FERC has created. PUCs will have no choice but to adopt more flexible, market-driven methods of regulating LDCs. Those new regulatory techniques will benefit all gas consumers. *See* Richard J. Pierce, Regulation and Competition in Natural Gas Distribution (1990).

FERC's extraordinary success in subjecting the gas industry to the unmatched discipline of a competitive market should be a source of many lessons that can be valuable in efforts to restructure other industries whose performance has been disappointing. The closely analogous electricity industry provides the most obvious candidate for similar restructuring. By restructuring that industry, we can improve the industry's performance dramatically and reduce the nation's electricity bill by approximately $24 billion a year. *See* Black and Pierce, The Choice Between Markets and Central Planning in Regulating the U.S. Electricity Industry, 93 Colum. L. Rev. 1339 (1993)....■

2. The Natural Gas Act of 1938: Public Utility Ratemaking for Pipelines—and Then Producers

The NGA of 1938 adopted cost-of-service ratemaking to control the monopoly power of pipelines, rather than the common carrier model of open access. Yet, until the Supreme Court's opinion in *Phillips Petroleum Co. v. Wisconsin*, 347 U.S. 672 (1954), Professor Pierce says that this policy choice was relatively harmless. Then, the Court interpreted the FPC's jurisdiction to include regulating the prices at which independent producers could sell their gas to pipelines. The FPC's jurisdiction is set out in section 1(b) of the Act (15 U.S.C. § 717b):

> [T]his chapter shall apply to the transportation of natural gas in interstate commerce, to the sale in interstate commerce of natural gas for resale for ultimate public consumption for domestic, commercial, industrial, or any other use, and to natural-gas companies engaged in such transportation or sale, but shall not apply to any other transportation or sale of natural gas or to the local distribution of natural gas or to the facilities used for such distribution or to the production or gathering of natural gas.

Phillips Petroleum was a gas producer engaged in the production, gathering, processing and sale of gas. It did not engage in the interstate transmission of gas, and it was not affiliated with any interstate pipeline company. Phillips simply sold its gas to five different interstate pipeline companies, which then transported and resold it to consumers and LDCs in 14 different states.

What prompted the state of Wisconsin to bring suit in the 1950s seeking FPC regulation of producers' prices at the wellhead? For more than two decades, many end-users had been buying gas under 20–year contracts at prices fixed in the 1930s when gas had been hugely in excess. Prices in many of these contracts were set at about one cent per thousand cubic foot (MCF). After World War II, new pipelines opened up the large Eastern markets. The demand for gas increased briskly, and the amount available to market slowed as producers reinjected gas back into reservoirs in order to increase oil recovery. Gas prices responded to the forces of supply and demand and started to advance. By the mid–1950s, many old gas contracts came up for renewal, and prices were jumping as much as ten-fold to about 15 cents per MCF. Lawyers in the cold state of Wisconsin argued that the FPC was required to regulate the wellhead price of gas under the language of section 1(b) quoted above.

The FPC issued an order denying jurisdiction over independent producers like Phillips, based on the express exemption of "production and gathering" in the statute. The FPC therefore refused to investigate the reasonableness of Phillips's gas prices. This set the stage for the Supreme Court's majority opinion interpreting section 1(b):

> In general, petitioners [Phillips, and the state of Texas] contend that Congress intended to regulate only the interstate pipeline companies since certain alleged excesses of those companies were the evil which brought about the legislation. If such were the case, we have difficulty in perceiving why the Commission's jurisdiction over the transportation *or* sale for resale in interstate commerce of natural gas is granted in the disjunctive. It would have sufficed to give the Commission jurisdiction over only those natural-gas companies that engage in "transportation" or "transportation and sale for resale" in interstate commerce, if only interstate pipeline companies were intended to be covered.

> Rather we believe that the legislative history indicates a congressional intent to give the Commission jurisdiction over the rates of all wholesales of natural gas in interstate commerce, whether by a pipeline company or not and whether occurring before, during or after transmission by an interstate pipeline company. There can be no dispute that the overriding congressional purpose was to plug the "gap" in regulation of natural-gas companies resulting from judicial decisions prohibiting on federal constitutional grounds, state regulation of many of the interstate commerce aspects of the natural-gas business. *Id.* 682–83.

> * * *

> Regulation of the sales in interstate commerce for resale made by a so-called independent natural-gas producer is not essentially different from regulation of such sales when made by an affiliate of an interstate pipeline company. In both cases, the rates charged may have a direct and substantial effect on the price paid by the ultimate consumers.

Protection of consumers against exploitation at the hands of natural-gas companies was the primary aim of the Natural Gas Act. *Id.* at 685.

■ DOUGLAS, J., dissented:

The sale by this independent producer is a "sale in interstate commerce ... for resale." It is also an integral part of "the production or gathering of natural gas." So we must make a choice....

There are practical considerations which ... lead me to conclude that we should not reverse the Commission in the present case. If Phillips' sales can be regulated, then the Commission can set a rate base for Phillips. A rate base for Phillips must of necessity include all of Phillips' producing and gathering properties; and supervision over its operating expenses.... The fastening of rate regulation on this independent producer brings "the production or gathering of natural gas" under effective federal control, in spite of the fact that Congress has made that phase ... exempt from regulation. The effect is certain to be profound.... The sales price determines his profits. And his profits and the profits of all the other gatherers, whose gas moves into the interstate pipelines, have profound effects on the rate of production, the methods of production, the old wells that are continued in production, the new ones explored, etc. Regulating the price at which the independent producer can sell his gas regulates his business in the most vital way any business can be regulated. That regulation largely nullifies the exemption granted by Congress. *Id.* at 690.

■ JUSTICES CLARK and BURTON also dissented, citing additional concerns:

By today's decision the Court restricts the phrase "production and gathering" to "the physical activities, facilities, and properties" used in production and gathering. Such a gloss strips the words of their substance. If the Congress so intended, then it left for state regulation only a mass of empty pipe, vacant processing plants and thousands of hollow wells with scarecrow derricks, monuments to this new extension of federal power.... The states have been for over 35 years and are now enforcing regulatory laws covering production and gathering ..., proration of gas, ratable taking, unitization of fields, processing of casinghead gas ... well spacing, repressuring, abandonment of wells, marginal area development, and other devices. There can be no doubt that federal regulation of production and gathering will collide and substantially interfere with and hinder the enforcement of these state regulatory measures. We cannot square this result with the House Report on this Act which states that the subsequently enacted bill "is so drawn as to complement and in no manner usurp State regulatory authority." *Id.* at 695–96.

3. THE NATURAL GAS POLICY ACT OF 1978: GRADUAL PRICE DECONTROL

The *Phillips* decision led to a dual system for selling natural gas: an intrastate and an interstate market. By 1978, producers' sales into the interstate market, with its low federally regulated prices, had dried up. Gas was available to intrastate users in the producing states, but only at a higher price. The 1976 shortages along the East coast led to the popular Texas bumper sticker "Drive 70 and freeze a Yankee in the dark." In 1978,

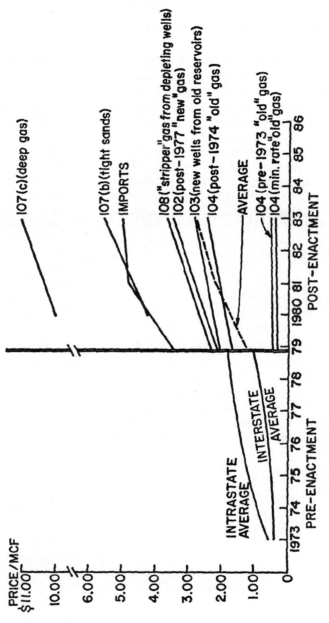

Figure 8–7

Price path of natural gas, before and after enactment of the Natural Gas Policy Act of 1978. After enactment of NGPA, intrastate gas was placed under federal control. The dashed line represents the common (interstate and intrastate) average price. The graph shows only a few of the many categories of gas established by NGPA.

Source: Connie C. Barlow & Arlon R. Tussing, Regulation and Deregulation of Natural Gas, in Free Market Energy, p. 63 (S. Fred Singer ed. 1984). (Universe Books).

Congress enacted a new regulatory pricing regime covering both the intrastate and interstate gas markets and established 27 different pricing categories for natural gas, depending on whether the gas came from existing wells, new wells, stripper wells, high-cost wells, offshore wells and a number of other factors. The different categories had different price escalators, so some gas was allowed to increase more in price than other gas (even though the molecules of gas were essentially identical). Congress also authorized the deregulation of some categories of gas, such as high-cost gas, as early as November 1979. **Figure 8–7**, above, shows the major categories of gas and the maximum legal prices allowed for each.

To what ends was this hydra-headed pricing system created? Congress attempted to achieve many goals:

1. First, the NGPA unified FERC control over all natural gas production, so that a national policy could be exerted over all gas sales.

2. The NGPA deregulated most gas prices gradually by January 1, 1985, giving consumers time to adjust to the forecast price increases. (Some high-cost gas was deregulated as early as November 1979, the date that FERC was to implement the "incremental pricing" rate design discussed below.) In particular, it sought to protect residential and commercial consumers from huge, abrupt price shocks.

3. The NGPA sought to prevent producers from collecting monopoly rents or excess profits on "old" gas from already existing wells, while at the same time encouraging producers to drill new wells to alleviate shortages by offering incentive prices on newly discovered gas, especially from high-cost areas.

4. It sought to promote the flow of gas into the interstate market where shortages were most severe.

In the long run, the most important achievement of the NGPA was to free natural gas prices from the utility-type, cost-of-service ratemaking imposed on it by the *Phillips* reading of the NGA. Congress itself determined what the just and reasonable rates were for different kinds of gas under the NGPA, and ultimately the market would be allowed to set this price without bureaucratic interference. The path to this end result was rocky, however, because of the $20 billion take-or-pay problem which grew out of the private system of long-term contracts that pipeline merchants had with producers.

4. TAKE-OR-PAY CONTRACTS IN TIMES OF SHORTAGE

Most contracts between selling producers and pipeline purchasers negotiated in the 1970s contained a provision similar to the following:

Seller agrees to sell and deliver to Buyer, and Buyer agrees to purchase and take, or pay for if available and not taken, Seller's pro rata part of the following quantities of gas produced from the reserves committed to this contract, to wit, a Quantity of gas equal to 85% of Seller's delivery capacity.[7]

Why would a purchaser sign an agreement to pay for gas that it doesn't take? The take-or-pay ("TOP") provision guaranteed producers a minimum cash flow in return for dedicating the producer's gas to one pipeline purchaser. Once dedicated, the gas could not be sold to others, even if the contracted purchaser did not take the gas. Producers wanted assurance against the risk that the dedicated purchaser would keep the gas in the ground, as a "bank" account of unproduced, reserve gas. If the purchaser did so, the TOP clause assured the producer that it would be paid anyhow. Also, in the energy shortages of the 1970s, interstate pipelines were desperate for additional gas supplies. They could not compete for more supplies on the basis of price because of federal price controls. Thus, they competed by giving producers other favorable contract provisions to lure them into signing up. Pipelines were happy to pay this non-price premium for gas because they expected to take all the gas that was dedicated and pay little or nothing as TOP payments. TOP percentages increased from 35% to 90% during the gas shortages of the 1970s. See John Lowe, Oil and Gas Law 288–90 (West 1995):

5.   TAKE-OR-PAY MEETS THE NGPA AND MARKET FORCES

Now let us hear from two economists how take-or-pay contracts combined with the NGPA and FERC's "rolled-in" gas pricing policy to produce the perverse market effect of rising gas prices at a time of excess gas supplies:

James M. Griffin and Henry B. Steele, Energy Economics and Policy

pp. 301–303 (Academic Press 1986, 2d ed.)

The general expectation of the 1978 act seems to have been that new gas prices would rise to their true competitive wellhead values, while old gas would continue to be underpriced for the benefit of the consumer as long as it lasted. These expectations were not to be realized. Gas prices increased more rapidly than had been anticipated, largely because pipelines with large quantities of cheap old gas could bid above-market prices for new gas and pass the higher average cost of supplies along to utility companies. The utilities in turn could cover these charges by averaging in the cost of this new gas with other old gas supplies they might have from other pipeline contracts and presenting a higher gas bill to their consum-

---

7. Delivery capacity was defined as the amount of gas which could be efficiently withdrawn from the wells on the lease under prudent operating practices and in accord with all applicable rules and regulations.

ers. Gas pipelines could do this because their profits depended upon maintaining a high percentage of pipeline capacity utilization, and not upon the margin between purchase cost and resale price, which was closely regulated. Natural gas prices also increased for other reasons. The Federal Energy Regulatory Commission (successor to the FPC in gas price control matters) favored gas price increases for reasons of economic efficiency, and took a number of steps to facilitate price hikes, especially for new gas. The most important categories of new gas were completely decontrolled by FERC action in 1979, . . . [Deregulated] deep gas had skyrocketed to over $9.00 per mcf by 1980, contrasted with certain vintages of old gas that were selling for $.50 per mcf. Thus . . . natural gas prices [increased] quite significantly during the period 1978–84, and it is very interesting to investigate the reasons for these increases.

Much of the blame for the rapid increase in the price of new gas has been directed at gas pipeline companies, particularly those with large supplies of underpriced old gas, but in a broader context these pipelines acted as agents rather than principals. The more fundamental causes of pipeline imprudence are (1) the whole scheme of gas price regulation, which over a period of years systematically underpriced new as well as old gas and hence created continual excess demand for any gas available at regulated prices; (2) inefficient price regulation of utility companies, which should have been required to charge prices based on the marginal cost of gas supplies rather than the weighted average cost; (3) less than optimal regulation of pipeline companies, such that their incentives to operate efficiently were impaired; and (4) a legal tradition of very inflexible long-term contracts for the sale of gas to pipelines. . . .

Since gas was persistently underpriced in the market, whatever could be produced could readily be sold. Regulated companies often lead a rather sheltered life. They focus their skills on the manipulation of the regulators, and not on keeping abreast of the whole market at all times. Why bother to pinpoint total potential gas demand when you can sell all you can produce, or resell all you can buy? Since the early 1960s, many forces had combined to produce an increasing excess demand for gas, including environmental regulations that placed a premium on gas as a fuel because of its freedom from major air pollution problems. Pipelines in particular were convinced as of 1978–80 that the gas shortage would be perpetual, since they felt oil prices would continue to rise over time, and under the new regulations, gas prices would never quite catch up. Thus it followed that they should control as many gas reserves as they could get the gas reserves under contract, regardless of price or contract terms.

After deregulation of high-cost new gas, supplies increased sharply in response to the very high prices offered by pipelines. A gas pipeline company with large reserves under contract at less than 50 cents per mcf could afford to contract for new reserves at $5.00 or more per mcf and still keep its weighted average of acquisition costs at or below the price that a utility company could pass on to its customers—at least, to its residential customers. [Ed. note: This method of averaging costs is called "rolled-in pricing"].

Not only did the price of new and deep gas increase sharply, but the gas producers insisted upon contract terms, other than price, that were very favorable to them: high deliverability rates, favorable "take-or-pay" provisions . . . , [and] "most favored nation" clauses, which guaranteed that higher prices paid to anyone else in a field would automatically trigger an increase to all producers in that field, and similar provisions.[8]

The pipeline companies' strategy was based on the assumption that gas consumption would never fall, since OPEC prices would always rise and gas prices would always lag behind oil prices. But gas consumption eventually fell. By the 1980s, high OPEC prices had induced energy conservation efforts everywhere. Initially oil consumption suffered before gas consumption declined. By late 1981 oil prices were slowly falling and gas prices were still rapidly increasing under the provisions of the 1978 gas act. It is apparent that some time in 1982 oil and gas prices converged and the gas market finally cleared. For the first time in roughly 20 years, excess demand for gas no longer existed. . . .

Within a surprisingly short period of time, gas prices came to be determined by competition and not by regulation. Under these circumstances, guaranteed price escalation under inflation adjustment clauses became a disadvantage, and the "take-or-pay" contracts signed in earlier years by pipeline companies became the casket in which pipelines were to be buried.

What did the pipelines do? Seemingly, the only option was to fight. If pipelines had to pay for gas they could not sell, it was clearly less expensive to them to pay for unpurchased cheap gas than for unpurchased expensive gas. So in the early 1980s, the natural gas market witnessed the paradox of low-cost reserves being shut-in or under-produced, while high-cost new gas was being produced as close to capacity as demand would permit. Such a policy maximizes total supply cost rather than minimizes it! Nevertheless, it was perfectly logical for pipelines to behave this way under existing legal, regulatory, and market constraints.

This was no solution, however, because as old gas was shut-in, the average price of gas to the consumer rose, causing additional reductions in natural gas consumption. As gas consumption fell further, pipelines were finally forced to cut purchases of high-cost new gas, in violation of contract terms, and lawsuits rapidly multiplied. If contracts on new gas were enforced, many pipelines faced bankruptcy. Bills were introduced in Congress to abrogate the terms of gas contracts already in existence, a rather novel proposal in the context of orthodox contract law. As the January 1,

---

8. A most favored nation clause reads: "If at any time after the execution of this contract, Buyer shall enter into a contract to purchase gas similar in quality at a price higher than the price hereunder, then Buyer shall immediately increase the price of gas received hereunder to equal the price under the other contract." This is a two-party favored nation clause. A third-party favored nation clause provides that the buyer will pay seller a price equal to the highest price paid by any buyer to any seller in the same area.

1985 deadline for gas price deregulation approached, demand was falling, prices to consumers were rising, gas producers were suffering from a burden of shut-in production, many pipelines were grasping at the straws of legal doctrines such as *force majeure* to save, them from ruin, and the FERC was having difficulties explaining how old gas prices could have risen so rapidly under continued price regulation.

The fundamental cause of all these market dislocations was the tradition of underpricing gas through regulation. As long as gas was underpriced, excess demand existed and it was obviously more important for the gas industry to forecast FERC policy than to forecast gas demand. Once the all-embracing nature of the regulatory context is understood, the self-confessed "imprudence" and "stupidity" of the pipelines becomes more comprehensible. . . .

It is straightforward to prescribe where policy should ultimately take us. It is less obvious how to get there. . . . [I]t should be clear that "rolled in" pricing coupled with differential pricing of new and old gas creates gross market distortions. . . . [P]olicy should aim for a single price of gas, irrespective of when it was found or how difficult it was to find. Does this mean immediate decontrol of all gas vintages still held under controls? In the event of complete decontrol, gas producers individually would be motivated to exploit all the terms in existing contracts to maximize price hikes, particularly those relating to receiving prices equal to the highest price received by any producer in a given field. If high-cost new gas production exists with contract prices well above competitive levels—and such production is rather widespread, . . . then gas producers will simply price themselves out of the market. [State utility commissions would probably not allow local gas distributors to pass along the high-cost gas prices to its customers; even if they did so allow, the high prices would cause the LDCs customers to reduce their demand for gas]. Industrial users would switch first, leaving residential users with a higher fixed cost allocation (for both pipeline and [LDC] investment) to be covered in their rates. This in turn would provoke revolt by residential users, with the probable passage of laws in some states that would regulate gas utilities more harshly. There would be demands everywhere for fresh legislation to "solve" the new gas price problems.

Thus a worst-case scenario can readily be devised that would result in disaster. On the other hand, gas producers as a group may see reasons to act more temperately. Since the gas pipelines are their only customers, it would not seem optimal to take steps that would destroy them. Voluntary renegotiations, contract by contract, might lead to more efficient resource allocation than the passage of extremely detailed national laws changing the terms of individual gas contracts. A major problem with voluntary renegotiations is that producers may be less willing to negotiate than pipelines. Existing contracts seem to give them an advantage in the event of decontrol; the market realities of excess supply at existing prices mean that they are likely to lose revenues at the present time, to the extent that prices are exposed to short-run competitive forces. Most producers believe that currently depressed prices will disappear in the long run as the present gas surplus is worked through, so they feel that delay will work in their interest. Under such circumstances negotiations may not begin readily or proceed rapidly.■

NOTES AND COMMENTS

1.   Do you understand why the natural gas market experienced such price rigidity between 1982 and 1985 (as shown in the price plateau in Fig. 8–5 *supra*), when gas shortages no longer existed? Was the effect caused solely by government regulation? After all, the NGPA set maximum legal prices, but producers could always sell their gas for less than the maximum if they wanted. Was the problem embedded in the private contracts between producers and purchasers? What particular clauses caused rigidities in price and quantity? Is there any indication that monopoly power by producers was causing too-high prices?

6.   PROTECTING THE RESIDENTIAL CONSUMER: ROLLED-IN PRICING

The rolled-in pricing discussed in the Griffin and Steele excerpt (which allowed a pipeline to sell gas by averaging the costs of old 50–cent gas and new $5.00 gas) was not without its critics or its legal battles. In *United Gas Pipe Line Co. v. FERC*, 649 F.2d 1110 (5th Cir. 1981), *reh'g denied*, 664 F.2d 289 (1981), the court upheld a FERC order that refused to allow rolled-in pricing for emergency gas purchases because such pricing was "unduly discriminatory" in violation of Section 5(a) of the NGA, 15 U.S.C.A. § 717d(a). In the mid–1970s, United Gas Pipe Line experienced such severe shortages of natural gas that it had to curtail deliveries. FERC approved a curtailment plan which divided United's customers into three classes according to end use. Residential consumers were Priority I; gas used as feedstock by direct industrial customers was Priority II; and gas for all other industrial users was Priority III.

FERC also allowed United to make emergency purchases of gas under a provision of the NGA, which it did, paying high prices for this gas. When United submitted new tariffs to recover the cost of the emergency gas on a rolled-in basis from all three classes of customers, Brooklyn Union Gas Company and Elizabeth Town Gas Company intervened and protested. They were LDCs which purchased the United gas. The LDCs insisted that proportional allocation of the cost of the emergency purchases among all customers was unduly discriminatory in light of United's curtailment plan. The demand of high-priority customers (like intervenors) could be satisfied from the gas supply normally available to United under long-term contracts at lower prices. Since the emergency purchases were made solely to meet the demand of low-priority customers, they should bear the burden of the premium price of the emergency gas. FERC agreed, and prohibited United from using rolled-in pricing to recover its emergency-gas costs "unless there is a direct benefit to all classes of customers."

FERC explained its reasons for disallowing rolled-in pricing in United's case: (1) it resulted in gross discrimination against high-priority customers, and (2) it failed to encourage efficient conservation of natural gas and substitution of more-abundant fuels. The Fifth Circuit court accepted FERC's explanation, as shown in the following excerpt from this case:

> When a curtailment plan groups customers according to their ability and willingness to find substitute fuel, the goal of encouraging efficient utilization of gas will be further served by allocating high cost gas to low priority customers. Although the Commission was not free to uncritically impose high cost gas on low priority customers, *cf. Elizabethtown Gas Co. v. FERC*, 575 F.2d 885 (D.C. Cir. 1978); *Fort Pierce Util. Auth. v. Federal Power Comm'n*, 526 F.2d 993 (5th Cir. 1976); *Mississippi Pub. Serv. Comm'n v. Fed. Power Comm'n*, 522 F.2d 1345 (5th Cir. 1975), *cert. denied*, 429 U.S. 870 (1976) . . ., here the Commission specifically found that allocating high cost emergency gas to United's low priority customers will encourage them to find substitute fuels and make more efficient use of the gas they do receive.

The NGPA provided a different mechanism, more regular than emergency purchases, for interstate pipelines facing shortages. In Sections 311 and 312 of the Act, intrastate pipelines were authorized to sell natural gas to interstate pipelines (at NGPA-controlled prices) without subjecting themselves to the full panoply of NGA jurisdiction over rates, entry, abandonment, etc. United stopped making emergency purchases and began making high-priced gas purchases under Sections 311 and 312. FERC allowed rolled-in pricing for this gas. Laclede, another LDC serving residential customers, argued that these types of gas purchases were merely a substitute for the prior purchases of emergency gas and rolled-in pricing should be prohibited, as in the *United Gas Pipe Line* case above. However, in *Laclede Gas Co. v. FERC,* 722 F.2d 272 (5th Cir. 1984), the court upheld FERC's rolled-in pricing under the NGPA. The court distinguished the policies behind emergency gas purchases and the NGPA's Sections 311 and 312 gas purchases. Emergency gas could be purchased only when the pipeline was in curtailment, when curtailment was imminent, or when the pipeline had to meet a sudden unexpected increase in demand. 18 C.F.R. § 157.46(a). By contrast, Sections 311–312 gas could be purchased at any time. Congressional policy behind 311–312 gas was to allow the surplus gas in the intrastate market to be sold to the interstate market, thereby facilitating the development of a national natural gas transportation network. Intrastate pipelines were unlikely to agree to such interstate sales if they then became wholly regulated by the FPC in addition to being regulated by their own state commissions. The statutory time frames of emergency gas and Sections 311–312 gas also differed. Emergency gas transactions were limited to sixty days, but Section 311 gas purchases could be as long as two years with additional two-year extensions and Section 312 did not limit the duration of an assignment of surplus gas from an intrastate pipeline. Because 311 and 312 purchases were intended to do more than forestall temporary emergency situations, FERC could conclude that this gas was an integral part of a pipeline's overall supply, purchased for the benefit of all customers. Thus the court upheld FERC's determination that it was just and reasonable for the cost of Sections 311–312 gas to be rolled-in to the costs of all customers.

On top of the 27 pricing categories for natural gas and FERC's policies for rolled-in (sometimes) prices, Title II of the NGPA introduced "incremental pricing", a rate design with the single goal of shifting the increased cost of gas from residential consumers to industrial users, but without driving industrial users to convert to other fuels. The legislative objective was to subsidize the favored class of residential gas users at the expense of the disfavored class, but not to the extent that industrial users would swing off of gas, thereby leaving no industrial buyers to bargain with pipelines to keep prices low as the pipelines bargained with producers for the newly deregulated gas. (Residential consumers or their representatives were not considered good bargaining agents because their demand for gas was inelastic; *i.e.*, they could not threaten to switch to another fuel if prices were raised too high). The intricacy of Congressional tinkering with this system of "ordering the market" defies summary description. If you want to try and make sense of either the economics or the politics of incremental pricing, read Carol Cormie, Incremental Pricing Under the Natural Gas Policy Act of 1978, 57 Denver L. Rev. 1 (1979); and William A. Mogel and William R. Mapes, Jr., Assessment of Incremental Pricing under the Natural Gas Policy Act, 29 Catholic U. L. Rev. 763 (1980). Even without reading these articles, compare FERC's decision to require fuel-switchable industrial users to bear 100% of the costs of emergency gas supplies in the *United* case *supra*. The "incremental pricing" provisions of the NGPA tried to arrest some of this switching, but still increase gas prices to industrial users. Clearly, policymakers were concerned that the industrial market for natural gas would completely dry up. In fact, much of the "excess" supply of natural gas in the 1980s came about not because more natural gas was found and produced but because gas demand shrank. Domestic production of natural gas peaked in 1973. (Review Section (A)(3) of this chapter).

As Griffin and Steele noted, rolled-in pricing does not accord with economically efficient markets, which should price gas or electricity to consumers at its long-run marginal cost. (Also review Chapter 2(B) *supra*). Rolled-in pricing is still an issue when pipelines expand an existing facility to serve new customers. Who should bear the costs of the expansion: all customers or only the new customers? See Section D(5) of this chapter *infra*.

7. FEDERAL PREEMPTION: THE NGPA AND STATE CONSERVATION LAWS

The inevitable conflict between federal regulation and then deregulation of natural gas prices and state conservation laws, presaged by the dissenting justices in *Phillips supra*, came to pass under the NGPA of 1978. In the following case, the U.S. Supreme Court had to determine whether Congressional policy had left room for state ratable-take laws to operate in the new federal scheme.

The facts in this case typified scenarios in gas fields throughout the United States at that time. To make the scenario more transparent, imagine that Transco pipeline signed long-term contracts during the gas-short years of the NGPA to buy gas from virtually all the producers in the Harper gas field for $5 an MCF with a 90% TOP provision. The gas is Section 107, high-cost gas under the NGPA's classification scheme shown in Figure 8–7 *supra*. The NGPA deregulated the price of this Section 107 gas completely in 1979, while allowing only gradual, controlled price increases for other gas categories. One producer, Spot Co., the owner of 5% of the reserves in the field refused to sign a long-term contract; instead it sold all of its gas to Transco on short-term contracts at a spot-market price. For a while after 1979, the spot market price rose to $8 per MCF, even higher than the long-term contract price of $5. However, the gas shortage then becomes a surplus. The spot market price drops to $2 an MCF. The LDC that bought Transco's gas for $5 and the $8 gas from Spot Co. has lost industrial customers that switched to other lower-priced fuels. Without this demand source, Transco no longer has a market to supply 90% of the deliverability of the wells in the Harper field. Transco needs to cut back production. If it reduces its purchases under the long-term contracts, it will still have to pay for the gas not taken under the TOP provision. So, Transco opts not to renew its short-term contract with Spot Co. Spot Co.'s wells are shut-in; there is no other pipeline purchaser serving Harper field and Spot Co. is being drained by adjacent producers. As Spot Co. heads for near-bankruptcy, it presses for relief at the state conservation commission (the Mississippi Board), under the state ratable-take law. Transco offers either to take Spot Co.'s gas, but only at the spot price of $2, or to transport the gas to any buyer that Spot Co. can secure for itself under any price that Spot Co. itself negotiates. Spot Co. refuses both alternatives.

The state commission issues a ratable-take order directing Transco to take Spot Co.'s gas ratably with gas from all other producers in the field, *i.e.*, 5% of the gas in Transco's pipeline must be Spot Co.'s gas. Spot Co., of course, wants Transco to pay it the same $5 per MCF price that the other producers in the field are getting for these sales. The Mississippi Supreme Court upholds the application of the state's ratable-take law to these interstate gas sales. In the opinion below the Supreme Court confronts the preemption issue [Ed. note: most citations have been omitted.]

Transcontinental Gas Pipe Line Corp. v. State Oil & Gas Board of Mississippi

474 U.S. 409 (1986).

■ BLACKMUN, J.

* * *

Under the NGA, the Federal Power Commission's comprehensive regulatory scheme involved utility-type ratemaking control over prices and supplies. The FPC set price ceilings for sales from producers to pipelines and regulated the prices pipelines could charge their downstream customers. But "[i]n the early 1970's, it became apparent that the regulatory structure was not working." *Public Service Comm'n of New York v. Mid–Louisiana Gas Co.*, 463 U.S. 319, 330 (1983). The Nation began to experience serious gas shortages. The NGA's "artificial pricing scheme" was said to be a "major cause" of the imbalance between supply and demand.

In response, Congress enacted the NGPA, which "has been justly described as 'a comprehensive statute to govern future natural gas regulation.'" *Mid-Louisiana Gas Co.*, 463 U.S., at 332, *quoting* Note, Legislative History of the Natural Gas Policy Act, 59 Texas L. Rev. 101, 116 (1980). The aim of federal regulation remains to assure adequate supplies of natural gas at fair prices, but the NGPA reflects a congressional belief that a new system of natural gas pricing was needed to balance supply and demand. The new federal role is to "overse[e] a national market price regulatory scheme." *See* S.Rep. No. 95–436, at 21 (NGPA implements "a new commodity value pricing approach"). The NGPA therefore does not constitute a federal retreat from a comprehensive gas policy. Indeed, the NGPA in some respects expanded federal control, since it granted FERC jurisdiction over the intrastate market for the first time. *See* the Act's §§ 311 and 312.

[The court then summarized the argument of the state Board that the NGPA's decontrol of high-cost gas prices in 1979 stripped FERC of jurisdiction over the Harper Sand pool gas, leaving the state free to regulate Transco's purchases through its ratable-take law. FERC's regulation of Transco's involvement with high-cost gas was now arguably limited to regulating Transco's sales to its end-use customers, not its purchases of new natural gas from its suppliers. Since the Board order concerned only this latter relationship, the state ratable-take order was not pre-empted by federal regulation. The Court responded:]

That FERC can no longer step in to regulate directly the prices at which pipelines purchase high-cost gas, however, has little to do with whether state regulations that affect a pipeline's costs and purchasing patterns impermissibly intrude upon federal concerns. Mississippi's action directly undermines Congress' determination that the supply, the demand, and the price of high-cost gas be determined by market forces. To the extent that Congress denied FERC the power to regulate affirmatively particular aspects of the first sale of gas, it did so because it wanted to leave determination of supply and first-sale price to the market. "[A] federal decision to forgo regulation in a given area may imply an authoritative federal determination that the area is best left *un*regulated, and in that event would have as much preemptive force as a decision *to* regulate" (emphasis in original). *Arkansas Elec. Coop. Corp. v. Arkansas Public Service Comm'n*, 461 U.S., at 384.

The proper question in this case is not whether FERC has affirmative regulatory power over wellhead sales of § 107 gas, but whether Congress, in revising a comprehensive federal regulatory scheme to give market forces a more significant role in determining the supply, the demand, and the price of natural gas, intended to give the States the power it had denied FERC. The answer to the latter question must be in the negative. First, when Congress meant to vest additional regulatory authority in the States it did so explicitly. Second, although FERC may now possess less regulatory jurisdiction over the "intricate relationship between the purchasers' cost structures and eventual costs to wholesale customers who sell to consumers in other States," *Northern Natural*, 372 U.S., at 92, than it did under the old regime, that relationship is still a subject of deep federal concern. FERC still must review Transco's pricing practices, even though its review of Transco's purchasing behavior has been circumscribed. In light of Congress' intent to move toward a less regulated national natural gas market, its decision to remove jurisdiction from FERC cannot be interpreted as an invitation to the States to impose additional regulations.

Mississippi's order also runs afoul of other concerns.... First, it disturbs the uniformity of the federal scheme, since interstate pipelines will be forced to comply with varied state regulations of their purchasing practices. In light of the NGPA's unification of the interstate and intrastate markets, the contention that Congress meant to permit the States to impose inconsistent regulations is especially unavailing. Second, Mississippi's order would have the effect of increasing the ultimate price to consumers. Take-or-pay provisions are standard industry-wide.... Pipelines are already committed to purchase gas in excess of market demand. Mississippi's rule will require Transco to take delivery of noncontract gas; this will lead Transco not to take delivery of contract gas elsewhere, thus triggering take-or-pay provisions. Transco's customers will ultimately bear such increased costs....

The change in regulatory perspective embodied in the NGPA rested in significant part on the belief that direct federal price control exacerbated supply and demand problems by preventing the market from making long-term adjustments. Mississippi's actions threaten to distort the market once again by artificially increasing supply and price. Although, in the long run, producers and pipelines may be able to adjust their selling and purchasing patterns to take account of ratable-take orders, requiring such future adjustments in an industry where long-term contracts are the norm will postpone achievement of Congress' aims in enacting the NGPA. We therefore conclude that Mississippi's ratable-take order is pre-empted.

The judgment of the Supreme Court of Mississippi is therefore reversed.■

NOTES AND COMMENTS

1. The finding of preemption rested on the narrowest of votes. Justice Rehnquist, joined by three other dissenters, found the ratable-take law to be consistent with the NGPA's purpose of decontrolling the wellhead price of high-cost gas. The 1938 NGA clearly had left no room for either direct or indirect state regulation of the prices of gas sold into the interstate market for resale; ratable-take laws, which indirectly affected gas prices, invaded

the federal agency's "exclusive domain" of sales regulation under the NGA. However, the NGPA's purpose of eliminating federal controls on the wellhead price gas did not conflict with traditional state conservation regulation that merely defined the correlative rights of owners of gas in a common field. In fact, Rehnquist noted: "Markets depend upon such rules to function efficiently." He continued:

> Ratable-take rules serve the twin interests of conservation and fair dealing by removing the incentive for "drainage." On its face, the ratable-take rule here is completely consistent with the free market determination of the wellhead price of high-cost gas. Like any compulsory unitization rule, it gives joint owners the incentive to price at the same level as a single owner. But it will not affect the spot market price of gas in any other way. It is similarly price neutral in the context of long-term contracting. The rule is merely one of a number of legal rules that regulates the contractual relations of parties in the State of Mississippi as in other States. * * *

> One may agree that Congress wished to return to the free market determination of the price of high-cost gas without concluding that Mississippi's ratable-take rule frustrates that wish.

2. Do the majority and the dissent disagree about the Congressional intent behind the NGPA's pricing policies? Does either opinion interpret the NGPA's goal as keeping gas prices low? What has the Supreme Court determined the NGPA policy to be regarding gas prices? If the policy was to ultimately let the market determine the price, then this price might be high or low, depending on supply and demand. How did the Mississippi ratable-take statute interfere with the forces of supply and demand in the gas market? Does the split in the Court reflect different views of federalism, of "state's rights," rather than a difference in interpreting the NGPA's pricing policy? Or did the dissent simply fail to recognize that the ratable-take rules could have a very real, albeit indirect, effect on natural gas prices?

3. Could Mississippi have accomplished the result it wanted by issuing a market-demand prorationing order rather than a ratable-take order? A prorationing order would restrict the producer from producing more than the market demanded. This type of order does not aim directly at interstate purchasers of gas. Yet the interstate pipeline is certainly affected by such an order. If the producers with whom the pipeline has long-term contracts can no longer supply the quantities demanded by the pipeline because their wells have been cut back by a state prorationing order, then the pipeline will have to buy gas from other non-contract producers. Doesn't this solve the correlative rights problem of drainage? How does this scenario affect the pipeline's take-or-pay liabilities? Can the pipeline be forced to pay for gas that it does not take because the state conservation agency prohibits producers from producing at their deliverability capacity and instead cuts producers to, say, 35 percent of capacity? Reread the take-or-pay clause quoted *supra* in the text at footnote 7 of this chapter. Now do you understand why pipeline companies with large take-or-pay liabilities pre-

ferred prorationing rules over ratable-take rules? Are state prorationing rules preempted under the reasoning of *Phillips* and the majority in *Transco?* See Smith & Weaver, 2 Texas Law of Oil and Gas § 8.5(C).

4. By 1985, natural gas production had basically been freed of the pervasive price regulation once imposed on gas producers. Now it was time to tackle the gas transportation sector. In 1985, FERC began issuing a series of orders to transform gas pipelines into open-access common carriers, the regulatory model which Congress had failed to enact in 1938, without waiting for Congress to amend the NGA. The story of this revolution is told in the next section.

D. THE TRANSITION TO A RESTRUCTURED PIPELINE INDUSTRY

Today the natural gas business would hardly be recognized by the people who knew it in the 1970s. A highly regulated, conservative industry has been transformed into a competitive business featuring entrepreneurs and marketers who would be equally at home on Wall Street. (Refer back to Figures 8–2 and 8–3 to view the changing landscape.)

1. THE 1982 "GAS BUBBLE" MEETS LONG-TERM CONTRACT RIGIDITIES

The underlying assumption of the NGPA was that shortages and high prices would be a fact of life for many years to come. However, domestic producers had responded to the increased incentives offered by the new federal pricing policies. Meanwhile, industrial end-users had often shifted to coal or heavy fuel oil rather than risk gas curtailments and the vagaries of federal pricing policies like incremental pricing. A "bubble" of excess gas appeared most unexpectedly in 1982, shortly after the Third Oil Shock. (Review Chapter 7(B) *supra.*) Conservation of oil by consumers and newly found oil supplies (developed around the world in response to the skyrocketing oil prices of the First and Second Oil Shocks) resulted in a dramatic drop in oil prices in 1981. The stage was set for the marketplace to reign in energy.

Residential consumers of gas, however, did not experience the benefits of any price decrease. The local distributing companies (LDCs) supplying residential customers had entered into long-term contracts to buy gas from the pipelines which were similar to the long-term contracts between the pipelines and the producers. The distributors typically had "minimum bill" contracts with the pipelines which functioned like take-or-pay contracts, *i.e.,* the distributors were required to pay for certain minimum amounts of gas whether or not they needed this amount to fill their customers' demands. LDCs, facing an oversupply of gas in a declining industrial market, had to raise rates to the captive residential consumer market to offset the withdrawal of industrial users from the market. This created the perverse effect of residential consumers' gas bills rising while the market price of gas was falling.

Many regulators found this situation discomforting—but the alternative of pipeline bankruptcy was equally distressing. And the potential of bankruptcy was very real for many pipelines, which would have meant that the pipeline bondholders and stockholders would take a big hit. LDCs and their investors were also suffering, so the pressure for relief was intense. FERC began to issue a series of orders that would allow flexible markets for gas to develop.

2.   RESTRUCTURING BEGINS: SPECIAL MARKETING PROGRAMS

FERC's initial attempt addressed one of the most contentious issues in the industry for many years: the complaint of big industrial customers that they were paying too-high prices for natural gas because LDCs wanted to keep gas prices lower for residential users. In other words, in designing rate structures to distribute the cost-of-service rates among different classes of customers, the LDCs forced the industrial sector to cross-subsidize the residential sector. Many industries were eager to negotiate their own purchases of gas directly from producers and to pay the pipelines for the cost of transportation only, thus leaving the LDC out of the transaction. And what producers might be eager for such a sale? The Spot Co.'s of the world, for one. The gas bubble was also forcing pipelines to shut-in the wells of producers with long-term TOP contracts, but the pipelines were breaching the TOP provision by not making payments for the gas not taken; thus contract producers also began to see their cash flow fall.

FERC's initial step toward creating more flexible markets by resolving and removing the price rigidities built into the long-term TOP contracts was to create a voluntary "Special Marketing Program," or SMP, between producers and industrial users. The program did not fare well in the following opinion by Judge (now Justice) Scalia, written when he was still on the D.C. Circuit:

Maryland People's Counsel v. FERC

761 F.2d 768 (D.C. Cir. 1985).

■ SCALIA, J. This is a challenge to the Federal Energy Regulatory Commission's approval of what it described as an experimental increase in [natural gas] pipeline competition. That increase was to be achieved by agreement of a pipeline and its producers to amend the high-priced gas purchase contracts entered into between them in earlier years, so as to permit the producers to sell the committed gas elsewhere (at current market prices), crediting the volume of such sales against the pipeline's high-priced purchase obligations. This challenge is brought, curiously enough, not by the competing pipelines or producers to whose flanks this new spur of competition is being applied, but by representatives of the putative beneficiaries, customers of the pipeline system. Their complaint is that, under the arrangements approved by the Commission, the only customers eligible to purchase the cheaper released gas are industrial users who would, at the higher gas prices agreed to in the original contracts, switch to an alternate fuel. They claim that because of this limitation "captive customers" of the pipeline—those who do not have alternate fuel sources to which they may turn—receive no net benefit, but to the contrary suffer a net loss from the arrangement. The principal issue before us is whether the Commission set forth a reasonable basis for believing that the program it approved will benefit all pipeline ratepayers.

A modest understanding of the complex regulatory background of this dispute is necessary to evaluate the arguments made before us. Pipelines regulated by the Natural Gas Act transport natural gas from producers to distributors and end-users in other states. Ordinarily (though not invariably) they purchase the gas on their own account and resell it to their customers. While they may transport gas purchased directly by distributors or end-users from producers, they have no common-carrier obligation to do so. Their rates to distributors (but not to end-users) are regulated by FERC. However, while that portion of the rate attributable to transportation costs (the fixed and incremental costs of constructing and operating the pipeline) is determined by standard public utility rate-making techniques, the much larger portion attributable to the cost of the transported gas is effectively unregulated at the pipeline stage. FERC permits that cost to be passed through, without assuring that the purchase price was a prudent one. A pipeline's purchase costs for all the gas it acquires are averaged to determine the appropriate gas-cost component of its rates.

Previously, lack of gas price regulation at the pipeline stage would have made little difference, since FERC ... regulated gas prices (for interstate gas) at the wellhead, controlling the maximum prices that producers could charge. Because it fixed those prices well below market, a large discrepancy developed between the price for interstate gas and the price for unregulated intrastate gas, and gas production was withheld from the interstate market. After the interstate gas shortages and curtailments of 1976–77, Congress almost entirely terminated Commission wellhead-price regulation, and provided in the Natural Gas Policy Act of 1978, 15 U.S.C. §§ 3301–3432 (1982) ("NGPA"), statutorily prescribed wellhead price ceilings for various categories of gas, in both inter-state and intra-state markets.

The problem ultimately giving rise to the present litigation is that the 1978 predictions of the 1985 market were much in error. Factors ranging from the increased wellhead prices and impending total decontrol, to greater energy conservation, to the lower prices of competing fuels, have turned the natural gas shortages of the 1970's into a natural gas surplus. Thus, as early as the summer of 1983—a year and a half before the scheduled deregulation of new gas—the formulary statutory maximum price for new gas had already reached or exceeded the market-clearing price in many geographic markets.... Pipelines, however, by reason of their practice of entering into long-term contracts with producers, were already locked into purchases, for years to come, of NGPA unregulated gas and new gas in volumes and at prices based upon the 1978 expectations.

If all natural gas customers were as a practical matter compelled to buy gas, the consequence of this miscalculation would merely be that they would be paying more for the gas they purchase than it is now "worth." In fact, however, many existing customers (and many would-be customers whose new business was contemplated in the pipelines' long-term purchases) can shift to alternate fuels that are cheaper than the gas that has been purchased by the pipelines (though not cheaper than the current market price of gas). The departure of these customers imposes two added burdens upon the customers that remain: (1) the "fixed cost" component of their rates will rise, because it must now be divided among a smaller number of ratepayers, and (2) the gas cost component of their rates will rise even further above its already-inflated level, since the pipelines' average gas cost per unit volume will be substantially increased by "take-or-pay" liabilities to producers—that is, liabilities under standard provisions of their long-term contracts requiring payment for a minimum volume of purchase whether or not it is in fact taken. Of course these additional increases make it worthwhile for even more customers to leave the system, so that the situation becomes still worse.

To meet this situation, one pipeline, Columbia Gas Transmission Corporation ("Columbia") concluded . . . an agreement with its largest supplier, Exxon Corporation. The core of the agreement was that Columbia would release its contract rights to certain categories of gas in specified Exxon fields (subject to retraction if Columbia should need the gas to fulfill its customer obligations), and would transport that released gas to direct purchasers from Exxon on Columbia's system; in exchange for which Exxon would credit Columbia's take-or-pay liability with the volume of released gas sold, on Columbia's system or elsewhere. Sales by Exxon to customers off Columbia's system would be subject to a right of first refusal by Columbia's customers.

[FERC approved this special marketing program ("SMP") subject to certain conditions: It required Columbia to permit all its gas suppliers, not merely Exxon, to participate in the SMP; and it expanded somewhat the category of eligible purchasers of the gas released from the TOP contract, although this category was still generally limited to customers with alternative sources of fuel. FERC also authorized other pipelines to initiate SMPs similar to Columbia's. Shortly thereafter, Maryland People's Counsel (MPC) filed a timely petition for review.]

The issue presented for our review is a narrow one. We have not been asked to pass on the Commission's general authority to approve SMPs such as Columbia's, but only on its power to permit exclusion, from the category of authorized purchasers of released gas under such an SMP, of the pipeline's captive customers or (as the Commission calls them) "core market"—i.e., those customers who have no readily available alternative source of fuel. . . .

* * *

The effect of this limitation of eligible participants is that captive customers of the Columbia system are excluded from purchasing the cheaper released gas.

The Commission recognized that [the SMP] raised substantial competitive concerns. Nonetheless, the Commission justified the program as essential to avoid saddling captive customers with an increased share of the fixed costs of gas pipelines as fuel-switchable customers left the system because of high prices. The Commission reasoned that if the SMP increased volumes of gas transported through the pipeline, the fixed costs could be spread over greater volumes, thereby lowering the costs assigned to each share. Thus, even though the SMP was limited to certain eligible customers, ineligible customers would benefit directly from the reduction in the portion of fixed costs they would be forced to bear. *See* Final Columbia SMP Order, *supra*, 26 F.E.R.C. (CCH) at ¶¶ 61,087–88.

MPC, however, raised several arguments not responded to by the Commission. Most important, the Commission's fixed cost saving rationale does not explain why such savings would not similarly accrue to the benefit of captive customers in the absence of the [SMP] limitation on eligible purchasers. Additional SMP sales would presumably still occur, and fixed costs would still be spread to the benefit of captive customers. . . .

On this appeal, the rationale the Commission advances most strenuously in defense . . . is that competition between pipelines for one another's "core" or captive market would not necessarily be in the public interest. The Commission's order expressed this point as follows:

> [W]e are not yet prepared to say that competition for the firm markets would achieve a net benefit. The pipelines have made long-term supply commitments, have designed their operations, and have major investments in pipeline capacity and other facilities, e.g., above ground and underground storage and synthetic gas, in order to serve these markets. Under competition, there would be winners and losers and the pipelines that lost firm markets would be forced to attempt to recover their costs from other captive markets that were unable to take advantage of competition. The shifting of these costs could constitute undue discrimination. On the other hand, failure to recover these costs could place the pipeline in financial jeopardy which could affect the reliability of service to those customers and consumers dependent upon the pipeline.

Final Columbia SMP Order, *supra*, 26 F.E.R.C. (CCH) at ¶ 61,087.

This "winners and losers" rationale plainly cannot support the [SMP] limitation. In the first place, in order to avoid competition between pipelines for "core" markets it was not necessary to exclude those markets entirely from the SMP. The same result could have been achieved by permitting each pipeline to transport only to its own captive customers the gas that is released from its system supply. . . . Moreover, even if competition between pipelines were allowed, it is quite possible that the downward pressure exerted by competition on gas prices (constituting 85 percent of the captive customers' rates) would outweigh any increased fixed cost burden—enabling even the "loser" pipelines to stay in business by charging their remaining customers higher fixed costs but overall lower rates. The Commission did not even consider this possibility. . . .

It would be an exaggeration to say that this petition for review has required us to evaluate whether the Commission had, if not the better side, at least a reasonable side, of the argument with MPC over the effects of these orders. On a number of obviously significant points that MPC raised, there is simply no argument to evaluate: the Commission proceeded on its course with no comment, or with comment that was patently unresponsive. As far as we can tell from the record before us, the Commission's decision was not "based on a consideration of the relevant factors," *State Farm*, 463 U.S. at 43, and was therefore invalid.

Since the orders at issue in this case have already expired, in lieu of mandate we will issue a certified copy of this opinion. As noted earlier, successor orders have already been challenged in other proceedings before this court. By accompanying orders, we are directing the Commission and intervenors on behalf of the Commission in those cases, *Maryland People's Counsel v. FERC*, 760 F.2d 318, and *Laclede Gas Co. v. FERC*, 760 F.2d 318, to show cause why the successor orders should not be vacated and remanded for reconsideration in light of this opinion.

Petition granted.

[In a companion case, the court also remanded to the FERC its new process for obtaining "blanket certificates," by which a pipeline could obtain the right to transport gas for others without obtaining FERC approval of each transaction. As with the Special Marketing Program, the court's objection was not to the process itself but to FERC's restriction of the process to large interruptible customers. *See* 761 F.2d 780.]■

NOTES AND COMMENTS

1. FERC's cautious approach, which the court criticized in the *Maryland Peoples' Counsel* opinion, reflected extreme nervousness in the financial markets about a switch to a competitive natural gas industry. The pipeline networks had been expensive to build and they were financed by bond purchasers. If a pipeline lost customers to competitors in a more flexible market, its bondholders—financial institutions, trusts, pension funds and individuals—would not receive their interest payments. Fortunately, by the 1980s, most of the pipelines had been in existence for many years and their bonds were being paid off as their terms expired, so concern for bondholders' investments was decreasing with time.

2. In general, the SMPs attempted to create a "win-win" opportunity to negotiate among all the parties caught in the Gordian knot of TOP contracts and the gas bubble. The shut-in or curtailed producer of high-priced gas could find new markets for large volumes of gas by dropping the price and selling directly to an industrial end-user of large volumes. This

end-user switched back to low-priced gas that was a cleaner, superior fuel to coal or oil. The switch back allowed the pipeline to ship greater volumes of gas, allowing it to lower its average cost of transporting each MCF or BTU and earn a decent rate of return. The pipelines had built up massive TOP liability to producers, and the SMP credited the volumes of gas released from the TOP contracts against the pipelines' obligations to take. Of course, both producers and pipelines would have been happier if gas prices had stayed high and end-users had kept buying all the gas that could be delivered, regardless of price. The market simply didn't allow this.

3. Open Access for All: Order 636

Following the court's lead in *Maryland Peoples' Counsel supra*, FERC began to expand the opportunities for producers and end-users to deal directly with each other in the purchase of gas, using the pipeline only as a transporter, not as the middleman merchant who first bought all the gas from producers and then sold it to LDCs to distribute to end-users. Increasingly, producers and end-users could now "bypass" the pipeline as a merchant. Industrial users also wanted to bypass the LDC (with its cross-subsidized rate structure favoring residential consumers) and ship gas directly from a producer to an industrial plant, using a small spur built off the pipeline's main transmission line. (This is called "industrial bypass," meaning the LDC is being bypassed in the gas sale.)

Full-scale restructuring of the industry demanded that all pipelines become open-access pipelines, obligated to transport the gas owned by others without discrimination, on the same basic rates and terms as any gas still owned by the pipeline as a merchant. From 1985 onwards, FERC orders continued to encourage open access until, in 1992, FERC issued its famous Order 636: full restructuring had arrived. Pipelines would become like railroads and trucks, carrying goods owned by others.

Before reading some major (but drastically shortened) parts of the 150–page opinion of the D.C. Circuit court reviewing Order 636, here is an overview of the key provisions and some of the jargon of Order 636:

a. Functional unbundling. The widely used term for the separation of one line of business from another is "unbundling." The pipelines were directed to separate their gas merchant sales services from their transportation services. This required changes in the internal organization of the companies which in the past had primarily transported only gas they bought and sold themselves. Because the pipelines were not required to actually divest themselves of one of these two divisions, Order 636 did not require a true unbundling, although the pipelines had the option to do so. The Order only demanded that an internal "Chinese wall" be created within the company to prevent the exchange of information between the two divisions except on the same terms as available to competitors. For this reason the process became known as "functional" unbundling.

b. Storage access. Most pipelines operate storage fields near their major markets, consisting of depleted oil or gas reservoirs into which gas can be pumped in the summer and withdrawn in the winter. Order 636 directed the pipelines to provide equal access to these storage fields to all shippers of gas and on terms comparable to the pipeline's own gas.

c.   Transportation access. The pipelines were required to file rate schedules ("tariffs") showing that all shippers of gas could buy transportation service from the pipeline at the same rate as the pipeline charged customers who bought gas owned by the pipeline.

d.   Electronic notification. Pipelines were required to install information technology that would give their customers equal and timely access to the prices and conditions of transportation service. These are referred to as "electronic bulletin boards" or "EBBs."

e.   Capacity release. Pipelines were required to implement a "capacity release" program so that firm shippers, *i.e.,* those who have committed to pay for reserved space in the pipeline, can release unneeded space to others who can use the capacity to ship their own gas. Contracts for pipeline capacity are bought and sold on the EBBs.

f.   Common rate design. All pipelines were required to compute their rates for transportation services on the basis of the same formula, a formula which ultimately shifted pipeline capital costs to the class of firm shippers rather than interruptible shippers.

The validity of Order 636 was upheld on appeal, although several minor issues were remanded to FERC for reconsideration. The following excerpts from the case first review some familiar background to Order 636 and its predecessor Order 436. This section of the opinion explains why Order 436 was only partially successful in providing open access, causing FERC to issue Order 636's mandatory unbundling to achieve full success. The excerpts then address three major parts of the order: First, how would curtailment work when unexpected events created a shortage in pipeline space? Previous curtailment policies had dealt with shortages in gas supplies, not in pipeline space. Second, did FERC have jurisdiction to regulate the newly created market in buying and selling pipeline space in the "capacity release" program? Third, and yet again, FERC still struggled with the issue of who would bear the burden of the costs of transition, mainly take-or-pay costs. The pipelines? All or some of their customers? Gas producers? Or should all interested groups share the costs somehow?

As you read these excerpts (from which most citations are deleted), note how the restructuring of the gas industry was a constant back-and-forth between FERC and the D.C. Circuit. The FERC in 1996 is clearly not as timid as it was in 1985 in *Maryland People's Counsel*. In fact, in the section on curtailment policies, FERC is cautioned by the court not to overly embrace markets, private contracts and self-help forms of relief in times when pipelines are constrained from carrying all of the gas demanded by its customers. [Eds. note: The original outline numbers and letters have been slightly changed to ease readability.]

United Distribution Companies v. FERC

88 F.3d 1105 (D.C. Cir. 1996).

■ Per Curiam. In Order No. 636, the Federal Energy Regulatory Commission (Commission or FERC) took the latest step in its decade-long restructuring of the natural gas industry, in which the Commission has gradually withdrawn from direct regulation of certain industry sectors in favor of a policy of "light-handed regulation" when market forces make that possible. We review briefly the regulatory background for natural gas [in Part I] . . . .

I.A. Background: Natural Gas Industry Structure

The natural gas industry is functionally separated into production, transportation, and distribution. Traditionally, before the move to open-access transportation, a producer extracted the gas and sold it at the wellhead to a pipeline company. The pipeline company then transported the gas through high-pressure pipelines and re-sold it to a local distribution company (LDC). The LDC in turn distributed the gas through its local mains to residential and industrial users.

The Natural Gas Act (NGA), (codified as amended at 15 U.S.C. §§ 717–717w (1994)), enacted in 1938, gave the Commission jurisdiction over sales for resale in interstate commerce and over the interstate transportation of gas, but left the regulation of local distribution to the states. The NGA was intended to fill the regulatory gap left by a series of Supreme Court decisions that interpreted the dormant Commerce Clause to preclude state regulation of interstate transportation and of wholesale gas sales. The overriding purpose of the NGA is "to protect consumers against exploitation at the hands of natural gas companies." *Federal Power Comm'n v. Louisiana Power & Light Co.*, 406 U.S. 621, 631 (1972) (*quoting Federal Power Comm'n v. Hope Natural Gas Co.*, 320 U.S. 591, 610 (1944)). Federal regulation of the natural gas industry is thus designed to curb pipelines' potential monopoly power over gas transportation. The enormous economies of scale involved in the construction of natural gas pipelines tend to make the transportation of gas a natural monopoly. Indeed, even with the expansion of the national pipeline grid, or network, in recent decades, many "captive" customers remain served by a single pipeline. Order No. 436, ¶ 30,665, at 31,473.

Even though the market function potentially subject to monopoly power is the transportation of gas, for many years the Commission also regulated the price and terms of sales by producers to interstate pipelines. Producer price regulation was widely regarded as a failure, introducing severe distortions into what otherwise would have been a well-functioning producer sales market. *See* Stephen G. Breyer & Paul W. MacAvoy, Energy Regulation by The Federal Power Commission 56–88 (1974). When a severe gas shortage developed in the 1970s, Congress enacted the Natural Gas Policy Act of 1978 (NGPA), 15 U.S.C. §§ 3301–3432 (1994), which gradually phased out producer price regulation. Under the NGPA's partially regulated producer-price system, many pipelines entered into long-term contractual obligations, in what were known as "take-or-pay" provisions, to purchase minimum quantities of gas from producers at costs that proved to be well above current market prices of gas.

The problem of pipelines' take-or-pay settlement costs has plagued the industry and the Commission over the last fifteen years. The Commission's initial response to escalating pipeline take-or-pay liabilities was to authorize pipelines to offer less expensive sales of third-party (non-pipeline-owned) gas to non-captive customers while still offering only higher-priced pipeline gas to captive customers. The court struck down these measures because the Commission "had not adequately attended to the agency's prime constituency," captive customers vulnerable to pipelines' market power. *Maryland People's Counsel v. FERC*, 761 F.2d 780, 781 (D.C. Cir. 1985) (MPC II); *see also Maryland People's Counsel v. FERC*, 761 F.2d 768, 776 (D.C. Cir. 1985) (MPC I). In response to the court's decisions in MPC I and MPC II, the Commission embarked on its landmark Order No. 436 rulemaking. *See* Order No. 436, ¶ 30,665, at 31,467.

B.   Order No. 436: Open–Access Transportation

In Order No. 436, the Commission began the transition toward removing pipelines from the gas-sales business and confining them to a more limited role as gas transporters. Under a new Part 284 of its regulations, the Commission conditioned receipt of a blanket certificate[9] for firm transportation of third-party gas on the pipeline's acceptance of non-discrimination requirements guaranteeing equal access for all customers to the new service. Order No. 436, ¶ 30,665, at 31,497–518. In effect, the Commission for the first time imposed the duties of common carriers upon interstate pipelines. *See Associated Gas Distribs. v. FERC*, 824 F.2d 981, 997 (D.C. Cir. 1987) (AGD I), *cert. denied*, 485 U.S. 1006 (1988). By recognizing that anti-competitive conditions in the industry arose from pipeline control over access to transportation capacity, the equal-access requirements of Order No. 436 regulated the natural-monopoly conditions directly. In addition, every open-access pipeline was required to allow its existing bundled firm-sales customers to convert to firm-transportation service and, at the customer's option, to reduce its firm-transportation entitlement (its "contract demand"). Order No. 436, ¶ 30,665, at 31,518–33. Moreover, the Commission established a flexible rate structure under which transportation charges were limited to the maximum approved rate (based on fully allocated costs) but pipelines could selectively discount down to the minimum approved rate (based on average variable cost). *Id.* at 31,533–49.

The court largely approved Order No. 436, but the principal stumbling-block was the unresolved problem of uneconomical pipeline-producer contracts in the transition to the unbundled environment. The Commission had decided not to provide pipelines with relief from their take-or-pay

---

9. Eds. note: A blanket certificate issued by FERC allows an interstate pipeline to apply for a one-time certificate that authorizes the transportation of gas for other pipelines, end-users, marketers, brokers and other shippers on a self-implementing basis rather than using individual, shipper-by-shipper certificates.

liabilities, even though the introduction of open-access transportation in Order No. 436 would likely exacerbate the problem by reducing pipeline sales. *AGD I*, 824 F.2d at 1021–23. After the court remanded the case on the ground that the Commission's inaction on take-or-pay did not exhibit reasoned decision making in light of open access, *id.* at 1030, the Commission adopted various interim measures in Order No. 500. First, it instituted a "crediting mechanism," under which a pipeline could apply any third-party gas that it transported toward the pipeline's minimum-purchase obligation from that particular producer. Order No. 500, ¶ 30,761, at 30,779–84. Second, the Commission adopted two alternative cost-recovery mechanisms. As customary, a pipeline could recover all of its prudently incurred costs in its commodity (sales) charges, although that could prove difficult for pipelines with shrinking sales-customer bases. In the alternative, under the equitable-sharing approach, a pipeline offering open-access transportation could, if it voluntarily absorbed between twenty-five and fifty percent of the [TOP] costs, recover an equal share of the costs through a "fixed charge" and recover the remaining amount (up to fifty percent) through a volumetric surcharge based on total throughput (and thus borne by both sales and transportation customers alike). *Id.* at ¶ 30,784–92; 18 C.F.R. § 2.104. Third, the Commission authorized pipelines not recovering take-or-pay costs in any other manner to impose a "gas inventory charge" (GIC), a fixed charge for "standing ready" to deliver gas—the sales analogue to a reservation charge. Order No. 500, ¶ 30,761, at 30,792–94; 18 C.F.R. § 2.105.

The Commission's alternative solutions to the problem of take-or-pay settlement costs in Order No. 500 fared poorly on judicial review. First, the court remanded the crediting mechanism for an explanation of whether the Commission had the requisite authority under § 7 of the NGA. *American Gas Ass'n v. FERC*, 888 F.2d 136, 148–49 (D.C. Cir. 1989) (*AGA I*). After the Commission explained its § 7 authority for the crediting mechanism in Order No. 500–H, the court upheld the crediting mechanism. *American Gas Ass'n v. FERC*, 912 F.2d 1496, 1509–13 (D.C. Cir. 1990) (*AGA II*). Second, the court struck down the equitable-sharing cost-recovery mechanism on the ground that the Commission's "purchase deficiency" method for calculating the "fixed charge," which assigned costs to each customer based on how much its purchases had declined over the relevant preceding period, violated the filed-rate doctrine. *Associated Gas Distribs. v. FERC,* 893 F.2d 349, 354–57 (D.C. Cir. 1989) (*AGD II*), *reh'g en banc denied*, 898 F.2d 809 (D.C. Cir.), *cert. denied*, 498 U.S. 907 (1990). The Commission responded to the invalidation of the "purchase deficiency" method in *AGD II* by adopting Order No. 528, which allowed pipelines, in the "fixed charge," to pass through a portion of costs to customers based on any of several measures of current (rather than past) demand or usage, with the intent of avoiding the filed-rate problem. Order No. 528, ¶ 61,163, at 61,597–98. Finally, the court struck down the Commission's approval of a GIC on a particular pipeline because it had given undue weight to the pipeline's customers' having agreed to the GIC and failed adequately to consider the interests of end-users. *Texas Power Corp. v. FERC*, 908 F.2d 998, 1003–05 (D.C. Cir. 1990).

Congress completed the process of deregulating the producer sales market by enacting the Natural Gas Wellhead Decontrol Act of 1989. As the House Committee on Energy and Commerce emphasized, the Commission's creation of open-access transportation was "essential" to Congress' decision completely to deregulate wellhead sales. The committee report declared also that "both the FERC and the courts are strongly urged to retain and improve this competitive structure in order to maximize the benefits of decontrol." *Id.* The committee expected that, by ensuring that "all buyers [are] free to reach the lowest-selling producer," *id.*, open-access transportation would allow the more efficient producers to emerge, leading to lower prices for consumers, *id.* at 3, 7.

C.   Order No. 636: Mandatory Unbundling

In Order No. 636, the Commission declared the open-access requirements of Order No. 436 a partial success. The Commission found that pipeline firm sales, which in 1984 had been over 90 percent of deliveries to market, had declined by 1990 to 21 percent. Order No. 636, ¶ 30,939, at 30,399 tbl. 1. On the other hand, only 28 percent of deliveries to market in 1990 were firm transportation, whereas 51 percent of deliveries used interruptible transportation. *Id.* at 30,399 & n. 61. The Commission concluded that many customers had not taken advantage of Order No. 436's option to convert from firm-sales to firm-transportation service because the firm-transportation component of bundled firm-sales service was "superior in quality" to stand-alone firm-transportation service. *Id.* at 30, 402. In particular, the Commission found that stand-alone firm-transportation service was often subject to daily scheduling and balancing requirements, as well as to penalties for variances from projected purchases in excess of ten percent. Moreover, pipelines usually did not offer storage capacity on a contractual basis to stand-alone firm-transportation shippers. *Id.* The result was that many of the non-converted customers used the pipelines' firm-sales service during times of peak demand but in non-peak periods bought third-party gas and transported it with interruptible transportation. The Commission found that "it is often cheaper for pipeline sales customers to buy gas on the spot market, and pay the pipeline's demand charge plus the interruptible rate, than to purchase the pipeline's gas." *Id.* at 30,400. Because of the distortions in the sales market, these customers often paid twice for transportation services and still received an inferior form of transportation (interruptible rather than firm). *Id.* Because of the anti-competitive effect on the industry, the Commission found that pipelines' bundled firm-sales service violated §§ 4(b) and 5(a) of the NGA. *Id.* at 30,405.

The Commission's remedy for these anti-competitive conditions, and the principal innovation of Order No. 636, was mandatory unbundling of pipelines' sales and transportation services. By making the separation of the two functions mandatory, the Commission expects that pipelines' monopoly power over transportation will no longer distort the sales market. Order No. 636, ¶ 30,939, at 30,406–13; Order No. 636–A, ¶ 30,950, at 30,527–46; Order No. 636–B, ¶ 61,272, at 61,988–92. To replace the firm-transportation component of bundled firm-sales service, the Commission introduced the concept of "no-notice firm transportation," stand-alone firm transportation without penalties. Those customers who receive bundled firm-sales service have the right, during the restructuring process, to switch to no-notice firm-transportation service. Pipelines that did not offer bundled firm-sales service are not required to offer no-notice transportation; but if they do, they must offer no-notice transportation on a nondiscriminatory basis.

[In contrast to the continued regulation of the transportation market, the Commission had essentially deregulated pipeline sales of natural gas by relying on producer competition at the wellhead to keep unbundled pipeline sales for resale within the NGA's "just and reasonable" standard.]

The Commission also undertook several measures to ensure that the pipeline grid, or network, functions as a whole in a more competitive fashion. First, open-access pipelines may not inhibit the development of "market centers," which are pipeline intersections that allow customers to take advantage of many more transportation routes and choose between sellers from different natural gas production areas.[10] Similarly, open-access pipelines may not interfere with the development of "pooling areas," which allow the aggregation of gas supplies at a production area. Finally, as part of the move toward open-access transportation, the Commission required Part 284 pipelines to allow shippers to deliver gas at any delivery point without penalty and to allow customers to receive gas at any receipt point without penalty.

Even though this is the court's first occasion to address Order No. 636, which was enacted in 1992, we do not write on a clean slate. Beginning with *MPC I* and *MPC II*, the court has consistently required the Commission to protect consumers against pipelines' monopoly power. No longer reluctantly engaged in the unbundling enterprise, the Commission has responded by initiating sweeping changes with Order No. 636. Accordingly, we review the Commission's exercise of its authority under the NGA in light of the principles that the court has already applied in this area.

        * * *

After two comprehensive rehearing orders, Orders No. 636–A and No. 636–B, the Commission denied further rehearing.... We ordered the petitioners to file briefs in consolidated industry groups: pipelines; local distribution companies (LDCs); small distributors and municipalities; industrial end-users; electric generators; and public utility commissions (PUCs).

The petitioners do not challenge the mandatory unbundling remedy itself. At issue on review are numerous other aspects of Order No. 636

---

10. These market centers are now called "hubs." They are locations where several pipelines meet and typically where large underground storage reservoirs exist so large volumes of gas can be traded, stored, temporarily "parked," and transferred to pipelines headed in another direction, creating a national network for gas flows throughout the U.S.

involving changes that the Commission undertook as part of its comprehensive restructuring of the natural gas industry. . . .

* * *

II.C.   Curtailment

When supply shortages arose in the natural gas industry during the 1970s, the Commission adopted end-use curtailment plans to protect high-priority customers from an interruption of supply. *See generally Consolidated Edison Co. v. FERC*, 676 F.2d 763, 765–67 (D.C. Cir. 1982); *North Carolina v. FERC*, 584 F.2d 1003, 1006–08 (D.C. Cir. 1978). In 1973, the Commission found itself "impelled to direct curtailment on the basis of end use rather than on the basis of contract simply because contracts do not necessarily serve the public interest requirement of efficient allocation of this wasting resource." Order No. 467, 49 F.P.C. 85, 86. The Commission's end-use curtailment schemes were essentially enacted into law by title IV of the Natural Gas Policy Act of 1978 (NGPA), which establishes the following priority system:

Whenever there is an insufficient supply, under the Act first in line to receive gas are schools, small business, residences, hospitals, and all others for whom a curtailment of natural gas could endanger life, health, or the maintenance of physical property. After these "high-priority" users have been satisfied, next in line are those who will put the gas to "essential agricultural uses," followed by those who will use the gas for "essential industrial process or feedstock uses," followed by everyone else. *Process Gas Consumers Group v. U.S. Dep't of Agriculture*, 657 F.2d 459, 460 (D.C. Cir. 1981) (*Process Gas I*).

With the introduction of stand-alone firm-transportation service in Order No. 436, the Commission distinguished for the first time between supply curtailment and capacity curtailment. Transportation service can suffer from a capacity interruption (such as a force majeure loss of capacity due to pipeline system failure or a pipeline's overbooking of capacity), whereas sales service can suffer from a shortage in the supply of gas. The Commission's subsequent approach was to allow pipelines to adopt pro rata capacity curtailment (allocation proportional to the amount reserved, without regard to end use), *see, e.g., Texas Eastern Transmission Corp.*, 37 F.E.R.C. ¶ 61,260, at 61,692–93 (1986), *order on reh'g*, 41 F.E.R.C. ¶ 61,015 (1987), *aff'd sub nom. Texaco, Inc. v. FERC*, 886 F.2d 749 (5th Cir. 1989), unless the parties agreed to end-use capacity curtailment on a particular pipeline, *see, e.g., Florida Gas Transmission Co.*, 51 F.E.R.C. ¶ 61,309, at 62,010–11, *order on reh'g*, 53 F.E.R.C. ¶ 61,396 (1990).

[The court then explained why supply curtailments due to shortages of natural gas often affected the parties differently from capacity curtailments due to a pipeline not having enough space for all its customers. Gas shortages usually affect a broader market and are longer lasting than a pipeline capacity shortage which is usually caused by some temporary bottleneck that appears unexpectedly in part of pipeline system. These capacity shortages often affect gas flows on only one segment of a pipeline and the customers can receive their gas by re-routing it to another pipeline or taking other self-help measures. The court had earlier ruled, in *City of Mesa v. FERC, 993 F.2d 888 (D.C. Cir. 1993)*, that FERC was not required to adopt the same sort of end-use curtailment policies for pipeline capacity shortages as FERC had adopted for natural gas supply shortages, because *e.g.,* an LDC that had contracted for pipeline service to serve its high-priority residential customers could better protect itself against the harmful effects of capacity interruptions. Nonetheless, the court, in reviewing Order 636, reminded FERC that it had a paramount duty to protect consumers under the NGA, and continued]:

[This court has] acknowledged that the NGA provided protections for capacity shortages. The court stated [in *City of Mesa supra*] that "implicit in the consumer protection mandate is a duty to assure that consumers, especially high-priority consumers, have continuous access to needed supplies of natural gas." 993 F.2d at 895. This duty arises because " 'no single factor in the Commission's duty to protect the public can be more important to the public than the continuity of service provided.' " *Id. (quoting Sunray Mid–Continent Oil Co. v. Fed. Power Comm'n*, 239 F.2d 97, 101 (10th Cir. 1956), rev'd on other grounds, 353 U.S. 944 (1957))....

In Order No. 636, which was issued before the court's decision in *City of Mesa*, the Commission continued without change its curtailment policies since Order No. 436 [which required end-use curtailment, placing high-priority customers at the top of the list to get gas].... Second, the Commission maintained that self-help measures would allow the consumer-protection mandate of the NGA to be satisfied by pro rata capacity curtailment:

The Commission believes that with deregulated wellhead sales and a growing menu of options for unbundled pipeline service, customers should rely on prudent planning, private contracts, and the marketplace to the maximum extent practicable to secure both their capacity and supply needs. In today's environment, LDC's [sic] and end-users no longer need to rely exclusively on their traditional pipeline supplier. Rather, to an ever-increasing degree they rely on private contracts with gas sellers, storage providers, and others; a more diverse portfolio of pipeline suppliers, where possible; local self-help measures (e.g., local production, peak shaving and storage); and their own gas supply planning through choosing between an increasing array of unbundled service options.

Id. at 30,590.

* * *

We [also] review the Commission's policy on pro rata curtailment to determine whether it is "just and reasonable" under § 4 and whether it serves the "present or future public convenience and necessity" under § 7(e). *See City of Mesa*, 993 F.2d at 895. The Commission decided that the consumer-protection mandate of the NGA did not require it to adopt end-use capacity curtailment across the board and promised to address the issue in each pipeline restructuring proceeding. Order No. 636–A, ¶ 30,950, at 30,591–92. Indeed, the Commission has broad latitude on whether to effectuate its policies in generic rulemakings or in individual-pipeline adjudications. *Mobil Oil*, 498 U.S. at 230. The issue presented to us, then, is whether the Commission's decision that the NGA does not require end-use curtailment in all circumstances is "reasoned, principled, and based upon the record."

The Commission explained that Order No. 636 had allowed the development of market structures that would enable customers to take independent, market-based steps to avoid the need for Commission-mandated end-use curtailment. Order No. 636–A, ¶ 30,950, at 30,590. Moreover, the Commission found that since the enactment of the NGPA in 1978 "the industry has not experienced shortages beyond isolated, short-lived dislocation," *id.* at 30, 591, and "gas has always flowed according to the dictate of the market, i.e., to the heat sensitive users who need it most and who are thus willing to pay the prevailing market price for it." *Id.* at 30,592. This experience with the industry provides substantial evidence for the Commission's conclusion that end-use curtailment is not required in all circumstances.

We are unpersuaded, particularly in light of the Commission's own actions in the restructuring proceedings, that pro rata capacity curtailment would adequately protect all high-priority customers on all pipelines. *Cf. City of Mesa*, 993 F.2d at 896–97. The Commission's market-based alternatives for customers to avoid curtailment fall into the following categories: (1) arrangements with other pipelines; (2) arrangements with other gas sellers; (3) arrangements for gas storage; (4) arrangements with other customers (including the capacity-release mechanism); and (5) "peak shaving."[11] First, arrangements with other pipelines are more widely available after Order No. 636, such as by using different pipelines that connect to one "market center," but a capacity constraint on a pipeline will still cut off delivery to any "captive customers," no matter how many transportation options some other customers may have. Second, arrangements with other gas sellers are by definition relevant only to supply curtailment, not to capacity curtailment. Third, arrangements for gas storage are unhelpful if the capacity interruption occurs at a point between the contract-storage area and the customer's receipt point. Fourth, obtaining gas from other customers, whether through the capacity-release mechanism or otherwise, depends upon the willingness of lower-priority customers to forgo deliveries. Fifth, practices such as "peak shaving" (letting a little gas go a longer way) can temporarily help to alleviate curtailment problems but cannot ensure continuous service if the interruption lasts too long. None of these market-based solutions, therefore, can guarantee continuous service to all high-priority customers in cases of capacity interruptions. Many of the market-based solutions fail to acknowledge that many customers have far less control over access to pipeline capacity than they do over gas supply. In

---

11.   [Ed. note]: Peak shaving adds propane air mixtures to augment supplies of natural gas during peak demand.

addition, some of the self-help mechanisms will be more readily available to larger pipeline customers. *City of Mesa*, 993 F.2d at 897.

[While FERC had clearly indicated that it strongly preferred pro rata curtailment to end-use curtailment in Order 636, the court noted that Order 636 did not preclude the use of curtailment plans that better protected high-priority customers. FERC had indicated that it would review each pipeline's curtailment policies on a case-by-case basis rather than in a generic rulemaking. In previous curtailment plans aimed at natural gas shortages rather than pipeline constraints, FERC had ordered pipelines to include provisions giving relief to any high priority shipper when that shipper had exercised all other self-help remedies in times of bona fide emergencies, or whenever necessary to avoid irreparable injury to life or property. FERC had even suggested that "there may be extraordinary circumstances when reasonable self-help efforts are insufficient, even for large customers," such that some emergency protections may always be required for certain force majeure capacity interruptions. El Paso, 69 F.E.R.C. ¶ 61,164, at 61,624; see also United Gas Pipe Line Co., 65 F.E.R.C. ¶ 61,006, at 61,092, *reh'g denied sub nom.* Koch Gateway Pipeline Co., 65 F.E.R.C. ¶ 61,338, at 62,630–31 (1993). Thus, the court concluded]:

We uphold the Commission's decision not to require end-use curtailment on a generic basis for capacity curtailment but to proceed instead on a case-by-case basis.

III.   Capacity Release

In this part of the opinion, we address challenges to the voluntary capacity release provisions of Order No. 636, which permit holders of firm transportation rights on a gas pipeline to resell them. 18 C.F.R. § 284.243 (1995). Petitioners challenge the Commission's jurisdiction to institute its capacity release program generally....

　　* * *

Among the central goals of Order Nos. 436 and 636 has been the conversion of bundled sales arrangements into separate transportation and gas sales transactions. On the transportation side, the Commission recognized that while much of the nation's interstate pipeline capacity was reserved for firm transportation, those transportation rights ultimately were not being utilized. *See supra* Part I.C. FERC therefore sought to develop an active "secondary transportation market," with holders of unutilized firm capacity rights reselling them in competition with any capacity offered directly by the pipeline. According to the Commission:

Capacity reallocation will promote efficient load management by the pipeline and its customers and, therefore, efficient use of the pipeline capacity on a firm basis throughout the year. Because more buyers will be able to reach more sellers through firm transportation capacity, capacity reallocation comports with the goal of improving nondiscriminatory, open-access transportation to maximize the benefits of the decontrol of natural gas at the wellhead and in the field.

Order No. 636, ¶ 30,939, at 30,418.

Understanding petitioners' challenges to the capacity release program requires a brief review of related policies that the Commission has employed in the past to accomplish a similar end.

If a firm capacity holder does not ship gas under its transportation right, it pays the pipeline a "reservation fee," but does not pay a "usage fee." Historically, FERC prohibited such holders of unutilized firm capacity rights from transferring those rights to other shippers, and shippers were therefore able to purchase capacity rights only directly from pipelines. *See generally United Gas Pipe Line Co.,* 46 F.E.R.C. ¶ 61,060 (1989) (approving first experimental capacity brokering program). Beginning with the *Texas Eastern Transmission Corp.* proceedings, 48 F.E.R.C. ¶ 61,248, *order on reh'g,* 48 F.E.R.C. ¶ 61,378 (1989), *order on reh'g,* 51 F.E.R.C. ¶ 51,170, *order on reh'g,* 52 F.E.R.C. ¶ 61,273 (1990), however, the Commission authorized shippers on some pipelines to engage in nondiscriminatory "capacity brokering." Brokering arrangements allowed a holder of firm capacity rights (the "releasing shipper") to sell those rights to a "replacement shipper." The transaction took place directly between the two parties, and the replacement shipper essentially stepped into the shoes of the releasing shipper.

Three years later, in the Order No. 636 and companion *Algonquin Gas Transmission Corp.* proceedings, 59 F.E.R.C. ¶ 61,032 (1992), FERC concluded that it could not ensure that the extant capacity brokering programs were operating in a nondiscriminatory manner. When transactions occurred directly and privately between shippers, there was no way to verify that certain purchasers were not being favored unreasonably over others. "Simply put, there [were] too many potential assignors of capacity and too many different programs for the Commission to oversee capacity brokering. . . ." Order No. 636, ¶ 30,939, at 30,416. In FERC's view, fairness could be secured only if capacity resale transactions were both centralized on each pipeline and subject to open bidding. Moreover, uniformity among the various pipelines was necessary to "prevent any pipeline or firm shipper from achieving an undue advantage, or incurring an undue disadvantage, compared to firm shippers on other pipelines." *Id.*

Accordingly, in Order No. 636, the Commission instituted a uniform national "capacity release" program, and exercised its power under NGA § 5 to conform pipelines' existing capacity brokering certificates to that program. *Id.* . . . Specifically, under capacity release, each interstate pipeline is required to establish and administer an electronic bulletin board ("EBB"), which is a computer through which putative releasing and replacement shippers may communicate. *Id.* at 30,418. The EBB carries information about available and consummated capacity release transactions. For example, holders of excess firm capacity rights may "post" their available capacity on the EBB. Further, they may establish nondiscriminatory conditions on the sale, including a minimum price and any terms under which the release may continue. Pipelines are also required to post on the EBB any firm capacity that they have available for sale, where the capacity competes for buyers against capacity made available for resale by shippers. "Potential purchasers of capacity will then be able to choose from among the pipeline and the releasers the service that best suits their needs." *Id.* at 30,419. In addition, shippers that wish to acquire firm capacity rights may post offers to purchase capacity on the EBB. 18 C.F.R. § 284.243(d); Order No. 636–A, ¶ 30,950, at 30,565.

With two exceptions, the pipeline must sell the capacity to the highest bidder. First, "short-term transactions," i.e., those for capacity releases of less than one month, may be arranged between shippers without competitive bidding. Second, a releasing shipper may identify a replacement shipper on its own and enter into a "pre-arranged" deal. In such a transaction, the selected replacement shipper need only match—rather than outbid—the highest offer made by any other shipper. 18 C.F.R. § 284.243(e). The net effect is that a shipper may ensure that it will receive certain capacity by entering into a pre-arranged deal that both conforms to the releasing shipper's conditions and matches the maximum allowable rate for the capacity. No matter what form the capacity release transaction takes, however, the purchase price for released capacity may not exceed the maximum rate set by FERC for the capacity. 18 C.F.R. § 284.243(e); Order No. 636, ¶ 30,939, at 30,420.

After the replacement shipper has been identified, the pipeline enters into a contract with it for firm capacity rights. The pipeline then may elect to excuse completely the releasing shipper's obligation to pay the reservation fee and related costs. Otherwise, the releasing shipper is credited for those costs unless the replacement shipper defaults. Order No. 636–A, ¶ 30,950, at 30,553. In no instance, however, is the releasing shipper liable for costs associated with the replacement shipper's transportation of gas.

[The court then addressed the jurisdictional challenges to the capacity release program]:

Various petitioners challenge both FERC's jurisdiction to institute a uniform capacity release program and its jurisdiction over specific transactions and entities. We begin, then, by outlining the Commission's jurisdiction under § 1(b) of the Natural Gas Act of 1938. Ultimately, we conclude that FERC's capacity release program is a legitimate exercise of its jurisdiction over the interstate transportation of natural gas.

... The [Natural Gas] Act, as provided in § 1(b), applies

[1] to the transportation of natural gas in interstate commerce, [2] to the sale in interstate commerce of natural gas for resale for ultimate public consumption for domestic, commercial, industrial, or any other use, and [3] to natural-gas companies engaged in such transportation or sale, but [does] not apply [4] to any other transportation or sale of natural gas or [5] to the local distribution of natural gas or to the facilities used for such distribution or [6] to the production or gathering of natural gas.

15 U.S.C. § 717(b).

Petitioners' jurisdictional challenges require us to interpret the first and fifth provisions of § 1(b), which address the interstate transportation and "local distribution" of natural gas. . . .

Petitioners' first jurisdictional challenge is the claim of the LDCs that FERC lacks any authority whatsoever to regulate shippers' resale of firm capacity rights. . . . As their theory goes, the Commission has jurisdiction over the pipelines' initial sales of transportation capacity—given that it is the pipelines that render transportation services—but is without jurisdiction over resales of those same capacity rights by third parties—given that those third parties do not render transportation services.

Initially, we believe that the distinction drawn by the LDCs between the "rights to" and "rendition of" interstate transportation services is not a meaningful one. While the pipeline provides transportation only when a party utilizes capacity rights to transport gas, the pipeline provides transportation services throughout the capacity release process. Specifically, the pipeline operates the electronic bulletin board on which all prospective transactions are posted and consummated. The pipeline also selects the winning bidder in the transaction. Moreover, unlike capacity brokering arrangements, which occur directly between releasing and replacement shippers, capacity release requires the pipeline to contract with the replacement shipper. "In effect, the pipeline is temporarily abandoning service to the releasing shipper and instituting service to the replacement shipper. Both of these activities are subject to the Commission's jurisdiction under NGA section 1(b). . . ." Order No. 636–A, ¶ 30,939, at 30,551. In sum, the capacity release regulations operate as a term or condition of pipeline service, with which its customers must comply.

As an entirely separate matter, the Commission's jurisdiction attaches to the subject of the capacity resale transaction: interstate transportation rights. "By controlling such capacity, the assignors are effectively determining by whom, and under what circumstances, gas will be transported and are using the pipeline's facilities as if they were the assignors' facilities." *Id.*. In contrast, under the regulatory system envisioned by the LDCs, holders of capacity rights could engage in resales without regard to the principles of open access and nondiscrimination that are at the heart of the uniform capacity release system. Such a result is directly contrary to Congress' intent in enacting the Natural Gas Act. Responding to the Supreme Court's conclusion that the Constitution's dormant Commerce Clause prohibited state regulation of the interstate transportation of natural gas, the federal government interceded to ensure stability and protect the interests of the consuming public. It thereby occupied the field, which necessarily includes both the sale and resale of interstate transportation rights. . . .

* * * We therefore conclude that the Commission has jurisdiction to require open, nondiscriminatory capacity release by municipalities. . . .

V.   Transition Costs [Ed. note: Part IV is omitted]

[The court first traces the history of FERC's handling of TOP costs as FERC restructured the pipelines. Order 436 had created massive TOP liabilities for those pipelines that had converted to open-access transportation service. Why? Because their once-bundled customers had mostly elected to convert bundled sales into a separate firm transportation contract and then make their own arrangements to buy cheaper gas from sources other than the pipeline's merchant gas. In a competitive natural gas market offering low prices, pipelines could not pass the costs of their TOP obligations along to end-users of gas.]

With purchases sharply reduced, pipelines owed massive "take-or-pay" liabilities to gas producers, which they had to either "buydown"—i.e., reduce—or "buyout"—i.e., eliminate. In Order No. 436, the Commission refused to set a general policy on whether or how pipelines could attempt to recover these costs. We vacated and remanded the Order, concluding that, in this regard, it was not based on reasoned decisionmaking, primarily because it appeared to grossly underestimate the financial impact of take-or-pay liability on pipelines. *Id.* at 1021–30. Of great concern to the court was the likelihood that even higher gas prices would simply cause more customers to switch suppliers, thereby exacerbating the take-or-pay crisis. This cycle of ever increasing prices and ever shrinking customer base—a phenomenon that petitioners label the "death spiral"—made it very unlikely that the pipelines would in fact recoup their take-or-pay liabilities absent some mechanism for separately passing those costs through to their customers.

In subsequent proceedings, the Commission adopted . . . [a policy that] a pipeline could agree to absorb between 25% and 50% of its take-or-pay costs in exchange for the right to bill [their transportation] customers an equal share through a fixed charge, and recover the remaining amount through a volumetric surcharge based on total throughput. Customers, and in turn the consuming public, ultimately reimbursed pipelines for approximately $6.4 billion in take-or-pay costs, while the pipelines themselves absorbed $3.6 billion.

After Order No. 436, all of the major interstate pipelines converted to open-access transportation. Not all customers on those pipelines, however, exercised their right to unbundle their sales agreements and reduce their gas purchase obligations. Several years later in Order No. 636, the Commission mandated unbundling and authorized sales customers to reduce their pipeline gas purchases. When customers exercised that right and secured gas supplies from other sources, the pipelines once again incurred substantial take-or-pay liabilities; though the Commission labeled these liabilities "gas supply realignment [GSR] costs" in Order No. 636, they arose from the same type of producer-pipeline contract provisions as the "take-or-pay" costs considered in Order No. 436.

In allocating recovery of GSR costs, however, the Commission adopted a policy more advantageous to the pipelines. . . . FERC authorized pipelines to bill their customers separately for 100% of their GSR costs. . . . The Commission set forth the mechanisms available to pipelines under Order No. 636 as follows:

. . . The Commission will permit pipelines full cost recovery of prudently incurred gas supply realignment costs deemed to be eligible under this rule. To recover those costs, a pipeline will be permitted to use either a negotiated exit fee, or a reservation fee surcharge recoverable from . . . firm transportation customers. . . .

On rehearing, FERC modified this ruling somewhat, and required pipelines to bill 10% of their GSR costs to interruptible transportation customers. . . .

[While acknowledging that the court owed FERC substantial deference in matters predictive and economic, the court continued]:

In this instance, we cannot discern the Commission's path from its view that interruptible transportation customers should bear some of the burden for GSR costs to the conclusion that the share should be 10%. *Cf.* Walt Whitman, Leaves of Grass, Darest Thou Now O Soul ("Darest thou now O soul, Walk out with me toward the unknown region, Where neither ground is for the feet nor any path to follow?"). And, while we are sympathetic to the Commission's view that "the task of determining fair allocations of transition costs is ultimately thankless, even though [it] brings all [its] experience and best judgment to bear on it," Order No. 636–B, ¶ 61,272, at 62,034, the law requires more than simple guesswork.

[The court then held that FERC did not err by imposing GSR costs on transportation customers rather than on gas producers, but remanded the case to FERC to further consider the appropriate share of those costs to be paid by interruptible transportation customers and the gas pipelines.]

VI.   Conclusion

In its broad contours and in most of its specifics, we uphold Order No. 636. However, we remand certain aspects of Order No. 636, . . . to the Commission for further explanation. . . .

Until the Commission takes final action on remand, however, we leave these measures in place as currently formulated.■

NOTES AND COMMENTS

1.   Despite its 150–page length, the D.C. Circuit opinion is largely congratulatory of FERC's effort to deregulate natural gas. On remand, FERC issued Order 636A responding to the few issues on which the court required rehearing. Order 636 was a great event in regulatory history and its appeal made for great theater. Roughly 250 parties intervened. The oral argument was allocated an entire day—375 minutes of scheduled argument by nearly two dozen lawyers on 22 issues grouped into six different categories. *See* Bruce D. Brown, Gashouse Gang, Legal Times, Feb. 26, 1996, at 6.

The D.C. Circuit plays an important policy-making role in administrative law, particularly in natural gas regulation where this court has often overruled FERC, as the opinion notes. FERC decisions are appealable directly to a circuit court of appeals, not to a district court. As a result of Byzantine multi-district litigation procedures, this case came to oral argument 3 1/2 years after Order 636 was issued and after most of the restructuring had already taken place.

2. Rate design had been a long-simmering issue in the pipeline industry until it was largely resolved by Order 636. Interruptible industrial customers had always complained that they should not be required to pay any of the pipelines' fixed costs because they were not guaranteed any capacity. Consumer groups and many state PUCs wanted to keep local rates down for heating users by making industrials pay some of these costs. FERC had sided with the consumer interests by making industrials pay some of the fixed costs through use of a "modified fixed variable (MFV)" rate design. But in Order 636, FERC switched to charging all of the fixed costs to firm users by adopting the "straight fixed variable (SFV)" rate design. The court upheld FERC's findings that SFV would increase efficiency and competition, as this excerpt shows:

> For several decades, FERC's ratemaking regime has included some portion of a pipeline's fixed costs in the pipeline's commodity and usage charges. Over the years, it varied the specific percentage of fixed costs actually included in those charges, but it generally followed the principle that some portion of fixed costs should be recouped through quantity-dependent charges.

> The PUCs argue that the switch to SFV rate design "will frustrate, rather than promote, the goals of maximizing efficiency and competition." Their complaint centers on the claim that because pipelines under SFV rate design will be able to collect all their fixed costs, including return on investment and taxes, in the demand charge, they will have no incentive to assure that gas actually flows through the pipeline under firm service arrangements. That is, because a pipeline will recover no fixed costs or return on investment through the commodity or usage charge, it will have no incentive to transport any gas.

> FERC recognized this potential incentive problem in Order No. 636, but determined that "the pipelines will now have much less influence on the use of their systems because they are transporting gas to, rather than selling gas at, the city-gate." Order No. 636, ¶ 30,939, at 30,436. Accordingly, "transportation volumes will mainly be a function of the needs of gas purchasers and the prices offered by gas sellers in the production areas." *Id.* In any case, "the goals to be accomplished via SFV outweigh generally the goal of allocating fixed costs to annual throughput." Order No. 636–A, ¶ 30,950, at 30,606. We find these explanations sufficiently convincing to meet the substantial evidence standard for rate design in the face of the PUCs' incentive argument. *United Distribution Companies v. FERC, supra* at 1167–69.

FERC adopted several measures to mitigate the effect of the rate design change on customers who would now bear a greater share of the pipeline's fixed costs. For example, if the switch to SFV resulted in a ten percent or greater rate increase for a particular customer class, FERC required that the pipeline phase in SFV rate design over four years for that class, to avoid "rate shock." The court upheld these mitigation measures. *Id.* at 1170–73.

3. Although producers and pipelines had settled many take-or-pay claims before Order 636, after the order more customers canceled contracts to buy gas from the pipelines, forcing the pipelines to pay more take-or-pay charges, now labeled "gas supply realignment costs" ("GSR" costs), to producers. This time, as noted in the excerpts, FERC authorized the pipelines to pass along all of these charges to customers, unlike the earlier orders which sought to force pipelines (and indirectly producers) to share some of the realignment costs. FERC's earlier policy had permitted pipelines to surcharge their transportation customers for take-or-pay costs only if the pipelines agreed to absorb between 25 and 50 percent of those costs.

In the end, it appears that many groups shared the TOP transition costs which totaled about $50 billion, or almost 60 percent of the 1985 value of final gas sales to final consumers. Interstate pipeline companies filed to recover about $10.4 billion in TOP costs, of which about $3.6 billion would be absorbed by the pipeline company shareholders. The bulk of the debt was negotiated away in settlements between the pipeline companies and producers over the years. In many cases, the gas producers, or the parties who held the gas contracts as collateral, had to accept lower values for the contracts they held. Some costs were spread to the creditors of those pipelines that went bankrupt, and some costs may have been partially shifted to general taxpayers if losses were used as credits in calculating income taxes. Margaret Jess, Restructuring Energy Industries: Lessons from Natural Gas, A Natural Gas Monthly Special Report available at: http://www.eia.doe.gov/pub/oil_gas/natural   _gas1F%/feature_articles/1997 /restructuring _energy_industries_lessons/html/peg.html

4. PAYING FOR TAKE-OR-PAY AT THE STATE LEVEL

The "pig-in-the-python" problem soon confronted state PUCs as pipelines settled and paid TOP liabilities to gas producers. Suppose, *e.g.*, the pipeline paid $500 million to producers to settle TOP lawsuits and that FERC allowed the pipeline to pass these costs along to its customers, many of whom were LDCs. Now, how would the LDC recoup these costs from its end-use customers? The following opinion nicely reviews some principles of ratemaking that appeared in Chapter 3. First, the court determines the total rate level, *i.e.*, the total amount of money that the LDC may pass to its customers; second, the court addresses rate design. *i.e.*, how classes of customers are allocated shares of the total rate increase allowed. The opinion also discusses the "filed-rate doctrine." Under this doctrine, the legality of rates that have been filed with and approved by the proper regulatory agency (and thereafter paid by users) cannot be subject to reopening in later proceedings; this would constitute invalid "retroactive ratemaking." Conversely, if a company agrees to provide a service to a particular customer at a rate different from the legally filed rate, then its promise is void. *American Tel. & Tel. Co. v. Central Office Tel., Inc.*, 524 U.S. 214 (1998).

Hamm v. Public Service Commission of South Carolina

425 S.E.2d 28 (S.C. 1992).

■ FINNEY, J. This is an appeal from a circuit court order reversing and remanding orders of the South Carolina Public Service Commission, which permitted a levelized surcharge based upon a combination of both the volumetric and deficiency-based systems to recover from retail gas customers take-or-pay charges incurred at the wholesale level. We affirm in part and reverse in part.

I.

On September 23, 1988, Appellant South Carolina Pipeline Corporation (Pipeline) filed an application with Appellant South Carolina Public Service Commission (Commission) for approval of a charge to be added to its customers' monthly cost of gas to empower Pipeline to recover TOP costs paid to its wholesale natural gas supplier.

Subsequently, Appellants South Carolina Electric & Gas Company and Respondents Piedmont Natural Gas Company, Inc. ("Piedmont"), South Carolina Energy Users Committee ("SCEUC"), and Steven W. Hamm, Consumer Advocate for the State of South Carolina ("Consumer Advocate"), were permitted to intervene. Thereafter, the American Gas Association was allowed to file an Amicus Curiae brief.

On April 3–6, 1988, the Commission conducted an evidentiary hearing during which the two controlling issues of this appeal were raised. First, how much, if any, of TOP costs should Pipeline be permitted to recover from its customers. Second, if permitted, by what method should TOP costs be allocated among Pipeline's customers. On May 31, 1988, the Commission issued Order No. 89–520 in which it approved the implementation of levelized billing on or after June 1, 1989, and imposed a collection methodology. [Ultimately, this appeal followed.]

II.

We address first the issue of whether Pipeline is entitled to recover from its customers the full amount of TOP charges. The circuit court found that TOP costs do not reflect purchased gas costs. Based upon its reasoning that TOP charges arise out of a failure to purchase gas, the court concluded there was no basis in fact or in law which would mandate their recovery through a purchased-gas expense recovery mechanism.

Appellants Commission and Pipeline argue that TOP costs approved by the Federal Energy Regulation Commission (FERC) may be treated as cost of gas under Pipeline's tariff and recovered from Pipeline's customers. We agree.

Mandated FERC rates may be passed on to customers pursuant to the filed-rate doctrine, a federal preemption rule which requires states to accord binding effect to filed rates approved by the FERC. *See General Motors Corp. v. Illinois Commerce Comm'n*, 143 Ill.2d 407, 574 N.E.2d 650 (1991); *Mississippi Power and Light Co. v. Mississippi*, 487 U.S. 354 (1988); *Nantahala Power and Light Co. v. Thornburg*, 476 U.S. 953 (1986).

Local gas companies are permitted to pass on to customers TOP charges if such charges are neither illegal, arbitrary nor unreasonable. Additionally, the Commission must authorize sufficient revenue to afford utilities the opportunity to recover expenses and the capital cost of doing business. *S. Bell Tel. & Tel. v. S.C. Pub. Serv. Comm'n*, 270 S.C. 590, 244 S.E.2d 278 (1978)....

The Commission found that because the rates and surcharges Pipeline pays for gas are federally approved and imposed as a cost of gas, the Commission was bound to allow Pipeline to recover from its South Carolina customers Pipeline's full gas costs in the absence of a Commission finding of imprudent purchasing practices. Specifically, Pipeline's existing tariff provisions permit Pipeline to pass on to its customers all costs and surcharges imposed on gas purchased from intrastate pipelines. Moreover, the record reflects no challenge by any party as to the prudency of Pipeline's purchasing practices.

We conclude that the record evinces substantial evidence to support the Commission's findings that Pipeline is entitled to recoup TOP costs in full and that, with regard to this issue, the record reflects neither arbitrariness nor capriciousness as a matter of law.

III.

We next consider whether the Commission's method of allocating TOP costs among Pipeline's customers is proper. The circuit court found that the deficiency-based portion of the Commission-authorized allocation constituted retroactive ratemaking. We agree.

The Commission adopted a 50% volumetric and 50% deficiency-based collection methodology, a combination of the collection methods supported by the parties. Under the volumetric system, TOP liability is reasonably apportioned according to the degree to which individual customers have benefitted from the recent restructuring of the natural gas industry. A deficiency-based allocation ascribes TOP liability according to the reasonable measure of an individual customer's responsibility for the incurrence of such costs.

The commission-approved method allowed Pipeline to prepay its lump sum direct bill liability and charge interest on the prepaid amounts pending collection. Ultimately, the volumetric provision would require Pipeline's customers to pay a surcharge on each unit of gas purchased by them in the future. The deficiency aspect would permit the allocation of TOP charges based on the customers' gas purchase "deficiencies" during the period 1982–1986 as compared with their 1981 purchases.

* * *

S.C.Code Ann. § 58–5–240 (Cum.Supp.1990) requires a public utility to have rates filed and approved by the Commission prior to implementation of such rates; the intent being to insure that customers know prior to purchase what rate is charged.

The Commission asserts that the deficiency method was approved by the FERC. However, in *Associated Gas Distributors* [893 F.2d 349 (D.C.Cir. 1989)], the United States Court of Appeals for the District of Columbia held that the deficiency allocation method approved by the FERC violates the filed-rate doctrine and constitutes retroactive ratemaking.

Appellants seek to distinguish this controversy by arguing that respondents were put on notice through Pipeline's tariffs, which permitted recovery of TOP costs as costs of gas. Even if notice to the respondents of the potential for TOP liability solved any conflict with the filed-rate doctrine, it cannot be argued that such notice apprized of any rate and method of recovery, or that retroactive recovery would be permitted. Pipeline's customers were entitled to rely on the contractual rates in effect at such time in the past as they chose to purchase or refrain from purchasing gas. This Court finds the deficiency-based collection methodology for recoupment of TOP charges to be arbitrary and capricious as a matter of law.

Accordingly, ... [w]e reinstate so much of the Commission's order as holds that Pipeline is entitled to recover from its customers 100% of its FERC-approved TOP costs.

We affirm so much of the circuit court's order as finds that a deficiency-based levelized charge to customers for TOP costs is prohibited in that it constitutes retroactive ratemaking. The issue of methodology for recoupment of FERC-approved TOP charges is reversed and remanded to the Commission for reconsideration consistent with the order of the circuit court.■

NOTES AND COMMENTS

1. The take-or-pay problem also caused a blizzard of law suits between the gas producer and the lessor from whom the producer had leased the tracts to explore for and develop oil or gas. The typical oil and gas lease grants the lessor a 1/8 royalty to be paid on oil or gas *"produced from said land"* or on *"production saved, removed or sold from the leased area."* (Review the lease provisions in Chapter 6(A)(1)(3) on Oil). If a lessee-producer sold gas to a pipeline purchaser in a long-term contract with a TOP provision and the pipeline makes TOP payments to the producer of, say, $5 million, for gas it has not taken, must the lessee-producer pay 1/8 of this sum to its lessors? Similarly, if the pipeline makes lump-sum payments in the millions of dollars to buy out (*i.e.,* terminate) or buy down (*i.e.,* reduce the contracted-for gas price) its TOP obligations, is the lessor entitled to a 1/8 share? Given the lease language quoted above, who do you expect would win these

TOP lawsuits? Hint: "Production" has been interpreted to mean the physical severance of gas from the underground reservoir. *See, e.g., Diamond Shamrock Exploration Co. v. Hodel*, 853 F.2d 1159 (5th Cir. 1988); *Condra v. Quinoco Petroleum, Inc.*, 954 S.W.2d 68 (Tex. App. 1997); *TransAmerican Natural Gas Corp. v. Finkelstein*, 933 S.W.2d 591 (Tex. App. 1996).

Would the result differ if the royalty clause required payment of "royalty on gas sold by Lessee of one-eighth of the amount realized at the well from such sales"? What if the court views the oil and gas lease as a "cooperative venture" or "symbiotic endeavor" in which the lessor contributes the minerals and the lessee contributes capital and expertise to develop the oil and gas for the mutual benefit of both parties? In a minority of states, royalty interest owners have won the right to share in some TOP payments based on lease language and construction such as this. *See, e.g., Frey v. Amoco Prod. Co.*, 603 So.2d 166 (La. 1992); and *Klein v. Jones*, 980 F.2d 521 (8th Cir. 1992), *aff'd on reh'g*, 73 F.3d 779 (8th Cir. 1996), *cert. denied*, 519 U.S. 815 (1996).

5.   CONTINUING ISSUES UNDER ORDER 636

The implementation of Order 636 has not been without its problems. This section discusses some of the more troublesome issues.

a.   FUNCTIONAL UNBUNDLING AND AFFILIATES

To comply with Order 636's functional unbundling requirements, most pipelines set up separate marketing entities. These marketing entities were not to receive any information from the pipeline that was not also made available to competitors. *See generally Tenneco Gas v. FERC*, 969 F.2d 1187 (D.C. Cir. 1992).

Compliance with this type of directive is understandably difficult even for a company with the best intentions. The employees of the marketing entity will probably be long-time former employees of the pipeline company and will have both a long institutional memory and close personal relationships with the employees who remain with the pipeline. If the pipeline is small, the practical necessity of sharing some employees complicates the problem. *See, e.g., In re Caprock Pipeline Co.*, 58 F.E.R.C. ¶ 61,141 (1992).

Shippers have filed a number of complaints with FERC alleging violations by pipelines and their marketing affiliates of the Chinese wall requirements. Many of these have been resolved through negotiations (*see, e.g., In re Transcontinental Gas Pipe Line Corp.*, 55 F.E.R.C. ¶ 61,318 (1991)), but a few have resulted in the assessment of penalties against the pipelines. For example, in *Amoco Prod. Co. v. Natural Gas Pipeline Co. of Am.*, 82 F.E.R.C. ¶ 61,038 (1998), shippers alleged that the pipeline had violated Standard of Conduct G which states that "to the maximum extent practicable [a pipeline's] operating employees and the operating employees of its marketing affiliate must function independently of each other." 18 C.F.R. § 161.3(g) (1997). FERC found that the pipeline had created a

System Optimization Group, composed of employees who had day-to-day duties and responsibilities for planning, directing, and carrying out gas-related operations including gas transportation, gas sales, or gas marketing activities, for both the pipeline (Natural Gas Pipeline Co.) and for MidCon Gas, its marketing affiliate. 82 F.E.R.C. ¶ 61,038.

FERC also found that the System Optimization Group decided whether to accept transportation discounts from nonaffiliated shippers, helped to determine whether the pipeline would conduct auctions, provided MidCon Gas with pricing inputs for its auction bids, and then evaluated all bids received by the pipeline. FERC assessed civil penalties of $8,840,000 against the pipeline but suspended half the penalty if the pipeline did not violate the rules again during the next two years. 83 F.E.R.C. ¶ 61,197 at 3 (1998).

Do you understand why the practices condemned above are anti-competitive?

Implicit in the natural gas restructuring policy discussion is the premise that unbundling, or separating, services traditionally performed by the same pipeline is desirable as a matter of economic efficiency. Order No. 636 unbundles pipeline sales and transportation, despite the fact that firms had historically found it to be efficient to provide both functions under the umbrella of the same corporation. As FERC noted, the rationale for unbundling was to minimize distortions in the sales market facilitated by the market power which pipeline companies had over transportation.

Yet, it is well recognized that vertical integration can be efficient. The major oil companies found efficiencies in developing their own crude oil supplies to feed their own refineries to supply their own service stations. Vertical integration internalizes within the firm those transactions costs which otherwise must be incurred through contracting in the open market. In industries that demand high degrees of fixed capital, the internalization of such transactions costs by building company-owned production or distribution infrastructures is often an efficient response to market uncertainties that cannot be easily contracted away. *See* Oliver E. Williamson, Transaction Cost Economics: The Governance of Contractual Relationships, 22 J. L. & Econ. 233 (1979); Ronald H. Coase, The Nature of the Firm, 4 Economica 386 (1937). Vertical integration is likely under circumstances in which assets are specific (or cannot be deployed to alternative uses because of sunk costs), transactions are frequent, and there is a high degree of uncertainty. *See* Oliver E. Williamson, The Mechanisms of Governance (1996).

In addition, operating and engineering (or network) efficiencies can be gained through vertical integration. For example, pipelines must coordinate the shipping of natural gas with expected demand patterns so that the two are continually matched. Changes in customer demand cannot be accurately foreseen. Many long-term purchase agreements in the natural gas industry are requirements contacts which obligate the pipeline to bear the risks of any increase in customer demand. To better cope with these risks, pipelines must keep gas reserves above current demands. If pipelines were allowed to provide both sales and transportation services, this business structure would let the pipeline spread the costs and risks of keeping such reserves among several sales markets, rather than building them into each sales contract.

Finally, a pipeline with integrated sales and transportation functions has internal information regarding changes in customer demand, facilitating the communication of such information to the valve operators and other engineers who physically direct the flow of gas through the lines. *See* Alfred E. Kahn, The Economics of Regulation: Principles and Institutions 157–58 (1988).

From the perspective of economic efficiency, then, the question is whether the costs of vertical integration exceed its benefits in the context of integrated pipelines sales and transportation. If so, then FERC's effort to unbundle are justified. Are you convinced? Might a pipeline company have a valid argument that its services are more efficient if bundled together?

b.   RATE DESIGN: ROLLED-IN RATES FOR NEW PIPELINE CAPACITY

Another issue of rate design that continues to be contentious is the issue of rolled-in versus incremental rates. When a pipeline builds a new segment of its system, should the cost of that segment be paid solely by the customers who will be served by it, or should those costs be "rolled-in" to the overall rate base and distributed among all of the pipeline's customers? *See, e.g., "Complex" Consolidated Edison Co. of N.Y. v. FERC,* 165 F.3d 992 (D.C. Cir. 1999).

In *Midcoast Interstate Transmission, Inc. v. FERC,* 198 F.3d 960 (D.C. Cir. 2000), the court held that FERC had properly authorized rolling-in the cost of new pipeline construction into a company's system-wide rates because there would be system-wide benefits to consumers and because the impact on system-wide rates would be minimal. This case starkly illustrates how the choice between rolled in and incremental rates can affect competing pipelines. Midcoast and Southern Colonial were both competing to bring new pipeline capacity to the same Alabama market. FERC granted Southern's application to construct a new pipeline. Midcoast appealed this FERC order as an aggrieved party. It argued that if FERC had required incremental pricing, Southern would have had to charge users of the new pipeline an incremental rate of $10.00 in addition to its system-wide rate of $8.80 per decatherm per month. Midcoast proposed to charge a total rate of only $8.60 to the users of the new pipeline. If Southern were allowed to roll in the costs of the new pipeline, rates would not rise by more than 5 percent because large pipeline systems like Southern's can spread the costs over its existing system-wide customers. The cost of the new facilities is subsidized by existing users, to the detriment of smaller competitors like Midcoast.

c.   SPOT AND FUTURES MARKETS: OVER-RELIANCE ON SHORT-TERM CONTRACTS?

Today, most natural gas is purchased through contracts of thirty days or less. This means that the price of gas can change dramatically in very short periods of time. As noted in Section (A)(4) of this chapter, price spikes have become part of the restructured gas markets, especially since the year 2000. All participants in the gas markets have had to radically readjust their thinking about gas prices since restructuring. Instead of negotiating twenty-year contracts, they have had to learn the ways of the commodity exchanges. Price volatility has become a significant business risk, leading to the creation of both a spot market and a futures market for natural gas. Spot market transactions are short-term (*i.e.*, for a term of less than a year, usually 30 days) and are generally interruptible. These factors make the contracts responsive to current market prices, but also expose the parties to the risks of price volatility or service interruption.

The New York Mercantile Exchange ("NYMEX") operates a natural gas futures market that allows buyers and sellers to hedge their price risks for up to 72 months into the future. Visit www.nymex.com/NG_spec.aspx. The NYMEX prices are quoted daily and provide reliable price signals for the operation of more complex futures transactions. These more complex transactions consist of a wide variety of over-the-counter derivatives offered by gas marketers. Derivatives are financial risk-management contracts, such as swaps, options, caps, floors, and collars. The details of the derivative market are beyond the scope of this book, but the bottom line is that LDCs and other large users of natural gas now have an array of products and services available to help them insure their business operations against losses from rapid future fluctuations in the price of natural gas.

The success of these new risk management tools was not tested until 2000 because prices were quite stable in the 1990s compared to the price shocks of the 1970s and 1980s.[12]

The switch to a competitive gas market became possible because so many new pipelines had been built that most market areas had reasonably good access to more than one pipeline and because pipeline capacity had largely caught up with demand. Thus, few pipelines had monopoly positions and there was less need for major new capital facilities that could be financed only on the basis of long-term contracts. But, will these conditions continue? Professor Richard Pierce, a long-time proponent of deregulation, argues that the spot market cannot be the permanent answer for the long-term future of the industry:

> A high proportion of transactions in the U.S. gas market today are made on the spot market or pursuant to short-term or interruptible contracts. A healthy U.S. gas market always will include considerable trade in these categories, but the U.S. market seems not yet to have reached a stable equilibrium in this respect. Increased use of long-term, firm contracts is required in the U.S. to encourage adequate

---

12. For a more complete analysis of natural gas derivatives, *see* Mark E. Haedicke & Alan B. Aronowitz, Gas Commodity Markets, in David J. Muchow & William A. Mogel, 4 Energy Law and Transactions, Ch. 88 (1999). Derivatives can create more efficient markets by transferring risk from hedgers to speculators, promoting information dissemination and price discovery, and promoting a broader, more liquid market.

investment in exploration and production, pipelines, and gas-burning combustion equipment.

Many participants in the U.S. market seem unusually reluctant to enter into long-term contracts at present. This reluctance is due to the bad experiences with long-term contracts many market participants had in the past. Regulators abrogated or modified contracts; changes in regulatory policies altered the effects of contracts; and many parties refused to comply with contracts because of changes in regulatory policies.

Richard J. Pierce, Jr., Experiences with Natural Gas Regulation and Competition in the U.S. Federal System: Lessons for Europe, in Natural Gas in the Internal Market 125 (Ernst J. Mestmäcker, ed., 1993).

6.   WHAT HAPPENS IN A SHORTAGE?

The potential problems which might arise because of over-reliance on short-term markets and unbundled sales naturally lead to the question: What will happen if gas shipments are curtailed because of force majeure events or other operational necessities? In this final case, the D.C. Circuit one more time remands aspects of FERC's curtailment policy for more reasoned decisionmaking. In defense of its order, FERC raises the issue of its ability to monitor conditions in the fast-changing gas markets. This issue becomes a very real one from 2000 onwards when the California energy crisis reveals major problems with relying on short-term gas and electricity markets.

Process Gas Consumers Group v. FERC

158 F.3d 591 (D.C. Cir. 1998).

■ WILLIAMS, J. In Order No. 636, FERC exercised its authority under § 5 of the Natural Gas Act, 15 U.S.C. § 717d, to require that natural gas pipeline companies unbundle their gas transportation and sales services and file tariffs in compliance with the order. The tariff filing at issue here provides that in the event of certain curtailments, customers with specified emergency conditions can secure exemption from curtailment. This of course increases the curtailment of the pipeline's other customers, which would otherwise have been pro rata. The tariff also calls for some compensation to be paid by the exempted customers to the customers who are additionally deprived. But the petitioners argue that the compensation approved by the Commission is so limited that it gives customers inadequate incentives to plan ahead to reduce the likelihood and severity of gas curtailment emergencies. As the Commission's explanation fails to come to grips with the petitioners' contentions, we remand the case for want of reasoned decisionmaking.

Texas Eastern Transmission Corporation ("Tetco") made its compliance filing in 1992. The proposed tariff would have allowed Tetco to curtail service—even to "firm" transportation customers—in certain situations of force majeure or operational necessity. Such "capacity curtailment" was to be borne pro rata with two exceptions: first, to protect high priority end-uses, as defined by §§ 401 and 402 of the Natural Gas Policy Act, 15 U.S.C. §§ 3391–92, and second, to provide gas to customers for "emergency" situations, defined as ones where gas was necessary "to avoid irreparable injury to life or property (including environmental emergencies) or to provide for minimum plant protection." Prompted by the comments of NUI Corporation (Elizabethtown Gas Division) ("NUI/Elizabethtown"), the Commission rejected Tetco's first proposed exception to pro rata curtailment, finding that the priorities in the NGPA did not apply to capacity curtailment. *See Texas Eastern Transmission Corp.*, 62 F.E.R.C. ¶ 61,015 at 61,119 (1993). The Commission allowed the second exception, but required that Tetco's revised tariff "include compensation by the customer seeking the short term [emergency] exception to any other customer receiving more than its pro rata share of the capacity curtailment." *Id.* Tetco filed a revised tariff, including such a compensation measure, in February 1993.

The compensation provided, however, was quite limited. The tariff calls for increases in the exempted customer's bill by "the aggregate curtailment adjustment quantity requested by the Customer pursuant to [the emergency exemption] multiplied by the Reservation Charge Adjustment for the applicable rate schedule per Dth [Dekatherm] for the applicable zone"; this amount is then distributed to the customers who were curtailed more than pro rata because of the exemption. As we understand this, it means that although the advantaged customers have already paid a reservation charge for their entitlement to transportation, they pay a premium, proportional to that charge, for the transportation they enjoy above pro rata curtailment levels by virtue of their emergency condition. The proceeds go to the more deprived customers, in proportion to their deprivation.

Despite the protests of NUI/Elizabethtown, The Process Gas Consumers Group, and The American Iron and Steel Institute (the latter two collectively "the Industrial Groups") that the compensation provided was inadequate, the Commission accepted Tetco's filing. Upon denial of their request for rehearing on this issue, NUI/Elizabethtown and the Industrial Groups petitioned for review in this court.

Petitioners objected below on two grounds. NUI/Elizabethtown argued that the compensation was inadequate, particularly for local distribution companies ("LDCs"). The increased curtailment for non-exempt customers removes these customers' regular access to part of their gas supply; this supply must be rerouted or replaced, often at a much higher cost. If no replacement can be found, the LDC customers lose the profit they would have made on the resale of the gas. NUI/Elizabethtown therefore proposed setting compensation either by these actual damage amounts (net replacement cost or lost margin) or by a "generic cost" calculated as "a stated percentage in excess of the spot gas price." The Industrial Groups raised an additional argument: that Tetco's compensation scheme gave bad incentives to its customers. Because an emergency exemption aids only customers without some backup capabilities of their own (such as "peak shaving" facilities), the low compensation rate allows these customers to free-ride on the costly contingency preparations of others. Between the grasshopper and the ant, in other words, Tetco's scheme favors the grasshopper and thus encourages his feckless ways. To correct this incentive problem, the Industrial Groups proposed compensation at "a predetermined amount that exceeds the cost of the most expensive gas sources or alternative fuels available to customers."

The Commission gave two reasons for rejecting these suggestions. First, the Commission pointed to the tariff's imbalance resolution procedures as an "adequate remedy" for the loss of gas supply. 63 F.E.R.C. ¶ 61,100 at 61,496; 64 F.E.R.C. ¶ 61,305 at 63,301. This seems to be a red herring. So far as appears, the imbalance procedures impose no cost on customers receiving emergency relief.

Second, the Commission claimed that "no party has put forth a plausible compensation scheme that could be adequately monitored by the Commission." 64 F.E.R.C. ¶ 61,305 at 63,301. But the Commission's two opinions say nothing to explain how any of the petitioners' proposals is either implausible or impractical to monitor. And, so far as concerns NUI/Elizabethtown's spot gas proposal, the Commission itself has in related contexts embraced a compensation device tied to the spot gas price: first in the very same proceeding, as the cash-out price used to resolve imbalances, *see* 62 F.E.R.C. ¶ 61,015 at 61,116–17, and second, in a later case, as compensation paid by those enjoying an emergency exemption from gas supply curtailment, *see Transcontinental Gas Pipe Line Corp.,* 72 F.E.R.C. ¶ 61,037 at 61,237–38 (1995). While we recognize that capacity curtailment and supply curtailment are not identical, *see, e.g., City of Mesa v. FERC,* 301 U.S. App. D.C. 226, 993 F.2d 888, 894–95 (D.C. Cir. 1993), the Commission has nowhere explained why the differences render use of a spot-price solution inappropriate here. *Cf. Florida Gas Transmission Co.,* 70 F.E.R.C. ¶ 61,017 at 61,063 (1995) (approving settlement providing capacity curtailment compensation based on alternative fuel cost). Nor, to repeat, has it offered any explanation of the supposed deficiencies of the petitioners' other proposals.

If the Commission had grounds to reject petitioners' proposed alternatives, it has not revealed them. We accordingly remand the case for reconsideration.

So ordered.■

7.   ASSESSMENT OF RESTRUCTURED GAS MARKETS: BEFORE THE CALIFORNIA ENERGY CRISIS

Has restructuring been a success? Professor Richard Pierce, whose article you read at the beginning of Section C on the Federal Framework of Natural Gas Regulation certainly thought so in 1995. Restructuring had brought a $5 billion *annual* improvement in aggregate efficiency; cleaner air; commercial and technical innovations; and competitive markets that performed well in the harsh winter of 1993–1994. Another enthusiastic supporter of FERC Order 636 marveled that federal regulators—of all people!—had restructured the pipelines into competitive entities, no longer operating under "incompetent regulation and redistributionist politics." Their former captive customers could now customize their own deals with gas producers, using the pipeline only for delivery. Moreover:

> Smaller producers and inexperienced customers have at their disposal a growing industry of gas marketers and brokers, who can familiarize them with the market and individualize their transactions. Over two-thirds of all gas sales are now effectively in "spot" markets, with terms of thirty days or less. Pipeline interconnections have grown in capacity and complexity to open up a national market. Futures contracts and options are traded on the New York Mercantile Exchange.

Robert J. Michaels, The New Age of Natural Gas: How the Regulators Brought Competition, Regulation, Winter 1993, at 68. This commentator warned LDCs and state utility commissioners that they would soon be forced to follow the federal path of open access and more efficient rate designs in their local franchise areas. Industrial customers would no longer tolerate cross-subsidies to residential consumers and industry would use the new federal open-access rules to bypass LDCs that did not adapt to more competitive markets. The LDCs should become open-access carriers themselves, allowing retail customers to choose their own gas supplier and use the local gas mains to have it delivered rather than be captive to the LDC's monopoly status.

Some commentators were not so happy about the changes. Joseph Fagan worried about the fate of the small consumer in the restructuring process. As industrial bypass occurs by large, sophisticated players, the cost of gas will increase for the captive consumer who lacks the flexibility to switch suppliers. This captive core will suffer a disproportionate share of transition costs. Allowing a pass-through of 100% of Gas Supply Realignment costs, coupled with the new SFV rate design, will "undermine FERC's statutory duty to protect the natural gas consumer." Fagan continued:

> The traditional linchpins of the industry, the interstate pipelines, have staggering costs, such as take-or-pay, which must be resolved before full deregulation can take hold. In a system of open access and unbundled service, the pipelines can only truly influence the behavior of the small customers. Yet, it is they who are the most vulnerable and the most incapable of bearing these transition costs.

Joseph Fagan, From Regulation to Deregulation: The Diminishing Role of the Small Consumer Within the Natural Gas Industry, 29 Tulsa L.J. 707 at 726–27 (1994).

Even Fagan agreed, however, that in the end, "a free, unregulated market for natural gas will benefit all concerned." But, the transition to this brave new world would be painful for the residential consumer.

NOTES AND COMMENTS

1. What is the best measure of the success of gas restructuring? A decrease in natural gas prices? Review Figures 8–4 and 8–5. What happened to the price of gas between 1985 and 1995? How do you know if pipeline restructuring was responsible for the trend? Perhaps it was the decontrol of natural gas prices at the producers' level that was key. Or was it the fall-off in demand as industrial users switched to lower-priced coal and consumers learned to conserve with better insulation, more efficient furnaces, etc.? How can you tell if prices would have fallen without restructuring?

Are there non-price factors that should be rated to measure the success of gas restructuring? What are they? Reliability? Reduced pipeline explosions and accidents?

In fact, big industrial users and power plants experienced much greater price reductions than retail consumers. Margaret Jess, Restructuring Energy Industries: Lessons from Natural Gas, A Natural Gas Monthly Special Report *supra*.

2. As Michaels noted in the excerpt above, it is possible to imagine greater competition in the local distribution of natural gas by allowing so-called "captive" consumers to break their bonds with the local gas distributing company and buy gas from independent suppliers; the LDC would provide open-access transportation only. The issues that arise in this type of retail competition will be discussed in Chapter 12 in the context of the electric industry, where such competition has advanced further than in the gas industry. Many of the issues discussed in this chapter on federal gas regulation have their counterpoint in electricity restructuring, such as who will bear the transition costs (also called "stranded costs"), rate design, curtailment policies, and the price volatility of spot markets in electricity. In other ways, electricity restructuring has proven to be significantly different and often more difficult at the wholesale level than gas restructuring.

E.   POTENTIAL PROBLEMS BECOME REAL: CALIFORNIA AND THE ENERGY CRISIS

1.   CONVERGENCE OF GAS AND ELECTRIC MARKETS

"Convergence" is an industry buzzword which describes a simple fact: the natural gas markets have become intertwined with electricity markets in far more pervasive ways as both sectors restructured. One reason is that 90% of all recent power generation built in the U.S. uses natural gas as its fuel source. Another reason is that both gas and electricity are traded in short-term markets and on the NYMEX futures market in similar ways. In addition, many restructured gas pipeline companies functionally unbundled by creating marketing affiliates that traded both gas and electricity; some companies also had affiliated generating facilities (many of which were merchant power plants, also called independent power producers, not regulated under traditional cost-of-service utility rate regulation, as you will soon see in Chapters 10–12), and some participants also had affiliated oil and gas producing arms.

This convergence has raised key issues of reliability in the supply of electricity for two reasons: First, many of the new gas-fired power plants have not contracted for firm transportation on the gas pipeline system, meaning that they will get "bumped" off the system if there is a shortage in pipeline capacity needed to serve firm customers (unless FERC curtailment regulations, possibly built into the pipeline's tariff structure, put these power plant customers back in at the front of the line; curtailment policies were discussed in Section D *supra*). Second, many of the new gas-fired plants lack fuel-switching capability. Thus, disruptions in the pipeline system will reverberate in the electricity sector. Yet the two sectors have different operational practices, time lines, and characteristics that can threaten reliability even if all parties maximize their efforts to coordinate the two. For example, electricity can travel at lightning speed over transmission wires and is bought and sold on an hour-ahead market that constantly balances supply and demand; it is impossible to schedule gas deliverability this way. Gas moves slowly, even in the high-pressure pipelines, and takes many days to reach distant locations.

The implications of these divergent characteristics in increasingly converging markets is well summarized in Ken Costello, Increased Dependence on Natural Gas for Electric Generation: Meeting the Challenge, Electricity J. 10 (June 2004). Under restructuring, merchant generators, free of state utility regulation, presumably have made a rational economic decision to purchase interruptible service (which is often available at 1/10 the price of firm service) without investing in dual fuel capability. Facing intense competition, many such generators must keep their costs as low as possible. How then, or rather—who then—will assure reliable electricity supplies? Will the regional system operators of the electricity grid (the RTOs that you will study in the upcoming chapters) account for this additional risk to reliability by requiring generators to sign firm contracts for gas transportation? This could drive up the price of electricity (although it would be "better quality" electricity), but it could also reduce the reliability of gas service to traditional gas customers using firm transportation (such as LDCs serving residential customers with space heating). Should regulators then force the new generators to invest in fuel switching capability at higher cost? What kind of a "market system" is this that so pervasively regulates individual choices of profit-minded businesses? Perhaps interruptible service is being priced too low relative to firm service, when the effects of reliability on an entire regional system are considered. Should FERC then step in and determine the "right" price? Maybe environmental and land use restrictions are retarding the development of dual fuel uses because communities refuse to allow coal burning or oil storage tanks near them or because Clean Air Act requirements prevent alternative fuel combustion. "Efficient energy policies" may require waivers of "efficient environmental policies." On a macro-level, if all costs and benefits of alternative fuel use are weighed against the costs and benefits of a less reliable gas-based electricity supply (brownouts and blackouts and extremely volatile gas and electric prices), what is the optimal balance?

The Costello article reviews a long list of reports by FERC, NERC, NAESB, RTOs, ISOs (you will learn these acronyms later), the National

Petroleum Council, the Edison Electric Institute, the American Gas Association, and the Electric Power Research Institute and concluded: "For the most part, ... they offer no concrete policy initiatives based on well-founded analysis of the associated costs and benefits," with the exception of the recommendation that electric power and gas pipeline operators communicate better with each other and perhaps even coordinate some of their operations. Costello, *id.* at 23.

Any solid analysis would depend, of course, on the accuracy of the data available to study, and in particular on the accuracy of the price data for gas used as an input to power generation. The link between dysfunctions in the gas market and dysfunctions in the electricity market became all too apparent during the California energy crisis in 2000–2001. A look at these linkages will focus on two problems highlighted at the end of Section D on restructuring: over-reliance on spot markets and prevention of affiliate abuse.

2.   PRICE INDICES AND COMMODITY MARKETS

a.   OVERVIEW OF COMMODITY MARKETS

We have already noted the increased volatility in spot prices for natural gas (review Figure 8–6) since 2000. The extraordinary price spikes in natural gas in the Northeast in the winter of 2000–2001 led to calls for an investigation from many legislators. The GAO undertook a three-part study of (1) the factors underlying the gas price spike; (2) FERC's role in ensuring that gas prices were being set in a competitive, informed marketplace and (3) the options available to gas distributing companies (LDCs) to mitigate the effects of price spikes on residential customers. In *Natural Gas: Analysis of Changes in Market Price* (GAO–03–46, Dec. 2002), the GAO concluded:

- Price spikes occur in natural gas markets because supplies cannot adjust quickly to demand increases and demand is inelastic. In the cold winter of 2000–2001, gas supplies were constrained and demand soared, leading to the "perfect environment" for price spikes. *Id.* at 5. The report noted that there were "some indications" that prices had been manipulated in the Western United States, where California had experienced a year of rolling brownouts and almost unimaginably high electricity price spikes, but other investigations of these Western markets were not yet complete; price manipulation could not be ruled out.

- FERC did not have an adequate monitoring system in place to provide assurance that gas prices were being set competitively. FERC's oversight initiatives were "incomplete or ineffective" and "served more to help educate FERC's staff about the new markets than [t]o produce effective oversight." *Id.* at 28. FERC staff had not used data available to it to conduct an investigation into allegations of market manipulation and FERC faced "significant human capital challenges" in acquiring a qualified staff that understood the restructured markets. FERC's belated investigation into improper behavior by energy companies such as Enron was "largely reactive to complaints" rather than pro-active, and relied heavily on requests for information from the energy companies because FERC itself lacked systems to collect or monitor market information. *Id.* at 29. FERC had agreed with an earlier GAO report that documented these problems at FERC. See GAO, Energy Markets: Concerted Actions Needed by FERC to Confront Challenges That Impede Effective Oversight (GAO–02–656, June 14, 2002).

- FERC's regulations governing the conduct of gas pipeline companies with affiliates were outdated. The 1988 rules did not reflect the significant changes in unbundling, capacity release, e-commerce and online trading systems, and market consolidation that had expanded the number and types of pipeline affiliates. *Id.* at 30.

- The Commodity Futures Trading Commission (CFTC) monitored trading in the NYMEX futures contracts, but other natural gas derivatives markets were not subject to CFTC regulation. Although the CFTC has general authority to investigate manipulation of commodity prices to prevent fraud, it had not yet concluded its investigations of "wash trades" and other complaints and it did not monitor derivatives markets on a daily basis.

The GAO report then provided a guide to local gas utilities describing tools that could be used to protect the LDC and its customers against price spikes. Physical tools include: (1) gas storage; and (2) fixed price contracts (also called forward contracts) to take physical delivery of a set quantity of gas over time at a set price. This price may, of course, be either higher or lower than spot prices at any specific time, but the fixed price provides price stability. Financial tools include: (1) futures contracts traded on NYMEX to lock in a future price for up to 72 months in the future; (2) option contracts that can be used to guarantee prices. (Utilities pay a premium for the option, much as you pay a premium to insure against accidental losses); and (3) swaps, which are futures contracts that are usually individually negotiated and traded in the OTC (over-the-counter) market rather than on an organized exchange like NYMEX. The report gives some basic examples: Suppose, *e.g.,* in March, a utility company wants to hedge against a possible future price increase by buying a futures contract for gas to be delivered the next January at $4.60 (per million BTUs). If the actual January cash price of gas later increases to $5.15, the company can buy the gas on the spot market at $5.15 and sell its futures contract on NYMEX for $5.15. Since it bought the futures contract for only $4.60, the company gains 55 cents on the futures contract in the financial markets, and the net price of the physical gas that is delivered to the utility is $4.60 (the $5.15 spot price in the physical market minus the gain of 55 cents in the financial market). Conversely, if the January cash price for gas has dropped to $4.25, the company can buy the gas at this spot price for delivery in the physical market that month, sell the futures contract at a loss of 35 cents, and still pay a net gas cost of $4.60. *Id.* at 35–37.

As is clear from the example, hedging does not guarantee the lowest gas price in the market. Rather, hedging allows the utility to mitigate price volatility and gain certainty with respect to its future gas costs. Minimizing gas prices by trying to "beat the market" is an entirely different strategy, one performed by "speculators" rather than "hedgers."

b. MANIPULATION OF PRICE INDICES

In March 2003, the FERC staff completed their fact-finding review and analysis of the California gas and electric markets. In its *Final Report on Price Manipulation in Western Markets* (Docket No. PA02–2–000), the FERC staff reported its key conclusion:

> [M]arkets for natural gas and electricity in California are inextricably linked, and ... dysfunctions in each fed off one another during the crisis. Spot gas prices rose to extraordinary levels, facilitating the unprecedented price increase in the electricity market. *Id.* at ES–1.
>
> * * *
>
> While soaring demand for gas and flawed electric power market rules were the primary drivers of high gas prices, spot market manipulations contributed significantly. *Id.* at I–1.

Here is a graph of the spot price of natural gas delivered from producing states like Texas at the Southern California Border. *Id.* at I–5:

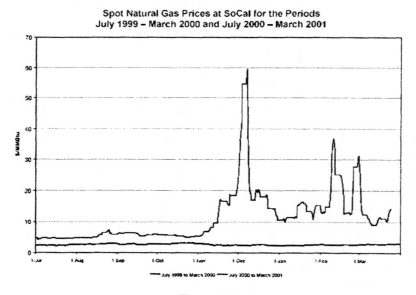

Figure 8–8
Spot Natural Gas Prices at SoCal for the Periods July 1999–March 2000 and July 2000–March 2001

How had spot gas prices, so crucial to the efficient (and fair) functioning of restructured gas and electric markets, been manipulated? The Report documented two ways:

First, trading in natural gas at Topock (a major delivery hub near the border where El Paso's interstate pipeline met the intrastate pipeline of Southern California Gas Company, a LDC), exhibited an anomalous pattern of "churning" between two traders—one from (the now infamously defunct) EnronOnline (EOL) and the other from Reliant Energy Services, a trading affiliate of a large Texas-based company that had restructured into a regulated utility company (called Centerpoint) and an unregulated affiliate (Reliant) that sought to provide new services to participants in new gas markets. Churning is the rapid execution of buy/sell trades between two traders in a very short period of time, designed to produce sharp upward price movements. (*E,g.,* on one day, Reliant traded gas at the rate of one transaction every 10 seconds over a 30–minute period.) These price movements were seen by all traders using the EOL electronic bulletin board (which was the dominant trading platform in the industry). These traders, not knowing that the price of gas was being churned, would start bidding up the gas price also, thinking that the price of gas they saw on EOL's screen reflected real market factors. Then, later, Reliant would profit as a net buyer of spot gas when the prices fell (which, of course, it knew they would). Enron traders used EOL to take large positions in the market as an active speculator. Enron had an enormous information advantage over other traders: it was both a buyer and seller on its EnronOnline trading platform. Using its information advantage from the physical gas trading market, Enron earned large profits in the derivatives and other financial products markets. (Enron earned more than $500 million in such profits in 2000 and 2001 during the California crisis). *Id.* at ES–12.[13]

The second method of manipulating the spot price of gas was far more widespread. Reliant and many other traders participated in false reporting of natural gas prices to the publishers of the gas price indices widely used by market participants to settle their contract obligations to buy and sell gas. Two trade publications, Platts *Gas Daily* and Platts *Inside FERC* were widely used by the industry to determine what gas had sold for on both a daily and monthly basis. To collect the data, Platts employees would call the trading desks of various energy companies that traded gas at hubs throughout the U.S. The traders would then report to Platts what the weighted average daily price had been that day (weighted by the volumes sold at each price in each trade) for gas bought and sold in the physical market. As FERC staff lamentably concluded in its investigation, false reporting was "epidemic" and "price index manipulation was part of the price formation process." *Id.* at Chapter III.

---

13. Interested readers should view the graphics and tables in the FERC Staff Report, available from the FERC Western Energy Crisis web page at http://www.ferc.gov/industries /electric/indus-act/wec.asp. The Report is definitely not "dry" reading. Chapter II explains the churning activity and its effects on profits and prices in detail. The FERC staff did a detailed analysis of the relationship between Reliant's purchases of physical gas on the spot market and Reliant's trades of financial gas derivative products. showing that Reliant traders made very large profits from financial trades based on Reliant's churning. *Id.* at II–9. The EOL/Reliant churning at Topock was actually large enough to affect the prices of natural gas at Henry Hub, the largest trading hub in the U.S. *Id.* at III–36, IX–12 to IX–24.

The motives for reporting false information were several: to influence the published price indices to enhance the value of the trading company's financial position in the derivatives markets or its purchase obligations; to increase reported volumes to create the impression of more liquid markets, thus attracting more customers; and to influence the spot market price of electricity which was based on the price of gas used by the generators, especially if the traders also sold power in California or were affiliated with such sellers. *Id.* at ES–6 and Chapter III. The false data reporting was not limited to the Western markets. El Paso Merchant's reported price trades in the Northeast and Gulf Coast failed to match actual trades 99% of the time. Instead, El Paso reported data according to its "book bias," *i.e.*, its trading book position in the financial markets.

In sum, the gas and electricity commodity markets that were so carefully created and nurtured by FERC over decades of sometimes painful transitioning to competitive markets were being manipulated by many in many ways to produce prices that were not "just and reasonable," as the federal statutory framework of the Natural Gas Act of 1938 still required. FERC's analyses found that the price of gas would have been lower by almost $8.54 per MMBtu in December 2000 if Reliant had not churned the market. Customers of Southern California Gas Co. paid hundreds of millions of dollars in excessive gas costs which, under reasonable assumptions, inflated electric prices by some $1.6 billion in December 2000 alone. *Id.* at II–60.

FERC's response to this Report is taken up in the Electricity chapters. One key reform was the creation by FERC of the Office of Market Oversight and Investigation (OMOI) staffed by highly qualified professionals (including some former employees of trading companies that were dissolved by their affiliated parents in the face of class action litigation, multi-agency investigations, and plummeting stock values).

3.   AFFILIATE ABUSE: ORDER 2004

As we have seen, FERC required only "functional unbundling," not the physical divestiture of pipelines, from the merchant trading arms. FERC's task was to enforce rules of nondiscrimination to prevent a pipeline company from favoring its own marketing affiliate with sweetheart deals that gave the affiliate an advantage in securing pipeline space, especially during shortages, or which gave price discounts only to its affiliate. In April 2000, a month before the California energy crisis began, the California Public Utility Commission (CPUC) complained to FERC that El Paso Pipeline and its affiliate were engaged in anticompetitive practices that violated FERC's Standards of Conduct for pipeline operations. El Paso Pipeline had put a large block of capacity up for auction. Two of its own merchant affiliates outbid other bidders and won all 1.22 billion cubic feet of capacity at rates below the level set in El Paso Pipeline's published tariff. The auction allowed El Paso Merchant to hold 1/6 of the pipeline capacity into California, alledgedly allowing El Paso to exercise market power and raise the price of gas to the state.

After months of hearings and media attention, the chief FERC administrative law judge concluded that while El Paso Pipeline and El Paso

Merchant had the ability to exercise market power, it was not clear that they had done so. However, clear evidence of affiliate abuse was found in transcripts of phone conversations between Pipeline personnel and Merchant personnel which violated the "firewall" that FERC rules required between the two. In March 2002, additional hearings generated 14 volumes of transcripts of evidence. The judge concluded that El Paso Pipeline had failed to post and schedule all the capacity that it controlled to transport available gas to California, thus artificially raising the price of natural gas delivered there. The pipeline had operated at only 78% of its capacity, even after accounting for the tragic pipeline rupture and explosion in New Mexico (discussed in Chapter 6(G)(3)).

The evidence also showed that El Paso officials discussed the "ability to influence the physical market to the benefit of any financial hedge/position" and ways to boost profits by "idling large blocks of transport." See Jacqueline Lang Weaver, Can Energy Markets Be Trusted? The Effect of the Rise and Fall of Enron on Energy Markets, 3 Hous. Bus. & Tax L. J. 1, at 55 (2003). Just days before FERC was to issue a final order on the case, El Paso agreed to a $1.7 billion payment to the state of California to settle the charges of withholding capacity to that state. At the same time, Williams Company agreed to pay a $20 million fine to FERC to resolve allegations that its Transco pipeline gave preferential treatment to its energy-trading affiliate. FERC had discovered that Williams' computer system allowed marketing personnel to gain access to Transco's confidential shipping information, giving it an advantage over other competitors. *Id.* at 56. As an American Bar Association report concluded, the lengthy hearings in the El Paso case showed the difficulty of detecting and proving the exercise of market power and affiliate abuse. ABA Section on Env't, Energy & Resources, Electric & Natural Gas Comm., Year in Review 2001 Report, Tab A, at 6–10.

To remedy these types of problems, FERC initiated a rulemaking that ended with the issuance of FERC Order 2004, imposing more stringent and detailed standards of conduct to govern the relationship between transmission providers (of both "pipes and wires," *i.e.,* both gas and electricity shippers). FERC Order 2004, Standards of Conduct for Transmission Providers, 68 Fed. Reg. 69,134 (Dec. 11, 2003) (to be codified at 18 C.F.R. Parts 37, 161, 250, 284, and 358, as amended by FERC Orders 2004a, 69 Fed. Reg. 23,562 and 2004b, 69 Fed Reg. 43,371). For example, the transfer of an employee from one affiliate to another must now be posted on the EBBs (the electronic bulletin boards) for FERC and competitors to see. The order broadens the definition of affiliate to cover a wider range of activities being performed by affiliates now engaged in the types of transactions, such as power marketing, that were only lightly regulated by FERC in the restructured markets. Weaver, *supra* at 96.

4. HAS RESTRUCTURING SUCCEEDED?

Surely, it is too early for the reader to answer this question without the benefit of studying the upcoming chapters on electricity restructuring—which we have learned are inextricably linked to gas markets. However, FERC's most recent *2004 State of the Markets Report for Natural Gas Markets*, prepared by the Staff of the Office of Market Oversight and Investigations in June 2005, cautiously asserts that gas markets are functioning well. Granted that natural gas prices had risen 63% in 2003 and another 7% in 2004, market forces were working: Gas producers were responding by increasing efforts to find new supplies, investment in gas pipeline infrastructure was proceeding, financial gas markets had developed new risk management tools, allowing traders and companies to hedge risks more robustly, and natural gas price indices had improved, although the collection and publication of key market data, especially reports on the amount of gas in storage, still needed improvement. *Id.* at 138. After the trading scandals were discovered, many traders had stopped reporting prices to Platts and the trade press. No statute required them to disclose their traded prices. Without this price information (accurately reported, of course), gas markets cannot operate well. (Imagine trying to decide if the time is right to buy or sell shares of Wal–Mart or Chevron if the stock markets only reported some of the trades in these stocks). FERC's 2004 Market Report stated that more traders were now participating in reporting gas prices to publishers under new procedures established by the trade press (with strong input and encouragement from FERC.) Still, "popular confidence in natural gas pricing remains uncertain. With rapid price increases in 2003 and 2004, pricing mechanisms remain under close scrutiny by policy makers in Congress and elsewhere." *Id.* at 147.

The Energy Policy Act of 2005 amends the Natural Gas Act in several ways that aim at increasing public confidence in natural gas markets and trading. Section 316 directs FERC to "facilitate price transparency in markets for the sale or transportation of physical natural gas in interstate commerce." FERC is given the power to obtain pricing information from participants in the gas markets and FERC may itself establish an electronic information system if it determines that existing price publications are not adequately providing price discovery or market transparency. In other words, if the gas industry and the price index publishers do not adequately police themselves, FERC will step in. Section 315 of the new Act amends the Natural Gas Act to prohibit any entity, directly or indirectly, from using "any manipulative or deceptive device or contrivance" in the purchase or sale of natural gas or gas transportation services in violation of any rules that FERC might prescribe as necessary to protect gas ratepayers. Finally, Section 314 amends the NGA by raising penalties for violations from $500 per day to $50,000 per day and authorizing a fine of up to $1 million (previously $5,000) against any person convicted of violating the NGA.

While FERC worked prodigiously from 2001 onwards to restore confidence in gas markets, it also focused tremendous efforts on facilitating the most promising new source of natural gas for U.S. consumers: LNG imported across hundreds of miles of ocean from gas fields in foreign lands. This is the topic of the last section of this chapter.

F.   LNG IMPORTS

As we have seen in Section A(5) of this chapter, domestic gas production is on a permanent decline, Canadian gas imports will not be available to bridge the gap between projected U.S. demand and supply, and the newly authorized Alaskan gas pipeline will not bring gas to the lower 48 states for at least 10 years. Yet electricity generation in the U.S is now keenly dependent on natural gas as are many homeowners and industries. LNG imports are to rescue us from the yawning gap between future demand and supply in the next few years. In 2002, LNG supplied 1% of our natural gas; by 2020, it could supply 20%. Daniel Yergin & Michael Stoppard, The Next Prize, 82 Foreign Affairs 103, at 111 (Nov./Dec. 2003). We will compete intensely with China, India, Japan, Korea and Europe for these imported gas supplies.

LNG is natural gas refrigerated to minus 260 degrees Fahrenheit to convert it into a liquid which can be shipped by tanker across thousands of miles of ocean. The LNG is regasified at receiving terminals and put into the existing (or newly built) infrastructure of gas pipelines. As a liquid, methane is 1/600 the volume of gas as gas. A single tanker cargo of LNG can deliver the equivalent of 5% of U.S. gas consumption on an average day. Id. at 107. In the past decade, striking technological improvements in engineering and construction of liquefaction plants and tankers have decreased the costs of LNG shipments by as much as 30%. In 1999, recall that forecasters predicted LNG would be profitable if the price of natural gas rose above $3.00/MCF. Gas prices since mid–2002 have been well above this price. On August 29, 2005, the futures prices for Henry Hub deliveries of natural gas ranged from $11.132/MMBtu (for 3–months futures) to $9.567 (for 24–months futures). Reliant Energy Market Notes, Aug. 30, 2005.

The siting and environmental issues related to LNG are discussed in the next chapter in Section 9(C). This concluding section of Chapter 8 discusses the business and regulatory models that will guide the LNG industry in the United States, tying the discussion to what you have learned in this chapter about FERC regulation of the gas industry and the role of long-term gas contracts and tying into the discussion of geopolitics in Chapter 7 on International Oil.

1. Will an OGEC join OPEC?

Because our new sources of gas will come from foreign countries, the first question arises: Will the LNG-exporting countries form an OPEC-like cartel that subjects LNG-importing countries to the same type of serious geopolitical risks and hazards that are documented in Chapter 7? Even if an Organization of Gas Exporting Countries (OGEC) is not likely to have the same power over world gas supplies as OPEC has over oil supplies, the geopolitics of dependence on unstable, undemocratic, unfriendly or corrupt nations are not easily dismissed. So—who has the gas? Here are the top holders of oil reserves compared to gas reserves in 2003. (The top 5 in gas are bolded):

	Oil	*Gas*
Saudi Arabia	25%	**4%**
Iraq	11%	2%
Iran	10%	**15%**
Kuwait	10%	—
UAE	6%	**4%**
Russia	6%	**31%**
Venezuela	5%	3%
Nigeria	3%	2%
Libya	3%	—
China	2%	1%
U.S.	2%	3%
Qatar	2%	**9%**
Algeria	1%	3%

Ronald Soligo & Amy Myers Jaffe, Market Structure in the New Gas Economy: Is Cartelization Possible?, available at the James A. Baker III Institute for Public Policy Energy Forum, Rice University, at www.baker-institute.org.

Clearly, Russia is the "Saudi Arabia" of gas. It already exports large volumes of gas to Europe via a 6,000–mile long pipeline network heading West from Siberia to the Atlantic, and its huge Sakhalin LNG project in far-eastern Russia will export LNG to Japan. How would you assess the likelihood of a successful gas-exporting cartel based on this data and your knowledge of OPEC? How many countries in the top gas reserve holders are already members of OPEC? How concentrated are gas reserves compared to oil reserves in just the top 2 countries? In the top 5 countries? How many of the top gas reserve holders are in the Middle East versus in other parts of the world? Which 3 countries are in the top 5 on both lists? Which country is most likely to be the "swing" producer in terms of having excess gas producing capacity relative to its own population needs? What are the key requirements for an effective cartel to be able to control output and prices? Are there key differences between gas production and LNG exports versus oil shipments that may affect the prospects of cartelization? *E.g.,* the liquefaction, shipping, and then regasification of LNG at receiving terminals require an investment of several billions of dollars for each project. Does this make it more or less likely that a country will hold excess capacity that it can turn on and off to affect market prices or drive out rivals? Which fuel source has more substitutes available to end-users to switch to? If Russia has a number of privatized gas production companies that compete with each other, does this make cartelization more or less likely?

In May 2001, the Gas Exporting Countries Forum (GECF) held its first ministerial meeting in Tehran to enhance consultation and coordination among gas exporters. GECF has met every year since then with about 12 to 14 countries attending, including some exporters not listed in the table above, such as Indonesia, Malaysia, Oman, Brunei, Norway and Turkmenistan, Bolivia, Egypt, and Trinidad–Tobago.[14] While professing to be unin-

---

14. Even a 1% share of world gas reserves has enabled some countries to become major gas exporters. *E.g.,* Australia exports LNG to Asian markets. Trinidad–Tobago (with 1/2 of one

terested in setting quotas, some GECF members clearly have promoted ideas that would restrict free markets in LNG, to the detriment of consumers. Soligo & Jaffe, *supra* in text at notes iv and v. In its April 2005 meeting, GECF members accounting for 70% of the world's gas reserves said they would seek a "fair price" for LNG, but would not "fix the price at this time." Greenwire, Apr. 28, 2005. The Soligo & Jaffe study offers the following conclusions to compare to your own:

- Russia will play an increasingly dominant role in international gas markets; its commanding share of the gas trade, now and even more in the future, will allow it to exert monopoly power. Russia can reach both Western and Eastern markets with pipeline gas which is still cheaper than LNG.

- However, for the next decade or so, Russia's power to price its pipeline gas above cost is limited by the fairly large number of other countries, including some Mideastern nations, which have substantial gas reserves to convert to LNG exports. LNG export costs will be a price ceiling on Russia's market power.

- In the longer term, say beyond 2030, as gas production capacity peaks in regions with limited reserves, these LNG exporters will have incentives to cooperate with Russia to keep gas prices high through a successful cartel.

- It is in Russia's interest to collude with OPEC to try and set prices for both oil and gas.

If you agree with these conclusions, what policy options would you recommend to gas importing countries like the U.S.?

2. THE BUSINESS AND REGULATORY MODEL FOR LNG

LNG's development as a global fuel began with Japan's efforts to reduce air pollution. Japan began to import LNG from Alaska in 1969 (and still does today). Yergin & Stoppard, *supra* at 107. After the 1973 OPEC oil embargo, Japan sought to import LNG from diverse countries such as Australia, Brunei, Indonesia, Malaysia in addition to Qatar and Abu Dhabi. Later, South Korea and Taiwan joined Japan as major LNG importers, and China and India are poised to become large importers soon. The U.S. also began importing LNG from Algeria as a post-embargo measure; ultimately four receiving terminals were built in the U.S., but the "gas bubble" of the 1980s caused such low gas domestic gas prices that 3 of the 4 terminals were mothballed until two years ago.

This early LNG trade developed using a business model called the "LNG paradigm." Yergin & Stoppard, *supra* at 108. A chain of long-term

percent of world gas reserves) is the largest exporter of LNG to the U.S. at this time, accounting for about 70% of our imports (Algeria and Qatar supply most of the remaining 30%.) One study warns that Islamic extremism is of concern in Trinidad–Tobago. Michael T. Burr, The Geopolitical Risks of LNG, Public Util. Fortnightly, Mar. 2005, at 28, citing Dept. of Energy, Energy Information Admin., The Global LNG Market: Status & Outlook, Dec. 2003.

contracts or vertically integrated activities linked LNG exporters to consuming importers at each stage of the LNG process. Specific gas reserves in the host country were tied to specific contracts of 25 years or more to send gas to specially built liquefaction plants which would then deliver the LNG in dedicated tankers that basically shuttled LNG to designated receiving terminals (the shuttling tankers were like floating pipelines). Gas prices were based on formulas linked to oil prices. Supply and demand were developed in tandem. *Id.* at 108. Financiers were unwilling to lend money to these huge projects unless long-term Sale and Purchase Agreements (SPAs) were in place and all steps in the LNG chain were developed together. This paradigm resulted because of LNG's huge capital costs (of $3 to $10 billion per project); no one would invest in LNG supply facilities unless the demand for LNG was guaranteed.

Clearly, this model mimics the old, pre-restructuring model under which domestic natural gas markets developed. Recall that gas pipelines are expensive to build; financing depended on guaranteed markets. All the gas from a field was dedicated to a single pipeline purchaser under long-term contracts; the merchant pipeline then sold the gas to LDCs under similarly matched long-term contracts. (Review Section C of this chapter). And yes, take-or-pay provisions are common in the long-term LNG sales and purchase agreements.

After FERC restructured the gas pipeline industry to become a more competitive, open access network, the old model gave way to short-term contracts, spot markets for gas, and direct bargaining between gas producers and gas users using the pipeline solely as an open access carrier. How can this newly structured gas market accommodate the needs of the LNG industry? In particular, based on your newly acquired knowledge of oil and gas markets, consider these questions:

- Should LNG receiving terminals, particularly those in the Gulf Coast area near Texas and Louisiana, be regulated as "open access" terminals, available to any importer that properly schedules space for its LNG tanker loads to be regasified? Or should they be regulated as "proprietary" terminals belonging to the investors that built them for their own specific contracts and markets without any duty to accept shipments from others?

- Should terminal rates be regulated by FERC under cost-of-service ratemaking or should FERC allow rates to be set by market forces as represented by privately negotiated contract terms? Should FERC have any role in guaranteeing profitability to private terminal owners who risk billion-dollar investments in such facilities?

- Should FERC use its regulatory staff to grant certificates of public convenience and necessity only to those terminals that FERC thinks are best sited, after conducting regional assessments of demand, comparative costs, environmental comparisons and other such public interest factors? Or should FERC grant permits to any qualified applicant and let the market sort out which competitors will ultimately win the race to supply U.S. markets? What institutions or laws are available at the federal, regional, or state level, then, to perform land use planning and comparative analyses of sites? (Chapter 9 takes up this question.)

When the electricity generation market was opened to independent power producers that could build power plants with little of the traditional federal or state public utility regulation, many new entrants and unregulated affiliates of the local utility companies constructed many new gas-fired power plants in a booming market—that soon turned to bust, leaving many of the companies in serious financial distress and many unhappy shareholders. In the 1970s, a similar boom in nuclear power plant construction also turned to bust, leaving both ratepayers and shareholders of the local utilities that ordered the plants to absorb billions of dollars of investments in unfinished and uncompetitive nuclear plants. Is it somehow better policy to let private investors "waste" capital by misreading market forces rather than to have the "waste" approved by regulatory authorities who misread the same markets and approved what turned out to be uneconomic facilities? Isn't the effect on the wetlands, coastal zones, prairies and deserts hosting these overbuilt or uncompetitive plants the same? Do you have any faith in planning processes that can mitigate overbuilding or should planning simply mitigate the environmental impacts of whatever private investors seek to build? How does the experience with the rush to develop coalbed methane in the Rockies (in Section B of this chapter) inform your opinion?

Faced with natural gas shortages and soaring prices, FERC responded quickly to the call for rapid development of LNG in U.S. markets and built an LNG regulatory paradigm designed to match what industry said it needed to develop expeditiously. How do you think FERC answered the questions posed above and what rationales did FERC offer to support its positions as reasonable? In the National Energy Act of 2005, Congress stepped in and affirmed much of what FERC had already decided in its LNG orders. Section 311 of the new Act reads, in part, as follows:

(B) Before January 1, 2015, the Commission shall not—

(i) deny an application solely on the basis that the applicant proposes to use the LNG terminal exclusively or partially for gas that the applicant or an affiliate of the applicant will supply to the facility; or

(ii) condition an order on—

    (I) a requirement that the LNG terminal offer service to customers other than the applicant, or any affiliate of the applicant, securing the order;

    (II) any regulation of the rates, charges, terms, or conditions of service of the LNG terminal; or

    (III) a requirement to file with the Commission schedules or contracts related to the rates, charges, terms, or conditions of service of the LNG terminal.

(C) Subparagraph (B) shall cease to have effect on January 1, 2030.

Is this "back to the future"? Why would Congress impose such strange dates of 2015 and 2030 in this section? Perhaps FERC and some industry members have warned that the current LNG paradigm will change over time as a huge global market in LNG trading develops with America's consumers as its most avid purchasers. Because of LNG, there is now the real possibility that a unitary world natural gas price will develop within the next decade. LNG could eventually be traded in tanker loads like crude oil, headed for the U.S. or Europe or Asia in response to price incentives that reflect differentials for transport costs and the heating value content of the LNG. How can such a market develop efficiently if LNG terminals are bottlenecks of monopoly power, refusing to offload the tankers of LNG cargo owned by independent or nonaffiliated gas marketers, end-users, or producers? Will the LNG paradigm of long-term contracts and take-or-pay provisions become relics of a much faster moving global market, forcing FERC to "restructure" the industry again?

Perhaps the possibility of a global market in LNG explains why FERC has reserved the right to file such supplemental orders as it finds necessary or appropriate if it receives complaints in the future of undue discrimination or other anticompetitive behavior by the owners of the proprietary terminals? See FERC's order approving an LNG terminal in Hackberry, Louisiana, 101 FERC ¶ 61,294, issued December 18, 2002.[15] How can there ever be undue discrimination if the terminal owner is expressly allowed to refuse service to others? Does this type of language in the FERC order prevent a company from asserting that it must be reimbursed from stranded costs that may arise if FERC later requires open-access terminals? *See* Blaine Yamagata & Joel A. Youngblood, Focus on LNG—Part I, Selected Current Regulatory Issues at pp. 3–4, 3d Ann. Gas & Power Inst. (Univ. of Texas and State Bar of Texas, Nov. 11–12, 2004) (FERC's opinion offers no guidance on this issue). For additional reading, *see* Gearold L. Knowles, Liquefied Natural Gas: Regulation in a Competitive Natural Gas Market, 24 Energy L. J. 293 (2003); and Ben Smith, Breaking the Chain: The Role of Short Term Trading in the LNG Markets of the Future, AIPN Advisor, Dec. 2004, at 8–10.

3.   SOME CONCLUDING THOUGHTS ON OIL, GAS AND GLOBAL MARKETS

Many of you readers have now studied Chapters 6, 7 and 8 on oil and gas. Even if you have not read all three, an inescapable fact frames our

---

15. The four LNG terminals that already existed in the U.S. before 1992 are still regulated under the pipeline utility model of cost-based rates and open-access service, under Section 7 of the Natural Gas Act which authorizes FERC to issue certificates of public convenience and necessity. The new LNG terminal orders are approved by FERC using only Section 3 of the Natural Gas Act which authorizes FERC to approve exports and imports of natural gas if not inconsistent with the public interest. Section 3 contains no federal right of eminent domain, while Section 7 has such a right. Might an LNG terminal investor prefer to file and receive both Sections 3 and 7 authorizations from FERC, as the four existing terminals did pre–1992?

energy future: The United States consumes more than 25% of the world's oil and natural gas production, yet our high-cost and relatively small domestic supplies of conventional oil and gas have peaked. We are competing with many other nations, both in Europe and Asia, for resources from Canada, South America, Russia, Africa, Australia, and, of course, the Mideast. Because LNG and gas-to-liquids technologies (which can produce a very clean diesel fuel) are proven technologies today, gas can substitute for oil in many uses. Isn't the Peak Oil debate on a global scale better framed, then, as a Peak Hydrocarbon scenario? It appears there are more diverse sources of natural gas, often in already-discovered stranded gas fields, available from a broader number of countries than exist for oil.

Put yourself in the position of one of today's supermajors, whether U.S.-owned (like ExxonMobil or Chevron) or European (like BP and Shell), competing against Chinese, Indian, and Korean[16] companies prowling the earth for resources for their own citizens. Your company has amassed many billions of dollars in cash from the past four years of high oil and gas prices. Where will you invest these billions—in deepwater OCS wells, Alaskan gas, LNG from foreign sources, gas-to-liquids facilities from foreign supplies, domestic or Canadian oil shale or tar sands, coal and ultimately coal gasification, nuclear, or renewables like solar, wind and biomass? Factor into your decision the very real possibility that increased combustion of carbon-based fuels contributes to global warming, first evidenced by the thawing of Siberian permafrost which has begun to release methane into the atmosphere. Also factor into your decision the assumption that Americans will find it unacceptable to decrease the air quality or visibility in national park areas.

Your company takes the plunge into LNG and coal gasification as its two major growth strategies, premised on the price of gas staying above $4.50/MCF and the price of oil above $28/barrel for the next 25 years. Other majors, independents, utility companies, and state oil companies choose to develop many of these other resources. Within seven years, Iraq, Saudi Arabia, Iran, Russia and Qatar have built up excess capacity in their gas facilities using their own vast holdings of increased dollars from higher oil and gas prices. Qatar and Russia decide to expand gas output to decrease prices and prevent coal-gasification gas and nuclear power from gaining too great a market share.[17] Much to everyone's surprise, the cost of

---

16. You will learn in Chapter 9 that South Korea is a major player in developing the gas reserves in the Peruvian Amazon at Camisea. This gas is expected to be used for LNG exports. Will Californians or Koreans receive this bounty from the rainforests?

17. Soligo & Jaffe, *supra* in text at notes xi to xiv. Saudi Arabia disciplined the market twice to punish its competitors: first during the 1980s when low oil and gas prices denied revenues to the Soviet Union, hastening its collapse (perhaps in cooperation with President Reagan's policies to force Russia to engage in an arms build-up); and in the 1998–99 when Saudi Arabia warned Venezuela to stop overproducing to expand its market share. Venezuela ignored the warnings, and the Saudis let the price of oil free-fall to $9/barrel. Venezuela plunged into financial trouble, its Western-friendly government was voted out and Hugo Chavez was voted in. He immediately reined in production; a workers' strike followed, and

nuclear power has dropped as dramatically and unexpectedly as did the costs of LNG in the 1990s because of better construction, engineering and technology, the federal insurance guarantees provided in the National Energy Act of 2005, and greenhouse gas trading credits. The price of natural gas on global markets falls to $2.90/MCF. Oil prices stay relatively high because the transportation sector is slower to adjust to high oil prices, and those majors who chose gas-to-liquids investments (which were more expensive than LNG in 2005) are profiting handsomely while your LNG investment is barely economic and the gas from coal is unprofitable. Those companies and municipalities that invested in gas from landfills in the U.S. are also surviving comfortably because "green" electricity marketers have successfully promoted the sale of electric power from renewable domestic sources to customers who strongly believe that the U.S. should not be dependent on polluting sources or on unfriendly foreign sources of petroleum. (Seven years from now we are spending about $60 billion/year in Iraqi reconstruction and stabilization and another $40 billion to station troops and military communication centers in certain Mideast and Caspian Sea areas.)

As a policymaker, would you support loan guarantees for the national coal gasification strategy proposed by William Rosenberg earlier in this chapter to match the loan guarantee already extended to Alaskan gas pipeline investors? Do national security concerns justify guaranteeing a price floor to U.S. producers of landfill gas, CBM, or gas from coal gasification? Do such concerns justify more royalty relief for domestic oil and gas producers so that they can continue to drill more wells, even if the wells are increasingly less productive? Do national security concerns or concerns about poverty, unemployment and overall industry competitiveness in a global society justify loosened environmental regulations in the U.S.? More public land access to energy resources, regardless of irreversible and unmitigatable land impacts? Would you support subsidies to U.S. consumers to buy energy-conserving products? Enforced building, appliance and vehicle standards for energy use? Or would you just let prices reflect market forces, including any oil or gas cartel power, and rely on our foreign policy (including our military power) to guide our energy relations with the world? As a citizen, what will you ask your legislators to promote on behalf of you, your children, and your grandchildren?

Venezuela's output fell from 3.7 million b/d to 2 million b/d in mid–2004. Prices started to soar.

CHAPTER 9

DEVELOPING ENERGY RESOURCES IN FRAGILE ENVIRONMENTS

Prior to the modern environmental movement, the location of large public or private works projects was not seen as a special legal problem. The dominance of engineers meant that there was little attention paid to the external environmental and social impacts of a project's location. The existing regulatory framework was generally weak and fragmented, and only a few scientists used terms like "sensitive environments" or "vulnerable ecosystems."

The environmental movement changed this state of affairs by making engineers talk to biologists, chemists, economists and the public generally. The passage of the National Environmental Policy Act, 42 U.S.C.A. § 4321

643

ff., brought about a multidisciplinary approach to the design of major projects, including those for energy resource production, transmission and distribution. Other statutes focused on particular kinds of sensitive areas and the construction of all types of project that impacted such areas; the Coastal Zone Management Act, discussed at Chapter 6.E, is one example. The concepts behind these laws spread rapidly throughout the world.

Resources for the efficient production of energy are scattered across the globe. Some are located in regions where the environment is sensitive to disruption. This sensitivity can arise from a number of causes. For example, Chapter 13 discusses the difficult issues posed by attempts to utilize the wind resources in the ocean offshore of tourist areas in New England, where the opposition focuses on the perceived threat to the aesthetics of the area. And the impact on migratory fish of dams producing hydroelectric power has produced long-running disputes involving biodiversity and Indian fishing rights (Chapter 4.C).

What sort of moral responsibilities does someone have when they seek to harness energy resources in a sensitive area? As an introduction to this topic, the first section of this chapter briefly sets out some ideas of a variety of people on the issue of moral responsibility. The remainder of the chapter will discuss how these ideas might apply to four areas in which the interaction between resource development and the natural and human environment has been particularly difficult to resolve: (1) The development of natural gas resources in the Peruvian Amazon; (2) The siting of liquefied natural gas import facilities along the coasts of North America; (3) The building of new electric transmission lines in the Florida wetlands; and (4) Exploration and production of oil in the Alaskan Arctic.

A. ISSUES OF RESPONSIBILITY

Consider the following points of view as you read the material on the four topics to be discussed in the remainder of the chapter:

Corporate Social Responsibility

Wikipedia, the Free Encyclopedia (a. July 28, 2005).

Corporate social responsibility ("CSR") is a company's obligation to be accountable to all of its stakeholders in all its operations and activities with the aim of achieving sustainable development not only in the economical dimension but also in the social and environmental dimensions.

A company's stakeholders are all those who are influenced by and can influence a company's decisions and actions, both locally or globally. Business stakeholders include (but are not limited to): employees, customers, suppliers, community organizations, subsidiaries and affiliates, joint venture partners, local neighborhoods, investors, shareholders (or a sole owner), and the environment.■

The Union of Concerned Executives

By the editors, The Economist, January 20, 2005.

On the face of it, questioning the efforts of companies to behave responsibly is an odd thing to do—unless you are accusing them of faking it, or of falling below some commonly agreed minimum standard. How could a company ever behave too responsibly? The very term "corporate social responsibility" endorses the actions to which it is applied. No doubt that is why companies fasten the label to a quite bewildering variety of supposedly enlightened, progressive or charitable corporate actions. . . .

Some executives think of their charitable donations—especially gifts such as sponsoring high-profile sporting or artistic events—as a kind of advertising. Others may feel that their companies, or their industries (oil, tobacco, pharmaceuticals), have such a poor image with the public at large that generous charitable donations are needed to redress matters. But straightforward corporate philanthropy of this kind is not woven into the way the firm manages its personnel, so the commercial benefits are probably limited. Most cash donations out of profits probably do represent a net loss of profits (even if the loss is less than the gross outlay).

Remember that corporate philanthropy is charity with other people's money—which is not philanthropy at all. When a company gives some of its profits away in a good cause, its managers are indulging their charitable instincts not at their own expense but at the expense of the firm's owners. That is a morally dubious transaction. When Robin Hood stole from the rich to give to the poor, he was still stealing. He might have been a good corporate citizen, but he was still a bandit—and less of one, arguably, than the vicariously charitable CEO, who is spending money taken not from strangers, but from people who have placed him in a position of trust to safeguard their property.

Note that the world's most spectacular philanthropists—think of the Bill & Melinda Gates Foundation, with its endowment of $27 billion—are not spending the profits of the companies they are associated with but their own private wealth. That is the real thing, true philanthropy, and is nothing but admirable, especially if the givers are taking care to ensure the money is spent wisely, as the biggest private foundations now do.

Philanthropy financed out of the profits of publicly owned companies is a quite different thing, ethically speaking. Shareholders might expect to be allowed to spend their money on good causes of their own choosing, rather than seeing the managers whose salaries they pay take that uplifting duty upon themselves.■

David B. Spence, The Shadow of the Rational Polluter

89 California Law Review 917, 919–920, 931–932 (2001).

If there is a foundation on which the traditional American environmental regulatory structure sits, it is the idea of the firm as a rational polluter.

The rational polluter as economic actor seeks to maximize its own pecuniary self-interest, and understands the payoffs associated with different courses of action. In order to maximize profit, the rational polluter will shift as many costs as possible to society; one way it does so is by discharging its wastes into the environment. Even though the rational polluter may prefer a clean environment to a dirty one, it is individually rational for each polluter to continue to pollute. . . .

Despite its impressive lineage, the rational polluter model has its critics. The strongest criticism challenges the rational polluter model as unrepresentative of reality and ultimately counterproductive. Critics charge that the environmental regulatory apparatus is so complex that compliance with regulatory requirements is unreasonably difficult. In a recent survey of corporate environmental managers, nearly half reported that their most time-and energy-consuming duty is trying to determine whether their companies are in compliance with the law, with seventy percent believing perfect compliance is impossible. As a result, critics claim most noncompliance results not from calculations by rational polluters, but rather from a lack of awareness or understanding of the rules. Consequently, say critics, the regulatory system is not producing as much environmentally beneficial behavior as it could.

This complexity critique is really several critiques, but includes at least four important elements. Critics complain that environmental regulatory requirements are (1) too numerous, (2) too difficult to understand, (3) too fluid, or ever-changing, and (4) too hard to find. Each of these characteristics, say critics, makes compliance difficult.■

Carol M. Rose, Property Rights and Responsibilities, in Thinking Ecologically: The Next Generation of Environmental Policy

(Marian R. Chertow and Daniel C. Esty, eds., Yale University Press, 1997).

Property rights—both private and public—are essential to a free enterprise system. The protection of both private and public rights is important because the goal of a free enterprise system, all other things being equal, is not simply to maximize the value of private goods. It is to maximize the value of *the sum of private and public resources.* Much of the recent discussion of takings points out the dangers to private owners from uncompensated public expropriations. Those dangers are real; public expropriations can unfairly single out particular private owners to pay for public benefits and, writ large, they mean that we could impoverish ourselves as a nation by discouraging enterprise and undermining commerce. . . .

But when diffuse public resources come under pressure from private piggybacked uses, the failure to manage private owners' uses presents a different kind of legislative failure. That failure too can impoverish us as a nation, by decimating resources that are diffuse and difficult to turn into private property, but that are still immensely valuable to the public as a whole, now (and it is to be hoped) in the future.■

Holmes Rolston, Environmental Ethics

(Temple University Press, 1988, p. 45).

"The question is not, Can they *reason?* nor, Can they *talk?* but, Can they *suffer?*" So Jeremy Bentham pinpointed half of a long-standing ethic toward animals. The other half is summarized by Aristotle: "Plants exist to give food to animals, and animals to give food to men—domestic animals for their use and food, wild ones, in most cases, if not in all, furnish food and other conveniences, such as clothing and various tools. Since nature makes nothing purposeless or in vain, all animals must have been made by nature for the sake of man." Thus the traditional ethic was rather simple: Use animals for your needs, but do not cause needless suffering.... Subject to prohibited cruelty, animals goods may be sacrificed for human interests. [Please note that Rolston is not *advocating* the traditional ethic, merely explaining it.]∎

Peter Singer, Animal Liberation

(Harper Collins Publishers, 3d ed., 2002, pp. 9, 219–20)

Most human beings are speciesists. Ordinary human beings—not a few exceptionally cruel or heartless humans, but the overwhelming majority of humans—take an active part in, acquiesce in, and allow their taxes to pay for practices that require the sacrifice of the most important interests of members of other species in order to promote the most trivial interests of our own species.

Among the factors that make it difficult to arouse public concern about animals perhaps the hardest to overcome is the assumption that "human beings come first" and that any problem about animals cannot be comparable, as a serious moral or political issue, to problems about humans.... How can anyone know that the problem is less serious than problems of human suffering? One can claim to know this only if one assumes that animals really do not matter, and that however much they suffer, their suffering is less important than the suffering of humans. But pain is pain, and the importance of preventing unnecessary pain and suffering does not diminish because the being that suffers is not a member of our species. What would we think of someone who said that "whites come first" and that therefore poverty in Africa does not pose as serious a problem as poverty in Europe?∎

Rick Potts, Humanity's Descent: The Consequences of Ecological Instability

(William Morrow and Company, 1996).

Homo sapiens owes its existence, at least in part, to the uncertainty and depth of nature's perturbations. The shifting, unforeshadowed settings of the Pleistocene favored faculties sensitive to environmental change and capable of stabilizing human needs. During hominid evolution, the mental, social, and ecological paradigms of our early ancestors were altered in ways that heightened the flexibility of response, the reading of environmental nuance, and the heterogeneity of behavior.

A species whose evolutionary history has been spurred by environmental disturbance over long spans of time is an organism designed to ensure its ultimate survival against those shocks, to exploit stability as fully as it can, and to modify the risks of a capricious natural world whenever possible.... Our impulse for innovation probes the environment on an expanded scale. The result is a species now standing squarely in the arena of habitat alteration. By a process of origin responsive to nature's whims, our kind has become an agent of environmental change.

That our species reflects the ecological conditions of its ancestry is no mere metaphor. We have deduced, in fact, a process by which environmental disparity has spurred the origin of our strongest defining characteristics. Variability selection refines any tendency or method that enables populations of organisms to modulate the disruptive effects of environmental extremes. It places a premium on any tendency to try out novel systems of behavior as insurance rated against an unstable ecological past. (pp. 243–244) The basic assumptions of variability selection are:

> First, each organism's genetic code is drawn from the gene pool of the population, which is shaped by random events involved in reproduction, and by a cumulative response to external conditions. All methods of survival that extend a population into future generations are the result of a lengthy history of response to these conditions.

> Second, in order to persist, all organisms must be malleable to variation in their habitats. Seasonal changes or any other regular variation in environments experienced during a lifetime are part and parcel of generation-by-generation Darwinian selection.

> Third, individual species may have long durations—in mammals, from hundreds of thousands to several million years. Over this span, a lineage may face wide differences in survival conditions, far exceeding seasonal variations.

> Fourth, certain novelties are favored because they enable the population to endure the widest environmental disparities. These include any attributes that enhance the tracking of resources as they move, shrink, or expand; the ability to buffer totally new habitat conditions; and the division of a species into diverse, far-flung populations, thus lessening the risk of extinction. (page 232)■

B.   PERUVIAN AMAZON

One of the most significant energy development projects in South America is nearing completion as this book is being written. Natural gas from Peru's huge Camisea field on the east side of the Andes Mountains is being pumped over the mountains to Lima and other coastal cities in Peru. The project has been in germination for decades, and illustrates the difficult issues involved in working in one of the world's most sensitive natural environments.

1. THE AMAZON RAINFOREST AND ITS PETROLEUM

The Camisea project is not the first oil and gas development project to take place in the Amazon Basin along the eastern slope of the Andes. Early development projects by major oil companies have been highly controversial, and some have led to extended litigation over their impact on the natural environment and on the indigenous population (see pp. 495–513).

The vast Amazon river basin in South America is often called the cradle of biodiversity. The number of species of plants and animals that remain undiscovered probably exceeds the total number of species found in many developed countries. The Amazon is also the home of many populations of indigenous people who continue to practice unique lifestyles of adaptation to the rainforest. In addition, the Amazon contains significant quantities of gas and oil, particularly along the portion of the rainforest that abuts the eastern slopes of the Andes Mountains.

Judith Kimerling, an attorney for the Natural Resources Defense Council, wrote a book titled "Amazon Crude" (NRDC, 1991), in which she chronicled many of the devastating effects of oil development on the lands and peoples of the rainforests of Ecuador and Peru. Parts of the book are excerpted in Judith Kimerling, "Disregarding Environmental Law: Petroleum Development in Protected Natural Areas and Indigenous Homelands in the Ecuadorian Amazon," 14 Hastings Int'l & Comp. L. Rev. 849 (1991). It is bleak reading, as shown by this brief excerpt:

> "During seismic studies, noisy helicopters carry equipment and work crews into the forests. They fell trees, clear trails and heliports, destroy crops, drill holes, and detonate explosives, typically without regard for the presence of homes, gardens, streams, lakes, or sacred areas. Indigenous people say these activities make wildlife act "crazy" and flee in terror, abandoning their young. Fish and wildlife also suffer from uncontrolled hunting and fishing (with explosives) by seismic workers. Clearing the forests destroys habitat, foods, medicines, and commercial woods. Erosion in cleared areas can degrade receiving waters....
>
> Before drilling a well, the oil company clears two to five hectares to build a drilling platform. [Ed. note: one hectare is about 2.5 acres]. Up to fifteen hectares of the surrounding forests are disturbed by logging for boards to lie beneath the platform. Wells are typically drilled without regard for the presence of settled areas.... For large helicopters additional lands are sometimes cleared for flight paths. Id. at 862.

In the Oriente, virtually all of the produced water wastes, along with spilled oil and chemicals, and wastes from well drilling and maintenance, enter the environment untreated. Most of these wastes initially are dumped into open pits, hundreds of which dot the region.... Rainwater freely enters the pits, swilling the contents and becoming contaminated as it mixes with the water.... Large artificial lakes of spilled petroleum are common near the pits.

Id. at 869.

Many multinational oil companies have tried to develop codes of conduct for their operations in fragile environments like the Amazon. Judith Kimerling returned to Ecuador to assess the code of conduct used by Occidental, then the largest U.S.-based producer of crude oil in Latin America, in its rainforest operations. Occidental's code is implemented through its petroleum contract with Ecuador which adopts Occidental's corporate Environmental Management Plan (EMP) as a legal standard. The EMP was to abide by "international standards" and "best practices."

Kimerling found that government officials and local communities did not know what these phrases meant in terms of actual standards which were to be used. Nor did they know what alternative standards might exist as a "best practice." Occidental originally appears to have adopted a "policy of equivalence" using the same level of protection required in the U.S., unless Ecuadorian standards are stricter. This policy was changed in 1995 to a "worldwide standard of care," but Occidental has not made public the standards which it uses to meet this contractual commitment. Kimerling also found that the company had not adequately disclosed or remedied an oil-related spill which occurred on a tribal hunting ground; and that the local community most directly affected by the petroleum activity had not been given a copy of the Environmental Management Plan.

Kimerling concluded that private environmental obligations in petroleum contracts require additional safeguards. First, they must clearly identify the standards being used and the source of these standards. Second, they must require compliance with these standards, and measure actual environmental performance against these standards. Third, they must have credible monitoring and review protocols that can ultimately be implemented by nationals, including public outreach and training programs for government officials, local community members, and NGOs. And, fourth, the findings of external experts and auditors must be accurately recorded and reported to the public. Otherwise, these codes may "legitimize norms defined by special interests" and legalize "environmental self-regulation."[1]

Kimerling's critical views about the need for external auditors of private activity are echoed by other long-term observers and experts on international petroleum contracts. Professor Thomas Walde notes that companies often oppose independent environmental audits on the grounds

---

1. Judith Kimerling, International Environmental Standards in Ecuador's Amazon Oil Fields: The Privatization of Environmental Law, 26 Colum.J. Envtl L. 289 (2001).

that they might reveal internal information which should not be released to competitors. Walde argues instead that companies should view external environmental audits like financial audits carried out by independent accounting firms.[2] Many large accounting firms now have environmental services groups or "Sustainability Advisory Services" which conduct field audits of their clients' environmental performance.[3]

2. Shell Oil explores Camisea

It was against this background of unfavorable commentary on the activities of oil companies that in 1981 Shell Oil began the exploration of a natural gas field in Eastern Peru that became known as the Camisea field. The field is located the remote rainforests of the Urubamba Valley in the southeastern Peruvian Amazon. The exploitation zone covers the legally recognized and titled territory of several nomadic, isolated, and uncontacted indigenous peoples, and the Smithsonian Institution, consultants to Shell and its partner Mobil, found that Camisea was in one of the richest areas of biological diversity in the world.[4] Moreover, to utilize any natural gas from the field would require building a pipeline over the Andes Mountains to the Peruvian coast.5

The Inter–American Development Bank, which provided some financing for the Camisea Project, has summarized four key issues the project must address:

> There are four noteworthy environmental and social aspects within in the influence of the Camisea Project:
>
> (1) the rainforest of the Lower Urubamba valley in the Urubamba Basin, recognized as an important global biodiversity "hotspot" because of its biological richness, high number of endemic species and the presence of threatened species; (2) the Lower Urubamba area, in terms of the approximately 22 native indigenous community settlements in the direct and indirect area of influence of the project and the noncontacted or voluntarily isolated groups that live in the lands reserved by the [Government] in benefit of the Nahua Kugapakori peoples; (3) the highlands area (Provinces of Huaytara, Cangallo, Huamanga, and La Mar in the Departments of Huancavelica and Ayacucho, respectively) in terms of the communities that live in extreme poverty, with very poor infrastructure, health services and economic opportunities, and have suffered decades of conflict and violence; and (4) the Paracas National Reserve located on the coast south of Pisco, which is Peru's only marine reserve, with part of Paracas Bay listed as a RAMSAR site (1971 Convention on Wetlands of International Importance Especially as Waterfowl Habitat and Reserve) and considered of ecological impor-

---

2. Thomas Walde, "Environmental Policies Towards Mining in Developing Countries," 10 J. Energy & Nat. Resources L. 327, 348 (1992).

3. Both Shell and BP use external auditors from firms like KPMG, Price Waterhouse and Ernst & Young and report value from these services.

4. Smithsonian Institution Research Report #94 (1998).

tance because it contains representative samples of natural formations and biological diversity (mostly fauna) found only in the Subtropical Pacific Deserts and the Warm Temperate Pacific Deserts of Chile and Peru.

Inter–American Development Bank. "Report Summarizing Performance of Environmental and Social Commitments in the Camisea Project." December 2004 (hereinafter IADB 12–04).

Many major oil companies, including Shell, have embraced the concept of sustainable development. Many in the industry have adopted the Brundtland Commission's definition of sustainable development as meeting "the needs of the present without compromising the ability of future generations to meet their own needs," and then translated it into a "triple bottom line" of accountability that meshes their business strategy with the three legs of the sustainable development tripod—economic progress, environmental progress, and social progress. The triple bottom line, or "TBL" congruence can be summarized as follows:[5] (1) economic growth, (2) environmental stewardship, as measured in terms of increased energy efficiency, pollution reductions, and mitigation projects, and (3) social progress, measured in terms of community outreach, human rights, labor standards, respecting diversity in the workplace, and preventing conflicts.

Insofar as the first bottom line—economic growth—is concerned, the Camisea Field has enormous potential. The proven volume of gas in Block 88 is 8.7 trillion cubic feet ("TCF"), with an estimated ultimate recovery of 6.8 TCF of natural gas plus 411 million barrels of associated natural gas liquids (propane, butane, and condensate). The estimated ultimate recovery considering the proven plus probable volumes is 8.24 TCF of gas and 482 million barrels of natural gas liquids. The Camisea reserves are ten times greater than all other existing natural gas reserves in Peru.[6]

Shell, in particular, has pledged a policy of openness and public participation in its practices. When it drilled exploratory wells in the Camisea area of Peru, it maintained an extensive website which broadcast briefing papers, photos, anthropologist's reports, environmental assessment reports, and speeches and contracts with the indigenous groups in the drilling area. In the latter years of the 20th century, major oil companies were just beginning to develop technologies for working in the Amazon. For example, ARCO's Villano project in Ecuador's installed the "small footprint" drillsite model now used in Alaska's North Slope and offshore. No roads access the area. All equipment was brought in by helicopter. The drill site is about 6.2 acres, and multiple wells extend from it. Produced water is reinjected. Production is remotely controlled from a central processing facility located 24 miles from the site next to an existing road in an area

---

5. Adapted from Conoco Sustainable Growth Report, p. 7 (June 2002). See generally, Martin Whittaker, "Emerging 'triple bottom line' model for industry weights environmental, economic, and social considerations," Oil & Gas J. 23 (Dec. 20, 1999).

6. Camisea Project. http://www.camisea.com.pe/project.asp (accessed March 27, 2005).

already disturbed by human intervention. Electricity is generated here and cabled to the drill site.

The company used new systems to transport the oil out of a roadless area with minimal impact. The usual pipeline right of way ("ROW") is 45 to 90 feet wide, and pipe is laid in trenches using heavy equipment, but ARCO determined that its 12–inch flow line to the central processing facility would not be buried because this caused erosion and damage to mature tree roots. Instead, it looked to densely populated countries in Europe and Japan for solutions and found a small, walking tractor-excavator used in the Alps on slopes of up to 45 degrees. It modified the machines with special attachments and cleared a ROW in the rainforest with a maximum width of 12 feet. It adapted a cogwheel-based monorack system used to transport harvest loads in vineyards and orchards on hilly slopes. The "invisible pipeline" now snakes through a "green tunnel" while the jungle canopy above the pipeline remains unbroken. A footpath of small logs follows the pipeline through the rainforest. Six small construction campsites remain with helipads to serve the six shutoff control valves, topped by solar power panels to power the valve.[7]

Experimentation with new technologies is bound to involve mistakes. Shell's briefing papers unflinchingly documented mishaps and problems, such as a cement spill near a creek, the need for greater erosion control at two well sites, and the anxiety of a local community over the criteria for awarding scholarships for higher education studies.[8] Shell pledged a standard of "sustainable development" in its Camisea agreements, defined as "improv[ing] the quality of life while ensuring that renewable resources remain vibrant to benefit future generations and nonrenewable resources are used wisely and efficiently with the benefit of future generations in mind."

Shell's greatest challenge was developing mechanisms to work with the indigenous groups. It hired environmental consultants to identify the stakeholders and NGO groups and involved them in meetings and workshops. As a result of these early consultations, Shell voluntarily modified the boundary of its concession to exclude a small area that intruded into a national park. Shell then undertook a "world class" environmental impact assessment. The Smithsonian Institution was invited to do an independent survey of the area to establish its biodiversity and to monitor any effects of the project. Shell undertook a study of the local population's health through the Royal Tropical Institute of Amsterdam and key Peruvian health agencies. It also studied the socio-economic base of the region. It agreed with Red Ambiental Peruana ("RAP"), an NGO network of 35 organizations, to perform independent monitoring work. In addition the

---

7. Bob Williams, "ARCO's Villano Project: Improvised Solutions in Ecuador's Rainforest," Oil & Gas J. Aug. 2, 1999 at 19.

8. Shell Prospecting and Development Peru maintained the Camisea website for several years at www.camisea.com, but the website was eliminated after Shell withdrew from the development stage of the Camisea project, having drilled three successful exploratory wells. The materials cited in this section are in Professor Weaver's files.

government performed quarterly audits of performance, which Shell requested be made public. Feedback from all of these studies and communication with all the stakeholders led to constant, iterative changes in the design of the project, a process called "adaptive management."

To minimize effects on the indigenous people, Shell developed a health passport of required inoculations for all workers going to Camisea. Anyone with signs of the flu or contagious illness could not travel to the project. Shell workers were restricted to project site areas. Only a few people called Community Liaison Officers met regularly with the native communities. Local native people were hired as guides or for field work, so that no settlers or outside workers would come up the river to look for work. This focus on health is due to the fact that a large number of Nahua Indians had died in 1984 from the spread of a western disease, seemingly contacted from loggers. Shell's Community Relations Guidelines, a code of conduct for all project workers at Camisea, were written by an independent anthropologist.

The Peruvian Hydrocarbon Law gives licensees the right of eminent domain to acquire surface access to acreage necessary for development. Shell promised in its Camisea agreement that its operation would involve the participation of the local indigenous people and that "net benefits" would accrue to them through contractual agreements for surface use, rather than using condemnation. In a Land Use Transfer Agreement between Shell and the Shivankoreni Native Community, Shell assumed a public commitment to carry out the project "in a sustainable manner, based on good operating practices, the fulfillment of the highest industry standards, and with a net benefit for the region with the dynamic participation and the cooperation of the surrounding communities to the area of the project." Shell agreed to "rigorously" fulfill the technical, safety and environmental protection standards in the EIA to prevent, minimize or eliminate negative impacts. Payment was to be in physical goods (such as medications, school supplies, water tanks, a community hall, sewing machines, machetes and shovels, mosquito netting, a solar-powered refrigerator to store medicines and vaccines, and modules for 100 laying hens) to be used as infrastructure for health, education, communication, water supply and the social well-being of the community (rather than as benefits to any one individual). In addition, Shell promised to finance the training of members of the Shivankoreni so that they would be able to operate and maintain the physical infrastructure and acquire a sense of autonomy with respect to their own development. The land use agreement could be nullified by the natives if Shell or its workers exceeded the limits of the acreage granted, failed to deliver the promised goods or programs, injured any member of the native group either "physically or morally," or failed to adhere to the stipulations of the environmental management plan for ecological protection. Shell invited SustainAbility, an independent NGO, to monitor the project's health, safety and environmental performance and make its report available to the public.

Two groups continued to oppose Shell's (and any other company's) drilling in the Amazon—the Rainforest Action Network ("RAN") and Project Underground. Shell's public website dialogue stated that RAN failed to acknowledge the support which Shell had from the local indigenous communities and the desire of these communities to make social and educational progress and to have an influential voice of their own. Mercedes Manriquez, legal advisor of CONAP (the confederation of Amazonian nationalities of Peru) spoke directly to the problem of achieving indigenous participation in the Camisea development. She documented the difficulties that native communities had in understanding Shell's EIA and responding to it. But, she also documented the problems that ensued when outside NGOs desiring to orient the communities as to the best way to face Shell ended up confusing the native viewpoint and limiting the joint initiatives that the natives wanted to establish. Manriquez concludes:

> The native communities need the interaction of national and international NGOs that identify with the indigenous cause, but will not impose upon our decisions, and will act in response to our needs. They must also be in agreement with the same principles of respect, consultation and participation that in support of us they demand from the State and the Oil Companies. Our options, priorities and the course of our destiny are decisions for us to make. We also have the right to make mistakes and learn from our errors.[9]

3. THE PROJECT FALTERS AND STARTS AGAIN

The Camisea project was put on hold during a long period of conflict between the Peruvian government and a group that called itself the Shining Path guerrillas. Eventually, Shell and Mobil formed a consortium that signed a two-year contract in 1996 to explore the Camisea field, but at the end of the contract they withdrew from Peru, citing guerilla violence and the inability to secure a long-term contract for the gas at a guaranteed price. Smithsonian researchers were disappointed. They found that the Camisea region is an amazingly rich storehouse of plant and animal species, and that Shell and Mobil had gone beyond the environmental requirements of the Peruvian government in seeking the Smithsonian's help and that of other national and international organizations to make the Camisea project as environmentally sensitive as possible, says Francisco Dallmeier, director of the Smithsonian Institution Monitoring and Assessment of Biodiversity program. The companies, he says, were very receptive to advice on siting facilities, minimizing impact and other issues.

9. Mercedes Manriquez, "Indigenous Participation in the Current Development Process of the Camisea Project," Camisea website document in author's files. For many thoughtful perspectives on both the positive and negative roles that environmental NGOs play in developing countries, see the symposium issue of 13 Colorado J. of Int'l Envtl L. & Policy, No. 1 (Winter 2002), titled "A Cartography of Governance: Exploring the Province of Environmental NGOs." For a stinging critique of the indifference of major environmental NGOs to the values of indigenous people in South America, see Mac Chapin, A Challenge to Conservationists, Worldwatch Magazine, Nov.-Dec. 2004.

The Peruvian government then held an auction for exploitation rights to Camisea. The successful bidder was a consortium led by Pluspetrol, an Argentinian company. The result was a Camisea project that is nearing completion as this is being written in mid–2005.

The Camisea gas extraction and pipeline project (Camisea Project) entails the construction of transportation infrastructure, wells, flow lines, a processing plant, and two pipelines running west through the Andes to Lima and Callao (the capital city and main seaport). It consists of two separate components: the Upstream Component and the Downstream Component.

The Upstream Component is the most sensitive part of the project due to its location in the remote rainforest. The Upstream Component includes a forty-year license for the exploration and exploitation of gas deposits in Camisea's Block 88, processing at Las Malvinas and a fractionation plant and marine terminal for natural gas liquid located south of Pisco, all under the responsibility of a multinational consortium led by Pluspetrol and financed in part by the Inter–American Development Bank. IADB 12–04 at iv.

The Downstream Component, which consists of the transport of natural gas from Las Malvinas to the City Gate in Lurín and natural gas liquids to a fractionation plant south of Pisco, is also problematic. It must cross the Andes Mountains over a pass over 15,000 feet high. IADB 12–04 at 3. The pipelines are the responsibility of Transportadora de Gas del Perú S.A ("TGP"), which was formed by the consortium specifically created for the development and operation of the Downstream Project. *Id.* The Downstream Project includes three different 33–year contracts: a contract for the transportation of gas from Camisea to Lima, a second one for the transportation of natural gas liquids from Camisea to the coast, and a third one for the distribution of gas in Lima and Callao. These contracts were awarded on the basis of the lowest service cost offered, which determined the natural gas transport and distribution tariffs.

Hunt Oil Company, a Texas-based company, is involved in the construction of the 700 km gas pipeline from the Camisea fields to the city of Lima and a 575 km liquids export line.[10] Peru LNG, which was created by Hunt Oil Company, SK Corporation, Pluspetrol and others, is developing a liquefaction facility located 169 kilometers south of Lima.[11] Hunt has completed the front-end engineering and design for this 4.4 million ton per annum liquefaction facility to export Camisea gas to Mexican and United States markets.

---

10.   Hunt Oil. "South America." <www.huntoil.com> (accessed July 28, 2005). Hunt is a famous name in Texas history. H.L. Hunt, the company's founder, was once listed as the richest man in the world by Fortune magazine, and was a major backer of Senator Joseph McCarthy during the years after World War Two. http://www.tsha.utexas.edu/handbook/online/articles/HH/fhu59.html H.L.Hunt.

11.   Peru LNG. "Environment." <http://www.perulng.com/env_siteselection.asp> (accessed June 27, 2005).

Natural gas will be transported to the main consumption center in Lima, where it will be used for residential and industrial purposes and to generate electricity, which will then be distributed nationwide through Peru's existing electrical transmission infrastructure. The savings in electricity prices will likely have its greatest impact on industry. For example, Peru's acrylic industry hopes to save 30% in energy costs, which will make it more competitive on the world market where it already exports to textile companies in countries including Chile, Ecuador, Bolivia, Brazil, Spain, Turkey, and China.[12] The estimate is that the Camisea Project will reduce electricity prices in Peru by 20–30%. Companies from Belgium and Panama have announced plans to build gas-fired power plants in coastal Peru.[13] The use of natural gas to produce electricity will reduce the dependence on diesel, which will benefit the environment because natural gas burns much more cleanly.[14]

The gas from Camisea should also reduce energy costs within Peru by reducing its need to import gas, thus saving local industry money. Pluspetrol predicts that Peruvian industry will save $275 million dollars a year in combustible purchases.[15] For example, in 2002 Peru had a hydrocarbon consumption deficit of $492 million. In 2003 that deficit had gone up to $724 million. Once the Camisea Project is fully operational, Peru will no longer have to import natural gas. The potential boost to the economy has the Minister of Energy and Mines saying that history will talk about Peru's economy in pre-Camisea and post-Camisea terms.[16]

Urban residents of Peru are expecting to be able to get natural gas. Some 90% of Peru's 28 million people use liquid petroleum gas tanks in their kitchens. It is estimated that by switching to piped-in natural gas the people would save 50% in costs.[17] However, as of May 2005, only 140 homes in Peru were hooked into the natural gas network. Despite that, by the end of 2005 it is hoped that 20,000 homes will be connected. It is slow going because the distribution infrastructure has to be laid, requiring installation in the homes. Many people are not sure how the system works, and are

12. Gas de Camisea: Con Camisea, Perú sueña dejar de ser pobre. August 23, 2004. <http://www.gasdecamisea.com/index.php?op=articulos&task=verart&aid=12>   (accessed June 20, 2005).

13. Firms Plan Camisea Plants, International Oil Daily, April 25, 2005.

14. Gas de Camisea. "Beneficios del gas de Camisea." August 30, 2004. <http://www.gasdecamisea.com/index.php?op=articulos&task=verart&aid=14> (accessed June 20, 2005).

15. Gas de Camisea: la gran esperanza para la economía Perú. August 23, 2004. <http://www.gasdecamisea.com/index.php?op=articulos&task=verart&aid=2> (accessed June 20, 2005).

16. Gas de Camisea: Con Camisea, Perú sueña dejar de ser pobre. August 23, 2004. <http://www.gasdecamisea.com/index.php?op=articulos&task=verart&aid=12>   (accessed June 20, 2005).

17. Gas de Camisea: la gran esperanza para la economía Perú. August 23, 2004. <http://www.gasdecamisea.com/index.php?op=articulos&task=verart&aid=2> (accessed June 20, 2005).

therefore reluctant to pay for the installation.[18]

4.   Camisea and the International Market

Camisea's gas is slated not only for domestic consumption, but also for export. In fact, the prospect of relatively quick receipts of foreign currency from exporting Camisea gas on liquefied natural gas ("LNG") tankers might well convince the government to give exports higher priority than the completion of the local distribution network. At least as early as August 2004, Mexico was in talks with Peru about purchasing its gas.[19] Peru's Minister of Energy (Quijandría) said that in 2007 Mexico will need about 650 million cubic feet per day, which is about the same as Peru's production. In June 2005, energy ministers from Argentina, Brazil, Uruguay, and Chile met with their counterpart in Peru to discuss buying natural gas.[20] These countries of the southern cone of South America could use up the reserve in 20 years.[21]

Hunt Oil also expects to export liquefied natural gas to both Mexico and the United States. A new LNG import terminal in Manzanillo, Mexico, will provide natural gas for parts of western Mexico, a country that now imports gas from the United States. Mexico hopes to use LNG to meet its own growing demand for gas and to export gas by pipeline to the United States.[22]

Such demand could have various effects. It will be likely to raise the asking price for the gas, thus reducing the chance that infrastructure will be built to accommodate the residential market for which, in part, it was originally slated. Moreover, the heavy demand for gas from multiple sources may tempt Peru to develop the gas quickly but inefficiently. Peru has already begun to let contracts for development of a second field, Block 56, that will have access to the same pipelines. Block 56, which is adjacent to the original Block 88, contains another three and one-half trillion cubic feet of gas that has been designated for export by the Peruvian government.

18.   Gas de Camisea. "Solo 140 hogares utilizan el gas natural de Camisea." May 28, 2005.   <http://www.gasdecamisea.com/index.php?op-articulos&task=verart&aid=45>   (accessed June 20, 2005).

19.   "Hoy Se Inaugura Camisea," *La Ultima* (though its source is *The Miami Herald*) August 5, 2004.   <http://www.laultima.com/noticia.php?id=8840&idcategoria=4>   (accessed June 26, 2005).

20.   Gas de Camisea. "Ministros se reúnen hoy para analizar compra de gas." June 13, 2005. Copied from *La Republica* (a Peruvian newspaper). <http://www.gas decamisea.com /index.php?op=articulos&task=verart&aid=47> (accessed June 20, 2005).

21.   Gas de Camisea. "Perú necesitará otro Camisea para atender creciente demanda de gas." June 15, 2005. Copied from *La Republica* (a Peruvian newspaper) (via *La Ultima*, a Peruvian   online   newspaper).   <http://www.laultima.com/noticia.php?id=12706&idcategoria=3> (accessed June 26, 2005).

22.   Peru LNG Eyes Mexican Manzanillo Facility as Top Market, International Oil Daily, May 13, 2005.

The development of this field involves negotiations with the indigenous Machiguenga people. At a public meeting in Lima held by the Inter–American Development Bank in February, 2005, many of the questions related to the environmental impact of the forthcoming development of Block 56. The minutes report that an "official of the Peruvian government" said that "the government is open to ideas for improving its environmental studies on Block 56, but a perfect document is unattainable and Peru needs to exploit its natural resources in a timely way to promote economic growth."[23]

Oil and gas reservoirs can be inefficiently produced if certain conservation principles, founded on petroleum engineering science, are not followed (see pp. 298–307). Some resource-dependent nations have adopted trust funds which place a certain percentage of the royalties and tax revenues from resource extraction into a fund reserved for future use. When the resource is depleted, the fund will continue to generate interest payments which can provide services to those citizens who can no longer benefit from the resource-generated rents enjoyed by earlier citizens. These trust funds can be useful devices to assure intergenerational equity, but they reduce the investment funds currently available for social infrastructure and economic diversification. At a minimum, sustainable development requires that such nations save and invest in social capital at a rate which replaces the natural resource capital being depleted.[24] Peru has promised shares of the royalty revenues from the Camisea project to a fund for the people of the Amazon area, but the exact funding process remains somewhat fluid.

The greatest difficulty remains the maintenance of the integrity of the natural and social environment affected by the project. To address the concern and pressure of environmental and social organizations, as well as to comply with governmental regulations, treaties, and demands from investors such as the Inter–American Development Bank, the oil companies have agreed to various mitigation requirements. First, they are taking an approach referred to as "offshore-inland." IADB 12–04 at 9 To minimize impact, gas processing facilities are concentrated and highly automated. No roads leading towards the Lower Urubamba area will be built. Only air and fluvial transport will be allowed to Lower Urubamba, with the resulting transportation being via helicopter and river barges. At a minimum, effluents will be treated based on international standards. *Id.*

Second, the land cleared for the right-of-way for the pipeline will be reclaimed and revegetated. Inspections will be carried out on foot and through aerial patrols. Outside pressure led the consortium to move the pipeline route away from the proposed Machiguenga Megatoni sacred grove and minimized its presence in the Apurimac Reserve Zone. The pipeline right-of-way was also the roadway used to transport personnel, materials,

23. Inter–American Development Bank, Summary of Public Meeting on Camisea, Held at IDB, Feb. 8, 2005, page 5.

24. Richard M. Auty and Raymond F. Mikesell, Sustainable Development in Mineral Economies at 47–80 (Clarendon Press, Oxford 1998).

and machinery to avoid the need for new roads. In the Upper Urubamba the project used existing access roads that were improved by the project. *Id.*

Third, active monitoring, using outside consultants and local people, is being undertaken by the oil companies, the government and the Inter–American Development Bank.

Fourth, the Peruvian government agreed to create a Camisea Fund, the purpose of which would be to return project benefits to the project areas for sustainable development. At a meeting in February 2005, an IDB official said that Peru's Congress had passed a law, known as FOCAM, which dedicates more resources for a Camisea development fund than was originally contemplated, but is deficient in autonomy and transparency and lacks provision for private sector participation.[25]

Despite extensive monitoring, a serious break in the natural gas liquids line occurred on December 22, 2004. The pipeline company's environmental manager said that the flow had been turned off within nine minutes of the discovery of the malfunction, but that the spill had left a residue of natural gas liquids 10 centimeters deep over an area of 50 square meters, killing some fish in Kemariato Creek but not affecting the Urubamba River into which it flows.[26] What actually goes on in the isolated tracts of the rainforest? We have assurances by the oil companies that they are doing their best, but one report states that tree cutting goes unchecked and the rivers continue to deteriorate. Helicopters arrive at all hours of the day, causing a racket which frightens the animals and causes taut nerves among the workers to break, producing fights between the Peruvian workers and the numerous Argentinian, Columbian, and Chilean workers who have been brought in to work in the jungle region.[27]

5. Rights of Indigenous Peoples

Camisea has, since the beginning, been under scrutiny because of the proximity of indigenous peoples to the field. International NGOs have pointed out that nearly 75 percent of gas extraction operations are located inside the Nahua Kugapakori State Reserve for indigenous peoples living with little or no contact with the outside world, including the Kugapakori, Nahua, Nanti, and other ethnic groups in voluntary isolation.[28] Reports

---

25. Inter–American Development Bank, Summary of Public Meeting on Camisea, Held at IDB, Feb. 8, 2005, page 1.

26. *Id.* at page 3.

27. Gas de Camisea. La verdad oculta sobre el gas de Camisea. August 23, 2004. <http://www.gasdecamisea.com/index.php?op=articulos&task=verart&aid=11> (accessed June 20, 2005).

28. Amazon Watch. Camisea Natural Gas Project: Project Overview. <http://www.amazonwatch.org/amazon/PE/camisea/index.php?page_number'99> (accessed March 27, 2005). Amazon Alliance. "The Camisea Project." <http://www.amazonalliance.org/camisea.html > (accessed June 28, 2005). Cultural Survival. "Peru: Camisea Gas Project Begins Operation." <http://www.culturalsurvival.org/publications/news/news/news_   article.cfm?id=33259512–097F–4665–AE2E–AB77B405082F&region_id=8&subregion_id=0&issue_id=3>   Citing

from people within the reserve indicate that there are still populations of uncontacted, nomadic indigenous people within this reserve.[29] It is estimated that in the Lower Urubamba area there are 22 native indigenous community settlements are in the direct and indirect area of influence of the project and the noncontacted or voluntarily isolated groups that live in the lands reserved by the government of Peru in benefit of the Nahua Kugapakori peoples. IADB 12–04 at 7.

Preliminary exploration for gas in the mid–1980s exposed indigenous people to diseases such as whooping cough, small pox, and influenza. These introduced diseases killed an estimated 50% of the Nahua population.[30] Exploration and development have led to the loss of food resources, the contamination of drinking water supplies, loss or damage to archeological sites, and changes to existing economic activity.[31]

The indigenous peoples of the Amazon rainforest have been the focus of a great deal of international attention. Joe Kane, a journalist-adventurer, lived with the Huaorani people for several months also wrote a riveting account of his experiences in "Savages" (Vintage Books 1996). He does not idealize the hunger, cold, disease and dangers of the Huaorani's natural environment, but the "savages" in the title to his book are clearly not the Huaorani. His book also gives a good account of the problems involved in working with native groups who live in small communities of a hundred or so members, scattered throughout dense rainforest. The book contains photos of the Huaorani and of the oil pollution. Judith Kimerling's work also paints a bleak picture of the effect of development on the health and culture of native communities and of the colonists who follow the roads and camps of the oil companies.[32]

In the U.S., clashes over Native American rights to land were ultimately resolved through the reservation system of setting aside specific land areas for the Indians, sometimes by forced removal of the Indians from their homelands. Unlike the English in North America, the Spanish conquerors of South and Central America adopted a strategy of assimilation, in which the native people were given the same rights as the Spanish settlers, at least on paper.

How would the Declaration of Principles appearing below resolve the rights of indigenous groups today? What if native groups want to maintain their identity rather than blend into a "melting pot." After reading the

source: Economist Intelligence Unit ViewsWire (part of *The Economist*), August 27, 2004. (accessed June 28, 2005).

29. Amazon Alliance. "The Camisea Project." <http://www.amazonalliance.org/camisea.html> (accessed June 28, 2005).

30. Amazon Watch. http://www.amazonwatch.org/amazon/PE/camisea /view_news.php?id=702 (accessed January 12, 2005).

31. Friends of the Earth, "Camisea Oil & Gas Project Peru," http://www.foe.org/camps /intl/institutions/camisea.htm (accessed January 12, 2005).

32. Judith Kimerling, "Disregarding Environmental Law: Petroleum Development in Protected Natural Areas and Indigenous Homelands in the Ecuadorian Amazon," 14 Hastings Int'l & Comp. L. Rev. 849 (1991).

Declarations, reconsider the problems of federalism that exist in developing and transporting energy resources in the United States, even with its strong centralized government. (Review, e.g., the cases on offshore oil and gas development at Chapter 6.E). How are power and financial benefits to be shared between the central government, provinces, and indigenous territories when oil and gas development occurs on native lands?

Declaration of Principles on the Rights of Indigenous Peoples

(as reprinted in S. James Anaya, Indigenous Peoples in International Law 190–91 (Oxford Univ. Press 1996)).[33]

1.   Indigenous nations and peoples have in common with all humanity, the right to life, and to freedom from oppression, discrimination, and aggression.

2.   All indigenous nations and peoples have the right to self-determination, by virtue of which they have the right to whatever degree of autonomy or self-government they choose. This includes the right to freely determine their political status, freely pursue their own economic, social, religious and cultural development, and determine their own membership and/or citizenship, without external interference.

3.   No State shall assert any jurisdiction over an indigenous nation and people, or its territory, except in accordance with the freely expressed wishes of the nation and people concerned.

4.   Indigenous nations and peoples are entitled to the permanent control and enjoyment of their aboriginal ancestral-historical territories. This includes air space, surface and subsurface rights, inland and coastal waters, sea ice, renewable and non-renewable resources, and the economies based on these resources.

5.   Rights to share and use land, subject to the underlying and inalienable title of the indigenous nation or people, may be granted by their free and informed consent, as evidenced in a valid treaty or agreement.

6.   Discovery, conquest, settlement on a theory *of terra nullius* and unilateral legislation are never legitimate bases for States to claim or retain the territories of indigenous nations or peoples.

7.   In cases where lands taken in violation of these principles have already been settled, the indigenous nation or people concerned is entitled to immediate restitution, including compensation for the loss of use, without extinction of original title. Indigenous peoples' right to regain possession and control of sacred sites must always be respected.

---

33. Adopted by representatives of indigenous peoples and organizations meeting in Geneva July 1985, in preparation for the fourth session of the United Nations Working Group on Indigenous Populations; as reaffirmed and amended by representatives of indigenous peoples and organizations meeting in Geneva, July 1987, in preparation for the working group's fifth session. Reprinted in U.N. Doc. ECN.4/Sub.2/1987/22, Annex 5 (1987).

8. No State shall participate financially or militarily in the involuntary displacement of indigenous populations, or in the subsequent economic exploitation or military use of their territory.

9. The laws and customs of indigenous nations and peoples must be recognized by States' legislative, administrative and judicial institutions and, in case of conflicts with State laws, shall take precedence.

10. No State shall deny an indigenous nation, community, or people residing within its borders the right to participate in the life of the State in whatever manner and to whatever degree they may choose. This includes the right to participate in other forms of collective action and expression.

11. Indigenous nations and peoples continue to own and control their material culture, including archaeological, historical and sacred sites, artifacts, designs, knowledge, and works of art. They have the right to regain items of major cultural significance and, in all cases, to the return of the human remains of their ancestors for burial according with their traditions.

12. Indigenous nations and peoples have the right to education, and the control of education, and to conduct business with States in their own languages, and to establish their own educational institutions.

13. No technical, scientific or social investigations, including archaeological excavations, shall take place in relation to indigenous nations or peoples, or their lands, without their prior authorization, and their continuing ownership and control.

14. The religious practices of indigenous nations and peoples shall be fully respected and protected by the laws of States and by international law. Indigenous nations and peoples shall always enjoy unrestricted access to, and enjoyment of sacred sites in accordance with their own laws and customs, including the right of privacy.

15. Indigenous nations and peoples are subjects of international law.

16. Treaties and other agreements freely made with indigenous nations or peoples shall be recognized and applied in the same manner and according to the same international laws and principles as treaties and agreements entered into with other States.

17. Disputes regarding the jurisdiction, territories and institutions of an indigenous nation or people are a proper concern of international law, and must be resolved by mutual agreement or valid treaty.

18. Indigenous nations and peoples may engage in self-defence against State actions in conflict with their right to self-determination.

19. Indigenous nations and peoples have the right freely to travel, and to maintain economic, social, cultural and religious relations with each other across State borders.

20. In addition to these rights, indigenous nations and peoples are entitled to the enjoyment of all the human rights and fundamental freedoms enumerated in the International Bill of Human Rights and other

United Nations instruments. In no circumstances shall they be subjected to adverse discrimination.

21. All indigenous nations and peoples have the right to their own traditional medicine, including the right to the protection of vital medicinal plants, animals and minerals. Indigenous nations and peoples also have the right to benefit from modern medical techniques and services on a basis equal to that of the general population of the States within which they are located. Furthermore, all indigenous nations and peoples have the right to determine, plan, implement, and control the resources respecting health, housing, and other social services affecting them.

22. According to the right of self-determination, all indigenous nations and peoples shall not be obligated to participate in State military services, including armies, paramilitary or "civil" organizations with military structures, within the country or in international conflicts.[34]■

NOTES AND COMMENTS

1. Of what force and effect are such declarations? Some commentators divide international law sources into "hard law" and "soft law." Hard law consists of binding international commitments such as treaties in force, decisions of international courts, and clear customary international law principles. Custom is defined as the general practice of sovereign states. For example, the law of the sea was derived almost entirely from custom before becoming codified in the 1958 and 1972 Conventions on the Law of the Sea. Custom is basically international "common law."

Soft law sources are nonbinding legal instruments that declare principles and aspirational goals or set voluntary standards. U.N. General Assembly Resolutions and declarations of international institutions and conferences generally fall into this category. However, some U.N. resolutions become authoritative evidence of international law as states conform their general practice to the resolution's principles. A resolution which is adopted unanimously, or by a large majority which includes the major powers, and which is relied upon by states can thus become "hard law."

As Professor Hickey writes: "In the energy field, [the generation of soft law] would include the 1990 Valdez Principles on corporate environmental conduct produced by the Coalition for Environmentally Responsible Economics [CERES][35], comprised of individual and corporate investors and environmental organizations. It would also include guidelines issued by the

---

34. Another declaration, the Declaration of San Jose, was adopted by the UNESCO Meeting of experts on Ethno–Development and Ethnocide in Latin America in 1981. UNESCO Doc. PS 82/WF.32 (1982), reprinted in Anaya, *supra* at 192.

35. CERES created the Valdez Principles after the Exxon Valdez oil spill; they pledge *inter alia* the sustainable use of natural resources and compensation for environmental harm,. The idea of such a code of conduct came from the Sullivan Principles which were written by a director of General Motors to bring about the end of apartheid in South Africa. *See* Daniel H. Pink, "The Valdez Principles: Is What's Good for America Good for General Motors?" 8 Yale L. & Pol'y Rev. 180 (1990).

International Maritime Organization ('IMO'), such as its 1989 Guidelines and Standards for the Removal of Offshore Installations and Structures on the Continental Shelf and on the Exclusive Economic Zone." James E. Hickey, Jr. "International Law," in Energy Law and Policy for the 21st Century at 4–18 (Rocky Mountain Mineral Law Foundation 2000). Soft law provisions are important because "they begin the process of hard law formation and provoke responses by states, by international organizations, and by other non-state international actors all of which help to shape future acceptable obligations." *Id.* at 4–19.

2. Multinational energy companies travel the globe to find and produce petroleum deposits. The host country may be a developing nation with relatively little environmental law on its books.[36] Even if such laws exist in a host nation's constitution or statutes, the country often has inadequate enforcement mechanisms and regulatory personnel to implement the laws. Sometimes, oil and gas reserves exist in "failed states," which have virtually no functioning government, and are plagued by civil wars, guerrilla fighting, massive corruption, and lack of any social infrastructure. Many developing countries granted near-monopoly control of their oil and gas resources to a state-owned company. These national oil companies often have had a far greater interest in providing revenues to the federal treasury than with environmental protection or local economic development.[37]

The national laws regulating the oil and gas industry can be broadly categorized into three approaches.[38] The first is represented by the U.S. and U.K. approach: a plethora of detailed, command and control statutes of considerable breadth and depth. The environmental framework generally regulates all industry broadly. There is relatively little unified legislation specifically designed for the oil and gas industry. The result is a complicated and sometimes confusing welter of laws, administered by many different agencies which sprang up incrementally over the years, sometimes in response to particular events such as the Exxon Valdez oil spill.[39] Developing nations may understandably decline to follow this pattern of detailed, but complex and uncoordinated, legislation.

A second model recently developed in some nations, particularly in South America, is to adopt environmental statutes that apply only to their petroleum sector. For example, Peru's petroleum law has 17 titles, 60

---

36. In general, environmental awareness was lacking in all countries, both developed and undeveloped, for most of the first half of the twentieth century. Environmental law only began as a field of law in the early 1970s and sustainable development did not become a mainstay of environmental law until the 1980s.

37. See Adriana Lieders, "A New Chapter in Brazil's Oil Industry: Opening the Market While Protecting the Environment," 13 Georgetown Int'l Envtl L. Rev. 781 (2001) for the sad environmental record of Petrobras, Brazil's national oil company.

38. Zhiguo Gao, Environmental Regulation of the Oil and Gas Industry, Discussion Paper DP16, University of Dundee Center for Energy, Petroleum and Mineral Law and Policy (1997) (hereinafter "Gao").

39. Until this spill occurred, virtually no national laws dealt with oil pollution in the U.S. The Oil Pollution Act was passed in 1990 to fill this gap.

articles, and many appendices with technical standards for discharges and emissions for all stages of petroleum operations. China adopted offshore petroleum regulations in 1982 which cover most environmental aspects of upstream operations, although no parallel onshore regulations have been enacted.[40] Indeed, one multinational company was taken by surprise at the stringency of some of China's offshore discharge requirements, and had to do expensive retrofitting of on-platform water treatment devices.[41] While this legislative approach appears to be spreading, it is still limited globally.[42]

In the past two decades, many developing nations have adopted some type of command-and-control environmental regulation. The requirement of an Environmental Impact Assessment, the most effective form of precautionary measure when accompanied by mitigation measures, has become nearly universal. Laws requiring environmental insurance, performance bonds, environmental audits,[43] oil spill response capability, and decommissioning and abandonment funds are becoming more common around the globe. Companies can anticipate that the enforcement devices used in many developed nations, such as suspension or cancellation of licenses, fines and criminal penalties, and environmental charges and taxes will spread to the developing nations. Indeed, foreign plaintiffs are already using the courts of a company's home nation to pursue litigation for environmental damages and human rights abuses committed by the company in the host country. See p. 477. Some of the impetus driving multinational energy companies and their industry associations to create private codes of conduct stems from an effort to avoid harsh and unreasonable laws that might otherwise be enacted. This is the third approach to national regulation of the petroleum industry: contracting for environmental protection.

3.   Dan Tarlock argues that contemporary science tells us that the "responsibility for managing rainforests should be shared between the nation-state in which the forest is located, indigenous peoples living in the forest, and the international community." Current doctrines of international law, however, make this impossible by effectively shielding "internal policies, such as natural resource management decisions from external standards regardless of the international spillovers." International law allows each nation to proclaim its own sovereignty, and thus to "shield internal development and management decisions from international law restraints

---

40.   Gao at 48–49.

41.   James D. Murphy and Stuart C. Williams, "International Environmental Issues and Strategies," at 333, in George E. Kronman, Don B. Felio & Thomas E. O'Connor (eds.), International Oil and Gas Ventures: A Business Perspective (2000 American Ass'n of Petroleum Geologists).

42.   Gao at 50.

43.   In Sustainable Development in Mineral Economies (1998), Richard Auty and Raymond Mikesell use environmental and natural resource accounting to measure the performance of many developing countries with resource economies. This accounting deducts the depletion of natural resources stocks and environmental degradation from a country's national product to give a more accurate measure of sustainability. This work contains useful case studies for students of international energy projects.

by equating exclusive territorial sovereignty with an absolute right to develop their natural resources. Rapid and intensive exploitation is an exercise of the right to develop—a right which has become an integral part of postcolonial international law." He argues that we can achieve the scientific objective only by modifying the concept of exclusive territorial sovereignty to make clear that nations have primary but not exclusive control over resource decisions with extraterritorial impacts and that nations owe duties to the international community. A. Dan Tarlock, "Exclusive Sovereignty Versus Sustainable Development of a Shared Resource: The Dilemma of Latin American Rainforest Management," Texas Int'l L.J. 37 (1997):

4. In 2004–05, high oil and gas prices have stimulated growing public unease in many South American countries over the extent to which the average resident is receiving a fair share of the benefits of the high prices. Peru's neighbor, Bolivia, has been severely disrupted by a revolt of Indian residents of the highlands who feel that the extensive natural gas deposits in the lowlands of eastern Bolivia are being controlled by non-Indian elites. Popular revolts have caused the resignation of two presidents. The Bolivian legislature has raised taxes on foreign energy companies sharply, disrupting projects that have yet to be completed. But antiglobalization groups in Bolivia say they will not be satisfied until all petroleum is nationalized and foreign companies driven out. See Juan Forero, Energy–Rich Countries Are Raising the Price of Foreign Admittance, New York Times, July 5, 2005, p. C1. The similarity to the unrest in the Middle East in the 1970s is obvious to all.

Could some of this reaction have been avoided if companies like Shell had gone forward with their elaborate proposals to insure that local people affected by energy projects received extensive benefits? Would the Peruvian government have accepted the idea that a foreign company should play such a significant role in the country's internal affairs?

It has long been acknowledged that many energy-producing countries are dominated by elites that cream large shares of the income from national energy resources. Are there ways in which foreign oil companies can assure that countries apportion petrodollars more fairly? Where governments have been democratically elected, as in Peru and Bolivia, should foreign companies be interfering in the countries' governing processes? If a major oil company such as Shell backs out of a country, won't its place be filled by smaller independents that have fewer scruples? The attempts of the industry to wrestle with the problem of corruption in developing are discussed more fully at Chapter 7.C.3.b.

Inter-American Development Bank, Report Summarizing Performance of Environmental and Social Commitments in the Camisea Project

December 2004.

Due to their complexity, large infrastructure projects invariably have some environmental and social issues that will arise during the construction and operation regardless of the breadth, adequacy and implementation of environmental and social design and mitigation measures. Given this reality, sound environmental and social management for large infrastructure projects includes two aspects. The first is a willingness and ability to adequately identify, understand and accept issues where they exist. The second is a willingness to take the necessary actions to properly address and resolve the identified issues. At this stage of the implementation of the Camisea Project (i.e., the early stage of operational phase) and notwithstanding the various measures and commitments established, the IDB has identified certain issues that require the IDB's special attention.

These include: (1) continuing to monitor erosion control and revegetation of the pipeline right-of-way and correction of any problems that may be identified; (2) full and continued implementation of the operational mitigation and monitoring plans, including staff training; (3) continuing to work with the [Government] in relation to its meeting the various commitments established for the Camisea Project; (4) continuing to work with civil society to address concerns and issues, in particular implementation of a supervision system to better satisfy the particular needs of civil society; and (5) maintaining the momentum in terms of actions resulting in positive impacts and effects including the Camisea Fund, Paracas Bay, and the Lower Urubamba area.

In retrospect based on the results of the Camisea Project construction, several positive aspects are especially noteworthy: (1) the amount of resources expended and the final results of the erosion control and revegetation programs especially given the difficult nature and characteristics of the pipeline ROW terrain; (2) the success and effectiveness of the compensation programs; (3) the amount of opportunity for stakeholder input related to the Camisea Project; (4) the success of the dredging and underground pipeline installation in Paracas Bay associated with the marine terminal; and (5) the nonoccurrence of the significant and major environmental and social impacts that had been identified prior to initiation of construction.

As with any project these are lessons learned that can be beneficial to future projects. In relation to the Camisea Project construction, examples of lessons learned include: (1) better pre-construction planning for erosion control associated with the pipeline construction; (2) better worker health and safety training during the early stages of pipeline construction; (3) better planning for work in the Nahua–Kugapakori reserve, especially in terms of establishing acceptance by stakeholders; (4) enhanced methods to communicate the actual results in the field to stakeholders' understanding and beliefs; (5) a more complete incorporation and consideration of all environmental and social impacts, risks and implications for the project of the Marine Terminal; and (6) a proactive, coordinated and effective communication strategy related to environmental and social aspects.

The IDB's support for Camisea represents a special approach toward private sector projects of this nature that responds adequately to legitimate environmental concerns and challenges, appropriately distributes economic benefits, protects social diversity and helps ensure long-term and sustainable development. By taking an integrated and innovative approach to problem-solving, the IDB believes it has leveraged its relatively small financial contribution (8 percent of total project cost) to achieve a greater good for Peru. (page 33)■

NOTES AND COMMENTS

1.   The "triple bottom line" efforts of Shell, ARCO, and other multinational oil companies deserve respect for their technical innovations, careful environmental planning, social infrastructure benefits, and training of nationals. This new approach to oil and gas development is far removed from the destructive practices often used before sustainable development became an industry pledge. These past practices have left a legacy of pollution in many parts of the world, and the existing petroleum infrastructure in many countries (often built by or with state oil companies or governments) will cause environmental problems for years to come. Petroleum operations will never be without some cost to the environment.

Are the smaller oil companies that are developing Camisea ideally suited for the project? Ironically perhaps, it appears that the best chance of getting high environmental standards applied in the oil and gas sectors of many countries is to involve large multinational companies in the projects. They can bring a level of expertise, capital and training that state oil companies and smaller-sized companies do not command. The worry is that these large companies have such strong bargaining power vis-a-vis developing nations that they can threaten to withdraw if the nations insist on standards other than those offered by the company. The nation may also prefer to trade higher revenues for lower environmental standards, as is its sovereign right. Smaller projects by smaller companies may not be as vigilantly monitored by international institutions or responsible NGOs, who learn about the problems too late to affect significant decisions. Even in those developing countries which have adopted sound petroleum laws and judicial systems, local regulatory officials will require training to build the expertise for effective monitoring and enforcement of the laws and contractual provisions for environmental protection. Until then, external monitoring by credible, experienced NGOs, international institutions, or non-industry experts is probably the only way to assure the global community that sustainable development is an "on the ground" reality, project by project.

2.   A World Bank study of a hectare of Peruvian rainforest calculated that the present value of harvesting the hardwood was $1000 but that the present value of a mix of fruit, latex, and selective timber harvesting was $6820. A contingent valuation study of the ecotourism value of the Montev-

erde Cloud Forest in Costa Rica produced a figure between $2.4 and $2.9 million. Tarlock, *supra* at 53.

What is a hectare of Amazon rainforest worth if it overlies a large oil or gas field? One industry expert posits a hypothetical 50 million barrel oil field which will cause 100 hectares of necessary forest destruction to develop. The project will also result in an additional 2000 hectares of destruction from squatters and loggers who gain access to new roads and from villagers who contrive crop destruction so that they can collect compensation from the oil company. The oil is worth about $1 billion. Of this, the host country will receive about $780 million in government take and local purchases. This amounts to $370,000 per hectare for all 2,100 destroyed hectares, or $7,800,000 per hectare for the project's necessary destruction. Richard Barry, The Management of International Oil Operations 70–72 (1994). Would Carol Rose's proposal to use a methodology that maximizes the sum of both public and private values lead to a different conclusion? See Section A, above.

3.   If humans are the prime examples of a species that has thrived because it has evolved myriad ways of adapting to changing environments, as Rick Potts suggests, does that mean that we should ignore those other species that seem to have trouble adapting to environmental change and seem likely to go extinct, such as the many species of animals and plants in the rainforest that appear to be unable to coexist with rapid development? How about human populations that have failed to adapt to today's conditions? Could the indigenous people of the Amazon be so classified?

Most biologists would argue that species that appear redundant at one point in time may be valuable as environmental conditions change. Princeton's Simon Levin argues that redundancy is an important value to protect for its own sake.[44] Species that may appear to be redundant at one point in time may turn out to be significant if environmental conditions change. American Chestnut trees were the dominant species in most forests in the Eastern United States until they were wiped out by a blight, after which oaks, elms and other species, which had been less common, became the dominant species, only to be threatened in turn by other disease outbreaks. After a disturbance, a species that formerly "appeared to be a small and functionally redundant part" of the ecosystem, may often become dominant in the reconstruction,[45] while a formerly dominant species, which might have driven other species to extinction in a stable environment, might find its dominance subdued by new environmental conditions. Can we imagine future circumstances in which people who have learned to survive in the rainforest would have advantages over people who think of themselves as more advanced?

44.   Simon A. Levin, Fragile Dominion: Complexity and the Commons 203 (1999).

45.   Judy L. Meyer, Conserving Ecosystem Function, in The Ecological Basis of Conservation: Heterogeneity, Ecosystems, and Biodiversity 136, 140 (Steward Pickett et al., eds., 1997).

4. International non-governmental organizations continue to have serious concerns about the wisdom of the Camisea Project. The rainforest of the lower Urubamba Valley in the Urubamba Basin has been called a biodiversity "hotspot" because of its biological richness, the high number of endemic species, and the presence of threatened and endangered species.[46] According to the environmental group Friends of the Earth, the project threatens a unique habitat for more than 800 species of birds and 45 species of orchids.[47] Endangered mammals such as the woolly monkey, giant anteater, giant armadillo and jaguar are also at risk in the region, it says.[48] Just west of the Camisea gas field in the Vilcabamba region the area is so remote that its biodiversity has not yet been catalogued by scientists.[49] The Downstream Component, located near Pisco, puts the Paracas National Reserve, Peru's only marine reserve, at risk. Paracas Bay contains critical feeding and resting areas for 216 species of migratory and local birds and also supports turtles, sea lions, and dolphins.[50] Current information on the Camisea project from this perspective can be found on the Amazon Watch website.[51]

What is the moral responsibility of international companies toward the animals and plants affected by the Camisea project? The traditional ethic toward animals would say that the animals may be sacrificed for human needs, as Rolston points out, unless we cause needless suffering. But a growing "animal liberation" movement, of which Peter Singer is a leader, argues that we must treat at least some categories of animals as equivalent to ourselves. How could you apply such an ethic in the context of such a large-scale development project as Camisea?

5. Shell pledged a standard of Corporate Social Responsibility, along the lines described at the beginning of this chapter, in its Camisea agreements. Has the Camisea project, as it has actually been implemented by other companies, met these expectations? To the extent that mistakes have been made in the implementation of the project, do you think they have been made by "rational polluters," as David Spence describes them, seeking single-mindedly to benefit their shareholders in the manner advocated by the editors of The Economist? Or can the oil companies legitimately argue that the environmental issues are so complex that no one could be expected to fully understand them?

46. Inter–American Development Bank. "Report Summarizing Performance of Environmental and Social Commitments in the Camisea Project." December 2004. p. 7.

47. BBC News World Edition, "Peru defends Amazon gas plans," September 5, 2003. <http://news.bbc.co.uk/2/hi/americas/3085490.stm>

48. BBC News World Edition, "Peru defends Amazon gas plans," September 5, 2003. <http://news.bbc.co.uk/2/hi/americas/3085490.stm>

49. Friends of the Earth, "Camisea Oil & Gas Project Peru," <http://www.foe.org/camps/intl/institutions/camisea.htm> (accessed January 12, 2005).

50. "Hoy Se Inaugura Camisea," La Ultima (though its source is The Miami Herald) August 5, 2004. <http://www.laultima.com/noticia.php?id=8840&idcategoria=4> (accessed June 26, 2005).

51. Amazon Watch. Camisea Natural Gas Project: <http://www.amazonwatch.org/amazon/PE/camisea> (accessed July 20, 2005).

In 1991, the Oil Industry International Exploration and Production Forum issued formal guidelines for operating in tropical forests. Can private codes of environmental conduct developed by multinational companies and their trade associations[52] provide the transfer of technological expertise necessary for sustainable development? Professor Baram writes that "[t]rade associations in particular are capable of weaving a global system of private codes that could be superior in many respects to public sector efforts, which have proven to be cumbersome and inefficient." Michael Baram, "Multinational Corporations, Private Codes, and Technology Transfer for Sustainable Development," 24 Environmental Law 33 (1994). His article discusses various strategies to extend the reach of private codes in the developing world, such as integrating and harmonizing codes into a quasi-regulatory international system which uses registration, progress reports, evaluations, and public access to monitor the performance of companies. He would have an international agency, such as the United Nations Environment Programme (UNEP), enforce the codes with sanctions such as de-registration and adverse publicity directed against companies that fail to make progress.

C. NORTH AMERICAN COASTLINES

Obviously, conflicts between the development of energy resources and protection of the environment are not limited to developing countries. The United States has its own share of fragile environments, both from an ecological and a human perspective. And the movement of energy around and through these fragile environments can generate controversy.

The exploration and production stages of energy resource development are not the only stages in which sensitive environments are encountered. Bringing energy to places with growing needs requires the provision of new transmission facilities. With oil, for example, the danger of oil spills from tankers has led to a variety of domestic and international legislation. (See Chapter 6.G). The unit trains that carry coal across the United States traverse a wide range of areas of special concern (see Chapter 5.C).

In recent years, attention has been directed to two other types of transmission facilities that will be the focus of this part of this chapter: (1) Terminals for the importation of liquefied natural gas, and (2) high-voltage electric transmission lines. The extent of the need for these facilities are discussed in chapters eight and thirteen respectively. This chapter will focus on the safety, environmental and jurisdictional issues that need to be resolved in the siting processes for these facilities.

52. An example is the International Organization for Standardization (ISO) which has developed widely used standards for environmental management, audits, labeling and life-cycle assessment. See, Paulette L. Stenzel, "Can the ISO 14000 Series Environmental Management Standards Provide a Viable Alternative to Government Regulation?" 37 Am. Bus. L. J. 237 (2000).

1. SWARMING ONSHORE

For reasons explained in the preceding chapter, the beginning of the twenty-first century has produced a large number of proposals to build terminals for the import of liquefied natural gas (LNG) into North America. Most observers believe that the market will sustain some, but not all, of the supply projected in these proposals.

The proposals fall into two categories: (1) Onshore terminals, which would consist of normal port facilities with special equipment for handling, storing and regasifying LNG; (2) Offshore terminals, which would be located in deep water beyond the limit of state jurisdiction, and would regasify the LNG and transmit the natural gas to shore by pipeline.

Regulation of the two types of terminal fall under the jurisdiction of two different agencies. The FERC has primary jurisdiction over onshore terminals, while the Maritime Administration (MARAD), a unit of the Department of Transportation, licenses offshore facilities.[53] Technical safety and environmental issues of some complexity will need to be resolved in each individual case because of the unique attributes of LNG.

Natural gas becomes a liquid when its temperature falls below about minus 160 degrees Celsius. At those temperatures, it occupies only about 1/600th of the space that it would occupy at normal temperatures. This makes it possible to transmit large quantities of natural gas economically if it can be carried in vessels designed to keep it very cold. There are now about 175 LNG tankers in operation throughout the world and many more under construction.

Cooling, storing and shipping takes a lot of energy and expensive equipment. In the past, the cost of these processes meant that LNG was produced only where a particularly strong demand for natural gas justified paying extra for it. During the gas shortages of World War Two, some distributing companies built liquefaction plants to store methane for distribution in peak winter months. One poorly constructed facility in Cleveland, Ohio leaked, creating a vapor cloud that filled the neighborhood and escaped into the storm sewer system. It ignited in the sewers, killing 128 people. This incident discouraged future use of LNG for storage until more reliable technologies were developed some two decades later.

In the 1970s, with natural gas supplies running short in the United States, Algeria, a country with extensive gas deposits and limited local markets, began exploring the export of natural gas. It signed a contract to deliver LNG to a newly-built terminal on Boston Harbor in Everett, Massachusetts. From there, the fuel would be delivered by specially-built LNG trucks to LNG storage facilities of local gas distribution companies and used to meet peak winter needs. Algeria made deliveries regularly until 1980, when the third oil shock reduced energy prices and made the

---

53. The MARAD siting process derives from the Deepwater Port Act of 2002 and is described at http://www.marad.dot.gov/dwp/. FERC will be issuing new regulations for its siting process under section 311 of the Energy Policy Act of 2005.

purchase uneconomic. As gas prices rose in later years, shipments to Everett have been resumed.

Other facilities built during the 1990s are at Cove Point, Maryland, Lake Charles, Louisiana, and Elba Island, Georgia. The Gulf Gateways Energy Bridge terminal offshore Louisiana also began operating in the Spring of 2005. Unlike Everett, all of these facilities regasify the LNG and distribute the gas through connections to major pipelines. Trinidad and Tobago, which has large gas deposits in offshore Caribbean waters and has recently built gas liquefaction facilities, has become a key supply source for United States LNG facilities.

As the development of new technologies for creating electricity from natural gas created a growing demand for gas, and the deregulation of the natural gas pipeline industry allowed the price to rise to market levels, the search for new sources of gas for the United States intensified. Domestic production has apparently been unable to keep up with the demand, and even increased imports from Canada did not stem the rising price of natural gas. This created a reinvigorated economic incentive for the import of LNG, leading to dozens of proposals to build new terminals on and off the shores of Canada, the United States and Mexico. These issues are analyzed more extensively in Chapter 8.F.

2.   SAFETY IN HANDLING LNG

Natural gas is a potentially dangerous substance even in normal use, but people have become accustomed to the limited risks and safety precautions associated with using it in their homes. When liquefied, gas is concentrated at six hundred times its normal volume, creating the need for additional precautions and magnifying the severity of any fire or explosion that might occur.

The oil and shipping companies that deal with LNG have been well aware of these risks, and have established international safety standards for all stages of the LNG process. LNG tankers are designed with heavy layers of insulation to keep the gas cold, and the gas is kept at normal pressures to reduce the risk of leakage. As of early 2005, some 33,000 tanker shipments of LNG had been made to ports all over the world (Japan and Taiwan are the leading consumers of LNG) without a single cargo explosion, fire or shipboard death.

Most attention has focused on the processes of liquefying and regasifying the gas, which takes place before and after the tanker delivers it. The safety record in these areas has also been exemplary, but two particular incidents have aroused some concern. The first was an explosion at the Cove Point terminal in Maryland in which a small leak from an improperly sealed line valve allowed gas to seep into a substation where it remained undetected until it ignited and exploded, killing one employee and severely injuring others. Since 1979, when this accident occurred, there have been no other major accidents at American import terminals.

In January 2004, a huge explosion occurred at the natural gas liquefaction plant in Skikda, Algeria, operated by the Algerian company, Sonatrach. Cold gas leaked and was blown into a high-pressure steam boiler used to power the liquefaction process by the boiler's combustion air fan. The boiler exploded, triggering an even larger explosion of the hydrocarbon vapors in the vicinity. Safety experts commented that high-pressure steam boilers are used to liquefy gas, not to regasify it, but the catastrophic nature of the resulting explosion makes it difficult to be sure how the original leak occurred and why it was not immediately detected.[54]

The Skikda explosion heightened the public concern about the safety of proposed new terminals. In states where oil and gas facilities were already commonplace, such as Texas and Louisiana, most people seemed unimpressed by the idea that new LNG terminals posed greater dangers than those to which they had become accustomed. But although there were proposals for new terminals in the Gulf Coast area, many importers wanted to bring LNG to the Atlantic and Pacific coasts, where the terminals would both be closer to markets and close to certain available sources of supply.

In New England, however, the Skikda explosion strengthened demands to close the existing import terminal at Everett. Dr. James A. Fay, an MIT scientist, argued that an accident to an LNG tanker in Boston Harbor could cause almost instantaneous fires that would be beyond the capabilities of any existing firefighting technique.[55] In response, federal and state agencies increased security precautions in the harbor, but did not close the facility.

The California state agencies have devoted extensive attention to the LNG issue, both before and after recent proposals to build terminals in the California area. Back in the 1970s, FERC and the California Public Utilities commission had actually approved a LNG terminal at Point Conception, west of Santa Barbara, but the project was abandoned when energy prices dropped sharply in the 1980's. In this century, the California Energy Commission has extensively analyzed the LNG safety issues, including the earthquake hazards for which the state is well known. California Energy Commission, Liquefied Natural Gas in California: History, Risks and Siting (2003).

3. ENVIRONMENTAL ISSUES

As fears about safety increased, proposals to site new terminals at locations far removed from human habitation began to receive more favorable attention. If the unloading and regasification could be conducted away from homes and valuable infrastructure, the potential damage from an accident could be greatly reduced, and the number of people who would fear injury would also be significantly less.

---

54. Testimony of Mark Robinson, Director of Energy Projects, FERC, United States Senate Comm. on Energy and Natural Resources, Feb. 15, 2005.

55. Fay's testimony can be found at http://www.lngwatch.com/lngwatch/docs /Fay_LNG_Fire_Impact.pdf.

The difficulty, of course, is that many of the coastal areas that are remote from human occupancy lack the conditions that would make navigation feasible. Unoccupied low-lying areas where ports could be built often perform valuable ecological or recreation functions with which the operation of a terminal might be incompatible. Coastal wetlands are extensively protected because of their role as a breeding ground for marine fish, among other reasons, and coastal islands often harbor important wildlife populations.

Most environmental issues relating to particular terminals are site-specific, but given enough of these constraints, the idea of locating terminals far offshore began to look better and better. The growing potential demand for gas and the increasing opposition to onshore sites led many companies to promote a variety of technologies to receive LNG shipments at a floating or fixed offshore facility, regasify them on the facility, and ship the natural gas to shore by pipeline. Offshore LNG terminals, however, require new technologies, since as of early 2005 no such facility currently existed. "There are a variety of different designs under development [including] ship-shaped hull designs similar to existing floating [oil production facilities], gravity based structures, and innovating docking structures that attach directly to the LNG carrier as it ties off to a single point mooring."[56] In addition, offshore terminals are feasible only when pipeline transportation is or can be made available, and cannot be used for truck transmission of LNG, as is done at Everett.

Although offshore terminals offer safety advantages, they pose problems of a different nature. Converting the LNG back to gas requires that it be gradually be exposed to a heat source until the gas reaches normal temperatures. At an offshore location, the heat source readily available is the seawater itself. Many of the offshore terminals are proposing to use large volumes of seawater to gradually warm the liquid gas. Not only does this process cool the seawater substantially, but to avoid contamination of their equipment, the operators propose to kill all of the organisms in the water before running it through their plant. This has attracted considerable opposition from commercial and sport fishing interests. Even along the Gulf coast, where public opposition had earlier been minimal, the offshore projects began to find opponents.

To get a sense of how the safety and environmental issues interact in these situations, both onshore and offshore, we will look briefly at three proposed new terminals: The Weavers Cove terminal in Fall River, Mass.; the Gulf Landing terminal off the shore of Louisiana; and the GNL Mar Adentro Baja California terminal proposed near the Coronado Islands in Mexican territory, just across the international boundary from the San Diego metropolitan area.

56. Testimony of Captain David Scott, Chief, Office of Operating and Environmental Standards, U.S. Coast Guard, United States Senate Committee on Energy and Natural Resources, February 15, 2005.

4. THREE EXAMPLES OF TERMINAL PROPOSALS

The following three examples are among over 50 proposals that have been made to site new LNG terminals. Each site presents its own local issues, but these examples provide a context for some of the types of issues that are being raised throughout North America.

a. WEAVERS COVE

The Weavers Cove terminal, to be built by a group of companies led by Amerada Hess, was approved by FERC on a 3 to 1 vote. 112 F.E.R.C. ¶ 61,070 (2005). The facility is located on a brownfields site in the heart of the City of Fall River, Massachusetts, formerly occupied by a Shell oil storage facility and subject to soil reclamation requirements. The neighborhood surrounding the terminal contains a mixture of industrial and residential uses. A major expressway and a commuter railway adjoin the site, while a coal and oil fired power plant is directly across the river.

From the terminal, two relatively short pipeline extensions would be built to transmit the regasified natural gas into the New England pipeline network. Facilities would also be available to truck liquefied natural gas to local storage sites. The project proposes to provide peak day sendout capacity of 800 mmcf per day.

Access to the site by tanker is along the Taunton River. Ships would travel 21 miles through the entrance to Narragansett Bay and up the river, passing under four bridges and alongside numerous cities and towns in both Rhode Island and Massachusetts. The project requires increasing the depth of the Taunton River and disposing of two to three million cubic yards of dredged material. The nature and extent of the disposal of the dredged material requires permits from other agencies.

This project is the first to be approved of a number of proposed terminals to serve the needs of the New England area, where doubts about the availability of future supplies of natural gas have been a major issue. Two offshore terminals are also under consideration. Other proposals include two facilities in the Maritime Provinces that have received Canadian government approval and a proposed pipeline to bring the gas into the United States. Another proposed LNG terminal on the Passamaquoddy Indian Reservation in Maine expects to connect to that pipeline. A number of other United States onshore proposals are also at various stages of preparation.[57]

Opponents of the Weavers Cove project asked the FERC to consolidate all of the proposals, including two offshore proposals, into a single proceeding instead of deciding them on a case-by-case basis, but the Commission denied the request "in view of the substantial construction period necessary for LNG projects, the substantial environmental compliance that must

---

57. A list of 55 such proposals throughout North America as of June 30, 2005 can be found on the Natural Gas Intelligence website: http://intelligencepress.com/features/lng/ (accessed August 1, 2005).

occur, and the other permits that must be obtained before construction can even begin." *Id.* at ¶ 30.

Among the facilities being proposed, Weavers Cove probably puts more people and infrastructure within the range of a potential fire or explosion than any other proposed terminal. Because the facility is located on a superfund site, and only minor filling of degraded wetlands is needed, the only serious issues relating to the natural environment are those relating to the proposal of dredged material, for which no specific plan has been identified. *Id.* at ¶¶ 106–109.

Fall River is suffering from a depressed economy, but the public opposition is still strong. The City of Fall River and the Attorneys General of both Massachusetts and Rhode Island have voiced strong opposition to the project and plan to appeal FERC's decision. In addition, Massachusetts congressmen cut the funding for the replacement of an existing bridge over the Taunton River that is not high enough to permit passage of tankers to the terminal site, and the Navy has asked FERC for a rehearing on the ground that LNG tankers would disrupt naval testing of submarines and torpedoes in nearby waters. Federal, State LNG Battle Joined in US, World Gas Intelligence, August 17, 2005. FERC estimates that the facility could enter service by 2010, but this could be delayed by litigation, other permit processes or market conditions.

b. GULF LANDING

Shell proposed the Gulf Landing offshore terminal late in 2003 and received approval from the Maritime Administration early in 2005. It is to be a fixed terminal located in 55 feet of water about 35 miles off the coast in the general area of the City of Lake Charles, Louisiana. It is located in a major gas production area and has access to five major interstate pipelines. It will have a peak day delivery capacity of 1.2 Bcf of gas.

Like other gulf coast offshore terminals, Shell's project originally aroused little public opposition. Somewhat late in the approval process, however, fishing and conservation groups expressed strong opposition when they realized the terminal's regasification system would destroy a significant amount of marine life. Like many proposed offshore terminals, Gulf Landing would use an open rack (ORV) vaporizer system to regasify the LNG. In such a system, the liquefied gas is piped out of the tanker through a rack surrounded by flowing seawater, the warmth of which gradually returns the gas to temperatures suitable for pipeline transportation. The operation of an ORV system requires the use of large volumes of seawater to circulate through the system. To prevent algae buildup on the equipment, the seawater is treated with chlorine to destroy all marine life in the water. The sterile seawater is then exhausted at a temperature some 20 degrees cooler than it was originally. The system is expected to require 136 million gallons of seawater per day. Screens would exclude larger marine animals from the system, but roe, plankton and small marine life would be destroyed.

Although the time for state objections under the Coastal Zone Management Act had passed before the opposition became organized, a long list of fishing and conservation groups in Louisiana have continued to express opposition to the project. Commercial and sport fishing groups joined with environmental groups in a "Gumbo Alliance for Safe LNG," and vowed to oppose any terminal facility that proposed to use the open rack system. State and federal wildlife agencies have also asked Shell to adopt a different type of regasification in which water is recirculated in a closed loop and heated by combustion of the LNG being transported.

However, the companies argue that the cost of such a system is three times as much as for an open rack system. In view of the highly competitive nature of the many LNG terminal proposals, the companies are reluctant to invest in this more expensive system unless required to do so. Shell said that it was confident that, using the open rack system, "we can operate Gulf Landing in a way that protects Louisiana's marine resources." " 'Gumbo Alliance' battling LNG projects in Gulf," Gas Daily, June 6, 2005.

Exxon–Mobil also proposes to use the open rack system at a terminal to be built 41 miles south of Cameron Parish, Louisiana. The company's spokesman said "In our view, the impact will be minimal." He noted that in the summer there was a "dead zone" in that part of the gulf due to excess fertilizer use and waste water disposal, and that by drawing water from below the forty foot level in the dead zone they would "avoid a lot of marine life that simply does not exist at that level." "LNG proposals encounter opposition along industry-friendly Gulf Coast," Inside FERC's Gas Market Report, June 3, 2005.[58]

BP had proposed to use the open rack system for its Bay Crossing terminal proposed for Pelican Island, near Galveston, Texas, but it backed off in response to objections from fishing and environmental interests. Its spokesman said that "When you look at the Galveston area and come to

---

58. The "dead zone" referred to above by Exxon–Mobil's spokesman is a serious problem, but the petroleum industry isn't to blame. "The failure to undertake control of nonpoint sources of nitrogen and phosphorus in the Mississippi River basin—primarily agricultural fertilizer—has resulted in a steady increase in the nutrient loading of coastal waters in an extensive area in the Gulf of Mexico where lower levels of the gulf waters are deprived of adequate oxygen every summer. Low oxygen has been documented as early as February and as late as October, but is most widespread, persistent and severe from May to September in water depths of five to thirty meters. Hypoxia [complete lack of oxygen] occurs mostly in the lower water column but may encompass as much as the lower half to two-thirds of the total water column." Nancy N. Rabalais, Hypoxia in the Gulf of Mexico, 12 Tul. Envtl. L.J. 321, 321–22 (1999). As the National Research Council pointed out, the "results of excessive nutrient loadings are seen in reduced water clarity; nuisance algal blooms, including species with toxic forms . . . , and hypoxic (low oxygen) bottom waters." The "decomposition of dead algae in bottom waters consumes oxygen, leading to loss of habitat for fish and other forms of life." Nat'l Research Council, Ecological Indicators for the Nation 84 (2000). One computer model has projected that continuing climate change will continue to produce heavier outflows from the Mississippi River and will increase the spread of the hypoxic area in both in space and time. Dubravko Justi et al., Effects of Climate Change on Hypoxia in Coastal Waters: A Doubled CO_2 Scenario for the Northern Gulf of Mexico, 41 Limnology & Oceanography 992, 1001–02 (1996).

understand the concerns or interest of the community, it did not seem to BP in this particular instance given this particular situation to proceed with the seawater option." *Id.*

In April, 2005, The Gulf Coast Restoration Network, the Sierra Club, and the Charter Boat Association petitioned the Fifth Circuit Court of Appeals to overturn the Gulf Landing Permit. The petitioners argued that Gulf Landing will cause undue harm to the fisheries by destroying millions of eggs and larvae. The groups are represented by the environmental law clinic at the Tulane Law School. *Id.*

c.   GNL MAR ADENTRO DE BAJA CALIFORNIA

As of January 2005, Chevron–Texaco had received regulatory approval in Mexico from the Secretariat of Environment and Natural Resources, the Regulatory Energy Commission, and the Communications and Transport Secretariat to build an offshore terminal 8 miles from the coast of Tijuana, Baja California, near the Coronado Islands, only about 11 miles south of the United States border . . . "LNG terminal off Mexico receives permits," Oil & Gas Journal, Jan. 15, 2005, p. 10. The terminal will be a fixed concrete structure with LNG storage tanks on the seabed in water 65 feet deep. LNG will be regasified in the structure and piped to Tijuana to connections with Mexican pipelines. Baja California currently imports natural gas from the United States.

The terminal platform will be located just east of the largest of the Coronado Islands, which will serve as a breakwater to protect operations. If operations go as planned, Chevron–Texaco will be bringing LNG from the stranded Gorgon gas field off the remote coast of northwestern Australia, where some 40 trillion cubic feet of gas is awaiting a market. The gas is said to be for use primarily in power plants in both Mexico and United States markets.

The four Coronado Islands are rocky outcrops visible from downtown San Diego and Tijuana. During prohibition, they were the famous site of a Mexican casino that attracted Hollywood celebrities. Today, the Mexican navy maintains a lighthouse and a small garrison near the site of the casino, which burned many years ago. Otherwise, the islands have no human occupants, and cannot be visited without Mexican government permission.

The islands are home to many nesting seabirds, including the region's largest breeding colony of the rare Xantus' murrelet. It contains rare coastal sage scrub habitat which has largely been destroyed in coastal areas. Harbor seals and sea lions live on the islands, and the waters surrounding them have long been attractive to scuba divers because of the variety of colorful fish. These waters are also part of the annual migration path of the gray whale. Diane Lundquist, "Nature vs. Natural Gas in Baja California," California Coast & Ocean, Autumn 2004, p. 30.

Opponents suggest that Chevron–Texaco is seeking to take advantage of lax enforcement of environmental regulations in Mexico. The company maintains, however, that its site is better than anything available north of the border. A spokesman says that the company is doing everything possible to accommodate the concerns of objectors. It has agreed to limit noise and lighting to avoid disturbing nesting seabirds. "We can be a facilitator in making the island a preserve." *Id. at 33.*

On May 3, 2005, Mexican and United States environmental groups filed a petition with the Commission for Environmental Cooperation, which was created in 1994 under a NAFTA side agreement. The petition alleges that the project violates Mexican environmental laws and thus presents a claim under NAFTA. The environmental side agreement to the NAFTA Treaty provides a process for a citizen of any of the NAFTA countries to challenge the failure of a country to enforce its environmental laws. Under this provision, known as Article 14, the petitioners challenge Mexico's failure to enforce its environmental laws in approving the Chevron–Texaco project. The petitioners allege that the bright lights needed for the terminal will interfere with the nesting of nocturnal seabirds, including the rare murrelet.

"ChevronTexaco's proposed terminal is an energy maquiladora that will pump natural gas to the United States while avoiding U.S. environmental laws and imperiling Mexico and its wildlife," said Arturo Moreno, Energy and Climate Change Program Coordinator of Greenpeace Mexico. The murrelets and other seabirds of the Coronado Islands would be harmed by the operations of the ChevronTexaco LNG terminal. "Nocturnal birds are attracted to lights like moths to a flame, and the result can be just as devastating" said Shaye Wolf, a Xantus's murrelet expert at the University of California, Santa Cruz. "When lights are added to these normally dark islands, murrelets are injured or killed when they fly into lighted structures and when chicks are separated from their parents. I have seen the light from a single bulb lure a murrelet chick away from its parents, which can lead to its starvation and death. The effects from all of the Chevron LNG terminal's lights would be absolutely devastating for the murrelets."

Environmentalists argue that the side agreement was supposed to prevent this "race to the bottom," and that the NAFTA side agreement recognized that cross-border environmental problems, such as those involving migratory birds, would never be redressed unless all three North American countries cooperated. Accordingly, the petitioners are also seeking to invoke Article 13 of the NAFTA side agreement, which allows the international tribunal to investigate issues where cross border cooperation is essential. "If the Commission for Environmental Cooperation does not prevent such a blatant example of a project that has fled across a border to avoid environmental laws, I don't know what purpose it fulfills other than to greenwash environmentally destructive free trade," said Jay Tutchton, Director of the University of Denver Environmental Law Clinical Partnership, which prepared the petition.[59]

---

59. http://www.lngwatch.com/race/pr_NAFTA.htm (accessed July 27, 2005). Copies of the petition, photographs of the Xantus murrelet and other supporting documents can be found at www.biologicaldiversity.org.

5.   TERRORISM CONCERNS

Although the overall safety record of the LNG industry is so good that it might induce a rational observer to conclude that the public concerns were simply the typical exaggerated fears associated with new technologies, the outbreaks of terrorism in the twenty-first century raised new fears of an intentional terrorist attack on an LNG tanker or terminal. The industry could not answer these arguments simply by pointing to safe conditions in the past, so the Department of Energy contracted with Sandia National Laboratories to analyze the risks associated with an intentional attack on a terminal or on a tanker approaching a terminal. Sandia released a report to the public on its conclusions, some of which are described in the following testimony by the report's lead investigator.

Testimony of Mr. Mike Hightower, Technical Staff Member, Sandia National Laboratories, before the Senate Committee on Energy and Natural resources, LNG Subcommittee, Hearing

February 15, 2005.

Based on available information, a range of historically credible and potential accidental and intentional events was identified that could cause an LNG cargo tank breach and spill.... From these analyses, the sizes of LNG cargo tank breaches for accidents were estimated to be less than 2 square meters. For intentional events, the size of the hole depends on its location on the ship and the source of the threat. Intentional breaches were estimated at 2 to approximately 12 square meters, with nominal sizes of about 5–7 square meters. These sizes are smaller than those used in many recent studies. Although smaller, the breach sizes estimated can still lead to large LNG spills....

Using structural fracture mechanics analysis, the potential for cryogenic damage to the LNG ship and other LNG cargo tanks was evaluated [and] cannot be ruled out, especially for large spills.[60] The degree and severity of damage depends on the size and location of the breach. Sandia considered cryogenic damage to the ship's structure and concluded that releases from no more than two or three tanks would be involved in a spill that occurs due to any single incident.

From the assessment conducted, thermal hazards will occur predominantly within 1600 meters [about one mile] of an LNG ship spill, with the highest hazards generally in the near field, approximately 250–500 meters of a spill [where] high thermal hazards are expected to occur. Major injuries and significant structural damage are possible in this zone. The extent of the hazards will depend on the spill size and dispersion from wind, waves, and currents. People, major commercial/industrial areas or

---

60.   Cryogenic damage refers to damage caused by the extremely cold nature of the LNG cargo.

other critical infrastructure elements, such as chemical plants, refineries, bridges or tunnels, or national icons located within portions of this zone could be seriously affected.... Beyond 750 meters for small accidental spills and 1600 meters for large spills, the impacts on public safety should generally be low for most potential spills.

[The hazard zones] are based on thermal hazards from a pool fire, because many of the events will provide ignition sources such that a fire is likely to occur immediately. In some cases, the potential exists for a vapor cloud to be created without being ignited. A vapor cloud from an LNG spill could extend to 2,500 meters, if an ignition source is not available. The potential thermal hazards within a vapor cloud could be high. Because vapor cloud dispersion is highly influenced by atmospheric conditions, hazards from this type of event will be very site-specific.

[For] areas in which LNG shipments occur in narrow harbors or channels, pass under major bridges or over tunnels, or come within approximately 500 meters of major infrastructure elements, such as military facilities, population and commercial centers, or national icons, ... the risk and consequences of a large LNG spill could be significant and have severe negative impacts. Thermal radiation poses a severe public safety and property hazard, and can damage or significantly disrupt critical infrastructure located in this area.

Risk management strategies for LNG operations should address vapor dispersion and fire hazards. The most rigorous deterrent measures, such as vessel security zones, waterway traffic management, and establishment of positive control over vessels are elements of the risk management process. Coordination among all port security stakeholders is essential. Incident management and emergency response measures should be carefully evaluated to ensure adequate resources (i.e., firefighting, salvage) are available for consequence and risk mitigation.■

NOTES AND COMMENTS

1. Mike Hightower was the principal researcher on the Sandia Laboratories report. Although he and the laboratory phrase their conclusions carefully and avoid using inflammatory language, many people interpret the report to mean that if an LNG tanker is hit by a bomb, plane or another ship, anything within about 7 football fields of it will be toast immediately, and anyone within a mile had better hope for very good luck. The full Sandia report is available at http://www.fe.doe.gov/programs/oilgas /storage/lng/sandia_lng_1204.pdf (accessed August 1, 2005)

2. Would it be possible to provide protection for LNG tankers that would prevent intentional attacks? In a report prepared for the Attorney General of Rhode Island, which was introduced in the Weavers Cove proceeding before the FERC, terrorism expert Richard A. Clarke concluded that there was no effective security against a terrorist attack on a tanker in Narragansett Bay. "Narragansett Bay is home to thousands of small craft. The USCG and other law enforcement agencies would be reluctant to use lethal

force against an apparently misguided pleasure craft. . . . To prevent the entry of weapons for land-based, stand-off attacks, all vehicles entering the littoral would have to be searched, not just during the tanker's transit, but at all times. . . . No air defense system is planned, nor is it easy to imagine a system that would authorize the use of deadly force against an aircraft that might appear to have unintentionally strayed into restricted air space."[61]

In its opinion approving Weaver Cove, the FERC majority expressed confidence that terrorism presented only minimal risks:

> "Unlike accidental causes, historical experience provides little guidance in estimating the probability of a terrorist attack on an LNG vessel or onshore storage facility. For a new LNG import terminal proposal having a large volume of energy transported and stored near populated areas, the perceived threat of a terrorist attack is a serious concern of the local population and requires that resources be directed to mitigate possible attack paths. While the risks associated with the transportation of any hazardous cargo can never be entirely eliminated, we are confident that they can be reduced to minimal levels and that the public will be well protected from them."

(p. 71 of opinion)

FERC also downplayed the conclusions of the Clarke Report because it did not take into consideration the Coast Guard's plan for mitigating intentional attacks. This plan is classified and not available to the public. Commissioner Kelly dissented, citing both safety and environmental concerns.

3. Some risks have a low likelihood of occurring but would have a devastating impact if they did occur. The deliberate attack by commercial airliner on the World Trade Center on September 11, 2001, is a prime example. How should the likelihood of such an event be balanced against the highly probable likelihood of environmental impacts that, although much less destructive immediately, may have disastrous cumulative effects in the long run?

6.   JURISDICTIONAL ISSUES

As the above examples indicate, the treatment that an applicant for a LNG terminal will receive may often depend on which level and agency of government calls the shots. At the international level, the NAFTA side agreement may provide a forum for addressing siting conflicts among Canada, Mexico and the United States, though its effectiveness remains to be seen. Otherwise, arguments among nations will continue to be resolved through diplomatic negotiations.

Within the United States, conflicts about LNG terminals among the federal, state and local governments are prevalent. FERC and MARAD

---

61. Clarke's report can be found at http://www.house.gov/mcgovern/GoodHarborreport.pdf (The quotes are from pages 5 and 6, accessed August 1, 2005).

have been concerned with meeting national gas supply needs, while some lower levels of government have been more worried about safety, terrorism and the environment. Understandably, therefore, the gas industry has pushed for centralizing control of the permitting process in a friendly federal agency to the extent possible, while state and local governments have sought to retain veto powers.

The first statute to attempt to clarify jurisdictional issues was the Marine Transportation Security Act of 2002, 116 Stat. 2064. This statute was primarily concerned with establishing the role of the new Department of Homeland Security in protecting ports against terrorist attacks, but it also amended the Deepwater Port Act of 1974, 33 U.S.C.A. § 1501 ff., to make that act applicable to LNG ports as well as oil ports. (The statute had originally been designed to deal with oil megatankers that needed to offload their cargo in deep water because they were too large to enter harbor facilities.)

The 2002 amendments made it clear that the FERC had no jurisdiction over deepwater LNG ports; these would remain under the jurisdiction of MARAD and the Coast Guard. FERC retained jurisdiction over any pipelines connecting deepwater LNG ports to interstate pipelines, but only if such connections were proposed. The statute also made it clear that deepwater LNG ports, unlike deepwater oil ports, were not required to serve as common carriers. This amendment was necessary in view of the well established business practice of trading in LNG through long-term contracts (see Chapter 8.F).

At the time the 2002 act was being debated, the interest in importing more LNG seemed largely theoretical to most people because natural gas was selling at $3 to $4 per thousand cubic feet. But price spikes in early 2003, followed by steady price increases in following years, quickly brought renewed interest in the establishment of LNG terminals, including both onshore and offshore terminals. Logically, one might expect that the federal government would try to develop a national policy designed to optimize the location of these terminals, but Congress had now established a bifurcated regulatory system in which onshore and offshore terminals were regulated by different federal agencies, neither of which had any obligation to undertake a comparative review of the many applications being submitted.

In addition to MARAD review, applicants for offshore terminals need to comply with environmental laws, but the application of other federal environmental statutes to offshore terminals can be difficult to determine since most of the statutes were written before such terminals were even conceived. The major environmental statutes, for example, contain language exempting ships from some air and water pollution controls that might or might not apply to LNG tankers engaged in regasification. See, e.g., 33 U.S.C.A. § 1362(12).

The role of state governments also varied depending on whether the terminal was onshore or offshore. Under the Deepwater Port Act, the governor of the state to which the port was adjacent is given an absolute veto power over any application for a federal permit, and this veto power was carried over to offshore LNG terminals. 33 U.S.C.A. § 1508. For onshore permits, the state must utilize the consistency procedures of the Coastal Zone Management Act ("CZMA") and demonstrate that the proposed terminal would be inconsistent with the state's coastal management plan, a more complex and less certain process. (See Chapter 6 for discussion application of the CZMA to oil facilities).

Congress attempted some clarification of the rules applicable to onshore LNG terminals in the Energy Policy Act of 2005, but basically left the existing separate procedures intact for both onshore and offshore terminals. Under section 311, FERC is given the "exclusive authority to approve or deny" applications for onshore terminals but "nothing in this Act is intended to affect otherwise applicable law related to any Federal Agency's authorities or responsibilities related to" such terminals, and the rights of states under the Coastal Zone Management Act, Clean Air Act and Clean Water Act remain the same.

Section 311 also requires FERC to adopt new NEPA regulations that are intended to provide an expedited process for reviewing the environmental impact of a proposed onshore terminal. The affected state is given tight time limits to provide safety information. The extent to which the statutory language is sufficiently clear to expedite anything remains to be seen.

As the law now stands, no provision is made for any agency to make comparative evaluations of competing applications for siting permits. Each is to be judged on its own merits under standards that give the agency a great deal of discretion. Each applicant is presumed to be willing to take the risk that continually rising demand for natural gas will make the construction of its facility economically prudent no matter how many other competing terminals may be built. And the state and federal agencies that will be providing security against terrorist attacks are assumed to be able to provide such security to however many terminals are built. This policy is consistent with the current trend toward deregulation, and one can only hope that it is based on sound assumptions.

D.   FLORIDA WETLANDS

Some controversies involving the transmission of energy attract national attention, like the infamous Exxon Valdez oil spill discussed at Chapter 6.G. But others get little noticed outside the immediate local area. Yet when the cumulative effects of these local controversies add up, the effect may have important national significance. Such is the case with the many local controversies that have prevented the construction of badly needed electric transmission lines.

1.   TRANSMITTING ELECTRICITY

As explained in Chapter 10, the North American electric systems have evolved from a collection of scattered independent projects serving individual urban areas into three large interconnected networks serving (1) the Eastern United States and Eastern Canada, (2) the Western United States, Western Canada and a part of Mexico, and (3) Texas. These networks consist of more than 150,000 miles of high-voltage transmission lines and associated equipment.

Network interconnections have brought significant advantages to consumers of electricity. The availability of backup power transmitted from adjoining regions during unexpected outages has reduced the need for each local community to build expensive backup generating capacity. Where adjoining regions have different seasons of peak usage, interconnections enable the trading of power to meet peak needs. And ample transmission capacity is essential if wholesale competition in the electric industry (see Chapter 11) is to be able to reduce prices to consumers.

But construction of new transmission lines has virtually come to a halt. Over the past 25 years, overall investment in electric transmission nationwide has been declining at the rate of $103 million per year. In 2000, the level of transmission investment was more than $2.5 billion below the level of investment in 1975, despite dramatic increases in electricity consumption.[62] In California, for example, transmission capacity has remained essentially unchanged for the last twenty years.[63] Throughout the country, transmission capacity additions are projected to continue to decline in relation to peak electricity demand.[64]

Why has transmission proved so difficult to build? The complex interplay among the various businesses involved in the wholesale electric market, and the lack of a clear division between state, federal and local jurisdiction are undoubtedly major factors[65] (see Chapter 11). But even when new transmission lines are approved by regulatory agencies, projects seem to be stalled. In 2004, FERC Commissioner Kelliher noted that the commission had approved eight transmission projects since 2000, but all but one of the projects were on hold or had been withdrawn, and the one that is operating—the Cross Sound Cable project between Long Island and Connecticut, discussed at Chapter 12.D—is in service only because the DOE issued emergency orders overruling Connecticut's objections.[66]

Fear of health risks from high voltage lines continues to cause local opposition. Despite the inability of physicists or biologists to conceive of any mechanism by which such lines could cause injury, studies continue to

---

62. Keystone Center, Regional Transmission Projects: Finding Solutions 13 (2005) (measured in 2001 dollars).

63. Brian Orion, Transmission in Transition: Analyzing California's Proposed Electricity Transmission Regulatory Reforms, 56 Hastings L. J. 343, 350 (2004).

64. See Eric Hirst, U.S. Transmission Capacity: Current Status and Future Prospects, Edison Electric Institute and U.S. Department of Energy, 2004.

65. See Charles H. Koch, Jr., Collaborative Governance in the Restructured Electricity Industry, 40 Wake Forest L. Rev. 589 (2005).

66. Joseph T. Kelliher, Transmission Investment, Restructuring, and the Future of the Electric Utility Industry: The Need for Mandatory Electric Reliability Standards and Greater Transmiccion Investment, 39 U. Rich. L. Rev. 717, 728 (2005).

indicate a correlation between residence near power lines and the development of childhood leukemia.[67] As a result of this opposition, engineers try to route transmission lines away from residential areas.

But moving transmission lines to natural areas often generates opposition of a different nature. High-voltage transmission lines have a significant impact on the terrain through which they pass. The wires must remain a safe distance from any obstruction that might cause the lines to short out. This requires a wide right of way free from vegetation, and regular maintenance to ensure that vegetation is kept under control. (Contact between trees and power lines was a principal cause of the extensive blackout of the Northeast in August, 2003, and of earlier blackouts in 1996.[68]) To understand why a transmission corridor may arouse objections because of its impact on wetlands requires an understanding of why wetlands are valuable.

2.   THE NATURE OF WETLANDS

The term "wetlands" has only recently become a part of our vocabulary; until the latter half of the twentieth century, there was no single common term used to describe what we now call wetlands. Instead, a variety of terms were used to describe different types of wetland, including "bog," "fen," "marsh," "mire," "muskeg," "slough," and "swamp." As suggested by these many names, there are many different kinds of wetlands. These differences have complicated regulation, and the definition of wetlands for regulatory purposes has been very controversial. The National Research Council's Committee on Wetlands Delineation has proposed the following scientific definition of wetlands to help clarify the question: "A wetland is an ecosystem that depends on constant or recurrent, shallow inundation or full saturation at or near the surface of the substrate. The minimum essential characteristics of a wetland are: (1) recurrent, sustained inundation at or near the surface, and (2) the presence of physical, chemical, and biological features reflective of recurrent, sustained inundation and saturation."

All categories of wetland maintain a basic system of energy flow in which sources of organic input, such as decaying vegetation, are converted into more and more concentrated forms of energy through a food web. If the biogeochemical cycles of the wetland are protected, a wetland can be extremely productive biologically. However, wetlands have historically been under-appreciated. In fact, wetlands were often the subject of ill-conceived legislative reclamation efforts to convert them to urban and agricultural land. This was particularly true in Florida, where many of the wetland areas were drained long ago.

---

67. A scan of the records of 9700 children with leukemia in England and Wales found that children who lived within 200 meters of a high-voltage power line at birth had a relative risk of leukemia of 1.69 compared to the general population of children. Gerald Draper et al., Childhood cancer in relation to distance from high voltage power lines in England and Wales: a case-control study, 330 British Medical Journal 1290 (2005).

68. Kelliher *supra* at 724.

Today, our view of wetlands has changed dramatically. Lands that were once thought to be worthless have in the last twenty years been recognized as increasingly scarce and valuable resources that need to be protected. We now realize that wetlands are the source of many important resource values, and provide vital ecosystem services.

> Wetlands provide fish and wildlife habitat, essential breeding and nursery areas for many species including economically-important shell-fish, and habitat and food for migrating birds; water supply protection through recharge; water quality protection through purification; flood control; erosion and shoreline protection by binding stream banks and absorbing wave energy; outdoor recreation opportunities for hunters and bird and wildlife watchers; and education and research benefits. Endangered species' use of and reliance on wetlands has been documented. A recent study documents [that] wetlands have significant effects on climate by moderating temperatures and protecting agricultural areas from freezes that damage crops. These facts point to an impressive array of values that bridge the economic and the aesthetic. We value the functions and services wetlands provide to broader ecosystems—both those functions and services that benefit humans directly (e.g., flood control and water purification) and those that may provide more indirect or intangible benefits (e.g., fish and wildlife habitat for species that have no economic or recreational value but which we value). There may be disagreement about why we care about these values—whether out of utilitarian impulses or an instinct to respect the intrinsic value of fish, wildlife, and the ecosystems on which they depend, for example. But the values themselves and the facts underlying these values are uncontested.

Alyson C. Flournoy, Section 404 at Thirty–Something: A Program in Search of a Policy, 55 Ala. L. Rev. 607, 637–38 (2004).

Our enlightened appreciation of these ecosystem values is manifest in recent statutory schemes. Modern legislation, both in the United States and throughout the world, emphasizes wetland protection, not wetland conversion.

In Florida, two types of wetland predominate: (1) the cypress swamp, consisting of a forest of cypress trees growing in shallow water, and (2) marshes, in which low-growing vegetation dominates. The value of both types of wetland are widely recognized today. The Everglades, a classic example of a marsh, is undergoing a major restoration efforts. And efforts have also been made to preserve some of the cypress swamps, such as the Big Cypress National Preserve. Throughout Florida, cypress swamps in their natural condition are becoming quite rare, as are some of the animals that occupy them, such as the wood stork. The ivory-billed woodpecker, which was thought to be extinct until recently, once occupied the cypress swamps of Florida and other southern states.

3. Lawyering in Sensitive Areas

The following case arose when the Florida Power Company wanted to build a new high-voltage transmission line to serve the southern part of the

Orlando area, one of the fastest growing regions in the country. It acquired a right of way through a wet cypress forest and cut down the trees. This left the land just as wet as it was originally, so the company assumed that it did not need a permit under the state's wetland statute. The regulators disagreed.

The central dispute between the company and the agency was whether the conversion of a wooded wetland to a grassy (herbaceous) wetland required a permit under the statute. The company argued that grassy wetlands were actually more efficient at the conversion of energy than wooded wetlands, while the agency argued that wooded wetlands were more uncommon and performed unique functions, and that the cumulative impact of the many other development activities in the Orlando area needed to be considered.

Florida Power Corp. v. State, Department of Environmental Regulation

638 So. 2d 545 (Fla. 1st D.C.A. 1994), review denied, 650 So. 2d 989 (1994).

■ BARFIELD, J. Florida Power Corporation ("FPC") appeals an order of the Department of Environmental Regulation ("DER") denying its application for a wetland resource permit, contending that DER improperly rejected the hearing officer's determination that FPC's project would have no adverse impacts and was not contrary to the public interest. . . .

FPC owns an easement over property in Reedy Creek Swamp, a large mixed wetland forest system in Osceola County, on which it seeks to install an electrical transmission line between Intercession City and Poinciana (the ICP line), which is expected to last at least thirty years. . . .

In December 1989, FPC filed an application with DER for a wetland resource permit to place 353.1 cubic yards of fill to support the transmission poles. The application stated that the fill would impact .0135 acres of jurisdictional wetlands. Prior to obtaining the permit, FPC undertook clearing activities during March–June 1990, cutting all vegetation within the sixty-foot transmission line corridor to the ground or water line. DER conducted a surveillance flight over the project site in June 1990 and visited the site in June and in August. The flight revealed the nearly completed clearing of the forested wetland, and the field appraisals indicated that some dredge and fill had occurred as a result of the land clearing activities. At an on-site meeting in late August 1990, the parties discussed mitigation. FPC eventually offered to preserve one acre of forested wetland, at a site east of the Intercession City substation near State Road 17/92, for each acre of forested wetland impacted.

In September 1990, DER issued a notice of intent to deny the permit request, finding that the proposed installation activities would actually impact approximately 6.01 acres, 5.997 acres of which were "secondary impacts" of the proposed construction (i.e., the clearing activities). It found that the wetland adjacent to State Road 17/92 "will be impacted by minor trimming of branches within the mature forested canopy and by removal of small subcanopy trees beneath the existing corridor," that the main crossing of the swamp "involves secondary impacts to a mature mixed forested wetland" (noting endangered and threatened orchids adjacent to the cleared corridor), and that the wetland south of the main crossing is a cypress community with saw grass as the primary understory. It found that the proposed alignment "has and will continue to result in disturbances to hydric soils and vegetation as a result of the tree cutting, installation and maintenance activities," that the power line "will result in a permanent change in the character of the wetland from a mature mixed forested canopy to a herbaceous wetland," and that this permanent change "is expected to diminish the overall productivity of the system and adversely affect wildlife utilization."

The title to chapter 84–79, Laws of Florida, which created the "Warren S. Henderson Wetlands Protection Act of 1984," Part VIII of chapter 403, Florida Statutes, now entitled "Permitting of Activities in Wetlands," reads ... "... it is the policy of this state to establish reasonable regulatory programs which provide for the preservation and protection of Florida's remaining wetlands to the greatest extent practicable, consistent with private property rights and the balancing of other vital state interests," and "it is the policy of this state to consider the extent to which particular disturbances of wetlands are related to uses or projects which must be located within or in close proximity to the wetland and aquatic environment in order to perform their basic functions, and the extent to which particular disturbances of wetland benefit essential economic development, ..."

Section 403.918, Florida Statutes (1989), which establishes the criteria for granting or denying permits under the Act, provides in part (emphasis supplied):

(2) A permit may not be issued under §§ 403.91–403.929 unless the applicant provides the department with reasonable assurance that the project is not contrary to the public interest. However, for a project which significantly degrades or is within an Outstanding Florida Water, as provided by department rule, the applicant must provide reasonable assurance that the project will be clearly in the public interest.

(a) In determining whether a project is not contrary to the public interest, or is clearly in the public interest, the department shall consider and balance the following criteria:

1. Whether the project will adversely affect the public health, safety, or welfare or the property of others;

2. Whether the project will adversely affect the conservation of fish and wildlife, including endangered or threatened species, or their habitats;

3. Whether the project will adversely affect navigation or the flow of water or cause harmful erosion or shoaling;

4. Whether the project will adversely affect the fishing or recreational values or marine productivity in the vicinity of the project;

5. Whether the project will be of a temporary or permanent nature;

6. Whether the project will adversely affect or will enhance significant historical and archaeological resources under the provisions of § 267.061; and

7. The current condition and relative value of functions being performed by areas affected by the proposed activity.

(b) If the applicant is unable to otherwise meet the criteria set forth in this subsection, the department, in deciding to grant or deny a permit, shall consider measures proposed by or acceptable to the applicant to mitigate adverse effects which may be caused by the project....

Section 403.919, Florida Statutes (1989), entitled "Equitable distribution," codifies the "cumulative impact doctrine" ...

[DER] Rule 17–312.300 et seq. establish the criteria for evaluating mitigation proposals. DER must first explore "project modifications that would reduce or eliminate the adverse environmental impacts of the project" and suggest any such modifications, either in addition to or in lieu of mitigation. It may not require mitigation, but it must consider "any mitigation proposed by a permit applicant in accordance with this rule." Rule 17–312.300(7) provides:

The amount, type and location of mitigation, if any, required of electric utilities conducting dredge and fill activities for the purpose of providing energy service shall be determined in conjunction with the criteria in Section 403.918, F.S., in recognition of the fact that such activities generally promote the public interest.

Rule 17–312.340 sets the standards for evaluating mitigation proposals, noting that they must be considered "on a case by case basis" and that offsetting adverse impacts "will usually be best addressed through protection, enhancement or creation of the same type of waters as those being affected by the proposed project."

In March 1991, FPC filed a request for formal administrative hearing ... The parties stipulated that the proposed project "benefits the public welfare by producing and providing for the reliable transmission of electricity to residents of the State" ... The five-day hearing centered on the relative condition of the area impacted and the impact of the clearing on the conservation of vegetation, fish and wildlife. FPC admitted that the canopy has been removed in a sixty-foot swath through the swamp and that maintenance activities will result in a change in the corridor from forested wetlands to herbaceous/shrubby wetlands, but it asserted that there has been "no adversity" resulting from the change in the character of the wetlands. DER argued that this was in effect "after-the-fact permitting," that six acres of forested wetland has been removed and will not be replaced, and that what is left is a disturbed herbaceous marsh that will, along with past, present, and future projects, have a cumulative negative effect on Reedy Creek Swamp as a whole....

[Company experts testified]that FPC had evaluated an alternate route which would have followed an existing roadway, but that this route would have been 2.5 miles longer and would have cost $700,000 more.... Vegetation would be cut to the ground or water level for seventeen feet on either side of the center line of the sixty-foot wide corridor. The remaining outer thirteen feet on each side would be allowed to regenerate, except for fast-growing trees expected to reach thirty feet or more in height, which would be girdled or treated with EPA approved herbicides by specific and selective application, and that all exotic or nuisance target species would be removed from the entire right-of-way....

Dr. William Dennis ... was presented as an expert in botany, wetland ecology, and wetland permitting. He testified that as a general rule, herbaceous wetlands are more productive (productivity measured by the amount of plant material accumulated per unit area over time) than forested wetlands. He testified that, while the habitat was definitely changed, he was not aware of any study showing any species adversely affected, and that quite a number of species (for example, wading birds) would be benefited....

[Steve] Godley [a biological expert for FPC] found that the mean "cover" was 85% in the corridor, higher than in the forest, and testified that a study showed that the net primary productivity of herbaceous wetlands is three times higher than in the adjacent flood plain forest, and that the decomposition rate is two or three times higher in the marsh....

As to endangered or threatened species, Godley found that the only endangered reptile, the indigo snake, would be positively affected, that none of the fish or mammals were listed as endangered or threatened, and that of the endangered or threatened birds, three were positively affected (wood stork, little blue heron, snowy egret) because they eat fish, and that the bald eagle, which prefers lakes, would be positively affected....

Godley stated that the ICP corridor had caused a change in the system, but that the wildlife utilization in the whole system is balanced across all kinds of animals and does not appear to have been negatively affected. He testified that the majority of the animal species are likely to be positively affected, and that the species which were negatively affected are "almost at the point of a de minimis effect." He testified that the corridor had not adversely affected recreation and had improved hunting.

Dr. Putz [an associate professor of biology and forestry at the University of Florida] testified [on behalf of DER] that forested wetlands in Florida are being lost faster than any other community type (15% between 1979 and 1987 according to one study of Florida and South Carolina wetlands), ... but he acknowledged a study by Randy Kautz with the Florida Game and Freshwater Fish Commission which found that there was no loss of lowland forest.

Bradley Hartman, with the Florida Game and Freshwater Fish Commission, testified as an expert in wildlife management. He and Stephen Lau, also with the Commission, wrote a report for DER in which they found that the wildlife population would be affected by the change in habitat (i.e., replacement of wooded wetlands by open marsh). He stated that there would be an increase in the number of individuals and the number of species because of two habitats located next to each other, but that population of forest animals would be lost because of losses of hardwood mast (seeds and nuts), high canopy, cavities and snags. He testified that they were more interested in regional diversity than in local diversity, and that the corridor could actually reduce the number of species in the regional area. He stated that while there was some additional feeding for the little blue heron and the snowy egret (special concern species), these species do not need more feeding area. He explained the LANDSAT habitat planning project which places emphasis on saving large tracts, more valuable because they buffer themselves. In his opinion, we are losing forested wetlands, resulting in a decline in forested species, some of which are the most rare. . . .

DER's Barbara Bass . . . testified that DER would have been happy to consider other proposals, but that none were submitted by FPC, and that rerouting the line along a road is a reasonable alternative. She stated that the 1:1 mitigation proposed by FPC is inadequate, that there should be at least a 10:1 ratio because of the quality of the swamp and its vulnerability to development, and that it would take sixty years to replace the mature system that was lost. She stated that other projects impact forested wetlands in Reedy Creek Swamp (Continental Development berms and roads, Owens commercial development and access road, Osceola County bridge, Wilderness Joint Venture enforcement case, Walt Disney access road, Walt Disney parking, Reedy Creek Improvement District (RCID) reuse pipeline and access road, RCID bridge, Parker Poinciana DRI, Johnson Island DRI, Pleasant Hill Point DRI, Oak Hill Estates DRI, Celebration Project DRI). She testified that she would prefer to see future crossings of the swamp adjacent to corridors, where disturbance has already occurred.

Dr. Herbert Kale, with Florida Audubon Society, was presented as an expert in ornithology. He testified that he has been to Reedy Creek Swamp many times and that he visited the ICP site in November 1991. He stated that the permanent loss of forested wetland affects woodpeckers and interior forest birds (red-eyed vireo, prothonotory warbler, hermit thrush, ovenbird, northern water thrush), that the corridor brings in wading birds, and that there is an "edge effect" 100–200 meters into the forest. He testified that the corridor is large enough to attract brownheaded cowbirds, who are nest parasites, and that the shiny cowbird is also moving in from the Caribbean. On cross-examination, he stated that the sixty-foot swath is not fatal to any of the forest birds, but "every time you make a cut you're creating problems and reducing habitat."

[The hearing officer recommended that the application for the permit be granted without mitigation.] On August 13, 1992, Secretary Browner issued a final order denying FPC's permit application. She accepted the [hearing officer's findings of fact] with the following exceptions: that "wetlands" were not destroyed; that the loss of six acres of forested wetlands is not permanent and that the "habitats which were affected when the clearing took place will regenerate and will be reestablished"; that the change from forested wetlands to herbaceous wetlands has not and will not adversely affect threatened plant species, fish or wildlife and that the edge effect "is at least neutral, and is generally positive"; and that there is no adverse impact when the project is considered cumulatively.

As to the hearing officer's finding that "wetlands" were not destroyed, the Secretary ruled that the finding was infused by a policy determination "that herbaceous wetlands are somehow environmentally equivalent to forested wetlands" and rejected this policy determination. She explained: "Forested wetlands are not environmentally equivalent to herbaceous wetlands. Each have their (sic) own unique environmental functions which are not interchangeable" and "the six acres of forested wetlands habitat is lost, i.e., destroyed, regardless of whether it is replaced by a different type of wetland system or by an asphalt parking lot." . . .

The Secretary reconsidered the balancing of the public interest criteria in section 403.918(2) in light of the rejected finding of no adverse impact. She determined that while there are no adverse impacts under criteria 1, 3, 4, and 6, the project has resulted in adverse impacts under criteria 2, 5, and 7. Balancing these adverse effects against the benefit provided, she found that the project is contrary to the public interest. She rejected several of the hearing officer's conclusions of law, and concluded that the mitigation proposed by FPC was not sufficient to offset the adverse impacts of the project. She denied the permit, noting:

> This project would have been permitted if FPC had offered sufficient mitigation in its application or during the hearing. Of course, this denial does not preclude FPC from reapplying with legally sufficient mitigation or a modified project.

The parties do not dispute that providing energy service promotes the public interest, that the ICP line must cross the Reedy Creek Swamp, and that some dredge and fill is therefore necessary, requiring a permit from DER. The statute makes it clear that before DER may grant this permit, FPC must provide it with reasonable assurance that the ICP project is not contrary to the public interest, and that in determining whether the ICP project is contrary to the public interest, DER must consider and balance the criteria set out in section 403.918, of which only (2), (5), and (7) are at issue in this case.

FPC admits that it cut down all vegetation to the ground in the ICP right-of-way, removing the forest canopy in a sixty-foot swath through the swamp, and that its proposed maintenance activities will result in a change in the corridor from forested wetlands to herbaceous/shrubby wetlands. . . . For purposes of considering and balancing the statutory criteria, there is little doubt that the ICP project will be more permanent than temporary (criterion 5). This leaves the other two criteria at issue: "whether the project will adversely affect the conservation of fish and wildlife, including endangered or threatened species, or their habitats" and "the current condition and relative value of functions being performed by areas affected by the proposed activity."

The parties do not dispute that there are significant differences between the condition of the site before FPC's clearing activities and the present condition of the site, the most notable being that all the large trees are gone, and that this difference will be maintained by FPC for at least the next thirty years if the permit is granted. The parties also do not generally dispute that, in addition to other wetland functions which remain relatively unchanged, the forested wetland which existed within the area at issue provided a habitat for various species of plants and animals which cannot live in the herbaceous/shrubby wetland resulting from FPC's clearing and maintenance activities, and that the clearing of the corridor affected many of the other plants and animals in the corridor and in the adjacent forest in various ways, some considered positive and some considered negative.

The issues to be resolved are first, the extent of the "adverse" effects on the plants and animals in the corridor and in the adjacent forest, and second, whether these adverse effects outweigh the public benefit which will result from the project, the provision of reliable electric power to the area south of the swamp. The first issue requires factual findings, while the second issue requires a balancing of the adverse effects which are found to exist against the public benefit, to determine whether the project is "contrary to the public interest." s. 403.918(2), Fla. Stat. (1989). In making the latter determination, however, DER must consider not only the impact of the ICP project, but also "the impact of projects which are existing or under construction or for which permits or jurisdictional determinations have been sought" and "the impact of projects which are under review, approved, or vested pursuant to s. 380.06, or other projects which may reasonably be expected to be located within the jurisdictional extent of waters, based upon land use restrictions and regulations." s. 403.919, Fla. Stat. (1989).

The hearing officer essentially dismissed the "cumulative impact analysis" in her recommended order, and Secretary Browner ruled that she had construed the "similarity" requirement too narrowly. When the Secretary remanded for a revised cumulative impact analysis, the hearing officer considered the existing and pending dredge and fill projects, but concluded that because wetlands were not destroyed in the ICP project and FPC provided reasonable assurance that its project will not violate state water quality standards or is not contrary to the public interest, "consideration of these additional projects does not change previous undisturbed findings of fact" (i.e., that the ICP project does not exacerbate the impacts from the other projects).

Secretary Browner correctly rejected the finding that wetlands were not destroyed, on the ground that it was based on a policy determination which she also rejected, "that herbaceous wetlands are somehow environmentally equivalent to forested wetlands." She also properly rejected the finding that there is no adverse impact when this project is considered cumulatively, which was based upon the hearing officer's rejected finding that there was no adverse impact from this project alone. We find that Secretary Browner's rulings were within her discretion in implementing the wetlands protection statutes.

The final order is affirmed.

■ ZEHMER, J., dissenting The lengthy recitation of the evidence in the majority opinion confirms my view that the findings of fact in the hearing officer's recommended orders are supported by competent, substantial evidence, and Secretary Browner was bound by these findings of fact. s. 120.57(1)(b)10, Fla. Stat. (1991); *Heifetz v. Department of Business Regulation*, 475 So. 2d 1277 (Fla. 1st DCA 1984). It is clear from the final order that the Secretary disagreed with the hearing officer's findings of fact and therefore modified certain facts to support her conclusion that the activity for which Florida Power sought a dredge and fill permit would result in adverse impacts contrary to the public interest. Yet, no authority permits the Secretary to make such changes in the facts when supported by competent, substantial evidence because of the provisions in subsection 120.57(1)(b)10.

Specifically, Secretary Browner's final order concluded that there is a major difference between forested wetlands and herbaceous wetlands, and that Florida Power had destroyed forested wetlands by clear cutting, thereby leaving instead herbaceous wetlands. This result, she opines, amounts to an adverse impact contrary to the public interest, irrespective of whether the hearing officer's recommended order found as a matter of fact, supported by competent, substantial evidence, that the altered conditions of the land did not factually result in adverse impacts. According to the majority opinion, the Secretary "determined that the public interest in the extent of the impact on the environment from this destruction of the forest was a policy matter for its determination and not a question of fact to be resolved by the hearing officer." Agreeing, the majority affirms the final order on this rationale.

I dissent because I do not agree that this determination is purely a matter of public policy reserved for exclusive decision by the Secretary; rather, the determination must be based on matters of fact determined by the hearing officer on the evidence presented in accordance with section 403.918.... Affirming the Secretary's ruling, the majority opinion notes that, "Secretary Browner correctly rejected the finding that wetlands were not destroyed, on the ground that it was based on a policy determination which she also rejected, 'that herbaceous wetlands are somehow environmentally equivalent to forested wetlands.'" [Emphasis added.] By characterizing this determination as one of policy rather than fact, the hearing officer's findings can be ignored. This is akin to designating the Secretary as the sole determinator of how land shall be used without regard to the statutory limitations in chapter 403.■

NOTES AND COMMENTS

1. The siting of new energy facilities often requires highly talented energy lawyers who need to have a basic understanding of many technical issues. The expert testimony quoted in this excerpt is only part of the expert testimony that the court analyzed. Obviously, this litigation was expensive and time consuming. Why do you think the company pursued this expensive litigation rather than abiding by Secretary Browner's interpretation of the statute?

Was this a situation in which the company simply faced such a confusing statute and set of regulations that it could not have been faulted for having made the wrong interpretation? Would you have been able to find a policy in favor of protecting forested wetlands over grassy wetlands in the language of the statute or regulations quoted in the case? In his article quoted in Section A, above, David Spence argues that many violations of environmental rules are the result of such complexity rather than the result of rational decisions made by companies to spend the least possible money on environmental protection?

Should a company have a responsibility to ask the agency what its policy is before taking action? If you had been Florida Power Company's attorney, would you have advised the company that it could proceed to clear the trees on this site without applying for a permit under the wetlands statute? Would you have made that decision on your own, or would you have consulted expert biologists? Would you have sought an informal opinion from the staff of the agency? (The opinion in this case does not tell us whether the company sought legal advice before cutting the trees).

2. The editors of The Economist argue that corporate managers use poor judgment if they give away corporate assets for charitable purposes. If the company had chosen to build the line along the road at an extra cost of $700,000, rather than cut through the swamp, would this argument be applicable? Keep in mind that Florida was (and still is) a state in which electric utilities are subject to the traditional type of rate regulation discussed in Chapter 3.

3. Carol Rose suggests that we should try to make land use decisions by maximizing the sum of all public and private resources, taking into account the impact on diffuse public resources from "private piggybacked uses." By constructing a power line, FPC is promoting additional growth in the region—growth that is piggybacking on the energy resources being made available by FPC. So should we charge FPC with the damage to all of the wetlands and other public resources that will be destroyed in the course of building the development that will use FPC's energy? Is FPC the proximate cause of all that development?

This issue of cumulative impact is a troublesome one throughout environmental and land use law. When one can foresee that a multiplicity of small projects will adversely impact the environment, but no single project can be shown to be the cause of significant damage, can individual projects be denied on the ground that they will contribute to the damage? The Supreme Court has suggested that consideration of cumulative impact may be constitutionally required, but it has been in dicta. *See Nollan v. Cal. Coastal Comm'n*, 483 U.S. 825, 835 (1987).

If you did try to put a dollar value on the public wetland resources that would be lost as a result of the cumulative effect of development, how would you make that computation? Recent literature devotes a great deal of attention to methodologies for the valuation of "ecosystem services," such as those provided by wetlands. *See e.g.* Gretchen C. Daily and Katherine Ellison, The New Economy of Nature (Island Press, 2002).

How fair is it to make energy providers responsible for cumulative impact? Can you make one developer responsible for cumulative effects for which earlier developers weren't held responsible? How do you predict what damage future developers will cause? There is no easy answer to these questions. The Council on Environmental Quality regulations require consideration of cumulative impact in NEPA processes, but they provide little assistance to those administering the process.

4.   By not choosing the alternate route that followed an existing road, FPC reduced the exposure of humans to any electromagnetic fields generated by the power line. Although FPC would certainly not have conceded that such fields have a harmful effect on human health, there is at least some evidence that suggests that such a risk may exist. How should the company evaluate the comparative risk of a slight possibility of damage to humans, against the rather certain destruction of specific plants and animals and the ecological functions of the cypress marsh? Peter Singer argues that it is "speciesism" if we always put humans first (see *supra*). Do you agree?

5.   Dissenting, Judge Zehmer addressed an important administrative law issue. Was the agency secretary acting properly by overruling the hearing examiner. The majority thought the issue was a question of law and thus within the secretary's power to decide, while the dissent thought it was a question of fact on which the hearing examiner's decision was supported by substantial evidence. Was the "fact" that the two kinds of wetlands are different a question of law? There is nothing in the language of the statute to suggest that the legislature had ever thought about the issue.

Do you agree with the dissenting judge that Secretary Browner was dissembling by purporting to use "policy" to overrule the hearing examiner's characterization of the factual evidence? Or do you think the hearing examiner was trying to make policy by the way she characterized the facts? Can you think of ways to clarify the distinction between fact and policy in this area?

6.   The above case arose under a state wetlands protection statute. Many construction projects in wetlands also require a federal "dredge and fill" permit under the Clean Water Act, 33 U.S.C. § 1344. Would clearing of vegetation constitute "dredging or filling" and thus trigger the permit requirement. See *Save our Wetlands, Inc. v. Sands*, 711 F.2d 634, 646–647 (5th Cir. 1983); Flournoy *supra* at 626.

7.   Assume that the forested wetland that pre-existed the power line was less efficient at converting solar energy than the shrubby wetland that was created by cutting down the trees. Is this a factor that should have been taken into consideration by the Department? Is energy conversion efficiency a value in and of itself? Or is there a presumption that the natural condition of the land is the most desirable from an ecological perspective? In many other parts of the state, people are trying to preserve and even create the same kind of grassy wetland that FPC created here. Why is it important that this wetland be woody? What if it were projected that rising water levels would drown the trees in 10 years? 30 yrs.?

8.   Many states have crafted statutes to coordinate the siting of facilities such as natural gas pipelines, power plants and electricity transmission lines. To help utilities cope with the permitting process for locating transmission lines, Florida, for example, enacted the Transmission Line Siting Act ("TLSA") in 1980. *See* Wade L. Hopping and Carolyn Songer Raepple, A Solution to the Regulatory Maze: The Transmission Line Siting Act, 8 Fla. St. U. L. Rev. 442 (1980). These statutes are discussed at Chapter 12.D. The nonpartisan National Commission on Energy Policy has noted that the growing interdependence of all North American regions makes it essential to incorporate regional and national perspectives into state and local siting procedures. Transmission siting should begin with a comprehensive review of alternatives, and if that review validates the need for new transmission lines, the siting process for a specific line segment should not allow for the reopening of broader system planning issues.[69]

E.   ARCTIC ALASKA

When large deposits of oil and gas were discovered in Alaska, the opportunity to provide new domestic sources of energy was greeted with pleasure by most Americans, especially those living in Alaska. But the petroleum was found in the northernmost part of Alaska, the country's northernmost state, which meant working in an environment that was not only extremely cold for much of the year, but was also a unique natural environment that was not easy to understand and appreciate.

1.   PRUDHOE BAY AND THE OIL PIPELINE

Oil industry exploration in Alaska began in the late 1950's when federal geological studies recognized that a large oil reserve existed in Arctic Alaska. The initial exploratory drilling in Prudhoe Bay began in 1967, and ARCO discovered the Prudhoe Bay oil field in 1968. Production at Prudhoe Bay began in 1977—since then more than 12 billion barrels of oil have been produced. The Prudhoe Bay oil field is the largest field in North America.

---

69.   The National Commission on Energy Policy, Ending the Energy Stalemate: A Bipartisan Strategy to Meet America's Energy Challenges 87 (2004).

Intensive exploration for oil and gas in the Alaskan Arctic has been going on for four decades, and has disturbed roughly thirty-five to forty thousand acres of the coastal plain on the North Slope, as the northern-most part of Alaska is called. Michelle A. Gilders & Matthew A. Cronin, *North Slope Oil Field Development, in* The Natural History of an Arctic Oil Field: Development and the Biota 15, 16 (Joe C. Truett & Stephen R. Johnson eds., 2000) (hereinafter "Truett & Johnson").

The current development of the Alaska oil fields was facilitated by the Trans–Alaska Pipeline, which brings the oil to market at Valdez. The pipeline begins on the tundra near Prudhoe Bay. It crosses the Brooks Mountain Range at Atigun Pass, passes over the Yukon River—a mile wide—and continues south to Valdez. Atlantic Richfield, Exxon and British Petroleum, the three main Prudhoe Bay oil companies, initially proposed the Trans–Alaska Pipeline in 1969. The pipeline was to be forty-eight inches in diameter and 800 miles long. The oil companies formed a company—Alyeska Pipeline Service Company, and began building the pipe-line in 1970, without waiting for the issuance of permits. Id. at, 79–81. However, the National Environmental Policy Act ("NEPA") had been passed in 1969. The Wilderness Society, Friends of the Earth, and the Environmental Defense Fund filed suit to try to stop the construction of the pipeline. *See Wilderness Soc. v. Hickel*, 325 F. Supp. 422 (D.D.C. 1970). While the legal challenges were being addressed, construction stopped on the pipeline, but after the 1973 oil embargo imposed by OPEC in retalia-tion for U.S. aid to Israel, Congress amended the Mineral Leasing Act and the Trans–Alaska Pipeline Authorization Act to make the construction permits immune from any legal challenges—including NEPA challenges— and the first construction permit was issued in 1974. *See* John Strohmeyer, Extreme Conditions 83–84 (Cascade Press 1997).

While the pipeline was being constructed, a bulldozer crushed one of the valves and 80,000 gallons of crude oil spilled onto the tundra. The pipeline also broke in 1979 at Antigun Pass and 210,000 gallons of oil spilled into the Antigun River. *See* Ken Madsen, *Under the Arctic Sun: Gwich'in, Caribou and the Arctic National Wildlife Refuge* 1, 45, 47 (Westcliffe Publishers 2002). The pipeline was finished in 1977. The total cost of the pipeline was $8 billion, which was more than nine times the original estimate. The Prudhoe Bay development was not truly profitable until the 1979 Iranian revolution, which tripled the cost of oil. *See* Stroh-meyer *supra* at 96.

The oil industry has created an enormous amount of revenue for Alaska. In 1982, the state of Alaska distributed $1,000 to every Alaskan citizen—the first installment of the Permanent Fund Dividend. Since 1982, Alaska has had no taxes on individuals—it has no statewide sales or income tax. Every year, each Alaskan citizen who has lived in Alaska for at least two years receives a Permanent Fund Dividend check. The amount of the dividend is calculated according to the number of eligible applicants and the earnings available for distribution. State of Alaska, Department of

Revenue, Permanent Fund Dividend Division, https://www.pfd.state.ak.us (last visited Feb. 9, 2004). In 2004, the dividend amount was $919.84. *Id.*

2.   LEARNING TO UNDERSTAND PERMAFROST

Recent interest in expanding the geographic scope of petroleum development in Arctic Alaska led Congress to commission the National Academies of Sciences and Engineering to undertake a study of the existing and probable future cumulative effects of such development on the physical, biological and human environment of Arctic Alaska. The National Acadamies' report was published in 2003. *See* National Research Council, Cumulative Environmental Effects of Oil and Gas Activities on Alaska's North Slope (National Academy Press, 2003) (hereafter "Cumulative Effects"). The findings in the report show how the industry has found ways to minimize its impacts, but they also show how recent warming of the climate, and projected future warming, will require continual research and development to cope with changing conditions.

The construction of both the oil fields and the pipeline took place on a landscape characterized by "permafrost," and the unique characteristics of permafrost continue to affect all existing and prospective future development activities on the North Slope. Soils containing permafrost cover about one-fifth of the earth's surface. Permafrost is permanently frozen subsoil that develops at temperatures below 0°C. Permafrost contains ice that occupies more space than the water-filled pores would occupy if the permafrost thawed. Thawing of the permafrost would thus result in uneven settlement of the surface and anything on the surface. *See* Cumulative Effects, Chapter 6.

Permafrost is absent under lakes and rivers that do not freeze to the bottom in the winter. Water in liquid form stores enough energy to keep the ground under it from freezing. Permafrost is also patchy south of the tundra zone. In some parts of the Arctic, permafrost persists because of the insulating effect of trees. If the trees are removed, the permafrost will thaw. *See* E.C. Pielou, *A Naturalist's Guide to the Arctic,* 31 (University of Chicago Press 1994).

The permafrost is insulated from the surface by an *active layer*. The active layer thaws during the summer from eight inches to more than two meters in some areas in the Arctic. On the North Slope, permafrost extends from 200–650 meters below the surface. The deepest permafrost occurs at Prudhoe Bay. *See* Cumulative Effects, Chapter 3. Melted water cannot filter through the impervious permafrost in the summer. The active layer sustains the tundra vegetation mat, which supports the land animals and controls erosion. The active layer also prevents the permafrost from warming in the summer.

The environmental effects of the oil and gas development can significantly change the active layer in ways that cause thawing of the underlying permafrost. While superficially it might seem desirable to get rid of all of that ice, the reality is quite different. The ice is the only solid ground in the

North Slope, and the only support for buildings and roads. If the permafrost were to melt, the North Slope would be one giant soupy wetland.

Changes to the active layer can be initiated by off-road traffic, removal of vegetation, addition of gravel, paving, oil and seawater spills, the deposition of dust, and the alteration of surface drainage. Changes in the condition of the permafrost surface affects the physical and biological environment, as well as the human environment. *See* Cumulative Effects, Chapter 6.

If disruption of the active layer begins to thaw the permafrost, *thermokarst* can occur. Thermokarst is the differential settling of the soil that creates pits, ponds, and mud flows. The thawed soil flows off of the active layer instead of remaining to insulate the ice below. Thermokarst occurs most often in disturbances of the active layer over *ice-wedge polygons—* cracks filled with a wedge of ice over a meter wide and several meters thick. The ice-wedges form because the cracks fill with water from melting snow in the spring, and then the crack expands in the winter because the water freezes.

In the early days of petroleum activity, before the companies began to understand the natural environment in which they were working, they often failed to provide the needed insulation of the ice and ended up with subsidence and sinkholes. This type of thermokarst is visible in early roads on the North Slope where the gravel compressed the active layer—destroying the insulating capacity of the active layer—and the thawed ice wedges formed trenches. Thermokarst also forms underneath heated buildings unless the buildings are elevated off of the ground. In the early days of oil exploration, the oil companies created roads by removing the active layer from each side of the road and piling it in the middle. These actions caused thermokarst that is still visible today. Cumulative Effects, Chapter 6.

Gravel roads will create thermokarst unless the gravel underneath the road is deeper than the depth of the summer thaw in the active layer. Often, thermokarst occurred because the drilling companies did not make the roads thick enough. In the Arctic coastal plain, roads must be placed on a layer of gravel up to two meters thick.

Permafrost also prevents the burial of pipelines. The warm fluids melt the permafrost and the resultant differential settlement strains the pipe. Because of this, pipelines must be elevated above the permafrost. *See* Cumulative Effects, Chapter 6. When the Alyeska Pipeline Service Company began to build the Trans–Alaska Pipeline, they discovered that the pipeline could not be buried in the permafrost. The elevation of the pipeline raised the cost from an original estimate of $900 million to $8 billion. *See* Cumulative Effects, Chapter 9.

Withdrawing fluids from underground can thaw the permafrost around the drilling wells—this is also known as a *thawed chimney*. This thawing generates three possible problems for the environment. First, the thawed permafrost is no longer impermeable to liquids, so it represents a potential path for fluids to reach the tundra surface. Second, the thawed chimney creates stress upon the casing around the drilling well. Finally, the thawed permafrost can lead to surface subsidence. *See* Cumulative Effects, Chapter 6.

Because of these many impacts that oil and gas exploration can have on the environment, the companies have had to develop new technology. Production well pads in the Arctic are typically 70% smaller than they were twenty years ago (13.5 acres vs. 43.7 acres). Production pads generally use 60% less gravel than twenty years ago (112,700 cubic yards vs.198,000 cubic yards). Wellheads are now separated by thirty-five feet rather than 135 feet for onshore production pads, and by 10 feet for some offshore wells. Gravel roads are used less often because of the availability of ice roads for winter construction. Some newer fields, including Northstar and Badami, have no gravel access roads. If Prudhoe Bay were built today, there would be 74% less surface area covered by pads and 58% less area covered by roads.[70]

3.   The Arctic National Wildlife Refuge and its Resources

The National Park Service ("NPS") began surveying what would become the Arctic National Wildlife Refuge ("Arctic Refuge") in the 1950's. The NPS recommended that the area be preserved as a wildlife refuge and as an area to protect indigenous culture. Later in the 1950's, the Conservation Foundation and the New York Zoological Society conducted a scientific expedition to the Arctic. Public support for preserving what would become Arctic Refuge grew. In 1960, President Eisenhower designated 8.9 million acres as the Arctic National Wildlife Range to protect its unique wildlife, wilderness, and recreational values. In 1980, the Alaska National Interest Lands Conservation Act ("ANILCA") (see p. 338) expanded the protected area to 19 million acres, and preserved it as a National Wildlife Refuge. Almost 8 million acres of the original "Range" was designated as wilderness.

Prudhoe Bay understandably focused oil industry attention on the rest of the north coast of Alaska. To the west of Prudhoe Bay is the National Petroleum Reserve, an area designated specifically for conservation of petroleum resources. Exploration of the reserve has led to production in a number of areas, and exploration is ongoing.

However, petroleum geologists believe that the Arctic Refuge, located just to the east of Prudhoe Bay, is the most promising area for future development. The Arctic Refuge is now managed by the U.S. Fish and Wildlife Service to protect wildlife, particularly large migrating herds of caribou. Under federal law, oil leasing is prohibited, because although Section 1002 of ANILCA specifically excluded 1.5 million acres of the Arctic coast from wilderness designation (*See* 16 U.S.C. § 3142) as part of the compromise necessary to pass the Act, Section 1002 also directed the Department of the Interior to inventory fish and wildlife resources, analyze

---

70.   BP Global, Using Technology to Reduce Impact, at http://www.bp.com/genericarticle /2016630 (accessed Mar. 1, 2004) [attested by Ernst & Young].

the potential impacts of oil and gas exploration and development on those resources, and identify the potential petroleum resources. Section 1003 of ANILCA prohibits oil exploration, leasing, and development unless Congress approves otherwise. *See* 16 U.S.C. § 3143.[71]

In 1986, the Interior Department presented its report to Congress. The report stated that oil development would have negative impacts on indigenous subsistence, caribou, musk oxen, water quality, recreation, and wilderness. Despite these finding, the Department of Interior recommended that the area be opened to oil and gas development. Madsen *supra* at 174–175. Congress was prepared to pass legislation opening the Arctic Refuge to drilling in 1989, but the *Exxon Valdez* spill turned public sentiment against drilling in the Arctic Refuge. Congress again attempted to pass legislation allowing drilling in the Arctic Refuge in 1995 by attaching the legislation as a "rider" to the budget proposal, but President Clinton vetoed the budget, citing the rider as one of his main reasons. *Id.* at 176.

While the debates over the future of ANWR were proceeding, the state government was seeking to lease submerged lands off ANWR for oil exploration. The United States claimed that certain submerged lands located within three miles of the Arctic coast were retained by the federal government, even though under the Equal Footing doctrine these lands typically would have been conveyed to Alaska at the time of statehood. In *United States v. State of Alaska*, 521 U.S. 1 (1997), the Supreme Court held that the federal government did not transfer title to these submerged lands to Alaska at statehood in 1959. The Court held that it was the intent of Congress to retain federal jurisdiction over offshore submerged lands within the boundaries of the Arctic National Wildlife Refuge and also within the boundaries of the National Petroleum Reserve. The decision was hailed by environmentalists because it blocked Alaska's claim of sole authority to open up ANWR's submerged lands to oil and gas development, and any discovery of oil in the submerged lands inevitably would pressure Congress to open up ANWR. The Alaskan Governor predictably vowed to continue to fight "for the rights of Alaskans to develop Alaska resources." BNA, Daily Executive Report, June 23, 1997, at A–7.

In April of 2002, Alaska's Senators proposed Amendments that would open all of the coastal plain of the Arctic Refuge to oil development. Senators Joe Lieberman and John Kerry, as well as thirteen other senators, threatened a filibuster. Two days later, the Senate voted 54–46 to *not* overturn the filibuster. (Sixty votes are needed to override a filibuster— filibusters are often used by the minority party to block controversial legislation.)

The USFWS currently manages the 1002 Area as a minimal management area. Minimal management involves the maintenance of the current conditions in areas that have high fish and wildlife values. Minimal management areas are suitable for wilderness designation. The Arctic

---

71. For further background, *see Natural Resources Defense Council v. Lujan,* 768 F.Supp. 870 (1991).

Refuge is open for public access, subsistence purposes, hunting, fishing, trapping, backpacking, river floating and camping. Motorized access also is allowed, as well as guiding and outfitting services and related temporary facilities.[72]

It is unclear in mid–2005 whether Congress will open the Arctic Refuge to oil and gas exploration. The Senate has included money for the Arctic Refuge development in the budget package for fiscal year 2006, which must be resolved in conference with the House. The many congressional committees with an interest in the bill have been given until mid-September, 2005, to report their instructions to the budget conference. Oil industry representatives hope for a resolution of the issue by the end of 2005. Nick Snow, ANWR leasing outlook hazy, Oil & Gas Journal, July 4, 2005, p. 42.

Under a very optimistic hypothetical scenario where the first federal lease sale is held in 2006, oil production could begin in 2013, and gas production could begin by 2020. The U.S. Geological Survey ("USGS") estimates that there is a technically recoverable reserve of 10.3 billion barrels of oil in the Arctic Refuge, and an economically recoverable reserve of 3.2 billion barrels of oil. The USGS estimates that there are 8.6 trillion cubic feet of gas in the Arctic Refuge, with no estimates of the economically recoverable reserve. *See* Cumulative Effects, Chapter 5. The USGS has estimated that the oil deposits in Arctic Refuge are spread over at least thirty-five locations. Roads and pipelines would connect these drilling areas. *See* Madsen, *supra* at 178.

The potential impacts of petroleum development on the refuge are real and serious, but the oil industry has greatly improved its understanding of the North Slope environment, and can certainly do a better job than it did when Prudhoe Bay was originally developed. To wilderness advocates, however, the nature and extent of the impacts is really a secondary issue. They argue that this is perhaps the last great natural area in the United States that is almost untouched by human activity, and that we need to leave it as a legacy for future generations. To the President of the Wilderness Society, it is "a Liberty Bell representing the idea of nature's freedom." Incommensurable positions like that leave little if any room for negotiation.

4.   THE INDIGENOUS PEOPLE OF ALASKA

Alaska has many populations of indigenous people scattered throughout the state. In the North Slope area, these people are Inupiaq Alaska Natives. They make up 70% of the North Slope Borough's population, and over 90% of the population of the smaller coastal villages other than Barrow. Just south of the North Slope, in the foothills of the Brooks Range, live a different group of indigenous people, the Gwich'in Indians.

All Alaska Natives have traditionally lived a subsistence lifestyle. People in the coastal villages rely heavily on the bowhead whale, which is

---

72.   See U.S Fish and Wildlife Service–Alaska, Management of the 1002 Area within the Arctic Refuge Coastal Plain, at http://arctic.fws.gov/1002man.htm (May 20, 2004).

the preferred food, accompanied by fish, birds, plants and caribou. Where bowhead whale is not available, ringed seal is substituted. For the Gwich'in people away from the coast, caribou is the most important subsistence resource, with lesser use of sheep, moose and fish. The Gwich'in maintain strong cultural and spiritual ties to the Porcupine Caribou Herd, which migrates between their territory and the Arctic Ocean. *See* Cumulative Effects, Chapter 2.

In the 1970's, Alaska's growing population led to tremendous increases in fishing and hunting. Many Alaskans felt that Alaska Natives had relinquished any ancestral rights to hunt and fish when the Natives received reparations under the Alaska Claims Settlement Act of 1971. However, most Alaska Natives did not contemplate that they were giving away these subsistence rights when they received the land and money. At the same time, environmentalists were concerned about the fact that many Native corporations were clear-cutting timber and engaging in other resource extraction activities. Strohmeyer *supra* at 197–198.

In response to these concerns, ANILCA established a priority for subsistence rights on all renewable resources on federal "public lands" in Alaska. All rural residents, both native and non-native, who depend upon non-wasteful subsistence uses are given priority if it is "necessary to restrict taking in order to assure the continued viability of a fish or wildlife population or the continuation of subsistence uses of such population." *See* 16 U.S.C. § 3112(2) (2000). The Alaska Natives argued that "public lands" included all navigable waters because they were subject to a federal navigation easement, but the Ninth Circuit in *Alaska v. Babbitt,* 72 F.3d 698 (9th Cir. 1995), reheard and affirmed en banc in *John v. United States,* 247 F.3d 1032, 1038 (9th Cir. 2001), held that these subsistence rights applied only to those navigable waters for which the federal governments had reserved water rights.

In response to The Interior Department's intention to open the Arctic National Wildlife Refuge to exploration in 1986, the Gwich'in Nation called for a gathering of the Arctic Village. This was the first such gathering in over a century. The Gwich'in passed a resolution opposing oil drilling in the Arctic and supporting Wilderness designation for the Arctic National Wildlife Refuge. The Gwich'in Nation has traditionally been nomadic—they have based their traveling patterns upon the migration of the Porcupine Caribou Herd. They have relied upon caribou for nutritional, cultural, and spiritual fulfillment for thousands of years. The Gwich'in Nation consists of fifteen villages, all of which are outside of the North Slope. However, the coastal plain of the wildlife refuge is the main calving ground for the Porcupine Caribou Herd. The Gwich'in believe that oil and gas development in Arctic Range would negatively impact the caribou, which in turn would negatively affect the Gwich'ins' quality of life. *See* Cumulative Effects, Chapter 9.

Debbie S. Miller,[73] Clinging to an Arctic Homeland

The Brooks Range separates traditional territories of two distinct cultures: The Gwich'in Athabascan Indians, forest dwellers to the south, and the Inupiat Eskimos, tundra dwellers and sea-faring people to the north. Like the Gwich'in, the once-nomadic Inupiat traveled extensively through their territory to hunt and fish. Both groups occasionally made long journeys over the crest of the mountains to trade with one another. Prior to 1850, battles and territorial skirmishes were not uncommon. Some Inupiat and Gwich'in bands fought over resources, such as the taking of caribou.

Lobbying on Capitol Hill, political demonstrations, and walks across America have replaced the more primitive warfare of the past. At issue is what lies on top, and what may lie beneath the Arctic Refuge coastal plain. For the Gwich'in the coastal plain is sacred ground, the place where the Porcupine caribou herd gives birth to tens of thousands of calves each year. The herd is the Gwich'in lifeblood, their most important cultural resource. They believe the vital birthplace of the herd should be left undisturbed. For the Inupiat, the coastal plain is an important hunting and fishing area, yet the corporate world has convinced many that, if developed, a promising storehouse of oil and gas beneath the tundra would bring them jobs, a fuel source, and millions of dollars. These differing views have polarized America's northernmost cultures.

Daniel Akootchook manifests his love for the outdoors in his happy outlook and a deep pride in his homeland. He has spent his entire life in Kaktovik, an Inupiat village on the Arctic coast, including a twenty-four year stint as a maintenance worker for a local school. When he began his job in 1964, prior to the Prudhoe Bay oil discovery, he earned two dollars an hour. When he retired in 1988, the oil-endowed North Slope School District paid him $27 an hour. Today, if he were still working, he would earn $41 an hour, or $80,000 per year. By comparison, the most a maintenance worker can earn in the neighboring Yukon Flats School District, which includes several Gwich'in villages, is about $19 an hour.

Yet, regardless of the wage-based economy, the Inupiat have continued to value their homeland and the resources that have sustained their traditional culture. The Inupiat will continue to hunt and fish, as sure as they will breathe. Daniel and other whalers are convinced that the loud seismic booming of offshore exploration once disturbed the bowhead whales' fall migration. To avoid the industrial noise, Daniel believes the whales moved farther offshore. The Inupiat villages of Alaska's North Slope, communities that depend on the whale for food, are united in their opposition to offshore oil drilling.

---

73. This is an abridged version of Ms. Miller's essay that appears in Subhankar Banerjee, Arctic National Wildlife Refuge: Seasons of Life and Land 132 ff. (Seattle: The Mountaineers Books, 2003). She is also the author of Midnight Wilderness: Journeys through Alaska's Arctic National Wildlife Refuge (Northwest Books, 2000) and other work described at www.debbiemilleralaska.com.

The Akootchooks and other families will soon have running water, as seventy homes will be hooked up to a new $60 million sewer and water system. This major construction project is providing many local jobs and is one example of the benefits that have come to the North Slope oil development. David's brother Isaac dreams of the day when Kaktovik residents will heat their homes with the natural gas that lies beneath them rather than barging in more costly fuel.

Yet there are other family members and villagers who feel differently, including Isaac's daughter, Jane, and her husband, Robert Thompson. They are outright opposed to any oil drilling in the Arctic Refuge. Robert, one of the most active hunters in the village, feels that the land environment is just as important as the sea, so he is opposed to any offshore or onshore oil development. "If they develop the coastal plain, huge areas will be off limits to hunting. Security guards will be telling us where we can and cannot hunt, I don't want to live in an oil field for the rest of my life," Robert says somberly.

* * *

The people of Arctic Village specifically call themselves the Nets'aii Gwich'in, which means "Mountain People," because they live in close proximity to the Brooks Range. Today the Gwich'in, at least seven thousand strong, live in fifteen scattered villages, in Alaska and in Canada's Yukon and Northwest Territories. As with the Inupiat in Kaktovik, much of the Gwich'in's traditional homeland is now protected in the Arctic Refuge. Additionally, the people of Arctic Village and Venetie, a nearby sister village, own title to 1.8 million acres of tribal lands that were initially set aside in 1934 as reservation lands under the Indian Reorganization Act.

Trimble Gilbert is a strong proponent of teaching youth about the Gwich'in culture through active, land-based learning. They study the historic caribou fences that were once used to funnel migrating caribou into keyhole-shaped corrals. Once the caribou entered the enclosure, hunters snared the animals and killed them with spears or bows and arrows. While the hunting technology has changed and wage jobs and store-bought food are readily available, the importance of the caribou has not diminished. The caribou provide as much as 80 percent of their diet, and the Gwich'in continue to make clothing from the hides and perform traditional caribou songs and dances. In addition to being people of the mountains, the Gwich'in commonly refer to themselves as "caribou people."

For this reason, the Gwich'in have strongly voiced their opposition to proposed oil development in the calving grounds of the Porcupine caribou herd. They consider the Arctic Refuge coastal plain sacred, calling it *Izhik Gwats'an Gwandaii Goodlit*, which means "the Sacred Place Where Life Begins." In 1988, Gwich'in leaders from Alaska and Canada gathered together in Arctic Village to form the Gwich'in Steering Committee, in an international effort to protect the caribou, their lands and their way of life. Since the 1988 gathering, dedicated Gwich'in leaders have worked tirelessly to protect the coastal plain from proposed development.

"Without the caribou, I don't think the Gwich'in people of Alaska and Canada would have survived for ten thousand years. No one should touch the birthplace of the herd. It is holy ground for the animals," Trimble says with reverence as strong as steel.

* * *

While the cash economy differs substantially between the North Slope Inupiat and the Gwich'in, I'm struck by the underlying similarities between the two cultures. Both the Inupiat and the Gwich'in are still deeply connected to the land and the waters around them. They share a profound love for their homeland. They both hunt and fish to feed their families and their neighbors. They share similar religious traditions. They both know that all the money in the world cannot replace a wilderness or a homeland, once it's lost. In one hundred years I hope that the caribou will still walk by the church window and the Gwich'in will sing their oldest songs, clinging to their precious wilderness and way of life.▪

NOTES AND COMMENTS

1.   Carol Rose argues that the goal of a free enterprise system should be to maximize the value of "the sum of private and public resources." The failure to take public resources into account, she says, "can impoverish us as a nation by decimating resources that are diffuse and difficult to turn into private property, but that are still immensely valuable ..." (see Section A, above). The bowhead whale and the caribou are certainly examples of such public resources. Is it possible to place a dollar value on such resources, given their central role in the cultures of the Inupiat and the Gwich'in? Can you identify other public resources in Arctic Alaska that are difficult to value?

2.   One way of valuing the whale and the caribou is by going to the store and finding the prices at which their products are being sold. We could then find the market price of substitute products—Big Macs instead of whale meat, polyester instead of caribou hide, etc. Classical economists refer to this as "substitution." Substitution is perhaps the most troublesome of classical economic concepts for many people. The concept of substitution is basically a simple one that we have all observed in practice. If a product becomes scarce, causing the price to rise, many people will choose to acquire a substitute product instead if it can provide an equivalent satisfaction at a lower price.

For example, when the housing market in Silicon Valley became tight and prices went through the roof, many people bought cheaper homes in Modesto and endured the long commute. As wild salmon became scarce and expensive, people began to buy the cheaper but relatively tasteless farmed product called euphemistically "Atlantic Salmon." If Coca Cola doubled its price, even confirmed Coke drinkers might switch to Pepsi.

No one doubts that substitution takes place. To classical economists, however, it is simply the natural operation of the market with no negative connotations. They simply assume away any problems by adopting the assumption that technological change can offset any limits to growth that might be associated with a finite supply of natural resources. *See, e.g.,* Robert M. Solow, Resources and Growth, 68 Amer. Econ. Rev. 5 (1978). If you hanker for wild salmon or a house in Silicon Valley, your nostalgia is simply a personal "taste" and thus does not deserve to be considered in economic calculations. As Robert Ayres puts it, "economists have preferred not to examine the concept of technological substitution too closely." Robert U. Ayres, Resources, Environment, and Economics 45 (John Wiley & Sons, 1978). *See also* Daniel S. Levy and David Friedman, The Revenge of the Redwoods; Reconsidering Property Rights and the Economic Allocation of Natural Resources, 61 U. of Chi. L. Rev. 493, 499–502 (1994).

Technology has undoubtedly provided us with substitutes for many resources that became scarce in the past. When whale oil declined it was replaced by petroleum derivatives. The niche formerly occupied by bison has been taken over by carefully hybridized cattle. Opportunities to hike in the wilderness are giving way to theme parks with virtual wilderness rides. To the classical economist this was simply progress, but today many people sense that progress may imply losses of ecological stability and resilience that deserve consideration. And people worry about the assumption that technology will always find a substitute for anything.

Not all economists today are blind adherents to classical theories, of course. A wide range of creative scholarship by economists and scientists from a variety of disciplines has addressed the perplexing issues related to declining resources and increasing waste. The relatively new field of ecological economics is devoted to such efforts.

> The environmental resource base upon which all economic activity ultimately depends includes ecological systems that produce a wide variety of services. . . . [One] useful index of environmental sustainability is ecosystem resilience, [which] is a measure of the magnitude of disturbances that can be absorbed before a system centered on one locally stable equilibrium flips to another. Economic activities are sustainable only if the life-support ecosystems on which they depend are resilient. . . . The loss of ecosystem resilience is potentially important for at least three reasons. First, the discontinuous change in ecosystem functions as the system flips from one equilibrium to another could be associated with a sudden loss of biological productivity, and so to a reduced capacity to support human life. Second, it may imply an irreversible change in the set of options open both to present and future generations (examples include soil erosion, depletion of groundwater reservoirs, desertification, and loss of biodiversity). Third, discontinuous and irreversible changes from familiar to unfamiliar states increase the uncertainties associated with the environmental effects of economic activities.

Kenneth Arrow *et al., Economic Growth, Carrying Capacity, and the Environment*, 268 Science 520 (April 28, 1995).

3. The Declaration of Principles on the Rights of Indigenous Peoples states that "Indigenous nations and peoples are entitled to the permanent control and enjoyment of their aboriginal ancestral-historical territories. This includes air space, surface and subsurface rights, inland and coastal waters, sea ice, renewable and non-renewable resources, and the economies based on those resources." (See Section A, above). Could the Inupiat argue that the coastal plain is their "ancestral-historical territory," and that they and not the Gwich'in are entitled to its "permanent control and enjoyment?" How might the Gwich'in respond to that argument?

4. In his book "Caribou Rising" (Sierra Club Books, 2004), Rick Bass quotes Calvin Tritt, a Gwich'in resident of Arctic Village as saying that the caribou make all of the Gwich'in stronger, not just the taking of them, but the eating. "We only harvest caribou during half of the year in autumn and winter, and we don't kill for sport or joy, but to sustain our people. Any other kind of meat doesn't give us the same energy." Bass says that "[later that afternoon two caribou] are butchered and cooked in the empty field across from the church. The severed heads are hung suspended from poles, tripods, to smoke above the coals. The wires and ropes from which they hand (a wire hook pierces their lips, like fish) are twisted so that the two heads spin slowly wreathed in that heat and smoke. The cheeks are the delicacy, as well as the eyes; there is nothing that is left unused, nothing wasted, and again, the relationship is so obvious, so simple, that even a first-time visitor can get it: the Gwich'in are the caribou, in almost every sense." How would Peter Singer and the animal liberation movement deal with the relative importance of the Gwich'in's desire to continue to live by hunting caribou and the caribous' presumed desire to continue their annual migration undisturbed?

5. THE CHANGING ARCTIC CLIMATE

The Arctic climate is currently warming and it is projected that the Arctic will get much warmer. The warming of the Arctic has already impacted the human environment. Arctic island communities are facing the possibility of evacuation. Higher temperatures have reduced the sea ice and thawed the permafrost along the coast. The decrease in sea ice has made the islands more vulnerable to storms, while the thawed permafrost has dramatically increased the erosion of the shoreline. Some communities, such as Shishmaref, Alaska, have lost fifteen meters of land in a single storm. See Elizabeth Kolbert, The Climate of Man, The New Yorker, April 25, 2005, pp. 56–58.

Indigenous people have reported that seasonal weather patterns are changing—snow quality is changing and there is more rain in winter. They also have noted that water levels in lakes are dropping and sea ice is declining. The ringed seal, upon which they depend for food, has become scarcer as sea ice has disappeared. Indigenous people also have stated that new species are appearing in the Arctic.

Annual average arctic temperatures are projected to rise 3–5°C over land, and up to 7°C over oceans. Winter temperatures are projected to rise even more dramatically, with increases of 4–7°C over land, and 7–10°C over the ocean. The Arctic Council completed a study in 2004 that determined that the amount, speed, and pattern of warming that has occurred in recent decades is unusual and is characteristic of the anthropogenic increase in greenhouse gases. The study relied on data that was gathered from ice cores and other sources. *See* Arctic Climate Impact Assessment, *Impacts of a Warming Arctic: Arctic Climate Impact Assessment*, 23 Cambridge University Press, (2004), available at http://www.acia.uaf.edu. (hereinafter "ACIA").

One of the key climate change indicators in the Arctic is sea ice because it is extremely sensitive to changes in air and water temperature. The ice cover over the Arctic Ocean has been decreasing by approximately 3% per decade. Sea ice has also become thinner—Arctic-wide the ice has thinned by 10–15%. Impacts of thinned sea ice include increased air temperature, decreased salinity of the ocean water, and increased coastal erosion. Additionally, the decreases in sea ice will amplify regional and global warming because of the reduced reflectivity of the ocean. Future declines of 10–50% in the sea ice are expected by the year 2100. If this trend continues, the sea ice could completely disappear in the summer. The loss of sea ice would reduce critical habitat for marine mammals and seabirds, including the ringed seals and polar bears that regularly occupy Arctic ice. *See* Cumulative Effects, Chapter 5. Snow cover in the Arctic has decreased by approximately 10% over the past thirty years. Models show that the snow cover will decrease by 10–20% more by the end of the century. Most of the decreases in snow cover are projected to occur in April and May. This earlier melting of the snow could lead to an earlier river runoff into the Arctic Ocean and coastal seas. *See* ACIA.

The warming of the Arctic will impact the Arctic ecosystem in many ways, including the vegetation, animal species diversity and survival, the permafrost, and the local and global climate. Additionally, the changing Arctic climate will affect the occurrence of catastrophic events—such as insect invasions and fires, and the human environment.

First, climate change will likely decrease plant species diversity. The projected losses of the species included whole groups of plants, such as all lichens, mosses or forbs[74]. Because the tundra has so few species, any loss of species has a proportionally greater impact on the community. This could have long-ranging impacts on animals and the soil. For example, caribou selectively graze forbs during lactation, while caribou depend upon lichen during the winter. *See* F. Stuart Chapin III, Joseph P. McFadden, & Sarah E. Hobbie, *The role of arctic vegetation in ecosystem and global processes, in* Ecology of Arctic Environments 97, 100 (Sarah J. Woodin & Mick Marquiss eds., 1997). [Special Publication Number 13 of British Ecological Society]

---

74. A broad-leaved herb other than a grass, especially one growing in a field, prairie, or meadow. *See* http://dictionary.reference.com/search?q=forbs (last visited Feb. 28, 2005).

Trees do not reflect sunlight as well as snow, which will result in increased thermal absorption. This warmer climate would then encourage more tree growth, creating a positive feedback. As vegetation increases northward, there will be an increase in carbon absorption. However, it is projected that this increase will not offset the increase in global warming from enhanced solar absorption. *Id.* at 106.

Second, the ACIA study found that warming of the Arctic will have an enormous impact on animal species. Several million birds migrate to the Arctic each year—the success of many species is dependent upon their breeding success in the Arctic. Breeding and nesting areas are likely to decrease significantly as the treeline advances farther north. Also, the increase in sea level will erode tundra in the north. The vegetation changes and the rising sea levels will contract the tundra to its smallest size in 21,000 years. It is projected that many bird species, including several endangered species, will lose more than 50% of their breeding areas during the next 100 years. Also, the warming of the climate could affect the timing of the insect hatching. In other words, the migration of the birds might no longer coincide with one of their major food sources.

The reduction of the tundra will reduce the grazing areas for many animals that depend upon the open areas of tundra and polar desert. Arctic species have adapted to the cold climate—these adaptations will limit the ability of these species to compete with invading, warmer-climate species. The quick pace of these projected changes will make it virtually impossible for the species to adapt to the warmer climate. Because of these factors, it is likely that species will react to the warming climate by relocating northward. As the species relocate northward—up to 1,000 kilometers in some cases—they will displace arctic species that are blocked from moving north by the Arctic Ocean. This process has already begun with some species of fish, birds, and butterflies. Because of these processes, many threatened species will go extinct, and some currently healthy populations of species are projected to decrease dramatically.

The ACIA study found that impacts of global warming have already been felt in the southernmost range of arctic animals, including polar bears. In the Hudson Bay area, there has been a 15% decline in both number of cubs born, and each cub's weight. Polar bears, seals, seabirds, and walruses are all dependent upon sea ice—they are unlikely to survive as a species if there is a complete loss of summer sea ice cover.

The changing climate also has impacted the Porcupine Caribou herd. Each year, the Porcupine Caribou Herd crosses the frozen Porcupine River to reach its calving grounds in the Alaska National Wildlife Refuge. Recently, the herd has been delayed when migrating north because deeper snow and freeze-thaw cycles have made their food less accessible, increased travel time, and weakened the health of the herd. The Porcupine River has been thawing earlier, which means that many cows have calved by the time they reach the river. Thousands of these newborn calves are washed away in the rushing river while trying to cross it.

Third, studies of the permafrost in the North Slope show that the near-surface temperature of permafrost has increased by 2–4°C in the century before the 1980's, and even more rapidly since then. *See* Cumulative Effects, Chapter 5. Permafrost will be strongly impacted by warming temperatures. The ACIA study projects that the southern limit of permafrost will shift northward by several hundred kilometers in the next century. Permafrost degradation is likely to occur over 10–20% of the present permafrost area. As the permafrost thaws, it is likely to affect buildings and structures because of uneven settlement. The uneven settling of permafrost will also impact forests.

The impact of the warming of permafrost will depend on whether the permafrost is continuous or discontinuous, i.e., permafrost interspersed with thawed ground. Continuous permafrost is stable—its temperature could rise several degrees before destructive thawing would begin. In the coastal plain and much of the foothills, the surface temperature of permafrost is generally $-6°$ to $-10°C$. This temperature is low enough that the permafrost would not start transitioning from continuous to discontinuous permafrost for several decades at the predicted rate of warming. However, sporadic permafrost with near-surface temperatures of 0°C is weak and more easily disturbed by warming. *See* Cumulative Effects, Chapter 5.

At current temperatures, the permafrost is receding an average of eight feet per year from the Beaufort and Chukchi Seas. This retreat can be expected to increase with a warming climate and retreating sea ice. The rapid withdrawal of the permafrost has resulted in the temporary persistence of areas of permafrost under the ocean for several miles offshore.

The offshore permafrost will be more vulnerable to engineering disturbance when it thaws. The temporary permafrost exists in an area of active exploration, including the Northstar project and the suspended Liberty project. The permafrost supports artificial islands, causeways, buried pipelines, and drill pads. The Northstar pipeline also is buried in the seabed for ten kilometers. The operating temperature of the pipeline is 85°F—oil began to flow through the pipeline in 2001. Heat from the oil will eventually thaw the permafrost and strain the pipeline. It is unclear when this will occur, or what the results will be. *See* Cumulative Effects, Chapter 5.

As permafrost warms, the ACIA study predicts that it will also impact the freshwater systems. Many shallow ponds and wetlands will dry out with the thawing of the permafrost. The ponds connect with groundwater when the permafrost thaws—the ponds are likely to drain if they lose more water through downward percolation and evaporation than they gain through snowmelt and precipitation.

A fourth impact from climate change will be a disturbance of local weather patterns. The Arctic climate is currently extremely dry. Most of the Arctic Islands receive less than 200 millimeters of precipitation annually. *See* E.C. Pielou, *A Naturalist's Guide to the Arctic* 1, 15 (University of Chicago Press 1994).

One effect of the global warming will be increased precipitation. This increased precipitation is due to the increased evaporation from the higher temperatures. Throughout the Arctic, the ACIA study estimates that precipitation—mainly in the form of rain—will increase by 20%. This increase in precipitation will occur mainly over coastal areas in the winter and autumn—at these times, the precipitation is projected to increase by over 30%.

Fifth, the ACIA study warns that warming of the Arctic will disrupt global climate patterns. The Arctic has a significant amount of control over the earth's climate. There are three processes by which the Arctic can cause additional climate change for the planet: (1) through albedo effects; (2) by affecting ocean circulation patterns; and (3) by changing the exchange of carbon between the atmosphere and arctic soils.

Snow and ice currently reflect most of the solar energy that reaches the Arctic. As the snow and ice begin to melt from rising temperatures, the land and water surfaces, which are much darker, will absorb more of the sun's energy. This is a feedback cycle—the absorbed energy warms the surface even more, which causes further melting, which then causes further warming. As stated above, the projected increase of forests at northern latitudes will also decrease reflectivity, because the trees will absorb more energy than the current tundra surfaces.

Arctic processes can alter ocean circulation patterns. The movement of ocean water transfers solar energy from the tropics to the poles. The current is driven by differences in heat and salts and is known as the *thermohaline circulation* ("thermo" for heat and "haline" for salt). If this thermohaline circulation is disrupted through decreased salinity of the ocean—from increased precipitation and river runoff, it will have two important impacts. First, the circulation currently carries carbon dioxide into the deep ocean—if it is interrupted, more carbon dioxide will build up in the atmosphere, leading to more global warming. Also, the disturbance of the current would slow the transportation of heat into the Atlantic, leading to cooling of Europe.

The third Arctic process that could affect the global environment is modification of the exchange of greenhouse gases between the atmosphere and arctic soils. The arctic peat holds some of the largest land-based stores of carbon. If the permafrost thaws because of the rising temperature, the organic matter will decompose, releasing methane and carbon dioxide into the atmosphere.

It is well known that large amounts of methane hydrates—methane in a solid frozen form—are associated with permafrost and cold ocean sediments. If the temperature of the permafrost or water near the ocean floor rises a few degrees, the ACIA study suggests that these hydrates could decompose, discharging methane, a powerful greenhouse gas, to the atmosphere.

Sixth, the warming of the Arctic will increase the occurrence of pollutants, insect species and forest fires. Increased precipitation in the

Arctic will likely increase the amount of persistent organic pollutants and mercury deposited in the Arctic. Additionally, the melting of accumulated snow and ice will release the pollutants contained within them. Non-native insect species from warmer climates will be able to survive in a warmer Arctic. Two such insects are the spruce bark beetle and the spruce budworm. The arctic trees are unable to resist these exotic species, which can have a significant deleterious effect on the forest health. With warming temperatures, catastrophic forest fires, such as those that plagued much of Alaska in the summer of 2004, are projected to increase. In the western United States, the amount of area burned has doubled over the last thirty years. These areas are projected to increase 80% over the next 100 years with the projected climate change.

6.   IMPACTS OF PETROLEUM PRODUCTION ON ALASKA'S ENVIRONMENT

Oil fields in arctic Alaska are bounded by the Colville and Sagavanirktok rivers on the arctic coastal plain and extend into the Beaufort Sea. Soils are frozen and snow-covered for eight or nine months out of the year. Surface waters of lakes and the coastal ocean are frozen nine months out of the year. The ice begins to form in early fall, and reaches its maximum thickness of two meters by March or April. *See* Joe C. Truett, Introduction 3, 5–6, in Truett & Johnson.

The effects from oil and gas development are numerous and diverse and somewhat difficult to categorize. The following section is divided into four general causes of environmental impacts: (1) spills, (2) waste disposal and habituation, (3) seismic exploration, and (4) oil field infrastructure. Additionally, there are also separate sections addressing caribou and restoration issues.

First, three substances are spilled most often in the Arctic: oil; diesel fuel, which is used for exploration; and saline water. The largest oil spill on the North Slope covered 18,300 square feet. The second largest spill after that was 5,400 square feet. *See* Cumulative Effects, Chapter 7. From July of 1995 to June 2001, there were 2,454 spills in Prudhoe Bay oil fields. *See* Ken Madsen, Under the Arctic Sun: Gwich'in, Caribou and the Arctic National Wildlife Refuge 1, 45, 47 (Westcliffe Publishers 2002).

Oil can kill most plant species in concentrations of twelve liters per square meter. Oil spilled on wet tundra can have a particularly severe effect—recovery can take ten or more years. When oil contaminates tundra ponds, it damages the birds that use the ponds. Recovery from these oil spills can often take several years. *See* Cumulative Effects, Chapter 8. Luckily, most spills on the North Slope have taken place on gravel pads supporting oil field equipment, and the gravel has minimized the extent of the impacts. *See* Cumulative Effects, Chapter 7.

Although the industry's record to date has been relatively good, the likelihood of spills caused by failure of the oil field infrastructure increases with the age if the field. The potential for failure is exacerbated by the fact that age-related maintenance costs will increase as the oil field's revenues decrease. Thus, there will be little economic incentive for oil companies to maintain declining fields. *See* Cumulative Effects, Chapter 4.

Future oil spills could have a significant impact on many animal species. If oil were spilled in broken ice, it would be hard to clean up, and bowhead whales would not avoid the oily water. Spilled oil harms the baleen apparatus of the whale—hair-like filaments that the whale uses to filter prey from the water. The oil would also erode areas of the skin, the conjunctival sac—the area around the whale's eye, and the whale's stomach. *See* Cumulative Effects, Chapter 8.

Studies of polar bears and oil spills have shown that oil ingested during grooming causes liver damage and eventually leads to death. Ringed seals absorb oil into their bloodstream, which also causes liver and kidney damage, eventually leading to death. *See* Cumulative Effects, Chapter 8.

In the period between 1986 and 1999, 929 seawater spills occurred because of North Slope oil and gas production. In total, 40,849 billion barrels of seawater have been spilled. Saltwater spills pose a problem because salts are not biodegradable, and are toxic to most plants. Although the spills of diesel fuel are not focused upon as much, the damage from these spills is persistent—diesel can remain in the soil for twenty years with little plant recovery. *See* Cumulative Effects, Chapter 7.

A second cause of environmental impacts in the Arctic is waste disposal and the attendant habituation. There are two main types of waste disposal—the injection underground of waste fluids, and the aboveground storage of solid wastes.

Fluid wastes are injected into previously undisturbed geological formations to dispose of them. A possible environmental effect from this practice is the escape of fluids to the surface. At least twenty wells in Prudhoe Bay have had fluid escape to the tundra surface. Ground water can also become degraded from the injection of waste. Not enough studies have been conducted on the sub-permafrost hydrologic system—it is thus unclear how often this contamination occurs. *See* Cumulative Effects, Chapter 6.

Solid waste disposal can contaminate the environment and affect the population dynamics of animals. *See* Cumulative Effects, Chapter 4. Some of the animals most impacted include grizzly, or brown bears, and arctic foxes. According to one study, grizzly bears that fed on anthropogenic food sources had lower cub mortality than bears that fed on natural food sources. However, once the offspring were weaned, they experienced a higher level of mortality. This mortality can be attributed to the habituation to humans. The habituation leads to the bears being killed by hunters near the Dalton highway, and in bear-human interactions near settlements and camps near oil fields. It is unclear whether this post-weaning mortality is affecting bears on a population level, although it has the potential to. *See* Richard Shideler & John Hechtel, *Grizzly Bear* 105, 127–28, in Truett & Johnson.

Arctic foxes have been affected in two main ways by oil field development. First, the presence of anthropogenic sources of food has modified the behavior of arctic foxes. The presence of human garbage has attracted arctic foxes to oil fields. Robert M. Burgess, Arctic Fox 159, 171 in Truett & Johnson. Second, oil field development has changed fox distribution and habitat use. Throughout the year, arctic foxes can be found in Prudhoe Bay camps, dumps, and worksites because of the availability of den sites. The increase in availability of food and shelter has led to an increase in the arctic fox population. A long-term increase in fox predation could decrease nesting success and population size of nesting shorebirds. *id.* at 159.

Seismic exploration is a third way that oil exploration can impact the arctic environment. Seismic exploration involves sending sound waves into the substratum so as to determine the oil potential of the area based on the rate and force of the returning echoes. Bowhead whales are likely to be affected by marine seismic surveys, exploratory and production drilling, boat and air traffic, discharges of pollutants, and island construction. As most seismic exploration is done in the open-water period, bowheads and seismic boats are in the same areas during fall migration. Bowhead whales avoid seismic ships in a zone of avoidance that extends for nine to fifteen miles around the ship. Noise from air and ship traffic displaces ringed seals as well as pregnant polar bears. Ringed seals have been shown to abandon breathing holes near seismic lines. *See* Cumulative Effects, Chapter 8.

Seismic surveys have had a long-term impact on the health of the vegetation. Some seismic trails from the 1940's are still visible in the Arctic. A U.S. Fish and Wildlife Survey in 1984–1985 of seismic trails in the Arctic National Wildlife Refuge has formed the basis for analysis of the impact of seismic trails. The original study looked at an aerial photo survey of 2,000 kilometers of seismic lines and 2,000 kilometers of trails used to move the support camps. Out of a random sample of 20% of the trails and lines, 57% had low disturbance, 27% had moderate disturbance, and 2% had high disturbance of the active layer and vegetation. In 1998, 15% of the trails showed disturbance from the air. In 1994, the active layer was thicker in about half of the disturbed plots than it was on adjacent control areas. The thickening of the active layer is the precursor to thermokarst. *See* Cumulative Effects, Chapter 7.

The potential for accumulation of permanently degraded seismic trails is great. Although only a small fraction of seismic trails fit into the "permanently degraded" category, a very large number of seismic trails— 32,000 miles from 1990 to 2001—are created. It is estimated that 27,000 miles of seismic trails will be created in the next ten years. If only 1% of the trails created in the next decade never recover—this is a conservative estimate, since the U.S. Fish and Wildlife Services ("USFWS") study showed that 3% of the seismic trails and 10% of the camp trails were still degraded after eight years—then 270 miles of permanently degraded land will be created in the North Slope ecosystem. *See* Cumulative Effects, Chapter 7.

The Alaska Department of Natural Resources engaged in a study of the impact of heavy equipment on North Slope tundra in 2004. The study, which was funded by the Department of Energy, concluded that snow is more important than ice in protecting the tundra during oil exploration. The study supports a change in policy that would open the exploration season much earlier in the winter. The old policy required six inches of snow, and twelve inches of frost before exploration could begin. The new standard still requires six inches of snow and twelve inches of frost, but it changes the definition of frost. If the standard had been in use in 2004, the tundra would have opened three to six weeks earlier than it did. *See* Yereth Rosen, Reuters, *Tundra Study Backs Longer Oil Search Season*, (Dec. 4, 2004).

Critics of the study have noted that the study was short-term and not peer-reviewed. Impacts on the tundra might take several years to be noticed. Additionally, the National Research Council found that even six inches of snow is not sufficient to protect the tundra in most of the North Slope. *See* Cumulative Effects, Chapter 7.

Oil field infrastructure, including gravel mining, is a fourth general cause of environmental impacts in the Arctic. Gravel for roads, causeways, islands, and other surface structures is mined from local riverbeds and gravel pits. The removal and placement of the gravel affects drainage patterns, the active layer, the movement of animals, the visual landscape, and snow accumulation. The highest flows in Arctic rivers occur when much of the floodplain is frozen. Because of this, areas modified by gravel mining take much longer to recover than comparable areas in lower latitudes. *See* Cumulative Effects, Chapter 4.

Billions of liters of freshwater are used to construct ice roads and pads in oil fields. Removing water from lakes can change the character of the lake. If the remaining water in the lake is so shallow that it freezes to the bottom, this can have a dramatic impact on organisms that depend on the lake for survival. Temporary ice structures in the ocean are used as causeways, islands, drilling platforms. These structures can alter ocean currents and fish migration. *See* Cumulative Effects, Chapter 4.

Construction infrastructure—roads, pipelines, buildings, and plat-forms—can alter animal migration. Both the physical presence of the infrastructure and the noise and traffic associated with the infrastructure have an impact on animal travel patterns. *See* Cumulative Effects, Chapter 4.

Vegetation is impacted by oil field infrastructure through the deposi-tion of dust and oil, and the compacting and removing of peat. Dust inevitably is created by the use of gravel roads. Studies have shown that all vegetation is eliminated from within sixteen feet of the most oft-used roads in Prudhoe Bay. The deposition of dust can affect the pH of the roadside areas, which changes the composition of the vegetative communities. *See* Cumulative Effects, Chapter 7.

Roads have many different impacts that combine to increase the thickness of the active layer and eventually produce thermokarst. The loss of the moss layer besides the road decreases the insulation of the active layer, while more snow accumulates along roads. The deeper snow keeps the surface warmer throughout the winter. The dust from the road is deposited on the snow; this dust absorbs more energy from the sun, which makes the snow melt earlier. All of these factors contribute to the thawing of the permafrost.

Roads often compact the active layer. Additionally, the construction of older roads involved removing the peat. Removing or compacting the active layer reduces the insulation, which results in the warming and eventual thermokarst of the permafrost. *See* Joe C. Truett, *Introduction*, 3, 5–6 in Truett & Johnson.

The indirect effects of oil fields, including dust, flooding, and thermokarst, have been estimated to be many times greater than the footprint of the infrastructure itself. Mapping studies from the 1980's show that wide areas along roads were affected by dust, thermokarst, intermittent flooding, gravel spray, vehicle trails, and trash. In heavily developed wet areas of the tundra, the ratio of the indirect affects of the road to the actual area of the road was 8.6:1. In heavily developed dry areas, the ratio of indirect affects to the area of the road was 2.4:1. The mean for all of the areas mapped was 6:1. *See* Cumulative Effects, Chapter 7.

Oil field infrastructure also has a negative impact on birds in the Arctic. Changes to the environment that affect birds—including shorebirds, Pacific loons, and others—have been classified as three types. The primary impacts are the actual footprint of facilities such as roads and gravel pads. Secondary impacts include modification of areas adjoining facilities due to drainage changes, dust, thermokarst, and human activity. Tertiary changes include habitat fragmentation from the oil field development and reduced nest success. *See* Declan M. Troy, *Shorebirds* 277, 292, in Truett & Johnson.

First, gravel placement results in direct habitat loss for most birds. However, gravel fill covers only a small percentage of the total area of the oil fields. Second, birds avoid developments such as roads and pads. During breeding and nesting, birds avoid the habitat near gravel fill. As the summer passes, birds avoid these areas less and less. Dust smothers vegetation, encourages alkaline plant development, and can increase nutrient availability. Greater densities of birds can be found in areas with high dust. Many birds appear to be attracted to these areas because of the earlier snowmelt caused by the dust. Some species of birds also frequent areas with thermokarst, while others avoid these areas. The effects of the tertiary impact of habitat fragmentation include inability to nest from habitat loss, and increased predation. *Id.* at 292–94. Nesting success for ground-nesting birds is exceptionally low in oil fields. *See* Cumulative Effects, Chapter 8. Spectacled and Steller's eiders are listed as threatened under the Endangered Species Act. Spectacled eiders have significantly lower nest success in oil fields, primarily due to predation. Reduced nest success has been enough in some cases to cause population declines, so any stability in oil field populations is the result of immigration. *See* Cumulative Effects, Chapter 8.

Caribou have been a major concern of both biologists and Alaska Natives. There are four[75] main identified caribou herds, distinguished by their different calving grounds. The largest is the Western Arctic Herd, which had 460,000 individuals in 2001. The other three are the Teshekpuk Lake Herd, with 27,000 individuals in 1999, the Porcupine Caribou Herd, with 123,000 in 2001, and the Central Arctic Herd, which had 27,000 individuals in 2000. All of the herds have been exposed to oil and gas development, but only the Central Arctic Herd has been continuously exposed to oil and gas activity. The calving and summer range of this herd lies in the Prudhoe Bay complex, and the rest of the year the herd is near the Dalton Highway and the Trans–Alaska Pipeline. *See* Cumulative Effects, Chapter 8.

During the summer, drilling sites and other infrastructure have a significant impact on caribou behavior.[76] Caribou avoid drilling sites completely within .7 miles of the site, and are less likely to use the area within two miles of a site. Those caribou that do enter the area within two miles of a drilling site spend less time sitting and lying down. Maternal caribou mainly avoid roads and pipelines within 1.2 miles of the infrastructure. *See* Cumulative Effects, Chapter 8. Older portions of the Prudhoe Bay Oil Field have a particularly negative impact on caribou because the low pipelines and infrastructure do not allow caribou to freely pass. *See* Stephen M. Murphy & Brian E. Lawhead, *Caribou* 59, 75–76 Truett & Johnson.

In late summer, the caribou are low on energy and nutrients. In particular, parturient and nursing caribou attempt to increase their caloric intake. The increased nutrition results in increased growth rates and survival of calves. Failure to gain enough weight in the summer can affect the ability of a caribou to conceive. One study showed that caribou that successfully conceived weighed significantly more than caribou that failed to conceive.

75. One researcher has stated that there were thirty-one recognized caribou herds in Alaska in 1997. Of these, twenty-five were stable or increasing, and six were stable or declining. *See* Warren B. Ballard, Matthew A. Cronin, & Heather A. Whitlaw, *Caribou and Oil Fields*, in Truett & Johnson.

76. In order to analyze the impact of oil and gas on animals, it is necessary to understand the concepts of *population dynamics*. First, the theory of *habitat selection* rests upon the idea that animals reproduce most successfully in the best available habitat. Thus, animals select the best available habitat for a particular use, and only choose poorer habitats when better habitat is not available. Also, when habitat selection is limited by population density, the population is likely to have a *source-sink population dynamic*. Source-sink populations occur when a species in a high quality habitat (*source*) has a higher reproductive rate than death rate. The extra individuals disperse into poorer quality habitats (*sinks*) that have a higher death rate than reproductive rate. Loss of source habitats can threaten the survival of the species even if much of the habitat occupied by the species remains intact. *See* Cumulative Effects, Chapter 8 at 98–99.

There are two ways that oil field disturbance could affect caribou at the population level. First, extra caloric output or failure to take in enough calories is the most likely way that oil fields will impact caribou at the population level. Caribou that encounter pipelines and roads spend less time lying down and more time walking and running. This increased activity burns more energy, which can affect the caribou's ability to gain enough weight. *Id.* Studies have shown that caribou are much more sensitive to not taking in enough energy than to expending too much energy. Thus, the inability to access high-quality forage would have a greater impact on caribou. Development affects this by preventing access to preferred habitat. Post-parturient caribou avoid roads and gravel associated with human activity for two or three weeks after birth. This avoidance of the road system forces the caribou into fragmented terrain farther away from oil field development. Oil field infrastructure can also reduce access to insect-relief and foraging habitats. The combination of the reduced forage and increased activity can affect the caribou's ability to conceive. The parturition rate of females exposed to oil field development from 1988 to 1994 was 64%, while females not exposed to development for the same period was 83%. High levels of insect harassment exacerbate the differences in parturition rates. *See* Cumulative Effects, Chapter 8.

A second consequence of avoidance of oil and gas infrastructure is a distribution into lower quality habitat, which can lead to increased exposure of predation. If caribou are displaced into habitat that has higher rates of wolves and grizzly bears, it could affect the population of the herd. The most vulnerable to predation are neonatal calves—the shift in location of calving activity has likely increased predation. *See* Stephen M. Murphy & Brian E. Lawhead, *Caribou* 59, 71–72 in Truett & Johnson.

7. FUTURE RESTORATION OF ARCTIC FACILITIES

Most of the environmental effects caused by oil and gas development accumulate because there is no scheme for restoration. Little progress has been made to restore older sites on gravel fill. Only approximately 1% of the 9,225 acres of land in the North Slope covered by gravel infrastructure has been rehabilitated. The Alaska Department of Environmental Conservation is aware of more than ninety contaminated sites from oil and gas development throughout the North Slope that have not been restored. The low rate of restoration is attributable to several factors, including the technical constraints imposed by the Arctic climate, the lack of regulatory demands for restoration, and the high cost of restoration. *See* Cumulative Effects, Chapter 7.

First, the exceptionally low temperatures, low precipitation, and short growing season in the Arctic all make restoration of vegetation difficult. Additionally, thermokarst is almost impossible to reverse, and can progress even after the primary disruption is finished. Second, restoration requirements for arctic oil and gas development are unclear. Section 404 of the Clean Water Act empowers the U.S. Army Corps of Engineers ("Corps") to issue permits for the placement of fill material into U.S. waters. Before

1979, the Corps did not utilize this authority, and it is estimated that about half of the gravel was filled without permits. The Corps does not have jurisdiction over these unpermitted sites. Even when the Corps does issue section 404 permits restoration is not mandatory. Less than 1% of the Corps' permits contain a restoration requirement with specific criteria for completion. Some permits—6%—require the permit holder to reuse gravel from existing sites. The Corps has posited that the landowner—the Bureau of Land Management, the state of Alaska, or the Mineral Management Service ("MMS")—has the proper authority to require restoration, rather than the Corps. *See* Cumulative Effects, Chapter 7.

The Environmental Protection Agency ("EPA") and the Corps have promulgated guidelines for the section 404 program that require "compensatory mitigation" for the destruction of wetlands throughout most of the United States. This mitigation includes the restoration of degraded wetlands, or the creation of artificial wetlands. However, the Corps and the EPA have stated that compensatory mitigation is not required on the North Slope. *See* Cumulative Effects, Chapter 7.

Federal agencies may require additional mitigation requirements in the leases they award on federal land. For example, no permanent facilities may be constructed in the National Petroleum Reserve–Alaska during the exploratory phase. Despite this, the Bureau of Land Management has not created any specific dismantlement, removal and restoration ("DRR") requirements in order to return the land to wildlife habitat and wilderness. *See* Cumulative Effects, Chapter 7. The MMS requires the removal of structures and the plugging of abandoned wells. However, in other parts of the United States, the MMS has required the removal of platforms and other obstructions. The MMS has no such requirement for North Slope gravel islands.

Exxon Mobil Corp. v. Commissioner of Internal Revenue

114 T.C. 293 (U.S. Tax Court, 2000).

■ SWIFT, J. In these consolidated cases, respondent determined deficiencies in petitioners' Federal income taxes for the years 1979 through 1982. [Exxon Mobil Corporation ("Exxon") accrued $204 million of dismantlement, removal and restoration ("DRR") costs during those years in regard to the anticipated expense of removing all facilities and equipment in the Prudhoe Bay Field when the field becomes unproductive in the year 2030. The Commissioner found that the accrual of these expenses was improper because the company had no legal obligation to dismantle its facilities and restore the site except for an obligation to plug abandoned oil wells.]

The Prudhoe Bay oil field is located in an extremely remote area 250 miles above the Arctic Circle on the North Slope of Alaska.... Because of its isolation and remoteness, labor, materials, equipment, and support services for major construction projects on the North Slope—in particular, for construction and installation of the Prudhoe Bay oil field equipment and facilities—must be imported, which significantly increases the costs of construction and of performing work on the North Slope. The oil companies' total $11 billion capital cost, in the 1970's and early 1980's, of installing and constructing the Prudhoe Bay oil field equipment and facilities was more than four times what the total cost would have been to install and construct a comparable oil field in the lower 48 States.

[Beginning in 1964, Exxon and other oil companies leased oil and gas rights from the owner of the Prudhoe Bay field, the State of Alaska, using the state's standard form for oil and gas leases, the DL–1 form. In 1967, the companies discovered] the largest oil and gas reservoir ever discovered on the North American Continent. As of 1967, the reservoir was estimated to contain 23 billion barrels of oil in place and 42 trillion cubic feet of natural gas.

In 1969, Exxon, ARCO, and BP announced plans to construct a 798–mile pipeline to transport oil recovered from the Prudhoe Bay oil field to the port of Valdez, Alaska, from which the oil would be shipped to the lower 48 States and to other destinations throughout the World. This pipeline came to be known as the Trans–Alaska Pipeline System (TAPS). TAPS was constructed under rights-of-way granted in 1974 by the Federal Government and Alaska to a group of seven pipeline companies, including subsidiaries of Exxon, ARCO, and BP.

The Prudhoe Bay oil field is laid out in a manner similar to an offshore oil field with centralized oil production facilities and isolated drilling locations. The oil well drilling equipment at the well sites rests on gravel pads called "well pads" from which multiple wells are drilled directionally underground into the oil reservoir. The six large production centers within the oil field are called "gathering centers" or "flow stations". Above-ground pipelines throughout the Prudhoe Bay oil field rest on vertical support members ("VSM's") and run from oil well drilling sites, to the production centers, and to TAPS. Pipelines within the Prudhoe Bay oil field are elevated on the VSM's above the ground at a sufficient height so that the tundra would not melt and so that moose and other wildlife would be able to traverse the pipelines. Due to the careful design, construction, and operation of the Prudhoe Bay oil field, the facilities and operations of the oil field have disturbed only 5,600 acres, or 2 percent, of the total land acreage at Prudhoe Bay.

In light of the costly and difficult construction conditions on the North Slope, the large industrial buildings and facilities at Prudhoe Bay (such as the flow stations and power plant), initially were constructed as large, modular buildings in plants near Bellingham and Seattle, Washington. The buildings, with the extensive equipment and facilities fully contained and installed therein, were then transported by special, oceangoing barges up the west coast of Canada through the Bering Sea to Prudhoe Bay where they were transported slowly over gravel roads to the installation sites in the Prudhoe Bay field.

To protect the North Slope tundra from thermal damage, the large plants and buildings constituting the oil production facilities at Prudhoe Bay were installed on pilings and gravel pads rising 4 to 6 feet above ground level. Once installed and in place at Prudhoe Bay, the modular segments of the large buildings were then joined together to form integrated facilities and buildings by connecting their structural components, piping, and electrical lines at interface points.

The oceangoing sealifts by which the equipment, buildings, and other facilities were transported by barge to Prudhoe Bay occurred in the 1970's and early 1980's. By July of 1984, construction, transportation, and installation costs of the wells, the equipment, the buildings, the pipelines, and the other facilities installed at the Prudhoe Bay field reflected, as indicated, a total capital cost to the oil companies of approximately $11 billion. The facilities included 645 wells drilled on 37 drilling sites, 980 acres of pits, 800 miles of above-ground pipelines, 3 flow stations, 3 gathering centers, a central power station, a central compressor plant, a base operations center, electrical lines and associated poles, switchgear, transformers, and an offshore seawater treatment plant completed in 1983 and connected to the mainland by a gravel causeway.

[Exxon and the other oil companies unitized the Prudhoe Bay field in 1977.[77]] The Unit Agreement incorporates therein whatever oil company DRR obligations existed under the DL–1 Leases with the State of Alaska. It also stipulates that no well site may be abandoned until "final cleanup and revegetation, if required, is approved in writing" by the State.... Current projections ... forecast that oil production from the Prudhoe Bay field will end approximately in the year 2030.

The [oil companies] originally believed that they might be able to recover and to market natural gas reserves located in the Prudhoe Bay field. To date, however, studies ... indicate that natural gas recovery from Prudhoe Bay will not be economically viable given the projected low price of natural gas relative to the high cost of recovering, producing, and transporting natural gas from the Prudhoe Bay field to world markets.[78] The extensive Prudhoe Bay oil field production facilities and the TAPS pipeline from Prudhoe Bay to Valdez, Alaska, were designed for the recovery, processing, and transportation of crude oil, not natural gas.... [and] it is anticipated that separate, new wells, processing, and transportation facilities would have to be constructed for the recovery from the Prudhoe Bay field of natural gas, if recovery of such natural gas someday would become profitable.

77. [Editor's Note: A unitization agreement obliges the various oil companies to share revenues and expenses in proportion to their share of ownership in the field. See pp. 310–16.]

78. Editors' note. In 2004, Congress authorized the construction of a pipeline to bring natural gas from Prudhoe Bay to the lower 48 states. Because private financing is required, it is unclear in mid–2005 whether the pipeline will be built. Exxon says that it is "focusing on securing the legislative and fiscal framework it needs to pursue the natural gas resources of Prudhoe Bay and Point Thompson in Alaska and the Mackenzie River Delta in Canada". http://www.exxonmobil.com/corporate/Newsroom/Publications/TheLamp_1_2005/html/story3B.asp (a. August 1, 2005).

The particular provisions of the DL–1 Leases that apply to DRR obligations of Exxon and of the other oil companies upon termination of oil production in the Prudhoe Bay oil field are vague and general. The principal language of the DL–1 Leases that describes what is to happen—upon termination of oil production at Prudhoe Bay—to the extensive oil production equipment and facilities located in the Prudhoe Bay field is found in paragraph 36, which reads oddly and ambiguously in terms of "rights" and "privileges" of the oil companies (not in terms of DRR "duties or obligations") as follows:

> RIGHTS ON TERMINATION. Upon the expiration or earlier termination of this lease as to all or any portion of said lands, * * * [Exxon] shall have the privilege at any time within a period of six months thereafter, or such extension thereof as may be granted * * * [by Alaska], of removing from said land or portion thereof all machinery, equipment, tools, and materials other than improvements needed for producing wells. Any materials, tools, appliances, machinery, structures, and equipment subject to removal as above provided which are allowed to remain on said land or portion thereof shall become the property of * * * [Alaska] upon expiration of such period; provided, that * * * [Exxon] shall remove any and all of such properties when so directed by * * * [Alaska]. Subject to the foregoing, * * * [Exxon] shall deliver up said lands or such portion or portions thereof in good order and condition. [Emphasis added.]

Language in paragraph 20 of the DL–1 Leases—pertaining generally to due diligence and to prevention of waste in the conduct of activities at Prudhoe Bay—does contain specific reference to Exxon's (and to the other oil companies') obligations to plug wells upon termination of oil production at the well sites. That language also makes general reference to Alaska regulations "relating to the matters covered by this paragraph" (namely, to due diligence and to waste). The language of paragraph 20, however, provides neither a description of DRR work that Exxon is or will be obligated to perform on leased property not associated with well sites nor specific reference to any Alaska regulations pertaining to broader fieldwide DRR obligations of the oil companies. Paragraph 20 provides, in part, as follows:

> DILIGENCE; PREVENTION OF WASTE. * * * [Exxon] * * * shall plug securely in an approved manner any well before abandoning it; * * * and shall abide by and conform to valid applicable rules and regulations of the Alaska Oil and Gas Conservation Commission and the regulations of * * * [Alaska] relating to the matters covered by this paragraph in effect on the effective date hereof or hereafter in effect if not inconsistent with any specific provisions of this lease. [Emphasis added.]

Language in paragraph 33 of the DL–1 Leases provides that Exxon (and the other oil companies), should it so choose, may abandon or surrender its interests in the leases to the State, provided it—

[places] all wells on the surrendered land * * * in condition satisfactory to * * * [Alaska] for suspension or abandonment; thereupon, * * * [Exxon] shall be released from all other obligations accrued or to accrue under this lease with respect to the surrendered lands * * *. [Emphasis added.]

In 1959, the new State of Alaska Constitution provided for "development, and conservation of all natural resources * * * for the maximum benefit of its people." Alaska Const. art. VIII, sec. 2. Alaska's land management policies generally allow development of Alaska's natural resources on condition that the environment be restored to the maximum reasonable extent upon completion of operations.

In 1967, the Alaska Oil and Gas Conservation Commission (AOGCC) issued regulations relating to plugging and abandonment of oil wells and to cleanup of oil well sites. These regulations are written only in terms of "plugging" the wells and cleaning up "loose debris" and restoring the well sites to a "generally level condition." The AOGCC regulations do not set forth or describe either specific or general DRR obligations of oil companies relating to the extensive Prudhoe Bay oil processing facilities not located at well drilling sites.

In 1972, in anticipation of oil production at Prudhoe Bay, a joint Federal–State commission was established to study Alaska land use issues. In 1979, the commission stated in its final report that development activities in the Arctic "should not lead to irreversible consequences" and that "areas impacted should be capable of restoration to a natural state upon the completion of development activities." (Emphasis added.)

In contrast to the generally vague language of the DL–1 Leases relating to oil company DRR obligations in the Prudhoe Bay oil field, language in the TAPS right-of-way provisions relating to DRR obligations of the oil companies which constructed and which operate TAPS is more specific. The Federal and Alaska right-of-way agreements for TAPS contain express language and provisions relating to oil company DRR obligations that specifically require the oil companies, upon termination of their use of the TAPS rights-of-way, to remove the facilities, improvements, and equipment. The Federal right-of-way agreements for TAPS state:

Stipulations for the Agreement and Grant of Right-of-Way for the Trans–Alaska Pipeline

1.10. Completion of Use

1.10.1. * * * [the oil companies] shall promptly remove all improvements and equipment, except as otherwise approved in writing by the Authorized Officer, and shall restore the land to a condition that is satisfactory to the Authorized Officer or at the option of * * * [the oil companies] pay the cost of such removal and restoration. * * * [Emphasis added.]

The State of Alaska right-of-way agreements for TAPS contain virtually the same language explicitly requiring the oil companies, upon shutting

TAPS down, to perform or to pay for the DRR work associated with dismantling and removing the pipeline and restoring the land.

As stated, the Federal right-of-way agreements and the permits relating to TAPS expressly require DRR work to be completed by the oil companies upon termination of pipeline operations. Also, in setting transportation rates for TAPS and other pipelines on the North Slope, the Federal Energy Regulatory Commission (FERC) has permitted owners of the pipelines to treat estimated DRR costs as capital costs of constructing the pipelines and therefore as costs that are recoverable ratably over the life of the pipelines through rate charges for transporting oil through TAPS and the other pipelines.

[During the relevant years, Exxon's policy was to accrue future restoration expenses only if they met the two-prong "all events test" test: (1) The work must be required as the result of local laws or regulations, or as part of a contractual agreement, and (2) The nature of the work is such that it is possible to estimate its cost. Thus, the law or agreement must specify the work to be performed or the conditions to be met.]

In preparing and filing its Federal corporation income tax returns for the years in issue, Exxon used the accrual method of accounting, and Exxon has consistently used the all-events test as the standard for determining when its liabilities accrue under the accrual method of accounting. On its consolidated Federal corporation income tax returns for the years in issue, Exxon accrued costs relating to its worldwide DRR obligations on the accrual method of accounting as its tax return preparers then understood the application to DRR costs of the all-events test of the accrual method of accounting. That is, DRR costs, for Federal income tax return purposes, were accrued only when the related DRR work was performed and then as current business expenses. As explained and as reflected in Rev. Rul. 80–182, 1980–2 C.B. 167, this was consistent with respondent's interpretation of how the all-events test of the accrual method of accounting applied to DRR costs.

In the 1980's, a Tax Court decision allowed, for Federal income tax purposes, the accrual of estimated future stripmining land reclamation costs relating to underground mines. See Ohio River Collieries Co. v. Commissioner, 77 T.C. 1369, 1981 WL 11319 (1981). As a result, in the late 1980's, Exxon raised in these pending cases with respondent via timely claims for refund the DRR cost accrual issue relating to estimated Prudhoe Bay DRR costs [but] respondent continues to disallow the accrual of estimated DRR costs.

Exxon's primary position in these cases is that estimated DRR costs relating to the oil-producing equipment and facilities located in the Prudhoe Bay field should be accruable, in the year such equipment and facilities are constructed and installed, as capital costs of the facilities and depreciated under the relevant tax depreciation system.

For Federal income tax purposes during the years in issue, an accrual basis taxpayer generally may accrue costs not yet paid in the year in which the costs satisfy the two-pronged all-events test of the accrual method of tax accounting; i.e., in the year in which all the events occur that establish the fact of the taxpayer's liability for the costs and in which the amount of the liability can be determined with reasonable accuracy. See *United States v. General Dynamics Corp.*, 481 U.S. 239, 243–244, 107 S.Ct. 1732 (1987*); United States v. Hughes Properties, Inc.*, 476 U.S. 593, 600, 106 S.Ct. 2092 (1986); United States v. Anderson, 269 U.S. 422, 437–438, 46 S.Ct. 131 (1926); sec. 1.446–1(c)(1)(ii), Income Tax Regs. As the Supreme Court has explained:

> It is fundamental to the "all events" test that, although expenses may be deductible before they have become due and payable, liability must first be firmly established. This is consistent with our prior holdings that a taxpayer may not deduct a liability that is contingent * * *. [United *States v. General Dynamics Corp., supra* at 243.]

The first prong of the all-events test looks only to whether the taxpayer's fact of liability for the costs in question has been established. This test may be satisfied even if it is not known when or to whom costs will be paid. A liability can be fixed even if there are procedural or ministerial steps that still have to occur before payment. Accrual should be deferred if the occurrence of those steps is sufficiently uncertain that they render the taxpayer's liability contingent. See, e.g., Continental Tie & Lumber Co. v. United States, 286 U.S. 290, 52 S.Ct. 529, 76 L.Ed. 1111 (1932). The mere speculative possibility that some future event will release the taxpayer from its liability does not prevent accrual. *See*, e.g., United States v. Hughes Properties, Inc., *supra* at 601–602, 606.

Exxon argues that the combination of the DL–1 Lease provisions, Alaska law, regulations, and oil industry practice, as of the end of each of the years 1979 through 1982, establish the fixed and definite nature of Exxon's future Prudhoe Bay DRR obligations regarding the entire Prudhoe Bay oil field. [Exxon's expert witness said that it] will have to plug all wells, close all reserve and containment pits, remove all above-ground pipelines and electrical lines, and remove all other structures, such as modular flow stations and gathering centers, ... dismantle, transport to barges, and transport off the North Slope the modules, pipelines, and electrical distribution systems, and leave the land in a clean and generally level condition. It is expected that Exxon ... will perform these DRR obligations around the year 2030.

In comparing the language of the right-of-way agreements relating to TAPS and to the other North Slope pipelines involved in the FERC rate-making proceedings, on the one hand, to the language of the DL–1 Lease agreements, on the other, Exxon's experts sense a common denominator or "idea" in the language of both sets of right-of-way agreements (namely, that removal of the equipment and related DRR work is "required" in each instance). We note simply that specific language relating to oil company DRR obligations is found in the TAPS right-of-way agreements, but, as we have explained, is not found in the language and provisions of the DL–1 Leases that relate to fieldwide oil production facilities at Prudhoe Bay.

Neither the language of paragraph 36 nor the language of paragraph 20 of the DL–1 Leases reflects fieldwide facility and equipment dismantlement, removal, or restoration obligations. As we have explained, paragraph 36 is written in terms of a "privilege" of the oil companies to remove equipment if they so choose or of an "option" of Alaska to have the equipment removed if it so elects. Paragraph 20 refers only generally to waste and due diligence, to preservation of the land, and to plugging abandoned wells. Fixed obligations to dismantle, remove, and restore the Prudhoe Bay fieldwide facilities and equipment are not reflected in the language of paragraph 20.

Further, as we have found, and contrary to Exxon's experts, AOGCC regulations in effect during the years in issue relate only to plugging, abandonment, and cleanup of oil well sites and do not apply to, and do not establish, DRR obligations of [Exxon] to the extensive Prudhoe Bay oil field equipment and facilities not located at oil well sites.

Again, we note that the right-of-way leases relating to TAPS and the regulations relating to oil well drilling sites reflect express language that imposes DRR obligations on the oil companies. The DL–1 Leases and the Alaska regulations, however, contain no such express language imposing fixed and definite DRR obligations on the oil companies relating to fieldwide production facilities located in the Prudhoe Bay oil field.

We believe the differences in language relating to DRR obligations are significant for purposes of the all-events test of the accrual method of accounting. We believe that specific DRR obligations relating to fieldwide oil production facilities could have been reflected in the DL–1 Leases or in the Alaska regulations were such obligations intended. Specific DRR language was used in the TAPS right-of-way provisions. No adequate explanation has been provided as to why specific language relating to DRR obligations . . . was not set forth either in the DL–1 Leases or in the Alaska regulations, other than that such DRR obligations with regard thereto, as of the years in issue, were not established. As the current Commissioner of the Department of Natural Resources for the State of Alaska acknowledged in his trial testimony herein, as late as 1997 no Alaska regulations specifically covered Prudhoe Bay fieldwide DRR obligations of the oil companies.

The 1979 joint Federal–State commission that studied Alaska land use issues and that concluded that development activities in the North Slope should not irreversibly damage the environment and that the environment should be "capable" of restoration upon completion of development activities imposed no fixed and definite DRR obligations on Exxon. An "expectation" of and the "capability" of restoration do not necessarily require restoration.

Exxon placed in evidence the extensive history, during the 1960's through the present, of the State of Alaska's supervision of oil company abandonment and cleanup operations of numerous North Slope exploratory well sites. Exxon emphasizes and argues that such history and practice and the AOGCC regulations (relating to abandonment of wells and to cleanup of well sites) together establish affirmative DRR obligations of the oil companies for all of the massive equipment and facilities located in the entire Prudhoe Bay oil field. One of Exxon's experts states in his report as follows: "The AOGCC's record of strict enforcement of cleanup requirements [for well locations] over the last thirty-one years * * * evidences the State's commitment to having its lands returned in good order and condition * * *." [Emphasis added.] We reject the equation, if that is what is intended by Exxon's expert, between well sites and the balance of the "lands" constituting the Prudhoe Bay oil field.

Contrary to our holding regarding fieldwide Prudhoe Bay DRR, we believe Exxon's Prudhoe Bay DRR obligations relating specifically to oil wells and to oil well sites are clearly set forth and established in the provisions of the DL–1 Leases and satisfy the first prong of the all-events test of the accrual method of accounting. Paragraph 20 expressly states that upon closing down wells, Exxon is to plug the wells and abide by Alaska regulations relating to such plugging. For the years in issue, Alaska regulations similarly required oil companies to plug and to clean up well drilling sites.

[The court also rejected Exxon's alternative argument that the future DRR costs should have been recognized as ordinary and necessary business expenses in the years the facilities were built.]■

NOTES AND COMMENTS

1. There are no complete estimates for the total cost of removing the approximately $50 billion worth of infrastructure on the North Slope. Phillips Petroleum has estimated that the cost of restoring the ninety-seven acre Alpine area will come to $50–100 million. Because this area has produced 30 million barrels, the restoration cost is equivalent to $1.67–3.33 per barrel. If this is an accurate estimate, the cost of restoring the 9,000 acres of the North Slope could range from $4.5–$9 billion. See Cumulative Effects, Chapter 7. State and federal bonds do not adequately cover the potential cost of restoration. The Alaska Department of Natural Resources requires $500,000 per company. The BLM requires bonds of $300,000 for the National Petroleum Reserve–Alaska, but the Army Corps of Engineers does not require any bonding. The Minerals Management Service requires $3 million bonds on the federal lands offshore, but even this amount is unlikely to cover the full costs of restoration. See Cumulative Effects, Chapter 7. Because restoration is technically difficult, not definitively required by the government, and expensive, it is unclear how much of the degradation caused by oil and gas development in Alaska will actually be restored.

2. To what extent is the Tax Court's decision relevant to the issue of whether restoration will actually take place in the year 2030 or whenever the fields are abandoned? Is the State of Alaska bound by the Tax Court's finding that the state leases don't require reclamation? The state was not a party to the litigation, although state agency witnesses testified that they

expected the oil companies to reclaim the site even though it was never specifically required. Does the court's decision have any effect on other oil companies who signed similar leases? (Complex issues of preclusion are beyond the scope of an energy law course.) In any event, when 2030 arrives, will anyone even remember that the decision took place?

3.   What will Exxon's moral responsibility be for reclaiming Prudhoe Bay when the company departs? Would David Spence's "rational polluter", who in order to maximize profit "will shift as many costs as possible to society," simply leave all of the buildings, roads and other facilities to weather the icy wind on their own? After all, the company has been told by a court that it has no legal duty to reclaim the site. Would the editors of the Economist say that it was improper corporate philanthropy to spend hundreds of millions of dollars of the shareholders' money on work they have no obligation to perform?

What would be the impact on the North Slope Environment of a failure to reclaim? Has most of the damage already been done? Or would the site turn into one of the nation's most difficult superfund sites requiring state and federal taxpayers to fund the cleanup? And what will the climate be like by that time? Will everything sink into the ooze that replaces the permafrost?

If you think that it is difficult to think so far ahead, skip to Chapter 14.D and read how a contemporary court deals with the issue of whether ten thousand years is a long enough time framework for consideration of the risks associated with the spent fuel rods of nuclear power plants.

One of the ironies of the North Slope is that the greatest risk to the environment of the Arctic may not come directly from petroleum industry operations but from a phenomenon that Exxon has long refused to recognize—the warming of the climate caused by the increasing use of fossil fuels and the release of methane. And because of the long lag time of greenhouse gases, the remediation of climate change may be much more difficult than even the mammoth task of reclaiming the surface of the North Slope. (See Chapter 16.)

In addition, scientists have discovered that the air and water currents in the Northern Hemisphere have had the effect of concentrating both heavy metals, such as mercury, and persistent organic pollutants, such as pesticide residues, in both human and other animal occupants of the Arctic. While the current status of the science makes it difficult to assess the long-term impact of these concentrations, they have become an issue of serious concern to the eight nations that occupy portions of the Arctic region. *See* Marla Cone, *Silent Snow: The Slow Poisoning of the Arctic* (Grove Press, 2005).

When humans cause disturbance outside the framework of historical precedent, the results are unpredictable. The key question is whether scientists can identify the limits beyond which we risk ecological collapse, and whether we can develop laws and policies that will keep us within those limits. Can we tell the difference between (1) human activities that merely imitate cyclical changes to which ecological systems are prepared to adapt, and (2) human activities that cause linear, unidirectional, continuous change that takes us into realms beyond the experience of ecological systems. We can hope to cope with cyclical changes in the natural world through a better understanding of ecological processes. But some of the changes humans are causing seem to be unidirectional rather than cyclical. The rate of increase of nitrogen in the water and carbon dioxide in the air, for example, seem to be steady and inexorable.

The first generation of environmental laws sought to ameliorate human activities that were making highly visible changes in the natural environment that seemed irreversible, such as opening new oil fields. Today, however, the gradual, insidious and seemingly inexorable change caused by human activities such as nitrogen deposition and greenhouse gas emission are among the most serious problems. Unless we can counteract such trends, we may be venturing into areas beyond the ability of science to foresee the effect on the natural world.

CHAPTER 10

INTRODUCTION TO ELECTRICITY

A. HISTORICAL DEVELOPMENT OF THE REGULATED UTILITY

We will now look at some of the key issues in the law relating to one of the most important forms of energy, electricity. The electric industry is in the midst of rapid and ongoing changes. To understand why these changes are taking place and what their impact will be it is necessary to understand some of the history of the industry.

1. INTRODUCTION OF ELECTRIC TECHNOLOGY

Water power, coal, oil and natural gas are primary forms of energy resources. They are found in nature and can be utilized directly into useable energy. Electricity is what is known as a secondary energy resource. Electricity is also found in nature, as Benjamin Franklin proved in the mid–18th century with his famous experiment in which he flew a kite during a thunderstorm to determine whether lightning was in fact electricity. But our ability to harness natural electricity has been very limited. For all practical purposes, we make our electricity from one of the primary energy resources listed above or from nuclear fission, to be discussed in Chapter 14.

James Trefil, A Scientist in the City

(Doubleday, 1994).

Electricity is different from other kinds of energy. When you turn on a light or use an electric tool, you don't need the source of the energy in the same building. In fact, the energy that drives the lights that allow you to read this book was probably generated some tens (if not hundreds) of miles from where you are sitting. Electricity provides a way of separating the generation of energy from its use.

Our modern electrically driven society owes its existence to an English scientist named Michael Faraday. In a series of experiments in 1831, he discovered that when a magnet is moved, an electric current will flow in wires near it. This discovery, part of Faraday's basic research into the nature of electricity, made it possible to build machines that could convert the energy stored in coal into electric energy carried in wires.

A simple generator [is] the device that carries out this conversion. A loop of wires is spun around between the poles of a magnet. From the point of view of someone on the loop, the magnet is always moving, so a current will always flow—first one way, then the other. This so-called alternating current (AC) can be run through wires to the place where it is to be used. To get the electricity from a power plant to your house may require that it travel through many miles of wire, from huge power lines on pylons to the smaller wires that bring it into your home to the little cord that runs from the wall to your lamp.

So long as you have an energy source that can make a shaft spin, you can use that energy to produce electricity. The most common technique is to boil water to make high-pressure steam and then squirt that steam against curved blades attached to the spinning shaft (a device like this is called a steam turbine). It makes no difference how you make the steam—it can be (and is) done routinely by burning coal, oil, or gas, or by extracting heat from a nuclear reactor. You can also turn the shaft by damming a river and then letting water fall from a great height onto the turbine blades.

Today, the advantages of electricity for supplying a city's energy are so obvious that there would seem little point in arguing about them. When electricity was first produced commercially in the late nineteenth century, however, it was far from clear that it would prevail over its competitors. The first use of electricity was for lighting, one of the landmarks of urban electrification occurring in Chicago on April 25, 1878, when a jury-rigged system of batteries and lamps lit up Michigan Avenue for the first time.

The demonstration showed up both the strengths and weaknesses of the new technology. The lights used weren't the steady incandescent lights we're accustomed to today but, rather, the kind of carbon arc lights now used only for searchlights and stage lighting. They produce light by passing an electric spark between two cone-shaped carbon rods. In the Chicago demonstration, the result was an intense light: the two electric lamps produced an illumination equivalent to over 600 gas lamps. But they required constant adjustment as the carbon rods burned down. In addition, electrical systems in those days were unreliable in the extreme. The night after that first successful illumination in Chicago, for example, the whole system burned out, and it was months before another demonstration could take place.

The first people to use electrical power in a big way were stores and hotels in downtown business districts. At this stage of development, the main question was whether electricity would be generated locally, by each user, or whether there would be a central utility selling electricity to customers. Many businesses (Wanamaker's store in Philadelphia and the Palmer House hotel in Chicago, for example) installed their own generators. The first central power station was built by Charles Brush in San Francisco in 1879, but at that time the price of copper wire was so high that it was only economical to deliver electricity about half a mile—8 city blocks.

You can't imagine a city with generating plants every 16 blocks. Before our modern system could emerge, with its far-flung power plants and long transmission lines, a huge number of engineering advances had to take place. There's no single thing you can point to and say, "Here's the invention that made it all happen." Instead, there was a steady progression of nickel-and-dime developments that made it possible to generate electricity in large amounts and send it out over long distances—a better valve on a generator here, a better switch on a transmission line there. In the end, such developments wound up not only beating out gas lamps but giving our cities an entirely new shape.

There is no question that electricity is the energy form of choice for urban America. The energy history of our cities over the past century has seen the constant displacement of direct burning of fuels by electricity. The gas lamps were the first to go, except in "olde townes," where they are kept for their historical associations. They were followed by steam-powered factories and steam locomotives, and it probably won't be long before the gasoline-powered automobile joins the list. Let's face it: there's something very attractive about having energy available when you want it, while someone else has to deal with the pollution and other social costs of its generation.■

2. The Growth of the Central Station

When we think of the history of electricity in the United States the first name on everybody's lips is that of Thomas Alva Edison. After hundreds of hours of failed experiments with different experiments with different materials, cotton sewing thread was carefully carbonized, inserted into a glass evacuated by suction pump and connected to electricity supply form a dynamo. The light bulb "burned like an evening star," and we have the exact beginning of a new era for civilization: October 21, 1879. Vaclav Smil, Energies 158–159, The MIT Press (1999).

The great inventor of the light bulb, the phonograph and countless other products was also a pioneer in the generation and distribution of electricity. In 1882, when his company's Pearl Street generating station first delivered electric light to buildings throughout Wall Street, he became a national hero. Neil Baldwin, Edison: Inventing the Century (Hyperion, 1995).

Edison's talents were more on the creative side than on the management side. Credit for the development of the management model for delivering electricity that prevailed throughout the 20th century—the vertically integrated public utility monopoly—is generally given to one of Edison's lieutenants, Samuel Insull, who left Edison's employ in 1892 to assume the presidency of Chicago Edison Co. The great depression of 1893 hit the company hard, but Insull pulled it out and led the company, which became Commonwealth Edison, until the depression of the 1930s, turning it into a widely copied model of corporate organization.

As you read the following excerpts from Harold Platt's book on Insull and his successors (a book that is well worth reading in full) ask yourself whether the key ideas that Insull developed are still appropriate to today's conditions; in particular, (1) the "central station" concept, in which electricity is generated at a central power plant and distributed to customers by wires, and (2) the demand/commodity rate design, which was discussed in Chapter 8.

Harold L. Platt, The Electric City

(University of Chicago Press, 1991).

In spite of Edison's faith in the central station concept, electrical technology seemed to contain inherent diseconomies of scale. Practical experience continued to accumulate in favor of the self-contained, "isolated" plant for the large consumer of electric lighting. Unit costs (and hence rates) were highest for small consumers, since they made the least efficient use of the station's generating equipment. As more lights were burned for longer periods, the cost of a unit of electricity—expressed as a kilowatt-hour (kWh)—declined. When the equipment was used more fully, the utility's huge capital costs were spread over more units of electricity, making each unit cheaper to generate. The resulting equation between rates and costs appeared to point irreversibly toward the eventual triumph of the self-contained system. As a customer's use increased, it would reach a point where significant savings could be gained from disconnecting the utility lines and purchasing a self-contained system of the appropriate size., In response, utility companies could offer discounts to large consumers, but at the expense of shifting a heavier burden of capital costs onto the small consumers. The result would be rates beyond the reach of most city dwellers who badly wanted to install the new technology.

More than any other individual, Samuel Insull solved the problems inherent in electrical technology and put the central station on a sound economic footing. Great ambition, international background, apprenticeship with Edison, and faith in technological progress combined to give the English immigrant a unique perspective on the problems facing local utility operators.... in the years leading up to his arrival in Chicago in 1892....

The state of the electrical industry in Chicago at the time of Insull's arrival can be described simply as one of chaotic growth. He would have to use all his considerable skills and talents to prove the superiority of the central station approach to meeting the city's electrical energy needs.... Within municipal borders alone, the city inspector's report of 1892 listed 18 central stations and 498 self-contained systems that were powering a total of 273,600 incandescent lights and 16,415 arc lamps.

The resulting crazy quilt of small distribution grids growing out from jerry-built central stations raised serious doubts about the ability of any single utility company to attain the economies of scale necessary to beat the competition of the self-contained system and cheaper sources of light and power. Perhaps the greatest shortcoming of the Edison system was its DC distributors. They used low voltage or "pressure," which made transmission at a distance extremely costly in terms of copper wiring and energy losses. The DC grid works much like a system of water mains. Larger and larger mains are needed to pump water to more distant points at a constant pressure, In a similar way, the diameter of the copper cables had to be enlarged in proportion to increases in both the size of the electrical load and the distance of transmission....

Operators of Edison systems faced a challenge even more threatening to their futures after the appearance in 1886 of an entirely new electrical technology using alternating current (AC). As the name implies, a generator creates a flow of electricity that rapidly alternates back and forth in a circuit. In contrast, in a DC system electricity flows in a single direction around a circuit. The critical, practical difference between the two was the unequivocal superiority of AC for transmitting electricity at a distance. Alternating current could be sent efficiently at high voltage or "pressure," which meant that comparatively inexpensive thin copper cables could be used without suffering unacceptable energy losses. The transmission of energy became increasingly efficient as the voltage was raised. To achieve high-voltage transmission, a passive device called a transformer was used, first to boost the voltages at the generator station for long-distance transmission and then to reduce it for local distribution at the service area.

Championed by George Westinghouse, the AC system threatened a fatal economic blow to the backers of Edison's DC technology. In the late 1880s, local companies using Westinghouse equipment began operating in middle-class communities such as Englewood on the South Side and Evanston on the northern border of the city. The applications of the early AC systems were restricted to incandescent lights and did not include practical motors or streetlamps, but the obvious advantages of the AC distribution grids made the technology ideal for the metropolitan area's vast expanse of low-density residential housing.

Over the next five years of depression and crisis between 1893 and 1898, Insull completed his plan to acquire all the central stations and their franchises in the Loop. Hard times undoubtedly helped persuade the small companies to sell out, especially since Insull followed a policy of offering generous terms. In most cases the equipment of these shoestring operators was simply junked, and the customers were connected to the Edison company lines. Added together with new light and power business in the Loop, the growth of the utility was extremely impressive during a period of general economic distress. For example, the Harrison Street Station had to be expanded by 167 percent from a maximum output of 2,400 to 6,400 KW to keep up with the peak demand. The use of electricity rose from 6.6 million kWh in 1893 to almost 11 million kWh in 1897, an average annual increase in consumption of about 18 percent.

But to Insull's dismay, generating all the CBD's electric business by a modern central station did not save enough to undercut the competition of self-contained systems, let alone gas lighting in the home. To be sure, the Harrison Street Station, with its more economical engines, generators, and fuel-handling equipment, could be expected to reduce the company's operating costs. And the growth of demand in the Loop would probably repay the investment capital sunk in the copper transmission line to link the riverfront plant to the Adams Street building. Yet, as Insull admitted, "no one in the central station business at that time really understood its fundamental economics."

During the depression, rates remained at luxury levels. Complaints from businessmen about high prices replaced the initial enthusiasm for the novel technology. Even in the homes of the affluent middle classes, the common practice was to use electric illumination only in the parlor when guests were present. After they left the light bulbs would be turned off, leaving the gas jets lit in the living quarters. The popularity of dual gas-electric chandeliers was a testament to the high cost of better lighting in the home.

The World's Fair of 1893, however, provided important clues on how to remove these supply-side constraints. For the electricians and the scientists, Chicago's exposition had technical as well as cultural lessons [that] demonstrated the principles of a universal system of distribution. Westinghouse employed a recent invention, the rotary convertor, to convert AC to DC for use by the intramural elevated railway. When coupled with the transformer, the rotary convertor provided a technological means of removing the constraints of restricted distribution areas. Electricity generated at a central station could now be boosted to high voltage by a transformer for long-distance transmission and then changed at local substations by transformers and convertors to meet the particular needs of the distribution area. The model city of 1893 taught Insull and other electrical men in Chicago that there was no real "battle of the systems" between AC and

DC. The most important lesson of the World's Fair was that the two systems could be harnessed together to deliver a complete range of electrical services throughout the city.

Insull soon applied the lessons of the model city to the real one, making Chicago Edison first or second to put the rotary convertor into commercial use. In August 1897 electricity from the Harrison Street Station was transmitted at 2,300 volts to the Twenty-seventh Street Station, converted back to DC, and fed to the homes and businesses of the Near South Side. Two years later the first true substation, containing no generating equipment, was jerry-built on the North Side to help handle periods of peak demand from 4:00 p.m. to midnight. Within a few months, the cost efficiencies convinced Insull to shut down the nearby Clark Street Station and convert it into a full-time substation.

More important, these experiments proved the feasibility of a metropolitan power network. Insull was quick to appreciate the economic implications of the new technology for supplying electrical energy at a price lower than previously possible. The combined AC–DC system suggested a hierarchy composed of a few efficient power plants and a citywide network of substations where electricity would be transformed to meet the needs of each local district. This novel concept of central station service led Insull almost immediately to expand his monopoly plans from the CBD to encompass the entire city. In just two years between 1897 and 1898, he was able to achieve this major goal owing to his control of key patent licenses and a measure of incredible good luck.... The resulting concept of a central station hierarchy, together with the monopoly he had obtained, put Insull on the threshold of creating a metropolitan network of power. Yet all this technical and business success would mean little unless Insull also found an answer to the riddle of rates for the large consumer as well as the small residential customer. Electric rates had to be cut sufficiently to compete with the self-contained system and cheaper sources of artificial illumination. Only then would the demand for electrical energy reach a point where true economies of scale could be achieved.

As with the rotary convertor, an invention helped Insull solve the equation of utility costs and consumer rates. But in contrast to the hardware displayed at the World's Fair, the Wright demand meter did not directly answer the question of how to undersell both the self-contained plant and the alternative sources of artificial illumination. Instead, this ingenious device provided Insull with an "aha" experience that suddenly made the pieces of the puzzle fit together. All the economic requirements to beat the competition fell into place once he grasped the peculiar, instantaneous relationship between supply and demand that is inherent in electrical systems. As Insull testified, the demand meter "first taught us how to sell electricity."

Insull first heard about the innovative measuring instrument in 1894 while visiting his homeland. Recently invented by Arthur Wright of Brighton, England, the meter recorded not only a customer's amount of consumption but also the timing and the maximum level of his demand.

Intrigued by the device, Insull returned to Chicago but sent his chief electrician, Louis Ferguson, to make a thorough study of its use in Brighton. The engineer returned with an enthusiasm for the metering system that soon infected Insull. In September 1897 the Chicago Edison Company started making a practical test of the measuring device. Within a few years, Wright's invention replaced most of the utility's other meters.

The demand meter showed Insull that electric companies did not work "just as the gas companies do." On the contrary, the two were fundamentally different. The storage tanks of the gas companies allowed them to even out their production schedules and make maximum use of the equipment on a twenty-four hour cycle. In this way gas companies could keep their capital investments in central station machinery to a minimum, because there was no need for expensive but little-used equipment to meet brief periods of peak demand on the system. In contrast, electric companies had to keep an instant balance between demand and supply or suffer service blackouts and equipment damage. To be sure, storage batteries could help meet periods of peak demand, but they had serious drawbacks of their own: they were expensive, cumbersome, dangerous, and very inefficient. Whether to purchase batteries or extra generating equipment to meet periods of maximum demand remained a problem.

Helping Insull break free of his mentor's teachings, the demand meter gave him the insight to recalculate the equation between the electric utility's costs and the customers' bills. Wright's invention suggested a new method of ratemaking with a two-part bill to replace the traditional flat charge. A customer's energy consumption (the number of kilowatt-hours of electricity recorded by the meter) corresponded to the company's operating expenses. The measure of peak demand on the meter represented the customer's share of the capital invested in generating equipment that had to stand ready to serve him. The utility would use each customer's maximum demand to apportion equally the cost of financing the utility's plants and equipment. This primary charge serviced the interest payments on the company's bonded indebtedness, which constituted about 70 percent of its total expenses. The demand meter would determine the number of kilowatt-hours for which to charge each customer at the higher primary rate. A much lower secondary charge would be levied for any consumption beyond that monthly minimum number of units of electricity. The primary rates were fixed for all customers, but the secondary rates were discounted on a sliding scale to encourage greater consumption.

In this way a two-tier rate structure promised to cut the bills of both the small household and the large commercial enterprise. In effect, residential customers would pay a smaller proportion of the utility's financial costs because they had relatively small peak demands. The net result of the two-tier system would be a lower effective rate for each kilowatt-hour of energy. For the most part, the heavy burden of the utility's interest payments would be absorbed by the large consumers of light and power. At the same time, they would benefit from the discounts for heavy use of the equipment, which would progressively reduce their net rate of charge for each kilowatt-hour of electricity. In this way a two-tier system of ratemaking was structured to encourage every type of consumer to use more energy.

During the second half of 1899, Insull not only talked about the future, he began taking practical steps to get there as soon as possible.... The Chicago utility announced a two-tier system of rates for light and power. For the average residential customer, the new method of billing translated into an immediate 32 percent savings, or a net reduction from 19.5¢ per kWh to 13.33¢. At the same time, the utility extended a special incentive to new customers by offering to install six lighting outlets free of charge.... During the crisis of the nineties, rapid improvements in central station service offered comforting reassurance to a nation torn with doubt about the power of technology to promote social justice and democracy.■

NOTES AND COMMENTS

1. Samuel Insull eventually built up a complex of holding companies that exercised operating control over most of the electric utilities in the United States by the 1920s. By making a large share of the stock in the actual operating companies nonvoting, Insull controlled half a billion dollars worth of electric utility assets in 1930 with a capital investment of about 27 million dollars. Leonard S. Hyman, America's Electric Utilities: Past, Present and Future 106 (Public Utilities Reports, Inc., 6th ed. 1997).

2. The Insull empire collapsed in the depression of the 1930s. Many of the operating companies went bankrupt and their stockholders lost their entire investment. In response, Congress passed the Public Utility Holding Company Act of 1935, which gave the Securities and Exchange Commission oversight responsibility for companies that owned ten percent or more of the shares of an electric or gas utility. 15 U.S.C. § 79.

3. ELECTRICITY GOES NATIONAL

Once the technology for sending electricity long distances was developed, it soon became clear that the state boundary lines often made no economic sense to an electron. Many communities and businesses found it more efficient to obtain their power from a nearby plant in another state rather than from a plant in their own state that might be farther away or more expensive.

Public Utilities Commission of Rhode Island v. Attleboro Steam and Electric Co.

273 U.S. 83 (1927).

■ SANFORD, J. This case involves the constitutional validity of an order of the Public Utilities Commission of Rhode Island putting into effect a schedule of prices applying to the sale of electric current in interstate commerce

The Narragansett Electric Lighting Company is a Rhode Island corporation engaged in manufacturing electric current at its generating plant in the city of Providence and selling such current generally for light, heat and power. The Attleboro Steam & Electric Company is a Massachusetts corporation engaged in supplying electric current for public and private use in the city of Attleboro and its vicinity in that State.

In 1917, these companies entered into a contract by which the Narragansett Company agreed to sell, and the Attleboro Company to buy, for a period of twenty years, all the electricity required by the Attleboro Company for its own use and for sale in the city of Attleboro and the adjacent territory, at a specified basic rate; the current to be delivered by the Narragansett Company at the State line between Rhode Island and Massachusetts and carried over connecting transmission lines to the station of the Attleboro Company in Massachusetts, where it was to be metered. The Narragansett Company filed with the Public Utilities Commission of Rhode Island a schedule setting out the rate and general terms of the contract and was authorized by the Commission to grant the Attleboro Company the special rate therein shown; and the two companies then entered upon the performance of the contract. Current was thereafter supplied in accordance with its terms; and the generating plant of the Attleboro Company was dismantled.

In 1924 the Narragansett Company—having previously made an unsuccessful attempt to obtain an increase of the special rate to the Attleboro Company—filed with the Rhode Island Commission a new schedule, purporting to cancel the original schedule and establish an increased rate for electric current supplied, in specified minimum quantities, to electric lighting companies for their own use or sale to their customers and delivered either in Rhode Island or at the State line. The Attleboro Company was in fact the only customer of the Narragansett Company to which this new schedule would apply.

The Commission thereupon instituted an investigation as to the contract rate and the proposed rate. After a hearing at which both companies were represented, the Commission found that, owing principally to the increased cost of generating electricity, the Narragansett Company in rendering service to the Attleboro Company was suffering an operating loss, without any return on the investment devoted to such service, while the rates to its other customers yielded a fair return; that the contract rate was unreasonable and a continuance of service to the Attleboro Company under it would be detrimental to the general public welfare and prevent the Narragansett Company from performing its full duty to its other customers; and that the proposed rate was reasonable and would yield a fair return, and no more, for the service to the Attleboro Company. And the Commission thereupon made an order putting into effect the rate contained in the new schedule.

From this order the Attleboro Company prosecuted an appeal to the Supreme Court of Rhode Island which [held] that the order of the Commission imposed a direct burden on interstate commerce and was invalid because of conflict with the commerce clause of the Constitution; and entered a decree reversing the order and directing that the rate investigation be dismissed. 46 R. I. 496.

It is conceded, rightly, that the sale of electric current by the Narragansett Company to the Attleboro Company is a transaction in interstate commerce, notwithstanding the fact that the current is delivered at the State line. The transmission of electric current from one State to another, like that of gas, is interstate commerce, and its essential character is not affected by a passing of custody and title at the state boundary, not arresting the continuous transmission to the intended destination.

The petitioners contend, however, that the Rhode Island Commission cannot effectively exercise its power to regulate the rates for electricity furnished by the Narragansett Company to local consumers, without also regulating the rates for the other service which it furnishes; that if the Narragansett Company continues to furnish electricity to Attleboro Company at a loss this will tend to increase the burden on the local consumers and impair the ability of the Narragansett Company to give them good service at reasonable prices; and that, therefore, the order of the Commission prescribing a reasonable rate for the interstate service to the Attleboro Company should be sustained as being essentially a local regulation, necessary to the protection of matters of local interest, and affecting interstate commerce only indirectly and incidentally.

The order of the Rhode Island Commission is not a regulation of the rates charged to local consumers, having merely an incidental effect upon interstate commerce, but is a regulation of the rates charged by the Narragansett Company for the interstate service to the Attleboro Company, which places a direct burden upon interstate commerce. Being the imposition of a direct burden upon interstate commerce, from which the State is restrained by the force of the Commerce Clause, it must necessarily fall, regardless of its purpose. It is immaterial that the Narragansett Company is a Rhode Island corporation subject to regulation by the Commission in its local business, or that Rhode Island is the State from which the electric current is transmitted in interstate commerce, and not that in which it is received. The forwarding state obviously has no more authority than the receiving State to place a direct burden upon interstate commerce. Nor is it material that the general business of the Narragansett Company appears to be chiefly local. The test of the validity of a state regulation is not the character of the general business of the company, but whether the particular business which is regulated is essentially local or national in character; and if the regulation places a direct burden upon its interstate business it is none the less beyond the power of the State because this may be the smaller part of its general business. Furthermore, if Rhode Island could place a direct burden upon the interstate business of the Narragansett Company because this would result in indirect benefit to the customers of the Narragansett Company in Rhode Island, Massachusetts could, by parity of reasoning, reduce the rates on such interstate business in order to benefit the customers of the Attleboro Company in that State, who would have, in the aggregate, an interest in the interstate rate correlative to that of the customers of the Narragansett Company in Rhode Island. Plainly, however, the paramount interest in the interstate business carried on between the two companies is not local to either State, but is essentially national in character. The rate is therefore not subject to regulation by either of the two States in the guise of protection to their respective local interests; but, if such regulation is required it can only be attained by the exercise of the power vested in Congress.

The decree is accordingly affirmed.

■ BRANDEIS, J., dissenting The business of the Narragansett Company is an intrastate one. The only electricity sold for use without the State is that agreed to be delivered to the Attleboro Company. That company takes less than 3 per cent. of the electricity produced and manufactured by the Narragansett, which has over 70,000 customers in Rhode Island. The problem is essentially local in character. The Commission found as a fact that continuance of the service to the Attleboro Company at the existing rate would prevent the Narragansett from performing its full duty towards its other customers and would be detrimental to the general public welfare. It issued the order specifically to prevent unjust discrimination and to prevent unjust increase in the price to other customers. The Narragansett, a public service corporation of Rhode Island, is subject to regulation by that State. The order complained of is clearly valid as an exercise of the police power, unless it violates the Commerce Clause.

The power of the State to regulate the selling price of electricity produced and distributed by it within the State and to prevent discrimination is not affected by the fact that the supply is furnished under a long-term contract. If the Commission lacks the power exercised, it is solely because the electricity is delivered for use in another State. That fact makes the transaction interstate commerce, and Congress has power to legislate on the subject. It has not done so, nor has it legislated on any allied subject, so there can be no contention that it has occupied the field. Nor is this a case in which it can be said that the silence of Congress is a command that the Rhode Island utility shall remain free from the public regulation—that it shall be free to discriminate against the citizens of the State by which it was incorporated and in which it does business. That State may not, of course, obstruct or directly burden interstate commerce. But to prevent discrimination in the price of electricity wherever used does not obstruct or place a direct burden upon interstate commerce. . . .

In my opinion the judgment below should be reversed.■

NOTES AND COMMENTS

1. Would the test proposed by Justice Brandeis, that a state could "prevent discrimination in the price of electricity wherever used," have been as effective a means of ensuring fair pricing as the creation of a federal regulatory system? Do the principles of rate design seem clear enough that they could serve as a constitutional standard?

2. After the Supreme Court limited the ability of the states to regulate interstate sales of electricity in the *Attleboro* case, Congress passed the Federal Power Act, which gave to the Federal Power Commission[1] the power to regulate the "sale of electric energy at wholesale in interstate commerce." 16 U.S.C. § 824.

3. By the 1950's, the nation was blanketed with a few hundred investor-owned electric utilities on the Insull model. In addition, there were a few large federal electric generation and distribution agencies, such as the Tennessee Valley Authority, a host of publicly owned municipal electric agencies (the "municipals") and hundreds of rural electric cooperatives created under the federal Rural Electrification Act (the "REA co-ops").

Each of the larger entities operated primarily as an independent, vertically integrated unit. It generated its own power, transmitted it over high voltage lines to its own substations, and from there distributed it along lower voltage wires to the end users. Most rural co-ops and some smaller utilities did not have their own generating plants and relied on power purchased from the larger entities.

Since the 1930s, the interconnection of these separate entities had been overseen by the Federal Power Commission. In the 1960s, the issue of interconnection assumed new importance as rapid economic growth left some areas subject to power shortages.

Throughout the 1950s and 1960s, demand for electricity was constantly increasing. Until approximately 1965, utilities were able to meet this increasing demand simply by expanding their base-load capacity and passing through these costs to customers in rate base. During this period, electricity generation was believed by regulators to have been characterized by significant economies of scale. Generation capacity was increased—often without question—to meet this demand. In 1965, the FPC published an extensive survey, the National Power Survey, which suggested that closely coordinated plant constructions and operations by electric utilities could produce power far more cheaply than expansions of capacity and operations by individual utilities.

Many regulators were becoming concerned that sufficient capacity did not exist to meet consumer demand. On November 2, 1965, a relay on the Ontario Hydro system broke. The system was tied into the network of interconnected lines that covered the entire Northeast United States and parts of Canada. Surges of power cascaded through the system, overloading lines and knocking them out of commission. The Northeast Blackout of 1965, as it came to be known, is one of the worst power failures the electric industry has ever seen. Within a quarter-hour over 30 million people lost their electricity. The FPC responded with recommendations to form "relia-

---

1. The Federal Power Commission was previously in existence, having been created under the Federal Water Power Act of 1920 to oversee the construction of hydroelectric dams on interstate rivers. *See* Chapter 4. The new statute was combined with the old into a new Federal Power Act. In a subsequent reorganization, the Commission's name was changed to the Federal Energy Regulatory Commission.

bility councils'' on a regional basis with representatives from the various utilities and government agencies.

Stephen Breyer[2] & Paul MacAvoy, Energy Regulation by the Federal Power Commission

Brookings Institution, 1974.

Electricity service is customarily viewed as consisting of (a) production of power by water or steam turbines, (b) transmission over high-voltage lines of the energy produced, and © local distribution for short distances over low-voltage lines to final consumers. By the accounting methods of the industry, more than half the costs are charged to production of electricity, one-eighth to transmission, and the rest to distribution. Several hundred firms owned by private investors provide approximately three-quarters of the nation's electricity supply. The remainder is produced by local, state, or federal installations. Nearly all private firms are vertically integrated, providing generating, transmitting, and distributing services as a single entity or through separate firms controlled by the same holding company . . .

. . . [C]hanging technology [in the electric utility industry] provoked similar change in the pattern of regulation. As technology made large-scale operation more efficient, competition between companies within a single city began to disappear, and municipalities sought to regulate prices and service quantity through their prerogatives in issuing franchises. Then, between 1905 and 1920, local franchising gave way to comprehensive control by state regulatory boards.

More recently, regulatory control has ceased to mirror the scale of operation that technology makes possible. . . . [T]oday as in the 1930s electricity regulation takes place primarily at the state level; state commissions control the prices of retail sales and review all construction plans. Restraints imposed by the commission or other federal agencies are typically viewed as supplementary forms of regulation.

With the growth of scale in capacity, power companies recognized the importance of coordinating generation and transaction by combining them across regions larger than the single retail distribution area. Recent technological change increasing the size of efficient generating units has in all probability increased the need for coordination. Operation of a group of generating units and a network of interconnecting transmission lines for service to multiple population centers as if the parts were one system can, in principle, produce cost savings in six categories.

Operating costs can be held to a minimum through a program to select for dispatch the power from the generators capable of producing it most cheaply. The program is formulated by tabulating the power stations in

---

2. Some two decades after co-authoring this book with economist Paul MacAvoy, Stephen Breyer was appointed to the Supreme Court of the United States by President Clinton.

ascending order of marginal operating costs the "first" station being the one with lowest marginal costs and then by loading the plants on the system in that order as demand increases. Each plant is "started up" for power production when total demand exceeds full capacity of the operating plants already on line with lower marginal costs.

Costs for meeting peak demands for electricity can be reduced by taking advantage of the fact that demand varies according to the time of day and the season of the year. Two regions in which peak demands occur at different times can save generating capacity by using the peaking capacity in one to supply some part of the peak demand in the other. If in winter demand peaks sharply at about 5:00 P.M., two adjacent systems in different time zones may be able to share the equipment needed to supply their respective peaks. The same principle suggests the possibility of exchanges between areas which have summer peaks because of air conditioning and those where peaks occur in winter because of heating demand. Coordination across companies with different peaks results in what is sometimes referred to as demand-diversity cost savings.

Reserve costs are also reduced by coordination. Reserve generating capacity is kept in case peak demand has been underestimated or in case operating units break down and for use during periods of maintenance. Interconnection can save on the capacity needed to allow maintenance work if firms in a coordination group can stagger their maintenance schedules to allow each to use the same spare generator to substitute for the generator being overhauled. Coordination can also reduce the risk of underforecasting demand. The larger the interconnected system, the more likely that the effect of unusual weather and changes in industrial demand in one place can be absorbed by reserve capacity from another place.

Coordinating the operations of several systems also reduces the need for breakdown reserves. Pooling reserve capacity allows each firm to call upon the reserves of other firms if a generator outage occurs. And the reserves of the others will be available unless several outages occur simultaneously a contingency that becomes more remote the larger the number of generators in the system. Sharing such capacity can reduce investment in reserve capacity by an amount sufficient to compensate for the increased costs of interconnecting transmission lines.

Generating costs can be reduced by coordination if it allows firms to take advantage of economies of scale in generator size. Since capacity depends on boiler and turbine volume while costs very roughly depend on metal surface areas, costs per unit of capacity decline with total outlay. The larger the generator, the more cheaply it can produce electricity at the margin. In fact, in estimating the elasticity of costs with respect to capacity, the consensus seems to be that costs increase by only 8 or 9 percent when capacity increases 10 percent. Thus the most efficient way to make electricity usually is to install the largest generator that technology permits a size that increased from roughly 400 megawatts (400,000 kilowatts) in the early 1960s to approximately 1,000 megawatts in the early 1970s. A large generating unit, however, requires a large backup unit in case it breaks down and recently larger units have tended to break down more frequently. Whereas a smaller firm may not face sufficient demand for its electricity to justify replacing a small generator with a large one, several small firms combined into a single system may be able to do so.

Transmission reliability costs can also be reduced through coordinated planning across a wide geographical area. When a generator breaks down, reserve generators must make up the deficit; but, during the first few seconds after a major breakdown (before the reserve generators can start up), more is needed. Power will rush into the deficit area, and the interconnecting transmission lines must be sufficiently strong to withstand the surge. Similarly, when a major line breaks down, power recoils and spreads itself out through the remaining interconnected lines of the system; those remaining lines must not break down, or they will aggravate the problem. Thus, once firms are interconnected at all, the generating or transmission plans of one will affect the need for lines elsewhere. Company X's installation of a large generator in State A may require the strengthening of Company Y's lines in State B, an area well outside Company X's service area. Unless Companies X and Y and others affected coordinate their plans, there is a risk of power failure, on the one hand, or waste, on the other.

Social costs, such as the adverse environmental effects from power generation, can also be reduced through coordination. Nearly every method of making electricity affects the environment in some way. Fossil-fuel plants pollute the air; nuclear plants heat nearby rivers and lakes; hydroelectric plants and their accompanying transmission lines disturb the biotic equilibrium and scenic attraction of wild areas. Coordinated planning over a wide geographic area can reduce total construction and help to locate the area's plants so as to produce the desired level of power at a lower cost to the environment.■

NOTES AND COMMENTS

1.   Throughout the late 1960s and the 1970s, blackouts and brownouts began to be a serious concern, especially during periods in which consumer demand "peaked"—such as Summer periods, in which residential and office air conditioning was added to normal demand. Most of us tend to take for granted the ability to throw a switch to provide light, power for appliances, or heat. We tend to underestimate the social impact of energy shortages. Another blackout of New York City on July 13 & 14, 1977, in addition to closing most public transportation facilities and businesses, led to communications shutdown (and the closing of Wall Street), riots and looting, prolonged fires, and many injuries and deaths. The Cost of an Urban Blackout, The Consolidated Edison Blackout, July 13–14, 1977, A Study for the Subcommittee on Energy and Power, Committee on Interstate and Foreign Commerce, United State House of Representatives (June 1978) at 4.

2. Writing in 1974 in the above-excerpted book, Breyer and MacAvoy went on to encourage the FPC to use its authority to require utilities to interconnect with each other in order to encourage the economies of scale that come with larger generating plants. They noted: "The most efficient way to make electricity usually is to install the largest generator that technology permits—a size that increased from roughly 400 megawatts (400,000 kilowatts) in the early 1960s to approximately 1,000 megawatts in the early 1970s." At that time, regulators were under intense pressure to increase utility capacity to supply electricity in order to meet expected shortages.

Recent economic studies suggest that the optimal size for coal and gas plants never exceeded 500 MW, although the optimal size for a nuclear plant was in the 900–1,100 MW range. *See* Paul L. Joskow & Richard Schmalansee, Markets for Power: An Analysis of Electric Utility Deregulation 51–54 (1983). If regulators during the 1970s were approving new plant construction on the basis of Breyer & MacAvoy's assumptions, would this be likely to lead to unnecessary capital expansion?

Today, the electric industry is the most capital-intensive industry in the U.S. economy: It currently requires $4 in capital investment for every $1 in annual revenues, as compared to a 3/1 ratio for the telephone industry and .6/1 for the automobile industry.

3. The size and impact of a major blackout in 2003 eclipsed the 1965 blackout: "On August 14 to August 15 of 2003, the northeastern U.S. suffered the worst electric power blackout in history. Over 50 million people in New York, Connecticut, Massachusetts, Vermont, New Jersey, Pennsylvania, Ohio, Michigan, and Ontario, Canada, went without electric power for up to 48 hours. Within nine seconds, an electric power surge had caused 100 power plants and 61,800 MW of electric generation to trip offline." James W. Moeller, Of Credits and Quotas: Federal Tax Incentives for Renewable Resources, State Renewable Portfolio Standards, and the Evolution of Proposals for a Federal Renewable Portfolio Standard, 51 Fordham Envtl. L. J. 69, 173 (2004). The 2003 blackout is discussed further in Chapter 11.

4. How a Modern Electric System Works

The physical equipment of a modern electric power system is divided into three basic categories: generation, transmission and distribution. Traditionally, in the territory of an investor-owned utility (IOU) or a large municipal utility, the same entity has owned and operated all three parts of the system. Today, however, an increasing share of the generation facilities are operated by independent power producers. And in the future, the transmission and distribution functions may increasingly be handled by separate entities, as discussed in Chapter 11.

a. GENERATION

Most electric power plants use either coal, oil, natural gas, or uranium as fuel. Some plants use renewable resources, such as hydro, geothermal, biomass, wind and solar energy. According to 2003 data, a bit more than half the electricity in the United States comes from coal-fired plants. About a fifth comes from nuclear power plants. Hydro furnishes less than ten percent, depending on the amount of rainfall that has taken place. The use of natural gas as power plant fuel is increasing and is now more than 15 percent. The use of fuel oil is dropping and now produces only about three percent. Power from renewable sources other than hydro is increasing, but still amounts to just a few percent. Statistics on power generation by source are available online at http://www.eia.doe.gov/neic/quickfacts/quickelectric.htm.

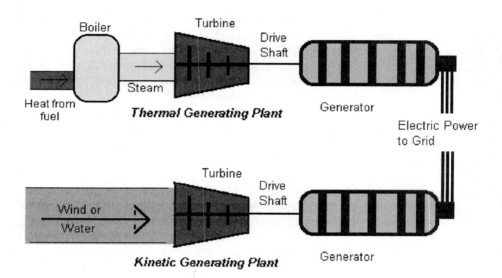

Figure 10–1
How to Make Electricity

The type of fuel, its cost, and generating plant efficiency can determine the way a particular generating plant is used. The demand for electricity varies considerably on both daily and yearly cycles. A large electric system will usually contain many different types of generating plant. The system operator will try to keep the mix of plants with the lowest operating costs running at any given time.

For purposes of deciding which plants to operate at any given time, power plants are generally classified into four categories: (1) base load "must run" plants, mostly nuclear or newer coal plants, which have low fuel costs and cannot be turned off and on rapidly; (2) variable "must run" plants, powered by hydro and wind, which have virtually no fuel costs but can operate only if the proper amount of water or wind is available; (3) intermediate load plants, often older coal plants that are more costly to operate than newer models; and (4) peaking plants, typically natural gas or diesel fueled, which have higher operating costs but are relatively inexpensive to build and can be taken on and off line quickly.

The need for this kind of careful balancing of the system results from the fact that electricity cannot be easily stored. This means that whenever customers turn the power on or off the generating load must be increased or decreased almost instantaneously to avoid affecting the voltage significantly.[3] Extensive research is underway in advanced battery design and superconducting magnetic energy storage, but progress is slow.

b. TRANSMISSION

Power plants are usually large and immovable[4], and its output must be moved from the generating plant site to the consumer. The transmission system accomplishes much of this task with an interconnected system of lines, distribution centers, and control systems. For example, the ERCOT transmission system that covers most of the state of Texas has over 48,000 miles of transmission lines, consisting of 7060 miles of 345KV lines, 16,538 miles of 138KV lines, and 11,456 miles of 69KV lines. Guide to Electric Power in Texas 5 (Center for Global Studies and Energy Institute, University of Houston, 2d. Ed., 1999).

To a degree, transmission expansion is a substitute for generation expansion. For example, if a utility expands its transmission resources, it may not need to build new generation facilities to serve customers but can transmit, or "wheel," power from another utility's generator.

Transmission lines are the lines commonly called "high-voltage" lines that are carried on high towers along wide rights of way. They form a spider web-like pattern on the landscape with many points of interconnection. When newly generated electricity is introduced into the network it will flow in whichever direction the lines are most lightly loaded. Similarly, where lines intersect, electricity will flow through the junction in a way that tries to even out the line loads. Thus if demand increases on a particular line, power will flow toward that line even if the generator assumed it was going to go somewhere else. This concept is known as "loop flow," and will be discussed in Chapter 11.

The transmission network must be operated in a way that keeps the voltage and frequency constant within very narrow limits. All systems keep a certain ratio of "spinning reserve;" *i.e.,* generating plants that are in operation and ready to be switched onto the network immediately if needed. In addition, a system needs "operating reserve" in the form of generation equipment or curtailable load that can be brought on or off line

3. The equivalent of storage can be obtained with "pumped hydro" plants, in which water is pumped up to the reservoir during periods when demand for electricity is low, and then released to generate power at peak times. However, there are few potential sites for such plants and the cost of operating them is not cheap.

4. The universality of this proposition is subject to change with the development of smaller scale plants known is the trade as "distributed generation." *See* Section E, *infra.* Nevertheless, for all practical purposes the great bulk of generating capacity will remain immovable for the foreseeable future.

within ten minutes or so. Finally, to operate properly the transmission system needs voltage control equipment dispersed throughout the system where voltage support is needed, and an overall system operator with authority to determine which generating units go on and off line at any time. These features of the transmission system are known in the trade as "ancillary services." *See* F.E.R.C. Order No. 888–A, 1997.

Standards for the operation of transmission systems have been set by the North American Electric Reliability Council (NERC), a consortium of various electric industry entities representing public and private utilities that account for virtually all of the electricity supplied in the United States and Canada. NERC's technical activities are carried out by committees on adequacy, security, and market interface. See www.nerc.com/about/.

The transmission systems of the United States and Canada are divided into three giant networks. (1) Beginning at about the Rocky Mountains and extending throughout the Western United States and Canada is the Western Interconnection. It's operation is governed by the Western Systems Coordinating Council, a non-profit entity controlled by representatives of the various utilities in the region. (2) Most of Texas has its own Texas Interconnection. These lines are operated by the Electric Reliability Council of Texas, a corporation created pursuant to state statute.[5] (3) The rest of the United States and Canada is part of the Eastern Interconnection, which is one giant network. Operation of the Eastern Interconnection is not centralized, however, but is managed by seven separate regional reliability councils. The future of the system of management of the transmission network is under considerable discussion (*See* Chapter 11).

Construction of transmission lines increased at a rapid rate during the 1970s but began to slow down after about 1985. Hyman, *supra.*, at 144, 161. Construction of new transmission lines today often encounters opposition from neighbors or environmental agencies, and may require a long period of negotiation. For discussion of this topic, see Chapter 9.

c.   DISTRIBUTION

Substations are located at various points on the transmission system. These substations contain transformers that reduce the voltage and send the power to the 120 and 240 volt lines that serve homes and businesses. (Large industries often bypass the distribution system and take electricity directly from the transmission network if they need higher voltages.)

The distribution system consists of the substations, poles and wires common to many neighborhoods as well as underground lines found in many other areas. Maintenance of these systems must respond to tree growth, sudden wind or ice storms, nesting eagles, and dozens of other local problems that frequently arise.

---

5.   Texas has traditionally tried to limit the interconnections between its lines and those of the rest of the country in order to discourage federal jurisdiction. *See generally* Guide to Electric Power in Texas (Center for Global Studies and Energy Institute, University of Houston, 2d. Ed., 1999)

The distribution function also includes the billing of customers, reading of meters, customer service, and many of the common activities that the average person associates with the work of an electric utility. As a public utility, the distributing company has an obligation to provide service to all customers at published rates. State laws sometimes make it difficult to terminate service to a customer even when he is not paying his bill.

Many rural cooperatives and small municipal utilities operate only a distribution system without either generating or transmitting power. They purchase power in "wholesale" transactions from other utilities or from Federal marketing entities.

B. CURRENT STRUCTURE OF THE INDUSTRY

The next two chapters will discuss the ongoing changes taking place in the electric industry. These include extensive mergers within the electric

Other Publicly Owned Utilities Other publicly owned utilities include: Municipals Public Power Districts State Authorities Irrigation Districts Other State Organizations There are 2,009 in the United States.	Are nonprofit State and local government agencies. Serve at cost; return excess funds to the consumers in the form of community contributions and reduced rates. Most municipals just distribute power, although some large ones produce and transmit electricity; they are financed from municipal treasuries and revenue bonds. Public power districts and projects are concentrated in Nebraska, Washington, Oregon, Arizona, and California; voters in a public power district elect commissioners or directors to govern the district independent of any municipal government. Irrigation districts may have still other forms of organization (e.g., in the Salt River Project Agricultural Improvement and Power District in Arizona, votes for the Board of Directors are apportioned according to the size of landholdings). State authorities, such as the New York Power Authority and the South Carolina Public Service Authority, are agents of their respective State governments.
Cooperatively Owned Utilities There are 912 cooperatively owned utilities in the United States, and they operate in all States except Connecticut, Hawaii, Rhode Island, and the District of Columbia.	Owned by members (rural farmers and communities). Provide service mostly to members. Incorporated under State law and directed by an elected board of directors which, in turn, selects a manager. The Rural Utilities Service (formerly the Rural Electrification Administration) in the U.S. Department of Agriculture was established under the Rural Electrification Act of 1936 with the purpose of extending credit to co-ops to provide electric service to small rural communities (usually fewer than 1,500 consumers) and farms where it was relatively expensive to provide service.
Power Marketers There are 194 active power marketers in the United States.	Some are utility-affiliated while others are independent. Buy and sell electricity. Do not own or operate generation, transmission, or distribution facilities.

Figure 10–2
Major Characteristics of Electric Utilities by Type of Ownership
Source: Energy Information Administration, Office of Coal, Nuclear, Electric and Alternate Fuels.

industry itself, both in the United States and overseas, as well as combinations of traditional electric companies with gas companies, energy market= ers and a wide range of other companies. And they also include the entry into the electricity business of a wide range of independent companies that may engage in more limited roles than the traditional vertically integrated electric utility.

As background for these changes, however, it is important to understand who the major players are as we enter this period of rapid change.

1.   THE PRESENT MIX

The electric utility industry is made up of five major groups of entities: (1) investor-owned utilities (IOUs); (2) federal agencies that generate, transmit or market power; (3) publicly owned systems, mostly operated by cities and known as "municipals" or "public power;" (4) rural electric cooperatives funded through the Department of Agriculture; and (5) power marketers. *See* **Figure 10–2**. In recent years, several new non-utility firms have also begun to provide services in the electric power industry. *See* **Figure 10–3**. To understand the legal issues facing the industry today, it is import to be familiar with each of these types of entities.

a.   INVESTOR-OWNED UTILITIES

In 1998 the 239 investor-owned utility (IOU) operating companies dominated the electric power industry, generating some 68 percent of the nation's power. Although referred to as *public* utilities, IOUs are private, shareholder-owned companies ranging in size from small local operations serving a customer base of a few thousand to giant multistate corporations serving millions of customers. The larger IOUs have always been vertically integrated, owning or controlling all the generation, transmission, and distribution facilities required to meet the needs of the customers in their assigned service area, although recent trends suggest that this vertical integration may become less prevalent. See Chapter 11.

IOUs can be found in every State except Nebraska. Their local operations and retail rates are usually highly regulated by State Public Utility Commissions, but their wholesale power sales and power transmission contracts fall under the jurisdiction of the Federal Energy Regulatory Commission (FERC).

Control over IOUs is further concentrated because many of them are actually subsidiaries of utility holding companies. Nearly one-quarter of the IOU operating companies are subsidiaries of electric utility holding companies. These were regulated under the Public Utility Holding Company Act of 1935 (PUHCA), 15 U.S.C. § 79, by the Securities and Exchange Commission and FERC, until repeal of that statute in the 2005 Energy Policy Act. Major utility holding companies included companies such as American Electric Power Co. and Entergy Corp.

b. FEDERAL POWER SYSTEMS

The Federal Government generates electric power at federally owned hydroelectric facilities. It is primarily a wholesaler, marketing its power through five Federal power marketing agencies: 1. Bonneville Power Administration, 2. Western Area Power Administration, 3. Southeastern Power Administration, 4. Southwestern Power Administration, and 5. The Alaska Power Administration. Together, federal systems accounted for just under 8 percent of the Nation's power generation in 1998. Federal power systems are generally required under existing legislation to give preference in the sale of their output to other public power systems and to rural electric cooperatives.

Federally owned or chartered power systems also include the Tennessee Valley Authority,[6] and facilities operated by the U.S. Army Corps of Engineers, the Bureau of Reclamation, the Bureau of Indian Affairs, and the International Water and Boundary Commission. Jurisdiction over Federal power systems operations and the rates charged to their customers is established in the various authorizing legislation in Title 16 of the U.S. Code.

c. PUBLIC POWER

The more than 2,000 public power systems include local, municipal, State, and regional public power systems ranging in size from tiny municipal distribution companies to giant systems like the Los Angeles Department of Water and Power. Some states, such as Nebraska and New York, operate electric systems that cover all (in the case of Nebraska) or part of the state. Public power systems generated about 9 percent of the Nation's power in 1998. Many public systems are involved only in retail power distribution; they purchase power supplies from other utilities. See **Figure 10–2**.

The extent of regulation of public power systems varies among states. In some states the public utility commission exercises jurisdiction in whole or part over operations and rates of publicly owned systems. In other states, public power systems are regulated by local governments or are self-regulated. Municipal systems are usually run by the local city council or an independent board elected by voters or appointed by city officials. Other public power systems are run by public utility districts, irrigation districts, or special state authorities.

d. RURAL ELECTRIC COOPERATIVES

Electric cooperatives are electric systems owned by their members, each of whom has one vote in the election of a board of directors. The Rural Electrification Act of 1936, 49 Stat. 1363, created the Rural Electrification Administration (REA) to bring electricity to rural areas and subsequently gave it broad lending authority to stimulate rural electricity use. The Act

---

6. The Tennessee Valley Authority is an independent government corporation that sells power within its statutory service area. 16 U.S.C. § 831.

authorizes federal loans at no interest or very low interest to cooperatives for the purpose of "financing the construction and operation of generating plans, electric transmission and distribution lines or systems for the furnishing of electric energy to persons in rural areas who are not receiving central station service." 7 U.S.C. § 904.

In the early 1930s, 9 out of 10 rural homes were without electric service. Today, 99% of rural homes have electricity service. Rural co-ops often act as buying and distribution agents for utility-generated power or for generation and transmission co-ops (G&Ts), which own both generating and transmission facilities. Early REA borrowers tended to be small cooperatives that purchased wholesale power for distribution to members. Over the past 20 years, however, many expanded into generating and transmission cooperatives in order to lessen their dependence on outside power sources.

Regulatory jurisdiction over cooperatives varies among the States, with some States exercising considerable authority over rates and operations, while other States exempt cooperatives from State regulation. In addition to State regulation, cooperatives with outstanding Federal loans fall under the jurisdiction of the Rural Utilities Service (RUS), successor to REA, which imposes various conditions intended to protect the financial viability of borrowers. *See* 7 U.S.C. § 901 et seq.

e. POWER MARKETERS

Since the passage of the Energy Policy Act of 1992, many new companies have been created to serve as marketers and brokers of electric power. These companies do not own or operate any electric facilities. They buy and sell electricity on the open market. Some IOUs have created subsidiaries to operate as marketers, but many marketers are independent. Marketers are discussed in Chapter 11.

f. INDEPENDENT POWER PRODUCERS

Most independent power producers—also known and "non-utility" generators—began operation because of the Public Utility Regulatory Policies Act of 1978 (PURPA) and its requirement that utilities purchase power from certain defined qualifying facilities (QFs). In addition, many state public utility commissions helped the independent power business by persuading utilities to put major generating capacity additions out to bid. Independents often found that they could underbid the traditional utilities, which brought even more independents into the business.

The National Energy Policy Act of 1992 extended the conditions under which an independent power producer could build and own projects itself without becoming regulated as a public utility. It encouraged the regulated utilities to set up their own unregulated subsidiaries to act as independent builders and operators of generating plants outside the utility's jurisdiction. And it gave FERC greater authority to compel utilities to provide transmission services for wholesale transactions between independent power producers and distant distributing utilities. Such service is known in the trade as "wheeling" and will be discussed in the next Chapter.

Table 5. Major Characteristics of U.S. Nonutilities by Type	
Type	**Major Characteristics**
Cogenerators (QF) (Combined Heat and Power)	Are qualified under PURPA by meeting certain ownership, operating, and efficiency criteria established by FERC. Sequentially produce electric energy and another form of energy, such as heat or steam, using the same fuel source. Are guaranteed that utilities will purchase their output at a price based on the utility's "avoided cost" and will provide backup service at nondiscriminatory rates.
Small Power Producers (QF)	Are qualified under PURPA by meeting certain ownership, operating, and efficiency criteria, established by FERC. Use biomass, waste, renewable resources (water, wind, solar), or geothermal as a primary energy source. Fossil fuels can be used but renewable resources must provide at least 75 percent of the total energy input. Are guaranteed that utilities will purchase their output at a price based on the utility's "avoided cost" and will provide backup service at nondiscriminatory rates.
Exempt Wholesale Generators	Creation authorized by 1992 EPACT. Were exempt from PUHCA's corporate and geographic restrictions. Are wholesale producers; do not sell retail. Do not possess significant transmission facilities. Utilities are not required to purchase their electricity. Are regulated but usually may charge market-based rates.
Cogenerators (Non-QF)	Are not qualified under the provisions of PURPA. Are nonutilities, utilizing a cogenerating technology, which may themselves consume part of the electricity they cogenerate.
Noncogenerators (Non-QF)	Are not qualified under the provisions of PURPA. Do not utilize a cogenerating technology.

QF = Qualifying facility (under PURPA).
Note: An entity can be any combination of cogenerator QF, small power producer QF, and exempt wholesale generator.
Source: Energy Information Administration, *Electric Power Annual 1995*. Volume II, DOE/EIA-0348(95)/2 (Washington, DC, December 1996).

Figure 10–3

2. JURISDICTIONAL ISSUES

The relationship of the investor-owned utilities with the federal agencies, municipals and REA co-ops has had its ups and downs. The cases that follow illustrate some of the issues that pervade the borderline between federal and state regulation of the electric industry.

Federal Power Comm'n v. Southern California Edison introduces the relationship of the various segments of the industry. Southern California Edison is a major investor-owned electric utility that generates, transmits, and distributes electricity. The federal government generates power from its hydroelectric facilities, some of which is sold to Edison. The City of Colton is a small municipally-owned facility; like many municipal utilities, it distributes, but does not generate, electricity. This case involves Colton's attempt to obtain federal regulation of the price it had to pay to buy power from Edison. The case involves the interpretation of the key statutory provisions in section 201 of the Federal Power Act, 16 U.S.C. § 824:

> (a) It is declared that the business of transmitting and selling electric energy for ultimate distribution to the public is affected with a public interest, and that Federal regulation of matters relating to generation to the extent provided in [cited sections] and of that part of such

business which consists of the transmission of electric energy in interstate commerce and the sale of such energy at wholesale in interstate commerce is necessary in the public interest, such Federal regulation, however, to extend only to those matters which are not subject to regulation by the States.

(b)(1) The provisions of this Part shall apply to the transmission of electric energy in interstate commerce and to the sale of electric energy at wholesale in interstate commerce, but except as provided in paragraph (2) shall not apply to any other sale of electric energy or deprive a State or State commission of its lawful authority now exercised over the exportation of hydroelectric energy which is transmitted across a State line. The Commission shall have jurisdiction over all facilities for such transmission or sale of electric energy, but shall not have jurisdiction, except as specifically provided in [cited sections], over facilities used for the generation of electric energy or over facilities used in local distribution or only for the transmission of electric energy in intrastate commerce, or over facilities for the transmission of electric energy consumed wholly by the transmitter....

(d) The term "sale of electric energy at wholesale" when used in this subchapter, means a sale of electric energy to any person for resale.

Federal Power Comm. v. Southern California Edison Co.

376 U.S. 205 (1964).

■ BRENNAN, J. Petitioner City of Colton, California (Colton), purchases its entire requirements of electric power from respondent Southern California Edison Company (Edison), a California electric utility company which operates in central and southern California and sells energy only to customers located there. Colton applies some of the power purchased to municipal uses, but resells the bulk of it to thousands of residential, commercial, and industrial customers in Colton and its environs. Respondent Public Utilities Commission of California (PUC) had for some years exercised jurisdiction over the Edison–Colton sale, but petitioner Federal Power Commission (FPC), on Colton's petition filed in 1958, asserted jurisdiction under § 201(b) of the Federal Power Act which extends federal regulatory power to the "sale of electric energy at wholesale in interstate commerce." 16 U.S.C. §§ 791a, 824–824h.

Some of the energy which Edison markets in California originates in Nevada and Arizona. Edison has a contract with the Secretary of the Interior under which, as agent for the United States, it generates energy at the Hoover power plants located in Nevada. This contract allocates to Edison 7% of the total firm generating capacity of Hoover Dam. Edison is also a party to a 1945 contract with the United States and the Metropolitan Water District of Southern California under which it is entitled to a portion of the unused firm energy allocated to the Water District from Hoover

Dam. Payment for this energy is made to the United States for the credit of the Water District. Also, Hoover Dam, Davis Dam in Arizona, and Parker Dam in California are interconnected by a transmission line from which Edison has drawn energy by agreement with the Water District.

The FPC found, on the extensive record made before a Hearing Examiner, that out-of-state energy from Hoover Dam was included in the energy delivered by Edison to Colton, and ruled that the "sale to Colton is a sale of electric energy at wholesale in interstate commerce subject to Sections 201, 205 and 206 of the Federal Power Act." 26 F.P.C. 223, 231.

The Court of Appeals did not pass upon the question whether the finding that out-of-state energy reached Colton has support in the record. The court assumed that the finding had such support, but held nevertheless that § 201 (b) did not grant jurisdiction over the rates to the FPC. It ruled that the concluding words of § 201(a)—"such Federal regulation, however, [is] to extend only to those matters which are not subject to regulation by the States"—confined FPC jurisdiction to those interstate wholesales constitutionally beyond the power of state regulation by force of the Commerce Clause, Art. I, § 8, of the Constitution. Accordingly, it held that the FPC had no jurisdiction because PUC regulation of the Edison–Colton sale was permissible under the Commerce Clause. Because of the importance of the question in the administration of the Federal Power Act we granted the separate petitions for certiorari of the FPC and Colton. 372 U.S. 958. We reverse. We hold that § 201(b) grants the FPC jurisdiction of all sales of electric energy at wholesale in interstate commerce not expressly exempted by the Act itself, and that the FPC properly asserted jurisdiction of the Edison–Colton sale.

The view of the Court of Appeals was that the limiting language of § 201(a), read together with the jurisdictional grant in § 201(b), meant that the FPC could not assert its jurisdiction over a sale which the Commerce Clause allowed a State to regulate. Such a determination of the permissibility of state regulation would require, the Court of Appeals said, an analysis of the impact of state regulation of the sale upon the national interest in commerce. The court held that such an analysis here compelled the conclusion that the FPC lacked jurisdiction, because state regulation of the Edison–Colton sale would not prejudice the interests of any other State. This conclusion was rested upon the view that the interests of Arizona and Nevada, the only States other than California which might claim to be concerned with the Edison–Colton sale, were already given federal protection by the Secretary of the Interior's control of the initial sales of Hoover and Davis energy. Since the first sale was subject to federal regulation, and since the energy subsequently sold by Edison to Colton for resale was to be consumed wholly within California, there was said to be a "complete lack of interest on the part of any other state," and the sale was therefore held to be subject to state regulation and exempt from FPC regulation. 310 F.2d, at 789.

The Court of Appeals expressly rejected the argument that § 201(b) incorporated a congressional decision against determining the FPC's jurisdiction by such a case-by-case analysis, and in favor of employing a more mechanical test which would bring under federal regulation all sales of electric energy in interstate commerce at wholesale except those specifically exempted, and would exclude all retail sales. In reviewing the court's ruling on this question we do not write on a clean slate. In decisions over the past quarter century we have held that Congress, in enacting the Federal Power Act and the Natural Gas Act, apportioned regulatory power between state and federal governments according to a test which this Court had developed in a series of cases under the Commerce Clause. The Natural Gas Act grew out of the same judicial history as did the part of the Federal Power Act with which we are here concerned; and § 201(b) of the Power Act has its counterpart in § 1(b) of the Gas Act, 15 U.S.C. § 717(b), which became law three years later in 1938.

The test adopted by Congress was developed in a line of decisions, [the last of which] and the one which directly led to congressional intervention, was *Public Utilities Commission of Rhode Island v. Attleboro Steam and Electric Co.*, 273 U.S. 83. There the Public Utilities Commission of Rhode Island asserted jurisdiction over the rates at which a Rhode Island company sold energy generated at its Rhode Island plant to a Massachusetts company, which took delivery at the state line for resale to the City of Attleboro. The Court held that the case did not involve "a regulation of the rates charged to local consumers," and that since the sale was of concern to both Rhode Island and Massachusetts it was "national in character." Consequently, "if such regulation is required it can only be attained by the exercise of the power vested in Congress." 273 U.S., at 89–90.

Congress undertook federal regulation through the Federal Power Act in 1935 and the Natural Gas Act in 1938. The premise was that constitutional limitations upon state regulatory power made federal regulation essential if major aspects of interstate transmission and sale were not to go unregulated. *Attleboro*, with the other cases cited, figured prominently in the debates and congressional reports. In *Illinois Natural Gas Co. v. Central Illinois Public Service Co.*, 314 U.S. 498, we were first required to determine the scope of the federal power which Congress had asserted to meet the problem revealed by Attleboro and the other cases. The specific question in that case was whether a company selling interstate gas at wholesale to distributors for resale in a single State could be required by that State's regulatory commission to extend its facilities and connect them with those of a local distributor, or whether such extensions were exclusively a matter for the FPC. The Court noted that prior to the Natural Gas Act there had been another line of cases which adopted a more flexible approach to state power under the Commerce Clause; these cases had been "less concerned to find a point in time and space where the interstate commerce in gas ends and intrastate commerce begins, and [have] looked to the nature of the state regulation involved, the objective of the state, and the effect of the regulation upon the national interest in the commerce." 314 U.S., at 505. But the Court held that Congress, rather than adopting this flexible approach, which was applied by the Court of Appeals in the instant case, "undertook to regulate ... without the necessity, where

Congress has not acted, of drawing the precise line between state and federal power by the litigation of particular cases." *Id.*, at 506–507. What Congress did was to adopt the test developed in the Attleboro line which denied state power to regulate a sale "at wholesale to local distributing companies" and allowed state regulation of a sale at "local retail rates to ultimate consumers." 314 U.S., at 504.

In short, our decisions have squarely rejected the view of the Court of Appeals that the scope of FPC jurisdiction over interstate sales of gas or electricity at wholesale is to be determined by a case-by-case analysis of the impact of state regulation upon the national interest. Rather, Congress meant to draw a bright line easily ascertained, between state and federal jurisdiction, making unnecessary such case-by-case analysis. This was done in the Power Act by making FPC jurisdiction plenary and extending it to all wholesale sales in interstate commerce except those which Congress has made explicitly subject to regulation by the States. There is no such exception covering the Edison–Colton sale.... [The Court also rejected the argument that Congress had exempted sales of Hoover Dam Power from FPC jurisdiction.]■

NOTES AND COMMENTS

1.   The terms "wholesale" and "retail" are important words of art in energy law. The rule in the Colton case still remains in effect under the Federal Power Act. A wholesale transaction is one between two entities who are not the ultimate users of the electricity. A retail sale is a sale directly to an end user. Wholesale sales are regulated by the Federal Energy Regulatory Commission (the successor to the FPC, *See* Chapter 4) while retail sales are regulated by the state in which the transfer occurs.

2.   The other qualifier that limits federal jurisdiction is that the sale must be in interstate commerce. When power is generated by a source that does not also own transmission lines, or by a source that owns transmission lines but these lines do not reach the geographic area in which customers are located, it is necessary for a utility to interconnect its lines with the source. In addition, as Breyer and MacAvoy note, it is common for adjacent utilities which own transmission lines to interconnect in order to coordinate power generation and distribution.

In *Federal Power Comm'n v. Florida Power & Light Co.*, 404 U.S. 453 (1972), the Supreme Court allowed the FPC to exercise jurisdiction over power sold by Florida Power & Light (FP&L), the major investor-owned utility serving South Florida. All of FP&L's generation and transmission facilities were located within the state of Florida and none of its facilities connected directly with out-of-state utilities, customers or power sources. Nevertheless, FPC contended that FP&L generated electrons reached the interstate market in Georgia since FP&L's transmission lines were connected with those of another Florida utility, Florida Power Corporation (Corp) which in turn connected with Georgia Power Company.

The Court addressed what would determine FPC jurisdiction over the interstate transmission of electricity:

... The FPC may exercise jurisdiction only if there is substantial evidentiary support for the Commission's conclusion that FP&L power has reached Georgia via Corp or that Georgia's power has reached FP&L because of exchanges with Corp. What happens when FP&L gives power to Corp and Corp gives power to Georgia (or vice versa)? Is FP&L power commingled with Corp's own supply, and thus passed on with that supply, as the Commission contends? Or is it diverted to handle Corp's independent power needs, displacing a like amount of Corp power that is then passed on, as respondent argues? Or, as the Commission also contends, do changes in FP&L's load or generation, or that of others in the interconnected system, stimulate a reaction up and down the line by a signal or chain reaction that is, in essence electricity moving in interstate commerce?

Federal jurisdiction clearly would have been present if FP&L directly exchanged power with Georgia. Jurisdiction would have also been present, the Court held, if Corp, the intermediate utility, "could be shown to be sometimes no more than a funnel." Even though neither of these circumstances was true in this case, the Court held that FP&L's power was commingled with Corp power and exported across the Georgia line. As the Court observed, "the elusive nature of electrons renders experimental evidence that might draw the fine distinctions in this case practically unobtainable." The Court upheld FPC's assertion of jurisdiction. (*See also* the *Fairfax Water Company* case in Chapter 4).

3.   Utilities from the State of Texas have exempted themselves from much federal regulation by avoiding the shipment of power across state lines. Many of their activities, however, are regulated by the Electric Reliability Council of Texas (ERCOT). In 1996 the Texas Public Utilities Commission established ERCOT as an Independent System Operator (ISO) that is separate from, and largely independent of, the utilities that own the transmission network. The reconstituted ERCOT board will establish policies for operating the transmission network on a nondiscriminatory basis for all power producers and users. The ERCOT board of directors has representatives from the IOUs, public power entities, coops, independent power producers and power marketers. See Guide to Electric Power in Texas, *supra*.

The following case, FPC v. Conway Corp., examines the scope of federal ratemaking authority and introduces the tensions between IOUs and smaller municipal and co-op systems that do not generate power. Although these municipals and co-ops tend to be small in relation to the typical IOU, they have always exerted considerable influence in the making of energy policy by congress and the executive branch through the American Public Power Association. See www.appanet.org.

Federal Power Commission v. Conway Corp.

426 U.S. 271 (1976).

■ WHITE, J. The question in this case is this: When a power company that sells electricity at both wholesale and retail seeks to raise its wholesale rates, does the Federal Power Commission (Commission) have jurisdiction to consider the allegations of the company's wholesale customers that the proposed wholesale rates, which are within the Commission's jurisdiction, are discriminatory and noncompetitive when considered in relation to the company's retail rates, which are not within the jurisdiction of the Commission? We hold that it does.

Arkansas Power & Light Co. (Company) is a public utility engaged in the sale of electric energy at wholesale in interstate commerce under the meaning of § 201 of the Federal Power Act, 16 U.S.C. § 824. Its wholesale rates are thus within reach of the Commission's powers under § 206(a) of the Act to establish rates which are just, reasonable, and nondiscriminatory. 16 U.S.C. § 824e(a). The Company also sells at retail and seeks industrial sales in competition with some of its wholesale customers. These wholesale customers include the seven municipally owned electric systems and the two electric power cooperatives which are respondents here. Each of these respondents (Customers) operates in the State of Arkansas and each borders on or is surrounded by the territory served by the Company.

In June 1973, the Company filed with the Commission a wholesale rate increase pursuant to § 205 (d). The Customers sought to intervene before the Commission, urging that the rate increase be rejected. Among other grounds, it was asserted that the Customers and the Company were in competition for industrial retail accounts and that the rate increase was "an attempt to squeeze [the Customers] or some of them out of competition and to make them more susceptible to the persistent attempts of the company to take over the public[ly] owned systems in the State." It was alleged that the proposed wholesale rates would make it "impossible for the [Customers] to sell power to an industrial load of any size at a competitive price with [the Company], since, in many cases, the revenues therefrom would not even cover the incremental power costs to [the Customers]." It was also asserted that the rate filing was "plainly discriminatory against the single class of customer which [the Company] has historically attempted to drive out of business, without justification on any ordinary cost of service basis...."

The Company opposed the petition. The Commission permitted the Customers to intervene but ruled that it would "limit Customers' participation in this proceeding to matters other than the alleged anti-competitive activities" because the Customers had failed to demonstrate that the relief sought was "within this Commission's authority to direct." The Commission also denied the Customers' amended petition to intervene, again refusing to consider the tendered anticompetitive and discrimination issues. Inasmuch as the Commission's authority is limited to wholesale rates and does not reach sales at retail, the Commission's opinion was that "the relief sought by [the Customers] is beyond the authority granted to us under the Federal Power Act."

Section 201(b) of the Act, 16 U.S.C. § 824(b), confers jurisdiction on the Commission with respect to the sale of electric energy at wholesale in interstate commerce. The prohibition against discriminatory or preferential rates or services imposed by § 205(b) and the Commission's power to set just and reasonable rates under § 206(a) are accordingly limited to sales "subject to the jurisdiction of the Commission," that is, to sales of electric energy at wholesale. The Commission has no power to prescribe the rates for retail sales of power companies. Nor, accordingly, would it have power to remedy an alleged discriminatory or anticompetitive relationship between wholesale and retail rates by ordering the company to increase its retail rates.

As the Commission is at great pains to establish, this is the proper construction of the Act, the legislative history of § 205 indicating that the section was expressly limited to jurisdictional sales to foreclose the possibility that the Commission would seek to correct an alleged discriminatory relationship between wholesale and retail rates by raising or otherwise regulating the nonjurisdictional, retail price. Insofar as we are advised, no party to this case contends otherwise.

Building on this history, the Commission makes a skillful argument that it may neither consider nor remedy any alleged discrimination resting on a difference between jurisdictional and nonjurisdictional rates. But the argument, in the end, is untenable. Section 205(b) forbids the maintenance of any "unreasonable difference in rates" or service "with respect to any . . . sale subject to the jurisdiction of the Commission." A jurisdictional sale is necessarily implicated in any charge that the difference between wholesale and retail rates is unreasonable or anticompetitive. If the undue preference or discrimination is in any way traceable to the level of the jurisdictional rate, it is plain enough that the section would to that extent apply; and to that extent the Commission would have power to effect a remedy under § 206 by an appropriate order directed to the jurisdictional rate. This was the view of the Court of Appeals, and we agree with it.

The Commission appears to insist that a just and reasonable wholesale rate can never be a contributing factor to an undue discrimination: Once the jurisdictional rate is determined to be just and reasonable, inquiry into discrimination is irrelevant for § 206(a) purposes, for if the discrimination continues to exist, it is traceable wholly to the nonjurisdictional, retail rate. This argument assumes, however, that ratemaking is an exact science and that there is only one level at which a wholesale rate can be said to be just and reasonable and that any attempt to remedy a discrimination by lowering the jurisdictional rate would always result in an unjustly low rate that would fail to recover fully allocated wholesale costs. As the Court of Appeals pointed out and as this Court has held, however, there is no single cost-recovering rate, but a zone of reasonableness: "Statutory reasonableness is an abstract quality represented by an area rather than a pinpoint. It allows a substantial spread between what is unreasonable because too low and what is unreasonable because too high." *Montana-Dakota Util. Co. v. Northwestern Pub. Serv. Co.*, 341 U.S. 246, 251 (1951). The Commission itself explained the matter in *In the Matter of Otter Tail Power Co.*, 2 F.P.C. 134, 149 (1940):

It occurs to us that one rate in its relation to another rate may be discriminatory, although each rate per se, if considered independently, might fall within the zone of reasonableness. There is considerable latitude within the zone of reasonableness insofar as the level of a particular rate is concerned. The relationship of rates within such a zone, however, may result in an undue advantage in favor of one rate and be discriminatory insofar as another rate is concerned. When such a situation exists, the discrimination found to exist must be removed.

The Commission thus cannot so easily satisfy its obligation to eliminate unreasonable discriminations or put aside its duty to consider whether a proposed rate will have anticompetitive effects. The exercise by the Commission of powers otherwise within its jurisdiction "clearly carries with it the responsibility to consider, in appropriate circumstances, the anticompetitive effects of regulated aspects of interstate utility operations pursuant to ... directives contained in §§ 205, 206...." *Gulf States Utilities Co. v. Federal Power Commission,* 411 U.S. 747, 758–759 (1973). The Commission must arrive at a rate level deemed by it to be just and reasonable, but in doing so it must consider the tendered allegations that the proposed rates are discriminatory and anticompetitive in effect.

We think the Court of Appeals was quite correct in concluding:

When costs are fully allocated, both the retail rate and the proposed wholesale rate may fall within a zone of reasonableness, yet create a price squeeze between themselves. There would, at the very least, be latitude in the FPC to put wholesale rates in the lower range of the zone of reasonableness, without concern that overall results would be impaired, in view of the utility's own decision to depress certain retail revenues in order to curb the retail competition of its wholesale customers.

510 F. 2d, at 1274. Because the Commission had raised a jurisdictional barrier and refused to consider or hear evidence concerning the Customers' allegations, the Court of Appeals could not determine whether a wholesale rate, if set low enough partially or wholly to abolish any discriminatory effects found to exist, would fail to recover wholesale costs. The case was therefore remanded to the Commission for further proceedings.

We agree with this disposition. It does not invade a nonjurisdictional area. The remedy, if any, would operate only against the rate for jurisdictional sales. Whether that rate would be affected at all would involve, as the Court of Appeals indicated, an examination of the entire "factual context in which the proposed wholesale rate will function." *Id.,* at 52, 510 F. 2d, at 1273. These facts will naturally include those related to nonjurisdictional transactions, but consideration of such facts would appear to be an everyday affair. As the Commission concedes, in determining whether the proposed wholesale rates are just and reasonable, it would in any event be necessary to determine which of the Company's costs are allocable to its nonjurisdictional, retail sales and which to its jurisdictional, wholesale sales—this in order to insure that the wholesale rate is paying its way, but no more....

Furthermore, § 206(a) provides that whenever the Commission finds that any rate, charge, or classification, demanded, observed, charged, or collected by any public utility for any transmission or sale subject to the jurisdiction of the Commission, or that any rule, regulation, practice, or contract affecting such rate, charge, or classification is unjust, unreasonable, unduly discriminatory or preferential, the Commission shall determine the just and reasonable rate, charge, classification, rule, regulation, practice, or contract to be thereafter observed and in force, and shall fix the same by order.

The rules, practices, or contracts "affecting" the jurisdictional rate are not themselves limited to the jurisdictional context. In the *Panhandle* case, supra, decided under the almost identical provision of the Natural Gas Act, 15 U.S.C. § 717d(a), the Court emphasized the same aspect of the section, and went on to hold that because it was "clear" that a gas company's "contracts covering direct industrial sales" are contracts "affecting" jurisdictional rates, [t]he Commission, while it lacks authority to fix rates for direct industrial sales, may take those rates into consideration when it fixes the rates for interstate wholesale sales which are subject to its jurisdiction. 324 U.S., at 646.■

NOTES AND COMMENTS

1. When one utility tries to pick off the best customers of another utility it is commonly referred to in the trade as "cherry-picking." The *Conway* case made it quite difficult for IOUs to pick off the best customers of the municipals by offering lower rates because they might be forced to offer the same rates to the municipal itself.

2. Municipal utilities sometimes get into conflicts with rural cooperatives as well as with investor-owned utilities. For example, if a city served by a municipal utility expands into an area formerly served by a rural cooperative, state statutes may authorize the municipal utility to use the eminent domain power to acquire the existing facilities of the co-op that are located in the expansion area. This can give rise to difficult issues of valuation of the acquired facilities and the measurement of the damages incurred by the co-op. *See, e.g., City of Stilwell v. Ozarks Rural Elec. Co-op. Corp.*, 166 F.3d 1064 (10th Cir. 1999).

3. REGULATION AND CONTRACT

Wholesale electricity rates are determined in two different ways: 1) by contracts between utilities, or between utilities and customer; or 2) by the regulatory provisions of the Federal Power Act. Traditionally, energy companies have relied heavily on long-term contracts. Financial institutions often insisted on such contracts as a condition for financing major capital facilities.

The United States Supreme Court has held that wholesale rates arrived at by contract are presumed to reflect fair bargaining. Therefore, under the Court's so-called "Mobile–Sierra doctrine," FERC cannot change a rate set by contract unless it first finds that the contract rate is "unjust, unreasonable, unduly discriminatory or preferential." *See United Gas Pipeline v. Mobile Gas Serv. Corp.*, 350 U.S. 332 (1956) and *Federal Power Comm'n v. Sierra Pac. Power Co.*, 350 U.S. 348 (1956). The Mobile–Sierra doctrine applies to both the gas and electric side of FERC's operations.[7]

Today, electric utilities are less likely to prefer long term contracts than they were in earlier times. The volatility of energy prices that began in the mid–1970s meant that many electric utilities, like the natural gas utilities, found themselves stuck with long-term contracts that had been entered into under much different market conditions. The *Mobile-Sierra* doctrine made it difficult to modify or terminate these contracts. The following case addresses the application of this doctrine in the context of a contract between two electric utilities.

San Diego Electric and Gas Co. v. FERC

904 F.2d 727 (D.C. Cir. 1990).

■ WILLIAMS, J. This dispute arises out of the lurching energy prices of the past two decades. An energy purchase contract that looked good for both parties on the date signed (November 4, 1985) soon afterwards looked dismal to the buyer. The Federal Energy Regulatory Commission declined to lower the price, but at the same time declined to relieve the seller from a delay of the effective date stemming from what may seem a technical default. We affirm the Commission against attack by both sides.

The contract obligates San Diego Gas & Electric Company to buy 100 megawatts of generating capacity and associated energy from Public Service Company of New Mexico for a 13–year period starting May 1, 1988. At the time it was entered into, the seller was awash in excess generating capacity and the state Public Service Commission had ordered the unnecessary capacity excluded from its retail rate base. Worse still, more unwanted capacity loomed from New Mexico's interest in a nuclear generating station whose three reactors would start up over the next two years. San Diego needed more capacity and wanted to diversify its mix of power sources by securing entitlements to power from coal and nuclear plants. The price offered by New Mexico was the most favorable available to San Diego and was in line with then prevailing market prices.

***

7. Today, wholesale contracts may specify that they are subject to FERC regulation. For example, in *Union Pacific Fuels v. FERC,* 129 F.3d 157 (D.C. Cir. 1997) the court upheld FERC's power to change the rate for transportation on the Kern River gas pipeline from modified fixed/variable to straight fixed/variable in response to the industry-wide shift mandated by Order 636. The Court held that where the contract between the shippers and the pipeline contained a clause specifying that rates were subject to FERC regulation, the Mobile–Sierra doctrine allowed regulatory rate revisions initiated by FERC even though the contract also contained a clause by which the parties agreed not to initiate any such changes themselves.

November 1985 proved, however, to be something of a crest in the wave of energy prices. Oil prices fell from nearly $30 a barrel in November 1985 to $12 in March 1986. J.A. 208. The plunge triggered a drop in the bulk electric power market as well. As oil is used to produce electricity, a fall in its price (and that of close substitutes such as natural gas, whose price is directly affected by that of oil) drives power production costs down; variable costs fall and electricity producers are able to shift away from relatively capital-intensive nuclear and coal sources.... New contracts in 1988 evidently called for much lower prices—with demand charges (the charge for the purchasing utility's entitlement to take electricity) about half or one-third that specified in the contract.

Under § 205 of the Federal Power Act, 16 U.S.C. § 824d (1988), New Mexico could not collect rates under the contract until it had been accepted for filing with the Commission. When New Mexico filed, San Diego tried to persuade FERC to reject the contract as unjust and unreasonable, but the Commission refused. On the other hand, it also refused New Mexico a waiver that proved necessary if New Mexico was to be able to collect the demand charge starting on the date provided by contract, May 1, 1988. As a result of the refusal New Mexico was unable to collect the $3.3 million contract demand charge accrued from May 1 to June 13. Both parties appeal....

San Diego claims that the Commission did not give enough weight to market changes between the execution of the agreement and the time for its performance. These changes were so great, it argues, as to require that the Commission set the contracts aside under its statutory obligation to ensure that interstate wholesale power rates are just and reasonable. *See* Federal Power Act § 205, 16 U.S.C. § 824d.

> In fact the Commission was far from blind to the prevailing market conditions: Given our statutory obligation to judge the justness and reasonableness of the rate in the Agreement, we are required to explore [San Diego's arguments]. The freedom of the parties to contract in this instance must yield to the Commission's duty to ascertain the justness and reasonableness of the rates.

Order, 43 F.E.R.C. at ¶ 62,153. Against this it placed great weight on the policy considerations behind contract stability:

> The certainty and stability which stems from contract performance and enforcement is essential to an orderly bulk power market. If the integrity of contracts is undermined, business would be transacted without legally enforceable assurances and we believe that the market, the industry and ultimately the consumer would suffer.

Id.

This has long been the Commission's position.... Indeed, the Supreme Court has insisted on great Commission deference to freely arrived at contract prices. *See United Gas Pipe Line Co. v. Mobile Gas Serv. Corp.*, 350 U.S. 332 (1956); *Federal Power Comm'n v. Sierra Pacific Power Co.*, 350 U.S. 348 (1956).

As the Commission recognized, the purpose of this contract was to allocate the risk of market price changes between the parties:

The volatility of oil and gas prices, often reflecting large and dramatic swings, is old news. Indeed, this is the very reason that San Diego pursued a long-term purchase from [New Mexico] at rates reflecting [New Mexico's] nuclear and coal units.

Order, 43 F.E.R.C. at ¶ 62,153.

San Diego wanted to diversify its mix of power sources, so to reduce the risk from further surges in the cost of oil and gas. J.A. 256. But each source carries its own set of risks. That is an inevitable part of energy production in a world where sources are varied and their relative prices subject to constant change. Scanning all the sources to which it had access, San Diego selected what it viewed as the optimal mix. On the other side, the contract gave New Mexico partial protection from the risk it had taken in investing heavily in precisely the sources that San Diego (in 1985) felt it needed. San Diego's current conclusion that it got the mix wrong is no reason to allow it to shift the risk (now the loss) back to New Mexico.

We note that New Mexico is no great winner either. The capital-intensive coal and nuclear plants to which it committed itself cannot generate the once-expected revenues. Nothing suggests that New Mexico is a more efficient bearer of the risks that the literal terms of the contract shifted to San Diego. Indeed, San Diego's participation in the 1985 contract as part of a systematic, deliberate program of diversifying risks would seem to mark it as an efficient risk bearer. See Richard A. Posner and Andrew M. Rosenfield, Impossibility and Related Doctrines in Contract Law: An Economic Analysis, 6 J. Legal Stud. 83, 91–92 (1977) (promisor's inferior ability to diversify risks may make it less efficient risk bearer and justify its discharge).

San Diego invokes our decision in *Associated Gas Distribs. v. FERC*, 824 F.2d 981 (D.C. Cir. 1987), where this court required FERC to proffer adequately "reasoned decisionmaking" for its decision not to use § 5 of the Natural Gas Act, 15 U.S.C. § 717d (1988), to relieve pipelines of enormous take-or-pay liabilities under contracts that had become uneconomic. But the root of that decision was the Commission's failure to face directly the effects of its own decision, Order No. 436, restructuring the gas pipeline industry and for the first time subjecting pipelines as gas-sellers to competition from gas sold by others but transported by the pipelines themselves.... Our ultimate conclusion was that on remand the Commission "must more convincingly address the magnitude of the problem and the adverse consequences likely to result from the nondiscriminatory access and CD adjustment conditions [i.e., the Commission's own regulatory interventions]." *Id.* at 1044. And, although asking for more reasoned decisionmaking, we acknowledged that even in the context of risks that the Commission itself had severely exacerbated, FERC's pro-contract policy arguments were "powerful and well grounded in the statutes it is authorized to enforce." *Id.* at 1027. San Diego here offers nothing remotely comparable to the AGD petitioners' plea for regulatory relief; the Commission's reasoning amply served the case at hand.

The petitions for review are Denied.■

NOTES AND COMMENTS

1.   As the above case illustrates, the oil shocks of the 1970s and 1980s had a significant impact on the electricity industry. Many utilities saw the rising fuel prices of the 1970s and early 1980s as a signal to increase their investment in nuclear power. When fuel prices fell in the mid 1980s, that signal changed, but many utilities thought they were too far down the nuclear road to respond. *See* Chapter 14.

2.   In an earlier case, *Metropolitan Edison Co. v. FERC*, 595 F.2d 851 (D.C. Cir. 1979) the court considered a contract entered into in the year 1906 by which an IOU agreed to provide electricity to the Borough of Middletown, Pennsylvania, for one cent per kilowatt-hour until such time as the Borough chose to terminate the contract. The court upheld FERC's determination that the contract was not subject to revision under the Mobile–Sierra doctrine despite the fact that the price was far below current market rates. The court found that the overall impact of the contract on the utility's revenues was minimal.

3.   As this case indicates, the courts tended to read the Natural Gas Act and the Federal Power Act *in pari materia*.

C.   EXTERNALITIES OF ELECTRICITY

Traditional rate regulation of electricity generation and transmission has, in recent years, been subject to criticism for not reflecting the full social costs of power production and delivery. These activities create externalities in two distinct respects: 1) they may impose costs on adjacent or nearby users by emitting pollutants, influencing property prices, or creating risks; and 2) they may fail to fully reflect the actual costs of the fuel inputs utilized for production, leading to overuse—and potential depletion—of certain energy inputs. In recent years, the generation and transmission of electricity has been subject to environmental regulation designed to internalize the full costs of production and delivery.

1.   GENERATION EXTERNALITIES

Electricity generation has a greater impact on air quality than any other single industry in the U.S. (other than the transportation sector, which is discussed in Chapter 15). Electricity generation accounts for approximately 63% of U.S. sulfur dioxide (SO_2) emissions. Local SO_2 emissions are associated with respiratory health problems and regional SO_2 emissions contribute to reduced visibility and acidic rainfall. Utility plants also emit significant quantities of toxic organics and metals such as mercury, cadmium, selenium, lead, arsenic, and beryllium.

The environmental impact of electricity is considered at a number of separate places in this book. The impact of coal-burning power plants on air quality was discussed in Chapter 5. Externalities created by nuclear generation are addressed in Chapter 14. Utilities also account for more than a third of man-made greenhouse gas (CO_2) emissions in the United States. This is discussed in Chapter 16.

2.   TRANSMISSION EXTERNALITIES

When the United States was founded, energy was highly immobile. If you wanted to build a factory, you built it at the specific site along the river where you could build a dam that would give you the water power to turn a mill.

The discovery of the steam engine provided more mobility. Coal and then oil could be brought to the site of the factory, though not without considerable expense. Over time, the technologies for shipping fossil fuels have reduced the cost of transportation. Safety and environmental impact, however, are problems that continue to plague such shipments. (*See* the discussion of transportation of oil by tanker in Chapter 6.)

During the last century, the ability to transmit electric current through wires at high voltage has made it possible to interconnect most of the nation's electric systems. Continuing improvements in the technology have steadily reduced the cost of long distance electric transmission. The ability to transmit energy over long distances at relatively modest cost has enhanced even further the mobility of industries, office complexes and residential communities. This dispersal of new development throughout the nation has had a major impact on American society.

In recent years, however, concern has been rising about the possibility that electric transmission lines have adverse health impacts. Biologists have discovered that proximity to certain types of electric current can cause changes in the formation of cells for reasons that no one can easily explain. This led to some initial studies that appeared to find "clusters" of cancer in a few areas near high-power lines, and these studies were widely reported in the media. The public fear of the electromagnetic field (EMF) created by high-voltage lines is a serious problem for the industry.

A number of scientific organizations have undertaken extensive studies of the EMF issue. A committee of the American Physical Society found no evidence that the electromagnetic fields that radiate from power lines cause cancer. The strength of magnetic fields is measured in "gauss". Magnetic fields radiating from power lines and appliances are measured in milligauss (thousandths of a gauss). A nearby powerline can radiate fields of 5 to 40 milligauss. By contrast, home appliances at a distance of one foot radiate fields from about 1 to 280 milligauss—the highest figure for an electric can opener. Council of the American Physical Society, Power Line Fields and Public Health, Public Statement issued April 22, 1995.

The National Research Council ("NRC") published a report in 1997 entitled "The Possible Health Effects of Exposure to Residential Electric and Magnetic Fields." In this report, the NRC concluded that the "current body of evidence does not show that exposure to these fields presents a human health hazard." The NRC found no conclusive and consistent evidence linking exposure to EMF's with cancer, adverse neurobehavioral effects, and reproductive and developmental effects. *See* Patsy W. Thomley, EMF at Home: The National Research Council Report on the Health Effects of Electric and Magnetic Fields, 13 J. Land Use & Envtl. L. 309 (1998).

In June 1998, another expert panel came to a different conclusion. A panel of experts from the National Institute of Environmental Health Studies ("NIEHS") recommended that low frequency EMF radiation be classified as "possibly carcinogenic" based on some potential correlation with incidence of childhood leukemia. Working Group Report, Assessment of Health Effects from Exposure to Powerline Frequency Electric and Magnetic Fields (Christopher Portier and Mary Wolfe, eds., 1998).

A study published in 2005 supports this claim. It found that children who lived within 600 meters of high voltage transmission lines at birth had a higher risk of childhood leukemia than those born further away. The study included 275 kv and 400 kv lines, as well as some 132 kv lines, in England and Wales. However, this study did not measure the magnetic fields from power lines and other sources, so it provides little risk that increased risk of cancer is due to magnetic fields. The causal mechanism of damage is unclear, but scientists claim reasonable certainty that it involves damage to DNA before birth, possibly in response to infection, chemicals, ionizing radiation, or other environmental exposures. *See* Gerald Draper et al, Childhood Cancer in Relation to Distance from High–Voltage Power Lines in England and Wales: A Case–Study Control, 333 British Medical Journal, June 4, 2005 at 1.

Legally, the EMF issue tends to arise in two different contexts. First, it arises when utilities seek to condemn land for a transmission line right of way. If landowners near the right of way claim that their property values have been reduced because of the public fear of EMF, should they be entitled to compensation even if the fear is unreasonable? For example, if an electric utility takes part of your land for a right-of-way, but leaves your home in usable condition, but you claim that the value of the home has been reduced because of the public's unwillingness to live near high-voltage lines, do you have to prove that the public's fear is a reasonable one? State courts have split on this issue. A minority view holds that damages caused by the public's fear are never compensable. An intermediate view holds that damages caused by the public's reasonable fear may be compensable. The majority view holds that damages caused by the public's fear are always compensable. *See* Comment, The Power Line Dilemma: Compensation for Diminished Property Value Caused by Fear of Electromagnetic Fields, 24 Fla. St. U. L. Rev. 125 (1996); David R. Bolton & Kent A. Sick,

Power Lines and Property Values: The Good, the Bad, and the Ugly, 31 Urb. Lawyer 331 (1999).[8]

A second and potentially even more serious problem for utilities is the possibility of damage awards based on theories of personal injury. Numerous personal injury suits have been filed against electric utilities, but few have been successful. EMF personal injury lawsuits generally allege that EMF exposure has caused various forms of cancer, although a few cases have alleged that EMF causes birth defects and other illnesses. The personal injury claims are toxic torts cases based on the theory that an EMF can be toxic. Exposure to ionizing EMF radiation can clearly be toxic, but the controversy in EMF litigation is over whether non-ionizing radiation produced by high-voltage lines is also toxic. Michael C. Anibogu, The Future of Electromagnetic Field Litigation, 15 Pace Envtl.L. Rev. 527 (1998).

In order to support their position, plaintiffs must be able to offer evidence that will pass the standard adopted by the Supreme Court in *Daubert v. Merrell Dow Pharm., Inc.*, 509 U.S. 579 (1993). Under *Daubert*, a trier of fact must consider several factors when determining the validity of scientific evidence: whether the evidence has been or can be tested; if the evidence has been subjected to peer review and publication; the potential or known rate of error; and whether there is general acceptance in the relevant scientific community. Plaintiffs have had difficulty finding expert EMF testimony that meets this standard. *See Indiana Michigan Power Co. v. Runge*, 717 N.E.2d 216 (Ind. App. 1999).

Most of the EMF personal injury claims to date have been negligence-based, with the plaintiff alleging a duty to warn of EMF health risks and/or a duty to take steps to mitigate such risks. Other lawsuits have raised strict product liability claims, emotional distress claims, and a variety of other claims. For example, in *Zuidema v. San Diego Gas & Electric Company*, the plaintiff, Mallory Zuidema, contracted a rare childhood kidney cancer known as Wilm's Tumor. The plaintiff alleged that SDG&E was negligent in failing to warn the Zuidemas of health risks attributable to EMF from power lines adjacent to the Zuidema home, and that but for SDG&E's alleged negligence the Zuidemas would have moved and Mallory would not have developed cancer. After four hours of deliberation, the jury returned a defense verdict on all counts. No appeal was filed. ABA Section of Public Utility, Communications and Transportation Law, 1996 Annual Report, p.201.

Electric utilities have often argued that tort claims based on EMF are within the primary jurisdiction of the state's public service commission. The California Supreme Court agreed with this argument in *San Diego Gas & Electric Co. v. Covalt*, 920 P.2d 669 (Cal. 1996). For a critique of the

---

8. Resistance to the construction of high-voltage lines may also arise from sources unrelated to EMF, including environmental agencies (*See* the *Florida Power* case discussed in Chapter 2) and neighbors who may think the new power lines will be taking away "their" power to benefit people elsewhere. *See* Robert Wasserstrom et al., Against the Odds: Building new power lines in a deregulated world, Electric Light & Power, June, 1999.

Covalt opinion *see* Paul Lacourciere, Environmental Takings and the California Public Utilities Commission: the *Covalt* Decision, 5 West by Northwest 115 (1998). An Indiana court came to the opposite conclusion. *Indiana Michigan Power Co. v. Runge*, 717 N.E.2d 216 (Ind. App. 1999).

Although EMF tort claims have floundered for the most part, the NIEHS report may provide plaintiffs' attorneys with support for continued pursuit of these claims, at least in childhood leukemia cases. Electric utilities have spent large sums on research, education programs, design changes, and litigation fees, which they recover from consumers through increased rates. *See* Lisa M. Bogardus, Recovery and Allocation of Electromagnetic Field Mitigation Costs in Electric Utility Rates, 62 Fordham L. Rev. 1705 (1994). A conclusive scientific determination of the health effects of EMF would save ratepayers a great deal of money, if it were favorable, or might dramatically reshape the industry, if it were not.

D. ENERGY CONSERVATION

Most of our fossil fuel reserves began to form over 500 million years ago, when the earth's oxygen content was too low to sustain mass fires and plant foliage was added layer by layer to the earth's surface. Since then, many areas with significant plant life have been developed or sustained mass fires on a regular basis and fossil fuel build-up has slowed to a snail's pace, while demand for fossil fuel has increased drastically—particularly in the last 300 years. On current estimates of supply and demand, the U.S. will exhaust most of its supply of petroleum and natural gas by the year 2050. While there will likely be adequate coal reserves to meet energy demand for several subsequent generations, wide-spread usage of coal is not without its impact on land and the environment (See Chapter 5).

Does the traditional system of ratemaking encourage electric utilities to invest more capital in generating facilities than is economically efficient, environmentally sound and socially desirable? Does traditional ratemaking push utilities to sell more electricity at a time when national policy suggests that the conservation of electricity is a more appropriate goal? Has the traditional pricing of fossil fuels encouraged over-consumption of these precious resources?

These questions have had a major impact on electric industry regulation in recent years. In particular, four regulatory mechanisms[9] have raised significant issues regarding the conservation of fossil fuels and usage of new fuel sources: 1) demand-side management (DSM): incentives designed to reduce the demand for electricity during peak periods or to conserve consumption generally; 2) cogeneration: the use of a single power source to generate heat and power; 3) integrated resource planning (IRP): programs which consider demand and supply options prior to approving utility

---

9. In many states, various combinations of, and variations on, these four regulatory mechanisms are used. There is a great deal of variation among the states, and the examples given in this book are illustrative only.

expansions; and 4) renewable portfolio standards: incentives for utilities and other power generators to utilize renewable sources rather than fossil fuels.

1. DEMAND-SIDE MANAGEMENT

Electric utility companies have promoted the use of electricity since the days of Thomas Edison and Samuel Insull. Traditional ratemaking methodologies have created an incentive for companies to exceed their own estimates for electricity sales each year because any such increase in sales directly improves that year's profits. And like most business people, utility executives like to believe they are producing a product that is of value to society.

During the 1960s, the electric utilities were being criticized for failing to provide adequate, reliable service. They naturally responded by significantly increasing the construction of new generating plants and other facilities. In the 1970s it came as a shock to the electric industry, therefore, when organized groups of ratepayers, such as major industrial users, began to complain that the utilities' emphasis on growth was driving up rates unnecessarily. If the utilities taught their customers to use electricity more efficiently, they argued, it would not be necessary to add so many expensive new power plants.

The ratepayers were supported in this argument by environmental groups that saw new nuclear power plants as too dangerous and new coal-fired plants as too dirty. When events in the Middle East brought home the possibility that our supply of imported petroleum might be at risk, the combination of these factors created strong pressures on the electric industry to consider ways by which the use of electricity could be conserved.

Today, most electric utilities have at least some programs designed to encourage their customers to either (1) reduce total electricity usage, or (2) reduce usage at peak hours. For example, Houston Lighting and Power Company works with home builders to encourage tighter, better insulated construction that will reduce the amount of electricity needed for both heating and air conditioning. It also offers incentives to air conditioning users who agree to cycle their air conditioning units on and off during periods of peak electricity demand.

The extent to which the electric utilities employ serious efforts toward these so-called "demand-side management" ("DSM") programs varies with the corporate culture of each company. The incongruity of using electric utilities to "anti-sell" their own product may be compared to using ice cream manufacturers to sell their customers on dieting. But the decision to use the utilities to promote DSM evolved as the result of many years of Congressional debate over various potential ways to promote energy conservation. Beginning with the Energy Policy and Conservation Act of 1975, 42 U.S.C. §§ 6201–6422, Congress almost annually tinkered with legislation designed to encourage users of electricity to use it more efficiently. Current policies for promoting conservation are found in the Public Utility Regulatory Policy Act ("PURPA") as amended by the Energy Policy Act of 1992, 42 U.S.C. §§ 6801–6892. This approach addresses the development and implementation of electric power rate structures with incentives for electric utilities to invest in energy conservation.

PURPA "encourages" the states to adopt regulatory policies that improve electric power conservation, encourage the efficient use of electric power generation facilities and fuels, and promote the adoption of equitable rates for electric power. PURPA outlined six fundamental policies for retail electric power rates and services: (I) rates should reflect the actual cost of electric power generation and distribution; (ii) rates should not decline with increases in electric power use unless the cost of providing the power decreases as consumption increases; (iii) rates should reflect the daily variations in the actual cost of electric power generation; (iv) rates should reflect the seasonal variations in the actual cost of electric power generation; (v) rates should offer a special "interruptible" electric power service rate for commercial and industrial customers; and (vi) each electric utility must offer load management techniques to their electric consumers that will be practicable, cost effective and reliable, as determined by the state public utility commission.

PURPA requires the state commissions to "consider each standard . . . and make a determination concerning whether or not it is appropriate to implement such standard . . . within three years from the law's enactment." PURPA also sets up five standards for retail electric power rates and services. First, the provision of services should ordinarily exclude the installation of "master meters" for multi-unit residential buildings. Second, the rates should not increase under automatic adjustment clauses, unless specific requirements are met. Third, services should provide information to electric utility customers concerning electric power rates. Fourth, the services may not terminate electric power service except in accordance with specified procedures. Finally, "[n]o electric utility may recover from any person other than the shareholders . . . of such utility any direct or indirect expenditure by such utility for promotional or political advertising." *See* Louis B. Schwartz *et al.*, Free Enterprise and Economic Organization: Government Regulation 806–829 (Foundation Press, 6th ed. 1985)

PURPA was upheld in *FERC v. Mississippi*, 456 U.S. 742 (1982). Mississippi and the Mississippi Public Service Commission argued that the statute usurped the traditional state prerogative to regulate the retail rates and services of public utilities in violation of the Constitution's Commerce Clause and the Tenth Amendment. With respect to the Commerce Clause, the Court first observed that, in Section 2 of PURPA, Congress had invoked "the proper exercise of congressional authority under the Constitution to regulate interstate commerce." The Court concluded that the legislative history of PURPA supported Congress' view that the policies and standards of Title I were needed to promote the conservation and efficient use of electric power, which were essential elements of interstate commerce.

With respect to the Tenth Amendment, the Court noted that numerous cases had upheld the federal government's power to compel the states to engage in regulatory activities. The Court said that "the commerce power permits Congress to preempt the States entirely in the regulation of private utilities." Therefore, Congress could choose not to preempt the traditional state prerogative to regulate the rates and services of public utilities, but choose instead to allow the states to take part in the adoption and implementation of federal policies and standards. Accordingly, the Court concluded that the requirements of Title I "simply establish requirements for continued state activity in an otherwise preemptible field."

The Energy Policy Act of 1992 added three new electric rate policies. First, that "[t]he rates allowed to be charged . . . shall be such that the utility's investment in and expenditures for . . . demand[-side] management measures are at least as profitable, giving appropriate consideration to income lost from reduced sales . . . as its investments in and expenditures for the construction of new generation, transmission, and distribution equipment." Second, that "[t]he rates charged . . . shall be such that the utility is encouraged to make investments in, and expenditures for, all cost-effective improvements in the energy efficiency of power generation, trans-mission and distribution." Third, that all electric utilities adopt least-cost or integrated resource plans.

An example of the type of programs typically set up in response to PURPA's policy of encouraging Demand Side Management is the following:

> Kauai Electric's (KE's) Commercial Retrofit (CR) Program is de-signed to promote energy efficiency improvements in existing commer-cial buildings. It targets all existing nonresidential customers. It offers energy audits (analysis), customer education, cash incentives, and low cost financing for energy efficiency measures. The primary program measures are high efficiency air conditioning systems and equipment, high efficiency lighting measures, solar water heaters and heat pumps, and energy management systems.
>
> Commercial customers are grouped into small, medium, and large customers. Those in the small customer category are users of less than 30 kilowatts (kW); those in the medium customer category are users of 30 to 100 kW; and those in the large customer grouping are users of over 100 kW. For small and medium-sized customers, KE will conduct on-site analyses of energy usage, identify energy efficient retrofit opportunities, and assist in implementing appropriate measures through qualified installation subcontractors. KE will buy-down the installed measure cost in an amount equivalent to a two-year customer payback and provide three-year financing of customer contribution at an 8.0 per cent annual rate, with no down payment or prepayment penalty. In the event that a measure does not qualify for an incentive because the payback is two years or less, KE will, nonetheless, provide financing.
>
> For large commercial customers, KE will conduct engineering studies to identify opportunities for increased energy efficiency and

develop a phased energy improvement plan. It will negotiate the measures to be installed and the incentives with each large customer. To avoid oversubscription to the program, KE intends to (1) set the initial incentives at a relatively low level and gradually increase them over time, (2) apportion the CR program budget over the three market segments, and (3) establish a cap on the amount of incentives that any one customer can receive in a year (without KE's review).

The CR program is KE's largest DSM program and is expected to account for over one-third of its total DSM savings. KE anticipates that this program will produce energy savings of 33,064,857 kilowatt-hours (kWh) per year and demand savings of 5,583 kW. KE estimates a net resource benefit of $11,460,000 and a benefit-cost ratio of 2.42. The budget for the first year of full scale operation of the CR program is $403,723.

Re Kauai Electric Division of Citizens Utilities Co. Hawaii Public Utilities Comm., Docket #94–0337 (August 5, 1997).

As indicated above, in 1992 Congress directed that the states should provide incentives for electric utilities to engage in DSM programs. Traditional ratemaking methods, however, discouraged utilities from undertaking programs that increased expenses and reduced revenues. State public utilities commissions were therefore required to re-examine their ratemaking methodologies to comply with the Congressional directive.

Georgia Power Co. v. Georgia Industrial Group

447 S.E.2d 118 (Ga. App. 1994).

■ POPE, C.J. Georgia Power appeals the superior court's order reversing three orders of the Georgia Public Service Commission (Commission) authorizing Georgia Power to recover through riders or surcharges the costs of certain energy conservation programs and "interruptible service credits" paid to customers to reduce their supply of electricity during peak periods.

The issue in this case is whether such costs may be recovered through riders or whether they must be recovered through base rates utilizing the accounting procedure specified in OCGA § 46–2–26.1 for determining the rates to be charged. This case arose out of the legislature's passage in 1991 of a statute that [the Integrated Resource Planning Act (IRP), OCGA § 46–3A–1 et seq. The IRP requires utilities to file long-range energy plans for review and approval by the Commission. OCGA § 46–3A–2. It also requires certification by the Commission before a utility can construct or sell an electric plant, enter into a long-term power purchase, or spend money on "demand-side capacity options" (programs that reduce the demand for electricity). OCGA §§ 46–3A–1(4); 46–3A–3(a). The IRP] allows a utility to recover, inter alia, its costs for any certified demand-side capacity option and an additional sum as determined by the Commission to encourage the development of such demand-side programs. OCGA § 46–3A–9.

... In September 1992, Georgia Power filed revised demand-side programs for its residential customers and sought a proposed residential demand-side cost recovery rider to recover the costs of such programs. The rider proposed to pass through to residential customers (except low income customers) the expected program costs through 1993, subject to a true-up against actual program costs in a future proceeding at the end of 1993. Any over or under collection would be used, together with projected costs for 1994, to set the rider for 1994.... On January 4, 1993, the Commission ... held that Georgia Power should be allowed to recover the costs of its "interruptible service credits" through a rate rider since the credits were relatively new and there would be a time period necessary to determine participation levels and customer responses.

Appellee Georgia Industrial Group appealed to the Superior Court of Fulton County [from the ruling that allowed] Georgia Power to recover the costs of its demand-side programs and its "interruptible service credits" through a rider mechanism. The superior court reversed the Commission's orders, finding that such expenses are recoverable only through the test year rate case procedure prescribed by OCGA §§ 46–2–25 and 46–2–26.1, which was not followed in this case. Georgia Power brought this appeal from the superior court's order, and we reverse.

Georgia Power argues ... that the superior court's ruling is erroneous because the future test year accounting method set forth in OCGA § 46–2–26.1 only applies to general rate cases, which these proceedings do not involve, and because [the IRP] requires use of an accounting method different from the test year statute since the test year statute bases rates on estimated costs and the new statute requires recovery of actual costs.

OCGA § 46–2–26.1 ("Accounting methods to be used by electric utilities in ratemaking proceedings") provides in pertinent part:

"(b) In any proceeding to determine the rates to be charged by an electric utility, the electric utility shall file jurisdictionally allocated cost of service data on the basis of a test period, and the commission shall utilize a test period, consisting of actual data for the most recent 12 month period for which data are available, fully adjusted separately to reflect estimated operations during the 12 months following the utility's proposed effective date of the rates...."

Thus, pursuant to this future test year method, utility rates are established after an analysis of combined revenue, expenses and investment forecasted for a future 12–month period. We agree with Georgia Power that § 46–2–26.1 sets forth the accounting method to be used in determining the general rates to be charged customers rather than issue-specific rates or riders to be charged a particular group of customers. In support of this conclusion, we note that Georgia Power has cited in the record to a number of occasions in which the Commission has approved rate riders without utilizing the test year method. For the reasons discussed below, we further hold that § 46–3A–9 of the IRP gives the Commission the authority to approve recovery of demand-side costs outside of a general rate case and the test year statute.

Traditionally, electric utilities have been concerned with selling electricity and building new power plants to meet increased demands for electricity. Thus, under traditional ratemaking principles (the test year method), a utility's revenues are tied directly to how much electricity it sells. With the advent of integrated resource planning, however, the focus has been on ensuring the efficient use of electricity and the resources used to produce it. As noted earlier, demand-side programs are those which encourage customers to reduce their demand for electricity; often they involve incentives paid to customers to buy more energy efficient equipment for their homes and businesses. However, because demand-side investments result in less electricity being sold, they necessarily reduce the utility's revenues and earnings. For this reason, the legislature enacted OCGA § 46–3A–9, which allows utilities to recover the cost of demand-side programs plus an additional amount as an incentive to develop such programs:

> "The approved or actual cost, whichever is less, of any certificated demand-side capacity option shall be recovered by the utility in rates, along with an additional sum as determined by the commission to encourage the development of such resources. The commission shall consider lost revenues, if any, changed risks, and an equitable sharing of benefits between the utility and its retail customers."

We read this provision to say that a utility may recover the actual or approved costs of its demand-side programs by passing along such costs directly to its ratepayers along with an additional sum or incentive (as determined by the Commission) to encourage it to develop such programs. It seems clear to us that the legislature intended to treat demand-side costs outside of general ratemaking procedures by virtue of the fact that it provided for the utility to recover through rates not only its costs of such programs but an additional financial incentive to develop such programs over and above its overall rate of return. We further note that in providing for utilities to recover the cost of constructing new power plants, the legislature specified in OCGA § 46–3A–7(a) that a utility should be permitted to include in its "rate base" the full amount of approved construction costs absent a showing of "fraud, concealment, failure to disclose a material fact, imprudence, or criminal misconduct." By contrast, § 46–3A–9 simply says that the utility shall recover its demand-side costs "in rates." Had the legislature intended for recovery of demand-side costs to be accomplished through traditional ratemaking principles, it would have specified that such costs could be put in the rate base as it did with power plant construction costs.

Finally, utilization of the test year method for calculating recovery of demand-side costs is unnecessary and would likely preclude the legislative mandate that utilities be allowed to recover their actual costs of such programs. OCGA § 46–3A–9. First, the purpose of the test year method is to analyze a utility's revenues, expenses and investment forecasted for an entire year and determine whether it is earning an appropriate return. *See* OCGA § 46–2–26.1. Since § 46–3A–9 authorizes a utility to recover the exact costs of its demand-side programs plus an incentive, there is no need to utilize the test year analysis to look at its overall earnings.

Second, use of the test year method will not allow a utility to recover its exact costs of such programs plus an additional amount as an incentive because the test year method is not tied to recovery of specific costs but to an overall rate of return. However, under the rider mechanism approved by the Commission, which contains a true-up provision for factoring in any over or under collection of program costs in setting the rider for the next year, the stated purpose of recovering the actual or approved costs of such programs will be met. *See* OCGA § 46–3A–9.

Because use of the test year statute for calculating recovery of demand-side costs would frustrate the legislature's stated intent in encouraging utilities to develop such programs, we conclude the superior court erred in holding recovery of such costs must be accomplished pursuant to OCGA § 46–2–26.1 and that the Commission could not effectuate recovery of such costs through the use of a rider mechanism.

Judgment reversed.■

NOTES AND COMMENTS

1.   An Illinois court construed the Illinois statutes to reach the opposite result in *A. Finkl & Sons Co. v. Illinois Commerce Comm'n*, 620 N.E.2d 1141 (Ill. App.1993) ("The rule against single-issue ratemaking recognizes that the revenue formula is designed to determine the revenue requirement based on the aggregate costs and demand of the utility. Therefore, it would be improper to consider changes to components of the revenue requirement in isolation.")

2.   How much energy are DSM programs actually saving? The question does not have an easy answer. As fuel prices and electricity rates have dropped beginning in 1986, the impetus behind DSM has been lessened. Most businesses have become aware of the value to them of energy efficiency, at least during times of high prices, and many businesses feel that the need for these programs has passed. For example, large industrial users in Minnesota are seeking an exemption from DSM requirements on the ground that they have exhausted all the possibilities for projects that make economic sense. Big Minnesota Industrials Opt Out Of State Energy Conservation Program, Industrial Energy Bulletin, March 5, 1999.

On the other hand, some companies believe that DSM programs are avoiding the need for new generating plant construction. For example, in projections filed with the Florida Public Service Commission, Florida Power and Light Co. says that it expects its DSM programs to reduce total peak summer demand by the end of the next decade by 765 MW. The company gives this as a reason for not constructing two new generating units that otherwise would have had to be put into service during that period. Conservation Plans Will Cut Demand Nearly 1,300 MW by 2009, Energy Services & Telcom Report, March 11, 1999. It is estimated that in Florida

DSM programs will reduce total peak demand by 5156 MW by 2013. See A Review of Florida Electric Utility 2004 Ten–Year Site Plans 8 (Florida Public Service Commission 2004), at http://www.psc.state.fl.us/general/publications/reports/elec-tysp2004.pdf.

The Energy Information Administration ("EIA") released in December 1997 its report entitled "U.S. Electric Utility Demand Side Management 1996." The EIA compiled information regarding the success of demand side management ("DSM") programs in six broad categories: (1) energy efficiency, (2) direct load control, (3) interruptible load, (4) other load management, (5) other demand side management, and (6) load building. In 1996, 1003 of 3199 electric utilities in the United States reported having one or more of these DSM programs. The 573 largest operators reported saving 61,842 million kWh. Consumer characteristics, which include knowledge, awareness, and motivation, often influence the success of a program. External influences, such as energy prices, technologies, and regulations, also affect the success of a DSM program.

(1) Programs relating to energy efficiency work to reduce the amount of energy consumed at specific end-use devices without considering the quality of the service provided. This is often achieved by substituting more advanced technology to use less electricity to produce the same levels of energy services. For example, use energy saving appliances and high-efficiency heating. It is common to use financial incentives to encourage participation.

(2) Direct load control involves consumer loads that can be turned off during peak load hours. The power utility operator directly shuts off the power supply to individual appliances or equipment, such as air conditioners.

(3) Interruptible load programs involve contractual agreements with the consumer that service can be interrupted during peak load hours, either by direct control of the utility operator or by the consumer at the request of the operator. For instance, large commercial and industrial consumers may get discounted interruptible rates for agreeing to reduce electrical loads upon request from the utility.

(4) Other load management programs include technologies that shift part or all of a load from one time of day to another and may affect overall energy consumption of space heating and water heating storage systems. If time-of-day metering is used, these programs can implement real time pricing. (5) Other demand side management programs include consumer substitution of other types of energy for electricity and self-generation of electricity. (6) Load building involves increasing the use of existing facilities instead of building new facilities.

3.   In the 1990s, the emphasis of national energy policy switched from electricity conservation to promotion of the restructuring of electric utilities to promote more competition. The impact of this restructuring on DSM will be discussed in Chapter 13.

2.   Cogeneration

In a traditional power plant, over half of the energy produced from the burning fuel is lost in the form of waste heat. Engineers have long recognized that if the power plant could be built at a place where additional heat was needed, the energy efficiency of the operation would be greatly improved. They began to develop smaller scale generating plants that could be located in large buildings such as industrial plants, hospitals, etc., where the heat could be used to heat the building or in industrial processes. This process is known as "cogeneration."[10]

Cogeneration has been one of the categories of independent power production encouraged under PURPA, and it has accounted for well over three-quarters of the independent power projects created under that statute. Builders of large buildings now routinely review the potential costs and benefits of cogeneration in comparison to purchased power. As will be discussed in Chapter 11, the interconnection between "cogen" projects and the electric utility's distribution network has sometimes been a contentious issue.

On a volume basis, the most extensive use of cogeneration is found in the wood and paper industries. For example, a lumber or paper mill can use heat to treat its products and use the same heat source to cogenerate their own electricity. If the process creates sawdust, it may be fed back into the process as fuel.

Independent power producers have argued that the monopoly powers of the regulated electric utilities are often used to discourage customers from building cogeneration projects. One such IPP executive, Thomas Casten, argues that the electric utilities became "stultified" prior to PURPA:

> "The original entrepreneurs who built electricity from a concept to one of the truly important businesses in every country are long since gone—dead and buried. The aggressive organization built by Samuel Insull took no prisoners and grew in every way possible. His excesses led to PUHCA in 1935, but he sped the development and availability of electricity. Forty years of regulated and protected monopoly prior to PURPA deadened that early entrepreneurial culture throughout the industry and replaced it with a risk-averse, caretaker culture."

Thomas Casten, Turning Off the Heat: Why America Must Double Energy Efficiency to Save Money and Reduce Global Warming 60 (Prometheus Books, 1998).

The incineration of municipal solid waste is another popular form of cogeneration. After the second oil shock on 1979, many local governments built waste-to-energy plants that would incinerate their solid waste and use the heat to generate electricity. Many of these plants are now in financial

---

10. A similar way of utilizing the heat produced in the generation of electricity is the combined-cycle gas generating facility, which has become increasingly popular for small plants. *See* Chapter 9.

difficulty because the rates they charge to solid waste haulers are not competitive with out-of-state landfills, and the Supreme Court has ruled that state and local governments may not favor local waste disposal sites over those from other states without violating the dormant commerce clause. *C&A Carbone, Inc. v. Town of Clarkstown*, 511 U.S. 383 (1994). Local governments that have invested large sums in solid waste combustion plants have tried a variety of maneuvers to maintain a supply of local trash despite the lower cost of other disposal methods, but many courts have tended to read the *Carbone* decision broadly. *See,* Comment, The Need for a Rational State and Local Response to *Carbone*, 18 Va. Envt'l L. J. 129 (1999).

In addition, suspicion has focused on the possible emission of toxic air pollutants from solid waste incinerators. For example, mercury from discarded flashlight batteries may end up in the air from incineration. The Toxic Release Inventory (TRI) established under the Emergency Planning and Community Right-to-Know Act of 1986 42 U.S.C. § 11001 *et seq.*, required all generating plants to report releases annually beginning in 1999.

3.   INTEGRATED RESOURCE PLANNING

While demand-side management has had modest success in promoting conservation by consumers, it was not directed toward promoting conservation by the utilities themselves. The program designed to do that goes under the name of "Integrated Resource Planning" (IRP).

Traditionally, state PSC's have regulated the supply of electricity provided by electric utilities. This was done, to a certain extent through rate regulation doctrines, such as the "used and useful" principle, as is discussed in Chapter 8. However, supply regulation has also historically been achieved through condemnation[11], siting, and permitting proceedings.

However, this is just the first step in the power plant or natural gas pipeline development process. Traditionally, most states have required electric utilities to obtain certificates-of-need (CONs) (sometimes called a CCN—"a certificate of convenience and necessity") before building power plants, transmission lines or pipelines. Typically, the CON is only issued following a siting proceeding—a hearing before the state PSC during which a utility makes its proposal and consumer and environmental groups may be allowed to participate as intervenors. Traditionally, the subject matter of power plant and transmission line siting proceedings was a specific utility-sponsored proposed project.

In recent years, states have begun to experiment with more comprehensive programs of evaluating supply-side alternatives. These are known as least-cost planning or integrated resource planning (IRP). As described

---

11. Ownership of land is often necessary for development of a power project by an electric utility. As is discussed in Chapter 3, in most states electric utilities have the power of eminent domain which is frequently used to build transmission lines for purposes of reaching consumers.

by one of the leading advocates of IRP, a utility's planning program should operate as follows:

The utility system must, in effect, take inventory of its residences, appliances, heating systems, commercial floor-space, and industrial processes, securing estimates of both absolute numbers and average efficiencies. Many utilities have made substantial progress along these lines already, although additional surveys may be needed.

The next step is to develop low and high case projections of additions to these inventories over the forecast period. The range should bound the universe of plausible growth rates for the major end use categories.... Electricity needs for the high and low scenarios should then be calculated by summing existing and new uses, less anticipated retirements, over the forecast period.

This calculation will yield a diverging "jaws" forecast comparable to that produced by the econometric methods reviewed earlier, with one crucial difference: the new forecast is rooted firmly in the instrumentalities of demand, allowing planners to track the effects of investments and policies designed to upgrade efficiencies of some or all of those instrumentalities. In parallel with this forecast, planners should develop a comprehensive assessment of opportunities for improving end use efficiencies. What is the "state of the art" existing and anticipated for delivering the services performed by the system's end uses at the lowest possible electricity consumption?

The question then shifts to how much of this unexploited conservation resource is worth attempting to secure. The answer requires a rigorous methodology for comparing the life-cycle costs of incremental amounts of conservation for each end use with the costs of the most expensive displaceable generating unit in the utility's acquisition plans. In performing that assessment, planners should explicitly credit conservation for its advantages on indices of scale, lead-time, and uncertainty-reduction; the cost column for both the conservation options and the generation alternative should also include quantifiable environmental costs associated with each. The calculation should take specific account of the avoidance of line losses, additional transmission construction, and additional reserve capacity that conservation makes possible when it displaces or defers a new power plant.

From this process will emerge a decision on which efficiency improvements are worth pursuing; it remains, however, to determine how much of the cost-effective conservation resource the system can count on securing. That inquiry focuses on mechanisms for getting the conservation installed; here planners can draw on numerous precedents. Options include state-imposed efficiency standards for some end uses, supplemented by direct utility investment through incentive programs. Planners must anticipate the success of such programs in convincing end users to take advantage of efficiency opportunities. Again, substantial empirical data are already available.

Using those predictions, planners can narrow the "jaws" of the forecast by inserting assumptions about increases in the efficiency of the end use inventories for the "high" and "low" forecasts. Both forecasts will drop, but the high forecast will drop by more because there are more end uses to upgrade. The high forecast then represents the maximum plausible "post-conservation" system needs: the low forecast represents the minimum requirements that will have to be met.

The gap between the two forecasts which conservation has narrowed but not eliminated represents a range of outcomes with which the utility must be prepared to deal. The enterprise is analogous to purchasing an insurance policy; the goal is to minimize the cost of coping with contingencies of varying probability. New generating units may be one element of the response, but other options will bear close scrutiny. Load management programs that shift consumption away from peak periods, without necessarily affecting total consumption, are an obvious example. Also worth investigating is the willingness of large industrial and commercial customers to sell interruption rights to the utility system, which would provide additional reserves in the event of unexpected shortfalls.

In addition, some options, clearly inferior on cost grounds to baseload generators if markets were assured, may look more attractive as a hedge against possible but unlikely growth in demand. Combustion turbines come readily to mind as a generating alternative with relatively high fuel costs, but shorter lead-times and lower capital costs than baseload plants. Obviously, the more certain the system is that it will need significant "post-conservation" additions of energy supply, the better the high-capital-cost, low-operating-cost baseload systems will look. But the converse is also true and most existing forecasts do not permit an informed evaluation of utilities' investment alternatives.

Ralph C. Cavanagh, Least Cost Planning Imperatives for Electric Utilities and Their Regulators, 10 Harv. Envtl. L. Rev. 299–324 (1986).

Bangor Hydro–Electric Co. v. Public Utilities Commission

589 A.2d 38 (Me. 1991).

■ WATHEN, J. Bangor Hydro–Electric Company (Bangor Hydro) appeals a final order of the Maine Public Utilities Commission (PUC) denying without prejudice Bangor Hydro's petition for certificates of public convenience and necessity for two independent hydroelectric generating projects. Bangor Hydro contends that the PUC arbitrarily ignored its own rules and precedents, made findings of fact that were not supported by the evidence, and erred in denying the certificates due to uncertainties created by their premature filing. Finding no error, we affirm the order of the PUC.

On November 22, 1989, Bangor Hydro filed petitions for certificates of public convenience and necessity requesting the PUC to approve three hydroelectric projects along the Penobscot River. The Basin Mills project, which was expected to provide 32 MW of additional capacity by 1999, involved the construction of a new dam and power facility. Construction on the project was not to begin until 1996. The Veazie project, which was expected to add 6 MW of capacity by 1996, and the Milford project, which was expected to add 2 MW of capacity by 1993, were to provide for an increase in the generating capability of currently existing hydroelectric facilities.

On August 17, 1990, the PUC denied without prejudice the Basin Mills and Veazie petitions [and approved only the Milford project]. *Re Bangor Hydro–Electric Company,* Nos. 89–193 and 89–195 (Me.P.U.C. Aug. 17, 1990). While the PUC found that this decision was warranted solely on grounds of the petitions' prematurity, it also cited Bangor Hydro's failure to pursue least-cost options and demand-side resource planning as an alternative to the projects. In its order, the PUC described the standard used in evaluating petitions for certificates of public convenience and necessity:

> [T]he utility must demonstrate that the power from the new source is needed and that the resource being considered is the most economical or at least it is a part of an overall least cost plan. In addition, the utility must demonstrate that the timing is reasonable. This ... standard ... is consistent with the PUC's longstanding policy of encouraging the development of qualifying facilities ("QFs")[12] while requiring utilities to pursue a least-cost plan as required by the Maine Energy Policy Act of 1988, 35–A M.R.S.A. § 3191 (Supp.1990) ("MEPA").[13]

Bangor Hydro argues that the PUC erred in finding that the company did not allow independent power producers to bid against the Basin Mills and Veazie projects and it did not use the bidding process to minimize costs.... The PUC found that, although Bangor Hydro had issued a

12. QFs are non-utility entities of cogeneration and small power production facilities which, as unregulated electric generation sources, market their power to electric utilities. In 1978, Congress enacted the Public Utilities Regulatory Policies Act, section 210 of which was designed to encourage the development of QFs. Pursuant to section 210, the Federal Energy Regulatory Commission promulgated regulations which, among other things, required electric utilities to purchase electricity from QFS at prices not to exceed their avoided costs and required state regulatory agencies to administer the rules. "Avoided costs" are the incremental costs to an electric utility of electric energy, capacity, load management, and/or conservation measures which, but for the purchase from the QF or QFs, such utility would obtain from another source. Public Utilities Commission Rules and Regulations Chapter 36 § 1(A)(3).

13. The MEPA states: The Legislature finds that it is in the best interests of the State to ensure that Maine and its electric utilities pursue a least-cost energy plan. The Legislature further finds that a least-cost energy plan takes into account many factors including cost, risk, diversity of supply and all available alternatives, including purchases of power from Canadian sources. When the available alternatives are otherwise equivalent, the commission shall give preference first to conservation and demand management and then to power purchased from qualifying facilities. 35–A M.R.S.A. § 3191.

request for proposals, the bidding and negotiation process was far from complete, and the company had no intention of completing the process until the PUC proceeding was over. The PUC could reasonably have based these findings on the evidence presented, including the testimony of Jeffrey A. Jones, Bangor Hydro's Manager of Power Supply, who stated that, although a bidding process had begun, it would probably not be completed before this case was concluded. He further admitted that the company had not given bidders an opportunity to bid against these particular hydro projects because these projects were already priced below the avoided costs. Thus, the PUC's findings of fact were basically supported by the totality of the evidence of record and not clearly erroneous. . . .

The "All Ratepayers Test" is an analysis of the overall economic efficiency of the use of ratepayer resources to produce end uses,[14] to determine whether the same end uses can be provided more efficiently with a demand side energy management program than without it, considering the costs and benefits of the program to the utility and to the ratepayers, taken together. A program satisfies this test if the present value of program benefits exceeds the present value of program costs, at the time of analysis.

Chapter 380 § 2(A). Under the MEPA, a DSM program satisfying the All Ratepayers Test should be implemented in preference to additional supply-side projects, including even QFS. Applying these standards, the PUC found that Bangor Hydro had not pursued its required least-cost plan in the area of conservation and demand-side management. Bangor Hydro argues on appeal that the PUC ignored its own rules and the evidence before it in making this finding. . . .

The PUC based its finding primarily on the testimony of Steve Linnell and Carroll Lee who presented Bangor Hydro's criteria for determining the cost effectiveness of DSM programs. Bangor Hydro had the burden of persuading the PUC that its proposed projects were superior to conservation or demand-side measures. The PUC's finding may not be overturned unless Bangor Hydro can demonstrate that the finding was unreasonable, unjust, or unlawful. Examining the totality of the evidence of record, we find no error.

Bangor Hydro fails to show that the PUC ignored the evidence regarding the manner in which the company screens DSM programs. Taken in its entirety, Lee's testimony supports the conclusion that Bangor Hydro conducts its DSM planning according to its own cost-effectiveness criteria, not in compliance with Chapter 380 or the MEPA. When asked whether Bangor Hydro viewed as its responsibility the obligation to implement all cost-effective programs that it could under the All Ratepayers Test, Lee responded, "No, I don't think that is correct." He also indicated that, "as a general rule, as long as long-run marginal rates exceed a utility's long-run marginal costs, it is not appropriate to pay customers to conserve." Be-

---

14. "An 'end use' is the light, heat, motor drive, industrial process, or other useful work resulting from electricity supplied by an electric utility or from a non-electric source provided through a demand side energy management program." Chapter 380 § 2(L).

cause, as Lee testified, Bangor Hydro's long-run marginal rates currently exceed its long-run marginal costs and are likely to continue to do so, the company would not purchase conservation even if the direct costs of conservation were less than the company's avoided cost. Linnell testified concerning the criteria Bangor Hydro uses in selecting programs for inclusion in the company's DSM plan. These criteria are clearly more stringent than the All Ratepayers Test. Bangor Hydro has failed to prove that the PUC erred in finding that its DSM resource planning was inadequate.■

NOTES AND COMMENTS

1.   Some IRP statutes require the public utility commission to evaluate potential new power sources in terms not only of their direct economic cost but in terms of the indirect costs of the environmental damage the source would create. Each year, power plants cause millions of dollars in damage to the environment but these costs, such as the medical costs produced by air pollution, are not included in the market price of electricity. The burden of "paying" for these environmental externalities falls on society in the form of increased medical expenses, depleted agricultural resources, and a reduced quality of life. Currently, in the United States, coal is the main source of electricity production and contributes significantly to air pollution.

One way to internalize these environmental costs is to add environmental cost values to each potential new source. Such values are sometimes referred to as "environmental adders." Currently about half of the state utility commissions take environmental externalities into consideration in their planning process. Of these, seven states have specified monetary externality values for designated air emissions from power plants. Energy Information Agency, Electricity Generation and Environmental Externalities: Case Studies (1998).

Two methods may be used to calculate the value of environmental externalities. One way is to calculate the environmental damage of a pollutant by examining the real world costs of future climate change, illness, and crop damage. This method is called "damage-cost estimate." Kenneth Rose, et al., The National Regulatory Research Institute, Public Utility Commission Treatment of Environmental Externalities 2 (1994). Public utilities commissions often use another method in which the externality values are based on the costs to the power plants of installing air emissions control technologies. This is called the "control cost method." Id. Proponents of these types of regulation argue that they will show that renewable power is really cheaper than fossil fuel when all costs are taken into account. The utility companies should want to choose the resource mix that will achieve the lowest cost, and therefore will be more attracted to renewable energy sources to meet future energy needs. Clinton A. Vince et al., Integrated Resource Planning: The Case for Exporting Comprehensive

Energy Planning to the Developing World, 25 Case W. Res. J. Int'l L. 371, 373 (1993).

Minnesota is one state that enacted renewable resource energy legislation. In 1991, Minnesota legislators passed a statute prohibiting new nonrenewable energy plants unless an applicant could demonstrate renewable energy alternatives were researched and the proposed plant was "less expensive (including environmental costs) than power generated by a renewable energy source." Minn. Stat § 216B.243(3)(a) (1994). The environmental externalities law requires the Minnesota Public Utilities Commission to "quantify and establish a range of environmental costs associated with each method of electricity generation." Minn. Stat. § 216B.2422(3)(a). Monetary values were set based on the values adopted by other jurisdictions and on a 1990 study of externalities. Re Quantification of Environmental Costs, 150 Pub. Util. Rep. 4th (PUR) at 137. The Minnesota courts upheld the values on appeal. *In the Matter of Quantification of Environmental Costs,* 578 N. W. 2d 794 (Minn. App. 1998). *See* Kirsten H. Engel, The Dormant Commerce Clause Threat to Market-based Environmental Regulation: The Case of Electricity Deregulation, 26 Ecology L. Q. 243, 282–287 (1999).

2.   Many states are now encouraging competition among electricity generators in order to bring about lower prices. Such competition allows individual customers to choose which electricity generator they want to buy power from. To what extent can IRP operate effectively in this type of competitive environment? The issue is discussed in the following article, and again in Chapter 13.

3.   In forecasting energy demand, should we assume that the increasing sophistication of information technology will increase energy efficiency and therefore slow the growth of demand? Joseph Romm, the Executive Director of the Center for Energy and Climate Solutions, argues that the increasing use of the internet has already increased energy efficiency and is likely to continue to do so. The Center's report on The Internet Economy and Global Warming is available at www.cool-companies.org.

4.   RENEWABLE PORTFOLIO STANDARDS

From earlier material, it is obvious that concern over the supply of fossil fuels and over the safety and reliability of nuclear energy have stimulated an extensive search for alternative energy sources. To the extent that the sources are renewable—i.e., do not deplete with use—they avoid some of the intergenerational issues discussed in Chapter 8.

An increasingly common practice of state public utility commissions is to require that all generators, or all sellers or both, obtain a certain percentage of their power from renewable resources. These rules are referred to as "renewable portfolio standards" (RPS) because they typically specify that a certain percentage of the company's product must be renewable, but allow the company to choose among a variety of sources. The following article describes how a national RPS program might operate, using existing state programs as a model. At the present time, the share of electric generation fueled by renewable resources other than hydropower is quite low. The challenge of increasing that share is thought to be dependent on the development of regulatory standards that would allow interstate trading of renewable shares.

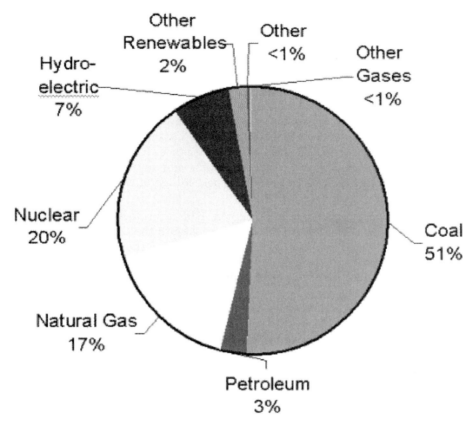

Figure 10–4

Source: U.S. Net Generation by Energy Source, 2003 (Energy Information Administration).

Brent M. Haddad & Paul Jefferiss Forging Consensus on National Renewables Policy

12 Electricity Journal No. 2, March, 1999.

The renewables portfolio standard requires all sellers (or generators) of electricity in the United States to show that they have provided a small but growing percentage of their sales from renewable-energy resources such as wind, solar, biomass, and geothermal. In this way, the RPS creates for electricity a widely used minimum-content-type standard similar to insulation requirements for new buildings and minimum standards for recycled paper content. More than this, the RPS is designed to use market forces to reduce the cost of the program in much the same way that the Environmental Protection Agency's SO[2] allowance trading system reduces the cost of the acid rain program, and that other programs use air pollution permit trading to reduce air emissions at the lowest possible cost.

It would be inconvenient to require every retail seller of electricity in the country to purchase renewably generated power up to a minimum standard. The RPS provides an alternative mechanism that provides minimal inconvenience and improved efficiency. First, a program administrator awards to producers of renewable-resource electricity currency-like renewable energy credits (RECs) that specify when, where, and how much renewable electricity they have generated, and what type of renewable resource was used. RECs represent all of the values of renewable energy not currently paid for by consumers [such as greenhouse gas mitigation and national energy independence]. Instead of having to generate or buy renewable energy, retail sellers could purchase RECs from renewable energy producers and submit them once each year to the program administrator in amounts equal to the required percentage of their total electricity sales.

For renewable energy producers, the RPS therefore creates a second commodity and a second market that supplements the income they receive from selling renewable power itself. They would sell their renewable power locally at the market rate, just like all other power producers. They would sell their RECs nationally to retail suppliers anywhere in the country who need RECs to comply with the law. The price of RECs is expected to be that increment of additional revenue needed to keep competitive renewable power producers in business and to attract new renewables producers into the business. New renewables development, up to the minimum standard, will take place wherever in the country that increment of revenue is lowest. As happened with SO[2] allowances, a vibrant market for RECs is likely to arise, driving their cost down, making renewable-resource generators more competitive, and lowering the cost of our national commitment to renewable energy.

When California's Public Utilities Commission became the first such commission to endorse the RPS, it was endorsing a concept, not a completed blueprint for a program. Now, after 3 years of development involving a collaboration of academic specialists, industry participants and representatives, NGO activists, and state and federal regulators, the concept of the RPS has been refined to the point where it can effectively deal with practical implementation issues. In the following paragraphs, we summarize these refinements and demonstrate how they not only overcome hurdles to implementation but do so in ways that enhance the overall efficacy and political viability of the policy.

One concern that has been raised is that it is difficult to predict or cap the cost of the program. The argument is that if there is a scarcity of renewable energy credits, then retail suppliers who need to purchase RECs may come up short. In this hypothetical scenario, retail suppliers who needed to buy RECs would then be forced to pay either exorbitant prices for scarce RECs or high penalties for non-compliance with the program.

Buyers of RECs can be fully protected from the risk of scarcity. First, we believe that it is quite possible to predict the cost of achieving particular standards in particular years, at least within a range. This means that policymakers can choose to set the initial level of the RPS and its subsequent ramp-up rate at levels that are unlikely to lead to credit scarcity or high prices. At the start, the level of the standard would be quite modest, increasing gradually but steadily over time in a manner consistent with a predetermined balance between our national commitment to renewable energy and our concern about limiting public expenditure. In practice, this means there will be ample advanced warning (years, in fact) to ramp up renewable-energy production to meet the growing requirement to purchase RECs. however, even if projections prove wrong, and credit shortages and high prices occur, a creative price-cap mechanism has been developed for the RPS. The proposed price-cap mechanism solves the issue of trading scarcity without reducing the effectiveness of the market mechanism. In the case of a national RPS, the RPS program administrator would issue a standing offer to sell "proxy" RECs to retail suppliers at a price administratively predetermined to reflect the maximum desired public expenditure on the whole program. If the price of RECs on the market remains below the capped price of the administrator's proxy RECs, retail suppliers will purchase those. But if for any reason (not just scarcity) the market price for RECs exceeds the capped price, retail suppliers can choose to purchase some or all of their requirement from the program administrator. The retail seller would fill out a one-page form stating how many RECs it wishes to purchase and would attach a check. Retail sellers will be able to identify in advance with complete precision their maximum cost of compliance simply by multiplying their REC-purchase requirement in KWHs by the price-cap price.

If retail sellers take advantage of the program administrator's standing offer, a fund would accumulate. The administrator would use this fund to purchase RECs on the market. Fewer RECs would be purchased than the required percentage, but the RPS market would consistently reward the least-cost generators of renewable energy until cost-cap funds run out. In the unlikely scenario that no RECs are available, the administrator could disburse the fund exactly like the trust fund, by auctioning production credits, or supporting R&D.

In practice, of course, retail suppliers will seek, and find, some lower-cost RECs on the market. In this way the certainty of a maximum cost turns the cost uncertainty of a market-based mechanism like the RPS into a defining virtue. The actual cost can only turn out to be equal to or less than the maximum. When one is faced with a choice between a fixed total cost and a maximum cost of equal value that is entirely likely to be much lower than the maximum, one would choose the latter option every time. This is the raison d'etre of market-based mechanisms. Society thus guarantees that it will achieve the goal it has set for itself (in this case, a minimum percentage of renewable-resource electricity as part of the overall electricity mix) at the lowest possible cost.

There is ample opportunity to structure a portfolio standard to ensure more even regional distribution of renewables development, an outcome that would spread out the economic and environmental benefits of renewables. With national credit trading and a relatively low RPS requirement, renewables development is likely to take place in locations where the difference between the local marginal cost of power and the cost of producing renewable energy is lowest. By creating an opportunity for "local content" in the federal program, states (or regions) could ensure that future renewable power development, with its attendant local benefits, occurs locally and, consequently, throughout the nation.■

NOTES AND COMMENTS

1.   As of 2005, 21 states have adopted renewable portfolio standards. *See* North Carolina State University, Database of State Incentives for Renewable Energy, http://www.dsireusa.org/summarytables/reg1.cfm?&CurrentPageID=7. *See also* Ryan Wiser et al., Emerging Markets for Renewable Energy: The Role of State Policies during Restructuring, Electricity Journal (January, 2000). To what extent will it be possible to trade credits under RPS programs on an interstate basis without violating the dormant commerce clause? *See* Engel, *supra* at 287–295. A number of other states have sought to promote renewable power through the use of "System Benefit Charges," through which all customers pay a fee based on volume of electricity used, which is collected at the state level and distributed to support renewable energy projects. Twelve states have adopted such programs. As of the end of 2003, about two dozen states had implemented systems benefit charges to pay for a variety of public programs, including renewable energy resources and energy efficiency. *See* American Coucil for an Energy–Efficient Economy, http://www.aceee.org/briefs/mktabl.htm. *See also* Wiser, *supra*.

2.   Financial investment in renewable resources by both the public and private sectors is continuing to increase. The federal government has announced a "Million Solar Roofs" initiative designed to encourage property owners to install solar systems on a million homes and businesses by the year 2010. The federal government has committed to install solar systems on 20,000 of its own buildings within this time period. Government-supported loans are available for program participants. *See* the Department of Energy's web site at http://www.millionsolarroofs.org.

Some of the major oil companies have made large investments in solar power technology because they are anticipating the expansion of the markets for such power in developing countries. Royal Dutch Shell has announced a plan to invest up to $250 million in its plant in the Netherlands to produce 100,000 square meters of solar cells each year. *See* Utility Environment Report, October 10, 1997, at 9.

3. The State of California has taken the lead in encouraging the use of wind power to generate electricity. Certain mountain passes in California offer some of the most reliable sources of consistently high winds. The California Energy Commission allocated $540 million in state funds in fiscal 1998 to support new renewable energy sources, much of which will be used for windpower projects. The Department of Energy also awards contracts to help develop improved technologies for the utilization of windpower.

Private utilities outside California are showing increasing interest in the development of windpower farms. Oregon utilities have built a $60 million windpower project in Wyoming that is designed to generate 41.4 MW of electricity. Sixty-nine wind turbines were erected on a 2100 acre tract of ranchland between Laramie and Rawlins, an area that has an average windspeed of 25 miles per hour. Foote Creek Rim 1 began operation April 22, 1999 (Earth Day). *See* http://www.eweb.org/home/windpower/wyoming/foote_creek.htm. Maximum generation output is 85 megawatts of electricity. *See* http://www.eweb.org/home/windpower/wyoming/index.htm.

E.   DISTRIBUTED GENERATION

There is a new group of smaller scale generation technologies on the horizon that are attracting a great deal of attention. By providing individual generating plants that are small enough to meet the needs of a home or business, they may reopen the issue that Samuel Insull thought he had settled: Is the central station the most efficient way to generate electricity?

These technologies have been grouped under the term distributed generation ("DG"). DG includes generation, generation-like and storage devices that are connected to the distribution grid on either the system side or customer side of the meter. These new technologies enable incumbent electric distribution utilities, their non-regulated utility affiliates, independent power producers and consumers to break from the central station paradigm of electricity generation and distribution.

Interest in DG is particularly keen in those businesses for whom a loss in power supply is especially costly. Banking and financial facilities, hospitals, manufacturing and assembly plants, grocery stores and restaurants are seen as the key market for DG, particularly in areas where older utility distribution systems have often caused blackouts. Distributed Generation Could Hit 20% of New Generation in 20 Years, Electric Utility Week, January 3, 2000.

DG includes small generating facilities that can be installed on-site or as part of the distribution network to generate additional power. DG technologies evolved from emergency back-up generators. Indeed, several DG technologies are just back-up generators re-engineered for constant generation at efficiencies comparable to larger central station generation, but others use a wide range of new technologies such as microturbines, reciprocating engines, fuel cells, and even the next generation of wind generators, photovoltaics, etc.

These units are usually generators ranging from about 1 megawatt down to a capacity sized for a single home. They can be used by industrial, commercial and residential customers. They are fueled by natural gas, oil, gas, solar and wind energy, of which natural gas is currently the most popular fuel.[15]

The future impact of the addition of DG on generation, distribution and independent power production systems may be significant. DG may be implemented in several different ways in the present distribution structure.

First, DG may take the form of an on-site generator owned by a single customer to meet its on-site needs. In that capacity, DG may also provide co-generated heat and emergency back up power. However, at the present state of the technology an on-site DG may not be an efficient way of meeting all of a customer's generation needs because, although on-site DG units can be used to meet the peak load of summer air conditioning, it is not economical to size a unit that can generate the far greater power needed to start up today's air conditioning units (ten times running load). A DG unit with sufficient capacity to meet such high loads would be under-utilized most of the time.

Second, DG could be interconnected to the distribution grid. A DG unit connected to the grid could generate all base load power, and draw off the grid for the critical cycling loads. Alternatively, a DG unit could be slaved to a certain device, such as a refrigerator or air conditioner and thereby flatten out the generation requirements of the customer throughout the year.

Third, DG could be bi-directionally interconnected to the grid. The bi-directional connection would allow the DG to generate power for the grid. In this role a network of on-site DG units can be used to generate peak-shaving power and voltage support.

Fourth, DG units can be directly installed by the electric utility as part of the distribution grid to perform peak-shaving and voltage support functions or other ancillary services. DG units could replace higher cost or aged peak-load generation facilities and allow utilities to incrementally raise generation to meet instant needs.

Fifth, DG may be used as an alternative to expansion of the distribution network or even the transmission network. Utilities can avoid the cost of constructing a new line to remote customers by siting DG close by them, thus avoiding line-losses resulting from long distance electricity transmis-

---

15. In addition, companies are developing fuel cells and ultra-capacitors for power storage that serves many of the same functions as DG. Fuel cells have made great improvements in efficiency, mostly due to the collateral benefits of research and development toward efficient automobile fuel cells. (See Chapter 15.) In addition, research into the development of a more efficient storage battery continues. Some commentators suggest that improved storage has even more potential than actual generation devices. Mark P. Mills, Micro Gen? Think Again, Public Utilities Fortnightly, June 1, 1999, at 16.

sion. Indeed, a nearby lower efficiency DG unit may be more efficient than a high efficiency central station generator several miles away.

Finally, one specific instance of this would be serving geographically remote customers by a single DG station in a distribution strategy called "islanding". "Islanding" could be especially beneficial for industrial parks and small communities, which could take advantage of the high efficiency co-generated heat. Such a generation island could be owned by the utility serving the territory, or, if state legislation permits, by an independent electricity service provider or by the community served.

Although DG is on the horizon, a number of important issues must be resolved before usage of DG becomes widespread. Technology and standards for uni-directional and bi-directional interconnection need to be fully developed. With current technology and under the present regulations, DG is limited to an unconnected back-up or full capacity generating unit for an unconnected customer, or to units owned by a utility and used as part of the distribution grid. Several things are required before other possibilities will be available.

First, there is a need to agree upon proven technology for either uni-directional or bi-directional interconnection of DG to the grid. Technologies must be developed to allow small scale interconnection. Uni-directional interconnection is the closest technology to realization, because it is the least different from traditional connection to the grid. Bi-directional, however, will be much more difficult to develop, because the utility will need to be able to control it for worker safety and for the anticipated sale of power or grid maintenance to the utility. Additionally, advanced metering technologies will be required to correctly bill customers for reduced use or credit them for grid benefits.

Second, regulations or standards for interconnection of DG are still developing. DG is analogous to the large generation connections to transmission required to implement PURPA contracts. The procedures under PURPA are too time consuming and expensive to be economically practical for small scale DG. Mindful of this concern, FERC has issued standard procedures for the interconnection of generators that are no larger than 20 megawatts, Order No. 2006, as well as for generators that are larger than 20 megawatts, Order No. 2003. *See* Order No. 2006, 111 F.E.R.C. ¶ ___ (2005), http://ferc.gov/EventCalendar/Files/20050512110357-order2006.pdf; Order No. 2003–C, 111 F.E.R.C. ¶ 61,401 (2005), http://ferc.gov/whats-new /comm-meet/061505/E–7.pdf. FERC's procedures provide for expedited procedures for the approval of interconnections and delimit standard cost-sharing responsibilities and a procedure for resolving disputes.

Third, electricity rates do not reflect the actual cost of generation and delivery of power for different times of day and year. Rather, all costs are aggregated into a single rate, thereby removing all price signals to customers. Without adequate price signals customers cannot determine whether DG is the more efficient manner of generation. Again this goes against the tenets of a competitive market. DG can only thrive in an environment where customers are subject to the actual cost of generation and distribution. Such rates would reveal when DG will be likely to be more efficient than peak power generation or remote customer distribution. Advanced metering technology will be necessary to implement actual time of day rates.

Finally, state commissions must address who may own and operate DG.[16] Specifically, to what extent utilities may do so, and what requirements they must meet. Related to this issue is the extent to which natural gas distributors will be allowed to enter the DG market. As the provider of the most prevalent DG fuel, natural gas distributors could have a substantial impact on the DG market.

If DG technology really becomes the wave of the future, electric utilities will face new "stranded cost" problems (see Chapter 12). And to what extent will they be compensated for maintaining "spinning reserves"?

DG offers the prospect of many new ways of providing power that depart from the central station model. The low capital investment and small generation capacity of DG makes it the ideal vehicle for independent electricity service providers to enter the electricity generation market. However, the current regulatory structure has long been geared toward large scale central station generation by regulated monopolies. The uncertainties cited above must be addressed before DG will be able to fulfill its potential in the coming competitive distribution market. *See* Chris Holly, Distributed Generation's Big Potential Faces Big Barriers, Energy Daily, June 24, 1999.

16. In California, independent power producers and industrial users have asked the California Public Utilities Commission to determine whether it would be fair to allow utilities to compete in the DG market. *See* www.cpuc.ca.gov./distgen. The independents and industries argue that under current regulations, utilities can refuse interconnection to any DG unit, but the utilities may install DG units for their own benefit. This seems to go against the competitive goals espoused by the California Commission. In order to remedy this, they argue, state commissions will have to mandate equal access for all DG units regardless of ownership in order to provide a level playing field for the new DG market. The independents claim that allowing utilities to compete and control interconnection will result in a fox guarding the henhouse scenario. If a competitive market is desired, an independent standard of interconnection must be created. Richard Stavros, Last Big Battle for State Regulators, Public Utilities Fortnightly, Oct. 15, 1999.

CHAPTER 11

WHOLESALE ELECTRIC POWER COMPETITION

A. COMPETITION IN ELECTRICITY IN GLOBAL CONTEXT

Electricity Reform Abroad and U.S. Investment Energy Information Administration, U.S. Department of Energy (1997)

<http://www.eia.doe.gov/emeu/pgem/electric/es.html>.

Over the past decade a number of nations have restructured their electricity industries. Several nations have also significantly reduced the government's role in the ownership and management of domestic electricity industries both at the state and at the national level. The Energy Information Administration selected Argentina, Australia, and the United Kingdom (UK) for this study partly because of the extent to which these nations have undergone electricity reforms but also because of the major role that U.S. companies have played as investors in these nations' reformed and privatized electricity sectors. Understanding how Argentina, Australia, and the United Kingdom each addressed the issues of primary importance to their country's electricity sector reform may be informative to those who will fashion the structure of similar reforms in the United States. This understanding may be all the more important because of the experiences that U.S. electric companies will have gained from their investments in these countries.

Since the early 1990's, investment in overseas electricity assets has been a rapidly growing target of U.S. companies' foreign investment. The predominant share of this investment has been directed at the United Kingdom and Australian electricity industries. The investment expenditures of U.S. companies in the electricity industries of the United Kingdom and Australia alone far exceed all U.S. overseas electricity investment in the rest of the world combined. Electric utilities from the United States have also been the most prominent foreign investors in the recently-privatized Argentine electricity companies although the dollar value of investment in Argentina's electricity industry has been smaller relative to the investment dollars flowing to Australia and the United Kingdom.

In Argentina, Australia, and the United Kingdom, electricity reform has involved a combination of the following issues:

— an unbundling of electricity assets;

— the creation of electricity pools;

— the creation of independent system operators;

— the privatization of electricity assets through sale or public auction;

— the deregulation of electricity and the implementation of a more restrained form of regulation where regulation was retained;

— the adoption of price cap regulation and movement away from rate-of-return regulation;

— the realization of a competitive market in generation;

— the separation of the "wires" function of distribution from the "marketing" function;

— the gradual introduction of competition in electricity marketing;

— an opening up of domestic electricity assets to foreign investment; and

— determination of the degree of recovery of stranded costs. In each of the three case study countries, issues surrounding electric industry restructuring, competitive electricity pools, privatization, deregulation, and stranded costs are unique to each country's electricity reform experience. However, there are often more commonalities than differences, particularly in the case of Australia and the United Kingdom. In all three countries, electricity reform involved a greater opening to foreign investment in electricity.

In Argentina, Australia, and the United Kingdom, electricity restructuring and privatization were carried out in an atmosphere of general economy-wide restructuring and privatization. In all three countries, a primary goal motivating electricity reform was to achieve lower electricity costs for consumers through encouraging efficiency improvements in the electricity industry. Reduced costs were also to serve the purpose of improving the efficiency of the overall economy. In all three countries, raising revenues for the treasury to reduce public borrowings was another overriding motive. In Argentina, obtaining badly needed capital for electricity infrastructure improvement and expansion was an additional motivating factor for reform and privatization. . . .

Figure ES3 [included as **Figure 11–1**] depicts a hypothetical "model" of what a national electric utility restructuring might look like. Figure ES3 shows an electricity industry as a single nationalized entity prior to the restructuring. The restructuring involved the separation of all electricity industry functions along separate lines of business (i.e., generation, transmission, distribution, and marketing) into newly created organizations. It should be stressed that Figure ES3 is a much simplified (and not entirely representative) model of restructurings that have taken place in several nations. Figure ES3 is more illustrative of the United Kingdom experience where the electricity industry prior to restructuring was owned and managed primarily by the central government. In contrast, in Australia statewide electricity restructuring largely preceded nation wide reforms and was predominate. Argentina is also distinct in that Argentina's restructuring involved a wide-scale consolidation of electricity operations.

In the United Kingdom, electricity reform initially involved the complete restructuring (unbundling) of the industry along segmental lines: electricity generation, transmission, distribution, and marketing all became separate operations. Prior to privatization, the United Kingdom created two large power generation companies, one national transmission company, and twelve regional generation companies. A newly-evolving electricity marketing segment was to be gradually developed, where sales, brokerage, and billing operations each became a separate function. In its restructuring, however, the United Kingdom created an industry that from its infancy was dominated by the two large generation companies whose predominant market share and predominant role in the electricity pool has often given rise to concerns over whether generation was adequately competitive.

Although Australian reforms borrowed heavily from the UK experience, there have been several notable distinctions. In contrast to reform in the United Kingdom, electricity reform in Australia was undertaken several years later and at both the state and national levels. In general, several of the Australian state governments restructured their electricity industries in a fashion similar to the United Kingdom: separating generation, transmission, distribution, and supply into different operations. However, although Australia's reform efforts are more recent (and therefore more difficult to appraise), it appears that Australia may have avoided the kind of public concerns that have occurred in the United Kingdom over a lack of competition in electricity generation. Victoria, the second most populous of the Australian states but with a population less than one-fifth that of the UK attempted to create more competition in generation through the creation of five generation companies. Various Australian governments have also encouraged the development of an independent electricity marketing function, thus as in the United Kingdom allowing customers to bypass traditional distribution companies.

In Argentina, as in the United Kingdom, restructuring was primarily a central-government-led operation. The Argentine government unbundled generation operations from transmission and distribution. Electricity marketing, however, was not separated out as a distinct business company or operation. However, due to the dispersed population concentrations in Argentina, several regional transmission companies were created. The regional companies act as spurs connecting otherwise isolated areas to the main electricity grids.

Competitive Electricity Pools

All three countries created national electricity pools. The United Kingdom was first to create a national electricity pool, which has been in operation since 1990. The UK electricity pool is operated by the National Grid Company, which is also responsible for electricity transmission. The UK pool has generally operated efficiently, although concerns have been raised over its tendency to produce price volatility and an unfair playing field between electricity suppliers (again, primarily the two now-privatized dominant generation companies) and electricity consumers. A secondary market, called a contract for differences market, has evolved in the United Kingdom. This secondary market allows participants to hedge a large fraction of their pool purchases.

In Australia, the National Electricity Pool was largely based on the UK model, but with some noteworthy variations. The Australian National Pool is a fairly recent operation, having started in May 1997. (Preceding the creation of the national pool, a couple of Australian state governments created their own electricity pools and these have been in operation for several years.) The Australian National Pool is operated by an independent system operator, the central-government-owned National Electricity Market Management Company, which is separate from any transmission operation. As in the United Kingdom, pool price volatility has been an important concern in Australia, and a contract for differences market has been created to manage this risk. However, due to the relatively large number of generators participating in the supply end of the business, less concern has been raised over a lack of competitiveness.

In Argentina, a national electricity pool was also based upon the UK model. Pool operations began in 1992, and pool prices have been considerably beneath the comparable wholesale price of electricity existing prior to the commencement of pool operations. Again in contrast to the United Kingdom, no generator in Argentina is allowed to control more than ten percent of the system's generation capacity. Further, in Argentina an independent system operator operates the pool.

Asset Privatization

In the United Kingdom, widespread privatization of electricity assets followed shortly after the restructuring. These privatization were achieved through public auctions. Eventually, virtually the entire UK electricity industry was privatized with the exception of some relatively old nuclear generation plants. Much controversy surrounded the sale of UK electricity assets. With the exception of the sale of nuclear assets, UK electricity auctions were oversubscribed, leading to allegations that the government had not obtained a fair value in the sale of public goods. Further, energy companies from the United States were eventually to acquire roughly one half of all UK electricity assets.

In Australia, only the state of Victoria has gone nearly as far as the United Kingdom in its privatization efforts. Other Australian state governments were either slower to privatize or decided to retain ownership while reducing control over their electricity industries. During the initial public auction of Victoria's electricity assets, U.S. companies purchased controlling interests in all five of the privatized regional distribution companies and three of the five generation companies. Sizable premiums over book value were paid in all cases, an indication of the relatively high value U.S. companies placed on these takeover targets.

The Argentine central government also employed an auction to transfer ownership of the national government's holdings in electricity companies to the private sector. Interestingly, in the Argentine auction, bidders were required to submit levels of service standards they were committing to meet along with bid prices. Again, U.S. companies were the dominant foreign investors in Argentine electricity.

Deregulation

All three governments employed a less intrusive form of regulatory authority than that which had existed in the past. The United Kingdom's electricity reform efforts embraced two fairly radical departures from previous electricity regulation. One involved the nature of the regulator. One of the first acts of electricity reform created a national electricity body, the Office of Electricity Regulation ("OFFER"). In order to reduce regulatory costs and allow industry more discretion in investment and operational matters, the OFFER was lightly staffed and was headed only by a single individual (not a commission). Similar institutions were adopted in Argentina and Australia.

A novel form of price-cap regulation was adopted in the United Kingdom and emulated in Argentina and Australia. Price-cap regulation attempts to restrain costs via the application of price ceilings. Price-cap regulation is a marked contrast to the rate of return regulation employed in the United States. In terms of encouraging efficiency, price-cap regulation appears to have been successful in all three nations but has become a highly controversial matter with regard to whether it promotes equity and fairness for consumers.

Energy Subsidies and Stranded Costs

In the United Kingdom, the issue of energy subsidies (mostly those related to coal) and the disposition of stranded costs (mainly nuclear-related) greatly complicated efforts at electricity privatization. The UK electricity industry had long sustained the UK coal industry through its purchases of domestic coal at highly inflated prices. As both industries became privatized and deregulated, these subsidies were severely reduced. The stranded costs associated with nuclear power investment in the United Kingdom represent the difference in the book value of nuclear power facilities and the market value of these facilities. In contrast to the situation in the United States, where the issue of who should bear the burden of stranded costs associated with nuclear power investments is between rate payers and shareholders, in the UK (where, prior to privatization, all nuclear generating assets were owned by the national government), the issue of allocating the burden of stranded costs was between rate payers and tax payers. In the end, both parties paid: tax payers through the government's auctioning off nuclear electricity assets at heavily discounted prices; and rate payers, through a nuclear surcharge attached to electricity bills.

In Australia, stranded costs were largely unimportant due to Australia's having a very competitive coal industry (by world standards) and never having developed a nuclear power industry. In Argentina, much as in the United Kingdom, part of the failure to successfully privatize the federal government's nuclear plants stemmed from the issue of stranded costs. However, unlike the United Kingdom, Argentina has had to resolve stranded costs associated with past investments in hydroelectric power as well. Even though the marginal costs of operating Argentina's two large binational (i.e., jointly held with Paraguay and Uruguay) hydroelectric facilities are low, it is doubtful that the Argentine government will be able to recover the large capital costs associated with these facilities because of their large construction cost overruns.■

NOTES AND QUESTIONS

1. This summary of an extensive report, prepared for the Department of Energy, discusses restructuring developments in other countries. Are there any institutional aspects of the U.S. energy sector that will make the implementation of competition in the U.S. more of a challenge for regulators? For example, how should the fact that we have so little government ownership of the electricity sector influence the regulatory solution in the U.S.?

2. In Australia, an independent system operator operates a "pool"—an arrangement that facilitates coordination of power transmission decisions and helps to ensure reliability and open access. The pool model is an approach to implementing competition that can involve both markets and government regulation, as regulators sometimes need to evaluate who participates in the pool, who makes decisions regarding the market, and how well the pool works at achieving regulators' goals. Later in this chapter, the independent system operator, a pooling approach endorsed by U.S. regulators, is discussed as a way of managing transmission. In Chapter 12, the power pool approach is discussed as an approach for implementing retail competition in states such as California.

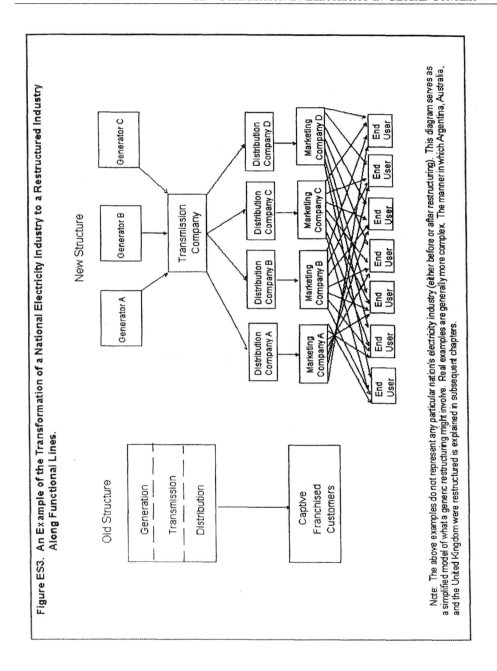

Figure ES3.   An Example of the Transformation of a National Electricity Industry to a Restructured Industry Along Functional Lines.

Note: The above examples do not represent any particular nation's electricity industry (either before or after restructuring). This diagram serves as a simplified model of what a generic restructuring might involve. Real examples are generally more complex. The manner in which Argentina, Australia, and the United Kingdom were restructured is explained in subsequent chapters.

Figure 11–1

3. Following the U.K.'s privatization and liberalization of its energy industry, foreign investors made large profits in the newly constituted energy services markets. In the late 1990s, the U.K. passed legislation designed to tax the profits of some these firms as "windfalls." This has created a large degree of uncertainty for investors regarding the risks in the restructured U.K. electric power market. For discussion, see Thomas W. Waelde & Abba Kolo, Renegotiating Previous Governments' Privatization Deals: The 1997 U.K. Windfall Tax on Utilities and International Law, 19 J. Intl. L. Bus. 405 (1999). Some investors have left the U.K. market due to this uncertainty.

4. The same restructuring trends have played out in the U.S., where debates over deregulation have taken on a distinctive political rhetoric. For an excellent discussion of the history of deregulation, see Richard F. Hirsh, Power Loss: The Origins of Deregulation and Restructuring in the American Electric Utility System (MIT Press 1999). Hirsh traces regulation to the passage of energy legislation in 1978, along with an unraveling of the "utility consensus" represented by rate regulation at the federal and state levels.

David Spence describes the impetus for restructuring of utility industries in the U.S. as follows:

> The theoretical case for restructuring was and is simple, straightforward, and based on two related propositions. First, the sale of electricity is not a "natural monopoly"; rather, it can and should be an industry in which sellers compete for customers. Second, and partly therefore, markets can set electricity prices better and more efficiently than governments can. Both of these propositions represent departures not only from traditional thinking but also from the assumptions that underlay the creation of the federal and state electric utility regulatory regimes during the first half of the twentieth century.

> Federal public-utility statutes like the FPA and its state analogs were created amid public worry over the concentration of economic power in the utility industries. Indeed, it is no coincidence that state regulation of electric utilities arose concurrently with American antitrust law. In the late nineteenth and early twentieth centuries, public demand for electric power grew, and electric systems grew up in major metropolitan areas. Some were publicly owned, others privately owned. Some used central-station technology, delivering power over a grid; others employed smaller, geographically distributed generators. A lengthy political fight eventually yielded the system we have today, dominated by state-chartered, vertically integrated, investor-owned utilities ("IOUs") providing monopoly electric service within their designated service areas, using their own central-station technology and distribution grid.

> However, the price of political victory included two important restrictions on IOUs' freedom: the obligation of universal service and limits on the sale price of electricity. Since IOUs were monopoly providers within their service areas, price regulation was necessary to

prevent the deadweight losses and producer surpluses associated with monopoly pricing. Thus, by 1930, state public-utility commissions had begun to regulate the rates charged by IOUs for electric service, using various forms of "cost-plus-fair-return" approaches. The "duty to serve" restriction forced IOUs to serve not only the most attractive customers—industrial users with large stable loads and geographically clustered residential and commercial customers—but also customers for whom the provision of service was more expensive. Since the tariffs according to which IOUs provided universal service did not permit price discrimination within customer classes, this duty to serve limited IOUs ability to control average costs. . . .

[Federal and State statutes] created a legal foundation for electricity pricing that remained fairly stable for the next five or six decades. State public service commissions regulated retail rates, and FERC regulated wholesale rates. Under this system, most twentieth-century IOUs were vertically integrated companies, generating most of their own power (and buying some power on wholesale markets), transmitting it over their own distribution system, and selling it directly to their retail customers. This remains the norm in most states today. Traditional regulation guarantees licensed monopoly electric service providers administratively established rates that allow the companies a "fair" return on their prudently made investments. In return, electric utilities agree to meet a variety of service obligations to the general public, including the obligation to serve all eligible customers and to provide a reliable source of supply.

The potential for inefficiency in this approach has long been evident. Regulators must depend upon the regulated to divulge their cost information. Commission staff and ratepayer advocate groups intervene in rate cases and review this information with a fine-tooth comb, but they cannot hope to overcome the information asymmetries inherent in the process. The regulated, in turn, have very little incentive to minimize costs, and every incentive to maximize the size of the rate base because under traditional ratemaking a larger rate base means more revenues. Finally, the regulatory oversight process entails its own considerable transaction costs. To its critics, a system characterized by high transaction costs, information asymmetries, and perverse incentives is bound to yield unnecessarily high electric rates in both wholesale and retail markets.

If the traditional system is inefficient, can the market do better? Yes, say proponents of restructuring. Traditional regulation has been based on a false premise: that the provision of electric service is a natural monopoly. That might be true if the sale and delivery of energy were one bundled product, but they are not. Rather, we can conceive of (and price) electricity sales, on the one hand, and the delivery of electricity, on the other, as two separate products. Delivery—transmission and distribution service—is a natural monopoly because the construction of duplicate electricity-delivery systems between two points is inefficient. However, the sale of the product that is delivered over such a system—electricity—is not a natural monopoly. We can unbundle sales and distribution so that buyers in wholesale and retail markets can choose their electricity supplier. Thus, said proponents of restructuring, transmission and distribution service should remain regulated, but prices of electricity sales should be set by the market. Competition among electricity sellers will force sellers to minimize (rather than maximize) costs, thereby driving prices down. The market will eventually weed out those who cannot provide reliable service at a competitive price, and consumers—broadly defined to include all consumer classes—will benefit. In this way, competitive markets should represent a Kaldor–Hicks improvement over regulated markets.

David B. Spence, The Politics of Electricity Restructuring: Theory vs. Practice, 40 Wake Forest L. Rev. 417 (2005).

5. What are the goals of restructuring, or so-called "deregulation"? The predominant populist measure of success is lower prices for consumers, but perhaps this criterion is too narrow a measure of success as some prices may increase while other decrease. There are many other goals, among them:

— Diversification of firms in the industry.

— Increased flexibility in firm investments.

— Increased adaptability to technological change.

— Increased efficiencies.

— Diversification of risk.

— Increased accountability and decreased reliance on government.

6. There are also many barriers to pursuing these goals as well as costs to deregulation. Among these are the following:

— Increased price volatility for consumers.

— Potential decreases in reliability.

— Reduced incentives for new entrants and innovation as price approaches marginal cost.

— Greater risks for investors and consumers.

— Potential concerns about consumer welfare and environmental programs.

— Increased costs of regulatory oversight for market conduct as firms increasingly engage in strategic profit-maximizing behavior.

— More intractable jurisdictional problems, as federal, state and local regulators each interact with the same firms.

Throughout this chapter and the next one, think carefully about how successful restructuring has been in the U.S.

B. U.S. Federal Regulation Before 1978

An economic basis for the treatment of firms in the electricity industry as regulated public utilities was because of the assumption that the industry constituted a "natural monopoly." However, in fact that monopoly was never complete. Since its initial development as an energy resource, competition has existed between electricity and alternative energy sources, such as oil and natural gas. For example, as the price of electricity rises, residential consumers in many areas have the option of switching to natural gas for purposes of heating and cooling. In this sense, the availability of alternative energy sources worked as a competitive check on electricity. In addition, competition among various suppliers of electricity has always existed to some degree.

The power of federal regulators to enhance competition in the electric utility industry is limited, largely because federal jurisdiction over competition policy has largely been restricted by statute to wholesale utilities and transactions. Nevertheless, federal regulators have played an integral role in redefining the structure of the utility industry. The application of the antitrust laws, designed to protect competition from monopolistic behavior, to the electricity industry was discussed by the Supreme Court in the landmark case of *Otter Tail Power v. United States*:

Otter Tail Power v. United States

410 U.S. 366 (1973).

[Otter Tail Power was the major IOU in Minnesota, North Dakota, and South Dakota. Like most IOUs, it engaged in the generation, transmission, and distribution of power. It served the large majority of towns in these three states, but in a number of towns power was distributed through a municipal power company which did not generate power itself. These municipal distribution utilities could purchase power at a low rate from federal Bureau of Reclamation projects. However, the purchased power had to be transmitted ("wheeled") over the lines owned by Otter Tail. The municipals alleged that Otter Tail had sought to take over service in the municipal areas by anticompetitive means in violation of the Sherman Act. The civil antitrust suit alleged that Otter Tail had refused to sell wholesale power, had refused to wheel power, had discouraged other suppliers from dealing with the municipals, and had begun litigation to delay the establishment of municipal power systems. The District Court found in favor of the U.S. and the municipals.]

I.

■ DOUGLAS, J. Otter Tail contends that by reason of the Federal Power Act it is not subject to antitrust regulation with respect to its refusal to deal. We disagree with that position.

"Repeals of the antitrust laws by implication from a regulatory statute are strongly disfavored, and have only been found in cases of plain repugnancy between the antitrust and regulatory provisions." *United States v. Philadelphia National Bank*, 374 U.S. 321, 350–351. *See also Silver v. New York Stock Exchange*, 373 U.S. 341, 357–361. Activities which come under the jurisdiction of a regulatory agency nevertheless may be subject to scrutiny under the antitrust laws.

In *California v. Federal Power Commission*, 369 U.S. 482, 489, the Court held that approval of an acquisition of the assets of a natural gas company by the Federal Power Commission pursuant to § 7 of the Natural Gas Act "would be no bar to [an] antitrust suit." Under § 7, the standard for approving such acquisitions is "public convenience and necessity." Although the impact on competition is relevant to the Commission's determination, the Court noted that there was "no 'pervasive regulatory scheme' including the antitrust laws that ha[d] been entrusted to the Commission." *Id.*, at 485. Similarly, in *United States v. Radio Corp. of Am.*, 358 U.S. 334, the Court held that an exchange of radio stations that had been approved by the Federal Communications Commission as in the "public interest" was subject to attack in an antitrust proceeding.

The District Court determined that Otter Tail's consistent refusals to wholesale or wheel power to its municipal customers constituted illegal monopolization. Otter Tail maintains here that its refusals to deal should be immune from antitrust prosecution because the Federal Power Commission has the authority to compel involuntary interconnections of power pursuant to § 202 (b) of the Federal Power Act. The essential thrust of § 202, however, is to encourage voluntary interconnections of power. *See* S. Rep. No. 621, 74th Cong., 1st Sess., 19–20, 48–49; H. R. Rep. No. 1318, 74th Cong., 1st Sess., 8. Only if a power company refuses to interconnect voluntarily may the Federal Power Commission, subject to limitations unrelated to antitrust considerations, order the interconnection. The standard which governs its decision is whether such action is "necessary or appropriate in the public interest." Although antitrust considerations may be relevant, they are not determinative.

There is nothing in the legislative history which reveals a purpose to insulate electric power companies from the operation of the antitrust laws. To the contrary, the history of Part II of the Federal Power Act indicates an overriding policy of maintaining competition to the maximum extent possible consistent with the public interest. As originally conceived, Part II would have included a "common carrier" provision making it "the duty of every public utility to ... transmit energy for any person upon reasonable request...." In addition, it would have empowered the Federal Power Commission to order wheeling if it found such action to be "necessary or desirable in the public interest." H. R. 5423, 74th Cong., 1st Sess.; S. 1725, 74th Cong., 1st Sess. These provisions were eliminated to preserve "the voluntary action of the utilities." S. Rep. No. 621, 74th Cong., 1st Sess., 19.

It is clear, then, that Congress rejected a pervasive regulatory scheme for controlling the interstate distribution of power in favor of voluntary commercial relationships. When these relationships are governed in the first instance by business judgment and not regulatory coercion, courts must be hesitant to conclude that Congress intended to override the fundamental national policies embodied in the antitrust laws. *See United States v. Radio Corp. of Am.*, supra, at 351. This is particularly true in this instance because Congress, in passing the Public Utility Holding Company Act, which included Part II of the Federal Power Act, was concerned with "restraint of free and independent competition" among public utility holding companies. *See* 15 U.S.C. § 79a(b)(2).

Thus, there is no basis for concluding that the limited authority of the Federal Power Commission to order interconnections was intended to be a substitute for, or to immunize Otter Tail from, antitrust regulation for refusing to deal with municipal corporations.

II.

The decree of the District Court enjoins Otter Tail from "refusing to sell electric power at wholesale to existing or proposed municipal electric power systems in cities and towns located in [its service area]" and from refusing to wheel electric power over its transmission lines from other electric power lines to such cities and towns. But the decree goes on to provide:

The defendant shall not be compelled by the Judgment in this case to furnish wholesale electric service or wheeling service to a municipality except at rates which are compensatory and under terms and conditions which are filed with and subject to approval by the Federal Power Commission.

So far as wheeling is concerned, there is no authority granted the Commission under Part II of the Federal Power Act to order it, for the bills originally introduced contained common carrier provisions which were deleted. The Act as passed contained only the interconnection provision set forth in § 202(b). The common carrier provision in the original bill and the power to direct wheeling were left to the "voluntary coordination of electric facilities." Insofar as the District Court ordered wheeling to correct anti-competitive and monopolistic practices of Otter Tail, there is no conflict with the authority of the Federal Power Commission.

III.

The record makes abundantly clear that Otter Tail used its monopoly power in the towns in its service area to foreclose competition or gain a competitive advantage, or to destroy a competitor, all in violation of the antitrust laws. *See United States v. Griffith*, 334 U.S. 100, 107. The District Court determined that Otter Tail has "a strategic dominance in the transmission of power in most of its service area" and that it used this dominance to foreclose potential entrants into the retail area from obtaining electric power from outside sources of supply. 331 F. Supp., at 60. Use of monopoly power "to destroy threatened competition" is a violation of the "attempt to monopolize" clause of § 2 of the Sherman Act. *Lorain Journal v. United States*, 342 U.S. 143, 154; *Eastman Kodak Co. v. Southern Photo Materials Co.*, 273 U.S. 359, 375. So are agreements not to compete, with the aim of preserving or extending a monopoly. *Schine Chain Theatres v. United States*, 334 U.S. 110, 119. In *Associated Press v. United States*, 326 U.S. 1, a cooperative news association had bylaws that permitted member newspapers to bar competitors from joining the association. We held that practice violated the Sherman Act, even though the transgressor "had not yet achieved a complete monopoly." *Id.*, at 13.

When a community serviced by Otter Tail decides not to renew Otter Tail's retail franchise when it expires, it may generate, transmit, and distribute its own electric power. We recently described the difficulties and problems of those isolated electric power systems. *See Gainesville Utilities v. Florida Power Corp.*, 402 U.S. 515, 517–520. Interconnection with other utilities is frequently the only solution. *Id.*, at 519 n. 3. That is what Elbow Lake in the present case did. There were no engineering factors that prevented Otter Tail from selling power at wholesale to those towns that wanted municipal plants or wheeling the power. The District Court found— and its findings are supported—that Otter Tail's refusals to sell at wholesale or to wheel were solely to prevent municipal power systems from eroding its monopolistic position.

Otter Tail relies on its wheeling contracts with the Bureau of Reclamation and with cooperatives which it says relieve it of any duty to wheel power to municipalities served at retail by Otter Tail at the time the contracts were made. The District Court held that these restrictive provisions were "in reality, territorial allocation schemes," 331 F. Supp., at 63, and were per se violations of the Sherman Act, *citing Northern Pacific Railroad Co. v. United States*, 356 U.S. 1. Like covenants were there held to "deny defendant's competitors access to the fenced-off market on the same terms as the defendant." *Id.*, at 12. We recently re-emphasized the vice under the Sherman Act of territorial restrictions among potential competitors. *United States v. Topco Associates*, 405 U.S. 596, 608. The fact that some of the restrictive provisions were contained in a contract with the Bureau of Reclamation is not material to our problem for, as the Solicitor General says, "government contracting officers do not have the power to grant immunity from the Sherman Act." Such contracts stand on their own footing and are valid or not, depending on the statutory framework within which the federal agency operates. The Solicitor General tells us that these restrictive provisions operate as a "hindrance" to the Bureau and were "agreed to by the Bureau only at Otter Tail's insistence," as the District Court found. The evidence supports that finding. . . .

V.

Otter Tail argues that, without the weapons which it used, more and more municipalities will turn to public power and Otter Tail will go downhill. The argument is a familiar one. It was made in *United States v. Arnold, Schwinn & Co.*, 388 U.S. 365, a civil suit under section 1 of the Sherman Act dealing with a restrictive distribution program and practices of a bicycle manufacturer. We said: "The promotion of self-interest alone does not invoke the rule of reason to immunize otherwise illegal conduct." *Id.*, at 375.

The same may properly be said of section 2 cases under the Sherman Act. That Act assumes that an enterprise will protect itself against loss by operating with superior service, lower costs, and improved efficiency. Otter Tail's theory collided with the Sherman Act as it sought to substitute for competition anticompetitive uses of its dominant economic power.

The fact that three municipalities which Otter Tail opposed finally got their municipal systems does not excuse Otter Tail's conduct. That fact does not condone the antitrust tactics which Otter Tail sought to impose. Moreover, the District Court repeated what we said in *FTC v. Nat'l Lead Co.*, 352 U.S. 419, 431, "those caught violating the Act must expect some fencing in." The proclivity for predatory practices has always been a consideration for the District Court in fashioning its antitrust decree. *See United States v. Crescent Amusement Co.*, 323 U.S. 173, 190.

We do not suggest, however, that the District Court, concluding that Otter Tail violated the antitrust laws, should be impervious to Otter Tail's assertion that compulsory interconnection or wheeling will erode its integrated system and threaten its capacity to serve adequately the public. As the dissent properly notes, the Commission may not order interconnection if to do so "would impair [the utility's] ability to render adequate service to its customers." 16 U.S.C. § 824a(b). The District Court in this case found that the "pessimistic view" advanced in Otter Tail's "erosion study" "is not supported by the record." Furthermore, it concluded that "it does not appear that Bureau of Reclamation power is a serious threat to the defendant nor that it will be in the foreseeable future." Since the District Court has made future connections subject to Commission approval and in any event has retained jurisdiction to enable the parties to apply for "necessary or appropriate" relief and presumably will give effect to the policies embodied in the Federal Power Act, we cannot say under these circumstances that it has abused its discretion.■

NOTES AND COMMENTS

1. The Sherman and Clayton Acts contain various sections that prohibit anticompetitive conduct. Section 1 of the Sherman act prohibits agreements in restraint of trade. Section 2 of the Sherman Act prohibits monopolization and attempts to monopolize. The Clayton Act condemns mergers that tend to substantially lessen competition.

In the *Otter Tail Power* case, Otter Tail claimed that it was exempt from the Sherman Act because of the regulated industries exception— where an enterprise's competitive activities are already scrutinized under a pervasive regulatory scheme, courts or agencies may, under the doctrine of primary jurisdiction, defer to that regulatory scheme rather than apply the antitrust laws. As the Court notes, however, such deference is unlikely where a regulatory scheme is not directly concerned with the anticompetitive implications of an enterprise's activities.

A similar exemption applies to regulated enterprises at the state level, where retail transactions in the electricity industry have historically been regulated. The state action doctrine exempts from federal antitrust laws anticompetitive conduct where a state has explicitly adopted an active regulatory policy to displace competition with regulation or a monopoly franchise. Thus, state PSC price regulation of a state-franchised public utility may be exempt from antitrust challenge. However, like the regulated industries exception, the state action doctrine is not automatic. *See, e.g., City of Lafayette v. Louisiana Power & Light Co.*, 435 U.S. 389 (1978); *Cantor v. Detroit Edison Co.*, 428 U.S. 579 (1976). The doctrine is discussed further in Chapters 3 and 12.

2. *Otter Tail* considered the authority of the FPC to order interconnection or wheeling of power. The benefits of interconnection are summarized in *Gainesville Utilities v. Florida Power Corp.*, 402 U.S. 515 (1971):

> The demand upon an electric utility for electric power fluctuates significantly from hour to hour, day to day, and season to season. For this reason, generating facilities cannot be maintained on the basis of constant demand. Rather, the utility's generating capacity must be geared to the utility's peak load of demand, and also take into account the fact that generating equipment must occasionally be out of service for overhaul, or because of breakdowns. In consequence, the utility builds certain "reserves" of generating capacity in excess of peak load requirements into its system. The practice of a utility that relies completely on its own generating resources (an "isolated" system in industry jargon) is to maintain equipment capable of producing its peak load requirements plus equipment that produces a "reserve" capacity equal to the capacity of its largest generating unit.

> The major importance of an interconnection is that it reduces the need for the "isolated" utility to build and maintain "reserve" generating capacity. An interconnection is simply a transmission line connecting two utilities. Electric power may move freely through the line up to the line's capacity. Ordinarily, however, the energy generated by each system is sufficient to supply the requirements of the system's customers and no substantial amount of power flows through the interconnection. It is only at the times when one of the connected utilities is unable for some reason to produce sufficient power to meet its customers' needs that the deficiency may be supplied by power that automatically flows through the interconnection from the other utility. To the extent that the utility may rely upon the interconnection to supply this deficiency, the utility is freed of the necessity of constructing and maintaining its own equipment for the purpose.

Gainesville Utilities upheld an FPC order that directed interconnection between a municipal utility and a larger, adjacent investor-owned system. The Court reversed the Court of Appeals' decision, which required the municipal system to provide substantially greater compensation for the interconnection than the FPC had required.

3.   The Public Utilities Holding Company Act of 1935 ("PUHCA"), 15 U.S.C. § 79 *et seq.*, mentioned in the Otter Tail case, regulated the ownership structure of public utilities. During the 1920s and 1930s, public utility holding companies had gained effective control over many operating electric utility companies, primarily by controlling voting with far less than 100 percent ownership. PUHCA was aimed at breaking up the trusts that controlled U.S. gas and electric utilities. At the time PUCHA was enacted into law, financial pyramid schemes were common. These schemes allowed utilities in many different areas of the country to fall under the control of a small number of holding companies. Before PUHCA, almost half of all electricity was controlled by three huge holding companies.

Samuel Insull's investments in the industry, a target during the hearing that lead to the enactment of PUHCA, are a good example:

> The Insull interests (which operated in 32 states and owned electric companies, textile mills, ice houses, a paper mill, and a hotel) con-trolled 69 percent of the stock of Corporation Securities and 64 percent of the stock of Insull Utility Investments. Those two companies togeth-er owned 28 percent of the voting stock of Middle West Utilities. Middle West Utilities owned eight holding companies, five investment companies, two service companies, two securities companies, and 14 operating companies. It also owned 99 percent of the voting stock of National Electric Power. National, in turn, owned one holding compa-ny, one service company, one paper company, and two operating companies. It also owned 93 percent of the voting stock of National Public Service. National Public Service owned three building compa-nies, three miscellaneous firms, and four operating utilities. It also owned 100 percent of the voting stock of Seaboard Public Service. Seaboard Public Service owned the voting stock of five utility operating companies and one ice company. The utilities, in turn, owned eighteen subsidiaries.

L.S. Hyman, America's Electric Utilities: Past, Present and Future 102 (5th ed. 1994).

The Securities and Exchange Commission ("SEC") was charged with the administration of PUHCA, including the regulation of holding compa-nies. PUHCA authorized the SEC to break up the massive utility holding companies by requiring them to divest their holdings until each was a single consolidated system serving a defined geographic area. PUHCA also limited the businesses that utility holding companies could engage in to utility-related functions. All holding companies were required to register with the SEC. Through the registration process, the SEC determined whether each holding company will be regulated or exempt from the requirements of PUHCA. The SEC defined a utility holding company as a company which directly or indirectly owns 10 percent or more of the outstanding securities of a single utility company. The SEC took a very aggressive approach to interpreting this requirement, but there was a safety valve in PUHCA for holding companies that are entirely intrastate in character. *See* Energy Information Administration, The Public Utility Holding Company Act of 1935: 1935–1992 (1993).

Congress repealed PUHCA in the Energy Policy Act of 2005. With PUHCA repeal, utilities and unregulated entities will be able to buy any utility asset or utility company regardless of location. Mergers between utilities that are located far from each other are possible for the first time since PUHCA was enacted. It will also be much less burdensome for multistate, for-profit transmission companies to form. The Energy Policy Act of 2005 also directed FERC to issue rules providing for expedited treatment of mergers, allowing for complete review of mergers with 360 days. For discussion of the significance of PUHCA as a barrier to mergers in the industry, see Judge Richard Cudahy, Consolidation: Key to the Future?, Public Utilities Fortnightly, August 2005, at 15.

C.   THE GROWTH OF WHOLESALE COMPETITION IN ELECTRIC GENERATION

Competition in electricity generation has brought about certain economic efficiencies, although the net degree of efficiency improvement is a subject of considerable controversy. A recent report by the Energy Information Administration concludes that if full scale competition in electricity generation began, retail prices for electricity would be reduced as much as 6 to 13 percent within 2 years compared to prices under the current approach to regulation. Under conditions of intense competition, the same study predicts that prices could fall as much as 24 percent. The study notes, however, that there are significant differences across regions of the U.S. *See* Energy Information Administration, Electricity Prices in a Competitive Environment: Marginal Cost Pricing of Generation Services and Financial Status of Electric Utilities—A Preliminary Analysis Through 2015 (August 1997).

To understand the current degree and future growth of competition in the electric power industry (which as a business area has now displaced its predecessor, the electric utility industry), it is useful to explore some of the legal and policy issues that have been addressed at the federal level since the 1970s. In evaluating these legal and policy issues, it is important to recognize how the services historically provided by a single, vertically-integrated utility—generation, distribution and transmission—are no longer regarded as possessing similar economic characteristics. Generation is seen as a structurally competitive industry, one that can accommodate multiple competing suppliers. Distribution and transmission, however, are considered to possess many natural monopoly characteristics.

1.   PURPA AND THE GROWTH OF INDEPENDENT POWER PRODUCERS ("IPPs")

The various factors that caused electricity prices to increase in the 1970s and 1980s—increased oil prices, environmental standards, and nuclear costs—increased pressure for competition in the electric industry for a number of reasons. First, increased costs did not impact electric utilities uniformly, increasing the disparity of electric rates among different utilities and causing some customers to look enviously at the rates their neighbors were paying. Second, new companies that were not burdened with old plants and had access to a fuel other than oil (such as natural gas) were in a position to build new plants and undercut the prices charged by the older utilities.

In 1978, Congress adopted the Public Utilities Regulatory Policy Act ("PURPA"), as a part of President Carter's national energy plan. PURPA's enactment in 1978 showed that Congress was responsive to the desire of customers to explore new options. According to Richard Hirsh, "Through its mostly unintended consequences, PURPA inaugurated the process by which the traditional structure of then the utility system disintegrated." Hirsh, *supra*, at 119. PURPA endorsed the potential for efficiency and conservation in the energy conversion process and the promotion of efficiency in the pooling, interconnection and "wheeling" (i.e., off-system customer or supplier transmission) of power. Two provisions in PURPA were of significance in jump-starting competition among wholesale power suppliers.

First, PURPA included provisions to encourage efficiency and conservation by non-utility generators of electricity. Section 210 of PURPA authorized FERC to prescribe rules to encourage cogeneration and small power production (known as "qualifying facilities", or QFs) by authorizing FERC to require utilities to purchase or sell electricity from such facilities. The statute provided that the rate of purchase from QFs 1) would be just and reasonable and in the public interest; and 2) shall not discriminate against cogenerators or small power producers. Rules FERC promulgated in 1980 encouraged the growth of QFs by requiring utilities to purchase their power at a price known as "avoided costs," requiring interconnection with the electric utility grid, and exempting the new facilities from certain federal and state regulations, including traditional rate regulation. *See* 18 C.F.R. Pt. 292. FERC's rules were challenged but upheld by the U.S. Supreme Court. *See FERC v. Mississippi*, 456 U.S. 742 (1982) (holding that Congress, in enacting PURPA, did not exceed its power under the Commerce Clause or violate states' rights under the Tenth Amendment); *American Paper Inst., Inc. v. American Elec. Power Serv. Corp.*, 461 U.S. 402 (1983) (holding that FERC's avoided cost rules are not arbitrary, capricious or an abuse of discretion).

PURPA's QF certification scheme jump-started the growth of an independent energy sector. After a period of decades of declining electricity prices, between 1973 and 1982 electricity prices increased by about 60 percent in real (inflation adjusted) terms. US DOE, DOE/S–0057, Energy Security, A Report to the President of the U.S., at 154 (1987). This created strong economic incentives for large consumers of electricity to reduce their energy costs. With PURPA's scheme cogeneration, which had supplied nearly 50 percent of power produced in the U.S. around the turn of the century, again became a viable economic alternative for many industrial and commercial energy users. By 1990, non-utility generation had grown to supply more than half of the marginal generation capacity added to the industry, and more than 10% of cumulative generation capacity. For a discussion of states' roles in implementing this aspect of PURPA, *see* Deirdre Callaghan & Steve Greenwald, PURPA from Coast to Coast: America's Great Electricity Experiment, Natural Resources & Environment, Winter 1996, at 17.

The second major competition-enhancing provision PURPA added to federal law authorized FERC to mandate wheeling for wholesale customers and suppliers. PURPA added Sections 211 and 212 to the Federal Power Act. As *Otter Tail* observed, the FPA did not originally authorize the Commission to require one utility to transmit off-system power. The sections added by PURPA in 1978 allowed FERC to mandate wholesale wheeling only where it would not result in a "reasonably ascertainable uncompensated economic loss" and would not place "an undue burden," "unreasonably impair the reliability of any electric utility," or will not impair adequate service to customers.

In part because of narrow agency and judicial interpretation, however, the version of Sections 211 and 212 enacted in 1978 was never fully utilized to require a utility to transmit power from an off-system source. The Second Circuit held that Section 211 clearly indicated that wheeling could not be ordered solely on the basis of the public interest and the enhancement of competition. *New York Elec. & Gas Co. v. FERC*, 638 F.2d 388, 402 (2d Cir. 1980). In addition, the Fifth Circuit rebuked an effort by FERC to foster competition through mandatory wheeling, noting that although FERC's goal was "laudable," the agency "is without authority under the FPA to compel wheeling." *Florida Power & Light Co. v. FERC*, 660 F.2d 668, 677–779 (5th Cir. 1981). Following these decisions, FERC itself interpreted Section 211 to "prohibit[] the issuance of wheeling orders that have a significant procompetitive effect." *Southeastern Power Administration*, 26 FERC ¶ 61,127 at 61,323 (1984). Although FERC noted that it may have been willing to require wholesale wheeling to address fuel shortages or to promote the coordination of electricity among utilities, *Southeastern Power Administration*, 25 FERC ¶ 61,204 at 61,539 (1983), FERC did not issue a single order requiring procompetitive wheeling.

Even though the 1978 version of Sections 211 and 212 were never directly used to enhance competition, they may have had some indirect effect on competition in the industry. First, the threat of compulsory wheeling may have nudged utilities to negotiate voluntary transmission agreements with other suppliers and wholesale customers.

Second, FERC used indirect regulatory mechanisms to implement section 211 and 212. FERC's ability to implement "open access" was severely limited by Section 211(c)(1) of the FPA, which barred FERC from requiring wholesale wheeling service "unless the Commission determined that such order would reasonably preserve existing competitive relationships." Despite FERC's narrow jurisdiction under the 1978 version of

Section 211 of the FPA to require wheeling, in recent years FERC has issued procompetitive transmission access orders in the adjudicative context as a voluntary condition to a benefit or approval conferred under other sections of the FPA.

For example, prior to 1996 FERC imposed open access transmission terms as a condition to approval of "market-based" rates under its general rate regulation authority, contained in sections 205 and 206 of the FPA. FERC initiated this policy with a flexible pricing experiment in bulk power transactions known as the "Southwest Experiment" in the early 1980s. Later, FERC developed a general market-based pricing policy in a number of adjudicative cases, routinely requiring wholesale transmission access as a condition to its approval of market-based rates.

FERC also used its merger approval authority to develop transmission policy on a case-by-case basis. In the 1980s, electric utility mergers increased dramatically and FERC took the opportunity to act on merger applications. These proceedings have served as an important vehicle for the development of transmission policy. FERC has consistently imposed "open access" transmission terms as a condition to its approval of mergers under section 203 of the FPA. *See* Jim Rossi, Redeeming Judicial Review: The Hard Look Doctrine and Federal Regulatory Efforts to Restructure the Electric Utility Industry, 1994 Wis. L. Rev. 763 (1994).

2. MARKET-BASED RATES AND OTHER REFORMS TO RATE REGULATION

With the growth of competition, federal regulators have considered moving away from the traditional approach of setting rates based on costs. *See* Chapter 3. Two approaches, still dependent on regulatory oversight by FERC or state commissions, are market-based rates and incentive rates.

a. MARKET-BASED RATES

In addition to transmission access, in the late 1980s, FERC adopted additional regulatory strategies to increase competition in the independent energy sector, jump-started by PURPA. Two significant measures adopted by FERC were: 1) the approval of market-based rates for independent power producers that lacked significant market power, effectively relieving these generators of the regulatory burden imposed by cost of service regulation; and 2) the exercise of "light-handed" regulation for independent power producers, which relieved these generators from other costly reporting requirements. Several states have adopted similar market-based rate and light-handed regulation mechanisms. In addition, state programs designed to encourage or require competitive bidding for approval of new generation capacity increased from only a few in 1988 to more than 30 by 1993. As is discussed in Chapter 3, market based rates remain an important tool for FERC, which engages in active monitoring of such rates to avoid opening up electric power markets to antitrust scrutiny. The *Dart-*

mouth Power case provides an overview of some of the concerns raised by market-based and light-handed regulation at the federal level:

Dartmouth Power Associates Limited Partnership

53 F.E.R.C. ¶ 61,117 (1990).

■ Before Commissioners: MARTIN L. ALLDAY, CHAIRMAN; CHARLES A. TRABANDT, ELIZABETH ANNE MOLER and JERRY J. LANGDON.

On March 21, 1990, as completed on October 5, 1990, Dartmouth Power Associates Limited Partnership (Dartmouth) submitted a Power Purchase Agreement (the Agreement) between Dartmouth and Commonwealth Electric Company (Commonwealth Electric), and an Amendment to the Agreement (Amendment). The rates from Dartmouth to Commonwealth Electric were negotiated between the parties and, as discussed infra, Dartmouth requests that the Commission find that its rates are just and reasonable as market-based rates. . . .

Negotiations leading up to the Agreement began in the spring of 1987. The Agreement was executed September 5, 1989, and was filed March 21, 1990. The Agreement originally provided that Dartmouth would construct, own and operate a 168.8–MW combined cycle, gas-fired unit, and would sell 50 MW of capacity and energy to Commonwealth Electric. Dartmouth states that in February 1990, it decided to reconfigure the unit to reflect a smaller, 67.6–MW combined cycle unit, and notified Commonwealth Electric of this proposed change. . . .

According to Dartmouth, the unit will be located in Commonwealth Electric's service territory and will be fully dispatchable by the New England Power Pool ("NEPOOL"). Dartmouth states that it will own only those transmission facilities used to interconnect the unit with Commonwealth Electric's system. . . .

Dartmouth is a limited partnership. Dartmouth's sole general partner, EMI Dartmouth, Inc., is a Massachusetts Corporation owned entirely by an individual, James Gordon. According to Dartmouth, Mr. Gordon "will also own at least 50% of the limited partnership interests in Dartmouth." Currently, five other individuals hold limited partnership interests in Dartmouth, and Dartmouth states that other limited partnership interests may be sold in the future. In this regard, the respective interests of Dartmouth's general and limited partners have yet to be determined.

Through Mr. Gordon, Dartmouth will be affiliated with Pawtucket Power Associates Limited Partnership (Pawtucket), an entity which will own a 62–MW cogeneration facility. Dartmouth states that Mr. Gordon owns a 100% interest in EMI Management, Inc. ("EMI"), the developer of Dartmouth and Pawtucket. According to Dartmouth, EMI has also developed a cogeneration facility which will sell electricity to Commonwealth Electric. . . .

Dartmouth states its price to Commonwealth Electric "was negotiated over an extended period of time," and that "[t]he history of the negotiations between [Commonwealth Electric] and Dartmouth and [Commonwealth Electric's] access to alternative sources of wholesale electric power demonstrate the existence of a competitive market supporting market-based rates." In this regard, in support of its request for approval of market-based rates, Dartmouth argues that the New England electricity market is characterized by an active market for new QF capacity, and that Commonwealth Electric participates in this market both through formal QF bid solicitations and through nonbid negotiations. . . .

Dartmouth argues that negotiations between Dartmouth and Commonwealth Electric took place in the context of a competitive market in which Commonwealth Electric had numerous supply alternatives. In this regard, Dartmouth notes that Commonwealth Electric has had numerous supply alternatives to choose from as evidenced by: (1) the responses to Commonwealth Electric's solicitation for QF capacity in RFP 1 (where bids totaling over 920 MW were received, constituting more than ten times the amount of capacity sought); (2) the responses eight other New England utilities received to 1987 and 1988 solicitations (where bids totaled over 11,000 MW, twelve times the capacity solicited); (3) the response Boston Edison Company (BECO) received in its fall 1989 QF solicitation (where bids totaled 2,837 MW, fourteen times the capacity solicited); and (4) the fact that, according to Dartmouth, 6,200 MW of independent power capacity is currently under construction or development in New England. . . .

Dartmouth argues that, since neither it nor its parent or affiliates own or control transmission facilities (other than those required to interconnect the facility with the purchaser's system), it cannot restrict Commonwealth Electric's access to competing suppliers. Furthermore, Dartmouth states that it does not control any other resources by which it could erect barriers against the entry of other suppliers. Dartmouth also states that it has no affiliations or business relationships which could result in self dealing.

Based on the foregoing arguments, Dartmouth concludes that it lacks market power over Commonwealth Electric, when its proposal is judged against the standards used by the Commission in approving other market-based rates.

Dartmouth requests that the Commission grant waivers of its regulations, considering the market-based nature of Dartmouth's rates. . . .

In Commonwealth Atlantic Limited Partnership (Commonwealth Atlantic), the Commission determined that market-based rates are acceptable if the seller can demonstrate that it lacks market power over the buyer. In addition, the Commission has carefully scrutinized transactions involving nontraditional sellers affiliated with franchised utilities, or affiliated with any other entities that own or control resources that could be used to create barriers to other suppliers who seek to enter the market. Accordingly, we have analyzed Dartmouth's proposal consistent with the analysis used in our prior cases.

In both Enron and Commonwealth Atlantic, the Commission noted that it had previously approved long-term power sales at market-based rates where the seller demonstrated that it had no market power over the buyer (or that the seller had adequately mitigated its market power) and where there was no evidence of potential affiliate abuse. *E.g., Enron*, 52 FERC at ¶ 61,708 & n.41 (*citing Commonwealth Atlantic*, 51 FERC ¶ 61,368 (1990); *Public Service Company of Indiana, Inc.*, 51 FERC ¶ 61,367 (1990); *Doswell Limited Partnership*, 50 FERC ¶ 61,251 (1990); *Ocean State Power Company*, 44 FERC ¶ 61,261 (1989)). In *Enron* and *Commonwealth Atlantic*, the Commission noted that it had previously stated that a seller has market power when it can significantly influence the price in the market by restricting supply or by denying access to alternative sellers. *E.g., id.* (*citing Commonwealth Atlantic*, 51 FERC at ¶ 62,244 & n.43; *Doswell*, 50 FERC at ¶ 61,757 & n.12 (1990); *Citizens Power & Light Corporation*, 48 FERC ¶ 61,210 (1989)).

Specifically, the criteria set forth in the Commission's prior decisions require that the seller provide evidence that: (1) neither the seller nor any of its affiliates is a dominant firm in the sale of generation services in the relevant market; (2) neither the seller nor any of its affiliates owns or controls transmission facilities which could be used by the buyer in reaching alternative generation suppliers, or they have adequately mitigated their ability to block the buyer in reaching such alternative suppliers; and (3) neither the seller nor any of its affiliates is able to erect or otherwise control any other barrier to entry. The Commission has also analyzed whether there is evidence of potential abuses of self dealing or reciprocal dealing. As discussed below, we find that Dartmouth's filing meets these standards, and thus we will accept Dartmouth's rates for filing. . . .

Neither Dartmouth nor its affiliates own or are affiliated with utilities that own transmission facilities in the region. Neither Dartmouth nor its QF affiliates can erect barriers preventing others from entering the relevant market; in this regard, Dartmouth has stated that it controls no major input factors (e.g., land sites, gas pipelines, or fuel supplies).

Finally, we find that there is no evidence of self dealing or reciprocal dealing abuse. Dartmouth is not affiliated with Commonwealth Electric. Although Dartmouth is affiliated with a developer which is constructing a QF which will serve Commonwealth Electric, there is no evidence that Dartmouth, because of this affiliation, was able to influence the price at which Commonwealth Electric purchased power. . . .

We find that Dartmouth's market-pricing proposal will result in rates to Commonwealth Electric that are within the legally mandated zone of reasonableness. We note that we will have the opportunity to reassess this finding if changes to the rate are proposed. The Dartmouth/Commonwealth Electric Agreement is a formula rate. While the rate charged Commonwealth Electric will vary over time, the adjustments will be pursuant to the approved formulae, which our review has shown were determined through negotiations in which Dartmouth lacked market power. The formulae cannot be changed without a further filing with the Commission. Accordingly, if Dartmouth in the future acquires market power over Commonwealth Electric and tries to exercise that power through modifications to the formula rate, it will need the Commission's approval for such changes. The Commission would review Dartmouth's proposal de novo in light of the then existing circumstances, and would not approve continuation of a market-based rate unless we were assured that Dartmouth continued to lack market power, or had adequately mitigated its market power.

■ CHARLES A. TRABANDT, Commissioner, concurring:

I join in approving the market rate that Dartmouth Power Associates Limited Partnership (Dartmouth Power) proposes to charge Commonwealth Electric Company under the contract before us. I write in order briefly to explain why.

[I take] issue with the majority's approach to approving market rates for independent power producers (IPPs), generators unaffiliated with utilities. [T]he Federal Power Act and the cases contain three requirements: finding a workable competitive market; imposing a just and reasonable price ceiling; and creating a monitoring mechanism to account for changed conditions. Specifically, I disagreed with the Commonwealth holding that we need not subject rates IPPs negotiate to just and reasonable ceilings.

Here, we all agree that the Dartmouth Power contract emerged from a competitive market. As to the second criterion, in this case, the majority keeps to its rejection of a rate ceiling. I adhere to my view. Nevertheless, I agree with approving the contract before us. . . . ■

* * *

b. INCENTIVE REGULATION

While FERC and many state PSCs will allow market based rates where a firm lacks market power, most utilities with market power continue to base rates on the cost of service. However, in recent years new regulatory mechanisms designed to encourage more efficient utility rate setting have emerged. One of the most popular of these is incentive rates.

In a policy statement issued in 1992, FERC announced that it will allow electric utilities with market power to propose incentive rate systems in order to advance two efficiency-enhancing results: lower rates to consumers and increase shareholder returns. *Incentive Ratemaking for Interstate Natural Gas Pipelines, Oil Pipelines, and Electric Utilities*, 61 FERC ¶ 61,168.

FERC's 1992 policy statement permitted electric utilities and natural gas pipelines to propose incentive rate mechanisms as alternatives to cost-of-service ratemaking. The Commission's incentive rate policy was premised on two overriding principles. First, incentive rate mechanisms should encourage efficiency by optimizing operating efficiency, allocating services to the highest valued uses, investing new capital when economically warranted, and capturing expanding markets. Second, the initial rates under the incentive rate mechanism must conform to the Commission's just and reasonable standard.

FERC required incentive rates to adhere to the five principles. They must:

1) be prospective;

2) be voluntary;

3) be understandable;

4) result in quantifiable benefits for consumers, subject to the constraint that they not exceed the rates that would apply under cost-of-service regulation; and

5) maintain or enhance incentives to improve the quality of service.

FERC indicated that it would rely on incentive rates on a case by case basis. To date, few utilities have availed themselves of the incentive rate mechanisms FERC has made available.

Most experimentation with incentive rates has occurred at the state level. In addition to cost of service regulation, discussed at length in Chapter 3, state PSC rate experiments include: benchmarking—giving rewards or penalties to a utility's earning opportunity based on comparison with a pre-set standard, the value of which become known in the future; and price caps—setting a maximum price to be charged which is determined by formula based on factors not within the utilities control, such as inflation, or factors under the utilities control, such as costs. *See* J. Robert Malko & Richard J. Williams, Traditional and New Regulatory Tools, 93, 99 in Reinventing Electric Utility Regulation (Gregory B. Enholm & J. Robert Malko, eds. 1995).

Although under the present laws states have jurisdiction over retail restructuring, discussed in Chapter 12, many states have also experimented with incentive rates. Like FERC's policy statement, many state efforts are designed to encourage more efficient internal decisionmaking by utility managers, resulting in lower customer rates and increased shareholder returns. These performance-based incentive rates come in a variety of different forms. Consider the following proceeding, which approves a form of performance-based incentive rates:

Re San Diego Gas and Electric Company

154 PUR 4th 313 (Cal. PUC 1994).

1. Summary

In this decision we consider a proposal by San Diego Gas & Electric Company ("SDG&E"), joined by Division of Ratepayer Advocates ("DRA") and Federal Executive Agencies ("FEA"), for an experimental base rates regulatory mechanism. . . .

We find that the current program for regulating SDG&E's gas and electric base rates through triennial general rate cases ("GRCs") may not provide the most appropriate or effective means of achieving our basic regulatory objective of the lowest reasonable rates consistent with safe, reliable, environmentally sensitive utility service. Moreover, traditional regulation may not be well-suited for the increasingly competitive energy services industry. The Joint Proposal represents an opportunity to take a conservative yet significant step away from traditional cost-of-service regulation. We find that, with minor modification, the proposed experimental, five-year base rates mechanism has a reasonable potential for improving on the attainment of our basic regulatory objective. While that result is not guaranteed, we are satisfied that the program does not represent a significant risk to ratepayers.

Key elements of the adopted experimental program are the following:

1. SDG&E is excused from filing a test year 1996 GRC. In the absence of this authorization, SDG&E would be required to file a GRC application later this year. Subject to further order of the Commission, SDG&E's next GRC will be for test year 1999.

2. During the 1994–1998 experiment, SDG&E's base rates will be capped by a revenue requirement formula which is comparable in some ways to the current operational attrition mechanism, but should yield more accurate revenue requirement forecasts.

3. A revenue-sharing mechanism which allows both shareholders and ratepayers to benefit when SDG&E's financial performance results in earnings in excess of the authorized rate of return plus 1%, yet requires shareholders to absorb the full impact of low earnings when the company earns less than its authorized rate of return.

4. A comprehensive system of performance incentives with as much as $19 million in rewards and $21 million in penalties at stake each year. This system is designed to provide SDG&E's management with additional incentives for reducing electric rates relative to a national rate index while maintaining system quality as represented by employee safety, customer satisfaction, and system reliability.

5. A program of monitoring and evaluation ("M&E") designed to ensure the availability of data that will be required to evaluate the experiment, and to systematically provide for such evaluation.

We emphasize our intent that the adopted experiment is applicable to SDG&E only. Southern California Edison Company ("Edison") and Pacific Gas and Electric Company ("PG&E") have now filed PBR proposals as well. Today's decision is not determinative of the appropriate PBR program components for other utilities....

We begin with a review of our fundamental and longstanding purpose for regulating monopoly utilities. "The function of the Commission is to regulate public utilities and compel the enforcement of their duty to the public." *Atchison, Topeka and Santa Fe Ry. Co. v. R.R. Comm'n* (1916) 173 C. 577, 582. "Created by the Constitution in 1911, the commission was designed to protect the people of the state from the consequences of destructive competition and monopoly in the public service industries." *California Motor Transp. Co., Ltd. v. R.R. Comm'n*, 30 C.2d 184, 188

(1947). The Commission regulates SDG&E's rates pursuant to the Public Utilities Act, whose "primary purpose is to insure the public adequate service at reasonable rates without discrimination . . ." *City and County of San Francisco v. Pub. Utilities Comm'n*, 6 C.3d 119, 126 (1971). . . .

Here, SDG&E perceives that under current regulation it has an incentive to focus too much on short-term savings, since longer-term savings are captured by ratepayers every third year of the GRC cycle. SDG&E sees this as a flaw of current regulation, and its primary reform objective is to lengthen its planning horizon. Its specific reform proposal is to eliminate its 1996 GRC. However, simply reducing or eliminating the Commission oversight that occurs in a GRC for a five-year period poses a risk to ratepayers (and to shareholders). One possible condition that could protect ratepayers, by compensating them for the assignment of greater risk, is a sharing mechanism that assures that ratepayers receive some of the benefit the utility expects to realize from its new-found impetus for longer-term planning and investment. Within this example, the point is that the sharing mechanism is not the primary objective of the experiment; it is a condition that we might attach to our approval. . . .

We find that current regulation either has caused or has failed to prevent a situation where SDG&E's rates are too high. The evidence is that SDG&E electric rates were recently 136% above the national average. Utility Consumers Action Network ("UCAN") witness Navarro reminds us that achieving the goal of least-cost, environmentally sensitive, reliable service "is not just a matter of fairness to ratepayers and the broader public . . . [i]t is a matter of economic survival for the state of California."

The evidence does not show that traditional regulation is solely responsible for high rates or a situation where SDG&E lacks the right incentives to control costs and reduce rates, and it does not show that the situation cannot be improved with continuation of traditional approaches to regulation. . . . The fact remains that high rates developed on traditional regulation's watch. There is little argument that the company can do better in reducing its costs and rates if given the right incentives. If more can be done, then more must done to reduce the company's rates. We therefore believe that reduction of SDG & E's rates, especially electric rates, is an appropriate and necessary objective for regulatory reform. In particular, we want to see a mechanism that provides greater incentive than the current system does for the company to reduce its rates. We agree with DRA's priorities, and hold this to be a primary objective for reform. And while we seek a reduction of SDG&E's rates, eventually to competitive levels, we do not, for purposes of specifying our objectives, require that reductions be accomplished by means of incentives or revenue-sharing. . . .

We find that current regulation places incorrect incentives before utility management to cut cost, find efficiencies, and reduce rates. It is time to place more emphasis on managerial performance in achieving efficiencies and cost reductions, and less emphasis on rate base expansion. Bearing both of these problematic areas of regulation in mind, and recognizing that any new regulatory program is bound to create a new set of incentives for managerial actions, some unintended, that could work at cross-purposes, we adopt as our second broad reform objective a more rational system of incentives to drive utility planning and investment which better serves the overall interests of ratepayers as well as shareholders and the public.

Meeting this second broad objective should help to create an environment which more closely replicates that of a competitive market. Thus, the proposed objective of preparing SDG&E for the increasingly competitive electric services industry is arguably subsumed within the broader objective of proper incentives.

Also, as we have already noted, SDG&E's management needs to respond to new challenges in the industry.... However, we also seek consistency and compatibility of this experiment with our restructuring efforts, whose theme is competition. Accordingly, we adopt the objective of preparing of the company for competition. This means that the company should be at greater risk for the consequences of its actions even as it stands to gain from those actions, and that there should be greater flexibility for management. SDG&E's objective of flexibility and UCAN's objective of loosened regulation are consistent with this objective.

Finally, we recognize that base rate regulation creates significant administrative costs for the utility, the Commission and its staff, and other parties. GRC proceedings, the hallmark of traditional base rate regulation, are burdensome and expensive. SDG&E needs to assemble a team of 150 to 200 people including support personnel to prosecute a GRC. DRA agrees that the regulatory process associated with GRCs has become "burdensome, litigious, and costly." Our own experience is that GRCs are major procedural events that sometimes require weeks of hearings; we have had to create a rate case processing plan to deal with scheduling impact of GRCs on the Commission and on parties. We agree with DGS that reducing this burden should not be the sole or even the primary purpose of this experiment, yet we think it is reasonable to search out ways to reduce the administrative burden and cost of regulation while pursuing the terms of the regulatory compact. That is our objective.

To summarize, our objectives for improving regulation with respect to SDG&E's proposed base rates experiment are as follows:

1. To provide greater incentive than exists under current regulation for the utility to reduce rates.

2. To provide a more rational system of incentives for management to take reasonable risks and control costs in both the long and short run. This includes extending the relatively short-term planning horizon associated with the three-year GRC cycle, and reducing the company's incentive to add to rate base to increase earnings.

3. To prepare the company to operate effectively in the increasingly competitive energy utility industry. This entails providing greater flexibility for management to take risks combined with a greater assignment of the consequences of those risks to the company.

4. To reduce the administrative cost of regulation....

The Joint Proposal includes three nonprice performance indicators which reward or penalize the utility's ability to control employee safety, system reliability, and customer satisfaction. There is also a price perform-ance indicator which sets rewards and penalties based on the utility's system average rate as compared to a national index. The maximum yearly reward under the Joint Proposal is $19 million, and the maximum yearly penalty is $21 million. . . .

. . . In addition to the aggregate limits on rewards and penalties noted above, each indicator has an individual limit on rewards and penalties. For employee safety, the maximum reward is $3 million and the maximum penalty is $5 million. The other indicators specify equal maximum rewards and penalties, which are, for customer satisfaction, system reliability, and rate comparison, $2 million, $4 million, and $10 million, respectively. . . .

As already noted, the overall concept of a performance incentives system with predetermined shareholder rewards and penalties that depend on utility management performance, and conditionality between price and nonprice performance, is uncontested. We deem such a system not only reasonable, but essential for achieving the objectives and criteria of regula-tory reform. The electric price performance indicator provides an important incentive for achieving the objective of rate reduction. It helps prepare the company for competition in that it begins to decouple rates from costs. Nonprice indicators are necessary to help assure that rate reductions and cost savings do not come at the expense of system quality in the short term or the long term. We will include a performance incentive system as part of the adopted base rates mechanism. . . .

We conclude that the Joint Proposal provides a balanced, appropriately conservative reform package which should prove to be an improvement over current regulation. Since there are risks to ratepayers and sharehold-ers in adhering to the status quo of current regulation, we conclude the only reasonable course of action is to approve the Joint Proposal with the few modifications discussed herein.■

NOTES AND COMMENTS

1.   Many other states have considered incentive rates. For example, Cen-tral Maine Power Co.'s incentive rates impose a price cap, utilizing current rates as a starting point. The utility is not able to recover dollar for dollar through its fuel adjustment clause or for purchased power, as it has in the past. The incentive rates contain a service reliability component which establishes an earnings-reduction mechanism, allowing imposition of penal-ties ranging from $250,000 to $3 million if net service quality or customer satisfaction declines. In addition, the utility is allowed to pass through to ratepayers a share of the savings and costs associated with the buyout of (QF) power purchase contracts. The utility has also secured a pricing flexibility component, which allows it to select from a variety of pricing options, typically between a marginal cost floor and the price cap, subject to safeguards designed to protect core customers, avoid undue discrimination,

and preserve its previously-established rate design policy. Docket No, 92–345, Jan. 10, 1995 (Maine PUC). A similar price flexibility program without a full-fledged price cap was approved in *Re Bangor–Hydro Electric Co.*, 159 P.U.R. 4th 460 (Me. PUC 1995).

2. Incentive rate mechanisms may run afoul of traditional cost of service principles. In *Stewart v. Utah*, 882 P.2d 141 (Utah 1994), the Utah Supreme Court held that incentive rates which were designed to encourage investment in the Utah telecommunications infrastructure by providing for an adjustable rate of return and revenue sharing between shareholders and customers of U.S. West, a regulated utility, violated cost-of-service principles:

> We turn now to the legality of the plan promulgated by the Commission under § 54–4–4.1(1). The Commission made no findings in support of the percentage breakdowns that determine the sharing of revenues between the utility and the ratepayers. Revenue sharing begins at a rate of return of 12.2%, the rate the Commission erroneously found to be just and reasonable based on cost-of-service standards. Under the plan, USWC [U.S. West Communications] retains 20% of all overearnings between 12.2% and 13.2%; 40% of all overearnings between 13.2% and 14.2%; and 50% of all overearnings between 14.2% and 17%. Earnings in excess of 17% were to be returned to the ratepayers. Thus, notwithstanding the 12.2% authorized rate of return fixed by the Commission, USWC has an incentive to earn up to a 17% rate of return.

> The Commission's order is defective for a number of reasons. First, it was entered without notice to any party or a hearing on the merits of the plan. Second, the plan essentially forsakes cost-of-service principles as required by Title 54 of the Public Utilities Code. The sharing of revenue begins at 12.2%, but all earnings over and above that percentage that USWC can retain are necessarily excessive because they are not justified by any cost-of-service principle. Nor can they be justified on the ground that they provide an "incentive" for USWC to invest in Utah.... In fact, the incentive to earn higher profits can be achieved as easily, or more easily, by false economics such as cutting maintenance expenses, reducing customer services, and deferring necessary investments. On that score, we emphatically note that the Commission has allowed USWC accelerated depreciation rates to induce USWC to invest in Utah and USWC has not made the investments contemplated. Unjustifiable accelerated depreciation rates translate into unjustifiable charges against ratepayers that inure to the benefit of the shareholders.

> Nor can the Commission's plan be justified on the ground that it enables ratepayers to share in some of USWC's excess earnings. Given the Commission's extraordinary default in the regulation of USWC's earnings over the past years, that might well seem a desirable objective, but it is hardly a rationale for institutionalizing and legalizing exorbitant rates. Even if it is possible to justify a sharing of earnings in

excess of an authorized rate of return because of a necessary and inevitable lag in rate-fixing procedures, it is certainly not justifiable for a utility to retain excess earnings in increasingly larger percentages above the authorized rate of return on equity. Finally, the Commission's plan in effect assumes that another rate-making proceeding need not take place unless and until USWC earns in excess of 17%, a prescription for regulatory neglect and exploitive rates.

For all the above reasons, the Commission's incentive plan is arbitrary, capricious, and unlawful.

3. Performance-based incentive rates focus on incentives for the utility to improve performance. Other "incentive" rates are more concerned with local economic development than improved utility performance. These economic development incentive rates are designed to entice new and preserve existing industries and business. To the extent that these allow the pricing flexibility necessary for utilities to continue to compete in emerging power markets, such rates are not necessarily inefficient. For example, Massachusetts Electric has filed an incentive rate plan, pursuant to Massachusetts Department of Public Utilities incentive ratemaking guidelines, that would increase customer rates by $30 million. The filing includes a discount program, based on participation in a real-time pricing program, for large industrial customers in the manufacturing, computer and biotech sectors of the economy. Massachusetts Electric Files State's First Incentive Rate Plan, Electric Light & Power, May 1995, at 4. The North Carolina Utilities Commission adopted interim guidelines for such economic development incentive rates to give utilities pricing flexibility necessary for competition. *Re Self-generation, Deferral Rates, Dispersed Energy Facilities and Economic Incentive Rates*, Docket No. E–100, Sub. 73, Nov. 28, 1994 (NC. U.C.).

3. THE ENERGY POLICY ACT OF 1992 AND THE EMERGENCE OF WHOLESALE SUPPLY COMPETITION

With the enactment of the federal Energy Policy Act of 1992 ("1992 EPAct"), a statute adopted following the U.S. crisis with Iraq, Congress gave even more emphasis to the promotion of competition among various components of the electric power industry. Two developments were significant in promoting more widespread wholesale power supply competition. First, the 1992 EPAct clarified and broadened FERC wholesale wheeling authority. Second, the 1992 EPAct removed some of the restrictions on the growth of the independent power industry imposed by PUHCA.

a. CLARIFICATION AND EXTENSION OF FERC's WHEELING AUTHORITY

Since passage of the Energy Policy Act, dozens of requests for wholesale transmission service have been filed with FERC. Despite a spirited opposition by the utility industry, FERC's initial treatment of these requests has erased any remaining doubt that it would, in certain circumstances, use its new authority under section 211 to push the industry towards open access and increased competition.

In a watershed decision issued in October 1993, FERC voted unanimously to require Florida Power & Light (FP&L) to provide network transmission service to members of the Florida Municipal Power Agency. *Florida Mun. Power Agency*, 65 F.E.R.C. ¶ 61,125 (1993) (granting request for transmission service as establishing further proceedings to investigate the rates, terms, and conditions of such service). Interpreting its new authority broadly, FERC noted that section 211(c)(2) of the FPA did not bar issuance of a wheeling order due to pre-existing transmission contracts, effectively allowing existing transmission customers the opportunity to "upgrade" the service they received under existing contracts. Given the FPA's purpose of "encourag[ing] the orderly development of plentiful supplies of electricity ... at reasonable prices," FERC found the public interest in favor of issuance of a wheeling order to be compelling under the circumstances:

> As a general matter, the availability of transmission service (or increased flexibility to use transmission) will enhance competition in the market for power supplies over the long run because it will increase both the power supply options available to transmission customers (thereby benefitting their customers) and the sales options available to sellers. This should result in lower costs to consumers. In addition, if a transmission customer determines that flexible service, such as network service, will allow it to serve its customers more efficiently, we believe that the public interest will be served by requiring that service to be provided so long as the transmitting utility is fully and fairly compensated and there is no unreasonable impairment of reliability.

Id. FERC's order emphasized that the rates, terms, and conditions under which the service is offered must be nondiscriminatory and comparable to what the utility provides other customers. This represents the first step in imposing on the industry the "comparability" standard FERC had adopted in the natural gas context. This precedent-setting decision was widely recognized by industry experts as a clear message that FERC was serious about "leveling the competitive playing field" between transmission users and transmission-owning utilities. FERC has continued to adopt competitive transmission mechanisms by requiring transmission to the distribution level and requiring the open access tariffs filed in merger proceedings to provide network service.

b. FURTHER PROMOTION OF POWER GENERATION BY INDEPENDENT POWER PRODUCERS (IPPs)

The 1992 EPAct also recognized the limits of PURPA for encouraging independent power production. PURPA applies only to certified QFs which met the strict small power production or cogeneration described in the statute and FERC's regulations. However, independent power producers which do not comply strictly with these criteria do not qualify for PURPA benefits. Prior to 1992, one significant impediment to the growth of non-PURPA independents was the regulatory morass of a New Deal statute, PUHCA. PUHCA required many power production projects to comply with costly SEC reporting regulations. The 1992 EPAct suspended PUHCA for certain independent power producers by creating what is known as a PUHCA exempt wholesale generator (or EWG, pronounced "e-wog"). (In the 2005 Energy Policy Act, Congress completely repealed PUHCA, making such EWG status irrelevant as of its effective date.)

By 1992, competition in the independent power production sector and open access transmission at the wholesale levels were common, but still not pervasive. In large part, the traditional single, vertically-integrated firm structure had been replaced with a multiplicity of power supply options provided through a single transmitting utility, typically an investor-owned utility (*see* **Figure 11–1**). In the U.S., most individual end use customers, such as residential users of electricity, do not have a choice from whom they purchase electricity. (The issue of retail competition is discussed in Chapter 12. Regardless of retail competition policies, if electricity prices were to become too high, consumers have the option, as they have in the past, to shift large-load appliances from electricity to natural gas). Large customers, such as industrial users, have many options: they can purchase from their local utility, self-generate pursuant to PURPA, or, if they are able to negotiate transmission terms, purchase their power requirements from an independent generator or other non-utility source.

By the 1990's, however, dissatisfaction with some of the approaches federal regulators embraced in encouraging the growth of the independent power production sector of the industry were widespread. Consider the following case, which discusses PURPA's QF certification criteria:

Brazos Electric Power Cooperative, Inc. v. FERC

205 F.3d 235 (5th Cir. 2000).

Tenaska is a privately-held partnership engaged in the production of wholesale electric power. Tenaska developed and owns a cogeneration plant in Cleburne, Texas. A cogeneration plant is a facility which produces electric energy and either steam or some other form of useful energy which is used for commercial, industrial, heating, or cooling purposes. See 16 U.S.C. § 796(18)(A). Brazos is an electric utility cooperative engaged in the generation and transmission of electric power. The utility is comprised of individual electric cooperatives in Texas and provides power to those cooperatives. Currently, Brazos is purchasing electricity from Tenaska pursuant to the facilities' Power Purchase Agreement. The Power Purchase Agreement was certified under a Texas statute that granted certification of such contracts only if the cogeneration facility met the requirements of the Public Utilities Regulatory Policies Act of 1978 ("PURPA"), 16 U.S.C. § 823a et seq. Brazos seeks to undo the contract, arguing that Tenaska no longer meets PURPA's requirements.

A further understanding of the facts of this case requires some explanation of the statutes and regulations that control the relationship between a private producer such as Tenaska and public utility corporation such as Brazos. PURPA was enacted in response to the nation's fuel shortage, and its primary aim was to promote conservation of oil and natural gas in electricity generation. *See FERC v. Mississippi*, 456 U.S. 742 (1982). To those ends, PURPA required FERC to promulgate rules encouraging the development of alternative generators of electricity, such as cogeneration facilities. *See* 16 U.S.C. § 824a–3(a). The rationale behind encouraging cogeneration is that the production of electricity frequently results in the production of thermal energy as a byproduct; by using small amounts of additional fuel, cogenerators can produce large amounts of thermal energy to be used in other processes. Congress created regulatory benefits to provide economic encouragement to such nontraditional power producers. For example, qualifying cogenerators are exempt from wholesale rate regulation under all federal and state public utility statutes, see 18 C.F.R. §§ 292.601, 292.602, and utilities can be compelled to interconnect with them, paying rates no greater than the utility's full avoided costs, see 18 C.F.R. §§ 292.303, 292.308, 292.101(b). In this way, PURPA ensures the cogenerator a market for its electricity production and allows it to make a profit when it can produce power at an average cost lower than the utility's avoided cost.

Of relevance to the instant appeal are PURPA's guidelines for the certification of facilities as "qualifying cogeneration facilities," and FERC's rules prescribing the standards for that certification. The statute defines "cogeneration facility" as one that produces "(I) electric energy, and (ii) steam or forms of useful energy (such as heat) which are used for industrial, commercial, heating, or cooling purposes." 16 U.S.C. § 796(18)(A). To determine which nontraditional power producers could receive benefits, PURPA created a category of "qualifying cogeneration facilities," or QFs, which includes any facility FERC determines has met the regulatory requirements. See 16 U.S.C. § 796(18)(B)(I).

FERC's regulations prescribe operating, efficiency, and ownership standards for facilities seeking QF status. See 18 C.F.R. § 292.205 (operating and efficiency standards); 18 C.F.R. § 292.206 (ownership criteria). Relevant here is the requirement that electric utilities hold less than 50% of the equity interest in the cogeneration facility. See 18 C.F.R. § 292.206. In addition, the cogeneration facility must "produce electric energy and forms of useful thermal energy (such as heat or steam), used for industrial, commercial, heating, or cooling purposes, through the sequential use of energy." 18 C.F.R. § 292.202© (emphasis added).

. . . [FERC] applies one of three economic tests in determining whether a thermal output is useful for purposes of QF certification. First, if a cogenerator proposes to use its thermal energy in a common industrial or commercial process, that energy is considered presumptively useful. *See id.* at ¶ 61,279. A process, or thermal application, will be deemed "common" after the Commission has received a satisfactory number of QF applications proposing the same use for the thermal output. *See Kamine/Besicorp Allegany*, L.P., 63 FERC ¶ 61,320, ¶ 63,158 (1993). The Commission reasons that, if a thermal application is a common one, the technology involved must be established and there must be a market for the application's end-product. *See Arroyo Energy, L.P.* (Arroyo II), 63 FERC ¶ 61,198, ¶ 62,545 (1993); *Polk Power Partners, L.P., et al.*, 61 FERC ¶ 61,300, ¶ 62,128 (1992). As such, when a facility's proposed use of thermal energy is common in the industry, FERC presumes the energy used in that application is useful and performs no further analysis regarding the economics of the thermal application. *See Bayside Cogeneration*, L.P. (Bayside II), 67 FERC ¶ 61,290, ¶ 62,006 (1994).

When the facility proposes an uncommon application, i.e., one that involves a new technology or creates an end-product without an established market, FERC's analysis is different. *See Electrodyne*, 32 FERC at ¶ 61,278. It employs separate analyses depending on whether the purchaser of the thermal energy—the "thermal host"—is an entity unaffiliated or affiliated with the cogenerator. If an independent entity, unaffiliated with the cogenerator, purchases the thermal energy, FERC considers the energy useful because it assumes no entity would purchase the thermal output, or the end-product produced with the aid of the thermal output, unless it served some legitimate purpose. *See Liquid Carbonic Industries Corp.* v. FERC, 29 F.3d 697, 700 (D.C.Cir.1994). In other words, purchase by the thermal host establishes that there is an arm's-length market for the output. *See Kamine*, 63 FERC at ¶ 63,158; *Electrodyne*, 32 FERC at ¶ 61,279. FERC, therefore, deems the thermal energy useful and performs no further analysis regarding the economics of the thermal application. *See LaJet Energy Co.*, 44 FERC ¶ 61,288, ¶ 61,194 (1988); *Electrodyne*, 32 FERC at ¶ 61,279. . . .

FERC's certification process occurs prior to the construction of the facility, and QF status is granted or denied based on the representations in a facility's application. The regulations provide, however, that FERC may revoke the QF status of a previously-certified facility if the facility, when operational, fails to comply with any of the statements in its application. *See* 18 C.F.R. § 292.207(d)(1).

Brazos challenges Tenaska's certification as a QF. Tenaska and Brazos entered their Power Purchase Agreement ("PPA") in 1993, which obligated Brazos to purchase electric power from Tenaska for twenty-three years, with a seventeen-year rollover, at prices fixed in the PPA. This was not a situation where Brazos was compelled under PURPA to purchase electricity from a QF. Rather, both parties were equally interested in Tenaska's becoming certified as a QF. Tenaska wanted to qualify for PURPA benefits. Brazos wanted the best rates. According to Philip Segrest, Brazos' attorney at the time, the only power sources in Texas were public utilities and QFs. As a QF, Tenaska would only be able to charge rates up to Brazos' avoided costs. The public utilities, however, were currently charging rates above Brazos' avoided costs. Thus, because Tenaska's rates were favorable and because the option of building its own plant was impractical, Brazos "insist[ed] that the PPA be certified by the [Public Utility Commission of Texas] pursuant to PURA [the Public Utility Regulatory Act]...." Under PURA, certification of power purchase agreements was permitted only if the power was being purchased from a QF, as that term was defined in PURPA. *See* Tex.Rev.Civ. Stat. Ann. art. 1446c (West Supp.1994) (repealed 1995).

Therefore, on October 20, 1994, Tenaska applied to FERC for QF certification, obviously with Brazos' blessing. According to its application, Tenaska intended to sell its electrical output to Brazos, while its thermal output, steam, was to be converted into distilled water for sale to "a third party." FERC published notice of Tenaska's application in the Federal Register but received no protests or requests for interventions to Tenaska's certification. Therefore, on January 13, 1995, the Commission granted Tenaska QF status. In doing so, FERC determined, in relevant part, that Tenaska fulfilled its ownership requirement that utilities own less than 50% equitable interest in the facility. More importantly, FERC also concluded that the conversion of steam to distilled water was a common industrial process and application of thermal energy for that use was, therefore, presumptively useful.

Tenaska entered into an arrangement with the City of Cleburne (the "City") in which Tenaska would (1) purchase the City's potable water for use in its steam generator, (2) recover the reject water stream from the steam generator's boiler makeup water treatment system and use it to supply the distilled water system, (3) sell the distilled water to the City, and (4) purchase effluent water from the City's wastewater treatment facility for use in its cooling tower. Under this arrangement, the City gave Tenaska a ten-dollar credit on its water bill for its production of the distilled water, and the City was obligated to construct the facilities necessary for transporting both the effluent water to Tenaska and the distilled water from Tenaska. The City was responsible for the initial financing of the construction, including the issuance of tax-exempt municipal bonds, for which Tenaska would reimburse the City in monthly payments when the debt service was owed. The facility became operational in January 1997.

The City had originally agreed to purchase Tenaska's distilled water in order to attract industries to an industrial park near Tenaska's facility, by offering the ready supply of distilled water for sale as process water. Water which was not resold was to be used to augment the flow of Buffalo Creek, a stream running near the City's business district whose stagnant waters were encouraging nuisance conditions and an increased mosquito population. While negotiations continued with potential occupants of the industrial park, the City ran into difficulty garnering permits from the Environmental Protection Agency to increase Buffalo Creek's flow with distilled water. Initially, therefore, the City had no specific use for the distilled water it was purchasing from Tenaska, and it released its purchase into the City's sewer system. An occupant of the industrial park began purchasing the distilled water in September 1997.

On August 22, 1997, Brazos filed with FERC a motion and petition for revocation of Tenaska's QF status. According to Brazos, the use of Tenaska's thermal output for the production of distilled water had not proven to be "useful." The presumption of usefulness on which Tenaska's QF status was certified, Brazos argued, was rebutted by actual operation of the facility—notably, by the fact that the City paid only ten dollars a month for thousands of gallons of water and then dumped the water in the sewer. Meanwhile, Brazos was being forced under the PPA to pay fixed rates which, five years into the deal, were no longer below the market price. In addition, Brazos contended that Tenaska did not satisfy the ownership requirements for QF status. Although utilities owned less than 50% of Tenaska, Brazos alleged that the utilities' 45% interest gave them effective control in a voting procedure requiring a 70% vote to take action.

FERC denied Brazos' motion. FERC stated that once it determines the proposed use of thermal energy is common, it presumes the thermal energy is useful. FERC would not inquire thereafter into how the thermal host used its purchase, nor would it question whether the cogeneration facility was actually making money from its sale. FERC also found that Tenaska satisfied the ownership requirements for QF status, noting that the utilities' 45% interest was insufficient to effect day-to-day action without the votes of 25% of the non-utility owners. Additionally, the Commission noted that Tenaska's ownership structure had not changed since its certification, and because Brazos failed to object then, its complaint now was untimely.

Subsequently, Brazos filed a request for rehearing and its request was denied. Brazos now petitions this Court for review of FERC's order denying the revocation of Tenaska's QF status.

We must affirm FERC's order unless it is "arbitrary, capricious, an abuse of discretion, or otherwise not in accordance with law." 5 U.S.C. § 706(2)(A). The scope of review under this standard is narrow; it does not authorize a reviewing court to substitute its judgment for that of the agency. *See Motor Vehicle Mfrs. Ass'n v. State Farm Mutual Ins.* Co., 463 U.S. 29, 43, 103 S.Ct. 2856, 77 L.Ed.2d 443 (1983). Rather, we must examine " 'whether the decision was based on a consideration of the relevant factors and whether there has been a clear error of judgment.' " *Id.* (quoting *Bowman Transp., Inc. v. Arkansas–Best Freight Sys., Inc.,* 419 U.S. 281, 285, 95 S.Ct. 438, 42 L.Ed.2d 447 (1974)). Where an agency has considered the relevant factors and provided a satisfactory explanation for its actions, its decision will be upheld.

Noting that FERC regulations allow for post-operational challenges to a QF's certification, Brazos maintains that Tenaska is not entitled to benefits under PURPA because, after its facility was certified and became operational, Tenaska failed to uphold the regulatory requirements for QF status in accordance with projections contained in its application for QF certification. Brazos advances the same arguments it did below: the Commission should revoke Tenaska's QF status because the production of distilled water has not proven to be useful, and because Tenaska does not meet PURPA's ownership requirements. We address each contention in turn.

A. Useful Thermal Output

The thrust of Brazos' argument is that the Commission's precedent has not established an irrebuttable presumption of usefulness. Brazos does not take issue with the use of the presumption during certification, before the facility is even built; then, Brazos reasons, the Commission is justified in relying on hypothetical facts and an applicant's claim that, because the proposed thermal use is common, the thermal energy will be useful. Rather, Brazos asserts that the Commission was obligated to consider post-operational facts that could rebut the presumption of a thermal output's usefulness. Specifically, Brazos avers first that, although Tenaska represented in its application for QF status that distilled water would be produced for sale to a third party, the sale of water to the City is a "sham" sale designed only to retain PURPA benefits; it is not a sale serving an independent business purpose that could be economically justified. Second, Brazos contends that the water was not useful because before the City found a purchaser, it was pouring the water in the sewer.

In response, FERC asserts that Tenaska continues to satisfy PURPA's regulatory requirements, as represented in its application for QF status. First, Tenaska's sale of water was one piece of a legitimate, integrated financing package. Second, Tenaska's thermal energy has been useful since the day it was certified, for Tenaska has used "an established technology to produce a common product with an existing market." *Arroyo*, 63 FERC at ¶ 62,545 n. 4. According to the Commission, there is no statutory or precedential requirement that, upon the facility's operation, it examine how each individual thermal host is using its purchases or how economically sound every transaction turned out to be. In fact, FERC argues, doing so would undermine its directives under PURPA, for conditioning the maintenance of QF status on investigations into the economics of a thermal host's purchase would impede the development of cogeneration. We agree that Brazos has misconstrued the Commission's prior holdings. Further, to the extent that the present factual scenario differs from that of the Commission's precedents, FERC's use of its presumption here furthers its congressional mandate under PURPA consistently with its regulations promulgated thereto. . . .

Given the consistency with which FERC has denied further inquiry into common thermal applications, nothing in these precedents persuades us that FERC's presumption of usefulness is rebuttable, even post-operation, by the two sets of facts Brazos presents. . . . The Commission has previously opined that treating its presumption as rebuttable would be inconsistent with PURPA's goals, in that "[p]roviding an opportunity for evidentiary hearings before the Commission . . . would seriously impede the very development of cogeneration . . . that Congress sought to facilitate." *Id.* at 62,006 n. 5 (*quoting American Paper Inst., Inc. v. American Elec. Power Serv. Corp.*, 461 U.S. 402 (1983)) (internal quotations omitted). Nonetheless, even if we were to look behind the presumption here, we, like the Commission, are not persuaded that the sale to the City is a sham. Tenaska correctly points out that it received much more than ten dollars in its transactions with the City, for the Distilled Water Supply Agreement was only one piece of their arrangement's puzzle: Tenaska purchased potable water from the City for use in its steam generator, the reject stream from the generator was turned into distilled water, the City purchased the distilled water to attract industrial customers to an adjacent industrial park, the plant's blowdown water was transported to the City's sewage treatment center, and Tenaska purchased the treated sewage effluent from the City for use in the cogenerator's cooling tower. In addition, Tenaska received tax abatements, as well as access to the City's debt for construction of its water facilities so all of this could take place. Seen in the context of a complex project financing, Tenaska's arrangement with the City garnered it more than ten dollars a month. Thus, as proposed in its QF application, Tenaska has sold its product to a third party.

In addition to the economics of Tenaska's transaction with the City, Brazos urges the Commission to examine the City's use of the distilled water during its first year of operation because, according to Brazos, the City's actual use would rebut the Commission's initial presumption of the thermal energy's usefulness. Relying heavily on *Arroyo II*, 63 FERC ¶ 61,-198 (1993), Brazos contends that, before determining that a thermal output is useful, the Commission must be satisfied that the thermal host's use of its purchase is a bona fide industrial or commercial use. When Tenaska first became operational, it was pouring its distilled water into a sewer, which Brazos maintains was not a bona fide use and renders the thermal energy used to create the water non-useful. Brazos contends that the Commission's failure to take into account the City's actual use of the water was an unexplained departure from its precedents.

In *Arroyo II*, the cogenerator's thermal output, steam, was to be used in absorption refrigeration (AR) equipment to provide ice to an adjacent ice rink. The utility complained that the use of thermal output to help create and maintain an ice rink was a novel use requiring application of the independent business purpose test. The Commission declined to apply the test because it found that AR technology was a common use for steam, and the steam was therefore useful. Brazos, however, relies on several passages in the opinion as evidence that the Commission has tempered its presumption of usefulness by also examining the proposed end-use to which the thermal product would be put:

> Our review of the evidence compiled in this proceeding confirms that the proposed use of the Arroyo [cogeneration] facility's thermal output for refrigeration purposes is indeed bona fide. SDG&E [the utility] presents us with no new reason to upset our earlier determination that the technology to be applied by Arroyo, as well as the end product, are established and, accordingly, that the thermal output of the facility is presumptively useful.

Arroyo II, 63 FERC at ¶ 62,545 (citation omitted) (Brazos' emphasis added). This passage does not support Brazos' contention that FERC examines the thermal host's end-use of its purchase in determining the usefulness of a cogenerator's thermal output. It is the cogenerator's use of thermal energy that must be bona fide, not the thermal host's end-use of the end-product, and the cogenerator's use is bona fide when it is common in the industry. Thus, the passage states that the thermal energy was useful because the thermal output (steam) was put to a bona fide use in a common application (AR technology) and created a common product (ice). This passage does not say that the cogenerator's thermal energy was useful because the thermal host's use of ice to build an ice rink was bona fide. The passage does not refer at all to the thermal host's end-use of the thermal product. Nor should it. As the Commission has noted, "if a cogenerator produces a product that has already met the Commission's usefulness requirement, there is no further inquiry to determine if the product is being used by the recipient for a common purpose." *Brooklyn Navy Yard*, 74 FERC at ¶ 61,046.

In this way, Brazos' complaint that the distilled water was not "useful" misses the point. The distillation of water is common, so the steam used to create it is useful. The use an unaffiliated thermal host makes of its arm's-length purchase is irrelevant. *See Arroyo I*, 62 FERC at ¶ 62,723 ("The fact that this is the first instance before the Commission in which this common refrigeration technology is associated with a common refrigeration product for end-use in an ice rink is irrelevant."). This is because the Commission, as the arbiter of "usefulness," has defined the concept in terms of economics. If an application is common, the technology is established and there is a market for the product. If the technology is established and there is a market for the product, that which is used in the application to create the product is "useful." Once the energy used in the established technology or the product with the established market is purchased by a thermal host, FERC has no further involvement. The purchaser bears the market risk of its purchase, not the seller, and whatever use or profit the purchaser makes of its purchase, whether by pouring it in a sewer or reselling it, is of no moment to the seller. *See Bayside II*, 67 FERC at ¶ 62,006 n. 7 (stating that "PURPA does not require that the Commission ensure that a thermal host make as much money as possible, or make any money at all; all PURPA requires is that the Commission ensure that the thermal host takes useful thermal energy that is used for industrial, commercial, heating, or cooling purposes." (internal quotations omitted) (emphasis added)). The point is that the seller has successfully sold its output in an arm's-length market and the purchaser has access to the same market for resale. There is, of course, proof of this point in the instant case—two weeks after Brazos filed its motion and petition for revocation, the City found a purchaser for its distilled water from among those industries it was trying to attract with the supply of that water. . . .

Although this case presents us with what, at first blush, appears to be the proverbial "peppercorn" scenario—a party paying ten dollars for thousands of gallons of distilled water that for nine months it poured into the sewer—we are, for a number of reasons, hesitant to look beyond FERC's presumption of usefulness to release Brazos from its contractual obligations. First, Tenaska and the City entered an arm's-length contract, one amongst many contracts in which the risks and benefits of the typical project finance arrangement were traded. That Brazos now finds itself paying above-market prices for electricity because it entered a "front-loaded" contract fails to undermine the utility of the Commission's presumption of the usefulness of thermal energy in common applications. A front-loaded contract means that the utility's payment rates are determined at the time the obligation to buy from the cogenerator is incurred, rather than at the time of delivery. Such contracts are often used because they allow the QF to finance the construction and operation of the facility in the early years of the contract. As the Ninth Circuit observed in *Independent Energy Producers Ass'n, Inc. v. California Pub. Util. Comm'n*, 36 F.3d 848, 858 (9th Cir.1994), such contracts have been upheld notwithstanding the recognized risk that the prices set by the contract might at times exceed the utility's actual avoided costs, because "certainty as to rate was important." By ensuring a predictable flow of income, such contracts encourage the development of alternative facilities that might never be built. In FERC's words:

> The Commission recognizes this possibility [that current avoided costs might be lower than the rates provided in the contracts] but is cognizant that in other cases, the required rate will turn out to be lower than the avoided cost at the time of purchase.... Many commentators have stressed the need for certainty with regard to return on investment in new technologies. The Commission agrees with these ... arguments, and believes that, in the long run, "over estimations" and "under estimations" of avoided costs will balance out.

Small Power Production and Cogeneration Facilities; Regulations Implementing Section 210 of PURPA, 45 Fed.Reg. 12224 (1980) (quoted in *Independent Energy Producers Ass'n*, 36 F.3d at 858).

Second, allowing post-operation rebuttal of FERC's presumption of a thermal output's usefulness on these grounds would impede the development of cogeneration facilities, a development PURPA was enacted to encourage. *See Arroyo II*, 63 FERC at ¶ 62,546 (explaining that performing economic analyses on common applications would discourage cogeneration). By sanctioning such rebuttal, we would ensure that every time the market for electricity fluctuated and the utility that was the QF's only market recipient was suddenly displeased with its rates, the utility could back out because it thought either the QF or the thermal host was not being as economically wise or efficient as it should be. This scenario poses several problems.

Owners of QFs would have little incentive to sell electric energy if they had to go through an evidentiary hearing before FERC in Washington, D.C., every time a utility claimed someone else was behaving inefficiently with a common application. ... Neither the statute nor the regulations insist or presuppose that FERC should engage in such heavy-handed oversight as to keep tabs on QFs' arm's-length purchasers. If we were to hold otherwise, we would embrace the very form of micro-management that the Commission has determined QFs are supposed to be freed from, and we would "impute to Congress a purpose to paralyze with one hand what it sought to promote with the other." *Clark v. Uebersee Finanz–Korporation, A.G.*, 332 U.S. 480, 489, 68 S.Ct. 174, 92 L.Ed. 88 (1947).

More importantly, FERC's presumption of usefulness is meant to enable cogeneration facilities to obtain financing. The presumption provides certainty for investors that their investment is duly certified under PURPA and entitled to the benefits of PURPA's statutory imperatives, including the presence of a utility to purchase the facility's output. Because the value of a facility's hard assets is usually less than the project debt, debt repayment and anticipated equity returns depend on performance under project contracts. The contracts constitute the framework for project viability because the ability of the project sponsor to produce revenue from project operation is the foundation of a project financing. The PPA is the principal source of project revenue. Therefore, banks lend money for construction and permanent financing on the strength of the utility's obligation to purchase power from a QF. Revocation of a facility's QF status releases the utility from its obligation under the PPA. It leaves the facility without a market recipient and thus without a revenue source for debt repayment. We would be hard pressed to imagine the investor who would contribute to a project so susceptible to such a scenario. In sum, both FERC's precedents and PURPA's mandates persuade us that Tenaska continues to produce useful thermal energy in accordance with the representations in its application for QF status.

B. Ownership Criteria

In order to obtain QF status under PURPA, a cogeneration facility must not be owned by persons primarily engaged in the generation or sale of electric power. *See* 16 U.S.C. § 796(18)(B). The Commission clarified this requirement, determining that electric utilities may own no more than 50% of the equity interest in a QF. *See* 18 C.F.R. § 292.206(b). FERC's regulations thus equate "ownership interest" with "equity interest," but they do not define the term "equity interest." *See Ultrapower 3*, 27 FERC ¶ 61,094, ¶ 61,183 (1984). Cases discussing the Commission's ownership criteria emphasize the stream of benefits accruing to each partner, but the voting interests of each partner have also been examined to avoid a utility partner's manipulation of those benefits. *See id.* at ¶ 61,184. Accordingly, "a utility partner may not have more than 50% control of a qualifying facility." *Brooklyn Navy Yard*, 74 FERC at ¶ 61,048.

According to Brazos, Tenaska has not satisfied the ownership criteria for QF status because utilities have effective control over the facility's operation. Affiliates of three utilities own a 45% interest in Tenaska and have a 38.9% voting interest in the facility, in conformity with the regulatory limits. Before FERC, however, Brazos contended that the utilities' 45% interest in the facility gives them effective control over the facility's operation, because a 70% vote of Tenaska's Executive Review Committee is needed to take significant actions. The Commission disagreed, pointing out that the utility affiliates would still need the approval of the non-utility owners to take significant action. The Commission also pointed out that Tenaska's ownership structure had not changed since it was certified as a QF. Because Brazos was listed as the utility-purchaser in QF application and failed to object when the application was noticed for comment, the Commission determined that Brazos' challenge was untimely.

.... We agree with the Commission that "[a]llowing such belated challenges to QF certifications despite unchanged facts would undermine the contractual reliance QFs need in order to finance and build their projects." *Brazos Elec. Power Coop. v. Tenaska IV Tex. Partners, Ltd.*, 85 FERC ¶ 61,097, ¶ 61,348 (1998)....

Briefly, even if we were to give Brazos the benefit of the doubt, its challenge is still without merit. As noted, FERC's ownership criteria are intended to prevent utilities from diverting to themselves the stream of benefits flowing from a QF, such that the utilities would gain some undue advantage vis-a-vis non-utility partners. *See Dominion Resources, Inc.*, 43 FERC ¶ 61,079, ¶ 61,251 (1988). In order to accrue such benefits, "control" requires action, not inaction. That is, a minority interest's ability to block significant actions does not garner the benefits the controlling interest can manipulate by taking significant actions. Furthermore, if the ability to block significant action constituted "control," then Brazos is actually contending that utilities may not have more than 30% control—a proposition that finds no support in the Commission's precedents. See id. at ¶ 61,251 (stating that "a facility will meet the ownership requirements of PURPA ... so long as the interest in the stream of benefits and control by a utility or utilities, by whatever mechanism used, does not exceed 50%"). The utility affiliates' equity and voting interests in Tenaska satisfy the Commission's ownership requirements for QF status.

■ EMILIO M. GARZA, CIRCUIT JUDGE, specially concurring:

The majority opinion reflects a wholesale endorsement of both the result reached by the Federal Energy Regulatory Commission ("FERC") and the methodology used to reach that result. I agree with the former, but not with the latter. Accordingly, I concur in the result reached by the majority, but write separately because the method by which FERC disposed of this case could, if repeated, produce results clearly in conflict with the language and intent of the Public Utility Regulatory Policies Act of 1978 ("PURPA"), 16 U.S.C. § 823a et seq.

In this case, the majority is correct in rejecting Brazos's claim that any "usefulness" from cogeneration in the Tenaska facility is "flushed down the sewer." The evidence shows that the thermal energy produced by the Tenaska facility is used to distill water which is sold to the city or directed into Buffalo Creek to attract customers to an adjacent industrial park. Accordingly, the thermal energy produced by Tenaska is "useful" in any sense of the word, and we defer to FERC's interpretation.

However, Brazos's allegations, when considered relative to FERC's treatment of petitions to revoke QF certification, beg the question: what if

Tenaska's cogenerated energy was used to distill water which was promptly flushed down the sewer? Clearly, nothing "useful" would result from the cogeneration, but since the cogenerated energy was "used in a common process," FERC would rely on its presumption of usefulness and the facility would retain QF certification. I fully agree with the majority's statement that "PURPA and its implementing regulations require only that the thermal energy be useful; they do not demand that the sale of every end-product be profitable." However, under FERC's procedural rationale, the Commission cannot ever be sure that the thermal energy is "useful" in the everyday sense of the word. In some cases, FERC's failure to even address claims that a facility's thermal energy is not "useful" could contravene both the language and the intent of PURPA. *See Liquid Carbonic*, 29 F.3d at 706 ("Congress intended PURPA to encourage the development of cogeneration facilities ... [but][t]he encouragement of the goal must, but its nature, limit entry to those who actually further the goal by producing useful energy.... ").

FERC's irrebuttable presumption of usefulness is justified in the context of petitions for initial certification, upon which financing to build such facilities often depends. As the majority notes, in this context "[p]roviding for evidentiary hearings before the Commission ... would seriously impede the very development of cogeneration ... that Congress sought to facilitate." However, FERC and the majority exaggerate the possibility that an evidentiary hearing years after a facility has been in operation to determine whether the facility truly produces "useful" thermal energy would impede the initial development of the facility. Any hesitancy that this potential future evidentiary hearing might produce is mitigated, if not eliminated, by the fact that FERC already performs evidentiary investigations into other issues of technical compliance (for example, into the 5% mandate). The alternative to allowing post-certification evidentiary hearings on "usefulness," which currently exists, allows facilities to retain QF benefits even if they are not (in fact, even if they never were) the type of facilities to which Congress wanted to afford such benefits. In many cases, this is a clear departure from the statutory mandate, and therefore an impermissible construction of PURPA.

Tenaska has proven that the energy it produces as a co-product to electricity is "useful" in producing distilled water which benefits the community at large, and thus that the benefits afforded it as a QF are justified. Accordingly, I concur in the decision allowing Tenaska's Cleburne facility to retain QF status. However, I cannot agree with the majority's endorsement of the procedure by which FERC summarily dismissed this case. Congress wanted to encourage the production of cogeneration facilities because, in developing alternative sources of "useful" energy while producing electricity, they improved the energy efficiency of electricity generation facilities in particular and the nation in general. By establishing an irrebuttable presumption that prevents it from ever examining whether a facility's co-produced energy is ever "useful," FERC has opened the door to facilities who meet FERC's technical requirements but defy the language and spirit of PURPA.■

NOTES AND COMMENTS

1.   The Fifth Circuit's decision focuses on FERC's very detailed operation and ownership criteria, which appear in PURPA, as well as FERC's regulations implementing the statute. Facilities that were built or remain in operation solely by virtue of the fact that they comply with PURPA's QF requirements—and thus qualify for PURPA benefits, such as avoided cost rates—are sometimes referred to as "PURPA machines." Do the benefits of such generation outweigh any imposition of their costs on utilities and/or consumers?

2.   While the facility at issue in the Firth Circuit decision was a PURPA cogeneration facility, similar issues arise in the context of FERC's approval process for small power production facilities that burn renewable fuels. Here reviewing courts have not always been as deferential towards FERC's approval process. PURPA defines a small power production facility as one that "produces electric energy solely by use, as a primary energy source, of biomass, waste, renewable resources, geothermal resources, or any combination thereof," 16 U.S.C. § 796(17)(A)(I). Some flexibility in fuel use is allowed to these facilities, subject to FERC's approval, in the event of express situations defined in PURPA, including shortages and to prevent electric power outages that affect the public safety, health, and welfare. FERC has adopted regulation that prohibits the use of oil, gas and coal by such a facility in excess of "25 percent of the total energy input of the facility during the 12–month period beginning with the date the facility first produces electric energy and any calendar year subsequent to the year in which the facility first produces electric energy." 18 C.F.R. § 292.204(b)(2).

While initially intended to provide flexibility in fuel use to promote innovative generation technologies, this requirement has recently posed a problem for some small power production facilities, particularly those burning waste and biomass. An example is Laidlaw Gas Recovery Systems, Inc., which owns and operates several landfill gas-to-energy plants which burn methane produced by decomposition to generate electricity. Laidlaw sought to permission to burn natural gas at an amount up to 25% of its output to increase operation of a plant from 17 to 20 MW, in order to alleviate the effects of forced outages and landfill maintenance. At the same time, Laidlaw was seeking a 20 MW output from the facility to meet its contractual supply obligations with a utility, Southern California Edison. Laidlaw also asserted that state environmental regulations in California limited its ability to influence the rate of decomposition and produce methane at its facility. FERC issued a declaratory ruling that would allow Laidlaw to burn natural gas, but Southern California Edison appealed FERC's decision. On appeal, a panel of the D.C. Circuit held that FERC's ruling violated the plain meaning of PURPA, which the court held expressly restricts the circumstances under which FERC can allow flexibility in fuel use for small power production facilities. The D.C. Circuit also rejected FERC's appeal to the general purpose of encouraging the development of small power production facilities. *See Southern California Edison Co. v.*

FERC, 195 F.3d 17 (D.C. Cir. 1999). Does the outcome of this case conflict with the Fifth Circuit's opinion? For an argument that FERC should have more flexibility in interpreting this provision of PURPA in order to encourage renewable and independent power generation, see Jim Rossi, Making Policy Through the Waiver of Regulations at the Federal Energy Regulatory Commission, 47 Admin. L. Rev. 255 (1995).

3. *Independent Energy Producers Ass'n, Inc. v. California Pub. Util. Comm'n*, 36 F.3d 848, 858 (9th Cir.1994), discussed in *Brazos*, addressed the issue of avoided cost rates set under PURPA. In Chapter 13, some of the problems in setting avoided cost rates under PURPA in the light of major changes in market conditions—including the introduction of wholesale and retail competition—are discussed.

A NOTE ON PURPA AND PUCHA REFORM

As the *Brazos* case illustrates, even after the 1992 EPAct a great deal of uncertainty revolves around the federal regulatory scheme designed to encourage IPPs. The uncertainty surrounds both PUHCA and PURPA.

While many believe that PUHCA worked to protect consumers in the mid-twentieth century, today utility industry investors are skeptical and Congress repealed the statute in 2005. With the rise of utility mergers, many made efficient with the growth of competition, it was believed that PUHCA more of a hindrance than a benefit to consumers, even given the reforms Congress adopted in the 1992 EPAct. The 2005 Energy Policy Act completely repeaed the statute. For discussion of some of the barriers PUHCA was enacting to utility mergers in a competitive environment see Judge Richard Cudahy, Consolidation: Key to the Future?, Public Utilities Fortnightly, August 2005, at 15.

PURPA QFs have spurned much competition in generation, but as the *Brazos* case illustrates, they have also created certain incentives for investment in QFs where other projects may have been more efficient. In addition, some utilities attribute a stranded cost problem to PURPA QFS, or see PURPA QFS as inhibiting competition [see Chapter 12]. The following excerpted chapter, prepared by the Energy Information Administration, summarizes some of the arguments for and against PURPA reform:

Federal Legislative Initiatives, Chapter 6 in the Changing Structure of the Electric Power Industry (2002)

available online at http://www.eia.doe.gov/cneaf/electricity/chg_stru_update/chapter6.html.

PURPA was born of the energy crises of the 1970s, which resulted in an intense desire by Congress to reduce the Nation's dependence on foreign oil (and fossil fuels in general) and to diversify the technologies used for electricity generation. PURPA's goal was to cultivate conservation and the efficient use of resources. It was successful in that it promoted cogeneration, the use of renewable resources, and other energy-efficient technologies, and it was fortuitous in that it also introduced competition by demonstrating that the generation of electricity is not a natural monopoly. But, like PUHCA, PURPA is now being targeted for repeal due to the industry's move to competition. There are many arguments on both sides of the debate over the prudence of eliminating PURPA immediately, eventually, or not at all.

Proponents of stand-alone PURPA-repeal legislation contend that the Act's mandatory purchase obligation is grossly anticompetitive and anticonsumer—anticompetitive because the Government created an artificial market by mandating that utilities buy from QFs, and anticonsumer because numerous studies have estimated that the Act caused utilities (and ultimately, consumers) to pay billions of dollars over present market prices for power. They claim that, although the Act introduced competition, it can hardly be said that it did so in an atmosphere of free market participation, a basic tenet of economic theorists who stress that the rules and prices must be established by the market—not by the Government. In addition they assert that, because of the 1992 EPACT's creation of EWGs and its incorporation of competitive policies, PURPA's QF concept has been overtaken by events, i.e., the industry now realizes that nonutilities can cleanly and efficiently provide additional generating capacity.

Those who want PURPA eliminated now say that its mandatory purchase clause is anticompetitive and is therefore impeding the transition to competition. Furthermore, QFs have been receiving long-run avoided-cost rates that today substantially exceed current market prices. These rates were based on past forecasts of sharply rising oil and natural gas prices as well as the expectation of future increases in the demand for electricity and construction of new generating capacity. By the late 1980s and early 1990s, however, oil prices had stabilized, natural gas prices had declined, and excess generating capacity in most regions of the country allowed utilities to buy capacity and energy at much lower prices than had been forecast a decade earlier. The utilities' actual avoided costs dropped lower than in the mid–1980s and were considerably lower than the levels required by the long-term contracts imposed by some State Commissions. Many utilities contend that PURPA has caused dramatic hikes in retail electric rates, and many groups along with these utilities now believe that new regulatory action must be taken to correct past misjudgments.

Forecasters predict that future power generation will be dominated by natural gas. Reformers argue that, based on these forecasts, PURPA becomes irrelevant because natural gas-fired power generation is relatively inexpensive and the most environmentally benign of all the fossil fuels used in electric power generation. As mentioned earlier, some groups contend that PURPA is no longer necessary because its goals have already been achieved—i.e., cogeneration using improved turbine techniques and the use of renewable resources has not only gotten a foothold but has claimed a rather significant share of electric power production. Proponents of repeal further contend that PURPA's environmental and fuel diversification goals will be maintained by the workings of a free market while others are not so sure. Although they may agree that a free market can provide a solution to many of the industry's problems, they seriously question the wisdom of relying on competition to continue the strides made in the use of renewables and cogeneration techniques. Energy conservation and diversification of generating fuels were mandated by Congress because of the growing dependence on foreign oil and the Nation's concerns about the energy crises of the 1970s. Those fears have faded with the passage of time, but it is argued that it is not out of the realm of possibilities that another crisis could occur. Indeed, some believe that it would be shortsighted and irresponsible to regard energy shortages as merely nightmares of the past and to gamble on the unlikelihood of a similar recurrence. They argue that the Nation cannot be without the ability to cope with such a situation in the future.

Even if dependence on foreign energy sources was not an issue, PURPA supporters stress that common sense dictates that energy be conserved and that electricity generation use more environmentally benign fuels in order to sustain a certain quality of life for future generations. In addition, some believe that QF policy corrects a market failure—i.e., the price of fossil or nuclear energy is too low based on the costly damage it does to the environment and the fact that those who create the pollution do not pay for it. In this context, some argue that conservation, diversification of fuels, and the use of renewable resources that are not depletable and other fuels that lessen the problems of acid rain and greenhouse gases must continue to be supported.

In addition to PURPA's merits regarding the environment and fuel diversification, its supporters point out that QFs bring increased reliability while decreasing the need for large, costly plants. They contend that today's utilities have too much market power, which makes it necessary for PURPA to continue to give nonutilities a competitive advantage, and until every electricity generator is playing on a level field, PURPA's QF provisions are justified.

There are also those who believe that, while PURPA repeal might be warranted in a competitive electricity supply scenario, such a scenario has not been realized yet. Just as some PUHCA reformers are against immediate piecemeal and stand-alone action, some PURPA reformers believe that repeal should be included in a comprehensive restructuring bill. They argue that there is no need to push a stand-alone repeal bill through Congress when there is currently other proposed electricity competition legislation that will comprehensively address the restructuring and regulatory issues that warrant legislative action, including repeal of PURPA.■

The Energy Policy Act of 2005 made significant changes to the rules for PURPA QFs. Among other things, that statute conditionally terminates mandatory purchase and sale obligations for new QFs and tightens the thermal output requirements for new cogeneration facilities to reflect technological changes. It eliminates statutory language that prevents owners of utilities from having an ownership share of grater than 50% in QFs.

Under the 2005 Energy Policy Act, if FERC finds that a new or existing QF has access to nondiscriminatory transmission service and competitive wholesale power markets (see below), electric utilities are no longer required to enter into new contracts to purchase power from it. Utilities are allowed to see service territory-wide relief from FERC by filing an application requesting FERC's determination that the required open access transmission and wholesale market access conditions are present. Also, if FERC finds that competing retail electric suppliers are willing and able to swell and deliver electric energy to QFs, and electric utilities are not required by state law to sell electricity in their service territories, the 2005 Energy Policy Act eliminates the requirement that utilities enter into new contracts to sell energy to QFs.

The 2005 Energy Policy Act does not affect any rights or remedies regarding the purchase or sale of electricity or capacity under existing contracts or contracts pending approval before state regulatory authorities. While the statute clearly repeals mandatory purchase obligations with respect to new facilities, the 2005 Energy Policy Act does not deprive QFs of the other regulatory exemptions that they currently enjoy. In fact, Congress extended an exemption top QFs from a statutory provisions giving FERC greater access to corporate books, records and accounts. It remains to be seen how beneficial QF status will continue to be in the future, and how many market participants will elect to apply for QF status, but the 2005 statute does give some suggestion that Congress intends to allow QF's to exist and intended FERC to continue to grant them at least some benefits not afforded to other market participants.

D.   ORDER NO. 888: OPEN ACCESS TRANSMISSION, UNBUNDLING, AND THE EMERGENCE OF NEW WHOLESALE POWER MARKETS

Creation of the EWG has spawned growth of many IPPs outside of the PURPA framework. The most significant class of new generators with EWG status are often referred to a "merchant" plants. Unlike traditional utilities, merchants plants do not have a duty to serve any retail load, and provide power primarily in the merging wholesale power markets. The relaxation of PUHCA's requirements in the 1992 EPAct and creation of the EWG allow many utilities, through affiliates, to begin supplying power in markets outside of their geographic service areas. An example, discussed further in Chapter 13, is the merchant plant proposed by Duke Energy, which was planned for siting in Florida. Merchant plants, which sell power at wholesale without the mandatory buyback benefits provided by PURPA, seem to have found an adequate market for their power without mandatory buyback at avoided cost rates, as was required under PURPA.

Regulatory developments after the 1992 EPAct have encouraged the development of markets for EWG power, as well as the development of merchants plants more generally. After the 1992 EPAct, competitive reforms of the electric power industry have proliferated in two respects. First, the 1992 EPAct fueled many reform efforts at the state level, as discussed in Chapter 12. Second, the 1992 EPAct shifted much debate over competition from wholesale transmission to retail transmission and other issues, by clarifying federal jurisdiction over wholesale transmission. As is discussed below, however, wholesale transmission reliability and pricing remain important federal regulatory issues. FERC endorsed each of these aspects of the movement to competition when it adopted Order 888 in Spring 1996, a massive set of regulations intended to restructure the electricity industry. (An appeal of Order No. 888 is pending. *See* petitions for review pending sub nom. *Transmission Access Policy Study Group, et al. v. FERC*, Nos. 97–1715, et al. (D.C. Cir., Mar. 30,1998)). Here are some excerpts from Order No. 888.

Federal Energy Regulatory Commission (FERC), 18 C.F.R. Parts 35 and 385, [Docket Nos. RM 95–8–000 and RM 94–7–001; Order No. 888], Promoting Wholesale Competition Through Open Access Non–Discriminatory Transmission Services by Public Utilities; Recovery of Stranded Costs by Public Utilities and Transmitting Utilities, 61 FR 21540, Friday, May 10, 1996

SUMMARY: The Federal Energy Regulatory Commission (Commission) is issuing a Final Rule requiring all public utilities that own, control or operate facilities used for transmitting electric energy in interstate commerce to have on file open access non-discriminatory transmission tariffs that contain minimum terms and conditions of non-discriminatory service. The Final Rule also permits public utilities and transmitting utilities to seek recovery of legitimate, prudent and verifiable stranded costs associated with providing open access and Federal Power Act section 211 transmission services. The Commission's goal is to remove impediments to competition in the wholesale bulk power marketplace and to bring more efficient, lower cost power to the Nation's electricity consumers.

EFFECTIVE DATE: This Final Rule will become effective on July 9, 1996.

In the year since the proposed rules were issued, the pace of competitive changes in the electric utility industry has accelerated. By March of last year, public utilities had filed wholesale open access transmission tariffs with the Commission. Today, prodded by such competitive changes and encouraged by our proposed rules, 106 of the approximately 166 public utilities that own, control, or operate transmission facilities used in interstate commerce have filed some form of wholesale open access tariff. In addition, since the time the proposed rules were issued, numerous state regulatory commissions have adopted or are actively evaluating retail customer choice programs or other utility restructuring alternatives. These events have been spurred by continuing pressures in the marketplace for changes in the way electricity is bought, sold, and transported. Increasingly, customers are demanding the benefits of competition in the growing electricity commodity market.

The Commission estimates the potential quantitative benefits from the Final Rule will be approximately $3.8 to $5.4 billion per year of cost savings, in addition to the non-quantifiable benefits that include better use of existing assets and institutions, new market mechanisms, technical innovation, and less rate distortion. The continuing competitive changes in the industry and the prospect of these benefits to customers make it imperative that this Commission take the necessary steps within its jurisdiction to ensure that all wholesale buyers and sellers of electric energy can obtain non-discriminatory transmission access, that the transition to competition is orderly and fair, and that the integrity and reliability of our electricity infrastructure is maintained.

In this Rule, the Commission seeks to remedy both existing and future undue discrimination in the industry and realize the significant customer benefits that will come with open access. Indeed, it is our statutory obligation under sections 205 and 206 of the Federal Power Act ("FPA") to remedy undue discrimination.

To do so, we must eliminate the remaining patchwork of closed and open jurisdictional transmission systems and ensure that all these systems, including those that already provide some form of open access, cannot use monopoly power over transmission to unduly discriminate against others. If we do not take this step now, the result will be benefits to some customers at the expense of others. We have learned from our experience in the natural gas area the importance of addressing competitive transition issues early and with as much certainty to market participants as possible.

Accordingly, in this proceeding and in the accompanying proceeding on OASIS, the Commission, pursuant to its authorities under sections 205 and 206 of the FPA:

- Requires all public utilities that own, control or operate facilities used for transmitting electric energy in interstate commerce

- To file open access non-discriminatory transmission tariffs that contain minimum terms and conditions of non-discriminatory service;

- To take transmission service (including ancillary services) for their own new wholesale sales and purchases of electric energy under the open access tariffs;

- To develop and maintain a same-time information system that will give existing and potential transmission users the same access to transmission information that the public utility enjoys, and further requires public utilities to separate transmission from generation marketing functions and communications;

- Clarifies Federal/state jurisdiction over transmission in interstate commerce and local distribution and provides for deference to certain state recommendations; and

- Permits public utilities and transmitting utilities to seek recovery of legitimate, prudent and verifiable stranded costs associated with providing open access and FPA section 211 transmission services.

Open Access

The Final Rule requires public utilities to file a single open access tariff that offers both network, load-based service and point-to-point, contract-based service. The Rule contains a pro forma tariff that reflects modifications to the NOPR's proposed terms and conditions and also permits variations for regional practices. All public utilities subject to the Rule, including those that already have tariffs on file, will be required to make section 206 compliance filings to meet the new pro forma tariff non-price minimum terms and conditions of non-discriminatory transmission. Utilities may propose their own rates in a section 205 compliance filing.

The Rule provides that public utilities may seek a waiver of some or all of the requirements of the Final Rule. In addition, non-public utilities may seek a waiver of the tariff reciprocity provisions.

The Final Rule does not generically abrogate existing requirements contracts, but will permit customers and public utilities to seek modification, or termination, of certain existing requirements contracts on a case-by-case basis. As to coordination arrangements and contracts, the Rule finds that these arrangements and contracts may need to be modified to remove unduly discriminatory transmission access and/or pricing provisions. Such arrangements and agreements include power pool agreements, public utility holding company agreements, and certain bilateral coordination agreements. The Rule provides guidance and timelines for modifying unduly discriminatory coordination arrangements and contracts, and specifies when the members of such arrangements must begin to conduct trade with each other using the same open access tariff offered to others. The Rule also provides guidance regarding the formation of independent system operators ("ISOs").

The Rule does not require any form of corporate restructuring, but will accommodate voluntary restructuring that is consistent with the Rule's open access and comparability policies. As discussed in the NOPR, not all owners or controllers of interstate transmission facilities are subject to the Commission's jurisdiction under sections 205 and 206 of the FPA and therefore are not subject to this Rule's open access requirements. Therefore, the Final Rule retains the proposed reciprocity provision in the pro forma tariff. Without such a provision, non-open access utilities could take advantage of the competitive opportunities of open access, while at the same time offering inferior access, or no access at all, over their own facilities. Thus, open access utilities would be unfairly burdened. We note that some non-jurisdictional utilities have expressed an interest in a mechanism for obtaining a Commission determination that their transmission tariffs satisfy the reciprocity provisions in the pro forma tariffs, and we provide such a mechanism in the Rule.

The Final Rule does not generically provide for market-based generation rates. Although the Rule codifies the Commission's prior decision that there is no generation dominance in new generating capacity, intervenors in cases may raise generation dominance issues related to new capacity. In addition, to obtain market-based rates for existing generation, we will continue to require public utilities to show, on a case-by-case basis, that there is no generation dominance in existing capacity. Further, in all market-based rate cases, we will continue to look at whether an applicant and its affiliates could erect other barriers to entry and whether there may be problems due to affiliate abuse or reciprocal dealing.

Finally, contemporaneously with this Rule the Commission issues an NOPR on capacity reservation tariffs as an alternative, and perhaps superior, means of remedying undue discrimination.

Conclusion

The Commission believes that the Final Rule will remedy undue discrimination in transmission services in interstate commerce and provide an orderly and fair transition to competitive bulk power markets.■

Following Order No. 888, FERC issued Order No. 889, requiring transmission utility participation in its Open Access Same–Time Information System (OASIS) electronic bulletin board system. The FERC's OASIS requirements apply to public utilities and non-public utilities that provide reciprocal open access transmission service, unless a waiver is granted. Order No. 889 requires that such utilities establish, maintain, and operate (either individually or jointly with other utilities) a real-time information network on which available transmission capacity will be posted and on which capacity reservations may be made. Information about a utility's transmission system must be made available to all transmission customers at the same times. OASIS makes that information available to all customers, ensuring that utilities do not use their ownership, operation, or control of transmission to unfairly deny access. Order No. 889 also requires that a public utility and non-public utility providing reciprocal service to adopt standards of conduct. These standards are designed to ensure that the utility's employees engaged in transmission system operations function independently of the utility's employees engaged in wholesale purchases and sales of electric energy in interstate commerce.

The Supreme Court unanimously upheld Order No. 888 in *New York v. FERC*, 535 U.S. 1 (2002). In so doing, the Court reaffirmed some of FERC's findings regarding changes to the industry:

> Since 1935, and especially beginning in the 1970's and 1980's, the number of electricity suppliers has increased dramatically. Technological advances have made it possible to generate electricity efficiently in different ways and in smaller plants. In addition, unlike the local power networks of the past, electricity is now delivered over three major networks, or "grids," in the continental United States. Two of these grids—the "Eastern Interconnect" and the "Western Interconnect"—are connected to each other. It is only in Hawaii and Alaska

and on the "Texas Interconnect"—which covers most of that State—that electricity is distributed entirely within a single State. In the rest of the country, any electricity that enters the grid immediately becomes a part of a vast pool of energy that is constantly moving in interstate commerce. As a result, it is now possible for power companies to transmit electric energy over long distances at a low cost.

As FERC has explained, "the nature and magnitude of coordination transactions" have enabled utilities to operate more efficiently by transferring substantial amounts of electricity not only from plant to plant in one area, but also from region to region, as market conditions fluctuate. In Order No. 888, FERC noted that the optimum size of electric generation plants has shifted from the larger, 500 megawatt plants (with 10–year lead time) of the past to the smaller, 50– to–150 megawatt plants (with 1–year lead time) of the present. These smaller plants can produce energy at a cost of 3–to–5 cents per kilowatt-hour, as opposed to the older plants' production cost of 4– to–15 cents per kilowatt-hour.

Despite these advances in technology that have increased the number of electricity providers and have made it possible for a "customer in Vermont [to] purchase electricity from an environmentally friendly power producer in California or a cogeneration facility in Oklahoma," public utilities retain ownership of the transmission lines that must be used by their competitors to deliver electric energy to wholesale and retail customers. The utilities' control of transmission facilities gives them the power either to refuse to deliver energy produced by competitors or to deliver competitors' power on terms and conditions less favorable than those they apply to their own transmissions.

Id. at 6–7.

* * *

It would be foolhardy to speculate about how the electricity industry will actually look in 25 years. However, following Order 888 federal regulators have focused on several issues, including unbundling and the development regional transmission entities. Although FERC has expressed a clear commitment to competition, Congress has considered federal legislation since 1992 and will likely continue to evaluate federal competition policy in the electric utility industry until consumers and the industry perceive clear and consistent courses of action for both federal and state policies.

1. UNBUNDLING OF WHOLESALE TRANSMISSION AND GENERATION

A significant issue regarding competition before FERC and many state regulatory commissions is the extent to which unbundling (applied by FERC to natural gas sales and transportation in Order No. 636) will work in the electricity industry. As discussed in Chapter 10, there are many economies to vertical integration of generation, transmission and distribution. However, vertical integration also acts as a significant barrier to enhanced competition. (Similar characteristics of the natural gas industry are discussed in Chapter 8.) So long as the utilities that own and operate bottleneck transmission and distribution facilities also own and operate generation, incentives for creating unequal access to transmission will exist. Unequal access to transmission facilities in inconsistent with the principle of comparability FERC endorsed in Order No. 888.

To disintegrate generation, transmission, and distribution, FERC could attempt to order formal disaggregation of functions through asset divestiture. Did it do this in Order No. 888? FERC's proposed rule on electricity restructuring, a slightly modified version of which was adopted as Order No. 888, discusses "functional unbundling" of generation and transmission:

Promoting Wholesale Competition Through Open Access Non-discriminatory Transmission Services by Public Utilities, 70 FERC ¶ 61.35 (March 29, 1995)

. . . Unless all public utilities are required to provide non-discriminatory open access transmission, the ability to achieve full wholesale power competition, and resulting consumer benefits, will be jeopardized. If utilities are allowed to discriminate in favor of their own generation resources at the expense of providing access to others' lower cost generation resources by not providing open access on fair terms, the transmission grid will be a patchwork of open access transmission systems, systems with bilaterally negotiated arrangements, and systems with transmission ordered under section 211. Under such a patchwork of transmission systems, sellers will not have access to transmission on an equal basis, and some sellers will benefit at the expense of others. The ultimate loser in such a regime is the consumer. . . .

As a result of Order No. 436, pipelines became primarily transporters of natural gas. However, in Order No. 636, the Commission noted that pipelines were still providing, albeit at a reduced level, a bundled, city gate, sales service in competition with third-party sales and transportation, and concluded that the competition was not occurring on an equal basis. The Commission also noted that pipelines' natural gas sales prices exceeded those of their competitors, much as electric utilities' embedded costs can exceed the cost of new generating capacity and excess generating capacity of others. In this regard, the Commission determined that the transportation service bundled with pipelines' sales service was superior to that made available to third parties and that pipelines and unregulated competitors were not selling the same product. Accordingly, in Order No. 636, the Commission found this behavior anticompetitive and required pipelines to "unbundle" their sales services from their transportation services and to provide open access transportation service that is equal in quality for all gas supplies whether purchased from the pipeline or some other supplier.

Our experience in the gas area influences our decision that, at a minimum, functional unbundling of wholesale services is necessary in order to obtain non-discriminatory open access and to avoid anticompetitive behavior in wholesale electricity markets. . . .

The Commission's preliminary view is that functional unbundling of wholesale services is necessary to implement non-discriminatory open access. Accordingly, the proposed rule requires that a public utility's uses of its own transmission system for the purpose of engaging in wholesale sales and purchases of electric energy must be separated from other activities, and that transmission services (including ancillary services) must be taken under the filed transmission tariff of general applicability. The proposed rule does not require corporate unbundling (selling off assets to a non-affiliate, or establishing a separate corporate affiliate to manage a utility's transmission assets) in any form, although some utilities may ultimately choose such a course of action. The proposed rule accommodates corporate unbundling, but does not require it.

Functional unbundling means three things. First, it means that a public utility must take transmission services (including ancillary services) for all of its new wholesale sales and purchases of energy under the same tariff of general applicability under which others take service. New wholesale sales and purchases are those under any contracts executed on or after the open access tariffs required by this proposed rule become effective. Non-discriminatory service requires that the utility charge itself the same price for these services that it charges its third-party wholesale transmission customers. We seek comment as to the appropriate means to enforce this requirement, such as a revenue crediting mechanism.

Second, functional unbundling means that a transmission owner must include in its open access tariffs separately stated rates for the transmission and ancillary service components of each transmission service it provides. The rates must satisfy the Commission's Transmission Pricing Policy Statement. Third, functional unbundling means that the public utility, in order to provide non-discriminatory open access to transmission and ancillary services information, must rely upon the same electronic network that its transmission customers rely upon to obtain transmission information about its system when buying or selling power.

For example, the proposed rule requires that a public utility unbundle its new wholesale requirements service contracts, and its new wholesale coordination purchase transactions, and take the firm network transmission component of those services under its own firm network transmission tariff. Similarly, the proposed rule requires that a public utility unbundle any new wholesale coordination sales transactions and take the point-to-point transmission component of that service under its own point-to-point transmission tariff. Finally, the proposed rule requires that a utility unbundle ancillary services and take these services under its network and point-to-point tariffs.

Public utilities also must authorize their power pool agents to offer any transmission service available under power pool arrangements to all transmission customers. In addition, public utilities that participate in a power pool that acts as a control area must authorize the power pool's control center to offer ancillary services under a filed tariff, and must take all of their control area services from that tariff. A public utility must take dispatch service and other ancillary transmission services on the same terms and conditions as those offered to its transmission customers.

The requirement to provide ancillary services and to take those services under a tariff is not intended to mandate any federal rules that would prescribe the actual merit order of dispatch. Rather, it is a requirement that public utilities ensure that dispatch practices and procedures applicable to them are also applied to third-party transmission customers.

The proposed requirement that a public utility take transmission service used for wholesale requirements service and wholesale coordination transactions under its own filed tariff means that all wholesale trade, both that of the public utility and its competitors, would be taken under a single wholesale transmission tariff. Our preliminary view is that such a requirement places the correct incentives on the public utility to file a fair tariff since it must live under those terms for wholesale purposes. The Commission invites comment on its approach to functional unbundling. Will it provide strong enough incentives for non-discriminatory access without some form of corporate restructuring? If utilities restructure, how will our proposed rules apply to different types of corporate structures?

While this approach to unbundling creates good incentives with respect to wholesale service, it omits retail service. In other words, it does not require the transmission owner to take unbundled transmission service under the same tariff as third parties in order to serve its retail customers. This will result in service under two separate arrangements—an explicit wholesale transmission tariff filed at the Commission and an implicit retail transmission tariff governed by a state regulatory body. It also raises the possibility that the quality of transmission service for retail purposes will be superior to the quality of transmission service offered for wholesale purposes.■

NOTES AND COMMENTS

1. In Order No. 888, FERC adopted the notion of "functional unbundling." Will functional unbundling work? Would FERC be required to monitor the communication between a utility's generation and transmission operations? Would it be better to erect a "Chinese wall" between the operations, or to require utilities to divest themselves of either their transmission or their generation assets as the courts required AT&T to sell off its local telephone service operations in 1984? For a discussion of how FERC was able to convince utilities of the benefits of unbundling, *see* Jim Rossi, Can FERC Overcome Special Interest Politics, Public Utilities Fortnightly, Oct. 15, 1995.

2. The industry was moving in the direction FERC anticipated even before Order No. 888 was promulgated. Around the time FERC was

considering announcement of its proposed rule, New England Electric System had announced a restructuring proposal that went a step beyond FERC's unbundling proposal. NEES proposed selling off its transmission assets at either replacement cost or original cost to a third party that had no generation assets and would ensure comparability of service. Proceeds from the sale would then be used to write-down NEES's stranded generating assets. NEES Restructuring Proposal Calls for Sale of Transmission Assets, Inside FERC, Nov. 7, 1994, at 4. (Stranded costs are discussed further in Chapter 12.)

3. Since Order No. 888's adoption, FERC has been presented with several proposals to sell off generation assets by utilities that intend to focus on transmission and distribution. *See, e.g., Bangor Hydro–Electric Co.,* 86 F.E.R.C. ¶ 61,044 (1999); *Central Maine Power Co.,* 85 F.E.R.C. ¶ 61,272 (1998). Some of these have involved nuclear plants. *See Boston Edison Co. & Entergy Nuclear Generation Co.,* 87 F.E.R.C. ¶ 61,053 (1999) (sale of Pilgrim nuclear unit); *Jersey Central Power & Light Co.,* 87 F.E.R.C. ¶ 61,014 (1999) (sale of Three Mile Island Unit No. 1). From the perspective of evaluating the asset sale, federal regulators have had a fairly easy task, given their commitment to increasing the number of generation sellers in different markets. Their decisions to approve such sales may have been aided, however, by the premium in excess of book value utilities have earned in generation asset sales. This premium can be used to retire stranded investments or to reduce rates to consumers. *See Duke Energy Moss Landing LLC,* 83 F.E.R.C. ¶ 61,318 (1998), *on reh'g,* 86 F.E.R.C. ¶ 61,227 (1999) (discussing acquisition premiums resulting from sale of generation assets at a price in excess of book value). Should FERC concern itself with the impact of asset spin-offs on customers of the purchasing utility? What safeguards might protect these customers from bearing the costs of uneconomic new purchases?

2. OPEN ACCESS WHOLESALE TRANSMISSION: INDEPENDENT SYSTEM OPERATORS AND REGIONAL TRANSMISSION ORGANIZATIONS

As discussed in Chapter 10, the transmission of electricity differs in many respects from the transportation of natural gas. Transmission lines, unlike natural gas pipelines, have no valves. Although it is technologically possible to install "phase shifters" to control the physical flow of power on transmission lines, extreme caution must be exercised to determine the optimum location and use of phase shifters to avoid sacrificing reliable service. Absent some sort of flow control, electrons flow in the path of least resistance. Thus, a transmission transaction that appears to involve the flow of electricity from New York to New Jersey may use transmission lines located in other states, such as Ohio, even though these states do not lie in the direct physical path between the generator and customer. Such physical geographical diversions in the transmission of electricity are called "loop flows".

Under traditional cost-of-service regulation, regulators have been able to avoid most of the economic, operational, and policy problems raised by loop flows. Because most utilities were vertically integrated and did not engage in a large number of transactions with third parties, this was not a significant issue. Where utilities were exchanging power, they tended to rely on informal cooperative mechanisms, such a regional power pools, to monitor loopflow problems.

The transition to competition, however, raises the specter of more system loop flow problems. While FERC has been able to implement competition in natural gas markets on a model of bilateral trading, in which consumers negotiate directly with pipelines for natural gas transportation, such a simple market model is likely to be problematic where transmission capacity constraints lead to large and constantly changing congestion costs.

U.S. regulators have looked to the experience of regulators in other countries as they attempt to implement power competition. Many countries have experimented with power pools, as the excerpt at the beginning of this chapter describes. The experience of other countries with transmission issues is of great importance to federal regulators in the U.S. as they attempt to implement the open access model in electricity. *See* Alex Henney, The Global Evolution of Competitive Power Markets, Public Utilities Fortnightly, January 15, 1995, at 38. Various alternative methods for the governance and regulation of power pools being used in Britain, Australia, Canada and Scandinavia are analyzed in James Barker, Jr., Bernard Tenenbaum and Fiona Woolf, Regulation of Power Pools and System Operators: An International Comparison, 18 Energy L. J. 261 (1997).

FERC has looked to the Independent Service Operator (ISO) as a way of ensuring transmission reliability in competitive markets. The concept has been described as follows:

ISOs are a new concept in the electric utility industry. Their purpose will be to manage the transmission network in such a way as to allow open and equal access to all electricity buyers and sellers. The FERC does not require utilities to have an ISO in order to ensure open and equal access to the transmission network, but by providing standards for approval, FERC encourages companies and regional power pools to explore the concept.

Questions arise as to what exactly an ISO will do to manage the transmission network, and how decisions will be made. The answers to these questions are being worked out by State commissions and utilities considering this option. It is clear, however, that the ISO will be responsible for reliability and security of the transmission system. The ISO will probably oversee all maintenance, even if the transmission owners provide day-to-day maintenance. The FERC guidelines, noted above, provide some light on other functions of an ISO. They include congestion management, administering transmission and ancillary pricing, making transmission information publicly available, and other activities. It is expected that these functions will not be performed by all ISOs; there will be differences from region to region.

The Changing Structure of the Electric Power Industry: An Update, Energy Information Administration, U.S. Department of Energy (1997) <http://www.eia.doe.gov/cneaf/electricity/chg_str/chapter9.html>.

As with the divestiture of assets, in Order No. 888 FERC did not require but encouraged the development of ISOs to assist with the management and operation of transmission networks. Independent, third-party operators of regional, multi-utility transmission systems offer assurance to customers of transmission that access is truly nondiscriminatory. Despite the structure of member utilities, since ISOs are independently operated, they have fewer incentives to favor the wholesale generation market of any incumbent utility.

In Order No. 888, FERC identified eleven principles of ISO governance and operation, in hopes that utilities would voluntarily develop and produce filings that satisfy these principles:

Federal Energy Regulatory Commission (FERC), 18 C.F.R. Parts 35 and 385, [Docket Nos. RM 95–8–000 and RM 94–7–001; Order No. 888], Promoting Wholesale Competition Through Open Access Non–Discriminatory Transmission Services by Public Utilities; Recovery of Stranded Costs by Public Utilities and Transmitting Utilities, 61 FR 21540, Friday, May 10, 1996

ISO Principles

The Commission recognizes that some utilities are exploring the concept of an Independent System Operator and that the tight power pools are considering restructuring proposals that involve an ISO. While the Commission is not requiring any utility to form an ISO at this time, we wish to encourage the formation of properly-structured ISOs. To this end, we believe it is important to give the industry some guidance on ISOs at this time. Accordingly, we here set out certain principles that will be used in assessing ISO proposals that may be submitted to the Commission in the future. These principles are applicable only to ISOs that would be control area operators, including any ISO established in the restructuring of power pools. We recognize that some utilities are exploring concepts that do not involve full operational control of the grid. Without in any way prejudging the merits of such arrangements, the following principles do not apply to independent administrators or coordinators that lack operational control. We do not have enough information at this time to offer guidance about such entities, but recognize that they could perform a useful role in a restructured industry. Because an ISO will be a public utility subject to our jurisdiction, the ISO's operating standards and procedures must be approved by the Commission. In addition, a properly constituted ISO is a means by which public utilities can comply with the Commission's nondiscriminatory transmission tariff requirements. The principles for ISOs are:

1. The ISO's governance should be structured in a fair and non-discriminatory manner. The primary purpose of an ISO is to ensure fair and non-discriminatory access to transmission services and ancillary services for all users of the system. As such, an ISO should be independent of any individual market participant or any one class of participants (e.g., transmission owners or end-users). A governance structure that includes fair representation of all types of users of the system would help ensure that the ISO formulates policies, operates the system, and resolves disputes in a fair and non-discriminatory manner. The ISO's rules of governance, however, should prevent control, and appearance of control, of decision-making by any class of participants.

2. An ISO and its employees should have no financial interest in the economic performance of any power market participant. An ISO should adopt and enforce strict conflict of interest standards. To be truly independent, an ISO cannot be owned by any market participant. We recognize that transmission owners need to be able to hold the ISO accountable in its fiduciary role, but should not be able to dictate day-to-day operational matters. Employees of the ISO should also be financially independent of market participants. We recognize, however, that a short transition period (we believe 6 months would be adequate) will be needed for employees of a newly formed ISO to sever all ties with former transmission owners and to make appropriate arrangements for pension plans, health programs and so on. In addition, an ISO should not undertake any contractual arrangement with generation or transmission owners or transmission users that is not at arm's length. In order to ensure independence, a strict conflict of interest standard should be adopted and enforced.

3. An ISO should provide open access to the transmission system and all services under its control at non-pancaked rates pursuant to a single, unbundled, grid-wide tariff that applies to all eligible users in a non-discriminatory manner. An ISO should be responsible for ensuring that all users have non-discriminatory access to the transmission system and all services under ISO control. The portion of the transmission grid operated by a single ISO should be as large as possible, consistent with the agreement of market participants, and the ISO should schedule all transmission on the portion of the grid it controls. An ISO should have clear tariffs for services that neither favor nor disfavor any user or class of users.

4. An ISO should have the primary responsibility in ensuring short-term reliability of grid operations. Its role in this responsibility should be well-defined and comply with applicable standards set by NERC and the regional reliability council. Reliability and security of the transmission system are critical functions for a system operator. As part of this responsibility an ISO should oversee all maintenance of the transmission facilities under its control, including any day-to-day maintenance contracted to be performed by others. An ISO may also have a role with respect to reliability planning. In any case, the ISO should be responsible for ensuring that services (for all users, including new users) can be provided reliably, and

for developing and implementing policies related to curtailment to ensure the ongoing reliability and security of the system.

5. An ISO should have control over the operation of interconnected transmission facilities within its region. An ISO is an operator of a designated set of transmission facilities.

6. An ISO should identify constraints on the system and be able to take operational actions to relieve those constraints within the trading rules established by the governing body. These rules should promote efficient trading. A key function of an ISO will be to accommodate transactions made in a free and competitive market while remaining at arm's length from those transactions. The ISO may need to exercise some level of operational control over generation facilities in order to regulate and balance the power system, especially when transmission constraints limit trading over interfaces in some circumstances. It is important that the ISO's operational control be exercised in accordance with the trading rules established by the governing body. The trading rules should promote efficiency in the marketplace. In addition, we would expect that an ISO would provide, or cause to be provided, the ancillary services described in this Rule.

7. The ISO should have appropriate incentives for efficient management and administration and should procure the services needed for such management and administration in an open competitive market. Management and administration of the ISO should be carried out in an efficient manner. In addition to personnel and administrative functions, an ISO could perform certain operational functions, such as: determination of appropriate system expansions, transmission maintenance, administering transmission contracts, operation of a settlements system, and operation of an energy auction. The ISO should use competitive procurement, to the extent possible, for all services provided by the ISO that are needed to operate the system. All procedures and protocols should be publicly available.

8. An ISO's transmission and ancillary services pricing policies should promote the efficient use of and investment in generation, transmission, and consumption. An ISO or an RTG of which the ISO is a member should conduct such studies as may be necessary to identify operational problems or appropriate expansions. Appropriate price signals are essential to achieve efficient investment in generation and transmission and consumption of energy. The pricing policies pursued by the ISO should reflect a number of attributes, including affording non-discriminatory access to services, ensuring cost recovery for transmission owners and those providing ancillary services, ensuring reliability and stability of the system and providing efficient price signals of the costs of using the transmission grid. In particular, the Commission would consider transmission pricing proposals for addressing network congestion that are consistent with our Transmission Pricing Policy Statement. In addition, an ISO should conduct such studies and coordinate with market participants including RTGs, as may be necessary to identify transmission constraints on its system, loop flow

impacts between its system and neighboring systems, and other factors that might affect system operation or expansion.

9. An ISO should make transmission system information publicly available on a timely basis via an electronic information network consistent with the Commission's requirements. A free flow of information between the ISO and market participants is required for an ISO to perform its functions and for market participants to efficiently participate in the market. At a minimum, information on system operation, conditions, available capacity and constraints, and all contracts or other service arrangements of the ISO should be made publicly available. This information should be made available on an OASIS operated by the ISO.

10. An ISO should develop mechanisms to coordinate with neighboring control areas. An ISO will be required to coordinate power scheduling with other entities operating transmission systems. Such coordination is necessary to ensure provision of transmission services that cross system boundaries and to ensure reliability and stability of the systems. The mechanisms by which ISOs and other transmission operators coordinate can be left to those parties to determine.

11. An ISO should establish an ADR process to resolve disputes in the first instance. An ISO should provide for a voluntary dispute resolution process that allows parties to resolve technical, financial, and other issues without resort to filing complaints at the Commission. We would encourage the ISO to establish rules and procedures to implement alternative dispute resolution processes.■

To date, many utilities have filed ISO proposals with FERC, including groups of utilities located in California, New York, New England, and the Mid–Atlantic (PJM) and the Midwest. In addition, many utilities have announced their intent to form single-utility or multiple utility "transcos," combining ownership with operational control of for-profit, stand-alone transmission companies.

An example of an ISO is the PJM ISO, created by the Pennsylvania–New Jersey–Maryland Interconnection. The PJM ISO is independent because its members are not affiliated with and are not controlled by market participants. Unlike the corporate board of a Transco, which answers first to shareholders, the PJM Board adheres to a public interest standard, regardless of the commercial interests of members. The ISO makes grid management decisions independent of the commercial interests of its members, and it has the authority to direct its members to construct upgrades or additional facilities. FERC approved the PJM ISO, as it complied with its Order No. 888 ISO principles. *See Pennsylvania–New Jersey–Maryland Interconnection*, 81 FERC ¶ 61,257 (1998).

By contrast, consider an alternative proposal submitted by Alliance Companies. The plan was to form two companies, Alliance Publico and Alliance Transco. Members would transfer their high-voltage transmission facilities to Alliance Transco, but no Alliance company would own more than 5 percent of Alliance Transco's stock. Alliance Publico, a registered public utility holding company, would operate as the managing member of the Alliance Transco. FERC conditionally approved the Alliance Companies request to form a for-profit Transco, but noted that the plan failed many of the eleven ISO principles in Order No. 888, including independence, financial interest, nondiscriminatory tariffs, efficient administration and pricing. *See Alliance Companies*, 89 FERC ¶ 61,298 (1999). FERC approved the arrangement, but encouraged the companies to consider an ISO arrangement over the Transco approach.

Does the distinction between an ISO and Transco matter? Although both may promote transmission coordination, many companies in the industry believe that it important whether FERC encourages ISOs only, or both ISOs and Transcos. Order No. 888 spoke primarily to the ISO. As a non-profit entity that separates ownership and control of transmission, the ISO is believed by some to be the best way of promoting the public interest in transmission.

Some utilities in the industry, however, favor a Transco approach on the grounds that the for-profit motive of the company that both owns and operates transmission will create an inherent incentive for the Transco to expand transmission capacity where this is needed. In many areas of the country, the expansion of transmission capacity will be integral to ensuring reliability in wholesale power markets. In addition, the Transco alternative may be more attractive to some companies, since a transmission-owning company may be more comfortable transferring its transmission facilities to a for-profit company over which it may have some influence. To the extent FERC does not have the authority to mandate transmission pooling, voluntary formation of transmission organizations is important so the Transco is not necessarily at odds with FERC's regulatory agenda. In addition, owners may fear that transfer of ownership of transmission assets to an ISO may jeopardize currently allowed rates of return, since a utility's passive ownership of resources under the control of an ISO may be viewed as a lower risk that justifies a lower rate of return. *See* Stephen Angle & George Cannon, Jr., Independent Transmission Companies: The For–Profit Alternative in Competitive Electric Markets, 19 Energy L.J. 229, 238 (1998).

With the proliferation of generation suppliers, many of whom do not own generation, transmission reliability remains a significant issue for federal regulators. FERC continues to evaluate its role in encouraging ISOs or more regional-based approaches to transmission management and operation. Its most recent effort, dubbed "Order 2000," focuses on the promotion of Regional Transmission Groups, which serve an overlapping function with ISOs in the promotion of wholesale competition. Below are excerpts from the proposed rule, which describes the necessity for FERC's rule, as well as a description of the final rule adopted in Order 2000 from FERC's order on rehearing on the rule.

Proposed Rules Department of Energy

Federal Energy Regulatory Commission
18 C.F.R. Part 35
[Docket No. RM99–2–000]
Regional Transmission Organizations; Notice of Proposed Rulemaking
64 Federal Register 31390

Thursday, June 10, 1999 The Federal Energy Regulatory Commission (Commission) is proposing to amend its regulations under the Federal

Power Act (FPA) to facilitate the formation of Regional Transmission Organizations ("RTOs"). The Commission proposes to require that each public utility that owns, operates, or controls facilities for the transmission of electric energy in interstate commerce make certain filings with respect to forming and participating in an RTO. The Commission also proposes minimum characteristics and functions that a transmission entity must satisfy in order to be considered to be an RTO.

As a result [of Order No. 888 and ensuing developments], the traditional means of grid management is showing signs of strain and may be inadequate to support the efficient and reliable operation that is needed for the continued development of competitive electricity markets. In addition, there are indications that continued discrimination in the provision of transmission services by vertically integrated utilities may also be impeding fully competitive electricity markets. These problems may be depriving the Nation of the benefits of lower prices, more reliance on market solutions, and lighter-handed regulation that competitive markets can bring.

If electricity consumers are to realize the full benefits that competition can bring to wholesale markets, the Commission must address the extent of these problems and appropriate ways of mitigating them. Competition in wholesale electricity markets is the best way to protect the public interest and ensure that electricity consumers pay the lowest price possible for reliable service. We believe that further steps may need to be taken to address grid management if we are to achieve fully competitive power markets. We further believe that regional approaches to the numerous issues affecting the industry may be the best means to eliminate remaining impediments to properly functioning competitive markets.

Our objective is for all transmission owning entities in the Nation, including non-public utility entities, to place their transmission facilities under the control of appropriate regional transmission institutions in a timely manner. We seek to accomplish our objective by encouraging voluntary participation. We are therefore proposing in this rulemaking minimum characteristics and functions for appropriate regional transmission institutions; a collaborative process by which public utilities and non-public utilities that own, operate or control interstate transmission facilities, in consultation with the state officials as appropriate, will consider and develop regional transmission institutions; a willingness to consider incentive pricing on a case-specific basis and an offer of non-monetary regulatory benefits, such as deference in dispute resolution, reduced or eliminated codes of conduct, and streamlined filing and approval procedures; and a time line for public utilities to make appropriate filings with the Commission and initiate operation of regional transmission institutions. As a result, we expect jurisdictional utilities to form Regional (RTOs).

As discussed in detail herein, regional institutions can address the operational and reliability issues now confronting the industry, and any residual discrimination in transmission services that can occur when the operation of the transmission system remains in the control of a vertically integrated utility. Appropriate regional transmission institutions could: (1) improve efficiencies in transmission grid management; (2) improve grid reliability; (3) remove the remaining opportunities for discriminatory transmission practices; (4) improve market performance; and (5) facilitate lighter handed regulation.

Thus, we believe that appropriate regional transmission institutions could successfully address the existing impediments to efficient grid operation and competition and could consequently benefit consumers through lower electricity rates resulting from a wider choice of services and service providers. There are likely to be substantial cost savings brought about by regional transmission institutions.

In light of important questions regarding the complexity of grid regionalization raised by state regulators and applicants in individual cases, we are proposing a flexible approach. We are not proposing to mandate that utilities participate in a regional transmission institution by a date certain. Instead, we act now to ensure that they consider doing so in good faith. Moreover, the Commission is not proposing a "cookie cutter" organizational format for regional transmission institutions or the establishment of fixed or specific regional boundaries under section 202(a) of the FPA.

Rather, the Commission is proposing to establish fundamental characteristics and functions for appropriate regional transmission institutions. We will designate institutions that satisfy all of the minimum characteristics and functions as Regional Transmission Organizations (RTOs). Hereinafter, the term Regional Transmission Organization, or RTO, will refer to an organization that satisfies all of the minimum characteristics and functions. . . .

In light of the comments received [from state regulators and other parties in a previous proceeding], we wish to respond to several concerns that were raised.

First, we are not proposing to mandate RTOs, nor are we proposing detailed specifications on a particular organizational form for RTOs. The goal of this rulemaking is to get RTOs in place through voluntary participation. While this Commission has specific authorities and responsibilities under the FPA to protect against undue discrimination and remove impediments to wholesale competition, we believe it is preferable to meet these responsibilities in the first instance through an open and collaborative process that allows for regional flexibility and induces voluntary behavior.

Second, the development of RTOs is not intended to interfere with state prerogatives in setting retail competition policy. The Commission believes that RTOs can successfully accommodate the transmission systems of all states, whether or not a particular state has adopted retail competition. However, for those states that have chosen to adopt retail wheeling, RTOs can play a critical role in the realization of full competition at the retail level as well as at the wholesale level. In addition, the Commission believes that RTOs will not interfere with a state's prerogative to keep the benefits of low-cost power for the state's own retail consumers.

Third, we propose to allow RTOs to prevent transmission cost shifting by continuing our policy of flexibility with respect to recovery of sunk transmission costs, such as the "license plate" approach.

Fourth, the existence of RTOs has not, and will not in the future, interfere with traditional state and local regulatory responsibilities such as transmission siting, local reliability matters, and regulation of retail sales of generation and local distribution. In fact, RTOs offer the potential to assist the states in their regulation of retail markets and in resolving matters among states on a regional basis. They also provide a vehicle for amicably resolving state and Federal jurisdictional issues.

Finally, we do not propose to establish regional boundaries in this rulemaking. Our foremost concern is that a proposed RTO's regional configuration is sufficient to ensure that the required RTO characteristics and functions are satisfied. To this end, the Commission proposes guidance regarding the scope and regional configuration of RTOs.

II. Background

In April 1996, in Order Nos. 888 and 889, the Commission established the foundation necessary to develop competitive bulk power markets in the United States: non-discriminatory open access transmission services by public utilities and stranded cost recovery rules that would provide a fair transition to competitive markets. Order Nos. 888 and 889 were very successful in accomplishing much of what they set out to do. However, they were not intended to address all problems that might arise in the development of competitive power markets. Indeed, the nature of the emerging markets and the remaining impediments to full competition have become apparent in the three years since the issuance of our orders.

A. The Foundation for Competitive Markets: Order Nos. 888 and 889

In Order Nos. 888 and 889, the Commission found that unduly discriminatory and anticompetitive practices existed in the electric industry, and that transmission-owning utilities had discriminated against others seeking transmission access. The Commission stated that its goal was to ensure that customers have the benefits of competitively priced generation, and determined that non-discriminatory open access transmission services (including access to transmission information) and stranded cost recovery were the most critical components of a successful transition to competitive wholesale electricity markets. [Stranded cost recovery is discussed in Chapter 12.]

Accordingly, Order No. 888 required all public utilities that own, control or operate facilities used for transmitting electric energy in interstate commerce to (1) file open access non-discriminatory transmission tariffs containing, at a minimum, the non-price terms and conditions set forth in the Order, and (2) functionally unbundle wholesale power services. Under functional unbundling, the public utility must: (a) take transmission services under the same tariff of general applicability as do others; (b) state separate rates for wholesale generation, transmission, and ancillary services; and © rely on the same electronic information network that its transmission customers rely on to obtain information about its transmission system when buying or selling power. Order No. 889 required that all public utilities establish or participate in an Open Access Same–Time Information System (OASIS) that meets certain specifications, and comply with standards of conduct designed to prevent employees of a public utility (or any employees of its affiliates) engaged in wholesale power marketing functions from obtaining preferential access to pertinent transmission system information. . . .

B. Developments Since Order Nos. 888 and 889

In the three years since Order Nos. 888 and 889 were issued, numerous significant developments have occurred in the electric utility industry. Some of these reflect changes in governmental policies; others are strictly industry driven. These activities have resulted in a considerably different industry landscape from the one faced at the time the Commission was developing Order No. 888, resulting in new regulatory and industry challenges.

Order Nos. 888 and 889 required a significant change in the way many public utilities have done business for most of this century, and most public utilities accepted these changes and made substantial good faith efforts to comply with the new requirements. Virtually all public utilities have filed tariffs stating rates, terms and conditions for third-party use of their transmission systems. In addition, improved information about the transmission system is available to all participants in the market at the same time that it is available to the public utility as a result of utility compliance with the OASIS regulations.

The availability of tariffs and information about the transmission system has fostered a rapid growth in dependence on wholesale markets for acquisition of generation resources. Areas that have experienced generation shortages have seen rapid development of new generation resources. For example, New England, where there was deep concern about adequacy of generation supply only three years ago, now has approximately 30,000 MW of generation proposed. That response comes almost entirely from independent generating plants that are able to sell power into the bulk power market through open access to the transmission system. Power resources are now acquired over increasingly large regional areas, and interregional transfers of electricity have increased.

The very success of Order Nos. 888 and 889 and the initiative utilities pursuing voluntary restructuring beyond the minimum open access requirements have put new stresses on regional transmission systems—stresses that call for regional solutions.

1.   Industry Restructuring and New Stresses on the Transmission Grid

Open access transmission and the opening of wholesale competition in the electric industry have brought an array of changes in the past several years: divestiture by many integrated utilities of some or all of their generating assets; significantly increased merger activity both between electric utilities and between electric and natural gas utilities; increases in the number of new participants in the industry in the form of independent power marketers and generators; increases in the volume of trade in the industry, particularly as marketers make multiple sales; state efforts to create retail competition; and new and different uses of the transmission grid.

With respect to divestiture, since August 1997, approximately 50,000 MW of generating capacity have been sold (or are under contract to be sold) by utilities, and an additional 30,000 MW is currently for sale. In total, this represents more than 10 percent of U.S. generating capacity. In all, according to publicly available data, 27 utilities have sold all or some of their generating assets and 7 others have assets for sale. Buyers of this generating capacity have included traditional utilities with specified service territories as well as independent power producers with no required service territory.

Since Order No. 888 was issued, there have been more than 20 applications filed with us to approve proposed mergers involving public utilities. Most of these mergers have been approved by various regulatory authorities, including the Commission, although a few have been rejected or withdrawn, and several mergers are pending regulatory approval. Most of these merger proposals have been between electric utilities with contiguous service areas, while some of the proposed mergers have been between utilities with noncontiguous service areas. The Commission has also been presented with merger applications involving the combination of electric and natural gas assets.

There has been significant growth in the volume of trading in the wholesale electricity market. In the first quarter of 1995, according to power marketer quarterly filings, marketer sales totaled 1.8 million MWh, but by the second quarter of 1998, such sales escalated to 513 million MWh. Many new competitors have entered the industry. For example, in the first quarter of 1995, there were eight power marketers (either independent or affiliated with traditional utilities) actively trading in wholesale power markets, but by the second quarter of 1998, there were 108 actively trading power marketers. The Commission has granted market-based rate authority to well over 500 wholesale power marketers, of which some are independent of traditional investor-owned utilities, some are affiliated with traditional utilities, and some are traditional utilities themselves.

[As discussed in Chapter 12, s]tate commissions and legislatures have been active in the past few years studying competitive options at the retail level, setting up pilot retail access programs, and, in some states, implementing full scale retail access programs. As of May 1, 1999, 18 states have enacted electric restructuring legislation, 3 have issued comprehensive regulatory orders, and 28 others have legislation or orders pending or investigations underway. Fifteen states have implemented full-scale or pilot retail competition programs that offer a choice of suppliers to at least some retail customers. Eight states have set in motion programs to offer access to retail customers by a date certain.

Because of the changes in the structure of the electric industry, the transmission grid is now being used more intensively and in different ways than in the past. The Commission is concerned that the traditional approaches to operating the grid are showing signs of strain. According to the North American Electric Reliability Council ("NERC"), "the adequacy of the bulk transmission system has been challenged to support the movement of power in unprecedented amounts and in unexpected directions." These changes in the use of the transmission system "will test the electric industry's ability to maintain system security in operating the transmission system under conditions for which it was not planned or designed." It should be noted that, despite the increased transmission system loadings, NERC believes that the "procedures and processes to mitigate potential reliability impacts appear to be working reliably for now," and that even though the system was particularly stressed during the summer of 1998, "the system performed reliably and firm demand was not interrupted due to transmission transfer limitations."

An indication that the increased and different use of the transmission system is stressing the grid is the increased use of transmission line loading relief (TLR) procedures.[16][1] NERC's TLR procedures were invoked 250 times between January 1 and September 1, 1998 to prevent facility or interface overloads on the Eastern Interconnection.

It appears that the planning and construction of transmission and transmission-related facilities may not be keeping up with increased requirements. According to NERC, "Business is increasing on the transmission system, but very little is being done to increase the load serving and transfer capability of the bulk transmission system." The amount of new transmission capacity planned over the next ten years is significantly lower than the additions that had been planned five years ago, and most of the planned projects are for local system support. NERC states that, "The close coordination of generation and transmission planning is diminishing as vertically integrated utilities divest their generation assets and most new generation is being proposed and developed by independent power producers."

The transition to new market structures has resulted in new challenges and circumstances. For example, during the week of June 22–26, 1998, the wholesale electric market in the Midwest experienced numerous

---

1. The TLR procedures are designed to remedy overloads that result when a transmission line or other transmission equipment carries or will carry more power than its rating, which could result in either power outages or damage to property. The TLR procedures are designed to bring overloaded transmission equipment to within NERC's Operating Security Limits essentially by curtailing transactions contributing to the overload. *See North American Electric Reliability Council*, 85 FERC 61,353 (1998) (NERC).

events that led to unprecedented high spot market prices. Spot wholesale market prices for energy briefly rose as high as $7,500 per MWh, compared to an average price for the summer of approximately $40 per MWh in the Midwest if the price spikes are excluded. This experience led to calls for price caps, allegations of market power, and a questioning of the effectiveness of transmission open access and wholesale electric competition.

The Commission's staff found that the market institutions were not adequately prepared to deal with such a dramatic series of events. Regarding regional transmission entities, the staff report observed: "The necessity for cooperation in meeting reliability concerns and the Commission's intent to foster competitive market conditions underscores the importance of better regional coordination in areas such as maintenance of transmission and generation systems and transmission planning and operation." Support for this view comes from many sources. For example, the Public Utilities Commission of Ohio, in its own report on the price spikes, recommended that policy makers "take unambiguous action to require coordination of transmission system operations by regionwide Independent System Operators."

On September 29, 1998, the Secretary of Energy Advisory Board Task Force on Electric System Reliability published its final report. The Task Force was convened in January 1997 to provide advice to the Department of Energy on critical institutional, technical, and policy issues that need to be addressed in order to maintain bulk power electric system reliability in a more competitive industry. The Task Force found that "the traditional reliability institutions and processes that have served the Nation well in the past need to be modified to ensure that reliability is maintained in a competitively neutral fashion;" that "grid reliability depends heavily on system operators who monitor and control the grid in real time;" and that "because bulk power systems are regional in nature, they can and should be operated more reliably and efficiently when coordinated over large geographic areas."[25][2]

The report noted that many regions of the United States are developing ISOs as a way to maintain electric system reliability as competitive markets develop. According to the Task Force, ISOs are significant institutions to assure both electric system reliability and competitive generation markets. The Task Force concluded that a large ISO would: (1) be able to identify and address reliability issues most effectively; (2) internalize much of the loop flow caused by the growing number of transactions; (3) facilitate transmission access across a larger portion of the network, consequently improving market efficiencies and promoting greater competition; and (4) eliminate "pancaking" of transmission rates, thus allowing a greater range of economic energy trades across the network.

---

2.   Maintaining Reliability in a Competitive U.S. Electricity Industry; Final Report of the Task Force on Electric System Reliability (Sept. 29, 1998) (Task Force Report). The Task Force was comprised of 24 members representing all major segments of the electric industry, including private and public suppliers, power marketers, regulators, environmentalists, and academics.

2. Successes, Failures, and Haphazard Development of Regional Transmission Entities

Since Order No. 888 was issued, there have been both successful and unsuccessful efforts to establish ISOs, and other efforts to form regional entities to operate the transmission facilities in various parts of the country. While we are encouraged by the success of some of these efforts, it is apparent that the results have been inconsistent, and much of the country's transmission facilities remain outside of an operational regional transmission institution.

Proposals for the establishment of five ISOs have been submitted to and approved, or conditionally approved, by the Commission. These are the California ISO, the PJM ISO, ISO New England ISO, the New York ISO, and the Midwest ISO. In addition, the Texas Commission has ordered an ISO for the Electric Reliability Council of Texas (ERCOT). Moreover, our international neighbors in Canada and Mexico are also pursuing electric restructuring efforts that include various forms of regional transmission entities.

The PJM, New England and New York ISOs were established on the platform of existing tight power pools. It appears that the principal motivation for creating ISOs in these situations was the Order No. 888 requirement that there be a single system wide transmission tariff for tight pools. In contrast, the establishment of the California ISO and the ERCOT ISO was the direct result of mandates by state governments. The Midwest ISO, which is not yet operational, is unique. It began through a consensual process and was not driven by a preexisting institution. Two states in the region subsequently required utilities in their states to participate in either a Commission-approved ISO (Illinois and Wisconsin), or sell their transmission assets to an independent transmission company (Wisconsin).

The approved ISOs have similarities as well as differences. All five Commission-approved ISOs operate, or propose to operate, as non-profit organizations. All five ISOs include both public and non-public utility members. However, among the five, there is considerable variation in governance, operational responsibilities, geographic scope and market operations. Four of the ISOs rely on a two-tier form of governance with a non-stakeholder governing board on top that is advised, either formally or informally, by one or more stakeholder groups. In general, the final decision making authority rests with the independent non-stakeholder board. One ISO, the California ISO, uses a board consisting of stakeholders and non-stakeholders.

Four of the five ISOs operate traditional control areas, but the Midwest ISO does not currently plan to operate a traditional control area. Three are multi-state ISOs (New England, PJM and Midwest), while two ISOs (California and New York) currently operate within a single state. The current Midwest ISO members do not encompass one contiguous geographic area and there are holes in its coverage. The ISO New England administers a separate NEPOOL tariff, while the other four administer their own ISO transmission tariffs.

Three ISOs operate or propose to operate centralized power markets (New England, PJM and New York), and one ISO (California) relies on a separate power exchange ("PX") to operate such a market. The Midwest ISO did not originally envision an ISO-related centralized market for its region. In addition, at least one separate PX has begun to do business in California apart from the PX established through the restructuring legislation.[35][3]

Not all efforts to create ISOs have been successful. For example, after more than two years of effort, the proponents of the IndeGO ISO in the Pacific Northwest and Rocky Mountain regions ended their efforts to create an ISO. More recently, members of MAPP, an existing power pool that covers six U.S. states and two Canadian provinces, failed to achieve consensus for establishing a long-planned ISO. In the Southwest, proponents of the Desert Star ISO have not been able to reach agreement on a formal proposal after more than two years of discussion.

Various reasons have been advanced to explain why it is difficult to form a voluntary, multi-state ISO. These include cost shifting in transmission capital costs; disagreements about sharing of ISO transmission revenues among transmission owners; difficulties in obtaining the participation of publicly-owned transmission facilities; concerns about the loss of transmission rights and prices embedded in existing transmission agreements; the likelihood of not being able to maintain or gain a competitive advantage in power markets through the use of transmission facilities; and the preference of certain transmission owners to sell or transfer their transmission assets to a for-profit transmission company in lieu of handing over control to a non-profit ISO.

Apart from these efforts to create ISOs, we have received proposals for other types of transmission entities. For example, in October 1998 a group of Arizona entities filed a request with the Commission to create an "independent scheduling administrator" (ISA) in Arizona. Unlike an ISO, this entity would not administer its own transmission tariff nor would it have any direct operational responsibilities. Instead, it appears that its functions would be limited to monitoring the scheduling decisions and OASIS site operation of the Arizona utilities that operate transmission facilities. In case of disputes, the ISA would provide a type of expedited dispute resolution process. The applicants state that the ISA would be a transitional organization that would ultimately evolve or be merged into a stronger, multi-state ISO. In other developments, one public utility has recently made a filing with us to sell its transmission assets to a newly formed affiliate. Another public utility recently filed a request for declarato-

---

3. The California PX offers day-ahead and hour-ahead markets and the ISO operates a real-time energy market. Participation in the PX market is voluntary except that the three traditional investor-owned utilities in California must bid their generation sales and purchases through the PX for the first five years. New York will offer day-ahead and real-time energy markets that will be operated by the ISO. PJM and New England offer only real-time energy markets, although PJM has proposed to operate a day-ahead market. The ERCOT ISO is the only other ISO that does not currently operate a PX.

ry order asking us to find that its proposal to transfer its transmission assets (in the form of ownership or a lease) to a "transco" in return for a passive ownership interest in the transco, would satisfy the Commission's eleven ISO principles.[4]

As part of general restructuring initiatives, several states now require independent grid management organizations. For example, an Illinois law requires that its utilities become members of a FERC-approved regional ISO by March 31, 1999, and Wisconsin law gives its utilities the option of joining an ISO or selling their transmission assets to an independent transmission company by June 30, 2000. In both states, the backstop is a single-state organization if regional organizations are not developed. Recently, Virginia and Arkansas have also enacted legislation requiring their electric utilities to join or establish regional transmission entities.∎

Regional Transmission Organizations

90 FERC ¶ 61,201
18 C.F.R. Part 35
(Docket No. RM99-2-001; Order No. 2000-A)
(Issued February 25, 2000) (order on rehearing)

The Federal Energy Regulatory Commission (Commission) reaffirms its basic determinations in Order No. 2000 and clarifies certain terms. Order No. 2000 requires that each public utility that owns, operates, or controls facilities for the transmission of electric energy in interstate commerce make certain filings with respect to forming and participating in an Regional Transmission Organization (RTO). Order No. 2000 also codifies minimum characteristics and functions that a transmission entity must satisfy in order to be considered an RTO. The Commission's goal is to promote efficiency in wholesale electricity markets and to ensure that electricity consumers pay the lowest price possible for reliable service.

In Order No. 2000, the Commission concluded that regional institutions could address the operational and reliability issues confronting the industry, and eliminate undue discrimination in transmission services that can occur when the operation of the transmission system remains in the control of a vertically integrated utility. Furthermore, we found that appropriate regional transmission institutions could: (1) improve efficiencies in transmission grid management; (2) improve grid reliability; (3) remove remaining opportunities for discriminatory transmission practices; (4) improve market performance; and (5) facilitate lighter handed regulation. We stated our belief that appropriate RTOs can successfully address the existing impediments to efficient grid operation and competition and can consequently benefit consumers through lower electricity rates and a wider choice of services and service providers. In addition, substantial cost savings are likely to result from the formation of RTOs.

Order No. 2000 established minimum characteristics and functions that an RTO must satisfy in the following areas:

---

4. Entergy Services, Inc., Docket No. EL99-57-000 (filed April 5, 1999).

Minimum Characteristics:

1. Independence
2. Scope and Regional Configuration
3. Operational Authority
4. Short-term Reliability

Minimum Functions:

1. Tariff Administration and Design
2. Congestion Management
3. Parallel Path Flow
4. Ancillary Services
5. OASIS and Total Transmission Capability (TTC) and Available Transmission Capability (ATC)
6. Market Monitoring
7. Planning and Expansion
8. Interregional Coordination

In the Final Rule, we noted that the characteristics and functions could be satisfied by different organizational forms, such as ISOs, transcos, combinations of the two, or even new organizational forms not yet discussed in the industry or Docket No. RM99–2–001–3 proposed to the Commission. Likewise, the Commission did not propose a "cookie cutter" organizational format for regional transmission institutions or the establishment of fixed or specific regional boundaries under section 202(a) of the Federal Power Act (FPA).

We also established an "open architecture" policy regarding RTOs, whereby all RTO proposals must allow the RTO and its members the flexibility to improve their organizations in the future in terms of structure, operations, market support and geographic scope to meet market needs.

In addition, the Commission provided guidance on flexible transmission ratemaking that may be proposed by RTOs, including ratemaking treatments that address congestion pricing and performance-based regulation. The Commission stated that it would consider, on a case-by-case basis, innovative rates that may be appropriate for transmission facilities under RTO control. Furthermore, to facilitate RTO formation in all regions of the Nation, the Final Rule outlined a collaborative process to take place in the Spring of 2000. Under this process, we expect that public utilities and non-public utilities, in coordination with state officials, Commission staff, and all affected interest groups, will actively work toward the voluntary development of RTOs. Lastly, under Order No. 2000, all public utilities that own, operate or control interstate transmission facilities must file with the Commission by October 15, 2000 (or January 15, 2001) a proposal to participate in an RTO with the minimum characteristics and functions to be operational by December 15, 2001, or, alternatively, a description of efforts to participate in an RTO, any existing obstacles to RTO participation, and any plans to work toward RTO participation. That filing must explain the extent to which the transmission entity in which it proposes to participate meets the minimum characteristics and functions for an RTO, and either propose to modify the existing institution to the extent necessary to become an RTO, or explain the efforts, obstacles and plans with respect to conforming to these characteristics and functions.■

NOTES AND QUESTIONS

1. Many commented on FERC's proposed rule to promote RTOs. The economist Paul Joskow argued that FERC's approach risks shortchanging consumers. His position has been summarized as follows:

> "Transmission regulatory reform," says Joskow, 'should not be viewed primarily as a "carrot" . . . to entice reluctant utilities to form and participate in RTOs.' " . . . "Regulators," Joskow notes, "will not be doing consumers any favor at all if the small price reduction they receive in the short run as a result of cutting a couple of points off the expected rate of return . . . destroys the transmission owner's incentives to invest." But even if the FERC should cave and offer higher ROEs, as the industry wants, Joskow still warns against putting too much faith in ROE incentives as a way of enticing grid expansion: "Indeed, proceeding under the assumption that, at the present time, 'the market' will provide needed transmission network enhancements is the road to ruin." There is abundant evidence that market forces are drawing tens of thousands of megawatts of new generating capacity into the system [but] there is not evidence that market forces are drawing . . . entrepreneurial investments in new transmission capacity."

See Bruce W. Radford, RTOs: Road to Ruin, Public Utilities Fortnightly, Sept. 15, 1999, at 4.

2. Other commentators focus on the form of the transmission operator. Professor Charles Koch favors the ISO over the for-profit Transco model, since he believes that the ISO will be less inclined to act as a monopolist. He argues, however, that ISOs need enhanced authority and carefully structured governance design. See Charles H. Koch, Jr., Control and Governance of Transmission Organizations in the Restructured Electricity Industry, 27 Fla. St. U. L. Rev. 569 (1999).

By contrast, Professor Robert Michaels believes that the ISO will face very similar incentives to the Transco, since the ISO is made up of for-profit firms who will face market incentives. He believes that the focus on the form of the transmission operator has focused too much on profit versus not-for-profit. Instead, he urges attention to the nature and consequences of the governance of ISOs and Transcos. According to Michaels, "ISOs are supported by those who have been best at playing the politics of traditional regulation, and opposed by those who have generally been less successful.'' Michaels fears that ISOs are likely to become barriers to entry (see discussion of California's ISO in Chapter 12), and that they may impair innovation vis-a-vis a Transco. *See* Robert J. Michaels, The Governance of Transmission Operators, 20 Energy L.J. 233 (1999).

In the end, does FERC favor either the ISO or Transco model? One author has argued that, despite Order No. 2000's professed neutrality on the ISO/Transco issue, FERC favors ISOs over Transcos. *See* Jeremiah D. Lamdert, Order 2000: A Subtle But Clear Preference for ISOs, Public Utilities Fortnightly, Mar. 1, 2000, at 36. But others, including a member of FERC during Order No. 2000's adoption, argue that FERC has paved the way for Transcos. See Curt L. Hebert, Jr. & Joshua Z. Rokach, Order 2000: Exposing Myths on What the FERC Really Wants, Public Utilities Fortnightly, Mar. 1, 2000, at 42.

3. The availability of transmission access means little to generators and customers who do not have information regarding a transmitting utility's transmission capacity and load. The 1992 EPAct also required FERC to promulgate rules on the reporting of transmission information. FERC's regulations require transmission-owning utilities to report hourly ''system lambda'' data, which is closely associated the marginal cost of producing power and provides a good indicator of the price for competitive energy. This information, once available only to the transmission owning firm and power pool operators, will undoubtedly provide vital information for both buyers and sellers of power. *See* William C. Booth & Judah L. Rose, Using Hourly System Lambda to Gauge Bulk Power Prices, Public Utilities Fortnightly, May 1, 1995.

4. As is discussed in opening excerpt to this chapter, one way in which most of the other countries experimenting with electricity markets have attempted to deal with transmission reliability problems is by creating pool-based electricity markets. Timothy Hogan, an economist, has proposed a model for implementing a pool-based market in the U.S. pool-based markets will contain both long-term contracts and spot markets. Long-term bilateral contracts, however, would exist for financial reasons only, not as mechanisms for controlling the physical delivery of electricity. A system of spot prices would reflect disparities in congestion conditions throughout the grid. The short-term transmission price from point A to point B would represent the difference between the location-specific spot price at each point. In congested time or areas, it would be very large, representing the difference between the marginal cost of a low cost generating unit that cannot operate because of transmission capacity constraints, and the marginal cost of the more expensive unit that displaces the lower cost option. *See* William H. Hogan, Electric Transmission: A New Model for Old Principles, Electricity Journal 18 (1993). Coupled with futures and options contracts, such markets could provide adequate incentives for investments in power plants. In the case of FERC's RTO rulemaking, Hogan's view has been described as follows:

> For Hogan, everything rests on efficiency of dispatch. He dismisses the Transco–ISO debate as a distraction, and tries to avoid using either

term: "With deference to Alfred Kahn, who popularized the practice when referring to a term of art that has become politicized, let us call the entity that provides these [grid] services a 'banana,' and explore what must be done." If nothing else, Hogan insists that the banana must coordinate generation prices with market interference caused by transmission constraints, . . ., with locational marginal pricing to allocate congestion rights. Do that, says Hogan, and everything falls into place, including the mystical debate between the transco and ISO models. He sees FERC's role as imposing the efficiency that's lacking when property rights are ambiguous.

See Bruce W. Radford, RTOs: Road to Ruin, Public Utilities Fortnightly, Sept. 15, 1999, at 4.

5. The implementation of RTOs has been one of the more challenging issues faced by FERC in the past ten years. Not every transmission owning utility has seen it beneficial to participate in RTOs. Many states, especially in the South, are resistant. As of 2005, FERC does not have plenary authority to mandate participation in RTOs, but FERC has a variety of powers which can be used to nudge utilities and states towards participation. Joel Eisen describes one high-profile conflict:

> Under the FPA, FERC has authority to review and approve mergers involving utilities under its jurisdiction. In 2000, FERC approved the proposed merger between AEP and Central and South West Corporation on the condition that AEP transfer operational control of its transmission facilities to a fully functioning FERC-approved RTO by December 15, 2001. AEP then made two unsuccessful attempts to join an RTO. FERC denied RTO status to the Alliance Companies, a group of companies (including AEP), and subsequently, AEP negotiated unsuccessfully to join the Midwest Independent System Operator. In April 2002, FERC ordered AEP to state which RTO it intended to join, and in response, AEP filed with FERC a document stating its intent to join PJM. Later that year, AEP filed for approval to transfer control of its transmission facilities to PJM, and FERC approved the application on April 1, 2003.
>
> AEP serves eleven states and needed approval from the PUCs in those states before control could be transferred. Two of those states— Kentucky and Virginia—took actions to block or delay the transfer. On April 2, 2003 (one day after FERC approved AEP's application to transfer control to PJM), Virginia amended its Restructuring Act to preclude Virginia incumbent electric utilities from transferring control of their transmission facilities to RTOs until July 1, 2004 but, interestingly, to require that they do so by January 2005. Three months later, the Kentucky Public Service Commission ("KPSC") denied AEP's request to transfer control of its Kentucky transmission facilities to PJM.
>
> At this point, the case became sui generis. AEP had been ordered to join an RTO (itself unusual) but then had been unable to do so. It now faced conflicting deadlines that could not be resolved. AEP was in

a pickle, to say the least. In response, FERC initiated an inquiry designed " 'to gather sufficient information for moving forward in resolving the voluntary commitment made by several entities to increase regional coordination by joining RTOs' and to 'explore ways to resolve the interstate disputes ... and enhance regional coordination to establish a joint and common market in the Midwest and PJM region.' " On November 25, 2003, FERC used section 205(a) of PURPA to make preliminary findings that the proposed transfer should be approved. This subsection authorizes FERC to exempt electric utilities, in whole or in part, from any provision of state law or regulation which prohibits "the voluntary coordination of electric utilities" if FERC determines that such voluntary coordination is "designed to obtain economic utilization of facilities and resources in any area." It contains a savings clause limiting FERC's authority to provide this exemption if the state law or regulation "is designed to protect public health, safety, or welfare, or the environment or conserve energy or is designed to mitigate the effects of emergencies resulting from fuel shortages."

Because FERC had thrown down the gauntlet to states using their power to oppose its drive toward mandatory RTO formation, the case quickly became a lightning rod for pro-deregulation and anti-deregulation states. Some, already suspicious of FERC's market initiatives, saw FERC's trumping of state law as diminishing their authority to regulate the industry and leading to a loss of cost control—historically the province of state regulators. The novel use of PURPA section 205(a) to achieve this purpose led other states to criticize FERC's reasoning. A number of Northern and Midwestern states (including Michigan, Indiana, Illinois, Pennsylvania, and New Jersey), however, supported FERC and called for regional coordination to take place without delay, which would prevent the benefits to be gained from integrating utilities into RTOs. The Texas PUC, not a player in this debate because of its unique status in the electricity regulatory environment, joined the battle anyway, arguing that RTOs "are a critical element for vibrant wholesale competition."

In March 2004, a FERC Administrative Law Judge ("ALJ") made an order rejecting the arguments of Virginia and Kentucky. The Virginia State Corporation Commission ("VSCC") had argued that PURPA was inapplicable, stating that "voluntary coordination" under PURPA meant only "the cost-based, tight power pools then known to the industry." The ALJ rejected this argument, stating that the transfer would create exactly the type of coordinated effort that Congress contemplated when it enacted PURPA a quarter-century earlier. The ALJ also rejected arguments by Virginia and Kentucky that AEP's decision to join was not voluntary because AEP had made other RTO proposals, stating it was "far more reasonable" to conclude that AEP was maneuvering to avoid "jurisdictional conflict." Virginia and Kentucky also claimed that the decision was not voluntary because AEP was forced to accept RTO membership as a merger condition. This argument, too, was rejected, with the ALJ noting that AEP was free to contest FERC's position in the courts.

Next, the ALJ turned to the central issue of whether the transfer would "obtain economic utilization of facilities and resources" in any area. This issue had generated reams of testimony from those (including the VSCC staff) who argued about the benefits of RTO membership. The ALJ disagreed with the VSCC on the proposed merger's benefits, finding that that there was "an impressive array of consistent expert testimony as to the benefits of the planned integration of AEP into PJM." Unfortunately, none of this testimony consisted of hard evidence. Instead, the ALJ relied on estimates from witnesses for PJM and AEP who argued that the proposed integration would result in a net efficiency gain under every conceivable forecasting scenario. The VSCC staff also argued that the costs of implementing the transaction had to be considered. The ALJ agreed with the VSCC staff and concluded that "consideration of the costs . . . that will result from the planned integration is a relevant and necessary element of a determination whether the planned coordination is designed to obtain economic utilization," but declined to find that this cost outweighed the benefits to be derived from integration.

The second major issue in the case—whether the state laws, rules, or regulations of Virginia and Kentucky were preventing AEP from fulfilling its voluntary commitment to join an RTO—was also decided in FERC's favor. The ALJ noted that while PURPA did not allow FERC to mandate coordination, it did grant FERC authority to prevent states from "blocking or frustrating coordination efforts." The ALJ concluded that the Virginia state law clearly impeded AEP from joining PJM and was "precisely the kind of state action that PURPA Section 205(a) was enacted to prevent—a state law, rule, or regulation which prohibits or prevents the voluntary coordination of electric utilities for the benefit of regional and national interests." The ALJ also concluded that while Kentucky did not directly prevent the transfer of control, its statement that it would not act in contravention of a state statute requiring preference to be given to native load customers "freezes integration in its tracks."

In June 2004, FERC affirmed the ALJ's decision, and the case took on an entirely new twist. Kentucky settled out of the case. The VSCC approved the integration of AEP into PJM, as its hands were effectively tied under Virginia's restructuring statute. At that point, a casual observer would be forgiven for thinking the case had become moot. But the VSCC, understandably, remained troubled by the existence of precedent under PURPA that would support orders to other utilities to join RTOs. It offered to settle the case with FERC, if FERC would vacate the opinion affirming the ALJ's decision. The VSCC argued that, "[i]f not vacated, Opinion No. 472 would represent an unfortunate precedent that will continue to contribute to federal-state tension and mistrust that will harm ongoing collaborative efforts between this Commission[, FERC,] and state utility commissions."

The VSCC's offer received a considerable number of comments from state PUCs and utility companies, including those that had intervened in the case originally. The intervenors generally supported the VSCC, arguing for the most part that FERC had achieved what it set out to do when Virginia approved the AEP–PJM integration and that leaving the opinion on the books was not necessary. Other commenters supported Virginia's position that vacating the decision would ameliorate federalism concerns and argued that because it had not been cited in any forum, vacating the decision would create a "no harm, no foul" case.

Not surprisingly, FERC disagreed. It issued an order dismissing the rehearing requests due to mootness, rejecting the settlement offer, and refusing to vacate the opinion. It also stated that "[o]ur decision not to vacate Opinion No. 472 does not reflect a retreat from our commitment to federal-state comity on RTO or other issues," which of course is a statement the VSCC and its allies are unlikely to endorse. But if the VSCC was to proceed further at this point, it would face a serious hurdle. PURPA section 205(a) gives administrative deference to FERC, allowing the exemption from state law which prohibits voluntary coordination of electric utilities "if the Commission determines" that such coordination is designed to obtain said benefits. And, of course, that is exactly what FERC has done. For this reason, the FERC staff's findings, confirmed by the ALJ, would almost certainly be given great latitude in any federal-court proceedings. It may well take another case to decide whether the evidence about problems in load pockets and potential price spikes in wholesale markets outweigh the forecasts of pro-deregulation proponents.

This hardly means, however, that this case was unimportant. In holding that the Virginia and Kentucky laws did not fit the PURPA savings clause, the ALJ revealed that the states disagreed strongly with FERC about the costs and benefits of RTO membership and thus highlighted a central issue. The ALJ believed Virginia wanted to amend its restructuring statute "essentially to prevent the integration of AEP into PJM" and "protect the economic interests of Virginia ratepayers by shielding them from the impact of the Commission's Standard Market Design ... [and to] maintain the preferential treatment for Virginia consumers in the *581 operation of an interstate transmission grid by securing an opportunity to second-guess the Commission's decisions on RTOs." The ALJ also held that the record demonstrated that "the primary reason KPSC denied AEP's application to join PJM was the KPSC's belief that costs to Kentucky's ratepayers would increase." According to the ALJ, the "KPSC's denial of AEP's application to transfer functional control of transmission assets from AEP to PJM was largely based upon AEP's alleged failure to show that Kentucky ratepayers would receive any benefits from such transfer." The ALJ further concluded that "while economic regulation may be a valid exercise of traditional state utility regulatory authority, in this proceeding, such state regulatory actions cannot be allowed to fall under the savings clause because those actions would prevent the voluntary coordination that is the purpose of PURPA Section 205(a)."

Because PJM uses LMP ["locational marginal pricing"] to make fundamental decisions, Virginia and Kentucky clearly viewed AEP's integration into PJM as the lamb lying down with the lion. The core of FERC's argument was the notion that RTOs yield economic benefits to consumers. But the ultimate point is not whether or not this will happen. It is that the parties are fighting at great length and over a period of years about whether RTOs will yield benefits. This fight is costly to ratepayers. The time and effort spent litigating this battle— not to mention the time and effort spent in earlier efforts to integrate AEP into an RTO—could have been spent far more productively in crafting an alternative scenario that would have been more palatable to the utility, FERC, and other stakeholders.

Looking at this outcome, Professor Pierce and others [see concluding section of this chapter] would probably blame the Southern states and their allies for dilatory tactics. The proceedings in The New PJM Cos. might indeed afford some support for this view that the protracted litigation was an example of state regulators captured by parochial interest groups. On reflection, that conclusion might be worth some re-examination. The states, it would seem, are not without blame. But neither is FERC. Its estimates that RTOs will yield benefits to the industry are just that—estimates—and have been challenged strongly. In the face of hard evidence, states should be entitled to assert their statutory and regulatory mandate to ensure that their ratepayers are protected.

It is perhaps even more revealing to look at the fate of the VSCC's settlement offer. Section 205(a) of PURPA is "obscure" and had not been relied upon in any recorded case since the 1980s, when the electric utility industry was far different from that of today. In these earlier cases, it was not used for the purpose advanced by FERC in The New PJM Cos. and of course could not have been, as the development and implementation of the concept of a regional transmission entity was still many years away. Even when the case was essentially over, it was not; FERC insisted on letting its decision stand as a message to later negotiators and litigants. And the message this sends is clear. FERC has exacerbated the difficulties of moving toward the market by taking the PJM model, making it the basis for the "one-size-fits-all" market design and promoting it to the rest of the country. The VSCC (and even the FERC ALJ, for that matter, in confirming some of the states' arguments) made it clear that the severe disagreements about this issue have been brought about in part by FERC's insistence on marginal price-based models for electricity markets. But its stance in this case is a signal from FERC that it believes in the economics of SMD so strongly that it will contest them in any forum—even with ill-fitting arguments if necessary—with anyone who disagrees. That only guarantees more time and effort will be spent hashing out this issue, rather than working toward constructive solutions.

Joel B. Eisen, Regulatory Linearity, Commerce Clause Brinkmanship, and Retrenchment in Electric Utility Deregulation, 40 Wake Forest L. Rev. 545 (2005).

3.   PRICE AND RELIABILITY IN COMPETITIVE WHOLESALE POWER MARKETS

Emerging wholesale electricity markets raise an operational challenge for buyers and suppliers, many of whom need to secure power on a firm basis to meet contractual obligations. Because the transmission system is interrelated in complex and interactive ways, supply and purchase arrangements do not operate in isolation, as they may in other contractual or market settings. Wholesale power markets have impacted both power prices and reliability.

To ensure power reliability and stable pricing, in 2002 FERC proposed a "Standard Market Design" (SMD) that would apply in all areas of the country. The SMD was comprised of portions of the various restructuring provisions that had been successful, drawing heavily on the PJM model RTO. FERC's SMD effort produced considerable opposition, and FERC has largely abandoned the effort to impose a uniform approach to all RTOs.

Despite the failure of SMD, FERC remains very interested in monitoring reliability and prices in deregulated wholesale markets.

* * *

As is mentioned in FERC's proposed rule on RTOs, the Midwest price spikes that accompanied a heat wave in Summer 1998 posed a particular stress to the wholesale transmission system. Did emerging new markets in power supply contribute to this problem, or did they help utilities avoid disaster?

As the events of Summer 1998 have been reported, operators for Commonwealth Edison Company, the utility that serves Chicago, faced some difficult choices. Although Commonwealth Edison owns many generation facilities, it still needs to depend on bulk power purchases to serve some of its customer load. With the heat wave during Summer 1998, Commonwealth Edison was required to purchase power on a short term basis from bulk power markets. In a single hour, Commonwealth Edison spent $4 million for power that would normally cost $200,000. At their extreme, prices surged to nearly 100 times their normal level. Utility managers faced the following choice: "either black out areas of Chicago to conserve power during a severe heat wave, just as storms had knocked out some plants and key transmission lines in the Midwest, or buy extra power at sky-high prices." *See* Agis Salpukas, Deregulation Fosters Turmoil in

Power Market, The New York Times, July 15, 1998, at D1. During the same period, other companies made some very profitable sales. Enron, a company that specializes in marketing and selling wholesale power, sold large amounts of power to utilities at high prices, and when it reported its earnings, it had a doubling of revenue to $5.86 billion, and an 85 percent rise in income, to $241 million. As has been described, "This was all a marked contrast with the old days, when utilities sold power to one another at reasonable prices during emergencies, and it provides a vivid glimpse of the challenges facing this industry." *Id.* While some of this volatility may be due to the growth of competition, there were other events contributing to the power shortage. "A heat wave was moving across the region, causing a surge in demand for electricity. Violent storms had knocked out key transmission lines and a nuclear plant in Ohio, causing further shortages." *Id.*

Following the Midwest power shortage, FERC investigated the reliability of emerging competitive markets in wholesale power. Following an investigation into the events, FERC issued a report. *See* Staff Report to the Federal Energy Regulatory Commission on the Causes of the Wholesale Electric Pricing Abnormalities in the Midwest During June 1998 available at <http://www.ferc.fed.us/electric/mastback.pdf>. FERC's report acknowledged that in competitive markets the price of wholesale power will be high in periods of peak demand, but determined that the conditions during the Summer of 1998 were "unusual." Some criticized FERC for downplaying the lesson of the Summer 1998 shortage, leading to some calls for more regulation of transmission and generation reliability, or alternative calls for more deregulation with warnings to the public about impacts on reliability:

> If we continue to move forward half-regulated and half-unregulated (i.e., with the wholesale market deregulated and the retail market regulated), then one of two transition strategies is required. Planning reserve margins sufficient to protect end users should be put in place and enforced with clear penalties, as in NEPOOL. In the alternative, policy makers should rely on the market alone to set reserves. If the market route is chosen, the public should be warned of the potential for rolling generation shortage-caused blackouts, especially in major urban areas, and especially during the transition.

Judah L. Rose, Missed Opportunity: What's Right and Wrong in the FERC Staff Report on the Midwest Price Spikes, Public Utilities Fortnightly, Nov. 15, 1998, at 48. Others saw the events of Summer 1998 as the new wholesale power market working itself pure:

> Certainly it is true that bulk power markets in the Midwest are relatively underdeveloped. However, our data show that they functioned quite effectively under extreme conditions. A relatively undeveloped market adapted quickly and efficiently to events never before seen. Buyers and sellers reacted rationally to those events in the face of great uncertainty and unfamiliar limits on their abilities to transact.

Robert J. Michaels & Jerry Ellig, Price Spike Redux: A Market Emerged, Public Utilities Fortnightly, February 1, 1999, at p. 40.

The debate over the Summer 1998 price spikes continues to have some impact on the regulatory discussion. The North American Electric Reliability Council (NERC) has proposed new procedures to relieve line overloading, known as transmission load relief protocols. The new TLR rules would relieve the impact of parallel flows on grid systems not located directly on the contract path of the curtailed transaction. FERC encouraged utilities to apply the TLR rules within the Eastern Interconnection pending a final decision, so they were in operation during the period of the Summer 1998 price spikes. The TLR procedures were a significant issue in the rulemaking that culminated in Order 2000, but FERC ultimately deferred to the voluntary approach of the North American Electric Reliability Council in setting protocols, rather adopting its own protocols. FERC's Order 2000 also requires transmission utilities that do not use the NERC TLR protocols to post their own protocol on FERC's OASIS system, so that customers have information regarding TLR.

Does FERC's lack of power over generation load impair its ability to ensure reliable transmission markets? TLR, if mandated, might result in a sort of rationing. Is it better to let a market determine the prices of transmission service? Can this happen? How should transmission be priced? Are there any other jurisdictional weaknesses that might make FERC's job in ensuring a reliable transmission market more difficult?

* * *

In 2003, another substantial blackout hit the Northeastern U.S. A Canada–U.S. Outage Task force report on the the blackout is available online at http://www.nrcan-rncan.gc.ca/media/docs/oneyear/oneyear_e.htm. The blackout was largely attributed to a single event: A coal-fired power plants operated by FirstEnergy Corp. began to behave oddly and had to be taken off-line, or "tripped". An hour later, one of the company's major transmission lines failed. The alarm system intended to warn the utility of such problems did not operate properly, so FirstEnergy did not give regional regulators and organizations in adjacent states any warning of the mishap. Over the next 45 minutes, three more transmission lines failed. The problem cascaded and, within hours most people in Ohio, Michigan, Ontario, New York State, New Jersey, and Connecticut were without power.

Consider the following assessment of the problems leading to the 2003 blackout:

Union of Concerned Scientists, Lessons from the August 2003 Blackout

http://www.ucsusa.org/clean_energy/renewable_energy/page.cfm?pageID=1248

The electricity blackout on August 14, 2003, highlighted the fragility of our electricity system and unleashed a torrent of proposals to upgrade it. Energy industry spokespeople have called for grid investments of $56 billion, $100 billion, and even as much as $450 billion in total electricity infrastructure investments. The White House and congressional leaders have also demanded higher rates of profit for transmission owners, federal eminent domain powers to site new transmission lines, and inclusion of electricity reliability measures in an overall energy bill loaded with tens of billion of dollars of additional incentives to the fossil fuel and nuclear industries, drilling in the Arctic National Wildlife Refuge, repealing consumer protections . . . and much more.

The fact that the specific cause of the blackout—and more importantly, the failure of mechanisms designed to prevent the loss of one or two transmission lines from triggering cascading outages across many states and power systems—are still unknown should give elected officials pause before using the blackout to justify huge investments in new wires, plants and conventional fuel sources. At this point, process and communication failures appear to be major contributors to the size of the blackout and priorities to fix. And there is no evidence that a lack of power plant capacity played a role.

Meanwhile, the one fix nearly everyone agrees upon—enforceable national reliability standards to replace current voluntary guidelines—is being held hostage to passing a controversial comprehensive energy bill. Mandatory reliability standards—which UCS endorsed as a participant in a Department of Energy Task Force on reliability five years ago—should be enacted now.

We also need to implement cost-effective energy efficiency and demand management measures through federal and state standards and incentives. These programs reduce stress and congestion on the transmission and distribution system, avoid the need to build new power plants and lines, reduce pollution, and pay for themselves in energy savings.

Some investments in upgraded existing transmission lines, building new lines, and implementing "smart grid" technologies will be necessary, but we need to establish fair, accountable, comprehensive regional planning processes that weigh the economic and environmental merits of all options for increasing reliability. As Amory Lovins has pointed out for decades, simply stringing together more central plants and wires can lead to a more brittle and vulnerable power system, whereas adding decentralized technologies for managing electricity demand and generating on-site power can increase the reliability and resilience of the system.

Decentralized, or distributed, resource options include targeted efficiency improvements, incentives for customers to reduce demand, and clean on-site power generation technologies such as fuel cells, micro-turbines, combined heat and power, solar, and small wind and bioenergy plants. We need to remove utility and regulatory barriers to the interconnection of clean distributed generation, and provide federal and state incentives to overcome market barriers to its adoption.

Finally, while it would not have prevented this blackout, diversifying our energy supply can also increase the reliability of our electricity system. We are becoming increasingly dependent on natural gas to generate electricity, increasing our vulnerability to supply shortages and price spikes. That is why the Federal Energy Regulatory Commission recently wrote, in supporting new rules for integrating wind energy into the grid, "Encouraging the development of intermittent generation will increase diversity in the resource base, thereby improving system reliability as a whole."

Wind, solar and other renewable energy resources can also reduce pollution and create tremendous new economic development opportunities, while enhancing the reliability and security of our energy system. A renewable electricity standard requiring utilities to increase their use of renewable electricity from a mere 2 percent today to at least 10 percent by 2020 was one of the few positive provisions in the energy bill recently passed by the Senate.

Reliability Problems

The nation's overreliance on large centralized power plants connected to high voltage transmission lines that bring power to consumers over long distances makes us vulnerable to the type of catastrophic failure in the system that occurred on August 14.

Reliance on large power plants and transmission lines also makes us vulnerable to blackouts from terrorist attacks and other security threats. The United States has nearly 500,000 miles of bulk transmission lines that carry high voltage electricity to consumers. It would be nearly impossible to monitor and protect all of these lines, as well as new lines and power plants, against potential security threats.

Improvements can certainly be made to lessen the likelihood of these events impacting such a large region in the future. Nonetheless, occasional unplanned blackouts, contained to small geographic areas, are unavoidable. Natural events, human error, and system failures cannot be completely engineered out of a system as complex and interdependent as the electric grid, where large generators in a network spanning more than half the continent must be synchronized to within one-sixtieth of a second.

Electricity deregulation has contributed to reliability problems in several ways:

1.   The deregulation of wholesale generation and some retail markets has resulted in a marked increase in power transfers over long distances. Since the blackout, a wide range of sources, including the utility-funded Electric Power Research Institute, the Pacific Northwest National Laboratory, and executives with major utilities have cited the problem that the grid was not designed to handle these flows.

2.   Many utilities have cut costs and staff to prepare for deregulation, including resources for maintaining transmission and distribution lines and for energy efficiency programs.

3.   The uncertainty created by the debate over transmission rules, rates, and governing bodies in an era of increasing competition has resulted in reduced investment in the transmission and distribution (T&D) system in some regions. Many analysts believe that additional

incentives to build transmission are not necessary. However, transmission owners are waiting to see if they will be allowed such incentives before they invest.

Blackout Solutions

Mandatory reliability standards. Strong, mandatory reliability standards should be established. The current voluntary standards, developed by the North America Electric Reliability Council (NERC), are not enough. Congress should not hold the reliability standards provision—twice passed by both the House and Senate—hostage to passing an overall energy bill.

According to NERC, roughly half of the 444 standards violations that occurred in 2002 could have caused a blackout. Mandatory standards with strong enforcement provisions are necessary to ensure the reliable operation of the nation's electricity system.

Energy efficiency. Increasing the efficiency of our homes and businesses is the fastest and cheapest way to ease pressure on the electricity system. This can be done by enacting tougher energy efficiency standards for appliances and buildings and increasing federal, state, and utility funding for energy efficiency. Federal standards to improve the efficiency of commercial air conditioners, residential furnaces, and distribution transformers could avoid the need to build 83 typical-size new power plants by 2020, and reduce transmission and distribution loads, while saving consumers $22 billion, according to the American Council for an Energy Efficient Economy. The standards for residential central air conditioners that were repealed by the Bush Administration would have saved the energy equivalent of another 48 power plants.

Consideration of diverse reliability options. Enhancing reliability must rely on a diversified approach that considers all alternatives before investing in new or upgraded transmission lines. This includes prioritizing targeted efficiency improvements, providing incentives to customers to wisely manage their loads (demand response programs), and developing clean decentralized generation when they are economically and environmentally preferable. There should be explicit opportunities for these options to compete against conventional transmission options.

Demand response programs. Demand response programs, in which customers receive financial incentives to reduce or shift their electricity use or switch on backup generators when power supplies are low or lines are congested, can be much less expensive than adding plants or wires to respond to peak demands on the electrical system. Demand response programs can also reduce vulnerability to corporate market abuses during power shortages. Without eligibility restrictions or environmental constraints, however, such programs can lead to increased use of highly polluting backup diesel generators.

Distributed generation. Distributed, or decentralized, generation sources can increase reliability for customers, avoid the need for new power plants and power lines, avoid power losses during transmission and distribution, decrease congestion on the grid, and bring many other benefits . . .

Net metering. National interconnection standards and net metering (allowing surplus generation to turn the electric meter backward) are needed to remove barriers to the development of distributed technologies. Congress should increase research and development spending and adopt financial incentives for distributed energy systems to help overcome market barriers to their introduction. Regulators need to assess and remove other utility, market, and regulatory barriers to distributed generation, and to account for the benefits of distributed generation in system planning . . .

Micro-grids. Distributed generation can be linked in local micro-grids to enhance reliability at the community level. A micro-grid under development by Northern Power Systems in Waitsfield, Vermont (in the Mad River Valley ski area), will initially use propane-fueled engines and microturbines, a photovoltaic array, and a small wind turbine, along with storage devices. It will provide power to 12 homes and five commercial and industrial facilities. It will also examine and potentially incorporate fuel cells, Stirling engines, and flywheels into the system.■

Fuel diversity. Renewable energy sources also increase system reliability because they diversify our resource base and do not use fuels that are vulnerable to periodic shortages or other supply interruptions. While some people think of solar and wind power as unreliable because they are intermittent generators, the Federal Energy Regulatory Commission (FERC) recently recognized the reliability benefit of wind in adopting new rules to facilitate integrating wind energy into the grid: "Encouraging the development of intermittent generation will increase diversity in the resource base, thereby improving system reliability as a whole."

Renewable energy incentives and standards. The most important ways to increase the use of renewable energy are through extending federal production tax credits and expanding their eligibility to all renewable resources, and through enactment of federal and state renewable electricity standards, also known as renewable portfolio standards. In July 2003, the Senate passed a renewable electricity standard requiring major electricity companies to obtain 10 percent of their electricity from renewable energy sources by 2020.

Upgrading existing transmission. Many technologies exist to significantly increase the capacity and efficiency of our existing transmission system, and new technologies have even greater potential. Priority should be placed on upgrading the existing system before building any new lines.

New transmission. Some new transmission will be needed to increase reliability and for other purposes. Some transmission upgrades and new lines will be needed to support wind power development, particularly in rural areas of the country. For example, the Minnesota Public Utilities Commission recently issued an order approving four new high voltage lines to support the development of 825 MW of wind power in southwestern Minnesota by 2006. Several consumer and environmental groups supported the development of these lines because they are being built primarily to support clean electricity from wind power.

RTOs. Regional transmission organizations (RTOs) can potentially have a positive, constructive role in enhancing reliability by facilitating regional planning, reliability assessment, and operational communication and by establishing market rules that treat renewable energy sources fairly. Effective RTOs should be open to all, governed independent of utility interests, work closely with multi-state agencies, and be accountable. Planning for system expansion or upgrades must be open, fair, and allow all options to compete. Rules should provide fair access to the transmission system and remove unfair scheduling penalties for variable-output resources such as wind power.

No across-the-board transmission incentives. Many analysts are not convinced that it is appropriate or legal for FERC to provide additional incentives to monopoly service providers, who already have an obligation to invest in transmission systems and receive a FERC tariff with a built-in profit margin. FERC's proposed across-the-board bonus approach will significantly increase costs to consumers, but may not produce system improvements in the most timely and cost-effective manner.

Analyze deregulation. Proponents of increased deregulation should provide thorough, open analysis of costs and benefits that accounts for the cost of upgrading the grid to achieve savings from purported increased efficiencies.■

* * *

With the rise of competitive wholesale power markets, FERC has begun to exercise jurisdiction over power marketers, such as Enron. EIA described the role power marketers are playing in the industry as follows:

> Power marketers are a relatively new type of firm in the electric power industry. They are different from traditional electric utilities. A power marketer buys electric energy and transmission and other services from traditional utilities, or other suppliers, and then resells these products. The concept of a power marketer first appeared in the mid–1980s. In October 1985, Citizens Energy filed a petition with the FERC seeking approval to purchase and resell electricity. This company was the first to file such a petition. In July 1987, the second petition to buy and resell electrical power was filed with the FERC by Howell Gas Management. It was not until August 1989, however, that the FERC approved a petition granting the right to buy and resell electric power to Citizens Power and Light. (*Citizens Power & Light Corp.*, 48 Federal Energy Regulatory Commission (FERC) 61,210 (August 8, 1989).) This order was particularly significant because the FERC recognized the existence of a new type of company in the wholesale marketplace and accepted the market-based rate schedules proposed by Citizens. That approval proved to be the foundation for subsequent applications for power marketing status.

Growth in the wholesale power market—estimated to be around 1,343 billion kWh in 1994—has spurred the increase in power marketing companies. EPACT and FERC's movement toward increased competition in the wholesale market by allowing market-based rates were also major factors in the increase in power marketers. Since the first approvals for power marketing status were granted, the number of companies obtaining approval has increased substantially. From a total of 9 in 1992, the number had grown to 180 by the end of December 1995. Most of the companies are gas marketers, who see power generation as a potentially lucrative market. Others types of companies getting into the power marketing business include brokers and financial firms, utility affiliates, independent entrepreneurs, commodity traders and manufactures, and independent power producers.

Presently, only a relatively small number of power marketers are active in the market, but the number of active companies is growing. In 1994, 9 firms sold 7.2 million MWh. In 1995, 40 power marketers sold 26.6 million MWh of electricity. Three companies—Enron Power Marketing, Lewis Dreyfus, and Electric Clearinghouse—accounted for 57 percent of the sales.

In summary, the growth of power marketers signals the potential for a fundamental change in the wholesale electricity business. Since the late 1980s the number of companies approved for power marketing has gone from a few to 180. Presently, only about 10 companies are active in the business of buying and reselling power. It is expected that, as access to transmission lines increases in a competitive environment, more companies will become active in the wholesale electric power business as power marketers.

As is now infamous, however, power marketers like Enron can manipulate markets. Historical prices in California had hovered at or below $50 per mega-watt hour, but in December 2002 wholesale prices on the California spot market reached monthly averages of nearly $400 per megawatt hour in December 2000 and average daily prices of nearly $1200 per megawatt hour. FERC conducted an investigation of Enron's role in California's deregulated wholesale power market, ordering Enron to refund more than $32 in profits it earned unjustly through the manipulation of wholesale markets supplying power to California utilities. At the same time, it is clear that the source of the difficulties in California extend far beyond Enron. See discussion in Chapter 12.

* * *

As wholesale competition evolves, new trading mechanisms are beginning to develop, providing stability against the type of situations that developed in the Summers of 1998 and 2003, as well as in California. Electricity is becoming a commodity like natural gas, petroleum products (e.g., crude oil, heating oil, gasoline), and other energy products. Electricity at wholesale value is now sold at market centers at market-based rates, and wholesale electricity prices are published daily. New electricity futures contracts have been introduced, which can help electricity buyers and sellers manage business risk.

Consider the following excerpt:

David Spence, The Politics of Electricity Restructuring: Theory vs. Practice

40 Wake Forest Law Review 417 (2005).

California's experience with a restructured electricity market is not representative of the restructuring experience of other states. Moreover, the California market was not simply atypical; it was atypical in ways that led directly to the crisis of 2000–2001. Simply stated, California's wholesale power market handed market power to major wholesale sellers on a silver platter. How? First, California had inadequate supply reserve margins in 2000, irrespective of the drought in the Northwest. According to FERC, California's average electricity demand grew by 11% during the 1990s, while installed generating capacity shrunk by about 2%. This reduced California's reserve margins to very low levels. Second, California forced wholesale buyers—providers of retail services to end users—to purchase nearly all of their power on the short-term markets. They were not permitted to enter into bilateral long-term power-purchase arrangements, thereby maximizing their exposure to price fluctuations in short-term markets. This was done in part to prevent the still somewhat vertically integrated, incumbent providers like PG&E and SCE from self-dealing in the contest for wholesale power from major generating units. Third, the California restructuring plan called for a cap on the retail rates incumbent providers could charge during the first phase of restructuring, which lasted until the incumbent had recovered all of its so-called "stranded costs" through rates. With hindsight, the errors of California's ways seem obvious. When reserve margins are low, supply is scarce. When supply is scarce, prices on the spot market will go up. Not only did this system offer large players in the spot market the opportunity to manipulate the market, but during periods of peak demand sellers of electricity from large plants could assume that their plants would be necessary to serve demand on the spot market and that their bids would be taken even if they demanded exorbitant prices (at least, by historical standards in California). Why? Price elasticity of demand for electricity is relatively low at certain points on the demand curve, because some consumers cannot effectively substitute other energy sources for electricity, at least in the short term. More importantly, retail price caps prevented end-user demand (and so, wholesale buyer demand) from responding to high wholesale prices. The price caps sustained high levels of demand, which helped to keep open the opportunities to manipulate the market and/or exact enormous scarcity rents.

Other restructuring states have taken a different path. All permit the participants in their wholesale markets to secure power through a combination of longer-term bilateral contracts and purchases on open short-term markets. Retail providers tend to secure most of their load from these long-term arrangements, relying on the spot markets to supplement their long-term contracts and to satisfy short-term fluctuations in demand. It is easy to see how this approach dampens the effects of price shocks on the short-term market compared to the California arrangement. Assume retail provider XYZ Electric buys 75% of its power—750 MWh per day—under a long-term contract establishing a fixed price of $40 per MWh. Assume further that XYZ Electric relies on the daily spot market to secure the remainder of its daily power needs (250 MWh per day), and that the spot market price fluctuates.

Over this ten-day period, XYZ Electric's total power purchase costs are $470,000 (the sum of the last row of [**Figure 11–2**]). The average spot market price over that period is greater than the fixed price under XYZ's long-term power purchase contract. If XYZ had been forced to rely exclusively on the spot market for all its power needs, then its costs would have been $680,000 (the sum of the products of the daily market prices multiplied by XYZ's 1000 MWh needs). On the other hand, when the spot market price is lower than the long-term contract price, XYZ's power purchase costs are more than if it had relied exclusively on short-term markets. Thus, while long-term bilateral contracts are not always cheaper than exclusive reliance on spot markets, their use provides more price certainty. Since most retail providers in restructured states enter into contracts with their customers to provide power at a specified rate, or according to a specified rate schedule, they welcome this additional price certainty on the wholesale market.

DAY	1	2	3	4	5	6	7	8	9	10
Spot Market Price ($/MWh)	30	30	40	40	60	100	180	110	50	40
Spot Market Purchase Costs ($) (250MWh/day x Spot Market Price)	7500	7500	10,000	10,000	15,000	25,000	45,000	27,500	12,500	10,000
Long-Term Power Purchase Costs ($) (750MWh/day @ $40/MWh)	30,000	30,000	30,000	30,000	30,000	30,000	30,000	30,000	30,000	30,000
Total Costs ($)	37,500	37,500	40,000	40,000	45,000	55,000	75,000	57,500	42,500	40,000

Figure 11–2
Power Purchase Costs for XYZ Electric

Just as importantly, buyers in the California market did not use commonly available financial techniques to hedge their price risk. Buyers on wholesale electricity markets can use option contracts, futures contracts and forward contracts to protect themselves against the risk of drastic price fluctuations. Electricity markets are ideal candidates for the use of options and futures to hedge against price risk because the price is volatile and the product (electricity) is fungible. In such a market, it makes sense for buyers to use these types of contractual instruments to secure rights to electricity in the future at reasonable rates. While the vast majority of these contracts are settled financially rather than executed, these contracts serve as a kind of insurance against drastic price increases in the future and are widely traded on major commodities exchanges. Buyers on the California wholesale markets had been precluded from using these hedging techniques until immediately prior to the crisis, leaving them almost fully exposed to the costs of the price spike on that market during the winter of 2000–2001. Other restructuring states encourage retail providers who must secure power on the wholesale market to meet their customers' needs to use these techniques for hedging price risk; indeed, they are widely used on U.S. wholesale electricity markets, including California's. Had PG&E and SCE protected themselves against price risk in this way, the damage done to their credit ratings (and the consequent exacerbation of the supply crisis that grew out of the credit problem) might have been reduced.

Even more important than PG&E's and SCE's inability to hedge against price risk in exacerbating the California crisis was the existence of retail price caps. These caps prevented demand from responding to price increases and facilitated the exercise (and misuse) of market power by sellers over an extended period of time. The consequent persistence of high wholesale prices meant persistent losses for the IOUs, further injuring their credit and causing sellers to add additional risk premiums to their prices. However, if retail prices had been permitted to float with wholesale prices, would demand have fallen? Critics of restructuring contend that the price elasticity of electricity demand is low, because electricity is a "necessity" for many people, and substitution of other energy sources is difficult or impossible for many users. However, economists have measured the price elasticity of demand, and have found that consumers do respond to electricity price increases by reducing demand. This was true (apparently) even during the California crisis, during which one retailer's customers were unprotected from price increases by retail price caps. The U.S. Congressional Budget Office noted that [i]n San Diego, where retail customers briefly faced market prices in the summer of 2000, evidence suggests that higher prices caused a decline in power use. A doubling of retail prices led to a drop in demand of between 2.2 percent and 7.6 percent, depending on the hour of the day. By September 2000, legislators had responded to public pressure by reducing and refreezing retail prices in San Diego, so customers there had no further incentive to curb their demand for electricity. Indeed, the opposite may have occurred, since consumers increased their use when prices dropped. Short-term price elasticity of demand for electricity may be low, but it is not zero. Presumably, short-term demand would have fallen in the PG&E and SCE service areas as well, and would have fallen more over the long term.

Thus, despite it's low reserve margins, bad weather, and droughts, the California electricity crisis might have been far less severe had the California wholesale power market been structured differently. When wholesale power purchasers can shield themselves against price risk through long-term and futures contracts, and share the risk of price increases with ratepayers (as they can in other restructuring states), the magnitude and duration of price spikes should be moderated accordingly. For these reasons, the California crisis does not undermine the economic rationale for restructuring.

E. THE LIMITS OF FEDERAL REGULATION

Under the Federal Power Act, FERC's authority over the electric power industry is limited to jurisdiction over wholesale transactions. Later statutes, such as the Energy Policy Act of 1992, continue to endorse jurisdictional limitations over FERC's power to completely deregulate the industry—especially regarding the provision of retail services (see Chapter 12, discussing state efforts)—but FERC has obviously played a major role in moving the wholesale power industry towards a competitive structure, much as it played a major role in restructuring natural gas.

Even with respect to FERC's jurisdiction over the wholesale operations of the industry, however, FERC's ability to successfully implement a competitive and reliable industry may fall short absent congressional expansion of its authority. The U.S. Supreme Court addressed two of these issues in its decision upholding Order No. 888.

New York v. Federal Energy Regulatory Commission

535 U.S. 1 (2002).

■ STEVENS, J. These cases raise two important questions concerning the jurisdiction of the Federal Energy Regulatory Commission (FERC or Commission) over the transmission of electricity. First, if a public utility "unbundles"—i.e., separates—the cost of transmission from the cost of electrical energy when billing its retail customers, may FERC require the utility to transmit competitors' electricity over its lines on the same terms that the utility applies to its own energy transmissions? Second, must FERC impose that requirement on utilities that continue to offer only "bundled" retail sales?

In Order No. 888, issued in 1996 with the stated purpose of "Promoting Wholesale Competition Through Open Access Non–Discriminatory Transmission Services by Public Utilities," FERC answered yes to the first question and no to the second. It based its answers on provisions of the Federal Power Act (FPA), as added by § 213, 49 Stat. 847, and as amended, 16 U.S.C. § 824 et seq., enacted in 1935. Whether or not the 1935 Congress foresaw the dramatic changes in the power industry that have occurred in recent decades, we are persuaded, as was the Court of Appeals, that FERC properly construed its statutory authority.

I

In 1935, when the FPA became law, most electricity was sold by vertically integrated utilities that had constructed their own power plants, transmission lines, and local delivery systems. Although there were some interconnections among utilities, most operated as separate, local monopolies subject to state or local regulation. Their sales were "bundled," meaning that consumers paid a single charge that included both the cost of the electric energy and the cost of its delivery. Competition among utilities was not prevalent.

Prior to 1935, the States possessed broad authority to regulate public utilities, but this power was limited by our cases holding that the negative impact of the Commerce Clause prohibits state regulation that directly burdens interstate commerce. When confronted with an attempt by Rhode Island to regulate the rates charged by a Rhode Island plant selling electricity to a Massachusetts company, which resold the electricity to the city of Attleboro, Massachusetts, we invalidated the regulation because it imposed a "direct burden upon interstate commerce." Creating what has become known as the *"Attleboro* gap," we held that this interstate transaction was not subject to regulation by either Rhode Island or Massachusetts, but only "by the exercise of the power vested in Congress."

When it enacted the FPA in 1935, Congress authorized federal regulation of electricity in areas beyond the reach of state power, such as the gap identified in *Attleboro,* but it also extended federal coverage to some areas that previously had been state regulated. The FPA charged the Federal Power Commission ("FPC"), the predecessor of FERC, "to provide effective federal regulation of the expanding business of transmitting and selling electric power in interstate commerce." Specifically, in § 201(b) of the FPA, Congress recognized the FPC's jurisdiction as including "the transmission of electric energy in interstate commerce" and "the sale of electric energy at wholesale in interstate commerce." Furthermore, § 205 of the FPA prohibited, among other things, unreasonable rates and undue discrimination "with respect to any transmission or sale subject to the jurisdiction of the Commission," and § 206 gave the FPC the power to correct such unlawful practices.

[I]n 1995, FERC initiated the rulemaking proceeding that led to the adoption of the order presently under review. FERC proposed a rule that would "require that public utilities owning and/or controlling facilities used for the transmission of electric energy in interstate commerce have on file tariffs providing for nondiscriminatory open-access transmission services." The stated purpose of the proposed rule was "to encourage lower electricity rates by structuring an orderly transition to competitive bulk power markets." Rather than grounding its legal authority in Congress' more recent electricity legislation, FERC cited § § 205–206 of the 1935 FPA—the provisions concerning FERC's power to remedy unduly discriminatory practices—as providing the authority for its rulemaking.

[FERC] found that electric utilities were discriminating in the "bulk power markets," in violation of § 205 of the FPA, by providing either inferior access to their transmission networks or no access at all to third-party wholesalers of power. Invoking its authority under § 206, it prescribed a remedy containing three parts that are presently relevant.

First, FERC ordered "functional unbundling" of wholesale generation and transmission services. FERC defined "functional unbundling" as requiring each utility to state separate rates for its wholesale generation, transmission, and ancillary services, and to take transmission of its own wholesale sales and purchases under a single general tariff applicable equally to itself and to others.

Second, FERC imposed a similar open access requirement on unbundled *retail* transmissions in interstate commerce.... FERC ultimately concluded that it was "irrelevant to the Commission's jurisdiction whether the customer receiving the unbundled transmission service in interstate commerce is a wholesale or retail customer." Thus, "if a public utility voluntarily offers unbundled retail access," or if a State requires unbundled retail access, "the affected retail customer *must* obtain its unbundled transmission service under a non-discriminatory transmission tariff on file with the Commission."

Third, FERC rejected a proposal that the open access requirement should apply to "the transmission component of bundled retail sales." Although FERC noted that "the unbundling of retail transmission and generation . . . would be helpful in achieving comparability," it concluded that such unbundling was not "necessary" and would raise "difficult jurisdictional issues" that could be "more appropriately considered" in other proceedings.

In its analysis of the jurisdictional issues, FERC distinguished between transmissions and sales. It explained:

> [Our statutory jurisdiction] over sales of electric energy extends only to wholesale sales. However, when a retail transaction is broken into two products that are sold separately (perhaps by two different suppliers: an electric energy supplier and a transmission supplier), we believe the jurisdictional lines change. In this situation, the state clearly retains jurisdiction over the sale of power. However, the unbundled transmission service involves *only* the provision of "transmission in interstate commerce" which, under the FPA, is exclusively within the jurisdiction of the Commission. Therefore, when a bundled retail sale is unbundled and becomes separate transmission and power sales transactions, the resulting transmission transaction falls within the Federal sphere of regulation.

With respect to various challenges to its jurisdiction, FERC acknowledged that it did not have the "authority to order, *sua sponte,* open-access transmission services by public utilities," but explained that § 206 of the FPA explicitly required it to remedy the undue discrimination that it had found. FERC also rejected the argument that its failure to assert jurisdiction over bundled retail transmissions was inconsistent with its assertion of jurisdiction over unbundled retail transmissions. FERC repeated its explanation that it did not believe that regulation of bundled retail trans-missions (*i.e.,* the "functional unbundling" of retail transmissions) "was necessary," and again stated that such unbundling would raise serious ju-risdictional questions. FERC did not, however, state that it had no power to regulate the transmission component of bundled retail sales. Rather, FERC reiterated that States have jurisdiction over the retail *sale* of power, and stated that, as a result, "[o]ur assertion of jurisdiction . . . arises only if the [unbundled] retail transmission in interstate commerce by a public utility occurs voluntarily or as a result of a state retail program." . . .

III

The first question is whether FERC exceeded its jurisdiction by includ-ing unbundled retail transmissions within the scope of its open access requirements in Order No. 888. New York argues that FERC overstepped in this regard, and that such transmissions—because they are part of retail transactions—are properly the subject of state regulation. New York insists that the jurisdictional line between the States and FERC falls between the wholesale and retail markets.

As the Court of Appeals explained, however, the landscape of the electric industry has changed since the enactment of the FPA, when the electricity universe was "neatly divided into spheres of retail versus whole-sale sales." As the Court of Appeals also explained, the plain language of the FPA readily supports FERC's claim of jurisdiction. Section 201(b) of the FPA states that FERC's jurisdiction includes "the transmission of electric energy in interstate commerce" and "the sale of electric energy at wholesale in interstate commerce." The unbundled retail transmissions targeted by FERC are indeed transmissions of "electric energy in interstate commerce," because of the nature of the national grid. There is no language in the statute limiting FERC's *transmission* jurisdiction to the wholesale market, although the statute does limit FERC's *sale* jurisdiction to that at wholesale. . . .

New York is correct to point out that the legislative history is replete with statements describing Congress' intent to preserve state jurisdiction over local facilities. The sentiment expressed in those statements is incor-porated in the second sentence of § 201(b) of the FPA, as codified in which provides:

> The Commission shall have jurisdiction over all facilities for such transmission or sale of electric energy, but shall not have jurisdiction, except as specifically provided in this subchapter and subchapter III of this chapter, over facilities used for the generation of electric energy or over facilities used in local distribution or only for the transmission of electric energy in intrastate commerce, or over facilities for the trans-mission of electric energy consumed wholly by the transmitter.

Yet, Order No. 888 does not even arguably affect the States' jurisdiction over three of these subjects: generation facilities, transmissions in intra-state commerce, or transmissions consumed by the transmitter. Order No. 888 does discuss local distribution facilities, and New York argues that, as a result, FERC has improperly invaded the States' authority "over facilities used in local distribution." However, FERC has not attempted to control local distribution facilities through Order No. 888. To the contrary, FERC has made clear that it does not have jurisdiction over such facilities and has merely set forth a seven-factor test for identifying these facilities, without purporting to regulate them.

New York also correctly states that the legislative history demonstrates Congress' interest in retaining state jurisdiction over retail sales. But again, FERC has carefully avoided assuming such jurisdiction, noting repeatedly that "the FPA does not give the Commission jurisdiction over sales of electric energy at retail." Because federal authority has been asserted only over unbundled *transmissions,* New York retains jurisdiction of the ultimate sale of the *energy.* And, as discussed below, FERC did not assert jurisdiction over bundled retail transmissions, leaving New York with control over even the transmission component of bundled retail sales. . . .

IV

Objecting to FERC's order from the opposite direction, Enron argues that the FPA gives FERC the power to apply its open access remedy to *bundled* retail transmissions of electricity, and, given FERC's findings of undue discrimination, that FERC had a duty to do so. In making this argument, Enron persistently claims that FERC held that it had no jurisdiction to grant the relief that Enron seeks. That assumption is incorrect: FERC chose not to assert such jurisdiction, but it did not hold itself powerless to claim jurisdiction. Indeed, FERC explicitly reserved decision on the jurisdictional issue that Enron claims FERC decided. See Order No. 888, at 31,699 (explaining that Enron's position raises "numerous difficult jurisdictional issues that we believe are more appropriately considered when the Commission reviews unbundled retail transmission tariffs that may come before us in the context of a state retail wheeling program"). Absent Enron's flawed assumption, FERC's ruling is clearly acceptable.

As noted above, in both Order No. 888 and rehearing Order No. 888–A, FERC gave two reasons for refusing to extend its open access remedy to bundled retail transmissions. First, FERC explained that such relief was not "necessary." Second, FERC noted that the regulation of bundled retail transmissions "raises numerous difficult jurisdictional issues" that did not need to be resolved in the present context. Both of these reasons provide valid support for FERC's decision not to regulate bundled retail transmissions.

First, with respect to FERC's determination that it was not "necessary" to include bundled retail transmissions in its remedy, it must be kept in mind exactly what it was that FERC sought to remedy in the first place: a problem with the *wholesale* power market. FERC's findings, as Enron itself recognizes, concerned electric utilities' use of their market power to " 'deny their *wholesale* customers access to competitively priced electric generation,'" thereby "'deny[ing] consumers the substantial benefits of lower electricity prices.'"

To remedy the wholesale discrimination it found, FERC chose to regulate all wholesale transmissions. It also regulated unbundled retail transmissions, as was within its power to do. However, merely because FERC believed that those steps were appropriate to remedy discrimination in the wholesale electricity market does not, as Enron alleges, lead to the conclusion that the regulation of *bundled* retail transmissions was "necessary" as well. Because FERC determined that the remedy it ordered constituted a sufficient response to the problems FERC had identified in the wholesale market, FERC had no § 206 obligation to regulate bundled retail transmissions or to order universal unbundling.

Of course, it may be true that FERC's findings concerning discrimination in the wholesale electricity market suggest that such discrimination exists in the retail electricity market as well, as Enron alleges. Were FERC to investigate this alleged discrimination and make findings concerning undue discrimination in the retail electricity market, § 206 of the FPA would require FERC to provide a remedy for that discrimination. And such a remedy could very well involve FERC's decision to regulate bundled retail transmissions—Enron's desired outcome. However, because the scope of the order presently under review did not concern discrimination in the retail market, Enron is wrong to argue that § 206 requires FERC to provide a full array of retail-market remedies.

Second, we can agree with FERC's conclusion that Enron's desired remedy "raises numerous difficult jurisdictional issues," without deciding whether Enron's ultimate position on those issues is correct. The issues raised by New York concerning FERC's jurisdiction over unbundled retail transmissions are themselves serious. It is obvious that a federal order claiming jurisdiction over *all* retail transmissions would have even greater implications for the States' regulation of retail sales—a state regulatory power recognized by the same statutory provision that authorizes FERC's transmission jurisdiction. But even if we assume, for present purposes, that Enron is *correct* in its claim that the FPA gives FERC the authority to regulate the transmission component of a bundled retail sale, we nevertheless conclude that the agency had discretion to decline to assert such jurisdiction in this proceeding in part because of the complicated nature of the jurisdictional issues. Like the Court of Appeals, we are satisfied that FERC's choice not to assert jurisdiction over bundled retail transmissions in a rulemaking proceeding focusing on the wholesale market "represents a statutorily permissible policy choice."

■ JUSTICE THOMAS concurred in part and dissented in part, joined by JUSTICE SCALIA and JUSTICE KENNEDY ... Given that it is impossible to identify which utility's lines are used for any given transmission, FERC's decision to exclude transmission because it is associated with a particular type of transaction appears to make little sense. And this decision may conflict with FERC's statutory mandate to regulate when it finds unjust, unreasonable, unduly discriminatory, or preferential treatment with respect to any transmission subject to its jurisdiction. FERC clearly recognizes the statute's mandate, stating in Order No. 888–A that "our authorities under the FPA not only permit us to adapt to changing economic realities in the electric industry, but also require us to do so, as necessary to eliminate undue discrimination and protect electricity customers." And it is certainly possible that utilities that own or control lines on the grid discriminate against entities that seek to use their transmission lines regardless of whether the utilities themselves bundle or unbundle their transactions. The fact that FERC found undue discrimination with respect to transmission used in connection with both bundled and unbundled wholesale sales and unbundled retail sales indicates that such discrimination exists regardless of whether the transmission is used in bundled or unbundled sales. Without more, FERC's conclusory statement that "unbundling of retail transmission" is not "necessary" lends little support to its decision not to regulate such transmission. And it simply cannot be the case that the nature of the commercial transaction controls the scope of FERC's jurisdiction.

To be sure, I would not prejudge whether FERC *must* require that transmission used for bundled retail sales be subject to FERC's open access tariff. At a minimum, however, FERC should have determined whether regulating transmission used in connection with bundled retail sales was in fact "necessary to eliminate undue discrimination and protect electricity customers." FERC's conclusory statement instills little confidence that it either made this determination or that it complied with the unambiguous dictates of the statute. While the Court essentially ignores the statute's mandatory prescription by approving of FERC's decision as a permissible "policy choice," the FPA simply does not give FERC discretion to base its decision not to remedy undue discrimination on a "policy choice."

. . . . By refusing to regulate the transmission associated with retail sales in States that have chosen not to unbundle retail sales, FERC has set up a system under which: (a) each State's internal policy decisions concerning whether to require unbundling controls the nature of federal jurisdiction; (b) a utility's voluntary decision to unbundle determines whether FERC has jurisdiction; and (c) utilities that are allowed to continue bundling may discriminate against other companies attempting to use their transmission lines. The statute neither draws these distinctions nor provides that the jurisdictional lines shift based on actions taken by the States, the public utilities, or FERC itself. While Congress understood that transmission is a necessary component of all energy sales, it granted FERC jurisdiction over all interstate transmission, without qualification. As such, these distinctions belie the statutory text.

As the foregoing demonstrates, I disagree with the deference the Court gives to FERC's decision not to regulate transmission connected to bundled retail sales. Because the statute unambiguously grants FERC jurisdiction over all interstate transmission and mandates that FERC remedy undue discrimination with respect to all transmission within its jurisdiction, at a minimum the statute required FERC to consider whether there was discrimination in the marketplace warranting application of either the OATT or some other remedy.

I would not, as petitioner Enron requests, compel FERC to apply the OATT to bundled retail transmissions. I would vacate the Court of Appeals' judgment and require FERC on remand to engage in reasoned decisionmaking to determine whether there is undue discrimination with respect to transmission associated with retail bundled sales, and if so, what remedy is appropriate.■

NOTES AND COMMENTS

1. Prior to the U.S. Supreme Court deciding this case, the Eighth Circuit held that FERC's attempt in Order No. 888 "to regulate the curtailment of electrical transmission on native/retail consumers is unlawful, as it falls outside of the FPA's specific grant of authority to FERC." *North States Power Co. v. FERC*, 176 F.3d 1090 (8th Cir. 1999). Consider the following assessment of the *Northern States Power* case:

> . . . if it survives, the Eighth Circuit's decision poses a serious threat of state interference with interstate transmission of electricity. The resulting balkanization of electricity markets would be a major setback both to existing electricity markets and to evolving electric power markets, ultimately undermining, not enhancing, service reliability for both wholesale and retail customers.

See William H. Penniman & Paul B. Turner, A Jurisdictional Clash Over Electricity Transmission: Northern States Power v. FERC, 20 Energy L.J. 205 (1999). Does this ruling survive *New York v. FERC*?

2. As the opening reading in this chapter hinted, restructuring of the European Union electric power market is also moving at a rapid pace. An E.U. directive issued in 1996 requires open access to transmission, establishment of a transmission system operator, and financial separation of generation, transmission and distribution activities. *See* Directive 96/92/EC, www.europa.eu.int/en/comm/dg17/gazel_en.htm. In addition to the U.K., whose competition plan is discussed in the opening readings of this chapter, Germany has implemented full wholesale and retail competition and Spain has implemented wholesale but not retail competition. The French government is actively studying competition for its markets, in part because the European Commission has taken legal action against France for its failure to end the monopoly of Electricite de France. The E.U. experience illustrates the practical implications of the legal constraints faced by federal regulators in the U.S.:

> The E.C.'s French compliance action illustrates one of the [] most striking differences in U.S. and E.U. power markets. In Europe, the E.C. has ultimate authority over member states to compel the market opening, whereas in the United States there is no national authority nor federal law to require states to open their retail markets. That is

rather ironic since a united Europe is a relatively new phenomenon by comparison to the U.S. federal structure.

Shannon Burchett, A Continent United? Some Thoughts on Prospects for a Single Energy Market in Europe, Public Utilities Fortnightly, Jan. 15, 2000, at 32.

3. For discussion of the legal barriers to restructuring at the federal level, see Richard J. Pierce, Jr., Completing the Process of Restructuring of the Electricity Market, 40 Wake Forest L. Rev. 452 (2005). More than a decade ago, Richard Pierce observed, "The FERC cannot control the path and rate of progress of the electricity transition to the extent it exercised control over the gas transition because it lacks many of the regulatory tools it applied to the gas industry." Richard J. Pierce, Jr., The State of the Transition to Competitive Markets in Natural Gas and Electricity, 15 Energy L. J. 323 (1994).

4. The 2005 Energy Policy Act made significant changes to federal jurisdiction, particularly over electric power transmission. As is discussed in Chapter 13, one of the most significant changes concerns federal jurisdiction over transmission siting in what DOE deems to be "national interest electric transmission corridors"—areas where, among other things, transmission congestion is a significant problem. The 2005 Energy Policy Act authorizes FERC "back stop authoirity" in limited circumstances to order the acquisition and siting of rights-of-way for developing transmission in these corridors.

The 2005 Energy Policy Act also amends the FPA to provide expansive new mandatory and enforceable electric reliability standards for interstate wholesale markets. Since 1968 NERC and regional reliability councils have relied on a voluntary, industry-based process to maintain reliability of the interstate transmission system. The new amendments to the FPA provide for FERC to certify an Electric Reliability Organization (ERO) with the authority to develop and enforce reliability standards, subject to FERC review.

NERC is likely to be accepted as the ERO. Among the rights and responsibility state for the ERO are the following:

— An obligation to maintain independence from users, owners and operators of the bulk power system while assuring fair stakeholder representation on its board of directors.

— The right to charge and collect fees, dues and charges from end user to pay for the ERO's administrative costs.

— A duty to promulgate reliability standards after notice and opportunity for public comments subject to FERC approval.

— The authority to impose penalties for violations of reliability standards, also subject to FERC review.

The ERO is authorized to delegate authority to develop and enforce reliability standards to a regional entity if the regional entity meets the same criteria as the ERO. (A regional entity may be governed by an independent stakeholder board or a balanced stakeholder board or both.) It is likely that extsing regional reliability councils will seek and obtain delegation agreements with the RTO.

The 2005 Energy Policy Act also bolsters FERC's enforcement jurisdiction by giving it jurisdiction over all users, owners, and operators of the "bulk power system," including traditional utilities, power marketers, independent power producers and utilities not otherwise subject to FERC jurisdiction (such as municipal systems and ERCOT utilities). The "bulk power system" is defined to include the interconnected transmission network as well as "electric energy from the generation facilities needed to maintain transmission system reliability." FERC is otherwise expressly denied jurisdiction over generation facilities and it remains to be seen how far FERC will move beyond the traditional generated-related reliability issue to address voltage control and operational reserves, as well as other issues. The statute did not give FERC authority over the adequacy of generation of transmission capacity and FERC cannot require the construction of enlargement of transmission facilities.

FERC is also given explicit authority to impose penalties if FERC finds that an user, owner or operator of the bulk power system has engaged in or is about to engage in any act that constitutes or will constitute a violation of an ERO reliability standard. FERC is authorized to impose civil penalties of up to $1 million per day for each day of a violation of any provision of the FPA continues, and criminal penalties and jail sentences are also available. The ERO, and regional entities by delegation from the ERO, also have the authority to impose penalties subject to FERC review, but only for actual violations.

A savings clause in the 2005 Energy Policy Act protects the rights of states to take actions to ensure the reliability of electric service within a state so long as the action is not inconsistent with the reliability standards promulgated by FERC or the ERO. The state of New York is granted special status allowing it to establish its own reliability rules so long as those rules provide for greater reliability within the state and no lesser reliability outside of New York.

Despite these significant changes to federal energy statutes, however, the limited jurisdiction of federal regulators in the U.S. remains a central issue. For example, proposals to authorize FERC to mandate RTO participation are controversial and have failed to pass into law.

CHAPTER 12

RETAIL COMPETITION IN ELECTRIC POWER

A. STATE RESTRUCTURING: THE GOALS AND THE PROMISE

Leading up to the mid–1990s, a number of forces combined to spur states to pursue competition in their retail electricity markets. As discussed in Chapter 11, PURPA's mandate that utilities purchase power from cogenerators and small power producers encouraged development of new technologies and alternative fuel sources. It also introduced a group of competitors to incumbent utilities in the generation market, where none had existed previously. The EPAct's provisions defining and promoting "exempt wholesale generators" allowed even more new, non-utility companies to generate and sell electricity. New generation technology based on cleaner-burning and (then) cheaper natural gas had emerged as an alternative to oil, coal, and nuclear power for generating electricity.

Deregulation was attractive to politicians who believed the economics literature extolling the efficiencies of the free market—and the inefficiencies of regulated industries. To them, traditional utilities, protected by the "regulatory compact" against competition in their service territories, had little incentive to provide better service or lower rates. There was even a blueprint of sorts for bringing about deregulation in the utility industry: the natural gas industry, once dominated by vertically integrated pipeline monopolies, had embarked on a course of deregulation. Some (but not all) states had high power costs, and restructuring proponents suggested that competition would lower them.

Responding to these developments, states sought to further the development of competition in retail power markets. The consumer would have choices as the industry opened up to competition, much as the cable, telephone, and airline industries had done. Consumers could select from a menu of different companies offering to deliver electricity to them, instead of having electricity delivered by the vertically integrated monopolist.

While FERC has extensive jurisdiction over interstate and wholesale sales of electricity, state PSCs took on the task of designing and implementing retail competition; states have authority over retail rates, local distribution of electricity, and construction and siting of power plants and transmission lines within their boundaries. Nearly one-half of all states have introduced retail competition, although the trend has slowed in recent years and in some states has even reversed itself. For a number of years, states had considered plans to implement retail wheeling, or direct access to electricity supply markets. Most of these plans focused on providing direct access for large retail customers such as industrial plants. By the mid–1990s, however, state retail wheeling plans were being displaced by much more comprehensive efforts to implement "retail competition." Unlike retail wheeling, which focuses solely on the issue of retail transmission access, retail competition plans address a range of additional issues, including consumer protection, stranded cost recovery, and green pricing. The basic approach has been to encourage competitive markets to evolve through the "unbundling" of generation, transmission and distribution: splitting the incumbent utility company into its component parts either functionally or legally.

Some aspects of this decentralized industry remain fully regulated by the states, and others are governed by new, market-oriented regimes. Thus, states' laws and regulations have not achieved complete deregulation; instead, states have pursued a hybrid called "restructuring." The two terms are often used (wrongly) as synonymous: "While policymakers sought to 'deregulate' the industry, the laws and regulations they used were intended and designed to 'restructure,' not deregulate, electricity." Joseph P. Tomain, 2002 Energy Law Symposium: The Past and Future of Electricity Regulation, 32 Envtl. L. 435, 437–38 (2002). In a competitive retail market, the DisCo (incumbent distribution utility) continues to provide service to retail customers and remains a regulated natural monopoly. On the other hand, retail customers are afforded the opportunity to choose the company that generates electricity and transmits it to them. This opens the incumbent utility's distribution network to access by its competitors, and introduces several levels of complexity in setting up restructuring plans. Think of the many questions involved in defining the relationship between the incumbent utility and the new entrants in the generation and transmission business. Under what terms and conditions would the incumbent utility provide open access? Could the incumbent utility keep some customers and jettison others? Regulators needed to carefully address these and many other issues.

As restructuring began, its proponents suggested it would lead to many beneficial outcomes, such as less expensive power for consumers, choices of electricity suppliers (including, perhaps, some that generated electricity in an environmentally-friendly manner), and innovations in generation and transmission grid technologies, that would not take place in a traditional regulatory environment. Has restructuring fulfilled any of these promises? Many would say no, and even the most ardent proponents of restructuring would conclude that at the very least we have a long way to go before a true competitive environment, yielding benefits to residential consumers, is in place. How did the movement toward retail competition get underway? What have the states done to bring about restructuring? Why has the transition to competition been so difficult?

The following excerpt discusses the reasons for the popularity of restructuring initiatives:

National Council on Electricity Policy, A Comprehensive View of U.S. Electric Restructuring with Policy Options for the Future 2–5 (2003) ("NCEP Report")

I. THE GOALS OF ELECTRIC INDUSTRY RESTRUCTURING

Electric restructuring focused on two areas: retail markets and wholesale markets. State policymakers retained primary responsibility for retail markets, defined as the sale of power directly to retail customers such as a house or a supermarket. State policymakers focus on whether or not to give retail electricity consumers the chance to choose their electricity provider and how to regulate retail electricity markets.... Lower-priced electricity was the most popular goal of electric restructuring advocates, but not the only one. Other primary goals included better service, improved innovation, and, for some advocates, improved environmental quality.... Some of these goals were based on realistic assumptions, others based on assumptions and hopes that may have been too optimistic.

GOAL 1: LOWER PRICED ELECTRICITY

Most lawmakers who voted to allow retail competition were convinced that electric rates would fall in restructured markets. Advocates of competition attacked high rates in order to encourage legislatures to address retail electric competition, warning legislators that failure to use retail competition to reduce rates would give the state a poor image in the business community. They pointed to the large disparity among rates across the U.S. and even within individual states and regions. Average electric rates in low cost states were less than half those of higher cost states. Advocates pointed to new, lower cost power sources that offered the promise of lower retail rates, though this promise could be delayed by decades because utility rates still had embedded within them the cost of older, more expensive generation. They also presumed that waste could be excised from utility operations.

Business Rate Discounts in Monopoly States

Before the first state adopted retail competition, larger customers were already winning lower rates. "Economic development" rate agreements, or "load retention" rate agreements became an issue of growing importance in many states.

Economic development rates present a trade-off between the interests of fairness among ratepayers and state economic development. A customer, typically a manufacturer, would tell state and utility officials that it would locate a facility in a given location, or make a significant expansion at an existing facility, if certain conditions were met by both sides. These conditions for the customer typically included a commitment to provide a minimum number of jobs, to employ energy efficient measures, and to stay for a minimum period.

Load retention rates present a more difficult policy choice. In this case, the customer offers nothing except the threat to move an existing operation elsewhere. The state is put in the difficult position of making a counter-offer to keep the customer and the jobs in the state. Because the revenue from existing load is reduced in a load retention rate, other customers must make up the difference consistent with normal utility cost recovery practices.

Some advocates for restructuring cited these situations as examples that the largest power users were already getting competitive benefits, and more sweeping changes were needed to make these opportunities available to all customers.

GOAL 2: BETTER SERVICE

Some advocates of retail competition suggested that monopoly utility service quality would improve under competition. These advocates cited examples of customer service centers that did not answer calls, or did so after too many rings; customer service agents who were uninformed or unhelpful; incomprehensible bills; and poor service quality (too many distribution maintenance outages, delayed restoration of service after outages). In addition, some customers wanted to buy power derived from sources, such as renewable energy, that they considered clean, but had no way to purchase through their utility. Collectively, these advocates of retail competition suggested that utilities made little or no effort to determine the different services and products customers might want, nor did they make a meaningful effort to deliver them. Utilities, for their part, had little incentive to provide exemplary service.

GOAL 3: SPUR INNOVATION

Advocates suggested that competition would spur innovation in the electric industry. Some critics tagged regulation with responsibility for a declining utility record in innovation. Traditional, regulation seemed to reward replacing and expanding the power system with traditional, not innovative technologies. At the same time, regulatory commissions that did not allow utilities to recover some of their investments in expensive nuclear units—and resulting write-offs—chilled the utility appetite for taking chances. Advocates of competition saw it as a way to spur innovation in several ways:

● A new fleet of highly efficient natural gas fired power plants would replace the older and less efficient generating facilities. Generators would compete on price and performance (efficiency, availability).

● Grid operators would deploy a host of new research and development technology and information systems on transmission and distribution to make the nation's grid of power lines operate more efficiently.

● Marketers would offer a host of new products supported by new information technologies that would encourage customers to be more efficient, to better respond to conditions in wholesale markets, to take advantage of new products to better meet their needs and to take advantage of ways to reduce their overall power costs.

GOAL 4: IMPROVE THE ENVIRONMENT

Some environmental advocates offered two reasons for supporting restructuring: accelerating the deployment of cleaner power, and enabling consumers to select cleaner power supplies.

Some environmental advocates embraced restructuring as a way to accelerate the deployment of efficient and low-emitting generation. New generation technology promised to lower emissions of acid rain and ozone precursors, SO_2 and NO_2. These power plants also emit lower levels of toxics, mercury, and particulates than the older power plants.

Environmental advocates also suggested that retail choice offered the chance for consumers to choose "green", "environmentally–friendly" products instead of power generated from traditional sources, creating demand for and promoting the construction of more sustainable electricity supplies, including resources on the customer side of the meter.

Not all environmental advocates welcomed restructuring. Environmental groups that opposed restructuring questioned whether customers would really make environmentally driven choices especially if they cost too much. They also worried that the expanded geography of interstate electricity markets would improve the ability of energy from inefficient and highly polluting energy stations to find economically driven customers several states away.

Another concern was the prospect that proliferation of customer-owned generation might take the form of polluting diesel engines, rather than cleaner systems, creating a new air quality challenge.∎

* * *

Major differences in several aspects of the utility industry have led different regions to have diverging views on the importance of restructuring:

> ... Generally, utilities in the Southeast, lower Midwest, and West are much larger than utilities in the Northeast and upper Midwest. The extraordinarily balkanized utility structure in the Northeast and upper Midwest limits severely the ability of the utilities in those areas to operate on an efficient scale, while large, multi-state firms like Pacificorp, American Electric Power, Entergy, and The Southern Company are in a much better position to take advantage of available economies of scale and coordination.
>
> The state regulatory environment in which utilities operate also varies greatly by region. Utilities in the Northeast and California were subjected to costly regulatory obligations to purchase high cost power from QFs and to make extravagant and inefficient investments in "conservation." Utilities in other parts of the country were not burdened with those costly regulatory obligations. Similarly, the massive investment disallowances of the 1980s were imposed disproportionately on utilities in California and northeastern states. Utilities in the lower Midwest and Southeast experienced virtually no disallowances. They remained profitable throughout the period in which utilities in the Northeast and California were experiencing severe problems retaining access to capital markets.
>
> Finally, utilities vary with respect to their access to subsidized resources. In particular, utilities in the Northwest have legally preferred access to the large quantity of federally-subsidized hydroelectricity that is generated by the dams owned and operated by the Bonneville Power Administration.
>
> The net effects of these differences included much higher electricity prices in California, the Northeast, and the upper Midwest than in the Northwest, lower Midwest, and Southeast. That, in turn, created a political environment in which there was much stronger popular and political support for restructuring in California, the Northeast, and the upper Midwest, than in the southeast, lower Midwest, and Northwest. People in the regions with low electricity prices ... were content with the status quo ante, and many feared that the restructuring movement was designed to allow outsiders to "steal" their low-cost resources....

Richard J. Pierce, Jr., Completing the Process of Restructuring the Electricity Market, 40 Wake Forest L. Rev. 101, 108–09 (2005) ("Completing the Process"). Some might disagree with Professor Pierce's contention that investments in conservation were "extravagant." *See* Chapter 13. However, his central point—that regional differences matter in restructuring—was and remains important in the restructuring debate. Some states, including several in the Southeast, continue to refer to themselves as "low cost power" states, suggesting that retail competition is far off on the regulatory horizon. Low cost power states see no need to restructure, as they do not believe that consumers will be better off with retail competition. Will these states be able to continue to avoid implementing retail access markets, or will the failure to do so impair the development of wholesale competition?

1.   MAJOR POLICY ISSUES IN RESTRUCTURING

States pursuing restructuring faced a bewildering array of complex policy questions. One primary set of issues involved consumer protection. Despite promises of lower prices, with the rise of retail competition many consumer protections taken for granted under the traditional approach to state utility regulation would be at risk. Under the traditional approach, as discussed in Chapter 2, regulation of utilities by state PSCs struck a balance between private gain and the public interest. The prospect of retail competition created a tension between these two interests, requiring regulators to reassess their role and transform their regulatory structures.

This in turn created major uncertainties. How would market mechanisms control supply and demand for the nation's most essential commodity? Would retail rates decrease or would consumers be vulnerable to price spikes in a restructured market? How would markets be structured so that participants would not take advantage of consumers? Would price signals from the market be sufficiently clear to encourage the appropriate level of investment in generation and transmission? Or would it be more likely that generators would have "strong incentives to limit capacity additions, and maximize profits"? Alan H. Richardson, Can A Free Market Work For Electricity?, Public Power, Nov.-Dec. 2000, at 6.

Another set of concerns came from utilities most directly affected by a transition from a regulated monopoly environment to a competitive marketplace. They contended they would not be able to recover investments they had made under the assumption that state regulation of their activities would continue. These so-called "stranded costs," they argued, needed to be accounted for in the restructuring process. If the states were to accept this argument and compensate utilities in whole or part for their stranded costs, who would bear the responsibility for paying them and by what mechanism would they be recovered? Would the recovery of stranded costs be limited to the period of transition to competition or would it last longer?

There were (and continue to be) issues related to the general division of power between the federal government and the states regarding competition policy. Would states modify or even scrap their traditional regulatory authority over utilities based in their states? In this transitional environment, what would be the limits of state ability to implement retail competition? What would be the relationship between FERC's initiatives to restructure the wholesale power market and state retail competition policies? There were other federalism issues to consider: Would federal antitrust laws continue to protect consumers in light of state restructuring, or would states need to develop their own active consumer protection programs to replace the traditional protections that accompanied price regulation?

In the quarter-century since the enactment of PURPA, a number of innovative programs had been developed to interject environmental concerns into the utility industry. These programs, such as "demand side management" (DSM) and "integrated resource planning" (IRP) (*see* Chapter 13), had just begun to be adopted on a widespread basis in the industry. Would restructuring and the advent of competition slow the adoption of these programs or stall it altogether? There were other environmental concerns, such as impacts on enforcement of the federal Clean Air Act (CAA) to reduce pollution from the utility industry. With the industry fragmenting and introducing a whole new set of competitors, how would better air quality be ensured? What if state regulations associated with power plant and transmission line siting posed a tension with federal or state competition policy? Would they yield or retain primacy?

2. COMMON FEATURES OF RESTRUCTURING PLANS

Twenty-six states (as of 2004) have looked at this myriad of issues and retained the traditional regulatory approach. No state has enacted a restructuring law since 2000, when 24 states had such laws in force (although some have studied whether to do so). These laws were complex and usually the result of lengthy discussions, negotiations, task force reports, and inevitable political compromises, given the billions of dollars at stake. As a result, the features of restructuring programs differ widely from state to state. On the whole, however, each state typically addressed the following common issues:

(1) *Choice of alternate provider*: Retail electricity customers in most states have their choice of electricity generators but no choice of distribution utility. In Texas, customers choose a "retail energy provider" (REP) that in turn selects generators and sells electricity to retail consumers.

(2) *"Standard offer" or "default" service and protections for customers not selecting alternate providers*: The "duty to serve" has evolved in the competitive environment (*see* discussion below), and states have used different ways of protecting customers who choose to stay with their incumbent electricity providers:

> Four models, with variations, illustrate the major approaches used thus far: (a) the incumbent utility continues to provide service [to non-switchers] under a rate that essentially passes through the utility's wholesale cost of power; (b) the utility remains a service provider to some customers but not to others; (c) the utility continues to provide service but does so under a rate structure designed to gradually wean customers away from utility service and towards market-based prices; and (d) the privilege of serving non-choosing customers is bid out, while the utility's role is to deliver power.

NCEP Report, *supra*.

(3) *Stranded costs*: Most states set up some sort of "competitive transition charge" ("CTC") that customers pay to incumbent utilities to cover stranded costs. The restructuring laws set up transition periods during which utilities are able to assess these charges; the charges end after the end of these periods. The CTC may apply to all consumers, or, in

states such as Virginia, only to those consumers who switch to another supplier of power.

(4) *Consumer rate protections*: Many state restructuring plans promised consumers rate reductions or attempted to hold residential consumers harmless, recognizing from the outset that retail power markets would not begin full operation immediately or for a period of years. Illinois and California, promised customers rate reductions with the adoption of retail competition. Many states, such as Virginia, established rate caps designed to last for the period of years during which the state was undergoing a transition to full competition.

These rate caps have had some successes. In Texas, for example, the caps prohibit incumbent utilities from lowering rates too much and driving out new competitors. Elsewhere, rate caps have been criticized for dampening the competitive market: if consumers have the protection of guaranteed low rates, what incentive is there to switch electricity providers? As customers leaving their current utilities would give up the rate caps' protection, it is not surprising that this has been a factor in keeping switching rates low. Yet if a state did not protect its consumers, it would be gambling that a new and untested retail market would keep rates low over time. States were unwilling to take this risk, as shown by subsequent events. When some rate caps were about to expire, states without viable competitive markets faced difficult choices, and some continued the rate caps for additional periods.

(5) *Other consumer protections*: Most restructuring states set up systems designed to protect consumers in their states from abusive behavior by marketers of electricity. As retail markets emerged, state regulators needed to actively police against abuses such as "slamming" and "cramming," common to competitive telecommunications markets. Practices like this have taken place in some states but are not common in the utility industry. However, states felt the need to put specific protections into place.

The Maine Public Utilities Commission's ("MPUC") scheme is typical. *See* http://www.state.me.us/mpuc/. Electricity marketers are required to secure a license from the state. To obtain the license, a marketer must show evidence of financial capability, demonstrate that it could enter into binding interconnection agreements with utilities that would transmit and distribute its power, disclose all pending legal actions or consumer complaints from the previous year, and disclose names of affiliates. Providers furnishing power to retail customers cannot terminate service without at least 30 days' notice, and cannot make telemarketing calls to those customers who have made written "do not call" requests. The MPUC may revoke a license of a marketer that violates its terms, and can impose penalties of as much as $5,000 per day for each violation. *See* Me. Rev. Stat. Ann. tit. 35–A, § 3203.

With the adoption of comprehensive retail competition plans, state regulators also embarked on massive consumer education programs.

(6) *System benefits charges*: Either in the restructuring law itself or in a separate law, a number of states established system benefits charges designed to ensure that the environmental programs underway in the electric utility industry would be continued in a restructuring environment. These charges, the current status of environmental mechanisms under restructuring, and the impacts of air quality regulation on the utility industry as it restructures are discussed further in Chapter 13.

(7) *Exit fees and switching penalties*: If too many customers "switch" (leave the incumbent utility to purchase in a competitive market) or switch power supply providers due to short term changes in price, this could cause serious problems with the reliability of distribution. What constraints, if any, are there on the customer's ability to leave or return to the original incumbent utility? One way some states are addressing this issue is to assess exit fees (also used to compensate for stranded costs), or penalties for customers who switch power suppliers too often and thus impose costs on other customers of the power distribution system. What impact will these fees have on "distributed generation"? *See* Chapter 13.

Other states require a minimum period of purchasing competitor's power. In Illinois, where power purchase options offered by utilities were required by law to run for at least twelve months, competitive markets were slow to develop because the prices for such contracts (determined by an independent consulting firm) were set at what many consider artificially low levels. This deterred many customers from leaving the incumbent utilities and encouraged some customers that once used other retail suppliers to return to their incumbent utility. *See* Steve Daniels, A Jolt to Electricity Deregulation: Pricing Glitch is Restoring ComEd's Market Power, Crain's Chicago Business, Mar. 13, 2000.

(8) *Functional separation (unbundling)*: States typically required that utilities separate the generation function of their businesses from the transmission and distribution functions, with detailed rules about conduct to prohibit inappropriate self-dealing. This was an attempt to control the potential exercise by utilities of their market power. For further discussion of this issue, *see* the analysis of the "state action doctrine," below in Section 2.b.

a. THE TREATMENT OF "STRANDED COSTS"

The "stranded cost" issue became one of the most contentious issues in restructuring the utility industry, because it involved the distributional impacts of retail competition plans to consumers, utilities, and investors at a scale of billions of dollars for individual utilities. Although competitive electricity markets might lead toward increased efficiencies and (perhaps) lower electricity prices overall, the move towards competitive markets is not what economists would call a "Pareto" move: competition would not make everyone better off and at least some persons or groups would be harmed in the transition.

The issue is not specific to energy, as it arose in the context of telecommunications, railroad and other industries. A utility may have incurred large costs under rate regulation, such as its investment in a power plant, expecting that these costs would be recovered through regulated rates over a long period of time, typically 20 to 50 years. The basic ratemaking principle that consumers who benefit from a plant pay for it requires long depreciation schedules. Yet a lot can happen in a time period that spans half a human life. The "stranded cost" problem arises as regulators announce new policies (such as restructuring plans) that do not guarantee rate base or other rate recovery of the costs of utilities' assets. "Stranded" is an apt metaphor for this phenomenon: these assets or costs are "shipwrecked," isolated from the traditional revenue streams used to pay for them. While this problem could exist in any industry (think about how the calculator displaced the slide rule), utility regulation may exacerbate the problem by setting rate recovery expectations over 20 to 50 years (allowing new entrants to undercut incumbents with new technology) and burdening incumbents with obligations, such as the duty to serve, not faced by new entrants.

Consider this simple example: if a large investor-owned utility, say Dominion Virginia Power ("DVP"), is required to "wheel" power from a competitive generator to Widgets Co., a manufacturer and former DVP customer, what is a fair rate for DVP to charge for the transmission service? Widgets Co. would probably concede that it should pay a share of the cost of operating and maintaining DVP's transmission lines, plus a return on the capital invested in those lines. DVP is likely to argue that the rate should be higher: Widgets Co. should continue to pay for its share of DVP's generating plants, even though the loss of Widgets' business might lessen the need for that generating capacity.

Not all utility expenses or investments qualify as stranded costs. Economically, stranded costs are those that arise because the cost to the incumbent utility is higher than those faced by new entrants. Stranded cost is not an absolute concept but requires an evaluation of the relative viability of a utility's investments in its specific region and market.

Gregory Sidak and Daniel Spurber, early advocates for stranded cost recovery, defined stranded costs as, "the inability of utility shareholders to secure the return of, and a competitive rate of return on, their investment." J. Gregory Sidak & Daniel F. Spulber, Deregulatory Takings and the Regulatory Contract 27 (Cambridge Univ. Press 1997). This definition would include both utilities' operating expenses and capital outlays. Timothy Brennan and James Boyd identified four basic types of stranded costs: "(1) Undepreciated investments in power plants that are more expensive than generators today. (2) Long-term contracts—most if not all mandated by the 1978 Public Utilities Regulatory Policies Act ("PURPA"). (3) Generators built but not used, primarily nuclear. (4) Expenses related to demand-side management ("DSM") and other conservation programs that, as substitutes for new plant construction, were charged to the generation side of the business." Timothy J. Brennan & James Boyd, Stranded Costs, Takings, and the Law and Economics of Implicit Contracts, 11 J. Reg. Econ. 41 (1997). Other commentators focused on capital outlays; Herbert

Hovenkamp defined stranded costs as "investments in specialized, durable assets that may seem necessary, or at least justifiable, when constructed and placed into service under a regime of price and entry controls but that have become underutilized or useless under deregulation." Herbert Hovenkamp, The Takings Clause and Improvident Regulatory Bargains, 108 Yale L.J. 801 (1999).

The U.S. Energy Information Administration (EIA) estimated that stranded costs could lead to an increase in bankruptcies in the industry if regulators could not find a way to address them. U.S. Department of Energy, Energy Information Administration, Electricity Prices in a Competitive Environment: Marginal Cost Pricing of Generation Services and Financial Status of Electric Utilities—A Preliminary Analysis Through 2015 ix (1997). Not surprisingly, then, utilities made vigorous arguments in favor of full or near-full recovery of stranded costs. Utilities and many commentators argued that compensation for these costs is efficient because it sends investors a signal that governmental commitments are credible and will be honored. Sidak and Spulber, *supra*. Some advocates believed that disallowing stranded costs recovery would put incumbent utilities at a competitive disadvantage with new entrants, working essentially as a "negative barrier to entry." *See* William B. Tye & Frank C. Graves, The Economics of Negative Barriers to Entry: How to Recover Stranded Costs and Achieve Competition on Equal Terms in the Electric Utility Industry, 37 Nat. Resources J. 175 (1997).

Sidak and Spulber advanced the most spirited argument in favor of full stranded cost recovery. *See* J. Gregory Sidak & Daniel F. Spulber, Deregulatory Takings and Breach of the Regulatory Contract, 71 N.Y.U. L. Rev. 851 (1996) ("Deregulatory Takings"). Following responses from some academic critics, they clarified their argument in 1997:

J. Gregory Sidak & Daniel F. Spulber

Givings, Takings, and the Fallacy of Forward–Looking Costs
72 N.Y.U. L. Rev. 1068, 1074–78 (1997).

A. Four Epigrams for Protecting Private Property in Network Industries

. . . We strongly favor moving from a regulated regime to a competitive market in the network industries as quickly as possible. That transition, however, means loosening regulatory controls not only on entry, but also on the incumbent utilities. The need to compensate the incumbent utility for past, present, or future regulatory obligations does not mean that competition should be delayed. Rather, it means that regulators should recognize the full economic costs of the services that are procured through regulatory fiat and the consequences of income transfers obtained through distorted rate structures. If the economic costs of regulation are explicitly recognized, rather than being obscured in a manner that facilitates income transfers to the investors of entrant firms and to some fortunate subset of the customers of incumbent utilities, then there will be greater political scrutiny of regulatory decisions, and policy makers will redesign or remove regulations accordingly....

Compensation for yesterday's investment does not insulate today's incumbent monopolist from the hazards of tomorrow's competitive marketplace. The decision to permit the incumbent utility the reasonable opportunity to recover the full economic cost of investments made to render service to the public was a decision made long ago, when the system of regulated utilities was instituted. Paying for the incumbent's stranded costs—that is, its expected earnings under regulation net of expected earnings under competition—addresses the problem of unamortized investment. Only a continuation of regulation would create de facto protections for incumbents. Going forward, after the resolution of outstanding regulatory obligations, the incumbent then confronts the same vagaries of the marketplace as do entrants.

The cost of compensation for takings need not prevent or delay deregulation. The economic benefits of competition provide a source of funds for compensating investors who relied on the regulatory contract. Cost efficiencies and innovative technologies brought by entrants lower industry costs. There is room for competitively neutral end-user charges to recover stranded costs while still allowing lower prices. That effect is similar to paying expectation damages for breach of contract. The returns to efficient breach cover the damage payment, yielding all of the efficiency gains as surplus. The faster regulators relax incumbent burdens, the greater the mitigation of damages that would otherwise arise from continuing regulatory asymmetry. The mere fact that companies can enter new lines of business, however, is not a sufficient quid pro quo for deregulation, for competitive firms already have the right to enter new markets. It is, instead, the relaxation of government-mandated cross-subsidies and other regulatory restrictions that minimizes the cost of compensating incumbents for the regulator's abrogation of the regulatory contract.

Thus, the "greater good" of competition does not necessitate a deregulatory taking, because paying compensation and moving to competition are compatible. Moreover, the inefficiencies of regulation do not provide a basis for refusing to compensate incumbents. The inefficiencies of regulation are manifest, including the transaction costs of regulatory hearings and regulatory accounting. The distortions in incentives created by rate-of-return regulation of capital intensive firms are generally understood. Moreover, the capital equipment of regulated firms cannot reasonably be expected to be free of technological obsolescence or to be immune from the possible superior performance of new entrants. Those inefficiencies are beside the point, however. Deregulation requires the state to compensate for past contractual obligations made to private investors and to think carefully before creating new ones.

Our analysis can be summarized in four familiar epigrams. First, "a deal is a deal." The government entered into a regulatory contract with utilities in the network industries consisting of entry controls, rate regulation, and obligations to serve. The contract can be renegotiated bilaterally to prepare the ground for competition, but the voluntary exchange inherent in such renegotiation will require compensating utility investors for the loss of their investment-backed expectations.

Second, "there is no such thing as a free lunch." Someone must pay the costs of publicly mandated services. The facilities of the regulated network industries did not fall like manna from heaven, but rather were established by incumbent utilities through the expenditures of their investors. Utilities made past expenditures to perform obligations to serve in expectation of the reasonable opportunity to recover the costs of investment plus a competitive rate of return. Investors must be compensated for those past costs; it follows a fortiori that investors must be offered additional compensation if existing responsibilities are perpetuated or new burdens are imposed. Reed Hundt, chairman of the Federal Communications Commission, revealed his lack of understanding of that principle when he declared at the end of 1996 that opening the local exchange should not be called a free lunch: "The rate payers paid for this network.... My argument is that it's been a nice lunch for the entire country."

Contrary to that reasoning, the benefits of deregulation are the result of free markets, not the expropriation of investor wealth. A telephone customer has acquired no ownership in the local exchange network by virtue of having paid regulated rates for service from an investor-owned LEC, just as he could not expect to have acquired any ownership interest in Texaco by virtue of having purchased gasoline from that company over a period of years. Chairman Hundt's comment fundamentally misapprehends the legal and economic significance, traceable to Munn v. Illinois and to earlier English common law, of dedicating private property to a public purpose. In addition, his remarks show that he does not recognize that investment in a network industry does not happen only once.

Third, "an ounce of prevention is worth a pound of cure." If regulators adopt the correct pricing policies for mandatory access to network facilities and accompany such pricing rules with competitively neutral and nonbypassable end-user charges, then they will avoid the takings issue. This advice is consistent with the prudential rule, commonly attributed to Justice Brandeis's famous 1936 concurrence in Ashwander v. Tennessee Valley Authority, that courts (and a fortiori regulatory agencies, we would add) should read statutes to avoid having to decide constitutional questions. The deregulation of network industries in the United States should not have come to this. Regulators should have taken care to read statutes, such as the local competition provisions of the Telecommunications Act of 1996, in a way that would have obviated litigation over takings questions that have arisen as a result of the FCC's actions. In short, this third epigram is necessary advice to dispense because the FCC and many state PUCs have ignored the constitutional precedent concerning regulated industries that makes clear that investors in public utilities are entitled to the reasonable opportunity to recover their investment and a competitive return.

Fourth, regulators should heed the advice, "look before you leap." Before creating new forms of regulation of network industries, such as the unbundling requirements of the Telecommunications Act of 1996, regulators should compare the costs and benefits. It does little good to protest the high cost of deregulation or the inefficiencies of regulation after the fact. Optimization is achieved as the result of decisions made before networks are created and costs are sunk. After costs are sunk, protections against regulatory opportunism and deregulatory takings come into play so as to preserve future incentives for private parties to invest in network infrastructure and to enter into efficient agreements with regulatory agencies. . . .

Protection of private property from government takings means protection of investors' residual returns, as well as protection of their residual control in the absence of just compensation. ∎

NOTES AND COMMENTS

1. Sidak and Spulber compiled their arguments in a book titled Deregulatory Takings and the Regulatory Contract: The Competitive Transformation of Network Industries in the United States (Cambridge Univ. Press 1997). Their book, with more than 500 pages of legal and regulatory analysis, has been invoked in regulatory proceedings and judicial cases across the country. It was compared in its importance to Robert Bork's The Antitrust Paradox (Basic Books 1978) as proposing a comprehensive reorientation of legal principles (in this case, those governing regulated industries). For reviews of the arguments made in the book, *see* Jim Rossi, The Irony of Deregulatory Takings, 77 Tex. L. Rev. 297, 311–13 (1998); Hovenkamp, *supra*.

2. Consider Sidak and Spulber's use of the term "regulatory contract" in the title of their book. Part of this traditional "bargain" between utilities, customers, and regulators was that utilities are allowed to recover prudently incurred costs through their rates. Utilities that own generation assets insist on stranded cost recovery in part because they expected the regulatory contract to continue.

But is it fair to provide stranded cost recovery no matter what the efficiency consequences? Sidak and Spulber's opponents, such as Oliver Williamson, argued that stranded cost compensation ignored "strategic opportunism" by utilities. Williamson stated that he was not necessarily convinced that investments by utilities were "prudently incurred" or that "regulated firms are operated in least-cost ways (*i.e.*, with an absence of slack)," and called Sidak and Spulber "unduly sanguine." Oliver Williamson, Response: Deregulatory Takings and the Breach of the Regulatory Contract: Some Precautions, 71 N.Y.U. L. Rev. 1007 (1996). As the Averch–Johnson effect suggests, utilities (with the acquiescence of regulators) may have overinvested in capital. If they were overcompensated, opponents of stranded cost recovery argued, they would be sent a signal that they could overinvest in the future. *See* Elizabeth Nowicki, Denial of Regulatory Assistance in Stranded Cost Recovery in a Deregulated Electricity Industry, 32 Loy. L.A. L. Rev. 431 (1999) (arguing that monopolists should not be rewarded for their inefficient investments). Opponents also felt that stranded cost recovery would recreate many of the same problems with ratemaking that led some to view restructuring and competition as potentially more efficient. As occurred with cost-of-service regulation, utilities might seek inclusion of many items in stranded cost recovery that consumer advocates and others might find questionable. *See* Robert J. Michaels, Stranded Investment Surcharges: Inequitable and Inefficient, Pub. Util. Fortnightly, May 15, 1999, at 21.

Putting all these arguments together, the case against stranded cost recovery was perhaps expressed best by Peter Bradford, a former state PSC chair in Maine and New York:

> I want particularly to dispel the claim that some societal "compact" compels the [regulator] to assure the recovery of every dollar not found to have been spent imprudently. My conclusion is based on several propositions:
>
> 1) There never was a regulatory compact.
>
> 2) Investors have long been aware that serious losses, even bankruptcy, were possible in the electric utility industry and that no compact protected them from technological or regulatory change.
>
> 3) Electric utility investors have for many years been compensated at levels sufficient to cover the risk of some loss of their strandable investment.
>
> 4) Not all strandable commitments were prudently incurred.

Peter Bradford, Testimony Before the Vermont PSB, Docket No. 5854 (1996).

3. Sidak and Spulber also refer to "deregulatory takings." This of course suggests a possible constitutional problem with denying a utility stranded cost recovery. In recent years the term "regulatory takings" has come in vogue in such Supreme Court cases as *Lucas v. South Carolina Coastal Council*, 505 U.S. 1003 (1992). It refers to governmental regulation that goes so far to deprive the regulated party of the economic value of its property interest as to be the equivalent of the government physically taking property for public use without just compensation (prohibited by the Takings Clause of the Fifth Amendment as applied by the Fourteenth Amendment to the states). Sidak and Spulber argued that deregulating the industry would operate as a "taking" if stranded costs were not completely recovered by utilities. Sidak and Spulber, Deregulatory Takings, *supra*, at 857–58.

However, the "regulatory takings" theory turned out to be overstated; in subsequent cases (*see In the Matter of Energy Ass'n of New York State v. Public Svc. Comm'n*, 169 Misc.2d 924, 653 N.Y.S.2d 502 (Sup. Ct., Albany Cty. 1996)) and commentary it was criticized as giving short shrift to the history of utility regulation. As one commentator put it, "the 'end results' test announced in Hope can be seen as a decision to allocate to the political institutions of government near total power to protect the constitutional values underlying the takings clause in the ratemaking context." Richard J. Pierce, Jr., Public Utility Regulatory Takings: Should the Judiciary Attempt to Police the Political Institutions?, 77 Geo. L.J. 2032 (1989); *see also* Jim Chen, The Second Coming of *Smyth v. Ames*, 77 Tex. L. Rev. 1555 (1999) (arguing that "Judicial endorsement of Deregulatory Takings would reinvigorate . . . the confiscatory ratemaking doctrine" [of *Smyth v. Ames*]); Hovenkamp, *supra*.

4.   Sidak and Spulber also argued that a breach of contract theory, based on *United States v. Winstar*, 518 U.S. 839 (1996), supported stranded cost recovery. The "contract" in this case is the regulatory contract, which led some commentators to criticize Sidak and Spulber on the basis that the contract supposedly breached was not spelled out in express terms. *See* William J. Baumol & Thomas W. Merrill, Deregulatory Takings, Breach of the Regulatory Contract, and the Telecommunications Act of 1996, 72 N.Y.U. L. Rev. 1037, 1045 (1997). Even assuming a "regulatory contract" established a contract between a government and a public utility, the "breach of contract" theory was still questionable in large part because deregulation did not necessarily result in a breach (*see Energy Ass'n*, *supra*, where the New York court rejected an argument that the "failure to guarantee full recovery of stranded costs constitutes breach of contract").

* * *

In Order No. 888 (*see* Chapter 11), FERC allowed utilities to recover a large portion of their stranded costs:

> With regard to stranded costs, the Final Rule adopts the Commission's supplemental proposal. It will permit utilities to seek extra-contractual recovery of stranded costs associated with a limited set of existing (executed on or before July 11, 1994) wholesale requirements contracts and provides that the Commission will be the primary forum for utilities to seek recovery of stranded costs associated with retail-turned-wholesale transmission customers. It will also allow utilities to seek recovery of stranded costs caused by retail wheeling only in circumstances in which the state regulatory authority does not have authority to address retail stranded costs at the time the retail wheeling is required. The Rule retains the revenues lost approach for calculating stranded costs and provides a formula for calculating such costs.

FERC's decision to allow stranded cost recovery for electric utilities appears to conflict with its policies in the natural gas market, where Order No. 500 articulated a principle for resolving how the costs of uneconomic "take or pay" contracts would be shared. In Order No. 500, FERC opted for cost sharing of the stranded costs in the natural gas pipeline industry pursuant to an equitable formula. FERC made pipelines and their shareholders absorb between 25% and 50% of high-priced natural gas costs and allowed them to pass on an equal amount to their customers through a fixed charge. Any residual costs (for instance, 50% if a pipeline chose to absorb just 25% and pass through 25%) could be added to the ordinary rate and recouped to the extent that customers would buy the pipeline's expensive gas. Order No. 500, 52 Fed. Reg. at 30,337. The difference between the two Orders led to criticism of FERC's allowance of stranded cost recovery in the electric utility industry. *See* John Burritt McArthur, The Irreconcilable Differences Between FERC's Natural Gas and Electricity Stranded Cost Treatments, 46 Buff. L. Rev. 71 (1998) (noting that, "such a marked difference in approach, with outcomes so contradictory, justifies at least the presumption that something is wrong with Order No. 888.").

* * *

Is stranded cost recovery either fair because of our societal obligations to utilities, or unfair because it rewards them for their past business mistakes? In the states, this question was addressed in highly charged, politicized proceedings. Most states chose to allow utilities to recover all or most of their stranded costs. The most common mechanism used, as noted above, was a nonbypassable charge imposed on all utility customers (typically known as a CTC or "wires charge") for a transitional period of time. Pennsylvania imposed a CTC on "every customer accessing the transmission or distribution network," but to end in 2005. 66 Pa. C.S. § 2808(a)–(b); *compare* Va. Code § 56–583 (imposing a "wires charge"). Regulators and legislatures also considered "exit fees" for customers leaving incumbent utilities and often combined stranded cost recovery with rate freezes or reductions for consumers. In Pennsylvania's case the rate cap lasted for nine years.

Differences among states primarily related to the process of calculating stranded costs and their amount. To some extent, states' restructuring laws listed specific categories of costs to be treated as stranded costs. Pennsylvania's law includes "regulatory assets and other deferred charges" and "the unfounded portion of projected nuclear decommissioning costs," among others, as allowable stranded costs. Other states (such as Virginia) left this decision to PSCs. States typically disallowed costs that were not prudent investments when made, and imposed a duty on utilities to mitigate their costs by reducing them as much as possible before claiming them (renegotiating above-market power supply contracts, for example).

Beyond this, there were differences in how stranded costs were to be calculated, which was not surprising given the massive uncertainty in forecasting them. Estimating a utility's cost profile in the competitive environment was difficult. What would a utility's assets be worth in the future? Didn't that depend on knowing how competition would turn out (and in turn on knowing who the utility's competitors would be and what their costs would be)? Forecasting could be done *ex ante* (before the start of competition) or *ex post*, after competition began. *See* U.S. Department of Energy, Energy Information Administration, The Changing Structure of the Electric Power Industry: An Update, Methodologies for Estimating Stranded Costs, Appendix E (1997) (modified 1999), http://www.eia.doe.gov. Using the *ex ante* approach could lead to windfall gains or losses if calculations were incorrect; using the *ex post* approach might be more accurate but left the uncertainty to be worked out down the line. Calculations could be done "bottom-up" (computing the value of each investment that would be stranded) or "top-down" (calculating the difference in revenue likely to occur with competition).

Not surprisingly, states used different means of calculation:

> Some states, like California, used an administrative determination of stranded costs. Others attempted to gather some specific market data, preferably based on sale prices for the assets in question. Massachusetts, for instance, established an administratively determined stranded cost number, but then adjusted it downwards once utilities sold their power plants for much more than had originally been anticipated. Because stranded costs calculations depended on not only an estimate of the value of power plants, contracts and other assets under utility control, but also depended on a comparison with an estimate of future market prices, any stranded cost estimate had a substantial element of uncertainty embedded in it. As a result many states opted to adjust the stranded cost recovery periodically.

NCEP Report, *supra*, at 31.

Case Study: PECO Energy

PECO Energy, a Pennsylvania utility, filed a plan with the Pennsylvania PUC (PPUC) in 1997, requesting a total of $6.8 billion in stranded costs:

Type of Stranded Cost	Amount Requested (in $billion)
Generating Plant Investment	$3.825
Regulatory Assets	$2.589
Regulatory Liabilities	($0.005)
Nuclear Plant Decommissioning	$0.236
Fossil Plant Decommissioning	$0.127
Other Transition Costs	$0.023
TOTAL	**$6.805**

See Anthony C. DeCusatis, The Next Step for PECO Energy in its Efforts to Recover Stranded Costs, http://www.morganlewis.com/pubs/103C3350–D2DF–469E–B42D57B3A6C812E5_Publication.pdf (June 1998). The lion's share of PECO's claim was for stranded plant investment and "regulatory assets." The latter are amounts due the utility, "such as deferred income tax liabilities, that regulators would have eventually allowed utilities to collect but that would not generate returns in a competitive market." *See* U.S. Congressional Budget Office, Electric Utilities: Deregulation and Stranded Costs (1998).

PECO's claim was actively contested by a number of parties, among them the Pennsylvania Office of Consumer Advocate ("OCA"), Philadelphia Area Industrial Energy Users Group ("PAIEUG", a group of large industrial electricity users), the PPUC's Office of Trial Staff (OTS), energy marketers (including Enron, whose subsidiary New Power eventually competed with PECO in the Pennsylvania market), environmental groups, the American Association of Retired Persons, and others. Some opponents (including the OCA and OTS) argued that the value of plants not "used and useful" should be excluded from recovery. Proposals advanced by the OCA, OTS, and PAIEUG all put the value of PECO's stranded plant investment at less than $2 billion. DeCusatis, *supra*. Meanwhile, PECO collected current market data showing its stranded costs had increased to $7.46 billion.

In August 1997, PECO and some objecting parties reached a Partial Settlement and filed it with the PPUC. Under the terms of this settlement, PECO would recover $5.46 billion in stranded costs through a CTC, writing off $2 billion. In return, PECO would reduce its rates by 10% across the board in 1998. Other significant provisions would require PECO to (i) transfer its generation assets, liabilities and wholesale power contracts to a separate corporate affiliate, (ii) unbundle and permit competition in providing metering, billing and collection services for customers with retail access, and (iii) expand its universal service program and its low-income weatherization program.

Enron and others, not parties to the proposed settlement, opposed it. Their principal objections were that:

(1) The generation rate cap created a "shopping credit" (benchmark price for competition; *see* the discussion of the "price to compare" below) that, in the marketers' view, was not sufficient to promote the development of competition.

(2) The CTC would recover more than the level of stranded costs stated in the Partial Settlement.

(3) The Partial Settlement did not provide for comparison of projected and actual CTC revenues.

(4) The transmission and distribution rates set forth in the Partial Settlement were overstated because PECO should have allocated more administrative and general expenses and common and intangible plant costs to the generation function.

Later in 1997, Enron asked the PPUC for authorization to purchase "default provider status" from PECO. Enron offered to serve the 80 percent of consumers not expected to switch their electricity provider; in return, Enron offered to issue bonds sufficient to pay $5.46 billion in stranded cost payments up front to PECO, and promised a 20% rate reduction to consumers. The PPUC rejected this offer.

The PPUC also rejected the Partial Settlement, in large part because it felt PECO's estimate of stranded costs was too high. PECO challenged this rejection in federal court, raising constitutional and other issues (including the deregulatory takings claim discussed above). In the end, the PPUC and PECO settled; PECO was allowed to recover $5.26 billion in stranded costs over a twelve-year period, using a 10.75% return, less than it had sought originally. The settlement provided that recovery would be "trued up" yearly to reflect actual electricity sales. PECO also agreed to the rate reduction for its customers through 2005 and the other conditions.■

NOTES AND COMMENTS

1.   The PPUC allowed $1.1 billion of PECO's stranded cost recovery to be "securitized," under a provision of the state's restructuring law allowing utilities to apply to the PPUC for an order whereby all or a portion of the utility's right to receive future competition transition charges could be converted into a current, fully vested property right that could be pledged or sold as security for the issuance of transition bonds. 66 Pa. C.S. § 2812.

Securitization of stranded costs enabled a utility to receive cash "today, as opposed to a revenue stream generated . . . over time." Calvin R. Wong, Emerging and Nonstandard Products: A Rating Agency's Perspective, 759 PLI/Comm 347, 371 (1999). Some utilities found this attractive. It also had some benefits from a cost mitigation perspective: proceeds from the sale of "rate reduction bonds" (bonds issued to finance the stranded costs) could reduce the utility's interest expenses. Because the legislature and the PSC guaranteed the CTC (and therefore the underlying revenue stream used to retire the bonds), the capital markets could provide certainty and lower interest rates. See J. Gregory Sidak & Daniel F. Spulber, Givings, Takings, and the Fallacy of Forward–Looking Costs, 72 N.Y.U. L. Rev. 1068, 1154–55 (1997).

While some states (including California, New Jersey, Pennsylvania, and Illinois) chose to allow securitization of their stranded costs, this was not universally done. NCEP Report, supra, at 31. Securitization was controversial for a number of reasons. It was different from conventional asset securitization in that traditional securitized assets are "already an enforceable contract right at the time of their securitization and require only collection by the servicing organization." Walter R. Hall, Securitization and Stranded Cost Recovery, 18 Energy L.J. 363, 385 (1997). Fixing the level of stranded costs up front, as would be necessary for securitization, had all the potential drawbacks of the ex ante estimation approach: if stranded costs turned out to be more or less than the fixed amount, there might be a windfall or loss to the utility. See Kenneth Rose, Securitization of Uneconomic Costs: Whom Does It Secure?, Pub. Utility Fortnightly, June 1, 1997, at 32. Consumer advocates and others objected to securitization because it gave utilities an immediate payment up front, removing any future risk. Another objection to securitization was that it would put incumbent utilities in a stronger competitive position than new entrants. Rose, supra, at 32.

Indianapolis Power & Light Company ("IPL"), an Indiana utility that wanted to sell power in Pennsylvania, appealed the PPUC's securitization decision to the Commonwealth Court of Pennsylvania, asserting that by permitting recovery of stranded costs, Pennsylvania was providing PECO with a substantial advantage in the electric generation market to the detriment of out-of-state electric utilities, in violation of the dormant commerce clause. The Pennsylvania court rejected this argument. *Indianapolis Power & Light Co. v. Pennsylvania Pub. Util. Comm'n*, 711 A.2d 1071 (1998). *See* Chapter 13 for a discussion of the dormant commerce clause and its intersection with electric utility competition.

2. A key provision of the PECO settlement addressed PECO's duty to serve retail customers as a default provider. If, by January 1, 2001, fewer than 35% of PECO customers had chosen a different electric supplier, customers would be assigned suppliers to bring the number up to 35% (rising to 50% by 2003). Additionally, in 2001, under Pennsylvania's "Competitive Default Service" program, competitive bidding would take place for 20% of residential service then offered by PECO. *See* Section B.2.

3. The "shopping credit" (more widely known as the "price to compare") is an important issue in restructuring states. This figure is designed to help consumers understand whether switching electricity suppliers will save them money. The price to compare, for a residential customer, is the amount the customer would ordinarily pay the incumbent utility for the portion of the total electric bill that is competitively priced. Thus, it is the breakeven point: a new electricity supplier must undercut this price for a consumer to save money.

States that have pursued retail competition typically require the incumbent utility to separate the distinct components of generation, transmission, distribution, and competitive transition charges on customers' bills. The price to compare only includes those components that would be priced by a new supplier (typically generation and transmission), not the total electricity bill. If a state has provided for a competitive transition charge, for example, that amount continues to be paid to the incumbent utility and is not part of the price to compare. John Hanger, Pennsylvania's Record, 7 Rich. J. L. & Tech. 2 (2000).

Here are two explanations of this approach. The first is from a utility that serves customers in Ohio:

WHAT IS INCLUDED IN PRICE TO COMPARE?

Your price to compare includes your generation and transmission costs. Your generation cost is what AEP currently charges for generating the power you use. The cost of the fuel used to generate your electricity is included in that charge. Depending on which tariff applies to your service, your generation charges may be a demand charge, an energy charge or both. These charges are included in your price to compare.

Your transmission cost includes charges for the transmission of electricity and related ancillary services. Depending on which tariff applies to your service, your transmission charges may be a demand charge, an energy charge or both. Transmission charges are included in the price to compare because either you or your supplier must arrange for transmission service.

WHAT ISN'T INCLUDED IN PRICE TO COMPARE?

The price to compare is for generation supply and transmission service only. It is not your total cost per kWh for electricity. Your total cost for electricity also includes:

—Distribution service and related charges including a distribution customer charge, a distribution demand and/or energy charge where applicable, the kWh tax, the Universal Service Fund rider, the Energy Efficiency Fund rider and other riders; and

—The Regulatory Asset Charge Rider (regulatory transition charge) which recovers expenses whose collection AEP has been authorized to defer over time.

Your total cost for electricity includes your price to compare (generation and transmission charges), distribution charges and transition charges as described above.

Note: In Ohio, AEP customers' price to compare includes the price of both generation and transmission service. Not all prices to compare of other companies or in other states are calculated this way. Always be sure that you are comparing figures that represent like costs.

American Electric Power, Electric Choice, http://www.aepcustomer.com /customerchoice/.

In Texas, the "price to beat" approach is different. Under the state's approach to restructuring, customers obtain electricity service from "retail electric providers," or REPs, which provide complete electricity service to their customers (including billing and collection). Thus, the "price to beat" is a benchmark that applies to utility-affiliated REPs' (in Texas' lingo, affiliated REPs, or "AREPs") total prices for electricity, with an initial 6% price reduction. The following excerpt explains this approach:

Under the state's restructuring plan, retail price caps were imposed on the prices charged by AREPs. In January 2002, AREPs were required to reduce the electricity prices charged to residential and small commercial customers by 6%, adjusted for fuel rate revisions and certain stipulated base rate reductions not yet in effect by January 1, 1999. The resulting price provides a benchmark PTB for potential competitors.

This PTB remains in effect for the first 5 years of retail competition. However, an AREP can begin charging lower rates other than the PTB after 36 months or when the AREP loses at least 40% of its residential and small commercial customer load to competitors. After either of these events occurs, the PTB establishes only a ceiling, and the AREP may also offer lower prices. Consumers on the PTB are free to leave the AREP to accept service from a competitive retailer (a "CREP") at any time.

Larger energy consumers in Texas (those with a billing demand that exceeds 1MW) received no price cap protection.

Adjustments to the fuel portion of the PTB are limited to two changes per year, unless an AREP is unable to maintain its financial integrity under the prevailing PTB rates or if transmission and distribution costs significantly change. While the AREP may rely on generation from a variety of fuels, all changes to the fuel component of the PTB are indexed to natural gas prices. Natural gas prices have been more volatile and have increased more than the cost of other fuels since retail competition was introduced.

Jay Zarnikau and Doug Whitworth, Has electric utility restructuring led to lower electricity prices for residential consumers in Texas?, www.pulp.tc/TXReport.pdf, at 3.

In Pennsylvania, the "price to compare" approach backfired when wholesale prices for generation rose in 2001, leaving competitive suppliers of electricity largely unable to undercut the price to compare. This had a disastrous impact on the number of competitive electricity providers in the Pennsylvania market, and dramatically reduced the number of retail consumers in Pennsylvania choosing an alternate provider.

4. Following the PPUC's decision, PECO took a $3.1 billion write-off, in anticipation of losses it claimed would result from the decision. PECO stock increased from $22.93 a share before the settlement was filed to $23.96 immediately afterwards, and $30 several months later. What does this suggest about any claim PECO might have had that its "regulatory contract" with the state was breached and that it suffered damages as a result?

b. CONSUMER PROTECTION IN RESTRUCTURING

While restructuring advocates felt consumers would be better off in a competitive market, others were not so convinced. Under the traditional approach to utility regulation, the states regulated utility rates to ensure that they were "just and reasonable." That is, they struck a balance between allowing the utility to earn a rate of return on its investment and protecting the consumer against high retail rates for electricity. With the advent of competition, restructuring advocates claimed retail rates would fall, but how that would happen, and what regulatory role the states would play in bringing that about (if any), was not clear. In addition, the historical "duty to serve" customers was potentially at odds with private companies' interests in serving customers who would be most profitable to them. Finally, as traditional state regulatory structures were transformed, new questions regarding the role of federal antitrust laws in protecting consumers arise.

i. *The duty to serve and retail competition*

In a competitive market, the notion of a guarantee of service from a utility, historically part of the regulatory compact, is almost "quaint." Susan Kelly, Wholesale Electric Restructuring: Was 2004 the "Tipping Point"?, The Electricity J., 22, 25 (2005). If consumers can switch from one company to another readily, would anyone insist on this guarantee? Yet it is equally obvious that competition could create serious risks for retail customers, who might find themselves without adequate service of an indispensable commodity. In a competitive environment, "an investor-owned utility could woo a commercial or industrial customer that uses a lot of power, then ignore surrounding consumers who [were] useless." Bill Knight, Power to the People, Illinois Issues, Jan., 1997 (quoting Susan Kelly).

In a competitive retail market, the incumbent utility would be the obvious candidate to assume the default obligation to serve all customers, as it remains a natural monopoly. But this raised numerous questions about the extent of the incumbent utility's obligation and the relationship between the incumbent utility and other actors in restructuring, as the following excerpt notes.

Jim Rossi, The Common Law "Duty to Serve" and Protection of Consumers in an Age of Competitive Retail Public Utility Restructuring

51 Vand. L. Rev. 1233 (1998).

Equal application of a duty to every institutional actor providing electric utility services in competitive retail markets will pose significant economic costs and may thwart the development of retail power markets. Regulators must acknowledge a need for new approaches to financing extraordinary service obligations. The introduction of competition will create a demand for distinct interim and longer-term mechanisms for financing the duty to serve....

... Current state retail wheeling plans require, at a minimum, that the power distribution sector of the industry assume some extraordinary service obligation. There is little agreement among the states, though, about whether the various market institutions interacting with the DisCo in retail markets should also bear extraordinary service obligations. After evaluating some various state approaches, I conclude that, in emerging retail power markets, a duty to serve can continue to apply in competitive retail power markets with little disruption to retail competition, but initially this obligation should be limited to DisCos. Efficient financing of this obligation will require an appropriately set system benefits charge ("SBC") on power distribution, unbundling or mandated use of a PoolCo power exchange to facilitate supply access, and properly set exit fees. The lesson of electricity markets is generalizable to other network industries, such as telecommunications and natural gas: In these industries, too, unbundling or the development of a robust supply competitive market clearinghouse, such as the PoolCo, can work to minimize the structural inefficiencies of imposing a duty to serve and concomitant financing mechanisms on incumbent distribution utilities....

A. Continuation of the Duty to Serve in Retail Markets: The Limits of Economic Efficiency and the Importance of Distribution

Wholesale transmission access and competition among wholesale suppliers has not posed any immediate threat to the public utility duty to serve, but the introduction of retail competition requires some reassessment of the intellectual foundations for and practical application of the traditional duty to serve. The California Public Utility Commission's first order leading to the adoption of retail choice legislation acknowledged the need for consideration of this issue as customers begin to shop for power:

> To allow eligible customers to choose without restriction between the regulated price for bundled utility service and the price offered by the generation services market may severely reduce the utility's ability to plan for, and reliably serve, its remaining customers. Absent modifications to the compact's traditional duty to service, consumers may make choices about electric services which they find economically attractive, but which are undesirable with respect to the broader goal of allocating society's resources efficiently. . . .

1. The Challenge of Simultaneous Competition and Access

Of course, perceived conflicts between vigorous retail competition and customer access can be avoided to the extent that one of these seemingly incompatible goals is simply abandoned. Because it is not likely that the movement towards retail competition in traditional public utility industries will cease, one option in the face of the tension between retail competition and common law service obligations is to abandon the duty to serve for electric power markets, treating electricity service as any other service in a competitive market. After all, as retail markets open up, it will be increasingly possible for suppliers and distributors to provide a variety of service qualities to end users. Without a duty to serve, the electricity market might operate much like other deregulated markets, such as trucking and banking, which rely on contractual obligations and general consumer protection laws to ensure service delivery. If a supplier refuses service to a customer, the customer must find alternative suppliers, and competition in power generation will likely provide customers a range of power supply qualities. And, should a power distributor refuse to extend or continue service to a customer because it is not profitable, the customer may attempt to find alternatives. For example, alternatives such as self-generation or wheeling around the DisCo may be cost feasible for large, heavy load customers of electricity. Markets, after all, flourish with bilateral relationships; the duty to serve imposes a unilateral obligation on the incumbent utility. Customers in such markets already have a variety of legal protections, including credit financing and consumer protection statutes, such as the Uniform Commercial Code.

Yet, though a challenge, it is not an impossible task for regulators to establish extraordinary service obligations in competitive retail industries. Many insurance industries provide for universal service through various sorts of assigned risk pools. For example, the property insurance industry has developed Fair Access to Insurance Requirements ("FAIR") plans. In the hospital industry, the obligation of hospitals to serve the indigent is explicitly made a condition in the awarding of federal construction grants.

Nonprofit health care providers take on an obligation to provide indigent health care, in part as a condition to the grant of certain governmental benefits, such as federal, state, or local tax benefits. Although it may be questionable how successful these approaches to promoting universal service have been, the experience in these industries suggests that the conflict between retail competition and universal service is not new. Those who look askance at the duty to serve in the age of competition refuse the enormous challenge it poses, but the challenge is not an insurmountable barrier.

To date, those states that have addressed retail competition in power markets express an awareness of the potential tension between the common law duty to serve and competitive retail markets without abandoning either goal. The preamble to California's 1996 retail wheeling legislation states, "(I)t is the further intent of the Legislature to continue to fund low-income ratepayer assistance programs ... in an unbundled manner" and maintains 1996–level low-income and universal service expenditures. New Hampshire, which considered similar legislation, is more explicit:

> A restructured electric utility industry should provide adequate safeguards to assure universal service. Minimum residential customer service safeguards and protections should be maintained. Programs and mechanisms that enable residential customers with low incomes to manage and afford essential electricity requirements should be included as a part of industry restructuring.

The task of formulating extraordinary service obligations should not preclude consideration of retail competition by states, nor should it necessarily lead to the abandonment of extraordinary service obligations. In fact, the introduction of retail competition may even lead to enhancement of consumer protection obligations, perhaps from fear of the abuses markets may yield. In Ohio, for example, the consideration of retail competition has mobilized consumer protection interests, leading to the proposal of minimum electricity service standards for the first time in the state's history.

2. Rationales for the Duty to Serve and Its Application to the DisCo

At least in the short run, for small load customers, such as residential customers, small business, and single location offices, power distribution is considered to remain a natural monopoly service. Put another way, a single utility will continue to provide distribution to power supply for the large bulk of power customers. So, for most smaller customers who do not have access to capital financing markets or own rights of way to build transmission lines, it is cost prohibitive to duplicate distribution lines if the incumbent DisCo itself owns the facilities. Thus, even in competitive retail markets, DisCos will initially remain natural monopolies for residential and small commercial customers, at least with respect to the horizontal distribution market. Following California's approach, to date every state retail wheeling plan treats power distribution in this manner by defining a de jure monopoly for distribution, subject to fairly traditional regulation, effectively defining a new regulatory compact that is limited to power distribution.

Further, to date every state that has seriously considered moving to retail competition in the sale of electricity has determined that the DisCo must provide a "basic service" option to those who do not choose an alternative supplier for electricity, are refused service by a retail supplier, or have been disconnected. In some states, this will be regulated at a rate established to be less than the rates immediately prior to competition, thus minimizing the impact of stranded costs on small residential customers.

For example, according to Vermont's retail competition restructuring order, "exclusive franchises for distribution" remain necessary. The DisCo "will retain its obligation to plan, build, and operate its local distribution system in a manner that ensures safe and reliable service to customers." Vermont defines the "Basic Service Offer" as "(s)ervice offered to customers by the distribution company but provided by a retail service provider through contract." This service "(m)ay be priced either to float with the spot market or fixed on a longer-term basis." After the transition to retail competition this offer, which is limited to franchised customers of DisCos, "will be made available over a contracted period" and "through a retail service provider."

Since retail competition envisions the fragmentation of utility service into different markets, from generation to transmission to distribution, the implications of continuing the duty to serve will need to be assessed in the context of each of these markets. Given power distribution's de jure monopoly status under state retail wheeling plans, most state regulators, with little or no analysis, look initially to the DisCo as the primary bearer of the traditional duty to serve. However, given the inapplicability of the traditional rate regulation framework for understanding service obligations in the competitive market structure and the mobilization of interests likely to support imposition of new service obligations, the economic efficiency rationales for continuing to impose an extraordinary service obligation on the incumbent utility require reassessment. . . .

Despite these structural and regulatory differences between a competitive market and the traditional regulated industry, some efficiency arguments support imposition of a service continuation obligation on the DisCo or other suppliers in a competitive environment. First, with respect to service discontinuation, the physics of power flow may require the DisCo to bear some responsibility if its grid has not been modernized. Once power is supplied to a distribution grid without computerized customer metering, the DisCo is automatically the supplier of last resort to the retail customer; the customer will continue to receive power until it is physically disconnected by the DisCo. In certain areas, technology may necessitate some DisCo service continuation obligation.

A second rationale for imposition of a service continuation obligation is that power markets may yield poor information. Assuming that customers have good information about power supply options and the terms of power supply sales contracts, when compared to the DisCo, the customer will be the superior bearer of the risks of service shut-off. The customer can purchase supply plans that provide for early warning or, if necessary, insurance to cover the risks of property or other damage due to a loss of power. Many customers, though, may not have adequate information about power supply markets so as to react to the risks of shut-off, particularly where shut-off is due to technological failure or emergencies. In addition, in competitive power markets, consumers are unlikely to immediately possess the knowledge or experience to react to this information when some action, such as the purchasing of power insurance or backup supply options, is in order. Poor information or consumer discounting of risks may require the DisCo or a supplier to assume some service continuation obligation, even in a competitive power supply market. This will especially be true as these markets initially evolve and as regulators embark on the task of educating consumers.

Further, given that a welfare system already exists in our market economy, the imposition of service continuation obligations in a competitive power supply market might work to mitigate the incentives the welfare system produces for taking excessive credit risks. As competitive power markets evolve, consumers are likely to be offered credit financing plans for electricity akin to many of the financing plans available for other purchases, such as purchase of an automobile. Offerers of such sales are likely to provide creative financing options, often offering consumers who are poor credit risks high-cost financing plans. Such risks, to the extent they are repeatedly presented to low-income consumers in a competitive power supply market, will also increase the incidence of default, especially because utilities will not face the same incentives as under rate regulation to continue service with acceptance of partial payment. As customers increasingly default and lose the basic necessities of life, such as electricity service, over time this could both drive up the cost of the welfare system and undermine its poverty reduction goal. Thus, imposition of a service continuation obligation, even in a competitive market, might be seen as a way of reducing the costs of other public welfare programs.

Though some reassessment is necessary, economic efficiency arguments for continuing with some extraordinary service obligations in competitive markets are not completely irrelevant. To the extent economic arguments exist, though, they relate primarily to horizontal integration and the quality of information consumers will likely possess, because with retail competition, the market facilitates many of the transactions which the traditional public utility previously coordinated within a single, vertically integrated firm. Weaknesses with the economic efficiency rationales for the traditional duty to serve aside, to the extent regulators continue to adhere to the constituent obligations of the common law duty to serve, they will also likely need to articulate non-efficiency justifications, such as fairness or distributive justice. In this sense, retail competition is likely to force more explicit discussion of the costs and benefits of extraordinary service obligations than occurred under the traditional regulatory compact. For example, in Ohio the discussion of consumer service protections has become explicit with the dawn of competition, while previously consumer protections were sometimes built into utility tariffs on a voluntary basis.

To the extent a duty to serve continues to apply to the industry, for whatever reasons, competitively priced retail power markets will work to minimize many of the price distortions of cross-subsidization historically associated with extraordinary service obligations. Under a rate regulation regime, utility service obligations were paid for through cross-subsidization, but rate regulation helped to minimize the market distortions caused by this practice. Utilities generally were not opposed to taking on service obligations, especially where they worked to enlarge the customer base, so long as they could recover the costs of these obligations from some customers. With retail competition and a movement to market-based pricing, cross-subsidization will continue to exist, but power supply markets will require DisCos to minimize the impact of subsidies on customers or risk losing customers, especially larger ones, to bypass or other suppliers wheeling on the DisCo system. Most DisCos are attempting to cover some or all of the cost of extraordinary access (along with the costs of environmental programs) through an SBC for which the retail customers who have power delivered via the distribution system pay. FERC has observed, "the authority of state commissions to address retail stranded costs is based on their jurisdiction over local distribution facilities and the service of delivering electric energy to end users." So long as states are regulating distribution service, there is some basis for a state-imposed charge and it is unlikely that this will be preempted under the Federal Power Act.

While imposition of extraordinary service obligations on the DisCo is a common and noncontroversial element of each state retail wheeling plan to date, its implementation poses new problems for regulators. First, is limiting imposition of extraordinary service obligations to the DisCo the best way to ensure an efficient power supply, or should regulators attempt to find ways to shift some of the extraordinary service obligations to power suppliers or marketers? Second, absent the traditional levels of vertical integration, how is the DisCo to obtain basic service power and ensure reliability for incumbent customers? Will it have an obligation to provide power supply from generators it owns or operates, or should the DisCo have some other mechanism for shifting the risk of supply shortage to power suppliers or others? If the former should be the case, residential and small commercial customers are unlikely to see many of the benefits of retail competition. However, because DisCos may have little notice of power needs—and no time to notify suppliers—it may be a challenge for them to plan for reliable power. Third, and most important, how will service obligations be paid for? Structuring this SBC is likely to be the subject of rate design debate, but in the long run the SBC will become unworkable if power distribution becomes structurally competitive. Regulators, then, will be required to look to alternative financing mechanisms for consumer access.■

NOTES AND COMMENTS

1. Why are power generation companies, suppliers, marketers and brokers different from distribution companies? Should these actors also bear a duty to serve? If so, how would this be implemented?

2.   How would power be provided for the "basic service" plan used to meet consumer service obligations in a competitive market? At the outset of restructuring, proposals focused on establishing a mandatory power supply pool (mimicking the telecommunications model) competitive bidding, allocating basic service based on market share, or pure competition through a power exchange. The mandatory supply pool would require each generating company wishing to compete in a retail market to set aside a portion of its capacity for "basic service." This approach is consistent with those who argue that "[a]ffirmative [service] obligations should attach to each part of the industry." *See* Roger D. Colton, The "Obligation to Serve" and a Competitive Electric Industry 45 (U.S. Department of Energy, Office of Economic, Electricity and Natural Gas Analysis, May 1997).

The telecommunications model, implemented by federal regulators following the breakup of AT&T, allows each customers to select its preferred long distance carrier. Applying their model to electricity supply, each customer could be mailed a ballot to select its power supplier; absent consumer selection of a power supplier, the customer's basic service plan would be assigned to the incumbent DisCo. Regulators could also conduct a competitive bidding procedure for basic service, choosing one or more basic service suppliers for a defined term. A fourth approach, endorsed by the National Consumer Law Center, would assign basic service obligations to generators based on market share. *See* Barbara Alexander, Consumer Protection Proposals for Retail Electric Competition 32 (1996). For discussion and criticism of the various approaches to ensuring basic service, see Rossi, *supra*, at 1301–14.

3.   With the rise of retail competition, consumer bills have become increasingly complex. In many states, consumers are sent a monthly bill that contains itemized accounts of generation, distribution, and transmission charges. If consumers choose an alternate electricity supplier, they continue to pay their local distribution utility for transmission and distribution, and pay the new supplier for generated electricity. Consumers may pay additional charges, such as a CTC or system benefits charge. These charges are listed together on one bill, which the consumer pays to the retail (distribution) utility. As noted above, states have used the common "price to beat" (or "price to compare") approach to allow consumers to decide if they will save money in this system.

4.   The rise of distributed generation (*see* Chapter 13) challenges the necessity of the DisCo's monopoly. What if distribution is no longer a natural monopoly? Have the economic arguments for service obligations lost their relevance? In the telecommunications industry, wireless services challenge the traditional monopoly that attached to the "wires" of the local telephone company, but universal service has survived. Why? Is a physical energy market, such as electricity or natural gas, any different? For criticism of the widely-held position that distribution remains a natural monopoly in a competitive power supply market, even without microturbines, *see* Vernon L. Smith, Can Electric Power "Natural Monopoly" Be

Deregulated?, *in* Making National Energy Policy (Hans H. Landsberg, ed. 1993).

ii. The State Action Doctrine; Protecting Against Market Power

The antitrust laws are designed to protect against anti-competitive and monopolistic conduct. The overarching purpose of antitrust law is to promote competition. Most modern antitrust laws in the United States derive from important antitrust statutes passed during the late nineteenth and early twentieth centuries, such as the Sherman Antitrust Act of 1890 ("the Sherman Act"). The wording of the Sherman Act's two substantive sections—Sections 1 and 2—reflects Congress's broad public policy against anti-competitive behavior. Another statute, the Clayton Act, was adopted several years later. A variety of offenses are included under the Sherman Act and Clayton Act, including combinations in restraint of trade, price fixing, price squeeze, and other anticompetitive acts. The antitrust laws also allow courts (and the Department of Justice) to scrutinize mergers; in the electric utility context, FERC has merger authority, which is discussed further in Chapter 11.

Unlike many industries, electric utilities have not been afforded an explicit exemption from antitrust liability. Instead, the industry had traditionally been granted immunity because of the view that the industry is comprised of natural monopolies—to the extent natural monopoly regulation dominates, the protection of competition under the antitrust laws is considered inappropriate. For this reason, the courts developed antitrust immunity for the activities of most electric utilities under the state action doctrine. The following case illustrates the application of this doctrine:

TEC Cogeneration, Inc. v. Florida Power & Light Co.

76 F.3d 1560 (11th Cir. 1996).

This is an appeal from the denial of a motion for summary judgment by the district court. Two questions are presented: first, whether a public utility is immune from antitrust liability under the state-action doctrine of Parker v. Brown, 317 U.S. 341, 63 S.Ct. 307, 87 L.Ed. 315 (1943), for its allegedly anti-competitive conduct concerning a cogenerator in the areas of wheeling, rates, and interconnection; and second, whether lobbying of a county legislative body by the utility is protected from antitrust liability under the Noerr/Pennington doctrine. *Eastern R.R. Presidents Conference v. Noerr Motor Freight, Inc.*, 365 U.S. 127, 81 S.Ct. 523, 5 L.Ed.2d 464 (1961); *United Mine Workers of America v. Pennington*, 381 U.S. 657, 85 S.Ct. 1585, 14 L.Ed.2d 626 (1965). The district court found that the utility was not entitled to immunity from antitrust sanctions for its actions. We disagree. The denial by the district court of the utility's motion for summary judgment is reversed.

Appellant Florida Power & Light Company ("FPL") is an investor-owned public electric utility engaged in three functions: generation, transmission, and distribution and sale of electric energy. It services southern and eastern Florida, including most of Dade [County]. FPL is regulated by the Florida Public Service Commission ("PSC"). It owns and controls ninety percent of the total electrical generating capacity in its service area and the electrical grid with which [the Miami Downtown Government] Center can interconnect. FPL has monopoly power within its service area both as to the purchase of wholesale power and the sale of retail power.

In 1981, Dade issued requests to bid on the Center cogeneration facility. Cogenerators' proposal was selected and in late 1983, Dade and the Cogenerators entered into contracts providing for the construction and operation of a twenty-seven megawatt cogeneration facility at Center and for the supply of cogeneration equipment for the project. The Cogenerators agreed to operate Center for Dade for sixteen years. The Cogenerators also contracted to supply electrical and thermal power to Dade. Dade and the Cogenerators were to share in the profits, if any, from operating the Center; the Cogenerators were to absorb the losses. The final contract allowed for excess power, if any, from Center, to be dispensed to Dade facilities outside Center, such as to the Jackson Memorial Hospital/Civic Center complex (Hospital). Practically speaking, excess power could be dispensed only one of two ways, either via a wheeling arrangement with FPL or by constructing a separate transmission line. A separate line would require the approval of the local legislative body, i.e., the Dade County Board of Commissioners (Commission). With these parameters in place, construction of the cogeneration facility commenced in mid–1984 and the facility became fully operational at the end of 1986.

To reduce their losses, the Cogenerators sought a logical use for the excess power. Under rules promulgated by the PSC, two options were immediately available: (1) the Cogenerators could either sell the surplus electricity to FPL at a rate equal to FPL's avoided cost; or (2) the Cogenerators could force FPL to transmit or wheel the excess power to another Florida utility, who in turn would purchase it at its own avoided cost rate.

At avoided cost rates, it appeared that the Cogenerators could not break even with either option. FPL alleges that the Cogenerators deliberately ignored their two legitimate options and pursued a third, allegedly illegitimate, alternative in order to obtain higher prices for their power: the Cogenerators approached FPL to wheel their surplus power to other Dade facilities outside Center, most notably, to Hospital, two miles northwest. Believing that the Cogenerators' request violated the PSC's self-service wheeling rules,[17][1] FPL declined to wheel.

---

1. Under PSC regulations, the Cogenerators can ask FPL to wheel electricity from Center to Hospital only if they qualify under the self-service wheeling rules: (1) there must be an exact identity of ownership between the generator and the consumer of the electricity; and (2) wheeling will not increase rates to utility, i.e., FPL ratepayers. Fla.Admin.Code R. 25–17.0882. Under Florida law, a cogenerator may not sell electricity at retail. PW Ventures, 533 So.2d at 281.

Rebuffed by FPL, the Cogenerators then turned to the best efforts clause in its contract with Dade. They directed Dade, in effect, to petition the PSC for an order compelling FPL to wheel power from Center to other Dade facilities, including Hospital.

After an eleven-month administrative proceeding, the PSC denied Dade's petition. The PSC found that Dade could not comply with the PSC's self-service wheeling rules because Dade did not actually own the generating equipment that produced the power to be wheeled; did not generate the power to be wheeled; and was contractually bound to purchase the electricity from the Cogenerators. Hence, the PSC found, by definition, that Dade could not "serve oneself." Petition of Metropolitan Dade County for Expedited Consideration of Request for Provision of Self–Service Transmission, Order No. 17510, Docket No. 860786–EI, 87 FPSC 5:32, 35–37 (May 5, 1987).

After the PSC wheeling disallowance, the Cogenerators played their fourth and final card: what can't be sent indirectly, send directly. They approached Dade with a proposal to construct a separate transmission line from Center to Hospital. A separate line would reduce surplus electricity without being dependent upon wheeling by FPL at avoided cost rates. A joint submission was made by the Cogenerators and Dade to Commission for its approval. The Cogenerators lobbied Commission for approval; FPL lobbied against. The Commission voted five-to-one against the construction of the separate transmission line.

Within weeks, the Cogenerators filed this suit....

FPL's motion for summary judgment relies principally on two immunity doctrines: the state action immunity doctrine and the Noerr/Pennington immunity doctrine. The district court denied summary judgment under both.

We review each of these findings de novo.

B. The State Action Immunity Doctrine

The Supreme Court first articulated the state-action immunity doctrine in *Parker v. Brown*, 317 U.S. 341, 63 S.Ct. 307, 87 L.Ed. 315 (1943). In Parker, the Court grappled with the applicability of the Sherman Act to a California agricultural statutory program intended to restrict competition among private producers of raisins in order to stabilize prices and prevent economic waste. Relying on principles of federalism and state sovereignty, the Court refused to find that the Sherman Act was "intended to restrain state action or official action directed by a state" and determined that "[t]here is no suggestion of a purpose to restrain state action in the Act's legislative history." Id. at 351, 63 S.Ct. at 313. The Court held, therefore, that federal antitrust laws were not intended to reach state-regulated anticompetitive activities. Id. at 350–52, 63 S.Ct. at 313–14; *City of Columbia v. Omni Outdoor Advertising, Inc.*, 499 U.S. 365, 370, 111 S.Ct. 1344, 1348, 113 L.Ed.2d 382 (1991).

Thirty-seven years later, in California Retail Liquor Dealers Ass'n. v. Midcal Aluminum, Inc., 445 U.S. 97, 100 S.Ct. 937, 63 L.Ed.2d 233 (1980), a unanimous Court established a two-pronged test to determine when private party anticompetitive conduct is entitled to state action immunity from antitrust liability: (1) the conduct had to be performed pursuant to a clearly articulated policy of the state to displace competition with regulation; and (2) the conduct had to be closely supervised by the state. Id. at 105, 100 S.Ct. at 943; see also F.T.C. v. Ticor Title Ins. Co., 504 U.S. 621, 112 S.Ct. 2169, 119 L.Ed.2d 410 (1992). These two prongs are addressed below.

1.   Clearly Articulated Policy of the State.

The Court set out the first element of state action immunity in *Southern Motor Carriers Rate Conference, Inc. v. United States*, 471 U.S. 48, 105 S.Ct. 1721, 85 L.Ed.2d 36 (1985). There, the Court determined that a private party acting pursuant to an anticompetitive regulatory program need not "point to a specific, detailed legislative authorization" for its challenged conduct. Id. at 57, 105 S.Ct. at 1726. As long as the State as sovereign clearly intends to displace competition in a particular field with a regulatory structure, the first prong of the Midcal test is satisfied. Id. at 64, 105 S.Ct. at 1730.

In this case, the district court found that Florida has two statutory policies regarding power generation and transmission: a policy favoring monopoly power in Florida electric utilities, and a policy of encouraging development of Florida cogeneration facilities, complemented by the implementation of PSC regulatory guidelines. Fla.Stat. § 366.051 (1991). The district court found that these statutes set out clearly articulated policies regarding utilities and cogenerators. Accordingly, the district court found that FPL had satisfied the first prong of the Midcal test, except as to its Strategic Energy Business Study or SEBS.

We agree with the district court that Florida has an obvious and clearly articulated policy to displace competition with regulation in the area of power generation and transmission and that FPL's conduct has been performed pursuant to that policy. The Florida legislature gave the PSC broad authority to regulate FPL. See Ch. 366, Fla.Stat. Further, the relationship between Florida utilities and cogenerators has been subject to pervasive state regulation through statute and regulatory rules. Fla.Stat. § 366.05(1), 04(1), (5), .06(1), .051 (1994); Fla.Admin.Code R. 25–17.080– .091 (1988). A myriad of agency proceedings have transpired. The field has not been left to the parties' unfettered business discretion. In addition, the Florida Supreme Court has been active in its role of judicial review. See *C.F. Indus., Inc. v. Nichols*, 536 So.2d 234 (Fla.1988) (standby rates for qualifying facilities); *PW Ventures, Inc. v. Nichols*, 533 So.2d 281 (Fla.1988) (third-party sales by qualifying facilities); *Storey v. Mayo*, 217 So.2d 304, 307 (Fla.1968), cert. denied, 395 U.S. 909, 89 S.Ct. 1751, 23 L.Ed.2d 222 (1969) ("The powers of the Commission over ... privately-owned utilities [are] omnipotent within the confines of the statute and the limits of organic law.").

We disagree, however, with the district court's exclusion of SEBS from its finding. It is clear that Florida intended to displace competition in the utility industry with a regulatory structure, Southern Motor Carriers, 471 U.S. at 64, 105 S.Ct. at 1730, and FPL's internal SEBS study has no relevance to the issue of Florida's clearly articulated policy of regulation. Contrary to the district court's ruling, we conclude that the first prong of the state action defense is satisfied here, without qualification, that is, including SEBS.

2. Conduct Actively Supervised by the State.

This second prong of the state action defense applies when the challenged conduct is by a private party rather than a government official. Ticor, 504 U.S. at 630, 112 S.Ct. at 2175. Active state involvement is the second precondition for antitrust immunity; the conduct by the private party has to be closely supervised by the state. Midcal, 445 U.S. at 105–06, 100 S.Ct. at 943–44. The active supervision requirement is designed to ensure that the state has "ultimate control" over the private party's conduct, with the power to review and disapprove, if necessary, particular anticompetitive acts that may offend state policy. *Patrick v. Burget*, 486 U.S. 94, 101, 108 S.Ct. 1658, 1663, 100 L.Ed.2d 83 (1988).

The district court considered FPL's conduct in three areas alleged to be anticompetitive by the Cogenerators: (1) FPL's refusal to wheel; (2) its use of rates; and (3) its alleged interference with interconnection. It determined that for FPL to meet the second prong of the state action defense, Florida, through the PSC, must have "actively supervised, substantially reviewed, or independently exercised judgment and control" over FPL's "overall anti-competitive campaign."

In each of the three areas, the district court found that, while the PSC had the power to review FPL's conduct, it was not given the opportunity to exercise its power to review FPL's conduct. Therefore, the district court determined that the PSC's regulatory authority (in application or as applied) did not satisfy the second prong of the state action immunity standard.

As we conclude that the PSC did in fact exercise active supervision over FPL, we do not discuss these areas separately, as the same rationale applies to each.

3. The Active Supervision in this Case.

In 1987, the PSC denied Dade's petition to allow the Cogenerators to wheel power to Hospital because they could not satisfy the PSC self-service wheeling rules. In re: Petition of Metropolitan Date County, Order No. 17510 (1987).

The district court notes that FPL stands behind this PSC ruling as conclusive evidence of active state supervision. The district court finds this reliance misplaced. It focuses instead on the circumstances leading up to the PSC hearing: FPL's acts that have their genesis in the embryonic stages of Center when FPL participated in the early negotiations of the Cogenerator–Dade agreement. That is, under an estoppel-like analysis, the district court found that, when FPL ostensibly gave its blessing to the contract (with full knowledge that it contemplated: (1) the wheeling of excess power by FPL to other Dade locations; (2) the conveyance of power to other Dade facilities through a direct transmission line; or (3) the sale of excess power to FPL at avoided cost rates), it can't be heard to complain now. The district court's determination is based, not on whether the PSC had the power to actively supervise and review FPL's conduct, but on whether it was ever given the opportunity to exercise its power to supervise and review (and possibly disapprove), these early acts of FPL.

That is not the issue. The issue is this: Has the State of Florida, through its state regulatory agency, the PSC, actively supervised FPL in the areas of wheeling, rates and interconnection? The answer is clearly yes, as to each. The fact that FPL didn't complain about wheeling or rates or interconnection when it first reviewed the Center contract is not material as to whether or not the PSC had the power to actively supervise FPL. That power is insulated. FPL's failure to object does not take away from the PSC its opportunity to exercise the power of active supervision. Failure by the parties to commence an action or proceeding (at the time when the district court apparently thought they should have objected), does not constitute the nullification of the PSC's power to act.

The PSC exercises its powers only when called upon to do so. No call was made. For example, the decisions of this circuit govern or control a plethora of legal issues—but if a particular issue is never brought before us—it doesn't mean we don't have control. We don't have opportunity—but we still have control. We still have active supervision.

The record is clear—the doors to the PSC were open to all with standing to complain. Being met with a complaint, the PSC had the full power to actively supervise. Whether or not the State, through the PSC, exercises its control sua sponte is not material, unless, of course, there is an apparent devious design to abdicate or obstruct control, and that is not the case here. The record shows that, when the PSC was called upon, they acted. We, the judiciary, do not have to take a walk with the PSC members to see if they visit FPL's offices every morning.

In sum, Florida has clearly articulated policies regarding the relationship between FPL and the Cogenerators. In addition, the record is clear that the PSC actively supervised all aspects of FPL's alleged anti-competitive conduct. We conclude, therefore, that both prongs of the state action immunity doctrine are satisfied here and FPL's conduct is immune from antitrust liability in each of the three areas of wheeling, rates and interconnection.■

NOTES AND COMMENTS

1. Would *TEC Cogeneration* be decided differently today in a state with a comprehensive retail competition plan? An official with the U.S. Department of Justice antitrust division has stated:

> "If a state opens its retail market to competition, then the state action doctrine would not apply to conduct that relates directly to retail

competition," says the attorney, Milton A. Marquis. "So I think it's becoming less relevant in electricity, certainly with respect to wholesale [power], which is not a state matter anyway, but with respect to retail competition in those states that have decided to open their retail markets to competition. Because you can't have both. You can't have the state action doctrine and retail competition."

Joseph F. Schuler, State Action Doctrine Losing Relevance, Department of Justice Attorney Says, Pub. Util. Fortnightly, May 15, 1999, at 70.

2. Despite the national movement towards competition, some appellate courts continue to decide cases consistent with the approach of the Eleventh Circuit in *TEC Cogeneration. See Trigen Okla. City Energy Corp. v. Okla. Gas & Elec. Co.*, 244 F.3d 1220 (10th Cir. 2001); *North Star Steer Co. v. MidAmerican Energy Holdings Co.*, 184 F.3d 732 (8th Cir. 1999) (examining Iowa's regulatory scheme and concluding that state action immunity applies).

Under the case law, however, the case for erosion of the state action doctrine for at least some aspects of the industry, if deregulated, seems strong. In *Cantor v. Detroit Edison Co.*, it was held that a utility could be subject to antitrust liability for illegally tying the "sale" of free light bulbs to the sale of electricity. 428 U.S. 579 (1976). There, the Court found the state action doctrine inapplicable for two reasons: (1) the decision to engage in the program and to recover the costs through the company's electric rates was more the decision of the company than the state public service commission; and (2) the bundling of light bulbs to electric sales, although approved and supervised by the state agency, was not integral to the state's interest and policy in the regulation of electric utilities.

Similarly, in *Columbia Steel Casting Co., Inc. v. Portland Gen. Elec. Co.*, 111 F.3d 1427 (9th Cir. 1996), a court found that the state action doctrine did not protect an agreement between two utilities to divide the city of Portland into separate service territories. The court observed that technology and deregulation have recently been exerting competitive pressures into markets where utility monopolies once dominated. The court determined that the state commission's orders were not specific enough to meet the clearly articulated policy requirement of the *Midcal Aluminum* test. In addition, the court looked to a city ordinance that disapproved of exclusive territories and instead favored competition.

3. For further discussion of application of the state action doctrine to a deregulated electric power industry, *see* Jeffery D. Schwartz, The Use of the Antitrust State Action Doctrine in the Deregulated Electric Utility Industry, 48 Am. U. L. Rev. 1449 (1999).

B. STATE RESTRUCTURING EXPERIENCE

By the late 1990s, many states had adopted competition plans. States with retail competition plans included a number of larger states, such as New York, Illinois, Texas, and Pennsylvania, and smaller states such as

New Hampshire. Because the states were grappling with a number of complex issues while deciding to pursue restructuring, it is not surprising that they moved in a slow, incremental manner. Suedeen Kelly, a FERC Commissioner and former regulatory commissioner in New Mexico, evaluated early restructuring efforts and suggested that this approach was well paced.

Suedeen G. Kelly, The New Electric Powerhouses: Will They Transform Your Life?

29 Envtl. L. 285 (1999).

Over the last thirty years the price of electricity has soared. This spurred experimentation with competition in the generation of electricity. In 1992, Congress promoted wholesale competition in the generation of electricity with the passage of the Energy Policy Act. The year 1999 finds seventeen states embarking on retail competition in generation. They are looking for choice, lower costs, and innovation—typical attributes of a competitive market—but they do not want to lose the reliability, universal service, and environmental protection that the regulated generation monopoly brought us. Trying to achieve all of these goals poses an enormous challenge for state policy makers. The issues they must resolve are difficult ones, and some of them are novel to regulatory policy. They include recovery of stranded costs, criteria for approval of mergers and acquisitions, and cost-shifting from large to small electricity consumers. So far the states have worked to solve these uncommon problems with uncommon sense. They are proceeding slowly, on a state-by-state basis, using consensus-building processes, and showing willingness to devise creative solutions that will also be politically acceptable. While this is the very process that foretells a successful transition to a restructured industry, it is threatened by objections that it is too slow, lacks uniformity, and results in solutions at odds with our economic models. These objections have merit. However, they should not be heeded because their merits are outweighed by their costs. . . .

A dream of many people is that the Summer of the Future in the electric industry can be even better than the Summer of' 98, and they have acted to realize that dream. To wit, twelve states [as of Summer 1999] have passed legislation to restructure their electric companies. These states include the usual suspect, California; but also the unusual, Arizona, Montana, and Oklahoma; and the unusually thoughtful, Connecticut, Illinois, Maine, Massachusetts, New Hampshire, Pennsylvania, Rhode Island, and Virginia; as well as the uncategorizable, Nevada.[44][2] Another five states

2.   Cal. Pub. Util. Code § 391 (West 1998); Ariz. Rev. Stat. Ann. § 30–803 (West 1998); Mont. Code Ann. §§ 69–8–101 to 69–8–104 (1998); Okla. Stat. tit. 17, §§ 190.1–190.9 (1998); Conn. Gen. Stat. Ann. § 16–244 (West 1998); 220 Ill. Comp. Stat. 5/16–101 to 5/16–130 (West 1998); Me. Rev. Stat. Ann. tit. 35–A, §§ 3201–3217 (West 1998); Mass. Gen. Laws ch. 164, § 1A (1998); N.H. Rev. Stat. Ann. § 374–F:1 to 374–F:7 (1998); 66 Pa. Cons. Stat. Ann.

are embarking on restructuring by regulatory order,[45][3] and at least seven other states have initiated pilot projects.[46][4]

The states that have developed restructuring plans have, by and large, tried to keep the benefits of regulation we have talked about (reliability, universal service, environmental protection) while also seeking the benefits of competition. Of course, it is one thing to want change and another thing to succeed with it. With the exception of California, none of these states has gone beyond the threshold of restructuring, so it is difficult to predict whether they will succeed. But, by and large, they seem to have gone about solving the problems associated with restructuring in a promising way.

A. Common Sense Can Be a Mistake

Always using common sense to solve problems is sometimes a mistake. I believe this is particularly true with the restructuring of the electric industry, where the goals are so uncommon. To succeed in this effort, we need decision makers with uncommon sense. There are three uncommon things going on in restructuring efforts across the states that lead me to believe we may succeed with reform.

1. Uncommon Characteristic Number One: Proceeding Slowly

First, we are proceeding very slowly—with, of course, the exception of California. However, we thank California for its bold experiments that so richly benefit the rest of us. Restructuring has been under consideration to some degree in most states since Congress passed the Energy Policy Act in 1992. While seventeen states have announced industry restructuring, sixteen of them are only just getting started. In short, there's been no rush to abandon the old and bring in the new, a sometimes uncommon response in the face of strong political pressure to change.

2. Uncommon Characteristic Number Two: Restructuring State-by-State

Second, we are restructuring on a state-by-state basis rather than at the federal level. Although there have been more than a dozen bills introduced in the House and Senate of Congress to restructure at the federal level, the word out of Washington is that, at least for the time being, the leadership is not going to move this legislation.

§§ 2801–2812 (West 1998); R.I. Gen. Laws § 39–1–43 (1998); 1998 Va. Acts ch. 633; Nev. Rev. Stat. Ann. § 704.976 (Michie1998).

3. These states are: Maryland, Michigan, New Jersey, New York, and Vermont. 181 P.U.R.4th 185 (Md. P.S.C. Dec. 3, 1997) (Nos. 8738, 73834); 177 P.U.R.4th 201, (Mich. P.S.C. June 5, 1997) (No. U–11290); Docket No. EX94120585Y (N.J.B.P.U. April 3, 1997); 168 P.U.R.4th 515 (N.Y.P.S.C. May 20, 1996) (Nos. 94–E–0952, 96–12); 174 P.U.R.4th 409 (Vt.P.S.B. Dec. 30, 1996) (No. 5854).

4. These states include: Idaho, Iowa, Missouri, New Mexico, Ohio, Texas, and Washington. See U.S. Energy Info. Admin., Status of Electric Industry Restructuring by State (last modified Feb. 1, 1999) <http://www.eia.doe.gov/cneaf/electricity/chg_str/tab5rev.html> [hereinafter U.S. Energy Info. Admin., Restructuring by State].

3.   Uncommon Characteristic Number Three: Using Consensus–Building Processes

Third, it seems in most states, reform is occurring through a variety of attempt-to-build-consensus processes. For example, even in California, which moved quicker than any other state, the administrative proposal was on the table for public comment and rearrangement for twenty months before a final administrative plan was adopted. Then, the legislature scrutinized it for nine months and replaced it with legislation that was the product of a three-week-long, eighteen-hour-a-day, give-and-take marathon negotiation among the California legislative leadership and all the stakeholders in the industry. The restructuring legislation ended up being passed unanimously by both houses of the legislature.

B.   Three Common Sense Threats to This Approach

This restructuring process, which involves moving slowly on a state-by-state basis and taking into account the interests of the many stakeholders in this business, holds promise for successful reform because it fosters novel and creative solutions to the many issues that are implicated by restructuring. However, this uncommon approach is being assaulted on three fronts by objections that are, arguably, common-sense ones.

First, the frustration of some with the slowness and diversity of a state-by-state process is creating pressure in Congress to mandate a universal solution. Second, the common knowledge that there is no pre-existing solution to some of these first-ever problems is creating pressure to duck these issues and restructure without first resolving all the problems. Third, the belief that some problems are plausibly susceptible to solution using existing models is creating pressure to abandon real problem solving and substitute "the model."

I'd like to discuss three restructuring issues that illustrate what I'm talking about, that is, successfully using uncommon solutions for a problem that, arguably and unsuccessfully, could be solved with common solutions.

1.   Uncommon Example Number One: Stranded Costs— Who Pays?

Common sense is the knowledge a person attains based on society's conventional wisdom. But, as Chris Marianetti, only sixteen years old but a national oratory finalist, put it, "Too often common sense serves as a sort of thoughtless mastery, and that is not an oxymoron." In electric industry restructuring, stranded costs are an uncommon problem that cannot be eliminated with a common solution. Stranded costs are what many of today's utility generators are going to have when competition comes to electricity. For example, today generators may need to be paid, say, six cents per kilowatt-hour ("KWH") to cover all the costs of having built, and now having to operate, an electric generator. Today, that's not a problem because they have a monopoly on the sale of electricity, and the regulator will set the price to allow them to recover the six cents per KWH they need. Tomorrow, however, when the competitive market takes hold and the lower cost generators start producing, the market price might well be just four cents per KWH. By market definition, today's utility will only be able to sell its power at four cents, although to make ends meet it needs to sell it at six cents. The two cents per KWH difference is the utility's stranded cost. Who is going to carry this loss? There are only three potential payers: the utility's shareholders, if it's an investor-owned utility, the consumers of electricity, or the taxpayer—or some combination of these.

Different states have approached this issue differently, and with unusual ideas. In California and Massachusetts, for example, utilities are potentially going to be able to recover all stranded costs associated with their own generation facilities from consumers. Although, in California the recovery period is four years, while in Massachusetts it is ten years.

In Connecticut, in order to recover from consumers the stranded costs associated with their generation facilities, utilities must first sell their generation assets. They must sell their nonnuclear generation by January 2000 and their interest in nuclear generation by January 2004. Each state has a variation on how stranded costs will be determined and how they will be recovered.

The threat to continuing to solve the stranded-cost problem in this case-by-case mode is the notion that a universal solution to this issue would expedite the restructuring process and add certainty of outcome for all stakeholders. Indeed, this is a common sense solution, but it is a thoughtless one because the issue of stranded costs is much more than an economics issue. It is a big values issue, especially to consumers. Many of today's consumer advocates were involved in administrative disputes in the 1970s and 1980s over the building of these generators. They took the position that they were too costly to build. They lost the cases then. Now they are in an "I told you so" mood. They are angry at having had to pay high costs, and they don't want to take it anymore. Many utilities with high-cost generation have suffered, too. Often, rates were set at a level insufficient to recover totally the costs they incurred and their stock values and bond ratings tumbled. They don't want to be handicapped with stranded costs at the same time they look to compete with new entrants in the generation market.

In short, the country's stranded cost problems are local, historical, and ideological, as well as economic. They need to be solved in individual and uncommon ways.

2. Uncommon Example Number Two: Utility Mergers— Good or Bad?

In order to achieve all the economic objectives of restructuring (i.e., choice, lower costs, and innovation) the market for generation has to work when all is said and done. Unfortunately, there is a lot we do not yet know about the relationship between the structure of a market and its performance. However, we do know that highly concentrated markets do not usually perform as well as less concentrated markets. If we are to have a competitive market in generation, we need to be concerned about the expected competitive effects of proposed utility mergers, especially with respect to likely future concentration. This is not an easy issue with which to grapple.

Although our antitrust history provides us with quite a bit of data regarding the likely competitive effects of proposed mergers in existing unregulated, competitive markets, there is little available on proposed mergers in new markets being formed by regulators out of regulated markets. This is different because when a market is just forming, particularly when it is forming under a regulatory regime, regulators can and will take regulatory actions that will affect it. For example, in the electric industry, if regulators are willing to take action to force utilities' transmission systems to eliminate transmission constraints regionally or nationally, the electricity market will be broadened and a particular merger might then pose less of a concentration threat.

The bottom line is that developing criteria for approving mergers in the emerging new market is going to be a difficult and complex undertaking. Today, most utility mergers must be approved by the Federal Energy Regulatory Commission ("FERC") as well as by the state public utility commissions of the states affected by the merger. FERC only looks at the likely effects of the merger on wholesale competition. The states have exclusive jurisdiction over the effects of the merger on retail competition.

Because this will be a difficult issue to decide, the danger is that state decision makers will forego a serious attempt at analysis and adopt a reflex reaction that could either be that bigger is better, or bigger is worse. Certainly, in some instances bigger will be better, like when it is necessary to create a new entrant in the market. But in some instances bigger will not be better because it will have an anticompetitive effect.

About a year ago, in one state, which should go nameless but which I can tell you is situated next to Washington, D.C., and is not Virginia, a merger of the two largest utilities in the state was approved with absolutely no evaluation of the likely effects on retail competition. It might be said that it was a common sense approach to the merger (not to analyze anticompetitive effects on retail competition) because the state did not have any retail competition in place. However, shortly after the commission approved the merger, which resulted in the newly combined utility serving over eighty percent of the state's market in generation, it announced that it was going to actively consider restructuring the industry in the state.

Needless to say, if the state had initially acted in considering the merger with some thoughtfulness, it likely would not have ended up with the handicap it now has in trying to introduce competition successfully into generation in the state. To quote John Wooden, UCLA's legendary coach with extraordinary success in competitive endeavors, "It's what you learn after you know it all that counts."

In restructuring the electric industry, we are likely going to face numerous problems whose solutions will demand knowledge beyond that which we already have acquired. Success will lie in forcing ourselves to learn more than we now know.

3. Uncommon Example Number Three: Cost–Shifting— From Regulated Rates to Market Rates, or Something In- Between?

In their book, For the Common Good, Herman Daly and John Cobb, Jr., have observed that "[o]utside the physical sciences no field of study has more fully achieved the ideal form of academic discipline than economics." And precisely because of its success, it has been particularly liable to the commission of the "Fallacy of Misplaced Concreteness." The fallacy of misplaced concreteness, as Daly and Cobb explain it, is the application of tried and true economic conclusions to the real world—without recognizing that the seemingly concrete conclusions are actually the product of a high level of abstraction and sometimes are not appropriately applicable. The fallacy of misplaced concreteness is a threat to devising creative solutions to the cost-shifting problem in electric industry restructuring.

The cost-shifting problem arises from the fact that electric utilities have forever been subject to rate regulation. Rate regulators do not like to raise rates, particularly residential rates, because of the political fallout that always occurs. I learned this lesson painfully with one of my decisions as a novice rate regulator. A particular utility had sought a rate increase. My fellow commissioners and I ultimately determined the facts necessitated a rate decrease. It would be the first time anyone could recall a New Mexico utility regulator ordering a rate decrease. We announced the decision with great relief that we did not have to order residential rates increased and deal with the usual attendant political fallout. Naively, we thought the residential customers would be happy. But we were quite anxious about the political fallout that might occur at the behest of angry shareholders. We were right to be anxious, but we were wrong about what to be anxious about. The State Attorney General, the advocate for residential consumers, was the angry and vocal one—for our failure to lower residential rates enough. Ah, the pitfalls associated with acting on misplaced conventional wisdom.

One more observation on the subject of residential utility rates: regulators almost universally have tried to keep residential rate increases to a minimum by raising industrial rates a bit more than a politically blind cost analysis would peg them. In economic terms, in today's regulated world, the larger consumers more often than not subsidize the smaller ones. When generation becomes competitive (i.e., when the market sets electricity rates) this will change. Smaller consumers will feel the burden of the shifting costs from the larger consumers to them.

Whether smaller consumers will actually feel a rate increase in a particular jurisdiction in a new market setting is difficult to predict. One New Mexico legislator has said that if it were to happen, it would be political suicide for the legislators or regulators deemed responsible for restructuring. Indeed, even the possibility that residential consumers might not see as big a rate decrease as industrial consumers is a big political concern. In sum, the fact that there will be cost-shifting is an issue that must be addressed in planning for restructuring.

The traditional economics-based solution would be to accept the shifting of costs to smaller consumers as a fact of economic life—indeed a necessary development of the efficient marketplace. "Homo economicus" would say the problem is not the shifting of costs but the negative perception of the shifting of costs. As "Hamlet the Economist" might argue "there is nothing either good or bad but thinking makes it so." The economist's response would be to focus on the negative perception as the problem and solve it by educating the public, or by spin-doctoring, or a combination of both. Thus, the economic argument goes, if the worst happens (such as the rates rise so that the most needy among us cannot afford the new cost of electricity), devise a safety net through the welfare or tax system. "Homo politicus" would respond that allowing the market to handle this issue as it saw fit would be committing the fallacy of misplaced concreteness, not to mention political suicide.

So far, most states have rejected the common sense economic solution of letting the market handle the cost-shifting issue in its conventional and efficient wisdom. For example, in California the legislature ordered all utilities to freeze customer rates at levels in existence on June 1996, except that rates for residential and small commercial customers must be lowered by ten percent. To allow utilities to accomplish this without losing money, the legislature authorized a secure stranded cost recovery mechanism that resulted in the utilities actually being able to lower their costs. In other words, as the restructured industry moves forward, small customers have been guaranteed a rate decrease.

Cost shifting has been held at bay by a guaranteed rate decrease in a number of states. It is not an elegant mechanism; it is not an efficient mechanism. It is an unconventional mechanism. Will it work? It is too soon to say, but I cannot help but think about the first air-conditioner that Arthur Miller described. A cooling machine rolling about on casters was certainly unconventional. Having to fuel it with pitchers of water was not very efficient. The fact that it spurted water everywhere upon its filling was hardly elegant. But it did come to change our lives, for the better.

Reordering an industry that began one hundred sixteen years ago, that came of age sixty years ago, and that hit productive middle age thirty years ago is an unconventional development. The process going on in the states to restructure the industry is likewise unconventional but seems to be working uncommonly well....■

NOTES AND COMMENTS

1. Kelly "thank[s] California for its bold experiments that so richly benefit the rest of us." In light of the catastrophic debacle that took place in that state shortly after the publication of this article, would she reevaluate that position today?

2. Market power problems have been identified in California and several other markets that have implemented retail competition. The disastrous experience with California's restructuring plan, particularly the demon-

strated ability of companies to manipulate the electricity market for private gain, shows that market power is an extremely important issue in restructuring and can produce serious problems in a state if the electricity marketplace is not set up appropriately:

> When many state policymakers looked hard at their power industry they saw one in which there was cause to worry about the ability of a small number of parties to control market prices. They further observed that even the ability ... to control market prices for a small number of hours during the day could be significant....
>
> As proof emerges showing the complex ways in which now-bankrupt Enron and other companies found ways to manipulate electricity markets, it ... is also clear that at least some of what one state— California—did to try to address market power did not work.

NCEP Report, *supra*. States employed different mechanisms to control market power. First, they required *functional separation ("unbundling")*: the electricity supply operation of a utility would be separated "functionally" (isolated, but not legally divested) from the transmission and distribution side of the business. Typically, utilities complied with this by creating affiliate organizations for the different functions. States took a number of precautions to make sure that the affiliates did not self-deal in ways that would allow for excess market power. They required utilities to file plans with the state PSC detailing how corporate structures, accounts and records would be maintained separately, and (in codes of conduct often governed by state rules) how they would avoid sharing of important information. *See* Va. Code § 56–590 and 20 VAC 5–202–10 *et seq.* (functional separation rules); W. Va. Code § 150–3–15. Functional separation has been criticized as an imperfect means of avoiding concentration of market power, as "it leaves in place the incentives to discriminate and cross-subsidize in an industry in which detection and documentation of violations may be difficult." Electric Restructuring, Comments of the Staff of the Bureau of Economics of the Federal Trade Commission Before the Michigan Public Utility Commission (Case No. U–11290, Aug. 7, 1998).

With the advent of competition, some utilities were almost certain to (and eventually did) spin off their generation businesses. Still, states were not quick to go beyond functional separation and require *full divestiture* of generation assets from transmission and distribution functions, viewing this as interfering inappropriately with utilities' business decisions. An exception to this was Maine, which required its utilities to divest generation from transmission and distribution. Me. Rev. Stat. Ann. tit. 35–A, § 3204. While California is often cited as a state that required divestiture, it did not; instead, it provided an incentive in the form of a higher rate of return on remaining assets for utilities that divested themselves of generation assets.

States cannot do all of the work in controlling market power, and this issue has been addressed in a number of ways at the federal level. FERC has two levers under the Federal Power Act to control utilities' market power. First, it can review and approve pending mergers in the utility industry. Second, it can take action to ensure that wholesale rates charged are "just and reasonable." Under the controversial process which FERC has undertaken to determine a utility's market power, it first applies various computational screens and then uses the results to bring individual proceedings. FERC uses the Supply Margin Assessment ("SMA"), as revised in a FERC Order from 2004 establishing two separate screens, the "Pivotal Supplier Analysis (PSA)" and "Market Share Analysis ("MSA")" against specific companies believed to be capable of exerting market power. A company that believes the screens are inaccurate may call for a "Delivered Price Test" for a more detailed analysis, or can bring other evidence to rebut the presumption of market power.

These mechanisms are discussed further in Chapter 3 and Chapter 11.

4. In many states, "pilot programs" were pursued as a gradual way of implementing retail competition. For example, in early May 1996, New Hampshire marketing groups began competing for 15,000 customers as a part of a two-year retail wheeling pilot program. *See* J. F. Schuler, Jr., Residential Pilot Programs: Who's Doing, Who's Dealing?, Fortnightly, Jan. 1, 1997. Pilot programs have also been used in states with restructuring plans that have found it difficult to transition to competition, with mixed results. *See* Greg Edwards, To market, to market: Deregulation hasn't sparked competition or lower prices, Richmond Times–Dispatch, Mar. 21, 2005, at D18 (noting that three pilot programs offered by Dominion Virginia Power, the state's largest utility, have attracted little interest).

1. SAMPLE STATE COMPETITION PLANS

The following excerpt describes the basic elements of restructuring plans in three states—Massachusetts, Texas, and Pennsylvania.

U.S. Department of Energy, Energy Information Administration, The Changing Structure of the Electric Utility Industry: An Update (2000)

This section presents the current status of restructuring in ... Massachusetts, Pennsylvania, and Texas.... Pennsylvania, and Massachusetts were chosen because they were among the first States to institute restructuring at the retail level and they did so differently. Texas has recently passed restructuring legislation and its utilities and public utility commission are planning for competition which will begin in 2002.

Texas

Much of Texas is unique in that it is not subject to the control of FERC.... Because utilities in the Texas Interconnected System are not connected with other utilities outside the State and electric trade does not cross State boundaries for these utilities, FERC does not have regulatory jurisdiction over them. In 1998, Texas was near the middle of the rankings of all States and the District of Columbia with respect to electricity rates. In 1998, the average revenue per kilowatthour was 6.07 cents, which ranked as the 25th lowest in the country. With prices in the middle of the range of States, it is not surprising that Texas recently passed restructuring legislation.

In 1995, Senate Bill 373, which became the Public Utility Regulatory Act of 1995, was enacted to restructure the wholesale electricity market in Texas consistent with FERC requirements for unbundled transmission service.... In 1996, the Public Utility Commission (PUC) of Texas issued rules implementing the legislation that required transmission-owning utilities in the State to provide open access to the transmission system and ancillary services. The rule also required separation of transmission, distribution, and generation costs and rates, and the establishment of the ERCOT ISO.

In 1999, Texas was the largest State to pass restructuring legislation. Governor George W. Bush signed Senate Bill 7 to introduce retail competition to Texas ... Retail choice will begin in 2002. The restructuring law freezes rates for 3 years or until 40 percent of a utility's customers have switched to an alternate provider, whichever comes first. The law is expected to give a boost to development of renewable energy sources. Utilities can recover an estimated $9 billion in stranded costs through securitization....

As of January 10, 2000, all Texas IOUs had filed detailed plans describing how they propose[d] to unbundle their operations.... The companies were also required to describe how they would separate their businesses into a retail provider, a generation company, and a transmission and distribution utility.... By September 2001, the PUC will begin to certify retail electricity providers. The Texas Pilot Program is scheduled to commence on June 1, 2001, and on January 1, 2002 retail choice is slated to begin with small commercial customer and residential electric rates decreasing by 6 percent. A proposal for a consumer education plan has been approved by State regulators....

The Texas approach to implementing competition has been cited as a good model for restructuring. The decision to deal with wholesale issues at the outset by leveling the playing field for equal transmission access "promises to create a strong retail market," according to one energy consultant. With regard to renewables, a new rule mandates the building of 2 gigawatts of new capacity fueled by renewable sources by 2009.... January 1, 2002, will mark the beginning of a Renewable Credits Trading Program in the State, which will continue until 2019. Retailers with insufficient credits will be penalized $50 per megawatthour or 200 percent of the average cost of traded credits of the year.

Massachusetts

On November 27, 1997, HB 5117, the Electric Utility Restructuring Act, was signed by Governor Paul Cellucci to restructure the industry in Massachusetts.... The Restructuring Act mainly affects the Commonwealth's eight investor-owned distribution companies, which supply 87 percent of the electricity in Massachusetts. Retail access was required by

March 1998, and a simultaneous rate cut of 10 percent to be followed 18 months later by an additional 5 percent cut was made law. Municipal utilities have the option to participate. Additionally, the divestiture of generation assets was encouraged. In 1996, Massachusetts had the eighth highest electricity rates in the Nation, which were most certainly a consideration in enacting the legislation the following year....

Three generation service options are available to consumers: (1) Standard Offer Service, provided by distribution companies; (2) Default Service, provided by distribution companies; and (3) Competitive Generation Service, provided by competitive suppliers. The price the customer pays for generation service is dependent on the type of service that the customer receives....

Competitive Generation Service will be provided by competitive suppliers and electricity brokers that have been licensed by the DTE.... As of May 2000, 33 authorized competitive suppliers/electricity brokers were located in Massachusetts.... Prices for Competitive Generation Service will be set by the competitive electricity marketplace; these prices will not be regulated by the DTE. Customers receiving generation service from a competitive supplier have two billing options: (1) complete billing, where a customer receives a single bill from the distribution company, including charges for generation service, and (2) pass-through billing, where a customer receives two bills—one from the distribution company for non-generation charges and another from the competitive supplier for generation service charges.

The generation portion of the electric industry is now virtually all owned by independent power producers. This extensive sale of power plants has significantly reduced the stranded cost obligations that would have been facing ratepayers. Massachusetts had awarded stranded costs if conforming utilities had demonstrated that they had divested all non-nuclear generation and attempted to mitigate all other costs. So far, approximately $2 billion of the total $6 billion that will eventually be paid has been transferred. Securitization then becomes permissible.

ISO New England received conditional FERC approval on June 25, 1997. Utilities in all six New England States created the ISO through a voluntary agreement. Additionally, proposed construction of more than 30 gigawatts of new power plants has been announced across the region, prompted by restructuring legislation enacted in most of the New England States. While not all proposals will come to fruition, it is likely that the increased competition from these new plants will force some of the existing, less efficient plants into retirement. Most of the new capacity will be fueled by natural gas and other low emission fuels; therefore air pollution should be lowered and customers will have the option to buy greener power from sources close to home.

Pennsylvania

Governor Tom Ridge signed the Electricity Generation Customer Choice and Competition Act into law on December 3, 1996. The law basically separates the generation of electricity from the services of transmitting and distributing it. The law called for a phase-in of retail choice with one-third eligible to choose by January 1998, another third by January 1999, and the remaining third by January 2000. Therefore, all customers in Pennsylvania can now choose the generator of their electricity, but they are still required to purchase the transmission and distribution components of their electricity from the local supplier. All utilities subject to the separation requirements were required to file their restructuring plans with Pennsylvania's Public Utilities Commission (PUC) in 1997. The PUC has established industry groups to provide recommendations on areas of concern that have arisen in the restructuring process. These areas include education, information and billing, universal service, conservation, reliability, direct retail access implementation scheduling, metering competitive safeguards, interaction between suppliers and utilities, and taxes. . . .

With regard to stranded costs, the PUC is authorized to determine the level of stranded costs that each utility is permitted to recover. . . . through a non-bypassable competitive transition charge ("CTC") that will be reviewed and adjusted annually for each customer who elects to receive service from an alternative generation supplier. . . .

Electric utilities are permitted to divest themselves of facilities or to reorganize their corporate structures, but unbundling of services is required. As a result of the new law encouraging outsiders to set up business within the Commonwealth (unlike Florida whose Supreme Court recently reaffirmed restrictions on merchant plants), interesting developments have occurred. For example, the largest wind farm in the eastern United States is now in Pennsylvania. GreenMountain.com, which completed the eight-turbine project in April 2000, is betting that customers will pay a slight premium to switch to power that is cleaner than the traditional source of Pennsylvania's electricity—coal.

Today, 52 suppliers are licensed to sell their generation in the Commonwealth. . . . One of the keys to Pennsylvania's successful transition to a competitive retail marketplace may have been its pilot program. The program provided an incentive to participate by guaranteeing a 10–to 13–percent discount off the electric distribution company charge for all classes of customers while establishing a generation credit that allowed customers to obtain electricity supply at 5 to 20 percent below the credit.■

NOTES AND COMMENTS

1. Massachusetts took a unique approach to the issue of service for customers who did not choose an alternate electricity provider. Originally, "Standard Offer Service" served all non-switching customers. A customer that did not select a competitive supplier by March 1, 1998 automatically received this service. Standard Offer Service was a transition generation service set to be phased out by mid–2005, with rates set in advance (reflecting the initial 10% rate reduction, increasing to 15% in 1999) and increasing gradually. In general, once customers selected a competitive

supplier, they were no longer eligible to return to Standard Offer Service. After the end of Standard Offer Service, all non-switching customers would be served by a second form of regulated service: Default Service, with pricing set on a benchmark not to exceed average New England market prices. Default Service provided two different pricing options: fixed (with prices averaged and held constant for 6–month periods) and variable (with prices changing monthly).

The hope was that more customers would be encouraged to select a competitive option, with Default Service serving as a transition to full competition. However, with switching customers precluded from returning to Standard Offer Service, Default Service became the service of last resort. By the end of 2004, only 4.7% of retail customers in Massachusetts had switched their electricity provider. *See* http://www.state.ma.us/doer. A number of factors accounted for the low switching rate. At the beginning of restructuring, few customers saw the need to choose competitors due to low Standard Offer rates; in 2000 only 7,302 of Massachusetts' 2.5 million electric customers had switched to competitors. EIA, *supra*. In a theme which would be repeated in other states, the volatility of wholesale market prices also played a part, with consumers opting for lower-priced default options over subjecting themselves to price spikes in the wholesale market. *Id.*

Does the Massachusetts experience suggest that it is impossible to balance rate protections for consumers during the transition to competition against the desire to develop a competitive market? If not, how could the state have gone about protecting its consumers while simultaneously developing the competitive market?

2.   The Texas retail market opened to full competition in 2002, except for those utilities such as municipals and small cooperatives that opted out of the program. By 2005, Texas could brag that it had the most competitive retail electric market in North America, and the third most competitive in the world. *See* Public Utility Commission of Texas, Report to the 79th Texas Legislature: Scope of Competition in Electric Markets in Texas (2005) (PUCT 2005 Status Report). Sorting through the evidence to date, Professor Jacqueline Lang Weaver concludes that "the consensus seems to be that Texas is doing 'OK'—not a resounding success, but certainly not a failure." Jacqueline Lang Weaver, Can Energy Markets Be Trusted?: The Effect of the Rise and Fall of Enron on Energy Markets, Houston Bus. and Tax L. J. 1, 130 (2004). In part, the relative success in Texas was due to the state's unique integration of retail and wholesale regulation under one state legislature and one state public utility commission, without FERC oversight or interstate conflicts. Texas Remains Retail Choice Leader, RED Index Shows, But U.S. Progress Stalled, Transmission & Distribution World, Oct. 30, 2002.

The wholesale market in Texas opened to competition in 1995, but it was the historic formation of the Electric Reliability Council of Texas (ERCOT) that catalyzed the development of a centralized market focused on competition. Shortly after the transition to a single control area, the retail market opened to competition on January 1, 2002. By September 2004, over one million retail customers had service from different electric providers than before. PUCT 2005 Status Report, *supra*.

A unique feature of the Texas retail competition plan, as noted above, is its reliance on retail energy providers (REPs), which purchase power and then sell it to retail customers. With the 6 percent cut in rates effective in 1999, Texas established a "price to beat" it believed new REPs could undercut. "AREPs," affiliated REPs or former IOUs, were required to charge their price to beat through January 2007 or until 40% of certain customer groups switched REPs. There was in fact considerable switching activity, but relatively few residential customers switched:

> From statistical data gathered as of May 2003 to provide a market "snapshot" and anecdotal evidence, it is apparent that large users (more than one ... MW) are shopping for competitive contracts and generating significant savings ... In contrast, small users (residential and commercial consumers with less than one MW of peak demand) are not switching electricity providers in significant numbers, and their savings are limited at best.... To the extent that fuel cost adjustments associated with higher natural gas prices have eaten into consumer savings, many consumers view competitive rates as rate increases that contravene the rate decreases many proponents of competition promised them and implemented.... Recently, retail providers began competing more aggressively on price, offering rates 15 to 20 percent below the rates of AREPs, especially in metropolitan areas....
>
> Overall, the competitive Texas Electric Choice program is moving forward fairly competently.... Large users are saving significant sums. But the potential outcome of retail competition for small users remains to be seen, and whether lack of results in terms of numbers of participating customers hampers the overall restructuring effort. Of concern also are natural gas supply and price trends. Natural gas generates more than 60 percent of electricity in Texas. If a $4 to $5 per MMBtu ... price range becomes the norm, as opposed to the $2 to $3 per MMBtu range of the past, electricity in general will be more expensive and new REPs, which depend largely on gas-fired power, may have difficulty competing in the market.

University of Houston Law Center, Institute for Energy, Law & Enterprise, Electricity Restructuring In Texas: A Status Report (2003). The relatively low switching rate for residential consumers is ironic, given that in many cases REPs offered competitive prices lower than consumers' current price to beat. Kelly, *supra*.

2. Case Study: Restructuring in Pennsylvania

In the mid–1990's, Pennsylvania was one of the first major states to move forward with a retail competition plan. At one point it could be said that, "In terms of numbers of customers that have switched suppliers,

Pennsylvania's restructuring program is the most successful in the Nation." EIA, *supra*.

Pennsylvania's retail electricity rates in the 1990s were 15% over the national average. According to data from the U.S. Energy Information Administration, in 1996 (at 7.96 cents/kWh) and in 1998 (7.86 cents/kWh), Pennsylvania had the eleventh highest average electricity price of the 50 states. *Id.* The Pennsylvania PUC believed that moving toward a competitive market might result in savings of as much as 25% for consumers in the state. The state proposed to allow consumers to choose an electricity generation supplier. A local DisCo would continue to provide transmission and distribution, and would continue to be regulated.

Hearing on Status of Electric Restructuring in Pennsylvania and H.B. 1841, Pennsylvania House Consumer Affairs Committee (Mar. 4, 2004)

Testimony of Sonny Popowsky, Consumer Advocate

Several weeks ago I had the opportunity to speak at a conference . . . that was entitled: Pennsylvania's *Electric Restructuring at its Midpoint: Is it on the Right Track?* As the statutory representative of Pennsylvania's electricity consumers, my answer to that question was: *Yes.* Now, if the question had been phrased differently, that is: *Is Pennsylvania Electric Restructuring on the Track That You Expected?*, my answer would have been: *No.*

So, how was it possible for me to conclude that we are going in the right direction, even though it is not the direction that I anticipated? I think . . . the framework that we developed has continued to work even as the retail market that we anticipated has not developed in the manner that many of us expected. I would contrast the Pennsylvania experience with the contemporaneous experience in California. . . . In Pennsylvania, we established a framework that may have lacked the ideological purity of the spot market design of California, but had a sufficient level of protection for consumers and flexibility for utilities that, even as unexpected setbacks occurred, the restructuring program as a whole has continued to advance. Also, it is important to note that we had the good fortune in Pennsylvania of building our restructured retail electric model on the foundation of what was at the time, and remains today, the most sophisticated and reliable wholesale electricity structure in the Nation—the PJM Interconnection.

So what did I expect would happen after 1996, and why do I think we are still on the right track even though it is not the track I expected us to be on? Basically, by 2004, I had expected that the majority of Pennsylvania consumers, including residential consumers, would be receiving their generation service from someone other than their local electric distribution company. In the electric pilot program in 1996, more than a million Pennsylvania consumers volunteered for the 230,000 slots in that program. There was a tremendous amount of excitement about electric choice, generated in part by a humorous and informative public education cam-

paign. Our utilities even insisted on a "phase-in" provision in the restructuring act so that no more than a third of Pennsylvania consumers would
be able to switch suppliers on the first day the market opened. Indeed,
some of those early expectations were not that far off. By April 2000, just
15 months after the market opened throughout Pennsylvania, more than
500,000 Pennsylvania consumers were being served by alternative providers, including more than 25% of the residential customers of Duquesne
Light Company and 15% of the residential customers of PECO Energy. In
the PECO service territory alone, there were 17 active electric generation
suppliers offering 23 different products to residential customers. As to
industrial customers, by April 2000, more than 60% of the industrial load
for PECO, PPL and GPU was being served by alternative suppliers.

By the beginning of 2004, however, most of the competitive suppliers
who had been serving residential customers in Pennsylvania had either
gone bankrupt or had simply abandoned the market. Except for PECO and
Duquesne, the combined market share of all the competitive suppliers in
the residential market of all the other electric utilities was less than 0.5%.
The industrial market share for competitive suppliers in the PECO service
territory dropped from 63% to less than 5%.

While I expect that shopping for industrial customers will rebound in
the future, I now believe that the vast majority of residential customers in
Pennsylvania will continue to receive generation service through their
electric distribution company indefinitely.

Is that such a terrible thing? Not in my opinion. As I mentioned
earlier, the Pennsylvania restructuring plan was flexible enough to protect
consumers even if things didn't work out the way we may have hoped or
expected. The most obvious protection was our long-term rate caps. . . .
With rate caps in place, customers have not suffered as a result of the lack
of robust retail competition. Rates paid by nearly all Pennsylvania electric
consumers are no higher than the rates paid by those customers in 1996. In
the case of Duquesne Light Company, where stranded cost recovery and the
initial rate caps expired in 2002, rates were actually reduced at that time to
a level that was more than 20% lower than they were prior to restructuring. In other words, just because the original rate caps expired, that didn't
mean that Duquesne ratepayers lost their regulatory protections. On the
contrary, Duquesne filed a new rate plan to serve those customers who did
not shop in the competitive market and the overall prices under that plan
were 20% less than they had been prior to the passage of our restructuring
law in 1996.

Some people have argued that our rate caps themselves prevent robust
competition and that we should let our utilities raise their prices as high as
the market will bear, and then competitors will appear. The problem with
that argument, I believe, is that it confuses ends with means. The goal of
restructuring was not to force consumers to pay ever higher rates to their
utilities until they were forced into the market. In my view, to the extent
that competitive suppliers offer benefits to consumers, either in the form of
lower prices or value-added services, such as "green" or renewable power,

then that is a benefit we should seek to obtain. But the "default" service that customers have a right to continue to receive from their utility under Pennsylvania law should be at least as good as the service they were receiving prior to restructuring. Our goal in 1996 was to make consumers better off, not worse off. And I think consumers are better off. As I said, customers across Pennsylvania today are paying no more than, and, in the case of Duquesne, substantially less than, they were paying under our prior form of regulation. In real, inflation-adjusted terms, of course, virtually all Pennsylvania consumers are paying lower rates today than they were in 1996.

While shopping has dropped substantially, nearly all Pennsylvania consumers continue to be able to choose a "green" alternative, and I believe more than 100,000 Pennsylvania consumers have taken advantage of that choice even though they recognize that the green supplier is typically more expensive than the standard utility service. I also do not think it is a coincidence that as generation choice became available to retail consumers in Pennsylvania, the choices made by generation builders in Pennsylvania changed as well. So today, when you drive along the Pennsylvania Turnpike, you can not only see smokestacks and cooling towers in the distance, but you can also see powerful windmills serving a still small but increasing portion of our electric needs. I would also add that a less-noticed provision of both our electric and natural gas restructuring laws in Pennsylvania was the addition of the concept of "universal service" to our energy vocabulary and a requirement that all of our utilities either maintain or expand vital programs needed to keep low-income and payment troubled customers connected to these vital life-giving services.

Finally, as I noted earlier, the Pennsylvania restructuring program has meshed well with the wholesale market that has thrived in the PJM Interconnection. I have long believed that the greatest benefits of generation competition would be reflected in the wholesale market. Those wholesale market benefits flow through directly to those retail customers who choose alternate suppliers. But even for customers who stay with their electric distribution company, a robust wholesale market will be essential when generation rate caps expire and the default service that is provided by our electric distribution companies will almost certainly be based in large part on wholesale market prices.

I am not testifying that everything has worked perfectly in Pennsylvania's electric restructuring. Far from it. I am particularly concerned that, despite the explicit requirement in our 1996 legislation that service reliability must be maintained at least at the levels that were present prior to restructuring, we have seen a deterioration in service quality statistics for some of our major utilities. The PUC has recently opened a formal investigation into that issue for three of our companies. I am also concerned about the impact on certain of our utilities resulting from unregulated investments around the Nation and around the world that have led to real damage to those companies' financial standing even as they have continued, to their credit, to meet their obligations to their Pennsylvania ratepayers. In the wholesale market, I am concerned with the continuing lack of a robust reliability and market structure in the Midwest region, which I believe contributed to the inexcusable Northeast Blackout of August 14, 2003. Finally, I am concerned that our increasing reliance on natural gas as the fuel of choice for nearly all new generating plants could leave electric consumers exposed to higher and increasingly volatile wholesale energy prices in the future and at the same time result in higher prices for natural gas customers who use natural gas for home heating and other industrial processes. Overall, however, I remain optimistic that we will continue on a track that will serve the long-term interests of Pennsylvania consumers and that the benefits of restructuring to consumers will continue to exceed the costs . . . ■

* * *

Kenneth Rose, 2004 Performance Review of Electric Markets, II–24 to II–32

http://www.scc.virginia.gov/caseinfo/reports/2004_rose.pdf.

Pennsylvania had, at one time, the most active retail access program in the country. In early 2000, PECO Energy alone, then the most active service area in the state (and the country), had 29 offers being made to residential customers about 20 of which were below the price-to-compare. Every service area in the state had at least two offers to residential customers that were below the price-to-compare. This changed dramatically by mid–2001, when many competitive suppliers reduced their offerings to customers or left the market entirely. . . .

[In] May 2003, the entire state had only one offer below the price-to-compare and none in 2004. In May 2002, the state had three such offers, all in PECO Energy's service territory. The number of competitive suppliers in each company's territory remained about the same and, with the exception of PECO Energy's area, the total number of offers from these suppliers also remained about the same. There offers were overwhelmingly for "green power" where at least some portion of the generation uses a renewable energy source. Of the 34 total offers in the state from competitive suppliers in July 2004, all but three had some portion of renewable resources use (the three non-renewable offers were all in PECO Energy's territory).

When energy prices reached over $50/MWh, as it averaged during December of 2000 and again in August of 2001, suppliers that need to secure [generating] capacity to serve a retail load in PJM would face a loss of at least 0.33 cents/kWh for each kilowatthour sold. This also leaves very little room for marketing costs, administrative costs, cost of risk management, or an adequate profit.

The decrease that occurred in 2001 in retail market activity can be seen in all three customer groups. Residential switching continues to decline or remain flat, with all but Duquesne Light and PECO Energy now below one percent of customers with an alternative supplier. There have been two assignments of residential customers in the PECO Energy area. The affect [*sic*] of the first assignment can be seen in the April 2001 percentage. While it drifted downward after the initial assignment, it dropped considerably in 2002 when the main supplier returned its customers back to PECO Energy (180,000 customers of NewPower, an affiliate of Enron, ceased to be a competitive supplier and transferred its customers back to PECO Energy in April 2002). The second assignment of residential customers in PECO Energy's territory can be seen in the January 2004 percentage, when it jumped back to about 20 percent of customers. It declined somewhat in April 2004, down to 17.7 percent. Without the assigned customers, PECO Energy residential customer switching for April was four percent.

With commercial customers . . . all areas, again except Duquesne Light and PECO Energy, are at or below one percent—PPL is reported at one percent and Allegheny Power, Met Ed/Penelec, Penn Power, and UGI are reported at 0.1 percent. Duquesne Light is at just above 20 percent and PECO Energy, with the assignment of its commercial customers, is at 38.5 percent. Without the customer assignment, PECO Energy commercial customer switching drops to 9.5 percent. Industrial customer switching in Pennsylvania . . . for all areas, except Duquesne Light, are well below five percent. Nearly 40 percent of the customers in Duquesne Light's territory are with an alternative supplier.

The peak [in switching] was reached in April of 2000, at 8,320 MW, fell to 5,509 MW in July 2000, then fell again to 2,039 MW in July 2001. Since then, total load served by an alternative supplier has climbed back to over 3,000 MW in 2004 (2,326 MW in April 2004 without the PECO Energy assigned residential and commercial load). This is about 10 percent of the state's total load.■

NOTES AND COMMENTS

1. Based on Rose's analysis, would you agree with Popowsky's optimism about the future of restructuring in Pennsylvania?

2. As part of the process of transitioning to retail competition, Pennsylvania required that utilities bid out the privilege of serving non-switching consumers. The "Competitive Default Service" program required 20% of a utility's residential customers—determined by random selection, including low-income and inability-to-pay customers—to be assigned to a default supplier other than the utility. A lack of interest in competitive bidding for these customers prompted PECO Energy to develop a program with PUC approval under which non-shoppers were assigned to a new supplier for service. In 2003, customers were randomly assigned to the winning bidders and received a 1.25 percent discount from PECO's generation and transmission rates for at least one year. Those who wished to decline the switch could do so with no penalty. As Rose points out, the switching figures in Pennsylvania include customers assigned in this fashion, and without taking this assignment into account the instance of voluntary switching by

residential consumers is very low. Rose, *supra*. One article explains with data from 2004,

> Overall participation dropped in Pennsylvania, from 426,102 [switching customers] at the end of the third quarter to 246,395 at the end of the year. But the earlier figure included 167,320 residential customers that PECO Energy bid out under its "market share threshold" program. Most of those were won by Dominion Retail, which could have continued serving them after the year-long program ended in late 2004, but only if it could beat PECO's rate. A Dominion spokesman said high wholesale prices prevent it from offering power at prices below PECO's rate so those customers went back to the utility.

Big customer switching in Northeast climbs, Power Markets Week, Jan. 10, 2005.

3. A number of Pennsylvania utilities belong to the Mid–Atlantic RTO, PJM Interconnection. Chapter 11 deals with issues relating to RTOs and the intersection between wholesale and retail competition. In 2001, as PJM's internal auditors noted, generators could exercise market power to increase the wholesale price of electricity, and thus make it difficult for competitors to beat the price to compare. *See* PJM Interconnection LLC, Market Monitoring Unit, 2003 Performance Review (2003). This issue of market power and increasing prices at the wholesale level was also problematic in the California electricity crisis.

4. While the name "Enron" is most often associated in electricity circles with energy trading, and especially the manipulation of the California market that helped contribute to the failure of retail competition in that state, Enron was also (briefly) an electricity supplier in Pennsylvania through its subsidiary The New Power Company:

> In November 1999, Enron Energy Services formed a new company called The New Power Company. Enron transferred its residential energy business to New Power. A few months later, America Online and IBM made equity investments in New Power totaling in the hundreds of millions of dollars. New Power was attempting to position itself as the energy "dot com" for residential and small commercial customers.
>
> New Power sold about 20 percent of its stock through an initial public offering (IPO) in October 2000 at $21.00 per share. After the IPO, Enron continued to own about 45 percent of the company, and New Power has entered into long-term contracts with Enron Energy Services—the company now in bankruptcy—to utilize Enron's expertise to purchase energy in the wholesale market and to manage its risks. . . . A few days after its IPO, New Power entered into an agreement with PECO Energy to become the default supplier of electricity for 299,000 PECO customers in the Philadelphia area.

Statement of Scott J. Rubin Before Pennsylvania Treasurer Barbara Hafer (Feb. 19, 2002). Unfortunately for Enron and New Power, this arrangement ended disastrously. When wholesale market prices spiked in 2000 and

2001, New Power became unable to profit while offering service at the discounted rates it had promised consumers, and suffered as well from financial problems associated with Enron. New Power eventually went out of business.

3. RESTRUCTURING'S COLLAPSE IN CALIFORNIA; ENRON'S ROLE

At the beginning of the movement toward restructuring, California was seen as a national and international innovator with its comprehensive plan for electricity restructuring. In the aftermath of the collapse of its electricity market in 2000 and 2001, however, the state is now best known as a model for how *not* to pursue restructuring. California's situation was somewhat unique. Some commentators believe its crisis was attributable in large part to the unique and flawed way it developed and operated its retail electricity market (and therefore the crisis that took place in California might be avoidable in other states). Pierce, Completing the Process, *supra*. Still, the spectacular failure of retail competition in the nation's largest state has had an undeniable retarding effect on progress nationwide toward retail competition.

a. CALIFORNIA'S RETAIL COMPETITION PLAN

In the 1990s, Californians paid more for electricity than their neighbors in Oregon and Washington. As in other states, the pressure to reduce electric rates in California came in the first instance from major industrial users that believed competition would lower their electric rates. California's efforts to adopt retail competition began in 1994, when the California Public Utilities Commission (CPUC) adopted a rule designed to allow all customers in the state a choice of their electricity supplier by the year 2002. In May 1995, after analysis of the changing electricity industry and many hearings around the state to get input from industry experts, utilities, consumer organizations, and the public, the CPUC proposed a policy for introducing competition in California's electric industry. Later that year, after additional public comment, the CPUC adopted a final policy and began to plan the transition to the new market.

In 1996, California Governor Pete Wilson signed AB 1890, a bill designed to facilitate the transition to retail competition in the state. The California act spelled out in detail provisions designed to address 1) stranded cost recovery, 2) organization of the new industry structure, 3) protection of system reliability, 4) funding of public purpose and environmental programs, and 5) consumer protection. To facilitate the transition to retail competition, the California act envisioned that state-chartered, non-profit institutions would play an integral role in the new industry structure. An Independent System Operator ("ISO") would "ensure efficient use and reliable operation of the transmission grid." A power exchange ("CalPX"), open to all buyers and sellers on a nondiscriminatory basis, would operate an "efficient, competitive auction" for the buying and selling of power. There would also be an Oversight Board for the ISO and the CalPX. The Act required both investor-owned and publicly-owned utilities to commit control of their transmission facilities to the ISO and jointly file transmission rates with FERC. After prolonged negotiations, the three major utilities and some larger electricity users agreed on a proposal for an ISO and submitted it to FERC for approval in April of 1996. The California legislature effectively endorsed that proposal by passing AB 1890.

Direct bilateral transactions between electricity suppliers and end-use consumers began in 1998. The three primary companies that distribute electricity in California were Pacific Gas and Electric Co. ("PG&E"), which covers northern California, Southern California Edison (SCE) and San Diego Gas & Electric ("SDG&E"), which serve the southern parts of the state. In addition, there are some substantial municipal systems, including the City of Los Angeles.

By law, PG&E, SCE, and SDG&E were required to reduce residential and small commercial electric rates by 10 percent on January 1, 1998. This seemed to provide protection to retail customers in California, and indeed was promoted that way. In addition, PG&E, Edison and SDG&E would now have to purchase electricity from the CalPX at market prices that fluctuated by the day, hour, and even by ten-minute segments, depending on demand and supply conditions.

The CPUC reviewed and approved incumbent utilities' stranded costs as reasonable, and authorized utilities to recover them through a competitive transition charge between 1998 and 2001.■

NOTES AND COMMENTS

1. Under California's restructuring act, PG&E, Edison, and SDG&E continued to own their transmission facilities, but turned operation of them over to the ISO. Because FERC regulates ISOs, it had a role to play in California's retail competition scheme. This became important later when the market collapsed and the state turned to FERC for intervention.

2. The Legislature and CPUC established public purpose programs to encourage energy conservation and efficiency, and research and development of energy efficient technologies and products. These programs were funded through a public goods charge, which all customers paid. *See* Chapter 13 for a description of these programs.

3. As in other states, the process envisioned by the Legislature was restructuring, not full deregulation. Distribution companies continued to have the obligation to serve the public, and were required to deliver electricity to customers regardless of who sold them electricity. The CPUC retained regulatory authority over transmission and distribution companies.

* * *

In two opinions in late 1996, FERC approved the basic structure of the ISO and the Power Exchange. *See Pacific Gas and Electric Company et al.,*

77 F.E.R.C. ¶ 61,204 (1996); *Pacific Gas and Electric Company et al.*, 77 F.E.R.C. ¶ 61,265 (1996). The following order describes the operation of the CalPX:

Pacific Gas and Electric Company et al.

77 F.E.R.C. ¶ 61,204 (1996).

PANEL: *Before Commissioners: Elizabeth Anne Moler, Chair; Vicky A. Bailey, James J. Hoecker, William L. Massey, and Donald F. Santa, Jr.*

I. Introduction

On April 29, 1996, Pacific Gas and Electric Company (PG&E), San Diego Gas & Electric Company (SDG&E), and Southern California Edison Company ("SoCal Edison") (collectively, the Companies) filed in Docket No. EC96–19–000 a Joint Application for Authorization to Convey Operational Control of Designated Jurisdictional Facilities to an Independent System Operator (ISO). Also on that date, the Companies filed in Docket No. ER96–1663–000 a Joint Application for Authority to Sell Electric Energy at Market–Based Rates Using a Power Exchange ("PX").

Overview of the Proposed PX in Docket No. ER96–1663–000

The Companies state that the PX will establish a competitive spot market for electric power through a day-ahead and hour-ahead auction of generation and demand bids using transparent rules and protocols. This auction will bring together buyers and sellers who have not arranged all of their needs through bilateral contracts. The auction will also allow the PX to reveal day-ahead and hour-ahead market-clearing prices in coordination with the ISO. According to the Companies, the day-ahead market is needed to accommodate the lead times required for start-up of fossil plants to meet load reliably, and the hour-ahead market provides flexibility to account for changed circumstances. Commitments will be treated as forward sales and purchases. They state that, "at times, the PX will need to iterate with the ISO to ensure that transmission constraints are not violated and over-generation conditions do not exist."

Day-ahead demand bids, and any associated price limits, will be submitted to the PX from buyers on behalf of their end-use customers or by end-use customers themselves. All generators wishing to supply energy may bid, including baseload, intermediate load, cycling units, and intermittent energy producers such as solar and wind units. Generation and demand bids will be binding on the bidders when they are submitted to the PX, although the generation and demand schedules are subject to adjustment by the ISO for reliability and congestion management purposes. The PX will conduct a day-ahead auction of bids from generators to serve the demand bids at or below the bid-in demand price.

The PX will rank and evaluate generation bids in merit order, based on both price and operational capabilities, and will then submit its preferred, balanced day-ahead schedules of generation, load, and associated transmission losses to the ISO. The PX's schedules will include generation, the

Companies' loads bid into the PX and which are not served by other means, together with demand bids submitted from other buyers, including but not limited to, municipal utilities, other scheduling coordinators, and utilities outside the ISO's control area. The PX's preferred schedules will also include reserve and regulation ancillary services sufficient to meet the PX's pro rata share of the requirements for the ISO's control area. The PX will bid both to supply ancillary services to, and to buy its full ancillary services requirements from, the ISO.

Prior to the PX's submission of its preferred schedule, the PX will participate in the ISO's management of over-generation conditions. The ISO will also receive balanced schedules from non-PX scheduling coordinators and will perform analyses to determine if transmission congestion will occur as a result of the combined schedules of the PX and other scheduling coordinators, and to arrange for required ancillary services. The scheduling coordinators will have an opportunity to adjust their schedules to account for transmission congestion. Upon final acceptance of all schedules by the ISO, the PX will notify the PX generators and buyers of the accepted generation and load schedules. These accepted schedules will become the day-ahead generation and load schedules and will be the basis on which the PX reveals the day-ahead market-clearing price in each zone and the corresponding price at each generator location in each zone.

The Companies state that a similar process, not including an iteration, will be used for hour-ahead scheduling. These final day-ahead and hour ahead schedules are used in the PX's settlement process, and are financially binding.

Participation in the PX will be voluntary, except that for a five-year transition period, the Companies must bid all of their generation into the PX and must purchase through the PX all of the electric energy required to serve their utility service retail customers. After the transition period, the Companies' participation in the PX will be voluntary.

Once the PX is in operation, the filing parties will authorize the PX to file on their behalf under section 205 any new rate schedules and amended contracts, rules, and protocols that change the rights, duties or operations of the PX. The PX will have exclusive filing authority, since the governing contracts will prohibit any party from making unilateral filings unless that party has exhausted its remedies under the PX's dispute resolution process.

The PX as an entity itself will be a public utility under section 201(e) of the FPA, 16 U.S.C. § 824(e) (1994). The PX will bill and collect revenue from energy purchasers at uniform marginal energy prices (averaged over a transmission zone) and disburse this revenue to the energy sellers and the ISO. All generators in a zone will be paid the bid price of the last winning marginal generator. The ISO will be paid for transmission losses, ancillary services, and congestion costs. Moreover, subject to the ISO's grid-management protocols, the PX auction will determine which buyers and sellers will sell or purchase through the PX, as well as the price and other terms under which these transactions will be made. In this sense, the PX will effectively exercise control, including unit-commitment and scheduling control, over transactions made through the PX. . . .

A variety of agreements and tariffs (ISO/PX Implementing Agreements) will include the rules, protocols or procedures which the PX will adopt to develop the preferred generation dispatch schedule in the forward market; and agreements between the PX and market participants dealing with entity-specific aspects of market participation. The Companies state that agreements between the PX and market participants will be standardized to the extent possible.

Bidding Rules and Bid Evaluation Procedures

The PX will evaluate generation and demand bids and establish a day-ahead preferred schedule by taking into account both the prices offered for service from each bid-in generating unit and the operating capabilities of each unit together with the demand bids for quantity of load and price. The PX will consider operating constraints, and it will not include in its final schedule any demand which had an associated bid price below the market-clearing price.

Based on the final PX dispatch schedule accepted by the ISO, the PX will reveal its market-clearing prices for PX energy. A uniform market-clearing price for PX buyers in a congestion-management zone will be established based on the cost of the marginal generator in that zone for each hour. Hourly prices will be established based on the PX's 24-hour optimization. However, the Companies state that notwithstanding the existence of different market-clearing prices in specific congestion management zones, the California Commission Decision envisions that the Companies will average the costs paid for energy within or among the utility service customers the Companies serve.

The PX price-determination methodology will establish a price in each hour that will match supply and demand according to five principles: (1) the loss-adjusted market-clearing price paid to the marginal generator in each hour will be no less than the combined energy and no-load bid price of the marginal generator; (2) the loss-adjusted market-clearing price may include all or a portion of the start-up cost of the marginal unit such that each generator scheduled to operate during the day will be paid no less than its full bid price for its scheduled operation; (3) no demand bidder whose demand is included in the schedule will pay more than its bid in each hour; (4) if supply is sufficient to meet demand at or below the demand price bid, (as defined by the Companies, a demand price bid states the maximum price for each hour at a which a customer is prepared to take a specified amount of energy in the day ahead schedule) the market-clearing price will be set by the marginal generating unit; and (5) if demand at a price exceeds supply, the market-clearing price will be set by the lowest winning demand price bid. In the absence of adequate demand price bids, demand will be curtailed to match supply, and the market-clearing price will be set equal to an administratively pre-determined cap . . . ■

NOTES AND COMMENTS

1. The CalPX began trading on April 1, 1998. Under its rules, distribution utilities that also own generation were required to sell their generated electricity to the power exchange and repurchase it at the spot market price prior to selling it to their incumbent customers. This paper transaction was meant to effectively unbundle generation and distribution. *See* Peter Fox–Penner, Electric Utility Restructuring: A Guide to the Competitive Era 211–13 (1997).

b. THE "PERFECT STORM" WRECKS CALIFORNIA'S PLAN

The years 2000 and 2001 were disastrous for California's electricity market. During the early summer of 2000, electricity prices began a rapid increase. The high prices and system emergencies threatened in the fall and winter of 2001 to send the state's electricity system into total failure. The crisis sent two of the state's largest companies to the edge of bankruptcy and derailed the state's retail competition plan. On September 20, 2001, the CPUC suspended retail competition in the state. Pac. Gas & Elec. Co., No. 01–09–060, *slip op.* (Sept. 20, 2001). In 2004, the CPUC advanced a "core/non-core" proposal, under which residential "core" customers would continue to get electricity from regulated utilities, and competition would be reintroduced for large industrial and commercial "non-core" customers. Mary O'Driscoll, California considers another run at retail competition, Greenwire, Apr. 16, 2004. Still, retail competition has yet to resume. In addition, the California electricity crisis thrust the future of restructuring across the nation into doubt.

Much has been written about the failure of retail competition in California, and the causes of the crisis are both well-known and multiple. So many events came together to bring the state into crisis that commentators have referred to them as the "perfect storm," after the then-popular movie of the same name. *But see* Nancy Rapoport, Enron, *Titanic*, and the Perfect Storm, 71 Fordham L. Rev. 1373 (2003) (arguing that this metaphor is inappropriate for Enron because "what brought Enron down ... wasn't a once-in-a-lifetime alignment of elements beyond its control."). California relied on electricity imported from other states for up to 25 percent of its generation needs. However, the surrounding states (which exported power to California) were growing rapidly themselves, and needed more power. Second, the Pacific Northwest, from which California bought power, experienced a drought which adversely affected generation of hydroelectric power at just the time that California needed it most.

Much of California's in-state electricity generation depends on natural gas, which skyrocketed in price during 2000–2001. California's gas prices rose to three and four times the national average, contributing to higher electricity prices. *See* Chapter 8 for a discussion of the reasons for this, including the effective abuses by utility affiliates. Restrictions on long-term contracts meant that the CalPX was a spot market, and the utilities could only buy power one day ahead, which exposed them even more to the fluctuations in electricity prices. California's largest utilities, encouraged by regulations to do so, had sold off their generation assets (although they were not required to do so), and that left them even more exposed to the spot market. The rate freeze protected customers from rising rates but put utilities in a terrible bind. When wholesale prices skyrocketed, the utilities were purchasing power at high wholesale rates, but selling it at low frozen retail rates. This situation became untenable.

Yet another set of problems chronicled in books, Congressional testimony, FERC investigative proceedings, television, and movies, relates to manipulation of the California market manipulation by Enron and other power traders and sellers. FERC's 2003 Final Report on Price Manipulations in Western Markets contains a somber analysis of the manipulative practices. Order Directing the Release of Information, Fact Finding Investigation of Potential Manipulation of Electric and Natural Gas Prices, 102 FERC ¶ 61,311 (2003) (2003 FERC Final Report).

The sections that follow analyze the California crisis and its aftermath. In hindsight, it is easy to criticize state legislators, regulators, utilities, FERC, power marketers and others, but what lessons should be learned, and what impact has California had on restructuring activities across the nation?

i. Market Collapse; FERC (In)Action, and Litigation

Steven Ferrey, The Eagles of Deregulation: The Role of the Courts in a Restructured Environment

32 Envtl. L. 297 (2002).

> Welcome to the Hotel California
> Such a lovely place, such a lovely face
> They're livin' it up at the Hotel California
> What a nice surprise. Bring your alibis.

In late calendar year 2000, California's restructured electric power market imploded. What really happened? The facile answer is that demand exceeded supply. But there is more.

A. The Restructuring

. . . Because California's concept of deregulation contained a ten percent price cut to pacify consumers, this discouraged consumers from shifting to alternative retail suppliers. Therefore, a vibrant retail market and significant customer choice did not become a reality. Only about two percent of customers—typically large customers—switched to other suppliers. The conventional utilities continued to supply more than ninety percent of the power being sold in the state. They had to do this after selling their generating assets . . .

After deregulation, the California [PUC] no longer assessed the state's need for power. Market participants, subject to regulatory siting approval, were responsible for supply. By law, deregulated power supply was bid to the [CalPX] daily, with the last/highest price accepted setting the price for all sales of power during that period. The utilities were required by regulatory authorities to buy a substantial amount of their power requirements on the "spot" market—day-to-day—rather than through hedged forward contracts. Rather than rely on hedged forward contracts to mitigate price swings, California sought the imposition of spot electric price caps as a means to control losses. This may work as a political solution, but it destroys the price signals that the market would otherwise send, as well as dampens conservation incentives. California was unique among the states in not allowing hedged forward power contracts for wholesale supply.

Approximately one-quarter of California's generating capacity is hydro-electric, which was susceptible to annual water flows that decreased. California's reservoirs were down to minimal levels, leaving little energy capacity from these hydroelectric resources in the system. Some of the problem in California was made more complex by unregulated companies and their affiliates controlling both some of the natural gas supply and a significant share of deregulated wholesale electric power producers. About half of California generation relies on natural gas, a great majority of which is not extracted in-state.

In California, the largest market participant has a share of only thirteen percent of the [generating] market. However, for purposes of exercising market power during certain hours in certain sub-markets, at times when demand is very inelastic, there could still be horizontal market power for a generator with less than a twenty percent share....

Some of the gas supply companies declined to sell natural gas to the cash-short integrated electric and gas utility companies in California that were required by law to serve residential and other natural gas customers. This drove the price of natural gas higher and, therefore, the cost of power produced at wholesale by natural gas-fired power generation technologies.

California's spot market began March 31, 1998. During summer 2000, spot market prices for electricity in California increased by 500%, and then doubled from that new plateau at the end of calendar year 2000. When spot market prices of wholesale power increased dramatically due to shortfall, this caused the ultimate cost of power needing to be passed on in retail rates or otherwise recouped to increase correspondingly. In response to ratepayer protest, the state ordered retail rates frozen at 6.5 [cents]/kilowatt-hour (kWh). Many of the investor-owned retail utilities were purchasing power at substantially higher wholesale spot market prices, but not allowed to pass on the higher acquisition cost in retail rates under this retail rate cap.

Thereafter, the revenue-strapped regulated California distribution utilities were unable to pay on time for their wholesale power acquisitions because of dwindling cash resources. The utilities teetered on the verge of bankruptcy. Over time, an increasing amount of total load was served through real-time spot market purchases, which reflected near-panic situations. The California ISO was allowed to purchase power from out-of-state suppliers at any price. A phenomenon known as "megawatt laundering" then ensued, where out-of-state suppliers could sell power to neighboring states, which could then be resold to the California ISO at inflated prices.

B. The Descent

There she stood in the doorway
I heard the mission bell
And I was thinking to myself
This could be Heaven or this could be Hell.

Rolling blackouts were visited on consumers during the off-peak winter and spring months of 2001. It is estimated that outages of electric supply, before adding the California experience, already cost the United States economy approximately $50 billion and could increase significantly in the future. A shortage of electricity has dire social and political consequences; a blackout has been equated to a natural disaster. Moreover, allowing rolling blackouts is a very inefficient way to balance electricity supply and demand differences. Not every consumer attaches the same value to electricity at a given hour. For some industries, even a short blackout can ruin millions of dollars of production; for others, it is a minor inconvenience. However, because of simple meters, no residential consumers see price signals that reflect the actual time-sensitive costs their consumption imposes on the system at any given time of day. This fixed retail rate, with no metering feedback system to retail consumers, excludes substantial amounts of retail electric consumption from any meaningful price response role in the deregulated market.

The situation in California became so extreme that President Clinton used a statute reserved for national emergencies, or when the national defense is threatened by foreign powers, to try to keep the lights on in California. Declaring a "natural gas supply emergency" under the Defense Production Act of 1950, which was enacted at the commencement of the Korean War to keep supplies flowing to the government, the President compelled unregulated out-of-state natural gas companies to keep selling gas to California utilities who were unable to pay for it and were on the verge of bankruptcy. The Clinton administration justified this action by claiming that, had the gas not been ordered moved to California, the California investor-owned utilities (IOUs) could have seized other gas in the pipelines to serve residential customers, cutting off federal military and NASA facilities.

This was an extraordinary exercise of national defense powers in peace time to cause private companies to act contrary to their market interests. President Bush allowed this order to expire after extending it once.

No state, particularly California, which imports power from eleven other states and Canada, is an island. This is especially true regarding electricity moving almost at the speed of light. As a practical matter, California energy requirements are such as to utilize all of the electric power exported by Arizona, Oregon, Montana, New Mexico, Utah, Washington, and Wyoming, as well as from Canada and Mexico.

The Clinton administration required neighboring western states to export power to California to limit California blackouts. This action spread concern regarding the operation of California's deregulated magnet market to several of the eleven states that export power to California.

As low-cost federal hydropower was exported to California, wholesale power costs for residual power in the Northwest rose. In the Pacific Northwest, the Bonneville Power Administration raised rates by seventy-five percent. Retail electricity prices in the state of Washington increased as much as fifty percent due to the ripple effects of scarce Northwest hydro-electric power being diverted to California. Louisiana–Pacific Co. had to close Northwest facilities; Boeing and Microsoft voiced corporate energy concerns. Ten aluminum smelters in the Pacific Northwest took advantage of increasing electricity prices by shutting down facilities and reselling their allotments of low-cost federal hydropower on the wholesale market. At a time of depressed aluminum prices and elevated electricity prices, this made eminent good sense and was economically rational. As prices receded in the latter half of 2001, these closures appeared less prudent.

California Governor Gray Davis sought additional federal intervention. FERC refused to restrain the operation of the market that California had created, other than to initially continue wholesale power sale "soft" price caps, and refused to approve in June 2001 a cap on spot market prices for all western power transactions occurring when reserve margins fell below seven percent.

The California ISO has had price caps that have descended over time from $750 per megawatt-hour ("MWh") in June 2000 to $500/MWh in July 2000, to $250/MWh in August 2000. However, the price caps that apply during certain periods of supply inadequacy do nothing to prohibit the recovery of otherwise excessive prices in other periods. This measure can occur in off-peak periods if the particular sub-market is dysfunctional. The New York ISO, ISO–New England, and the Pennsylvania–New Jersey–Maryland Interconnection ("PJM") ISO have each approved price caps of approximately $1000/MWh, applicable during certain temporary conditions to protect consumers. Trades do continue, but the price is capped in lieu of halting trades... ∎

NOTES AND COMMENTS

1.   The shortages and high electricity prices had devastating consequences for Californians dependent on electricity. In 2001, the Los Angeles Times published a harrowing account of California residents who relied on electricity to keep their life-saving machines in operation. These people were forced to move to hospitals to stay alive. Bob Pool, Power for Survival, L.A. Times, Jan. 26, 2001.

2.   The design of California's retail access plan contemplated that the PX and the ISO, as non-profit companies working in tandem, would prevent market manipulation. However, both entities lacked appropriate mecha-

nisms to combat gaming practices by marketers, traders and other market participants:

> In January 2001, two reports appeared analyzing the post-May 2000 power crisis ... Robert McCullough ... attributed the price spikes to the California ISO's letting itself be gamed by the merchant power plant generators that did not have an obligation to serve a franchised area ... The mystery, to McCullough, was why the ISO allowed itself to be so repeatedly deceived. The ISO board did consist of a substantial number of representatives from generating companies, calling into question its status as an "independent" system operator.

> The ISO and [PX] did not exchange data between them, and they operated on automatic pilot, rather like Hal the computer in the movie 2001: A Space Odyssey. Divestiture had put generating capacity in the hands of only a few companies. Generators could simply reverse-engineer the computer software and game the system with strategic bidding. Indeed, the ISO collected and distributed the hourly operating data for its generating suppliers, so each company knew the production levels of its competitors....

> [In] 2002, McCullough revisited his earlier study.... His report again lambastes the California ISO for its passive market surveillance [and] FERC for its "appalling indecision." The ISO had no good log of plant outages and did not know if electricity was being exported out-of-state (to avoid price caps) or if generating units were experiencing abnormal bouts of maintenance shutdowns....

Weaver, *supra*.

In June 2004, the ISO's Board of Governors released a report detailing its errors during the crisis, admitting that some of its employees took "questionable steps" (including participation in a conference call in which "fictitious load"—the alleged purchase of unnecessary power—was scheduled) and were "less than forthcoming" with state investigators. Report By the California ISO Board of Directors Regarding Matters Raised By the Senate Select Committee to Investigate Price Manipulation of the Wholesale Energy Market (2004).

3.   On April 6, 2001, PG&E, California's largest IOU, filed for Chapter 11 bankruptcy protection. On December 18, 2003, after extensive settlement negotiations, the CPUC (on a 3–2 vote) approved an agreement between the CPUC and PG&E that permitted the utility to emerge from its bankruptcy proceeding; in 2004, the federal bankruptcy court entered a confirmation order implementing the agreement. *See In re PG&E Co.*, 304 B.R. 395 (Bankr. N.D. Cal. 2004); *Lynch v. Cal. Pub. Util. Comm'n*, 311 B.R. 798 (Bankr. N.D. Cal. 2004) (granting motion to dismiss the appeal of the two objecting commissioners). The plan provided for PG&E to freeze its rates through the end of 2003, and achieve savings of about $1 billion by refinancing its $13 billion of unpaid power bills resulting from the California crisis over a nine-year period through the use of asset-backed securities.

4. A small silver lining in the California crisis was the recognition that state residents practiced energy conservation to a considerable degree, even if doing so under crisis conditions, and that it worked to reduce the worst impacts of the crisis. Californians reduced overall energy use by 7.1% in the summer of 2001, and the state paid $90 million in rebates to energy-saving ratepayers in July 2001. *See* Kevin Starr, Coast of Dreams: California on the Edge 1990–2003 599 (Knopf, 2004). *See* Chapter 13 for a detailed discussion of energy conservation techniques.

5. Numerous lawsuits followed in the aftermath of the California crisis, between 2000 and 2005. Wholesale power suppliers sued utilities, seeking payment for power purchased. The California ISO sought refunds from suppliers for overcharging the state. Numerous parties (including the San Francisco City Attorney, several municipal utilities, and private individuals on their own behalf and in class action lawsuits) sued electricity suppliers, alleging conspiracies to fix prices and to manipulate the CalPX. PG&E sued the state's Victim Compensation and Government Claims Board in 2002, seeking $4.1 billion in damages relating to the alleged failure of the state to allow it to include certain amounts in its stranded cost recovery. California's Attorney General, Bill Lockyer, sued Mirant and Reliant in state court for more than $1 billion for "controlling" California electricity supplies and exercising market power. *See* Steven Ferrey, Inverting Choice of Law in the Wired Universe: Thermodynamics, Mass, and Energy, 45 Wm. & Mary L. Rev. 1839, 1848–52, 1855–61 (2004), for summaries of these and other lawsuits through 2004.

The state brought an action before FERC in 2001, involving all of the competitive wholesale suppliers as respondents, to recover $9 billion in refunds. In March 2001, FERC ordered thirteen companies (including Dynegy Power Marketing, Duke Energy Trading & Marketing, Reliant Energy Services, Williams Energy Services, and Enron's Portland General Electric Company) to justify that the rates they had charged in the unregulated California market were "just and reasonable." In 2004, the U.S. Court of Appeals for the Ninth Circuit ordered FERC to begin refund proceedings of $2.8 billion for California ratepayers. *California ex rel. Lockyer v. FERC*, 383 F.3d 1006 (9th Cir. 2004); the subsequent proccedings involving Enron are discussed below.

Dynegy eventually was ordered to pay $281.5 million to satisfy claims that the company manipulated California's electricity and natural gas markets. Mary O'Driscoll, FERC approves $281.5 million Dynegy settlement with California, Greenwire, Oct. 26, 2004.

* * *

FERC came under considerable criticism for its role in the failure of retail access in California. At first, as Professor Ferrey notes, FERC refused to intervene in the market that California had designed. Its subsequent action (until mid–2001, when it finally imposed wholesale price caps on the entire eleven-state western region) was too late to avert disaster, as Professor Jacqueline Lang Weaver notes:

FERC's first major order, issued in final form on December 15, 2000, acknowledged that it had a duty to assure that wholesale prices were just and reasonable and then stated that the current California rates—which were the unregulated, market-based rates granted to the now-independent generators—were not just and reasonable. The November/December orders did not offer price relief to California in the form that it sought: maximum ceiling prices on wholesale electric prices (popularly called price caps). However, the order did set up some "price mitigation" measures along with operational changes in the market design.

The December order did not succeed in either taming prices or stabilizing the market. In fact, things got worse. Even though far less electricity was consumed in January 2001 than in August 2000 (when no emergencies or rolling blackouts actually occurred), January prices were much higher and emergencies or rolling blackouts occurred with frequency. Many economists, especially those in the think tanks that became a growth industry unto itself during the era of deregulation, had a ready explanation, true to their trust in free markets: Price caps always back-fire and result in shortages and higher prices.

The [December] order also addressed the issue of whether FERC was authorized under the Federal Power Act to refund to consumers that portion of the rates charged by generators that were found to be unjust and unreasonable. Despite having found that rates since May 2000 were not just and reasonable, FERC's legal analysis of the Federal Power Act concluded that FERC had no authority to issue retroactive refunds. The "filed rate doctrine" is a well established principle of federal rate regulation. Under this doctrine, a regulated utility cannot charge rates other than those properly approved and filed with FERC as being just and reasonable. A corollary of the doctrine is that FERC only has the authority to change rates prospectively, after it has found that the existing rates are no longer just and reasonable.

The most that FERC could legally do, according to its analysis, was to establish a "refund effective" date of October 2, 2000 (sixty days after San Diego Gas & Electric Company had filed its complaint that wholesale rates were not just and reasonable, initiating the investigations that led to the order). If subsequent investigation proved that rates were not competitive or that market power was being used to produce unjust rates, then FERC could require refunds for sales made from that date forward. This left five long months of soaring prices and steeplelike price spikes, from May to September 2000, outside of FERC's refund power.

California's response, in turn, was to blame "outsiders"—merchant power generators and energy traders like Enron, headquartered in Houston, Texas—for the spikes in wholesale prices and to blame FERC for failing to control them. When little help from FERC was forthcoming, the state took active steps to try to manage its way out of the chaos. In January 2001, it authorized a small, 7 to 12 percent increase in retail rates to residential users. In February, it authorized the Los Angeles Department of Water Resources to enter into long-term, bilateral contracts to purchase electricity on behalf of the utilities (which were either in or close to bankruptcy) so that consumers would no longer be dependent on the volatile spot market, and arranged for the bonding authority to pay for these contracts. The state also mandated conservation efforts, provided monetary incentives to conserve, and expedited the construction of new generating plants. In late March 2001, the state raised retail rates significantly.

FERC's December order was followed by an April order, which marked a somewhat more aggressive stance. The "soft" price mitigation measures had clearly not worked, so FERC's April order set another, more sophisticated, method of mitigating prices through proxy prices, although it still did not impose a maximum price cap on wholesale prices. FERC did, however, begin an investigation of power markets in the entire Western region. By now, FERC understood the obvious: What was happening in California had large ripples, indeed waves, in energy markets, electricity prices, industries and jobs in states like Nevada, Oregon and Washington. California was part of an interconnected grid, and all the western governors, even conservative Republicans, wanted federal action to end the crisis. After the April order, electricity prices in California dropped significantly.

Finally, on June 19, 2001, FERC issued a strong and comprehensive order, relying on the price drop that had followed its April order as justification. FERC extended its price mitigation plans to the entire western region. This order, for the first time, prevented "megawatt laundering"—shipping electricity out-of-state and then reselling it back to California to avoid price mitigation measures for sales within California. The crisis ended.

Weaver, *supra.*

As Robert McCullough reported in 2002, the timing of FERC's inaction was critical: "If FERC had intervened knowledgably in the California markets in May 2000 and imposed a western-wide price cap and a 'must offer' rule to counter the generators' strategic withholding of bids and supplies, the entire California energy crisis would have been avoided." Weaver, *supra.*

Another author agrees that FERC could have acted sooner:

FERC was, from the inception of California's deregulation efforts, advised about the potential problems that might arise in that market. It obtained reports as early as 1996 commenting on the potential for price manipulation and weakness in California's deregulation scheme. FERC ignored all of these reports and signed off on California's deregulation plan. A recent report notes how few resources FERC then spent (and currently spends) on controlling anti-competitive behavior in the energy market. FERC blamed on all of the flaws in the design of the California system on the California CPUC, California PX, and California ISO, thus deflecting attention from its own deficiencies and culpability in approving such a system.

Other federal agencies were critical of FERC's poor performance in dealing with the California market. In June 2001, the General Accounting Office (GAO) released a report assessing why energy prices in California had increased so dramatically. The report criticized FERC's study of outages, stating that it was not thorough enough to support the conclusions that generators had not withheld supply. In November 2002, the Senate Committee on Governmental Affairs released a report regarding FERC's oversight of Enron. The Report found that FERC "was no match for a determined Enron."

Had FERC acted in a timely manner, "it could have saved Californians billions of dollars." At the most critical moment of the California crisis, FERC abandoned its role as a regulator, leaving the market vulnerable to massive profiteering. FERC chose to investigate the various schemes being used to game the California energy market, only after the disclosure of an internal legal memo at Enron. Sadly, prior to the release of that memo, FERC was convinced that California's problems were merely the result of poor design and a supply and demand imbalance.

Jeffrey D. Van Niel, Enron—The Primer, *in* Enron: Corporate Fiascos and Their Implications 23–25 (2004).

There was a separate problem that FERC belatedly discovered. In the Galinas Report, FERC "discovered that natural gas prices, the key input in the cost of generating electricity, had been misreported and manipulated to favor the trading positions of traders in the gas markets." *Id*. This led eventually to criminal proceedings against some parties for their involvement in manipulating the natural gas market. *See* Chapter 8.

Why did FERC fail to stem the California crisis? Some pointed to political differences between "red state" Texas (the home state of President George W. Bush, who took office in 2001) and "blue state" California:

[T]he gulf between Sacramento and the George W. Bush White House—which is to say, the gulf between California and Texas—on the entire energy question could not be wider. . . . By spring 2001 there had emerged a rapidly developing energy showdown: a shootout at the energy corral, if you will, with Governor Davis demanding wholesale price caps and refunds from the boys in Texas and their cohorts in the energy business. The whole energy crisis, Davis told *Time* magazine, represented "a massive transfer of wealth from the ordinary citizens of California to rich energy barons in Houston, Charlotte, and Atlanta." . . . It came as no surprise, when the White House released its supply-side-oriented energy plan in May 2001, that it made no provisions for California, although in discussing the plan both Bush and [Vice President] Cheney frequently referred to the state as an example of how not to conduct energy policy. . . . As Congressman Brad Sherman (D–

Thousand Oaks) put it, the Bush energy plan could be summed up quite simply: "Bush to California—Drop Dead!"

Which was not an unfair characterization. Already, the previous February, FERC had not renewed its emergency order requiring suppliers to sell electricity to California. A Stage Three alert and two days of rolling blackouts followed in mid-March. . . . On April 25, 2001, FERC, on a divided vote, had offered a highly qualified temporary cap on wholesalers only, not producers, and only in emergency circumstances. . . .

The stage was set for Bush's first postelection visit to California on May 29. . . . "The last time I looked," Davis told reporters in anticipation of the president's visit, "California was still part of the United States of America. We have contributed disproportionately to the economic growth of this country. There is no reason why a president should not respond to a legitimate request [for caps] from the chief executive of the largest state in the union." . . .

In mid-June, Governor Davis did not get exactly what he wanted—comprehensive caps—but he did get something from FERC: the extension of the soft cap from peak hours to twenty-four hours a day. This concession represented a break on the part of the Bush administration from its hard-line stance, and thus a personal victory for Davis. . . .

Starr, *supra*, at 599–601. The political ramifications of the California electricity crisis did not end there; Davis was defeated in a special California gubernatorial election in 2003 (following a statewide recall campaign) by the former actor Arnold Schwarzenegger.

The ideological belief among many in the supremacy of free markets was also a factor:

This ideology explains FERC's long reluctance to intervene in the chaos of California and California's own embrace of a Power Exchange as the ultimate market of all power markets. The California crisis precipitated an extraordinary round of competing "manifestos" by prominent economists. The true believers urged officials to resist any form of price cap, while those who recognized the reality of dysfunctional markets urged regulatory intervention.

Weaver, *supra*.

An additional factor was the application of the "filed rate doctrine," as noted above and as discussed in Chapter 3. Under this doctrine, a utility's tariff filed with FERC is treated as "a firm-specific regulation, freezing in place the tariff's rates and other conditions and precluding their modification by anyone other than the agency or (with a new tariff filing) the regulated firm." Jim Rossi, Lowering the Filed Tariff Shield: Judicial Enforcement for a Deregulatory Era, 56 Vand. L. Rev. 1591 (2003). Discussing and criticizing the reasoning of *Duke Energy Trading and Marketing, L.L.C. v. Davis*, 267 F.3d 1042 (9th Cir. 2001), Professor Rossi notes that the filed tariff doctrine was applied to bar Governor Davis "from commandeering contracts to deliver wholesale electric power to utilities, favoring federal regulation over the state's approach to crisis management." Professor Rossi also points to the "significant" application of the filed tariff doctrine in *Pacific Gas and Elec. Co. v. Lynch*, 216 F. Supp. 2d 1016, 1048–49 (N.D. Cal. 2002), and concludes that, "[T]o the extent that an agency, such as FERC, does not even assert jurisdiction over deregulated market actors in compliance with filed rates, the agency may lack any remedies at all for abuses of deregulated power markets." He proposes that "It is time for the filed tariff shield to surrender to a dual enforcement regime that includes common law and statutory remedies enforced by courts."

ii.   Enron's Role: Of "Death Star" and "Fat Boy"

The involvement of Enron and other power marketers and sellers created four separate problems in California, each of which has been the subject of extensive after-the-fact investigation: (1) Gaming of the flawed regulatory system; (2) Withholding of generating capacity; (3) Affiliate abuse of pipeline capacity; and (4) Manipulation of gas and power price indexes. Weaver, *supra*, at 29. The following excerpt describes Enron's gaming practices and their devastating impact on the California market.

Jeffrey D. Van Niel, Enron—The Primer, *in* Enron: Corporate Fiascos and Their Implications 18–25 (2004)

California's market design had flaws, but the crisis was caused more precisely by a failure to understand the inherent rationale of regulation or to regulate despite those flaws. Some of Enron's schemes appear to violate ISO rules, which expressly prohibit gaming the system. The ISO tariff prohibits (1) "gaming" (defined as "taking unfair advantage of the rules and procedures") of either the PX or ISO; (2) "taking undue advantage" of congestion or other conditions that may affect the grid's reliability or render the system "vulnerable to price manipulation to the detriment of [the ISO Markets'] efficiency"; or (3) engaging in anomalous market behavior, such as "pricing and bidding patterns that are inconsistent with prevailing supply and demand conditions" Contrary to these express prohibitions, Enron and other companies created and tested techniques that did all of the above. These techniques had names like Death Star (a phantom power transfer), Fat Boy (an artificial increase in demand), Ricochet (see Ricochet Chart and description below), Load Shift (megawatt laundering see Load Shift Chart below) and others to extract huge profits from the California market. Let's look at some of these games in a bit more detail.

Under several of the schemes, companies would intentionally over-schedule power into a transmission and power transfer interface in order to take advantage of the most obvious loophole in the system, in which the ISO would pay congestion relief charges to companies that failed to deliver power to the interface. In other words, the companies would schedule loads for delivery that they had *no intention* of providing, so that they could be paid by the ISO not to deliver that power. Enron called this particular scheme "Load Shift." Chart C illustrates this scheme.

Chart C. Load Shift Chart

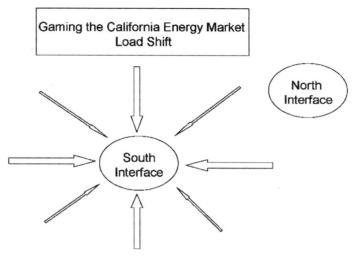

Enron creates an artificial load schedule at the South Interface by intentionally overscheduling load at the interface. No load is scheduled to the North Interface, and the California ISA pays Enron a congestion management fees to eliminate the congestion on the grid.

Figure 12–1

Chart D. Ricochet Chart

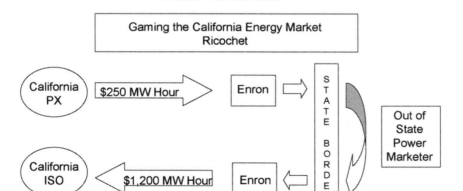

California PX sells power to Enron, who ships power to out-of-state entity. Shortage of power in California triggers buying obligation by ISO, which shops for power out of state. Enron waits until prices peak on the California Grid, has the out-of-state entity ship power back to Enron, who then re-sells the same power back to ISO for up to 20 times the price that was paid that same day to bring the power out of California. The out-of-state entity charges Enron a fee to take power and return it the same day

Figure 12–2

Enron had another game called "Ricochet." Enron and others simply bought power from the PX, shipped it out of state to a confederate, then when prices were high enough in California, wheeled that same power back into California at prices that were sometimes 200 times higher than the price that was paid for the same power earlier that day. See Chart D below. Simply put, Enron and other power suppliers exploited the system.

One of the most popular abuses employed was "wash trades," "swap trades," or "roundtrip trades." Under this mechanism, there appears [sic] to be two purchases and two sales between two market participants. In reality, these trades exist only on paper: no power or money ever changes hands, as the two transactions take place simultaneously and cancel each other out completely. See Chart E below. Electricity was not the only commodity manipulated using the roundtrip trade method; roundtrip trading was also used for natural gas and broadband capacity. Dynegy, AEP, CMS, El Paso, and Williams admitted that some of their traders had engaged in roundtrip trades.

Chart E. Wash Trades Charts

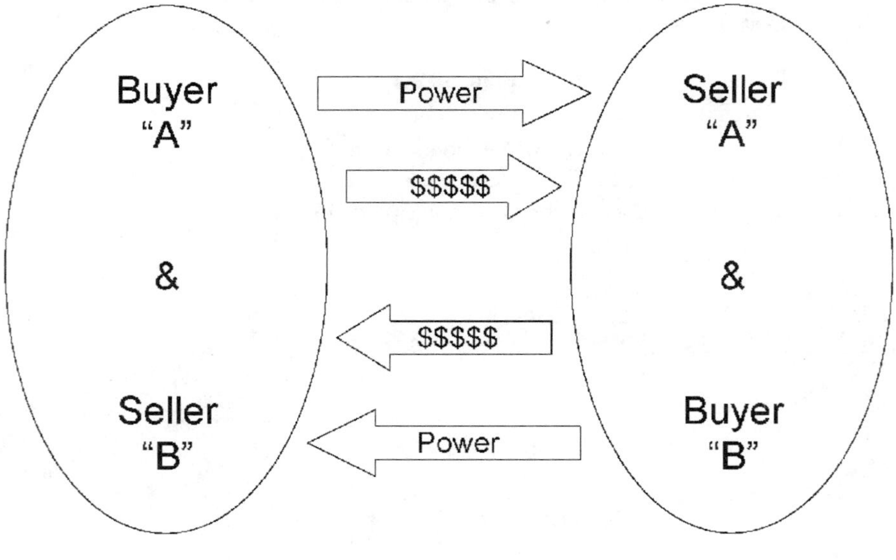

Figure 12–3

NOTES AND COMMENTS

1. In response to manipulation of the natural gas market, the federal Commodity Futures Trading Commission launched a very broad investigation of various energy trading schemes. *See* Chapter 8.

* * *

The aftermath of the Enron debacle featured high-profile investigations of the company's practices, with the company's bankruptcy proceeding and corporate scandals dominating national news for a considerable period of time. Much of what embroiled the seventh-largest publicly traded company in the U.S. in scandal and eventual collapse was due to accounting-related matters and other practices that went well beyond the manipulation of California's electricity market. *See generally* Enron: Corporate Fiascoes and Their Implications, *supra*.

A Senate Select Committee to Investigate Price Manipulation of the Wholesale Energy Market investigated Enron and subsequently recommended criminal charges against individual employees. In August 2004, in but one of these criminal proceedings, John Forney, the former manager of Enron's trading desk and inventor of the "Death Star" scheme, pled guilty to one count of conspiring to commit wire fraud in exchange for his cooperation in other investigations. Forney faced a maximum sentence of five years in prison and $250,000 in fines. Inventor of Enron "Death Star" trade accepts plea agreement, Greenwire, Aug. 6, 2004.

The 2003 FERC Final Report was a major factor in showing that Enron's business practices were predatory. It concluded that dysfunctional design and operation of the California market made market manipulations possible, with the adverse effects of poor design and operation exacerbated by the spike in natural gas prices. But soaring natural gas prices were not solely to blame, as Enron and other companies violated California ISO and CalPX tariffs by engaging in practices that constituted gaming, with prices in the CalPX being artificially inflated by these gaming practices. As a result, the 2003 FERC Final Report recommended proceedings (subsequently undertaken) to force the named companies to disgorge their profits earned as a result of the gaming practices.

The litigation involving the Public Utility District No. 1 of Snohomish County, Washington ("SnoPUD") illustrates the far-reaching impacts of Enron's involvement in the California electricity crisis. At the height of the California crisis, the SnoPUD canceled its nine-year contract to purchase 25 MW of power from Enron, and Enron sought to recover $122 million as a termination fee. SnoPUD argued that Enron's market manipulation negated the contract's legality, and sought refunds from Enron. Initially, FERC rejected the objections of SnoPUD and the city of Tacoma, Washington to proposed settlements between California and energy suppliers on the grounds that they did not provide for refunds to wholesale purchasers of electricity outside of California who were harmed by price manipulation in the wholesale markets. *El Paso Electric Co. et al.*, 104 FERC ¶ 61,115 (2003).

In 2003, FERC began an investigation of the impacts of the California crisis on the Pacific Northwest, and on July 22, 2004, the Commission issued an order in *El Paso Electric Co, et al.* 108 FERC ¶ 61,071 (2004), that "... Enron potentially could be required to disgorge profits for all of its wholesale power sales in the Western Interconnect for the period January 16, 1997 to June 25, 2003." *Id.* FERC initially ruled that an initial $32.5 million should be returned, and in 2005 FERC analysts recommended that Enron disgorge as much as $1.87 billion. Mary O'Driscoll, FERC proposes record penalty for Enron's market manipulation, Greenwire, February 1, 2005. However, it was unclear that any of this amount might ever be recovered, given Enron's bankrupt status: "Yet whatever the final number, it is questionable whether Enron will be able to pay it in full. The company, still operating under federal bankruptcy protection, has many claims remaining against it and is expected to settle them for pennies on the dollar." *Id.*

The SnoPUD had been active in uncovering Enron's misdeeds. In 2004, it released a series of taped conversations between Enron day traders, acquired from the U.S. Department of Justice (in its ongoing criminal investigation of several Enron employees) that were full of vulgarities and hilarity over how much money the company was making at the expense of individual ratepayers. *See* http://www.snopud.com. In 2005, SnoPUD released Enron company documents and telephone transcripts purporting to show that even before California deregulated its electricity market, Enron had tried the same "Death Star" and "Ricochet" gaming techniques in Alberta, Canada, and in Nevada (thus making it responsible for disgorging profits between 1997 and 2003). Newly released Enron documents show longer market manipulation, intentionally shut plants, Greenwire, Feb. 4, 2005.

The July 2004 ruling regarding the disgorgement of Enron's profits did not end the matter, for FERC had not clarified whether the termination fee was counted in the profits Enron was required to disgorge. In March 2005, however, a FERC administrative law judge ruled that the contract termination fee sought by Enron should be considered "unjust profits." Christopher Schwarzen, Snohomish County PUD may be off hook in Enron lawsuit, Seattle Times, Mar. 14, 2005. For SnoPUD's customers, this ruling was significant: to pay Enron the $122 million, PUD officials stated, they likely would have to charge each of its 290,000 customers an additional $400. Instead, Enron might be liable to SnoPUD: "This is very significant for us," said PUD attorney Eric Christensen. "We put in an extensive body of evidence on the last day of January saying that Enron was committing violations all the way through the period beginning in 1997." Christensen added, "If the case comes out as we expect, we would have a claim for some dollar amount against [Enron]." *Id.*

iii. *Market Abuse vs. Scarcity Rents*

The California debacle has highlighted an important question: how do fluctuating market-based rates square with the Federal Power Act's long-standing requirement that rates be "just and reasonable"? Is the problem merely one of policing markets to prevent and punish the kinds of collusive and anticompetitive behavior we associate with antitrust violations? Or is the problem deeper than that? Can electricity markets work as intended and still comply with the "just and reasonable" rate requirement? Consider the following hypothetical situation adapted from the California experience.

In State X, the electric power market has been restructured, and sellers are permitted to charge market rates for power. Retail rates in the state are capped at the seemingly generous level of $120 per megawatt-hour ("mwh"), more than three times the historical average. Acme Power Sales sells power to retail electricity providers on the short-term spot market as well as through bilateral long-term power sales agreements. It sells power from its Springfield natural gas power plant on the spot market, and has sold power from that facility for between $30 and $40/mwh for the last six months of the calendar year. In July, however, demand for power has increased steadily in the state market as temperatures have soared into the 90s and higher. Several other plants (not owned by Acme) have been shut down for maintenance, exacerbating the imbalance between supply and demand. Simultaneously, the price of natural gas has spiked due to market conditions in natural gas markets. Acme's asking price on the state spot markets for power from the Springfield plant has risen steadily under these conditions, as have those asked by owners of other natural gas-fired power plants.

Fearing an electricity supply shortage in the state, FERC orders Acme to offer to continue to sell its power on the State X spot market (as FERC did during the California crisis) rather than elsewhere; Acme, for its part, worries about the ability of its customers (retail electricity providers) to pay for the power Acme is selling them: Acme fears that retail price caps in State X will prevent its customers from making enough money to honor their power purchase contracts. On the 20th of July, Acme offers to sell power in the daily spot market at $260/mwh, an unprecedented rate more than six times the historical average. That rate is nevertheless low enough to be accepted by customers desperate for power. However, when the bills for the July 20th power subsequently come due, the buyers refuse to pay, contending that the price was "unjust" and "unreasonable" under the Federal Power Act.

Investigations reveal the following components of the $260/mwh rate:

1. $35/mwh for natural gas fuel costs (which is more than double historical rates in the state)

2. $5/mwh for nitrogen oxides emissions credits, which are required under environmental laws and which have become scarce as natural gas-fired power plants run at full capacity to take advantage of profit opportunities in the tight power sales markets

3. $90/mwh "scarcity rent," representing the amount of profit Acme believed it could extract from any buyer given the relative shortage of electricity on that day's spot markets, and

4. $130/mwh representing a 100 percent "risk premium" charged by Acme because Acme feared that the buyer would be unable to pay, since it could not charge enough for retail power to cover its wholesale power purchase costs

In this hypothetical, Acme has not colluded with other sellers to fix prices, nor has it contributed to the supply shortage by shutting down any of its plants. Rather, it has simply responded to market conditions like a good utility-maximizing firm. Which portions of this $260/mwh rate, if any, are unjust and unreasonable?

With respect to the first two components of the rate, we might assume that Acme is entitled to recover these costs since Acme cannot influence the market prices in the natural gas and emissions markets, and these sorts of cost increases would have been passed along to ratepayers under traditional cost-of-service regulation. However, what if Acme is also a seller of natural gas, and benefits from the increase in the market price of natural gas? Does that fact make the inclusion of these costs in power sales rates unreasonable in some way? Similarly, is the fourth component of the rate, the 100 percent risk premium charged by Acme, reasonable under these circumstances? Remember FERC requires Acme to make this sale. Would the risk premium be reasonable if FERC had not ordered Acme to sell power on the spot market? What do you think? Even more important and difficult are the questions surrounding the third component of the $260/mwh rate, the scarcity rent. Is it unjust for Acme to charge a scarcity rent representing such a large portion of the price? The rationale of market-based electric rates contemplates that scarcity rents will sometimes be available to sellers, and assumes that new firms will enter the market precisely in order to capture those rents, driving the price back down. Because it takes months or years to bring most electric generating plants online, one would expect scarcity rents to be available for extended periods on short-term markets before the presence of new entrants can have a corrective effect on price. How should FERC view this state of affairs? FERC seems to draw a distinction between prices inflated by the exercise of market power and prices inflated by scarcity. However, where exactly is that line?

In this hypothetical, Acme has a scarce good in a market characterized by high barriers to entry (in the short term) and inelastic demand. Acme can increase its selling price secure in the knowledge that it will not be undercut by existing competitors or new entrants. Is Acme engaging in the (presumably permissible) capture of scarcity rents, or the (impermissible) exercise market power?

If the market responds slowly to price spikes, as in California, does the poorly designed market mean that prices are automatically unjust and unreasonable? Does it matter why the market isn't working? What if the reason is the state's interference in the market—that is, what if the state imposes regulatory barriers to the construction of new capacity and retail price caps which make retail demand unresponsive to wholesale price fluctuations? Should regulators step in whenever prices get too high for too long? If so, will market-based pricing have the desired effects in the long run? Can FERC shave the tops off the highest or widest peaks in the price curve and still attract sufficient investment in generation to bring long-run average prices down to efficient levels? Wouldn't that sort of intervention in the market mark a return to the traditional "cost plus fair return" regulation the FERC abandoned in favor of market-based rates? We do not yet have sufficient experience with electricity markets, or with FERC's and the courts' regulation of electricity markets, to know the answers to these questions.

C. THE FUTURE OF STATE RESTRUCTURING

Following the California debacle and other events, there is substantial uncertainty whether restructuring will be beneficial in the long run. There is a high degree of agreement that the road to the marketplace will be bumpy, and the jury is still out on the ability of state regulators and legislatures to successfully realize restructuring's promise. Innovations such as aggregation, real-time pricing (using an advanced meter to allow customers to see the price of electricity in "real time" and correspondingly reduce demand when prices are highest), and net metering may help reduce the adverse effects of the transition to market prices for electricity. Real-time pricing is considered in Chapter 13 along with other measures designed to enable conservation of energy use.

Many observers think that these programs are important for the future of retail competition. However, given their limited use to date, they are hardly a panacea for the problems facing retail competition plans.

1. AGGREGATION AND NET METERING

Aggregation gives small customers buying power in an aggregated group, which presumably can get a better price for its members than an individual can get. This buying power may also allow aggregators to negotiate for additional benefits for the group's members, such as consolidated billing, energy management services, and energy use analysis.

A few states allow municipalities, counties and other local government units to engage in aggregation, combining the electricity loads of entire communities to purchase power and even join with other communities to form a larger purchasing block. (This is different from "municipalization," in which the city or county operates the distribution system and either generates power or purchases it elsewhere, in that the government is only a buying agent for its citizens.) There are two forms of aggregation: *opt-in* (each customer is allowed to choose whether to sign up for the program); and *opt-out* (customers are automatically enrolled unless they individually choose not to be included). Opt-in aggregation can be done by private entities (such as trade associations or nonprofit groups), which then must convince each customer to agree to become part of the buying group.

Ohio's law allows for local government aggregation by cities, townships or counties, with "opt-in" or "opt-out" provisions for their consumers. *See* Ohio Energy Choice, Aggregation: Joining a Buying Group, http://www.ohioelectricchoice.com/residential/aggregation.asp. The plan must include all rates and terms for customers to consider when deciding to join. If the local government chooses opt-in aggregation, it can proceed to develop a plan, become certified and start signing up customers. All aggregators must be certified by the Public Utilities Commission of Ohio ("PUCO") to make sure they are qualified to provide electricity in Ohio.

Aggregation accounts for most customers switching electricity providers in Ohio. The Ohio PUC reported at the end of 2004 that except for government aggregation, "the competitive electric market has not developed as expected," even with a transition period scheduled to expire at the end of 2005. Aggregation made up the bulk of switching residential and small commercial consumers. By 2004, nearly 170 cities, counties, and townships had been aggregated. A total of 858,549 Ohioans had switched electric providers through aggregation as of the end of 2004, almost 95% of all switching consumers; nearly 44,000 customers of the utility Dayton Power & Light took advantage of a new auction-based opt-in aggregation program. 106,697 commercial consumers, or 88% of all switching commercial consumers, had switched through aggregation. Aggregation, however, made up for less than 9% of all switching industrial consumers. Public Utility Commission of Ohio, 2004 End of Year Review and Aggregation Activity in Ohio, http://www.puco.ohio.gov.

Aggregation may have succeeded in Ohio for reasons not easily replicated in other states. *See* NCEP Report, *supra*, at 42–43 (describing Ohio's allocation of "market support generation" power and the requirement in the state's restructuring law that stranded cost recovery was only allowed after a utility had divested itself of 20% of its customers). There have been some aggregation successes elsewhere. *Id.* (discussing aggregation in Massachusetts). In Texas, "[a]ggregators appear to have had limited success in enrolling residential customers." 2005 PUCT Status Report, *supra*, at 70. However, more than 190 school districts benefit from aggregation efforts through the Texas Association of School Boards ("TASB")' "BuyBoard." *See* Texas Ass'n of School Boards, Cooperative Purchasing: Electricity Aggregation Program, http://www.tasb.org/services/cooperative_purchasing/electricity_aggregation/index.aspx. The TASB estimates that school districts save $30 million annually in this program.

* * *

Net metering allows individual customers who generate electricity onsite through some form of distributed generation ("DG," *see* Chapter 13), typically small systems powered by renewable resources, to earn credit from their utility against their electric bills. In effect, a customer using net metering is spinning the meter backward during the time that customer is generating electricity and exporting it to the grid. While net metering is not currently in extensive use, one author terms its potential nothing short of revolutionary due to its ability to reduce the price of electricity for end consumers. Steven Ferrey, Nothing But Net: Renewable Energy and the Environment, Midamerican Legal Fictions, and Supremacy Doctrine, 14 Duke Envtl. L. & Pol'y F. 1, 119 (2003). Net metering also serves an incentive generally for promoting DG; Chapter 13 explores this issue in more depth.

U.S. Department of Energy, Energy Efficiency and Renewable Energy, Net Metering

http://www.eere.energy.gov/

Description

Net metering allows consumers to offset the cost of electricity they buy from a utility by selling renewable electric power generated at their homes or businesses. In essence, a customer's electric meter can run both forward and backward in the same metering period, and the customer is only charged for the net amount of power used. Net metering programs adopted in many states offer the potential for consumers to gain greater financial benefits from installing renewable energy systems.

Implementation

Here's how it works in a hypothetical case. In California, where the legislature adopted net metering in 1995, residents can receive the full retail value of electricity generated by solar-powered systems (about 12 cents to 15 cents per kilowatt-hour [kWh]) and use existing electric meters to measure the flow of electricity between their home and the utility company. On sunny days, the resident's solar system is often able to provide all the household electric needs and generate excess electricity to sell to the utility. In the evenings or on cloudy days, the household will often use power from the utility. Since the consumer sells power and buys power at the same rate, the utility bill is calculated only on the net electricity that the consumer bought from the utility. Metering is usually done monthly, although occasionally the period extends for a full year.

Rate Impact

According to the California Solar Energy Industries Association, a homeowner with a monthly electric bill of around $50 (350 kWh per month) can use a three kilowatt photovoltaic system to bring electric bills to zero under net metering. This will vary depending on the site of the installation.

States with Net Metering

A total of 23 states have adopted some type of net metering provision, either through law or administrative rule....

Arguments for Net Metering

—Net metering adds a significant financial incentive to customers who install renewable energy systems, particularly on systems in which the timing of electricity generation does not match the household usage.

—Programs limited to small systems have little overall financial impact on utilities, assuming these systems are not a major part of the customer base. When an installed system has a peak output less than or comparable to the customer's peak demand, no modifications to utility systems are needed.

—These customers tend to see lower bills with net metering, but the payment system is rarely disrupted. The utility has the advantage of no longer having to account separately for electricity produced by customer-generators. This accounting includes reading second meters sometimes installed at the residences of net metering participants, calculating the payment due, and processing and mailing the payment to customers. Generally, net metering customers do not produce more electricity than they consume during billing periods. Thus, the customer only pays a reduced bill.

—Net metering participants are more aware of energy consumption, and tend not to consume all the energy being generated. Many studies, including some sponsored by utilities, have shown that direct, measurable benefits exist for having generation located close to the end user.

Arguments Against Net Metering

—Net metering has the potential to be a bad deal for utilities. If market penetration of solar and other renewable energy-powered buildings becomes substantial, utilities are likely to become concerned with revenue losses. The utility will then be forced to seek higher rates from its remaining customers to recover fixed costs. Migration away from utility-generated power can leave certain disadvantaged customers holding the bag as rates continue to rise.

—Net metering may involve legal problems under [PURPA], according to an analysis by the Renewable Energy Policy Project. . . . ■

NOTES AND COMMENTS

1.   States vary widely in the structure of their net metering programs. California, Maryland, and New York limit their net metering program to residential customers, but other states allow broader participation. States also vary in fuel types allowed for net metering credit, the capacity of systems, and the types of renewable resources that qualify. Some states limit net metering to certain types of renewable resources, such as solar or wind. Vermont, which enacted a net metering law in 1998, allows solar, wind, fuel cells using renewable fuel, and systems powered through anaerobic digestion to receive net metering credits. Capacity is limited to 15 kilowatts or less, except 100 kilowatts or less for systems using anaerobic digesters. Washington's net metering law, also enacted in 1998, includes solar, wind, and hydropower and includes all customer classes. Arizona allows renewables and cogeneration and makes its program available to all customer classes.

2. According to a November 2002 report, the total number of utility customers with net metering was still small. In California, the state with the largest number of net metering customers, a total of 1,416 net metered systems had been approved and 994 net metered systems are pending. Other states had smaller totals. Nat'l Renewable Energy Laboratory, The Effects of Net Metering on the Use of Small–Scale Wind Systems in the United States (2002).

* * *

PURPA requires utilities to purchase power from "qualifying facilities" (QFs) at the utilities' "avoided cost." To avail itself of this provision, the facility must meet certain requirements to be treated as a QF. Would a net metering customer spinning the meter backward need to meet those requirements or be precluded from providing power to the utility? In 1998, the MidAmerican Energy Company, a utility in Iowa, invoked PURPA to challenge that state's net metering statute. After a series of state and federal proceedings, FERC issued a decision that ended the dispute.

MidAmerican Energy Co.

94 FERC ¶ 61,340 (2001).

In this order, we deny the request of MidAmerican Energy Company (MidAmerican) for a declaratory order that certain orders of the Iowa Utilities Board (Iowa Board) are preempted by Federal law.

MidAmerican's Petition

On October 8, 1998, as amended on November 3, 1998, MidAmerican filed a petition for enforcement pursuant to section 210(h) of the Public Utility Regulatory Policies Act of 1978 (PURPA), 16 U.S.C. § 824a–3(h) (1994), and also for a declaratory order. MidAmerican asked the Commission to undertake enforcement action against the Iowa Board, or to issue a declaratory order.

MidAmerican objects to the Iowa Board's implementing final orders (issued pursuant to Iowa's Alternate Energy Production (Alternate Energy) Statute and § 199–15.11(5) of the regulations thereunder) directing MidAmerican to interconnect with three Alternate Energy facilities and to offer net billing arrangements to those facilities.

Under the net billing arrangements, a single meter measures both energy delivered by MidAmerican to an Alternate Energy facility and energy delivered in the other direction by the Alternate Energy facility to MidAmerican. This single meter offsets the two quantities over the billing period and indicates the net quantity delivered by one to the other. Under the Iowa Alternate Energy statute, an Alternate Energy facility may or may not be a QF. MidAmerican complains that net billing arrangements will result in MidAmerican paying in excess of its avoided costs for power produced by those Alternate Energy facilities which are QFs.

MidAmerican explains:

Assume a QF customer that is an [Alternate Energy] producer consumes 2000 kWh in a month and generates 1000 kWh in the same month. Further assume that the retail rate for electric service is 7¢ per kWh and MidAmerican's avoided cost is 2¢ per KWh. Under the requirements of PURPA, MidAmerican would pay the customer $20 for that month's generation, i.e., for the avoided cost of energy received, and bill the customer $140 for retail electric service provided by MidAmerican. The difference is obviously $120. But, under net billing, the meter registers a net 1000 kWh during the month. MidAmerican's bill for retail services under the net billing scheme is only $70.

MidAmerican concludes that the Iowa Board's actions require MidAmerican to pay in excess of avoided cost for QF power and thus is preempted by PURPA. MidAmerican also claims that when the Alternate Energy facility is not a QF, net billing results in the Iowa Board setting rates for wholesale sales by a public utility, which is preempted by the Federal Power Act.

Interventions

... The Iowa Board filed a notice of intervention and protest. The Iowa Board states that its orders are permissible implementations of state energy policy and are not in conflict with Federal law. The Iowa Board states that it understands that a small producer that qualifies as an Alternate Energy facility under state law must also meet the requirements of PURPA or the FPA to make sales to MidAmerican. The Iowa Board claims that any sales from Alternate Energy facilities pursuant to net billing requirements would meet the requirements of PURPA. It quotes from one of its orders requiring net billing:

One argument made by MidAmerican, however, warrants further comment. MidAmerican claims net billing would require it to pay MidAmerican's retail rates for all power generated by Clarion–Goldfield's alternate energy production ("AEP") facility. This is not how net billing works.

Net billing involves only one meter and one net transaction. Under net billing, the AEP produces power primarily for the owner's needs. However, at times the AEP generates "excess" power which is supplied to the utility through the single meter. Other times, the AEP may not generate sufficient power for the owner's needs and the AEP draws power from the utility through the single meter. Electricity flows through the meter in both directions and is netted out and one meter reading made at the end of a billing period. Strictly speaking, MidAmerican only "pays" for the net negative kWhs, if any, recorded by this single meter. MidAmerican's PURPA tariff, Rider No. 54, applies only if net negative kWhs are recorded in a given billing month.

The Iowa Board further explains that the net billing cases it has addressed have arisen in the context of small power producers. It also states that it is aware that some Alternate Energy facilities are covered by the Federal Power Act, but that such larger producers rarely present a net billing issue. The Iowa Board further argues that the current case before the Commission does not involve "pricing or rates or federal preemption over them. It involves the measurement of power used by a retail customer operating in parallel with the utility."

... [The] ... National Association of Regulatory Utility Commissioners ("NARUC") argues that state programs to address these issues are consistent with the Commission's pro-competitive policies for bulk power markets and should be supported by the Commission. Others point out that most of the net billing and metering programs involve small retail consumers who utilize small sized facilities (often wind or solar) to supply a portion of their own electric power needs and that few of the net billing programs will result in net sales to utilities.

Many intervenors also argue, inter alia, that:

(1) where there is no net sale in a billing period Federal law is not involved;

(2) net billing and metering decisions relate exclusively to the states' regulation of retail sales;

(3) most net billing and metering regulation relates to QFs and is consistent with PURPA; and

(4) where PURPA is not involved, any net sale involved is so minimal, and so related to the state retail policies, that this Commission's jurisdiction under the Federal Power Act is not involved.

NIMO states that it has worked hard to restructure its QF contracts, which it characterizes as uneconomic, and that it fears that it will be economically harmed by any Commission decision that would approve a state program like Iowa's.

Discussion

... MidAmerican argues that every flow of power constitutes a sale, and, in particular, that every flow of power from a homeowner or farmer to MidAmerican must be priced consistent with the requirements of either PURPA or the FPA.

We find no such requirement. This case presents an issue similar to that in our recent decision addressing the netting of station power used at a generating station against certain wholesale sales from the generating station. See PJM Interconnection, L.L.C., 94 FERC ¶ 61,251 (2001)(PJM). In that case, in the context of the FPA, the Commission found that there is no sale (for end use or otherwise) between two different parties when one party is using its own generating resources for the purpose of self-supply of station power, and accounting for such usage through the practice of netting. Id., slip op. at 20. In the case before us we find likewise that no sale occurs when an individual homeowner or farmer (or similar entity such as a business) installs generation and accounts for its dealings with the utility through the practice of netting. In implementing PURPA, the

Commission similarly recognized that net billing arrangements like those at issue here would be appropriate in some situations, and left the decision of when to do so to state regulatory authorities.

There may be, over the course of the billing period, either a net sale from the individual to the utility, or a net purchase by the individual from the utility. When there is a net sale to a utility, and the individual's generation is not a QF, the individual would need to comply with the requirements of the Federal Power Act. According to the Iowa Board, however, facilities which are not QFs rarely, if ever, have net billing arrangements with a utility. When there is a net sale to a utility, and the individual's generation is a QF, that net sale must be at an avoided cost rate consistent with PURPA and our regulations implementing PURPA. We note that from the description of the three facilities that were the subject of the Iowa Board's orders, however, each appears to be a QF. . . .

The Commission orders:

MidAmerican's request for a declaratory order is hereby denied, as discussed in the body of this order.■

NOTES AND COMMENTS

1. Commenting on *MidAmerican Energy Co.*, Professor Steven Ferrey terms the decision "surprising" for its avoidance of the central issue: whether the transaction in which the customer transfers excess power to the utility is a "sale" within FERC's jurisdiction. Ferrey, *supra*. Professor Ferrey asserts that FERC's holding is contrary to those in other cases involving FERC's jurisdiction over sales of electricity in interstate commerce. *See* Chapter 11.

2.   CAUTION ABOUT RETAIL COMPETITION'S FUTURE

Retail competition has been slow to develop even in states that were early adopters of competition plans, with Texas perhaps standing as a notable exception. Factors such as a continuing volatility in natural gas prices (which affects consumers' willingness to switch from incumbent utilities that guarantee stable electricity rates), an inadequate transmission system and (in some parts of the country) immature wholesale power markets, a continuing squabble between the states and federal government about the contours of jurisdiction over restructuring policy, and other factors such as a dearth of consumer knowledge about utility choice have all added up to put restructuring in a holding pattern. The following excerpt summarizes the status of competition nationwide:

Kenneth Rose, 2004 Performance Review of Electric Markets ii–vi

http://www.scc.virginia.gov/caseinfo/reports/2004_rose.pdf.

Since the price run-ups in California and the West beginning in mid–2000 and into 2001, the electric supply industry has not been able to return to a relative stable or calm period of time. The industry's problems continued after the western power crisis with Enron's disclosures and collapse in late 2001, revelations of market price manipulation strategies, disclosures of accounting improprieties and data misreporting, the continuing "credit crunch," and, the major event of 2003, the most extensive blackout in North American history.

In the face of this turmoil, most states have decided to either discontinue their efforts to implement retail access or have stopped considering adopting it altogether. The overall picture of which states have adopted retail access has not changed substantially in the last few years. Sixteen states and the District of Columbia have fully implemented their legislation and commission orders and currently allow full retail access for all customer groups. Two states allow retail access for larger customers only; Nevada, that modified its original law to limit access to just larger customers and Oregon, whose original law limited retail access to larger customers. Six states that passed restructuring legislation later delayed, repealed, or indefinitely postponed implementation. Oklahoma and West Virginia passed restructuring legislation but stopped short of implementation, Arkansas and New Mexico have repealed their laws, California suspended the retail access program it already had implemented in September 2001, more than one year after the beginning of the California and western power crisis. Montana, has also been dealing with the severe aftermath of the western power crisis, has extended the transition period to retail access for smaller customers. They implemented retail access for large industrial customers in July 1998, but residential access originally scheduled to begin by July 2002 was postponed to 2027. While there are some large retail customers in western state retail markets active in the market (in California, Montana, and Oregon), in general, these retail markets have not yet fully recovered from the western power crisis.

Twenty six states are no longer considering restructuring at this time and none of these states appear to be near passage of restructuring legislation or working in any meaningful way toward passage at this time. In fact, no state has passed restructuring legislation since June of 2000, when the California and western power crisis was just beginning to take shape. These states that did not pass legislation but were in the process of considering it either gradually lessened their efforts to allow time to consider what was occurring in the west or they abruptly stopped any activity that was ongoing at the time. A total of 32 states have repealed, delayed, suspended or are now no longer considering retail access.

For the 16 states and D.C. that have continued with retail access, many retail markets have remained relatively inactive, particularly for smaller residential customers.... Of the 63 distribution companies represented in [these states], 43 or over two-thirds of the companies, had less than one percent of the customers choosing an alternative, most (27) were zero. Only seven have greater than 20 percent of the residential customers receiving power from alternative suppliers. Three of those seven distribution companies are in Ohio where nearly 95 percent of the residential switching in the state has been through the state's aggregation program. Two of the remaining four distribution companies were in relatively higher priced states, Pennsylvania and New York (although not the highest priced distribution companies in the state, each were the second highest priced distribution company in their state) and the two Texas distribution companies had the highest "price-to-beat" (the price-to-compare for residential customers) in the state.

. . . While there are seven states where there are more than 20 percent of the total state load now being served by competitive suppliers, no state has reached that point for residential load. Only two states and D.C. have surpassed 10 percent of residential load, one of these states is Ohio, which again is mainly attributable to the state's aggregation program. Five of the seven states (including D.C.) where total load was greater than 20 percent were in relatively higher priced regions. The two exceptions were Texas, where again a substantial portion of the retail activity has been in the higher priced distribution companies of the state, and Montana, which began restructuring as one of the lowest-priced states in the country and where retail access is limited to only large customers. However, due to the western power crisis of 2000 and 2001, those customers that entered the power market paid considerably higher prices than they had before restructuring began.

Several states are now also using bidding or auctions to procure power supply for their non-choosing customers. The Maine Public Utilities Commission has conducted four rounds of competitive bidding since March 2000. Currently, all customers not receiving power from a competitive supplier are on competitively-determined standard offer price, this includes nearly all residential customers in the state. New Jersey has had three auction rounds of an Internet-based, simultaneous, multi-round, and descending clock auction. The "Basic Generation Service" load is auctioned simultaneously for all four New Jersey electric utilities. Maryland had its first round of competitive bidding for two distribution companies in 2004.■

NOTES AND COMMENTS

1.   In addition to the states mentioned by Rose, there is activity underway in Ohio and Michigan to either amend or repeal the state restructuring plans. Kelly, *supra*.

2.   In some states with competition plans, switching rates are low because there are no meaningful opportunities for competitive choice at all, and none likely to materialize for quite some time. *See* Virginia Energy Choice, http://yesvachoice.com.

3.   Maine, Maryland, and New Jersey (all mentioned in the Rose excerpt) are but three of the states that have addressed a difficult question: with residential and small commercial switching rates being low in virtually every state, most of these customers will be served for the foreseeable future by their current (incumbent) utilities. States must decide who will supply power to these customers, and under what conditions. With whole-

sale markets evolving in many parts of the nation, should utilities use these markets to obtain power they distribute at retail to non-switching residential and commercial customers?

Assume for the moment that distribution utilities could purchase power in well-run wholesale markets, though that is hardly the case in all parts of the nation. *See* Chapter 11. If DisCos simply passed through the wholesale price to their customers, that leaves those customers subject to potential price volatility. Most residential customers have limited ability at present to respond to changing electricity prices without engaging in conservation measures (*see* the discussion of real-time pricing, *supra*), and customers such as those with lower incomes could be severely harmed by fluctuating prices. As one author notes, this is not the only risk of relying on wholesale markets: "It is unclear that markets alone will support the needed construction of new sources of power when they are needed. Certainly the implosion of many of the early participants in the new wholesale markets and the recent difficulties in raising capital for any power plant construction raises serious doubt as to whether investors have confidence in these markets." Barbara R. Alexander, Managing Default Service to Provide Consumer Benefits in Restructured States: Avoiding Short–Term Price Volatility, Nat'l Center for Appropriate Technology (2003), http://neaap.ncat.org/experts/defservintro.htm. The prospect of political and consumer backlash to relying exclusively on wholesale markets, as took place in California, is not appetizing.

States have adopted a number of different approaches to address these issues. In general, however, there are two basic models (outside of Texas, where the retail and wholesale markets, as noted above, are closely linked):

(1) The DisCo purchases power from the wholesale market, either with or without state regulation of the results; or

(2) The DisCo enters into contracts in advance, at prices fixed for specific periods of time, to serve a percentage of load (that is, a certain number of customers), and then purchases power to supply these customers.

Michael Schnitzer, The POLR Procurement Puzzle, Ill. Commerce Comm'n, Post 2006 Symposium (2004), at 4, http://www.icc.illinois.gov/ec /docs/040503ecPostSchnitzer.pdf. Schnitzer terms the first approach "resource procurement" and the second "full requirements procurement." A state adopting a "resource procurement" approach (with regulation) is Montana, which has modified its retail competition law to require incumbent utilities to provide "adequate and reliable default supply service at the lowest long-term total cost." Mont. Code Ann. § 69–8–102; Alexander, *supra*.

The "full requirements procurement" approach has a major advantage for the DisCo: it can make its own decisions about the resources it will use to supply customers. From a consumer's perspective, it can be beneficial if it shifts some or all of the risk of price fluctuations to the utilities from individual customers. For these and other reasons, states have moved increasingly toward it.

New Jersey uses a unique auction process for full requirements procurement to serve customers who receive its default service, called "Basic Generation Service" ("BGS"). The state's retail competition law was enacted in 1999, with competition beginning in August 1999. Under this statute, mandated rate reductions and rate caps expired in August 2003. The state's Board of Public Utilities ("BPU") adopted a unique "auction" process to govern the purchase of power during the transition period, and later extended it to govern additional years beyond 2003:

> In December 2001 the BPU determined that for year 4 of the transition period (i.e., August 2003–August 2004), electric utilities should continue to provide BGS, with the procurement of the generation supply to be achieved by means of an auction process. The auction was held in early 2002 pursuant to a multi-day electronic auction process supervised by a consultant to the Board. All the utilities were required to accept the result of this action and enter into full requirements contracts with the auction winners pursuant to the Master Supply Agreement that had previously been negotiated by the parties and approved by the Board. The auction divided the customer load that must be served into 170 "tranches" (slices of customer load) to allow for multiple rounds of bidding by a wide range of licensed suppliers.

> This auction was conducted as a "simultaneous declining block" auction. All the load of the electric utilities was bid out at the same time (approximately 18,000 MW), but the retail load of each EDC [*electric distribution company*] was considered a separate "product" for which a supplier could bid to serve all or part ("tranche" or fixed percentage share of a utility's load). The auction is "descending" because the going prices are gradually reduced during the term of the auction. The auction ends when the total number of tranches bid equals the number of tranches that the Auction Manager (as the agent of the Board) has set as the auction volume. The bidders that hold the final bids when the auction closes are the winning bidders. The resulting bids are averaged for each utility's tranches so that the resulting prices for generation supply service vary among the different utilities. As a result of the auction conducted in 2002 for Year 4, the closing prices were PSE&G–5.11 [cents/kWh]; Jersey Central–4.87; Conectiv–5.12; and Rockland–5.82.

> After an extensive proceeding in 2002, the Board approved essentially the same approach for pricing BGS for the post–2003 period. The Board approved the same type of auction process, but required that a separate auction for Fixed Price service be conducted to obtain two-thirds of the utility load eligible for this service for 10 months and one-third of the fixed price load for a 34–month period. The results of these two sub-auctions will be blended in a single price for fixed price customers, notably residential and small commercial customers, for a full year (August 2003 until May 31, 2004). Other larger customers will

obtain BGS service via an Hourly Energy Price auction and be required to take service through interval meters. The Board reserved for a later time its decision about the procurement process for a subsequent year (June 2004 through May 2005).

This auction was conducted in early 2003 and announced on February 5, 2003. According to the BPU, customer rates will increase on average 7.3 percent as a result of the auction. Individual utilities will experience different results: PSE&G–6.54 percent increase; Jersey Central–7.3 percent increase; Conectiv–4.5 percent increase; Rockland–4.3 percent decrease. These results do not include the base rate increases sought by the utilities (in the range of 8 to 12 percent) which will be decided this summer, along with the rate impact of deferred balances.

Alexander, *supra*.

Note that the winning bidder for supply of a specific tranche need not be a utility that owns generating capacity: it could be a financial company that believes it can make a profit buying power on the wholesale market and selling it to consumers for the defined price. Schnitzer, *supra*, at 11. For example, in the 2005 auction for Fixed Price load, the Morgan Stanley Capital Group was the successful bidder to supply five slices of customer load. *See* http://www.bpu.state.nj.us/wwwroot/energy/BGS_FP05.pdf.

Believing the process to be successful, the BPU extended it through the supply year beginning in mid–2006. N.J. Bd. of Public Util., Order in Docket No. EO05040317, May 5, 2005. One author, however, advises caution:

The New Jersey approach reflects the most sophisticated effort to attain "true" wholesale market prices based on competitive bidding. The fact that the entire utility customer load is available during one auction process is likely to draw the largest pool of suppliers and supply resources to this effort. On the other hand, the auction process itself reflects only short-term market trends, which in the PJM area is in a wholesale surplus situation. As a result, there is no long-term price stability, resource acquisition, or portfolio management occurring in New Jersey. New Jersey has truly put all its electricity eggs in the hands of the wholesale market for generation, and the fact that the vast majority of the customer load is bid out at the same time is a very risky business. While the PJM wholesale market has been relatively stable, at least compared to Western energy markets, the changes that are likely to occur as a result of the expansion of PJM to include New York and other large Midwestern utilities (such as Commonwealth Edison in Illinois) may result in unforeseen changes in electricity prices in the short term. Furthermore, the risk that the auction will be conducted during a time of market instability due to either a true shortage or market manipulation should also be considered.

Alexander, *supra*.

Other states—notably Illinois—have contemplated following the New Jersey auction process. The proposal of utility Commonwealth Edison to purchase power through a wholesale auction starting in 2007 was opposed by the Illinois attorney general's office, the Cook County state's attorney's office and the Citizens Utility Board. Robert Manor, Auction aids ComEd, foes charge, Chicago Tribune, June 10, 2005. In his 2004 presentation to the Illinois Commerce Commission (the state's PSC), Michael Schnitzer explained one concern with administering an auction in Illinois: the universe of potential competitors in the New Jersey auction process was much greater than in Illinois. Schnitzer noted that a "substantial number of winning bidders" in New Jersey are financial companies that do not own generating capacity, which he believed made for a more robust competitive process. By contrast, in Illinois there were "only two large owners of generators, and one is a ComEd affiliate" (the Exelon Corp., the owner of nuclear plants in the state and corporate parent of ComEd). Schnitzer, *supra*. In 2004, however, Commonwealth Edison was integrated into PJM—the regional wholesale market used to supply New Jersey customers. Commonwealth Edison Successfully Integrated Into PJM, Transmission & Distrib. World, May 3, 2004, http://tdworld.com.

Could Commonwealth Edison argue that PJM's market monitoring procedures will protect Illinois consumers against price spikes? Or should the potential risks of relying on the wholesale market—even one as currently stable as PJM, as described by Barbara Alexander above—weigh against extending the auction process?

a.   IS RESTRUCTURING YIELDING BENEFITS?

With low levels of customer switching, it is reasonable to wonder whether more than a decade of restructuring has accomplished much, if anything. As one observer puts it, the answer is different for different classes of electric customers:

> The "power to choose" has turned out in many cases to be overrated, at least for residential and small commercial electric customers. The vast majority of such customers never really asked for retail choice in the first place. Large industrial customers, and the marketers that wanted to serve them directly, were the driving force behind retail access in those states that implemented it.

Kelly, *supra*.

If large numbers of residential customers are not switching, have there at least been sufficient benefits for those who have done so such that one could conclude the experiment in competition is worth continuing? Are residential consumers saving on their electric bills? Or have savings been confined to larger industrial customers? The choice of fuel used to generate electricity (and its cost) can be vitally important to this inquiry:

> A common theme that most wholesale markets shared in the last two years is the substantial impact that the price of natural gas now has on power prices. In particular, the natural gas price spikes that occurred across the country in early 2003 and in the northeast region of the country in early 2004, led to corresponding power price spikes in these

regions. Even when natural gas is not the most commonly used fuel to generate power in the region, because it is often the marginal fuel used and because many power contracts have the price for power pegged to natural gas prices, natural gas and power prices now generally move in tandem.

Rose, *supra*.

The experience in Texas is telling. Wholesale and retail electricity prices have increased significantly since 2002, and the Public Utility Commission of Texas found that the state's electricity rates have risen at a faster pace than those of the rest of the nation as a whole. PUCT 2005 Status Report, *supra*. That rise has been attributable in large part to increases in the market price of natural gas, because the majority of generation in ERCOT is fueled by natural gas. Since the 2002 opening of the retail market to competition, natural gas prices have increased approximately 150% and wholesale electricity prices have also more than doubled. *Id*. According to University of Texas statistician Jay Zarnikau, switching customers have been the *most* adversely affected by these trends. Zarnikau found that restructuring in Texas has led to rate increases of 43 percent between January 2002 to October 2004 for switching customers, 17 percent increase for non-switching customers, and 9 percent for customers of rural electric cooperatives. Deregulation raises rates for Texas residential, small business consumers—study, Greenwire, May 20, 2005.

A 2004 report by the National Association of State PIRGs (Public Interest Research Groups) concludes that nationwide, residential customers have not benefited much from restructuring, noting that "[a] decade of electric industry restructuring has led to few benefits for the majority of consumers, and any benefits consumers have experienced are likely to be short-lived." Toward A Consumer–Oriented Electric System: Assuring Affordability, Reliability, Accountability and Balance After a Decade of Restructuring (2004) ("PIRG Report"). Specific findings included the following:

• Retail electricity rates for residential consumers declined by 18.3 percent in inflation-adjusted terms between 1993 and 2002—a decline broadly consistent with long-term historical trends. In 2001 and 2003, however, residential rates increased in inflation-adjusted terms—the first such year-to-year increases in nearly two decades.

• Declining real energy prices—particularly for coal—appear to have played a major role in causing the rate decline. Coal prices declined by about 40 percent in real terms between 1993 and 2002. Natural gas prices were at their lowest point since the mid–1970s for several years during the 1990s, before spiking in 2000.

• States in which consumers may choose their retail electricity provider experienced greater reductions in residential electricity rates than states without retail choice (21 percent vs. 16 percent) between 1993 and 2002. But the restructured states experiencing the greatest decreases were those in which very few consumers chose competitive suppliers, leading to the conclusion that other factors—including the imposition of mandatory rate reductions that accompanied restructuring in most states and the fact that most restructured states had higher rates to begin with—are responsible for the greater rate of decrease in restructured states.

● The gap between the rates paid by residential customers and those paid by industrial customers has been rising. In 1993, the average residential customer paid 71.5 percent more per unit of electricity than the average industrial customer. By 2002, residential customers were paying 74.9 percent more for each unit of electricity they used. *Id*. The PIRG Report also notes that restructuring has had other costs, such as a 38% decrease in spending on state-and utility-sponsored energy efficiency programs between 1993 and 2000. *See* Chapter 13 for a description of these programs.

A report by the Center for the Advancement of Energy Markets ("CAEM") found that in 2002, restructuring led to "more than $3 billion in total savings in 2002 in the Mid–Atlantic (PJM) region," and that the average household in Pennsylvania saved $117 on its electricity bill due to restructuring. *See* Benefits of Competition in the Mid–Atlantic, http://www.caem.org. However, this conclusion is attributed more to the development of a functioning wholesale market (PJM) than to Pennsylvania's retail competition plan. As the PIRG report observes, if there are benefits from restructuring in the form of lower retail electricity prices, they are often attributable to the caps which keep rates low. *See* T.M. Sell, What if you deregulated a market, and no one cared?, Salon.com, May 24, 2004 (discussing this with respect to Pennsylvania).

The rate caps and transition periods in restructuring states were designed to mark the time when fully competitive markets would be operational. Thus, many states face hard policy choices about continuing the transition to competition (as in Virginia, which extended rate caps to 2010) or ending it and exposing consumers to the market. NCEP Report, *supra*. With many rate caps still in place, however, it is difficult to make a nationwide comparison between electricity prices in restructuring states and those which have retained traditional bundled service. Nonetheless, it is highly unlikely that removal of rate caps will help a situation in which the evidence to date already suggests that consumers are not seeing lower electricity prices as a result of restructuring. Removal of the rate cap in New Jersey in 2003—and the implementation of the wholesale market-based auction process for obtaining power for customers served by default service—led to an immediate 19 percent increase in rates. PIRG Report, *supra*.

Finally, even if competitive markets were fully operational, states would continue to struggle with designing appropriate market monitoring mechanisms to protect consumers from abuses such as those that took place in California.

b.   CAN ENERGY MARKETS BE TRUSTED?

Surveying the current status of restructuring, Professor Jacqueline Lang Weaver is not sanguine about the future of restructuring and the ability of the marketplace to deliver promised benefits to consumers.

Jacqueline Lang Weaver, Can Energy Markets Be Trusted? The Effect of the Rise and Fall of Enron on Energy Markets.

1 Houston Bus. & Tax L. J. 131–140 (2004).

After California, retail electricity deregulation is a much harder political sell. But even before that state's chaos made headlines for so many months, thoughtful commentators had questioned whether the small consumer would benefit from deregulated energy markets in contrast to large industrial and commercial users. It is very difficult to allow incumbent utilities to recover their stranded costs and also prevent prices to the consumer from rising, while simultaneously providing enough profit margin for new competitors to enter the markets and erode the monopoly power of the local incumbent. Even for larger users, price volatility is a serious business risk for companies that no longer rely completely on long-term contracts for their energy supplies. Risk management tools may not be adequate to hedge against risk that extends beyond a few years.

Small wonder, then, that in electricity—with its peculiar needs for spare capacity and real-time balancing of the grid minute by minute—the transition to competitive markets will be much more difficult than in other industries. The federal/state jurisdictional issues, stranded costs, inelastic demand for electricity, and the ineffectiveness of antitrust laws and other regulatory reviews to assess and curb monopoly power add enormously to the complexity of the sheer physics of electricity markets. In a widely publicized report, Consumers Union looked at the effects of deregulation in the airlines, trucking, cable TV, banking, telephone, and electricity markets, and scored deregulation in terms of price savings, consumer rights, safety, consumer choice, and innovation. All industries present a mixed picture, ranging from the woeful $160 billion government bailout of 1,600 bank failures in the savings-and-loan crisis of the early 1990s, to the success of Southwest Airlines as an efficient, low-cost carrier. Yes—prices have dropped in most of the deregulated industries, but prices were falling before deregulation, often at a faster rate, a fact seldom recognized by proponents of deregulation.

In longer reports, this consumer organization looked more closely at electricity deregulation. Electricity deregulation in many states, not just California, had been too often accompanied by abuse of market power, excessive scarcity overcharges, inefficient transactions costs of coordinating the complex system, and a sharp increase in the cost of capital, all of which may have swamped any conceivable efficiency gains. Lower electricity prices to date are often due to mandated regulatory price decreases, not to deregulation. In major respects, the Consumer Federation is right: deregulation has produced decidedly mixed results. The question is: Do we move forward in electricity markets, learning from past mistakes, or do we go back to a less complex system that, whatever its inefficiencies, never produced the chaos that now enshrouds the entire industry? The public utility model, for all its faults, generally delivered reliable power and reserve margins at reasonable prices. How can competition and deregulation provide this essential reliability without a high degree of coordination, interrelatedness, and centralized planning? Even the top utility regulator in Texas sounded like a central planner the minute that power companies in the state started shutting down plants in the midst of a surplus of generating capacity, saying, "We can't take for granted these blessed reserves," so new rules would be needed to protect against future power shortages. In essence, have markets met their match in electricity?

VIII.   CAN ENERGY MARKETS BE TRUSTED?

... So, should we plunge forward, as Alfred Kahn suggests, or engage in dialogue first about the morality and rationality of markets? ... The ultimate test of electricity markets will be how industry participants, regulators, and consumers react to shortages that may arise after 2005. It is relatively easy to regulate when excess capacity exists—and quite difficult when it disappears, as California discovered. It is still not clear whether FERC's proposed Standard Market Design or Wholesale Market Platform has provided adequate market incentives and regulatory mandates to assure investment in transmission assets and reserve generating capacity.

... The new paradigm views the goals of regulation as the promotion of competition and consumer choice. Once in place, competition and choice will police the markets without much need for a regulatory bureaucracy. "Light-handed" regulation will suffice. The reasons for this paradigm shift have been found to be twofold: first, key interest groups, notably large business interests, discovered that deregulation was to their advantage; and second, economists and other policy elites reached an ideological consensus that the risks of regulatory failure under the original paradigm exceeded the risk of market failure under the new paradigm.

As noted earlier, large industrial and commercial users are the chief recipients of benefits from competition in electricity and natural gas (although these lower prices should ultimately "trickle through" to lower-priced manufactured products for consumers). Furthermore, there is so much money being spent on political lobbying by every major group within the electricity industry that cynics say Congress has little incentive to resolve energy issues quickly. As to the ideological consensus, strongly fostered by economists, that markets are superior to regulation, there is little doubt that that this has been a major factor in electricity restructuring. This ideology explains FERC's long reluctance to intervene in the chaos of California and California's own embrace of a Power Exchange as the ultimate market of all power markets. The California crisis precipitated an extraordinary round of competing "manifestos" by prominent economists. The true believers urged officials to resist any form of price cap, while those who recognized the reality of dysfunctional markets, including Alfred Kahn, urged regulatory intervention. Another manifesto was issued in early 2003, urging California to create commodity market institutions, to implement real-time pricing, and to "rely on markets whenever possible."

But when are markets "possible"? . . . The primary lesson of California is that . . . light-handed regulation combined with the entrepreneurial, profit-maximizing behavior of private participants in electricity markets does not serve the public well. So, can electricity markets be trusted? Here again is Fukuyama's definition of trust as "the expectation that arises within a community of regular, honest, and cooperative behavior." I think the easy answer is: no. They cannot be trusted to work without a high degree of government intervention that true believers will continue to find "offensive" and continue to criticize as retarding the "dazzling benefits" that markets can provide. In this conclusion, I have the company of others:

> [T]he process of deregulation is more corruptible than the process of regulation. . . . [I]t is absolutely clear that if we are to pursue "deregulation," then we must be willing to regulate deregulation.

Alan Richardson, American Public Power Association President, June 2002.

> The curious paradox of a market-based regulatory reform [in electricity] is that we may end up with more rather than less regulation.

Joseph P. Tomain, Dean and Professor of Law, 2002.

And will the government intervention be well-designed even when it incorporates lessons learned from experience? FERC has learned this lesson from its study of market problems in California and the Northeast:

> Small details of market design can turn out to have major effects on market performance.

FERC's proposal for Standard Market Design, July 2002.

If the "devil is in the details," but the details are so difficult to get right because electricity has such unique attributes, then it is time to say that markets have met their match in this arena. In even simpler markets, such as one-time auctions for the telecommunications spectrum, "disastrous" results have occurred because "superficially trivial" distinctions between policy proposals were actually quite important and because the economic consultants' market design, while sound in theory, could not translate into good policymaking, given real-world political pressures, including lobbying from the regulated industry.

Certainly, electricity markets can and will be designed to avoid the more obvious flaws in California's noble, but failed, experiment. But, the real question is whether deregulated energy markets will produce a better grade than the C+ that [FERC Chairman] Pat Wood gave to traditional utility regulation. The FERC Chairman is hoping for a grade of B for restructured markets. In my mind, the mid-term grade to date for deregulation is a U for "unsatisfactory." Residential consumers have for too long been wooed with hyperbolic promises of great benefits from electricity deregulation—lower rates, more reliability, and greater choice. There is little evidence that restructured markets will reduce electricity rates in any meaningful amount for the residential consumer.

The poor performance of retail competition hinders the development of wholesale markets by undermining investment incentives for distribution companies and other retail providers to enter into long-term contracts with new investors for generation and transmission service. Without new entrants, incumbents are left with market power that regulators will intervene to suppress when prices rise as supply margins narrow. Reliability becomes more precarious as the industry "de-integrates" into competitive rather than coordinated units. In addition, no one in these new markets—except traders, sometimes—appears to like the volatility that has accompanied deregulation. The dreadful "Averch–Johnson inefficiency" of regulated utilities does not seem to have been so large that deregulation will capture significant gains that regulators were not already capturing through incentive-based performance standards, mandatory competitive bidding by utilities for new generation supplies, and other mechanisms that were lowering electricity rates before restructuring began.■

NOTES AND COMMENTS

1.   Professor Richard Pierce, whose analysis of the future of restructuring focuses mainly on wholesale markets, agrees that the California power crisis still looms over the restructuring of the industry. However, he argues that entrenched competitors in the electricity business and their political supporters in Southern and Western states have seized on the California fiasco as a means to ward off restructuring efforts they oppose for completely different reasons. There is no doubt, in Pierce's view, that the California experience was horrible. He argues that nonetheless the causes of the California debacle are well known and will, if heeded (and more importantly, avoided in the future), make future restructuring efforts productive. Pierce, Completing the Process, *supra*.

John Anderson, Executive Director of ELCON, the national organization of large industrial users of electricity and a proponent of restructuring since the mid–1980s, agrees with Pierce, saying that, "Basically, we are in a transition. One that will last a long time [a]nd won't be pleasant or easy. But I am cautiously optimistically that we will succeed—the only question is when. [The] problems were caused by both state regulators and legislators. Prodded, of course, by those with very strong interests and tremendous resources—primarily the incumbent utilities." Anderson, *supra*.

As industry expert Susan Kelly notes, wrangles over jurisdictional turf persist in the wake of *New York v. FERC* (*see* Chapter 11). Kelly states, "The strongly expressed preferences of state public utility commissioners to maintain their jurisdiction over bundled retail transmission service" may well be responsible for the dearth of RTO formation at the wholesale level and a corresponding correlation to states that have not implemented retail competition. Kelly, *supra*. In his analysis of the litigation between FERC and the Virginia State Corporation Commission and other states' agencies over the application of utility American Electric Power to join the PJM Interconnection RTO, Professor Joel Eisen places blame both on the states and FERC for engaging in "Commerce Clause brinksmanship" that has continued the climate of uncertainty in restructuring. Joel B. Eisen, Regulatory Linearity, Commerce Clause Brinksmanship, and Retrenchment in Electric Utility Restructuring, 40 Wake Forest L. Rev. 545 (2005).

2. Interest groups as widely divergent in their perspective on governmental regulation as the libertarian think tank Cato Institute and the consumer group National Association of State PIRGs have criticized retail competition in electricity. The Cato report from 2004, "Rethinking Electricity Restructuring," prefers full deregulation of the industry but, noting it would be politically difficult, calls for the electric power industry to embrace an updated version of its former regulated, vertically integrated structure because restructuring has led to spectacular failures in the states. *See* http://www.cato.org/pubs/pas/pa530.pdf. Laura Murrell and Ken Malloy, Center for the Advancement of Energy Markets, Throwing the Baby out with the Bathwater: A Rebuttal to Cato's Report "Rethinking Electricity Restructuring" (2004), http:www.caem.org, criticizes the Cato report:

> "Adam Smith must be rolling over in his grave.... Rather than constructively engaging on making the open access model work—a model of competition that is both politically feasible and has delivered significant benefits to in telecom and natural gas—CATO takes the bizarre position that the U.S. return to the monopoly model," said Malloy.
>
> The open access model in electric has unquestionably suffered setbacks in the last several years. "This is no time to cut and run. It is a time for the supporters of competitive electric markets to regroup and develop an action plan that learns from the past setbacks. The Cato report is a wake-up call that we have a lot of work to do," said Malloy.

The PIRG Report, discussed above, concludes that the U.S. electric system is "on the verge of a crisis," with consumers trapped between a regulated system with high levels of consumer protection and emerging market-based structures that offer little in the way of certainty. PIRG Report, *supra*. The report calls for regulators to acknowledge that retail competition is unlikely to provide significant benefits to small power consumers, and for the government to focus on wholesale market policies that will benefit consumers and measures designed to produce long-term benefits, including programs for energy efficiency, distributed generation and renewable energy—the subject of Chapter 13. *Id.*; *see* American Public Power Association, Restructuring at the Crossroads—FERC Electric Policy Reconsidered (2004) for another critical analysis of restructuring's impacts.

CHAPTER 13

ENVIRONMENTAL ISSUES IN ELECTRIC POWER GENERATION

Traditional rate regulation of electricity generation and transmission has been criticized for not reflecting the full social costs of power production and delivery. These activities create externalities in two distinct ways: 1) they may impose costs on adjacent or nearby users by emitting pollutants, influencing property prices or creating risks; and 2) they may fail to fully reflect the actual costs of the fuel inputs utilized for production, leading to overuse—and potential depletion—of these inputs. In recent years, the generation and transmission of electricity has been subject to environmental regulation designed to internalize the full costs of production and delivery.

Electricity generation has a greater impact on air quality than any other single industry in the U.S. (other than the transportation sector, discussed in Chapter 15). The environmental impact of electricity is considered at a number of separate places in this book. The impact of coal-burning power plants on air quality was discussed in Chapter 5. Externalities created by nuclear generation are addressed in Chapter 14. Utilities also account for about a third of man-made greenhouse gas (CO_2) emissions in the United States, a subject discussed in Chapter 16. The impact of hydro-electric generation on wildlife habitat and commercial fishing was discussed in Chapter 4.

Widespread competition will also have significant impacts on environmental regulation of the industry. This chapter addresses those impacts.

A. AIR POLLUTION REGULATION

Some believed competition in the electric power industry would lead to a reduction in air pollution. One author argued that competition would encourage the development of more efficient combined-cycle generation technologies, which would displace obsolete and inefficient technologies, such as single-cycle coal generation. *See* Thomas R. Casten, Turning Off the Heat: Why America Must Double Energy Efficiency to Save Money and Reduce Global Warming (Prometheus Books 1998). Many others, however, are not as optimistic about the prospects of competition for environmental regulations. Recall from Chapter 5 that the Clean Air Act regulates air emissions from major new or modified sources of pollution, including coal- and gas-fired power plants. With the rise of competition, it was feared that power produced from low-cost coal fired plants in the Midwest could find its way to the Northeast, where electricity producers are at a disadvantage compared to Midwestern producers who have access to low-cost, high sulfur coal. In addition, competition could make it economical for utilities to run cheaper, dirtier, coal-fired power plants mothballed for years. These dynamics could lead to increased emissions of particulates, ozone and other pollutants in the Midwest would travel to the Northeast, exacerbating air quality problems there:

Congressional Research Service (Larry Parker and John Blodgett), Report 98–615: Electricity Restructuring: The Implications for Air Quality (1998)

http://www.ncseonline.org/nle/crsreports/energy/eng-43.cfm.

In general, older facilities that have been fully depreciated would tend to have market values greater than their current book value under regulation; in contrast, newer, capital intensive facilities (such as some nuclear plants) would have market values less than their current book value. (Case-by-case valuation would be affected by location, availability of alternatives, and electricity demand.) In addition, the Clean Air Act typically imposes its most stringent pollution controls on new powerplant construction, permitting existing capacity to meet less stringent and less costly standards. This differential impact may give some older facilities a competitive operating cost advantage to complement their low, depreciated cost basis.

The new valuation, combined with low operating costs, would encourage operators to maximize generation from their existing facilities. For example, over one-half the increase in electricity generation projected for 2005 (about 64,000 MW) could be obtained if operation of coal-fired capacity increased from its 62% capacity factor in 1995 to 75%. However, the economic and environmental advantages of new technology, such as natural gas-fired, combined-cycle technology (a very clean technology) may be sufficient in some case to overcome the advantages of expanding use of existing plants.

Environmental Implications. It is this renewed attractiveness of existing capacity under restructuring, specifically of coal-fired capacity, along with the potential that demand for electricity may rise (and energy conservation slacken) if prices decline, that raises environmental concerns. Absent effective controls, burning more coal will produce more emissions than alternative sources of electricity generation—and much of that coal capacity is in the Midwest, which is currently a center of attention for reducing NOx emissions.

Except for CO_2, the regulatory regimen of the Clean Air Act provides authorities for controlling the potential increase in emissions—assuming they are effectively implemented. Existing controls "cap" SO_2 emissions in the 48 contiguous states and the District of Columbia, and there is no reason to question the effectiveness of the cap in the future, regardless of the changes underway in the utility industry. For NOx emissions, control and implementation is more complicated, primarily because implementation of much of the process lies with the states. Any increase in NOx emissions in the Midwest could complicate an already difficult process underway to reduce the region's NOx emissions, which contribute to ozone nonattainment in the Northeast. How this regional, state-implemented process would be affected by restructuring is not certain.

CO_2 is not currently regulated. Any increase in fossil fuel-fired generation will increase CO_2 emissions ... unless Congress ratifies the Kyoto Agreement and enacts implementing legislation (an uncertain prospect)....

The current attention on increased emissions from coal-fired generation may address the clearest and most quantifiable risk to the environment from restructuring, but with so many changes underway, the ultimate outcome remains uncertain. Some trends are already manifest, such as renovation of existing coal-fired capacity. Others are just emerging, such as a "green market" in California, in which consumers can take into account environmental costs in their purchasing decisions. Some effects remain to be determined in the future, such as the implications of new price signals for demand and conservation; the implication of new cost valuations for the choice of new generating technologies; developments in transmission capacity; and the effectiveness of ongoing environmental programs.■

NOTES AND COMMENTS

1. The Federal Energy Regulatory Commission (FERC) addressed the environmental transition costs of wholesale power competition in Order No. 888:

> [T]he relative future competitiveness of coal and natural gas generation is the key variable affecting the impact of the Final Rule. If competitive conditions favor natural gas, the Rule is likely to lead to environmental benefits. Both EPA and the Commission staff believe this projected scenario is the more likely one. If competitive conditions favor coal, the Rule may lead to small negative environmental impacts. However, even using the most extreme, unlikely assumptions about the future of the industry, the negative consequences are not likely to occur until after the turn of the century. Because the impacts will remain modest at least until 2010, there is no need for an interim mitigation program. In addition, even if the data showed more significant negative consequences requiring mitigation, the Commission does not have the statutory authority under the Federal Power Act or the expertise to address this possible far-term problem. The Commission believes, however, that there is time for federal and state air quality authorities to address any potential adverse impact as part of a comprehensive NO[X] regulatory program under the Clean Air Act.
>
> ... [T]he preferred approach for mitigating increased NO[X] emissions generally is a NO[X] cap and trading regulatory program comparable to that developed by Congress to address sulfur dioxide emissions in the Clean Air Act Amendments of 1990. ...

Initially, the Environmental Protection Agency (EPA) disagreed with FERC, deciding in May 1996 not to approve FERC's final environmental impact statement on Order No. 888. The EPA's major concern was that competition would result in increased generation at higher polluting power plants, resulting in greater emissions of pollutants such as nitrogen oxides. *See* Stephen C. Fotis & Ann P. Southwick, The Price of Switching, Legal Times, May 13, 1996, at 23. As a result, the EPA requested that FERC include environmental mitigation measures in Order No. 888. This resulted in a referral of FERC's actions to the White House Council on Environmental Quality (CEQ), as is allowed under the National Environmental Policy Act. FERC maintained, however, that it did not have the jurisdiction under the Federal Power Act to impose such measures on the industry, and that the EPA was the appropriate agency to adopt mitigation measures.

2. Chapter 5 describes the ongoing dispute over so-called "new source review," the question of when older power plants must comply with stricter, new source standards because they have been "modified." Can you see how and why restructuring and the move to competitive markets has increased the intensity of that dispute? If grandfathered sources (a) are cheaper to operate, and (b) emit more pollution per unit of energy generated, restructuring might bring a more pollution-intensive energy mix. If those grandfathered sources can be treated by regulators as "new or

modified" sources subject to stricter pollution control standards, perhaps the pollution impacts of increased reliance on coal-fired plants can be minimized. What does this battle mean for communities struggling to comply with the EPA's ozone standards? Remember that NOx is a precursor of ground-level ozone (smog).

3. Remember that the new source review issue concerns the regulation of conventional pollutants like SO_2, NOx, and particulate matter. With respect to SO_2 emissions, many large coal-fired plants are subject to regulation under the Clean Air Act's acid rain program, which is also described in Chapter 5. For purposes of the acid rain program, it does not matter whether a plant is new or old, or whether it has been modified or not. Many otherwise grandfathered plants are part of the acid rain program, are allocated annually tradeable acid rain allowances, and must acquire or retain sufficient allowances each year to cover their SO_2 emissions. What will the move to competition mean for these facilities? If the electricity market buys more coal-fired power, what will that mean for the price of acid rain allowances?

4. Coal-fired power plants emit a variety of toxic pollutants as well. The battle to force the EPA to regulate mercury emissions from coal-fired plants as toxic emissions under the Clean Air Act is described in Chapter 5. If mercury is treated as a toxic pollutant under the Clean Air Act (as the Clinton Administration proposed), the Act would restrict emissions from new and grandfathered sources alike, since the Act's regulation of toxic pollutants under Section 112 applies to both types of sources. On the other hand, if mercury emissions are regulated as a conventional pollutant, emissions from older plants might escape regulation, depending upon whether those plants are subject to new source review.

5. Perhaps the most controversial air pollution issue triggered by restructuring concerns global warming. Since CO_2 emissions from all coal-fired plants in the United States remain unregulated, increased reliance on coal-fired power will mean increased emissions of CO_2 from coal-fired plants. For a discussion of global warming, greenhouse gases, and regulation of CO_2 emissions generally, see Chapter 16.

6. For a summary of the Clean Air Act issues triggered by electricity restructuring, *see* Arnold W. Reitze, Jr., 2002 Energy Law Symposium: State and Federal Command-and-Control Regulation of Emissions From Fossil–Fuel Electric Power Generating Plants, 32 Envtl. L. 369 (2002).

7. In recent years, both the Bush Administration and members of Congress have proposed "multipollutant" legislation which would revise the current approach to air pollution control by implementing a single program to deal with all power plant emissions (much like the way that motor vehicles are regulated). The Bush Administration and environmentalists have clashed over this legislation. In 2002, Senator James Jeffords of Vermont proposed the "Clean Power Act," that would have set caps for mercury and CO_2 emissions as well as for SO_2 and nitrogen oxides. The Bush administration has touted its proposal, the "Clear Skies Act," as a dramatic improvement in air pollution reduction. However, this bill stalled

in the Senate, with its critics objecting to its two principal differences from the Clean Power Act's approach: it does not propose regulating CO_2 emissions and it sets less stringent caps. *See* Utility Pollution Bill Stalls in Senate Committee, Reuters, Mar. 10, 2005. For a further discussion of the various multipollutant legislative proposals, *see* Chapter 5.

B. RENEWABLE ENERGY AND CONSERVATION PROGRAMS

The possibility of a more sustainable energy economy in the future, based on renewable resources and energy conservation programs, is beginning to seem a little less like an environmentalists' pipe dream. As technologies have matured, renewable resources such as solar and wind power have garnered more popular support and come closer to the goal of mass commercialization than ever before.

Competition in the electricity industry in the U.S. has had transformative effects on programs adopted since the enactment of PURPA to promote renewables and conservation. In some cases, utilities view these programs as unduly expensive to maintain in a competitive environment, and states have filled the gap with new requirements and policies designed to integrate renewable resources into electric generation portfolios.

1. RENEWABLE ENERGY RESOURCES

The extent to which energy resources are "renewable" depends on the time scale you use. The sun itself will presumably fade gradually over millions of years. Uranium and related minerals usable as fuel for nuclear power might be exhausted in a few millennia. Coal resources will apparently last for a century or more. Oil and natural gas, however, may have a life span measured in decades at current rates of use.

In today's terminology, renewable energy resources have come to be defined as those that can be utilized without any discernable reduction in their future availability. Since medieval times, inventors have constantly been searching for cheaper and more reliable sources of renewable energy. Modern technology has made the prospect of renewable energy more realistic than before, though still far from broad public acceptance.

Renewable energy resources are often classified into two basic categories: (a) cool resources, which can produce energy without being burned; and (2) hot resources, which require combustion.

a. COOL RENEWABLES

i. *Solar Energy*

Solar energy is the prototype of a cool renewable energy resource. This may seem odd given the heat of the sun's rays, but that heat means that solar energy does not have to be burned and is thus classified as a cool resource. Increasing development of small scale solar energy sources has made such energy available for a wide range of uses where relatively small amounts of energy are needed in remote locations, such as camp stoves, communications satellites, highway sign lighting, and pocket calculators.

The United States Department of Energy, whose mission includes the promotion of economical ways to conserve energy, uses the following pamphlet to explain solar heating of ordinary homes in simple terms:

United States Department of Energy Solar Energy and You (1993)

Solar energy is heat and light that comes from the sun. Thousands of years ago some people used this energy to heat their homes. Today, solar energy is again helping to heat buildings.

The sun is a giant heat source. If you can collect enough solar heat, you can use it instead of the heat from a furnace. One way to collect heat is to trap solar energy with **solar collectors.** An example of how a solar collector works is a car that has dark seat covers and has all its windows closed tightly. When sunlight passes through the glass windows of the car, it is **absorbed** (taken in) by the dark seat covers and walls and floor. Light that is absorbed changes into heat. If the seat covers are a pale color, such as white or yellow, they would not absorb as much sunlight. So pale colored seats do not become as hot as dark seats.

Now here is an interesting fact about glass: it lets light in, but it does not let all the heat out. Even if it is cold outside, the inside of the car will be warm from the trapped heat. So a solar collector does three things: 1) it allows sunlight inside through glass (or plastic); 2) it absorbs the sunlight and changes it into heat; and 3) it traps most of the heat inside.

Solar collectors become so hot that they can be used as heat sources for a building. There are two kinds of buildings that use solar collectors as heat sources: passive solar buildings and active solar buildings.

In some cases, a whole house itself is a solar collector (just like the car). These houses are called **passive** solar homes because they don't use any special **mechanical equipment** such as pipes, ducts, fans, or pumps. Since the sun shines from the south in North America, passive solar houses are built so that most of the windows face south. They have very few or no windows on the north side.

Some passive homes have greenhouses attached to them to let in light and trap the heat. The greenhouse is also used to grow plants because its many windows provide a lot of sunshine for the plants. Passive houses use walls and floors to absorb solar energy and turn it into heat. Passive homes do not use a mechanical heat distribution system. Instead, a passive home works because hot air is lighter than cold air. Because it is lighter, the hot air will naturally rise to the top of a room, leaving the cold, heavy air near the floor. In a passive home, air that is heated downstairs will naturally flow upstairs. Cold air will flow downstairs and will be heated up again.

To control the amount of heat in a passive solar house, people close doors and windows to keep heated air in and open doors and windows to let heated air out. At night, special heavy curtains or shades are pulled over the windows to keep the daytime heat inside the house. In the summertime, awnings or roof overhangs help to cool the house by shading the windows from the high summer sun.

Some buildings do use special mechanical equipment to collect and distribute solar heat. These buildings have **active** solar heating systems. Active systems use collectors which look like boxes covered with glass. Dark colored metal plates inside the boxes absorb sunlight and change it into heat. Air or water flows through the collectors and is warmed by this heat. The warmed-up air or water is then distributed to the rest of the house just like in an ordinary furnace system. Thermostats are also used to control the delivery of heat in active solar heating systems. Active solar collectors are usually placed high up on roofs where they can collect the greatest amount of sunlight. They are put on the south side of the roof in a place where no trees or tall buildings will shade them.

Solar energy systems must include some ways of storing the heat that was collected during sunny weather.

In active systems, either hot water is moved to large tanks of water, or hot air is moved to bins of rocks beneath the building. When it is needed, the hot water or air is taken back out of storage and sent to the living areas.

In a passive house, heat is absorbed by the thick walls and floors during the day. At night, when it becomes cold outside, warm walls and floors release their heat back into the room. If you have ever leaned up against a sunny brick wall or dark rock on a cold day, you were leaning on warm solar storage.

Houses with active or passive solar heating systems also have a furnace, wood burning stove, or some other heat source to provide heat in case there is a long period of cloudy weather. This is called a backup heating system.

Solar energy can be used in many other ways besides heating buildings. Solar **photovoltaic cells** change sunlight directly into electricity; solar energy heats water for homes and businesses; and sunlight can even be used to cook food. As our supplies of precious gas and oil get smaller, we will find new uses for energy from the sun.■

* * *

Producing electricity with solar energy through the use of photovoltaic (PV) devices has considerable environmental benefits. It is pollution-free (except in the device manufacturing process) and relies on an inexhaustible resource. Yet solar energy accounts for only a small fraction of the nation's electricity generation. According to the U.S. Department of Energy's Energy Information Administration ("EIA"), less than 400 megawatts (MW) of solar capacity were in place in the U.S. in 2002. *See* Renewable Energy

Annual 2003, http://www.eia.doe.gov/. In 2004, Tucson Electric Power announced it would build the nation's largest solar power plant in Springerville, Arizona, but at four megawatts it would produce considerably less than 1 percent of Arizona's total demand for electricity on a summer day. T.R. Reid, Western Station Transforms Sunbeams Into Electricity, Wash. Post., July 25, 2004. One obstacle to widespread commercialization of solar technology for use in electricity generation is cost. The Solar Energy Industries Association ("SEIA"), the leading trade association for the solar industry, notes that, "photovoltaic technologies have declined in price every year since they were introduced onto the market, driven by improved research and development, and most of all by steady increases in sales volume." See http://www.seia.org/. Still, solar power remains expensive by contrast with other resources used in generating electricity.

Passive solar technology is finding increasing use in residential and commercial buildings. In regions a long way from the equator, reliance on solar energy as a sole source for heating a home would be impractical, but builders are discovering that passive solar heating can dramatically reduce heating costs. Active solar technology's current promise is great in a wide variety of applications. The fastest growth is in "grid connected" systems in residential or commercial applications where rooftop solar panels are in place, but the homes or businesses remain connected to the electrical grid. See Tom Abate, Solar energy's cloudy past: Advocates say 50–year-old industry is finally in a position to heat up, S.F. Chronicle, Feb. 16, 2004.

California has been a leader in the use of "grid connected" systems. The environmental group Greenpeace called San Diego a "national leader in clean energy" for its program that sets a goal of using renewable energy to generate 10 percent of the energy used at any new or remodeled city-owned buildings that are 5,000 square feet or larger. Kathryn Balint, City could fall victim to its solar successes, San Diego Union–Tribune, Mar. 28, 2004. At the Oakland International Airport, the shipping company FedEx has planned a 904–kW array of solar cells that will be the largest solar system in the state and "generate nearly enough electricity to make the facility self-sufficient," according to the company. Jim Herron Zamora, FedEx to build solar power system at Oakland airport hub, S.F. Chronicle, Oct. 19, 2004.

In his election campaign, Governor Arnold Schwarzenegger promoted statewide incentives that would achieve a goal of 50 percent of new homes in California being built with solar power. In 2004, the California Assembly considered S.B. 1652, the "Million Solar Homes Initiative," which would require builders in the state to install two-kilowatt PV systems for heating, cooling, and running appliances on five percent of new homes by 2010, and 50 percent of homes by 2020. Opposition came from several different corners, including lawmakers who claimed solar power was too expensive, and builders who opposed the mandate to build a specific percentage of solar systems. They claimed solar power would add $20,000 or more to the cost of already expensive new homes in California and stated that the bill would require training of installers because not enough building tradesmen had familiarity with solar systems.

The Assembly Appropriations Committee declined to vote on S.B. 1652 in August 2004, effectively postponing its consideration. Don Thompson, California Legislature defeats incentives to spur solar homes, Reno Gazette–Journal, Aug. 12, 2004. In 2005, the Assembly reconsidered the Million Solar Roofs Initiative, which continued to have the goal of one million solar roofs but dropped the mandate that builders install solar systems, instead proposing subsidies to achieve the goal. The rewritten bill, S.B. 1, would require the California Public Utilities Commission to fund enough subsidies so that the goal could be reached by 2018. Craig D. Rose, Solar energy efforts heat up, San Diego Union–Tribune, Mar. 13, 2005.■

NOTES AND COMMENTS

1. A 1999 study found that a PV system's payback period (time to recoup its original cost) is as little as one to four years. Nat'l Renewable Energy Laboratory, Energy Payback: Clean Energy From PV, http://www.nrel.gov /docs/fy99osti/24619.pdf. That payback period can be shorter if state "net metering" laws, which allow generators of power using renewable resources to sell their excess power back to the utility, are taken into account. Daniel Shugar, president of PowerLight, a Berkeley, California firm that installs solar systems, terms net metering "a revolution in solar affordability." *See* Abate, *supra*. The California net metering law has been a factor in promoting solar installations, up to a point:

> California law obligates utilities to purchase excess power from solar providers up to a specified level. But the level for San Diego Gas & Electric Co. is capped at 19.5 megawatts of solar power, meaning the state's electricity grid is not obligated to purchase excess solar power once production reaches that level. Currently, the county is close to producing 8 megawatts. Local officials are lobbying members of the state Legislature to raise or remove the cap. Irene Stillings, executive director of the San Diego Regional Energy Office, said without the financial incentives, most customers will avoid using solar power, which is a more costly energy source.

Balint, *supra*. Net metering is covered in more detail in Chapter 12.

* * *

Who Owns Sunlight?

Many nations have treated the sunlight that naturally reaches a piece of land as a form of property belonging to the landowner. This is particularly true in countries in the higher latitudes where sunlight seems more precious than it does in more tropical areas. In Japan, for example, construction of an office building requires extensive negotiations with any landowners whose sunlight would be reduced during prime daylight hours. In England, the common law once recognized a doctrine of "ancient lights," which treated the right to receive sunlight as an easement appurtenant to real property. This doctrine has been abandoned in England and in most of the American states. *See Fontainebleau Hotel Corp. v. Forty–Five Twenty–Five, Inc.*, 114 So.2d 357 (Fla. App. 1959).

In 1982, the Wisconsin Supreme Court interpreted the common law of that state to provide a potential action in nuisance against a person who built a structure that interfered with the operation of a solar collector. *Prah v. Maretti*, 321 N.W.2d 182 (Wis. 1982). Although a number of states have dealt with this issue by statute, relatively few have adopted the Wisconsin rule as a part of the common law. One of those that did is New Hampshire, in the following opinion written by Justice (now United States Supreme Court Justice) Souter:

Tenn v. 889 Associates, Ltd.

500 A.2d 366 (N.H. 1985).

■ Souter, J. The plaintiff, Sylvia Tenn, owns a six-story office building constructed in 1891 at 907–913 Elm Street in Manchester, New Hampshire, known as the Pickering Building. Its south wall is built to the southerly line of its lot. A neighboring building formerly located to the south of the plaintiff's property was built to the same lot line and to a height of nearly four stories, so that up to that height, the south wall of the Pickering Building had no windows. Above the fourth story, a total of twelve windows faced south, as did the glazed south wall of a light shaft, capped with a skylight, which provided light for the offices and halls. Several of the south windows held room air conditioners.

The defendant, 889 Associates, Ltd., now owns the lot south of the Pickering Building. In November, 1983, the defendant's president and treasurer, Michael Ingram, wrote to a representative of the plaintiff, Dr. James Tenn, informing him of the defendant's plans to demolish the existing four-story structure and to replace it with a new one. The letter indicated that the defendant intended to construct the new building, like the old one, to abut the south wall of the Pickering Building, but to a full height of six stories, so that the Pickering Building's room air conditioners would have to be removed. Mr. Ingram offered to meet with Dr. Tenn to describe the plans in more detail.

When they met in December, 1983, Dr. Tenn objected to the plans to block the Pickering Building's south windows and asked Mr. Ingram to redesign the new building with an accommodating set-back of several feet. Mr. Ingram declined to do so and proceeded to seek the requisite zoning variances and building permits.

On April 19, 1984, nearly five months after learning of the defendant's plans, and after demolition of the existing building had already begun, the plaintiff filed the present bill in equity. To the extent that the new building would block the windows and the wall of the light shaft, the plaintiff claimed that it would be a private nuisance.

[T]he substantial issues in this appeal [are] whether the law of private nuisance is broad enough to comprehend a claim of interference with light and air, whether the court correctly applied that law in this case and whether there was a prescriptive right to maintain the air conditioners. In considering the applicability of nuisance law to the interests at stake, it will be helpful to start by canvassing the alternative possibilities that the parties have discussed.

At one extreme there is the English common law doctrine of ancient lights, under which the owner of a window that has enjoyed unobstructed access to sunlight for a sufficient period of time can acquire a prescriptive easement entitling him to prevent an adjoining landowner from obstructing the accustomed light. Comment, Solar Rights: Guaranteeing a Place in the Sun, 57 Or. L. Rev. 94, 108–09 (1977). While in the early days some American courts adopted a similar rule, it fell into disfavor during the nineteenth century. By 1977 "no American common-law jurisdiction affirmatively recognize[d] an ability to acquire an easement of light by prescription," Comment, supra at 112 (footnotes omitted), and "very few, if any, American courts today would uphold a prescriptive right to light," Pfeiffer, Ancient Lights: Legal Protection of Access to Solar Energy, 68 A.B.A.J. 288, 289 (1982).

Historically, there have been three principal reasons for the unpopularity of the doctrine of ancient lights: a desire to foster unimpeded development of real estate, a belief that in an age of artificial illumination light should be classed as an aesthetic rather than a property interest, and a suspicion that the enjoyment of light was so far from a characteristically adverse use that it could not fall within the basic concept of prescriptive use. *See* Comment, *supra* at 110–11; *Prah v. Maretti,* 321 N.W.2d 182, 189 (Wis. 1982).

While time has not weakened the third of these historical reasons, the first and second have definitely begun to wane. The desire to encourage unrestricted development has receded as zoning and planning regulations have become more comprehensive, and access to natural light can be expected to justify an increasing degree of protection as the technology of solar energy develops. It does not follow, however, that we should turn to the doctrine of ancient lights to accomplish this purpose. Because the law of zoning is itself one means to recognize an interest in access to light and air, and because, as we will discuss below, the law of nuisance is another, we reject the argument that a prescriptive right to light or air should be recognized at this time. *Cf. Morton v. State,* 181 A.2d 831, 835 (N. H. 1962) (assuming possibility of conveyance of rights to light, air, etc.).

At the other extreme among the positions taken in this litigation is the rule customarily identified with *Fontainebleau Hotel Corp. v. Forty–Five Twenty–Five, Inc.,* 114 So.2d 357 (Fla.App.1959), *cert. denied,* 117 So.2d 842 (Fla.1960). In that case the court dissolved a trial court's preliminary injunction against construction of a building that would have cast a shadow over the cabana, pool and sunbathing areas of a neighboring hotel. The court ruled out the possibility of proving a nuisance on the facts before it by affirming Florida's traditional rule, that in the absence of a zoning restriction, a property owner could build up to his property line and as high as he chose. The rule in Fontainebleau thus stands at the furthest remove from the doctrine of ancient lights. Where the latter would limit the neighbor's right to build, the former never would.

The present defendant urges us to adopt the Fontainebleau rule and thereby to refuse any common law recognition to interests in light and air, but we decline to do so. If we were so to limit the ability of the common law to grow, we would in effect be rejecting one of the wise assumptions underlying the traditional law of nuisance: that we cannot anticipate at any one time the variety of predicaments in which protection of property interests or redress for their violation will be justifiable. For it is just this recognition that has led the courts to avoid rigid formulations for determining when an interference with the use of property will be actionable, and to rest instead on the flexible rule that actionable, private nuisance consists of an unreasonable as well as a substantial interference with another person's use and enjoyment of his property. *See Robie v. Lillis*, 299 A.2d 155, 158 (N. H. 1972). That is, because we have to anticipate that the uses of property will change over time, we have developed a law of nuisance that protects the use and enjoyment of property when a threatened harm to the plaintiff owner can be said to outweigh the utility of the defendant owner's conduct to himself and to the community. *Id.* at 159.

Viewing the elements and concept of private nuisance as thus formulated in Robie, there is no reason in principle why the law of nuisance should not be applied to claims for the protection of a property owner's interests in light and air, and for reasons already given we believe that considerations of policy support just such an application of nuisance concepts. We therefore hold that the law of private nuisance as expressed in Robie provides the appropriate standard for passing on a property owner's claims of interference with interests in light and air. *See Prah v. Maretti*, 321 N.W.2d 182, 191 (Wis. 1982).

Since this is the course that the trial court followed, the third of the substantial issues before us is whether the evidence supported the court's finding that the defendant's building would not be a private nuisance.... The court found, first, that the threatened interference would not be unreasonable. It based this conclusion on findings that nearly all the affected office windows had previously been covered with translucent but not transparent plastic sheets or were blocked by heavy drapes. The southerly openings to the light shaft were covered by translucent but not transparent glass, which admitted substantially less light than the clear skylight above it. It was uncontested that virtually every affected office would continue to receive light from the shaft or from the east or west windows of the building.

The court addressed both the issues of reasonableness and of substantiality when it further found that such interference as there would be would not exceed what was normal under the circumstances. The sites were in the downtown commercial area of Manchester, where buildings commonly buttress and block the sides of adjacent structures. Moreover, the defendant proposed to do no more than the plaintiff's own predecessor had done, by building right to the lot line and to a height of six stories. If, as the plaintiff claimed, this would require expenditures for additional artificial lighting and ventilation systems, she failed to present any evidence that the costs would exceed what was customarily necessary for such buildings.

The court again alluded to the element of substantiality of the threatened interference when it expressly found that little weight should be accorded to the evidence that the Pickering Building would drop in value. This finding was warranted both by the plaintiff's unconvincing evidence on the point, and by this court's holding in Robie that evidence of depreciation in value is to be given little weight in the law of nuisance, since "the law cannot generally protect landowners from fluctuating land values which is a risk necessarily inherent in all land ownership." *Robie v. Lillis,* 299 A.2d at 160.

Thus on the issues of unreasonableness and substantiality the evidence supported the findings. The evidence also supported the court in its more general conclusion under Robie, that the utility to the defendant and to the public of a new office building would outweigh the burden to the plaintiff of installing additional lighting and ventilating equipment. The court therefore was warranted in finding that the building as planned would not be a private nuisance.

We turn now to the final issue of substance. Quite apart from her claims to have protectable interests in light and air, the plaintiff claimed to have an easement to use the defendant's air space for the air conditioners that protruded from the windows. There was no evidence of any express or implied grant of such an easement. Assuming, then, that such an easement could arise by prescription, it was necessary for the plaintiff to "prove by a balance of probabilities twenty years' adverse, continuous, uninterrupted use of [defendant's property] in such a manner as to give notice to the record owner that an adverse claim was being made to it. The nature of the use must [have been] such as to show that the owner knew or ought to have known that the right was being exercised, not in reliance upon his toleration or permission, but without regard to his consent." *Ucietowski v. Novak,* 152 A.2d 614, 618 (N. H. 1959) (emphasis added) (citations omitted).

Whether the plaintiff satisfied this standard was an issue of fact to be determined by giving consideration to the peculiar circumstances of an alleged use of small amounts of air space several stories above the ground. *See Ucietowski v. Novak, supra,* 152 A.2d at 618. Thus, acts that might be obtrusive and ostensibly adverse at ground level would not necessarily have the same character high above the street.

Considering these circumstances, the record supports the trial court's finding that the plaintiff did not carry her burden. The evidence indicated that for the required twenty-year period only two or three portable air conditioners had been so placed as to extend several inches into the air space, and that each of these was twelve feet or more above the roof of the building formerly on the defendant's lot. There was no evidence that these air conditioners were or appeared to be permanently installed, that they interfered in any way with the then-current use and enjoyment of the defendant's property or that they physically intruded onto an appreciable portion of defendant's space. In the absence of any such evidence, the trial court was not compelled to conclude that the defendant or his predecessors knew or should have known that the plaintiff was claiming a right to use the defendant's air space for the placement of the air conditioners. Thus, under Ucietowski the trial court reasonably found that no easement had arisen by prescription. *Cf. Matthys v. Swedish Baptist Church of Boston*, 112 N.E. 228 (Mass. 1916) (roof of church which extended four feet over property line, from which snow and ice regularly fell onto adjoining land, held sufficiently adverse to create prescriptive easement).

The trial court did not err in dismissing the bill in equity.

Affirmed.■

NOTES AND COMMENTS

1. A variety of states and localities have laws designed to provide for solar or wind easements or access rights. Easements are agreements between two or more property owners that allow for the rights to access to a renewable resource a property owner to transfer to another property owner. The easement grantor's uses of his property are restricted to allow the easement holder access to the renewable resource. This easement may be transferred with the property title.

In addition, some states prohibit neighborhood covenants that preclude the use of renewables. At the local level, communities use many different land use techniques to protect access to renewable resources, including solar access ordinances, development guidelines, zoning ordinances with building height restrictions, and solar permits.

ii. *Windpower*

Windpower has become one of the most attractive sources of renewable energy in windy parts of the world. Huge farms of windmills with blades exceeding 100 feet in length are used to generate electricity. The use of windpower for electricity generation has been growing at a rapid rate in the past decade, albeit from a low baseline.

About 2% of the solar energy that reaches the earth is ultimately converted to the kinetic energy of wind. Joseph M. Moran *et al.*, Meteorology: The Atmosphere and the Science of Weather 204 (5th ed., 1997). Wind blows when there is uneven air pressure. Variations in the temperature in the Earth's atmosphere cause differences in air pressure. Movement of air closer to the earth is affected by friction; the wind rubs against trees, hills, buildings, etc., which tend to slow wind down. In the upper atmosphere, the air flow is much smoother. Winds tend to be gustier where terrain is rough and the temperature contrasts between a warm surface and cooler air are common. *See* George Bomar, Texas Weather 176–198 (University of Texas Press, 1995).

The use of windpower for the generation of electricity has become a big business. Giant "wind farms" that contain dozens of linked windmills have been erected in many locations. Wind power has its greatest potential where average wind speeds are relatively strong and consistent in direction. In the U.S., such "regions include the western High Plains, the Pacific Northwest coast, portions of coastal California, the eastern Great lakes, the south coast of Texas, and exposed summits and passes in the Rockies and Appalachians." Moran *et al.*, *supra*, at 205. Projects for wind farms were either planned or under construction in a number of states between 2000 and 2005. In 2003, the nation added 438 MW of windpower capacity. Renewable Energy Annual 2003, *supra*. In 2004, the federal Bureau of Land Management (BLM) released an environmental impact statement for a program that proposed adding as much as 3,240 MW of windpower projects on federal lands in the West by 2025, or about half the entire installed current capacity in the nation. *See* http://www.windeis.anl.gov/documents/dpeis/index.cfm. That same year, the town of Moab, Utah became the nation's first "Green Power Community" under an EPA program for its use of wind-generated electricity. Lisa Church, EPA designation puts wind in Moab's environmental sails, Salt Lake Tribune, Oct. 24, 2004.

Still, at present wind contributes only 0.3% of domestic electricity generation. Renewable Energy Annual 2003, *supra*. The American Wind Energy Association predicts, however, that percentage will rise to 6 percent by 2020. Jeff Donn, Wind power buffeted by technical and economic challenges, Associated Press, June 12, 2004. Unfortunately, windpower facilities are not without their drawbacks, as the following critic of wind farms claims:

R. Dobie Langenkamp, Sustainable Development–Renewable Energy and Reality

Duke Envtl. L. & Pol'y F. (2004) Symposium paper.

Once again, with oil prices rising, the excitement over these "clean" and "sustainable" forms of energy is intense. But hydrogen is still 10–20 years in our future—about the same as it was when I testified on the matter before Congress in 1979. Wind turbines are much larger and more efficient, but the source is of limited benefits . . .

Since the early '70s renewables have been the politically correct solution both to the problem of "sustainability" and to the environmental problems. Now, three decades and billions of dollars of subsidies later, what is the usage? Solar and wind combined equal less than .2 of 1% of U.S. energy production. (This is .2% of electric power and doesn't refer to all energy. This is 1/46th of the energy provided by the largely moribund nuclear industry.)

THE POSTER CHILD OF RENEWABLE SUSTAINABILITY—WIND POWER

Let's look at the facts. PSO just announced that it seeks to manufacture and distribute wind power in the amount of 107 mw. A suitably attractive photo of the turbines at sundown is provided. Power for 31,000 homes was predicted. Wow. "This is just the kind of thing we need more of" is the response of most Americans. Oklahomans ought to take a little longer look at this energy source.

1.   COST AND PRICE: This 20–year PSO contract is conditioned on an extension of the 1.8 cents per kilowatt tax credit for generated wind power. (This 1.8 is the approximate total cost of conventionally coal-generated power.) A tax credit is like cash—from the taxpayers of the nation—to the generating company. The power company wants to be a good citizen and support renewables, but even the tax credit is not enough to stimulate this altruism; they get to pass the higher generation cost along to the consumers. The consumers pay twice—first the tax credit, which is a taxpayer burden, and second, the higher cost which is passed on to them. Texas requires a 3–cent wind power premium that is paid by the customer in addition to the 1.8–cent tax credit, putting wind at about a nickel per kwh above conventional power.

2.   QUANTITY AND RELIABILITY: Power from this PSO project would add only .0046% to Oklahoma's power capability (46/1000). To generate just 10% of Oklahoma's electric power needs, we would have to site and build 1,600 of the largest turbines, requiring 64,000 acres (100 square miles). It would take about 4,000 turbines to supply the Tulsa metropolitan area's 3 gigawatts of electric power. If the amount of wind power in the U.S. were quintupled, it would still contribute only about 1% of the U.S. power generated. A combined cycle gas turbine power plant similar to several built in Oklahoma recently can produce 1,000 megawatts from about 15 acres. Another issue is reliability. Wind is notoriously fickle. When the wind does not blow consistently at a speed needed to make the turbine operative (14 mph), no power is generated. When the wind is blowing too hard (60 mph), the turbine has to shut down. Since the power grid cannot rely on the wind power, fossil fuel spinning reserve power has to be maintained in the full amount of the wind power.

3.   BIRDS: The impact on birds can be devastating. This is a great embarrassment for wind advocates and they attempt to minimize the impact. The wind towers in the Altamont Pass in California have on average killed 200–300 red tail hawks and 40–60 golden eagles each year. According to the California Energy Commission, 7,000 migrating birds are killed each year by wind turbines in southern California. In the UK and the Netherlands, many sites have been rejected because of proximity to wildlife refuges. The problem is primarily nighttime contact with the 1.5–ton, 747–sized blades, the tips of which are traveling at 180 mph.

4.   NOISE: Although engineering has sought to cut down on the noise, it still remains a serious problem in some locations. In the UK, environmental officers have taken action "against the noise nuisance." "For

existing wind farms we are satisfied that there are cases of individuals being subject to near-continuous noise during the operation of the turbines ... which are clearly disturbing and may have some psychological effects." One farmer who lived 350 meters from one turbine and 750 from others complained of "sickening sound waves" and "disruption" of sleep even with the windows closed. From 1,000 meters the sound was so great according to one complaining group that "those of us who are unfortunate enough to be closest are experiencing a barrage of noise pollution, actually making some of those worst affected physically ill." (There is no evidence to date of noise complaints in Oklahoma.)

5. HEIGHT: Three hundred feet is the equivalent of a 30-story building. Some of the largest turbines in Germany are 500 feet high, equal to a 50-story building. Historian David McCullough is protesting the installation of turbines in and around Cape Cod. These turbines would be 410 feet tall. "I'm not against wind turbines. I'm against 130 of them over 400 feet tall right smack in the middle of one of the most beautiful places in America." (Actually there are 612 planned for Cape Cod and Narragansett Bay.) The "Cape Wind Project" alone involves 130 turbines that will be spaced 880 yards apart over a 24-square-mile area four miles offshore.

6. AESTHETICS: Most photography of wind turbines deserves an artistic prize. Never has one seen so many sunsets and lush, rolling grass fields with well-groomed cattle. The pristine white sculpted structures in the background look like some kind of avant-garde artwork. The reality is that these structures are large industrial machines that can be seen for 20 miles or more. They also often claim the most conspicuous and picturesque high ground. The British and Dutch fear that their cliffs and coastline will be covered with these large towers. In the U.S. many sites are less picturesque than Cape Cod. Few would argue that the plains of Woodward County resemble the blue seas off Hyannis Port. Still, how many 30-to 50-story towers do you want on your neighbor's land?

7. TV RECEPTION: Each turbine leaves a "shadow" of as much as 10 km radius and will also interfere with microwave transmissions. Some in England have complained of complete loss of their TV reception.

8. SAFETY: The 1.5-ton blades travel at 180 mph at the extremity and on occasion shatter or break off. When they do, the parts or pieces fly almost a quarter mile and hit with a 170-mph impact. In Palm Springs the traffic safety authorities insisted the turbines be at least a half-mile from the highway. In cold climes ice chunks on the blades can break off and are like shrapnel to nearby persons. Suspected metal fatigue has caused the shutdown of several UK turbines. The British Horse Society insists that riding trails be 1,000 to 1,200 feet from the towers due to danger to horse and rider. Most turbines have a maximum wind speed beyond which operations are not safe. At this point power generation ceases.

9. JOBS: The largest wind "farm" in Germany has three full-time employees; many have just one.

10. OTHER ENVIRONMENTAL IMPACTS: To support a tower the height of two Statues of Liberty, a huge, swimming pool-sized cement foundation is required. Not only must the concrete be trucked in, but the fill needs to be trucked out. There have been complaints that the large foundations have interfered with groundwater flows. The large trucks require heavy all-weather roads.

RENEWABLES—A FEEL–GOOD DISTRACTION

Wind power is the most oversold energy source since the solar craze of the '70s. This is not to say that wind will not make any contribution to the energy needs, but just that it really isn't anything serious people in the energy business get worked up over. "Renewable energy ... is a showy way for politicians to prove that they are doing something." As the British opponents of wind power put it: "Tinkering at the edges of the problem by supporting a technology like wind, which is unpredictable, intermittent and dependent on machines whose output is derisory, is a dangerous distraction and a piece of 'green' window dressing designed to allow the government to avoid the problem." ...■

NOTES AND COMMENTS

1. Windpower projects pose a dilemma for some environmental organizations. They support windmills as a renewable source of energy, but in some cases they oppose wind farms that may result in harm to wildlife. A notorious example of this is the wind farm at Altamont Pass, east of San Francisco, California. An Energy Department study concluded that this installation, which has operated for decades, has the worst bird-kill problem among the world's wind farms. In 2004, the environmental group Center for Biological Diversity brought a lawsuit against the wind farm's operators after they filed for local permits to upgrade their equipments, charging them with violations of the federal Migratory Bird Treaty Act for alleged kills of as many as 1,000 eagles, hawks, and owls annually. Jane Kay, Bird killings at Altamont Pass, S.F. Chronicle, Jan. 13, 2004. Altamont Pass, noted Jeff Miller, a spokesman for the group, "has become a death zone for eagles and other magnificent and imperiled birds of prey. Birds come into the pass to hunt and get chopped up by the blades." *Id.*

2. The federal Endangered Species Act, 16 U.S.C. §§ 1531–1544, is a potentially powerful obstacle to construction of a windpower facility. When a species (or a subspecies or population of a species) is listed under the Act, all federal agencies must consult with the United States Fish and Wildlife Service before taking any action that might harm the species. Moreover, any person that harms a listed species may be guilty of "taking" the species, which carries criminal penalties under the act. Destruction of the habitat of a listed species can also constitute a taking. For a thorough analysis of the Endangered Species Act, *see* J.B. Ruhl and John Cameron Nagle, The Law of Biodiversity and Ecosystem Management (Foundation Press 2002).

The discovery of an endangered species near a proposed windpower facility can have a dramatic impact. The Enron Corporation agreed to relocate a planned wind farm in California after the National Audubon Society objected that the turbines might pose a threat to the endangered California Condor. Andrew Broman, Environmentalists Pressure Houston–Based Firm to Drop Plans for Wind Farm, Houston Chronicle, Nov. 4, 1999.

Case Study: The Cape Wind Energy Project

The Cape Wind project would create the first offshore wind farm in the U.S., with a planned capacity of 420 MW to be generated by 130 wind turbines located five miles off the Cape Cod shore in Massachusetts. According to the project developer, Cape Wind Energy, these turbines would generate sufficient electricity to meet 75% of the demand on the Cape and nearby islands. See http://www.capewind.org. David K. Garman, Assistant Secretary for Energy Efficiency and Renewable Energy, termed the Cape Wind project "important to our national interest and a critical first step to building a domestic, globally competitive wind industry," and added that, "Success in this project could also lay the foundation for a focused national investment to develop offshore wind technology in the coming years." See Letter to U.S. Army Corps of Engineers, http://www.capewind.org.

The proposed project has generated an intense level of controversy, which is not surprising as it raises a number of the issues that impact development of offshore wind farms. Concerns for wildlife and navigation, primary arguments made by project opponents, are balanced against the need for clean, renewable energy. Democratic and Republican Senators, and both Massachusetts Governor Mitt Romney and the state's Attorney General have weighed in against the project. Federal agencies (most notably the EPA and Army Corps of Engineers) disagree about the project's environmental impacts. A coalition of regional environmental groups lined up in support of the project, while a local group formed in opposition to Cape Wind, the Alliance to Protect Nantucket Sound (Alliance), raised millions of dollars from large and small donors and pursued a variety of means to block Cape Wind. See http://saveoursound.org.

As a "major federal action[ ] significantly affecting the quality of the human environment" under the National Environmental Policy Act ("NEPA"), see 42 U.S.C. § 4332(2)(C), the Cape Wind project requires an Environmental Impact Statement ("EIS"). The 3,800–page draft EIS (DEIS) prepared by the U.S. Army Corps of Engineers addressed the project's scope and expected environmental impacts.

U.S. Army Corps of Engineers, Cape Wind Energy Project

Draft Environmental Impact Statement 1–3 to 1–4 (2004).

1.5.1 Project Overview

The proposed Wind Park will consist of 130 WTGs [*wind turbine generators*] located at the applicant's proposed location on Horseshoe Shoal in Nantucket Sound, Massachusetts (**Figure 13–1**). The WTGs will be arranged to maximize the Wind Park's energy generating capacity in order to achieve a maximum potential electric output of approximately 454 MW of renewable power. The wind-generated electricity from each of the turbines will be transmitted via a 33 kV submarine transmission cable system to the Electric Service Platform ("ESP") centrally located within the WTG array. The ESP will then transform and transmit this electric power to the Cape Cod mainland via two 115 kilovolt ("kV") alternating current (AC) submarine cable circuits. These submarine cable systems will make landfall in the Town of Yarmouth (Lewis Bay). From this landfall, an upland transmission system will be installed in an underground conduit system within exiting roadways and right-of-way ("ROW") where it will intersect with the existing NSTAR Electric ROW near Willow Street in Yarmouth. The upland transmission line will continue within the ROW to the Barnstable Switching Station. The Project's interconnection with the existing NSTAR electric transmission line will allow wind-generated energy from the WTGs to be transmitted and distributed to users connected to the New England transmission system, including users on Cape Cod and the Islands. These areas in their entirety constitute the Project area.

The Project has been designed with sufficient spacing between WTGs (a minimum of 0.34 nautical mile (629 meters) × 0.56 nautical mile (1,000 meters) grid) so that the construction and operation of the proposed Project will not preclude or prohibit traditional uses of the water-sheet area within or around the Wind Park turbine array. Use of the water sheet area within the turbine array would include the continuation of general commercial and recreational navigation, commercial and recreational aviation, commercial and recreational fishing, and other traditional water-based activities that promote the use and enjoyment of this area of Nantucket Sound.

1.5.2   Project Location

The proposed location of the Wind Park will be located on Horseshoe Shoal in Nantucket Sound. As shown in **Figure 13–1**, the northernmost WTGs will be approximately 4.7 miles from the nearest point of land on the mainland (Point Gammon), the southeastern portion of the Wind Park will be approximately 11 miles from Nantucket Island (Great Point), and the westernmost WTGs will be approximately 5.5 miles from the island of Martha's Vineyard (Cape Poge).

The proposed submarine cable system route is approximately 12.2 miles in length (6.6 miles within the Massachusetts 3–mile territorial line) from the ESP to the landfall location in Yarmouth. The submarine transmission lines would travel north to northeast in Nantucket Sound into Lewis Bay past the westerly side of Egg Island, and then make landfall at New Hampshire Avenue. The submarine transmission lines would transition to the upland transmission line by using horizontal directional drilling ("HDD") methodologies to a transition vault situated at the end of New Hampshire Avenue.

Upon making landfall, the proposed transmission line route would then follow New Hampshire Avenue north, merging with Berry Avenue. The route continues north on Berry Avenue, crossing Route 28 and continuing north on Higgins Crowell Road to Willow Street. Continuing north on Willow Street, the route passes under Route 6, to the proposed intersection point with the existing NSTAR Electric 115 kV transmission line ROW, approximately 500 feet north of Summer Street. The route then turns westerly within the NSTAR Electric's existing ROW to the Barnstable Switching Station, crossing under Route 6. The proposed upland transmission line would be located entirely within existing public roadways for a length of approximately 4.0 miles from landfall to the NSTAR Electric transmission line ROW located on the west side of Willow Street. The upland transmission line would then proceed underground approximately 1.9 miles along the existing NSTAR Electric ROW to the Barnstable Switching Station.

* * *

A summary prepared by Cape Wind of the environmental effects studied in the DEIS includes the following:

Air Quality/Global Warming—The project will reduce operations of fossil fuel power plants, thereby reducing air pollution and improving air quality. There will be a reduction in greenhouse gas emissions of over a million tons a year.

Health—Cape Wind could have an annual cumulative beneficial effect on public health estimated at approximately $53 million dollars resulting from reduced power plant pollution.

Energy—Cape Wind will reduce energy costs in several ways including offsetting the burning of expensive fossil fuels, reducing New England's dependence on natural gas, and reducing the cost of compliance with the Renewable Energy Portfolio Standards ("RPS") for Massachusetts electricity consumers. Cape Wind will reduce the regions reliance on imported fossil fuels.

Jobs—The project will create 600–1,000 new construction jobs and 154 new permanent jobs.

Economic—The direct, indirect and induced effects of Cape Wind would generate permanent economic changes in Massachusetts, most of which would be concentrated in Barnstable County that will result in annual permanent increases of $21.8 million in economic output; $10.2 million in value added; and, nearly $7 million in labor income.

Fishing—There will be minimal or no adverse impacts on fishing. Due to the wide spacing for the wind turbines, the physical presence of these structures should not interfere with fishing activity. The presence of the turbines may enhance fishing for certain species such as Atlantic cod, black sea bass, and scup.

Sea Navigation—Due to the spacing between the turbines, it is expected that the construction and operation of Cape Wind will not substantially adversely impact general commercial/recreational vessel navigation or ferry operations.

Air Navigation—The FAA issued a Determination of No Hazard to air Navigation.

Birds—Detailed bird activity mapping in Nantucket Sound from radar, boat and aerial observations are provided in the DEIS. There is less bird activity over Horseshoe Shoal than in many other areas of Nantucket Sound. The estimated small number of birds killed by wind turbines is unlikely to cause bird population declines.

Noise—Based upon modeling, people onshore will not hear the operations of the wind turbines or the foghorns that will be used when needed for marine safety that will have a range of one half mile. No noise impacts from the operations of the wind turbines are expected for boaters approaching Horseshoe shoal.

Alternative Sites—Seventeen sites were evaluated in New England for wind power . . . Horseshoe Shoal was shown to be technically, environmentally and economically preferable to other alternative sites.

Cape Wind Energy, Notable Findings in the Draft EIS, http://www.capewind.org/article72.htm#DEIS.

The Corps received more than 3,500 comments on the DEIS. A coalition of environmental groups led by the Conservation Law Foundation and Massachusetts PIRG lined up in support of the project. *See* http://www.capewind.org/article47.htm. However, others criticized the DEIS. The Alliance issued an 800–page report, bolstered by the findings of 30 technical consultants, in which it stated that the DEIS "promotes the project, rather than analyzing it critically and objectively under federal and state laws." Kevin Dennehy, Critics Assail Corps' Review, Cape Cod Times, Feb. 24, 2005. Robert W. Varney, the Regional Administrator for the EPA, wrote to the Corps that its "review lacked information about environmental conditions, impacts of the proposed project, and whether alternatives—such as a scaled-down version of the wind farm—could avoid or minimize those impacts." Theo Emergy, EPA Calls U.S. Army Corps Review of Wind Farm Project Inadequate, Boston Globe, Feb. 25, 2005. The Interior Department also criticized the Corps' findings, in a sharply worded memo in which the Department sought additional information on the likelihood of birds colliding with the proposed turbines and on impacts on wildlife migration.

To what extent is the Corps required to halt the Cape Wind project if other federal agencies believe the project would be damaging to the environment? Regulations promulgated by the Council on Environmental Quality under NEPA require the DEIS to be furnished to a federal agency that has "jurisdiction by law or special expertise" for their comments, and the agency preparing the EIS has a duty to assess and consider those comments. *See* 40 C.F.R. §§ 1503.2–1503.4. On the other hand, if after reviewing these comments the Corps decides to issue a permit, well-established case precedent under NEPA precludes substantive review of the decision.

See Strycker's Bay Neighborhood Council, Inc. v. Karlen, 444 U.S. 223 (1980).

NOTES AND COMMENTS

1. While the turbines would be located in waters over which the federal government has jurisdiction, transmission cables and other equipment will cross state waters, tidal areas and lands, and nine different state agencies have jurisdiction over part of the project. Playing the State Card, Cape Cod Times, Feb. 26, 2005. The project was subject to tougher state scrutiny after the state's request to change its borders to include some of Cape Wind's turbines in state waters was granted by the federal Minerals Management Service, which maps state and federal boundaries. Kevin Dennehy, Bay State Gets a Bit Bigger, Cape Cod Times, Feb. 23, 2005.

2. Senator John Warner (R–VA), the Chair of the Senate Armed Services Committee, proposed an amendment to the Defense Authorization Act that would have imposed a moratorium on Cape Wind and all other offshore wind farms, but later withdrew it in the face of opposition. Beth Daley, Tough Language Dropped in Cape Wind Farm Plan, Boston Globe, Oct. 8, 2004. For more on the roles of state and federal regulators and Congress in Cape Wind, *see* Carolyn S. Kaplan, Congress, the Courts, and the Army Corps: Siting the First Offshore Wind Farm in the United States, 31 B.C. Envtl. Aff. L. Rev. 177 (2004).

3. Offshore wind farms are planned for other locations in the U.S. In New York, the Long Island Power Authority plans to build a 100 MW facility about three miles off the south shore of Long Island, near the renowned Jones Beach. Utility to announce contractor for construction, operation off N.Y. beach, Greenwire, May 3, 2004. Along the Gulf Coast of Louisiana, developers GT Energy and Wind Energy Systems Technology moved forward with a plan to build 500 MW of windpower capacity, including the possible use of inactive offshore oil and gas platforms to locate some turbines. Ben Geman, Planned Gulf project may use oil and gas platforms, Greenwire, Nov. 10, 2004.

However, two proposals for wind projects off the coast of New Jersey ran into opposition in 2004, as acting Governor Richard Codey announced a moratorium on state funding and permitting for offshore wind farms, and Representative Frank Pallone stated he planned to introduce legislation in Congress to extend the moratorium throughout the mid-Atlantic region. New Jersey governor to put moratorium on offshore projects, Greenwire, Dec. 9, 2004.

4. Which federal agency or agencies have responsibility for permitting and overseeing construction of offshore wind farms? As the Cape Wind saga unfolded, several different agencies, including the Interior Department, Army Corps of Engineers, and FAA became involved, each with different responsibilities and powers. The 2004 final report of the U.S. Commission on Ocean Policy finds this fragmentation typical of development on the Outer Continental Shelf (OCS), and calls for a national ocean policy that

would feature more coordination among agencies. An Ocean Blueprint for the 21st Century, http://www.oceancommission.gov/. *See* Chapter 9.

5.   While controversy rages over offshore wind farms in the U.S., they are well underway in Europe. Germany and Denmark, in particular, have substantial installed capacity; Denmark gets more than 15 percent of its electricity from the wind. Donn, *supra*. A report in 2004 claimed that European nations could have enough wind turbine capacity by 2020 to meet 23% of projected demand for electricity. Sea Wind Europe, http://www.greenpeace.org.uk/MultimediaFiles/Live/FullReport/6204.pdf.   The United Kingdom, according to the British Wind Energy Association (BWEA), "has potentially the largest offshore wind resource in the world, with relatively shallow waters and a strong wind resource extending far into the North Sea." *See* http://www.bwea.com. The British government has proposed a target of 10 percent of electricity generation from renewable resources by 2010, and the BWEA expects that projects underway or planned will contribute as much as 7.2 GW, or 7% of U.K. supply and nearly half of the renewable energy target. North Hoyle, the first offshore wind farm in the U.K., began operation in 2004.

iii.   Subterranean Energy; The Tragedy of the Commons

Geothermal energy is another cool renewable resource. In those limited locations in which underground steam produces hot springs or geysers, this steam can be used for electric generation. It is generally believed, however, that all of the locations in the United States where it would be practical to harness geothermal energy have already been exploited. Geothermal heat originates from the earth's core, where temperatures reach over 9,000 degrees F. Magma that remains beneath the earth's crust heats rock and water. The hot water sometimes travels to the earth's surface as hot springs and geysers, although most stays underground in cracks and porous rocks. Such a formation is known as a geothermal reservoir, and such reservoirs, where available, provide a source of geothermal energy.

In the past, people used geothermal energy from hot springs to bathe and heat buildings. Native Americans used hot springs for cooking and medicine. Today, we drill wells into the geothermal reservoirs to bring the hot water to the surface. Once the water travels to the surface, it is used to generate electricity or for other energy saving measures not related to electricity generation.

Geothermal power plants use steam, heat or hot water from the geothermal reservoirs to spin turbine generators which produce electricity. The water is then returned through an injection well to be reheated and sustain the reservoir. There are three kinds of geothermal power plants. A "dry" steam reservoir produces steam, but very little water. The steam is piped into a "dry" steam power plant that provides the force to spin the turbine generator. A "flash" power plant uses water ranging from 300–700 degrees F. The water is brought to the surface through a production well where some of the water "flashes" into steam, which powers a turbine. A binary power plant uses water that is not hot enough to flash into steam.

The water is passed through a heat exchanger, where the heat is transferred to a second liquid that has a lower boiling point than water. The binary liquid flashes to vapor when heated and is used to spin the turbine. The vapor is then condensed and used again.

Geothermal power is a very clean source of energy. The land required for geothermal power plants is generally smaller per megawatt than most any other type of power plant. There is also much less physical damage to the environment. Rivers do not need to be dammed or forests cut down. Geothermal power is reliable-the plants are located on top of the power source. This eliminates the uncertainties associated with weather and natural disasters, and possible political conflicts that often affect the importation of fossil fuels.

Relatively few places in the world happen to be situated in locations where geothermal energy is available sufficiently close to the surface of the earth that it can be utilized efficiently with current technology. Where it is available, the rights to access this energy have sometimes created disputes not unlike those involving the right to sunlight. *See Parks v. Watson*, 716 F.2d 646 (9th Cir. 1983).

NOTES AND COMMENTS

1. Geothermal energy is found only in a relatively small number of places, and thus is most efficiently utilized by the use of large facilities which provide economies of scale. However, this has often meant monopolization of the resource by a single supplier, which reduces competition and the economies that competition typically creates. This issue reappears throughout the book.

2. To what extent is it appropriate for public agencies to develop and control energy resources? In many countries, energy development and distribution is controlled by public entities. For example, the Comision Federal de Electricidad of Mexico operates geothermal energy facilities with a combined capacity of 843 MW, with another 110 MW of capacity planned; geothermal plants satisfy 2.5% of the country's electricity demand. Mexico Country Analysis Brief, http://www.eia.doe.gov; Program Partners in Mexico, http://www.re.sandia.gov/en/pb/nl/4/nl4–rt.htm.

Where the federal government grants a patent for title to land to an individual, reserving "all the coal and other minerals in the land so entered and patented, together with the right to prospect for, mine, and remove same . . . ," does the patentee get the right to use geothermal steam under the land or has that right been reserved to the federal government by the quoted language? *See Rosette, Inc. v. United States*, 64 F.Supp.2d 1116 (D.N.M. 1999).

The issue of public versus private ownership of energy facilities has recurred from time to time in the United States, and can be seen today in disputes over hydroelectric projects (*see* Chapter 4). As a capitalist country, the United States has opted for private control of most of our energy resources, but at various times in our history we have been persuaded that public ownership of certain resources distributes the costs and benefits more fairly throughout the population. For example, we provide tax advantages for public ownership of facilities and resources by allowing state and local governments to sell bonds free from federal income taxation. As with so many issues, our national policy on public ownership is not necessarily internally consistent.

3. Sometimes attempts by state or local governments to monopolize a particular energy resource may raise a constitutional issue under the interstate commerce clause if it results in discrimination against people from other states. For example, municipal solid waste is an energy resource that can be burned to generate electricity. It is economical to do so, however, only if a large volume of waste can be assembled at a single incinerator. Some local governments have tried to ensure that a large volume of waste would be available by prohibiting their residents from delivering their waste to anyone but the local government, but the Supreme Court held that this discriminated against waste haulers from other states in violation of the commerce clause. *C & A Carbone, Inc. v. Town of Clarkstown*, 511 U.S. 383 (1994) The incineration of municipal solid waste is a popular form of cogeneration, discussed below in section B.2, "Energy Conservation."

4. The Energy Information Administration reported that 13.7 trillion kWh of electricity was generated from geothermal sources in 2001, considerably less than the 17.32 trillion kWh of electricity generated as recently as 1993. Renewable Energy Annual 2003, *supra*. While government programs at the Department of Energy and Bureau of Land Management promote geothermal exploration and development, they are less robust than those for other renewable resources. Tom Gardner, Geothermal exploration underfunded, BLM tells Reno gathering, Las Vegas Sun, Jan. 28, 2004.

* * *

In 2001, almost all of the geothermal energy utilization was in California, and production at larger fields there has dropped considerably over time. Renewable Energy Annual 2003, *supra*. To a great extent, the rapid depletion of some of these geothermal fields reflects the fact that the geothermal energy is in the form of a "common-pool resource" that becomes the property of anyone who obtains access to it. In the absence of regulation, such common-pool resources may become rapidly depleted because each user will rush to increase his share. This phenomenon has become known as the "Tragedy of the Commons."

In a famous essay, Garrett Hardin argued that when resources exist in a common pool, without individual ownership, they are likely to become victims of "The Tragedy of the Commons." Garrett L. Hardin, The Tragedy of the Commons, 162 Science 1243 (1968). He described this phenomenon by using the example of medieval English farmers who could not prevent overgrazing of common lands because each individual peasant would benefit by grazing one more cow despite that cow's contribution to the overall malnutrition of the herd:

> Picture a pasture open to all. It is to be expected that each herdsman will try to keep as many cattle as possible on the commons.... Explicitly or implicitly, more or less consciously, he asks, "What is the utility to *me* of adding one more animal to my herd?" This utility has one negative and one positive component.

The positive component is one additional animal. The negative component is that all of his animals are a bit weaker. But since "the effects of overgrazing are shared by all the herdsmen," the negative component is overshadowed by the positive benefits of an additional animal.

> Therein is the tragedy. Each man is locked into a system that compels him to increase his herd without limit—in a world that is limited. Ruin is the destination toward which all men rush, each pursuing his own best interest in a society that believes in the freedom of the commons. Freedom in a commons brings ruin to all.

From his parable Hardin drew the conclusion that we must "explicitly exorcize" the "invisible hand" when dealing with problems involving commons. For commons that could not be privatized he favored "coercion." Hardin's metaphor has become widely used to describe a problem that often arises when resources, including energy resources, are commonly owned.

Classical economic theory advocates the privatization of common property as a means of avoiding the kind of problems that Hardin describes. *See, e.g.*, Carol Rose, Property and Persuasion 105–108 (1994). But as she points out, not all common-pool resources easily lend themselves to that kind of division. For some types of energy resources, in particular, division of the resource into private allotments has proven quite difficult.

In the 1980s, institutions like the World Bank that finance development in third world countries began to express interest in systems to manage common-pool resources. Many of these countries had traditionally relied on common resources as an important element in the local economy. Attempts to intervene in these countries without understanding the existing systems by which common resources were managed sometimes proved to be counterproductive.

In 1985, the National Research Council of the National Academies of Science and Engineering brought together a Panel on Common Property Resource Management to "assess systematically differing institutional arrangements for the effective conservation and utilization of jointly managed resources." National Research Council, Proceedings of the Conference on Common Property Resource Management vii (1985). Out of this conference came a research program to study common lands, energy and water resources and "other jointly held resources that constitute the global commons." *Id.*

Current research has found many instances of resource-using communities developing their own informal norms for apportioning common rights effectively. In some cases they found that Hardin's famous "tragedy of the commons" had indeed occurred, but in other instances they found systems of managing common property that appeared to be working well. For example, common grazing lands provided Hardin's example of potential disaster, but a study of common grazing lands in Morocco found that a highly complex body of rules had evolved out of agreements to resolve conflicting claims of nearby villages and tribes. By strictly limiting the seasons of use, the rules allowed the Berber communities to maintain a highly productive and sustainable resource in common ownership. Daniel W. Bromley, ed., Making the Commons Work 229 (San Francisco: ICS Press, 1992).

Many of the common-pool resource studies have looked at third world locations, but other studies found similar examples in highly developed countries. In the Alps of Switzerland, effective rules for the management of common grazing land have been adopted through the processes of Swiss direct democracy. Fikret Berkes, Common Property Resources: Ecology and Community Based Sustainable Development 15 (London: Belhaven Press, 1989). *See generally* Glenn G. Stevenson, Common Property Economics (Cambridge University Press, 1991). Other studies reached similar conclusions in modern American settings. For example, a study of several ground-water systems in semiarid portions of California concluded that locally accepted and managed regulations can sometimes control sharing behavior effectively. Elinor Ostrom, Governing the Commons (Cambridge University Press, 1990).

Because so much of our energy comes from common-pool resources, the study of methods of managing such resources is a potential source of applications that may become useful in the development of energy law. If resources exist as a common pool, to which no one has individual property rights, unique resource management problems are presented. For example, petroleum is usually found underground in reservoirs that have the characteristics of common-pool resources; *i.e.,* the ownership of the resource is divided among a number of separate owners of the land surface but each owner does not have a separately identifiable share of the oil. The resolution of these relationships is a major task of oil and gas law. *See* Chapter 6.

Many other types of resources also exist in common-pool form. When the tanker *Exxon Valdez* cracked open in Alaska's Prince William Sound in 1989 it produced an oil slick that spread for hundreds of miles, devastating the wildlife and natural resources of the Sound. Negligence could easily be established, but who could be a plaintiff? And how could you quantify the damages? The common law had great difficulty in dealing with injuries to common-pool resources because no individual person had a quantifiable share of the right to use such resources. *See Alaska Sport Fishing Ass'n v. Exxon Corp.,* 34 F.3d 769 (1994).

iv.   *Other Resources*

Deepwater energy is an experimental form of renewable energy. Two forms have been the subject of various test projects: (a) tidal power plants, if located in areas where there is a big range in the tides, could be built to operate on the energy generated by the tidal movement; and (b) convection plants, which would build up a circulation of cold deep water that could be used to cool buildings. In 2004, the British government announced a project to harness the power of the tides. The prototype Pelamis "wave energy converter," deployed off the coast of Scotland, is estimated to have power at full capacity comparable to that of a wind turbine. Andrew Freedman, New marine wave device generates power for U.K., Greenwire, Sept. 2, 2004. At present there is little interest in wave energy in the U.S.

Hydropower is by far the largest source of cool renewable energy currently being used. Water stored behind dams is released to turn turbines that generate electricity. Because of the extensive environmental impacts of these facilities, however, they are often controversial. The topic of hydropower is the subject of Chapter 4.

Hydrogen-powered fuel cells are currently the form of cool renewable technology that is attracting the most attention.

> Fuel cells use an electrochemical process that combines hydrogen and oxygen, producing water and electricity. Avoiding the inherent inefficiency of combustion, today's top fuel cells are roughly twice as efficient as conventional engines, have no moving parts, require little maintenance, are silent, and emit only water vapor. Unlike today's power plants, they are nearly as economical on a small scale as on a large one. Indeed, they could turn the very notion of a power plant into something more closely resembling a home appliance.

Brown *et al., supra,* at 28–29. Whether this assessment is overly optimistic remains to be seen. Fuel cell technology is discussed in more detail in the chapter on transportation, Chapter 15, and the chapter on global climate change, Chapter 16.

b.   HOT RENEWABLES

Among the so-called hot renewable resources, the term "biomass" is used to include a wide variety of plant materials that can be burned to provide energy. In the U.S., the Biomass Research and Development Initiative is a multi-agency effort established in 2000 to coordinate bioenergy research and development. This program provides financial assistance to institutions of higher education, national laboratories, federal research agencies, state research agencies, private sector entities, and nonprofit organizations.

In primitive regions, wood is often still used as a primary source of energy. Is wood a renewable resource? It is if used in moderation and accompanied by effective replanting of trees. In many poor regions, however, the wood is being depleted faster than it is being replaced.

The burning of waste vegetation from agricultural crops is also a potential energy source that is beginning to be utilized commercially. In tropical climates, for example, sugar cane fields convert solar energy to biomass at very high rates. When the sugar is extracted, the remainder of the plant has traditionally been burned. If this combustion can be converted to electricity it would be renewable as long as the soil would continue to produce crops.

A hot renewable resource attracting increased attention is "biodiesel," fuel derived from waste vegetable oils or animal fats for use in vehicles. Biodiesel itself contains no petroleum products, but can be used alone or in combination with other fuels to power vehicles, in many cases without any modifications to the vehicles. Unless used in its "neat" form (B100, or pure biodiesel), biodiesel is not strictly speaking a purely renewable resource because vehicles running on it also burn a petroleum product. However, there are environmental benefits associated with the use of the "B20" blend (fuel that is 20% biodiesel and 80% regular diesel fuel), particularly in reducing air emissions associated with diesel engines. A one-year biodiesel tax incentive went into effect in 2005, and about 500 fleets and 400 retail stations across the nation offer biodiesel. *See* Douglas E. Faulkner, Bush Highlights Biodiesel's Role in Energy Security, Richmond Times–Dispatch, May 19, 2005, at A13 (describing President Bush's visit to a Virginia biodiesel production facility). The singer Willie Nelson formed a company in 2005 to promote a B20 blend called "BioWillie," and announced plans to contract with an Oklahoma City-based chain of truck stops to carry the fuel at its 169 locations across the nation. Matt Curry, Willie Nelson's new gig: Biodiesel, Associated Press, Jan. 14, 2005.

NOTES AND COMMENTS

1.   There has been a dramatic increase in the extent of private sector investment in research and development of renewable power sources. Major oil and auto companies and electric utilities all have put significant capital into a wide variety of renewable technologies, including multimillion-dollar initiatives to develop hydrogen-powered fuel cell automobiles. *See* Chapter 16.

c.   INCENTIVES FOR RENEWABLES; PURPA's AVOIDED COST REQUIREMENT

i.   *Federal and State Incentives*

Federal policies promoting renewables with research and development funding, tax credits, and accelerated depreciation rates are critical to the industries' success. The production tax credit (PTC) for power produced from renewable resources (including solar and windpower) stands at 1.8 cents per kWh after its renewal through 2008 in section 1301 of the Energy Policy Act of 2005. The importance of this incentive is demonstrated by events after the end of 2003, when the PTC temporarily expired. *See* Working Families Tax Relief Act of 2004, Pub. L. No. 108–311, 118 Stat. 1166 (2004) (restoring PTC retroactively to January 1, 2004); American Jobs Creation Act of 2004, Pub. L. No. 108–357, 118 Stat. 1418 (2004) (expanding resources eligible for PTC). One year later, with its renewal uncertain at that time, windpower projects slated to add 2,000 MW of new domestic capacity at a cost of $2 billion were postponed, according to an industry spokeswoman. *See* Industry growth slowed by cost hurdles, Greenwire, June 14, 2004; Jeff Nesmith, Some see a way to produce new energy at competitive rates, but investors are few because a tax credit has expired, Atlanta Journal–Constitution, Sept. 13, 2004 (discussing a project in Oklahoma put on hold). The PTC garners criticism from those who see it as a pure subsidy to the industry, *see* Langenkamp, *supra*, but without it renewables producers claim they would not succeed.

A second federal incentive for windpower under consideration is an "interconnection" policy allowing windpower producers to connect to the grid on an equal footing with other producers of electricity. From the standpoint of the grid controller, whether that entity is a regional transmission organization ("RTO") or other control operator (*see* Chapter 11), windpower is problematic. Like most renewable energy resources, it is both diffuse, that is, thinly scattered; and sporadic, that is, variable over time. The sun doesn't shine reliably everywhere and all the time, nor does the wind always blow. This lack of "dispatchability" (the ability to count on being able to dispatch power to meet demand at any given time) is a major handicap for renewable resources. The high cost of capital investment to build plants that produce dispatchable power to back up the unreliable renewable sources remains a disincentive to the use of renewables. Also, as a result of the lack of dispatchability, windpower producers pay higher effective charges for transmission than other producers. Finally, as wind farms must be sited where the wind blows, they may be located at a distance from transmission lines, requiring expensive infrastructure to connect to the grid. A FERC staff report prepared in 2004 concluded that wind sites are on average 500 miles from major metropolitan centers and require transmission interconnections of longer than 10 miles to reach the grid.

In 2003, FERC had proposed a rule for interconnection of small generators (those generating less than 20 MW). Standardization of Small Generator Interconnection Agreements and Procedures, 60 Fed. Reg. 49,-974 (Aug. 19, 2003). After considerable discussion with a variety of stakeholders, including wind energy producers and the AWEA, FERC issued a second proposed rule in early 2005. Interconnection for Wind Energy and Other Alternative Technologies, 70 Fed. Reg. 27,935–01 (May 16, 2005) (*to be codified at 18 C.F.R.*). This proposed rule would set standards applicable to wind farms as an appendix to the Large Generator Interconnection Agreement (LGIA), which contains standard interconnection procedures for large generators required by FERC's Order No. 2003. For additional details on interconnection procedures and the LGIA, *see* Chapter 11.

Federal subsidies for renewable energy R&D were included in the Energy Policy Act of 1992 ("EPAct"), Renewable Energy and Energy Efficiency Technology Competitiveness Act of 1989, Solar Energy and Energy Conservation Act of 1980, Solar Photovoltaic Energy Research, Development, and Demonstration Act of 1978, Solar Energy Research Development and Demonstration Act of 1974. The amounts of these subsidies, however, have been small compared to long-term federal subsidies for coal and nuclear power. In 2002, the Union of Concerned Scientists noted that the nuclear power industry received 25 times more federal funding than the solar and wind industries combined from 1943–1999. Union of Concerned Scientists, Clean Energy: The Renewable Electricity Standard (2002).

Other federal financial incentives for renewables include a five-year program of the U.S. Department of Agriculture ("USDA") under section 9006 of the Farm Security and Rural Investment Act of 2002 (the "farm bill"). This program is intended to provide funding to help farmers, ranchers and small rural businesses develop renewable energy projects and make energy efficiency improvements to their operations. *See* http://www.rurdev.usda.gov/rbs/farmbill/. In a 2004 report, however, the federal General Accountability Office criticized the USDA for its failure to adequately implement the program. *See* http://www.gao.gov/new.items/d04756.-pdf. Other programs guarantee bank loans that can be used to purchase or refinance homes or businesses using renewable energy, often targeting specific income levels or communities where applicants would not otherwise be approved for a loan. USDA, Single Family Housing Loan Guarantees, http://www.rurdev.usda.gov/rhs/ProgramBriefs/brief_rhguar.htm. A new federal incentive for a consumer's purchase of renewable energy technology is the concept of an "energy efficient mortgage." EEMs make it easier for prospective home buyers to purchase houses by increasing the maximum borrowing amount allowed by lenders ("PITI," or principal, interest, taxes and insurance) by an amount equal to the estimated energy savings through the use of specified technologies. *See* http://www.energystar.gov.

NOTES AND COMMENTS

1. The Database of State Incentives for Renewable Energy's (DSIRE) Web site (http://www.dsireusa.org) maintains a complete summary of federal, state, local, and utility incentives and programs that promote renewable energy. For thorough analyses of the major laws affecting renewable resources, *see* Richard L. Ottinger & Rebecca Williams, Renewable Energy Sources for Development, 32 Envtl. L. 331 (2002); Suedeen G. Kelly, Alternative Energy Sources, in James E. Hickey, Jr. et al., Energy Law and Policy for the 21st Century, Ch. 13 (Rocky Mountain Mineral Law Foundation, 2000). Financing programs are discussed in John A. Herrick, Federal Project Financing Incentives for Green Industries: Renewable Energy and Beyond, 43 Nat. Resources J. 77 (2003).

2. State renewable energy programs established during the advent of competition, such as system benefits charges and renewable portfolio standards, have had an impact on the promotion of electricity generated from solar, wind, and other renewable resources. Other state incentives include state tax credits and deductions for consumers' purchases of qualifying equipment using renewable resources.

ii. PROPOSED REPEAL OF PURPA SECTION 210

Promotion of power generated from renewable resources intersects with restructuring policy through proposals to repeal or modify the "avoided cost" provision of PURPA, discussed in Chapter 11. Under PURPA, small independent power facilities are entitled to sell their power to utilities at "avoided cost" if they fit within the statutory definition of a "qualifying facility" (QF). One test for qualification is whether the facility will produce energy from renewable resources. *See, e.g., Wyoming Wind Power, Inc.,* 34 F.E.R.C. ¶ 61,152 (1986) (application granted for certification of a windpower facility as a qualifying small power production facility); *Southern California Edison Co. v. FERC,* 195 F.3d 17 (D.C. Cir. 1999) (QF status improperly granted where facility supplemented renewable energy with natural gas). The Federal Energy Regulatory Commission (FERC) makes the determination of whether a facility qualifies upon application by the builder of the proposed facility.

Many have complained that PURPA's avoided cost rates increase consumer electricity rates because utilities are contractually required to continue purchasing power at these rates even though the costs of generating electricity have subsequently dropped significantly. In many states, consumers are bearing the cost of long-term contracts with non-utility generators at avoided costs. As competition becomes more pervasive, mandatory buyback programs risk becoming a type of stranded cost.

While it was decided before California's ill-fated experimentation with restructuring and retail choice for consumers, the following case illustrates the origins of the conflict between competition and PURPA's avoided cost scheme:

Southern California Edison; San Diego Gas & Electric Co.

70 F.E.R.C. ¶ 61,215 (1995).

Introduction

On January 6, 1995, Southern California Edison Company (Edison) filed a petition for enforcement pursuant to section 210(h) of the Public Utility Regulatory Policies Act of 1978 (PURPA), 16 U.S.C. § 824a–3(h) (1988). On January 18, 1995, San Diego Gas & Electric Company (San Diego) filed a petition for enforcement pursuant to section 210(h) of PURPA or, in the alternative, for a declaratory order.

Both utilities state that the California Public Utilities Commission (California Commission) has ordered them to sign long-term, fixed-priced contracts with qualifying facilities (QFs) to purchase significant amounts of unneeded QF capacity at prices far in excess of their avoided costs. They argue that this new directive is in violation of PURPA and this Commission's implementing regulations. The California Commission responds that the two utilities challenge only a small part of a complex and comprehensive resource plan that is entirely within its implementation role under

PURPA. Numerous intervenors support or challenge all or portions of the challenged program.

While we have grave concerns about the need for this capacity and the staleness of the data relied upon by the California Commission, we do not reach a definitive conclusion on these issues because we decide the cases on other grounds. We do, however, find that the California program at issue violates PURPA and our implementing regulations because the California Commission did not consider all sources in reaching its avoided cost determinations.

Edison's Enforcement Petition

Edison states that the California Commission has ordered Edison to sign long-term, fixed-price contracts with QFs to purchase 686 MW of new capacity that will come on line in 1997–1999. Edison states that these contracts will require payments demonstrably more expensive than alternative sources of power, will require Edison to purchase capacity before it is needed, and will dramatically increase stranded costs in a soon-to-be-restructured electric utility industry.

Edison explains that these obligations are the result of the California Commission's Biennial Resource Plan Update ("BRPU"), which, pursuant to section 210(f) of PURPA, implements this Commission's rules governing the purchase by electric utilities of electricity from QFs. According to Edison, the BRPU has three stages. First, following the latest projections of energy and capacity needs of California utilities (Edison, San Diego, and Pacific Gas and Electric Company ("PG&E")) made by the California Energy Commission ("CEC"), the utilities file a resource plan identifying potential resource additions. The California Commission examines these plans and determines what new resources the utilities would add. Second, after the utilities have supplied certain data, the California Commission determines the utilities' assumed costs, known as "benchmark prices", for these resource additions, and determines which of the additions could be avoided. Third, QFs are then allowed to bid against the utilities' benchmark prices for the new resources. If bids received by the QFs are below the utilities' benchmark prices for the new resources, the utilities are then directed by the California Commission to enter into standard contracts (called "Final Standard Offer 4" or "FSO4" contracts) with the winning bidders with respect to each avoided resource. The winning bidders are paid the price bid by the second lowest bidder with respect to each avoided resource. (This procedure is referred to as a second-price auction.) Certain winning bidders receive additional payments to reflect the assumed value to society of reduced air emissions.

Based on the CEC's 1990 electricity report, the California Commission concluded in 1992 that Edison would construct 624 MW of new generation from 1997 to 1999 as follows: two new geothermal plants, one wind farm, and the repowering of an existing steam plant. The California Commission also estimated Edison's costs for construction of each of these projects, which were given the name "Identified Deferrable Resources" ("IDRs"). Edison states that even though the estimated costs were many times larger than the capital costs of constructing new gas-fired turbines, the California Commission concluded that the IDRs were economic by imputing massive environmental compliance costs to the alternative, gas-fired resources.

In 1993, pursuant to California Commission directive, Edison solicited bids for 624 MW of new capacity, broken down into four separate IDRs. Only QFs were allowed to bid. The California Commission, in implementing a California statute, required that half of the capacity for three of the four IDRs be reserved solely for renewable bidders. The solicitation produced bids lower than the IDR benchmarks.

Edison argues that the California program is in conflict with PURPA and the Commission's rules implementing PURPA. Edison states that a fundamental flaw in the solicitation structure is its assumption that any QF contract that is priced below the utility's assumed cost of providing the same power to itself through the construction of new resources (the benchmark price) is necessarily below avoided cost. Edison states that the California Commission ignores this Commission's regulations, which define avoided costs as the costs of replacement energy the utility could generate itself or "purchase from another source." 18 C.F.R. § 292.101(b)(6)(1994). Edison also states that lower-cost alternatives were readily available for 4.0 cents/kWh or less, even though it was required to execute contracts with QFs at initial rates as high as 6.6 cents/kWh.

Edison argues that this result also is the product of the California Commission's intention to favor "renewable" QFs. Edison explains that the California Commission segmented the solicitation into four separate IDRs (274 MW repower, 50 MW wind, 100 MW geothermal, and 200 MW geothermal), and that a QF was required to bid separately against each IDR. Compounding this segmentation, half of the renewable IDR capacity was set aside for bidding only by renewable QFs. A related flaw, in Edison's opinion, was the mandate that winning bidders be paid an air emissions adder/subtracter based on the difference in projected emissions between the bid-winning QF project and the IDR. Edison also criticizes the California Commission for failing to determine the utility's avoided cost calculated at the time the power is delivered or "at the time the obligation is incurred." 18 C.F.R. § 292.304(d)(2)(ii) (1994). Edison claims that the California Commission's avoided cost determination was made with stale data.

Finally, Edison argues that the California QF program is inconsistent with the California Commission's ongoing proposal to restructure the electric utility industry, whereby certain retail customers will be able to opt for "direct access", i.e., retail wheeling. Edison states that the failure to address the effect of restructuring on avoided costs, and the failure to allow a means to address stranded costs in the standard offer contracts, violates PURPA and the Commission's implementing regulations.

Edison states that it is required under the BRPU to execute contracts with the QFs by March 29, 1995. Edison requests that the Commission act as expeditiously as possible. Specifically, Edison asks that the Commission either relieve it of its obligation to enter into contracts with the QFs by March 29, 1995 or, if the Commission declines to take action, to issue a notice of intent not to act in time to allow Edison to seek appropriate injunctive relief from a federal district court before it is required to sign the contracts. . . .

Discussion

When Congress enacted PURPA in 1978, there was very little non-utility generation. In 1978 virtually all new generating capacity was provided by traditional electric utilities. In fact, one of the principal reasons Congress adopted section 210 of PURPA was because electric utilities had refused to purchase power from non-utility producers. In contrast to 1978, non-traditional producers, including QFs, now provide well in excess of half of all new generating resources, and the Commission has determined that there is no longer any dominance in the provision of new generating capacity.

One of the reasons for the dramatic growth of the QF industry was the Commission's policy decision in 1980 to set the maximum rate permissible under PURPA section 210(b), i.e., a full avoided cost rate. While such rates do not result in direct benefits to ratepayers, they nevertheless are fully consistent with PURPA section 210(b)'s requirement that the rates be just and reasonable to ratepayers and in the public interest. Nevertheless, PURPA does not permit either the Commission, or the States in their implementation of PURPA, to require a purchase rate that exceeds avoided cost.

Since 1980, the Commission has given the States wide latitude in implementing PURPA. We have done so partly in recognition of the important role which Congress intended to give the States under PURPA, as well as to avoid unnecessary interference with state efforts to maximize the development of QFs. However, as noted above, the QF industry is now a developed industry and the need for integration of policy objectives under PURPA and other federal electric regulatory policies is pronounced. This is particularly the case given the fact that the electric utility industry is in the midst of a transition to a competitive wholesale power market, and some States, including California, are considering direct access for retail customers.

As the electric utility industry becomes increasingly competitive, the need to ensure that the States are using procedures which ensure that QF rates do not exceed avoided cost becomes more critical. This is because QF rates that exceed avoided cost will, by definition, give QFs an unfair advantage over other market participants (non-QFs). This, in turn, will hinder the development of competitive markets and hurt ratepayers, a result clearly at odds with ensuring the just and reasonable rates required by PURPA section 210(b).

We believe it is incumbent upon regulators, Federal and State, to avoid the creation of transition costs where possible. California's decision to consider a major restructuring of its retail electricity market significantly heightens our concern with stranded costs arising from above-avoided-cost rates. We believe it is inconsistent with our obligation under PURPA to ensure just and reasonable rates, and our goals to encourage development of competitive bulk power markets, to permit the use of PURPA to create new contracts that do not reflect market conditions for new bulk power supplies.

Finally, in acting today, we acknowledge California's ability under its authorities over the electric utilities subject to its jurisdiction to favor particular generation technologies over others. We respect the fact that resource planning and resource decisions are the prerogative of state commissions and that states may wish to diversify their generation mix to meet environmental goals in a variety of ways. Our decision today does not, for example, preclude the possibility that, in setting an avoided cost rate, a state may account for environmental costs of all fuel sources included in an all source determination of avoided cost. Also, under state authority, a state may choose to require a utility to construct generation capacity of a preferred technology or to purchase power from the supplier of a particular type of resource. The recovery of costs of utility-constructed generation would be regulated by the state. The rates for wholesale sales would be regulated by this Commission on a cost-of-service or market-based rate basis, as appropriate. Our decision here simply makes clear that the State can pursue its policy choices concerning particular generation technologies consistent with the requirements of PURPA and our regulations, so long as such action does not result in rates above avoided cost.

Commission Response

. . . While we are reluctant to interfere in California's implementation of PURPA and our regulations, as we explained in *Connecticut Light and Power Company*, 70 FERC ¶ 61,102 (1995) ("CL&P"), PURPA expressly directed this Commission, and not the states, to prescribe rules governing QF rates. PURPA gave the states responsibility for "implementing" the statute and the Commission's rules. As a result, a state may prescribe a particular per unit charge only if the process it uses to establish the per unit charge is in accordance with the Commission's rules.

Section 210(b) of PURPA explicitly provides that no Commission rule on QF rates "shall provide for a rate which exceeds the incremental cost to the electric utility of alternative energy." The "incremental cost of alternative electric energy" is defined in section 210(d) of PURPA as "the cost to the electric utility of the electric energy which, but for the purchase from such cogenerator or small power producer, such utility would generate or purchase from another source." The Supreme Court stated that PURPA "sets full avoided cost as the maximum rate that the Commission may prescribe." The Commission's regulations, tracking the statutory language, in turn expressly provide that QF rates must "be just and reasonable to the electric consumer of the electric utility" and "not discriminate against qualifying cogeneration and small power production facilities," and that "nothing in [the Commission's regulations] requires any electric utility to pay more than the avoided cost for purchases." The Commission's regulations define avoided costs as "the incremental costs to an electric utility of electric energy or capacity or both which, but for the purchase from the qualifying facility or qualifying facilities, such utility would generate itself or purchase from another source."

As pointed out by the California Commission, IEP, and numerous other intervenors, the Commission gives great latitude to state commissions as to procedures selected to determine avoided costs. The Commission has not, and does not intend in the future, to second-guess state regulatory authorities' actual determinations of avoided costs (i.e., whether the per unit charges are no higher than incremental costs). Rather, the Commission believes its role is limited to ensuring the process used to calculate the per unit charge (i.e., implementation) accords with the statute and our regulations.

As noted above, under PURPA an avoided cost (incremental cost) determination must permit QFs to participate in a non-discriminatory fashion and, at the same time, assure that the purchasing utility pays no more than the cost it otherwise would incur to generate the capacity (or energy) itself "or purchase from another source" (the language of section 210 of PURPA, emphasis added). Congress in this language did not in any way limit the sources to be considered. The consequence is that regardless of whether the State regulatory authority determines avoided cost administratively, through competitive solicitation (bidding), or some combination thereof, it must in its process reflect prices available from all sources able to sell to the utility whose avoided cost is being determined. If the state is determining avoided cost by relying on a combination of benchmark and bidding procedures, as here, this means that the bidding cannot be limited to certain sellers (QFs); rather, it must be all-source bidding.

For this reason, we find that the California Commission's process of determining avoided costs did not comply with PURPA. Under the California Commission's procedures, as explained above, a benchmark price was determined for the acquisition of certain capacity. Only QFs were then permitted to bid against the benchmark. Such a procedure could not properly determine avoided costs, because it excluded potential sources of capacity from which the utilities could purchase, in contravention of the requirements of section 210 of PURPA and our regulations.

Because the California Commission's procedure was unlawful under PURPA, Edison and San Diego cannot lawfully be compelled to enter into contracts resulting from that procedure. At this juncture, there are no executed contracts. However, in order to avoid parties spending further time and resources in pursuing contracts that would be unlawful under PURPA, we believe it would be appropriate for the California Commission to stay its requirements directing Edison and San Diego to purchase pending the outcome of further administrative procedures in accordance with PURPA. We also encourage the utilities and QFs to reach a settlement that would be consistent with PURPA.

Finally, based on the record before us at this time, we have grave concerns about the need for this capacity and the staleness of the data relied upon by the California Commission. Because we are deciding these cases on other grounds, we do not need to reach a definitive conclusion on these issues.

Applicability of Decision

Many other states now also use some sort of bidding procedure to establish avoided cost. We do not know whether these states engage in all-source bidding procedures, or whether they, as California, limit bidding to QFs. However, we do not believe it would be in the public interest to invalidate the QF contracts that have resulted from prior solicitations in California or elsewhere that have not been challenged and are pending. Consistent with our recent order in CL&P, we will not entertain requests to invalidate preexisting contracts in which avoided costs were established pursuant to a state bidding procedure that did not allow all-source bidding unless such issue has been raised and is pending or is raised in a timely appeal of a state decision. We believe that the appropriate time in which to challenge a state-imposed rate for a QF purchase is up to the time the purchase contract is signed, not years into a contract.

■ WILLIAM L. MASSEY, COMMISSIONER, concurring: I concur in today's order. My concurrence is driven by essentially two factors. First, as competition emerges, the QF contracts at issue here would increase the amount of stranded costs ultimately borne by the utilities' ratepayers and/or share-holders. That is a step in the wrong direction. Stranded cost is the central issue in the debate over the future structure of the electric industry and it is time for regulators, federal and state, to face it squarely and boldly. We need to find ways to reduce, not increase, the industry's potential stranded cost problems.

Second, in today's wholesale market, QFs should compete head-on with other power suppliers. The power supply industry has become much more competitive since the enactment of PURPA. PURPA has been a success in this respect. The QF industry has matured sufficiently that QFs can and should compete on the merits with other supply options. QFs can, for example, often assist utilities to meet long-term environmental compliance requirements, and I believe the market and state regulators can recognize and integrate the value of such assistance in the all-source determination process.

Our order stands for two principles. First, while avoided costs may be determined administratively, through bidding or some combination thereof, the determination must consider prices available from all sources able to sell to the affected utility. Thus, our order does not preclude administrative determinations of avoided costs, so long as all sources are considered. I believe bidding may be the best way for states to comply with PURPA, but it is not the only way. Second, if avoided costs are determined through a combination of bidding and benchmark procedures, the bidding phase must be open to all sources, not just QFs. The parties addressed many other issues but, beyond establishing these two principles, we do not resolve those issues in this order.

I want to underscore that our decision today does not preclude states from considering environmental costs in determining avoided costs under PURPA. The order expressly leaves open the possibility that states may account for the environmental costs of all fuel sources included in an all-source determination. The order also says that states can pursue their policy choices concerning particular generation technologies consistent with PURPA and our regulations, so long as such action does not result in rates above avoided cost. Indeed, a primary purpose of PURPA is to encourage the development of alternative generation, including non-fossil generation, and today's order must be read with that in mind.

The consideration of environmental costs and other non-price factors under PURPA is consistent with a recent amendment to PURPA. In the Energy Policy Act of 1992, Congress amended PURPA to require states to consider mandating the use of "integrated resource planning." The amendment of PURPA to include this requirement supports construing PURPA's avoided cost standard as allowing consideration of the non-price factors essential to integrated resource planning.

The consideration of environmental costs and other non-price factors under PURPA is also consistent with this Commission's past statements. In proposing procedures in 1988 to allow bidding under PURPA, the Commission stated:

Terms and conditions for electricity production and delivery cannot be described by a single facet of the sale, such as price. Rather, a variety of factors which affect the continued security and operational integrity of the purchasing utility's system, including fuel diversity and reliability, must be taken into consideration in selecting purchases. Congress was aware that many attributes need to be taken into account in determining the value of purchases from QFs.

The Commission also stated then that one permissible way to rank bids under PURPA would be based on price alone, but "there are severe drawbacks to focusing solely on price because of the multiple attributes of electricity." The Commission stated: "It is precisely for this reason that this rulemaking proposes to condition the use of bidding on nonprice factors being taken into account in the selection of winning bids." While the Commission has since terminated the 1988 [competitive bidding] rulemaking, the Commission has never disavowed its interpretation of PURPA as allowing consideration of nonprice factors, and does not do so in today's order.

One shortcoming I see in today's order is the lack of guidance to the states on how to determine avoided costs. We tell California they did it wrong. But we offer little guidance on how to do it right. I support opening a generic proceeding, to elicit input from all interested parties and to explore fully how PURPA should work in a competitive power supply industry. One of PURPA's primary goals is to encourage the development of alternative fuel generation such as geothermal, wind power and others. As long as PURPA is the law of the land, we owe it to the state regulators, the QFs and the utilities to provide additional guidance with respect to how PURPA's goals can be accomplished in a competitive era.

In hindsight, the Commission should have initiated a generic proceeding sooner. If we had, perhaps we could have avoided the surprise that some will argue we are imposing today. We should flesh out a number of issues by rulemaking to give the states guidance on how to implement PURPA in a lawful manner. Providing such guidance will help to ensure that this Commission is not regularly called upon to second-guess state decisions under PURPA.

Finally, our order in no way affects the authority of states to adopt and implement power supply policies outside of PURPA. Our order today construes only the requirements of PURPA, and does not (indeed, could not) purport to limit the authority of states beyond the context of PURPA. Our order says only that states cannot act under PURPA to require utilities to pay more than their avoided costs.■

NOTES AND COMMENTS

1. By the late 1990s, a wide variety of stakeholders advocated repeal of the PURPA Section 210 mandate, believing (as described in *Southern California Edison*) that market forces and the advent of competition made a mandatory requirement to purchase power at specific rates obsolete. Specific conditions in the electric industry during the 1990s (particularly "bad deals" made by utilities that locked into long-term contracts with QFs at above-market rates) exacerbated the problem:

> By the late 1980s and early 1990s, however, oil prices had stabilized, natural gas prices had declined, and excess generating capacity in most regions of the country allowed utilities to buy capacity and energy at much lower prices than had been forecast a decade earlier. The utilities' actual avoided costs dropped lower than in the mid–1980s and were considerably lower than the levels required by the long-term contracts imposed by some State Commissions. Many utilities contend that PURPA has caused dramatic hikes in retail electric rates, and many groups along with these utilities now believe that new regulatory action must be taken to correct past misjudgments.

U.S. Energy Information Administration, The Changing Structure of the Electric Power Industry 2000: An Update, http://www.eia.doe.gov. While FERC had taken action in some cases, it had expressly refused to overturn utilities' contracts with QFs "simply because avoided-cost rates have changed and the deals have gone sour in changing electricity markets." Michael J. Zucchet, Renewable Resource Electricity in the Changing Regulatory Environment, U.S. Department of Energy, Energy Information Administration (1995).

By 2000, most federal legislative proposals to restructure the electric utility industry included some provisions for repeal of PURPA avoided cost benefits for QFs. Congress finally took action in 2005. *See* Chapter 11 for a discussion of the provisions of the Energy Policy Act of 2005 modifying PURPA benefits.

2.   As Commissioner Massey acknowledged presciently in his concurrence in *Southern California Edison*, long-term contracts for power from QFs eventually did become a major form of "stranded costs." *See* Chapter 12.

2.   ENERGY CONSERVATION

Most of our fossil fuel reserves began to form over 500 million years ago, when the earth's oxygen content was too low to sustain mass fires and plant foliage was added layer by layer to the earth's surface. Since then, many areas with significant plant life have been developed or sustained mass fires on a regular basis and fossil fuel build-up has slowed to a snail's pace, while demand for fossil fuel has increased drastically—particularly in the last 300 years. On current estimates of supply and demand, the U.S. will exhaust most of its supply of petroleum and natural gas by the year 2050. While there will likely be adequate coal reserves to meet energy demand for several subsequent generations, widespread usage of coal has adverse impacts on land and the environment (*see* Chapter 5).

For these and other reasons, state and federal energy policies since the oil crisis of the 1970s have promoted energy conservation. "Conservation" is popularly used to refer to two different ideas: (1) cutting back on consumption of energy (conservation), and (2) making energy-consuming processes more efficient (energy efficiency). Public appetite for conservation has waxed and waned over the past few decades, largely in response to market prices of energy resources, economic conditions, and perceptions of crisis conditions in energy availability. The early years of the 21st century have seen less emphasis on conservation than in the past. The famous image of President Jimmy Carter wearing a sweater in the Oval Office to demonstrate a commitment to conservation has been replaced by a national preference for energy-gulping "mega-mansions" and SUVs. Still, the public can conserve when it perceives it to be necessary. During California's electricity crisis in 2000–2001, discussed in Chapter 12, the state implemented a 20/20 program, which offered 20 percent rebates to households and commercial users that used 20 percent less electricity during the crisis than in the previous year. This program has been credited with averting more widespread blackouts than would otherwise have been the case. *See* Jerry Hirsh, Lessons From the Energy Frontlines, L.A. Times, Oct. 28, 2001, at C1.

A wide array of energy efficiency techniques has been developed at the state and federal level over the past few decades. The Department of Energy's Office of Energy Efficiency and Renewable Energy ("EERE") divides energy efficiency measures by the sectors of the economy affected by them: Buildings, Industry, Power, and Transportation. *See* http://www.eere.energy.gov/. Some of the best-known and most innovative efficiency programs in the Buildings, Industry and Transportation sectors include the following:

Buildings: A recent trend in building energy efficiency is wider availability of voluntary standards-based programs that certify environmentally friendly and energy efficient qualities of buildings and their contents (such as appliances). The "Energy Star" label has become a familiar seal of approval of lower-power consuming buildings, appliances and computers. The U.S. Green Building Council, a coalition of building industry leaders, uses the "Leadership, Energy and Environmental Design (LEED)" certification for green buildings such as Weinstein Hall, the social sciences building at the University of Richmond that opened in July 2003. The LEED certification is a complete framework for assessing building performance and meeting sustainability goals. A building meeting LEED standards is required to meet benchmarks in such areas as energy efficiency and materials and water usage. *See* http://usgbc.org; Weinstein Hall at University of Richmond Receives Environmental Certification, Sept. 24, 2004, http://oncampus.richmond.edu/news/press/sept04/WeinsteinHall.html. In 2005, Washington state adopted a green building law that requires all public agency facilities exceeding 5,000 square feet to meet the LEED standards.

Industry: Efforts to increase energy efficiency in the industrial sector tend to be targeted to individual industries and have focused on individual industries such as metals manufacturing, where large amounts of energy are used per unit of output. In certain sectors, there has been dramatic improvement in this measurement since the 1970s.

Transportation: The Corporate Average Fuel Economy ("CAFE") standards established in the Energy Policy and Conservation Act of 1975 set mileage standards for the vehicle fleet. *See* http://www.fueleconomy.gov. Many observers believe the current standards are too low and full of loopholes that allow lower-mileage vehicles on the roads, and a variety of proposals is under consideration to raise the standards. Techniques to achieve greater fuel economy are discussed further in the transportation chapter, Chapter 15, and the chapter on global climate change, Chapter 16.

* * *

In the electric power industry, four regulatory mechanisms have raised significant issues about the conservation of fossil fuels and usage of new fuel sources: 1) demand-side management ("DSM"): incentives designed to reduce the demand for electricity during peak periods or to conserve consumption generally; 2) cogeneration: the use of a single power source to generate heat and power; 3) integrated resource planning ("IRP"): programs which consider demand and supply options prior to approving utility expansions; and 4) renewable portfolio standards: incentives requirements for utilities and other power generators to utilize renewable sources rather than fossil fuels. In addition, distributed generation, or "DG" (small-scale electric generation, typically less than 50 MW in size, located closer to the load being served by it) can serve an efficiency function, and is discussed in this section.

Does the traditional system of ratemaking encourage electric utilities to invest more capital in generating facilities than is economically efficient, environmentally sound and socially desirable? Does traditional ratemaking push utilities to sell more electricity at a time when national policy suggests that the conservation of electricity is a more appropriate goal? Has the traditional pricing of fossil fuels encouraged over-consumption of these precious resources? As restructuring has brought fundamental changes to the industry, the answers to these questions have evolved as well.

a. DEMAND–SIDE MANAGEMENT

Electric utility companies have promoted the use of electricity since the days of Thomas Edison and Samuel Insull. Traditional ratemaking methodologies have created an incentive for companies to exceed their own estimates for electricity sales each year because any such increase in sales directly improves that year's profits. And like most business people, utility executives like to believe they are producing a product that is of value to society.

During the 1960s, the electric utilities were being criticized for failing to provide adequate, reliable service. They naturally responded by significantly increasing the construction of new generating plants and other facilities. In the 1970s it came as a shock to the electric industry when organized groups of ratepayers, such as major industrial users, began to complain that the utilities' emphasis on growth was driving up rates unnecessarily. If the utilities taught their customers to use electricity more efficiently, they argued, it would not be necessary to add so many expensive new power plants.

The ratepayers were supported in this argument by environmental groups that saw new nuclear power plants as too dangerous and new coal-fired plants as too dirty. When events in the Middle East brought home the possibility that our supply of imported petroleum might be at risk, the combination of these factors created strong pressures on the electric industry to consider conservation techniques.

Today, most electric utilities have at least some programs designed to encourage their customers to either (1) reduce total electricity usage, or (2) reduce usage at peak hours. For example, Houston Lighting and Power Company works with home builders to encourage tighter, better insulated construction that will reduce the amount of electricity needed for both heating and air conditioning. It also offers incentives to air conditioning users who agree to cycle their air conditioning units on and off during periods of peak electricity demand.

The extent to which the electric utilities employ serious efforts toward these so-called "demand-side management" (DSM) programs varies with the corporate culture of each company. The incongruity of using electric utilities to "anti-sell" their own product may be compared to using ice cream manufacturers to sell their customers on dieting. But the decision to use the utilities to promote DSM evolved as the result of many years of Congressional debate over various potential ways to promote energy conservation. Beginning with the Energy Policy and Conservation Act of 1975, 42 U.S.C. §§ 6201–6422, Congress almost annually tinkered with legislation designed to encourage users of electricity to use it more efficiently. Current policies for promoting conservation are found in PURPA as amended by the EPAct.

PURPA "encourages" the states to adopt regulatory policies that improve electric power conservation, encourage the efficient use of electric power generation facilities and fuels, and promote the adoption of equitable rates for electric power. PURPA outlined six fundamental policies for retail electric power rates and services: (i) rates should reflect the actual cost of electric power generation and distribution; (ii) rates should not decline with increases in electric power use unless the cost of providing the power decreases as consumption increases; (iii) rates should reflect the daily variations in the actual cost of electric power generation; (iv) rates should reflect the seasonal variations in the actual cost of electric power generation; (v) rates should offer a special "interruptible" electric power service rate for commercial and industrial customers; and (vi) each electric utility must offer load management techniques to their electric consumers that will be practicable, cost effective and reliable, as determined by the state public utility commission.

PURPA requires the state commissions to "consider each standard . . . and make a determination concerning whether or not it is appropriate to implement such standard . . ." within three years from the law's enactment. PURPA also sets up five standards for retail electric power rates and services. First, the provision of services should ordinarily exclude the installation of "master meters" for multi-unit residential buildings. Second, the rates should not increase under automatic adjustment clauses, unless specific requirements are met. Third, services should provide information to electric utility customers concerning electric power rates. Fourth, the services may not terminate electric power service except in accordance with specified procedures. Finally, "[n]o electric utility may recover from any person other than the shareholders . . . of such utility any direct or indirect expenditure by such utility for promotional or political advertising." *See* 16 U.S.C. §§ 1623–25. PURPA was upheld in *FERC v. Mississippi*, 456 U.S. 742 (1982), against challenges that it usurped the traditional state prerogative to regulate the retail rates and services of public utilities in violation of the Constitution's Commerce Clause and the Tenth Amendment.

The EPAct added three new electric rate policies. First, that "[t]he rates allowed to be charged . . . shall be such that the utility's investment in and expenditures for . . . demand[-side] management measures are at least as profitable, giving appropriate consideration to income lost from reduced sales . . . as its investments in and expenditures for the construction of new generation, transmission, and distribution equipment." Second, that "[t]he rates charged . . . shall be such that the utility is encouraged to make investments in, and expenditures for, all cost-effective improvements in the energy efficiency of power generation, transmission and distribution." Third, that all electric utilities adopt least-cost or integrated resource plans. *See* 16 U.S.C. § 2621. *Re Kauai Electric Division of Citizens Utilities Co. Hawaii Public Utilities Comm.*, Docket #94–0337 (Aug. 5, 1997) describes a typical program set up in response to the PURPA and EPAct mandates.

While Congress directed that the states should provide incentives for electric utilities to engage in DSM programs, traditional ratemaking methods discouraged utilities from undertaking programs that increased expenses and reduced revenues. State PSCs were therefore required to reexamine their ratemaking methodologies to comply with the federal directive. *See, e.g., Georgia Power Co. v. Georgia Indus. Group*, 447 S.E.2d 118 (Ga. App. 1994) (reversing lower court's order disallowing Georgia PSC authorization to utility Georgia Power to recover costs of DSM programs); *A. Finkl & Sons Co. v. Illinois Commerce Comm'n*, 620 N.E.2d 1141 (Ill. App.1993) (reaching an opposite result).

In 2002, the EIA released information regarding the success of DSM programs in six broad categories:

(1) Energy efficiency includes programs relating to energy efficiency work to reduce the amount of energy consumed at specific end-use devices without considering the quality of the service provided. This is often achieved by substituting more advanced technology to use less electricity to produce the same levels of energy services. For example, use energy saving appliances and high-efficiency heating. It is common to use financial incentives to encourage participation.

(2) Direct load control involves consumer loads that can be turned off during peak load hours. The power utility operator directly shuts off the power supply to individual appliances or equipment, such as air conditioners.

(3) Interruptible load programs involve contractual agreements with the consumer that service can be interrupted during peak load hours, either by direct control of the utility operator or by the consumer at the request of the operator. For instance, large commercial and industrial consumers may get discounted interruptible rates for agreeing to reduce electrical loads upon request from the utility.

(4) Other load management programs include technologies that shift part or all of a load from one time of day to another and may affect overall energy consumption of space heating and water heating storage systems. If time-of-day metering is used, these programs can implement real time pricing.

(5) Other demand side management programs include consumer substitution of other types of energy for electricity and self-generation of electricity.

(6) Load building involves increasing the use of existing facilities instead of building new facilities.

In 2000, 962 electric utilities in the United States reported having one or more DSM programs. The 516 largest operators reported saving 53.7 million kWh. Consumer characteristics such as knowledge, awareness, and motivation often influence the success of a program. External influences, such as energy prices, technologies, and regulations, also affect the success of a DSM program. U.S. Department of Energy, Energy Information Administration, U.S. Electric Utility Demand Side Management 2000 (2002) ("EIA DSM Report 2002").

* * *

How much energy are DSM programs actually saving? The question does not have an easy answer, and the answer is different for industrial and residential customers. DSM programs are saving millions in dollars for savvy industrial and commercial customers that have become aware of the value of energy efficiency at times of high prices. These customers can reduce their demand at specific times, use backup equipment located at their sites, or otherwise plan to save electricity.

For residential customers, there has been much hope for DSM, particularly the use of market-based or "real-time pricing" ("RTP") of electricity. In theory, RTP is quite simple. The standard electric meter gives no information to consumers about the price of the product they are consuming. If consumers had price signals in "real time"—as they do for other products like hamburgers or handkerchiefs—they could adjust their behavior accordingly. In particular, if prices were high, they could cut their demand for electricity. Professors Sidney Shapiro and Joseph Tomain view RTP as a cornerstone of a "smart" approach to electricity regulation that would replace the "traditional" model. Joseph P. Tomain and Sidney A. Shapiro, Rethinking Reform of Electricity Markets, 40 Wake Forest L. Rev. 100 (2005). There have been estimates that it could yield billions of dollars in savings for individual consumers. *See* Jeffrey M. Jakubiak, Time–Of–Use Electricity Pricing Should Be Mandated As A Public Good, http://library.findlaw.com/2003/Mar/6/132618.html (summarizing findings of various studies).

In its August 2004 report, the federal General Accountability Office (GAO) studied whether demand response programs have reduced demand and saved customers money on their electric bills. U.S. General Accountability Office, Consumers Could Benefit from Demand Programs, but Challenges Remain (2004) (GAO Report). The GAO reviewed studies of actual and planned DSM programs and found some successes, particularly for industrial and commercial customers, as the following table indicates:

Table 1: Studies of the Benefits of Existing Market-Based Pricing Programs for Regions and Specific Programs (selected programs)

Study title, author, date	Results/conclusions
"The Economics of Real-Time and Time-of-Use Pricing for Residential Consumers," King, June 2001	Pacific Gas and Electric has operated a time-of-use program since 1982, with about 85,000 participants as of 2001. Consumers have reduced their electricity usage during peak periods by 18%. As of the early 1990s, 80% of participants were saving $240 per year through the program, or about $16 million per year. The utility has also benefited from the shift in demand to off-peak.
"Evaluation of the Energy-Smart Pricing Plan: Final Report," Summit Blue Consulting for Community Energy Cooperative, Mar. 2004	Community Energy Cooperative of Chicago's demand-response program had 750 participating residential customers, representing a wide variety of neighborhoods and types of homes, in 2003, its first year of operation. Under day-ahead pricing, these customers saved an average of 19.6% on their energy bills, or more than $10 per month in 2003, for modestly cutting back on consumption during approximately 30 hours of peak demand during the summer months.
"Industrial Response to Electricity Real-Time Prices: Short Run and Long Run," Schwarz, et al., Oct. 2002	Real-time pricing by Duke Power in the Carolinas induced demand reductions of about 70 MW, or approximately 8% of consumption during four summer months of peak demand. This translates into long-term savings of about $2.7 million per year for the 110 industrial customers who participated during the period 1994 to 1999.
"Customer Response to Electricity Prices: Information to Support Wholesale Price Forecasting and Market Analysis," Braithwait for EPRI, Nov. 2001	Georgia Power's real-time pricing program, with about 1700 participants representing about 5,000 MW of demand, can count on a demand reduction of at least 750 MW when capacity is constrained and wholesale markets are tight. On a few days in summer 1999, Georgia Power's real-time prices reached levels as much as twice as high as those seen in previous years. Prices were moderately high on several days and spiked to an extremely high level on a few days. The very large industrial customers on hour-ahead rates reduced their purchases by about 30% from their normal rate on the moderately high-priced days and by nearly 60% during the two high-cost, capacity-constrained episodes.
"Analysis for 2002 GoodCents Select Program Critical Calls," Gulf Power, May 2003	Customers participating in Gulf Power's critical peak pricing program in 2002 on average consumed 50 percent less electricity during "critical periods"—when price was higher—than did a similar group of nonparticipating consumers. Participants also paid 11 percent less in total electricity bills because their total electricity expenditures rose slower than the similar group of nonparticipants.
"Demand Responsiveness in Electricity Markets," Lafferty, et al. for FERC, Jan. 2001	Residential customers in the Wisconsin Public Service Corporation's peak-load pricing program who faced a peak price that was double the off-peak price reduced their consumption during summer peak periods by about 12%, while those facing a peak price that was 8 times the off-peak price reduced their consumption by 15% to 20% during summer peak periods. At peak hours during heat waves, consumption was reduced by 31% relative to nonpeak noncritical days.

Figure 13–1

Some utilities believe these programs are avoiding the need for additional generating plant capacity. According to the GAO, the utility Georgia Power could plan for reductions of about 750 MW of power during high-priced hours (and reduced peak demand of up to 17 percent on critical days), lessening the need for costly peaking plants. *Id.*

On the whole, however, successes for residential customers have been much more limited. The GAO found that RTP has not achieved widespread use:

Overall, the use of market-based pricing is rather limited, generally affecting only certain types of customers and some areas and accounting for a small share of overall demand, with most customers paying prices that are not market-based. Time-of-use pricing programs are available from many utilities, but participation is generally limited to some commercial and industrial customers. However, in some parts of the country some customers have been required to pay time-of-use rates. For example the California Public Utility Commission requires large customers of the state's public utilities to be on time-of-use pricing plans. Real-time pricing programs are available in only a few locations, and the number of customers enrolled in these programs is generally small.

Id.

This lack of widespread acceptance of RTP is perhaps not surprising, given the implementation hurdles for RTP programs to overcome:

In 2002, Puget Sound Energy was praised for its notable program of "Personal Energy Management" which offered time-of-use rates for residential customers. A month later, people were quitting the PSE program in droves and another bold experiment in retail electric markets in the western states ended with customers feeling conned and duped.

In retrospect, even though PSE customers adjusted their life styles, shifted about 5 percent of their demand away from peak hours, and reduced their overall electricity use, the administrative costs of the program were too high and the savings too low to provide any net benefits to the consumer. In general, there is a serious question whether the costs of advanced meters, which consumers will ordinarily be expected to bear in markets served by competitive suppliers, will be low enough to benefit small consumers. One-time meter costs can range from $450 to $1,500 with installation. Monthly fees for small users range from $10 to $300, even with cheaper time-of-use meters versus real-time meters. In short, it may not be cost-effective for the typical household to use dynamic pricing or advanced meters. California's catchy 20/20 program, which gave 20 percent rebates to households and commercial users that used 20 percent less electricity during the crisis than in the previous year, cost the state $285 million, or about $200 for every megawatt-hour saved, a steep price compared to the $35 spot price for electricity in April 2002.

Weaver, *supra.* Professor Weaver concludes, "It may well be that dynamic pricing only makes sense for large industrial users that may adopt it voluntarily in response to the increased volatility of power markets." *Id.*

* * *

In the 1990s, the emphasis of national electricity policy switched to promotion of the restructuring of electric utilities to promote more competition. This tectonic shift in the industry had major implications for DSM programs. To what extent can DSM programs operate effectively in a restructuring electric utility industry? One possible response is that they are no longer necessary and are even antithetical to a competitive environment. A number of utilities took this position:

> Electric utilities had built up a substantial research and development effort by the early 1990s, and had also been investing a great deal of funding into energy efficiency, renewable energy, and low income customer programs. When the power industry started its transformation to competition, these were among the first programs to be cut; they were long-term investments that did not mesh well with the utilities' short-term competitive strategies and their worries about stranded cost recovery. Some utilities were uncertain they would be allowed to recover these costs over time, as had been standard practice. Utilities' budgets for such programs fell precipitously: The budget for Florida Power efficiency programs fell by 53 percent, that of Central Vermont Public Service fell by 73 percent and that of PacifiCorp fell by 88 percent. Nationally, utility energy efficiency budgets fell by over 50 percent.

National Council on Electricity Policy, A Comprehensive View of U.S. Electric Restructuring with Policy Options for the Future 45 (2003) (NCEP Report).

As the NCEP notes, states recognize the value in DSM programs and have found ways to continue them. The most significant way in which this has been done is with statewide funding for programs previously funded by utilities. In California, for example, "the California Board for Energy Efficiency (CBEE) was created to fund energy efficiency programs that had previously been funded by electric utilities. Utilities in California report their costs associated with and energy savings resulting from CBEE programs." EIA DSM Report 2002, *supra*. The EIA discontinued its DSM reporting after 2002 and today system benefits charges and funds, and other mechanisms are more important at promoting efficiency, conservation and renewable resources in a competitive environment.

b. COGENERATION

In a traditional power plant, over half of the energy produced from the burning fuel is lost in the form of waste heat. Engineers have long recognized that if the power plant could be built at a place where additional heat was needed, the energy efficiency of the operation would be greatly improved. They began to develop smaller scale generating plants that could be located in large buildings such as industrial plants, hospitals, etc., where the heat could be used to heat the building or in industrial processes. This process is known as "cogeneration." A similar way of utilizing the heat produced in the generation of electricity is the combined-cycle gas generating facility, which has become increasingly popular for small plants. *See* Chapter 8.

Cogeneration is a category of independent power production encouraged under PURPA, and it has accounted for well over three-quarters of the independent power projects created under that statute. Builders of large buildings now routinely review the potential costs and benefits of cogeneration in comparison to purchased power. On a volume basis, the most extensive use of cogeneration is found in the wood and paper industries. For example, a lumber or paper mill can use heat to treat its products and use the same heat source to cogenerate their own electricity. If the process creates sawdust, it may be fed back into the process as fuel. As discussed in Chapter 11, the interconnection between "cogen" projects and the electric utility's distribution network has sometimes been a contentious issue.

Independent power producers often believe the monopoly powers of the regulated electric utilities are often used to discourage customers from building cogeneration projects. One IPP executive, Thomas Casten, argued that the electric utilities became "stultified" prior to PURPA:

> "The original entrepreneurs who built electricity from a concept to one of the truly important businesses in every country are long since gone—dead and buried. The aggressive organization built by Samuel Insull took no prisoners and grew in every way possible. His excesses led to PUHCA in 1935, but he sped the development and availability of electricity. Forty years of regulated and protected monopoly prior to PURPA deadened that early entrepreneurial culture throughout the industry and replaced it with a risk-averse, caretaker culture."

Casten, *supra*, at 60.

The incineration of municipal solid waste is another popular form of cogeneration. After the second oil shock on 1979, many local governments built waste-to-energy plants that would incinerate their solid waste and use the heat to generate electricity. Many of these plants are now in financial difficulty because the rates they charge to solid waste haulers are not competitive with out-of-state landfills, and the Supreme Court has ruled that state and local governments may not favor local waste disposal sites over those from other states without violating the dormant commerce clause. *C&A Carbone, Inc. v. Town of Clarkstown* 511 U.S. 383 (1994). Local governments that have invested large sums in solid waste combustion plants have tried a variety of maneuvers to maintain a supply of local trash despite the lower cost of other disposal methods, but many courts have tended to read the *Carbone* decision broadly. *See* Comment, The Need for a Rational State and Local Response to *Carbone*, 18 Va. Envt'l L. J. 129 (1999).

In addition, suspicion has focused on the possible emission of toxic air pollutants from solid waste incinerators. For example, mercury from discarded flashlight batteries may end up in the air from incineration. The Toxic Release Inventory (TRI) established under the Emergency Planning and Community Right-to-Know Act of 1986, 42 U.S.C. §§ 11001–11050, required all generating plants to report releases annually beginning in 1999.

c. INTEGRATED RESOURCE PLANNING

DSM promotes conservation by consumers, but was not directed toward promoting conservation by utilities themselves. The program designed to do that is known as least-cost planning or integrated resource planning (IRP). Traditionally, state PSC's have regulated the supply of electricity provided by electric utilities. This was done to a certain extent through rate regulation doctrines, such as the "used and useful" principle discussed in Chapter 3. However, supply regulation has also historically been achieved through condemnation, siting, and permitting proceedings. In the 1980s and 1990s, states experimented with more comprehensive programs of evaluating supply-side alternatives, generally known as IRP, and a number of states enacted statutes to require IRP. *See Georgia Power Co. v. Georgia Indus. Group,* 447 S.E.2d 118 (Ga. App. 1994) (observing that Georgia's IRP statute allowed a utility to recover "its costs for any certified demand-side capacity option."

What (if any) vitality is left for IRP in the restructuring environment?

* * *

As described by one of IRP's leading advocates, a utility's planning program should operate as follows:

The utility system must, in effect, take inventory of its residences, appliances, heating systems, commercial floor-space, and industrial processes, securing estimates of both absolute numbers and average efficiencies. Many utilities have made substantial progress along these lines already, although additional surveys may be needed.

The next step is to develop low and high case projections of additions to these inventories over the forecast period. The range should bound the universe of plausible growth rates for the major end use categories.... Electricity needs for the high and low scenarios should then be calculated by summing existing and new uses, less anticipated retirements, over the forecast period.

This calculation will yield a diverging "jaws" forecast comparable to that produced by the econometric methods reviewed earlier, with one crucial difference: the new forecast is rooted firmly in the instrumentalities of demand, allowing planners to track the effects of investments and policies designed to upgrade efficiencies of some or all of those instrumentalities. In parallel with this forecast, planners should develop a comprehensive assessment of opportunities for improving end use efficiencies. What is the "state of the art" existing and anticipated for delivering the services performed by the system's end uses at the lowest possible electricity consumption?

The question then shifts to how much of this unexploited conservation resource is worth attempting to secure. The answer requires a rigorous methodology for comparing the life-cycle costs of incremental amounts of conservation for each end use with the costs of the most expensive displaceable generating unit in the utility's acquisition plans.

In performing that assessment, planners should explicitly credit conservation for its advantages on indices of scale, lead-time, and uncertainty-reduction; the cost column for both the conservation options and the generation alternative should also include quantifiable environmental costs associated with each. The calculation should take specific account of the avoidance of line losses, additional transmission construction, and additional reserve capacity that conservation makes possible when it displaces or defers a new power plant.

From this process will emerge a decision on which efficiency improvements are worth pursuing; it remains, however, to determine how much of the cost-effective conservation resource the system can count on securing. That inquiry focuses on mechanisms for getting the conservation installed; here planners can draw on numerous precedents. Options include state-imposed efficiency standards for some end uses, supplemented by direct utility investment through incentive programs. Planners must anticipate the success of such programs in convincing end users to take advantage of efficiency opportunities. Again, substantial empirical data are already available.

Using those predictions, planners can narrow the "jaws" of the forecast by inserting assumptions about increases in the efficiency of the end use inventories for the "high" and "low" forecasts. Both forecasts will drop, but the high forecast will drop by more because there are more end uses to upgrade. The high forecast then represents the maximum plausible "post-conservation" system needs: the low forecast represents the minimum requirements that will have to be met.

The gap between the two forecasts which conservation has narrowed but not eliminated represents a range of outcomes with which the utility must be prepared to deal. The enterprise is analogous to purchasing an insurance policy; the goal is to minimize the cost of coping with contingencies of varying probability. New generating units may be one element of the response, but other options will bear close scrutiny. Load management programs that shift consumption away from peak periods, without necessarily affecting total consumption, are an obvious example. Also worth investigating is the willingness of large industrial and commercial customers to sell interruption rights to the utility system, which would provide additional reserves in the event of unexpected shortfalls.

In addition, some options, clearly inferior on cost grounds to baseload generators if markets were assured, may look more attractive as a hedge against possible but unlikely growth in demand. Combustion turbines come readily to mind as a generating alternative with relatively high fuel costs, but shorter lead-times and lower capital costs than baseload plants. Obviously, the more certain the system is that it will need significant "post-conservation" additions of energy supply, the better the high-capital-cost, low-operating-cost baseload systems will look. But the converse is also true and most existing forecasts do not permit an informed evaluation of utilities' investment alternatives.

Ralph C. Cavanagh, Least Cost Planning Imperatives for Electric Utilities and Their Regulators, 10 Harv. Envtl. L. Rev. 299–324 (1986).

As Chapter 12 notes, many states are now encouraging competition through restructuring of their electric utility industry, which replaces vertically integrated utilities with a free market in generation. The modern restructured environment contemplates a split of the industry into generation, transmission, and distribution companies. This development, coupled with the emergence of new entities such as regional transmission organizations (*see* Chapter 11) with responsibilities for procurement of power, called into question the continued necessity of IRP programs. If one utility no longer controlled decisions with respect to generation, transmission, and distribution was there any relevance for IRP? In a competitive environment, where generation is purchased in the marketplace, it is feasible or even appropriate to engage in the sort of long-range forecasting demanded by the IRP approach? The following excerpt discusses these issues.

Bernard S. Black & Richard J. Pierce, Jr., The Choice between Markets and Central Planning in Regulating the U.S. Electricity Industry

93 Colum. L. Rev. 1339 (1993).

The structure, methods of operation, and forms of government intervention that have dominated the electricity industry since its birth are no longer viable. The industry has begun a period of radical change. When that process is complete, the electricity industry and its regulation will bear little resemblance to the patterns that have become familiar over the past century. The defenders of the old regime, recognizing that the status quo ante is dead, have changed their allegiances to one of two competing revolutionary armies. Those armies, led by policy wonks with radically different visions of the post-revolutionary state of the industry, are assaulting the ramparts at state utility commissions, state legislatures, a variety of federal agencies, and the U.S. Congress.

The results to date are surprising. Both armies have won almost every battle! Over the past five years, government institutions have begun to implement a combination of four revolutionary changes in the structure, operation, and regulation of the electricity industry. These changes are competitive contracting for electric power, negawatt acquisition programs (NAPs) (utility subsidies for energy-efficiency investments by their customers), market-based environmental regulation (emission fees and marketable pollution permits), and environmental adders (shadow prices reflecting pollution harm that utilities add to power costs when choosing new power sources).

These revolutions cannot continue indefinitely on their present paths. Neither large-scale negawatt programs nor environmental adders can coexist with competitive retail power markets. Environmental adders double-count pollution harm for most pollutants given market-based methods of controlling pollution that are already in place. Taken together, NAPs and environmental adders undermine our ability to achieve the economic gains from competitive contracting and market-based pollution control, while offering small environmental gains.

We must choose between two revolutionary visions of the future of the electricity sector of the U.S. economy. The first vision, embodied in competitive contracting and market-based environmental regulation, relies where possible on markets, private incentives, and decentralized decisions to produce optimal pricing and consumption of electric power and least-cost pollution control. This vision resembles the deregulatory trend that has produced huge benefits in the telephone, transportation, and natural gas sectors of our economy. The second vision, embodied in NAPs and environmental adders, distrusts consumer choice and relies on central planners, housed in regulated utilities, state utility commissions, and federal regulatory agencies, to correct perceived large-scale imperfections in the electricity market. This vision's faith in central planning ("integrated resource planning" is the new phrase) bears an uncomfortable resemblance to the systems previously used to govern the economies of eastern Europe and the former Soviet Union.

As this analogy suggests, we have strong views concerning the best path for revolutionary change.■

NOTES AND COMMENTS

1.   The restructuring activities of the late 1990s were accompanied by a transition away from the centralized planning approach of IRP. *See* Best Practices Guide: Integrated Resource Planning For Electricity, http://www.iie.org/programs/energy/pdfs/IntegResourcePlanning.pdf (noting that as a result of restructuring, "the selection, construction, and operation of generation facilities was left largely to private investors responding to their perceptions of the market for power output."). Texas, for example, repealed its IRP statute and rules in 1999.

The decline of IRP represented a fundamental philosophical shift in the utility industry:

> The model of "integrated resource planning" first developed in California in the 1970s as the CEC set the existing regulation paradigm on its head. "Integrated resource planning" was subsequently challenged in the early 1990s by a new paradigm promoting deregulation of wholesale electricity markets and reduced industry oversight by public utilities commissions. Deregulation was consistent with the social and political climate of the day, as this was "the age of market triumphalism" when "markets were the answer, government was the problem, and anybody who thought otherwise was either Rip Van Winkle or a card-carrying liberal clinging to the past." By the mid–1990s deregula-

tion had replaced "integrated resource planning" and California became the poster child of the new order.

Brian Orion, Note, Transmission in Transition: Analyzing California's Proposed Electricity Transmission Regulatory Reforms, 56 Hastings L.J. 343, 365–66 (2004).

2. Given the collapse of California's restructuring program (*see* Chapter 12), would some form of IRP make a comeback? Yes, says one author, pointing to California's actions after the end of retail access:

> The CPUC adopted procedures for the state's investor-owned utilities to resume full energy procurement responsibilities on Jan. 1, 2003, removing the state from power-buying responsibilities. The rule marks a return to state-supervised, long-term integrated resource planning and also includes a ratemaking balancing account mechanism to track utility power purchase costs. The CPUC said that it is now developing a long-term planning process to ensure that sufficient new resources are developed to provide a low-cost, reliable electric system for California consumers. The rule calls for the "upfront" approval of the utilities' procurement processes and plans, which should minimize the need for any after-the-fact review of the resulting purchases, the CPUC said. [Re Policies and Cost Recovery Mechanisms for Generation Procurement and Renewable Resource Development, 220 PUR4th 377 (Cal.P.U.C.2002).]

Phillip S. Cross, Retail Energy in 2002: A Regulatory About–Face, Fortnightly, Jan. 15, 2003.

Long-term planning also remains important in states that have not yet restructured. *See* Utility resource planning back in style, NW Energy Coalition Report (June 2003) (discussing plans prepared by Pacific Northwest utilities PGE, Puget Sound Energy and PacifiCorp). Some believe IRP has continued relevance for decisions by utilities in restructuring states other than the acquisition of generation. *See* Best Practices Guide, *supra* (noting that "if competitive generation markets exist only at the wholesale level, while electricity users must still purchase power at retail from distribution utilities, then IRP can still be applied at the utility system level [for] the selection of investments in transmission and distribution systems, end-use distribution options, and that mix of power available at wholesale which best satisfied IRP objectives.").

But others see less reason for optimism. Expressing concern about planning for the future of the transmission grid in the wake of the 2003 blackout, a representative of the Consumer Union testified before a Senate subcommittee that while "public investment [in transmission capacity] is best carried out within the framework of a comprehensive plan . . . integrated resource planning is harder to implement in the deregulated model, if it is not abandoned altogether." Statement of Dr. Mark N. Cooper, The Federal Response to the 2003 Blackout: Time to Put the Public Interest First, U.S. Senate Subcommittee On Oversight Of Government Management, The Federal Workforce And The District Of Columbia Committee On

Governmental Affairs, Sept. 10, 2003. With decision-making about transmission increasingly moving from utilities to regional organizations, is there any future for IRP in these decisions?

3. In their analysis, Black and Pierce refer to "environmental adders." Each year, power plants cause millions of dollars in damage to the environment but these costs, such as the medical costs produced by air pollution, are not included in the market price of electricity. The burden of "paying" for these environmental externalities falls on society in the form of increased medical expenses, depleted agricultural resources, and a reduced quality of life. Currently, in the United States, coal is the main source of electricity production and contributes significantly to air pollution.

One way to internalize these environmental costs is to add environmental cost values to each potential new source. Such values are sometimes referred to as "environmental adders." Two methods may be used to calculate the value of environmental externalities. One way is to calculate the environmental damage of a pollutant by examining the real world costs of future climate change, illness, and crop damage. This method is called "damage-cost estimate." Kenneth Rose *et al.*, The National Regulatory Research Institute, Public Utility Commission Treatment of Environmental Externalities 2 (1994). PSCs often use another method in which the externality values are based on the costs to the power plants of installing air emissions control technologies. This is called the "control cost method." *Id.* Proponents of these types of regulation argue that they will show that renewable power is really cheaper than fossil fuel when all costs are taken into account. The utility companies should want to choose the resource mix that will achieve the lowest cost, and therefore will be more attracted to renewable energy sources to meet future energy needs. Clinton A. Vince *et al.*, Integrated Resource Planning: The Case for Exporting Comprehensive Energy Planning to the Developing World, 25 Case W. Res. J. Int'l L. 371, 373 (1993).

Without IRP, environmental values (such as the environmental merits of renewable power sources) might not be counted as readily in utility decisions: "Because public utility commissions will no longer have oversight authority over resource decisions of power generators following restructuring, IRP will become a less common means of promoting renewables." The Database of State Incentives for Renewable Energy: State Programs and Regulatory Policies Report (1998), http://www.dsireusa.org. *But see* NW Energy Coalition Report, *supra* (IRP used in 2002 to integrate renewables and conservation into 3 utilities' plans).

Black and Pierce suggest the appropriate way to integrate environmental concerns in a restructuring environment is through the use of direct regulatory approaches such as air pollution regulation, not through programs to promote renewables and conservation. Based on the discussions of competition's impact on air pollution regulation earlier in this chapter and in Chapter 5, do you agree?

d. DISTRIBUTED GENERATION

"Distributed generation" (DG) involves power generated locally on a customer's premises, rather than transmitted and distributed from a central power station. This represents a reversal of sorts of utility industry history: "When Edison flipped the switch at Pearl Street Station in New York City in 1882, the first electricity company went into operation and did so on a small scale." Tomain and Shapiro, *supra*, at 143–44. DG can take a lot of forms, including solar cells and wind turbines, gas or diesel-fired engines, small turbines, fuel cells, and photovoltaic cells. Some DG technologies capture both heat and power, increasing energy efficiency. *Id.*

The U.S. Congressional Budget Office recently studied DG, and issued a report that described its potential benefits and the barriers to more widespread implementation of it.

U.S. Congressional Budget Office, Prospects for Distributed Electricity Generation

(2003).

Distributed generation refers to the production of electricity at or near the place of consumption. Examples of distributed generation include backup generators at hospitals, solar photovoltaic systems on residential rooftops, and combined heat and power (CHP) systems (also known as cogeneration) in industrial plants and on university campuses. Those applications differ from the infrastructure for supplying electricity that utilities in the United States have built over the past five decades. Under that infrastructure, utilities typically have built power plants away from centers of consumption, on the basis of such factors as fuel transportation costs and environmental regulations, and then moved that electricity long distances over high-voltage transmission lines to local distribution systems, which then reduce the voltage and deliver the power to retail consumers.

Total customer-owned generation as a percentage of all output is small. The Energy Information Administration (EIA) estimates that in 2000 (the latest year for which data are available), only 0.5 percent of total U.S. electricity generation (21 billion of 3,800 billion kilowatt-hours) was from "nonutility generation for [customers'] own use." In addition, cogeneration systems in the commercial and industrial sectors produced 135 billion kilowatt-hours (3.6 percent of U.S. generation) for their own use. Three basic characteristics differentiate most distributed generation from traditional electricity supply: location, capacity, and grid connection. Distributed generators are located at or near the point at which the power is used. They are typically on-site generators, owned and operated by retail customers, that are used to meet a portion of the customers' demand or to provide backup service for customers that need highly reliable power.

Electric utilities can also install their own small generators near customers. Such installations relieve congestion in power lines during periods of peak demand, helping to defer investments in additional transmission and distribution capacity. They may also be used to boost the quality and reliability of local electricity service by providing voltage control and backup power to customers who require such "premium" service. The second defining characteristic of most distributed generation is its size. Generation capacities of customer-owned units, used primarily to meet on-site requirements, typically range from a few kilowatts to several hundred kilowatts.

The level of their connection with the local or regional electric grid is the third characteristic that distinguishes distributed generators from traditional suppliers. Traditional suppliers are connected to the grid at the transmission level (the high-voltage portion of the delivery network). If distributed generation came into widespread use, most distributed generators would be connected to the grid at the distribution level.

How Distributed Generation Contributes to the Nation's Power Supply

The applications that account for the largest portion of the customer-owned power production by distributed generation in the United States are cogenerators used in industrial or commercial operations or primarily to generate electricity for sale. After cogeneration, backup units that are operated only in emergencies account for the most distributed generation capacity. According to a 1995 survey by the EIA, nearly one-fourth of the commercial floor space in the country had some capacity to generate electricity on-site. But less than 1 percent of that capacity was ever used to generate electricity to meet peak demand or to operate continuously; in essence, it constitutes a large reservoir of capacity that is virtually untapped as a regular source of power.

Looking to the future, there are reasons to expect that distributed generation could meet a significantly greater portion of future electricity demand in the United States, at costs that could compete with those of generation from new central power plants. The first reason is the existence of the considerable amount of backup generation capacity that represents a sunk cost to its owners, who have typically installed the generators to meet reliability needs or building code requirements. In the absence of environmental prohibitions or other restrictions, many of those generators could be adapted to operate regularly, at the cost of modest investments in improved electronic power controls and pollution control equipment.

A Description of Selected Electricity Generation Technologies

Several technologies are frequently mentioned as well suited to small and medium-sized distributed generation applications. Among the technologies fueled by fossil energy are conventional steam turbines, combustion turbines, internal combustion engine generators, microturbines, and fuel cells. The renewable technologies are photovoltaic cells, wind-powered generators, and biomass-fueled generators.

Conventional steam turbines and combustion turbines are well-developed technologies that are widely used for medium-sized and large power systems (more than 500 kilowatts). In very large systems, typically built by commercial generators, combustion turbines are often operated in tandem with steam turbines that use waste heat from the combustion turbine to fire a boiler (that combination is referred to as a combined-cycle system). Conventional combustion turbines produce low emissions, given standard control equipment, and they have low maintenance and operating costs relative to those of most other generating technologies. Those characteristics, along with the short lead times needed to build units, make them the preferred technology for most conventional generation applications requiring more than several megawatts of power. . . .

Microturbines are small combustion-turbine generators that were developed on the basis of the turbocharger technology used in trucks and airplanes. The capacity range of microturbines (30 kilowatts to 400 kilowatts) covers the average load requirements (consumption needs) of most commercial and light industrial customers. Microturbines have low emissions of pollutants, especially nitrogen oxides, which would permit their installation in urban areas with restrictive emissions standards. Microturbine electricity generators are in the early stages of commercial development; studies commissioned by DOE predict that their installed equipment costs (costs of equipment plus installation) will fall significantly in the future.

Fuel cells use an advanced electrochemical process to generate electricity. . . .

Photovoltaic cells convert sunlight directly into an electric current. . . . Photovoltaic systems can be small, which is why they are widely used in residential settings, particularly in the Southwest and California. Because photovoltaic systems, by their nature, produce electricity intermittently, they require battery storage or a supplemental power source to provide continuous electricity service. . . .

Most analysts would not consider large wind turbines to be a type of distributed generation because they are not typically located near customers. . . .

Small wind turbines designed for residential and rural applications to date account for only a limited share of the market. Because of the large amount of space they require, small wind generators are generally appropriate for applications in rural areas with good wind resources.

Biomass refers to a renewable fuel rather than to a particular technology. The EIA defines biomass as "organic nonfossil material of biological origin constituting a renewable energy source." Wood products, animal and plant agricultural waste, and municipal solid waste are all examples of biomass. Electric generators use biomass as fuel, often mixed with other fossil fuels.■

The Cost Structure of Distributed Generation

The direct costs of distributed generation to customers include the installed cost of the equipment, fuel costs, nonfuel operation and maintenance (O&M) expenses, and certain costs that the customers' utility imposes.

Capital Costs

The costs of acquiring and installing a generating unit vary widely, depending on technology, capacity, and other factors. The Department of Energy estimates that the typical installed capital costs for distributed generators range from under $1,000 per kilowatt for a combustion turbine to almost $7,000 per kilowatt for a solar photovoltaic system. Among small-capacity technologies, internal combustion engines (fueled by diesel and gasoline) have the lowest capital costs and highest operating costs. Renewable technologies (using wind and solar power) have the highest capital costs and lowest operating costs. New high-efficiency technologies (microturbines and fuel cells) fall in between.

For customers who maintain emergency backup generation on-site, the relevant capital cost for choosing the least expensive source of electricity is not the total cost but rather the additional investment needed to operate an on-site generator at the same time they are connected to the utility network (termed parallel operation). That extra investment may include such costs as equipment upgrades to meet environmental requirements for regular operation and additions of power controls and metering to permit parallel operation.

Long-Run Costs of Production

The most cost-competitive distributed generation technologies are fossil-fuel engines—diesel motors (internal combustion engines) and microturbines—in combined heat and power configurations. Other distributed generation technologies have electricity costs that are more than twice those of the combined-cycle technology. Nonetheless, the costs of some distributed generation technologies, especially those in combined heat and power systems, are below the retail price of utility-supplied electricity in many parts of the United States. That comparison may explain much about the contrasting incentives of utilities and customers to invest in distributed generation. Regulated utilities are concerned about retaining their sales base in order to recover the costs of past investments. Customers are concerned about lowering their electricity costs without sacrificing the reliability of their utility service connection.

Trends in Costs

The capital and operating costs of certain distributed generation technologies have fallen significantly in recent years and can be expected to continue to do so. In the case of one technology, photovoltaic systems, the cost per delivered kilowatt-hour in suitable applications has plummeted by almost 70 percent since 1980, and it is projected to decline by another 70 percent from current levels by 2020. Similarly, developers forecast that fuel cells will improve in performance and decline in cost over the next several years to the point that they will soon be suitable for widespread use in distributed generation. . . .

Whether the direct costs of distributed generation will continue to fall relative to the costs of utility-supplied power is another matter.

Other Economic Considerations in Installing Distributed Generators

... [C]ertain distributed generation technologies or energy sources can benefit from existing federal and state incentives (including investment tax credits or mandates on utilities to purchase power generated from renewable sources).

Commercial and small industrial customers with significant hot-water needs can use microturbines in combined heat and power configurations. Customers who have on-site emergency backup generators may be able to run them regularly during periods of peak demand, when wholesale prices are high. Customers in environmentally sensitive areas can use fuel cells that produce extremely low emissions and no noise. Photovoltaic systems and wind turbines can be used in rural applications, reducing the need for capital spending to extend power lines to remote sites.

Distributed generation can also protect against service interruptions or variations in voltage or frequency that can harm equipment.... The value of backup capability would be great wherever a manufacturing process depended on the continuous operation of power-sensitive equipment, such as in the production of computer chips. Generally, those backup units would be available to operate whenever interruptions occurred in utility-supplied power.

... [S]ome owners of distributed generators might be able to earn money by selling their excess power to the utilities. At the federal level, the Energy Policy Act of 1992 provides tax credits for certain investments in solar, wind, and biomass-fueled electricity generation. At the state level, renewable portfolio standards mandate that a certain percentage of electricity generation come from renewable energy sources. Several states, including New York and California, have adopted such renewable portfolio requirements.

The Benefits and Risks of Distributed Generation ...

Lower Costs of Generation

If customers can be induced to install and run distributed generators when their operating costs are lower than the utilities' wholesale costs, the retail price of electricity will fall for all customers. Systemwide savings may be enhanced if the generation of electricity for customers' own use is flexible—the generator can increase output at certain times of the day or in certain seasons, when the demand from all customers for utility-supplied power is greatest. Additional savings will result because utilities generally operate their most expensive power plants during those peak periods.

Avoided Investment and Operating Losses in Transmission and Distribution

Distributed generation can reduce the need for sometimes significant investment in transmission and distribution lines and equipment to meet growing loads or to relieve congestion at certain points in the electric system. The costs of those investments can add significantly to the price of power delivered by utilities to retail customers. For example, in regions where transportation charges are broken out from the charges for the electric power itself, the average charge for transmitting and distributing the electricity (2.4 cents per kilowatt-hour) is more than 30 percent of the average price of delivered electricity (7.9 cents per kilowatt-hour).

Retail electric utilities as well as their customers could use distributed generators to avoid or defer investments at the local level. Utilities have recognized that small generators can be used to relieve periodic local congestion in the subtransmission and distribution portions of the electricity network. Such use can be a cost-effective alternative to investment in additional transformer capacity and other distribution infrastructure—often delaying the need for such upgrades.

In other cases, local utilities may want to install and operate distributed generators because building new transmission capacity raises environmental concerns. That use of distributed generation could prove especially valuable in places where opposition from environmental groups was constraining or delaying the construction of additional transmission capacity.

Wider adoption of distributed generation also would reduce power losses from the transmission and distribution of electricity between central power plants and customers. Those losses result from electrical resistance in the transmission and distribution system and from changes in voltage as the power approaches the point of consumption.

Additional Savings from Incentives for Adjusting Demand

Customers who need highly reliable power can install distributed generators, allowing them to obtain uninterrupted service without imposing their requirements and associated costs on other customers. The potential for using distributed generation to meet reliability needs could be enhanced through measures that permitted nonemergency operation of the units. Such an approach would allow owners to operate their generators when it was cost-effective and to reduce the net cost of reliable service.

Reductions in the Volatility of Wholesale Prices

If retail customers had the capability to adjust their net demand for utility-supplied power through distributed generation and had the necessary incentives to do so through time-varying tariffs, such as real-time pricing or time-of-use tariffs, then wholesale prices would be less volatile and lower, on average. During periods of peak demand, even modest changes in the demand for and supply of wholesale power could significantly reduce electricity prices in regional spot markets. For example, one study estimated that a 5 percent reduction in peak demand in California during 2000 would have lowered wholesale spot prices by more than 50 percent.

Potential Benefits for the Environment and National Security

Many environmental and energy-conservation advocates believe that distributed generation could offer significant benefits—ones that are not fully reflected in the value of that electricity to the market. Distributed generation technologies that relied on renewable energy sources could yield environmental benefits in the form of reduced emissions of pollutants and greenhouse gases if those technologies displaced utility-supplied power, much of which is generated from coal. Technologies that relied on conventional fuels would yield environmental benefits if they resulted in a shift to less-polluting energy sources—for example, natural gas rather than coal. High-efficiency technologies could yield benefits by reducing the amount of energy required to produce a unit of electricity.

Security benefits of distributed generation relate to the current vulnerability of the nation's electricity infrastructure to terrorist attacks. If more of the nation's electricity supply originated in the homes and businesses where it was consumed, the adverse consequences of any attack that disrupted the network would be diminished.

Uncertainties and Risks

This new source of electricity poses a distinct risk of negative impacts that may be difficult to anticipate or expensive to avoid. Measures to mitigate those adverse impacts could significantly limit the adoption of distributed generation or increase costs to the point at which most applications would no longer be financially viable. In fact, many restrictions on the use of distributed generators have been imposed.

Threats to the Performance of Electric Systems

Without adequate upgrades to the electricity supply network, widespread adoption of distributed generation could adversely affect regional electricity distribution systems. For example, with many customers switching their generators on and off, the quality of the power and the reliability of the systems could be degraded. Moreover, because utilities could have difficulty pinpointing the sources of the degradation, they might not be able to allocate to the owners of distributed generators the costs of preventive actions.

Risks to Air Quality and National Security

The distributed generation technologies with the greatest market potential are probably those fueled by fossil energy (backup generators powered by diesel fuel and cogenerators powered by natural gas), not renewable energy. Thus, the immediate promise of improved air quality from wider adoption of distributed generation may be limited, and improvements would probably come primarily from substituting natural gas-and diesel-fired generators for coal-fired generators. On the downside, those new generators might end up displacing power from units that were already fired by natural gas. And if some generators switched from relatively clean-burning natural gas to diesel, local air quality could worsen.

Barriers That Impede Widespread Adoption of Distributed Generation

Advocates of distributed generation contend that many industry practices and government restrictions discourage investment in customer-owned generators. Four areas of contention are frequently mentioned: requirements and charges for the installation of protective equipment as a precondition to interconnection with the grid; surcharges on the electricity bills of operators of distributed generators (those who remain utility customers); prices established for the distributed power that utilities purchase; and environmental siting restrictions and permitting requirements.

The stated purpose of the technical interconnection restrictions and requirements is to ensure the safety and quality of the electric power system and to avoid possible damage to equipment. Those restrictions often prohibit small generators from connecting to the grid at the distribution level of the network. In the absence of outright prohibitions, however, operators of distributed generation units may want to remain connected to the grid while producing power (termed parallel operation). In that case, utilities generally require operators to install additional controls and equipment in order to protect the network from feedbacks or disturbances. Utilities may also require upgrades to the distribution system to support the power supplied by the distributed generators and to protect neighboring customers. Operators typically bear the cost of such site-specific equipment and any system upgrades, too. Many observers argue that those technical and contractual interconnection requirements are often excessive.

Utility Surcharges: Paying for Stranded Costs and Standby Service

Under the electric utility regulations in most states, utilities may levy surcharges on customers who install distributed generators and operate them regularly. Typically, the surcharges take the form of flat monthly charges based on customers' past maximum usage. Monthly charges may be used to help utilities cover the costs of public benefits programs (such as purchasing renewable power or providing service to remote customers). Regulators in every state require utilities to conduct such programs, which are otherwise financed by electricity sales. More commonly, however, monthly charges are used to pay for past capital investments and for standby service. Proponents of distributed power argue that the unrecoverable (or "stranded") costs covered by exit fees often do not reflect the actual costs of past investments, which have become uneconomic with the drop in customer demand.

The more common purpose of the recurring monthly charge that some utilities impose on operators of distributed generators is to pay the utility's cost of maintaining standby generating capacity and distribution lines to serve that household or business. If those surcharges exceed the cost to the utility of providing standby service, they will discourage the efficient siting of distributed generators. Proponents of distributed generation argue that standby charges often overstate the cost of the service provided by the retail utility and fail to account for the benefits that distributed generators provide to the system.

PURPA-mandated purchases and net-metering tariffs create the only organized markets for the sale of excess power from most operators of small distributed generators in the United States today. For operators who do not qualify for those markets (because their generators use conventional technologies such as internal combustion engines), often no outlet exists through which they can sell excess power. That limitation will constrain customers to considering generators that serve only their needs, even though larger-capacity generators could be more cost-effective, both for the customer and for all ratepayers.

Environmental Concerns: Siting Restrictions and Permitting Requirements

Almost all states, counties, and cities regulate the installation and operation of electricity generators. Those regulations, which vary widely across the country, are often enforced by multiple, and sometimes overlapping, jurisdictions. Some analysts argue that the lack of standardized environmental regulations for distributed generation inappropriately hinders its development by making it impossible for national manufacturers to design equipment to meet a set of clear, uniform requirements. They also contend that most air quality programs fail to recognize the environmental benefits of distributed generation in reducing emissions from other sources that may be less efficient, including central power plants and customer-owned boilers.

[S]ome observers argue that the existing regulations governing distributed generation are often too broad or are inconsistent from site to site. The NREL study on environmental regulations and distributed generation concluded that "the complex, case-by-case permitting process designed for 'large' generators is inherently incongruous with application to small, standardized distributed generation technologies." Examples of such regulations include blanket prohibitions on electricity generation, limits on operation of backup generators, and height restrictions on towers needed for wind generators.■

NOTES AND COMMENTS

1. Interconnecting DG to the existing distribution system often poses technical challenges: Most distribution systems are designed to accept power at a single point from higher voltage transmission systems, usually at a distribution substation, and then distribute the power in a single direction along radial feeders to customers. With distributed generation, however, the unidirectional nature of power flow on distribution circuits can be changed with potentially significant effects on voltage regulation, the behavior of the system during faults, system protection, and safety procedures. Because the distribution system is the portion of the power system that is closest to customers, its performance under the presence of

distributed generation directly influences the quality and reliability of power delivered to customers.

> Because voltage regulation and protection devices are coordinated under the assumption that power flows in one direction only, distribution equipment, controls, and operating procedures may require modification under the presence of distributed generation. The impact of distributed generation on feeders, and the extent to which modifications are required, will depend on the saturation and location of distributed generation units. Even at low penetrations, care must be taken to ensure that appropriate system protection and safety procedures are in place. Of particular concern is the possibility of "islanding," a condition in which a distributed generator energizes a portion of a distribution system at a time when the remainder of the system is de-energized. Unintentional islanding can result in safety hazards and damage to customer equipment.

Vermont Public Service Board, Distributed Utility Planning: An Introduction to Concepts and Issues, http://www.state.vt.us/psd/Menu /EE_and_Renewable/ee-DUP.htm. In Los Angeles, which has one of the nation's largest DG programs with over 125 MW of capacity installed in the past 15 years (representing nearly one quarter of all new generating capacity), the Department of Water and Power has experimented somewhat successfully with techniques designed to prevent islanding. Robert Castro, DG Islanding Rescue, Distributed Energy, Mar./Apr. 2005.

2. A wide variety of laws and policies can have impacts on the viability of DG. Many of those are discussed elsewhere in this book, including net metering (*see* Chapter 12), state and federal policies promoting the use of small renewable power facilities (*see* Section B.3 of this chapter), air pollution regulation (*see* Section A of this chapter and Chapter 5), small generator interconnection policies and rules (*see* Chapter 11), and state and local power plant siting rules (*see* Section C of this chapter). *See also* Anthony Allen, The Legal Impediments to Distributed Generation, 23 Energy L.J. 505 (2002).

Professors Tomain and Shapiro include DG as part of their "Smart Model" to replace the "Traditional Model" of generating electricity:

> DG and micropower are dependent upon significant technological improvements throughout electricity production, transmission, distribution, storage, and consumption. Most simply, the scale of generation units is reduced significantly, and they are widely dispersed. "Smart energy" technologies are intended to reduce the size of power generation units, to be closer to the source of consumption, to utilize "Smart Grids" which will transmit power more efficiently, and to use "smart meters" which will provide consumers with more information about their consumption patterns and about their choice of providers.

Tomain and Shapiro, *supra*. What changes to existing laws (or new laws) might be necessary to make the grid a "Smart Grid"?

3. As discussed in the next section of this chapter, states have funded renewable and conservation programs with system benefits charges, small fees levied on all utility customers. Because operators of DG generate electricity "off the grid," could they avoid paying these charges? If a state attempted to compensate for this by a surcharge on DG, would that lessen the financial attractiveness of investment in DG?

4. Some states impose "exit fees," one-time fees paid by certain customers who choose electricity providers other than their incumbent utilities. The purpose of an exit fee is to compensate the incumbent utility for the departing customer's share of stranded costs. If the exit fee is imposed because the customer is choosing to rely exclusively on DG, would that fee act as a disincentive to DG? *See* Steven Ferrey, Exit Strategy: State Legal Discretion to Environmentally Sculpt a Deregulating Electric Environment, 26 Harv. Envtl. L. Rev. 109 (2002). California imposed an exit fee in its restructuring scheme but allowed an exemption for customers relying on DG; several other states imposed exit fees on certain customers even if the reason for switching was to use DG. *Id.*

5. Not all DG is beneficial to the environment, and environmentalists would almost certainly support some "barriers" to DG. An example is the CAA's NSR program, that forces major new sources of air pollution in areas not meeting federal air quality standards to obtain permits, typically from a state agency, that require them to use technology-based controls that achieve the "lowest achievable emission rate" in practice and purchase pollution offsets from other sources of the same pollutant. *See* Section A, and Chapter 5.

3. NEW "GREEN" PROGRAMS; DORMANT COMMERCE CLAUSE AND PREEMPTION CONCERNS

During the advent of competition in the utility industry, states have been active in continuing to promote environmental values. Because centralized decisions by the states about the resource mix of individual utilities have less relevance in states that have moved toward the marketplace, this function has been replaced in large part by statewide laws (such as those establishing system benefits charges) that promote environmental values. This section describes the various state programs and the tension between them and the competitive environment.

a. STATE RENEWABLES AND CONSERVATION PROGRAMS

As regulators are attempting to ensure the coexistence of retail competition and environmental protection, they have devised ways to maintain energy efficiency and renewable energy programs, or even provide additional funding for technologies and programs that might otherwise become "stranded benefits" in a competitive environment. There are a number of recognized programs for achieving these goals. The Database of State Incentives for Renewable Energy (DSIRE) maintains a state-by-state map with current information about state programs. *See* http://www.dsireu-sa.org.

A *system benefits charge* (alternatively known as a "public benefits fund" or "renewable energy trust fund") is established in sixteen states and the District of Columbia through a non-bypassable fee imposed on all customers' bills, regardless of the entity selling power to those customers. The provision establishing the system benefits charge was often included in a state restructuring law. While the fee imposed is typically small, the funds raised can amount to millions of dollars.

States use these funds for purposes perceived to benefit the entire public, such as rebates on renewable energy systems, funding for research and development of renewable energy, and development of renewable energy education programs. The design of the program (particularly the size of the fees imposed and the purposes for which the funds are used) varies considerably from state to state:

A system benefits charge will raise the following issues: the level of the charge, the allocation to classes of customers, the rate design, the programs to be implemented, and the ongoing process for oversight and management of the fund. Between 1998 and 2012, approximately $3.5 billion will be collected by sixteen states with existing renewable energy funds. More than half the amount collected—at least $135 million per year—comes from just California. The funding levels range from $0.07/MWh in Wisconsin up to almost $0.6/MWh in Massachusetts. Most only provide assistance to new projects and not to existing renewable projects.

The form of administration of renewable trust funds varies. Many states administer them through a state agency, while others use a quasi-public business development organization. Some funds are managed by independent third-party organizations, some by existing utilities, while two states allow large customers to self-direct the funds. For distribution, some states utilize an investment model, making loans and equity investments. Other states provide financial incentives for production or grants to stimulate supply-side development. Some other states use research and development grants, technical assistance, education, and demonstration projects.

Steven Ferrey, Sustainable Energy, Environmental Policy, and States' Rights: Discerning the Energy Future Through the Eye of the Dormant Commerce Clause, 12 N.Y.U. Envtl. L.J. 507, 523–25 (2004). Two typical funds are the Connecticut Clean Energy Fund (CCEF) and the Massachusetts Renewable Energy Trust (RET). The CCEF has operated since 2000, with funding expected to be $100 million between 2005–2010. It has invested in biomass gasification projects, fuel cell companies, and ocean wave technologies. The RET was created in 1993 as part of Massachusetts' restructuring law, and is funded with approximately $27 million annually. It has invested in solar PV manufacturers, fuel cell companies, and provided $54 million for a waste-to-energy program affecting 138 communities.

Philip J. Deutch, Renewable Energy in the 21st Century: Why States Lead the Way, Fortnightly, Mar. 1, 2005.

A number of other state laws and policies work to encourage renewables and conservation. These include net metering and aggregation (discussed in Chapter 12), and legislative mandates and local codes regarding "green buildings" (discussed above in "Energy Conservation"). A common form of mandate is a *renewable portfolio standard* (RPS), that typically requires a specified percentage of the power sold by retail electricity suppliers operating in a state to be derived from renewable power sources. Many of these portfolio plans are accompanied by a market in renewable credits, allowing suppliers with an excess to sell credits and those with a deficit to buy them. The following readings explore the design of RPS and their impact on promoting renewable energy.

R. Wiser et al., Evaluating Experience with Renewables Portfolio Standards in the United States

Lawrence Berkeley National Laboratory (2004).

2. The RPS in Context

2.1 What is an RPS?

The RPS is a policy that requires retail suppliers of electricity (otherwise referred to as loadserving entities, or "LSEs") to meet a specific portion of their energy supply needs with eligible forms of renewable energy. RPS policies are generally designed to maintain and/or increase the contribution of renewable energy to the electricity supply mix. The RPS establishes numeric targets for renewable energy supply, applies those targets to retail electricity suppliers (i.e., LSEs), and encourages competition among renewable developers to meet the targets in a least cost fashion. RPS purchase obligations generally increase over time, and LSEs typically must demonstrate compliance on an annual basis. The administrator of an RPS frequently levies penalties on those suppliers that fail to meet their renewable energy purchase obligations. Because the RPS sets quantitative targets for the supply of renewable energy, but allows electricity suppliers flexibility in how to meet those targets, it is expected that a properly designed RPS will lead to strong incentives for cost reduction.

LSEs can meet their RPS requirements with renewable energy facilities that they already own or that they construct, or through bilateral purchases of renewable electricity from independent generators. In some jurisdictions, LSEs can use tradable renewable certificates ("TRCs")—also known as "green certificates" or "renewable energy credits"—to comply with their RPS requirements. A TRC is created when a megawatt-hour of renewable energy is generated, is a purely financial product, and can be traded separately from the underlying electricity generation, much like tradable emissions permits. TRC transactions create a supplemental revenue stream for renewable generators, and allow LSEs to demonstrate compliance with the RPS by purchasing TRCs in lieu of directly purchasing renewable electricity. In theory, TRCs should trade at a price that represents the incremental cost (relative to conventional power) of the marginal renewable generator needed to meet RPS requirements (see, e.g., Morthorst 2000). [Instead of] tracking actual renewable electricity contracts to verify compliance with an RPS, the use of TRCs can create liquidity and depth in the renewable energy market, increase compliance flexibility, and ease administrative burdens by simplifying compliance demonstration.

2.2 Comparing the RPS to Other Policy Approaches

... The use of an RPS to support renewable energy development does have some *theoretical* appeal:

- The RPS can drive a known quantity of new renewable development, based on the specific standards that are established, and can ensure that there are buyers for that renewable energy.

- It can help lower the total cost of that development by giving LSEs the flexibility to meet their purchase targets in the way they deem best, and by encouraging competition among renewable developers for contracts with LSEs.

- An RPS can be competitively neutral if it is applied equally to all retail electricity suppliers.

- An RPS imposes relatively low administrative burdens and direct administrative costs on those responsible for overseeing the policy, because LSEs have the burden of contracting with renewable generators.

- An RPS can be applied in both restructured and monopoly electricity market contexts.

While the RPS has some theoretical advantages, the RPS also has some potential disadvantages:

- As documented in this report, due to its complexity, an RPS can be difficult to design and implement well.

- The exact cost impacts of an RPS cannot be known with certainty in advance, and will depend on the results of LSE efforts to comply with the policy.

- If an RPS does not lead to the availability of long-term power purchase agreements, the ability to finance new renewable projects will be limited and compliance costs may increase.

- An RPS may be less flexible in offering targeted support to renewable energy than policies that provide greater discretion to government regulators to oversee specific policy supports.

- An RPS is not necessarily suited to supporting diversity among renewable technologies (because it will encourage least-cost renewable supply options), although an RPS can be designed to do so through the use of "resource tiers" or "credit multipliers."

- Operating experience with the RPS remains limited, and lessons on the appropriate design of an RPS are only beginning to emerge.

3.1   State RPS Policies and Their Design

The U.S. Congress has considered applying an RPS on a federal level in the United States, and a number of other countries have recent experience with the policy; countries with operating RPS policies include Australia, Belgium, Italy, Sweden, and the United Kingdom.

The most extensive and diverse base of experience with the RPS on a worldwide basis arguably exists in the United States, however, where 13 states have created some form of RPS policy: ... Electricity suppliers in these states collectively serve over 30% of total U.S. electricity consumption. More than half of these existing RPS policies are located in states that have restructured their electricity markets, opening those markets to retail competition. Nonetheless, a growing number of state RPS policies have been established in traditional, still-regulated monopoly electricity markets.... [Few] of the states have more than four years of experience with their RPS programs, ...

... [E]ach of the 13 states has crafted their RPS policies differently, sometimes radically so. The percentage purchase obligation, for example, increases to just 1.1% in Arizona, but to 20% in California. While wind, solar, and geothermal energy are eligible under most of the RPS policies, criteria for the eligibility of biomass and hydropower varies considerably across states. Some of the key design choices for an RPS are listed in Text Box 1.

TEXT BOX 1:

RPS DESIGN ELEMENTS

Structure, Size, and Application of the RPS

- Percentage purchase obligation targets over time
- Start date for purchase obligations
- Duration of purchase obligations
- Structure (e.g., single equirement, or multiple % requirements for each technology group)
- Renewable resource diversity requirements or incentives
- Application to LSEs—who must meet the obligations
- Product-or company-based application

Eligibility

- Resource type eligibility
- Allow imports, or just in-state facilities
- Eligibility of existing renewable generation
- Definition of new/incremental generation
- Eligibility of customer-sited renewable facilities

Administration

- Regulatory oversight body(ies)
- Verifying compliance—TRCs or contract-path
- Certification of eligible generators
- Compliance filing requirements
- Enforcement mechanisms (i.e., penalties)
- Existence of cost caps
- Compliance flexibility mechanisms
- Contracting standards for regulated LSEs
- Cost recovery for regulated LSEs

Interactions Between the RPS and Other Policies

- Interactions with other renewable energy policies
- Linkages with emissions credits policies

3.2   The Impacts of State RPS Policies

. . . RPS policies have the potential to stimulate over 16,000 MW of new renewable energy capacity by 2017 (and support the continued operation of over 7,000 MW of existing generation capacity). This is comparable to the total amount of existing, non-hydro renewables capacity currently in place in the U.S. [and] would represent approximately 1.7% of current electricity sales in the entire U.S.

. . . [T]hese policies are already beginning to have an effect; this is especially apparent for wind power. In Texas, 915 MW of wind power came on line in 2001 in large part to serve the state's RPS; another 204 megawatts came on line in 2003. . . . The Massachusetts RPS, though it began in 2003, has already resulted in some merchant landfill gas activity, some incremental production at existing biomass plants, and increased site prospecting by wind, landfill gas, and biomass developers. . . . New Jersey's RPS has contributed somewhat to the increased renewable development efforts of renewable companies in the mid-Atlantic region.■

NOTES AND COMMENTS

1.   The provision of accurate information is critical to the success of an RPS program.

State RPS operate at the state level: the state requires each utility subject to its jurisdiction to prove that it has generated a sufficient amount of power from renewable resources (or has sufficient credits to cover a shortfall). However, utilities are increasingly purchasing power in regional marketplaces. This raises a number of complex informational issues:

> How should a regional market be structured to allow a utility to meet the relevant state RPS? The operational aspects of this inquiry are complex. It is impossible to "tag" a unit of electricity, so an LSE

cannot determine at any given moment whether the electricity it just delivered was generated by a nuclear plant or a wind farm. Nor can the RTO know the environmental attributes of the power it is transmitting about the grid, unless it has some form of accounting. And then there's the matter of the reckoning: how does the state know at the end of the year that the utility has complied with the RPS?

Some regions have made considerable progress toward establishing a market for the attributes of electricity wholly separate and independent from that for the electricity itself. PJM Interconnection, the large RTO in the Mid–Atlantic region, has developed a "GATS" (Generator Attribute Tracking System) with a sophisticated design. In it, each generator would have an account into which certificates would be deposited as electricity was generated. These certificates would contain relevant data about the nature of the generation (*e.g.*, the fuel used). LSEs would also have GATS accounts, and they would obtain certificates from PJM generators, who would have to sell or transfer certificates to them. At the end of the year, if the LSEs did not have certificates that matched their load served, they would be allocated them from a "residual mix" pool of unsold and unused certificates. Once all certificates had been allocated reports could be generated to determine whether LSEs met the RPS requirements.

Joel B. Eisen, The Environmental Responsibility of the Regionalizing Electric Utility Industry, 15 Duke Envtl. L. & Pol'y F. 295 (2005). A technical assistance report for New Jersey on harmonizing the state RPS with PJM's GATS program posed the following questions:

(1) What power should count toward the RPS? As noted above, Constitutional problems would arise if a state determined that only in-state power would count. But could a state set *any* limitations on power generated too remotely from the state? Would it have to credit wind power generated in North Dakota, for example? Would this issue have to be revisited if, as is the case at present, the regional market continued to expand?

(2) If it is desirable that only power from "new" renewable facilities counts toward the RPS, how should that be defined?

(3) If other states in the region adopt RPS, would that lead toward a possible shortage of REC's, and what would be done to address this shortage? Should a state consider altering its RPS in light of the actions of neighboring states that are also part of the regional market?

(4) If a shortage of credits persisted, could a utility satisfy its requirement through some sort of alternative mechanism such as a payment into a state's clean energy fund, or would that have the effect of discouraging the market for green power?

(5) Should the state have its own accounting system for REC's or should it simply rely on the regional one?

National Council on Electricity Policy, Regulatory Assistance Project, Technical Assistance for the New Jersey Renewable Energy Task Force (2003), http://www.ncouncil.org/rap.pdf.

The question raised by item (1) above—the intersection of the dormant commerce clause and state policies promoting renewables and conservation—is discussed in the next section.

2.   One frequent objection to RPS is that they set a target that can be viewed at worst as arbitrary (*see* Langenkamp, *supra*) or at best, as set without knowing how much of electricity generated from renewable energy is available in the market. Ferrey, *supra*. How would you respond to this criticism?

3.   An RPS that allows only new sources to qualify will obviously have more of an effect on new development of renewable energy facilities; if existing sources may be counted the RPS is easier to meet. On the other hand, if existing sources are not counted, those sources may not be competitive in a wholesale power purchasing environment. NCSL, *supra*. Which approach do you find the most desirable?

4.   The idea of a regional or national goal for renewables has found recent support (though the U.S. Senate's provision to set a national RPS was rejected in the conference report on the Energy Policy Act of 2005). A bipartisan resolution of the Western Governors' Association, co-sponsored by Governors Bill Richardson and Arnold Schwarzenegger, calls for the Western region to develop 30,000 MW of capacity for power generated from solar, wind, geothermal, biomass, clean coal and advanced natural gas technologies by 2015, and increase energy efficiency by 20 percent by 2020. *See* www.westgov.org/wga/policy/04/clean-energy.pdf. On the international level, a number of countries, especially in Europe, have had considerable success setting national targets. Germany's Renewable Energy Sources Act of 2000 set a goal of doubling the country's share of electricity derived from renewable sources by 2010. In 2004, wind, hydroelectric, and other renewable plants produced a total of fifty-six terawatt hours ("TWh") of electricity, or 9.3 percent of the power consumed in Germany. German Environmental Ministry, http://www.bmu.de.

Should this idea become mandatory—that is, should the state RPS be replaced in the U.S. with regional or national standards? If so, how would they be designed and administered? Would it be easier administratively to do this than use the current state standards?

5.   Do mandates for the purchase of renewable power, and other state programs designed to promote public purposes in a competitive environment, resemble the "centralized planning" of IRP? As one author notes,

From a long-term perspective, retail access has effectively ended the traditional service obligation that underpinned investments in generation facilities. Thus, it has become necessary to try to develop surrogates to replace the now-quaint "obligation to serve"—installed capacity markets, locational capacity markets, state sponsored auctions to provide default service, resource adequacy requirements, and the like. Add to this concerns by state regulators about generation fuel diversity, environmental "collateral damage," and the corresponding need to foster the use of renewables, and soon you have increasingly elaborate generation portfolio regimes that start to look and smell like the "integrated resource planning" programs of old.

Susan Kelly, Wholesale Electric Restructuring: Was 2004 the "Tipping Point"?, The Electricity J., Mar. 2005, at 22.

* * *

With restructuring, "green pricing" programs for residential, commercial, and industrial consumers have also emerged as a way to promote environmentally safer ways of generating electricity. These programs allow customers to choose to purchase an electricity product based on its environmentally friendly attributes (particularly its fuel source and emissions profile). They also offer a potential market solution to the funding of future renewable technologies. Consumers willing to pay a price premium for renewable energy participate in a program that allows them to add some incremental amount of money to their regular electricity bills, with the added amount going to support renewable energy.

More than 500 utilities, including investor-owned, municipal utilities, and cooperatives, offer or plan to offer "green pricing" programs. These work in one of two fundamental ways:

1. As actual kWh sales where electricity and its "green" attributes are bundled together as a single product in a single transaction; there, the purchaser switches from conventional power to a bilateral contract with the "green" energy supplier.

2. [As a] sale only of the "green" attributes without purchasing the actual kilowatt hours; the retail customer does not need to switch from buying conventional power but only purchases the renewable certificate.

Ferrey, *supra.*

An early market survey concluded that customers were willing to pay $10 more per month to purchase green power. *See* Kari Smith, Customer Driven Markets for Renewably Generated Electricity, California Regulatory Research Project (CRRP/1–96 August 1996). The top ten green pricing programs as of December 2004 (in terms of the number of the utility's customers participating) included the following:

Total Number of Customer Participants (as of December 2004)			
Rank	Utility	Program Name(s)	Participants
1	Xcel Energy	*WindSource Renewable Energy Trust*	40,990
2	PacifiCorp	*Blue Sky Block Blue Sky Usage Blue Sky Habitat*	36,125
3	Portland General Electric	*Clean Wind Green Source Healthy Habitat*	33,491
4	Sacramento Municipal Utility District	*Greenergy PV Pioneers I*	28,527
5	Los Angeles Department of Water & Power	*Green Power for a Green L.A.*	27,293
6	National Grid	*GreenUp*	14,978
7	Puget Sound Energy	*Green Power Program*	14,074
8	Alliant Energy	*Second Nature*	11,544
9	We Energies	*Energy for Tomorrow*	11,120
10	Florida Power and Light	*Sunshine Energy*	10,674

See Green Power Network, http://www.eere.energy.gov. The lowest ten price premiums for green pricing programs ranged from 0.33 to 1.0 cents per kWh. *Id*. A recent study confirms that smaller utilities (such as municipals) typically have greater percentages of their customers choosing green pricing options. R. Wiser *et al.*, Utility Green Pricing Programs: A Statistical Analysis of Program Effectiveness, Lawrence Berkeley National Laboratory (2004). On the other hand, larger utilities could find more of their customers signing up for green pricing. Factors such as a utility's long-term commitment to green pricing are important; each additional year of a green pricing program yields an increase of 0.25% or more of a utility's customers choosing it. *Id*.

In general, "green pricing" is still a relatively new concept in the U.S. Its voluntary nature (states may require utilities to offer green pricing but do not compel consumers to choose it) limits its effectiveness. In the long run, it is not likely to be as successful as specific targeted mandates such as renewable portfolio standards in encouraging the development of renewable energy:

> The drawback of green power marketing is that it relies on individual consumer decisions to create a public good. The environmental benefits of green power consumption are not internalized to the consumer who elects to pay a premium for green power, but rather are shared by all in the region. This allows "free riders" who benefit but do not pay or contribute. This raises equity and efficiency issues. Therefore, green power marketing suffers from individual consumer motivation and equity impediments that are not raised by a portfolio standard, which imposes requirements on energy producers rather than consumers.

> Ferrey, *supra*.

An important element of any "green pricing" program is information. Consumers need to know that "green power" is what they are in fact getting. Also, it is important to be able to ensure that those marketing "green" power are not deceiving consumers. However, the nature of electricity and the grid makes this difficult, as it is impossible to prove that actual electrons flowing to a consumer came from "green" sources. A number of states have disclosure rules designed to address this issue through provision of labels to consumers about the "green" attributes of electricity delivered to them:

> Disclosure labels do not claim to track emissions from the power physically delivered to the customer. Rather, it tracks [*sic*] the contractual flow of dollars from the customer to generators from which the load serving entity has acquired the attributes of power. As a result, if a customer buys power from a source claiming to be 100 percent "green," it means the supplier has contracted to buy power attributes from a source somewhere in the relevant power grid that is "green." The actual electrons serving the individual customer will almost certainly be generated from the same power plants as before.

NCEP Report, *supra*. States' disclosure rules work in tandem with certification programs such as the Green-e stamp, independent assessments of "green" power products that ensure that the power provided is in fact "green." *See* http://www.green-e.org. The DSIRE and the Department of Energy's "Green Power Network" maintain comprehensive lists of states' disclosure provisions. DSIRE, *supra*; EERE, http://www.eere.energy.gov.

b.   DORMANT COMMERCE CLAUSE AND PREEMPTION CONCERNS

While states' system benefits charges, renewable portfolio standards and other statewide programs to promote renewables and conservation are increasingly popular, do they violate the dormant commerce clause, which protects commerce from protectionist regulation by states?

The following article explains the impact of the Dormant Commerce Clause on state "green" programs.

Kirsten H. Engel, The Dormant Commerce Clause Threat to Market–Based Environmental Regulation: The Case of Electricity Deregulation

26 Ecology L.Q. 243 (1999).

If a governor, under pressure during hard economic times to save her state's struggling dairy industry, signed into law a bill banning the import of out-of-state milk products, such a law would surely be struck down in court under the dormant Commerce Clause. Indeed, the principle against protectionism in interstate trade applies to all articles traded in interstate commerce, including those related to the environment.

Imagine instead that two states, for example, California and Maine, wish to reduce local levels of pollutants attributable to the generation of electricity from fossil fuels. They therefore adopt programs to foster their states' renewable power industries. According to each program, ten percent of the energy supplied to end-use customers within the state must consist of renewable power such as wind, solar, geothermal, or biomass. In developing strategies to implement this renewable power mandate, each state toys briefly with a traditional regulatory approach according to which each individual energy retailer must alter its energy sources to ensure that a minimum percentage of its portfolio consists of renewable power. Each state rejects this option, however, due to opposition from a subset of suppliers obligated under long-term fossil fuel supply contracts. Instead, each state implements a tradable obligation mechanism, a variation on the increasingly popular emissions trading programs recently adopted by federal, state, and local governments. Under such a program, energy retailers can meet renewable energy requirements through the purchase of renewable energy credits from other generators or retailers without altering their own energy portfolio. Conversely, retailers who overcomply by purchasing more renewable power than the mandated minimum percentage may sell their extra credits to suppliers whose percentage of renewable power falls below the minimum. Marketable renewable energy credits thus efficiently spread the cost of satisfying the ten percent renewable requirement among the state's energy retailers.

Suppose that sometime later a California energy retailer purchases renewable energy credits from a biomass company in Maine and proffers such credits under California's minimum renewable energy mandate. Upon learning of the sale, the California legislature prohibits the use of out-of-state renewable energy credits under the California standard. California's legislators reason that accepting out-of-state credits will undermine the state's objective of improving air quality. Upset that the legislature has spoiled their trade, both the California energy credit importer and the Maine energy credit exporter sue California, claiming that the state's ban violates the dormant Commerce Clause.

What result? Can California's hypothetical ban on importing out-of-state renewable energy credits be distinguished from the New Jersey ban on importing out-of-state waste that was struck down in Philadelphia v. New Jersey? Both constitute facial discrimination against articles of commerce, which the Supreme Court has generally held "virtually per se" invalid. Nevertheless, California is guilty of nothing more than trying to ensure clean air in an efficient manner. California provides such clean air benefits when it adopts a renewable energy mandate, and it provides those benefits more efficiently by using a tradable obligation mechanism to implement that mandate. If California does not also prohibit credits from out-of-state renewables generators, it may subsidize clean air in distant areas such as Maine. To be sure, California could capture the clean air benefits simply by refusing to use a tradable obligation mechanism, but it would then lose the efficiencies gained by such a market-based approach. If California's ban on out-of-state credits is considered facial discrimination, the Commerce Clause would require California to choose either inefficient regulation that provides clean air only within the state or efficient regulation that may improve the air quality of distant states ...

States have many options for retaining the environmental or economic benefits of an incentive-based mechanism while deregulating their electricity industries. [M]any of these options are constitutionally permissible. Others, however, unavoidably burden interstate trade and hence could be struck down under the dormant Commerce Clause under either the test for regulation that is facially discriminatory or the test for regulation that is facially neutral and yet places an excessive burden on interstate trade.

Application of these tests reveals that state market-based environmental legislation may be invalidated under the dormant Commerce Clause in at least three situations. First, a state acts unconstitutionally if it creates a marketable permit or obligation scheme and employs facial discrimination to retain the environmental public goods for its own residents. A state might, for example, restrict its energy credit program to renewables generators located within its boundaries. Second, a state violates the dormant Commerce Clause if it requires that the environmental costs of economic activity be internalized, and such internalization results in a significant discriminatory effect against out-of-state producers. Mechanisms such as nondiscriminatory environmental externality values, emissions portfolio standards, and hybrid emissions and consumption taxes raise such problems. Third, a state might unconstitutionally divert funds generated through a nondiscriminatory tax to a subset of local industry, as with a system benefits charge used to subsidize in-state renewables generators.

A state probably does not act unconstitutionally if it takes a less burdensome approach. For example, a state might restrict the legal value of a tradable environmental permit according to the location of the ultimate use of the permit (for example, limiting renewable energy credits that satisfy a renewable portfolio standard to credits that are sold to in-state consumers). Similarly, a state might subsidize environmentally sensitive industries through general tax revenues, rather than through a system benefits charge. A state might thus implement some of the incentive-based options in a manner that minimizes the constitutional risk. Nevertheless, these approaches are not foolproof, and a state may still fear constitutional challenges to such regulations.

For this reason, many policymakers wish to adopt a nonregulatory approach to reduce the environmental threats of electricity deregulation. Green marketing is such an approach. Through green marketing, corporations encourage consumers to patronize environmentally sensitive products by using standard marketing techniques to emphasize a good's environmental advantages. Green marketing is premised on the idea that fully informed consumers will switch to less polluting and habitat-destroying products. As a consequence, it is believed, producers will shift their purchases away from environmentally destructive production processes and toward environmentally benign processes because environmental consciousness will be more profitable. Green marketing thus moves environmental protection away from the realm of government regulation to individual choice in the marketplace.

Many large electricity companies are pursuing green marketing as a business strategy. At least twelve United States electric utilities support renewable power generation through "green pricing," and another thirty have considered, or are planning to offer, such an option. Nevertheless, fewer than twenty megawatts of renewable electricity are currently supported through green pricing programs. Perhaps more promising are the green marketing proposals of electricity retailers in states that have already deregulated their electricity industry. Deregulated retailers might be expected to market green power more aggressively than would a monopolistic public utility.

Unfortunately, economics and equity prevent the successful substitution of green marketing for state incentive-based environmental regulation. As a stand-alone mechanism to reduce the harmful environmental impacts of electricity production, green marketing suffers from numerous drawbacks. The first problem is that the benefits of renewable power, clean air, for instance, are public goods. Hence consumers have little incentive to purchase renewable power, given that they can enjoy (that is, free-ride off of) this clean air benefit when renewable power is purchased by others. The result of the free-riding activity associated with purchases of public goods such as renewable power is that the good will be under-supplied in relation to its net social benefits. The simple economic lesson here is that renewable power will be under-supplied if its support is left solely to the workings of the market.

Various pilot programs intended to test the demand for green power have demonstrated this basic law of economics. Although as many as seventy percent of residential customers claim that they are willing to pay more for renewable power, utility green pricing programs typically draw less than three percent of residential customers and an even smaller percentage of commercial customers. In a Massachusetts electric retail competition pilot program, residents were offered a choice between various energy options, some of them consisting of green power sources, and were provided with complete and comparable information about each option. Only four percent of eligible residential customers chose to participate in the Massachusetts pilot program. Of the four percent who enrolled, thirty-one percent chose a green option. Overall then, slightly more than one percent of eligible consumers subscribed to a green power option. In short, while people support clean energy, they have little incentive to purchase it out of their own pocketbook, since they can always enjoy its benefits if it is purchased by someone else.

Green marketing also raises equitable considerations. First, because the benefits of green energy are public goods, all of society gains from the purchasing decisions of a subset of environmentally conscious consumers. Thus, those who are willing to pay for environmental benefits subsidize a clean environment for those who are not. Second, industrial energy purchases have the largest environmental impacts (simply as a result of their larger energy demand), but green marketing appeals are not likely to make much of a difference in corporate decision making. To date, interest in environmentally friendly electricity is found primarily among residential consumers. Because it relies solely on individual choice to shape the energy market, green marketing ensures that residential consumers will pay to offset the environmental harms caused by the largest electricity consumers. Not only is funding for renewable power likely to decrease in such a scenario, but it is plainly inequitable for those least responsible for the environmental problems of electrical production to pay for the environmental restorative measures of those who are most responsible. For that reason, green marketing can be seen as a reversal of the principle endorsed by most environmental groups—the polluter pays principle. Despite this reversal, several prominent environmental organizations are promoting green marketing as a key component of their strategy to combat the possible adverse environmental impacts of electricity deregulation, prompting a vigorous debate within the environmental community.

The above criticisms all assume a green marketing mechanism that is functioning perfectly. But for a market to be efficient, consumers must have access to complete and accurate information concerning the goods being traded. Generators must inform consumers about the source of the energy offered as well as the impacts of its generation upon the environment. Obtaining such information is extremely difficult. In promotional literature, electricity companies stress their reliance upon renewable power and their record of environmental leadership. Many of the claims of green marketers, however, may be misleading, and purchasers of green energy may provide no net improvement in environmental quality.

Given these controversies, consumer groups are advocating truth-in-advertising laws specifically related to the green marketing claims made by retailers of electricity. Such laws would supplement the Federal Trade Commission's general restrictions upon green marketing claims. States are beginning to respond. Recently, California passed a law requiring that entities offering electric services disclose accurate, reliable and easy-to-understand information on the generation attributes of the electricity they propose to sell. Under this law, electricity suppliers must disclose this information to all potential end-use consumers "in all product-specific written promotional materials" distributed to consumers through print or electronic media. Moreover, several attorneys general recently urged states to adhere to consumer protection green marketing guidelines in electric industry restructuring legislation.

Other proposals include certification programs in which sellers of green energy compete for a seal or other stamp of approval from regulators. Certification programs call for a state agency or private organization to verify that the type and percentage of renewable power being advertised by retail sellers corresponds to the characteristics of their actual renewable power supplies. Green power certification programs are now being implemented in several states. California has enacted one of the most aggressive of such programs. Under California's electricity restructuring law, the state is required to "implement a process for certifying eligible renewable resource providers." Customers who purchase certified renewable resources gain earlier access to the deregulated market. Certification programs advance not only consumer right-to-know objectives but also the marketing goals of retail sellers by assuring customers of the true greenness of the products they purchase.

Green marketing alone is thus an insufficient and, arguably, even inequitable method of addressing the environmental problems caused by the deregulated electricity market. If green marketing cannot provide the answer, is there any way to avoid the problems for incentive-based environmental regulation posed by the dormant Commerce Clause? . . .

The desirability of state market-based environmental regulation warrants several reforms in the Court's current tests for identifying unconstitutional burdens upon interstate commerce. First, state market-based mechanisms that employ facial discrimination should not be presumed invalid where the discrimination is part of a state's attempt to correct for market failures that create or exacerbate environmental degradation and where the discrimination is necessary to prevent a state from losing to other jurisdictions the benefits associated with correcting a market failure. Second, the market participant exception should be expanded to encompass state legislation dictating particular consumer preferences and again designed to prevent the loss to other jurisdictions of public environmental goods. Finally, the rule prohibiting extraterritorial regulation should be expanded to allow state decision makers to consider the environmental costs of their decisions, regardless of whether these costs will be incurred within or without the state's territory.■

NOTES AND COMMENTS

1. Professor Engel proposes some modifications to how courts apply the dormant commerce clause analysis. Do you believe that these modifications are necessary? How would you assess the constitutionality of the hypothetical program Professor Engel presents at the beginning of her article?

2. How would actual programs designed to implement the two most popular means of encouraging renewables and conservation—the system benefits charge and renewable portfolio standard—fare under dormant commerce clause analysis? That depends greatly on the design of the states' programs:

> The fact that the charge to fund the renewable trust fund is imposed only on in-state consumers is irrelevant, as every state tax can be imposed only within that state. The . . . discriminatory impact on commerce, not the ultimate burden of the tax, is the impermissible element. . . . While most states' renewable trust fund legislation does not distinguish at what stage of commerce the tax or charge will be imposed, this may make a difference. If a state were savvy, it could elect to impose the tax on the local distribution service, rather than on the sale of the electric good or service. This result might make the tax more acceptable: the state would be taxing a purely in-state service, rather than taxing interstate sales of power, which can be regarded as a commodity.

> . . . With a renewable energy trust fund, only certain in-state generators receive subsidies. Moreover, some minority of the funds raised in certain of the states employing a renewable energy trust fund will be used for public information and promotion, where no individual power generator directly is subsidized. This creates two types of selective subsidy: Only some in-state renewable energy generators benefit, and

only some renewable energy projects benefit. More importantly, it decouples the subsidy from direct proportionate receipt by all in-state market participants. This discriminatory subsidy, standing alone, should be within state policy discretion and not violate the Commerce Clause.

Ferrey, *supra*.

A RPS is problematic if it limits its scope to in-state generating resources. However, in a restructuring environment, with power increasingly being purchased outside of the state, that limitation would be difficult if not impossible for the state to impose. It is not good policy, either: "There are few compelling local police power justifications, aside from economic protectionism for host-state interest, for limiting a renewable portfolio or tradable portfolio credits to in-state resources." *Id.*

3. The Pennsylvania Public Utility Commission (PPUC) issued an order under the state's restructuring law (*see* Chapter 12) authorizing PECO Energy, a Philadelphia-based electric utility, to recover stranded costs from transmission customers through a transition charge. Indianapolis Power & Light Co., an Indiana utility that wanted to sell power in Pennsylvania, appealed the PPUC's decision to the Commonwealth Court of Pennsylvania, arguing that it violated the dormant commerce clause because it discriminated against companies from outside Pennsylvania. The Court upheld the order, saying that the power to authorize the recovery of these costs came within the scope of the regulatory powers traditionally assigned to the states. *Indianapolis Power & Light Co. v. Pennsylvania Pub. Util. Comm'n*, 711 A.2d 1071 (1998).

C.   SITING DECISIONS

Traditionally, most states have required electric utilities to obtain certificates-of-need (CONs) (sometimes called a CCN—"a certificate of convenience and necessity") before building power plants, transmission lines or pipelines. Typically, the CON is only issued following a siting proceeding—a hearing before the state PSC during which a utility makes its proposal and consumer and environmental groups may be allowed to participate as intervenors. Many states actively police the environmental aspects of utility regulation through statutes that govern the siting of power plants and transmission lines, and through integrated resource planning statutes. Such regulatory proceedings may also include some assessment of the "need" for power plants or transmission lines. However, if markets, rather than regulation, are the norm for decisions about power supply, does discussion of "need" continue to make sense? Moreover, given that new power plant and transmission line projects are often stymied by "NIMBY" opposition by state and local interest groups, what is the best course of action to ensure that what one author has termed "state parochialism" does not hamper the development of otherwise worthy projects?

Richard J. Pierce, Jr., Environmental Regulation, Energy, and Market Entry, 15 Duke Envtl. L. & Pol'y F. 167 (2005).

These issues are the subject of this section, with a case study focusing on the Cross Sound Cable project, the proposal to bury a new transmission line under Long Island Sound from Connecticut to Long Island in New York.

1. REGULATION OF POWER PLANT SITING

The advent of competition in the electric utility industry has fundamentally changed the nature of siting decisions:

> During most of the twentieth century, state and local regulatory bodies coordinates the siting of power plants and transmission lines. These bodies focused on two important issues: 1) the determination of "need," so as to avoid unnecessary economic duplication of costly infrastructure; and 2) environmental protection, so as to provide local land use and other environmental concerns input on the placement of necessary generation and transmission facilities. With the rise of deregulated wholesale power markets, the issue of need is increasingly determined by the market, not regulators. Environmental concerns with siting, however, frequently remain contested—especially locally—but the regulatory apparatus for processing these concerns faces new challenges in deregulated markets. Environmental concerns in transmission line siting will increasingly be addressed at the federal level, with federal concerns predominating consideration of the issues. The dormant commerce clause does much of the work towards making this a predominantly federal concern, but eventually FERC's jurisdiction over such issues will need to be expanded by statute.

Jim Rossi, Transmission Siting in Deregulated Wholesale Power Markets: Re-Imagining the Role of Courts in Resolving Federal–State Siting Impasses Law, 15 Duke Envtl. L. & Pol'y F. 315 (2005).

The following case was decided against the backdrop of such concerns in Florida. Pay close attention to the state statutes and their role in the siting decision.

Re Duke Energy New Smyrna Beach Power Company, L.L.P.

193 P.U.R.4th 181 (Fla. PSC, Mar. 22, 1999).

ORDER granting a joint petition for a determination of need for a proposed "merchant" electrical power plant.

On August 19, 1998, the Utilities Commission, City of New Smyrna Beach, Florida, and Duke Energy New Smyrna Beach Power Company Ltd., L.L.P. filed a Joint Petition For Determination Of Need For An Electrical Power Plant pursuant to Section 403.519, Florida Statutes. The proposed plant is a 514 megawatt natural gas fired, combined cycle plant together with a natural gas lateral pipeline and associated transmission facilities to be located in Volusia County, Florida, adjacent to Interstate 95. The Utilities Commission, City of New Smyrna Beach, a municipal electric utility within the meaning of Section 366.02(2), Florida Statutes, has an entitlement to 30 megawatts of the proposed plant's capacity and energy associated with the capacity. The City will use the capacity and energy to serve its retail customers. Duke New Smyrna will build, own, and operate the plant and will market the balance of the capacity and energy (approximately 484 MM) on the wholesale power market. As such, except for the 30 megawatts entitlement provided to the City, the proposed plant will be a merchant plant. The term "merchant plant" as used in this order is a power plant with no rate base and no captive retail customers....

Need determination proceedings in Florida are governed by Section 403.519, Florida Statutes, Exclusive Forum For Determination Of Need. In order to analyze the extensive legal arguments made by the parties in conjunction with the Motion To Dismiss, it is instructive to summarize the terms contained in the statute relative to entities which may initiate need proceedings.

> Section 403.519, Florida Statutes, provides in pertinent part On request by an applicant or on its own motion, the commission shall begin a proceeding to determine the need for an electrical power plant subject to the Florida Electrical Power Plant Siting Act.... The commission shall be the sole forum for the determination of this matter.... In making its determination, the commission shall take into account the need for electric system reliability and integrity, the need for adequate electricity at a reasonable cost, and whether the proposed plant is the most cost effective alternative available. The commission shall also expressly consider the conservation measures taken by or reasonably available to the applicant or its members which might mitigate the need for the proposed plant and other matters within its jurisdiction which it deems relevant. The commission's determination of need for an electrical power plant shall create presumption of public need and necessity....

Section 403.503(4), Florida Statutes, defines an "applicant" as:

> any electric utility which applies for certification pursuant to the provisions of this act.

"Electric utility" is defined in Section 403.503(13), Florida Statutes, as follows:

> cities and towns, counties, public utility districts, regulated electric companies, electric cooperatives, and joint operating agencies, or combinations thereof, engaged in, or authorized to engage in, the business of generating, transmitting, or distributing electric energy.

Section 403.519, Florida Statutes, was enacted in 1980, Chapter 80–65, Laws of Florida, and amended in 1990, Chapter 90–331, Laws of Florida. The Florida Electrical Power Plant Siting Act, was enacted in 1973, Chapter 73–33, Laws of Florida, and amended in 1976, Chapter 76–76,

Laws of Florida, and in 1990, Chapter 90–331, Laws of Florida, Sections 403.501–403.518, Florida Statutes. Section 403.519, Florida Statutes, is not part of the PPSA.

Need determination proceedings in Florida are also governed by Rule 25–22.081, Florida Administrative Code. The Rule provides in pertinent part:

> Petitions submitted to commence a proceeding to determine the need for a proposed electrical power plant ... shall contain the following information:
>
> (1) A general description of the utility or utilities primarily affected....
>
> (2) A general description of the proposed electrical power plant....
>
> (3) A statement of the specific conditions, contingencies or other factors which indicate a need for the proposed electrical power plant.... If a determination is sought on some basis in addition to or in lieu of capacity needs, such as oil backout, then detailed analysis and supporting documentation of the costs and benefits is required.
>
> (4) A summary discussion of the major available generating alternatives....
>
> (5) A discussion of viable nongenerating alternatives....
>
> (6) An evaluation of the adverse consequences which will result if the proposed electrical power plant is not added....
>
> (7) If the generation addition is the result of a purchased power agreement between an investor-owned utility and a nonutility generator, the petition shall include a discussion of the potential for increases or decreases in the utility's cost of capital....

FPL [Florida Power & Light] argues that the Joint Petition does not meet the requirements of Florida Statutes or Florida Administrative Code and therefore, must be dismissed. With respect to Florida Statutes, FPL states that the Joint Petition fails to allege with specificity the manner in which it meets the statutory criteria. With respect to the rule requirements, FPL argues that the Joint Petition fails to satisfy the criteria of Rule 25–22.081, Florida Administrative Code.

By contrast to FPL's criteria-specific attack on the Joint Petition, FPC's arguments for dismissal are based on its global construction of the statutory framework of generation siting and planning. FPC's first argument is that the Florida Energy Efficiency and Conservation Act's limitation to retail utilities, likewise limits Section 403.519 to only retail utilities. Therefore, only retail utilities may be applicants for a need determination. FPC's second statutory argument for dismissal relates to the 1973 enactment of the Power Plant Siting Act which included the Ten Year Site Plan (TYSP) requirements....

Joint Petitioners' arguments supporting their status as applicants are compelling. Joint Petitioners argue that, individually and collectively, they are proper applicants within the broader regulatory framework as well as the specific provisions of Section 403.519, Florida Statutes. Joint Petitioners also effectively rebut FPL and FPC's arguments to the contrary. . . .

It is uncontroverted that the City is a proper applicant for a need determination. The City is a retail-serving municipal electric utility and thus, one of the seven enumerated entities within Section 403.503(13). The City has an entitlement to 30 megawatts of the Project's capacity and has the contractual right to purchase energy associated with that capacity. The City will use the capacity and energy to serve the needs of its retail customers.

Duke New Smyrna is also a proper applicant for a need determination. Duke New Smyrna maintains that it is a proper applicant for a need determination both as a joint applicant with the City, and individually as a "regulated electric company". Duke New Smyrna argues that it is an "applicant" in its own right based on the plain meaning of the definitions contained in the PPSA and the Grid Bill. In addition, Duke New Smyrna alleges that the Project is a Joint Electrical Power Supply Project within the meaning of Chapter 361, Florida Statutes.

As set forth above, Section 403.503(13), Florida Statutes, defines "applicant" as any "electric utility" which, in turn, is defined, among other things, as "regulated electric companies". Thus, a regulated electric company is a proper applicant pursuant to the plain language of the statute.

Duke New Smyrna is both "regulated" and an "electric company" and therefore clearly meets the statutory definition of applicant. Duke New Smyrna is a public utility pursuant to the Federal Power Act, 16 U.S.C. § 824(b)(1) ("FPA") and an EWG pursuant to the Public Utility Holding Company Act of 1935, 15 U.S.C. §§ 79z–5a. As a public utility and an EWG, Duke New Smyrna is regulated by the Federal Energy Regulatory Commission.

In addition to being a regulated electric company, Duke New Smyrna will be engaged in at least one of the qualifying activities listed in Section 403.503(13). The definition is phrased in the disjunctive. An "electric utility" is one of the enumerated entities which must be engaged in the business of generating, transmitting, or distributing electric energy. "In its elementary sense, the word 'or,' as used in a statute, is a disjunctive article indicating an alternative." TEDC/Shell City, Inc. v. Robbins, 690 So.2d 1323, 1325 FN4 (Fla. 3rd DCA 1997) quoting 49 Fla. Jur.2d Statutes s 137, at 179 (1984). Clearly, the Legislature intended the Power Plant Siting Act to govern electric utilities performing one or more of those functions. Duke New Smyrna proposes to engage in generation, and to a limited extent, transmission, of electricity. It therefore complies with the functional requirement of the statute.

FPL's and FPC's arguments that Duke New Smyrna should not be granted applicant status require us to add limiting language to the PPSA statutory definitions. FPL's argument is that "regulated electric company" means "state regulated electric company". FPC's argument is that "electric utility" means "retail electric utility". In combination, FPL and FPC would require that in order to build a power plant in the State of Florida, it is necessary to be a vertically-integrated utility, serving retail customers, subject to traditional rate regulation of the Commission. We find that the argument is not supported by the facts or the law. FPL's interpretation is based primarily on its analysis of decisional law and is addressed in a different section of this order. FPC's argument is discussed below.

Section 403.503(13), Florida Statutes, does not use the word "retail" before the phrase "electric utility". Yet, FPC argues that the word "retail" should be read into the statute. To reach its conclusion, FPC analyzes the enactment of Florida Energy Efficiency and Conservation Act and submits an "interchangeable definition" argument. Section 403.519, Florida Statutes, was enacted in 1980 as part of FEECA. According to FPC, because Section 366.82, Florida Statutes, limits the definition of "utility" to a retail provider, that same limitation applies to the definition of "applicant" as that term is used Section 403.519, Florida Statutes. "The most reasonable construction of these terms is that the Legislature used the words 'electric utility,' 'utility,' and 'applicant' interchangeably for purposes of electric industry need proceedings...." FPC's conclusion is that Duke lacks standing to bring the instant proceeding because it is a wholesale and not a retail power producer.

FPC's analysis is incorrect. First, while Section 403.519, Florida Statutes, is not part of the PPSA, its definitions are governed by the PPSA, not FEECA. Section 403.519 Florida Statutes, states, in part: "On request by an applicant ... the commission shall begin a proceeding to determine the need for an electrical power plant subject to the Power Plant Siting Act...." (emphasis added) The PPSA defines and governs "applicants". By contrast, FEECA defines and governs "utilities". Neither the PPSA nor Section 403.519 Florida Statutes, use the word "utility" as a defining entity and, thus, are not governed by the FEECA definition.

Second, FPC's assertion that "applicants" are the same as FEECA "retail utilities" utterly disregards the law relative to entities required to file need determinations under the PPSA. Section 366.82 of FEECA exempts small electric cooperatives and municipalities with sales of less than 2,000 gigawatt hours. The cities of Tallahassee, Lakeland and Kissimmee, and Seminole Electric Cooperative are all exempt from FEECA. Notwithstanding that, all four entities must file for need determinations with this Commission. The City of Lakeland currently has a petition for need determination pending before us. (Docket No. 990023–EM) The City of Kissimmee was granted a need determination in late 1998. (Docket No. 980802–EM, Order No. PSC–98–1301–FOF–EM, issued October 7, 1998) The City of Tallahassee was granted a need determination in the summer of 1997. (Docket No. 961512–EM, Order No. PSC–97–0659–FOF–EM, issued June 9, 1997) Seminole Electric Cooperative was granted a need determination in 1994. (Docket No. 931212–EC, Order No. PSC–94–0761–FOF–EC, issued June 21, 1994) Under FPC's construction of FEECA, none of these entities would have to file petitions for need determination. Clearly FPC's analysis is inconsistent with the requirements of the PPSA.

Third, the FPC's interchangeable definition argument ignores two fundamental tenets of statutory construction. When a definition of a word or phrase is provided in a statute, that meaning must be ascribed to the word or phrase whenever it is repeated in the statute unless contrary intent clearly appears. Vocelle v. Knight Brothers Paper Company, Inc., 118 So.2d 664 (Fla. 1st DCA 1960) In addition, when different definitions are provided for different sections, the distinctions must be presumed to be intentional. Florida State Racing Commission v. Bourquardez, 42 So.2d 87 (Fla. 1949) (The presence of a provision in one portion of a statute and its absence from another are an argument against reading it as implied by the section from which it is omitted). The greater weight of authority is clearly in favor of refraining from amending the statute by administrative decision as advocated by FPC. Thus, we hold that it is not necessary to be a retail electricity provider to be an applicant under the PPSA. . . .

The negative or dormant Commerce Clause prohibits state regulation that discriminates against, or unduly burdens interstate commerce thereby impeding free private trade in the national marketplace. General Motors Corporation v. Tracy, 519 U.S. 278 (1997). The crucial inquiry is determining whether a protectionist measure can fairly be viewed as protecting legitimate local concerns, with effects on interstate commerce that are only incidental. But, "where simple economic protectionism is effected by state legislation, a virtually per se rule of invalidity has been erected." City of Philadelphia v. New Jersey, 437 U.S. 617, 624 (1978). The dormant Commerce Clause restriction on state regulatory authority evolves from the Constitution and, therefore, applies even in the absence of any federal statute preempting a particular state regulation. Atlantic Coast Demolition & Recycling, Inc. v. Board of Chosen Freeholders of Atlantic County, 48 F.3d 701, 710 (3d Cir. 1995).

The parties argue animatedly either for or against application of the dormant Commerce Clause and federal preemption on the issue of whether an EWG can be required to enter into a contract with a retail utility before applying for a need determination. A contract requirement, opine Joint Petitioners, makes the regulated utilities the gatekeepers of the wholesale power market in Florida. Joint Petitioners and Amicus cite numerous United States Supreme Court cases in support of their position that such an application of state regulation is economic protectionism and per se invalid. FPL and FPC counter with a series of United States Supreme Court cases they allege validates their construction.

Having considered the well-reasoned arguments of counsel and authority cited by them, we find that while it is incumbent upon us to remain cognizant of Commerce Clause analysis, is not appropriate for us to reach a decision on the issue because there is insufficient evidence in the record to fully adjudicate it. Likewise, to arrive at a decision on the Motions To Dismiss, it is not necessary for us to reach a definitive conclusion on federal preemption. The decision as to whether Joint Petitioners are applicants for a need determination in the absence of a contract with a retail utility can be made by construing Florida's existing statutory, regulatory framework for retail and wholesale generation being mindful of, but without resort to, a finding of federal preemption.

[The portion of the Commission's order applying the criteria of the power plant siting act is deleted.]

DISSENTS

COMMISSIONER CLARK:

I dissent from the majority's decision to deny the Motions to Dismiss filed by Florida Power and Light Company (FPL) and Florida Power Corporation (FPC). Neither the legislative history of the Power Plant Siting Act, nor the logic and legal analysis of the majority's decision convinces me that Duke New Smyrna is a proper applicant for a determination of need. The Motions to Dismiss should be granted because Duke New Smyrna is not a proper applicant under Section 403.519, Florida Statutes.

The majority concludes that Duke New Smyrna is a "regulated electric company" and is therefore included in the definition of "applicant" in Section 403.503(13), Florida Statutes, which in turn applies to Section 403.519, Florida Statutes. Close inspection of legislative history and case law refutes this conclusion.

The Power Plant Siting Act was first enacted in 1973. The legislative intent for the Act recognized the need for a statewide perspective on the selection and utilization of sites for generating facilities given the "significant impact upon the welfare of the population, the location and growth of industry and the use of the natural resources of the state." 1973 Fla. Laws Section 1, Chapter 73–33. Initially, the Commission's role was simply to prepare a "report and recommendation as to the present and future needs for electrical generating capacity in the area to be served by the proposed site . . ." 1973 Fla. Laws Section 1, Chapter 73–33.

Then, in 1980, as part of the Florida Energy Efficiency and Conservation Act (FEECA), the Legislature changed the requirement of a "report and recommendation" to a proceeding resulting in a determination of need. Because of the rapid rise in the cost of electric power production resulting from the dual impact of inflation and effects of the Arab Oil Embargo, the Legislature found it in the public interest to vigorously pursue energy efficiency and conservation measures. The Legislature gave the Commission the responsibility of requiring utilities to pursue energy efficiency and conservation to reduce growth rates of consumption. As part of the responsibility to encourage energy efficiency and conservation, the Legislature required the Commission to increase its scrutiny of the need for prospective power plants. The Commission was directed to review proposed new plants to ensure that they were needed for system reliability and integrity, that their cost was reasonable and cost effective, and that the utility had undertaken all conservation measures that could reasonably be employed to mitigate the need for the new plant. 1980 Fla. Laws Section 5, Chapter 80–65. . . .

By seizing on the term "regulated" as including regulation by the FERC (and presumably regulation by any other governmental authority), the Commission is relying on a federal act, not the laws of Florida, for its authority. It is unlikely that the legislature delegated to the federal government the authority to determine who might come within the definition of applicant, but that is precisely the effect of the majority's decision. Duke New Smyrna is an Exempt Wholesale Generator (EWG), a category of electric generators that was created by the Energy Policy Act of 1992. Clearly, this category of generators was not in existence when the Power Plant Siting Act was created in 1973. Nonetheless, the majority concludes it is within the definition of applicant because the federal government has subsequently decided to authorize this category of generators.

This Commission has previously tried to rely on federal acts to broaden its authority, and the Florida Supreme Court overturned that decision. In Florida Power and Light Company v. Florida Public Service Commission, 5 FALR 227-J (4/4/83), 471 So. 2d 526 (Fla. 1985), the court reversed a decision adopting rules on the purchase of power from cogenerators and small power producers. The adoption of rules was precipitated by the Public Utilities Regulatory Policy Act enacted by Congress in 1978. The act directed FERC to adopt rules encouraging cogeneration but gave the states the task of implementing that policy particularly by setting the price to be paid by utilities for cogenerated energy. The court found the Commission lacked state statutory authority to implement the directives of PURPA.

The need for the Commission to give careful consideration to legislative authority is even more important today given the 1996 amendments to the [Florida] Administrative Procedures Act. The majority has acknowledged the need to further develop policy with respect to merchant plants. To codify that policy into rules will require specific authority. It will not be enough that the rules are reasonably related to enabling legislation or founded on an expression of legislative intent.

[*Opinion of Commissioner Jacobs, dissenting in part and concurring in part, is omitted.*]∎

NOTES AND COMMENTS

1. Two issues are raised by the Florida PSC in its opinion, but not discussed at length: 1) whether using a state siting statute to preclude approval of a merchant power plant owned by an out-of-state utility violates the dormant commerce clause; and 2) whether the federal policy of competition in the Energy Policy Act of 1992 preempts state consideration of nonenvironmental factors (e.g., reliability and "need") in power plant siting.

Regarding the Constitutional issues, one author concludes that, "While the dormant commerce clause may be a necessary limit on state ability to limit siting, [it] will invalidate only the most blatantly protectionist state regulations." Rossi, *supra,* at 17.

In its appeal of this decision, New Smyrna presented a challenge to the Florida state siting statute based on the dormant commerce clause, arguing that prohibiting Duke Energy, its out-of-state partner, "from applying directly for a need determination would violate the dormant Commerce Clause of the United States Constitution because such action would unconstitutionally discriminate against out-of-state commerce and burden interstate commerce." *Tampa Elec. Co. v. Garcia*, 767 So.2d 428 (Fla. 2000). In its appeal, New Smyrna also contended that the EPAct preempted Florida's requirement that Duke contract with a Florida retail utility to build its plant. *Id.* The Supreme Court of Florida rejected these arguments, stating, "We find no merit in the constitutional arguments advanced by New Smyrna. As to any alleged preemption or interference with interstate commerce, we find that power-plant siting and need determination are areas that Congress has expressly left to the states." *Id.*

2. For further discussion of this case, *see* Jeffery S. Dennis, Federalism, Electric Industry Restructuring, and the Dormant Commerce Clause: *Tampa Electric Co. v. Garcia* and State Restrictions on the Development of Merchant Power Plants, 43 Nat. Resources J. 615 (2003).

3. To many commentators, the reason for applying the dormant commerce clause to override state siting policies is simple: state policies have the effect of creating a parochial climate in which only benefits to individual states are considered, even though projects may benefit the nation as a whole. Professor Richard Pierce cites *Tampa Electric Co. v. Garcia* as one situation (among others) where states are using "a wide variety of subtle and not so subtle means to protect their utilities from having to compete with other electricity wholesalers" and therefore impeding progress toward electricity restructuring. He criticizes Florida because it "refuses to authorize construction of merchant generating plants ... With no non-utility generating plants and limited transmission capacity allowed into the state, competition in the wholesale market is ineffective." Pierce, *supra*.

4. Is *Tampa Electric Co. v. Garcia* an example of the well-known national trend of "NIMBY-ism," in which projects can easily be stopped or (perhaps) diverted elsewhere by local or state opposition? The "environmental justice" movement—one response to "NIMBY-ism"—arose in large part due to studies pointing out that often-unwanted facilities such as landfills and power lines were situated disproportionally in states and areas that do not have the political muscle to object to them. *See* Vicki Been, What's Fairness Got to Do With It? Environmental Justice and the Siting of Locally Undesirable Land Uses, 78 Cornell L. Rev. 1001 (1993).

5. A number of authors have argued that FERC's jurisdiction over siting issues should be expanded by statute. *See* Rossi, *supra*; Pierce, *supra*. One commentator noted that federal power over siting has worked well for the natural gas industry, and similar authority could be invoked to promote new electricity transmission projects. Cassandra Burke Robertson, Bringing the Camel into the Tent: State and Federal Power Over Electricity Transmission, 49 Clev. St. L. Rev. 71 (2001).

Section 1221 of the Energy Policy Act of 2005 added a new section 216 to the Federal Power Act on siting. Here is part of that proposed new section:

SEC. 216. SITING OF INTERSTATE ELECTRIC TRANSMISSION FACILITIES.

"(a) Designation of National Interest Electric Transmission Corridors.—(1) Not later than 1 year after the date of enactment of this section and every 3 years thereafter, the Secretary of Energy (referred to in this section as the 'Secretary'), in consultation with affected States, shall conduct a study of electric transmission congestion.

"(2) After considering alternatives and recommendations from interested parties (including an opportunity for comment from affected States), the Secretary shall issue a report, based on the study, which may designate any geographic area experiencing electric energy transmission capacity constraints or congestion that adversely affects consumers as a national interest electric transmission corridor....

"(4) In determining whether to designate a national interest electric transmission corridor under paragraph (2), the Secretary may consider whether—

"(A) the economic vitality and development of the corridor, or the end markets served by the corridor, may be constrained by lack of adequate or reasonably priced electricity;

"(B)(i) economic growth in the corridor, or the end markets served by the corridor, may be jeopardized by reliance on limited sources of energy; and

"(ii) a diversification of supply is warranted;

"(C) the energy independence of the United States would be served by the designation;

"(D) the designation would be in the interest of national energy policy; and

"(E) the designation would enhance national defense and homeland security.

"(b) Construction Permit.—Except as provided in subsection (i), the Commission may, after notice and an opportunity for hearing, issue 1 or more permits for the construction or modification of electric transmission facilities in a national interest electric transmission corridor designated by the Secretary under subsection (a) if the Commission finds that—

"(1)(A) a State in which the transmission facilities are to be constructed or modified does not have authority to—

"(i) approve the siting of the facilities; or

"(ii) consider the interstate benefits expected to be achieved by the proposed construction or modification of transmission facilities in the State;

"(B) the applicant for a permit is a transmitting utility under this Act but does not qualify to apply for a permit or siting approval for the proposed project in a State because the applicant does not serve end-use customers in the State; or

"(C) a State commission or other entity that has authority to approve the siting of the facilities has—

"(i) withheld approval for more than 1 year after the filing of an application seeking approval pursuant to applicable law or 1 year after the designation of the relevant national interest electric transmission corridor, whichever is later; or

"(ii) conditioned its approval in such a manner that the proposed construction or modification will not significantly reduce transmission congestion in interstate commerce or is not economically feasible;

"(2) the facilities to be authorized by the permit will be used for the transmission of electric energy in interstate commerce;

"(3) the proposed construction or modification is consistent with the public interest;

"(4) the proposed construction or modification will significantly reduce transmission congestion in interstate commerce and protects or benefits consumers;

"(5) the proposed construction or modification is consistent with sound national energy policy and will enhance energy independence; and

"(6) the proposed modification will maximize, to the extent reasonable and economical, the transmission capabilities of existing towers or structures.

How would this provision affect FERC's existing authority to deal with a state that refused to approve a transmission line siting proposal, if the proposal was intended to alleviate congestion in the transmission system? As you read the following case study of the Cross Sound Cable, consider whether this provision would have affected the outcome.

2. CASE STUDY: THE CROSS SOUND CABLE

The 330–MW power cable under Long Island Sound between Connecticut and New York's Long Island, proposed by the Massachusetts-based company TransEnergie U.S. (owned by Canadian utility Hydro–Quebec), was the first proposal for a "merchant transmission" line (built by a private company) in the nation. After the summer heat waves of 1999, power supply on Long Island became a major issue, and the Long Island Power Authority utility invited power producers to build new plants on Long Island. TransEnergie offered a different source of power: access to relatively inexpensive power in New England. It would create a subsidiary (the Cross Sound Cable Company) that would build a transmission line under Long Island Sound at its own expense and rent capacity on the line to the utility. FERC welcomed the Cross Sound Cable as a necessary development in a competitive environment. However, the project generated opposition, most notably from Connecticut's Attorney General, Richard Blumenthal.

Five years after it had been proposed, an agreement was signed to allow the cable to begin operation, but this development had not taken place without considerable controversy and project delay.

Regional Energy Reliability and Security: DOE Authority to Energize the Cross Sound Cable

U.S. House of Representatives, Energy and Commerce Committee, Hearing of the Subcommittee on Energy and Air Quality.
(May 19, 2004).

Testimony of Jeffrey A. Donahue, President and CEO, Cross Sound Company, LLC

II.   DESCRIPTION OF THE CROSS SOUND CABLE

The CSC is a 330 megawatt bi-directional, high voltage direct current and fiber optic cable system that runs under Long Island Sound and can transmit electricity in either direction between New Haven, Connecticut and Brookhaven, Long Island, New York. CSC LLC commissioned the Project in August 2002. CSC LLC is a joint venture between TransÉnergie U.S. Ltd., a wholly-owned subsidiary of Hydro–Québec, and United Capital Investments, Inc., a non-regulated business unit of UIL Holdings, Inc., which owns the United Illuminating Company, a regulated utility in Connecticut.

III.   HISTORY OF THE CROSS SOUND CABLE

On June 1, 2000, the Federal Energy Regulatory Commission ("FERC") granted the CSC project sponsors the first-of-its-kind authorization to make sales of electric transmission capacity in interstate commerce at negotiated rates. TransEnergie U.S. Ltd., 91 FERC ¶ 61,230 (2000). FERC granted this authorization because the full financial risk for the project costs is borne by the developer (i.e., CSC LLC) rather than captive ratepayers, and because the project "enhances competition and market integration by expanding capacity and trading opportunities between the New England and New York markets." Pursuant to an "open season" auction process, the Long Island Power Authority ("LIPA") subscribed to the full capacity of the CSC.

CSC LLC then began the process to obtain the required state and federal permits. The New York State Public Service Commission ("NYPSC") granted a certificate of environmental compatibility and public need on June 27, 2001, finding that the CSC will "enhance regional and local competition in the electric power industry and [] improve system reliability." The Connecticut Siting Council ("Siting Council") followed suit on January 3, 2002, finding that "the proposed project would enhance the inter-regional electric transmission infrastructure and improve the reliability and efficiencies of the electric system here in Connecticut as well as in New York."

Then, in March 2002, the U.S. Army Corps of Engineers ("Army Corps") and Connecticut Department of Environmental Protection ("DEP") issued the necessary permits for CSC LLC to install the Project. The permits each included an identical condition that, within the Federal Navigation Channel ("Federal Channel") in New Haven Harbor, the Project's cable system must be buried to a depth no less than the deeper of six feet below the seabed or 48 feet below mean lower low water. The reason for this requirement was to accommodate the possible future deepening of the Federal Channel by the Army Corps, although the Army Corps currently has no plans to deepen the Federal Channel. ... For the areas outside the Federal Channel, the Army Corps and DEP permits required cable system burial depths of at least 4 feet and 6 feet, respectively, below the seabed of the Sound....

IV. OPERATION OF THE CSC PROVIDES SIGNIFICANT AND SUBSTANTIAL BENEFITS TO CONNECTICUT, NEW YORK AND THE REGION

Upon being energized pursuant to the Secretary of Energy's orders in the wake of the August 2003 blackout, the CSC assisted in restoring power to and stabilizing the transmission system in the northeastern United States. The Secretary's order allowed the CSC to transmit and deliver power and to provide critical voltage support and stabilization services to the transmission systems in Connecticut and New York....

Since September 1, 2003, the CSC has been operating with excellent consistency and has been recognized for its value in ensuring a reliable power supply in both Connecticut and New York. ISO–New England (the independent operator of the New England transmission system) directs the operators of the CSC when to transmit power over the CSC and when to provide (simultaneously or separately) voltage support to the neighboring transmission systems. The inherent capability of the high voltage direct current cable system allows it to act immediately and automatically to help smooth out the aftershocks of electric system spikes and other disturbances in Connecticut and New York, which in turn lowers the risk of other transmission lines switching off and magnifying a system problem.

While the CSC operated full time pursuant to the DOE order, CSC LLC responded to 108 requests by ISO–New England and 9 requests by the New York Independent System Operator ("NYISO") to help maintain a steady operating voltage on the Connecticut and New York transmission systems, respectively. Importantly, the CSC's capability to respond to these grid operators' requests for voltage stabilization not only provides reliability benefit, but also provides environmental benefit, as it reduces the need to start up less efficient and dirtier power plants (including plants in New Haven) that would otherwise be needed to provide the same level of service....

In addition to stabilizing the regional transmission system, the CSC has been used as an operating reserve in times of power scarcity. In fact, when Connecticut's energy supply was at dangerously low levels during an extreme cold spell in January 2004, the CSC was on standby at ISO–New England's request to export 200 megawatts over the CSC from Long Island to Connecticut. ... Southwest Connecticut has been widely identified as one of the most transmission-deficient and capacity-constrained areas in the U.S. transmission system. Long Island has exported power to Southwest Connecticut many times in the past, including during the July 2, 2002 heat wave, using the existing "1385" submarine cable between Norwalk, Connecticut and Northport, New York. Last fall, ISO–New England and NYISO coordinated a successful test that sent power from New England over the Cross Sound Cable to Long Island while simultaneously returning power from Long Island over the 1385 cable to Connecticut.

Energy exports out of New England have no impact on the reliability of the New England system. In fact, ISO–New England will not schedule any exports out of New England if the transfer of such power would degrade the reliability of the New England system. Energy flows over the CSC are jointly controlled by the NYISO and ISO–New England under the same reliability rules applied to all other interconnections between New York and New England. Under those rules, energy flows over any transmission line will only occur if such flows do not jeopardize the electric system of the exporting region....

[The] CSC is expected to provide reliability and economic benefits of approximately $40 million per year to electricity market participants in New York and New England.... Clearly, the public interest benefits of the continued operation of the CSC are tangible and substantial ... Regulatory agencies with direct responsibility and jurisdiction over the CSC have recognized the significant economic benefits to Connecticut provided by the CSC. These independent agencies include the Connecticut Siting Council, the FERC, and the NYPSC.

The Connecticut Siting Council, after a full consideration and review, unanimously concluded that the CSC would provide a public benefit to Connecticut. Specifically, the Siting Council found that "the wholesale price of electricity in New England should not increase with the export of up to 330 MW of electricity from Connecticut to Long Island." The Siting Council further found that the CSC "could increase the competition and markets available to electric generators in New England and Long Island" and that "an open competitive market for electricity, enhanced by the increased capability for trade [provided by the CSC], will result in increased private investment in infrastructure, and lower electricity costs for the region." Further evidence of the CSC's benefits to Connecticut is the FERC's approval of the CSC. In its order approving rates for the CSC, FERC stated that the CSC "enhances competition and market integration by expanding capacity and trading opportunities between the New England and New York markets." FERC further found that the CSC "will provide benefits to electric consumers and producers in both markets while impos-ing no risk or cost on captive customers in any market."

V. OPERATION OF THE CSC HAS NO ENVIRONMENTAL OR NAVI-GATIONAL IMPACT

Both Federal and State agencies have confirmed that operation of the CSC "as is where is" neither causes any harm to the environment nor poses any threat to navigation. Specifically, neither the Army Corps nor the DEP have raised any environmental or substantive objection to operating the CSC at its current depth. DEP itself describes its objection as procedur-al, driven by a concern about the scope of Connecticut's legislative morato-rium on Long Island Sound energy projects, not by environmental is-sues. . . .

The Army Corps has determined that operation of the cable as install-ed would cause no environmental harm or interference with navigation. Accordingly, the Army Corps has expressly authorized operation of the CSC while CSC LLC continues work toward attaining the required depth. . . .

The DEP made a similar determination of no environmental harm from operation of the cable system as installed. Shortly after CSC LLC notified DEP that the cable could not buried to the permitted depth in a few locations, DEP Commissioner Arthur J. Rocque responded in a June 13, 2002 letter to a letter from Richard Blumenthal, Attorney General of Connecticut, by placing the environmental impacts in appropriate perspec-tive and expressing his concern about the "published rhetoric" about such impacts:

I would be remiss if I did not note my disappointment in your characterization of the impacts associated with both the installation of the cable and the failure to attain greater depths in part of the federal channel as serious, critical and devastating environmental impacts. . . . From an environmental perspective, this cable project pales in comparison to even maintenance dredging of the federal navigational channel in New Haven Harbor. . . . [P]ublished rhetoric has eclipsed facts on this project, at least from an environmental impact standpoint.

However, in contrast to the Army Corps, the DEP stated that, as a matter of procedure, it would not permit operation of the CSC while CSC LLC was endeavoring to meet the burial depth requirements. Nor would the DEP permit CSC LLC to work to meet the burial depth requirement. According to the DEP, the Connecticut legislative moratorium on agency consideration of proposed crossings of Long Island Sound by utility projects (including interstate transmission lines) prevents DEP from allowing CSC LLC (by permit modification or by new permit) either to continue working to meet the burial condition or to allow operation of the CSC in its current location—effectively denying CSC LLC any recourse to the gradual loss of its permit rights. The CSC had by this time become a highly politicized project in Connecticut. As a result, while construction was completed and there remained no substantive objections to operation of the CSC, the CSC had not operated for an entire year until directed to do so by DOE's post-blackout orders. . . .

VI. CONNECTICUT'S "CATCH–22" EFFECTIVELY BLOCKS OPERATION OF THE CSC WITHOUT REGARD TO THE PROJECT'S SUBSTANTIAL BENEFITS, LACK OF IMPACTS, AND CSC LLC'S RIGHTS UNDER THE PROJECT'S PERMITS

CSC LLC has submitted five (5) separate proposals to DEP to either bury the cable to its permitted depth or operate the CSC in its current location with no environmental impact. Despite acknowledging the lack of environmental impacts from operation, DEP has refused to let CSC LLC either bury the cable system deeper or operate, thus creating the classic "Catch 22" situation in which CSC LLC finds itself, as outlined below. Connecticut enacted legislation specifically targeted to prevent CSC from complying with its permits and block the Project from operating. While preventing CSC LLC from complying with or seeking waiver from its permits, Connecticut contemporaneously authorized a major dredging project in the same harbor (New Haven) with exponentially larger environmental impacts, and supports a plan to dump dredge spoils in Long Island Sound.

In the spring of 2002, while the Connecticut Attorney General's appeal of the Siting Council approval of the CSC was pending (and ultimately dismissed), the Connecticut legislature passed Public Act 02–7 ("P.A. 02–7"), which enacted a moratorium on the consideration of new applications for electric transmission cables and gas pipelines crossing the Sound and, moreover, retroactively voided permits already granted for electric transmission cables (but not gas pipelines) that had not yet been installed—which was Cross Sound Cable's situation at that time. The class of entities affected by the retroactive provision was a class of one: Cross Sound Cable. The Governor of Connecticut vetoed P.A. 02–7 on April 19, 2002, recognizing in his formal veto message the grave constitutional infirmities of "unfairly penaliz[ing] a company that has followed the [agency approval] process set up by the General Assembly." The legislature sustained the veto on April 24, 2002.

The legislature then revised the vetoed act and passed a new bill, now Public Act 02–95 ("P.A. 02–95" or the "Moratorium Law"). The Governor signed P.A. 02–95 on June 3, 2002, and the law went into effect on that date, after CSC LLC had obtained all necessary permits to install and operate the cable, and after its initial burial of the cable was completed on May 28, 2002. The Moratorium Law forbade state agencies from "consider[ing] or render[ing] a final decision for any applications relating to electric power line crossings, gas pipeline crossings or telecommunications crossings of Long Island Sound" for one year from the effective date of the statute, during which period a task force was to complete a comprehensive environmental assessment and plan. The law provided that after the task force completed its work, "[a]ny application for an electric power line . . . crossing of Long Island Sound that is considered by any state agency" is to be additionally evaluated based on the results of the task force's study.

The task force released its report on June 3, 2003—the day the moratorium was set to expire. On June 26, 2003, Connecticut enacted legislation that extended the original one-year duration of the moratorium another full year to June 2004. In September 2003, subsequent to the energization of the CSC pursuant to the Secretary of Energy's orders after the August 14, 2003 blackout, Connecticut Governor Rowland called for an evaluation of the impacts of operating the CSC in its present location. DEP responded on October 31, 2003 by issuing a request for proposals from consulting firms to provide an evaluation of the impacts of operating the CSC in its present location. The deadline for responses to this solicitation was December 2003; however, to our knowledge DEP has yet to select a consultant to perform this evaluation. Finally, just this month (May 5), the Connecticut legislature again extended the moratorium by another full year, to June 2005. The Connecticut legislature approved extension of the moratorium in spite of the opposition from both the DEP and the Connecticut Department of Public Utility Control ("DPUC").

Testimony of Richard Blumenthal, Attorney General, State of Connecticut

The Cross–Sound Cable ... threatens to divide us and endanger vital common interests. These pet projects of major energy companies, if spared careful long-range planning and vigorous scrutiny, may wreak havoc in Long Island Sound. We must seek regional cooperation—not confrontation and conflict. We share critical environmental and consumer values, much as we share Long Island Sound, a precious and precarious natural treasure.

Connecticut has been willing to assist Long Island in addressing its electricity shortfalls. We have actively sought to upgrade the existing 1385 cable from Norwalk to Northport in order to stop damaging pollution caused by the present damaged oil-leaking cable. This upgrade will significantly increase the amount of electricity available to Long Island from this cable line. We are also building a 345 KV transmission from Bethel, Connecticut on the border of New York to Norwalk, Connecticut, the site of the 1385 cable. Finally, the Connecticut Siting Council and the Connecticut Department of Environmental Protection approved permits for the Cross–Sound Cable, provided it met strict safety and environmental protection standards.

This subcommittee should work to develop legislation that encourages public officials to build consensus and to jointly and fairly share the burdens and benefits of siting efficient and environmentally-sound generating and transmission facilities. It should not support hasty, ill-considered suggestions to jettison a carefully crafted and well established state-federal permitting program that has worked effectively for decades.

Regional cooperation and long-range planning to provide safe, efficient and reliable electric power is obviously a desirable goal, which I fully support. Three core conditions are essential to any regional plan or system:

1. The plan must recognize that states are best positioned and equipped to evaluate and assess all of the environmental and economic impacts of specific projects.

2. Insofar as a plan imposes direct or indirect costs on ratepayers in one state to help support reliability elsewhere, the benefits of the plan should be shared by ratepayers in both states. The system must be totally transparent and accountable to the states, not just federal regulators. Indeed state consent and advice must be at its core. Consensus is a key precondition, achieved by state agreement and support, not federal edict or preemption.

3. Any plan must respect the fact that states own—indeed, actually hold legal title to—the seabed of Long Island Sound in a public trust, as they have since the founding of the Republic. This public trust means that the federal and state governments must seek to minimize or eliminate environmental disruption or damage.

The Cross Sound Cable, unfortunately, has so far failed to meet any of these three core conditions. It poses real dangers to Long Island Sound and to economically critical shipping and navigation. It effectively robs Connecticut ratepayers to subsidize Long Island's failure to plan and meet its energy needs, and it attempts to wrest legal control of the Connecticut seabed away from its protection as a "public trust" under state and federal law.

In fact, the Cross–Sound Cable, in its present state, suffers from numerous critical flaws, including the following:

- It creates a serious and substantial hazard to economically critical shipping and navigation.

- It poses a severe threat to the environment by the need to blast the seabed in order to place the cable at the federally required depth.

- It is patently illegal.

- It costs Connecticut ratepayers millions of dollars to unfairly subsidize Long Island ratepayers and the cable owners.

- It undermines incentives for Long Island to meet its obvious and growing energy needs, while Connecticut is taking the tough steps needed for safe and reliable electric supply.

- It provides negligible reliability benefits to Connecticut.

Shipping and navigation in New Haven Harbor is critical to Connecticut's economy. About 75% of our critical supplies of gasoline and fuel oil arrive by this route. In 2002, the United States Army Corps of Engineers (Army Corps) approved the first ever longitudinal laying of cable in a navigational channel—in the center of New Haven Harbor's federal navigation channel only after Cross–Sound agreed to a number of conditions. The conditions were to mitigate the possibility that a ship might accidentally drop an anchor onto the cable—such incidents have occurred many times in Long Island Sound, some disastrously—or some other navigational accident. The Army Corps, therefore, ordered the cable sunk a minimum of 6 feet below the Long Island Sound seabed, a depth that Cross–Sound accepted as both feasible and appropriate. This depth requirement is not arbitrary. It is needed to ensure navigational safety in the most important energy supply port in the region. . . .

Following this determination of the Army Corps, the Connecticut Department of Environmental Protection, acting under state and federal law, approved a permit allowing the construction of the cable as long as the construction was consistent with the Army Corps six foot depth requirement.

Cross–Sound, after agreeing to meet this important safety condition, failed to do so, claiming that unanticipated obstructions prevented its compliance with the permit requirement. These supposed unanticipated obstructions included bedrock ledge—well and widely known for many years. . . .

Connecticut refused to issue a permit to operate the cable because it failed to meet the federal safety standard. Connecticut's Department of Environmental Protection has treated Cross–Sound Cable like any other applicant that fails to meet permit conditions required to safeguard the environment and public safety. Despite Cross–Sound's efforts, the Army Corps has steadfastly refused to weaken the 6 foot requirement.

Turning to the second problem—environmental damage—the company concedes that the only way to bury the cable to a safe depth in the harbor would be by blasting the bed of the Sound, drilling holes in the bedrock, filling them with explosives such as dynamite or ammonium nitrate fuel oil and detonating it. In addition, the National Marine Fisheries Service has required as part of its permit for the Cross–Sound Cable that such cable be buried at least 4 feet below the sea floor in order to minimize adverse impacts to essential fish habitat. The cable does not currently meet this requirement.

As to the illegality of the cable, the violation is clear. The relevant Federal law—section 404 of the Clean Water Act—appropriately gives Connecticut the legal authority to protect its coastal waters by setting conditions before issuing permits for cable construction. As I have explained, Cross–Sound agreed to and then failed to meet a critical condition—burial at least six feet under the seafloor.

Under the Federal Power Act, the Secretary of Energy has the legal authority to override this law, but only in a genuine emergency. In the past, when the Secretary has invoked this power briefly in a genuine emergency, I have not opposed it. Unfortunately, after the August, 2003 blackout ended, Secretary Abraham attempted to use it as an excuse to order the indefinite routine operation of the Cross–Sound Cable. He did so knowing that the cause of the blackout related to the Midwest power grid, and that no evidence has ever existed that the presence or absence of the Cross–Sound cable connection had anything to do with the blackout. Only after I challenged his order in court, and only days before I was scheduled to seek a stay of his order from the Second Circuit Court of Appeals, did

Secretary Abraham rescind his illegal and unjustified order, effectively conceding its illegality. . . .

Long Island's current power deficit is entirely of its own making. LIPA has failed to develop and build new generating and transmission facilities—not one major plant in more than 10 years—or develop any long term plans. LIPA admitted that it seeks to increase power transmission to Long Island in order to avoid building needed generators on Long Island. LIPA looks to everyone else to site its power plants—a classic NIMBY approach.

In contrast to LIPA, the State of Connecticut has recently developed more than 2,000 megawatts of additional electrical power and is upgrading approximately one hundred miles of transmission lines to more efficiently move electricity throughout the state. The idea that Connecticut ratepayers should be effectively compelled to subsidize LIPA's arrogant improvidence is completely unacceptable, even outrageous.

. . . No one disputes the Secretary of Energy's existing legal authority to act quickly in a real emergency to prevent a blackout on Long Island. In fact, Cross Sound seeks to operate the cable routinely, moving electric voltage to Long Island and money to itself. It offers no answer to Long Island's self-inflicted problems.

Congress should learn from our experience with the Cross–Sound Cable and enact common-sense energy policies that would require public officials to build consensus and jointly and fairly share the burdens and benefits of siting efficient and environmentally sound generating and transmission facilities.■

NOTES AND COMMENTS

1.   On June 24, 2004, Cross Sound Company, New York, and Connecticut (through the DPUC) reached a settlement allowing for reenergizing of the Cross Sound Cable. However, Attorney General Blumenthal opposed this settlement, and the Cable "remains in a state of legal limbo." Pierce, *supra*.

Professor Pierce points to the Cross Sound case as an example of the need for federal policy on siting of transmission lines:

The [Cross Sound] case illustrates well the difficulty of attempting to reduce transmission constraints into load pockets. The New York metropolitan area, including Long Island, is a classic load pocket that is subject to severe and growing transmission constraints . . .

[The] fate of the Cross–Sound project has sent a clear message to anyone else who was considering whether to propose a transmission expansion project to reduce the transmission bottlenecks into the New York Metropolitan area. That message is: don't even think about it. Given the powerful opposition to all above-ground transmission lines, underwater lines were viewed as the only hope to reduce the extreme level of transmission congestion into the New York metropolitan area. If a project sponsor cannot even convince state authorities to allow it to operate a critically-needed underwater transmission line in circumstances in which every agency has determined that activation of the line will have no adverse effect on the environment, other transmission expansion projects have no realistic chance of being approved.

The conflict between state and local environmental regulation of transmission lines and pursuit of national energy goals is already costing consumers many billions of dollars per year. If it is not resolved in the near future, it will produce even higher electricity costs and frequent blackouts. The conflict can be eliminated by conferring on a federal agency or federal courts authority to override the decisions of state and local governments when those decisions interfere with pursuit of national energy policy goals.

Id.

2. Would the new section 216 of the Federal Power Act have given FERC the authority to force energizing of the Cross Sound Cable?

3. Getting the Cable energized was expensive for TransEnergie:

For TransEnergie, the victory had come at a high cost—about $20 million in legal bills, lobbying efforts, and extra engineering costs on top of the cable's original $125 million price tag, not to mention lost momentum in its bid to lead the emerging merchant transmission market.

TransEnergie: Playing Two Power Games, Technology Review, Apr. 2005, at 32.

4. FERC Commissioner Joseph T. Kelliher calls for performance-based rates and other incentives to encourage transmission investment. Joseph T. Kelliher, The Need for Mandatory Electric Reliability Standards and Greater Transmission Investment, 39 U. Rich. L. Rev. 717 (2005). Commissioner Kelliher is not sanguine about the prospects for merchant transmission projects, however, citing the Cross Sound Cable and other examples. *Id.*

CHAPTER 14

Nuclear Energy

A. THE EARLY DEVELOPMENT OF NUCLEAR POWER

The growing nuclear weapon capabilities of Asian countries have brought renewed media attention to nuclear energy. But although peaceful uses of nuclear power attract less attention, nuclear energy continues to be used throughout the world for a wide variety of purposes ranging from nuclear medicine to the generation of electricity in nuclear power plants.

Radiation has only been known since 1895 when Wilhelm Roentgen discovered X-rays. David Bodansky, Nuclear Energy: Principles, Practices and Prospects 57 (Springer–Verlag, 2d ed., 2004.) Nuclear energy in explosive form was first brought into being in the latter days of World War Two when the atomic bomb was invented and then quickly used against the Japanese cities of Hiroshima and Nagasaki. In retrospect, these events made "environmental" concerns a serious domestic issue for the first time, as Judge Richard Cudahy recalls:

> In the war years, a healthy environment was one free of five hundred pound bombs and long-range artillery fire. There was a flickering of concern about radioactivity when A-bombs and H-bombs began exploding. In fact, I think in principle nuclear explosions raised the basic environmental question. Here was an awesome source of primal energy released by sophisticated human calculation, but spreading a whole battery of mysterious and severe health hazards in its wake.

Richard D. Cudahy, Coming of Age in the Environment, 30 Envtl. L. 15 (2000).

In the aftermath of the war, the United States emphasized the importance of peaceful uses of atomic energy. One of the most obvious possibilities was the use of nuclear fission as a source of heat for commercial power plants. In the years immediately following the war, the United States was the only nation that had demonstrated its ability to create nuclear fission. The government hoped that it could maintain that monopoly, but it soon became apparent that the Soviet Union was also capable of producing nuclear weapons. As nuclear capabilities spread, the United States gave up hope of isolating nuclear technology and decided to encourage the spread of peaceful uses of nuclear energy. The "Atoms for Peace" program, initiated by President Eisenhower shortly after his election, transferred nuclear technology from the military to private companies that began to specialize in power plant construction, such as Westinghouse, General Electric, and Babcock & Wilcox.

From the outset, the federal government regulated all domestic uses of this energy under the Atomic Energy Act of 1954, 42 U.S.C. § 2011 et seq., which encouraged the private development of nuclear power as regulated by the Atomic Energy Commission (now the Nuclear Regulatory Commission). In 1957, Congress passed the Price–Anderson Act, which capped the liability of private companies and provided federal reinsurance for the nuclear industry. It not only limits liabilities arising out of any "nuclear incident or precautionary evacuation," 42 U.S.C. § 2014(w), it also provides a mechanism for consolidating all claims in the nature of "any public liability action arising out of or resulting from a nuclear accident" in a single federal court proceeding. 42 U.S.C. § 2210(n)(2). Congress extended these protections until the end of 2025 in Section 602 of the Energy Policy Act of 2005.

The first American nuclear power plant came on line in 1957 in Shippingport, Pennsylvania, near Pittsburgh. Stephen E. Atkins, Historical Encyclopedia of Atomic Energy 329–330 (Greenwood Press, 2000). In the late 1950s and early 1960s some three dozen small nuclear plants were built in various parts of the world. Initial experience with these plants suggested that the resulting cost of nuclear power would decline steadily with improvements in the technology. In the mid–1960s, optimistic supporters of nuclear power extrapolated that decline into the future and bragged that soon nuclear power would be "too cheap to meter."

Power companies throughout the world then rushed to jump on the bandwagon. From 1965 until 1975, they ordered almost 300 nuclear power plants. Companies in Japan, Sweden, Britain, France, Germany and Canada joined four big American companies in the race to build nuclear plants as fast as the orders could be filled. In the United States, nuclear power was seen as an important element in the ability of America to maintain energy self-reliance. With existing and potential regional wars disrupting world trade, American industry was increasingly nervous about its growing reliance on oil that had to be imported from the Middle East.

Ample deposits of uranium, the metal used to make nuclear power plant fuel, were found in Southeast Utah, where huge piles of tailings along the bed of the Colorado River remain as the residue of mines and mills that produced uranium oxide. The uranium oxide is enriched to increase the percentage of the isotope uranium 235 and eventually transformed into "fuel rods" that produce the heat that boils water and creates steam that drives the turbines that generate electricity. The boilers and turbines, two of the main elements of a nuclear power plant, are essentially the same as those in all other steam generating plants. It is in the source of the heat that creates the steam that the nuclear power plant is unique.

The uniqueness of nuclear power's heat source did not go unnoticed. Throughout this period the United States was continuing to develop and test nuclear weapons, including a "hydrogen bomb" that far exceeded the power of the weapons used on Japan in 1945. Moreover, other nations including the Soviet Union, China and France were actively testing such weapons.

Public reaction to nuclear power plants was initially dominated by patriotic pride in American technology that submerged the nagging fears about accidental or hostile misuse of the power. As the public became aware of the long range impact of radiation sickness on residents of Hiroshima and Nagasaki, the fear of nuclear power plants began to spread more widely in the United States, and an increasing number of people began to doubt their safety.

The Nuclear Regulatory Commission, created by the Energy Reorganization Act of 1974, (codified as amended at 42 U.S.C.A. §§ 5801–79), reacted to the growing doubts about the risks associated with nuclear power by repeatedly adding new safety requirements, which were often applied to plants already under construction. The procedures for licensing of new plants involved a multitude of layers, and the NRC responded to anti-nuclear groups by permitting them to intervene at many stages of the process.

In addition, the wild fluctuations in the costs of competing energy sources that took place during this period caused electricity users to institute conservation measures, thus reducing the demand for electricity. This made some of the power plants under construction appear to be unnecessary, and a number of plants were canceled before they were completed.

The utilities were forced to raise electric rates sharply during this period, both to cover the costs of the nuclear plants and the rise in the prices of other fuels. Consumer resistance to these increases put great pressure on state utility commissions, which often forced utility shareholders to swallow expenditures for plants that went dramatically over budget or were never completed. The result was that many electric utilities were forced to cut dividends and face the wrath of both unhappy shareholders and unhappy customers. And their attempts to challenge regulatory cutbacks in court proved fruitless after the Supreme Court's *Duquesne* decision (p. 101 *supra*).

The events of September 11, 2001, have brought back fears of nuclear war that had been almost forgotten during the 1990s. In 1945, initial attention focused on the explosive power of the nuclear reaction, which was awesome. But as the stories of radiation sickness from Japan became better known, attention shifted to the invisible nature of nuclear radiation. People became aware that there could be "something in the air" that you could not see or feel but could cause lingering, painful death. This awareness had a powerful impact on the development of environmental policy generally. In 2000, Congress passed the Radiation Exposure Compensation Act (P.L. 106–245) belatedly establishing procedures to provide compensation for people who suffered radiation damage from early development and testing of nuclear weapons. Recent fears about a "dirty bomb," which would spread radiation without the powerful explosion that accompanies nuclear weapons, has renewed those concerns.

B. THE FUTURE OF NUCLEAR POWER

In 2002, nuclear power provided about 16% of the world's electricity. The world's nuclear industry operates a total of 443 commercial nuclear generating units with a total capacity of about 364.9 gigawatts. David Bodansky, Nuclear Energy: Principles, Practices and Prospects 177 (Springer–Verlag, 2d ed., 2004). In the United States, the first generation of nuclear power plants in the United States are providing about 20% of the nation's electricity. The American nuclear industry now needs to decide what to do in the future.

1. RELICENSING AND EXPANSION OF EXISTING NUCLEAR PLANTS

In the early 1990s it was generally assumed that most nuclear power plants would be closed and dismantled when the original terms of their licenses ran out early in the 21st century. Although a few plants have closed, many more plant owners are applying for extension of the licensing term through the NRC's relicensing process set forth in 10 CFR Part 52. As of August 3, 2004, there were 104 commercial nuclear generating units fully licensed by the NRC to operate in the United States. The last reactor to come on line in the United States was the Watt's Bar reactor in Tennessee in May 1996. Nevertheless, US commercial nuclear capacity has increased in recent years through a combination of license extensions and uprating (upgrading) of existing reactors. http://www.eia.doe.gov/cneaf/nuclear/page/nuc_reactors/reactsum.html (a. June 8, 2005).

As of February, 2005, completed applications for license renewal had been filed for 14 reactors, 9 more were under staff review, and the NRC had received letters of intent for 23 more license renewal applications.[1]

U.S. commercial nuclear capacity has also increased in recent years through a combination of license extensions and uprating (upgrading of the reactor's maximum output) of existing reactors. Although the uprates are usually less than 10 percent, they are quite significant in the aggregate. If all of the proposals are implemented, nuclear capacity would increase by more than the construction of any new reactor design now under consideration.   http://www.eia.doe.gov/cneaf/nuclear/page/nuc_reactors/reactsum html (a 2–19–05). Applicants are "taking advantage of NRC's more flexible 'risk-informed, performance-based' regulatory posture to apply for relief from overly conservative requirements that can be shown ... to have minimal safety benefit." The agency's new policy considers "the probability and consequence of a potential safety problem, together with other factors," such as operating experience, in its "risk-informed regulation." Neil J. Numark & Robert D. MacDougall, Nuclear Power in Deregulated Markets, 14 Tulane Envtl. L. J. 463, 472–73 (2001).

2.   NEW POWER PLANT CONSTRUCTION

Should another generation of nuclear plants, perhaps incorporating new safety and economy features, be started? The major designers of such plants believe that they can now build plants that avoid the mistakes of the past and produce safe and economical power. But the electric utilities' worry about the economics of such plants, combined with public fear of their safety, have held back construction. Nevertheless, preliminary steps are underway to build new nuclear power plants in the United States.

As of early 2005, utilities were considering building or restarting up to eight reactors in Mississippi, South Carolina, Alabama, Virginia, Idaho and Illinois. Robert Manor, After 30 Years in Exile, Nuclear Power is Back, Chicago Tribune, January 20, 2005. Because individual utilities are reluctant to be the first to put up the capital for what is likely to be a drawn-out and expensive regulatory and court battle, groups of utilities have formed consortiums to proceed jointly through the early stages of the NRC's regulatory process in which generic issues of plant design and safety can be settled.[2] The DOE's "Nuclear Power 2010" program is prepared to split the

---

1.   http://www.nrc.gov/reactors/operating/licensing/renewal/applications.html#plant (a 2–19–05).

2.   http://www.eia.doe.gov/cneaf/nuclear/page/analysis/nucenviss2.html.

costs with the utilities for engineering and licensing expenses, subject to Congressional budget approval.[3]

The Energy Policy Act of 2005 provided additional support to the industry by enacting Section 638, "Standby Support for Certain Nuclear Plant Delays." The Act authorized DOE to enter into up to six "contracts" with sponsors of new nuclear power plants under which the federal government will guarantee to pay certain costs incurred by the sponsors in case full power operation of the plant is delayed by either the failure of the NRC to meet deadlines set forth in the license, or litigation that delays the commencement of full power operation. Costs that may be recovered include "principal or interest on any debt obligation" and "the incremental difference between (1) the fair market price of power purchased to meet the contractual supply agreements that would have been met by the [plant] but for the delay, and (2) the contractual price of the power from the advanced nuclear facility subject to the delay." The DOE is to pay 100% of these costs up to a limit of 500 million dollars per reactor for each of the first two licensed reactors, and 50% of the costs up to a limit of 250 million dollars after a 180 day delay for the next four reactors. The sponsor's obligation is to use due diligence to minimize delay.

For individual projects, the NRC has established an Early Site Permit (ESP) program that is intended to resolve in advance all on-site environmental issues associated with the licensing of a new reactor at a particular site. The agency has accepted applications for three ESPs, each for an existing nuclear plant site that had originally been designed for more reactors than were eventually built: Exelon's plant site in Clinton, Illinois, Dominion Resources' site in North Anna, Virginia, and Entergy Nuclear's site in Grand Gulf, Mississippi. Nuclear News, July 2005, p. 11.[4]

The economic profitability of nuclear power remains hard to predict. *See* Special Report: Nuclear Power, The Economist 58 (July 9, 2005). A 2004 study by the Argonne National Laboratory, carried out in cooperation with the University of Chicago's Department of Economics, the Graduate School of Business, and the Harris School of Public Policy, concluded that new nuclear power plants could be economically competitive if the government provided investment and production tax credits. University of Chicago, The Economic Future of Nuclear Power (2004).

The expansion of nuclear power may be moving slowly in the US, but many Asian countries find it an attractive and affordable solution to their growing need for electrical power. Of the 31 nuclear plants most recently connected to the electric grid, 22 have been in Asia, as are 18 of the 27 under construction in 2004. Experts Assess Prospects for Nuclear Power, Nuclear News, Aug. 2004, p. 33. China now has nine nuclear reactors in operation and two under construction. To meet government targets, China

---

3. http://nuclear.gov/nucpwr2010/NucPwr2010.html (2–19–05).

4. The isolated town of Galena, Alaska, population 700, has agreed to acquire a Toshiba 4S nuclear reactor if it can get NRC approval, but the reactor design has yet to be evaluated by the NRC. Jenny Weil, small reactor project in Alaska moved forward, Nucleonics Week, June 9, 2005, p. 1.

will need to build 2 or 3 reactors per year from 2008 to 2020. Steve Kidd, China: A Drop in the Ocean, Nuclear Engineering Intl., August 31, 2004, p. 8.

Although most countries that are building nuclear power plants rely heavily on central planning rather than free market policy, a new reactor has been ordered in Finland, where electricity rates are market-driven. The economic performance of Finland's four existing reactors has been favorable, and much of the country's industry is heavily dependent on long-term baseload electricity. Steve Kidd, Can New Units Start Up in Liberalised Markets?, Nuclear Engineering Intl., December 31, 2004, p. 14.

The multilateral Convention on Nuclear Safety (CNS), which entered into force on October 24, 1996, set forth internationally recognized nuclear safety standards. CNS, adopted on June 17, 1994, IAEA Doc. IN-FCIRC/449/Annex, 33 I.L.M. 1518. The objective of the agreement is to regulate international nuclear energy through the use of the peer review process under the auspices of the autonomous intergovernmental organization International Atomic Energy Agency (IAEA). Both general and specific safety standards are set out that guide radiation protection, emergency preparedness, siting, design, construction, and operation of nuclear power plants. CNS, art. 17, INFCIRC/449/Annex at 6, 33 I.L.M. at 1521. Additionally, each nation must rely on a separate regulatory body, one *not* concerned with the promotion of nuclear energy, for licensing, inspection and enforcement. *Id.* at art. 8. The benefit of peer review lies in its voluntary nature. The review process consists largely of national reports and review meetings and, when practiced, feels more like persuasion than compulsion. *See* Note, The Practice of Peer Review in the International Nuclear Safety Regime, 72 N.Y.U. L. Rev. 430 (1997).

3. ADVANTAGES AND DISADVANTAGES OF NUCLEAR POWER

The strong emotions evoked by nuclear energy make it difficult to find objective appraisals of its advantages and disadvantages, but one of the nation's leading energy scholars, Donald Zillman, suggests that it is time to re-examine the beneficial attributes of nuclear power. "Global warming can produce as catastrophic harms to the earth as significant radiation release from a nuclear accident," he points out. "Increased use of nuclear energy may be the most practical current method of reducing consumption of fossil fuels." He says that nuclear energy was overpraised in the 1950s and over-condemned in the 1980s but that "it might take its place as a technology in which the real risks are outweighed by the benefits in the new century." Donald N. Zillman, Nuclear Power, in James E. Hickey, Jr. et al., Energy Law and Policy for the 21st Century 10–2 (Rocky Mountain Mineral Law Foundation, 2000).

a. ADVANTAGES OF NUCLEAR POWER

Why is there now renewed interest in nuclear power? Its air quality advantages offer one significant reason. None of the waste that nuclear power plants generate is released into the environment, while a typical

1000–megawatt coal-burning plant emits 100,000 tons of sulphur dioxide, 75,000 tons of nitrogen oxides, and 5000 tons of fly ash into the environment every year. In addition, such plants also emit great quantities of carbon dioxide, which is a contributor to climate change. Bodansky *supra* at 11–21. Energy analyst Vaclav Smil says that even if the full energy chain is evaluated, nuclear generation produces only about 9 grams of CO_2 per kilowatt-hour. "If all of the electricity generated by nuclear plants was to be produced by burning coal, the world's CO_2 emissions would rise by an equivalent of more than one-third of the total produced by fossil fuel combustion in the year 2000." Vaclav Smil, Energy at the Crossroads 313 (MIT Press, 2002).

In addition, the fuel used in nuclear power plants exists in abundant supply. Assuming a conservative estimate of 20 million tonnes of uranium available, this could sustain four times the current rate of use for about 80 years. Bodansky, *supra* at 225. And some observers see a role for new nuclear plants in the production of hydrogen for use in fuel-cell vehicles. See Charles W. Forsberg, What is the Initial Market for Hydrogen from Nuclear Energy?, Nuclear News, January 2005, p. 24.

All existing commercial nuclear reactors operating in the United States fall into two broad categories, pressurized water reactors (PWR) and boiling water reactors (BWR).[5] Because both types of reactors are cooled and moderated with ordinary "light" water, the two designs are often grouped collectively as light water reactors (LWR). New designs for reactors employing nuclear fission propose to reduce safety and terrorism risks and increase economic efficiency. The DOE has issued an evaluation of four company's advanced reactor designs.[6] Most proposals for plants to be constructed in this decade involve relatively modest changes in LWR technology, emphasizing improved safety management and economical design.

But the most important reason for the renewed interest in nuclear power is the rapidly rising cost of alternative sources of generation. As Business Week recently noted, "Not long ago, nuclear power in the U.S. seemed dead, buried by memories of Three Mile Island, Chernobyl, and the mammoth cost overruns that pushed utilities to the brink of bankruptcy. But as the price of oil soars, the onetime pariah is making a comeback." John Carey with Michael Arndt, With Oil over $50, Nukes are Back, 3907 Business Week 59 (November 8, 2004).

---

5. Of these 104 reactors, the EIA categorizes 69 as pressurized water reactors (PWRs) totaling 65,100 net megawatts, and 35 units are boiling water reactors (BWR) totaling 32,300 net megawatts. For a discussion of the distinction, see Bodansky supra at 171–92.

6. http://nuclear.gov/nucpwr2010/ConSchEvalofCandidateRDReportpage.html (a. 2–19–05). In addition, The DOE's "Next Generation Nuclear Plant Project," to be led by the Idaho National Laboratory and "a consortium of appropriate industrial partners," is set to build a prototype plant at the Idaho facility that will "determine whether it is appropriate to combine electricity generation and hydrogen production in a single ... plant." See sections 641–645 of the Energy Policy Act of 2005.

Despite some apparent advantages of nuclear power, electric companies in the United States have been reluctant to begin construction of new nuclear units. The arguments against such construction can be divided into two categories: arguments based on (1) cost and (2) risk.

b.   HISTORY OF COST OVERRUNS

The financial problems experienced by many electric utilities in connection with the construction of the first generation of nuclear power plants were discussed in Chapters 3 and 12. In general, these projects were plagued by complex health and safety regulations that were often applied retroactively to plants under construction. Lawsuits by project opponents and multi-level review procedures at the NRC resulted in expensive delays at a time of rising construction costs.

The rush to embrace the new technology produced economic factors that drove up costs. The shortage of trained labor led to enough faulty construction to scare even advocates of nuclear power. And the dominance of a few firms limited competition and contributed to dramatic cost increases. *See generally* Robert J. Duffy, Nuclear Politics in America (University Press of Kansas, 1997). By the 1990's, it appeared that nuclear power had become an economic disaster:

> The nuclear power plant debacle destroyed the status quo ante in the electricity industry. In the 1970s, with enthusiastic encouragement from state and federal regulators, utilities began construction of over one hundred nuclear power plants. Utilities and regulators predicted continuation of the historic pattern of a doubling in electricity demand every decade. Moreover, nuclear plants were expected to drive the cost of electricity to new lows. The massive nuclear construction program, predicated on forecasts of low costs and high demand, became instead an economic nightmare for all concerned. Actual costs of nuclear power plants vastly exceeded estimates, sometimes by as much as 1000%. At the same time, electric rate increases dramatically slowed the growth in demand for electricity. As the power plants approached completion, it became apparent that they were both unneeded and extravagantly expensive. Consumers were outraged at the huge rate increases that would result from letting utilities recover their massive investments in nuclear power plants. Regulators and their political superiors responded to the outpouring of populist sentiment by disallowing tens of billions of dollars in utility investments—approximately 20% of total utility investments in nuclear power plants. Most utilities suffered significant financial harm from these disallowances.

> The massive disallowances of utility investments in nuclear power plants dramatically changed utility incentives. The high perceived risk of future disallowances reversed utilities' incentives to overinvest, and made utilities extremely reluctant to build new power plants. Shareholders are not compensated for this risk through the allowed rate of return. Disallowances also place utility managers' jobs in jeopardy. As a result, utilities now systematically underestimate future demand to

justify not building new generating capacity. The unwillingness of utilities to invest in new power plants created a void that must be filled with a new industry structure and new forms of government oversight.

Bernard S. Black & Richard J. Pierce, Jr., The Choice Between Markets and Central Planning in Regulating the U.S. Electricity Industry, 93 Colum. L. Rev. 1339 (1993).

Some utilities became insolvent as a result of investments in nuclear facilities. One such utility is a rural cooperative in Louisiana, Cajun Electric Power Cooperative. Like all cooperatives, it received financing from the Department of Agriculture on very favorable terms. When Cajun's nuclear investments proved unmanageable, the Department demanded that Cajun raise its rates to enable it to pay off its federal loan, but the Louisiana PSC refused to allow the rate increases. The U.S. sued, claiming that the Rural Electrification Act gave the Secretary of Agriculture the authority to demand that a co-op raise its rates, but the Fifth Circuit held that the federal statute did not allow the secretary to preempt state rate regulation—at least not on a case-by-case basis. *In re Cajun Electric Power Cooperative*, 109 F.3d 248 (5th Cir. 1997). The company was in bankruptcy proceedings, and the magnitude of its financial problems were set out in another Fifth Circuit opinion (*In re Cajun Electric Power Cooperative*, 119 F.3d 349 (5th Cir. 1997)) approving a settlement of the bankruptcy:

> Cajun's largest creditor is the federal government's Rural Utilities Service ("RUS") (formerly the Rural Electrification Administration), which provided Cajun with loans and loan guarantees for its investment in the River Bend nuclear plant. RUS asserts that it has secured claims against Cajun of $4.2 billion. Cajun's second-largest creditor is the nuclear plant's builder and principal owner, Gulf States Utilities Co. ("Gulf States"), which through its corporate successor, Entergy Gulf States, Inc., asserts unsecured claims of $400 million.
>
> The Committee representing the trade creditors [who had claims totaling about $7 million] requested that the court defer approval until confirmation of a bankruptcy plan, or, in the alternative, approve the settlement conditionally, pending confirmation of a plan. The district court denied these requests and approved the settlement on August 27, 1996. The Committee appeals....

The appellate court held that the bankruptcy court correctly decided that the settlement was fair and equitable. The court noted that past precedent required that the court "consider the reasonable views of a majority of the creditors," and that "the vast numerical majority of creditors is represented by the Committee [of trade creditors], which opposes the settlement.... The appellees point out, however, that the trade creditors' aggregate claim against Cajun is only a drop in the bucket—by some estimates less than one percent of Cajun's total debt." And, said the court, "given also the relatively small amount of the trade creditors' claims, the district court did not clearly err by finding the settlement in the creditors' interests. In any event, given that all of the other factors in the equation overwhelmingly favor the settlement, the wishes of the trade creditors do not compel us to reject the settlement."[7]

c. THE RISK FACTOR

A 1979 accident at the Three Mile Island plant near Harrisburg, Pennsylvania, brought extended media attention to the risks associated with the potential malfunction of nuclear power plants. The accident also resulted in tort litigation.

In re TMI Litigation

193 F.3d 613 (3d Cir. 1999), cert. den. 530 U.S. 1225 (2000).

■ McKEE, J. [Plaintiffs sued the owners, operators and contractors of the Three Mile Island nuclear power plant, alleging that they suffered neoplasms as a result of radiation released into the environment as a result of an accident at the plant. For background purposes, the court described the accident as follows:] What has been described as the "nation's worst nuclear accident"[8] began at about 4:00 a.m. on Wednesday, March 28, 1979. Ironically, the "nation's worst nuclear accident" grew out of a minor malfunction, or transient that occurred in the nonnuclear part of the system. For some reason, several feedwater pumps, that normally drew heat from the pressurized water reactor's (PWR's) cooling water, shut-off automatically. The system was designed so that when the feedwater pumps tripped, the main turbine and electrical generator also tripped. Thus, by design, the turbine and generator tripped approximately one second later. Three seconds after the turbine tripped, the pressure in the reactor coolant system increased to a level that caused the power-operated relief valve (PORV) to open in order to release the pressure. When the PORV opened, the fission process in the reactor core automatically shut down. Consequently, the heat generation in the reactor core dropped to decay heat levels.

However, the PORV did not close as it should have when the system pressure was reduced to acceptable levels. Instead, it remained open for approximately 2 hours. Unfortunately, the personnel operating Unit 2 did not realize that the PORV had not closed. They believed that it had automatically closed when the system was depressurized. Because the PORV remained open, reactor coolant water flowed from the reactor

---

7. The history of the Cajun Coop's involvement with nuclear power is discussed in Matt J. Farley, The Regulatory Approval Issue in Cajun Electric Power Corp., Inc., 40 Loyola L. Rev. 331 (2000).

8. [note 74 of opinion] Prior to the TMI–2 accident, there were "major" reactor accidents at the National Reactor Testing Laboratory in Idaho in 1955 and 1961, at the Fermi Reactor in Detroit, Michigan in 1966 and at Browns Ferry 1 in Alabama in 1975. Major accidents outside of the United States occurred at Chalk River, Canada in 1952, Windscale, England in 1957, Lucens, Switzerland in 1969 and, perhaps the most famous of all reactor accidents, at Chernobyl, in Ukraine about 30 miles south of the border with Belarus, (both of which were then part of the former USSR) in 1986.

coolant system into the reactor coolant drain tank, which is designed to collect reactor coolant that is released from the reactor coolant system through the PORV during power operation. The continued flow of reactor coolant water into the reactor coolant drain tank caused a safety valve to lift on the drain tank and a drain tank rupture disk to burst. This rupture disk burst allowed the reactor coolant water to be discharged directly into the reactor building, which overfilled along with its sump pumps. The reactor building sump pumps were on automatic and aligned with the auxiliary building sump tank. When the reactor building sump pumps overfilled, some coolant water was transferred to the aligned auxiliary building sump tank. For some reason, there was no rupture disk on the sump tank and reactor coolant water was discharged directly into the auxiliary building. The contaminated coolant water continued to flow from the reactor building into the auxiliary building for several days. Estimates of the amount of radioactive water discharged into the reactor and auxiliary buildings range from 700,000 gallons to 5,000,000 gallons.

Approximately 2 minutes into the accident, the emergency core cooling system ("ECCS") began pumping water into the reactor core. However, operations personnel, still believing that the PORV had closed, and therefore unaware that reactor coolant water was escaping from the reactor coolant system, turned off most of the water flowing to the core through the ECCS. They did so believing that they were preventing the reactor system from becoming filled with water—a condition they were required to prevent.

However, there was not enough coolant water being circulated through the reactor coolant system to cool the reactor core because reactor coolant water was being discharged into the reactor building. Consequently, the core reaction was producing more heat than the coolant system was removing, and the core began to heat up. The loss of reactor coolant water allowed the reactor core to become uncovered. Within three hours of the beginning of the accident, as much as two-thirds of the twelve-foot high core was uncovered. Temperatures reached as high as 3500 to 4000 degrees Fahrenheit or more in parts of the core during its maximum exposure.

About 2-1/2 hours into the accident, some of the fuel rods in the reactor cracked, releasing xenon and other fission product gases, which had accumulated in the fuel rod gap between the fuel and the cladding, into the coolant water. Over the next few hours, more fuel rods cracked, releasing radioactive iodine and cesium into the primary coolant water as well as additional noble gases.

A series of events then unfolded involving various reactions, valves and controls. The end result was that, nearly 10 hours into the accident, there was a sudden spike of pressure and temperature in the reactor building. Initially, the spike was dismissed as some type of instrument malfunction. However, operations personnel learned on March 29th that the spike was caused by the explosion of hydrogen gas in the reactor building. Fears of another hydrogen explosion developed when a hydrogen gas bubble was later found in the reactor system. Presumably, there was a concern that another hydrogen explosion would damage the reactor vessel, leading to further releases of radioactive material. However, the fears about another hydrogen explosion were later learned to be unfounded.

During the last days of March and the first week of April, operations personnel began to regain control and contain the radioactive releases caused by the accident. However, it was not until the afternoon of April 27, 1979 that stable conditions were finally established in TMI–2.

The parties generally agree that the radioactive fission products released to the environment as a result of the accident escaped from the damaged fuel and were transported in the coolant through the letdown line into the auxiliary building. Once in the auxiliary building, the radioactive fission products were released into the environment through the building's ventilation system. Because of the volatility of noble gases and radioiodines, those elements were the primary radionuclides available for release from the auxiliary building. Two krypton isotopes, 87 and 85, were not released in significant quantities because of the short half-life of 87Kr and because of the small amount of 85Kr in the reactor core. Nonetheless, despite the various filters, radioiodines were released. After the first day, the quantities of 88Kr and 135Xe were reduced by radioactive decay. All of the 133I contained in the coolant which was released to the auxiliary building eventually decayed to 133Xe and 133mXe. These radionuclides were the predominate ones released from the plant to the environment. TMI–2 also contained a treatment system, called the "liquid radwaste treatment system", which was designed to collect, process, monitor and recycle or dispose of radioactive liquid wastes prior to discharge to the environment. After the system processed the liquid radwaste, it was discharged into the Susquehanna River. However, because the primary coolant water flowed into the auxiliary building during the accident, the liquid radwaste treatment system was overwhelmed and radioactive materials were released to the Susquehanna River. The Nuclear Regulatory Commission's Special Inquiry Group concluded that the quantity of radioactive materials contained in the liquid released into the Susquehanna River was not significant. None of the plaintiffs here claim harm as a result of the releases of liquid radwaste into the river.

[In an exhaustive opinion, covering 116 pages in the Federal Reporter, the court of appeals affirmed the district court's grant of summary judgment in favor of defendants in regard to ten plaintiffs that had been selected as trial plaintiffs. It held that the district court acted properly in excluding much of plaintiffs' expert testimony under the standard set forth in *Daubert v. Merrell Dow Pharm., Inc.*, 509 U.S. 579 (1993).]■

NOTES AND COMMENTS

1. A thorough analysis of the TMI accident and its aftermath is found in J. Samuel Walker, Three Mile Island: A Nuclear Crisis in Historical Perspective (University of California Press, 2004). See also Bonnie A. Osif et al., TMI 25 Years Later (Penn State University Press, 2004). Although

these and most other assessments of the impact of TMI have found no evidence of long-term health impacts, critics of nuclear power maintain that "remarkably few questions about the health effects of that near-catastrophe have been asked—let alone answered." Joseph Mangano, Three Mile Island: Health Study Meltdown, 60 Bull. of the Atomic Scientists 30 (2004).

A study of nuclear power plant safety by social anthropologist Constance Perin concludes that the command-and-control structure of the nuclear industry has tended to foster a mode of thinking about parts, components and assemblies, which is appropriate in the construction of plants but not in their operation. It ignores the fact that plant operation is a "peopled technology" in which operators of varying technical backgrounds have learned invaluable technical and contextual knowledge about a plant's condition. Constance Perin, Shouldering Risks 211–213 (Princeton University Press, 2005).

2.   The Three Mile Island accident also focused attention on the issue of emergency evacuation of the area around a nuclear power plant in case of an accident. In 1980, Congress added new requirements for emergency evacuation plans as a condition for the issuance of power plant licenses. This led to a series of conflicts between utilities and nearby local governments that opposed the plant and sought to torpedo the evacuation plan by refusing to participate in the planning process. The Shoreham nuclear plant on the south shore of Long Island was abandoned after completion because the local governments were unable to come up with an evacuation plan (and didn't want to). The Seabrook plant took so long to build the company went bankrupt; the neighboring states held it up by refusing to participate in evacuation planning.

Eventually, after additional legislation, the NRC adopted the so-called "realism doctrine" and concluded that the Commission could assume that each local government would really cooperate in the utility's evacuation plan if an emergency arose, even if the local government claimed that it wouldn't. The NRC rules incorporating these assumptions were upheld in *Massachusetts v. United States*, 856 F.2d 378 (1st Cir. 1988).

3.   In 1986, an explosion at the Chernobyl nuclear power plant in the Ukraine caused the release of large amounts of radiation into the atmosphere. Some thirty people died as a result of the explosion and acute radiation poisoning in the immediate neighborhood. Radiation in amounts that caused concern spread over much of Northern and Eastern Europe. The Chernobyl reactor, like many Russian-constructed reactors, was in the open rather than in a pressurizable containment structure used in American nuclear plants. Nevertheless, the Chernobyl accident heightened public fears of nuclear power plants throughout the world. Atkins, *supra* at 81–84.

In 2002, the OECD's Nuclear Energy Agency released an update on the health and environmental impacts from Chernobyl. The instance of thyroid cancer increased in Belarus and the Ukraine. The number of thyroid cancer cases in children increased from about 5 per year before the explosion to over 600 in 1998 in Belarus. In particular, one area in Belarus, the Gomel

Oblast, has over 50% of all of the cases. About half of the childhood cancer cases are in children who were between one and four years of age at the time of the accident. However, the incidence of childhood leukemia has not changed in the ten years since the accident. The update also states that the International Agency for Research on Cancers conducted a review that found no harmful effects on congenital abnormalities or pregnancy outcomes.

Several psychological and social health effects are prominent. Anxiety and stress are prevalent from the massive evacuations and relocations that occurred after the accident. The relocations disrupted social networks and traditions. Some common symptoms are headaches, depression, sleep disturbances, emotional imbalance, and the inability to concentrate. The report concluded that the accident had a significant, long-term effect on the psychological health effects and the quality of life.

After the accident, the main cause of exposure to radiation was from the consumption of contaminated food. An area of 4000 km² forbids all agricultural activities and transfers of products. This exclusion zone is with Belarus, Ukraine, and Russia. Drinking water is not a problem, but may become one in the future within the basins that are downstream from Chernobyl. Also, contaminated fish may become a long-term problem in the future. *See* Nuclear Energy Agency, Chernobyl Assessment of Radiological & Health Impacts 2002 Update of Chernobyl: Ten Years On. http://www.nea.fr/html/rp/chernobyl/c05.html (a. Aug. 6, 2005).

The book Voices from Chernobyl, (Dalkey Archive Press, 2005), presents a more human and less statistical view of the accident. It contains interviews with people affected by Chernobyl conducted by Svetlana Alexievich in 1996. The translator, Kieth Gessen, writes "that Chernobyl, while an accident in the sense that no one intentionally set it off, was also the deliberate product of a culture of cronyism, laziness, and a deep-seated indifference toward the general population. The literature on the subject is pretty unanimous in its opinion that the Soviet system had taken a poorly designed reactor and then staffed it with a group of incompetents. It then proceeded, as the interviews in this book attest, to lie about the disaster in the most criminal way." *Id.* at ix.

On September 5, 2005, the United Nations' Chernobyl Forum released reports on the environmental, health and socio-economic impacts of the Chernobyl explosion. The Chernobyl Forum reports included work by more than 100 scientists and was sponsored by numerous U.N. and national agencies. The reports are available at http://www.iaea.org/NewsCenter/Focus/Chernobyl/index.shtml (accessed Sept. 6, 2005).

4. The chief conservationist of the International Union for the Conservation of Nature has noted one beneficial, if ironic, side effect of the accident. "Chernobyl has now become the world's first radioactive nature preserve.... 200 wolves are now living in the nature reserve, which has also begun to support populations of reindeer, lynx and European bison, species that previously were not found in the region. While the impact on humans was strongly negative, the wildlife is adapting and even thriving on the site

of one of the 20th century's worst environmental disasters." Jeffrey A. McNeely, Energy and Biodiversity: Understanding Complex Relationships, in Energy Law and Sustainable Development (Adrian J. Bradbrook & Richard L. Ottinger, eds., IUCN Environmental Policy and Law Paper #47, 2003).

5.   The fear of accidents at nuclear power plants has spawned a subspecialty of risk evaluators who have tried to develop credible means of predicting the likelihood of such accidents. *See* National Research Council, Risk Assessment in the Federal Government: Managing the Process (National Academy Press, 1993). Other studies have evaluated why our psychological sense of danger often seems different than would be expected from what the experts tell us. See, e.g., Howard Margolis, Dealing with Risk (University of Chicago Press, 1996). In addition, a new field of "risk communication" has arisen, involving specialists in informing decisionmakers and the public about the relative likelihood and gravity of various kinds of risks. National Research Council, Understanding Risk: Informing Decisions in a Democratic Society (National Academy Press, 1996).

6.   Like any factory, a nuclear power plant has a limited life expectancy. How long will the existing plants continue to operate safely and economically? Some nuclear power plants have been retired by their operators before the end of their expected lives. In 1998, two units at Zion, Illinois, and a unit at Millstone, Connecticut, were retired prematurely because of high costs. The San Onofre plant on the California coast was dismantled in 2000, in part because of worries about earthquake risks.

What do you do with an abandoned nuclear power plant? The cost of removing irradiated materials and making the site available for other uses is estimated to be in the range of $400 to $600 million per plant. To assure that funds will be available to cover these costs, ratepayers served by nuclear plants have been paying special fees into trust funds which are intended to accumulate enough money to be able to pay these costs of decommissioning when they occur.

The problems of decommissioning a nuclear power plant are severely complicated by the difficulties associated with the disposal of both the highly radioactive fuel rods and the large volumes of less radioactive "low-level" waste found in any nuclear facility. See *Citizens Awareness Network v. Nuclear Regulatory Comm'n*, 59 F.3d 284 (1st Cir. 1995)(requiring completion of a decommissioning plan before any waste material can be removed from a plant site). These issues are discussed at greater length later this chapter. The existing rules requiring funding for decommissioning nuclear power plants are found in 10 C.F.R. § 50.75. After the *Citizens Awareness Network* decision, the Commission amended its rules relating to the decommissioning process in SECY–96–086.

4.   Advanced Nuclear Technologies

Nuclear engineers have remained busy during the long down-side of the power plant construction cycle. New designs for reactors employing nuclear fission propose to reduce safety and terrorism risks and increase economic efficiency. And a coalition of governments is conducting research on the dramatic possibility of producing usable power from nuclear fusion.

Substantial efforts are underway to "develop next-generation reactors that would usher in a Second Nuclear Era." Bodansky *supra* at 439. These include high-temperature gas-cooled reactors and liquid metal reactors. *Id. at 449–477.* The South African government has approved a five-year financing strategy for a "pebble-bed reactor" design near Cape Town. See also Daniel Clery, Nuclear Industry Dares to Dream of a new Dawn, 309 Science 1172 (Aug. 19, 2005).

Practically all of the energy available on earth comes from the nuclear fusions by which the sun creates its energy. E. C. Pielou, The Energy of Nature 148 (University of Chicago Press, 2001). Nuclear scientists managed to replicate nuclear fusion for the development of the hydrogen bomb. Is it possible to harness this force for the production of electricity, or do we run the risk that, like Icarus, flying too close to the sun will cause a meltdown?[9]

A coalition of eight industrialized countries have agreed to develop a prototype facility to generate electricity from nuclear fusion, known as the ITER project, at a site in southern France.[10] The ITER budget is projected to be 10 billion euros (13 billion dollars) over the next 30 years, including 4.7 billion euros to build the reactor. The European Union plans to finance 40 percent of the total. The project, emulating the sun's nuclear fusion, is not expected to generate electricity before 2050.

5.   THE EFFECT OF ELECTRICITY RESTRUCTURING

As the restructuring of the electric power industry gives companies more options, the question of whether to buy or sell nuclear power plants has become a reality for many companies for the first time. A few electric utilities have apparently decided to shop around to purchase nuclear power plants owned by other utilities, hoping that economies of scale can be achieved through management of a sizable number of plants. AmerGen Energy Company, a U.S.-British joint venture, purchased the first Three Mile Island unit from General Public Utilities, and the holding company, Entergy Corporation, bought the pilgrim nuclear plant from Boston Edison. Exelon Co. is the result of a merger between Commonwealth Edison and PECO based largely on a common desire to operate a fleet of nuclear plants.

With increasing competition in the electricity market, the Nuclear Regulatory Commission has had to evaluate the extent to which new players in the market are qualified to operate nuclear power plants. Studies of other deregulated industries suggest that financial problems stemming

---

9.   For a relatively simplified discussion of fusion, see http://crppwww.epfl.ch/crppfusion/ (2–19–2005).

10.   Nuclear Ambitions: Fusion Power, The Economist, July 2, 2005. The project website is www.iter.org.

from deregulation are statistically associated with increasing safety problems. Vicki M. Bier et al, Effects of Deregulation on Safety: Implications Drawn from the Aviation, Rail and United Kingdom Nuclear Power industries (Kluwer Academic Publishers, 2003).

In addition, the extent to which unregulated companies will be responsible for the financial obligations of decommissioning has raised new issues regarding proof of financial responsibility. Originally, it was always assumed that the operators of nuclear plants would be regulated utilities that would be able to pass along to their customers any costs imposed by NRC rules. What happens if ownership passes to a non-regulated company?

In the Matter of North Atlantic Energy Service Corp., (Seabrook Station, Unit 1)

49 N.R.C. 201 (1999).

The Montaup Electric Company ("Montaup") seeks to transfer its 2.9–percent ownership interest in Seabrook Station, Unit 1, to the Little Bay Power Corporation ("Little Bay"). Montaup is one of eleven co-owners of the Seabrook Station, Unit 1. Little Bay is a wholly-owned subsidiary of BayCorp Holdings, Ltd. ("BayCorp"), which is also the holding company for the Great Bay Power Corporation (the holder of a 12.1–percent ownership interest in Seabrook). On Montaup's behalf, Seabrook's licensed operator, the North Atlantic Energy Service Corporation ("NAESCO"), submitted the transfer application to the Commission for approval. The Atomic Energy Act ("AEA") requires Commission approval of transfers of ownership rights. See AEA, § 184, 42 U.S.C. § 2234. Recently-promulgated NRC regulations ("Subpart M") govern hearing requests on transfer applications. See Final Rule, "Public Notification, Availability of Documents and Records, Hearing Requests and Procedures for Hearings on License Transfer Applications," 63 Fed. Reg. 66, 721 (Dec. 3, 1998), to be codified at 10 C.F.R. §§ 2.1300 et seq.

Pursuant to Subpart M, the New England Power Company ("NEP")— a 10–percent co-owner of the Seabrook plant—has filed a timely intervention petition opposing the Montaup-to-Little Bay transfer application as well as a petition for summary relief or, in the alternative, a request for hearing.

Pursuant to Section 184 of the AEA and section 50.80 of our regulations, Montaup and Little Bay seek approval of the proposed transfer as part of Montaup's efforts to divest all of its electric generating assets pursuant to the restructuring of the electric utility industry in Massachusetts and Rhode Island. Under the transfer arrangement, Little Bay would (among other things) assume full responsibility for Montaup's remaining share of Seabrook's future costs ... Little Bay submits estimates for the total operating expenses at Seabrook attributable to Montaup's 2.9–percent ownership share of Seabrook for the first five years of Little Bay's ownership and the sources of funds to cover those costs. Little Bay also proffers favorable revenue predictions for the future, based on the assumptions that Seabrook will operate until its current license expires in 2026 and that market revenues through the year 2026 should be sufficient to cover Little Bay's share of the plant's decommissioning expenses and operating expenses, even if the estimates for those costs are later revised upward. As a further indication of the adequacy of Little Bay's financial assurances, the application points out that Little Bay's take-or-pay sales contract with Great Bay requires the latter to pay for all of Little Bay's Seabrook-related costs, whether or not Great Bay succeeds in reselling the electricity it buys from Little Bay.

Our grant of NEP's hearing request by no means suggests that NEP necessarily will succeed in its challenge to the transfer application. It faces a formidable task in persuading us that factors peculiar to Seabrook call for modification or rejection of what NEP acknowledges are financial qualification plans of the type ordinarily found acceptable by the Commission. Some aspects of NEP's position seem to us particularly troublesome. We will set out our concerns to guide the parties as they proceed to a hearing in this case.

First, as a general matter, NEP cannot insist that applicants provide the impossible: absolutely certain predictions of future economic conditions. To be sure. safe operation of a nuclear plant requires adequate funding, but the potential safety impacts of a shortfall in funding are not so direct or immediate as the safety impacts of significant technical deficiencies. Generally speaking, then, the level of assurance the Commission finds it reasonable to require regarding a licensee's ability to meet financial obligations is less than the extremely high assurance the Commission requires regarding the safety of reactor design, construction, and operation. The Commission will accept financial assurances based on plausible assumptions and forecasts, even though the possibility is not insignificant that things will turn out less favorably than expected. Thus, the mere casting of doubt on some aspects of proposed funding plans is not by itself sufficient to defeat a finding of reasonable assurance.

At the same time, though, funding plans that rely on assumptions seriously at odds with governing realities will not be deemed acceptable simply because their form matches plans described in the regulations. Relying on affidavits and various forms of financial data, NEP asserts that Little Bay's cost-and-revenue estimates fail to provide the required assurance because they do not reflect a realistic outlook for Little Bay itself or for the nuclear power industry in New England. As in other cases (e.g., *River Bend*, 40 NRC at 51–53), we cannot brush aside such economically-based safety concerns without giving the intervenor a chance to substantiate its concerns at a hearing, but we note that NEP's arguments ultimately will prevail only if it can demonstrate relevant uncertainties significantly greater than those that usually cloud business outlooks.

Finally, we cannot accede to NEP's seeming view that Little Bay inherently cannot meet our financial qualification rules because its rates are not regulated by a state utilities commission. This view runs counter to the premise underlying the entire restructuring and economic deregulation of the electric utility industry, i.e., that the marketplace will replace cost-of-service ratemaking. In our view, unregulated electricity rates are not incompatible with maintaining sufficient financial resources to operate a nuclear power reactor.[11]■

NOTES AND COMMENTS

1. "Last year was either the worst or the second-worst year in history for power industry common stocks, depending on which index one looks at. The Dow Jones Industry Group Performance Index for electric utilities saw its worst percentage drop ever. And 11 companies reduced or eliminated dividends, the most ever," said Electric Utility Week on January 6, 2003. "Last year's best percentage gainer was BayCorp Holdings Ltd., which closed Dec. 31 at $14.74, up 56.8% in a year. BayCorp is a holding company with two power subsidiaries, Great Bay Power Corp. and Little Bay Power Corp [which] sold their 15% share of the Seabrook nuclear plant to FPL Group on Nov. 1 . . ."

2. New England Power is now a subsidiary of National Grid Group plc, an English corporation. Beginning in the 1990s, many United States electric companies expanded through acquisition of companies abroad, and a number of foreign energy companies began to acquire electric companies in the United States. For a survey of the national security implications of foreign purchase of nuclear power plants see Energy Information Agency, Foreign Direct Investment in United States Energy in 2000 (August 2002): http://www.eia.doe.gov/emeu/finance/fdi/advance/index.html (accessed 2–19–05)

3. Under 10 C.F.R. § 50.75(e) of the Commission's regulations, a company acquiring an interest in a nuclear power plant has five different options for demonstrating that it will be financially responsible for meeting its decommissioning obligations. For a non-regulated company, prepayment may be the only feasible option, since it cannot count on ratepayers' legal obligations in the way that is possible for regulated public utilities. In the above proceeding, the NRC found that Little Bay had met that requirement by prepaying 11.8 million dollars to cover decommissioning expenses.

4. The continuing financial stability of existing public utility operators of nuclear power plants is also a matter of concern as competition has brought new independent generating sources into the market. As more and more independent companies get into the electricity business, regulators have worried whether the new companies would have (1) the technical expertise, and (2) the financial backing, to meet their obligations as an operator. Regulated utilities were assumed to have the ability to pass along any costs to the public in the rate-making process, but in a free market that assumption may no longer be valid, and certainly isn't valid for IPPs, as the financial problems of Enron and other independent generators have demonstrated.

---

11. Further proceedings in this dispute are found at 50 N.R.C. 257 (Oct. 25, 1999).

The NRC intends to monitor the financial condition of existing operators and to request additional financial assurances if needed to assure that decommissioning obligations are met. SECY–98–164, Final Rule on Financial Assurance Requirements for Decommissioning Power Reactors, July 2, 1998. The NRC plans to maintain continuing oversight to ensure that operators' budgets for maintenance and safety, for example, are not unduly reduced. Nuclear Regulatory Commission, Final Policy Statement on Restructuring, 62 Fed. Reg. 44,071 (Aug. 19, 1997). The General Accounting Office suggested that NRC should clarify the standards and criteria by which it will be reviewing the financial reports of the operators. GAO, Nuclear Regulation: Better Oversight Needed to Ensure Accumulation of Funds to Decommission Nuclear Power plants (May, 1999).

5.   In November, 2004, the Public Service Commission of Wisconsin initially rejected the proposed sale by two Wisconsin utilities of an aging nuclear power plant in Kewaunee, WI, to Dominion Resources, Inc., an out-of-state firm, finding that the sale was not in the public interest because it would have resulted in the power plant being turned over to a unregulated entity, reducing the PSC's ability to regulate the facility. In March, 2005, the commission reversed course and approved the sale after the buyer offered to attach some conditions.

> The conditions convinced the three-member panel March 17 that the sale was in the public interest. The utilities and Dominion offered to give the utilities a right of first refusal to buy the Kewaunee plant if Dominion sells the plant to another party. The right of first refusal would require any purchaser to agree to be bound by all of the conditions agreed to by Dominion in the current sale, according to the PSC. For example, waste created at another nuclear power plant could not be stored at the Kewaunee site. Also, Dominion said it would return any excess decommissioning funds to WPS and WP&L customers following completion of all decommissioning activities. Dominion also agreed to increase the total level of Dominion's guaranty under the purchased power agreement (PPA) for selling the plant's output to the utilities through 2013. The guarantee is designed to protect the utilities in case Dominion doesn't perform under the PPAs. The exact level of the guarantee is confidential, but it is twice the industry standard, according to the PSC. Overall, the sale is an economic benefit to Wisconsin ratepayers, said Burnie Bridge, PSC chairwoman. The sale does not signal the beginning of deregulation in Wisconsin, she said.[12]

C.   FEDERAL PREEMPTION OF NUCLEAR SAFETY REGULATION

Nuclear energy was initially developed during World War II as part of the federal government's national defense effort. The concern about the potential conversion of nuclear energy to military purposes by foreign

---

12.   Electric Utility Week, March 21, 2005.

governments or guerilla groups remains an important issue. Consequently, the federal government continues to play a key role in the control of nuclear energy. The dominant nature of this federal role has led to a series of cases testing the extent to which the federal government has pre-empted the field and barred state and local regulation affecting the industry.

The Atomic Energy Act specifically said that a federal agency (now the NRC) would have the exclusive authority to regulate safety of nuclear facilities. State and local governments retained, however, the right to enforce all other forms of regulation. In regard to nuclear power plants in particular, it was recognized that the electric industry was heavily regulated by state public utility commissions, and Congress intended to leave this regulatory system in place. The line between safety and other regulatory objectives is not crystal clear, and the following case indicated that the Supreme Court was willing to interpret the distinction generously in favor of state regulation.

Pacific Gas and Electric Co. v. Energy Resources and Development Commission

461 U.S. 190 (1983).

■ WHITE, J. The turning of swords into plowshares has symbolized the transformation of atomic power into a source of energy in American society. To facilitate this development the Federal Government relaxed its monopoly over fissionable materials and nuclear technology, and in its place, erected a complex scheme to promote the civilian development of nuclear energy, while seeking to safeguard the public and the environment from the unpredictable risks of a new technology. Early on, it was decided that the States would continue their traditional role in the regulation of electricity production. The interrelationship of federal and state authority in the nuclear energy field has not been simple; the federal regulatory structure has been frequently amended to optimize the partnership.

This case emerges from the intersection of the Federal Government's efforts to ensure that nuclear power is safe with the exercise of the historic state authority over the generation and sale of electricity. At issue is whether provisions in the 1976 amendments to California's Warren–Alquist Act, Cal. Pub. Res. Code Ann. §§ 25524.1(b) and 25524.2 (West 1977), which condition the construction of nuclear plants on findings by the State Energy Resources Conservation and Development Commission that adequate storage facilities and means of disposal are available for nuclear waste, are pre-empted by the Atomic Energy Act of 1954, 68 Stat. 919, as amended, 42 U.S.C. § 2011, et seq.

A nuclear reactor must be periodically refueled and the "spent fuel" removed. This spent fuel is intensely radioactive and must be carefully stored. The general practice is to store the fuel in a water-filled pool at the reactor site. For many years, it was assumed that this fuel would be reprocessed; accordingly, the storage pools were designed as short-term

holding facilities with limited storage capacities. As expectations for reprocessing remained unfulfilled, the spent fuel accumulated in the storage
pools, creating the risk that nuclear reactors would have to be shut down.
This could occur if there were insufficient room in the pool to store spent
fuel and also if there were not enough space to hold the entire fuel core
when certain inspections or emergencies required unloading of the reactor.
In recent years, the problem has taken on special urgency. Some 8,000
metric tons of spent nuclear fuel have already accumulated, and it is
projected that by the year 2000 there will be some 72,000 metric tons of
spent fuel. Government studies indicate that a number of reactors could be
forced to shut down in the near future due to the inability to store spent
fuel.

There is a second dimension to the problem. Even with water pools
adequate to store safely all the spent fuel produced during the working
lifetime of the reactor, permanent disposal is needed because the wastes
will remain radioactive for thousands of years. There are both safety and
economic aspects to the nuclear waste issue: first, if not properly stored,
nuclear wastes might leak and endanger both the environment and human
health; second, the lack of a long-term disposal option increases the risk
that the insufficiency of interim storage space for spent fuel will lead to
reactor shutdowns, rendering nuclear energy an unpredictable and uneconomical adventure.

The California laws at issue here are responses to these concerns. In
1974, California adopted the Warren–Alquist State Energy Resources Conservation and Development Act, Cal. Pub. Res. Code Ann. § 25000–25986
(West 1977 and Supp. 1983). The Act requires that a utility seeking to
build in California any electric power generating plant, including a nuclear
power plant, must apply for certification to the State Energy Resources
Conservation and Development Commission (Energy Commission). The
Warren–Alquist Act was amended in 1976 to provide additional state
regulation of new nuclear power plant construction.

Two sections of these amendments are before us. Section 25524.1(b)
provides that before additional nuclear plants may be built, the Energy
Commission must determine on a case-by-case basis that there will be
"adequate capacity" for storage of a plant's spent fuel rods "at the time
such nuclear facility requires such ... storage." The law also requires that
each utility provide continuous, on-site, "full core reserve storage capacity"
in order to permit storage of the entire reactor core if it must be removed
to permit repairs of the reactor. In short, § 25524.1(b) addresses the
interim storage of spent fuel.

Section 25524.2 deals with the long-term solution to nuclear wastes.
This section imposes a moratorium on the certification of new nuclear
plants until the Energy Commission "finds that there has been developed
and that the United States through its authorized agency has approved and
there exists a demonstrated technology or means for the disposal of high-
level nuclear waste." "Disposal" is defined as a "method for the permanent
and terminal disposition of high-level nuclear waste ..." Cal. Pub. Res.

Code § 25524.2(a), (c). Such a finding must be reported to the state legislature, which may nullify it.

Petitioners Pacific Gas and Electric Company and Southern California Edison Company filed this action . . . alleging that the two provisions are void because they are preempted by and in conflict with the Atomic Energy Act . . . The Court of Appeals for the Ninth Circuit held that the California statutes . . . were not preempted because §§ 271 and 274(k) of the Atomic Energy Act, 42 U.S.C. §§ 2018 and 2021(k), constitute a Congressional authorization for states to regulate nuclear power plants "for purposes other than protection against radiation hazards."[13] . . .

From the passage of the Atomic Energy Act in 1954, through several revisions, and to the present day, Congress has preserved the dual regulation of nuclear-powered electricity generation: the Federal Government maintains complete control of the safety and "nuclear" aspects of energy generation; the States exercise their traditional authority over the need for additional generating capacity, the type of generating facilities to be licensed, land use, rate making, and the like . . .

The above is not particularly controversial. But deciding how § 25524.2 is to be construed and classified is a more difficult proposition. At the outset, we emphasize that the statute does not seek to regulate the construction or operation of a nuclear powerplant. It would clearly be impermissible for California to attempt to do so, for such regulation, even if enacted out of nonsafety concerns, would nevertheless directly conflict with the NRC's exclusive authority over plant construction and operation. Respondents appear to concede as much. Respondents do broadly argue, however, that although safety regulation of nuclear plants by States is forbidden, a State may completely prohibit new construction until its safety concerns are satisfied by the Federal Government. We reject this line of reasoning. State safety regulation is not pre-empted only when it conflicts with federal law. Rather, the Federal Government has occupied the entire field of nuclear safety concerns, except the limited powers expressly ceded to the States. When the Federal Government completely occupies a given field or an identifiable portion of it, as it has done here, the test of pre-emption is whether "the matter on which the State asserts the right to act is in any way regulated by the Federal Act." Rice v. Santa Fe Elevator Corp., *supra* 331 U.S., at 236. A state moratorium on nuclear construction grounded in safety concerns falls squarely within the prohibited field.

---

13. Section 271, 42 U.S.C § 2018, provides that: "Nothing in this chapter shall be construed to affect the authority or regulations of any Federal, State or local agency with respect to the generation, sale, or transmission of electric power produced through the use of nuclear facilities licensed by the Commission: Provided, That this section shall not be deemed to confer upon any Federal, State or local agency any authority to regulate, control, or restrict any activities of the Commission." Section 274(k), 42 U.S.C. § 2021(k), provides that: "Nothing in this section shall be construed to affect the authority of any State or local agency to regulate activities for purposes other than protection against radiation hazards." The role of these provisions in the federal regulatory structure is discussed *infra*, at 1724–1726.

We should not become embroiled in attempting to ascertain California's true motive. First, inquiry into legislative motive is often an unsatisfactory venture. *United States v. O'Brien*, 391 U.S. 367, 383 (1968). What motivates one legislator to vote for a statute is not necessarily what motivates scores of others to enact it. Second, it would be particularly pointless for us to engage in such inquiry here when it is clear that the States have been allowed to retain authority over the need for electrical generating facilities easily sufficient to permit a State so inclined to halt the construction of new nuclear plants by refusing on economic grounds to issue certificates of public convenience in individual proceedings. In these circumstances, it should be up to Congress to determine whether a State has misused the authority left in its hands.

Therefore, we accept California's avowed economic purpose as the rationale for enacting § 25524.2. Accordingly, the statute lies outside the occupied field of nuclear safety regulation.

Finally, it is strongly contended that § 25524.2 frustrates the Atomic Energy Act's purpose to develop the commercial use of nuclear power. It is well established that state law is pre-empted if it "stands as an obstacle to the accomplishment and execution of the full purposes and objectives of Congress." *Hines v. Davidowitz*, 312 U.S. 52, 67 (1941).

There is little doubt that a primary purpose of the Atomic Energy Act was, and continues to be, the promotion of nuclear power ... [But] the promotion of nuclear power is not to be accomplished "at all costs." The elaborate licensing and safety provisions and the continued preservation of state regulation in traditional areas belie that. Moreover, Congress has allowed the States to determine—as a matter of economics—whether a nuclear plant vis-a-vis a fossil fuel plant should be built. The decision of California to exercise that authority does not, in itself, constitute a basis for pre-emption. Therefore, while the argument of petitioners and the United States has considerable force, the legal reality remains that Congress has left sufficient authority in the States to allow the development of nuclear power to be slowed or even stopped for economic reasons. Given this statutory scheme, it is for Congress to rethink the division of regulatory authority in light of its possible exercise by the States to undercut a federal objective. The courts should not assume the role which our system assigns to Congress.

The judgment of the Court of Appeals is: Affirmed.

■ BLACKMUN, J., with whom JUSTICE STEVENS joins, concurring in part and concurring in the judgment: I join the Court's opinion, except to the extent it suggests that a State may not prohibit the construction of nuclear powerplants if the State is motivated by concerns about the safety of such plants. Since the Court finds that California was not so motivated, this suggestion is unnecessary to the Court's holding. [The dissent went on to explain why it believed California could prohibit nuclear power plants even if it were motivated by safety concerns.]■

NOTES AND COMMENTS

1. The background of the events that led to this case is discussed in Thomas R. Wellock, Critical Masses: Opposition to Nuclear Power in California, 1958–1978 (University of Wisconsin Press, 1998).

2. Given the Court's limited interpretation of Congress' intent to preempt state regulation, is it likely that any state that wants to prevent the construction of additional nuclear power plants will be able to do so? Do you agree with Donald Zillman's observation that "It does not take a very adept state legal counsel to advise the Legislature how to draft a 'no more nukes' statute that would be based on economic or planning reasons rather than on safety concerns."? Zillman, *supra* at 10–23. See also *Kerr-McGee Chemical Corp. v. City of West Chicago, 914 F.2d 820 (7th Cir. 1990)* (federal statute does not preempt a municipal ordinance that on its face targets only health and safety hazards unrelated to hazards created by radiation). Are there sound policy reasons why Congress might want to override state objections to nuclear power plants? See David B. Spence & Paula Murray, The Law, Economics, and Politics of Federal Preemption Jurisprudence: A Quantitative Analysis, 87 Calif. L. Rev. 1125 (1999).

3. Unlike regulatory issues, jurisdiction over damage actions alleging liability to the public for radiation-related damages is strictly preempted to actions in the federal courts under the Price–Anderson Act, which the supreme court has characterized as invoking "complete preemption doctrine" that converts an ordinary common law complaint into a federal cause of action. *El Paso Natural Gas Co. v. Neztsosie, 526 U.S. 473 (1999).* On the other hand, the Court upheld an award of damages under state law to an *employee* of a nuclear fuel fabrication facility licensed by the NRC. *Silkwood v. Kerr–McGee Corp.*, 464 U.S. 238 (1984). See also *English v. Gen. Elec. Co., 496 U.S. 72 (1990).*

D. DISPOSAL OF NUCLEAR WASTES

The most troublesome issue dogging nuclear power continues to be the disposal of nuclear waste. Almost thirty years have passed since the adoption of the California statute at issue in the *Pacific Gas & Electric* case, *supra*, but the industry is still unable to predict with assurance what will be done with used fuel rods. In addition, the disposal of less radioactive forms of radioactive waste continues to pose difficult political and legal problems.

1. THE NATURE OF NUCLEAR WASTES

The process by which nuclear fuel is created leaves radioactive waste behind at various stages of the process. The mining and milling of uranium creates piles of debris known as mill tailings, which contain small amounts of radioactive material. The handling of the material during the various stages of the process turns clothing, tools etc. into low-level sources of radioactivity. And when the fuel loses enough of its potency that it must be replaced, it still remains highly radioactive. See generally Bodansky *supra* at 193–251.

As the cases in the previous section indicate, concern with the disposal of waste materials from operations using nuclear energy have had a major impact on the willingness of people to develop new facilities using such energy. As radioactive material emits radiation it gradually loses its radioactive property. Some materials lose almost all of their radioactivity within a matter of days, while other materials will remain dangerously radioactive for thousands of years.

Humans and other animals are exposed to radioactivity in small amounts in everyday life from cosmic rays, elements such as radon in the soil, and other sources. But when radiation exceeds certain levels it can be very hazardous to health. In some cases, the gradual accumulation of radioactivity in the body can cause radiation sickness in people who never even knew they had been exposed. Although nuclear power plants emit no radiation to the outside environment that exceeds background levels, and although they have a much better safety record than most other power plants, many people remain overly fearful that accidents involving nuclear power could cause serious illness. Robert C. Morris, The Environmental Case for Nuclear Power.

When radioactive materials are used for medical or industrial purposes, they typically exhaust their productive radioactive capability over a period of time. At the end of that time they remain radioactive, though no longer producing the kind of radiation needed to perform the tasks for which they were intended. At that point, the user often seeks to dispose of the material, and it becomes categorized as radioactive waste. For almost half a century, Americans have been debating what to do with radioactive waste.

Under United States law, various categories of radioactive waste are treated under separate statutes and regulations. In general, the categories consist of (1) the waste from uranium mining, (2) military waste, (3) low-level waste, and (4) high-level waste.

2.   URANIUM MILL TAILINGS

When ore is processed to remove uranium, the ore that remains is referred to as uranium mill tailings. Such tailings contain low but significant levels of radioactivity. Most uranium mining in the United States has ceased production, but huge piles of uranium mill tailings remain near the mining sites.

The Uranium Mill Tailings Radiation Control Act of 1978, 42 U.S.C. § 2000 *et seq.*, provides that the Nuclear Regulatory Commission is to control the disposal of radioactive waste from uranium mill tailings. The Environmental Protection Agency adopted standards to be met by such disposal facilities (*see American Mining Cong. v. Thomas*, 772 F.2d 640 (10th Cir. 1985), cert. denied 476 U.S. 1158 (1986)), but it is the NRC that issues the permits. The ninth circuit rejected arguments of a citizen group that disposal of uranium mill tailings required an NPDES permit under the

Clean Water Act. The court found that the legislative intent of Congress in adopting the Uranium Mill Tailings Radiation Control Act of 1978 precluded joint jurisdiction under the Clean Water Act. *Waste Action Project v. Dawn Mining Corp.*, 137 F.3d 1426 (9th Cir. 1998).

Probably the most controversial uranium mill tailings site is located in Moab, Utah, and is now owned by Atlas Minerals Corporation, which is bankrupt. The site is adjacent to the bed of the Colorado River, and there are questions about the extent to which the site is contributing radioactivity to the waters of the river. Moab is a center for a growing tourist economy in southeast Utah, so the community is eager to see the problem resolved.

The company originally proposed a plan to decontaminate the tailings pile on-site by capping it. Opponents demanded that the tailings be moved to a site away from the river. On January 14, 2000, the Department of Energy announced that it would ask Congress for $300 million to remove the 10.6 million tons of tailings to a site away from the River. On November 9, 2004, the DOE published a draft EIS. http://www.antenna.nl /wise/uranium/udmoa.html.

3.   MILITARY RADIOACTIVE WASTE[14]

Large amounts of radioactive waste are being stored at the various sites used for defense-related research and development activities. Most of these sites are under the control of the Department of Energy. The DOE has begun shipments of this radioactive waste to the Waste Isolation Pilot Plant (WIPP) near Carlsbad, N.M. This is an underground storage facility located in a salt formation. *See* www.wipp.carlsbad.nm.us. The facility has been designed to store both transuranic waste (primarily materials contaminated by plutonium from weapons plants) and "mixed waste," defined as a mixture of hazardous chemicals and low-level radioactive waste. Transuranic waste is a residue of DOE military programs. The term refers to elements with an atomic number greater than 92.

Initially, WIPP is receiving shipments from Los Alamos, N.M., the Idaho National Engineering and Environmental Laboratory, and the Rocky Flats site near Denver. Eventually, shipments will come from DOE sites in 15 states. The material is being shipped by truck. The regulations provide for tracking of the trucks by satellite, and call for cooperation with state and local authorities to ensure the safety of the shipments. Some New Mexico state officials sought to prevent shipments to the plant but without success. *State of New Mexico ex. rel. Madrid v. Richardson*, 39 F.Supp. 2d 48 (D.D.C. 1999).

The costs of clean-up at commercial power plants pales in comparison to the cost of cleaning up some of the sites where early military nuclear work was done, such as Hanford, Washington and Rocky Flats, Colorado.

---

14. For a more complete analysis of the entire complex interrelationship of the military services with the environment, see Stephen Dycus, National Defense and the Environment (University Press of New England, 1996).

See Michele Stenehjem Gerber, On the Home Front: The Cold War Legacy of the Hanford Nuclear Site (University of Nebraska Press, 2d. Ed., 1997). Programs for military purposes have created some of the most contaminated sites in the country with cleanup costs in the billions of dollars. The estimate for cleaning up the Rocky Flats plant, near Denver, is $7.3 billion. More than a ton of plutonium is unaccounted for and believed to be lodged in the equipment and the ducts of the buildings. For a discussion of the cleanup problems at Hanford, *see* Gerald F. Hess, Hanford: Cleaning Up the Most Contaminated Place in the United States, 38 Ariz. L. Rev. 165 (1996); John S. Applegate & Stephen Dycus, Institutional Controls or Emperor's Clothes? Long–Term Stewardship of the Nuclear Weapons Complex, 28 Envt'l L. Rptr. 10631 (1998).

The Department of Energy seeks to store some high-level military waste in concrete-sealed storage tanks on the site of weapons plants. The district court in Idaho blocked this effort, and DOE has appealed and is also seeking specific authorization from Congress for such on-site storage.

4.   LOW-LEVEL RADIOACTIVE WASTE

Low-level radioactive wastes ("LLRW") are divided into four classes: Class A, B, C, and greater-than-C. The classes are ranked in order of their hazard level. Class A is the least hazardous and greater-than-C is the most hazardous. Class A and Class B wastes will decay during the 100–year period. 10 CFR § 61.7(b)(4). Class C waste will not decay to an acceptable level within 100 years. *Id.* at (b)(5). The majority of Class A waste has a half-life of less than five years.

Low-level radioactive waste includes lab coats, cloths, and other materials used where radioactive material is present, materials from hospitals used with radioactive material, carcasses of animals treated with radioactive materials, and research equipment from laboratories. Examples of Class A waste include materials such as trash, paper, plastic, medical and institutional wastes having low concentrations of radionuclides. Class B waste includes evaporator concentrates, resins and filters from medical isotope production facilities and from nuclear power plants. Class C contains mostly waste from nuclear power plants.[15]

a.   CURRENT STATUS

Currently, three active LLRW sites are located in the United States. They are located in South Carolina, Washington, and Utah. Disposal at all three sites grew in volume by about 12 million cubic feet in 2003. This volume is a 200% increase over the amount disposed of in 1999. Classes A, B, and C are disposed of at all three sites, but the Utah site takes most of the Class A waste while most of the Class B and C waste is sent to South Carolina. Class A waste composed 99% of all waste in 2003. United States Regulatory Commission, http://www.nrc.gov/waste/llw-disposal.html. None

---

15. See What is Low–Level Radioactive Waste, Ohio State University, http://www.ag.ohio-state.edu/?rer/rerhtml/rer_10.html (a. June 8, 2005).

of the sites are currently expected to close, but in 2008, the South Carolina site will no longer accept waste from states that are not in its compact. However, South Carolina's position with regards to accepting waste from other states has changed before. Government Accountability Office, Disposal Availability Adequate in Short Term, but Oversight Needed to Identify any Future Shortfalls, GAO–04–604 (June, 2004).

In May, 2005, a new LLRW site in Andrews, Texas, began taking waste from the Fernald, Ohio uranium processing plant. Greenwire, July 6, 2005. The newly Republican-dominated Texas legislature has supported such a facility as a potential revenue source for the state, but arguments remain about the categories of waste to be stored.[16]

b. INTERSTATE COMPACTS

Congress, through the Low–Level Radioactive Waste Policy Amendments Act of 1985, 42 U.S.C. § 2021b *et seq.*, tried to implement a national policy for low-level nuclear waste disposal without preempting all of the states' traditional authority over the use of land within their jurisdictions. Relying largely on a report submitted by the National Governors' Association, Congress declared a federal policy of holding each State "responsible for providing for the availability of capacity either within or outside the State for the disposal of low-level radioactive waste generated within its borders," and found that such waste could be disposed of "most safely and efficiently ... on a regional basis." § 4(a)(1). The 1980 Act authorized States to enter into regional compacts that, once ratified by Congress, would have the authority beginning in 1986 to restrict the use of their disposal facilities to waste generated within member States. § 4(a)(2)(B). The 1980 Act included no penalties for States that failed to participate in this plan.

By 1985, only three approved regional compacts had operational disposal facilities, and these were pre-existing facilities in South Carolina, Nevada, and Washington. No new facilities had been sited. The 1980 Act would have given these three compacts the ability to exclude waste from nonmembers, and the remaining 31 States would have had no assured outlet for their low level radioactive waste. To avoid that prospect, Congress passed the Low–Level Radioactive Waste Policy Amendments Act of 1985.

The 1985 Act was again based largely on a proposal submitted by the National Governors' Association. It required the existing facilities to continue to accept waste from any other state for seven years, but after 1992 "Each State shall be responsible for providing, either by itself or in cooperation with other States, for the disposal of ... low-level radioactive waste generated within the State," 42 U.S.C. § 2021c(a)(1)(A), with the exception of certain waste generated by the Federal Government, §§ 2021c(a)(1)(B), 2021c(b). The Act authorizes States to "enter into such

---

16. For background on the site and speculation about future plans for it, see Randy Lee Loftis, Nuclear disposal deal in the works, Dallas Morning News, March 12, 2005, page 1A.

[interstate] compacts as may be necessary to provide for the establishment and operation of regional disposal facilities for low-level radioactive waste." § 2021d(a)(2). After the seven-year transition period expires, approved regional compacts may exclude radioactive waste generated outside the region. § 2021d(c).

The Act provides three types of incentives to encourage the States to comply with their statutory obligation to provide for the disposal of waste generated within their borders. (1) Monetary incentives. One quarter of the surcharges, which states in which disposal facilities are located are entitled to collect, is to be transferred to other states that meet certain statutory deadlines. § 2021e(d)(2)(A). (2). Access incentives. The second type of incentive involves the denial of access to disposal sites. States that fail to meet the statutory deadlines may be denied access to disposal facilities thereafter. § 2021e(e)(2). (3) The take title provision. The Act provides: "If a State (or, where applicable, a compact region) in which low-level radioactive waste is generated is unable to provide for the disposal of all such waste generated within such State or compact region by January 1, 1996, each State in which such waste is generated, upon the request of the generator or owner of the waste, shall take title to the waste, be obligated to take possession of the waste, and shall be liable for all damages directly or indirectly incurred by such generator or owner as a consequence of the failure of the State to take possession of the waste as soon after January 1, 1996, as the generator or owner notifies the State that the waste is available for shipment." § 2021e(d)(2)(C).

Despite the fact that the statute was written by the state governments themselves, the Supreme Court held that the Tenth Amendment was violated by the section of the act that would have required each state government to "take title" to all low-level waste in the state if it could not find a workable disposal site. *New York v. United States*, 112 S. Ct. 2408 (1992):

> The take title provision appears to be unique. No other federal statute has been cited which offers a state government no option other than that of implementing legislation enacted by Congress. Whether one views the take title provision as lying outside Congress' enumerated powers, or as infringing upon the core of state sovereignty reserved by the Tenth Amendment, the provision is inconsistent with the federal structure of our Government established by the Constitution....

> Respondents note that the Act embodies a bargain among the sited and unsited States, a compromise to which New York was a willing participant and from which New York has reaped much benefit. Respondents then pose what appears at first to be a troubling question: How can a federal statute be found an unconstitutional infringement of State sovereignty when state officials consented to the statute's enactment?

> The answer follows from an understanding of the fundamental purpose served by our Government's federal structure. The Constitu-

tion does not protect the sovereignty of States for the benefit of the States or state governments as abstract political entities, or even for the benefit of the public officials governing the States. To the contrary, the Constitution divides authority between federal and state governments for the protection of individuals. State sovereignty is not just an end in itself: "Rather, federalism secures to citizens the liberties that derive from the diffusion of sovereign power." *Coleman v. Thompson*, 111 S. Ct. 2546, 2570 (1991) (Blackmun, J., dissenting). "Just as the separation and independence of the coordinate Branches of the Federal Government serves to prevent the accumulation of excessive power in any one Branch, a healthy balance of power between the States and the Federal Government will reduce the risk of tyranny and abuse from either front." *Gregory v. Ashcroft*, 111 S. Ct. 2395, 2400 (1991). *See* The Federalist No. 51, p. 323.

Where Congress exceeds its authority relative to the States, therefore, the departure from the constitutional plan cannot be ratified by the "consent" of state officials. . . .

The Court said that state officials could not negate the Constitution's allocation of authority by purporting to submit to the direction of Congress to avoid the appearance of personal responsibility.

Whether the Act would have succeeded in obtaining approval of numerous disposal sites if the take-title provision had been upheld is a question that will remain unanswered. What is clear is that in the absence of that provision the Act has not provided enough carrots or sticks to persuade state and local government officials to take the unpopular step of approving the permits necessary to bring these sites into operation.

A study by the General Accounting Office in 1999 found that "the efforts by states to develop new disposal facilities have essentially stopped." GAO, Low-level Radioactive Wastes: States Are Not Developing Disposal Facilities (Sept., 1999). For example, the Central Interstate Low–Level Radioactive Waste Compact Commission ("Commission") was formed with five states, including Nebraska. *Entergy Arkansas, Inc. v. Nebraska*, 358 F. 3d 528, 532 (2004). The Commission chose Nebraska as the site of a future LLRW facility. *Id.* The licensing application process and approval by Nebraska took over eight years and cost over $88 million. *Id.* at 535–536. The Commission had to pay all of the costs associated with the licensing application process, but Nebraska controlled the length of the process. *Id.* at 536. Since the Commission could not afford the licensing costs, it entered into an agreement with LLRW generators where the generators prepaid for disposal services. *Id.* at 537–538. When Nebraska ultimately denied the license for the LLRW facility, the Commission and the generators brought suit. *Id.* at 538.

The district court found for the Commission and the state of Nebraska and its government offices ("Nebraska") appealed. The 8th Circuit Court of Appeals affirmed. *Id.* The court held that Nebraska did not have the right to a jury trial under the Seventh Amendment because this action did not arise from state common law, but from federal law because Congress approved the Commission. *Id.* at 542. Further, the Commission was not a private litigant, and this suit is more comparable to an action between sovereigns, which historically have no juries. *Id.* at 544.

The court also held that the proper focus when reviewing Nebraska's licensing process was whether it acted in good faith and not whether it acted arbitrarily and capriciously. *Id.* The district court found that Nebraska did not base its license denial on the technical aspects, but rather on the administration's bias against building the facility in Nebraska. *Id.* at 551. Because of the facts, the court of appeals held that Nebraska breached its good-faith obligation under the compact. *Id.* at 553. Further, the court held that monetary relief was the appropriate remedy for the good-faith breach and that the Commission could recover damages for all work and money put into the licensing process. *Id.* at 555. The court held that since Nebraska "waived its sovereign immunity from an award of damages, it also has no immunity from the assessment of interest." *Id.* at 556.

The court ultimately affirmed the district court's judgment against Nebraska for a total of $151,408,240.37. *Id.* at 540. Nebraska then accepted a settlement with the Commission under which it will pay $141,000,000 plus interest. Robin M. Nazzaro, Testimony before the Senate Committee on Energy and Natural Resources, GAO–04–1097T September 30, 2004. For a discussion of other state attempts to bar LLRW, see Melissas Beutler Orien, Battle over Control of Low–Level Radioactive Waste: Some States Are Overstepping Their Bounds, 2005 B.Y.U.L. Rev. 155 (2005).

c.   GREATER THAN CLASS C WASTE

Greater-than-C waste is to be disposed of by the Department of Energy because of the high radiation levels. While the DOE has not yet provided a waste site for the greater-than-C waste, it has begun the environmental analysis to build a permanent disposal facility. Robin M. Nazzaro, Testimony before the Senate Committee on Energy and Natural Resources, GAO–04–1097T September 30, 2004.

The Department of Energy is required to submit to Congress a report on a permanent disposal facility for greater-than-class-C waste by August 2006. Meanwhile, Congress has asked DOE to submit a plan to ensure "the continued recovery and storage of greater-than-class-C low-level radioactive sealed sources that pose a security threat until a permanent disposal facility is available." *See* Section 631 of the Energy Policy Act of 2005.

5.   HIGH-LEVEL NUCLEAR WASTE

The problems associated with the disposal of low-level nuclear waste have been frustrating. The gravity of the low-level waste issue, however, pales in comparison to the problem of disposal of high-level waste.

a.   HOW HIGH-LEVEL WASTE IS CREATED

High-level radioactive wastes are the byproducts of the reactions that occur inside nuclear reactors. "The spent fuel is commonly referred to as 'waste,' although some of the radionuclides have potentially useful applications and it has been argued that spent fuel is a resource, not a waste product." Bodansky *supra* at 231–32.

The waste is highly radioactive and comes in two forms. One is spent waste, which is the reactor fuel that is ready to be disposed. 42 U.S.C. § 10101(12). The other is the waste materials that remain after reprocessing spent fuel in defense or energy department facilities.[17] The high-level radioactive waste is thermally hot and potentially harmful. US Nuclear Regulatory Commission, http://www.nrc.gov/waste/high-level-waste.html (a. June 8, 2005).

The US Nuclear Regulatory Commission estimates that about 45,000 tons of spent fuel from nuclear power plants are in the United States. The waste is stored in 160,000 spent fuel assemblies. About 156,500 assemblies are stored at nuclear power plants and 3500 are in other storage facilities that are away-from-reactor facilities. Most of the assemblies in away-from-reactor facilities are in wet storage and only about 5% of those are in dry storage.[18]

b. CURRENT STORAGE METHODS FOR HIGH LEVEL WASTE

Currently, spent fuel is being stored in water pools on the site of each nuclear power plant in which the fuel had been used. To the extent that the capacity of the water pool is used up, the firm switches to dry cask storage.

Water pool storage of spent nuclear fuel uses water to cool the fuel and to shield from radiation. One of the potential dangers of wet storage is an uncontrolled nuclear reaction, which is called criticality. In order to prevent criticality, the pools require constant supervision and operation of the cooling, filtration, and cleaning systems. This constant supervision results in high operating and storage costs for water pool storage systems.

As the interim storage of high-level waste began to outgrow the water-filled pools that were included as part of the plants' original designs, the NRC authorized the use of dry cask storage, which can be undertaken by a plant operator if an NRC-approved cask design is used. *See Kelley v. Nuclear Regulatory Comm'n*, 42 F.3d 1501 (6th Cir. 1995). These casks are kept above ground on the power plant site. Dry cask storage uses concrete or steel containers to shield from radiation and the fuel is cooled by inert gas or air. The fuel is cooled in water pools for several years before being placed in the dry casks. The casks are created to resist temperature extremes, floods, tornadoes, and projectiles. *See* US Nuclear Regulatory Commission Fact Sheet, Dry Cask Storage of Spent Nuclear Fuel. Because dry cask storage does not require any electricity, water, or maintenance, its

---

17. Some of the government's high-level radioactive waste is in South Carolina, Idaho, Washington, and at the Nuclear Fuel Services Plant in West Valley, New York, where the waste is stored underground on the federal reservations. Ninety-nine percent of the high-level radioactive waste is from defense related activities. EPA Spent Nuclear Fuel and High–Level Radioactive Waste, http://www.epa.gov/radiation/docs/radwaste/snf_hlw.htm.

18. U.S. Nuclear Regulatory Commission, http://www.nrc.gov/reading-rm/doc?collections /nuregs/brochure/br0216/r2/#hlw.

operating costs are much lower than that for water pool storage. The dry casks do require monitoring and surveillance, but not the constant supervision and operation that water pools require.

Since September 11th, 2001, security at nuclear power plants has been questioned. In September 2003, the US General Accountability Office (GAO) conducted a study on the NRC's regulation of plant security. The GAO concluded that the security at commercial nuclear power plants needed to be strengthened. The GAO report identifies three areas that are problematic. First, the NRC often identifies security problems as "non-cited violations" if the problem did not result in any immediate consequences or if the problem was not frequently identified in the past. A non-cited violation does not require the NRC to verify that the problem was corrected. In addition, the violating nuclear power plant does not have to provide a written response to the violation. For example, non-cited violations were issued for a security guard who had been asleep for over thirty minutes and for inspectors who failed to physically search individuals that set off the metal detectors. Those individuals were then allowed to access the protected areas of the plant without any escorts.

Second, the NRC has no method for collecting and disseminating important information to the power plants. No process exists to characterize problems that may be common to many plants or to provide information on how past problems were resolved.

Third, NRC's force-on-force exercises, which are simulated attacks on the nuclear power plants to test their security, are not realistic for several reasons. During the exercises, the nuclear power plants had a larger number of security personnel than normal. The GAO found that an average of 80% more guards were used for these exercises than what the power plant's security plan included. The individuals conducting the security exercises are not trained in terrorist tactics. Also, rubber guns are used, which do not simulate actual gunfire. The rubber weapons make it difficult to determine if the intended target was hit. In addition, after conducting the force-on-force exercises, the plants were required to submit an Operational Safeguards Response Evaluation. About 60% of these reports were not submitted to the NRC within the required time period, which results in less effective feedback and slower reactions to any needed changes. For the previous reasons, the GAO determined that the NRC needed to increase security at commercial nuclear power plants. *See* Nuclear Regulatory Commission, Oversight of Security at Commercial Nuclear Power Plants Needs to Be Strengthened, September 2003.

In addition to the GAO report, critics of nuclear power plant security cite other reasons for security concerns. The Physicians for Social Responsibility state that there have been credible threats to nuclear power plants not only since September 11th, but also before. *See* http://www.psr.org //print.cfm?id=pressroom18&ignore=page_check. One potential problem with the nuclear power plants is that they were not tested to withstand the type of attack that occurred on September 11th because it was not considered to be likely that terrorists would take over and pilot a jet airliner. Some critics assert that if an airplane could hit the containment structure and introduce jet fuel, it could cause a severe explosion and fire. Furthermore, the Physicians for Social Responsibility say that since 1991, about 47% of nuclear plants failed to pass the NRC mock terrorists attacks, even with months of warning and the extra security force employed to respond for such tests. The Union for Concerned Scientists also states that nuclear power plants need more security because they are vulnerable not only to attacks by land, but also by air and water. *See* http://www.ucsu-sa.org/news/press_release.cfm?newsID=415 (a. June 8, 2005).

Given these concerns, Congress asked the National Research Council (an arm of the National Academy of Sciences and the National Academy of Engineering) to study the safety risks associated with the continued storage of spent fuel at power plant sites. The classified report of the study was delivered to the Nuclear Regulatory Commission in 2004. After long debates between the Academies and the Commission, a censored version was released to the public in 2005.

National Research Council Safety and Security of Commercial Spent Nuclear Fuel Storage: Public Report (2005)[19]

In the Fiscal Year 2004 Energy and Water Development Conference Report, the U.S. Congress asked the National Academies to provide independent scientific and technical advice on the safety and security of commercial spent nuclear fuel storage in the United States, specifically with respect to the following four charges:

(1) Potential safety and security risks of spent nuclear fuel presently stored in cooling pools at commercial reactor sites.

(2) Safety and security advantages, if any, of dry cask storage versus wet pool storage at these reactor sites.

(3) Potential safety and security advantages, if any, of dry cask storage using various single-, dual-, and multi-purpose cask designs.

(4) The risks of terrorist attacks on these materials and the risk these materials might be used to construct a radiological dispersal device.

Congress requested that the National Academies produce a classified report that addresses these charges within 6 months and also provide an unclassified summary for unlimited public distribution. The first request was fulfilled in July 2004. This report fulfills the second request.

Spent nuclear fuel is stored at commercial nuclear power-plant sites in two configurations: (1) In water-filled pools, referred to as *spent fuel pools,* and (2) in *dry* casks that are designed either for storage (single-purpose casks) or both storage and transportation (dual-purpose casks). There are

---

19. As of July 2005, the report is available only on the internet, but National Academies Press says it will publish it as a book. The internet site is http://www.nap.edu/openbook /0309096472/html/1.html.

two basic cask designs: bare-fuel casks and canister-based casks, which can be licensed for either single-or dual-purpose use, depending on their design.

Spent fuel pools are currently in use at all 65 sites with operating commercial nuclear power reactors, at 8 sites where commercial power reactors have been shut down, and at one site not associated with an operating or shutdown power reactor. Dry-cask storage facilities have been established at 28 operating, shutdown, or decommissioned power plants. The nuclear industry projects that up to three or four nuclear power plants will reach full capacity in their spent fuel pools each year for at least the next 17 years.

The congressional request for this study was prompted by conflicting public claims about the safety and security of commercial spent nuclear fuel storage at nuclear power plants. Some analysts have argued that the dense packing of spent fuel in cooling pools at nuclear power plants does not allow a sufficient safety margin in the event of a loss-of-poolcoolant event from an accident or terrorist attack. They assert that such events could result in the release of large quantities of radioactive material to the environment if the zirconium cladding of the spent fuel overheats and ignites. To reduce the potential for such fires, these analysts have suggested that spent fuel more than five years old be removed from the pool and stored in dry casks, and that remaining younger fuel be reconfigured in the pool to allow more space for air cooling in the event of a loss-of-pool-coolant event. * * *

The committee's findings and recommendations from *this analysis* are provided below, organized by the four charges of the study task. The ordering of the charges has been rearranged to provide a more logical exposition of results.

CHARGE 4: RISKS OF TERRORIST ATTACKS ON THESE MATERIALS AND THE RISK THESE MATERIALS MIGHT BE USED TO CONSTRUCT A RADIOLOGICAL DISPERSAL DEVICE

The concept of risk as applied to terrorist attacks underpins the entire statement of task for this study. Therefore, the committee examined this final charge first to provide the basis for addressing the remainder of the task statement. The committee's examination of Charge 4 is provided in Chapter 2. On the basis of this examination, the committee offers the following findings and recommendations numbered according to the chapters in which they appear:

FINDING 2A: The probability of terrorist attacks on spent fuel storage cannot be assessed quantitatively or comparatively. Spent fuel storage facilities cannot be dismissed as targets for such attacks because it is not possible to predict the behavior and motivations of terrorists, and because of the attractiveness of spent fuel as a terrorist target given the well known public dread of radiation. Terrorists view nuclear power plant facilities as desirable targets because of the large inventories of radioactivity they contain. While it would be difficult to attack such facilities, the committee judges that attacks by knowledgeable terrorists with access to appropriate technical means are possible. It is important to recognize, however, that an attack that damages a power plant or its spent fuel storage facilities would not necessarily result in the release of *any* radioactivity to the environment. There are potential steps that can be taken to lower the potential consequences of such attacks.

FINDING 2B: The committee judges that the likelihood terrorists could steal enough spent fuel for use in a significant radiological dispersal device is small. Removal of a spent fuel assembly from the pool or dry cask would prove extremely difficult under almost any terrorist attack scenario. Attempts by a knowledgeable insider(s) to remove single rods and related debris from the pool might prove easier, but the amount of material that could be removed would be small. Moreover, superior materials could be stolen or purchased more easily from other sources. Even though the likelihood of spent fuel theft appears to be small, it is nevertheless important that the protection of these materials be maintained and improved as vulnerabilities are identified.

RECOMMENDATION: The Nuclear Regulatory Commission should review and upgrade, where necessary, its security requirements for protecting spent fuel rods not contained in fuel assemblies from theft by knowledgeable insiders, especially in facilities where individual fuel rods or portions of rods are being stored in pools.

FINDING 2C: A number of security improvements at nuclear power plants have been instituted since the events of September 11, 2001. However, the Nuclear Regulatory Commission did not provide the committee with enough information to evaluate the effectiveness of these procedures for protecting stored spent fuel. Surveillance and other human-factors related security procedures are just as important as the physical barriers in preventing and mitigating terrorist attacks. Although the committee did learn about some of the changes that have been instituted since the September 11, 2001 attacks, it was not provided with enough information to evaluate the effectiveness of procedures now in place.

RECOMMENDATION: Although the committee did not specifically investigate the effectiveness and adequacy of improved surveillance and security measures for protecting stored spent fuel, an assessment of current measures should be performed by an independent organization.

CHARGE 1: POTENTIAL SAFETY AND SECURITY RISKS OF SPENT NUCLEAR FUEL STORED IN POOLS

The committee's examination of Charge 1 is provided in Chapter 3. On the basis of this examination, the committee offers the following findings and recommendations:

FINDING 3A: Pool storage is required at all operating commercial nuclear power plants to cool newly discharged spent fuel. Freshly discharged spent fuel generates too much decay heat to be passively air cooled. This fuel must be stored in a pool that has an active heat removal system (i.e., water pumps and heat exchangers) for at least one year before being moved to dry storage. Most dry storage systems are licensed to store fuel that has been out of the reactor for at least five years: Although spent fuel younger than five years could be stored in dry casks, the changes required for shielding and heat-removal could be substantial, especially for fuel that has been discharged for less than about three years.

FINDING 3B: The committee finds that, under some conditions, a terrorist attack that partially or completely drained a spent fuel pool could lead to a propagating zirconium cladding fire and the release of large quantities of radioactive materials to the environment. Details are provided in the committee's classified report.

FINDING 3C: it appears to be feasible to reduce the likelihood of a zirconium cladding fire following the loss-of-pool-coolant event using readily implemented measures. The following measures appear to have particular merit: Reconfiguring the spent fuel in the pools (i.e., redistribution of high decay-heat assemblies so that they are surrounded by low decay-heat assemblies) to more evenly distribute decay-heat loads and enhance radiative heat transfer; limiting the frequency of offloads of full reactor cores into spent fuel pools, requiring longer shut downs of the reactor before any fuel is offloaded, and providing enhanced security when such offloads must be made; and development of a redundant and diverse response system to mitigate loss-of-pool-coolant events that would be capable of operation even if the pool or overlying building were severely damaged.

FINDING 3D: The potential vulnerabilities of spent fuel pools to terrorist attacks are plant-design specific. Therefore, specific vulnerabilities can only be understood by examining the characteristics of spent fuel storage at each plant. As described in Chapter 3, there are substantial differences in the designs of spent fuel pools that make them more or less vulnerable to certain types of terrorist attacks.

FINDING 3E: The Nuclear Regulatory Commission and independent analysts have made progress in understanding some vulnerabilities of spent fuel pools to certain terrorist attacks and the consequences of such attacks for releases of radioactivity to the environment. However, additional work on specific issues is needed urgently. The analyses carried out to date provide a general understanding of spent fuel behavior in a loss-of-pool-coolant event and the vulnerability of spent fuel pools to certain terrorist attacks that could cause such events to occur. The work to date, however, has not been sufficient to adequately understand the vulnerabilities and consequences of such events. Additional analyses are needed to fill in the knowledge gaps so that well-informed policy decisions can be made.

RECOMMENDATION: The Nuclear Regulatory Commission should undertake additional best-estimate analyses to more fully

understand the vulnerabilities and consequences of loss-of-pool-coolant events that could lead to a zirconium cladding fire. Based on these analyses, the Commission should take appropriate actions to address any significant vulnerabilities that are identified. The committee provides details on additional analyses that should be carried out in its classified report. Cost-benefit considerations will be an important part of such decisions.

RECOMMENDATION: While the work described in the previous recommendation under Finding 3E, above, is being carried out, the Nuclear Regulatory commission should ensure that power plant operators take prompt and effective measures to reduce the consequences of loss-of-pool-coolant events in spent fuel pools that could result in propagating zirconium cladding fires. The committee believes that there are at least two such measures that should be implemented promptly: (1) Reconfiguring of fuel in the pools so that high decay-heat fuel assemblies are surrounded by low decay-heat assemblies. This will more evenly distribute decay-heat loads, thus enhancing radiative heat transfer in the event of a loss of pool coolant. (2) Provision for water-spray systems that would be able to cool the fuel even if the pool or overlying building were severely damaged.

Reconfiguring of fuel in the pool would be a prudent measure that could probably be implemented at all plants at little cost, time, or exposure of workers to radiation. The second measure would probably be more expensive to implement and may not be needed at all plants, particularly plants in which spent fuel pools are located below grade or are protected from external line-of-sight attacks by exterior walls and other structures.

The committee anticipates that the costs and benefits of options for implementing the second measure would be examined to help decide what requirements would be imposed. Further, the committee does not presume to anticipate the best design of such a system whether it should be installed on the walls of a pool or deployed from a location where it is unlikely to be compromised by the same attack—but simply notes the demanding requirements such a system must meet.

CHARGE 3: POTENTIAL SAFETY AND SECURITY ADVANTAGES, IF ANY, OF DIFFERENT DRY CASK STORAGE DESIGNS

The third charge to the committee focuses exclusively on the safety and security of dry casks. The committee addressed this charge first in Chapter 4 to provide the basis for the comparative analysis between dry casks and pools as called for in Charge 2.

FINDING 4A: Although there are differences in the robustness of different dry cask designs (e.g., bare-fuel versus canister-based), the differences are not large when measured by the absolute magnitudes of radionuclide releases in the event of a breach. All storage cask designs are vulnerable to some types of terrorist attacks, but the quantity of radioactive material releases predicted from such attacks is relatively small. These releases are not easily dispersed in the environment.

FINDING 4B: Additional steps can be taken to make dry casks less vulnerable to potential terrorist attacks. Although the vulnerabilities of current cask designs are already small, additional, relatively simple steps can be taken to reduce them as discussed in Chapter 4.

RECOMMENDATION: The Nuclear Regulatory Commission should consider using the results of the vulnerability analyses for possible upgrades of requirements in 10 CFR 72 for dry casks, specifically to improve their resistance to terrorist attacks. The committee was told by Nuclear Regulatory Commission staff that such a step is already under consideration.

CHARGE 2: SAFETY AND SECURITY ADVANTAGES, IF ANY, OF DRY CASK STORAGE VERSUS WET POOL STORAGE

In Chapter 4, the committee offers the following findings and recommendations with respect to the comparative component of Charge 2:

FINDING 4C: Dry cask storage does not eliminate the need for pool storage at operating commercial reactors. Under present U.S. practices, dry cask storage can only be used to store fuel that has been out of the reactor long enough (generally greater than 5 years under current practices) to be passively air cooled.

FINDING 4D: Dry cask storage for older, cooler spent fuel has two inherent advantages over pool storage: (1) It is a passive system that relies on natural air circulation for cooling; and (2) it divides the inventory of that spent fuel among a large number of discrete, robust containers. These factors make it more difficult to attack a large amount of spent fuel at one time and also reduce the consequences of such attacks. The robust construction of these casks prevents large-scale releases of radioactivity in all of the attack scenarios examined by the committee in its classified report.

FINDING 4E: Depending on the outcome of plant-specific vulnerability analyses described in the committee's classified report, the Nuclear Regulatory Commission might determine that earlier movements of spent fuel from pools into dry cask *storage* would *be* prudent to reduce the potential consequences of terrorist attacks on pools at some commercial nuclear plants. The statement of task directs the committee to examine the risks of spent fuel storage options and alternatives for decision makers; not to recommend whether any spent fuel should be transferred from pool storage to cask storage. In fact, there may be some commercial plants that, because of pool designs or fuel loadings, may require some removal of spent fuel from their pools. If there is a need to remove spent fuel from the pools it should become clearer once the *vulnerability* and consequence analyses described in the classified report are completed. The committee expects that cost-benefit considerations would be a part of these analyses.

[In a brief section not included in this excerpt, the committee also recommended that the Commission improve the sharing of safety and security information among the commission staff, plant operators and storage system vendors.]■

NOTES AND COMMENTS

1. As the report suggests, the on-site water pool storage of spent fuel rods raises the greatest security concerns in plants where the spent fuel rods are stored above the reactor. The spent fuel pools are not as protected as the reactor and the NRC has acknowledged that a large enough plane could penetrate the roof. Another concern is the fear of a terrorist attack that drained water or stopped the cooling system, which could possibly cause the zirconium cladding of the fuel rods to ignite.

2. Section 170E of the Energy Policy Act of 2005 requires the Nuclear Regulatory Commission to undertake a "design basis threat rulemaking" process that will address the various risks of intentional attack against a nuclear facility. It also instructs the NRC to employ a federal security coordinator at each regional office of the Commission monitor security at nuclear facilities within the region.

3. The environmental group, Greenpeace, had been one of the most vocal in arguing that spent fuel should be stored in dry casks to the extent possible. They have argued that if an accident did occur at a nuclear power plant, it would be very hard, if even possible, to maintain the adequate water requirements to keep the reactor pools safe.[20] The National Research Council's report appears to provide strong support for their position, at least in regard to plants in which the water pool is not adequately protected.

c. THE NUCLEAR WASTE POLICY ACT OF 1982

The policy of the United States government since the late 1970s has been based on the desire to bury all of the fuel rods from nuclear power plants at an underground disposal site. The Nuclear Waste Policy Act of 1982 (NWPA) 42 U.S.C. § 10101 *et seq.*, gave the Department of Energy the responsibility of finding a site for the permanent disposal of high-level nuclear waste. DOE selected five potential sites in 1986: Richton Dome, Mississippi; Yucca Mountain, Nevada; Deaf Smith, Texas; David Canyon, Utah; and Hanford, Washington. Of these five sites, the Secretary recommended and the President approved for site characterization studies the three sites in Nevada, Texas, and Washington.

Congress reacted to a storm of opposition to these sites by narrowing the selection to the single site at Yucca Mountain. *See* 42 U.S.C. § 10172 (1987). After exploratory work at the site satisfied the DOE, NRC and EPA that the site was safe, President George W. Bush submitted to Congress a recommendation that the site be approved, which Congress accepted.

---

20. See Greenpeace, Dry Storage of Spent Nuclear Fuel: The Safer Alternative to Reprocessing, http://www.greenpeace.fr/campagnes/nucleaire/dossiers/OSPARfairlie.pdf   (a. June 8, 2005).

Under the statute, this authorized the DOE to proceed with an application to the NRC for a license. The total amount of spent fuel held at power plants and destined for Yucca Mountain is scheduled to reach the congressionally mandated cap of 63,000 tons by 2010, which is the year the repository is nominally scheduled to begin receiving waste. David Bodansky, Nuclear Energy: Principles, Practices and Prospects 235 (2d ed., Springer–Verlag, 2004).

d.   PROTECTING FUTURE GENERATIONS: THE CLOUDY CRYSTAL BALL

Underground burial of nuclear waste reflects a kind of natural logic. "The uranium at the heart of those wastes was once an ore brought up from deep beneath the ground, and even though humankind has fired that ore into something truly awesome, it seems to make intuitive sense to put it back. Ashes to ashes, dust to dust. Besides, we are creatures of the surface in much the same way that aquatic animals are creatures of the deep and we find it easy to suppose that we have disposed of something, rid ourselves of something, if it is lifted above or sunk below the plane on which we live." Kai Erickson, 12,000 A.D.: Are You Listening?, The New York Times Magazine, March 6, 1994.

Permanent underground disposal also offers perhaps the best security against potential terrorist attempts to use nuclear waste. The Swedish government's concern has led it to test a site on the Simpevarp Peninsula as a potential site for disposal of the waste from Sweden's 11 nuclear power plants. Richard Stone, Deep Repositories: Out of Sight, Out of Terrorists' Reach, 303 Science 161 (2004). The managing the atom project at Harvard University argues that permanent entombment is far more cost-effective than any other alternative disposal method. See Managing the Atom Project, The Economics of Reprocessing vs. Direct Disposal of Spent Nuclear Fuel, December, 2003.

Throughout the discussions of permanent disposal one issue has been dominant: How far into the future should the government need to plan to ensure the safety of the burial site?

Nuclear Energy Institute, Inc. v. EPA

373 F.3d 1251 (D.C. Cir. 2004).

■ PER CURIAM. Having the capacity to outlast human civilization as we know it and the potential to devastate public health and the environment, nuclear waste has vexed scientists, Congress, and regulatory agencies for the last half-century. After rejecting disposal options ranging from burying nuclear waste in polar ice caps to rocketing it to the sun, the scientific consensus has settled on deep geologic burial as the safest way to isolate this toxic material in perpetuity. Following years of legislative wrangling and agency deliberation, the political consensus has now selected Yucca Mountain, Nevada as the nation's nuclear waste disposal site.

In this case, we consider challenges by the State of Nevada, local communities, several environmental organizations, and the nuclear energy industry to the statutory and regulatory scheme devised to establish and govern a Yucca Mountain nuclear waste repository. Petitioners challenge regulations issued by the three agencies with responsibility for the site: the Environmental Protection Agency (EPA), the Nuclear Regulatory Commission (NRC or Commission), and the Department of Energy (DOE).

Since the dawn of the atomic age, the United States has used nuclear fission to generate electricity. Today, approximately twenty percent of the nation's electricity comes from nuclear power. *See* Recommendation by the Secretary of Energy Regarding the Suitability of the Yucca Mountain Site for a Repository Under the *Nuclear Waste Policy Act of 1982* at 1 (Feb. 2002), *available at* http://www.ocrwm. doe.gov/ymp/sr/sar.pdf [hereinafter "Secretary's Recommendation"]. Although nuclear power burns without emitting harmful greenhouse gases, it produces a potentially deadly and long-lasting byproduct: highly radioactive spent nuclear fuel.

At massive levels, radiation exposure can cause sudden death. National Institutes of Health, Fact Sheet: What We Know About Radiation, *at* http://www.nih.gov/health/chip/od/radiation (last visited May 28, 2004). At lower doses, radiation can have devastating health effects, including increased cancer risks and serious birth defects such as mental retardation, eye malformations, and small brain or head size. *See Environmental Radiation Protection Standards for Yucca Mountain, Nevada, 64 Fed. Reg. 46,976, 46,978 (Aug. 27, 1999)*.

Radioactive waste and its harmful consequences persist for time spans seemingly beyond human comprehension. For example, iodine–129, one of the radionuclides expected to be buried at Yucca Mountain, has a half-life of seventeen million years. *See* Comm. on Technical Bases for Yucca Mountain Standards, Nat'l Research Council, Technical Bases for Yucca Mountain Standards 18–19 (1995) [hereinafter "NAS REPORT"]. Neptunium–237, also expected to be deposited in Yucca Mountain, has a half-life of over two million years. *Id.* at 19.

As currently designed, the Yucca Mountain waste repository will house up to 70,000 metric tons of radioactive waste deep underground. *See 66 Fed. Reg. at 32,081.* DOE projects that ninety percent of the waste destined for Yucca Mountain will be spent nuclear fuel from commercial nuclear power plants. *See id.* The remaining ten percent will be high-level radioactive waste left over from the nation's nuclear weapons program. *See id.*

To isolate this waste for the epochal years required—by comparison, human history has been recorded for only 5000 years, *see id. at 32,099*—the disposal system's overall design contemplates two types of barriers. First, "engineered" barriers, which include waste packages consisting of metal cylinders protected by drip shields, will surround the waste and protect it from water infiltration. These packages will sit in a complex of over fifty horizontal tunnels, each over sixteen feet wide, 2000 feet long, and reinforced with steel sets, rock bolts, and wire mesh. These tunnels are designed not only to keep water and falling rocks from reaching the waste canisters, but also to manage the heat the waste will generate. Second, the disposal system's "natural" barriers, *i.e.*, the characteristics of the rock formations under Yucca Mountain, are intended to protect the waste from water infiltration and to dilute radiation releases expected to occur from leakage of the engineered barriers or from their failure thousands of years from now. DOE plans to construct the repository tunnels in a thick layer of rock 1000 feet below the surface and 1000 feet above the water table. The Energy Department expects that this surrounding rock will both limit water from seeping into the waste packages and delay radioactive particles from migrating into the human environment. Decades or even centuries after beginning to bury waste at Yucca Mountain, DOE will permanently close the repository by sealing off all openings to the surface.

Through the 1992 Energy Policy Act [EnPA], Congress required EPA to establish site-specific standards for a repository at Yucca Mountain. The statute provides:

> The [EPA] Administrator shall, based upon and consistent with the findings and recommendations of the National Academy of Sciences, promulgate, by rule, public health and safety standards for protection of the public from releases from radioactive materials stored or disposed of in the repository at the Yucca Mountain site. Such standards shall prescribe the maximum annual effective dose equivalent to individual members of the public from releases to the accessible environment from radioactive materials stored or disposed of in the repository. The standards shall be promulgated not later than 1 year after the Administrator receives the findings and recommendations of the National Academy of Sciences ... and shall be the only such standards applicable to the Yucca Mountain site.

EnPA *§ 801(a)(1).*

Acting pursuant to this authority, EPA promulgated a rule, codified at *40 C.F.R. part 197,* establishing a trio of public health and safety standards to govern DOE's nuclear waste disposal activities at Yucca Mountain. Together, these standards are designed to protect both individuals living near the disposal site and local ground-water supplies from excessive radiation contamination.

The rule begins by prescribing an "individual-protection standard" that requires the Energy Department, as a condition of receiving an NRC license, to show that the Yucca Mountain disposal system will sufficiently contain radiation to protect a hypothetical person living adjacent to the site from excessive exposure to radiation releases. The standard provides:

> The DOE must demonstrate, using performance assessment, that there is a reasonable expectation that, for 10,000 years following disposal, the reasonably maximally exposed individual receives no more than an annual committed effective dose equivalent of 150 microsieverts (15 millirems) from releases from the undisturbed Yucca Mountain disposal system. The DOE's analysis must include all potential pathways of radionuclide transport and exposure.

40 C.F.R. § 197.20 (2004). This "reasonably maximally exposed individual" (RMEI) represents a theoretical person living in the "accessible environment," *id. § 197.21 (2004)*, i.e., any point outside the "controlled area," an area no greater than 300 square kilometers around the repository, *id. § 197.12 (2004)*. The RMEI is designed to have lifestyle characteristics (such as water and food consumption habits) that would expose him or her to "reasonably maximal" exposure levels. *See 66 Fed. Reg. at 32,092.* The individual-protection standard expresses the maximum doses the RMEI may incur in terms of an "annual committed effective dose equivalent," a methodology that calculates an overall exposure dose by assigning weighting factors to account for organs' relative sensitivities to radiation. *See 40 C.F.R. § 197.2 (2004)* (defining "effective dose equivalent" as "the sum of the products of the dose equivalent received by specified [human body] tissues following an exposure of, or an intake of radionuclides into, specified tissues of the body, multiplied by appropriate weighting factors").

The rule's second standard, the "human-intrusion standard," requires DOE to show, among other things, a reasonable expectation that the RMEI will receive no more than a specified dose of radiation even if humans drill, intentionally or otherwise, into a waste package during the 10,000–year period immediately following disposal. *Id. § 197.25(a) (2004)*.

The third standard, the "ground-water-protection standard," requires DOE to demonstrate that the Yucca Mountain disposal system will contain radiation sufficiently well to protect ground water outside the controlled area from excessive contamination. Specifically, the rule provides:

> The DOE must demonstrate that there is a reasonable expectation that, for 10,000 years of undisturbed performance after disposal, releases of radionuclides from waste in the Yucca Mountain disposal system into the accessible environment will not cause the level of radioactivity in the representative volume of ground water to exceed the limits in . . . Table 1.

Id. § 197.30 (2004). Table 1, in turn, specifies maximum permitted contamination levels for three different types of radionuclides, which correspond to the maximum contaminant levels (MCLs) that EPA established under the Safe Drinking Water Act (SDWA), *42 U.S.C. §§ 300f to 300j–26 (2000)*. *See 66 Fed. Reg. at 32,106.*

To obtain a license to dispose of waste at Yucca Mountain, the Energy Department "must demonstrate to NRC that there is a reasonable expectation of compliance" with each of these three protection standards. *Id. § 197.13 (2004)*. To account for changing conditions during the 10,000 years following disposal, EPA requires DOE to "vary factors related to geology, hydrology, and climate based upon cautious, but reasonable assumptions." *Id. § 197.15 (2004)*. In contrast, the Energy Department must hold constant "changes in society, the biosphere (other than climate), human biology, or increases or decreases in human knowledge or technology." *Id.*

As to the period beyond the first 10,000 years, the rule requires DOE to calculate the maximum radiation exposures the RMEI will incur and then include the results of this calculation in its environmental impact statement as an indicator of long-term disposal system performance. *Id. § 197.35 (2004).* "No regulatory standard," however, "applies to the results of this analysis." Id.

In their petition for review, the State of Nevada, the Natural Resources Defense Council (NRDC), and the other environmental groups (throughout section II of this opinion, we shall refer to this set of petitioners as either "Nevada" or "the State") first challenge *part 197*'s 10,000–year compliance period, claiming that it both conflicts with EnPA and is arbitrary and capricious.

Nevada first challenges EPA's decision to establish a compliance period that extends only 10,000 years into the future. According to Nevada, the 10,000–year marker violates EnPA *section 801(a)* and is arbitrary and capricious under the Administrative Procedure Act (APA), *5 U.S.C. § 706(2)(A) (2000).* We begin and end with Nevada's EnPA challenge.

Section 801(a) of the Energy Policy Act requires EPA to promulgate public health and safety standards for Yucca Mountain "based upon and consistent with the findings and recommendations of the National Academy of Sciences." Chartered by Congress during the Civil War, the National Academy of Sciences (NAS or Academy) serves as the federal government's scientific adviser, convening distinguished scholars to address scientific and technical issues confronting society. *See* NAS REPORT at vi. EnPA directs EPA to contract with NAS to conduct a study to provide "findings and recommendations on reasonable standards for protection of the public health and safety" from the potential hazards posed by a Yucca Mountain repository. EnPA *§ 801(a)(2).* To undertake the necessary study, NAS convened a committee organized under the auspices of its principal operating arm, the National Research Council. NAS REPORT at vi-vii. That committee retained two consultants, conducted five open meetings to which it invited over fifty scientists and engineers, and reviewed publicly available research compiled by federal, state, and local agencies, among others. *Id.* at viiviii.

The Academy's work culminated in a 1995 report entitled "Technical Bases for Yucca Mountain Standards." With respect to the length of the compliance period, NAS found "no scientific basis for limiting the time period of the individual-risk standard to 10,000 years or any other value." *Id.* at 55. According to the Academy, "compliance assessment is feasible for most physical and geologic aspects of repository performance on the time scale of the long-term stability of the fundamental geologic regime—a time scale that is on the order of 106 [one million] years at Yucca Mountain." *Id.* at 6. NAS also explained that humans may not face peak radiation risks until tens to hundreds of thousands of years after disposal, "or even farther into the future." *Id.* at 2. Given these findings—and central to the issue before us—NAS "recommended that compliance assessment be conducted for the time when the greatest risk occurs, within the limits imposed by the long-term stability of the geologic environment." *Id.* at 6 (emphasis omit-ted). That said, NAS explained that "although the selection of a time period of applicability has scientific elements, it also has policy aspects that we have not addressed," such as the goal of establishing consistent policies for managing various kinds of long-lived, hazardous materials. *Id.* at 56.

Following issuance of the NAS Report, EPA promulgated its draft *part 197* standards in which it proposed a 10,000–year compliance period. In so doing, EPA "requested comments upon the reasonableness of adopting the NAS-recommended compliance period or some other approach in lieu of the 10,000–year compliance period which we favor...." *64 Fed. Reg. at 46,995.* DOE, responding to EPA's request, supported the 10,000–year compliance period, claiming that a "significantly longer time period for assessing compliance would be unprecedented, unworkable, and probably unimple-mentable."

After the comment period closed, EPA promulgated its final rule, in which it adopted a 10,000–year compliance period. Expressly acknowledging that NAS had recommended that the compliance period cover the time when the greatest risk of radiation exposure occurs and that the Academy had found it scientifically possible to predict repository performance for approximately one million years, EPA nevertheless concluded that "such an approach is not practical for regulatory decisionmaking." *66 Fed. Reg. at 32,097.* The agency explained:

> Despite NAS's recommendation, we conclude that there is still consid-erable uncertainty as to whether current modeling capability allows development of computer models that will provide sufficiently mean-ingful and reliable projections over a time frame up to tens-of-thou-sands to hundreds-of-thousands of years. Simply because such models can provide projections for those time periods does not mean those projections are meaningful and reliable enough to establish a rational basis for regulatory decision-making.

Id. Moreover, EPA maintained that selecting a compliance period for the individual-protection standard "involves both technical and policy consider-ations ... In addition to the technical guidance provided in the NAS Report, we considered several policy and technical factors that NAS did not fully address, as well as the experience of other EPA and international programs." *Id. at 32,098.* According to EPA, five considerations guided its decision: (1) the agency uses 10,000 years for programs involving the disposal of other long-lived, hazardous materials, (2) the individual-protec-tion requirements in 40 C.F.R. part 191, EPA's generally applicable nuclear waste disposal standards, use such a time frame, and "consistency [is] appropriate because both sets of standards apply to the same types of waste," (3) many international geologic disposal programs use 10,000 years, (4) setting the standard to peak dose times "could lead to a period of regulation that has never been implemented in a national or international radiation regulatory program," and focusing on 10,000 years forces more emphasis on features that humans can control such as repository design, and (5) projecting human exposure levels over long periods of time involves great uncertainty. *Id. at 32,098–99*. On this last point, EPA stated that "we believe that NAS might not have fully addressed two aspects of uncertainty," specifically (1) "the impact of long-term natural changes in climate and its effect upon choosing an appropriate RMEI," and (2) "the range of possible biosphere conditions and human behavior." *Id.*

In the final rule's preamble, EPA also explained why it believed that *part 197* complied with EnPA's requirement that the rule be "based upon and consistent with" NAS's findings and recommendations. *Id. at 32,082–84*. That mandate, EPA stated, "does not bind us absolutely to follow the NAS Report. Instead, we used it as a starting point for this rulemaking ... We do not believe the statute forces our rulemaking to adopt mechanically NAS's recommendations as standards." *Id. at 32,083*. Thus, because *part 197* was "guided by the [Academy's] findings and recommendations [in light] of the special role Congress gave it," *id.*, EPA concluded that it had acted in accordance with EnPA's directive.

It would have been one thing had EPA taken the Academy's recommendations into account and then tailored a standard that accommodated the agency's policy concerns. But that is not what EPA did. Instead, it unabashedly rejected NAS's findings, and then went on to promulgate a dramatically different standard, one that the Academy had expressly rejected. Although *section 801*'s "based upon and consistent with" standard does not require EPA to walk in lock-step with the Academy, we think it entirely unreasonable for EPA to have acted *inconsistently* with NAS findings and recommendations.

In sum, because EPA's chosen compliance period sharply differs from NAS's findings and recommendations, it represents an unreasonable construction of *section 801(a) of the Energy Policy Act*. Although EnPA's "based upon and consistent with" mandate leaves EPA with some flexibility in crafting standards in light of NAS's findings, EPA may not stretch this flexibility to cover standards that are *inconsistent* with the NAS Report. Had EPA begun with the Academy's recommendation to base the compliance period on peak dosage and then made adjustments to accommodate policy considerations not considered by NAS, this might be a very different case. But as the foregoing discussion demonstrates, EPA wholly rejected the Academy's recommendations. We will thus vacate *part 197* to the extent that it requires DOE to show compliance for only 10,000 years following disposal. On remand, EPA must either issue a revised standard that is "based upon and consistent with" NAS's findings and recommendations or return to Congress and seek legislative authority to deviate from the NAS Report. It was Congress that required EPA to rely on NAS's expert scientific judgment, and given the serious risks nuclear waste disposal poses for the health and welfare of the American people, it is up to Congress—not EPA and not this court—to authorize departures from the prevailing statutory scheme.

Because EPA's 10,000–year compliance period violates EnPA *section 801*, we have no need to consider Nevada's alternative argument that the standard is arbitrary and capricious under the APA.■

NOTES AND COMMENTS

1. In response to the court's opinion, EPA published a new proposed rule for radiation standards for Yucca Mountain. 70 Fed. Reg. 49104 (August 22, 2005). The new rule retains the prior rule's standard for the first 10,000 years but adds a second, more relaxed standard for the post–10,000 year period. Whereas the DOE must show that the mean projected release of radiation during the first 10,000 years will not exceed 15 mrem per year, for the post–10,000 year period it need only show that the median of projected radiation will not exceed 350 mrem per year. EPA says that the natural background radiation in the area around Yucca Mountain is about 350 mrem per year. The State of Nevada says it will challenge the proposed rule in court if it is adopted. Elaine Hiruo, Draft EPA standard hit with immediate criticism, Nuclear Fuels, August 15, 2005, p. 1.

2. Our legal system has a history of ignoring some risks because the impact of them is thought to be too far in the future to worry about, although our decision whether or not to postpone an issue is often puzzling. For example, it has been estimated that asteroid 1950 DA has a 0.3% possibility of hitting the earth on March 16th, 2880, less than 900 years from now. Modelers have predicted that if it landed in the Atlantic Ocean it could create tsunami waves about 100 meters high, but the issue has yet to make it to the top of any legislative agenda. Andrea Milani, Extraterrestrial Material—Virtual or Real Hazards, 300 Science 1882 (2003). For an argument that it should, see Evan R. Seamone, The Duty to Expect the Unexpected: Mitigating Extreme Natural Threats to the Global Commons Such as Asteroid and Comet Impacts with the Earth, 41 Columbia J. of Transnational Law 735 (2003).

The threat of an asteroid strike is not merely science fiction. NASA has a Near Earth Object Program designed to evaluate and monitor asteroids and comets that could possibly hit Earth. As of September 2004, 3047 Near–Earth objects have been identified. Of the 3047 identified, 734 have a diameter of 1 kilometer or larger and 634 are labeled as Potentially Hazardous Asteroids.[21]

Asteroids larger than 50 meters can cause regional disasters or tidal waves and occur an average of every one hundred years. Global disasters could occur from asteroids larger than one kilometer. The instance of these asteroids possibly hitting the Earth is about every few hundred thousand years. However, the effects could include acid rain, firestorms from debris, partial blocking of sunlight and tsunamis.[22] In 1908 an asteroid or comet about 130 feet wide hit Siberia and destroyed 500,000 acres of uninhabited forest.[23] Also, around September 28, 2004, Toutatis, an asteroid measuring 3 miles at its longest point, passed within 963,000 miles of the Earth's

21. See NASA's Near Earth Object Program FAQs http://neo.jpl.nasa.gov /faq/#how many.

22. See NASA's Near Earth Object Program http://neo.jpl.nasa. gov /neo/target.html.

23. See http://www.cnn.com/2002/TECH/Space/11/20/asteroid.threat/; Threat of Killer Asteroids Downgraded, by Richard Stenger, November 20, 2002.

center. Toutatis' orbiting path is well tracked and scientists state that it will not pass this closely to Earth for another 500 years.[24]

Clark Chapman of the Southwest Research Institute has testified that, in his opinion, the chance of being killed by the impact of an asteroid or comet is about the same as the chance of being killed in a plane crash—1 in 20,000.[25] However, in an article by Linda M.V. Martel at the Hawaii Institute of Geophysics and Planetology, she states that the chances of being in an area destroyed by an asteroid are 1 in 500,000. The Meteor Crater in Arizona devastated an area about 800–1500 kilometers squared and every 1000 to 2000 years an impact that could create a comparable devastation occurs. Taking the chances of being in that area with the frequency of the impact occurring, she concludes that there is a 1 in 7.5 billion chance of being killed by an asteroid. In addition, the chances of an impact occurring that causes a global disaster are once every 500,000 years. If you assume that 1 in 4 people would die in that instance, there is a 1 in 2 million chance of dying during the next year from an asteroid impact big enough to cause a global disaster.[26]

Is the question of whether we should be planning for asteroid impacts that may occur in the next 1000 years fundamentally different from the question of whether we should plan for possible leaks of radioactivity that might occur over 10,000 years in the future? Does our responsibility for having concentrated the radioactivity put us under a greater responsibility to assess risks to future generations—assuming humans continue to exist—than to assess the risks of extraterrestrial objects over which we may have no control?

3.   The National Research Council released a report on temporary storage at Yucca Mountain. NRC proposed implementing an adaptive staging process involving stages and decisions that can be modified as the process continues. Several advantages of adaptive staging are the ability to incorporate new knowledge throughout the process, flexibility, reversibility, and responsiveness to act on new information. The current design for Yucca Mountain leaves the repository open for 300 years, at which time any projects could be reversed if needed. Also, a pilot stage of testing can be conducted during the licensing time to test the process and learn of any potential problems.

Throughout the adaptive staging process, re-evaluations will occur to decide if the current plan needs to be modified in any way. NRC also states that security at Yucca Mountain would be underground and therefore

---

24.   See http://neo.jpl.nasa.gov /news/new144.html; Asteroid (4179) Toutatis to Pass Closely By Earth on Wednesday, September 29, 2004, by Don Yeomans and Paul Chodas, NASA's Near Earth Object Program Office.

25.   http://impact.arc.nasa.gov/congress/1998 _may/chapman.html; U.S. Congressional Hearings on Near–Earth Objects and Planetary Defense; May 21, 1998 (continued); Statement on the Threat of Impact by Near–Earth Asteroids by Dr. Clark R. Chapman, Southwest Research Institute.

26.   See http://solarsystem.nasa.gov/scitech/display.cfm?ST_ ID=345; Damage by Impact—The Case at Meteor Crater, Arizona, by Linda M.V. Martel.

better than what could be maintained at nuclear power plants. This process also allows for cost-reduction because potential problems are identified before they become expensive and time consuming. New scientific knowledge and new technological advances can be applied to the stages of development. The report also states that the Department of Energy has recognized potential advantages of staging, such as its flexible repository design. Further, security and safety are more prominent because of the re-evaluations during the process and its focus on technical and societal concerns. Overall, the adaptive staging process allows for a continuous learning process. *See* National Research Council, One Step at a Time: The Staged Development of Geologic Repositories for High–Level Radioactive Waste Committee on Principles and Operational Strategies for Staged Repository Systems, 2003.

Currently the federal statutes specifically forbid the development of a temporary storage facility in the state of Nevada. However, the government has solicited bids for a "waste aging facility" to be constructed above-ground near the Yucca Mountain site. The independent National Commission on Energy Policy has recommended the construction of two temporary aboveground storage sites, one east and one west of the Mississippi River. National Commission on Energy Policy, Ending the Energy Stalemate (2004).

4.   Other scientists favor a different approach, recycling fuel rods through the use of "breeder reactors." Atkins, *supra* at 59–60. India has such a reactor in operation and is bringing a larger one on line in order to use its plentiful supply of thorium as a fuel. Peter E. Hodgson, Nuclear Power, Energy and the Environment 59 (Imperial College Press, 1999). Many other countries have used this method to avoid the need either to mine new uranium or to dispose of used fuel rods. The British operate a facility on the shore of the Irish Sea at Sellafield that recycles fuel from many countries, but the facility has been a source of concern to the Irish government. Colum Kennedy, Fearing Sellafield, (Gill & Macmillan, 2003).

Although the supply of uranium is plentiful given the size of the current market, if a substantial expansion of nuclear power generation occurs, attention will need to be paid to the adequacy of the fuel supply.

> "the most uranium-efficient fuel cycle is the breeder cycle. The prospect of breeders elicits enthusiasm in some circles, because it offers a virtually unlimited energy source. It raises concern in others, because it may allow more ready access to plutonium for nuclear weapons. A decision on breeder reactors could be deferred for a long period of time, even if a substantial nuclear expansion begins. However, ultimately it is an important, high stakes decision."

David Bodansky, Nuclear Energy: Principles, Practices and Prospects 598 (2d ed., Springer–Verlag, 2004).

5.   Meanwhile, scientific support for the idea of permanent burial of nuclear waste may be weakening. Some analysts believe that a wiser policy would be to leave the waste on the surface so that it can be more easily

monitored or modified. Bodansky, *supra* at 281–84, 359–361. The 2004 National Research council study of spent fuel security endorsed the safety of dry cask storage, lending support to temporary storage options. Safety and Security, p. 1155 *supra*, finding 4D.

There is increasing interest in technologies to convert some of the long-lived radioactive material into more benign forms. Murray, *supra* at 342–47. See National Research Council, Nuclear Wastes: Technologies for Separations and Transmutation. (National Academy Press, 1995). If the longest-lived radionuclides in spent fuel were to be transmuted into other nuclides by exposure to high fluxes of neutrons produced in a reactor or accelerator, then the long-term radioactivity of the spent fuel could be reduced dramatically. If successful, the waste "would contain only relatively short-lived fission products that would go into a repository and decay to the background level of high-grade uranium ore in about 250 years." Patricia A. Baisden, A Renaissance for Nuclear Power?, in National Research Council, Energy and Transportation: Challenges for the Chemical Sciences in the 21st Century (National Academy Press, 2003). By heating certain radioisotopes in the spent fuel in what is called a "burner," one could destroy problem isotopes such as cesium–137 and strontium–90 that contribute to heating in the early period and neptunium–237, technetium–99, and iodine–129 that dominate the hazard at long times. "These constitute only about a percent of the waste stream. If they are removed, the remaining waste needs to be secure for only about 100 years rather than the 10,000 years for spent fuel." Murray, *supra* at 347.

e.   WHO SHOULD PAY FOR ONSITE STORAGE?

Indiana Michigan Power Co. v. Department of Energy
88 F.3d 1272 (D.C. Cir. 1996).

■ SENTELLE, J. The Nuclear Waste Policy Act (NWPA) of 1982 authorized the Secretary of Energy (Secretary) to enter contracts with owners and generators of high-level radioactive waste and spent nuclear fuel (SNF) under which the private parties were to pay the Secretary statutorily imposed fees in return for which the Secretary, "beginning not later than January 31, 1998, will dispose of the high-level radioactive waste or [SNF] involved...." 42 U.S.C. § 10222(a)(5)(B) (1994). Petitioners are utilities and state commissions who paid fees to the Secretary under the statute. They seek review of the Department of Energy's ("DOE") final interpretation declaring that the Department has no obligation to perform its part of the contractual bargain. We conclude that the Department's interpretation is not valid and we therefore allow the petition for review.

In the NWPA, Congress created a comprehensive scheme for the interim storage and permanent disposal of high-level radioactive waste generated by civilian nuclear power plants. NWPA establishes that, in return for a payment of fees by the utilities, DOE will construct repositories for SNF, with the utilities generating the waste bearing the primary responsibility for interim storage of SNF until DOE accepts the SNF "in accordance with the provisions of this chapter." 42 U.S.C. § 10131(a)(5).

The NWPA requires the utilities to enter into standard contracts with DOE for the disposal of the waste. According to the statute, the contracts shall provide that "the Secretary shall take title to the high-level radioactive waste or spent nuclear fuel" and "in return for the payment of fees established by this section, the Secretary, beginning not later than January 31, 1998, will dispose of the high-level radioactive waste or spent nuclear fuel as provided in this subchapter." 42 U.S.C. § 10222(a)(5). The final standard contract adopted by DOE, following notice and comment, states that "the services to be provided by DOE under this contract shall begin, after commencement of facility operations, not later than January 31, 1998 and shall continue until such time as all SNF . . . from the civilian nuclear power reactors specified . . . has been disposed of." 10 C.F.R. § 961.11, Art. II (1996).

In February 1994, DOE's Secretary, Hazel O'Leary, indicated that, while at the time NWPA was enacted DOE "envisioned that it would have a waste management facility in operation and prepared to begin acceptance of [SNF] in 1998," DOE subsequently concluded it did not have "a clear legal obligation under the [NWPA] to accept [SNF] absent an operational repository or other facility constructed under the [NWPA]." . . . On April 28, 1995, DOE issued its Final Interpretation (Final Interpretation of Nuclear Waste Acceptance Issues, 60 Fed. Reg. 21,793 (1995)) that it would not be able to begin taking SNF by January 31, 1998, that it did not have an unconditional statutory or contractual obligation to accept high-level waste and spent fuel beginning January 31, 1998 in the absence of a repository or interim storage facility constructed under the NWPA, [and] that it had no authority under the NWPA to provide interim storage in the absence of a facility that has been authorized, constructed and licensed in accordance with the NWPA.

Petitioners and intervenors then filed their petitions for review of the Final Interpretation. In reviewing an agency's construction of a statute entrusted to its administration, we follow the two-step statutory analysis established in *Chevron U.S.A., Inc. v. Natural Resources Defense Council, Inc.*, 467 U.S. 837, 842–43 (1984). First, we ask whether Congress has spoken unambiguously to the question at hand. If it has, then our duty is clear: "We must follow that language and give it effect." *Wisconsin Elec. Power Co. v. Dep't of Energy*, 778 F.2d 1, 4 (D.C. Cir. 1985). If not, we consider the agency's action under the second step of *Chevron*, deferring to the agency's interpretation if it is reasonable and consistent with the statute's purpose. We now apply that review to the Department's interpretation of section 302(a)(5)(B).

Section 302(a)(5)(B) states that "in return for the payment of fees . . . [DOE], beginning not later than January 31, 1998, will dispose of the [SNF]. . . ." The states and utilities contend that this provision means what it says: in return for the payment of fees to the utilities, DOE will begin accepting SNF not later than January 31, 1998. DOE argues that this language does not in fact require it to begin to dispose of SNF by January 31, 1998; rather, the agency contends that this obligation is further conditioned on the availability of a repository or other facility authorized, constructed, and licensed in accordance with the NWPA. DOE contends that this is the only interpretation possible when one examines the statute as a whole.

To support this interpretation, the Department first argues that Congress's use of the term "dispose" in section 302(a)(5)(B), which provides that DOE "will dispose of the high-level radioactive waste or spent nuclear fuel involved as provided in this subchapter," presupposes the availability of a repository. Although conceding that the statute does not define "dispose," DOE notes that the statute does define "disposal" as "the emplacement in a repository of . . . spent nuclear fuel . . . with no foreseeable intent of recovery." 42 U.S.C. § 10101(9). DOE contends that "dispose" is simply a different grammatical form of "disposal," and that Congress must have intended the two terms be interpreted consistently. Thus, it argues, section 302 must require a repository be operational before DOE may begin accepting SNF.

We disagree. The phrase "dispose of" is a common term. It has a common meaning. For example, Webster's Third New International Dictionary Unabridged 654 (1961) defines it as meaning, among other things, "to get rid of; throw away; discard." Admittedly, that and other dictionaries list other definitions. Each of those definitions, however, is consistent with the one set forth and not consistent with a limitation for placing the object of the phrase "in the disposal." There is no indication in the statute that Congress intended the words to be used in any but their common sense. Indeed, the very fact that Congress defined "disposal" restrictively and did not define "dispose" bears mute testimony to the strong possibility that Congress intended the former as a term of art, the latter as common English. . . .

DOE next argues that subsections (A) and (B) of 302(a)(5) are not independent provisions, but rather must be read together because taking title to the waste cannot be separated from the disposal activities. To support this proposition, DOE cites section 302(a)(1), which describes the Standard Contract as "for the acceptance of title, subsequent transportation, and disposal of such waste or spent fuel" and section 123, which provides that "delivery and acceptance by the Secretary, of any high-level radioactive waste or spent nuclear fuel for a repository constructed under this part shall constitute a transfer to the Secretary of title to such waste and spent fuel." 42 U.S.C. § 10143. Respondent contends that these provisions evince Congress's intent that DOE take title to the waste before proceeding with disposal. According to DOE, any other interpretation of these sections would result in an anomaly in which one party would have ownership of the SNF while another party would have physical control of it.

We do not find this argument persuasive. Sections 302(a)(5)(A) and (B) clearly set forth two independent requirements. These separate obligations are independent of whether DOE holds title to SNF when it begins to dispose of the material. The duties imposed on DOE under subsections (A) and (B) are linked to different events and are triggered at different times. DOE's duty under subsection (A) to take title to the SNF is linked to the commencement of repository operations and is triggered when a generator or owner of SNF makes a request to DOE. DOE's duty under subsection (B) to dispose of the SNF is conditioned on the payment of fees by the owner and is triggered, at the latest, by the arrival of January 31, 1998. Nowhere, however, does the statute indicate that the obligation established in subsection (B) is somehow tied to the commencement of repository operations referred to in subsection (A). . . .

The Department's treatment of this statute is not an interpretation but a rewrite. It not only blue-pencils out the phrase "not later than January 31, 1998," but destroys the quid pro quo created by Congress. It does not survive the first step of the *Chevron* analysis. 467 U.S. at 842–43. Under the plain language of the statute, the utilities anticipated paying fees "in return for [which] the Secretary" had a commensurate duty. She was to begin disposing of the high-level radioactive waste or SNF by a day certain. The Secretary now contends that the payment of fees was for nothing. At oral argument, one of the panel compared the government's position to a Yiddish saying: "Here is air; give me money," and asked counsel for the Department to distinguish the Secretary's position. He found no way to do so, nor have we.

It is premature to determine the appropriate remedy, particularly as to the interaction between Article XI and Article XVI of the Standard Contracts, as DOE has not yet defaulted upon either its statutory or contractual obligation. We therefore will remand this matter for further proceedings consistent with this opinion.

In conclusion, we hold that the petitioners' reading of the statute comports with the plain language of the measure. In contrast, the agency's interpretation renders the phrase "not later than January 31, 1998" superfluous. Thus, we hold that section 302(a)(5)(B) creates an obligation in DOE, reciprocal to the utilities' obligation to pay, to start disposing of the SNF no later than January 31, 1998. The decision of the Secretary is vacated, and the case is remanded for further proceedings consistent with this opinion.■

NOTES AND COMMENTS

1. Is the court's reasoning persuasive in regard to legislative intent? Do you think the Congress intended that the DOE would take control of the spent fuel before there was anywhere to put it? How would it have exercised that control? Is the court's use of private contract interpretation principles to determine legislative intent appropriate?

2. In a subsequent order issued on November 14, 1997, the D.C. Circuit decided that the appropriate remedy was an action for damages against the DOE for breach of contract: "Although petitioners have a clear right to

relief, and the Department has a clear duty to act, we decline to issue the broad writ of mandamus sought by petitioners because they are presented with another potentially adequate remedy. Although the statute does not prescribe a particular remedy in the event that the Department fails to perform on time, the Standard Contract does provide a scheme for dealing with delayed performance. 10 C.F.R. § 961.11, Art. IX." *Northern States Power Co. v. Dep't of Energy, 128 F.3d 754 (D.C.Cir. 1997).*

3.   The Indiana Michigan Power Company then sued the Department of Energy in the United States Court of Federal Claims for damages under the contract. In 2004, the court dismissed its complaint:

> Defendant breached the Standard Contract in 1998. Plaintiff has not shown that it incurred damages related to the breach to date, however. Defendant's delay has not impaired DOE's ultimate performance of the Standard Contract so far as this plaintiff is concerned. Indiana Michigan continues to expect compliance from the Department of Energy. We did not discuss repudiation or anticipatory breach in detail because plaintiff did not argue those theories of recovery. Plaintiff seeks its costs of mitigation. Repudiation was implicit in plaintiff's evidence and testimony supporting some of its past costs, however. Its decision to rerack[27] is an example. Plaintiff decided to rerack years before defendant's breach and well before DOE stated that it would not meet the contract deadline. Government statements in the late 1980's expressing doubt that DOE would meet the 1998 deadline did not rise to the level of repudiation. Indiana Michigan's decision in 1989 to rerack was made for sound business reasons. The claim for partial breach of contract focuses on the years 1998 through 2004, the period between the breach and the trial. The utility accumulated tons of nuclear waste that DOE should have collected during those years, but plaintiff's case included little testimony or other evidence of costs associated with that period of time. Plaintiff emphasized instead costs that it incurred well before the breach, in 1993 and 1994; and possible costs in 2005 or 2006, extending forty years or more into the future. Future costs are not allowable for the reasons stated in the Opinion. Defendant testified that it will comply with the Standard Contract by beginning to collect spent nuclear fuel from the utilities in 2010. One of plaintiff's experts attempted to show that defendant may not meet that deadline. Defendant has not promised to comply in 2010, however. When Indiana Michigan can show that it has incurred costs related to defendant's breach, plaintiff may have causes of action that are not speculative. A non-breaching party "may elect to regard the breach as partial, proceed with his own performance, sue for the partial injury, and maintain a second suit in case a further breach occurs." 9 Corbin on Contracts § 946, at 720 (interim ed.). Defendant represented before trial that such causes of action would be appropriate if applicable. If DOE begins compliance with the Standard Contract soon enough,

---

27.   Editors' note: Reracking is a process for expanding the capacity of the storage pool to hold more fuel rods.

Indiana Michigan may not need to build a dry storage facility. This would reduce plaintiff's potential damages substantially.

Count I of the Complaint states, "Indiana Michigan reserves its rights to recover presently unascertainable damages that may be caused by DOE's future partial breaches of the Standard Contract." Plaintiff asks that we retain jurisdiction to hear partial breaches of contract that may occur in the future. The Clerk of Court may treat such claims as related cases pursuant to the rules of this court. The Clerk will dismiss Count I of plaintiff's Complaint. No costs.

Indiana Michigan Power Co. v. United States, 60 Fed.Cl. 639, 664–665 (2004).

f.   A PRIVATE STORAGE ALTERNATIVE

Fed up with the long delays in the Yucca Mountain project, some utilities have been supporting a private venture to store fuel rods on Indian lands in Northwestern Utah. *See* www.privatefuelstorage.com. A band of the Goshute Indian Tribe has approved a plan by a Wisconsin company, Private Fuel Storage, to store spent nuclear power plant fuel on the Goshute Indian Reservation in Skull Valley, Utah. The company is a joint venture of Northern States Power Co. and seven other electric utilities. The lease to the company has been approved by the Bureau of Indian Affairs, and the project was approved by the Nuclear Regulatory Commission on September 9, 2005. Utah state authorities have vowed to fight the project, but their direct control over reservation land is limited.

Skull Valley Band of Goshute Indians v. Nielson
376 F.3d 1223 (10th Cir. 2004).

■ HENRY, J. The Governor and Attorney General of Utah, along with Utah environmental and transportation officials, appeal the district court's ruling that the state's statutes regulating the storage and transportation of spent nuclear fuel are preempted by federal law. See Skull Valley Band of *Goshute Indians v. Leavitt, 215 F. Supp. 2d 1232 (D. Utah 2002).*

In light of the D.C. Circuit's recent resolution of the Utah officials' challenge to federal statutes and regulations concerning spent nuclear fuel, see *Bullcreek v. Nuclear Regulatory Comm'n, 360 U.S. App. D.C. 184, 359 F.3d 536 (D.C. Cir. 2004),* we further conclude that the case is now ripe for review.

This case is one of many arising out the vexing problem of transporting and storing the spent nuclear fuel (SNF) that is generated by nuclear power plants. Because SNF remains radioactive for thousands of years, long-term storage strategies are essential. However, the search for the safest solution has been long and difficult.

In 1982, Congress passed the Nuclear Waste Policy Act (NWPA), *42 U.S.C. §§ 10101–10270.* The NWPA requires the United States Department of Energy to construct a permanent storage facility for the disposal of

SNF. The NWPA also establishes a federally monitored temporary storage program in the event that a permanent facility is not available by the deadline.

Under NWPA, the United States Department of Energy and various utility companies controlling nuclear reactors entered into agreements to accept SNF no later than January 31, 1998. However, the Department of Energy has estimated that, at the earliest, it will not have a permanent repository to receive SNF until 2010. See *Final Interpretation of Nuclear Waste Acceptance Issues, 60 Fed.Reg. 21,793, 21,794 (May 3, 1995).* Unless Congress, the Department of Energy, and the Nuclear Regulatory Commission (NRC) take heroic steps, even this date is optimistic. See John Karl Gross, *Nuclear Native America: Nuclear Waste and Liability on the Skull Valley Goshute Reservation, 7 B. U. J. SCI & TECH. L. 140, 147–48 n.64 (2001)* (reporting estimates that a permanent storage facility may not be available until 2015 or perhaps 2025).

PFS is a consortium of utility companies, which formed in order to seek temporary storage options for the SNF storage problem. In May 1997, PFS entered into a lease of Skull Valley Band tribal land located fifty miles from Salt Lake City. PFS sought to build an SNF storage facility there. The Bureau of Indian Affairs of the United States Department of Interior has conditionally approved the lease, and PFS has submitted an application for licensure of the facility with the NRC, which remains pending. Under the federal regulations, the proposed facility is characterized as an "independent spent fuel storage installation," see *10 C.F.R. § 72.3*, and must satisfy detailed requirements before it may be constructed. See *10 C.F.R. § 72.1* (noting that "the regulations in this part establish requirements, procedures, and criteria for the issuance of licenses to receive, transfer, and possess" SNF).

The Utah officials intervened in the NRC proceedings, arguing that the NRC lacked the authority to license the proposed facility. The NRC rejected that argument, concluding that "Congress, in enacting the *Atomic Energy Act*, gave the NRC authority to license privately owned, away-from-reactor facilities and did not repeal that authority when it later enacted the Nuclear Waste Policy Act of 1982." *In re Private Fuel Storage, L.L.C., 56 N.R.C. 390, 392 (2002).* The Utah officials appealed that ruling, and the D.C. Circuit has recently affirmed the NRC's decision. See *Bullcreek v. Nuclear Regulatory Comm'n, 359 F.3d 536 at 541–43 (D.C. Cir. 2004).*

In addition to contesting the licensing proceedings before the NRC, the state of Utah passed a series of statutes between 1998 and 2001 that regulate the storage and transportation of SNF. As the district court explained, the statutes are comprised of four general categories: (1) amendments to Utah's Radiation Control Act, which establish state licensing requirements for the storage of SNF, and which revoke statutory and common law grants of limited liability to stockholders in companies engaged in storing SNF; (2) "the County Planning Provisions," *Skull Valley, 215 F. Supp. 2d at 1248–49,* which require county governments to impose regulations and restrictions on SNF storage; (3) "the Road Provisions," id., which vest the Governor and the state legislature with authority to regulate road construction surrounding the proposed SNF storage site on the Skull Valley reservation; and (4) "the Miscellaneous Provisions," *id. at 1250*, which require drug and alcohol testing of employees of companies engaged in SNF storage and which authorize litigation to determine water rights in areas under consideration for SNF storage. As the district court held that "the Miscellaneous Provisions" did not violate the *Commerce Clause*, and PFS and the Skull Valley Band do not challenge that ruling on appeal, only the first three categories are at issue here.

We now proceed to the merits of this dispute.... Federal regulation of privately-owned nuclear power facilities began with the Atomic Energy Act of 1954 [which] gave the Atomic Energy Commission "exclusive jurisdiction to license the transfer, delivery, receipt, acquisition, possession, and use of nuclear materials." *Pacific Gas & Elec. Co. v. State Energy Res. Conservation & Dev. Comm'n, 461 U.S. 190, 207 (1983)*.

Congress amended the Atomic Energy Act in 1959. Congress specifically directed the Atomic Energy Commission to

> retain authority and responsibility with respect to regulation of ... the construction and operation of any production or utilization facility ... and ... the disposal of such ... byproduct, source or special nuclear material as the Commission determines ... should, because of the hazards or potential hazards thereof, not be so disposed of without a license from the Commission.

Pacific Gas, *461 U.S. at 209* (quoting *42 U.S.C. § 2021(c)*).

In 1982, Congress enacted the Nuclear Waste Policy Act, *42 U.S.C. §§ 10101–10270*. That act was passed "in response to 'a national problem' created by the accumulation of spent nuclear fuel from private nuclear generators, as well as radioactive waste from reprocessing such fuel, activities related to medical research, diagnosis, and treatment, and other sources." *Bullcreek, 359 F.3d at 538* (quoting *42 U.S.C. § 10131(a)(2)*). Noting that previous efforts of the federal government to find a permanent solution to the problem of storing SNF have been inadequate, the NWPA establishes a schedule for developing a permanent federal repository. Id. (discussing *42 U.S.C. §§ 10131–10145*). As an alternative to a permanent facility, the statute also establishes a federally-monitored temporary storage program. Id. (discussing *42 U.S.C. §§ 10161–10169*). Congress also found that those who generate SNF have " 'the primary responsibility to provide for, and ... to pay the costs of, the interim storage of such ... spent fuel,' " and it thus "limited the federal government's obligation to assist private nuclear generators with interim storage." Id. (quoting *42 U.S.C. § 10131(a)(5)* and discussing *§ 10151(a)(1)*). Accordingly, the NWPA requires private operators of nuclear facilities to exhaust on-site options for storage. Id. (discussing *42 U.S.C. §§ 10155(b)(1), 10151(a)(1), and 10152*).

Pursuant to these statutes, the Atomic Energy Commission and the NRC have promulgated detailed regulations regarding the operation of nuclear facilities, including the storage of SNF. See *10 C.F.R. Part 72;*

Bullcreek, 359 F.3d at 538 (stating that the 1954 Act "authorized the NRC to regulate the possession, use, and transfer of the constituent materials of spent nuclear fuel, including special nuclear material, source material, and byproduct material" and that "while the [Atomic Energy Act] does not specifically refer to the storage or disposal of spent nuclear fuel, it has long been recognized that the [Atomic Energy Act] confers on the NRC authority to license and regulate the storage and disposal of such fuel"). These regulations establish requirements for the licensing of spent nuclear fuel storage facilities both at and away from the reactor site. The regulations also establish recordkeeping and inspection requirements, site evaluation criteria, design requirements, quality assurance, and training and certification of personnel.

* * *

The Utah officials challenge the district court's merits ruling regarding the County Planning Provisions, [which] allow a county to either (a) adopt an ordinance barring the transportation and storage of SNF, or (b) allow such transportation and storage, but only if the county adopts a comprehensive land use plan containing detailed information regarding the effects of any proposed SNF site upon the health and general welfare of citizens of the State. See *Utah Code Ann. § 17–27–301(3)(b), 17–27–301(3)(a)(i–iii)*. Counties are indemnified if they choose the former option. *Id. § 17–27–308*. The County Planning Provisions also prohibit counties from providing "municipal-type services," including fire protection, garbage disposal, water, electricity, and law enforcement, to SNF transportation and storage facilities within the county. *Id. § 17–34–1(3)*. According to the Utah officials, the district court erred in holding that these provisions are preempted by federal law.

We agree with the district court that the County Planning Provisions are preempted. In requiring county land use plans to "address the effects of the proposed [SNF storage] site upon the health and general welfare of the citizens of the state," including "specific measures to mitigate the effects of high-level nuclear waste . . . [to] guarantee the health and safety of citizens of the state," *Utah Code Ann. § 17–27–301(3)(a)*, these provisions address matters of radiological safety that are addressed by federal law and that are the exclusive province of the federal government. See *Pacific Gas, 461 U.S. at 205*.

Finally, we disagree with the Utah officials that the County Planning Provisions are not preempted because they concern "areas that characteristically have been governed by the States." Pltfs' Br. at 88 (quoting *Pacific Gas, 461 U.S. at 205–06*). Although it is true that the County Planning Provisions address law enforcement, fire protection, waste and garbage collection and other similar matters that have been traditionally regulated by local governments, that fact does not trump the preemption analysis that the controlling Supreme Court decisions require us to undertake. Under that analysis, we consider the purpose and effect of the state law at issue, and, as a result, a state cannot use its authority to regulate law enforcement and other similar matters as a means of regulating radiological hazards. That is what the County Planning Provisions attempt to do, and they are thus preempted by federal law.

Next, the Utah officials argue that the Unfunded Potential Liability Provisions are not preempted. At issue here are the sections of the Utah licensing scheme that require the operator of a SNF storage facility to pay to the state of Utah an amount equal to at least 75% of the "unfunded potential liability" of the project. *Utah Code Ann. § 19–3–319(3)*. That amount is determined by the Department of Environmental Quality, based upon "the health and economic costs expected to result from a reasonably foreseeable accidental release [of SNF]." Id. *§ 19–3–301(5)*.

Under the federal licensing scheme however, it is not the states but rather the NRC that is vested with the authority to decide under what conditions to license an SNF storage facility. The Utah statutes are thus preempted by federal law.

Next, the Utah officials argue that the district court erred in holding that federal law preempts the state statute abolishing limited liability for stockholders in companies operating SNF storage facilities, *Utah Code Ann. § 19–3–316*.

By upending a fundamental principle of corporate law as applied to SNF storage facilities, *§ 19–3–316* disrupts the balance that Congress sought to achieve. In light of the conflict between the state statute and federal objectives, we agree with the district court that it is unnecessary to consider evidence of the specific costs imposed upon PFS by the elimination of limited liability.

The Utah officials argued that the four Road Provisions are not preempted. As we have explained, these provisions amend the Utah statutes by (1) requiring the concurrence of the governor and the legislature to resolve disputes arising out of the request to construct a railroad crossing made by an entity engaged in SNF storage and transportation; (2) designating certain county roads and trails near the Skull Valley Reservation as "statewide public safety interest highways," and providing that the state Department of Transportation has jurisdiction and control over them, *Utah Code Ann. § 72–3–301*; (3) removing control of the only road permitting access to the Skull Valley Reservation and PFS's proposed facility from the county by designating it as a state highway; and (4) requiring the consent of the governor and the state legislature before the Department of Transportation may grant a right of way to a company engaged in the transportation or storage of SNF. See id. *§§ 54–4–15, 72–3–301, 72–4–125(4), and 54–4–15(4)(b)*.

Here, the evidence cited by the district court indicates that the Road Provisions were enacted in order to prevent the transportation and storage of SNF in Utah. See *Skull Valley, 215 F. Supp. 2d at 1248 n.10*. The state legislator who sponsored the Road Provisions explained that they established a "moat" around the proposed SNF site, and the Governor added that the Road Provisions "will add substantially to our ability as a state to protect the health and safety of our citizens against the storage of high-level nuclear waste." Id. (internal quotation marks omitted). In the 1999 State of the State address, the Governor announced that he would deny permission for the rail crossings needed to provide access to the proposed SNF facility. Aplts' App. at 583.

The Utah officials do not attempt to contest any of this evidence; nor is it likely that they could. The record thus establishes that the Road Provisions were enacted for reasons of radiological safety and are therefore preempted. Cf. *Pacific Gas, 461 U.S. at 213* (observing that "[a] state moratorium on nuclear construction grounded in safety concerns falls squarely within the prohibited field"). Moreover, as the district court concluded, by jeopardizing access to the proposed SNF storage facility, the Road Provisions directly and substantially affect decisions regarding radiological safety levels by those operating nuclear facilities.

Finally, the Utah officials challenge the district court's ruling as to certain provisions in Part 3 of the state's Radiation Control Act. The licensing provisions set forth in Part 3 of Utah's Radiation Control Act are "grounded in [radiological] safety concerns," *Pacific Gas, 461 U.S. at 213*, and also have "some direct and substantial effect on the decisions" regarding radiological safety levels of SNF in Utah. As a result, the licensing provisions are preempted by federal law.

In holding the Utah statutes preempted, we do not denigrate the serious concerns of Utah's citizens and lawmakers regarding spent nuclear fuel, a matter which presents complex technological, economic, and political challenges to those seeking effective solutions. However, in the matter of nuclear safety, Congress has determined that it is the federal government, and not the states, that must address the problem. We also note that many of the concerns that Utah has attempted to address through the challenged statutes have been considered in the extensive regulatory proceedings before the NRC, as well as in appeals from the NRC's decisions. We are hopeful that Utah's concerns-and those of any state facing this issue in the future-will receive fair and full consideration there.

We thus AFFIRM the district court's decision.■

NOTES AND COMMENTS

1. Utah filed a petition for certiorari. In January, 2005, the Court asked the United States Department of Justice to submit its views on the case. *Nielson v. Private Fuel Storage, L.L.C.,* 125 S. Ct. 945 (2005). As of August, 2005, the Court had not acted on the petition.

2. In *United States v. Kentucky, 252 F.3d 816 (6th Cir. 2001)*, the court held that the State of Kentucky could not impose conditions on the disposal of radioactive waste in a landfill operated by the DOE because such conditions were preempted by the Atomic Energy Act. The court distinguished *United States v. New Mexico, 32 F.3d 494 (10th Cir. 1994)*, where the court had held that such state-imposed conditions were permitted under specific provisions of the Resource Conservation and Recovery Act,

42 U.S.C. §§ 6901–6992k. The Sixth circuit said that the United States did
not raise the preemption issue in the earlier case.

3.   In a rare application of the Bill of Attainder clause of the Constitution
(Art. 1, sec. 10), the Second Circuit struck down an act of the New York
legislature that purported to bar Consolidated Edison from recovering from
the ratepayers any costs caused by a temporary outage at the Indian Point
nuclear power plant, which had been caused by failure to replace a
defective generator. Consolidated Edison Co. of N.Y., Inc. v. Pataki, 292
F.3d 338 (2d Cir. 2002).

g.   REPROCESSING

Although all spent fuel contains some plutonium, and is thus theoretically susceptible to theft by terrorists seeking to use the plutonium for
bombs, the extraction of the plutonium from the spent fuel requires
complex reprocessing involving large and conspicuous facilities. It is generally assumed, therefore, that the risk of terrorists using spent fuel is slight.

Some countries, however, have been engaged in extensive reprocessing
of spent fuel for reuse in power plants, including the United Kingdom,
France, Russia and India. These facilities produce a mixture of uranium
oxides and plutonium oxides that can be mixed with standard uranium
oxide to create new reactor fuel. The United States had begun to operate a
reprocessing facility in West Valley, New York, in the 1960s, but the facility
was phased out in the 1970s due to a concern about the worldwide risks
posed by the possibility that reprocessing facilities would contribute to
potential bomb manufacture.

Some scientists favor reexamination of this decision. These scientists
believe that the United States decision in the 1970s to forego reprocessing
of nuclear fuel was a serious mistake. Morris, supra at 168. India has such
a reactor in operation and is bringing a larger one on line in order to use its
plentiful supply of thorium as a fuel. Peter E. Hodgson, Nuclear Power,
Energy and the Environment 59 (Imperial College Press, 1999). Many
other countries have used this method to avoid the need either to mine new
uranium or to dispose of used fuel rods. The British operate a facility on
the shore of the Irish Sea at Sellafield that recycles fuel from many
countries, but the facility has been a source of concern to the Irish
government. Colum Kennedy, Fearing Sellafield, (Gill & Macmillan, 2003).

h.   TRANSPORTING SPENT FUEL

When spent fuel is moved from a power plant site, it must be encased
in an NRC-approved cask. The casks that have been approved for transportation weigh about 40 tons (for road transport) and 100 tons (for rail
transport). Through the end of 1995, approximately 1300 shipments of
spent fuel have been made, about 90% by road and 10% by rail. Accidents
occurred on four of these shipments, but in none of them were the contents
of the casks released.[28] Spent fuel is loaded into casks by remote handling

---

28. Presentation by James D. McClure, Sandia Laboratories, to the Nuclear Waste
Technical Review Board, Nov. 19, 1997. For a summary of the complex federal laws governing

equipment. The casks provide substantial shielding. The high radiation levels from unshielded spent fuel provide important protection against theft by people who do not have the elaborate equipment and facilities required to handle the fuel assemblies. Bodansky, supra at 244.

One of the most intensive programs for the movement of spent fuel occurred when the Shoreham nuclear power plant on Long Island was closed down after it had been loaded with fuel and tested. (The plant was closed because of uncertainties about the ability to evacuate people from the heavily populated neighborhood in which it was located.) The fuel, which had been used only in the start-up tests, was transported by barge around Long Island and up the Delaware River to a power plant in Philadelphia. From there it was transferred to special railroad trains that carried it through central Philadelphia to the Limerick power plant. The movement of 560 fuel assemblies was completed over a one-year period in 1993–94 without serious incident. For the history of the ill-fated Shoreham project, see Joan Aron, Licensed to Kill? The Nuclear Regulatory Commission and the Shoreham Power Plant (University of Pittsburgh Press, 1998).

At nuclear power plants where the quantity of spent fuel has outrun the capacity of the pools in which the fuel was originally stored, the NRC has approved the use of dry cask storage, but the casks used for such storage differ from those that would be used for transportation of the spent fuel. Applications are currently pending before the NRC for the approval of a cask that would serve both the needs of storage and those of transportation.

When the time comes to move the spent fuel now stored at nuclear power plants to a central disposal site, the shipments will extend over a long period of time. Some shipments will go by rail and some by truck. The State of Nevada has estimated that close to 80,000 truck trips and almost 13,000 rail trips would be needed if the shipments took place in 1999. While this estimate may be high, the volume of traffic will certainly be substantial enough to attract a great deal of public attention.

Many state and local governments have adopted regulations designed to exercise supervision over, or prohibition of, the transportation of nuclear materials. In a number of instances the courts have held that such regulations are preempted by federal law. See e.g. Washington State Building and Construction Trades Council v. Spellman, 684 F.2d 627 (9th Cir. 1982). However, as the prospect of actual transportation looms, the elected officials of the states through which the material must pass may grow increasingly nervous.

the transportation of radioactive waste, see Dan W. Reicher, Nuclear Energy and Weapons, in Celia Campbell–Mohn et al., Environmental Law: From Resources to Recovery 559, 609–613 (West Publishing, 1993).

CHAPTER 15

ENERGY IN TRANSPORTATION

A.   TRANSPORTATION'S ROLE IN ENERGY CONSUMPTION

American-born columnist Bill Bryson, who worked in England for twenty years before returning temporarily back to the United States in 1995, noted that "Not long after we moved here we had the people next door round for dinner and—I swear this is true—they drove. I have since come to realize that there was nothing especially odd in their driving less than a couple of hundred feet to visit us. Nobody walks anywhere in America nowadays." Bill Bryson, Notes from a Big Country 131 (1998).

Most Americans own a vehicle. In fact, most likely either you or someone in your family owns at least one car or truck. Do you know how your driving habits affect energy use? How often do you think about energy consumption when you get into your vehicle? While on a short trip to the grocery store? While on an errand to the bank? Most Americans do not think about energy consumption in any way unless the price of gas is continuing to rise. Yet, even then, the rising cost often does not decrease the amount of driving we do. The average American makes 87% of all of their daily trips in vehicles. *Bureau of Transportation Statistics*, National Household Travel Survey (2004)[1].

Americans take 1.1 billion trips a day—which averages to four trips daily per person. Where do we go? Almost half of all trips are for shopping, about one fourth are for recreation, and the rest are commuting. What do we drive? Over half of all drivers have cars or station wagons. About 20% drive SUVs and 19% drive light trucks. Each driver, on average, spends a little less than an hour in their vehicle each day and drives 29 miles a day. *Id*. As you can see, transportation plays a major role in energy consumption.

In the United States, transportation consumes about 28% of the nation's total consumption of energy of all types.[2] In addition, the energy demand from the transportation sector is expected to grow from 27.5 quadrillion Btu in 2003 to 40 quadrillion Btu by 2025. *Energy Information Association*, Annual Energy Outlook 2005[3]. The demand for light-duty vehicles is also expected to increase from 16.2 quadrillion Btu to 24.5 quadrillion Btu from 2003 to 2025. *Id*.

Of particular importance for national security is the dominance of transportation in the consumption of petroleum, most of which is now imported. About two-thirds of all petroleum used in the United States is consumed by the transportation sector. Energy Information Agency, Oil Market Basics.[4]

But with the energy demand increasing so significantly, can new technologies keep up? Motor vehicle fuel economy is predicted to increase from 25.1 miles per gallon to 26.9 miles per gallon in 2025.[5] But will this be enough? These numbers are also just predictions. What if the energy demand increases faster than the technology? This chapter will address these issues by looking at the different engines and fuels in relation to new engine technology and air pollution controls. In addition, future trends in energy consumption will also be discussed.

Why do we drive so much? Other countries, especially European countries, drive far less than Americans. However, European countries are smaller in area than the United States. From the early days of European colonization of North America, concern about linkage among the widespread sections of the country has been a matter of national debate. Could the interests of the separate colonies be unified without an efficient transportation network? Could we realize our "manifest destiny" of controlling the western part of the continent without effective ways to move

---

1. http://www.bts.gov/programs/national_household_travel_survey/daily_travel.html (a. June 9, 2005)

2. Data as of calendar year 2004. *See* www.eia.doe.gov/emeu/mer/consump.html (a. June 9, 2005)

3. http://www.eia.doe.gov/oiaf/aeo/demand.html#trans (a. June 9, 2005)

4. http://www.eia.doe.gov/pub/oil_gas/petroleum/analysis_publications/oil_market_basics/default.htm (accessed August 6, 2005).

5. http://www.eia.doe.gov/oiaf/aeo/demand.html#trans. (a. June 9, 2005).

people and goods there? How much energy should we expend in integrating the different parts of the country?

The growth of the transportation sector in the United States has led to troublesome increases in certain air pollutants. This has led to tighter regulation of both vehicles and fuels in efforts to stem the increases of these pollutants. And the growing concern about the impact of greenhouse gases on the changing climate has drawn attention to the major role that transportation plays in the emission of such gases.

This chapter looks at the way that debates about transportation have shaped, and are continuing to shape, energy law and policy. It begins with a reminder that the technology of engines and fuels has always set the parameters of potential policy, a topic of particular relevance today as we may be nearing new breakthroughs in automotive engine technology. Will such technology succeed in producing a more efficient and less polluting motor vehicle that captures a large share of the market?

The chapter then looks at the present pattern of highway-oriented transportation with its high energy consumption ratio and serious air pollution consequences. After briefly summarizing the social and economic factors that have produced the current pattern, it looks at our attempts to use the law to ameliorate the pollution and energy consumption problems resulting from our current patterns of transportation and development.

B. ENGINES AND FUELS IN TRANSPORTATION

One of the key factors that affects the use of energy in transportation is the kind of engine being used and the type of fuel consumed by that engine. The twentieth century saw a gradual shift from coal-fired steam engines to internal combustion, jet and diesel engines fueled by petroleum derivatives, so that by the end of the century these oil-based engines drove virtually all forms of transportation. This means that as domestic oil supplies have leveled off, and we have become increasingly dependent on foreign oil, the dependency of our transportation sector on these overseas oil supplies has played a major role in our international relations. See Chapter 7, *supra.*

1. THE EMERGENCE OF AUTOMOTIVE DOMINANCE

From a broad historical perspective, the use of energy in transportation has gone through three phases. In each phase there has been one dominant form of power used to propel transportation. In the first phase animals dominated. In the second phase the steam engine; today it is the internal combustion engine. Whether we are at the dawn of a new phase remains to be seen.

The pre-industrial era. In the early days of the republic, animal power and wind power were the predominant sources of energy for transportation. Oxen pulled the covered wagons that brought settlers to the

West; mules towed barges along the Erie Canal; horse-driven coaches carried the mail. Western cowboys managed cattle drives on horseback.

In urban areas, horses were everywhere, especially after about 1840 when the horse-drawn streetcar began to be the most popular form of urban transportation. The livery stable, with its noise and odors, became a common target of nuisance litigation. *See, e.g., Sheldon v. Weeks*, 51 Ill. App. 314 (1893). Even well into the late 19th Century, horse-drawn railways were one of the main forms of urban transportation. And we still use "horsepower" as a measure of the ability of an engine to perform work.

On the oceans, transportation and trade were carried on by "tall ships" that captured the wind with dozens of sails. The ability to use our sailing vessels to trade with Europe and the Caribbean was one of the goals of the American Revolution. Clipper ships from American ports carried goods all over the world in the mid 19th Century.

Internally, an intricate network of canals was built in the first half of the nineteenth century to transport goods to and from the interior of the country. Along the towpaths, mules pulled the barges at a stately pace. By mid-century, however, there were clear signs that animals would no longer remain the dominant form of transportation either on water or on land.

The industrial revolution. Steam engines fueled by coal were developed late in the 18th century, but it wasn't until the first half of the 19th Century that they were installed on wheeled vehicles that came to be known as railroad trains. Peter Cooper attracted national attention to steam railroad engines when he made a widely publicized bet that his locomotive, Tom Thumb, could win a race with a horse-drawn wagon. In 1830, the race was a "media event" that attracted national attention. The locomotive was in the lead but a broken drive belt gave the horse the victory. Nevertheless, the event made the public aware of the steam engine's capabilities. Russell Bourne, Americans on the Move 69 (Fulcrum Publishing, 1995).

It was not the speed of the railroad engine but its power that proved to be the key factor in establishing the railroads' dominance in the period after the Civil War. The railroads revolutionized transportation by making it possible to carry heavy loads over long distances much faster and cheaper than older forms of transportation.

In the cities, electricity became the driving force in rail transportation as the old horse-drawn streetcars were replaced by electrified trolleys. Between 1890 and 1920, the use of electric streetcars rose from 2 billion to 15.5 billion trips annually. Mark S. Foster, From Streetcar to Superhighway 14 (Temple University Press, 1981).

Passenger travel on long distance railroads also became common. The trains provided increased comfort and convenience in comparison to the stagecoaches they replaced, and the volume of passengers and speed of travel was increased while the cost was substantially reduced. In 1882, just three years after the intercontinental railroad was completed, a million passengers rode between Omaha and San Francisco. Bourne, *supra* at 97.

The steam engine also had a significant impact on water travel. Robert Fulton first attracted wide attention to the possibility of steamboats when he made his well publicized journey up the Hudson River from New York to Albany in 1807. Within a few decades the paddlewheel steamboats became a familiar sight on rivers such as the Ohio and Mississippi, carrying passengers and towing barges. Towards the end of the century, steamships became the dominant force in international travel as well.

The automotive era. The end of the nineteenth century saw the development of the internal combustion engine using gasoline as a fuel. Internal combustion ushered in the third phase of American transportation, as automobiles and trucks began to supplant steam-driven railroads except for the heaviest loads or the most frequently used routes.

In 1886, when Carl Benz obtained a German patent on a motorcar with an internal combustion engine of his design and named the car after a friend's daughter, Mercedes, few people recognized the revolution that was to come. Autos began to be made in the United States during the next decade; the Duryea Brothers opened the first American automobile manufacturing plant in 1895, followed quickly by a number of others, and by 1905 the most popular song in the country had everyone singing "Come away with me Lucille ... in my merry Oldsmobile." Three years later, Henry Ford started producing the Model T, and the auto industry never looked back. Clay McShane, The Automobile 19–39 (Westport, Ct.: Greenwood Press, 1997).

It didn't take long to begin putting the internal combustion engine in trucks as well as cars, and the newly formed trucking industry quickly began to compete with railroads and barge lines for the transport of goods. In the 1950s, the efficiency of trucking was further enhanced by the widespread use of diesel engines and diesel fuel, a more economical method of transporting heavy cargoes. Between 1965 and 1980, the number of tractor-trailers in the national fleet nearly doubled, and their total miles traveled per year grew at a rate nearly double that of passenger car travel, which was itself growing significantly. National Research Council, Transportation Research Board, Toward a Sustainable Future 41 (National Academy Press, 1997).

In the air, early airplanes used internal combustion engines that relied on gasoline. In the mid–20th century, jet engines using jet fuel began to replace the older propeller driven planes. Today, mid-size jet planes are increasingly taking over shorter routes formerly being flown by propeller aircraft.

There are a great many engineering differences among automobile, truck and airplane engines, but they have one important thing in common. They all run on fuel derived from petroleum. Diesel engines have also replaced steam engines on ships and railroad trains, reducing the coal-fueled steam engine to the status of a nostalgic toy for rail buffs. This means that as the 21st Century begins, virtually all of the mechanized transportation in the world is dependent on petroleum.

2. THE DISTRIBUTION AND MARKETING OF PETROLEUM

Modern automobile and truck transportation has been possible because gasoline and diesel fuel are readily available all over the nation, and throughout most of the world. If changes are to be made in the engines and fuels used on the highways, they will need to take into account the existing system through which motor vehicle fuels are distributed.

Early in the Twentieth Century, when it became apparent that the gasoline-fueled automobile was going to be a major source of business for the oil companies, each of the major oil companies began creating a network of "gas stations" to sell their product. These vertically integrated companies wanted the oil that they explored for and produced to remain within the company's control until it actually reached the consumer.

The result was the competing networks of gas stations that are familiar sights all over the world. Most early gas stations not only sold gas but performed repair work as well. Early autos needed lots of work, and the gas station operator was often a skilled mechanic. Gas stations contained bays for car repair and carried an extensive selection of tools and parts. Many gas stations operated tow truck fleets to bring stranded motorists to the facility.

After World War II, the major oil companies competed ferociously with each other for the best locations for gas stations. Frequently the location of gas stations became an issue under local zoning laws. Many communities tried to use zoning to limit the number of gas stations, both to preserve the land for other uses and to respond to pressure from the local operators of the stations who complained that the bitter rivalry among the oil companies for more stations meant that local operators were making less profit. Local governments passed laws providing that no new gas station could be built within, e.g., 500 feet of any other gas station. *Compare Stone v. City of Maitland*, 446 F.2d 83 (5th Cir. 1971) (upholding such an ordinance) with *City of Miami v. Woolin*, 387 F.2d 893 (5th Cir. 1968) (striking down an ordinance requiring an even greater separation).

As oil and gasoline prices fell in the 1980s, most of the major oil companies lost some of their competitive zest in marketing. Most companies cut back on the number of regions in which they operated to reduce distribution costs. Local operators began to complain about the closing of gas stations rather than the proliferation of them. In addition, local dealers have complained that the major oil companies are increasingly opening company-owned stations that compete with their own dealers. Some states have passed laws that try to protect local dealers. Divorcement—the prohibition of refiners from direct operation of gasoline stations—has been in effect for a number of years in Connecticut, Delaware, Maryland, Nevada, and the District of Columbia. Some commentators suggest that these laws tend indirectly to increase prices and reduce service.[6]

---

6. The most carefully studied experience of divorcement relates to Maryland, where divorcement legislation prohibiting refiners from directly operating retail gasoline stations was enacted in 1974 and has been in force since 1979. About 200 stations (less than 100% of the

Modern cars need repairs less often, with the result that the nature of the modern gas station has become quite different from its original counterpart. Self-service gas pumps have replaced attendants, and an increasing number of stations provide facilities for inserting credit cards right at the pump, which has made the purchase of gas less time-consuming for the customer. On the other hand, the number of retail gasoline outlets has been declining rapidly, from about 210,000 in 1990 to less than 176,000 in 1999. See Energy Information Agency, Restructuring: The Changing Face of Motor Gasoline Marketing (2001).[7]

In addition, gas stations today often obtain a large share of their revenue from selling other commercial products. The major oil companies' share of gasoline marketing has been declining, so that branded outlets directly supplied with gasoline by major oil companies amounted to only 30% of all retail outlets, although the branded outlets supplied 62% of the gasoline sold. *Id.* The line between the traditional convenience store and the gas station has become blurred as many traditional convenience stores have started to sell gas while many gas stations sell the products typically found at convenience stores. *Id.* This has led to local zoning battles over whether a facility zoned for a gas station could operate a convenience store as an "accessory use" (*See, e.g., Exxon Co. v. Bd. of Standards & Appeals,* 542 N.Y.S.2d 639 (App. Div. 1989)) and whether convenience stores could install gas pumps as an accessory use in areas that were not zoned for gas stations (*See, e.g., Eubanks v. Bd. of Adjustment,* 768 S.W.2d 624 (Mo. App. 1989)).

The difficulty of predicting the future of the gas station is underscored by the complex mixture of federal, state and local laws and regulations governing gas station operations, and by questions about the nature of the fuels that will be needed for new engines that will be developed in the twenty-first century.

Oil companies often operate some gas stations themselves, but a large proportion of the gas stations are still operated by local franchisees, who operate them pursuant to a contract that requires them to sell the company's products. Such franchising arrangements are quite common in other retail businesses such as restaurants. It is estimated that over one third of all of the retail sales of all kinds in the United States are made at franchised outlets. Robert W. Emerson, Franchise Terminations: Legal Rights and Practical Effects When Franchisees Claim the Franchisor Discriminates, 35 Amer. Bus. L. J. 559, 561 (1998).

Maryland market) were affected. The best available empirical evidence on the effects of divorcement comes from a study by Barron and Umbeck [who] found that divorcement caused full service gasoline prices to rise 5–7 cents per gallon at the stations subject to forced divestiture, and about 1 cent per gallon at the competitor stations. The also found that hours of operation fell about 8–9 hours per week at the stations subject to divorcement. Thus, this study indicates that, while the competitors of integrated stations benefited, it was the consumers who were harmed by Maryland's divorcement law. Larry Goldstein et al., Divorced from the facts, The Oil and Gas Journal, Nov. 9, 1998.

7. http://www.eia.doe.gov/emeu/finance/sptopics/downstrm00/index.html (a. June 9, 2005).

Relationships between the franchisee and the franchisor are not always harmonious. The franchisees often feel overwhelmed by the size and expertise of the large companies with which they deal. And the oil companies are sometimes frustrated when they need to modify national marketing strategies to adapt to the franchisees' local problems. In the field of gasoline retailing, the franchisees have persuaded Congress to adopt a federal statute, the Petroleum Marketing Practices Act, 15 U.S.C. § 2801 *et seq.*, that limits the right of the oil companies to terminate a franchise agreement in certain circumstances, and provides that if the agreement is terminated the company must offer to sell the property to the franchisee.

Although the issues under the PMPA may seem trivial today, the importance of legal control of the fuel distribution network may increase significantly if new engines are developed that use fuels other than gasoline. Assume, for example, that major car manufacturers were prepared to develop virtually pollution-free automobiles that were fueled by liquid hydrogen. In order to make it practical to use such engines for anything except very localized transportation, it would be necessary either to arrange to supply the needed fuel throughout the existing network of gas stations, or else to set up an independent network of stations. This issue may need examination relatively quickly if technological advances in engine design proceed on their current course. See § 3, *infra.*

As part of its general relaxation of earlier strict antitrust principles, the Supreme Court has held that it is not an antitrust violation for an oil company to fix the price at which its franchisee may sell gasoline or other fuels. *State Oil Co. v. Khan*, 118 S.Ct. 275 (1997). Will the ability to exercise this power have an effect on the future availability of alternative fuels at gas stations? *See also Portland 76 Auto/Truck Plaza, Inc. v. Union Oil Co. of Cal.*, 153 F.3d 938 (9th Cir. 1998) (franchisee's lease of truck stop was not a "facility" within the protection of the Robinson–Patman Act.)

State legislators have sometimes tried to respond to complaints by gas station operators about their treatment by the oil companies, but the oil companies have challenged rules that appear to favor local interests. In *Chevron U.S.A. Inc. v. Bronster*, 363 F.3d 846 (9th Cir. 2004), the 9th circuit court of appeals held invalid a Hawaii statute that limited the rents that oil companies could charge dealers. The Supreme Court reversed in the following opinion:

Lingle v. Chevron USA, Inc.

125 S.Ct. 2074 (2005).

■ O'CONNOR, J. The State of Hawaii, whose territory comprises an archipelago of 132 islands clustered in the midst of the Pacific Ocean, is located over 1,600 miles from the U.S. mainland and ranks among the least populous of the 50 States. Because of Hawaii's small size and geographic isolation, its wholesale market for oil products is highly concentrated. When this lawsuit began in 1997, only two refineries and six gasoline wholesalers were doing business in the State. As of that time, respondent

Chevron U.S.A. Inc. was the largest refiner and marketer of gasoline in Hawaii: It controlled 60 percent of the market for gasoline produced or refined in-state and 30 percent of the wholesale market on the State's most populous island, Oahu.

Gasoline is sold at retail in Hawaii from about 300 different service stations. About half of these stations are leased from oil companies by independent lessee-dealers, another 75 or so are owned and operated by "open" dealers, and the remainder are owned and operated by the oil companies. Chevron sells most of its product through 64 independent lessee-dealer stations. In a typical lessee-dealer arrangement, Chevron buys or leases land from a third party, builds a service station, and then leases the station to a dealer on a turnkey basis. Chevron charges the lessee-dealer a monthly rent, defined as a percentage of the dealer's margin on retail sales of gasoline and other goods. In addition, Chevron requires the lessee-dealer to enter into a supply contract, under which the dealer agrees to purchase from Chevron whatever is necessary to satisfy demand at the station for Chevron's product. Chevron unilaterally sets the wholesale price of its product.

The Hawaii Legislature enacted Act 257 in June 1997, apparently in response to concerns about the effects of market concentration on retail gasoline prices. See 1997 Haw. Sess. Laws no. 257, § 1. The statute seeks to protect independent dealers by imposing certain restrictions on the ownership and leasing of service stations by oil companies. It prohibits oil companies from converting existing lessee-dealer stations to company-operated stations and from locating new company-operated stations in close proximity to existing dealer-operated stations. Haw. Rev. Stat. §§ 486H–10.4(a), (b) (1998 Cum. Supp.). More importantly for present purposes, Act 257 limits the amount of rent that an oil company may charge a lessee-dealer to 15 percent of the dealer's gross profits from gasoline sales plus 15 percent of gross sales of products other than gasoline. § 486H–10.4(c).

Thirty days after Act 257's enactment, Chevron sued the Governor and Attorney General of Hawaii in their official capacities (collectively Hawaii) in the United States District Court for the District of Hawaii, raising several federal constitutional challenges to the statute. As pertinent here, Chevron claimed that the statute's rent cap provision, on its face, effected a taking of Chevron's property in violation of the Fifth and Fourteenth Amendments. Chevron sought a declaration to this effect as well as an injunction against the application of the rent cap to its stations. Chevron swiftly moved for summary judgment on its takings claim, arguing that the rent cap does not substantially advance any legitimate government interest. Hawaii filed a cross-motion for summary judgment on all of Chevron's claims.

To facilitate resolution of the summary judgment motions, the parties jointly stipulated to certain relevant facts. They agreed that Act 257 reduces by about $207,000 per year the aggregate rent that Chevron would otherwise charge on 11 of its 64 lessee-dealer stations. On the other hand, the statute allows Chevron to collect more rent than it would otherwise charge at its remaining 53 lessee-dealer stations, such that Chevron could increase its overall rental income from all 64 stations by nearly $1.1 million per year. The parties further stipulated that, over the past 20 years, Chevron has not fully recovered the costs of maintaining lessee-dealer stations in any State through rent alone. Rather, the company recoups its expenses through a combination of rent and product sales. Finally, the joint stipulation states that Chevron has earned in the past, and anticipates that it will continue to earn under Act 257, a return on its investment in lessee-dealer stations in Hawaii that satisfies any constitutional standard.

The District Court granted summary judgment to Chevron, holding that "Act 257 fails to substantially advance a legitimate state interest, and as such, effects an unconstitutional taking in violation of the Fifth and Fourteenth Amendments." *Chevron U.S.A. Inc.* v. *Cayetano*, 57 F. Supp. 2d 1003, 1014 (1998). The District Court accepted Hawaii's argument that the rent cap was intended to prevent concentration of the retail gasoline market—and, more importantly, resultant high prices for consumers—by maintaining the viability of independent lessee-dealers. *Id.*, at 1009–1010. The court concluded that the statute would not substantially advance this interest, however, because it would not actually reduce lessee-dealers' costs or retail prices. It found that the rent cap would allow incumbent lessee-dealers, upon transferring occupancy rights to a new lessee, to charge the incoming lessee a premium reflecting the value of the rent reduction. Accordingly, the District Court reasoned, the incoming lessee's overall expenses would be the same as in the absence of the rent cap, so there would be no savings to pass along to consumers. *Id.*, at 1010–1012. Nor would incumbent lessees benefit from the rent cap, the court found, because the oil company lessors would unilaterally raise wholesale fuel prices in order to offset the reduction in their rental income. *Id.*, at 1012–1014.

On appeal, a divided panel of the Court of Appeals for the Ninth Circuit held that the District Court had applied the correct legal standard to Chevron's takings claim. *Chevron U.S.A. Inc.* v. *Cayetano*, 224 F.3d 1030, 1033–1037 (2000). The Court of Appeals vacated the grant of summary judgment, however, on the ground that a genuine issue of material fact remained as to whether the Act would benefit consumers. *Id.*, at 1037–1042. Judge William Fletcher concurred in the judgment, maintaining that the "reasonableness" standard applicable to "ordinary rent and price control laws" should instead govern Chevron's claim. *Id.*, at 1048.

On remand, the District Court entered judgment for Chevron after a 1–day bench trial in which Chevron and Hawaii called competing expert witnesses (both economists) to testify. 198 F. Supp. 2d 1182 (2002). Finding Chevron's expert witness to be "more persuasive" than the State's expert, the District Court once again concluded that oil companies would raise wholesale gasoline prices to offset any rent reduction required by Act 257, and that the result would be an increase in retail gasoline prices. *Id.*, at 1187–1189. Even if the rent cap did reduce lessee-dealers' costs, the court found, they would not pass on any savings to consumers. *Id.*, at 1189. The court went on to reiterate its determination that Act 257 would enable incumbent lessee-dealers to sell their leaseholds at a premium, such that incoming lessees would not obtain any of the benefits of the rent cap. *Id.*, at 1189–1190. And while it acknowledged that the rent cap could preclude oil companies from constructively evicting dealers through excessive rents, the court found no evidence that Chevron or any other oil company would attempt to charge such rents in the absence of the cap. *Id.*, at 1191. Finally, the court concluded that Act 257 would in fact decrease the number of lessee-dealer stations because the rent cap would discourage oil companies from building such stations. *Id.*, at 1191–1192. Based on these findings, the District Court held that "Act 257 effected an unconstitutional regulatory taking given its failure to substantially advance any legitimate state interest." *Id.*, at 1193. The Ninth Circuit affirmed. 363 F.3d 846 (2004). We granted certiorari and now reverse.

There is no question that the "substantially advances" formula was derived from due process, not takings, precedents.... The "substantially advances" formula suggests a means-ends test: It asks, in essence, whether a regulation of private property is *effective* in achieving some legitimate public purpose. An inquiry of this nature has some logic in the context of a due process challenge, for a regulation that fails to serve any legitimate governmental objective may be so arbitrary or irrational that it runs afoul of the Due Process Clause. See, *e.g.*, *County of Sacramento* v. *Lewis*, 523 U.S. 833, 846 (1998) (stating that the Due Process Clause is intended, in part, to protect the individual against "the exercise of power without any reasonable justification in the service of a legitimate governmental objective"). But such a test is not a valid method of discerning whether private property has been "taken" for purposes of the Fifth Amendment.... [T]he "substantially advances" inquiry reveals nothing about the *magnitude or character of the burden* a particular regulation imposes upon private property rights. Nor does it provide any information about how any regulatory burden is *distributed* among property owners. In consequence, this test does not help to identify those regulations whose effects are functionally comparable to government appropriation or invasion of private property; it is tethered neither to the text of the Takings Clause nor to the basic justification for allowing regulatory actions to be challenged under the Clause.

Chevron appeals to the general principle that the Takings Clause is meant " 'to bar Government from forcing some people alone to bear public burdens which, in all fairness and justice, should be borne by the public as a whole.' " Brief for Respondent 17–21. But that appeal is clearly misplaced, for the reasons just indicated. A test that tells us nothing about the actual burden imposed on property rights, or how that burden is allocated cannot tell us when justice might require that the burden be spread among taxpayers through the payment of compensation. The owner of a property subject to a regulation that *effectively* serves a legitimate state interest may be just as singled out and just as burdened as the owner of a property subject to an *ineffective* regulation. It would make little sense to say that the second owner has suffered a taking while the first has not. Likewise, an ineffective regulation may not significantly burden property rights at all, and it may distribute any burden broadly and evenly among property owners. The notion that such a regulation nevertheless "takes" private property for public use merely by virtue of its ineffectiveness or foolishness is untenable.

Instead of addressing a challenged regulation's effect on private property, the "substantially advances" inquiry probes the regulation's underlying validity. But such an inquiry is logically prior to and distinct from the question whether a regulation effects a taking, for the Takings Clause presupposes that the government has acted in pursuit of a valid public purpose. The Clause expressly requires compensation where government takes private property *"for public use."* It does not bar government from interfering with property rights, but rather requires compensation "in the event of *otherwise proper interference* amounting to a taking." *First English Evangelical Lutheran Church*, 482 U.S., at 315 (emphasis added). Conversely, if a government action is found to be impermissible—for instance because it fails to meet the "public use" requirement or is so arbitrary as to violate due process—that is the end of the inquiry. No amount of compensation can authorize such action.

Chevron's challenge to the Hawaii statute in this case illustrates the flaws in the "substantially advances" theory. To begin with, it is unclear how significantly Hawaii's rent cap actually burdens Chevron's property rights. The parties stipulated below that the cap would reduce Chevron's aggregate rental income on 11 of its 64 lessee-dealer stations by about $207,000 per year, but that Chevron nevertheless expects to receive a return on its investment in these stations that satisfies any constitutional standard. Moreover, Chevron asserted below, and the District Court found, that Chevron would recoup any reductions in its rental income by raising wholesale gasoline prices. In short, Chevron has not clearly argued—let alone established—that it has been singled out to bear any particularly severe regulatory burden. Rather, the gravamen of Chevron's claim is simply that Hawaii's rent cap will not actually serve the State's legitimate interest in protecting consumers against high gasoline prices. Whatever the merits of that claim, it does not sound under the Takings Clause. Chevron plainly does not seek compensation for a taking of its property for a legitimate public use, but rather an injunction against the enforcement of a regulation that it alleges to be fundamentally arbitrary and irrational.

Finally, the "substantially advances" formula is not only *doctrinally* untenable as a takings test—its application as such would also present serious practical difficulties. [It] can be read to demand heightened means-ends review of virtually any regulation of private property. If so interpreted, it would require courts to scrutinize the efficacy of a vast array of state and federal regulations—a task for which courts are not well suited. Moreover, it would empower—and might often require—courts to substitute their predictive judgments for those of elected legislatures and expert agencies.

Although the instant case is only the tip of the proverbial iceberg, it foreshadows the hazards of placing courts in this role. To resolve Chevron's takings claim, the District Court was required to choose between the views of two opposing economists as to whether Hawaii's rent control statute would help to prevent concentration and supracompetitive prices in the State's retail gasoline market. Finding one expert to be "more persuasive" than the other, the court concluded that the Hawaii Legislature's chosen regulatory strategy would not actually achieve its objectives. See 198 F. Supp. 2d, at 1187–1193. Along the way, the court determined that the State was not entitled to enact a prophylactic rent cap without actual evidence that oil companies had charged, or would charge, excessive rents. See *id.*, at 1191. Based on these findings, the District Court enjoined further enforcement of Act 257's rent cap provision against Chevron. We find the proceedings below remarkable, to say the least, given that we have long eschewed such heightened scrutiny when addressing substantive due process challenges to government regulation. See, *e.g.*, *Exxon Corp.* v. *Governor of Md.*, 437 U.S. 117, 124–125 (1978). The reasons for deference to legislative judgments about the need for, and likely effectiveness of, regulatory actions are by now well established, and we think they are no less applicable here.

For the foregoing reasons, we conclude that the "substantially advances" formula is not a valid method of identifying regulatory takings for which the Fifth Amendment requires just compensation. Since Chevron argued only a "substantially advances" theory in support of its takings claim, it was not entitled to summary judgment on that claim.

We hold that the "substantially advances" formula is not a valid takings test, and indeed conclude that it has no proper place in our takings jurisprudence. Because Chevron argued only a "substantially advances" theory in support of its takings claim, it was not entitled to summary judgment on that claim. Accordingly, we reverse the judgment of the Ninth Circuit and remand the case for further proceedings consistent with this opinion.

■ **Kennedy, J., concurring:** This separate writing is to note that today's decision does not foreclose the possibility that a regulation might be so arbitrary or irrational as to violate due process. *Eastern Enterprises* v. *Apfel,* 524 U.S. 498, 539 (Kennedy, J., concurring in judgment and dissenting in part). The failure of a regulation to accomplish a stated or obvious objective would be relevant to that inquiry. Chevron voluntarily dismissed its due process claim without prejudice, however, and we have no occasion to consider whether Act 257 of the 1997 Hawaii Session Laws "represents one of the rare instances in which even such a permissive standard has been violated." *Apfel, supra,* 524 U.S., at 550. With these observations, I join the opinion of the Court.■

NOTES AND COMMENTS

1. Is the Court opinion consistent with its earlier opinions in the *Hope Natural Gas* case (see p. 82) and the *Duquesne* case (see p. 101) ? The

Court suggests that Chevron should have brought its claim under the due process clause. Do you think it is likely that the Court would have ruled in Chevron's favor on such a claim?

2. *Lingle* is one of the few cases in the recent history of the Supreme court in which the court has decided a case involving regulatory takings by an opinion in which all nine justices joined. Time will tell whether the case becomes a major precedent or simply reflects the rather astonishing weakness of Chevron's substantive complaint.

3. The United States Environmental Protection Agency has been trying to deal with the millions of underground gasoline storage tanks at gas stations around the country that were beginning to corrode. A number of celebrated incidents occurred in which gasoline from rusted tanks leaked into drinking water wells or caused serious explosions underneath buildings.

Beginning in 1984, the Resource Conservation and Recovery Act ("RCRA") authorized a special Underground Storage Tank ("UST") program targeted specifically on this problem. 42 U.S.C. § 9001 *et seq.* State governments may assume responsibility for administering the program if their program is approved by the EPA. 42 U.S.C. § 9007. The EPA regulations adopted in 1988 gave gas station owners ten years to either upgrade their existing tanks, install new tanks meeting EPA standards for corrosion protection, or close down. 40 C.F.R. Part 280 and Part 281. Thus towards the end of the year 1998 gas stations all over the country were being ripped apart and put together again. Over a million tanks were closed between 1990 and 1998 and over 300,000 cleanups were undertaken. Bureau of Transportation Statistics, Annual Report 132 (1999).

Although there were some significant instances in which leaking underground tanks caused major health and safety problems, these were a very small percentage of the tanks that had to be replaced. The industry felt that the cost of the cleanup efforts required by the EPA far exceeded the relatively small amount of property damage that typically occurred.

> [A California study by Lawrence Livermore laboratory found] that, to recover a perceived property-value loss of a few tens of thousands of dollars, cleanup efforts can cost millions of dollars at a site with groundwater that poses a minimal risk or has limited beneficial use. The average cost of pump-and-treat groundwater cleanups has been $637,000/acre-ft of California water. New water supply sources can normally be developed at a cost of $700–900/acre-ft in California. The water that is affected by leaking underground fuel tanks is almost always shallow groundwater that was originally not recommended for use due to susceptibility to contamination from sewers, septic fields, etc. The total volume of California groundwater affected by leaking underground fuel tanks is less than 0.0005% of California's groundwater resources.

Craig S. Marsen, Costs of remediating underground storage tank leaks exceed benefits; Oil and Gas Journal, Aug. 9, 1999.

Litigation over the leaking underground tanks has been particularly prevalent in those parts of the country in which methyl tertiary butyl ether ("MTBE") has been added to gasoline in order to meet federal air quality requirements. In New York, over 13,000 spills of MTBE have occurred. Further, at least 28 states have groundwater contaminated with MTBE. The costs associated with clean-up for the nation are $30 to $100 billion. Over 150 lawsuits against oil companies are currently pending nationwide. One part of the dispute is that since oil companies were required by the EPA to use an oxygenate additive and most chose MTBE, the companies argue that they are not accountable for the cleanup costs. *See* The New York Times, *A Gasoline Additive Lingers in New York's Drinking Water*, by Ian Urbina, Oct. 31, 2004.

Ever since the oxygenation rules went into effect, they have been the basis for the addition of either ethanol or MTBE to gasoline. However, scientific support for the use of oxygenation as a pollution reducer has been slim. "Motor-vehicle emissions of chemicals that form ozone pollution have decreased in recent years," said [National Research Council] committee chair William Chameides, Regents Professor of Earth and Atmospheric Sciences at the Georgia Institute of Technology, Atlanta. "But that's largely because of better emissions control equipment and components of reformulated gasolines—other than oxygen additives—that improve air quality. Although additives do reduce some pollutants from motor vehicles emissions, the oxygenates appear to have little impact on lowering ozone levels." http://www4.nationalacademies.org/news.nsf/isbn/0309064457 ?OpenDocument (a. 8–21–05)

Section 1504(a) of the Energy Policy Act of 2005 eliminated the Clean Air Act's requirement that reformulated gasoline contain specific oxygen levels. Instead, the Energy Policy Act of 2005 mandates the increasing use of ethanol in gasoline not because it reduces pollution, but because it is deemed to be a renewable fuel; i.e., one that is "produced from grain, starch, oilseeds, vegetable, animal or fish materials including fats, greases, and oils, sugarcane, sugar beets, sugar components, tobacco, potatoes, or other biomass." Section 1501(a)(1)(C)(I). MTBE would not qualify.

By eliminating the statutory requirement that oxygen be added to gasoline, Congress has removed the MTBE suppliers' best defense to lawsuits seeking to recover damages for water pollution created when MTBE leaked into drinking water systems. When the new law takes effect, they will no longer be able to argue that they were merely using their best efforts to meet a legal mandate. As a result, production of MTBE may decline rapidly, putting pressure on suppliers of alternatives. Ron Gold et al, Energy Policy Act of 2005 leaves US with open issues, Oil & Gas Journal, August 22, 2005, pp. 20, 25. A consolidated multi-district proceeding in the Southern District of New York is handling complaints removed to the federal courts from state courts in Connecticut, Florida, Illinois, Indiana, Iowa, Kansas, Louisiana, Massachusetts, New Hampshire, New Jersey, New York, Pennsylvania, Vermont, Virginia and West Virginia. *See* In re Methyl Tertiary Butyl Ether (MTBE) Products Liability Litigation,

379 F.Supp.2d 348 (S.D.N.Y. 2005) (analyzing product liability law of the various states).

3.   DEVELOPMENTS IN ENGINE TECHNOLOGY

In the final decades of the twentieth century the automobile industry significantly improved the efficiency of auto and truck technology. They improved the rolling resistance of tires and added lockup torque conversion to transmissions to eliminate slippage at highway speeds. Engines have been improved by switching from carburetors to fuel injection, improving combustion control, and adding valves to improve engine breathing. These efficiency gains were offset, however, by consumer switches to larger vehicles. Bureau of Transportation Statistics, Annual Report 105 (1999).

Continuing concern over air pollution from gasoline-burning internal combustion engines, aggravated by the awareness that over a quarter of United States greenhouse gas emissions come from the transportation sector's consumption of petroleum, has led to extensive research and development efforts to find clean, efficient substitutes for the traditional automobile and truck engines. These efforts have included attempts to produce electric cars and cleaner burning diesel engines, but at the present time the two most promising technologies appear to be (a) hybrid vehicles, that combine an electric motor and an internal combustion engine, and (b) fuel cell vehicles.

a.   HYBRID VEHICLES

The Galt Motor Company produced a hybrid automobile in 1914. It was powered by a small gasoline engine that turned a Westinghouse electric generator. It was reported to get 70 miles per gallon, but its top speed of 30 miles per hour was a deterrent to sales. Judy Anderson and Curtis D. Anderson, Electric and Hybrid Cars: A History 34–35 (McFarland & Company, 2005). Interest in hybrid vehicles was not reinvigorated until the gasoline price increases of the 1970s. In 1976, Congress passed the Electric and Hybrid Vehicle Act which authorized the DOE to set up a demonstration project, but when gasoline prices dropped in the 1980s interest in alternative fuels evaporated. *Id.* at 67.

The primary source of support for alternate-fueled vehicles then passed to the California Air Resources Board ("CARB"), which began to require that a certain percentage of cars to be sold in future years be Zero Emission Vehicles ("ZEVs"). During the 1990s, CARB's emphasis was on cars which were exclusively powered by electric motors, which would be recharged by plugging the vehicle into the electric network. But the public never supported electric cars, and over time CARB's interest in hybrid vehicles grew as Japanese auto manufacturers began introducing hybrid models in Japan. CARB now gives manufacturers a choice of two options for meeting their low-emission vehicle requirements: (1) meeting part of their ZEV obligations by making AT–PZEVs (vehicles earning advanced technology partial ZEV credits), i.e. advanced hybrids; or (2) meeting part of their ZEV requirement by producing a sales-weighted market share of 250 fuel cell vehicles by 2008 (increasing to 2,500 from 2009–11, 25,000 from 2012–14 and 50,000 from 2015 through 2017).

As of 2005, the hybrid cars on the market in the United States fell into two categories, the mild hybrid and the full hybrid. A mild hybrid uses a powerful electric starter motor to begin operation of the internal combustion or diesel engine prior to fuel injection. The internal combustion engine is shut down whenever the car is coasting, braking, or stopped but the accessories can continue to run on electrical power. Honda uses this technology in its Insight, Accord Hybrid and Civic Hybrid models, and General Motors in its 2005 Silverado and Sierra hybrid trucks.

A full hybrid begins to propel the vehicle using the electric motor, and the gasoline engine kicks in when more power is needed. The Toyota Prius and the Ford Escape hybrid SUV are examples of this type of hybrid vehicle, and Toyota has also introduced a hybrid Highlander SUV and a Lexus RX400h luxury SUV. The Prius has generated a lot of consumer demand, with waiting lists a common phenomenon; Toyota plans to introduce hybrid versions of most of its models in the near future. Full hybrids achieve better gas mileage than mild hybrids for vehicles of the same weight category. *See* http://www.fueleconomy.gov/feg/hybrid_news.shtml (a. June 9, 2005)

The National Commission on Energy Policy suggests that renewed attention should be paid to a type of vehicle that the automakers have been avoiding, the "plug-in hybrid." The hybrids currently on the market recharge the battery internally, and neither need to be, nor can be, plugged in to the electrical network. Given the public's distaste for electric cars, automakers have found it important to distinguish the new hybrids from the unpopular plug-ins. But the Commission pointed out that adding plug-in capability to a modern hybrid increases its energy efficiency:

> "Plug-in" hybrids are a logical extension of the current technology. These vehicles would carry more robust battery packs and be capable of being charged using the electricity grid. Since most trips are relatively short, these vehicles could operate using grid-provided electricity much of the time, while retaining the flexibility consumers desire for being able to travel longer distances without the need to recharge. To the extent they would operate more often than conventional hybrids in a pure-electric mode, plug-in hybrids could provide additional oil security and fuel diversity benefits.

National Commission on Energy Policy, Ending the Energy Stalemate 91 (2004). Section 706 of the Energy Policy Act of 2005 set up a small grant program to improve technologies for plug-in hybrid or combination hybrid/flexible fuel vehicles that would achieve not less than 250 miles per gallon of petroleum fuel consumption. Under Section 721, grants are available to state and local governments for the purchase of hybrid and advanced diesel vehicles meeting certain requirements.

Tax incentives for purchasers of new products can be strong motivators of consumer behavior. As of 2005, qualifying hybrid vehicles were eligible for a federal "clean fuel" deduction of $2,000 if placed in service by the end of 2005, or $500 if placed in use during 2006. *See* http://www.fueleconomy.gov/ (a. June 9, 2005). Section 1341 of the Energy Policy Act of 2005 provides a complex formula for tax credits for future years based on the extent to which the vehicle achieves fuel economy.

Incentives for hybrids are not universally popular. A letter writer to a Richmond, VA newspaper called the $2,000 deduction for a Lexus RX400h hybrid SUV an "unfair tax cut for the affluent." Letters to the Editor, Richmond Times–Dispatch, May 19, 2005. Some states have another incentive for the purchase of hybrid vehicles: laws that allow the use of high-occupancy vehicle (HOV) lanes by solo hybrid vehicle drivers (which of course has the drawback that it encourages single-occupant driving). However, when hybrids became popular in the Washington, D.C. area HOV lanes, slowing traffic in those lanes, other commuters criticized the incentive. Steven Ginsburg and Carol Morello, As Hybrid Cars Multiply, So Do Carpooling Gripes, Wash. Post, Jan. 7. 2005, at A01.

b.   FUEL CELL CARS

Although fuel cells have been in widespread use for specialized applications, attempts to design automobile engines based on hydrogen fuel cell technology were widely assumed to be far from any current relevance.[8] In 1999, these assumptions began to change, when Daimler–Chrysler demonstrated a model of a fuel cell car that was much farther along than others in the industry had expected. The reaction in the industry was immediate: The Wall Street Journal said "not long ago, the fuel cell was dismissed as an environmentalist's pipe dream [but now] it is the subject of a heavily-financed research-and-development race among some of the world's biggest auto makers" Wall Street Journal, March 15, 1999, at 1.

The growing emphasis on fuel cell vehicles responds to three important areas of concern: (1) we are increasingly forced to import oil to meet our growing needs, and most of that oil goes into the transportation sector; (2) over a quarter of United States greenhouse gas emissions come from the transportation sector's consumption of petroleum (see Chapter 16), and (3) increasing automotive air pollution creates a need to find clean, efficient substitutes for the traditional automobile and truck engines.

Fuel cells have been in widespread use for specialized applications ever since they began to be used in the space program. http://www.americanhistory.si.edu/csr/fuelcells/index.htm (a. June 9, 2005) A fuel cell is a device

---

8.   Some industry segments believe that burning hydrogen in internal combustion engines will be more efficient that using fuel cells. Bavarian Motor Works (BMW) has been an advocate of this position. BMW has built a small fleet of model 750HL cars in which the internal combustion engine can be fueled by liquid hydrogen. The 750hL has a 12 cylinder engine capable of running on either gasoline or hydrogen using two independent, electronically controlled fuel induction systems. Running on hydrogen, the car has a range of 400 kilometers. *See* BMW 750hl—The Ultimate Clean Machine, http://www.bmwworld.com/models/750hl.htm (a. June 9, 2005). So far, there seems to have been little interest in this technology in the United States.

that generates electricity from chemical reactions other than combustion. A wide variety of fuel cell technologies exist, but the technology generally used in automotive applications is the proton exchange membrane ("PEM") fuel cell. PEM fuel cells use a polymer electrolyte consisting of a thin, permeable sheet that works at low temperatures. The electrolyte of the PEM must allow hydrogen protons to pass through but not electrons and heavier gases. To speed the reaction a platinum catalyst is used on both sides of the membrane. Hydrogen atoms are stripped of their electrons at the anode, and the positively charged protons pass by diffusion through one side of the porous membrane and migrate toward the cathode. The electrons pass around the electrolyte from the anode to the cathode through an exterior circuit and provide electric power along the way. At the cathode, the electrons, hydrogen protons and oxygen from the air combine to form H_2O–water.[9]

PEM fuel cells require highly purified hydrogen as a fuel. Thus to create a PEM fuel cell vehicle, pure hydrogen must be available onboard the vehicle. As a source of energy, hydrogen is famous for its role in the hydrogen bomb—the most powerful of nuclear weapons, but hydrogen has been used as a fuel in many small scale applications as well. It has the highest energy content per unit of weight of any known fuel, and when burned produces no pollution. If it is used to power a fuel cell, its only byproduct is pure water. A fuel cell is far more efficient than internal combustion or steam engines, as the latter involve an intermediate mechanical step and high heat loss. As with electricity, hydrogen is a secondary energy resource, meaning that it must be made from another fuel. Because hydrogen can be produced from a wide variety of energy resources, including fossil fuels, nuclear power, renewable resources and even water, hydrogen is seen as an opportunity for the United States to reduce its reliance on foreign oil.

Initial development of fuel cell vehicles in the United States focused on buses. Georgetown University has built and operated a fuel cell bus pursuant to a Federal Transit Administration demonstration grant, and the Chicago Transit Authority operates three hydrogen-powered fuel cell buses that store compressed hydrogen in roof-mounted tanks that are centrally refueled by liquid hydrogen.[10] The Department of Energy can enter into grants or cooperative agreements with units of local government to promote the use of fuel cell transit buses and school buses. *See* sections 741 and 743 of the Energy Policy Act of 2005. In addition, the Department of Transportation has been authorized to undertake a fuel cell bus technology development program by section 3045 of the 2005 Transportation Act.

In his 2003 State of the Union Address, President Bush brought hydrogen to public attention by unveiling a $1.2 billion Hydrogen Fuel Initiative aimed at developing the technology needed for commercially viable hydrogen-powered fuel cells. Through partnerships with the private

9. PEM fuel cells are also currently being used for distributed generation of electricity. See Chapter 13.

10.   http://www.fta.dot.gov/11325_11358_ENG_HTML.htm (a. June 9, 2005).

sector, this program seeks to develop hydrogen, fuel cell, and infrastructure technologies needed to make it practical and cost-effective for large numbers of Americans to choose to use fuel cell vehicles by 2020. *See* U.S. Department of Energy, Hydrogen, Fuel Cells, and Infrastructure Technologies Program.[11] Under section 1341 of the Energy Policy Act of 2005, buyers of fuel cell cars will eventually be eligible for tax credits.

The Hydrogen Fuel Initiative, which works in parallel with the Department of Energy's "FreedomCAR Partnership," formed in 2002, is the Bush Administration's showcase R&D program for new vehicles. It has been disparaged in some quarters for two principal reasons. First, critics argue that new funding of $720 million over five years for hydrogen research is far less than would be needed to speed up development of hydrogen fuel cell vehicles. Second, as hydrogen-fueled vehicles are, under any scenario, years away from mass commercial acceptance, there is a perceived lack of near term initiatives to reduce GHG emissions. "President Bush's new, 'big' idea allows this former Texas oil man to give the auto and oil industries exactly what they want—an opportunity to continue to profit from highly inefficient, polluting cars," according to Dr. Brent Blackwelder, president of the environmental group Friends of the Earth. "Any increase in funding for cleaner cars must be viewed as part of a much broader budget context that is terrible news for the environment." J.R. Pegg, Bush Hydrogen Fuel Proposal A Sham, Critics Say, Monitor, Feb. 6, 2003.

But support for fuel cells is bipartisan. In 2005, Senator Hillary Clinton toured a Rochester, New York manufacturing plant that produced the world's first fuel cell-powered truck, a modified Chevrolet Silverado, intended for military use. According to General Motors, it is on track to have technology in place so it can commercially manufacture viable fuel cell vehicles by 2010. Clinton: Build fuel cell auto "right here in the Rochester area," Rochester Democrat and Chronicle, Apr, 2, 2005. Most other auto companies are emphasizing research into the use of hydrogen fuel cells in motor vehicles, and the President's Hydrogen Fuel Initiative envisions a mass market for fuel cell vehicles by 2020. Hydrogen Fuel Initiative, *supra*.

California has also played a leading role in promoting fuel cell vehicles. The California Fuel Cell Partnership (CaFCP) is a joint venture between the state and a number of fuel cell manufacturers, auto manufacturers and oil companies aimed at getting fuel cell vehicles into production. The CaFCP plans to test fuel cell vehicles under real day-to-day driving conditions by placing up to 300 fuel cell cars and buses into fleets and promoting the development of hydrogen fueling stations. *See* http://www.fuelcellpartnership.org/ (accessed August 6, 2005). The governor of California has issued an Executive Order committing the state to "achieving a clean energy and transportation future based on the rapid commercialization of hydrogen and fuel cell technologies." Executive Order S–7–04 (2004). The order designated twenty-one California highways as the "California Hydro-

---

11.   http://www.eere.energy.gov/hydrogenandfuelcells/presidents_initiative.html   (a. June 9, 2005).

gen Highway Network," and committed the state to take a number of actions to ensure a "rapid transition to a hydrogen economy."

There are a number of important issues, however, that must be resolved successfully for hydrogen-fueled vehicles to find widespread acceptance. First is the cost. Currently, fuel cells are up to ten times more expensive than internal combustion engines, and hydrogen is three to four times as expensive to produce as gasoline (when produced from its most affordable source, natural gas). Research is underway to reduce the cost to affordable levels. Another important issue is safety. Hydrogen is non-toxic and much lighter than air, so it will dissipate rapidly when it is released. On the other hand, it is a flammable fuel, and has been suffering an image problem since the Hindenburg caught fire and burned in New Jersey in 1937. However, it is not any more flammable than gasoline or similar fuels, and the risk could be managed. William Vincent, Hydrogen and Tort Law, 25 Energy L. J. 385 (2004). The basic issue is that hydrogen is an unknown to most people compared to gasoline.

A difficult issue is developing a hydrogen storage tank that will store the amount of hydrogen required for a conventional driving range. This has proven technically challenging due to hydrogen's inherent properties. Prototype hydrogen vehicles use compressed hydrogen, stored onboard at about room temperature and under moderate pressure. Unfortunately, these moderate pressures lead to large fuel tanks and/or limited driving range because the energy density of hydrogen is lower than the energy density of gasoline. Because all gases occupy less volume at colder temperatures, compressed hydrogen can be stored more compactly when cryogenically cooled, but that introduces other challenges (imagine driving around American cities with supercold fuel tanks).

Liquid hydrogen is even more compact than cryogenic hydrogen, but because hydrogen's boiling point is lower than that of any substance except helium, liquefying hydrogen is complicated and not energy efficient. Liquid hydrogen is relatively easy and safe to store and transport, but it is extremely sensitive to heat, expanding significantly when warmed only a few degrees. Evaporation losses increase sharply if the car is driven less. In a parked car, an entire tank of liquid hydrogen fuel will completely evaporate in just 3 weeks. Technology development is actively underway to address these challenges. *See* Toyota Develops High-pressure Hydrogen Tanks for Fuel Cell Vehicles, The Auto Channel, May 16, 2005.

Even if efficient fuel cell engines can be developed for automotive use, however, the biggest hurdle to overcome is developing a network of technologies to get the hydrogen into the vehicle's engine.

c.   THE FUELS OF THE FUTURE

If hydrogen proves to be the next big thing, the key question is: Where will the hydrogen come from? The demonstration of the prototype fuel cell car by Daimler–Chrysler led the refiners' trade journal *Octane Week* to editorialize that this "amazingly compact, fuel-efficient, prototype 2004 model year hydrogen fuel cell car signals a potentially devastating future for oil refiners. Unless they can come up with a fuel cell friendly fuel, such as zero-sulfur, zero-aromatics naphtha or a similar 'gasoline,' refiners may be unwise to assume the gasoline/diesel infrastructure guarantees their products have a place in the fuel cell fleet of the future." Fuels Industry May Be Turned Upside-down by Fuel Cell Revolution, Octane Week, March 22, 1999. On the other hand, the Oil Daily quoted the chairman of Chevron: "People have been predicting the death of the internal combustion engine for a very long time, and it hasn't happened.... But as I've said for years, if automobiles are going to run on milk, then we'll be in the milk business." Analysts Have Trouble Predicting Future Route for Fuel Cell Vehicles, 49 Oil Daily #60, March 30, 1999.

Milk is not currently in the cards, but extensive research is underway on virtually every other possible fuel alternative. The fuel cells being developed for motor vehicles use pure hydrogen as fuel. Most observers have assumed that the cheapest source of hydrogen for use in fuel cells would be natural gas. A substantial amount of hydrogen is currently being produced from natural gas for industrial use. But the cost of natural gas has tripled in recent years, and the United States is expecting to rely on increasing imports of natural gas to meet existing needs. (See Chapter 8). This has led to intensive exploration of other methods for obtaining the high volumes of hydrogen that would be needed to supply transportation needs if fuel cell cars are to become widely used.

Auto manufacturers originally hoped to develop technologies for fuel cell cars that would allow drivers to continue to use gasoline by installing "reformers" that would convert the gasoline to hydrogen onboard the vehicle. So far, the efficiency of this technology has not been satisfactory, and the DOE has ceased funding research in this area. *See* On-board Hydrogen Reformation Deemed No More Efficient than Hybrids, Inside Fuels and Vehicles, August 26, 2004.

Methanol is another alternative source of hydrogen. Currently, methanol is being refined for use in the gasoline additive MTBE that is required in areas with high ozone pollution. That additive is likely to be phased out because of concern about its potential for causing water pollution (*see* § 4, *infra*), which will force closing of methanol production facilities unless new uses are found. This has stimulated research into the use of methanol as an on-board fuel for fuel cell cars.[12]

Some industry executives suggest that ethanol may prove to be the most efficient and economical source of hydrogen. " 'Ethanol is the least costly way to make hydrogen,' Sandy Thomas, a veteran hydrogen expert, told a session at the Society of Automotive Engineers' Government/Industry Meeting in Washington, D.C. last week. John Brady, an official with oil industry giant ChevronTexaco working on hydrogen, seconded the assertion in the same session: The fuel that jumps out at us [for making

---

12. The Los Alamos National Laboratory has a model available for licensing http: / /www.lanl.gov/partnerships/license/technologies/index.php?fuseaction=home.viewTechnology&id=500 (a. June 9, 2005)

hydrogen] is ethanol. He went on to describe how one hydrogen production device would 'be able to switch to ethanol from natural gas.' " Experts See Ethanol as Cheapest Route to Renewable Hydrogen, Energy Washington Week, May 18, 2005.

Other sources of hydrogen for transportation that could be the beneficiaries of scientific breakthroughs include nuclear reactors. The DOE's "Next Generation Nuclear Plant Project," to be led by the Idaho National Laboratory and "a consortium of appropriate industrial partners," is set to build a prototype nuclear plant at the Idaho facility that will test technologies for high-temperature hydrogen production. See sections 641–645 of the Energy Policy Act of 2005. Other possibilities include coal, propane, and new varieties of diesel fuel. *See generally* Daniel Sperling and James S. Cannon, eds., The Hydrogen Energy Transition: Moving toward the Post Petroleum Age in Transportation (Academic Press, 2004). And every environmentalist dreams of the possibility of developing efficient techniques to separate hydrogen from H_2O economically. *See* John A. Turner, Sustainable Hydrogen Production, 305 Science 972 (August 13, 2004). Section 801 ff. of the Energy Policy Act of 2005 authorizes $160,000,000 for the fiscal year 2006, and more for later years, to the DOE to fund the research and development of hydrogen and fuel cells for both vehicular and stationary uses.

However, many observers believe that the extensive promotion of hydrogen for use in vehicles is misdirected. Robert F. Service, The Hydrogen Backlash, 305 Science 958 (August 13, 2004). The National Academies of Science and Engineering have emphasized the need for long years of relatively basic research before proceeding toward development of an extensive hydrogen infrastructure for transportation. National Research Council, The Hydrogen Economy (National Academies Press, 2004). Joseph Romm, who headed the DOE's hydrogen research program in the Clinton administration, believes that it is much more likely that hydrogen can provide an efficient and economical source for electrical generation than for transportation. Joseph Romm, The Hype About Hydrogen (Island Press, 2004). Romm suggests that the loss of energy efficiency during the various conversions of energy resources necessary to deliver hydrogen to an onboard fuel cell would mean that those resources could be used much more economically in centralized facilities. *Id.* At present, hybrid vehicles may be able to produce energy efficiencies at least as good as fuel cell vehicles. Nurettin Demirdöven and John Deutch, Hybrid Cars Now, Fuel Cell Cars Later, 305 Science 974 (August 13, 2004). But a spirited defense of the use of hydrogen in vehicles by Amory Lovins of the Rocky Mountain Institute can be found at http://www.rmi.org/sitepages/pid171.php#20H2Myths (a. June 9, 2005).

If fuel cells truly become a common technology for motor vehicle engines, many familiar laws, regulations and business practices will need to be reexamined. If our transportation sector is to operate efficiently and equitably in a sustainable environment it is not too early to explore the impact of the fuel cell automotive engine, and to think about how existing rules and practices may need to be modified to maximize the benefits of the new technology and minimize any adverse impacts. The difficulties experienced with ill-prepared revisions to the laws relating to electricity distribution, as in California, exemplify the need for early consideration of the legal issues affecting any major technological and economic advance.

1. Monopoly or competition. With competing technologies using different fuels, it may be difficult to provide a fuel distribution network that will satisfy consumers that they will be able to find the fuel they need. Should the government guarantee a "natural monopoly" for one type of fuel cell? Or would this stifle the entrepreneurial ingenuity that has brought the technology so far so rapidly?

2. Control of gas stations. Whether one or more new fuels are required, the control of existing networks of gasoline stations will be an important factor in determining when or how the fuel will be available. In recent years, the major oil companies have been reducing their control of gas stations. And more gasoline is being sold by independents and convenience store chains. In addition, franchisee operators have obtained legislation protecting their interests against the majors. Do we need additional laws to encourage these various parties to cooperate in a system to make new fuels available?

3. Federalism. Our existing air pollution legislation allows California to set its own standards for motor vehicle air pollution. If there is going to be a need for major investment in new fuel and engine production technologies, is it still appropriate to allow California to set its own rules? Does this competition between regulators encourage creativity? Or would it be more effective to have a single national standard?

4. Recycling refineries. If gasoline begins to lose market share significantly, how can the significant investments in existing refineries be protected from becoming stranded costs? Similarly, if methanol is no longer used to produce MTBE, and does not become a fuel of choice for fuel cells, can the methanol production facilities be recycled? Does the government need to assist refinery operators in converting to other uses?

5. Climate change. Fuel cell technologies differ in the extent to which they create greenhouse gases. Should we create incentives to promote those technologies that minimize additional greenhouse effect? If so, should the incentives go for research by manufacturers, subsidies for users, reduced rates for fuel, or some other alternative?

6. Customer choice. If competing technologies vary in the nature and degree of their impact on the environment, is it desirable to give consumers a choice of the type and degree of environmental protection they wish to support? Will individual consumers pay more for cars that run on "green fuel?"

7. Safety. Many of the potential fuels for fuel cell vehicles are more flammable or explosive than the existing fuels found at gasoline stations. Can we rely on the existing public and private standard-setting organizations to develop safety standards for the storage, transportation and

distribution of these fuels? Or will new laws be needed to assign safety responsibilities?

8. Liability. Will insurance companies be willing to insure the operators of a system for distributing new fuels that may have volatile characteristics? Will insurance be available to vehicle owners at reasonable rates? Should some sort of government-supported reinsurance system be created?

4. AIR POLLUTION CONTROLS

Research and development of engine technology has been driven by two objectives, which are sometimes compatible but at other times seem to work at cross purposes. One is economic efficiency, heightened by the desire to reduce dependence on overseas sources of petroleum; the second is concern with air pollution caused by motor vehicles. The pollution-reduction objective is the charge of the United States Environmental Protection Agency, which lacks a strong mandate to improve energy efficiency. That goal is in the purview of the United States Department of Energy. The private sector sometimes finds itself pulled in two different directions by these two agencies.

The EPA is authorized by the Clean Air Act to regulate emissions of harmful pollutants from mobile sources (motor vehicles). The Act gives the EPA the general power to promulgate "standards applicable to the emission of any air pollutant from any class or classes of new motor vehicles or motor vehicle engines, which in the EPA Administrator's judgment cause, or contribute to, air pollution which may reasonably be anticipated to endanger public health or welfare." 42 U.S.C. § 7521(a)(1). These standards apply for the useful life of the car. Currently that life is ten years or 100,000 miles starting in 1990, but vehicles are not tested after 7 years or 75,000 miles.

The EPA originally was slow to establish sulfur and particulate emissions standards as required by the 1977 amendments to the Clean Air Act. Indeed, the EPA failed to set such standards for over six years for autos, and for even longer periods for heavier vehicles, necessitating litigation by environmental organizations that forced EPA to meet court-imposed timetables. *See, e.g., Natural Resources Defense Council v. Thomas,* 805 F.2d 410 (D.C. Cir. 1986).

The EPA has now promulgated separate standards for light duty passenger vehicles, light duty trucks, heavy duty vehicles and motorcycles. The Act requires that standards for carbon monoxide, hydrocarbons, nitrous oxides and particulates mandate the greatest degree of emission reduction technologically achievable. Indeed, EPA may set standards that are currently technologically feasible, or promulgate a higher technology-forcing standard. *Natural Resources Defense Council v. EPA,* 655 F.2d 318 (D.C. Cir. 1981). However, the EPA must consider whether these emission standards will be cost-effective, or endanger public safety.

Every new vehicle model and new emission control device must be tested by the EPA. § 206(a)(1),(2). The EPA may also randomly test new vehicles that have already been certified in conformity with the standards. If the vehicle does not pass, the EPA may suspend or revoke the certificate of conformity unless the manufacturer pays a non-conformance penalty ("NCP"). An attempt by EPA to avoid recall of nonconforming vehicles by requiring offsetting reductions of future year models was held invalid by the D.C. Circuit, but the court indicated that EPA had some discretion to consider offsets as part of an enforcement policy. *Center for Auto Safety v. Ruckleshaus,* 747 F.2d 1 (D.C. Cir. 1984).

The Act preempts state regulation of mobile source emissions with the exception of California. (§ 209(a)) California may promulgate different emission standards subject to a waiver from EPA standards. The EPA may not require other states to adopt the California standards, *Virginia v. EPA,* 108 F.3d 1397 (D.C. Cir. 1997), but any state may voluntarily choose to adopt the California standards. The EPA addresses vehicles and engines, along with the fuels used to operate them, as a single system. This integrated approach to combine technology advances with cleaner fuels results in greater emissions reductions. *See* Environmental Protection Agency, *Mobile Source Emissions—Past, Present, and Future.*[13]

a. VEHICLE REGULATIONS

In § 202 of the 1990 Clean Air Act amendments, Congress directed EPA to initiate Tier I standards for light-duty vehicles and light-duty trucks beginning with the 1994 model year, and set the stage for EPA to adopt Tier II standards for the 2004 and following model years. The EPA adopted its Tier II standards in 2000 *(68 Fed. Reg. 6698)*. Because new emission control technologies had been developed, these standards are considerably more stringent than the Tier I requirements. They are also applicable to a wider range of vehicles, including many minivans and SUVs that were not covered by Tier I. *See* The Clean Air Act Handbook, 2nd Edition, by Robert J. Martineau, Jr. and David P. Novello, 2004 American Bar Association, p. 328–330. Tier II standards began applying to vehicles in model year 2004 and apply to both light-duty vehicles and light-duty trucks. 40 C.F.R. § 86.1811–04(a)(1). The fleet average for Tier 2 should be 0.7 g/mi of NOx. 40 C.F.R. § 86.1811–04(d)(1)(I).

Congress and the EPA waited a long time to regulate heavy-duty trucks. The nature of diesel fuel with its heavy sulfur content, and the difficulty of adapting catalytic converters to diesel engines, created techno-logical challenges. Eventually the EPA and the automobile manufacturers agreed that the mandatory use of low-sulfur diesel fuel was the only way to provide cost-effective control of emissions. Now the EPA treats the heavy-duty vehicles, engines, and fuel as a combined system when promulgating regulations.

Diesel exhaust contains many fine particles which become airborne, and medical science has increasingly pinpointed ultrafine particles (less than one micrometer in diameter) as one of the most serious airborne

---

13.   http://www.epa.gov/otaq/invntory/overview/solutions/index.htm (a. June 9, 2005).

pollutants. Jocelyn Kaiser, Mounting Evidence Indicts Fine–Particle Pollution, 307 Science 1858 (March 25, 2005). Carbon particles appear to be the most unhealthy. Diesel exhaust exacerbates asthma attacks, heart attacks, and respiratory problems. More severely, the particle pollution lessens the lifespan of individuals with lung cancer and increases the risk of getting lung cancer. Diesel particles also impact premature deaths, chronic bronchitis, can restrict physical activity, increase the incidence of stroke, and cause respiratory damage. Other systems, such as immune, endocrine, reproductive, developmental, and nervous systems, are also negatively affected. *See* Clean Air Task Force, Diesel and Health in America: The Lingering Threat (2005).[14]

The new standards reduce PM and NOx emissions by 90 percent for heavy-duty trucks and by 95 percent for buses. Further, the EPA will reduce the level of sulfur in diesel fuel from the current level of 500 ppm to 15 ppm by the year 2006. A credit option is available to refineries that meet the requirements ahead of time. These credits can be used by the refinery to average emissions, saved for the future, or sold. Martineau, Jr. and Novello, *supra* at 385–386.

National Petrochemical & Refiners Association v. Environmental Protection Agency

287 F.3d 1130 (D.C. Cir. 2002).

■ PER CURIAM We have here a set of challenges to an EPA rule affecting diesel fuel and engines. The rule requires drastic reductions in exhaust emissions starting in 2007 (for some emissions 95% lower than current standards). To aid in the achievement of the new emission standards, the rule also requires a 97% reduction in the sulfur level in diesel fuel. Numerous parties, including engine manufacturers (including Cummins Inc.), automobile makers, and fuel refiners, challenged the rule on various grounds, while others, including environmental groups and states, defended it. We deny the petitions.

I.   The Regulations

Diesel engines emit nitrous oxides ("NOx"), non-methane hydrocarbons, and particulate matter ("PM"), all of which are harmful to the environment and human health (as no party disputes). Fulfilling its duty under the Clean Air Act to set emission standards that "reflect the greatest degree of emission reduction achievable" through cost-effective technology, *42 U.S.C. § 7521*(a)(3), the EPA decided on dramatic reductions of diesel engine emission standards, issuing a final rule on January 18, 2001: Control of Air Pollution from New Motor Vehicles: Heavy–Duty Engine and Vehicle Standards and Highway Diesel Fuel Sulfur Control Requirements, *66 Fed. Reg. 5002 (2001)* (hereinafter "2007 Rule").

---

14.   http://www.catf.us/publications/reports/Diesel_Health_in_America.pdf (Accessed August 6, 2005).

The 2007 Rule sets the following standards for diesel engines: 0.01 grams per brake-horsepower-hour (g/bhp-hr) for PM, 0.20 g/bhp-hr for NOx, and 0.14 g/bhp-hr for nonmethane hydrocarbons. *66 Fed. Reg. at 5005; 40 C.F.R. § 86.007–11(a)(1)*, (3). For PM and NOx, the new standards are "90 percent and 95 percent below current standard levels, respectively." *66 Fed. Reg. at 5002.* Engine emissions are to be measured by the Federal Test Procedure, see *40 C.F.R. § 86.1301–90 et seq.*, as well as two other test procedures that are not at issue in this case.

The standard for PM takes full effect in 2007. *66 Fed. Reg. at 5005.* The standards for NOx and non-methane hydrocarbons, however, will be phased in as follows: 50% of a manufacturer's sales for 2007, 2008 and 2009 engines and 100% of sales for 2010 and following. *Id.; 40 C.F.R. § 86.007–11(g).* During the phase-in period, manufacturers will be allowed to participate in an averaging, banking, and trading ("ABT") program. This program allows the generation of credits from engines that beat the standards; the credits can then be applied to engines that may not be able to meet the 2007 standards right away. *66 Fed. Reg. at 5109–11; 40 C.F.R. § 86.007–15.* A crucial distinction is made here: Averaging across service classes (e.g., between light heavy-duty engines and heavy heavy-duty engines) is allowed, but not banking or trading. 66 Fed. Reg. at 5110.

The 2007 Rule also eliminates a preexisting exception—available only for turbocharged heavy-duty diesel engines—for emissions from engine crankcases. *66 Fed. Reg. at 5040; 40 C.F.R. § 86.007–11(c).* As a result, any crankcase emissions not eliminated count against a vehicle's emission limit.

High pollutant levels in fuel make it impossible or at least far more difficult to achieve low emissions. Thus, under its authority to regulate any fuel components that significantly impair "the performance of any emission control device or system," *42 U.S.C. § 7545*(c)(1)(B), the EPA also decided to require "a 97 percent reduction in the sulfur content of diesel fuel." *66 Fed. Reg. at 5002.* As of 2006, the maximum sulfur content of diesel fuel will be reduced from 500 ppm to 15 ppm. (Under a 15 ppm cap, the EPA predicts that the average sulfur level in diesel will actually be 7 ppm. Response to Comments at 3–50.) Under its "Temporary Compliance Option," the EPA actually requires that only 80% of fuel from any given refinery meet the 15 ppm cap in years 2006–08. Any overachieving refiner will generate credits, which it can then use to average with another refinery owned by that refiner, bank for future years, or sell to another refiner. *66 Fed. Reg. at 5065.*

II.   The Emissions Standards

We review the 2007 Rule under the arbitrary and capricious standard of *42 U.S.C. § 7607*(d), which is indistinguishable from the Administrative Procedure Act equivalent. See *Ethyl Corp. v. EPA, 51 F.3d 1053, 1064 (D.C. Cir. 1995); Small Refiner Lead Phase–Down Task Force v. EPA, 705 F.2d 506, 519 (D.C. Cir. 1983).* Deference is particularly great where EPA's decision is based on complex scientific or technical analysis. *Appalachian Power Co. v. EPA, 251 F.3d 1026, 1035 (D.C. Cir. 2001).*

A. Background on Emissions Control Technology

Diesel exhaust emissions can be controlled through the use of catalytic emission control devices in the vehicle's exhaust system. *66 Fed. Reg. at 5007.* These resemble the familiar catalytic converters found on ordinary automobiles. *Id.* Current control devices for diesel engines work less well than they do for gasoline engines, because of diesels' "oxygen-rich and relatively cool ... exhaust environment." *Id. at 5009.* PM emissions are also more difficult to control in diesel engines because of the soot formed during diesel combustion. *Id.* Compounding the difficulties is the fact that "historical diesel NOx control approaches tend to increase PM and vice versa, but both are harmful pollutants that need to be controlled." *Id.*

Thus, in order to achieve drastic—and simultaneous—reductions in PM, NOx, and non-methane hydrocarbons, engine manufacturers will need technical innovations in emission controls. The EPA predicts that two relatively new technologies will aid in achieving the 2007 reductions: the catalyzed diesel particulate filter ("particulate filter") and the NOx adsorber. *66 Fed. Reg. at 5036.* In the following paragraphs, we explain briefly—and to the best of our understanding—how each technology works on the targeted emissions.

Particulate matter is made up of three things: Unburned carbon particles (or soot), unburned hydrocarbons (also called the "soluble organic fraction"), and sulfates (resulting from the oxidation of sulfur in the engine's exhaust). *66 Fed. Reg. at 5047.* The majority of diesel PM is soot. Catalyzed particulate filters work by passing the exhaust through a ceramic or metallic filter that captures soot and other PM.

Particulate filters eventually become plugged up with particulate matter, at which point the collected particles (mostly carbon) have to be burned off (or oxidized). *Id.* The burning-off process is called "regeneration," and the result (from oxidizing carbon) is of course carbon dioxide. *Id.* The EPA was convinced that precious metal catalysts would make regeneration possible at the low temperatures typical of diesel engines, and that such catalysts could thus be used on a continuous basis throughout the life of the trap. *Id.*; see also Regulatory Impact Analysis ("RIA") III–6.

NOx adsorbers do their work by storing NOx during the normal oxygen-rich conditions of diesel engine operation. RIA III–18. Over time, the adsorber becomes full of the stored NOx, thus requiring regeneration. During regeneration, the excess NOx is burned off; technically, it is reduced to N[2] by an interaction with carbon monoxide across a catalyst system that typically contains platinum and rhodium; the less-harmful gases that result are N[2] and CO[2]. *Id.* Like NOx, sulfur from the fuel accumulates over time by bonding to the NOx adsorber's catalysts, and must be burned off during a "desulfation" process (more on that below). The EPA suggests the use of dual-bed NOx adsorbers (for a diagram, see RIA III–23), which involve splitting of the exhaust stream into two pipes, each of which has an adsorber bed. The benefit of such an arrangement is that regeneration and/or desulfation can be conducted in one bed while nearly all the exhaust stream is directed to the bed that is still in adsorbtion mode, thus maintaining a consistent level of performance. RIA III–22 to III–25.

Crankcase emissions are emitted from the vehicle's crankcase, having gotten there by leaking from the combustion chamber through the piston rings. *66 Fed. Reg. at 5040.* The EPA's elimination of the previous exception for such emissions is a "performance requirement," leaving the solution entirely up to manufacturers. *Id.* The EPA predicts that manufacturers will either filter crankcase gases and route them back into the engine intake, or route the gases into the exhaust stream (upstream of any emissions control devices). RIA III–78–79. Another option would be to vent crankcase gases directly to the atmosphere; this is an unlikely choice, because the combined emissions from exhaust and crankcase together would have to fall within the exhaust emissions standards. *66 Fed. Reg. at 5040.*

B. Cummins's Challenges

1. Feasibility of NOx and PM Standards

Cummins argues that the EPA acted arbitrarily and capriciously in concluding that engine manufacturers will be able to develop emissions-control systems satisfying the new rule. According to Cummins, the EPA failed to make "reasonable extrapolations," Cummins's Opening Brief at 5 (quoting *Natural Resources Defense Council v. Thomas, 805 F.2d 410, 432 (D.C. Cir. 1986)),* or to "provide a reasoned explanation for believing that its projection is reliable," *id.* (quoting *National Resources Defense Council, Inc. v. EPA, 655 F.2d 318, 328 (D.C. Cir. 1981)).*

In reviewing these issues, we note that EPA was "not obliged to provide detailed solutions to every engineering problem," but had only to "identify the major steps" for improvement and "give plausible reasons for its belief that the industry will be able to solve those problems in the time remaining." *Husqvarna AB v. EPA, 254 F.3d 195, 201 (D.C. Cir. 2001)* (quoting *Natural Res. Def. Council, 655 F.2d at 333).* Since the EPA is authorized to adopt "technology-forcing" regulations, see *Natural Res. Def. Council, 655 F.2d at 333; Sierra Club v. Costle, 657 F.2d 298, 364 (D.C. Cir. 1981),* a petitioner's evidence that current technology is inadequate is not enough to show that the EPA was arbitrary in predicting future success. [The court found that EPA had adequately shown that all of its technological research met that standard in regard to the feasibility of NOx and PM regulations.]

III. Diesel Fuel Sulfur Standard

Under *42 U.S.C. § 7545*(c)(1), EPA is empowered to regulate fuel content if the Administrator either determines that (A) "any emission product of such fuel ... causes, or contributes, to air pollution which may reasonably be anticipated to endanger the public health or welfare," or (B) "emission products of such fuel ... will impair to a significant degree the performance of any emission control device or system which is in general use, or which ... would be in general use were such regulation to be promulgated." *42 U.S.C. § 7545*(c)(1)(A) & (B). We first consider whether EPA's 15 ppm sulfur rule is justified as protecting public health or welfare under § 7545(c)(1)(A). . . . EPA's justifications for a 15 ppm sulfur rule in this proceeding belie its post-hoc assertion that it was regulating pursuant to its authority under § 7545(c)(1)(A). Although the Agency cited general health and environmental effects of diesel exhaust, as well as sulfur dioxide formation, *e.g. 66 Fed. Reg. 5002, 5021–23 (2001),* it explicitly declared that "we are requiring significant reductions in diesel fuel sulfur *to enable certain emission control devices to function properly." Id. at 5034* (emphasis added). Indeed, EPA justified the 15 ppm standard (as opposed to some other concentration) as necessary for effective operation of the NOx adsorber and PM trap. See *id. at 5053; id. at 5047.* . . . It could hardly be clearer—EPA is regulating sulfur *because* of its effects on emission-control devices, and not for health and welfare reasons. Therefore, the 15 ppm sulfur rule either rises or falls with EPA's justification under *42 U.S.C. § 7545*(c)(1)(B).

NPRA argues that EPA's 15 ppm sulfur requirement is arbitrary, capricious, and contrary to law because EPA has failed to show that the emission-control technology requiring ultra-low sulfur fuel is in or near general use. Specifically NPRA contends that NOx adsorption technology requiring 15 ppm sulfur diesel fuel will not be "in general use" even if this fuel standard is adopted. Further, NPRA argues that the PM control technology does not require ultra-low sulfur fuel. As discussed in Part II.B, *supra,* EPA has reasonably determined that NOx adsorption technology will be available. The record contains ample support for EPA's conclusion that NOx adsorbers will be available by 2007 if fuel sulfur is regulated. Although some research remains to be done to solve the problem of catalyst sintering (deterioration caused by desulfation—high temperature operation to remove sulfur building up on the catalyst), petitioners have identified no theoretical barriers to the development of NOx adsorbers. "In the absence of theoretical objections to the technology, the agency need only identify the major steps necessary for development of the device, and give plausible reasons for its belief that the industry will be able to solve those problems in the time remaining." *Natural Res. Def. Council, 655 F.2d at 333.* Here EPA notes that NOx adsorbers are used in gas turbine systems and natural gas fired powerplants. EPA claims that the "differences between these current applications of the NOx adsorber technology and the future use of NOx adsorbers to control NOx emission from diesel engines lies only in the need to adapt the diesel engine operation to the NOx adsorber performance." It is only necessary that a desulfation cycle be developed—and EPA cites evidence that such research is under way. EPA has evidence that application of this technology is feasible, appears to have set forth an engineering path rather than mere optimism, and has given a reasoned explanation why it believes this path can be followed. See *66 Fed. Reg. at 5052.* That is sufficient: "EPA is not obliged to provide detailed solutions to every engineering problem posed in the perfection of the [technology]." *Natural Res. Def. Council v. Thomas, 805 F.2d 410, 434 (D.C. Cir. 1986)* (quoting *Natural Res. Def. Council, 655 F.2d at 333).*

EPA's determination that NOx adsorption technology is viable and necessary justifies the 15 ppm sulfur diesel fuel standard; therefore, we need not consider whether the diesel fuel standard is necessary for the operation of PM control technology.

IV. Mack Truck Petition

Petitioner Mack Truck challenges EPA's changes to its Averaging, Banking and Trading ("ABT") program. This program allows engine manufacturers who produce engines cleaner than those required by the regulations to generate "credits" that they may then use to offset higher emitting engines ("averaging"), save for future use ("banking"), or sell to other manufacturers ("trading"). See *40 C.F.R. § 86.004–15*. Traditionally, EPA has prohibited engine manufacturers from applying credits generated by light heavy-duty or medium heavy-duty engines to heavy heavy-duty engines. See *40 C.F.R. § 86.004–15(d)*, (e), (f)(3). The new rule allows such cross-subclass averaging, but only during the 2007–09 phase-in period. See 2007 Rule, *66 Fed. Reg. at 5164* (to be codified at *40 C.F.R. § 86.007–15(m)(10)*). Furthermore, when manufacturers use credits from one diesel engine class in calculating the emissions of another diesel engine class, credits are discounted by 20%. *Id. at 5163* (to be codified at *40 C.F.R. § 86.007–15(m)(3)*, (4)). Cross-subclass banking and trading remain prohibited. *Id. at 5164* (to be codified at *40 C.F.R. § 86.007–15(m)(10)*).

Mack's complaint about these new provisions stems from the fact that it makes only heavy heavy-duty engines. According to Mack, because manufacturers cannot make a compliant heavy heavy-duty engine without sacrificing some fuel efficiency and because Mack's customers are extremely sensitive to cost increases generated by decreased fuel economy, the new rule will likely force Mack to purchase emissions credits from manufacturers of the same engine class. Mack contends that the agency failed to provide a reasoned explanation for its "sudden reversal of its previous, long-standing position against cross-class averaging." Mack Truck's Opening Br. at 10. As EPA points out, however, a provision that temporarily allows cross-subclass averaging from 2007 through 2009, but retains the prohibition against banking and trading, can hardly be considered a wholesale reversal of a general policy against cross-subclass averaging, banking, and trading. Respondent's Br. at 60. In any event, EPA fully explained its decision, noting that the revised ABT program adds flexibility during the transition to the new emissions standards. Any adverse environmental effects, EPA observed, would be eliminated by the temporary nature of the cross-subclass averaging and by the 20% discount applied to credit use. Responding to the claim of anti-competitive effects, EPA explained that although it "tries to avoid introducing competitive . . . disadvantages when it establishes new emissions control programs, it is not a result [EPA] can ensure; nor is that the primary goal for EPA under the statute." EPA Resp. to Mack Truck's Req. for Recons. at 12.

Conclusion: The petitions for review are denied.∎

NOTES AND COMMENTS

1.   Opponents of the new diesel fuel regulations continue to argue that the rule could disrupt the supply of diesel fuel. A report by the National Petroleum Council warns that the low-sulfur fuel may become contaminated with higher sulfur fuel during transfer in pipelines. The contaminated fuel could not be used and would reduce supplies. *See* The Wall Street Journal, "Oil Group Says Diesel Rules May Crimp Supply," December 2, 2004.

2.   The EPA also regulates evaporative emissions, which are the emissions from fuel that evaporates during refueling and while the engine is operating, and in high ambient temperatures even when it is not operating. The EPA imposed a limit on gasoline service stations to allow only ten gallons of gas per minute to be dispensed. Martineau, Jr. and Novello, *supra,* at 333–334.

3.   Mobile Source Air Toxics ("MSATs"), as the name implies, are air toxics from mobile sources, such as motor vehicles. It is estimated that air toxics from mobile sources account for between 21 and 42 percent of all toxic substances in urban air. Transportation Research Board, Surface Transportation Environmental Research: A Long–Term Strategy 35 (2002). To combat MSATs, the EPA has established limits on gasoline volatility, required reformulated gasoline in certain area, and limited sulfur in diesel fuel. *See* EPA, Environmental Fact Sheet, Air Toxics from Motor Vehicles. In 2001, the EPA promulgated a final rule establishing a list of MSATs and new toxic emission levels for reformulated gasoline and regular gasoline. 66 FR 17230. In *Sierra Club v. EPA*, 325 F.3d 374 (D.C.Cir. 2003), the Sierra Club and others brought suit arguing that certain EPA provisions did not reduce MSATs sufficiently. The petitioners argued that the rule failed to be technology-forcing and put too much emphasis on costs, but the court rejected the claims and held that the EPA's interpretation of the statute was not arbitrary and capricious.

4.   The regulations for on-road vehicles will continue to decrease mobile source emissions for the future. The EPA estimates that without the regulations, emissions levels in 2020 would be 20 times greater for carbon monoxide, 50 times greater for hydrocarbons, and 10 times greater for particulate matter. Further, nitrogen oxide emissions in 2020 will be less than 1970 levels, which is a reduction of 20 times what the levels would be without the regulations. *See* EPA, *Mobile Source Emissions, On–Road Sources.*[15]

5.   Agricultural interests have been promoting the idea of "biodiesel," a form of diesel fuel made agricultural material. Biodiesel can be made from many different kinds of vegetable oils. Jon Van Gerpen and Gerhard Knothe, Basics of the Transesterification Reaction, in Gerhard Knothe et al, eds., The Biodiesel Handbook 26 (Champaign, IL: AOCS Press, 2005).

15.   http://www.epa.gov/otaq/invntory/overview/results/onroad.htm (a. August 6, 2005).

Greg Pahl, Biodiesel: Growing a New Energy Economy 42–45 (Chelsea Green Publishing, 2005). Alcohol is added to the vegetable oil together with a catalyst, such as sodium hydroxide (commonly called caustic soda). This initiates a process known as transesterification in which the triglycerides in the vegetable oil are converted into alkyl esters that can be used to fuel diesel engines.

Biodiesel can be used alone or in combination with petroleum diesel to power vehicles, in many cases without any modifications to the vehicles. Unless used in its "neat" form (B100, or pure biodiesel), biodiesel is not strictly speaking a purely renewable resource because vehicles running on it also burn a petroleum product. At present the manufacturers of diesel engines say that their engine warranties are voided if pure biodiesel is used. Beginning in 2006 the DOE is to include biodiesel testing in its studies of engine technology. *See* section 757 of the Energy Policy Act of 2005.

The use of the "B20" blend (fuel that is 20% biodiesel and 80% regular diesel fuel) is becoming more common. B20 provides additional lubrication that is needed when sulfur is removed from diesel fuels, and helps reduce some air emissions associated with diesel engines. A one-year biodiesel tax incentive went into effect in 2005, and about 500 fleets and 400 retail stations across the nation offer biodiesel. *See* Douglas E. Faulkner, Bush Highlights Biodiesel's Role in Energy Security, Richmond Times–Dispatch, May 19, 2005, at A13 (describing President Bush's visit to a Virginia biodiesel production facility).

Biodiesel is becoming widely used in Europe, where the use of diesel engines in passenger cars is widespread. Most of the biodiesel in Europe is made from rapeseed oil (canola oil), while in the United States almost all of the biodiesel is made from soybeans. However, there are efforts to design new crops specifically aimed at producing the product. Pahl, *supra* at 46–50.

The singer Willie Nelson formed a company in 2005 to promote a B20 blend called "BioWillie," and announced plans to contract with an Oklahoma City-based chain of truck stops to carry the fuel at its 169 locations across the nation. Matt Curry, Willie Nelson's new gig: Biodiesel, Associated Press, Jan. 14, 2005.

Manufacturing biodiesel can be a very simple or a very sophisticated process. In agricultural areas, many people make it in the farmyard in old 55 gallon drums and use it in old tractors that are no longer under warranty. Larger industrial operations use additional treatments to meet industry standards.

School bus fleets in farming communities are a key market for biodiesel. Not only are local farmers provided with a market, but the consumption of carbon-intensive vegetation does not add to the total amount of carbon dioxide that would otherwise be created. As a locally-derived fuel, biodiesel avoids adding to reliance on petroleum imports, and there are indications that it can have aggregate air quality benefits. Efforts are underway to broaden the market for biodiesel. See National Biodiesel Board, Biodiesel, On the Road to Fueling the Future.[16]

6. For non-road sources, such as spark-ignition engines, marine engines, locomotives, and compression-ignition engines, the EPA set standards for CO, hydrocarbon ("HC"), PM, NOx, and smoke (59 *Fed.Reg.* 31,306) and the standards have been upheld by the D.C. Circuit. *Engine Mfrs. Ass'n v. EPA, 88 F.3d 1075 (D.C. Cir. 1996). See also Husqvarna AB v. EPA, 254 F.3d 195 (D.C.Cir. 2001).* Regulations for nonroad vehicles, including tractors, bulldozers, locomotives, and barges, require full compliance by 2012, and are intended to reduce emissions from new engines by more than 90 percent. *See* New York Times, "Tougher Emission Rules Set for Big Diesel Vehicles," by Michael Janofsky, May 11, 2004. The EPA estimates that non-road emission sources are over twice the levels in 1970. However, emissions controls are expected to cut 2020 levels of hydrocarbon emissions and nitrogen oxides by half of their expected levels without regulation. PM 2020 levels are expected to remain at the current level, but that level is about two-thirds of what would be expected without regulations. *See* EPA, *Mobile Source Emissions–Non–Road Sources.*[17]

b. GASOLINE REGULATIONS

Section 211 of the Clean Air Act ("CAA") (42 U.S.C. § 7545) gives the EPA authority over the composition of fuels. Historically, this section of the CAA was first used to ban the sale of leaded gasoline. *Ethyl Corp. v. EPA,* 541 F.2d 1 (D.C. Cir. 1976). Presently, every fuel manufacturer must register all fuels and additives that it wishes to sell. The manufacturer must provide the EPA with the name of each additive contained in the fuel, the concentration of that additive, and purpose for which the additive was added. Where the EPA finds that a fuel or additive may detrimentally effect the public health or the emission control system of any vehicle, it may control or prohibit its manufacture or sale.

The EPA's ability to prevent the use of certain additives under the CAA was challenged in *Ethyl Corp. v. EPA,* 51 F.3d 1053 (D.C. Cir. 1995) (preventing use of MMT). While the court found that the EPA had improperly relied on a provision requiring that an additive not damage or impair a vehicle's emission control system (sec. 211(f)(4)), an earlier case between the same parties held that the EPA had the duty to consider public health in the evaluation of additives under section 211(a) and (c). *Ethyl Corp. v. EPA,* 541 F.2d 1 (D.C. Cir. 1976) (regarding EPA's ability to ban lead as gasoline additive). That interpretation of the CAA was reiterated by the 1977 amendments to the CAA which explicitly authorized the EPA to regulate fuels or fuel additives "which may reasonably be anticipated to endanger the public health or welfare." H.R. Rep. No. 95–294, 95th Cong. 1st Sess. 43–50 (1977). Current EPA regulations adopted pursuant to

---

16. http://www.biodiesel.org (a. June 9, 2005).

17. http://www.epa.gov/otaq/invntory/overview/results/nonroad.htm (a. June 9, 2005).

§ 211(f)(1)(B), added in 1990, impose numerous restrictions of fuel additives for the purpose of protecting emission control devices.

In apparent contradiction to their early stance of opposition to emission reductions, the auto manufacturers currently support the EPA's plan to require oil refineries to retool to produce lower sulfur gasoline. This would enable manufacturers of light trucks to lower emissions without applying new technologies because sulfur has been shown to inhibit the performance of catalytic converters. However, auto manufacturers insist that advanced emission-control technologies being developed can only achieve lower emissions with even lower sulfur gasoline. Indeed, both domestic and foreign auto manufacturers have asked the EPA to further reduce allowable sulfur levels.

In addition to regulating additives, the EPA enforces the requirements that reformulated gasoline ("RFG") be used in specified non-attainment areas. RFG must not have greater emissions than conventional gasoline, and must contain some form of detergent to prevent efficiency damaging deposits. Additionally, RFG may not contain any lead or other heavy metals, cannot contain more than 1.0% benzene by volume, and cannot exceed an aromatic hydrocarbon content of 25% by volume. Finally, during the high ozone season RFG volatile organic compound emissions must be 15% lower than that of conventional gasoline, and year round toxic emissions must be 15% lower than conventional gasoline. Manufacturers that exceed these minimum requirements are granted credits, which may be used for future production or sold to other manufacturers for the same non-attainment area.

In some states, ethanol manufactured from corn is used to meet RFG requirements. (Can you guess which states?) Oil companies have voiced strong objections to regulations requiring the use of ethanol. Ethanol cannot be distributed by pipeline because of its chemical composition, so it must be transported by truck or railroad tank car at considerable expense. Since currently used ethanol is made from corn, this imposes additional economic burdens on those regions far removed from corn-growing areas, such as the West coast.

Ethanol mixed with gasoline is used in Flexible Fuel Vehicles ("FFVs"). EPA, Clean Alternative Fuels.[18] In February 2004, the government extended an ethanol credit for auto makers that make FFVs for another four years. Some responses were critical because many FFVs end up only using gasoline. *See* The Wall Street Journal, *Bush Plans to Extend Ethanol Credit*, by Stephen Power, Feb. 19, 2004. However, if traditional fuel costs continue to rise, ethanol may become a money-saving option for the owners of these vehicles. *See* Special Report: Biofuels, The Economist, May 14, 2005, p. 71. Manufacturers will be required to attach a label to the fuel compartment of any dual-fueled vehicle manufactured after September 1, 2006, notifying the owner that the vehicle can be operated on an alternative fuel. *See* section 759 of the Energy Policy Act of 2005.

---

18.   http://www.epa.gov/otaq/consumer/fuels/altfuels/420f00035.pdf (a. June 9, 2005).

Currently, a new blend of ethanol is being made from plant waste after farmers' harvest. The new blend provides income to the farmers, reduces exhaust emissions, and when the reduction in emissions is combined with the carbon dioxide reduction from the plant waste used, the reduction can be 90% or greater. The new blend is called cellulosic ethanol and may cost less than 80 cents a gallon by 2020. *See* BusinessWeek, *Not Your Father's Ethanol; A new blend could reduce U.S. dependence on oil and cut greenhouse gas emissions*, by Otis Port, vol. 3921, Feb. 21, 2005. The National Commission on Energy Policy's 2004 report puts much emphasis on research and development of cellulosic ethanol. National Commission on Energy Policy, Ending the Energy Stalemate 70–84 (2004). Section 1501 of the Energy Policy Act of 2005 includes special incentives for the development of cellulosic ethanol as part of its general requirements that refiners increase their use of ethanol.

The future of the RFG gasoline program is in some doubt because of growing concerns that MTBE (methyl tertiary butyl ether), which has been the additive favored by the oil industry for meeting oxygen requirements, has been the source of water pollution problems. In response to a recent University of California study concluding that adding MTBE to gasoline produces significant health risks while only minimally reducing emissions, California banned the use of MTBE from gasoline sold in the state beginning in 2002, and the ban was upheld in *Oxygenated Fuels Association Inc. v. Davis*, 331 F.3d 665 (9th Cir. 2003). The refiners claim that MTBE cannot readily be replaced. In the Energy Policy Act of 2005, § 1504, Congress removed the requirement that gasoline contain oxygen at certain levels in certain areas. Instead, the Act mandates that refiners add ethanol to motor fuel in amounts rising from 4 billion gallons in 2006 to 7.5 billion gallons in 2012. See § 1501.

The volatility, or tendency to evaporate, of fuel is also regulated. Volatility is gauged by the pounds per square inch (psi) of Reid Vapor Pressure ("RVP"). The higher a RVP a fuel has, the more volatile it will be. The EPA promulgated a regulation prohibiting the sale of gasoline containing over 9.0 psi during the summer months, or the high-ozone season. More stringent standards apply to non-attainment areas. *See* Martineau, Jr. & Novello, *supra* at 378.

c. CALIFORNIA REGULATIONS

The Clean Air Act contained a special provision allowing California to set its own mobile source standards without being preempted by the federal legislation Other states may opt into California's exception if they: 1) adopt standards identical to California's; 2) California receives a waiver from EPA for those standards; and 3) both California and opting state give manufacturers at least two model years to comply with new standards The opt-in states may still vary the target number of sales as long as the vehicle standards are equal to California's. *See American Auto. Mfrs. Ass'n v. Cahill*, 973 F. Supp. 288 (N.D.N.Y. 1997) was later reversed by *American Auto. Mfrs. Ass'n v. Cahill*, 152 F.3d 196, 200 (2d Cir. 1998).

A number of Northeastern states have followed the California ZEV rule. *See* Rona Cohen, States Vote For Cleaner Cars, Council of State Governments, Eastern Regional Conference, Environmental Issue Brief, May 2004. They are permitted to do this under the CAA (*see* 42 U.S.C. § 7507(1)). A state may adopt the standards for new motor vehicles if "such standards are identical to the California standards for which a waiver has been granted." This section ensures that automakers need only worry about designing and manufacturing vehicles for one of two standards—the national standards or the California standards. Courts have unanimously determined that the ZEV sales mandate is an "emission standard" subject to § 177. *Assoc. of Int'l Auto. Mfrs. v. Massachusetts DEP*, 208 F.3d 1, 6–7 (1st Cir. 2000).

California has set a fleet average requirement for non-methane organic ("NMOG") emissions, which becomes stricter each year. Auto manufacturers may meet these requirements by selling Low Emission Vehicles ("LEV"). The manufacturers also earn credits for selling more LEVs than required to meet the NMOG standard. The manufacturer may use these credits to offset future fleet emissions. In addition, unlike the federal fuel efficiency credits, the manufacturer may sell the emission credits to other manufacturers.

California developed a three phase program to implement cleaner gasoline. Phase 1, effective in 1992, banned all lead in gasoline and required that gasoline evaporate less readily. Phase 2, effective in 1996, reduced toxic air emissions from gasoline by 40 percent and smog-inducing emissions by 15 percent. Phase 3 eliminated MTBE beginning January 1, 2003. The sulfur content and levels of benzene in gasoline will also be reduced. *See* California Air Resources Board, Phase 3 Cleaner–Burning Gasoline.[19]

A substantial obstacle to lower mobile source pollution is the proliferation of minivans and sport utility vehicles ("SUVS"), which are currently regulated under the lower light truck standard for emissions. California has already brought light truck emission standards up to that of passenger cars for 2004, and Ford currently produces SUVs that meet those standards. Therefore it may be difficult for the other manufacturers to argue the technological unfeasibility of the higher standards. Indeed the California Air Resources Board (CARB) states that the new standards are attainable for $60 for passenger cars and $220 for SUVs.

California also has its own standard for on-board emission diagnostic devices (OBDs). These devices monitor the operation of the emission control system and warn motorists if the system is not working properly by flashing a "check engine" light on the dashboard. Equipment manufacturers challenged certain anti-tampering provisions of the rules, but the rules were approved by EPA and upheld by the D.C. Circuit. *Motor & Equipment Manufacturers Ass'n v. Nichols*, 142 F.3d 449 (D.C. Cir. 1998).

---

19.   http://www.arb.ca.gov/newsrel/ph3cbg.htm (a. June 9, 2005).

California has also adopted special standards applicable to all fleet vehicles. A challenge to these standards reached the Supreme court in 2004.

Engine Manufacturers Ass'n v. South Coast Air Quality Management District

541 U.S. 246 (2004).

■ Scalia, J. Respondent South Coast Air Quality Management District (District) is a political subdivision of California responsible for air pollution control in the Los Angeles metropolitan area and parts of surrounding counties that make up the South Coast Air Basin. It enacted six Fleet Rules that generally prohibit the purchase or lease by various public and private fleet operators of vehicles that do not comply with stringent emission requirements. The question in this case is whether these local Fleet Rules escape pre-emption under *§ 209(a) of the Clean Air Act* (CAA), 81 Stat 502, as renumbered and amended, *42 U.S.C. § 7543(a)*, because they address the purchase of vehicles, rather than their manufacture or sale.

The District is responsible under state law for developing and implementing a "comprehensive basinwide air quality management plan" to reduce emission levels and thereby achieve and maintain "state and federal ambient air quality standards." *Cal. Health & Safety Code Ann. § 40402(e) (West 1996)*. Between June and October 2000, the District adopted six Fleet Rules. The Rules govern operators of fleets of street sweepers, of passenger cars, light-duty trucks, and medium-duty vehicles, of public transit vehicles and urban buses, of solid waste collection vehicles, of airport passenger transportation vehicles, including shuttles and taxicabs picking up airline passengers, and of heavy-duty on-road vehicles. All six Rules apply to public operators; three apply to private operators as well.

The Fleet Rules contain detailed prescriptions regarding the types of vehicles that fleet operators must purchase or lease when adding or replacing fleet vehicles. Four of the Rules (1186.1, 1192, 1193, and 1196) require the purchase or lease of "alternative-fuel vehicles," and the other two (1191 and 1194) require the purchase or lease of either "alternative-fueled vehicles" or vehicles that meet certain emission specifications established by the California Air Resources Board (CARB). CARB is a statewide regulatory body that California law designates as "the air pollution control agency for all purposes set forth in federal law." *Cal. Health & Safety Code Ann. § 39602 (West 1996)*.

In August 2000, petitioner Engine Manufacturers Association sued the District, claiming that the Fleet Rules are pre-empted by *§ 209 of the CAA*, which prohibits the adoption or attempted enforcement of any state or local "standard relating to the control of emissions from new motor vehicles or new motor vehicle engines." *42 U.S.C. § 7543(a)*. The District Court granted summary judgment to respondents, upholding the Rules in their entirety. It held that the Rules were not "standard[s]" under *§ 209(a)* because they regulate only the purchase of vehicles that are otherwise certified for sale in California. The District Court recognized that the First and Second Circuit Courts of Appeals had previously held that *CAA § 209(a)* pre-empted state laws mandating that a specified percentage of a manufacturer's in-state sales be of "zero-emission vehicles." See *Association of Int'l Auto. Mfrs., Inc. v. Commissioner, Mass. Dep't of Environmental Prot., 208 F.3d 1, 6–7 (1st Cir. 2000)*; *American Auto. Mfrs. Ass'n v. Cahill, 152 F.3d 196, 200 (2d Cir. 1998)*. It did not express disagreement with these rulings, but distinguished them as involving a restriction on vehicle sales rather than vehicle purchases: "Where a state regulation does not compel manufacturers to meet a new emissions limit, but rather affects the purchase of vehicles, as the Fleet Rules do, that regulation is not a standard." *158 F. Supp. 2d 1107, 1118 (CD Cal. 2001)*.

The Ninth Circuit affirmed on the reasoning of the District Court. *309 F.3d 550 (2002)*. We granted certiorari.

Section 209(a) of the CAA states:

"No State or any political subdivision thereof shall adopt or attempt to enforce any standard relating to the control of emissions from new motor vehicles or new motor vehicle engines subject to this part. No State shall require certification, inspection, or any other approval relating to the control of emissions ... as condition precedent to the initial retail sale, titling (if any), or registration of such motor vehicle, motor vehicle engine, or equipment." 42 U.S.C. § 7543(a).

The District Court's determination that this express pre-emption provision did not invalidate the Fleet Rules hinged on its interpretation of the word "standard" to include only regulations that compel manufacturers to meet specified emission limits. This interpretation of "standard" in turn caused the court to draw a distinction between purchase restrictions (not pre-empted) and sale restrictions (pre-empted). Neither the manufacturer-specific interpretation of "standard" nor the resulting distinction between purchase and sale restrictions finds support in the text of § 209(a) or the structure of the CAA.

"Statutory construction must begin with the language employed by Congress and the assumption that the ordinary meaning of that language accurately expresses the legislative purpose." Today, as in 1967 when § 209(a) became law, "standard" is defined as that which "is established by authority, custom, or general consent, as a model or example; criterion; test." Webster's Second New International Dictionary 2455 (1945). The criteria referred to in § 209(a) relate to the emission characteristics of a vehicle or engine. To meet them the vehicle or engine must not emit more than a certain amount of a given pollutant, must be equipped with a certain type of pollution-control device, or must have some other design feature related to the control of emissions. This interpretation is consistent with the use of "standard" throughout *Title II of the CAA* (which governs emissions from moving sources) to denote requirements such as numerical emission levels with which vehicles or engines must comply.

Respondents, like the courts below, engraft onto this meaning of "standard" a limiting component, defining it as only "[a] production mandat[e] that require[s] manufacturers to ensure that the vehicles they produce have particular emissions characteristics, whether individually or in the aggregate." Brief for Respondent South Coast Air Quality Management District 13 (emphases added). This confuses standards with the means of enforcing standards. Manufacturers (or purchasers) can be made responsible for ensuring that vehicles comply with emission standards, but the standards themselves are separate from those enforcement techniques. While standards target vehicles or engines, standard-enforcement efforts that are proscribed by § 209 can be directed to manufacturers or purchasers.

The distinction between "standards," on the one hand, and methods of standard enforcement, on the other, is borne out in the provisions immediately following § 202. These separate provisions enforce the emission criteria—i.e., the § 202 standards. *Section 203* prohibits manufacturers from selling any new motor vehicle that is not covered by a "certificate of conformity." *42 U.S.C. § 7522(a). Section 206* enables manufacturers to obtain such a certificate by demonstrating to the EPA that their vehicles or engines conform to the § 202 standards. *§ 7525. Sections 204 and 205* subject manufacturers, dealers, and others who violate the CAA to fines imposed in civil or administrative enforcement actions. *§§ 7523–7524.* By defining "standard" as a "production mandate directed toward manufacturers," respondents lump together § 202 and these other distinct statutory provisions, acknowledging a standard to be such only when it is combined with a mandate that prevents manufacturers from selling non-complying vehicles.

That a standard is a standard even when not enforced through manufacturer-directed regulation can be seen in Congress's use of the term in another portion of the CAA. As the District Court recognized, *CAA § 246* (in conjunction with its accompanying provisions) requires state-adopted and federally approved "restrictions on the purchase of fleet vehicles to meet clean-air standards." *158 F. Supp. 2d, at 1118* (emphasis added); see also *42 U.S.C. §§ 7581–7590* (Respondents do not defend the District's Fleet Rules as authorized by this provision; the Rules do not comply with all of the requirements that it contains.) Clearly, Congress contemplated the enforcement of emission standards through purchase requirements.

In addition to having no basis in the text of the statute, treating sales restrictions and purchase restrictions differently for pre-emption purposes would make no sense. The manufacturer's right to sell federally approved vehicles is meaningless in the absence of a purchaser's right to buy them. It is true that the Fleet Rules at issue here cover only certain purchasers and certain federally certified vehicles, and thus do not eliminate all demand for covered vehicles. But if one State or political subdivision may enact such rules, then so may any other; and the end result would undo Congress's carefully calibrated regulatory scheme.

The courts below held all six of the Fleet Rules to be entirely outside the pre-emptive reach of *§ 209(a)* based on reasoning that does not withstand scrutiny. In light of the principles articulated above, it appears likely that at least certain aspects of the Fleet Rules are pre-empted. It does not necessarily follow, however, that the Fleet Rules are pre-empted in toto. We have not addressed a number of issues that may affect the ultimate disposition of petitioners' suit, including the scope of petitioners' challenge, whether some of the Fleet Rules (or some applications of them) can be characterized as internal state purchase decisions (and, if so, whether a different standard for pre-emption applies), and whether *§ 209(a)* pre-empts the Fleet Rules even as applied beyond the purchase of new vehicles (e.g., to lease arrangements or to the purchase of used vehicles). These questions were neither passed on below nor presented in the petition for certiorari. They are best addressed in the first instance by the lower courts in light of the principles articulated above.

The judgment is vacated, and the case is remanded for further proceedings consistent with this opinion.

Justice Souter dissented.■

NOTES AND COMMENTS

1.   The California Air Resources Board develops programs to reduce greenhouse gases and other pollutants. One regulation prohibits any modifications to a motor vehicle that result in increased emissions. Another regulation embodies a diesel risk reduction plan to retrofit existing diesel engines to reduce diesel emissions. Other regulations reduce evaporative emissions, include inspections to test for excessive emissions and regulations for both on-road and off-road emission sources. Emission reduction programs also exist for school buses.[20]

2.   In September 2004, California passed a new greenhouse gas emission regulation that will become effective for cars and trucks by the 2016 model year. Auto manufacturers in California will be required to reduce emissions by about 30 percent. This regulation is discussed in Chapter 16.

C.   THE ENERGY COST OF "SPRAWL"

Technological changes in transportation have greatly influenced patterns of land development in the United States. The greater mobility that people obtain from modern transportation technology has led to a dramatic change in the American landscape. Americans are increasingly living in thinly scattered and decentralized locations, with the result that Americans each year expend more energy getting from place to place. Awareness of the influence of transportation on the quality of life has grown gradually:

20.   *See* http://arb.ca.gov /msprog/msprog.htm ?PF=Y (a. June 9, 2005).

Transportation planning tends to be oriented to future conditions, because new projects take so long to build. But it is difficult to get the public interested in long-term plans if no problem exists currently. The public generally responds best when there is a crisis. Traffic congestion became that crisis in the 1980s, especially in those new suburban centers that blossomed.... The traffic attracted to edge cities and the new fringe beehives of business and commerce quickly expanded to fill up the remaining highway capacity, and caused lengthy traffic delays. Traffic congestion became a media topic, locally and nationally.

Robert T. Dunphy, Moving Beyond Gridlock: Traffic and Development 1–2 (Urban Land Institute, 1997). Ironically, the construction of those office and commercial complexes on the urban fringe was originally stimulated by the hope of attracting employees who wanted to avoid the traffic congestion that they then associated with the older cities.

At the present time, the transportation sector uses 28% of all of the energy consumed in the United States, and 67% of the petroleum consumed in the United States. This means that transportation uses the equivalent of all of the domestically produced oil and nearly half of our oil imports. Bureau of Transportation Statistics, Annual Report (2004).[21]

Studies of alternative transportation patterns employing higher building densities and more mass transit suggest that dramatic savings in energy use would be achieved by changes in land use patterns. Analyses of European cities that use such patterns, and model simulations of American cities, all suggest that substantial savings could be achieved. *See* Judy S. Davis & Samuel Seskin, Impact of Urban Form on Travel Behavior, 29 Urban Lawyer 215 (1997). Whether such changes can be accomplished, however, is a serious question.

1. Automobile-Oriented Decentralization

In modern times, land development has been extending far out into the countryside as residential and commercial developers open up new areas to the driving public. People are driving longer and longer distances and the traffic is continually getting worse. This pattern of decentralized urbanization is commonly referred to as "sprawl."

Modern development patterns contrast sharply with those that prevailed when the country was founded. The cities of the eighteenth century tended to be small and compact. Horsedrawn vehicles' limitations made it impractical to travel long distances to work on a daily basis.

In the nineteenth century, railroads made it possible to move goods to central locations for consolidation and transshipment. This spurred the expansion of port cities such as New York and San Francisco. And "Chicago's location at the breaking point between eastern and western rail

---

21. http://www.bts.gov/publications/transportation_statistics_annual_report/2004/html /chapter_02/transportation_sector_energy_use.html (a. June 9, 2005).

networks ... maintained Chicago's railroad hegemony for the rest of the century." William Cronon, Nature's Metropolis 83 (Norton, 1991).

The most significant technological innovation that triggered the expansion of cities was the streetcar. Development of land on the outer fringes of urban areas was stimulated by the availability of streetcar lines that made it easy to reach the downtown area.

Automobiles brought a new mobility, unhindered by the need for extensive track systems. As the road network grew, buses replaced streetcar lines as the most common form of mass transportation. As more people acquired their own automobiles, the pattern of urban development began to change.

Many promoters of road construction saw themselves as providing a healthier alternative to the "teeming cities," which they saw as increasingly overcrowded. Henry Wallace, the Secretary of Agriculture in President Roosevelt's cabinet, said that "decentralization properly worked out in connection with concrete roads and electricity will have a lot to do with providing a more satisfactory life for the next generation." Lewis, *supra* at 52. Roads were widened into highways and connected by interchanges that greatly increased the speed of travel, but only for a while. Retailers began to move out of downtown areas into new shopping centers scattered throughout the urban areas. Jackson, *supra* at 257–261.

Meanwhile, the federal government stimulated new housing developments in outlying areas through federally guaranteed home loans. Federal tax laws, which permitted homeowners to take a tax deduction for home mortgage interest, stimulated families and individuals to invest in a home. And if they sold the home, they were required to invest the proceeds in another equally expensive home or pay capital gains tax, thus providing further stimulation to the housing market. Christine A. Klein, A Requiem for the Rollover Rule: Capital Gains, Farmland Loss, and the Law of Unintended Consequences, 55 Wash. & Lee L. Rev. 403 (1998).

High inflation in the 1970–85 period further stimulated homeownership as the values of homes went up dramatically. An entire generation came to believe that the best way to keep up with inflation was to buy a home because home prices always went up at a rate exceeding the inflation rate.

Most of the new homebuilding was in outlying areas rather than in the cities. Older housing in the cities was suffering from neglected maintenance during the depression and the war, and urban renewal programs were seen as ways to clear out the slums so that people could move to a better life in new housing. Robert Moses, the master builder of transportation facilities, saw highway building as one element in a desirable program to replace slums with highways, move slum dwellers into better high rise public housing, and open up the suburbs for the middle classes.

Office buildings also started seeking locations on the fringes of urban areas where land was less expensive. As traffic generators scattered throughout metropolitan areas, the radial network of rail and road ways that had been typical of early 20th century cities became unsuited to the non-radial travel patterns that were becoming typical. Frequently a "beltway" circling the metropolitan area became one of the most heavily traveled routes. Highways that were built to bring workers downtown ended up carrying their heaviest traffic in the opposite direction as city workers commuted to suburban jobs. Dunphy, *supra* at 33–35.

In summary, current patterns of land development emphasize single family homes at relatively low densities in developments designed on the assumption that virtually all residents would travel by private automobile. The great amount of space needed to accommodate this pattern has meant that the mileage traveled per household has increased rapidly. And with trucks replacing railways as the primary means of goods transport, the road network has absorbed a growing share of American energy consumption.

2. FACTORS THAT HAVE FOSTERED CURRENT TRENDS IN TRANSPORTATION

In the twentieth century, Americans' energy choices have affected every area of production and consumption, but it is in transportation where these choices have most dramatically increased our energy consumption. As David Nye puts it, "Most farmers abandoned horses and oxen for tractors, [and] motorists preferred large cars with poor fuel economy; [while the federal government] spent billions of dollars on interstate highways instead of on mass transit. And during the 1970s the federal government signally failed to develop a coherent energy policy. As the result of all these decisions, made by the people or their institutions, the United States became the largest consumer of energy in the world's history." David Nye, Consuming Power 255–56 (MIT Press, 1998).

The reasons why the people of the United States have chosen to expend such a large share of their budgets for transportation are many and complex. Any listing of them would include the following dozen:

[1] **Automobile merchandising.** The American's reputed love affair with the automobile is often cited as the cause of our increasingly decentralized pattern of development. In comparison with other industrialized countries, such as Japan or the European countries, Americans take far fewer trips by public transportation. Is our lifestyle simply a matter of what the economists would call a "taste" for private transportation? Or are there factors about American society at the turn of the millennium that make our development pattern more efficient than its critics recognize?

[2] **Growth in trucking.** It was the trucking industry's powerful political support for federal gasoline taxes to fund federal spending on highways has facilitated the rapid development of the federal interstate highway network. Although automobile drivers must share the network with more and heavier trucks, the network's increased efficiency has made it possible to extend significantly the mileage that drivers are willing to commute, thus greatly increasing total energy consumption.

The volume of truck movements has also grown as a result of the increased emphasis in American industry on the use of sophisticated logistics to move resources and products so that they are the right place at the right time. *See* W. Bruce Allen, The Logistics Revolution and Transportation, 553 Annals of the American Academy of Political and Social Science 106 (1998). The growth of the trucking industry was been facilitated by the deregulation of most shipments and the development of more entrepreneurial management. The deregulation of the trucking industry has brought about significant competition in trucking while railroad ownership is becoming increasingly concentrated.

[3] Workforce expansion. Another factor that has driven up the usage of energy in transportation is certainly the growth of the workforce. The so-called baby boom generation began to reach driving age in the 1960s and began entering the workforce around 1965. The number of licensed drivers doubled between 1960 and 1980; and between 1965 and 1985 the labor force grew at a rate of 2.1% per year, nearly twice the rate of growth from 1950 to 1965. Sustainable Future, *supra* at 44–45.

Equally striking was the increase in two-income families. In early 1999, 46.4% of the working population was female, and the ratio has been increasing steadily. Bureau of Labor Statistics, Employment and Earnings (February, 1999) p. 8. With two people in the household traveling to employment, a homesite located near one particular jobsite becomes less important than a location conveniently situated for access to the overall highway network. Anthony Downs, Still Stuck in Traffic: Coping with Peak–Hour Traffic Congestion 234, 237 (Brookings Institution Press, 2004).

And the automobile makes it possible to combine trips for work and shopping or pleasure in ways that are difficult on public transportation; this efficiency is particularly valuable to the time-sensitive two-income family. Among two-parent families with children, the amount of time spent on paid work increased by 18% between 1969 and 1996. Council of Economic Advisers, Families and the Labor Market, 1969–1999: Analyzing the "Time Crunch" (May, 1999).

[4] Privacy and security. Traditionally, Americans have sought a higher degree of personal space and privacy than people in other cultures, and the private automobile satisfies this desire. Charles L. Wright, Fast Wheels, Slow Traffic 115–118 (1992). Psychologists have observed, for example, that a group of Americans who converse with each other will stand farther apart than similar groups from most other cultures. This demand for more private space is rewarded on American roadways where the vast majority of cars carry a single occupant.[22]

---

22. "At first, electricity and the automobile enlivened the city, reinforcing its density and bringing mobility and kinetic excitement to its daily round. Eventually, however, they were used to undermine the central city as Americans moved to suburbs and embraced a more private form of popular culture." Nye, *supra* at 158.

[5] **The climate-controlled lifestyle.** The pervasiveness of air conditioning in homes and businesses has also increased the demand for the kind of air conditioned door-to-door travel that the automobile can provide. The EIA's 1997 Residential Energy Consumption Survey showed that 72% of American households have air conditioning. The downtown business districts of cities with climates as varied as Minneapolis and Houston have invested significant sums in the creation of enclosed walkways among office buildings that preserve the climate-controlled environment, and the indoor regional shopping mall has become a fixture throughout the country.

These trends are responding to the fact that white collar workers, who make up a growing segment of the population, seek to avoid exposure to weather-related inconveniences. The executive who commutes from the climate-controlled garage attached to her single-family house to the climate-controlled garage attached to her office building may be able to dress with complete disregard for outside weather conditions.

[6] **Perception of safety.** Although nearly 50,000 people each year are killed in auto accidents in the United States, people tend to downplay the danger. Howard Margolis, Dealing With Risk 38 (University of Chicago Press, 1996). Despite the high risk of automobile accidents, many Americans say that they actually feel safer in their car than in public transportation. Accidents involving public transportation tend to receive more media coverage than the routine fatalities in auto accidents. And the fear of contact with criminal behavior on public transportation is one of those risks that ranks higher in public perception than statistics would support.

[8] **Job-shifting.** Increasing job mobility has accentuated the need for flexibility in housing location. Downs *supra* at 234. The number of people who predict that they will remain at the same job for a long period of time has been declining steadily, and the 1990s' downsizing of large corporations and growth of entrepreneurial start-ups has continued to encourage the trend to seek flexibility over stability in home location.

[9] **Greater affluence.** Reliance on the private automobile is also simply a product of increased wealth. All industrialized countries have seen increases in automobile ownership, but the increase in the United States has been particularly notable. In 1950 there were just under 7 automobiles in the United States for every 10 licensed drivers; by 1980 the ratio had passed 1 to 1. Sustainable Future, *supra* at 41.

Although many of the newly affluent are more conscious of environmental issues than members of preceding generations, that has not necessarily lead to reduced energy consumption. Every improvement in gas mileage was counteracted by more cars and more mileage driven per car. In the decade preceding 1997 annual motor vehicle travel increased nearly 30%. *Id.* Environmentalists might jog for their health but rarely walked to work, and a love for the outdoors often meant wanting to live as far from the city as possible.

[10] **Information technology.** The rapid growth of advanced information technology in the 1990s has also contributed to new transportation and development patterns. The need for centralized locations for "office work" has begun to diminish, and increasing numbers of people work at home for part of the week. Dunphy, *supra* at 36–37.

As this trend continues it will reduce the importance of home-to-work transportation in the selection of a residence, which may benefit both rural and urban locations at the expense of traditional suburbs. A growing number of individuals who work in e-commerce out of their homes have wide-ranging choices of where to live. Some Western states that once relied on resource extraction as their economic base are coming to realize that it is "resource attraction" that is bringing in new entrepreneurs who can work from any place that a satellite can see. *See* Thomas Michael Power, Lost Landscapes and Failed Economies 41–43 (Island Press, 1996).

[11]   **Cheap land.** Much new development takes place at the edge of metropolitan areas in "a peripheral zone, perhaps as large as a county, that has emerged as a viable socioeconomic unit. Spread out along its highway growth corridors are shopping malls, industrial parks, campuslike office complexes, hospitals, schools and a full range of housing types. Its residents look to their immediate surroundings rather than to the city for their jobs and other needs; and its industries find not only the employees they need but also the specialized services." Robert Fishman, Bourgeois Utopias: The Rise and Fall of Suburbia 184 (Basic Books, 1987). The name "edge city" has become commonly used for these areas. *See* Joel Garreau, Edge City: Life on the Urban Frontier (Doubleday, 1991).

[12]   **The highway lobby.** Such a wide range of interest groups are so well organized in support of government money for road construction that it has long been difficult to obtain support for any other mode of transportation. Automobile manufacturers, oil companies, truckers, farmers, land developers; all are comfortable with a system that provides extensive financial support for the maintenance of the network on which the existing pattern of development is dependent. *See* Dunn, *supra* at 23–30.

* * *

All of these factors have stimulated increasing movement into formerly rural areas, thereby stretching out the time of travel if not its frequency. If we are going to reduce our consumption of energy for transportation, we must either begin to reverse these development patterns, or find new technological ways of traveling within the current pattern without using so much energy, or both.

Americans' preferences for sprawling growth, automotive movement, and individualistic heating and housing impose conditions on their future energy choices. As the United States prepares to enter a new century, the federal government and the major automobile manufacturers are investing billions of dollars in electric cars, hybrid cars, solar cars, and smart cars that will drive themselves. Such planning makes sense so long as consumers choose to remain spread out. Nye, *supra* at 257–58.

But are current trends inevitable? Dissatisfaction with existing modes of transportation and development patterns is increasing for a variety of reasons.

3. FACTORS CREATING PRESSURE FOR CHANGES IN TRANSPORTATION

Despite the reasons for continuing support of a pattern of development of spread-out living with ever-increasing reliance on automobiles and trucks to connect everything together, a backlash has been gradually developing. It has developed on two fronts: (a) attempts to accommodate to the current development pattern but expend less energy, and (b) attempts to promote a more concentrated development pattern that would facilitate more use of mass transit.

[1] **Air pollution.** Motor vehicles are recognized as a serious source of air pollution. Motor vehicle exhaust includes carbon monoxide, nitrogen oxides, volatile organic compounds and particulate matter. Nitrogen oxides and volatile organic compounds are the major contributor to smog, which can be hazardous to people with many common breathing disorders, as can particulate matter. In the concentrations found in some traffic "hot spots," carbon monoxide can slow peoples' reflexes and contributes to safety problems.

[2] **Climate change.** Recently attention has been focused on the extent to which transportation is responsible for the emission of greenhouse gases that may be contributing to climate change (see Chapter 16). If future trends continue, transportation within the United States will be contributing a third of the nation's emissions of atmospheric carbon dioxide, the most prevalent of the greenhouse gases. James J. MacKenzie, Driving the Road to Sustainable Ground Transportation 121, 126–27 in Frontiers of Survival (World Resources Institute, 1997).

[3] **Concern about oil imports.** Americans have been nervous about the extent to which the national economy, and particularly the transportation system, has become increasingly dependent on imported oil. The overall transportation system is the largest user of oil in the U.S. economy and is almost completely dependent (97%) on oil. About two thirds of the oil we use goes directly into transportation. And, as indicated in Chapter 6, the percentage of our oil that comes from overseas is projected to rise each year.

Our reliance on imported oil has led us to become involved diplomatically and at times militarily in the affairs of those parts of the world from which we get our oil. This has not only contributed to high defense budgets but has frequently embroiled us in hostile relations with countries that have turned potential trading partners into enemies.

[4] **Safety.** Highway safety became a growing concern of the federal government under pressure from Ralph Nader whose book Unsafe at Any Speed (Grossman, 1965) attained wide popularity. Congress created the National Highway Traffic Safety Administration and authorized it to set

safety standards and order recalls. The automobile manufacturers were required to install airbags and undergo safety testing of vehicle models. In 1974, Congress adopted national speed limits designed to increase safety and reduce energy consumption in response to the first oil shock, but these were relaxed after gasoline prices came down.

[5]   Noise. People who live near transportation facilities have become increasingly vocal objectors as transportation volumes have increased. Most large scale forms of transportation create noise that can be unpleasant at close range. Residents of areas near airports have often persuaded authorities to impose curfews and specific takeoff and landing patterns designed to reduce noise. Highway departments are increasingly installing sound barriers alongside freeways to reduce the noise level in residential neighborhoods.

[6]   Traffic congestion. The users of the highways are also expressing frustration with steadily growing traffic congestion and increased home-to-work travel time. In 2001, it took 39% longer to make the average peak period trip in the average urban area as it would have without highway congestion. Bureau of Transportation Statistics, Annual Report (2004). In large metropolitan areas, the congestion is increasing even more markedly. The Texas Transportation Institute estimates that in 2003 each resident in one of the 13 largest metropolitan areas lost an average of 61 hours a year due to traffic congestion. Even in mid-sized cities like Indianapolis, Providence and San Antonio the average resident lost over 30 hours per year to congestion. http://mobility.tamu.edu/ums/congestion_data/tables/national/table_1.pdf (accessed August 6, 2005).

[7]   Alienation. Concern about loss of a sense of community is also part of the growing dissatisfaction with current land use patterns. It is commonly believed that people are spending less time in social or civic pursuits and more time alone. A "tendency for social life to become 'privatized,' and to a reduced feeling of concern and responsibility among families for their neighbors ..." has been noted by many observers. Jackson, *supra* at 272.

[8]   Lack of open areas. In many parts of the country, voters are beginning to protest the lack of open space and natural habitat in metropolitan areas. Throughout the West, for example, people speak of their fear of their community becoming "Los Angelized." In the late 1990s, voters began to show solid support for bond issues to protect open space through land acquisition.

[9]   Sprawl. The word "sprawl" has become a common opprobrium for the pattern of land development that relies on the private automobile for transportation. Voters have been expressing a growing dissatisfaction with the phenomenon of widely dispersed low-density land development. "Sprawl is self-perpetuating: the dominance of the automobile among our transportation choices makes low-density development possible; low-density development, in turn, makes us more dependent on automobiles for access to increasingly dispersed locations for employment, services, and recreation. This is bad news for all, but especially for those who are unable to use cars as a primary mode of transportation, including the poor, the disabled, the elderly, and children." F. Kaid Benfield, Running on Empty: The Case for a Sustainable National Transportation System, 25 Envtl. L. 651, 657 (1995).

Although the interrelationship of highway projects and sprawling development is widely assumed[23], few governmental units in the United States have successfully managed systems for identifying and regulating the growth-inducing impacts of transportation projects. Marie L. York, Dealing with Secondary Environmental Impacts of Transportation, 51 Land Use L. & Zoning Digest 3 (March, 1999).

[10] Tax resistance. Perhaps the most important cause of dissatisfaction with the existing patterns of transportation and land development has simply been the voters' resistance to spending money on the public works projects that would be needed to reduce congestion and improve efficiency. During the first two oil shocks between 1979 and 1981, the high rates of inflation doubled the cost of highway construction and maintenance, causing great political reluctance to raise the taxes needed to keep highway construction going. Mark H. Rose, Interstate: Express Highway Politics, 1939–1989 113 (University of Tennessee Press, rev. ed., 1990).

This aversion to expenditures affected public works projects of all sorts. Lester Thurow points out that "public infrastructure investment has been cut in half over the past twenty-five years and has fallen to the point where the stock of public capital is now declining relative to the GDP— falling from 55 to 40 percent of GDP in the last decade. Less is being invested in public infrastructure in the United States than in any of the [developed] countries—one third as much as Japan." Lester Thurow, The Future of Capitalism 291 (1996).

During the Reagan administration, a policy decision was made to use virtually all federal highway funds for repairs rather than new roads, with the result that between 1981 and 1989 total highway mileage increased only 0.6% while total vehicle miles driven went up over 33%. Anthony Downs, Stuck in Traffic: Coping with Peak–Hour Traffic Congestion 11 (Brookings Institution, 1992). Most capital spending today is on renovation, rehabilitation and widening of existing highways rather than on new route construction. Sustainable Future, *supra* at 51.

D. FEDERAL LEGISLATIVE RESPONSES

In response to these concerns, Congress has adopted a number of new programs designed to reduce the energy consumption and pollutant output of motor vehicles. Congress has been very reluctant to address the issue of land use patterns[24], which has traditionally been considered an area of

---

23. Not everyone shares the conviction that the automobile is primarily to blame for decentralization, which in fact began a century ago. *See* Dunn, *supra* at 146–147.

24. The indirect impact of federal programs on patterns of land development is significant but also complex. *See* William W. Buzbee, Urban Sprawl, Federalism, and the Problem of Institutional Complexity, 68 Fordham L. Rev. 57 (1999).

state and local policy, and some state and local governments have also begun to address these issues.

1.   FUEL ECONOMY STANDARDS

In response to the first oil shock, the Congress adopted in 1975 the Corporate Average Fuel Economy (CAFÉ) program designed to require vehicle manufacturers to sell more fuel-efficient automobiles. The program set minimum miles-per-gallon requirements for automobile and light truck manufacturers based on total vehicle sales. It requires auto manufacturers to produce a total output of cars that averaged over the minimum standards for miles-per-gallon, but left the companies the discretion to create whatever mix of vehicles they chose as long as the average complied with the standard.

In 1975, the federal government set the average fuel economy for passenger automobiles, at 27.5 miles per gallon (mpg). 49 U.S.C. § 32902. This regulation went into force for the 1985 model year. The fuel economy program enumerated exceptions for emergency vehicles, dedicated alcohol or natural gas vehicles and manufacturers of less than 10,000 autos per year. More importantly, the program provided mechanisms to modify the average mpg across the board or to provide exemptions from the national standard for individual manufactures to reflect the maximum feasible average for that model year. The Secretary of Transportation could lower the average down to 26.0 mpg before she must submit an amendment to Congress. Any increase above 27.5 must also be submitted before Congress for approval. *Id.* The Secretary lowered the average down to 26.0 in 1986, but the average has remained at 27.5 since 1990.

Where a manufacturer is unable to meet the national standard it must either pay a $5 fine for each .1 mpg that the manufacturer's fleet is below the standard multiplied by the number of cars in the fleet (49 U.S.C. § 32912) or it can elect to submit a plan to the Secretary of Transportation. This plan provides for efficiency credits, whereby a manufacturer earns credits for exceeding the national standard, which may be used to remedy past standard violations. The plan must demonstrate that the manufacturer will, within the next three model years, earn enough efficiency credits to cover its deficiency for the current year. The program also allows a manufacturer to apply credits to any of the three consecutive model years following the year the credits are earned, but may only do so if it has already met the national standard, by meeting the standard or applying credits, for any preceding three consecutive model years: 49 U.S.C. § 32903. These credits are only available for the same class of automobile.

This program also factors in the benefits to the manufacturers' fleets derived from electric cars (49 U.S.C. § 32904) and hybrid vehicles. 49 U.S.C. § 32906. However, the program limits a manufacturer's fleet average increase due to hybrid vehicles to .9 mpg until 2008. Presently those limits are not in danger of being met. In terms of current development, purely electric cars are taking a backseat to the new hybrid vehicles, but even these hybrids have only been introduced for a short time.

The federal program preempts state law in this area unless the state adopts identical standards. The only exception to this rule allows states to mandate a different efficiency standard for automobiles obtained for the state's own use. 49 U.S.C. § 32919.

Competitive Enterprise Institute v. National Highway Safety Admin.

45 F.3d 481 (D.C. Cir. 1995).

■ GINSBERG, J. The Competitive Enterprise Institute and Consumer Alert (hereinafter referred to jointly as the CEI) petition for review of the National Highway Traffic Safety Administration rulemaking setting the corporate average fuel economy (CAFÉ) standard for 1990 passenger cars. The petitioners claim that the agency arbitrarily and capriciously failed to acknowledge significant adverse safety effects of setting the standard at 27.5 rather than 26.5 miles per gallon or somewhere in between. Finding that the agency adequately rooted its decision in the record of the rulemaking, we deny the petition for review.

In response to the then-restricted world supply of oil, the Congress enacted the Energy Policy and Conservation Act of 1975, which was intended, among other things, to induce automobile manufacturers to improve the fuel economy of their cars. The Act set a CAFÉ standard for passenger cars that increased several times and then leveled off at 27.5 miles per gallon for model years 1985 and beyond. 15 U.S.C. § 2002(a)(1). The NHTSA is authorized to raise or lower the standard for a particular model year, however, in order to achieve the "maximum feasible average fuel economy," taking into account technological feasibility, economic feasibility, the effect upon fuel economy of other federal motor vehicle standards, and the need of the nation to conserve energy. *See* 15 U.S.C. § 2002(e) (listing factors); *15 U.S.C. § 2002*(a)(4) (granting Secretary of Transportation discretion to amend CAFÉ standard); 49 C.F.R. § 1.50(f) (delegating authority to NHTSA). Although the Act does not list safety as a factor that the agency is to consider in setting the CAFÉ standard, the NHTSA has previously considered safety as an aspect of technological or economic feasibility. *See Competitive Enter. Inst. v. Nat'l Highway Traffic Safety Admin.*, 956 F.2d 321, 322 (D.C. Cir. 1992) ("CEI II").

Under the Act, a manufacturer that fails to meet the CAFÉ standard is liable for a monetary penalty. *15 U.S.C. § 2008*(b)(1). A manufacturer may, however, offset its shortfall in meeting the CAFÉ standard one year with credits it earns by exceeding the standard in other years. *15 U.S.C. § 2002(l)*. A manufacturer may carry credits backward or forward up to three model years.

Each manufacturer must meet the CAFÉ standard separately for its domestically manufactured fleet and for its "not domestically manufactured" fleet, which is defined to exclude cars built in the United States from imported parts. In 1988 the NHTSA was concerned that the 27.5 mpg standard might lead American automobile manufacturers to shift some of their large-car manufacturing activity overseas in order to average the fuel economy of those cars with more of their small cars, thereby raising the average fuel economy of their domestic fleets and lowering the comfortably high average fuel economy of their non-domestic fleets. Notice of Proposed Rulemaking: Passenger Automobile Average Fuel Economy Standards for Model Years 1989 and 1990, 53 Fed. Reg. 33,080, 33,080–81 (1988). Foreseeing the job loss and "potential economic harm" that might occur, the NHTSA proposed to lower the MY 1989 and 1990 CAFÉ standards from 27.5 mpg to not less than 26.5 mpg. *Id. at 33,083.*

Later in 1988 the NHTSA lowered the CAFÉ standard for MY 1989 from 27.5 mpg to 26.5 mpg. Final Rule: Passenger Automobile Average Fuel Economy Standards for Model Year 1989, 53 Fed. Reg. 39,275 (1988). We affirmed. *See Competitive Enter. Inst. v. Nat'l Highway Traffic Safety Admin.*, 901 F.2d 107, 110 (D.C. Cir. 1990) ("CEI I"). In 1989, however, the agency terminated the MY 1990 aspect of the rulemaking without changing the CAFÉ standard for that year. "This decision [was] based largely on the increasing need of the nation to conserve energy and a conclusion by the agency that retention of the 27.5 mpg standard for MY 1990 [would] not have a significant adverse effect on U.S. employment or on the competitiveness of the U.S. auto industry." Termination of Rulemaking: Passenger Automobile Average Fuel Economy Standard for Model Year 1990, 54 Fed. Reg. 21,985, 21,989 (1989). The NHTSA also concluded, contrary to the submission of the CEI, that leaving the MY 1990 CAFÉ standard at 27.5 mpg would not have an adverse effect upon automotive safety. *Id.* at 21,992–94. [On review, the D.C. Circuit remanded the MY 1990 standard to the agency to address the issue of whether the standard would cause manufacturers to discourage purchase of larger cars by raising their price. *CEI II, supra.* The agency reopened the rulemaking but concluded that there would be no such impact. CEI now petitions for review of that decision]

The CEI contends that the NHTSA, on remand, failed to give adequate consideration to the petitioners' contention that retaining the statutory CAFÉ standard for MY 1990 would have significant adverse safety effects. Specifically, the CEI claims that the agency failed to consider that (1) the CAFÉ standard causes automobile manufacturers to downsize passenger cars, resulting in significantly more traffic fatalities because larger, heavier cars are safer than smaller, lighter cars; and (2) the CAFÉ standard constrains automobile manufacturers from upsizing cars, thereby pricing consumers out of the market for larger, heavier, and (presumably) safer cars. The substance of the CEI's position is intuitively appealing. We must deal here, however, not with our intuition and not with the petitioners' position in the abstract, but with the concrete record before us and with the conclusions that the agency drew from it. That record adequately supports the NHTSA's conclusion that maintaining the 27.5 mpg CAFÉ standard for MY 1990 would not significantly affect the safety of the motoring public.

First, the NHTSA reasonably concluded from the evidence before it that the MY 1990 CAFÉ standard did not cause automobile manufacturers either to downsize or to refrain from upsizing their cars. In its notice reopening the rulemaking proceeding, the agency asked commenters to address:

> What specific actions [manufacturers would] actually take, if any, depending upon whether the MY 1990 CAFÉ standard remained at 27.5 mpg or were reduced to some level between 26.5 mpg and 27.5 mpg? If the standard remained at 27.5 mpg, would manufacturers downsize vehicles, refrain from upsizing vehicles[,] or change the mix or pricing policies of the vehicles they offer for sale?

Reopening of Rulemaking Proceeding: Passenger Automobile Average Fuel Economy Standard for Model Year 1990, 57 Fed. Reg. 48,777, 48,778 (1992). Further, recognizing that a regulatory change made in 1992 would not affect the production of vehicles in MYs 1990–92, the NHTSA asked the automobile manufacturers to state what specific actions they would take with respect to any model year (presumably by carrying credits backward or forward) were the agency to lower the 1990 standard. *Id.*

No manufacturer identified any change that it would make in the size or weight of its vehicles, in its product mix, or in its pricing strategy—for any model year—if the NHTSA were to lower the MY 1990 CAFÉ standard. In fact, the Ford Motor Company asserted that it "did not reduce its average car size over what would have been offered absent such 1990 standard." The General Motors Corporation stated that "relaxing the standard could in some cases generate credits giving manufacturers more flexibility to offer larger, safer cars in later model years," but did not go so far as to suggest that it would be one of the beneficiaries. Accordingly, the NHTSA reasonably decided that maintaining the MY 1990 CAFÉ standard would have no appreciable effect upon the size or weight of automobiles offered for sale in any model year.

Second, the factual record simply does not support the CEI's contention that consumers are priced out of the market for larger, heavier cars by reason of the 27.5 mpg standard. As part of the rulemaking for the MY 1986 CAFÉ standard, the NHTSA analyzed the cost-effectiveness of various technological changes that manufacturers have used to meet fuel economy standards. That analysis showed that most of the technological changes paid for themselves with fuel savings over the first four years of ownership and that all but one were cost-effective over the life of the vehicle. *See* Final Regulatory Impact Analysis for MY 1986 Passenger Car CAFÉ Standard III–32, III–33 (1985). Moreover, the NHTSA noted that the technological changes—including improved aerodynamics, substitution of lighter materials, fuel injection, electronic engine control, wide ratio gearing, reduced lubricant viscosity, and reduced rolling resistance—are widely available on large and small cars alike. Therefore, any increase in the purchase price of cars owing to those features would not impose a relative penalty upon the purchase of a large car. Finally, while the NHTSA recognized that a manufacturer could attempt to induce a shift in its product mix either by reducing the price of its small cars or by increasing the price of its large cars (or both), *see* 58 Fed. Reg. at 6944, the agency noted that no manufacturer commented in the rulemaking on remand that it had taken either step in order to meet the MY 1990 CAFÉ standard of 27.5 mpg.

Finally, the NHTSA considered the study upon which the CEI rested its contention that the MY 1990 CAFÉ standard had a significant effect on safety. *See* Robert W. Crandall & John D. Graham, The Effect of Fuel Economy Standards on Automobile Safety, 32 J. of L. & Econ. 97, 109–10 (1989). That study suggests that in the 1980s manufacturers significantly reduced the average weight of their cars due to the CAFÉ standards. Using a model describing the relationship of automobile weight to safety, and explaining weight as a function solely of CAFÉ regulation and of the expected prices of gasoline and steel (as forecast four years in advance), Crandall and Graham estimated that the CAFÉ program caused a "500–pound or 14 percent reduction in the average weight of 1989 cars," which was "associated with a 14–27 percent increase in occupant fatality risk." *Id.* at 111.

The NHTSA did not directly dispute the general finding of the Crandall and Graham study, i.e., that there is a relationship between safety and the size or weight of automobiles. *See* 58 Fed. Reg. at 6946 ("The agency ... fully agrees ... that all other things being equal, a large car is safer than a small car"). Instead the agency faulted Crandall and Graham for failing to take account of factors in addition to gasoline and steel prices—namely, "technological advances," "increased competition," and "changes in consumer preferences"—that in the agency's view would explain almost all of the average car's weight loss that the authors instead attributed to the CAFÉ standard. (Indeed the agency even suggested that "any CAFÉ standard effect [on weight] is negligible." Id.)

Although phrased in a variety of ways, the NHTSA's response to Crandall and Graham comes down to suggesting that a change in consumers' preferences, rather than any constraining effect of the CAFÉ standards, accounts for vehicle downsizing over the period that they studied. (After all, "increased competition" only facilitates the satisfaction of consumers' preferences; nor, if manufacturers were not constrained by the CAFÉ standards to adopt them, are "technological advances" relevant unless consumers demanded them). While the agency speculated that consumers might have preferred "downsized vehicles [because they] offered better handling, easier parking, and potential cost savings associated with reduced materials usage," it offered no reason whatsoever to think that consumer preferences actually did change at all during the relevant time, much less that they changed in the direction of preferring smaller and apparently more dangerous cars. Merely to assert the existence of another possible explanation, which is all that the NHTSA has done, does nothing to undermine the significance of the findings carefully documented by Crandall and Graham. It is like asserting that regulation of the airlines had no effect because it occurred at a time when all consumers preferred amenities such as gourmet meals rather than cheaper fares; that is, of course, possible, but the only evidence is to the contrary.

The NHTSA's failure adequately to respond to the Crandall and Graham study is troubling, but it is not a basis, upon this record, for overturning the agency's decision to adhere to the 27.5 mpg CAFÉ standard for MY 1990. The overwhelming fact is that no automobile manufacturer is on record stating that it would have added weight to its automobiles (or taken any other action) in any model year had the NHTSA relaxed the 1990 CAFÉ standard. Therefore, record evidence documenting a correlation between the safety and the size or weight of a vehicle, and the contribution of the CAFÉ standard to determining size or weight, while potentially relevant to any future decision to retain or amend the CAFÉ standard, simply does not require the NHTSA to amend the MY 1990 CAFÉ standard.

The NHTSA has identified sufficient support in the record for its decision not to amend the MY 1990 CAFÉ standard. The manufacturers did not assert in their comments to the agency on remand that they would implement any design or product mix changes if the NHTSA amended the MY 1990 CAFÉ standard and there is no hard evidence in the record that the MY 1990 CAFÉ standard caused any manufacturer to price any consumers out of the market for larger, safer cars. The petition for review is therefore Denied.■

NOTES AND COMMENTS

1. If you were the attorney for an automobile manufacturer, and your client had received an inquiry from a federal agency asking, in effect, whether your client could build cars that are safer than they are now building them, how would you have advised your client to answer? Was Judge Ginsberg (soon to become Justice Ginsberg) being fair in basing her decision on the automobile manufacturers' responses to such a loaded question?

2. The safety argument advanced by the CEI in the MY 1990 lawsuit continues to be the issue creating "the most strident public debate" over CAFE standards. National Research Council, Automotive Fuel Economy: How Far Should We Go? (1992). The Transportation Research Board's 2002 report discusses the conflicting views and studies on this issue. TRB, *supra*. John Graham, the co-author of the rejected study discussed in the above case, was appointed to oversee all federal regulatory activities by President George W. Bush in 2001.

3. New vehicle fuel economy hit an all-time high of 28.8 MPG in 1988, but has not improved since then. *See* Transportation Research Board, Effectiveness and Impact of Corporate Average Fuel Economy (CAFE) Standards 17 (2002) ("TRB"). Since then, the shift in consumer preferences to SUVs and other less efficient vehicles has prevented an increase in efficiency, and average overall fuel economy has actually declined. *Id.*

4.   Light truck fuel economy requirements were first established for MY 1979 (17.2 mpg for 2–wheel drive models; 15.8 mpg for 4–wheel drive). Standards for MY 1979 light trucks were established for vehicles with a gross vehicle weight rating ("GVWR") of 6,000 pounds or less. Standards for MY 1980 and beyond are for light trucks with a GVWR of 8,500 pounds or less. The light truck standard progressively increased from MY 1979 to 20.7 mpg and 19.1 mpg, respectively, by MY 1991. From MY 1982 through 1991, manufacturers were allowed to comply by either combining 2– and 4–wheel drive fleets or calculating their fuel economy separately. In MY 1992, the 2– and 4–wheel drive fleet distinction was eliminated, and fleets were required to meet a standard of 20.2 mpg. The standard progressively increased until 1996, when the Appropriations prohibition froze the requirement at 20.7 mpg. The freeze was lifted by Congress on December 18, 2001. On March 31, 2003, NHTSA issued new light truck standards, setting a standard of 21.0 mpg for MY 2005, 21.6 mpg for MY 2006, and 22.2 mpg for MY 2007.[25]

5.   In an evaluation of the CAFÉ standards program, the Transportation Research Board concluded that the standards have led to reduced petroleum use but "the magnitude of the effect is subject to debate" because "motorists may respond to higher fuel economy by driving more" and thus might counteract the program's benefits. Sustainable Future, *supra* at 117. A subsequent economic analysis of surveys of motor vehicle use concluded that motorists do drive more when gasoline prices drop or fuel economy improves, and that this phenomenon reduces energy savings of fuel economy improvement by about 20%. David L. Green et al., Fuel Economy Rebound Effect for U.S. Household Vehicles, 20 Energy Journal 1 (1999). In 2005, Congress directed the National Highway Traffic Safety Administration to conduct and submit to Congress by August, 2006 a study of alternatives to the existing CAFÉ standards system. See section 773 of the Energy Policy Act of 2005.

6.   The American Council for an Energy–Efficient Economy has stated, "Increasing the fuel economy of light duty vehicles is the single most effective energy-saving policy the federal government could adopt." *See* Vehicle Fuel Economy Standards: Big Energy Savings at a Modest Cost, http://www.aceee.org/energy/cafe.htm (a. June 9, 2005). A Sierra Club proposal in 2001 suggested that it is entirely feasible both economically and technically for auto makers to meet a much stricter 40 MPG standard by 2012 and 55 MPG by 2020, and that even attaining the 40 MPG standard would save more oil than the U.S. would get from the Persian Gulf, California offshore drilling and the Arctic National Wildlife Refuge combined. Higher Miles Per Gallon Standards Would Save Californians More Than $1 Billion Dollars Annually, http://www.sdearthtimes.com/et0701 /et0701s16.html (a. June 9, 2005).

Some proposals for more rigorous fuel economy standards would tailor the program more closely to reductions in greenhouse gas emissions, for

---

25.   http://www.nhtsa.dot.gov/cars/rules/cafe (a. August 6, 2005).

example by converting existing standards into standards based on CO_2 equivalent emissions, or even transforming their nature altogether. See Chapter 16.

2.   TRANSPORTATION PLANNING REQUIREMENTS

The historic compromise that produced the Interstate Highway Act of 1956 was interpreted by the "road lobby" as a guarantee that all of the taxes on gasoline and related equipment were to be sequestered in the Highway Trust Fund where they would be used only for road construction. Advocates of other modes of transportation soon began to cast a covetous eye on this fund, arguing that if the fund were used to finance subways, for example, the result would be to reduce the need for highway construction by taking people off the roads.

The auto manufacturers, trucking companies and oil companies adamantly resisted these attempts. There continues to be a strenuous debate between those who think that the existing system contains built-in subsidies for automobiles (*see, e.g.,* World Resources Institute, The Going Rate: What it Really Costs to Drive (1992)) and those who believe that the publicly owned transit systems are an inefficient waste of public funds (*see, e.g.,* Clifford Winston & Chad Shirley, Alternate Route: Toward Efficient Urban Transportation (Brookings Institution Press, 1998)).

This debate has also been regularly heard in the halls of Congress. Since 1962, federal law has required the states to engage in a highway planning process for "urbanized areas" of more than 50,000 people. In response to the desire of local governments to play a greater role in the planning of highways, highway trust funds were given to the states to finance the creation of Metropolitan Planning Organizations, which included representatives of local governments as well as state agencies. These MPOs were staffed with engineers and planners who worked closely with state and federal highway officials in approving the layout of the highway system.

a.   THE 1991 ISTEA LEGISLATION

During the 1990s, Congress began to increase the funding for alternative modes of transportation. Responding to the argument that the construction of new highways just seemed to create more traffic and more traffic jams, Congress passed new legislation in 1991 and again in 1998 that tried to stimulate "multi-modal" transportation planning that considered not only roads but mass transit and other modes of transportation.

The ready availability of cash from the highway trust fund has frequently meant that the highway planners have had better financing than the planners of other types of public facilities. This led to many complaints that highways were being built without consideration of alternative modes of transportation, particularly rapid transit. In addition, the growing concern about air pollution from motor vehicles meant that state environmental agencies were required by the Clean Air Act to engage in a separate planning process to try to attain the standards for ozone and nitrogen oxides established by the U.S. Environmental Protection Agency.

Congress responded to these concerns in 1991 by passing the Intermodal Surface Transportation Efficiency Act of 1991, commonly called "ice tea" ("ISTEA"). The act adopted the policy that transportation planning should consider not only roads but travel by train, bus, bicycle and on foot. It substantially increased the funds available for non-highway modes of transportation. It also required the states to make many detailed changes in the planning process, which were designed to ensure that all modes of transportation were given fair consideration and to integrate the transportation planning with air quality planning. 23 U.S.C. § 135. Comparable changes to the air quality planning requirements were made in the Clean Air Act amendments of 1990. 42 U.S.C. § 7506(c).

Different urbanized areas developed their own administrative structures to carry out these planning processes. Some saw the need for change as a high priority, while others tried to change as little as possible. On balance, the ISTEA legislation produced a number of significant plans that brought attention to a greater variety of modes of transportation. *See* Daniel Carlson et al., At Road's End: Transportation and Land Use Choices for Communities (Island Press, 1995).

In general, ISTEA represented a move away from the complete dominance of the highway in transportation planning. The new buzzword became "intermodalism," meaning that planners should consider all different modes of transportation and how they interrelate. Terminals at which people could interchange among transit, highway, bicycle and pedestrian facilities were encouraged.

The act also sought to increase the role of state and local governments in the decisionmaking process with the objective of reaching an earlier consensus among affected groups; "partnerships" became the preferred way of making decisions. State and local agencies were encouraged to "leverage" their funds in combination to maximize the efficiency of federal funding.

But although ISTEA was "a significant symbolic achievement for the anti highway forces" it did not cause dramatic shifts of money from highways to transit. Dunn, *supra* at 43. Its long term impact is likely to result from opening up the planning process to new ideas and new people who approach transportation issues from a broader perspective than traditional highway engineers.

b.   THE 1998 TEA–21 LEGISLATION

In 1998, Congress was presented with a potential surplus in the federal budget for the first time in many years. It responded by passing legislation appropriating significantly increased funds for highways and other transportation projects and making further changes in the transportation planning process. Public Law 105–178 was given the high-sounding name of the

Transportation Equity Act for the Twenty-first Century, and is referred to as TEA–21.

The TEA–21 legislation included a variety of initiatives directed to the full range of transportation alternatives, including highways, mass transit, and bicycle paths. 23 U.S.C. § 133. New programs were established for the design and demonstration of advanced technologies, such as fixed guideway vehicles, fuel-cell powered transit vehicles, and magnetic levitation technologies for urban public transportation. The DOT's ITS (Intelligent Transportation Systems) program for advanced transportation technologies for the movement of goods between states and across borders received an authorization of over a billion dollars. Some $9 billion was allocated to individual "demonstration projects" in the districts of influential members of Congress.

As in the 1991 legislation, particular emphasis was given to the coordination of transportation planning and the reduction of air pollution. Section 1110 of the Act authorized over $8 billion for the CMAQ (Congestion Mitigation and Air Quality Improvement) program to fund projects and programs that help meet the requirements of the Clean Air Act in areas that are or were failing to attain the National Ambient Air Quality Standards.

The Department of Transportation was also charged with writing regulations with the goal of reducing delay in the environmental review process, using the environmental review process under NEPA as a vehicle for integrating other required environmental reviews and analyses related to the proposed project, including reviews under other relevant state and local laws. TEA–21 also included a specific provision to require the early identification of all federal agencies, and, in certain instances, state agencies, with jurisdiction by law over issues related to a proposed project. Cooperating agencies can participate in the NEPA process as soon as the identification of a proposal has occurred and they can also assume responsibility for preparation of a portion of the analyses within their area of expertise. Section 1309 also mandated the establishment of timelines, in consultation with all involved federal agencies, and incorporated the criteria set forth in the CEQ regulations for determining appropriate time limits for projects. It also authorized the Secretary, at the request of a State, to allow federal-aid highway funds to be used to meet the provisions for enhanced environmental streamlining.

c. SAFETEA–LU OF 2005

In August, 2005, President Bush signed the "Safe, Accountable, Flexible, Efficient Transportation Equity Act: A Legacy for Users," officially known as "SAFETEA–LU". The act contains a number of provisions intended to speed up the process of review of proposed transportation projects. Section 6002(j) authorizes grants to state and local governments and other federal agencies if they need additional funds to complete their review of a project. Section 6004 authorizes delegation to the states of the power to designate types of construction that would be categorically excluded from the applicability of the National Environmental Policy Act, and section 6005 authorizes a pilot program for delegating all NEPA authority to the states.

The Act also authorizes the waiver of existing requirements that special studies be undertaken where a project impacts parks, recreation areas, wildlife refuges and historic sites. The waiver is available in cases in which the Secretary of Transportation finds that the impact of the project will be "de minimis." See 23 U.S.C. § 138 as amended by section 6009 of the Act. But the Act does require that the impact of projects on wildlife be taken into consideration in the planning process. *See* section 6008.

The major thrust of the legislation is the authorization of billions of dollars worth of transportation projects—primarily highways but including other surface transportation as well. It is by far the most expensive transportation legislation ever enacted, and includes money for many projects earmarked for the home districts of particular members of Congress.

E.   FUTURE TRENDS

Throughout the United States a great deal of creative energy is being devoted to devising ways of producing a more energy-efficient, pollution-resistant pattern of transportation and land development. Among the research topics of interest are the following:

Brownfields development. Energy efficiency is one of the objectives of government programs for the promotion of "infill" development; i.e., the encouragement of new development on vacant or underused land within existing cities. When "brownfields" sites, which have been abandoned by earlier industries, are redeveloped they can take advantage of existing transportation networks and proximity to existing housing. Robert A. Simons, Turning Brownfields into Greenbacks (Urban Land Institute, 1998). If the indirect costs of fringe area development were taken into account, redevelopment of inner city sites may be the more economically efficient alternative. Joel B. Eisen, Brownfields of Dreams: Challenges and Limits of Voluntary Cleanup Programs and Incentives, 1996 U. Ill. L. Rev. 883, 1025–26 (1996).

Improved mass transit. The use of light rail transit rather than heavier subway construction has made transit cost-effective in many new communities. Funding for mass transit has been a significant goal for those who seek to improve energy efficiency. The 1998 TEA–21 law provided a very substantial increase in funding for mass transit. The Federal Public Transportation Act of 2005's major contribution was to change the term "mass transit" to "public transit" throughout the federal legislation. Transit trips nationally increased by 20% between 1995 and 2002. Still, the federal budget for fiscal 2003 gave highways was almost 31 billion dollars compared to 8.2 billion dollars for transit. Bureau of Transportation Statistics, Annual Report (2004).

Increased urban densities. Land developers have expressed a growing interest in promoting more dense urban development. Downs 2004, *supra* at 265–71. Some architects and planners advocate a "new urbanism" in development design. The concept of new urbanism, sometimes referred to as "neotraditional" development, is based on a desire to reduce the need for automobile travel and to create communities with more social interaction. Neighborhoods are dotted with businesses accessible by foot; networks of bike paths encourage people to leave their cars at home. *See generally* Peter Katz, The New Urbanism: Toward an Architecture of Community (1994).

To date, only a relatively few communities designed according these principles have been completed, and it is too early to evaluate their success. The Disney Company's town in Florida called Celebration has attracted the most attention. But unless these design principles become the new norm among developers, a few demonstration communities are unlikely to have any real influence on patterns of sprawl. Dunn *supra* at 152–155. For information promoting the use of community designs that minimize automotive travel, *see* www.carfree.com (a. August 6, 2005).

Meanwhile, a significant number of older cities are experiencing extensive revitalization as developers convert older buildings to modern housing and build new condominiums. This has attracted both young people who are bored with the suburban lifestyle and older people seeking to have more convenient access to urban amenities. Many neighborhoods in places such as Brooklyn, Chicago and Washington have been dramatically transformed by this "gentrification," though not without criticism from some of the poorer tenants displaced by the process.

More rail shipments. Increased use of rail for shipments rather than trucks has been one of the goals of environmental groups. *See* Benfield, *supra* at 673. But the Transportation Research Board has concluded that diversion of truck traffic to rail is unlikely to have a significant effect on fuel use and pollution emissions. Sustainable Future, *supra* at 122–123.

Peak-hour pricing. Economists have long advocated the establishment of higher prices for traveling at peak times as a way of reducing traffic congestion and improving the overall efficiency of the transportation system. *See* Downs 2004, *supra* at 152–179. A few communities have undertaken limited experiments with such programs. Felicia B. Young & John T. Berg, Value pricing helps reduce congestion, 62 Public Roads #5 (1999) at 47. Some transit systems do provide discounts for off-peak travel, as do some toll roads and bridges (*see* Robert W. Poole Jr. and C. Kenneth Orski, HOT Networks: A New Plan for Congestion Relief and Better Transit. Reason Foundation, 2003), but the technical problems of implementing such a system on a large scale for automobile travel are daunting. Tirza S. Wahrman, Breaking the Logjam: The Peak Pricing of Congested Urban Roadways under the Clean Air Act to Improve Air Quality and Reduce Vehicle Miles Traveled, 8 Duke Env. L. & Pol'y F. 181 (1998).

Intelligent vehicles. The U.S. Department of Transportation continues to fund research on intelligent vehicle highway systems. *See* SAFE-

TEA–LU sections 5301–07. Such systems would combine electronic sensors in highways and vehicles with centralized management of traffic flows. Lewis T. Branscomb & James H. Keller, Converging Infrastructures: Intelligent Transportation and the National Information Infrastructure (MIT Press, 1996). This and other uses of systems engineering are attracting attention in urban areas all over the world. Downs 2004, *supra* at 197–99, 294–96. An Intelligent Transportation Systems Society holds semiannual conferences to review current research and development on these topics. *See* http://www.ewh.ieee.org/tc/its/ (a. June 7, 2005).

Conclusion. Is our present system of virtually total reliance on the automobile a policy that can be sustained indefinitely? In his history of American energy consumption, David Nye summarizes:

> The energy choices of the past have brought the United States prosperity, but no more than was achieved by some other countries that use far less. The choices made at the end of the twentieth century will determine whether the US continues to consume more power per capita than any other country. Americans must choose whether to tax gasoline in order to stimulate conversion to alternative energies. They must choose whether deregulation will be used simply to save money in the short term or whether it can be part of a larger strategy of becoming more efficient. They must choose whether to make environmental economics the basis of policy. Individually, they must choose whether they want to drive or to take mass transit, whether they will buy ever-larger houses, how well they will insulate their homes, whether they will invest in low energy light bulbs and appliances, and whether they will adopt solar water heating, heat pumps, and other energy-saving technologies. In designing their cities, Americans can decide whether to encourage cycling, pedestrian traffic, and local shopping. In the workplace, they must decide to what extent computers will be used to reduce commuting. At the polls, they must decide whether to endorse recycling, research on alternative energies, and more fuel-efficient vehicles. In short, they must decide whether they think energy choices matter now, or whether they expect ingenious technologies so solve emerging problems later. They can even choose to believe in technological determinism, which will apparently absolve them from any responsibility to make choices. Whatever Americans decide, in the twenty-first century their economic well-being, the quality of their environment, how to travel, where and how they work, and how they live together will be powerfully shaped by their consuming power. Nye, *supra* at 273–74.

James Dunn, on the other hand, argues that the "automobile system has been nothing if not sustainable for about a century now," having survived depressions, wars, and energy and pollution crises. Throughout the world, automobiles are "the most popular form of transportation, with people scrambling to own a car in spite of high taxes and bad roads." The "intense popularity and durability" of the automobile means that "calling an as yet nonexistent future system with fewer automobiles more sustainable than the present one would be laughable."

CHAPTER 16

THE CLIMATE CHANGE ISSUE

A. CLIMATE CHANGE AND THE ENERGY SECTOR

No environmental issue poses as many potential difficulties for the energy industries as the possibility that the combustion of fossil fuels is

1243

contributing to a change in the world's climate: a change predicted to cause a gradual increase in the temperature levels each year for a century or more.

The key points of mainstream scientific opinion on climate change can be summarized succinctly: The combustion of fossil fuels containing carbon (coal, oil and natural gas) emits greenhouse gases ("GHG") such as carbon dioxide ("CO_2") to the atmosphere. These emissions have increased the levels of carbon dioxide (CO_2) in the atmosphere. Carbon dioxide lets radiant energy into the atmosphere more freely than it lets it out. The effectiveness of this atmospheric heat retention increases with increases in CO_2. This increase has the potential to warm the earth's climate, and computer models predict that the climate will warm significantly over the next century.

There is growing evidence of a warming climate over the past 100 years that is consistent with the progressively increasing concentration of GHG, especially CO_2, in the atmosphere. *See* Gayle Christianson, Greenhouse 167 (Walker & Co. 1999). Although scientists do not yet know how much of the current climatic change is natural and how much is due to human activity, there is no question that the burning of fossil fuels is the dominant mode of human CO_2 production. Because the amount of CO_2 in the atmosphere far exceeds that of the other GHGs, many studies of the problem have focused solely on CO_2, assuming that if it can be controlled the problem will largely be solved.

1.   GHG EMISSIONS FROM POWER PLANTS

U.S. greenhouse gas emissions in 2003 were 6,115.2 million metric tons CO_2 equivalent. This total was 13.4 percent higher than 1990 emissions, or an average annual increase of 1.0 percent. Power plants that generate electricity from fossil fuels emit a substantial amount of this total. The combustion of fossil fuels in the generation of electricity accounted for approximately 2,249 million metric tons of carbon dioxide in 2002, or 39.3 percent of total U.S. CO_2 emissions. EIA, *supra*. This was the largest share of total CO_2 emissions of any industrial sector in the U.S. and had been for the previous five years. *See* Energy Information Administration (EIA), Emissions of Greenhouse Gases in the United States 2003, http://www.eia.doe.gov; EPA U.S. Emissions Inventory 2003, http://yosemite.epa.gov/oar/globalwarming.nsf/. *See also* Pew Center on Global Climate Change, Global Warming Basics, http://www.pewclimate.org.

The amount of GHGs a power plant emits depends upon the type of fossil fuel it burns to generate electricity. Coal is the primary energy source for U.S. electricity generation, providing 50 percent of total generation in 2002. It is a plentiful natural resource in the United States but creates the most significant emissions of all GHGs, including CO_2; coal-fired power plants accounted for 83.4 percent of electric power industry CO_2 emissions in 2002, and coal has the highest rate of CO_2 emissions per unit of energy used among fossil fuels. Since 1990, CO_2 emissions from the electric power industry have increased by 25.3 percent (or twice as fast as overall growth), a trend that reflects U.S. economic growth and corresponding increases in fossil fuel consumption in the electric power sector. EIA, *supra*.

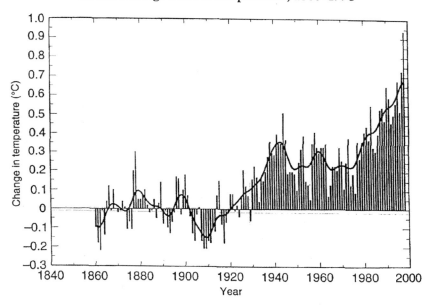

Figure 16–1

Source: Hadley Centre, *Climate Change and its Impacts*, Bracknell: UK Meteorological Office, 1998.

Note: The bars show the annual global average surface temperature; the smoothed curve represents the 5–year average.

2.   Positions of Energy Industries on Climate Change

When the concern about global warming began to be voiced in the 1980s, the energy industries sought out people who had serious questions about the mainstream theories. Funding for the work of many of these skeptics was provided by the Global Climate Coalition ("GCC"), a joint venture financed primarily by the oil, coal, and automobile industries which styled itself as a "voice for business in the global warming debate." Mainstream scientists were quite disdainful of these industry-funded experts. *See* Ross Gelbspan, The Heat Is On: The High Stakes Battle Over Earth's Threatened Climate (Addison–Wesley 1997).

The position of energy industries on climate change is less consistent than it was in the early 1990s, when the industry almost uniformly dismissed concern about the issue as premature. The GCC has been "deactivated," claiming it achieved its objective of "contributing to a new national approach to global warming" by taking part in the development of the Bush administration climate change policy. *See* http://www.globalclimate.org. As the Bush policy has been criticized as ineffective, some would find this not much of a step forward. However, the GCC's demise does suggest less resistance on industry's part to discussing the issues. Some former members have pledged to reduce GHG emissions. British Petroleum (BP), for example, has committed to reduce 353,000 tons of CO_2 equivalent emissions and has joined the emissions trading scheme administered by the U.K. Department of Food, Environment, and Rural Affairs (Defra) (*see* Section E.2, below). The American Petroleum Institute lists a number of voluntary greenhouse gas reduction strategies by its members. *See* www.api.org/globalclimate. The Business Roundtable, an association of CEOs of America's leading corporations, announced in 2004 that 70 percent of its member companies—representing every sector of the U.S. economy—had embraced voluntary actions to reduce GHG emissions in its "Climate RESOLVE" program. Business Roundtable, Every Sector, One RESOLVE (Sept. 2004). While some skeptics see these actions as hedging against future regulation, other commentators generally praise the efforts.

A growing number of utility companies are acknowledging the threat of climate change and pledging to take action. Cinergy CEO James Rogers wrote to the company's shareholders in 2005 that "avoiding the debate over global climate change and failing to understand its consequences are not options for us." AP/MSNBC Online, Apr. 7, 2005. Cinergy and American Electric Power ("AEP") both issued reports in 2004 detailing their plans to reduce GHG emissions. These two utilities and others (including TXU and Southern Company) announced in 2004 that they would publish reports estimating the financial risk to their companies if carbon regulations took effect. Brian Stempeck, Two electric utilities agree to assess impact of global warming regs, Greenwire, Feb. 20, 2004. This development is attributable in part to campaigns by company shareholders to force reports filed with the Securities and Exchange Commission about public companies' "contingent liabilities" (situations involving risk to balance sheets) to include this information. *See* Gregory A. Bibler and Nathan J. Brodeur, Assessing SEC Disclosure Requirements after Kyoto, Mondaq Bus. Briefing, Mar. 9, 2005.

The Voluntary Reporting of Greenhouse Gases Program maintained by the EIA is a key element of the Bush Administration climate change strategy. In 2002, 80 companies in the electric power industry reported to the EIA that they had projects to reduce GHG emissions underway or planned. These projects included fuel switching, power plant availability improvements (displacing fossil-fueled plants with other plants that generate fewer GHGs, including nuclear plants), and increases in deployment of low-or zero-emitting generation capacity. *See* http://www.eia.doe.gov. A trend increasing in popularity is for companies to disclose their GHG emissions through a registry, instead of solely through their own reports. An example of a third-party organization of this sort is the California Climate Action Registry, created in 2001. *See* http://www.climateregistry.org.

Although the views of energy companies are now more diverse, this does not mean that they are less concerned about the accuracy and the impact of global climate projections. Even now, industry organizations such as the American Petroleum Institute continue to insist that "U.S. oil and natural gas companies believe that uncertainties about climate change make it hard to justify mandatory, severe, near-term emission reductions." *See* www.api.org/globalclimate. Nor does the GCC's demise mean the skeptics of mainstream positions on global climate change have disappeared. There continue to be active organizations funded by energy companies and others that sponsor research by academic skeptics and advocate publicly for caution about responding to climate change. *See* Chris Mooney, Some Like It Hot, Mother Jones, May/June 2005.

B. Has the Earth Become Warmer?

Records of temperatures at the earth's surface have been kept in great detail throughout the world in recent years. The farther back in time one searches for such records, the more questionable they become. Nevertheless, most scientists are confident that we have reliable temperature records at least for the twentieth century. And modern scientific methods of examining ice cores and other buried materials give us increasing confidence that we can estimate climate conditions even in prehistoric times.

1. Geological Time

Geologists, paleontologists and astronomers all have produced theories about why the earth's climate appears to have fluctuated dramatically over hundreds of thousands of years. Astronomers, for example, believe that glaciers have advanced and retreated based on slight changes in the earth's axis and orbit, producing cycles that last 41,000, 23,000 and 19,000 years. William K. Stevens, A Change in the Weather 24–26 (Delacorte Press, 1999). Fluctuations on this kind of time scale seem irrelevant for practical purposes.

The completion of two sets of ice core records from locations in Greenland has given scientists one of the best sets of climate records that go back about 110,000 years. These records indicate that there have been abrupt climate shifts in the last few thousand years, and that these shifts have often occurred within a decade or lass and have often lasted for centuries. National Research Council, Global Environmental Change: Research Pathways for the Next Decade 131, 237 (National Academy Press, 1999) ("Research Pathways"). Similar records of warming since the end of the "little ice age" of the fourteenth through the sixteenth centuries are found in the studies of Antarctica's paleoclimatic ice-core record. C. Lorieus et al., The ice-core record: climate sensitivity and future greenhouse warming, 347 Nature 139 (1990).

The National Research Council has concluded that the recent paleoclimatic data is more consistent with the mid- to upper-range of consensus estimates of climate sensitivity to increases in carbon dioxide. Research Pathways, *supra,* at 266. Few people argue, however, that we can derive principles to guide today's actions solely from the observations of millennia past. Instead, much current thinking focuses on changes that took place in the twentieth century.

2.   THE PAST QUARTER CENTURY

In 1996, the computer models suggested that over the past century, Earth's surface has warmed by about 0.5 degrees C (± 0.2 degrees C). In January 2000, a panel of the National Academy of Sciences reviewed the data and agreed that the earth's surface temperature had increased by between 0.4 and 0.8 degrees C in the past century. National Research Council, Reconciling Observations of Global Temperature Change (National Academy Press, 2000).

The fact that the climate at the surface of the earth has warmed over the period of a century is not really seriously debated, though the extent of that increase is still subject to differing views. But until recently, there was great doubt that the activities of humans could have any discernible impact on Earth's climate. Some doubt still remains, but the events of the last quarter century have swung scientific and public opinion heavily toward the view that humans are at least partially responsible.

Data from the U.S. National Climactic Data Center show that the ten warmest years in history have all been since 1990. As of mid–2004 the warmest year on record since 1861 was 1998, but the next three warmest were 2002, 2003 and 2001. Global temperatures in 2002 and 2003 were 1.01°F above the long-term (1880–2001) average, tying them for the second warmest year in the last 123 years, exceeded only by 1998. http://www.ncdc.noaa.gov/. During the period from 1980 to 1999, the world, and particularly the Northern Hemisphere, experienced the hottest years in the twentieth century. The 1990s were the warmest decade ever recorded; the top 6 warmest years of the century were in the 1990s, and each year in the decade of the 1990s ranked among the top 15 in the century. *Id.*

When ocean temperatures are factored in, 1998 and 1997 were the two warmest years in the 20th century, but 1999 remains the 5th warmest year even taking account of the cooling effect of dramatic changes in the Pacific ocean oscillation. Scientists have noted that these unusually warm temperatures include especially warm winter temperatures in the Northern Hemisphere. This is referred to as the cool ocean warm land (COWL) pattern. Periods of these COWL conditions have occurred in the past, and it is not clear to what extent this current episode has been aggravated by greenhouse gas emissions. Research Pathways, *supra,* at 137–147.

Scientists are quick to point out that a few years or even a couple of decades is too short a time to be confident that a long term trend has been observed. When global temperatures dipped in the early 1990s, the skeptics saw support for their argument that global warming is far from imminent. However, atmospheric scientists argued that the eruption of Mount Pinatubo in the Philippines, and the consequent rise in sulfate aerosols, explained this apparent cooling trend. Stephen Henry Schneider, Laboratory Earth 64 (Weidenfeld & Nicholson, 1996). Overall, during the 1990s public opinion swung sharply toward support of the mainstream scientific theory that supports human responsibility for global warming. Although most journalists still feel they must not discuss climate change without giving equal time to interest groups that seek to discredit mainstream theories, that position is weakening. *See* Chris Mooney, Blinded By Science: How "Balanced" Coverage Lets the Scientific Fringe Hijack Reality, Colum. Journalism Rev., Mar./Apr. 2004.

C.   What Causes Climate Change?

Although the fact that the climate has warmed is generally accepted, the cause of the warmer temperatures is still debated. The great majority of climate scientists believe that human-caused GHG emissions are a major factor, but the extent of that relationship is difficult to prove, and some scientists argue that the relationship is either unproven or at best minor. Before trying to understand the dissenters, who expound a variety of different theories and often disagree among themselves, it is necessary to appreciate the position of the great majority of the scientific community.

1.   Climate Models: The IPCC

The growing recognition in the 1970s and 1980s of the possibility that increases in greenhouse gases were triggering climate change came at the time that high-powered computer modeling was beginning to be widely used. In various parts of the world, global climate models began to be developed by academic and governmental institutions. These institutions realized that there was a need for international cooperation if the scientific research was to proceed efficiently.

Much of the science of global warming has been developed by the International Panel on Climate Change ("IPCC"), established in 1988 by the World Meteorological Organization ("WMO") and the United Nations Environment Program ("UNEP"). *See* http://www.ipcc.ch/. The IPCC includes thousands of scientists from around the world, representing the model builders and other academic and governmental agencies with expertise in climate science.

The IPCC was directed to prepare a report every five years that would indicate the consensus of the views of the expert community about the extent of climate change that was likely to take place, and its causes. The IPCC's first report was issued in 1990, and its second report in 1995 reflected the development of new data and analyses that improve our understanding of climate change. In its 1995 report, the IPCC determined that there is a discernible human influence on climate and a link between the concentration of CO_2 and increases in temperature. Summary for Policymakers: The Science Of Climate Change IPCC Working Group I, Chapter 8 (John T. Houghton et al., eds., Cambridge University Press 1996). In 2001, the IPCC released its Third Assessment Report, Climate Change 2001: The Scientific Basis ("IPCC 2001 Report").

The IPCC reports are based on sophisticated computer climate models that seek to replicate the forces that affect climate on a global basis and distinguish between natural and anthropogenic influences on climate. The models are updated and recalibrated through a constant process of comparing modeled and observed spatial and temporal patterns of climate change. In the United States, some prominent models are located at the National Center for Atmospheric Research, the Lawrence Livermore Laboratory, the Goddard Institute for Space Studies, and the Geophysical Fluid Dynamics Laboratory. Other models are operated by institutions in other countries. The National Research Council has suggested that more money needs to be invested in climate models that will be sufficiently fine-tuned to produce accurate results. Research Pathways, *supra*.

Spirited and occasionally acrimonious colloquy, has ranged over many aspects of the credibility (or lack thereof) of the mathematically and physically based climate models used to project the climate changes resulting from a sustaining buildup of atmospheric CO_2. Some skeptics ask why should we believe such models' attempts to describe changes in such a dauntingly complex system as Earth's climate, especially given the difficulty they have had in simulating present temperature conditions without making arbitrary "flux corrections." Although arguments about the models will persist, given the staggering array of variables with which they must deal, mainstream scientists such as Princeton climatologist Jerry Mahlman say that there are no credible alternatives. To Mahlman, "the climate models do a reasonably good job of capturing the essence of the large-scale aspects of the current climate and its considerable natural variability on time scales ranging from 1 day to decades, while recognizing that the models contain weaknesses that add important uncertainty to the very best model projections of human-induced climate changes." J.D. Mahlman, Uncertainties in Projections of Human–Caused Climate Warming, 278 Science 1416 (Nov. 21, 1997). For an explanation of the mechanics of the climate models, *see* Martin Parry and Timothy Carter, Climate Impact and Adaptation Assessment: A Guide to the IPCC Approach (Earthscan Publications, 1998).

The IPCC's projections are based on modern computer models, which in turn are based on an underlying scientific theory known as the "greenhouse effect," that has been known and accepted for a long time.

2.   THE GREENHOUSE EFFECT

The "greenhouse effect" is one of the most well-established theories in the atmospheric sciences. It is the name given to the process that occurs when greenhouse gases accumulate in the atmosphere and trap heat at the surface of the earth, thus contributing to increases in temperature levels.

Jean–Baptiste–Joseph Fourier hypothesized its existence in the 1820s, *see* Christianson, *supra,* at 11–12, and the Swedish chemist Svante Arrhenius was awarded the Nobel prize for his calculations of the greenhouse effect as early as 1903. *Id.* at 105–115.

In addition to CO_2, other greenhouse gases include N_2O, SO_2, chlorofluorocarbons (CFCs) and tropospheric ozone. Methane, the chemical name for natural gas, is itself a powerful greenhouse gas that on a molecule for molecule basis has ten times the heat retention power of carbon dioxide. Christianson, *supra,* at 219–221.

Energy from the sun enables life to exist on the planet. The net effect of the greenhouse gas accumulation is that the earth's atmosphere acts as a blanket to retain the sun's heat and maintain the earth's average surface temperature of about 15°C. This heat retention is principally due to the action of the particles and gases that give rise to the greenhouse effect. Carbon dioxide, and certain other gases, preferentially allow sunlight to filter through to the surface of the planet relative to the amount of radiant energy that the atmosphere allows to escape back up through the atmosphere to space. A certain amount of greenhouse gas is needed to keep a planet at a habitable temperature; the earth would be much colder in the absence of any greenhouse warming. But when the amount of greenhouse gases increase, there is an increase in the planet's temperature because more heat is trapped.

To summarize, the unchallenged facts about the greenhouse effect include three key propositions: (1) atmospheric levels of greenhouse gases are increasing because of human activities; (2) greenhouse gases absorb and re-radiate infrared radiation in a way that heats the planet; and (3) atmospheric changes are long-lasting, because the major greenhouse gases remain in the atmosphere for periods ranging from a decade to centuries, and the climate itself has considerable inertia, mainly because of the high heat capacity of the world ocean. Mahlman, *supra,* at 1419.

3. OTHER POSSIBLE CAUSATIVE FACTORS

There is little dispute that the increased atmospheric concentration of greenhouse gases is largely attributable to human activities like the burning of fossil fuels. The debate hinges on the impact of these increased concentrations. What is being extensively debated is (1) the *degree* to which the greenhouse effect is causing the observed climate changes; (2) whether the greenhouse effect will be counteracted by other changes in world climate; and (3) what we should do about it, if anything.

Some critics challenge the IPCC's predictions because they believe it is virtually impossible to accurately predict the behavior of the global climate, and that the recent warming trend may simply be simply Earth's natural variation at work. For journalistic advocacy based on some of the skeptical views, *see* Antony Milne, Beyond The Warming: The Hazards Of Climate Prediction In The Age Of Chaos (Prism Press 1996); M. L. Parsons, Global Warming: The Truth Behind The Myth (Plenum 1995).

Other commentators accept the possibility that the models may be correct, but argue that (1) future warming will probably be slow, small, and partly beneficial, or (2) the accuracy of computer models is not yet sufficiently great to justify large expenditures in reliance on them. Stevens, *supra* at 242–243. Murray Weidenbaum, a former chairman of the Council of Economic Advisers, says: "Clearly, the massive and unprecedented scale of emissions of CO_2 (the major and most durable greenhouse gas) into the atmosphere is a source of genuine worry." But he suggests that the "effects of those human-originated emissions ... can be and often have been swamped by serious natural fluctuations, such as activity related to the sun." He finds this to be just one of "many continuing uncertainties involved in developing global warming policies." Murray Weidenbaum, An Agnostic Examination of the Case for Action on Global Warming (National Policy Association, 1997). One of the most difficult arguments to either prove or disprove is that the trends in climate change are not largely influenced by natural climatic variation that has produced cycles of warm and cold periods in the past. The natural variability of climate adds confusion to the effort to diagnose human-induced climate changes. Apparent long-term trends can be artificially amplified or damped by the contaminating effects of undiagnosed natural variations.

Some astronomers who study the sun's sunspot cycles have speculated that there may be a connection between these cycles and climate change. Jerry Mahlman says that it "is difficult, but not impossible, to construct conceivable alternate hypotheses to explain this observed warming. Using variations in solar output or in natural climate to explain the observed warming can be appealing, but both have serious logical inconsistencies." Mahlman, *supra,* at 1420. But some studies of tree-ring records suggest that the climate models do need to be adjusted both for changing solar variability and for periods of high-level dust following major volcanic eruptions. Rosanne D'Arrigo *et al.*, Northern Hemisphere Temperature Variability for the Past three Centuries: Tree-ring and Model Estimates, 42 Climate Change 663, 671–73 (1999).

One of the more difficult issues posed for the model builders is to explain the discrepancies between temperature levels at the surface of the earth, which have been rising, and temperatures in the troposphere, which have been almost steady.

> Since 1979, polar orbiting satellites have monitored atmospheric temperatures on a global scale.... There is an apparent difference between the thermometer-estimated surface warming of roughly 0.20 degree Celsius per decade since 1979 and the much smaller temperature trend in the lower troposphere estimated from satellites and radiosondes.

B.D. Santer *et al.*, Interpreting Differential Temperature Trends at the Surface and in the Lower Troposphere, 287 Science 1227 (Feb. 18, 2000).

Surface temperatures impact human activities, of course, but if the increased heat is caused by the greenhouse effect, then the temperatures in the upper air should be rising also. Mainstream scientists have been puzzled by these differences, and some skeptics have argued that satellite data suggest that no real increase in global temperature has been observed. However, other analysis of the satellite data indicates that when gradual changes in the satellites' orbits are taken into consideration, the data does show a steady increase. Frank J. Wentz & Matthias Schnabel, Effects of Orbital Decay on Satellite–Derived Lower–Tropospheric Temperature Trends, 394 Nature 661 (Aug. 13, 1998).

Nevertheless, scientists still cannot fully explain why the differences exist. A review by a panel of the National Academy of Sciences concluded that the differences between surface and upper air measurements are real and not simply data glitches. The committee concluded that "major advances are needed in our modeling and interpretation of temperature profiles, along with considerable improvements in data acquisition, documentation and distribution of the data, and their analysis by the scientific community worldwide." David E. Parker, Temperatures High and Low, 287 Science 1216, 1217 (Feb. 18, 2000).

4. Skepticism About the Models

Scientists agree that additional research is desirable to improve the accuracy of global climate models. The computer modelers are the first to admit that the science of modeling is still relatively young and will undoubtedly improve with time. The Bush administration supports research to improve the models, and formed the Climate Change Science Program ("CCSP") in 2002. Its task is to "measurably improve the integration of scientific knowledge, including measures of uncertainty, into effective decision support systems and resources." See http://www.climatescience.gov/. For a critique of the CCSP's research agenda, see National Research Council, Implementing Climate and Global Change Research: A Review of the Final U.S. Climate Change Science Program Strategic Plan (2004).

An example of the sort of "uncertainty" often cited by scientific skeptics of mainstream theories of climate change is that the greenhouse effect may (according to them) be largely negated by other changes in climate that will be taking place. Any warming will have a variety of "feedback" effects that will themselves affect future warming, in ways that are difficult to determine. See National Research Council, Understanding Climate Change Feedbacks (2003). These feedback effects could accelerate or slow down the warming process.

Some skeptics have seized upon this and suggested that increased cloudiness will counteract greenhouse heating. The most prominent of these is MIT meteorology professor Richard Lindzen.

> According to Lindzen and scientists of a like turn of mind, additional cloud cover will boost negative feedback by reflecting more light and cooling the planet, thus short-circuiting the glum scenario advanced by environmentalists. Yet many of Lindzen's peers are skeptical. Their research indicates that a substantial increase in clouds will contribute

to a warming of the air and sea, bringing about a number of positive feedbacks such as the melting of the polar ice.

Christianson, *supra,* at 202–203.

The substitution of cloudier weather for warmer weather does not necessarily cheer the average person. In any event, the climate models do not agree with Lindzen's predictions, and Lindzen does not have his own computer model of the impact of greater cloud cover. There has apparently been no consensus on what the impact of increased cloud cover would be if it occurred. Christianson, *supra,* at 201–203. Nevertheless, we know that changes in other radiatively active substances offset somewhat the warming effect of increased greenhouse gases. There have been decreases in lower stratospheric ozone and increases in sulfate particles, and both of these factors should produce cooling effects in the stratosphere, and such a trend has been observed, consistent with model predictions. The impact that these effects will have on the surface, however, is uncertain. "Significant reduction of key uncertainties will require a decade or more. The uncertainties concerning the responses of clouds, water vapor, ice, ocean currents, and specific regions to increased greenhouse gases remain formidable." Mahlman, *supra,* at 1420.

* * *

In 2004, the George C. Marshall Institute and the U.K.-based Scientific Alliance of London released "Climate Issues and Questions," a report purporting to undermine all of the major mainstream assumptions about global climate policy. Andrew Freedman, Report questions science behind GHG regulation, Greenwire, Dec. 8, 2004. As several critics of that report note, it goes against the weight of mainstream scientific expertise, and as both of these institutions are heavily funded by industry, its conclusions are at best suspect. *See* Mooney, *supra.* The CCSP's 2004 report was the Bush Administration's first admission that GHG emissions will rise considerably to 2020 and that increased levels of CO_2 are the most likely explanation of global warming since 1950. U.S. Climate Change Science Program, Our Changing Planet (2004), http://www.usgcrp.gov/. However, the Administration has repeatedly stated that mandatory GHG reductions are not necessary until more is known about global warming.

On balance, then, do the skeptics' views raise sufficient questions about mainstream climate change theory and models that they do not produce reliable evidence for reliance by policy makers? The popular novelist Michael Crichton would say "yes." In his "Author's Message" at the end of his fictional book State of Fear, which conjectures an apocalyptic scenario based on acceptance of warming and alarming the public, he states, "Before making expensive policy decisions on the basis of climate models, I think it is reasonable to require that those models predict future temperatures accurately for a period of ten years. Twenty would be better." Michael Crichton, State of Fear 570 (HarperCollins 2004). However, given the overwhelming weight of evidence brought forth by the IPCC in its three reports and criticism of Crichton's arguments, it is difficult to support this wait-and-see approach. *See* Pew Center on Global Climate Change, Comments On "State of Fear," http://www.pewclimate.org (noting that "the novel contains a number of strawman arguments, misinterpretations of the scientific literature, and even a few misleading statements drawn from the so-called 'skeptics,'" and stating that "Crichton has a less-than-commanding understanding of climate change science").

D. Possible Impacts of Climate Change

Concern about future warming of the planet has led to a good deal of speculation about its likely effects. One obvious category of direct effects is changes in crop yields and the range or numbers of pests that affect plants, or diseases that threaten animals or human health. Water supplies may be affected by changes in the probability of catastrophic episodes of drought and flooding if climate warming alters the number and character of destructive storms. The effect on natural ecosystems, such as the tropical forests, has also been a matter of concern.

1. Temperature and Rainfall Changes

The aspect of climate change that has captured most of the public attention is the idea that there will be "global warming." This sound bite fails to capture the complex nature of the scientists' predictions, either at the global level or at the regional level. Nevertheless, it is accurate to say that on average the mainstream theory predicts that there will be a gradual increase in average global temperature as the accumulation of greenhouse gases in the atmosphere increases.

a. GLOBAL AVERAGES

The 2001 IPCC report reaffirms in much stronger language than previous reports that the climate is changing in ways that cannot be accounted for by natural variability and that global warming is happening. The current IPCC projection (based on scenarios derived from the computer models) is that temperatures will rise between 1.4 and 5.8 degrees Celsius by 2100. This wide range is due to variations in the level of GHG emissions assumed by each scenario and to the designs of the individual computer models. Scientists also predict that, on the global scale, increases in temperature will be accompanied by comparable increases in precipitation.

Jerry Mahlman has criticized some assertions that the number of tropical storms, hurricanes, and typhoons will increase from warming activity as lacking scientific support. Mahlman, *supra*, at 1418. In 2004, however, some scientists, including Dr. Paul Epstein, associate director of the Center for Health and the Global Environment at the Harvard Medical School, suggested that the barrage of hurricanes (four in a five-week span) that hit south Florida that fall may have happened as a result of climate change occurring faster than predicted. These reports were later criticized for many of the same reasons as earlier predictions regarding tropical storms, but the issue continues to be of considerable concern. Dennis O'Brien, A Storm Over Global Warming: Some Link Temperature to '04 Hurricanes, Seattle Times, Nov. 7, 2004. Controversy also erupted about links (if any) between global warming and the damage caused by Hurricanes Katrina and Rita in Fall 2005.

b. REGIONAL EFFECTS

A person might well take a different view of climate change if he lived on the plains of Saskatchewan than if he lived on the Maldive Islands. The prospect of a longer growing season in Canada might bring both economic and lifestyle advantages, although that is by no means certain, but the prospect of rising sea levels on low-lying islands would surely mean disaster. How can these regional differences be analyzed and taken into account?

Climatologists are much less confident about their abilities to predict the extent to which particular regions will be more or less affected by climate change than they are about the likelihood of change: "[U]ncertainty tends to increase going from global to regional scales. Regional information is highly relevant to policy, but is ... less precise and can be ambiguous and confusing, thus a careful balance is needed when considering the scale at which policy relevant information can be provided." *See* IPCC Workshop on Describing Scientific Uncertainties in Climate Change to Support Analysis of Risk and of Options (2004). In general, however, scientists predict that the change will be greater in the Northern Hemisphere than in the Southern, and particularly great in the Arctic region. Recognizing that the Arctic region will bear a disproportionate impact from climate change, the Inuit Circumpolar Conference (representing 150,000 Inuit within the Arctic rim) announced in 2003 that it was developing a human rights petition to be submitted to the Inter–American Commission on Human Rights ("IACHR"). The basis of the claim is that "the United States has effectively violated their fundamental human rights by refusing to cut the country's [GHG] emissions and by reneging on its international commitments to address climate change." Juliette Niehuss, Litigation Update: Inuit Circumpolar Conference v. Bush Administration, Sustainable Dev't L. & Pol'y, Spring 2005, at 66. Enforcement of any finding of a human rights violation would be in the Inter–American Court of Human Rights, which does not have jurisdiction over the U.S. Therefore, "[t]he Inuit's claims against the U.S. have the best chance of being recognized through a nonbonding declaration or ruling by the IACHR." *Id.*

Additional scientific data documenting the warming that has already taken place in the Arctic, and projecting further increases, came in 2004 from scientists in the countries with Arctic territory, who released an extensive report. *See* Arctic Climate Impact Assessment, http://www.acia.uaf.edu/default.html. At a U.S. Senate hearing on the report, Senator Ted Stevens of Alaska said that, "Alaska is literally being reshaped by warming temperatures that are melting permafrost, causing glaciers to retreat and disrupting indigenous people's traditional ways of life." Andrew Freedman, Sens. Stevens, McCain sound alarm over Arctic warming, Greenwire, Nov. 17, 2004.

The interdisciplinary Pew Center of Global Climate Change has attempted to forecast the effect of climate change on the United States. Its report illustrates the complexity of making these predictions at a national or regional level, particularly because the extent to which changes in temperature forecasts can produce large changes in the anticipated impacts is not well known and depends on a wide variety of factors. See Pew Center on Global Climate Change, A Synthesis of Potential Climate Change Impacts on the U.S. (2004). Much greater fidelity of calculated local climate impacts will require large improvements in computational power and in the physical and biological sophistication of the models. For example, the large uncertainty in modeling the all-important responses of clouds could become even harder at regional and local levels. Major sustained efforts will be required to reduce these uncertainties substantially. Mahlman, *supra*, at 1421.

Regional studies to date suggest that it is likely, though by no means certain, that the temperate regions of the Northern Hemisphere will experience decreases in soil moisture in response to increases in summer temperatures. This result remains somewhat sensitive to the details of predicted spring and summer precipitation, as well as to model assumptions about land surface processes and the offsetting effects of airborne sulfate particles in those regions. Mahlman, *supra* at 1420. Studies showing warming temperatures in Arctic regions have raised concerns about the impact of melting permafrost that could become an impenetrable morass. Christianson, *supra* at 216–217. By 2050 or so, the high latitudes of the Northern Hemisphere are also expected to experience temperature increases well in excess of the global average increase. In addition, substantial reductions of northern sea ice are expected. Precipitation is expected to increase significantly in higher northern latitudes. This effect mainly occurs because of the higher moisture content of the warmer air as it moves poleward, cools, and releases its moisture. Mahlman, *supra* at 1420; *see also* Robert T. Watson, ed., The Regional Impact of Climate Change: an Assessment of Vulnerability (Cambridge University Press, 1998).

2. SEA LEVEL RISE

Climate-induced increases in sea level are caused by thermal expansion of the oceans and melting of land ice and ice sheets. Projections from different models vary on the details, but all of the models predict that there will be gradual but eventually significant sea level increases. The IPCC's projections of 50 ± 25 cm by the year 2100, at a gradual rate of 5 millimeters a year, reflect primarily the thermal expansion of sea water. Small island nations, such as the Bahamas or the Maldives, have been particularly concerned about the potential of rising sea levels. Long-term melting of landlocked ice carries the potential for considerably higher increases, but with less certainty. Mahlman, *supra*, at 1419.

Concern about potential sea-level rise is the dominant theme of a group of small island states that have formed a coalition to participate in the international negotiations over climate change issues. For example, 80% of the Bahamas are five feet or less above sea level, and about 35 other countries find themselves in roughly similar positions. Stevens, *supra,* at 258–259

3.   PLANT GROWTH

The higher concentrations of carbon dioxide in the air should stimulate greater plant growth. A study by the U.S. Department of Agriculture predicts that overall crop production will increase, due to the beneficial effects of elevated CO_2 on crop yields and to marked precipitation increases. These two factors will counterbalance negative effects of warmer temperatures on crop yields. *See* U.S. National Assessment Technical Report— Effects of Climate Change on U.S. Crop Production, http://www.usgcrp.gov /usgcrp/nacc/agriculture/TubielloEtal–2000.pdf. This will have both beneficial and adverse impacts on agriculture. Some agronomists point out that plant growth is limited by available nutrients like nitrogen and phosphorus, not to mention water (although carbon dioxide stimulation also makes plants use water more efficiently). Faster growth may simply make plants less nutritious, "diluting the nutrient content. The need for fertilizer and pesticides would increase." Finally, some scientists believe that eventually a saturation point is reached, at which forest trees and perennial plants gain no more benefit from more carbon dioxide. Stevens, *supra,* at 247.

The ranges of insects and other pests are likely to spread as the climate warms. *See* M. Gabriela Bidart–Bouzat, Herbivory modifies the lifetime fitness response of arabidopsis thaliana to elevated CO_2, 85 Ecology 297 (2004). The complex interrelationship of all of these and other factors make it difficult to predict the extent to which a particular regional impact will be beneficial or harmful. Christianson, *supra,* at 251–253. In a special 1998 report, a panel of the IPCC concluded that the ability of agricultural interests to adapt to changing climate conditions would vary greatly from one part of the world to another. It suggested that the areas that would be most vulnerable would be those that (1) are already having difficulty coping with extreme weather events, (2) lack good markets or other institutions to facilitate redistribution of deficits and surpluses, or (3) lack resources to finance adaptation. Watson, *supra* at 6; *see generally* George Frisvold & Betsey Kuhn, Global Environmental Change and Agriculture: Assessing the Impacts (Edward Elgar, 1999).

4.   ENERGY DEMAND

In regions where temperatures become warmer, the growing season will increase and the cost of heating will be reduced. On the other hand, energy costs for air conditioning, which accounts for peak usage in most parts of the United States, will increase. A consortium of Texas academics concluded that that state would experience substantial increases in energy demand. Clarkson *et al.*, *supra,* at 179–181.

Macroeconomists have found it difficult to model the impact of climate change on energy usage, concluding that the relationship between energy consumption and carbon dioxide emissions must be analyzed in terms of individual fuels. In addition, the capital intensive nature of the energy industries makes short term shifts in fuel usage complex and difficult. Terry Barker *et al.*, Global Warming and Energy Demand 311–312 (Routledge 1995).

5.   BIODIVERSITY

In 2004, mussels were found growing on the seabed just 800 miles from the North Pole, in what scientists claimed was a likely sign of global warming. Alister Doyle, Mussels Found Near North Pole, Reuters, Sept. 17, 2004. This is but one example of the many considerable effects on biodiversity that might be attributable to climate change. Studies have led to "an impressive array of data suggesting that climate changes big and small can have profound effects on species. Climate's fingerprints are turning up in observations compiled over years and decades." Bernice Wuethrich, How Climate Change Alters the Rhythms of the Wild, 287 Science 793 (February 4, 2000). A panel of the IPCC Working Group identified many regions in which ecosystem shifts were a serious concern. Watson *et al.*, *supra,* at 4–5.

A review of the various studies by Adam Markham and Jay Malcolm concluded that eight categories of ecosystem were most at risk: (1) mangrove forests, (2) boreal forests, (3) tropical forests, (4) alpine/montane ecosystems, (5) Arctic ecosystems, (6) coastal wetlands, (7) coral reefs, and (8) island ecosystems. Adam Markham and Jay Malcolm, Biodiversity and Wildlife: Adaptation to Climate Change, in Adapting to Climate Change: An International Perspective 384 (Joel B. Smith et al., eds., Springer, 1996).

In some parts of the world the changes in climate that have already taken place have produced noticeable changes in the composition of natural areas. In the sub-Arctic regions of North America, for instance, the warming of the 1980s and 1990s have produced substantial changes in forest composition. "The permafrost is thawing, and clouds of insects that have been proliferated in a warmer climate are killing vast stretches of Alaska's evergreen forest." Stevens, *supra,* at 173. Subtropical areas also stand to lose significant ecological values. *See* Eugene O. Box et al., Predicted Effects of Climatic Change on Distribution of Ecologically Important Native Tree and Shrub Species in Florida, 41 Climate Change 213, 238 (1999). In 2001, Japan's Environment Ministry released a report blaming global warming for making the cherry blossoms bloom earlier than ever in the nation and for melting the ice on the sea of Okhotsk, calling this evidence that climate change has taken a foothold in Japan. The Daily Yomiuri (Tokyo), Apr. 27, 2001.

6.   IS THERE A RISK OF SUDDEN CATASTROPHE?

The changes most scientists predict are very gradual in nature. Although steady and inexorable, they hardly lead the average person to imagine the apocalyptic scenario portrayed in the recent movie "The Day After Tomorrow." Some commentators have suggested, however, that more catastrophic results of climate change are possible. In 2004, an unexplained and unprecedented rise in carbon dioxide at the Mauna Loa Observatory monitoring station in Hawaii for two years running raised fears about rapid climate change. Scientists were baffled why the quantity of CO_2 had leapt in a two-year period and were concerned that the Earth's natural systems were no longer able to absorb as much as in the past. *See* Rise in CO_2 at Mauna Loa station warrants close future scrutiny, Guardian, Oct. 11, 2004.

Although most scientists discount possible disaster scenarios, there is some scientific support for the suggestion that at least two of these theories are possible: (1) collapse of Antarctic ice shelves, and (2) sudden shifts in ocean currents. *See* Abrupt Climate Change: Should We Be Worried?, Robert B. Gagosian (presentation at the World Economic Forum, Davos, Switzerland, Jan. 27, 2003).

a.   ANTARCTIC ICE FIELD COLLAPSE

One possibility is that large ice shelves in the Antarctic will collapse into the sea, causing an immediate and catastrophic rise in sea levels all over the globe. Some scientists are concerned that sudden loss of Greenland or Antarctic ice could produce a sudden rise in sea levels, but the majority of scientists don't think this is likely. Most of the Arctic polar ice is already floating in the ocean, so if it melts it would not cause the sea to rise. But much of the ice in Antarctica rests on land, as does the ice cap that covers most of Greenland. The Greenland ice cap has shrunk markedly during the 1990s, but the IPCC's forecasts suggest that in the future this may be partially offset by precipitation increases in Greenland. Stevens, *supra,* at 260.

Recent research has raised new concerns about the Antarctic, however. Ice shelves off the Antarctic Peninsula have disintegrated, causing glaciers to surge toward the sea. *See* H. De Angelis and P. Skvarca, Glacier Surge After Ice Shelf Collapse, 299 Science 1560 (Mar. 7, 2003).

b.   OCEAN CURRENT SHIFTS

Another widely discussed possible result of climate change is a sudden change in ocean currents. The example often cited is the possibility that the Gulf Stream might change, robbing the Northeastern United States and all of Europe of its moderating influence.

"Wally Broecker of Lamont–Doherty has been the chief proponent of the idea that the on-again, off-again behavior of the ocean conveyor was responsible for sharp, rapid climatic changes in the past.... If the world warms as much as the IPCC projects, he says, it could set in motion a train of events that would weaken or halt the conveyor. Some computer models have supported this hypothesis."

Stevens, *supra,* at 285. The projected precipitation increases at higher latitudes act to reduce the ocean's salinity and thus its density. This effect inhibits the tendency of the water to sink, thus suppressing the overturning circulation. Mahlman, *supra,* at 1420. Subpolar seas bordering the North Atlantic have become noticeably less salty since the mid–1960s, especially in the last decade. This is the most dramatic oceanic change ever measured in the era of modern instruments and suggests there may be some validity in this theory.

Another big question mark is the interrelationship between climate change and *el niño* events. The repeated onset of extremely powerful *el niño* events during the 1980s and 1990s led some observers to hypothesize that the warming of the earth's climate was responsible for the trend. Scientists have not documented any clear evidence that the overall climate change contributed to the warming of the Pacific Ocean that triggers *el niños,* but their studies have confirmed the correlation. Richard A. Kerr, Big *El Niños* Ride the Back of Slower Climate Change, 283 Science 1108 (Feb. 19, 1999). The ability of scientists to predict *el niños* continues to improve, so that they now feel confident of their ability to predict these events a year in advance. Research Pathways, *supra,* at 87.

E.   ATTEMPTS TO CONTROL CLIMATE CHANGE

Are the likely impacts of greenhouse gas build-up so serious that we should take immediate steps to change our patterns of energy use? In any event, are the impacts at least sufficiently inevitable and serious that we need to try to adapt to the changing conditions we will be encountering? If so, what should those efforts entail?

The choices range from massive alteration of lifestyles to complete inaction. The issue has taxed the creative minds of some of the best scientists, economists and engineers. Proposed responses tend to fall into two categories: (a) prevention strategies, which would reduce the amount of greenhouse gas buildup in the atmosphere, and (b) adaptation, which would reduce the adverse effects of the greenhouse gas buildup.

1.   DOMESTIC PREVENTION AND MITIGATION STRATEGIES

As the twenty-first century begins, federal and state governments in the United States have adopted relatively few legal rules and principles based on the objective of avoiding climate change. But some other nations are moving forward more aggressively, and the industry no longer assumes that the possibility of United States laws on the topic is more remote than a cold day in the nether worlds.

a. VOLUNTARY OR MANDATORY REDUCTIONS?

Although many nations, particularly in Europe, have developed mandatory programs designed to reduce GHG emissions, the United States has shown little appetite for them. In the United States, federal effort has centered almost exclusively on voluntary reduction programs. The Bush Administration's 2004 CCSP report detailed the risks of increasing GHG levels, but the federal government has no plans to entertain mandatory GHG reduction strategies. In 2002, President Bush committed the United States to reduce the GHG intensity of the American economy by 18 percent over the next 10 years. The White House said it aims to fight climate change through voluntary programs and technology improvements in such areas as clean-burning coal, advanced nuclear power and hydrogen fuel cells. *See* U.S. Dep't of State, Fact Sheet: U.S. Climate Change Policy, http://www.state.gov/g/oes/rls/fs/2004/36425.htm. An example of a federal government technology improvement program is the "Clean Coal Technology Program," co-funded by the DOE and the coal industry, and managed by the National Energy Technology Laboratory, that seeks to demonstrate and deploy advanced clean coal technologies that meet strict environmental standards. *See* http://www.lanl.gov/projects/cctc/.

While the Bush administration claimed its commitment would prevent more than 500 million metric tons of carbon-equivalent emissions through 2012, the plan has been consistently ridiculed by environmentalists who see it as a strategy of avoidance. David Hawkins, director of the air and energy programs at the Natural Resources Defense Council, observed in an interview before the November 2004 Presidential election that businesses may even begin to exert pressure on the White House to enact GHG restrictions so that they can have more regulatory certainty. "There are likely to be a variety of forces inside and outside the administration arguing that further delay does not serve business interests let alone environmental interests," Hawkins said. Andrew Freedman and Brian Stempeck, Bush to face added international pressure on GHG regulation, Greenwire, Nov. 4, 2004.

As the Kyoto Protocol (*see* below) was being ratified in 2005, and the U.S. stood virtually alone among developed nations in refusing to adopt it, the Bush administration continued to insist that its voluntary greenhouse gas reduction efforts would have a salutary effect. James Connaughton, chairman of the White House's Council on Environmental Quality, stated, "The U.S., in the last three years of the Bush administration, has dedicated more resources to the issue of climate change than any other nation of the world and most other nations of the world combined." Other nations were not quick to agree. "141 countries have not allowed this process to be blocked by the unilateral power play of one country," responded German Environment Minister Juergen Trittin. *See* Alistair Doyle, Feted and Hated, Kyoto Global Warming Pact Starts, Reuters, Feb. 17, 2005.

In his first visit to Europe after his second inauguration, President Bush told the European Union that, "Emerging technologies, such as hydrogen-powered vehicles, electricity from renewable energy sources (and) clean coal technology will encourage economic growth that is environmentally responsible.'' This message was not well received. The EU's Environment Commissioner, Stavros Dimas said, ''Technologies are important and the European Union has always been keen for progress in this area [but] to combat climate change, this is not enough. Action is needed now. Significant reductions in emissions worldwide must be agreed.'' A Greenpeace climate expert, Mahi Sideridou, put it even more bluntly, saying technology is key is ''as groundbreaking as saying that Brussels has bad weather and good chocolate.'' *See* Bush Disappoints Europe With Climate Change Ideas, Reuters, Feb. 22, 2005.

b.   MANDATORY REDUCTION PROPOSALS—FEDERAL GOVERNMENT

In the early 21st century, the U.S. stands apart from its principal international allies on the question of using mandatory schemes to reduce GHG emissions. Despite widespread opposition to them and a lack of political will to implement them, however, proposals continue to emerge for mandatory federal GHG reduction programs.

i.   *Direct Regulation of GHG Emissions*

Some proposals would involve direct regulation of CO_2 emissions under the federal Clean Air Act (CAA). The CAA regulatory scheme focuses on ''criteria pollutants'' and ''hazardous air pollutants.'' *See* Chapter 13. If GHGs met either of these definitions, then the EPA would have the authority to regulate them directly. *See* Nicholle Winters, Note, Carbon Dioxide: A Pollutant in the Air, But Is the EPA Correct That It Is Not An ''Air Pollutant''?, 104 Colum. L. Rev. 1996 (2004). In 2003, the EPA's general counsel, Robert Fabricant, reversed a position taken by the agency's two previous general counsels on this issue. He declared that the EPA does not have the authority to regulate CO_2 under the CAA and that CO_2 does not fall under the CAA's definition of an air pollutant, because the CAA does not authorize regulation of climate change. On the same day, the EPA also denied a request that it regulate CO_2 emissions in automobiles, stating it did not have the authority to do so. *See* Control of Emissions From New Highway Vehicles and Engines, 68 Fed. Reg. 52,922 (2003).

Twelve states and numerous other parties filed petitions with the U.S. Court of Appeals for the D.C. Circuit, challenging these actions. In early 2005, the D.C. Circuit heard oral arguments in the case. Massachusetts Assistant Attorney General James Milkey argued that the CAA requires EPA to regulate pollutants that have an adverse affect on public health and welfare (*see* 42 U.S.C. § 7521(a)(1)), which includes CO_2 and other GHGs gases because they lead to the ''precise harms that the act sought to prohibit.'' ''You don't have to look very far to find the authority that EPA claims is missing,'' Milkey said. Michael Janofsky, 2 Sides Do Battle in Court on Whether E.P.A. Should Regulate Carbon Dioxide, N.Y. Times, Apr. 9, 2005. Later in 2005, the appellate court rejected the states' arguments. Massachusetts v. EPA, 415 F.3d 50 (D.C. Cir. 2005). The D.C. Circuit held that the EPA properly exercised its discretion to deny the rulemaking petition and accepted its position that the effects of GHGs are sufficiently scientifically uncertain that regulation is not required at this time. In his dissent, Judge David Tatel stated that the EPA misinterpreted the scope of its statutory authority and failed to provide a statutorily based justification for refusing to make an endangerment finding.

Who has standing to sue the EPA (or any other agency) to force it to address GHG emissions—or for damage caused by GHG emissions? To bring an action in federal court, a plaintiff must demonstrate an "injury in fact" that is "concrete and particularized" and either "actual or imminent," a "causal connection between the injury and the conduct complained of," and a likelihood that a decision in his favor would redress his injury. *Friends of the Earth, Inc. v. Laidlaw Environmental Services (TOC), Inc.*, 528 U.S. 167 (2000). There are also "prudential limitations" on standing; for example, under section 702 of the Administrative Procedure Act as interpreted by the Supreme Court, the plaintiff's suit must fall within the "zone of interests" protected by the specific statute or regulation. *Bennett v. Spear*, 520 U.S. 154 (1997). Because global warming affects the entire planet, a plaintiff seeking direct regulation of GHG emissions may be no more affected than anyone else on Earth, and the Supreme Court has stated that a "generalized grievance" is not suitable for federal court. *Id.* One author, however, concludes that "at least some plaintiffs with concrete injuries, such as Alaska Natives, have standing to file global warming suits under either the National Environmental Policy Act of 1969 (NEPA) or the CAA." Bradford C. Mank, Standing and Global Warming: Is Injury to All Injury to None?, 35 Envt'l L. 1 (2005).

Other proposals targeted to regulating GHG emissions include those for "multipollutant legislation." These proposals would create a single program to deal with all power plant emissions, much like the way that motor vehicles are regulated. However, the Bush administration proposal, the "Clear Skies Act," does not include CO_2 controls. The EPA has proposed regulations (the "Clean Air Interstate Rule") that would try to accomplish multipollutant reductions without changing the Clean Air Act, and without regulating CO_2. *See* Chapters 5 and 13 for discussions of these proposals.

ii.   Cap–and–Trade Proposals

Economists have long advocated flexible, market-based processes for dealing with environmental issues. In 2003, U.S. Senators John McCain and Joseph Lieberman introduced S. 139, the "Climate Stewardship Act," legislation featuring a GHG emissions "cap-and-trade" scheme.

S. 139 would have required the EPA Administrator to promulgate regulations to limit greenhouse gas emissions from the electricity generation, transportation, industrial, and commercial economic sectors (but not the agricultural or residential sectors), accounting for about 85% of the overall U.S. emissions in the year 2000. The bill also would have provided for the trading of emissions allowances and reductions through a "National Greenhouse Gas Database" containing an inventory of emissions and registry of reductions. The bill would have capped the 2010 aggregate emissions level for the covered sectors at the 2000 level, with certain subsectors being exempt if the Administrator determined that it was not feasible to measure their GHG emissions. The Commerce Department would have had the task of biennially re-evaluating the level of allowances to determine whether it was consistent with the objective of stabilizing GHG emissions at a level that will prevent dangerous anthropogenic interference with the climate system.

An entity that was in a covered sector, or that produced or imported synthetic GHGs, would have been subject to the requirements of S. 139 if it (a) owned at least one facility that annually emitted more than 10,000 metric tons of GHGs (measured in units of carbon dioxide equivalents–$MTCO_2E$); (b) produced or imported petroleum products used for transportation that, when combusted, would emit more than 10,000 $MTCO_2E$; or (c) produced or imported HFC, PFC and SF_6 that, when used, would emit more than 10,000 $MTCO_2E$. Each covered entity would be required to submit to the EPA one tradeable allowance for each $MTCO_2E$ directly emitted. Each petroleum refiner or importer would be required to submit an allowance for each unit of petroleum product sold that, when combusted, would emit one $MTCO_2E$. Each producer or importer of HFC, PFC, and SF_6 would be required to submit an allowance for each unit sold that, when used, would emit one $MTCO_2E$. The Administrator would determine the method of calculating the amount of GHG emissions associated with combustion of petroleum products and use of HFC, PFC, and SF_6.

The Secretary of Commerce would determine the amount of allowances to be given away or "grandfathered" to covered entities and the amount to be auctioned. The Secretary's determination would be subject to a number of allocation factors identified in the bill. Proceeds from the auction would be used to reduce energy costs of consumers and assist disproportionately affected workers. Covered entities would have had flexibility in acquiring their allowances. In addition to the allowances grandfathered to them, they could trade with other covered entities to acquire additional allowances, if necessary. Also, any entity would be allowed to satisfy up to 15% of its total allowance requirements by submitting (a) tradeable allowances from another nation's market in GHGs; (b) a net increase in sequestration registered with the National Greenhouse Gas Database; (c) a GHG emission reduction by a non-covered entity registered with the Database; and (d) allowances borrowed against future reductions (as described below). A covered entity that agreed to emit no more than its 1990 levels by 2010 would be allowed meet up to 20% of its requirement through (a) international credits, (b) sequestration, and (c) registered reductions, but not (d) borrowed credits. An entity planning to make capital investments or deploy technologies within the next 5 years would be allowed to borrow against the expected GHG emission reductions to meet current year requirements. The loan would include a 10 percent interest rate.

Any covered entity not meeting its emissions limits would have been fined for each ton of GHGs over the limit at the rate of three times the market value of a ton of GHG.■

NOTES AND COMMENTS

1. On October 30, 2003, a substitute amendment to S. 139 was defeated by a vote of 43 to 55 in the full Senate, but a number of news accounts noted the historic occasion of the vote (the first ever in the U.S. Senate on a program designed to regulate greenhouse gas emissions) and the growing bipartisan support for a strong U.S. climate change policy. *See* Senate rejects McCain–Lieberman greenhouse gas effort, but advocates say tally is progress, Electric Utility Week, Nov. 3, 2003. Senators McCain and Lieberman reintroduced their bill in the following Congress, but neither it nor any comparable bill was included in the Energy Policy Act of 2005.

2. The 2004 report of the bipartisan National Commission on Energy Policy recommends implementing a mandatory, economy-wide GHG cap-and-trade system. Nat'l Comm'n on Energy Policy, Ending the Energy Stalemate: A Bipartisan Strategy to Meet America's Energy Challenges (2004).

3. There are two principal options for a cap-and-trade program: a "downstream" program (applying to sources of emissions and requiring them to have allowances equal to their emissions) and an "upstream" program (applying to fuel suppliers and requiring them to have allowances covering the carbon content of the fuels they distribute). Robert R. Nordhaus and Kyle W. Danish, Designing a Mandatory Greenhouse Gas Reduction Program For the U.S., *in* A Climate Policy Framework: Balancing Policy and Politics (Aspen Inst. 2004). Which of these would have been established by S. 139? Which do you believe is best, and why?

iii.   GHG Tax Proposals

Carbon taxes have been discussed in the U.S. since the early 1990s (*see* U.S. Congressional Budget Office, Carbon Charges as a Response to Global Warming: the Effects of Taxing Fossil Fuels (1990)), but have generally fallen out of favor because of their political unpalatability and their tendency to aggravate distortions associated with remaining taxes on investment or labor (even though this impact could perhaps be minimized). Nordhaus and Danish, *supra*.

The first major attempt to institute a "carbon tax" in the U.S. was rejected. In 1993, the Clinton administration put forth legislation that called for a general tax on all energy products based on the heat content or "Btu" (British Thermal Unit) of the particular fuel. The tax would have been imposed on coal, natural gas, liquified petroleum gases, natural gasoline, nuclear-generated electricity, hydroelectricity, and imported electricity at a base rate of 25.7 cents per million Btus (p/MBtu). Thomas W. Lippman, Energy Tax Would Touch All, Wash. Post, Feb. 18, 1993, at A1. The Administration believed that a Btu approach was a relatively neutral proposal on a regional basis and that its impact was balanced on all market shares of energy sources.

The tax proposal immediately met with stiff opposition. Citizens for a Sound Economy's economist, Paul Merski, claimed the tax was regressive, stating that "families living on $20,000 or less spend twice as large a share of their income on gasoline as families living on $50,000 or more." *See* Chris Bredehoeft, TED Case Study—U.S. Btu Tax (1995), http://www.amer-ican.edu/TED/usbtutax.htm. The Mobil Oil Co. placed a full page ad in the *New York Times* comparing the energy tax to the Edsel, noting "both looked good on paper." *Id.* The National Association of Manufacturers actively lobbied key members of the House and Senate, claiming the Btu tax would seriously affect the competitiveness of U.S. companies. In the end, the proposal was withdrawn. Lippman, *supra*, at A4.

Since this debacle, there have been few attempts to institute taxes on GHG emissions in the U.S., although tax proposals occasionally surface. In April 2005, CEO Paul Anderson of utility Duke Energy announced his company would push for a tax on CO_2 emissions to combat climate change. Anderson acknowledged that he did not expect to see a carbon tax enacted while President Bush remains in office. "The next couple of years are about getting the debate out in the open and getting the sides lined up," Anderson stated, adding, "Personally, I feel the time has come to act—to take steps as a nation to reduce the carbon intensity of our economy [and] actions must be mandatory, economy-wide and federal in scope." David Mildenberg, Duke CEO to put energy into environment, Charlotte Bus. J., Apr. 7, 2005.

c.   REGULATION BY THE STATES

A few states, such as Minnesota, have regulated CO_2 as a pollutant. In 1998, a Minnesota court upheld a utility commission rule that treats CO_2 as a pollutant in choosing among potential power plant types.

In the Matter of the Quantification of Environmental Costs Pursuant to Laws of Minnesota 1993, Chapter 356, Section 3

578 N.W.2d 794 (Minn. Ct. App. 1998).

■ RANDALL, J. The Minnesota Legislature directed the Minnesota Public Utilities Commission (the commission) to determine environmental cost values for each method of electricity generation and required utilities to use those values in proceedings before the commission. The commission set interim environmental cost values for five air pollutants on March 1, 1994, including carbon dioxide (CO_2). The commission also initiated a contested case proceeding to set final environmental cost values and appointed an administrative law judge ("ALJ") to preside over the proceedings. On January 3, 1997, the commission set final values for six air pollutants. The commission established four separate geographic ranges to more accurately represent environmental costs corresponding to pollutants emitted in ur-ban, metropolitan fringe, rural areas, and areas "within 200 miles of the Minnesota border." Several parties objected to the commission's decision concerning the value set for CO_2 and requested reconsideration. Upon reconsideration, the commission removed the cost value for CO_2 in the 200 mile range, but did not change the values for other pollutants in that range. The relators filed a certiorari appeal alleging that the commission's decision to set values for CO_2 was improper. Other parties filed notices of review on separate issues. We affirm.

The relators, Lignite Energy Council (LEC), and the Environmental Coalition (the "EC") assert challenges to the commission's order setting environmental cost values for CO_2. The relators argue that (1) the commission should not be entitled to great deference because the commission was acting outside of its realm of expertise; (2) the commission decision to set values for CO_2 was not supported by substantial evidence and/or its decision was arbitrary and capricious because the testimony of Dr. Ciborowski, an expert witness, (and the bases for his testimony) was grounded in incomplete data, speculation, conjecture, and uncertainty; and (3) there is no substantial evidence that CO_2 causes or contributes to serious environmental damage. We address each contention in turn.

Was the commission acting within its realm of expertise? The relators argue that no special deference is due to the commission because it was not acting within its realm of expertise in evaluating global economic conditions, the scientific properties and analysis of CO_2, and the effects of CO_2 on the environment. We disagree. Here, the legislature assigned the task of determining environmental cost values to the administrative agency it presumably thought would be most appropriate to take on this responsibility. There is no challenge that the legislature made an improper delegation of authority to the agency, and it is fundamental that the courts cannot take on the functions of administrative agencies without violating the separation of powers. Thus, this court will not substitute its judgment for the commission's in such a situation.

Was the commission's decision concerning the CO_2 values proper? There is considerable debate as to which standard of review applies. Here, the ALJ heard evidence in the form of oral and written testimony, weighed the evidence on a preponderance of the evidence standard, and made findings of fact concerning environmental cost values. Further, the commission chose to employ a contested case procedure. Given these circumstances, the commission acted in a quasi-judicial capacity in determining facts and in resolving the rights of the parties, and as such, its decision is subject to the substantial evidence test.

The relators argue that the speculative nature of the evidence (specifically Dr. Ciborowski's testimony) on which the commission relied in setting the CO_2 values shows that commission's decision is not supported by the record. We disagree. Here, the record shows that Dr. Ciborowski's testimony and recommendations, as relators contend, are based on some assumptions, speculations, and uncertainties in data. But the ALJ conducted a careful review of (1) Intergovernmental Panel on Climate Change (IPCC) research and the peer review process; (2) research on CO_2 values by other scientific review panels; (3) the uncertainties in the scientific reports and how the uncertainties are acknowledged in the scientific community; (4) Dr. Ciborowski's testimony and the basis for his testimony; (5) damage estimates; (6) discount rates; (7); the Minnesota Pollution Control Agency's and the Attorney General's recommended values; and (8) several parties' recommendations that a zero value be used. The ALJ determined that some testimony and suggestions were supported by the evidence and others were not, and explained the bases for his determinations.

Further, the ALJ noted that the parties had a sufficient opportunity for thorough cross-examination in his determination that Dr. Ciborowski was qualified to give an expert opinion. This determination appears to be within the ALJ's broad discretion.

Furthermore, in its order, the commission explained its decision to set the values on the following factors (1) the IPCC report was the most accurate and useful source available; (2) some expert testimony and suggested ranges were more strongly supported by the evidence than others; (3) Dr. Ciborowski's approach was supported by the evidence; (4) the experiences of New York in setting environmental costs; and (5) the uncertainties inherent in the research would be taken into account by using a lower estimate of global damage and a higher damage discount rate. The commission also argues that it believed it should attempt to do what was practicable, given the uncertainties, instead of doing nothing as LEC's argument implies. Under these circumstances, the commission based its decision on sufficient evidence in the record (primarily the IPCC report and Dr. Ciborowski's testimony and recommendations) and has given an adequate and reasonable explanation of its decision.

Was the commission's decision that CO_2 negatively affects the environment supported by the evidence? Given the above analysis, the commission properly relied on Dr. Ciborowski's expert testimony and the IPCC report. Here, the ALJ and commission made findings of fact and adequately explained the basis underlying the determinations. Additionally, the commission acted pursuant to a valid delegation of authority from the legislature in an area in which the courts are not accustomed to dealing. Accordingly, we conclude that the commission's determination that CO_2 negatively affects the environment was proper.

While we acknowledge the concerns about the uncertain and speculative nature of the available data, we are disinclined to prohibit the state from directing its instrumentalities to engage in environmentally-conscious planning strategies. Hopefully, the administrative process ensures the use of the best information available and takes precautions to guard against the dangers surrounding the use of such data. Here, the process adequately explained its decisions. . . .

Affirmed and motion granted.■

NOTES AND COMMENTS

1. In the 1990s, a number of states used a procedure similar to Minnesota's in which the decision to build a particular type of electric generating facility must take into consideration the environmental externalities of the

various alternative technologies. After the advent of competition in the electric utility industry, this type of process was revamped. *See* Chapter 13.

2. The coal industry presented expert testimony by a number of the prominent skeptics about climate change in the administrative proceeding that led up to this Minnesota litigation, and all of the witnesses were subject to extensive cross-examination. Some of this testimony is discussed critically in Gelbspan, *supra,* at 39–61.

* * *

Other states and localities have taken action to reduce GHG emissions. In 2001, Massachusetts issued a rule capping total CO_2 emissions from the six highest-emitting power plants in the state. Wisconsin, Oregon, and New Hampshire have adopted comparable rules requiring reductions or offsets of CO_2 emissions from power plants. San Francisco's "climate action plan" of 2004 seeks to slash annual CO_2 emissions by 2.5 million tons by 2012, a 20 percent cut below 1990 emissions. In May 2005, a coalition of 131 mayors from around the U.S. pledged their cities would meet Kyoto Protocol reduction targets for GHG emissions. *See* Eli Sanders, Rebuffing Bush, 132 Mayors Embrace Kyoto Rules, N.Y. Times, May 14, 2005, at A9.

A group of nine Northeastern states have formed the "Regional Greenhouse Gas Initiative," working toward developing a cap-and-trade system for CO_2 emissions from power plants, with plans to expand it later to cover other CO_2 emitters. Freedman and Stempeck, *supra.* This regional program could serve as a model for a nationwide system, as has happened before in air pollution regulation. *See* Kyle W. Danish, Linking a U.S. Federal Climate Program With International and Sub–Federal Climate Programs, *in* Aspen Institute, *supra* (exploring implementation issues associated with expanding a regional program to the national level). New Jersey has proposed regulations to classify CO_2 as an "air contaminant," which would make it subject to the full range of regulatory requirements of the state's air pollution control law. John Spinello et al., The Changing Tides of Regulating Greenhouse Gases, New Jersey's Proposed Carbon Dioxide Regulation May Have Far–Reaching Implications For Corporations, 179 N.J.L.J. 604 (Feb. 7, 2005).

In 2004, eight states and New York City launched an unprecedented civil action against five of America's largest power companies, using theories of "public nuisance" laws to attempt to force reductions of GHG emissions from the utilities' power plants. *Connecticut v. Am. Elec. Power Co.,* No. 04–CV–05669, 2004 WL 1685122 (S.D.N.Y. July 21, 2004). David Doniger, policy director for the Natural Resources Defense Council (which filed a parallel suit) stated that, "We don't want a single penny [and] [a]ll we ask is that these companies begin curbing their carbon dioxide emissions." Greenhouse polluters face the law: top cops bring the fight against global warming to a new battleground, OnEarth, Sept. 22, 2004. The chief counsel for Cinergy, one of the defendants, called the suit a "publicity stunt." Utilities Ask Judge To Dismiss State Climate Change Lawsuit, Clean Air Rep., Oct. 7, 2004.

For updates on these and other state and local activities relating to reductions in GHG emissions, *see* http://www.pewclimate.org/what_s_being_done/in_the_states/.

d. REDUCING EMISSIONS THROUGH ENERGY CONSERVATION

Because of the unlikelihood that Americans would opt for sharp reductions in fossil fuel usage, attention has been focused on efforts to reduce emissions in less spectacular fashion through energy conservation and the sequestration of greenhouse gases. An early study by the National Academy of Sciences recommended that the best strategy for addressing climate change, given the uncertainties that surround it, is simply to generate, distribute, and use energy as efficiently and cleanly as possible. National Academy of Sciences, Policy Implications of Greenhouse Warming (1991). Energy efficiency is a "tie-in strategy" because climatic change is only one of several good reasons to consider a policy of energy efficiency. What would be wasted by an energy efficiency strategy if serious global warming never materialized?

A number of measures and programs underway in the industrial, buildings (residential and commercial) and electric utility sectors of the economy are featured in Chapter 13's discussion of energy conservation. An industrial conservation program tailored to GHG reductions is the EPA's "Climate Leaders" initiative, a voluntary-based emissions reduction program encouraging individual companies to develop long-term, comprehensive climate change strategies. Under this program, partners set corporate-wide GHG reduction goals and inventory their emissions to measure progress. More than 50 major companies are now participating, including General Motors, Alcoa, BP, Pfizer, Staples, International Paper, IBM, Miller Brewing, Eastman Kodak, and Target. The program reported in 2004 that five companies—DuPont, Alcan Inc., BT Group PLC, IBM and Norske Canada—had each been able to lower their GHG emissions by at least 60 percent and had saved a combined $5.5 billion through improved energy efficiency, fuel switching and reduced waste output. *See* http://www.epa.gov/climateleaders/. The Climate Leaders program has encountered some criticism, notably for being slow to reconcile the multiple different reporting systems of the various partner companies. Brian Stempeck, EPA Voluntary Emission Program's Progress Still a Mystery, Greenwire, Jan. 27, 2005.

Another possibility mentioned increasingly more in recent years is reconsidering the licensing and operation of new nuclear power plants, which emit no CO_2 during actual plant operation. Also, because nuclear power plants are invariably large baseload facilities, even a fairly small switch to nuclear (such as improving the availability of existing nuclear plants) can lead to a sizable reduction in fossil fuel consumption. EIA, *supra*. However, is there a greater risk from enormous volumes of low-activity waste (CO_2) or small volumes of high-activity waste (fission products)? *See* Chapter 14.

Other technologies may also hold promise for the generation of electricity without GHG emissions. In 2003, President Bush announced that the United States would sponsor, with international and private-sector partners, a $1 billion, 10–year demonstration project to create the world's first coal-based, zero-emissions electricity and hydrogen power plant. This initiative is part of an international Carbon Sequestration Leadership Forum, chaired by the Secretary of Energy, to work cooperatively on research, development and deployment of carbon sequestration technologies in the next decade (*see* the discussion of sequestration below). For decades, scientists have attempted to harness fusion energy, the same form of energy that powers the sun, without success. In 2003, President Bush committed the United States to participate in a $5 billion fusion research project, and if successful, this project would advance progress toward producing clean, renewable, commercially available fusion energy by the middle of the century. Participating countries include the United Kingdom, Russia, Japan, China, and Canada.

* * *

The transportation sector of the economy offers considerable promise for GHG reductions, as 26% of GHGs emitted in this country come from motor vehicles. EIA and EPA, *supra.* The Transportation Research Board has identified four basic types of strategies for reducing motor vehicle GHG emissions: (1) reducing vehicle emissions directly; (2) reducing the demand for transportation; (3) increasing vehicle fuel economy standards; and (4) other measures (for example, switching to alternative fuels for transportation). Transportation Research Board, Toward a Sustainable Future (1997).

i.   *Reducing Motor Vehicle GHG Emissions*

In early 2002, California passed the first law in the nation to regulate CO_2 emissions by vehicles. Two years later, the California Air Resources Board (CARB) adopted rules that require reduced emissions of CO_2 for new passenger cars, SUVs and pickup trucks sold in California starting in model year 2009. *See* http://www.arb.ca.gov/regact/grnhsgas/grnhsgas.htm. Under the rules, slated to take effect in 2006, the average reduction of greenhouse gases from new California cars and light trucks will be about 22 percent in 2012 and about 30 percent in 2016, compared to today's vehicles. *Id.* The additional cost per vehicle that would be necessary to meet these rules is a point of dispute. The state estimates it at around $1000 when the rules are fully implemented in 2016, while the auto industry puts it at about $3000. *See* Danny Hakim, Schwarzenegger Vows to Defend Emissions Law, N.Y. Times, Dec. 8, 2004, at C1. California auto dealers and auto manufacturers have challenged the rules in both state and federal courts. The plaintiffs in *Central Valley Chrysler–Jeep Inc. v. Witherspoon* (the federal lawsuit) argue the state isn't regulating pollution, which it may do, but setting fuel economy standards, which the federal Clean Air Act preempts. *Compare* Automakers and Dealers Cite Federal Law, Marketplace Principles in Challenging Carbon Dioxide Law, http://www.autoalliance.org/archives/000163.html (auto industry position) with Big Auto Fights California's

Landmark Global Warming Law, http://www.nrdc.org/globalWarming/fau-to.asp (opposing view). Ann E. Carlson, Federalism, Preemption and Green-house Gas Emissions, 37 U.C. Davis L. Rev. 281 (2003), discusses the legal issues raised by the California rule.

Several Northeastern states and states in the Pacific Northwest may adopt California's rules, although these states are undoubtedly awaiting the results of the California lawsuit before taking any action. Meanwhile, in Canada, the federal government and major automakers Ford, General Motors and DaimlerChrysler reached an agreement in 2005 under which the companies would voluntarily reduce the GHG emissions of their vehicles by 5.3 million metric tons by the end of 2010. Ian Austen, Canada and Automakers Agree to Emissions Reductions, N.Y. Times, Apr. 6, 2005, at C5. The irony of this action did not go unnoticed in California. Jason Mark of the Union of Concerned Scientists stated, "The same automakers who are suing California over its clean car standards are agreeing to essentially the same level of reductions in Canada." Id. The automobile companies have responded that Canada's requirements are less stringent than the ones they would be required to meet in California.

ii.   Reducing Travel Demand

Americans' love affair with the automobile is well documented. Motor vehicle fuel use (and, as a result, GHG emissions) has increased considerably since 1970. See U.S. Department of Transportation, Bureau of Transportation Statistics, http://www.transtats.bts.gov/. This is in large part due to increases in car ownership and miles traveled. Between 1970 and 1990, the number of cars on the road increased by more than 75 percent to 189 million while population increased only 23 percent during the same period. Miles traveled increased substantially as well. Id.

Over the past several decades, transportation planners have recognized that very little travel is done for pleasure. Americans travel for work, family business, and recreation, and existing settlement patterns, economic activity, and available roads and other forms of transportation (such as mass transit) all play a part in determining how much we use our cars. Americans have a strong preference for driving in their cars and small trucks over taking mass transit, and tend to drive alone. In 2002, seventy-seven percent of commutes to work in America were made in an automobile occupied by the driver alone. Only ten percent of American commuters carpooled to work, and five percent took public transportation.

Controlling travel demand, as measured by the number of vehicle miles traveled (VMT), would have a substantial effect on reducing GHG emissions. OTA, supra, at 154–55. Strategies developed by transportation planners to reduce VMT (collectively known as transportation control measures, or TCM) include improving mass transit, encouraging employer ridesharing and mass transit incentives, managing urban parking through higher fees or eliminating free parking and other subsidies, encouraging bicycling (through such means as dedicated lanes), restricting auto use (through schemes such as London's fee-based scheme for managing congestion in central London), and setting aside high-occupancy vehicle (HOV) lanes. TCM programs have to be tailored to individual areas, and their popularity varies widely as a result. *See* Chapter 15.

Land use patterns also play a role in determining how people will use their cars. People who live close to their workplace might walk, ride a bike, or take public transit, and the "New Urbanism" school of architecture has capitalized on this to recommend more compact urban design. However, Americans have generally resisted living in compact spaces, opting for the "sprawl" so familiar across the landscape. The importance of lifestyle choices and land use patterns in transportation planning is discussed further in Chapter 15.

iii. Increasing Fuel Economy Standards

The new car fuel economy standards, known as corporate average fuel economy ("CAFE") standards, have doubled since their inception in the mid–1970s. Between 1975 and 1984, through a variety of fuel efficiency improvements (not all of which are attributable to the CAFE standards), fuel efficiency of cars sold in the U.S. increased by sixty-two percent without a reduction in vehicle performance. *See* Joel Ban, NEPA Review of CAFE: An Opportunity Lost, 23 Temp. Envtl. L. & Tech. J. 121, 137 (2004). However, motor vehicle fuel use continues to rise. One reason for this is that the added weight of popular SUVs (which are held to the less stringent light truck CAFE standard) and trucks has more than offset increased vehicle efficiency. Also, sales of heavier vehicles continue to outpace those of lighter, more efficient vehicles (although the first few months of 2005 saw a slight reversal of this trend); in 2001 light duty trucks outsold cars for the first time ever.

Another reason is that the standards themselves have not increased much in the past two decades. The U.S. Senate rejected a proposal in 2002 that would have required automobile manufacturers to produce fleets averaging thirty-six miles per gallon ("MPG"). Some proposals for more rigorous fuel economy standards would tailor the program more closely to reductions in GHG emissions, for example by converting existing standards into standards based on CO_2 equivalent emissions, or even transforming their nature altogether. In 2004, participants in a Climate Change Policy Dialogue sponsored by the Aspen Institute and Pew Center on Global Climate Change pondered the idea of a cap-and-trade emissions trading system applying to the transportation sector. Eileen Claussen and Robert W. Fri, A Climate Policy Framework: Balancing Policy and Politics, in Aspen Institute, *supra*. The participants discussed whether a cap would apply to fuel suppliers, vehicle manufacturers, or both, concluding that a dual approach "would not only signal a future (and increasing) carbon constraint on fuel but also a program to promote vehicle efficiency and thus provide consumers with the means to adapt."

Participants in the Dialogue acknowledged that "political and practical obstacles exist to curbing the growth in [vehicle] emissions." *Id.* A cap-and-trade system for vehicle manufacturers would almost certainly encounter as much or more resistance as proposals to increase fuel economy standards. For this and other reasons, some studies have explored a "hybrid" approach in which existing fuel economy standards could be maintained or upgraded at the same time that economic forms of GHG control (tax or trading) are implemented. *See* U.S. Congressional Budget Office, Reducing Gasoline Consumption: Three Policy Options 17 (2002).

For further discussion of CAFE standards, *see* Chapter 15.

iv. *Other Fuel Economy Measures*

New vehicle technologies such as the deployment of hybrid vehicles (vehicles with both gasoline and electric power plants) and vehicles powered by fuel cells or directly by hydrogen may well play a major role in reducing GHG emissions in the U.S.

In the 1990s, many felt electric vehicles held the most promise for reducing GHG emissions in the near term. The 1991 report of the U.S. Office of Technology Assessment ("OTA") on reducing GHG emissions evaluated the potential of only two alternatives to gasoline in its "Tough" scenario (projection yielding the most reductions by 2015): methanol and electricity. U.S. Office of Technology Assessment, Changing By Degrees: Steps To Reduce Greenhouse Gases (1991). While automakers offered them in the 1990s, electric vehicles never really took off in the U.S., primarily due to their limited range. General Motors only leased 800 of its all-electric EV1 between 1996 and 2004. The EV1 was hailed at the time of its unveiling as a state-of-the-art vehicle, but its range was only 55 to 95 miles on a full charge, making it impractical for most consumers. *See* EV1: Lessons Learned, http://www.gm.com. In addition, if the electricity used in an electric vehicle was generated from fossil fuels, GHG emissions would not necessarily be reduced. OTA, *supra*.

Another possibility is reducing GHG emissions through the use of internal combustion engine vehicles fueled by a source other than gasoline, such as ethanol, compressed natural gas (CNG), biodiesel (*see* Chapter 15), or hydrogen. In 1991, the OTA categorized hydrogen as the "least technologically advanced" of any of the options under consideration. OTA, *supra*. However, it has attracted considerably more attention since then. In his 2003 State of the Union Address, President Bush announced a $1.2 billion Hydrogen Fuel Initiative aimed at developing the technology needed for commercially viable hydrogen-powered fuel cells. Through partnerships with the private sector, this program seeks to develop hydrogen, fuel cell, and infrastructure technologies needed to make it practical and cost-effective for large numbers of Americans to choose to use fuel cell vehicles by 2020. *See* U.S. Department of Energy, Hydrogen, Fuel Cells, and Infrastructure Technologies Program, http://www.eere.energy.gov/hydrogenandfuelcells/presidents_initiative.html.

Hydrogen has many potential advantages in a GHG reductions scenario. It has the highest energy content per unit of weight of any known fuel, and when burned in an engine, it produces effectively zero emissions. If it is used to power a fuel cell (a device in which fuel and oxygen are combined to produce chemical energy converted directly into electrical energy, in a manner analogous to living cells), its only by-product is pure water. A fuel cell is far more efficient than internal combustion or steam engines, as the latter involve an intermediate mechanical step and high heat loss. As with electricity, hydrogen is a secondary energy resource, meaning that it must be made from another fuel. Because it can be produced from a wide variety of energy resources, including fossil fuels, nuclear power, and renewable resources, hydrogen is viewed by many as a means to allow the United States to wean itself from dependence on foreign oil. Again, as with electricity, the source of the hydrogen is important in calculating eventual GHG reductions, because using fossil fuels to make it would offset hydrogen's environmental benefits. Hydrogen and fuel cell vehicles are discussed further in Chapter 15.

Additional GHG emissions reductions might be achieved by using fuel cells in generating electricity for residential or commercial uses. Stationary fuel cells could be one of several options used to supply the power for "distributed generation" (DG) installations. Regulatory changes that would be necessary to encourage DG through the use of fuel cells are discussed in Andrew R. Thomas et al., Regulation of Power Generated By Stationary Fuel Cells in the United States, 18 Tul. Envtl. L.J. 141 (2004). *See* Chapter 13.

An interim solution to reduce GHG emissions has achieved some prominence in recent years: the increased use of gasoline hybrid-electric vehicles, which are becoming more widely available to consumers today. A hybrid car is one that has both gasoline and electrical power plants. *See* Chapter 15.

e. OTHER MEANS OF GHG REDUCTION

i. *Sequestration*

One appealing but questionable potential response to greenhouse gas buildup that is undergoing intense scientific study is "carbon sequestration" through the planting of more forests. *See* Robert N. Stavis and Kenneth H. Richards, The Cost of U.S. Forest-based Carbon Sequestration (Pew Center on Global Climate Change, 2005). Forests, and to a lesser extent other forms of plant life, are known to absorb CO_2 in the process of photosynthesis. Some studies suggest that the total impact of forests is significant while other studies view it as relatively minor. Studies suggest that in the 1990s the forests sequestered between 1 and 2 billion tons of carbon annually, but in the 1980s very little sequestration took place, suggesting that sequestration is highly variable. Carbon sinks large but unreliable, says science, Electricity Daily, March 31, 2000. Another potential problem, according to the Pew Center report, is that forest sequestration would take up large land areas and might cost as much or more than other mitigation options. *See* Brian Stempeck, Carbon storage would require vast forest tracts, report says, Greenwire, Jan. 19, 2005.

A number of large multinational corporations have instituted sequestration forestry projects in the hopes that they will be able to offset the benefits from such projects against their own CO_2 emissions or use them in some future emissions trading program. Vanessa Houlder, Emissions Trading: Salvation or Hot Air, Financial Times, Apr. 15, 1999. However, many biologists have expressed concern about whether the potential replacement of the natural landscape with plantation forests may lead to a loss of biodiversity or other unforeseen ecological effects. Joy E. Hecht and Brett Orlando, Can the Kyoto Protocol Support Biodiversity Conservation?, 28 Envt'l L. Rptr. 10508 (1998).

Another way of preventing CO_2 from reaching the atmosphere is to sequester it underground or in the oceans. CO_2 is sometimes used in the secondary recovery of oil fields. The gas is pumped into oil-bearing formations in order to increase the amount of oil that can be recovered (*see* Chapter 6). More CO_2 could be disposed of if it were injected into other sealed aquifers independent of oil production needs. Since 1996, the Norwegian oil company Statoil has been piping a million tons of CO_2 per year into a salt dome under the North Sea. Karen Schmidt, A Way to Make CO_2 Go Away: Deep–Six It, 281 Science 505 (July 24, 1998). In 2004, officials from the U.S. Department of Energy and EPA began work to figure out how deep geologic formations might be used for sequestration of CO_2. Brian Stempeck, DOE, EPA consider regulations for underground CO_2 storage efforts, Greenwire, Nov. 1, 2004.

Some scientists have suggested adding iron to the oceans to help plankton absorb more CO_2, but there is likely to be strong opposition to the idea because of concern about unforeseen chemical and biological consequences. Vanessa Houlder, Carbon Sequestration: Not Yet Out of the Woods, Financial Times, Apr. 15, 1999. Other experiments designed to pipe the gas into deep ocean waters are also being explored. Peter G. Brewer *et al.*, Direct Experiments on the Ocean Disposal of Fossil Fuel O_2, 284 Science 943 (May 7, 1999).

In June 2003, the inaugural Carbon Sequestration Forum meeting was held in Virginia, and attended by representatives of Australia, Brazil, Canada, China, Colombia, India, Italy, Japan, Mexico, Norway, Russian Federation, the United Kingdom, and the European Commission. These global partners signed the first international charter setting the framework for international cooperation in research and development. *See* http://www.fe.doe.gov/programs/powersystems/futuregen/.

ii.   Geoengineering

Could modern engineering technology counteract the effect of greenhouse gases by reconstituting the atmosphere? Relatively little serious attention has been paid to a variety of ideas to counteract the greenhouse effect by the physical emission into the atmosphere of substances that would have the effect of blocking sunlight, thus counteracting the warming influence of the greenhouse effect.

iii.   Methane Control

One of the simplest ways to cut GHG emissions is to encourage the use of natural gas in the generation of electricity and discourage the use of coal, which emits twice as much CO_2 per unit of energy produced as does natural gas. Switching from coal to natural gas lowers carbon dioxide emissions because of the lower carbon content of natural gas relative to other fossil fuels. For example, switching from bituminous coal to natural gas can reduce carbon dioxide emissions per unit of energy consumed by approximately 43 percent. EIA, *supra*. However, it will be important to ensure that uncontrolled release of methane, itself a powerful greenhouse gas, is adequately controlled.

Methane is ordinarily burned rather than emitted into the atmosphere. While modern methods of using natural gas can reduce unintentional methane emissions, the cumulative effect of the emissions can be substantial. And the slight leakage of natural gas that typically accompanies every stage of its use from extraction to combustion also adds substantial amounts of methane to the atmosphere, as do the operation of hog farms and cattle feedlots. Dr. James Hansen of the Goddard Center has suggested that we could more effectively and quickly reduce methane emissions than those of other greenhouse gases. If sources of methane and tropospheric ozone were reduced, along with a reduction in particles of black carbon and modest carbon dioxide gas emissions, climate change could eventually be stabilized. James Hansen, 97 Proc. Nat'l Acad. of Sciences 9875, Sept. 29, 2000.

Methane is released in much smaller quantities into the atmosphere than CO_2. EIA, *supra*. However, it is 23 times more potent than CO_2 when it comes to trapping heat in the atmosphere. *Id*. In 2004, together with the U.K., Japan, Brazil, China and nine other countries, the EPA embarked on a "Methane to Markets" Partnership, aiming to capture methane emissions from landfills, coal mines and other sources. The EPA says this program will aim to reduce methane emissions by 50 million metric tons per year by 2015, the equivalent of removing 33 million cars from the nation's roadways. Administrator Mike Leavitt called methane "the only greenhouse gas you can reduce at a huge profit," because it is the key component of natural gas. Brian Stempeck, U.S. officials cast doubt on post–2012 global warming talks, Greenwire, Nov. 17, 2004.

2.   INTERNATIONAL GHG REDUCTION STRATEGIES

When the scientific community began to reach a consensus about the causes of climate change, the major nations of the world began to react. Could international law provide a vehicle by which nations could agree upon a coordinated approach to the climate change issue? The first steps in getting them together to formulate a consensus on the issue were taken by various United Nations organizations.

a.   THE INTERNATIONAL POLITICS OF CLIMATE CHANGE

At the 1992 United Nations Conference on Environment and Development, the world's industrial leaders and developing nations pledged to reduce greenhouse gases emissions. However, implementation of the goal to reduce emissions to 1990 levels by the year 2000 voluntarily proved ineffective.

The following book review summarizes some of the political issues that made diplomatic negotiation so difficult.

Alan E. Boyle, Book Review: Negotiating Climate Change: The Inside Story of the Rio Convention

(Irving M. Mintzer and J. Amber Leonard, eds., Cambridge University Press 1994).
89 Amer. J. Int'l L. 864 (1995).

The development of a body of international law dealing with the environment is one of the more remarkable features of international law in the past twenty-five years. Starting almost from nothing, it is today an increasingly large and complex subject; its global dimensions are apparent in the instruments of the 1992 UN Conference on Environment and Development (UNCED) in Rio de Janeiro, and it has implications at various levels for North–South relations, international trade, economic development and human rights.

One of the reasons for the importance of the Rio Conference instruments, including the Climate Change Convention, is that together they set out a framework of global environmental responsibilities, distinct from earlier concerns with merely regional or transboundary responsibilities. The nature of these global environmental responsibilities is subtle and not easily expressed in terms of rights and obligations. They involve notions of sustainability and intergenerational equity; a recognition of the limitations of science and prediction, in the form of a precautionary approach to the control of potential global risks; and the institutionalization of a North–South relationship, expressed in the principle of "common but differentiated responsibility." This principle is a recognition of the reality that the contributions of developed and developing states to global environmental problems are historically different, and that their economic and technical capacity to tackle these problems also varies widely.

The Climate Change Convention, whose negotiation is the subject of this book, exemplifies these elements of global environmental responsibility. Although at one level it is correct to see the Convention as part of a lawmaking process, comparable to others that constitute most of contemporary international environmental law, the Convention is arguably much more significant for what it says about international political and economic relations than for its international law. This is most obvious in (1) its formulation of the common but differentiated responsibilities of developed and developing states; (2) the limited commitments made by developing states; and (3) the provision for access to funding and technology on which these commitments are expressly conditional. An understanding of the Convention thus requires, rather more than a lawyer's skills of interpretation, an appreciation of its political, scientific and economic context and of the dynamics of the negotiation process....

Jean Ripert of France, Chair of the Intergovernmental Negotiating Committee, poses at the outset the still-unanswered question whether the universality of support for a Convention concluded after very difficult negotiations reflects a real balance of interests or merely "a legal void created by agreement to a text of no significance." The committee's Vice–Chair, Ahmed Djoghlaf, while emphasizing the important role played by developing states, remarks also on their inability to reach coordinated positions. Divisions of policy between oil producers like Saudi Arabia and the members of the Association of Small Island States were clearly apparent in the negotiations.

The developed states found it no easier to coordinate their positions. Speaking for India, Chandrashekhar Dasgupta gives a good account of how these various differences were overcome, partly because of the high political priority attached to agreeing to a text for UNCED, and partly because of the negotiating process, with its use of consensus procedures, small working groups and activist Chairs (reminiscent of the UNCLOS negotiations). This view is echoed by Bo Kjellen from Sweden, who, like others, points to the many and complex unresolved issues, which will require continuing negotiation. Goldenberg, from Brazil, points out the most important omission of all—"without 'targets and timetables' the implementation of the Convention will depend on the goodwill of OECD countries." That so much depends on good will is a measure of the success of the United States in resisting any concrete commitments; but, as Nitze observes, this will be a continuing source of tension in U.S. foreign policy. Precisely because the lack of concrete commitments is the largest part of the problem, the United States must also be the largest part of the solution if the Convention is to stand any chance of success.

Thus, the prospects for the Convention, which several authors address in the latter part of the book, remain clouded and contingent on maintaining a coalition of interests that is at the same time capable of moving things forward. The process is one of "equitable dialogue" among diverse interests, but the problem is one of avoiding an outcome similar to that of UNCLOS III, without abandoning the goal of universality and common commitments. What this book does make clear about the Climate Change Convention is that, as with the French Revolution, any assessment of its long-term significance is still very premature.■

NOTES AND COMMENTS

1. At the present time, the United States and European countries are the largest generators of GHG emissions. However, developing countries are increasing their energy consumption as they industrialize. As a result, countries in Asia, including India and China, have been increasing their

share of GHG emissions to a very significant extent. Mark Clayton, New coal plants "bury" Kyoto, Christian Sci. Monitor, Dec. 23, 2004 (noting that China and India have 775 coal-fired power plants planned, with expected CO_2 emissions exceeding the reductions achieved from Kyoto); *see also* Greenhouse Gas Emissions by Source, Earth Trends, World Resources Institute. http://earthtrends.wri.org; Note, The Kyoto Protocol and China: Global Warming's Sleeping Giant, 11 Geo. Int'l Envtl. L. Rev. 401 (1999). These countries are largely unwilling to give up cheap resources of fossil fuel in exchange for nuclear or renewable technologies. However, in 2004, the Chinese government imposed fuel economy standards on new cars, sport utility vehicles and vans for the first time. Keith Bradsher, China Tries to Reduce Thirst for Gas: Government Imposes Strict Fuel–Economy Standards, Int'l Herald Tribune, Sept. 23, 2004.

The unwillingness of developing countries to make commitments to stem future GHG emissions has been a major stumbling block to meaningful participation by the United States government in programs to reduce emissions. *See* Paul G. Harris, Common but Differentiated Responsibility: the Kyoto Protocol and United States Policy, 7 N.Y.U. Envtl. L.J. 27, 30–31 (1999).

Is the developing countries' argument—that the industrial nations caused the problem and must remedy it—a persuasive one? For the view that equity requires that developing countries have a right to increase greenhouse gas emissions as a corollary of their right to economic development, *see* Christine Batruch, "Hot Air" as Precedent for Developing Countries: Equity Considerations, 17 UCLA J. Envtl. L. and Pol'y 45 (1998–1999).

* * *

The "Rio Plus 5," a special session of the U.N. General Assembly five years after the Rio Conference, ended without substantive commitments to GHG reductions. This led to the third conference of the parties (COP) to the U.N. Framework Convention on Climate Change ("FCCC"), held in Kyoto, Japan in December 1997, and the adoption of the "Kyoto Protocol."

ABA Section of Natural Resources, Energy and Environmental Law

Special Committee on Climate Change and Sustainable Development.
1997 Annual Report.

On December 11, 1997, in Kyoto Japan, the Conference of Parties to the UN Framework Convention on Climate Change (FCCC) unanimously adopted the "Kyoto Protocol to the United Nations Framework Convention on Climate Change" (Kyoto Protocol). The FCCC concluded nearly two years of international negotiations involving various FCCC subsidiary bodies and resulted in an international agreement calling for binding obligations on Annex I Parties (developed countries) to reduce their greenhouse gas emissions at least five percent below 1990 levels by 2008–2012.

The U.S. will have, during the first commitment period of 2008–2012, binding obligations to reduce its 1) carbon dioxide, methane and nitrous oxide emissions seven percent below 1990 levels and 2) hydrofluorocarbon, perfluorocarbon and sulfur hexafluoride emissions seven percent below 1990 or 1995 levels. The same base years or base periods apply to all Annex I Parties except for countries with economies in transition (EITs), which are allowed some flexibility in the selection of a base year or base period. The "assigned amounts" (targets) are set forth in Annex B to protocol and include the following:

Iceland	110%
Australia	108%
Norway	101%
Russia, Ukraine, New Zealand	100%
Croatia	95%
Japan, Canada, Poland, Hungary	94%
U.S.	93%
European Union (EU) collectively, Switzerland, other EITs	92%

Targets and timetables and binding obligations. Known as Quantified Emission Limitations and Reduction Objectives (QELROs), the binding commitments and targets and timetables for Annex I parties are set forth in Article 3 and Annexes A and B. The key compromise was the EU as a bloc agreeing to a collective eight percent reduction under its so-called "bubble" (*see* Article 4 and discussion in I.A.2, *infra*), with the U.S. agreeing to a seven percent reduction level and Japan agreeing to a six percent reduction level. Thus, the commitments are politically differentiated but were not determined by any formulaic means.

Critical components of the agreement on targets and timetables were agreements on coverage of gases—the so-called "basket" approach—and "sinks," or forestry-based offsets. Coverage of all six gases was crucial to the U.S. The option of being able to elect a different baseline for the second set of gases was important to Japan and other countries. No clear consensus could be reached on sinks, so the Parties agreed to limit removals by sinks to afforestation, reforestation and deforestation since 1990, subject to later decisions by the conference, taking into account work by the Intergovernmental Panel on Climate Change. *See* Articles 3.3, 3.4 and 3.7.

"Banking" of excess reductions from the first commitment period to meet obligations in a subsequent commitment period was allowed, but "borrowing" of reductions from a subsequent commitment period to meet obligations in the first commitment period was not. *See* Article 3.13.

Policies and measures, and the EU bubble. Under Article 4, the EU received its bubble, under which it collectively will be responsible for an eight percent reduction but will also have the flexibility to assign different targets to individual Parties. Thus, some EU countries will be able to increase their emissions, while others (such as the United Kingdom and Germany) will bear a larger share of reductions. Failure by the EU to meet the collective eight percent target will mean that each Party shall be responsible for meeting its own level of emissions set out in the EU agreement. *See* Article 4.5. However, the EU was only able to obtain a weakened version of policies and measures ("PAMs") in Article 2. While there is still mandatory language in Article 2, implementation or "elaboration" of such PAMs appears to be discretionary in accordance with individual Parties' national circumstances.

Emissions trading and commitments for developing countries. These two issues threatened to crater the negotiations in the early hours of December 11. Ultimately, the U.S. and other Annex I Parties insisted on emissions trading, and the non-Annex I Parties (developing countries) acceded in order to avoid total collapse of the negotiations. Later, however, although many Annex I Parties and some non-Annex I Parties sought to include a U.S.-sponsored provision so that advanced developing countries could "opt in" to Annex I commitments, the U.S. acceded to developing countries' insistence that the protocol exclude binding obligations for developing countries, the opt-in provision, and even establishment of a process for developing such commitments for developing nations.

Emissions trading, joint implementation and the Clean Development Mechanism. Because no clear consensus could be forged on many critical issues, numerous framework, shell or placeholder provisions are scattered throughout the Kyoto Protocol. Notable among these are the following provisions: emissions trading (Articles 3.10, 3.11 and 16 bis); joint implementation among Annex I Parties (Articles 3.10, 3.11 and 6); the so-called Clean Development Mechanism (Articles 3.12 and 12), which became a substitute for joint implementation between Annex I and non-Annex I Parties and for the Brazil-sponsored Clean Development Fund; credit for early action from the year 2000 (Article 12.10); and enforcement and noncompliance (Article 17).■

NOTES AND COMMENTS

1. An extensive analysis of the Kyoto Protocol is found in Michael Grubb *et al.*, The Kyoto Protocol: A Guide and Assessment (Royal Institute of International Affairs, 1999). Perhaps the key question in the international politics of climate change is whether the developing countries will remain unified in their present posture. At one point during the Kyoto negotiations, some 35 developing countries supported a proposal to provide an explicit path by which developing countries might voluntarily adopt quantified commitments, but Brazil, India, China and the OPEC countries lined up solidly against it and it was withdrawn. Grubb, *supra* at 110. For a relatively optimistic look at the possibilities for reductions by developing countries, *see* Jonathan Baert Wiener, On the Political Economy of Global Environmental Regulation, 87 Geo. L. J. 749 (1999). For a critique of Kyoto from a deep ecology perspective, see Prue Taylor, An Ecological Approach to International Law: Responding to Challenges of Climate Change (Routledge, 1998).

2. The United States, the world's biggest GHG emitter, explicitly rejected the Kyoto Protocol in 2001. President Bush said Kyoto was too costly,

based on unreliable science and unfairly excluded big developing nations like India, China and Brazil which account for a third of the world's population. In 2005, on the occasion of President Bush's visit to Europe, British Prime Minister Blair promised to try to persuade the U.S. to rethink. "The truth of the matter is without America there is no deal. We have got to do our best and use our relationship with America to try and make sure they come into agreement with us. Whether I will be able to achieve it or not, I don't know," he told Channel Five TV. Doyle, *supra*. Australia, the only big developed nation on the sidelines with the United States, said it had no plans to sign up. "Until such time as the major polluters of the world, including the United States and China, are made part of the Kyoto regime it is next to useless and indeed harmful for a country such as Australia to sign up to the Kyoto Protocol," Prime Minister John Howard told the Australian Parliament. *Id.*

3.   In July 1997, the only vote in the U.S. Senate on the Kyoto Protocol took place. By a unanimous vote of 95–0, the U.S. Senate adopted S. Res. 98, the so-called Byrd–Hagel Resolution. S. Res. 98, 105th Cong., 143 Cong. Rec. S8138–39 (daily ed. July 25, 1997). S. Res. 98 stated that the United States should not be a signatory to any protocol to, or other agreement regarding, the Climate Convention that would (A) mandate new commitments to limit or reduce greenhouse gas emissions for the Annex I [developed country] Parties, unless the protocol or other agreement also mandates new specific scheduled commitments to limit or reduce greenhouse gas emissions for Developing Country Parties within the same compliance period, or (B) would result in serious harm to the economy of the United States.

One argument cited by a number of Senators was the same one later made by President Bush: that the Kyoto Protocol would put an unfair burden on developed countries, particularly the United States. In order for the Senate to ratify Kyoto and agree on legislation to implement it, developing countries would need to share in reductions, which they were not required to do.

b.   RATIFICATION OF THE KYOTO PROTOCOL

In 2004, Russia ratified the Kyoto Protocol, and it went into effect. *See* Doyle, *supra*. A key consideration in Russia's decision to ratify the Protocol was its position as a likely net exporter of CO_2 allowances after the collapse of Soviet-era industries reduced GHG emissions in the nation. In Moscow, Russian electricity giant Unified Energy, which accounts for 2 percent of world GHG emissions, said it was close to signing 30 deals to cut emissions. *Id.*

Scientists have stated that the Protocol's goal of reducing GHG emissions by 5.2 percent from 1990 levels is just a first step, and a cut of at least 60 percent is needed to prevent catastrophic impacts of climate change this century. *See* Clouds Gather Over Future of Kyoto Climate Pact, Reuters, Feb. 11, 2005. Even if fully implemented, Kyoto would slow rising temperatures by just 0.18 F (0.1 C) by 2100, according to figures from the IPCC, and this would be a small dent in rising temperatures compared to the IPCC's forecasts of an overall rise of 1.4–5.8 degrees Celsius this century. *See* IPCC 2001 Report, *supra*.

NOTES AND COMMENTS

1. Canada announced in early 2005 that it would spend between $8–10 billion (Canadian) by 2012 on its efforts to meet targets under the Kyoto Protocol. The majority of the money would be split into two projects: a $1 billion Climate Change Fund to create an emissions credit-trading program for private industry and a partnership fund for provincial clean-air efforts. Canadians also would be encouraged to reduce their energy consumption, and oil, gas and other large industries would cut GHG emissions with new clean-air equipment. CBC News Online, Apr. 8, 2005. Emissions trading is discussed further in the next section.

2. The Kyoto Protocol gave support to "joint implementation," a system where industrialized countries receive benefits from helping developing countries with their emissions reduction commitments. Kyoto Protocol Annex I countries can undertake emissions reduction projects in other Annex I countries and receive a negotiated share of the emissions reductions generated by the projects. Some commentators suggest that this may present a "free-rider" problem. *See* Hanafi, *supra* at 460, 467–69. For additional commentary on joint implementation, *see* Note: Joint Implementation: Legal and Institutional Issues for an Effective International Program to Combat Climate Change, 22 Harv. Envtl. L. Rev. 441 (1998).

3. The Kyoto Protocol created the Clean Development Mechanism (CDM) to foster collaborative projects to reduce emissions or sequester carbon in developing countries. It allows an industrialized country that must reduce its emissions under the Protocol (an Annex I country) to invest in a project in a developing country without a target (non-Annex I), and claim credit for the emissions that the project achieves (known in CDM parlance as "Certified Emission Reductions"). In theory, this is done if it is easier and cheaper for the Annex I nation to meet its GHG reduction target in this fashion; at the same time, a developing country host can benefit from new investment that increases economic productivity and may reduce local environmental problems. *See* Sophie Smyth, The Prototype Carbon Fund: A New Departure in International Trusts and Securities Law, Sustainable Dev't L. & Pol'y, Spring 2005, at 28.

Article 12 of the Kyoto Protocol established three bodies to oversee the CDM: the representatives of the COP, an executive board established by the COP, and independent auditors to verify project activities. However, the Protocol provided almost no guidance on what exactly the CDM would do or how it would operate. Instead, the structure and authority of supervisory bodies and the CDM were left for future negotiation. The final rules for the CDM were agreed to at the 7th COP in Marrakech in 2001, with the exception of rules on carbon sinks, which were completed at the 9th COP in 2003, and some details about CDM project approval, which were delegated to the newly formed CDM Executive Board. *See* CDM Watch, The Clean Development Mechanism (CDM) Toolkit, http://www.cdmwatch.org/files/CDMToolkitVO19–02–04.pdf, for a complete description of the project application process; Annual report (2003–2004) of the Executive Board of the clean development mechanism to the Conference of the Parties, http://unfccc.int/resource/docs/cop10/02a01.pdf. The World Bank has three carbon funds for the financing of CDM projects. *See* http://www.carbonfinance.org. The operational details of the "Prototype Carbon Fund" are described in Smyth, *supra*.

A "CDM Scorecard" is maintained by the group CDM Watch. *See* http://www.cdmwatch.org/. One observer notes that the CDM "remains under-resourced and its lethargic approval process has only sanctioned several projects to date," and recommends more involvement from private sector firms with experience in emissions trading finance. Stephen Tully, Commercial Contributions to the Climate Change Regime: Who's Regulating Whom?, Sustainable Dev't L. & Pol'y, Spring 2005, at 14, 22.

The CDM overlaps with the European Union's emissions trading scheme (discussed below); CO_2 emissions reduction projects undertaken outside the EU pursuant to JI and CDM may qualify for allowances that can be bought and sold within the ETS. However, one report notes that over 800 CDM projects—significantly more than the number currently approved—would be necessary to meet European reductions targets. Pew Center on Global Climate Change, The European Union Emission Trading Scheme: Insights and Opportunities (2005), http://www.pewclimate.org ("Pew EU–ETS Report").

For a discussion of the possible conflict between the CDM and world trade rules, *see* Andrew Green, Climate Change, Regulatory Policy and the WTO, 8 J. Int'l Econ. L. 143 (2005).

4. The tenth session of the COP was held in Argentina in 2004, and produced a number of decisions aimed at strengthening the climate change framework. *See* http://unfccc.int/. However, negotiations on commitments to GHG reductions after the Kyoto period were rejected by the U.S. as premature. Tully, *supra*, at 23.

c.   EMISSIONS TRADING

Emissions trading, a market-based mechanism for pollution control, has been widely discussed as a means of GHG reduction. *See* Jonathan B. Wiener, Global Environmental Regulation: Instrument Choice in Legal Context, 108 Yale L. J. 677 (1999); David M. Driesen, Free Lunch or Cheap Fix? The Emissions Trading Idea and the Climate Change Convention, 26 B.C. Envtl. Aff. L. Rev. 1 (1998); Comment: An Analysis of a Global CO_2 Emissions Trading Program, 14 J. Land Use & Envtl. L. 125 (1998). CO_2 and other GHGs have the same effect wherever they are emitted, but compliance costs differ dramatically across sources and there is therefore considerable potential for a trading system to yield gains. While formal regulatory schemes are for now stymied in the U.S., emission trading has moved ahead in Europe, where a sophisticated scheme went into effect in 2005.

Emission trading for GHGs has not been without its critics. A strong majority of the countries represented at the Kyoto conference had been opposed to the idea of emission permits that could be traded internationally. Many developing countries saw the idea as "a way for rich countries to export their pollution and evade their obligations," Vanessa Houlder, Emissions Trading: Salvation or Hot Air, Financial Times, April 15, 1999. International tradable permits are occasionally thought of as only attractive to private industry because the system creates a tradable asset, as opposed to taxes which create only liabilities. Christiaan Vrolijk, The Kyoto Protocol: Implications for the Electricity Sector, Power Economics, January 31, 2000; *see also* Anne Petermann & Orin Langelle, UN Global Warming Convention Meets US Resistance

While Activists Criticize Carbon Trading As "Privatization of the Atmosphere," Z, Feb. 2005.

An emission trading scheme for GHG emissions would be a novel regulatory mechanism with numerous questions to be resolved in designing and implementing it. In 2000, University of Dundee law professor Peter Cameron summarized the difficulties of moving toward a multinational trading scheme:

> (1) Will such a trading system evolve? Most observers believe that there are a number of significant and difficult problems that must be settled before progress can be made. (2) If you have an emissions trading scheme, to what extent will that fit with existing regulatory mechanisms'? (3) Should a trading permit be a transferable property right? (4) How should permits for emissions trading be allocated and how can they be traded in an international marketplace? (5) How will a domestic emissions trading scheme mesh with regional and international emissions trading? (6) How will it be possible to ensure that emissions trading is transparent, low-cost and efficient? (7) How can verification of greenhouse gas emissions or sinks be ensured? (8) How can compliance with an international emissions trading regime be enforced?

Peter Cameron, From Principles to Practice: The Kyoto Protocol, 18 J. of Energy & Natural Resources Law 1, 17–18 (2000).

The world's first large-scale GHG trading program, the European Union Emissions Trading System (EU–ETS), opened for business in 2005, covering around 12,000 installations in 25 countries and 6 major industrial sectors. Under the Kyoto treaty the existing 15 member nations of the EU agreed to meet a commitment of an 8% reduction in GHGs collectively. Despite considerable reductions in the U.K and Germany, by 2000 many EU countries had difficulty slowing and reducing their GHG emissions. As a result the EU developed a range of policy measures to reduce GHGs and meet the Kyoto targets, one of which was the EU–ETS. In May 2004, ten nations from Central and Eastern Europe joined the EU, and the EU–ETS was expanded to 25 nations to include them.

The EU–ETS is up and running with significant trading volumes. It consists of a first phase from 2005–2007 and then successive five-year periods, with the second phase from 2008–2012 set to coincide with the Kyoto compliance period.

As you read the following description of the EU–ETS, consider how the questions raised by Professor Cameron and others have been addressed.

The EU Emissions Trading Scheme

http://europa.eu.int/comm/environment.

Trading emissions to cut costs and reduce emissions worldwide

The European Union is committed to global efforts to reduce the greenhouse gas emissions from human activities that threaten to cause serious disruption to the world's climate. Building on the innovative mechanisms set up under the Kyoto Protocol to the 1992 United Nations Framework Convention on Climate Change ("UNFCCC")—joint implementation, the clean development mechanism and international emissions trading—the EU has developed the largest company-level scheme for trading in emissions of carbon dioxide (CO_2), making it the world leader in this emerging market. The emissions trading scheme started in the 25 EU Member States on January 2005.

A key aspect of the EU scheme is that it allows companies to use credits from Kyoto's project-based mechanisms, joint implementation (JI) and the clean development mechanism (CDM), to help them comply with their obligations under the scheme. This means the system not only provides a cost-effective means for EU-based industries to cut their emissions but also creates additional incentives for businesses to invest in emission-reduction projects elsewhere, for example in Russia and developing countries. In turn this spurs the transfer of advanced, environmentally sound technologies to other industrialised countries and developing nations, giving tangible support to their efforts to achieve sustainable development.

The EU system is open to cooperation with compatible schemes in other countries that have ratified the Protocol. This has the potential to enlarge the market for trading. Focused initially on big industrial emitters which produce almost half of the EU's CO_2 emissions, the scheme gives European and foreign-owned businesses based in the EU a "first-mover" advantage through the invaluable early experience they are gaining. Due to mandatory monitoring and reporting of emissions, companies are establishing CO_2 budgets and carbon management systems for the first time.

Because CO_2 has a price, companies are engaging the ingenuity of their engineers to identify cost-effective ways to reduce their emissions, both through improving current production processes and investing in new technologies. A whole range of new businesses is emerging in Europe as a result of the EU carbon market: carbon traders, carbon finance specialists, carbon management specialists, carbon auditors and verifiers. New financial products such as carbon funds are entering the market.

Creating the emissions trading scheme and linking it to JI and CDM has been identified by the European Climate Change Programme as a particularly cost-effective way to reduce greenhouse gas emissions.... The 15 Member States that made up the EU until its enlargement to 25 countries on 1 May 2004 are committed to reducing their combined emissions of greenhouse gases by 8 %From 1990 levels by the end of the Protocol's first commitment period between 2008 and 2012. This overall target has been translated into differentiated emission reduction or limitation targets for each Member State under a "burden sharing" agreement. The 10 new Member States are not covered by the EU target but in most cases have their own reduction target of 6% or 8% under the Protocol. They are full participants in the EU trading scheme ...

The EU emissions trading scheme

The EU emissions trading scheme (ETS) is based on a recognition that creating a price for carbon through the establishment of a liquid market for emission reductions offers the most cost-effective way for EU Member States to meet their Kyoto obligations and move towards the low-carbon economy of the future. The scheme should allow the EU to achieve its Kyoto target at a cost of between 2.9 and 3.7 billion annually. This is less than 0.1% of the EU's GDP. Without the scheme, compliance costs could reach up to 6.8 billion a year.

The ETS has been established through binding legislation proposed by the European Commission and approved by all EU Member States and the European Parliament. The scheme is based on six fundamental principles:

—It is a "cap-and-trade" system

—Its initial focus is on CO_2 from big industrial emitters

—Implementation is taking place in phases, with periodic reviews and opportunities for expansion to other gases and sectors

—Allocation plans for emission allowances are decided periodically

—It includes a strong compliance framework

—The market is EU-wide but taps emission reduction opportunities in the rest of the world through the use of CDM and JI, and provides for links with compatible schemes in third countries.

What the scheme covers

While emissions trading has the potential to involve many sectors of the economy and all the greenhouse gases controlled by the Kyoto Protocol (CO_2, methane, nitrous oxide, hydrofluorocarbons, perfluorocarbons and sulphur hexafluoride), the scope of the ETS is intentionally limited during its initial phase while experience of emissions trading is built up. Consequently, during the first trading period, from 2005 to 2007, the ETS covers only CO_2 emissions from large emitters in the power and heat generation industry and in selected energy-intensive industrial sectors: combustion plants, oil refineries, coke ovens, iron and steel plants and factories making cement, glass, lime, bricks, ceramics, pulp and paper. A size threshold based on production capacity or output determines which plants in these sectors are included in the scheme.

Even with this limited scope, more than 12 000 installations in the 25 Member States are covered, accounting for around 45% of the EU's total CO_2 emissions or about 30% of its overall greenhouse gas emissions. The scheme will be reviewed around mid–2006 to allow fine-tuning in the light of experience gained and to consider whether it should be extended to other sectors, such as chemicals, aluminium and transport, and to more greenhouse gases.

How does emissions trading benefit companies and the environment?

Companies A and B both emit 1000 0000 tonnes of CO_2 per year. In their national allocation plans their governments give each of them emission allowances for 950,000 tonnes, leaving them to find ways to cover the shortfall of 5,000 allowances. This gives them a choice between reducing their emissions by 5,000 tonnes, purchasing 50,000 allowances in the market or taking a position somewhere in between. . . .

Emission allowances

At the heart of the ETS is the common trading "currency" of emission allowances. One allowance represents the right to emit one tonne of CO_2. Member States have drawn up national allocation plans for 2005–07 which give each installation in the scheme permission to emit an amount of CO_2 that corresponds to the number of allowances received. Decisions on the allocations are made public. The limit or "cap" on the number of allowances allocated creates the scarcity needed for a trading market to emerge. Companies that keep their emissions below the level of their allowances are able to sell their excess allowances at a price determined by supply and demand at that time. Those facing difficulty in remaining within their emissions limit have a choice between taking measures to reduce their emissions, such as investing in more efficient technology or using a less carbon-intensive energy source, buying the extra allowances they need at the market rate, or a combination of the two, whichever is cheapest. This ensures that emissions are reduced in the most cost-effective way.

Most allowances are allocated to installations free of charge—at least 95% during the initial phase and at least 90% in the second phase from 2008 to 2012. Though only plants covered by the scheme are given allowances, anyone else—individuals, institutions, non-governmental organisations or whoever-is free to buy and sell in the market in the same way as companies.

National allocation plans

Member States' national allocation plans ("NAPs") have to be based on objective and transparent criteria, including a set of common rules that are laid down in the legislative framework establishing the ETS. The most important of these rules are as follows: An allocation plan has to reflect a Member State's Kyoto target as well as its actual and projected progress towards meeting it. The total quantity of allowances allocated is key in this regard. Allocating too many allowances would mean that greater efforts to cut emissions would have to be taken in economic sectors not covered by the scheme, in potentially less cost-effective ways than trading. Allocations to installations must take account of their potential for reducing emissions from each of their activities, and must not be higher than the installations are likely to need.

Where Member States intend to use JI and CDM credits—thereby giving their companies more scope to emit—to help them reach their national emission target, these plans must be substantiated, for example through budgetary provisions. The European Commission has issued specific guidance on how these rules are to be applied by Member States. The Commission assesses NAPs on the basis of these rules, as well as EU rules on State aids and competition, and has the power to require changes or even to reject them altogether.

Ensuring compliance

Appropriately for a market-based instrument that makes it possible to put a price on carbon, the ETS incorporates a robust framework of measures to ensure compliance that also gives a central role to economic incentives. After each calendar year, installations must surrender a number of allowances equivalent to their verified CO_2 emissions in that year. These allowances are then cancelled so they cannot be used again. Those installations with allowances left over can sell them or bank them for the future.

Those that have not produced enough allowances to cover their emissions will have to pay a dissuasive fine for each excess tonne emitted. In the initial phase the penalty is 40per tonne, but from 2008 it will rise to 100. Operators also have to obtain allowances to make up the shortfall in the following year, and they will be "named and shamed" by having their names published. Member States are also required to lay down dissuasive penalties for any infringements of the ETS rules at national level.■

NOTES AND COMMENTS

1.   The national allocation plans (NAPs), the backbone of the EU–ETS, have not always been developed smoothly or timely. In January 2005, the EU sued Belgium, Finland, Greece and Italy in the European Court of Justice for not submitting their NAPs. E.U. sues four nations over national allocation plan, Greenwire, Jan. 20, 2005. In Italy, the EU's fourth-largest CO_2 emitter, a dispute had arisen over whether companies could put all of their industrial sites into a pool (or "bubble"), which was an important issue to utilities.

The U.K., meanwhile, was embroiled in a dispute with the EU over its plan. The EU approved its plan in July 2004, but critics charged that a revised plan released in October would not enable the U.K. to meet its

Kyoto target. The revised U.K. NAP set a goal of reducing CO_2 emissions by 5.4 percent, but the U.K.'s target was a 12.5% reduction. U.K. threatens E.U. with legal action over emissions plan approval, Greenwire, Jan. 10, 2005.

2.   While the EU–ETS is ambitious, economic pressures may make it difficult to meet the Kyoto targets in Europe:

> Although overall considerable progress appears to have been made in reducing GHG emissions, this overall result is skewed by the fortuitous reductions by Germany and the UK. Emission levels in other EU nations, especially the southern European countries, have increased considerably. Overall, an upward pressure on GHG emissions levels will remain as the EU economy continues to expand, and this realization was a major impetus in the implementation of the EU–ETS as a cost-effective policy lever to reduce GHG emissions. . . . Achievement of the overall reduction goal has been helped by the accession of 10 new countries from Eastern Europe whose aggregated emissions are considerably less than their own Kyoto targets following their economic restructuring. . . . It should be noted however that as the accession countries' own economies grow, their available emission allowances for sale will be reduced (e.g., Hungary and Slovenia).

Pew Center EU–ETS Report, *supra*. The "fortuitous reductions" in Germany and the U.K. included a large-scale switch from coal to natural gas for generating electricity in the U.K. and the modernization of ex-communist East Germany, both one-time opportunities for GHG reductions.

3.   As the first large-scale complex, market-based GHG control program, the EU–ETS will almost certainly yield a wealth of practical information on the design and implementation of GHG economic control programs and on such variables as the cost of emissions reductions, the impacts on industries, and the development of new GHG control technologies. At the program's outset, there were the inevitable predictions of gloom and doom from business groups that the EU–ETS would cause dramatic job losses and higher electricity prices. However, other observers noted that with the second phase of the scheme kicking in only a few years later, businesses should use the first phase as a chance to learn more about how to curb emissions. Brian Stempeck, First year of CO_2 trading likely to be industry's "learning phase," Greenwire, Jan. 4, 2005.

4.   Economists in both the developing and the developed countries have questioned the advisability of using a system of permits that could be traded internationally. P.K. Rao believes that the high transaction costs and the high degree of uncertainty "suggest that the principle of market-based emission trading may have a long way to proceed before being effective in any sense." P.K. Rao, The Economics of Global Climate Change 128–131 (M.E. Sharpe, 2000). Murray Weidenbaum suggests that an economic analysis of the distributional effects of international emissions trading "shows the unexpected result that emissions trading among nations is, in effect, a massive shift of income and wealth from the economi-

cally advanced societies of the West to China, India, and other poor but rapidly growing nations. I do not see any support among Americans for that type of stealthy cross-border philanthropy." Weidenbaum, *supra,* at 7. Would the EU–ETS be subject to this sort of criticism?

5.   The Chicago Climate Exchange (CCX), a voluntary, U.S.-based market representing the world's first "multi-national and multi-sector market for reducing and trading greenhouse gas emissions," opened in September 2003, and recently passed the 1 million metric ton mark in carbon trades. *See* http://www.chicagoclimatex.com/.

d.   INDIVIDUAL NATIONS' ACTIONS TO CONTROL GHG EMISSIONS

Some countries have begun rather extensive efforts to cut back on fossil fuel usage. In March 1990, the British government proposed very large cuts in greenhouse gas emissions, hoping to reduce emissions to 21.5% below 1990 levels by the year 2010 (although it may not meet this target, according to the most recent data):

> U.K. carbon dioxide emissions dropped dramatically from 1990 to 1999, nearly 15 percent, due to a major shift from coal to natural gas in electric power production. But, facing complaints from coal miners, the British government essentially put a hold on new gas-fired generation. As a result, CO_2 emissions are projected to begin rising next year. The proposed new measures include an energy tax; negotiated agreements with energy-intensive sectors, including electric power; a voluntary agreement already secured with European car manufacturers to reduce carbon dioxide by 25 percent in new cars; and a requirement that sources of electricity include 10 percent from renewables. Continuing increases in a controversial petrol tax escalator are also on the table, the government says.

Brits Outline Massive Cuts in CO_2 Emissions, Electricity Daily, Mar. 15, 2000.

Although these proposals were initiated by the Labor government, it was Margaret Thatcher, the long-time Conservative prime minister, who initiated serious research into the climate change issue in Britain back in the 1980s. Mrs. Thatcher, whose background was in chemistry, was responsible for the creation of the Hadley Center for Climate Prediction and Research, one of the leading centers for climate research. Stevens, *supra,* at 162.

The U.K. now has its own emissions trading scheme, operated by the Department for Food, Environment, and Rural Affairs (Defra). The U.K. emissions trading scheme was the world's first economy-wide GHG emissions trading scheme, and began in March 2002. Thirty-one participants have voluntarily taken on emission reduction targets to reduce their emissions against 1998–2000 levels, delivering 11.88 million tons of additional CO_2 equivalent emission reductions over the life of the scheme (2002–2006). The scheme is also open to the 6,000 U.K. companies with Climate Change Agreements. These negotiated agreements between business and Government set energy-related targets. Companies meeting their targets will receive an 80% discount from the Climate Change Levy, a tax on the business use of energy. These companies can use the scheme either to buy allowances to meet their targets, or to sell any over-achievement of these targets. Anyone can open an account on the registry to buy and sell allowances. *See* http://www.defra.gov.uk/.

In 2004, British Prime Minister Tony Blair officially launched The Climate Group, a new coalition of states, cities, nongovernmental organizations ("NGOs") and businesses that aims to reduce greenhouse gas emissions. The Climate Group brings leaders from corporations, governments and financiers from across the globe to meet at international "Conferences of the Reducers" to demonstrate how they are taking practical action to drastically reduce their greenhouse gas emissions. This group included representatives from business (including BP, Lafarge and DuPont) and the British and Canadian Federal governments. *See* theclimategroup.org.

Despite the U.K.'s leadership on greenhouse gas reductions, by 2005 the nation was on the verge of being unable to meet even its Kyoto target to reduce emissions of GHGs to 12.5 percent below 1990 levels by 2009–2012. According to the environmental group Friends of the Earth, government figures showing a rise in emissions by 1.5 percent in 2004 over 2003 levels put the U.K.'s emissions for 2004 just 12.6 percent below 1990 levels. The main culprits blamed for this performance were the industrial and transportation sectors. *See* UK Emissions Rise Again, May Miss Kyoto Target, Reuters, Apr. 1, 2005.

There has been little public skepticism in Europe about the potential problem of climate change. Elsewhere in the world, however, the prospect of drastic reductions seems quite unpalatable.

3.   THE COST AND EFFECTIVENESS OF CONTROLS

Many economists have analyzed the economic impact of a cap on carbon dioxide. "It is no surprise that each analyst comes up with a different set of numbers," since they make different assumptions and use different data and models, says Murray Weidenbaum. "Yet, one overriding point emerges from examining these impact studies: the costs of meeting the proposed caps on carbon dioxide usage will be very substantial, ranging from tens of billions to hundreds of billions of dollars a year." Weidenbaum, *supra,* at 5.

Most estimates of the implementation cost of greenhouse gas reduction have focused on reductions by large emitters, such as power plants. *See* Hanafi, *supra,* at 450–57. As the EU's emissions trading scheme acknowledges, these are also the sources that are typically least difficult to control. But to achieve the kinds of reduction called for by advocates of major change, it would be necessary to regulate the small scale emissions of individual buildings and vehicles, which are responsible for the great majority of carbon dioxide emissions. The cost of measuring and monitoring reductions of small sources is an imposing hurdle for any system to overcome. Hanafi, *supra,* at 488–95. David Fleming, the director of the Lean Economy Initiative, a British environmental group, has proposed a system of "Domestic Tradable Quotas" that would allow the "industrial economy to reinvent itself with a completely new way of meeting its energy needs," Every person would be given a Domestic Tradable Quota (DTQ), which would be an "equal per capita entitlement of 'carbon units' to cover domestic needs for fuel for all purposes, including private transport," People could trade their units in the market. Over time, the total quantity of carbon units made available would be gradually reduced. Carbon units "would be surrendered—as virtual ration coupons—to cover the purchase of all types of fuel and domestic energy," The greater the carbon emissions of the fuel or energy source, the more carbon units would have to be surrendered. "The whole transaction and all the calculations needed would be carried out using technology which is already commonplace for credit cards and direct debit systems," David Fleming, Your Climate Needs You, Town & Country Planning 302, Oct. 1998.

Fleming's proposal illustrates the fact that the ubiquitous nature of carbon dioxide emissions means that virtually every aspect of our lives has some impact on the problem. Unlike the acid rain program, which is often discussed as a model for an international emissions trading program, it would be difficult to provide meaningful and equitable remedies by focusing only on the largest polluters.

It is not easy to imagine public acceptance of a regulatory system as pervasive and Orwellian as the one Fleming proposes, but can meaningful reductions of CO_2 be achieved without affecting such basic activities as home heating and automobile driving? Will advances in technology make it possible to achieve reductions at this scale without the kind of restrictions that Fleming advocates? How would we design such a comprehensive scheme and measure its effectiveness? The following excerpt addresses this issue.

Robert R. Nordhaus and Kyle W. Danish, Assessing the Options For Designing a Mandatory U.S. Greenhouse Gas Reduction Program

32 B.C. Envtl. Aff. L. Rev. 97 (2005).

III. Design Criteria for a Domestic GHG Regulatory Program

Evaluating different GHG regulatory program options involves a number of considerations. The first design decision is establishing the program's emissions reduction objective. Once an emissions reduction objective is set, policy-makers have to design a regulatory program to meet it. Key design criteria include environmental effectiveness, cost, administrative feasibility, distributional equity, and political acceptability. The sections that follow elaborate on each of these criteria.

The emissions reduction target for a domestic program establishes the level and timing of reductions at the national level. The target can be set for purposes of compliance with an international obligation or could be established as a matter of domestic policy, independent of any international obligations. Moreover, it could take the form of a cap on domestic GHG emissions or a limit on GHG emissions per unit of output (also referred to as an "emissions intensity" target). It could establish a GHG reduction target for an initial compliance period, or it could establish a long-term emissions reduction path, phasing in progressively more stringent targets over an extended period of time. . . .

The criteria for evaluating design options are described below.

A. *Environmental Effectiveness: How Effective Is the Program in Meeting Its Emission Reductions Target?*

A regulatory program's effectiveness in meeting its target is a function of a number of factors, including its coverage of sources throughout the economy, its certainty in meeting a particular emissions target, and its provisions for enforcement.

1. Coverage: Are All Sources and Gases Covered?

A program's coverage refers to the extent to which it directly or indirectly regulates sources of GHG emissions throughout the U.S. economy and applies to the full range of GHGs. Broad coverage is preferable from an environmental perspective (but may have to be balanced by considerations of administrative cost). . . . Programs with only partial coverage (including opt-ins) also risk "leakage." Leakage occurs when a regulatory program encourages shifting of emission-generating activities from regulated to non-regulated firms.

2. Environmental Certainty: Will the Program Ensure That the Emission Reductions Target Will Be Met?

Some program designs provide greater certainty that total emissions from regulated firms will not exceed a particular level. For example, a "quantity-based" approach, such as a conventional cap-and-trade program, enforces an overall limit on emissions from the covered firms. By contrast, "price-based" approaches, such as emission taxes or trading programs with a "safety valve", do not place a precise limit on total emissions but instead impose a particular price or price limits on a ton of emissions. . . . However, because it is cumulative rather than annual emissions that are important, taxes or standards should be able to provide almost equivalent environmental certainty if there is political will to adjust them over time.

3. Enforcement: Is the Program Enforceable?

Any regulatory program's overall success in reducing emissions also is a function of its enforcement mechanisms. Enforcement is, in turn, a function of clear rules, precise and effective measurement of emissions, pursuit of violators, and having non-compliance penalties high enough to exceed any benefits associated with non-compliance.

B. *Cost-Effectiveness: Will the Program Design Allow Cost–Effective Compliance?*

A key consideration in evaluating a GHG regulatory program is whether it permits compliance with the program's target at least cost to the U.S. economy-what we refer to as "cost-effective" compliance. The first cost-related issue is the direct cost of complying with the program.... Another key cost-related consideration is administrative cost. Finally, some program designs raise revenue, which, as explained below, could be used to offset part of the overall cost of the program by reducing "distortionary" taxes on capital and labor.

1. Flexibility: Will the Program Provide Flexibility as to How, Where, And When Emissions Reductions Are Attained?

A cost-effective program will provide wide flexibility to regulated firms in determining how to reduce emissions to meet the program target ("what" flexibility), where to reduce them ("where" flexibility), and within limits, when to reduce them ("when" flexibility). "What" flexibility implies that a firm can comply by implementing any of the full range of GHG mitigation measures, including increasing energy efficiency; switching fuels; reducing consumption; adopting land use, land-use change, and forestry ("LULUCF") measures (including agriculture); or taking other action to reduce or sequester GHGs. Second, it implies that firms can comply through reductions in any of the major GHGs. Third, it implies that firms that can achieve low-cost reductions will undertake a greater proportion of emission reductions than firms that achieve reductions at higher costs. Many different kinds of firms and activities generate emissions of different GHGs; their costs of reducing those emissions and the means of reduction available to them vary widely. A program with maximum "what" flexibility has the effect of equating marginal costs of mitigation across all firms subject to the program, thereby generating the lowest-cost distribution of abatement activities throughout the economy....

"Where" flexibility implies that the program will recognize reductions achieved throughout the world. A domestic GHG program that is integrated with the emerging international market in GHG emission reductions almost certainly will have lower compliance costs than a program that credits only reductions made within the United States. Studies have suggested that opening up a U.S. climate program to trading even with just the industrialized countries that are subject to Kyoto Protocol emission limits could reduce a U.S. program's marginal (incremental) abatement cost by anywhere between 13 percent and 68 percent....

"When" flexibility provides the regulated firm with choices as to the timing of emission reductions.... A multi-year approach gives firms the flexibility to manage their emissions over time and avoids penalizing them for emissions changes caused by difficult-to-control fluctuations in business cycles and the weather.

Other "when" flexibility measures include "banking" and "borrowing." Programs can be designed so that firms that over comply can "bank" emission credits and use them in a subsequent compliance period or sell them at a later date when prices in the trading market might be higher. A "borrowing" provision would allow a firm to comply with its obligations in one compliance period in part by committing to even deeper-than-required reductions in the subsequent compliance period.... A firm's ability to borrow has to be limited, however, lest it become a means of simply avoiding reductions.

  2. Cost Predictability: Are costs of Compliance Reasonably Predictable?

A regulatory program also can be designed so that total compliance costs are capped. As discussed above, "price-based" approaches, such as emissions taxes, do not provide assurances that a particular level of emission reductions will be achieved. On the other hand, such programs do provide assurances that the costs of compliance will not rise above a particular per-ton level. This kind of certainty about costs generally is not possible with a quantity-based program, such as a traditional cap-and-trade program, where it is implied

that the quantitative limit on emissions will be enforced regardless of compliance costs. To address the risk of spiraling compliance costs associated with a cap-and-trade program, some have proposed a "safety-valve" mechanism, in which additional allowances would be made available at a pre-set price representing the maximum acceptable cost.

  3. Raising Revenue: Will the Program Raise Revenues That Can Be Used to Offset a Portion of Its Costs?

Some program designs that raise revenue, such as GHG taxes or allowance auctions, offer an opportunity to offset economic costs of the program borne by particular sectors through financial assistance programs or reduce the overall cost of the program through a reduction in federal taxes. Economic analysis indicates that programs that recycle the revenue to reduce distortionary taxes on capital, labor, or income have significant potential to reduce overall costs of a GHG regulatory program to the economy. However, it may prove politically difficult to implement tax cuts that increase economic efficiency. The revenues raised could just as easily be spent in activities that reduce, or have no impact on, economic efficiency as on activities that improve it.

  4. Long–Term Incentives: Will the Program Induce Key Sectors to Begin Investing in Low–Emission Technologies and Practices?

Most climate change analysts agree that moderating the increase in atmospheric concentrations of GHGs ultimately will require a substantial transformation in the way that industrialized countries like the United States produce and use energy. Near-term policy choices will have a major impact on the cost of such a long-term effort. The reason is that energy-producing and energy-using technologies involve long-term capital investments that are not readily converted to other uses. Therefore, a domestic program needs to send a credible long-term signal to key sectors of the economy that encourages a shift toward lower-carbon technologies and lower-emitting practices. A domestic program that leaves certain sectors uncovered could result in those sectors "locking in" higher-emitting technologies and practices, potentially increasing the cost of achieving more substantial economy-wide GHG reductions in the future.

C. *Administrative Feasibility: Can the Program Be Administered and Does It Minimize Administrative and Transaction Costs?*

A key consideration in designing any regulatory program is whether it is feasible to administer. A program that is infeasible to administer will be both environmentally ineffective and economically inefficient. . . .

Another particularly important administrative criterion for a climate change policy is adaptability, given the necessary duration of any effort to stabilize concentrations of GHGs in the atmosphere. A U.S. climate change policy framework needs to be able to evolve over time to accommodate adjustments in the emission reduction commitments as new information becomes available and as the U.S. economy changes. In addition, because stabilization of GHG concentrations ultimately will require global efforts, the policy framework will have to be flexible enough to provide for coordination with other countries.

D. *Distributional Equity: Is the Burden of Compliance with the Program Fairly Apportioned?*

Another consideration in designing a regulatory program is how its costs are distributed across society. . . . All other things being equal, a regulatory program that aims to reduce GHG emissions will tend to impose its largest costs on firms and households that produce fossil fuels or are heavily dependent on them. A GHG regulatory program also will tend to be relatively more costly for low-income individuals because they spend a greater proportion of their total income on energy.

Some regulatory programs provide opportunities for modifying these distributional impacts. For example, in an emissions trading program, the government could allocate allowances on a cost-free basis to firms that would bear the brunt of regulatory compliance costs. Alternatively, the government could auction allowances and use the revenue to compensate those particularly burdened by the regulatory program through targeted tax breaks or lump-sum payments. Emissions tax programs hold similar revenue recycling potential.

E. *Political Acceptability: Are There Elements of Program Design That Affect Its Political Acceptability?*

Program designs that promise relatively greater environmental effectiveness, lower costs, and a more equitable distribution of regulatory burdens will be more likely to obtain more political support than other designs. However, the U.S. experience with environmental and energy policy suggests that other factors also affect a program's political acceptability. Indeed, considerations of political acceptability may lead policymakers away from what could otherwise be an optimal program design with respect to environmental effectiveness, cost, and equity.

For example, 25 years of environmental and energy policy experience suggests that it is difficult to gain public support for a program that relies principally on direct increases in the price of energy-either through taxes or regulatory measures-even where such a program arguably is more cost-effective or will result in a more equitable distribution of regulatory burdens than other approaches. Even in times of most compelling national circumstances, such as the 1973 Arab oil embargo, Congress was unwilling to use energy price increases to rein in consumer demand. On the other hand, program designs involving emissions trading or emissions charges offer the opportunity to develop what may be a politically-attractive policy package, *i.e.*, using the revenue raised from regulation of GHG emissions as a basis for reducing taxes on income.■

F.   ADAPTATION TO A CHANGING CLIMATE

The other major category of potential responses to greenhouse gas buildup is adaptation. Many energy industry analysts argue that democratic societies will never accept the cost of major reductions in fossil fuel consumption. They say that the prudent course of action is carefully planned adjustment to environmental changes. Even people who advocate prevention strategies often agree that those strategies may take effect so far in the future that some degree of adaption is also necessary. Some economists believe that the gradual nature of the changes in climate will allow us to cope with many of the changes without undue disruption. *See* Robert Mendelsohn & James E. Neumann, The Impact of Climate Change on the United States Economy 321 (Cambridge Univ. Press 1999).

The key element of the adaptation argument is that in comparison with the naturally rapid rate at which society rebuilds and changes, the relatively slow rate of predicted climate change should not be very serious. By phasing in adaptive measures over many decades the cost of the adjustment could be significantly reduced.

1.   AGRICULTURAL READJUSTMENT

One of the most obvious areas in which there are possibilities for adaptation is agriculture. Some forms of adaptation may be relatively easy to implement; *e.g.*, planting alternative crop strains that would be more suited to a wide range of plausible climatic futures, or building coastal barriers to block the advance of a rising ocean. But the application of these strategies may encounter strong opposition if they are perceived as having other adverse impacts. Construction of seawalls, for example, often destroys coastal wetlands.

A study by two economists of the potential impact of climate change on the United States (funded by the Electric Power Research Institute) suggests that if sensible adaptation measures are implemented gradually, "moderate warming over the next century would result in a much diminished economic impact compared to" previous estimates. They suggest the agricultural sector would benefit, while the impact on energy prices and the availability of water resources would be adverse. Mendelsohn & Neumann, *supra,* at 328. Other studies suggest the center of the United States would suffer the most because of drought. Kathryn S. Brown, Taking Global Warming to the People, 283 Science 1440 (Mar. 5, 1999).

2.   PROTECTING NATURAL AREAS

Most of our governmentally protected natural areas have been selected to preserve the type of habitat that was present in the area at the time protection was initiated. What will happen if climate change effectively moves habitats to new locations?

Studies of the impact of climate change on animal species are beginning to show significant geographical movements already taking place that appear to be the result of changes in climate. For example, amphibians in Costa Rican cloud forests have significantly declined in the face of warmer and drier conditions. A study of 34 European butterfly species found that their ranges had shifted to the north by from 35 to 240 kilometers. And the worldwide decline of several coral species has been linked by some scientists to climate change. Wuethrich, *supra* at 795.

Could we redesign our methods for protecting natural areas to cope with the needed changes? Flexible location of reserve boundaries is an appealing idea in principle, but it "has little precedent in the real world." Markham & Malcolm, *supra* at 392. Corridor systems that connect natural areas may become particularly important, and "fragmentation" of habitats may be "the single biggest barrier to ecosystem adaptation to a changing climate." *Id.* At 392–393.

G.   CONCLUSION

It is clear that much is known about the climate system and about how that knowledge is expressed through the use of physically based coupled models of the atmosphere, ocean, ice, and land surface systems. This knowledge makes it obvious that human-caused greenhouse warming is not a problem that can rationally be dismissed or ignored. However, the remaining uncertainties in modeling important aspects of the problem make it evident that we cannot yet produce a sharp picture of how the warmed climate will proceed, either globally or locally.

None of these recognized uncertainties can make the problem go away. It is virtually certain that human-caused greenhouse warming is going to continue to unfold, slowly but inexorably, for a long time into the future. "The decades-long lag between emission of the gases and their effect on the atmosphere has not yet been fully played out. Moreover, it seems unlikely at best that atmospheric concentrations of greenhouse gases are going to stop building up anytime soon." Stevens, *supra* at 309. The severity of the impacts can be modest or large, depending on how some of the remaining key uncertainties are resolved through the eventual changes in the real climate system, and on our success in reducing emissions of long-lived greenhouse gases.

*

INDEX

References are to pages.

†